NINTH EDITION
Managing Stress

Principles and Strategies for Health and Well-Being

Brian Luke Seaward

Paramount Wellness Institute
Boulder, Colorado

JONES & BARTLETT
LEARNING

World Headquarters
Jones & Bartlett Learning
5 Wall Street
Burlington, MA 01803
978-443-5000
info@jblearning.com
www.jblearning.com

Jones & Bartlett Learning books and products are available through most bookstores and online booksellers. To contact Jones & Bartlett Learning directly, call 800-832-0034, fax 978-443-8000, or visit our website, www.jblearning.com.

Substantial discounts on bulk quantities of Jones & Bartlett Learning publications are available to corporations, professional associations, and other qualified organizations. For details and specific discount information, contact the special sales department at Jones & Bartlett Learning via the above contact information or send an email to specialsales@jblearning.com.

13796-5

Production Credits
VP, Executive Publisher: David D. Cella
Publisher: Cathy L. Esperti
Editorial Assistant: Carter McAlister
Director of Production: Jenny L. Corriveau
Senior Production Editor: Nancy Hitchcock
Director of Marketing: Andrea DeFronzo
Production Services Manager: Colleen Lamy
VP, Manufacturing and Inventory Control: Therese Connell
Composition: S4Carlisle Publishing Services
Cover Design: Kristin E. Parker
Director of Rights & Media: Joanna Gallant
Rights & Media Specialist: Wes DeShano
Media Development Editor: Troy Liston
Cover Images (Title Page): © Inspiration Unlimited. Used with permission.
Printing and Binding: LSC Communications
Cover Printing: LSC Communications

Library of Congress Cataloging-in-Publication Data
Names: Seaward, Brian Luke, author.
Title: Managing stress : principles and strategies for health and well being
 / Brian Luke Seaward.
Description: Ninth edition. | Burlington, MA : Jones & Bartlett Learning,
 [2018] | Includes bibliographical references and index.
Identifiers: LCCN 2017010699 | ISBN 9781284126266
Subjects: | MESH: Stress, Psychological--therapy | Adaptation, Psychological
 | Mind-Body Therapies--methods | Psychophysiology--methods
Classification: LCC RA785 | NLM WM 172.4 | DDC 616.9/8--dc23
LC record available at https://lccn.loc.gov/2017010699

6048

Printed in the United States of America
21 20 19 18 17   10 9 8 7 6 5 4 3 2 1

To all my friends and family,
and to the many great people I have encountered
who have served as dynamic inspirations in my own life journey,
thanks for making this a better world in which to live.

A portion of the royalty derived from the sale of
this book will be donated to several nonprofit
organizations dedicated to environmental conservation
and health promotion.

"No problem can be solved from the same level of consciousness that created it."
— *Albert Einstein*

"Your time is limited, so don't waste it living someone else's life. Don't be trapped by dogma, which is living with the results of other people's thinking. Don't let the noise of others' opinions drown out your own inner voice. And most important, have the courage to follow your heart and intuition. They somehow already know what you truly want to become. Everything else is secondary."
— *Steve Jobs*

Brief Contents

PART 1

The Nature of Stress 1

1 The Nature of Stress 2
2 The Sociology of Stress 27
3 Physiology of Stress 44
4 Stress and Disease 61

PART 2

The Mind and Soul 97

5 Toward a Psychology of Stress 98
6 The Stress Emotions: Anger, Fear, and Joy 125
7 Stress-Prone and Stress-Resistant Personality Traits 146
8 Stress and Human Spirituality 167

PART 3

Coping Strategies 209

9 Cognitive Restructuring: Reframing 214
10 Healthy Boundaries: Behavior Modification 229
11 Journal Writing 241
12 Expressive Art Therapy 255

13 Humor Therapy (Comic Relief) 269
14 Creative Problem Solving 291
15 Communication Skills in the Information Age 308
16 Resource Management: Managing Time and Money 325
17 Additional Coping Techniques 342

PART 4

Relaxation Techniques 359

18 Diaphragmatic Breathing 362
19 Meditation and Mindfulness 370
20 Hatha Yoga 394
21 Mental Imagery and Visualization 410
22 Music Therapy 427
23 Massage Therapy 446
24 T'ai Chi Ch'uan 464
25 Progressive Muscular Relaxation 475
26 Autogenic Training and Clinical Biofeedback 485
27 Physical Exercise, Nutrition, and Stress 503
28 Ecotherapy: The Healing Power of Nature 532

Contents

Foreword xi
Preface xii
Acknowledgments xvi
How to Use This Book xvii
Student & Instructor Resources xix
Praise for Managing Stress xxii
Introduction xxiv

PART 1
The Nature of Stress   1

1   The Nature of Stress 2
    Times of Change and Uncertainty 2
    Definitions of Stress 5
    The Stress Response 6
      Tend and Befriend 7
    Types of Stress 8
    Types of Stressors 10
      Bioecological Influences 10
      Psychointrapersonal Influences 11
      Social Influences 11
    Social Stress in America: A Twenty-first
      Century Look 11
    The General Adaptation Syndrome 13
    Stress in a Changing World 15
    Stress and Insomnia 15
      College Stress 17
    A Holistic Approach to Stress Management 19
    Summary 24
    Study Guide Questions 24
    References and Resources 25

2   The Sociology of Stress 27
    Technostress 29
      Digital Toxicity, FOMO (Fear of Missing Out),
        and Digital Dementia 32
    A Decline in Civility 33
    Environmental Disconnect 35
    Occupational Stress 39
    Race and Gender Stress 40
    Summary 42
    Study Guide Questions 42
    References and Resources 42

3   Physiology of Stress 44
    The Central Nervous System 45
      The Vegetative Level 45
      The Limbic System 45
      The Neocortical Level 46
    The Autonomic Nervous System 47

    The Sympathetic and Parasympathetic
      Nervous Systems 47
    The Endocrine System 50
    The Neuroendocrine Pathways 52
      The ACTH Axis 53
      The Vasopressin Axis 54
      The Thyroxine Axis 55
    A Parable of Psychophysiology 55
    Three Decades of Brain Imaging Research 56
    Summary 58
    Study Guide Questions 58
    References and Resources 59

4   Stress and Disease 61
    Theoretical Models 62
      The Borysenko Model 63
      The Pert Model 67
      The Lipton Model 69
      The Gerber Model 70
      The Pelletier Premodel 78
      DNA, Telomeres, Stress, and Aging 82
    Target Organs and Their Disorders 82
      Nervous System–Related Disorders 84
      Immune System–Related Disorders 87
    Summary 91
    Study Guide Questions 91
    References and Resources 92

PART 2
The Mind and Soul   97

5   Toward a Psychology of Stress 98
    Freud and the Egg 99
    Jung and the Iceberg 102
    Elisabeth Kübler-Ross: The Death
      of Unmet Expectations 106
    Viktor Frankl: A Search for Life's Meaning . . . 108
    Wayne Dyer: Guilt and Worry 110
      The Sin of Guilt 111
      The Art of Worrying 111
    Leo Buscaglia: The Lessons of Self-Love 112
    Abraham Maslow: The Art of
      Self-Actualization 115
    Martin Seligman: Optimism and the
      Art of Being Happy 118
    A Tibetan Perspective of Mind and Stress 120
    Some Theoretical Common Ground 121
    Summary 122
    Study Guide Questions 122
    References and Resources 123

6   The Stress Emotions: Anger, Fear,
    and Joy 125
    The Anatomy of Anger..................... 126
        Gender Differences......................... 127
        Physiological Responses 129
        The Myth of Catharsis 129
        Anger Mismanagement Styles................ 131
        Creative Anger Strategies................... 132
    The Anatomy of Fear 134
        Basic Human Fears........................ 135
        Fear, Vulnerability, and Shame 137
        Strategies to Overcome Fear 138
    Depression: A By-Product of Anger
        or Fear? 138
    Joy, Eustress, and the Art of Happiness 139
    Summary................................. 142
    Study Guide Questions 142
    References and Resources 143

7   Stress-Prone and Stress-Resistant
    Personality Traits 146
    Type A Behavior 148
        Hostility: The Lethal Trait of Type A's 149
        Behavior Modification for Type A Behavior 150
        Social Influences on Type A Behavior 150
    Did Someone Say Type D Personality? 151
    Codependent Personality Traits.............. 151
    Helpless-Hopeless Personality 155
    Resiliency: The Hardy Personality 156
    Survivor Personality Traits.................. 158
    Sensation Seekers......................... 160
    Self-Esteem: The Bottom-Line Defense 161
    Summary................................. 164
    Study Guide Questions 164
    References and Resources 165

8   Stress and Human Spirituality 167
    A Spiritual Hunger? 168
    A Turning Point in Consciousness 169
    Definition of Spirituality................... 171
    Theories of Human Spirituality.............. 172
        The Path of Carl Jung...................... 173
        The Path of M. Scott Peck 175
        The Path of Hildegard von Bingen 177
        The Path of Black Elk 177
        The Path of Matthew Fox 179
        The Path of Joan Borysenko 181
        The Path of Deepak Chopra 182
        The Path of Jesus of Nazareth............... 184
        The Path of Joseph Campbell 186
        The Path of Lao Tzu 188
        The Path of Albert Einstein................. 189
    Common Bonds of Human Spirituality 191
        Centering Process (Autumn) 192
        Emptying Process (Winter) 192
        Grounding Process (Spring)................. 193

        Connecting Process (Summer)................ 194
    A Model of Spirituality for Stress Management ... 194
        Internal and External Relationships 194
        Personal Value System 196
        Meaningful Purpose in Life 197
        The Divine Mystery 199
        Spiritual Potential and Spiritual Health......... 199
        Roadblocks and Interventions 199
        Current Research on Spirituality and Health 200
    Summary................................. 203
    Study Guide Questions 204
    References and Resources................... 204

PART 3
Coping Strategies   209

    Expecting the Unexpected 212
    Conclusion 213
    References and Resources................... 213

9   Cognitive Restructuring: Reframing 214
    A Thinking-Process Model 215
    Two Minds Are Better Than One 216
    Toxic Thoughts 217
    The Choice to Choose Our Thoughts......... 221
    Acceptance: An Alternative Choice........... 224
    Steps to Initiate Cognitive Restructuring 225
    Some Additional Tips for Cognitive
        Restructuring 226
        Best Application of Reframing 226
    Summary................................. 227
    Study Guide Questions 227
    References and Resources................... 228

10 Healthy Boundaries: Behavior
    Modification 229
    Behavior as a Component of Personality 230
    The Behavior Modification Model 231
        A Second Behavior Modification Model:
            Stages of Change....................... 233
        Is Stress a Trigger for Relapse? 234
    Assertiveness............................. 235
    Assertiveness Skills 236
    Steps to Initiate Behavior Modification........ 238
    Summary................................. 239
    Study Guide Questions 239
    References and Resources................... 239

11 Journal Writing......................... 241
    Historical Perspective 242
    Journal Writing as a Coping Technique....... 243
    Steps to Initiate Journal Writing 247
        Journal Writing Styles, Themes, and Ideas 250
        Best Tips for Journal Writing as
            a Coping Technique..................... 251
    Best Application of Journal Writing 252

Summary..................................253
Study Guide Questions....................253
References and Resources.................253

12 Expressive Art Therapy.................. 255
Origins of Art Therapy...................256
Clinical Use of Art Therapy..............257
Steps to Initiate Art Therapy............262
    Artistic Roadblocks......................262
    Materials...............................262
    Illustrative Themes.....................263
    Interpretations.........................265
Best Application of Art Therapy..........265
Summary..................................267
Study Guide Questions....................267
References and Resources.................267

13 Humor Therapy (Comic Relief)........ 269
Historical Perspective...................270
Theories of Humor........................272
    Superiority Theory......................272
    Incongruity (Surprise) Theory...........272
    Release/Relief Theory...................273
    Divinity Theory.........................274
Types and Senses of Humor................275
    Types of Humor..........................275
    Senses of Humor.........................279
    Group Laughter = Laughter Yoga..........280
Humor Therapy as a Coping Technique......280
The Physiology of Laughter...............281
Steps to Initiate Humor Therapy..........282
Best Application of Comic Relief.........286
Summary..................................288
Study Guide Questions....................288
References and Resources.................288

14 Creative Problem Solving.............. 291
Think Like da Vinci!.....................293
The Creative Process.....................293
    Players on the Creativity Team..........294
    The Myths of Creativity.................296
Obstacles to the Creative Process........299
    The Right Answer........................299
    I'm Not Creative........................300
    Don't Be Foolish........................300
    To Err Is Wrong.........................300
From Creativity to Creative Problem Solving..302
Steps to Initiate Creative Problem Solving.....302
    Description of the Problem..............302
    Generating Ideas........................303
    Idea Selection and Refinement...........303
    Idea Implementation.....................303
    Evaluation and Analysis of Action.......303
Best Application of Creative Problem Solving....304
Summary..................................305
Study Guide Questions....................305
Appendix: Answers to Creative Problems.....305
References and Resources.................306

15 Communication Skills in the
    Information Age........................ 308
High-Tech Communication: Welcome
    to Information and Communication
    Overload...............................309
    High-Tech Miscommunication..............310
The Technology Gap.......................310
Anger and Fear Influences with High-Tech
    Communication..........................310
    Smartphones, Dumb Messages..............310
    How to Incorporate Effective Communication
        Skills into Your Life Routine.......312
The Basics of Face-to-Face Communication
    Skills.................................313
Conversational Styles....................314
Verbal Communication.....................314
Communicating Ideas and Feelings.........315
Nonverbal Communication..................316
    Physical Elements.......................316
    Nonphysical Elements....................317
Listening, Attending, and Responding
    Skills.................................318
Conflict Resolution......................319
Conflict-Management Styles...............320
Steps to Enhance Face-to-Face
    Communication Skills...................320
Best Benefits of Effective High-Tech
    Communication Skills...................322
Summary..................................323
Study Guide Questions....................323
References and Resources.................324

16 Resource Management: Managing
    Time and Money........................ 325
Money Matters............................326
Mass Marketing to Your Ego...............326
The Psychology of Poverty................327
Money Problems? Try This.................327
    Tips for Financial Freedom..............327
The Hands of Time........................328
Roadblocks to Effective Time
    Management.............................330
Personality Styles and Behaviors.........331
Distractions: Roadblocks on the Time
    Management Highway.....................333
    Estimated Time of Completion............334
Steps to Initiate Good Time-Management
    Techniques.............................334
Additional Time-Management Ideas.........336
Best Application of Time-Management
    Skills.................................339
Summary..................................340
Study Guide Questions....................340
References and Resources.................340

17 Additional Coping Techniques.......... 342
  Information Seeking 342
  Social Orchestration...................... 343
  Friends: Social-Support Groups............. 345
  Hobbies 347
  Forgiveness............................. 348
    Ho'oponopono: Forgiveness Hawaiian Style.....348
  Dream Therapy 349
  Prayer and Faith......................... 351
    Types of Prayer 351
    Of Prayer and Meditation 351
    Research on Prayer and Faith 352
    Prayers for Non-Believers 353
    Ways to Pray............................354
  Summary................................ 355
  Study Guide Questions 355
  References and Resources.................. 356

PART 4
Relaxation Techniques   359
  References and Resources................... 361

18 Diaphragmatic Breathing 362
  The Mystery of Breathing.................. 363
  Breathing and Chronic Pain................ 364
  Steps to Initiate Diaphragmatic Breathing..... 364
    1. Assume a Comfortable Position 364
    2. Concentration..........................364
    3. Visualization...........................366
  Summary................................ 368
  Study Guide Questions 368
  References and Resources.................. 368

19 Meditation and Mindfulness........... 370
  Historical Perspective 371
  Types of Meditation...................... 373
    Exclusive Meditation......................373
    Transcendental Meditation 375
    The Relaxation Response 376
    Inclusive Meditation 376
    Zen Meditation 377
  Split-Brain Theory....................... 379
  Left Brain, Right Brain, Top Brain,
    Bottom Brain 382
  Altered State of Consciousness.............. 383
  Physiological and Psychological Effects
    of Meditation 385
  Neuroplasticity: The Neuroscience
    of Meditation 386
  Meditation and Brain Imaging Research 386
  Meditation and Chronic Pain............... 387
  Steps to Initiate Meditation................ 387
    Grand Perspective Mental Video.............387
    Mindfulness 387
  Best Application of Meditation 389

  Summary................................ 390
  Study Guide Questions 390
  References and Resources.................. 390

20 Hatha Yoga 394
  Historical Perspective 395
  Physiological and Psychological Benefits 396
  Hatha Yoga and Chronic Pain............... 397
  Steps to Initiate Hatha Yoga................ 397
    The Art of Breathing 397
    The Art of Conscious Stretching.............398
    The Art of Balance 399
    Salute to the Sun (Surya Namaskar)..........399
    Hatha Yoga Asanas.......................402
    Sample Workout 405
  Additional Thoughts on Hatha Yoga 405
  Best Application of Hatha Yoga.............. 405
  Summary................................ 407
  Study Guide Questions 407
  References and Resources.................. 407

21 Mental Imagery and Visualization....... 410
  Historical Perspective 411
  Mental Imagery Research 412
  Mental Imagery as a Relaxation Technique.... 415
    Tranquil Natural Scenes....................416
    Behavioral Changes.......................416
    Internal Body Images 419
  Color Therapy 421
  Mental Imagery and Chronic Pain 421
  Steps to Initiate Mental Imagery 422
  Best Application of Mental Imagery 423
  Summary................................ 424
  Study Guide Questions 424
  References and Resources.................. 424

22 Music Therapy........................ 427
  Historical Perspective 428
  From Sound to Noise to Music 429
  Music as a Relaxation Technique............. 431
  Biochemical Theory....................... 431
    Entrainment Theory.......................433
    Metaphysical Theory......................435
  Psychological Effects of Music 436
  Visualization and Auditory Imagery.......... 439
  Music Therapy and Chronic Pain 440
  Steps to Initiate Music Therapy 440
  Best Application of Music Therapy........... 441
  Summary................................ 442
  Study Guide Questions 442
  References and Resources.................. 442

23 Massage Therapy 446
  Historical Perspective 447
  The Need for Human Touch................ 447
  Massage Therapy Research 448
  Types of Massage 449

Shiatsu...................................450
Swedish Massage...........................451
Rolfing...................................453
Myofascial Release........................454
Sports Massage............................454
Other Touch Therapies 455
Physiological and Psychological Benefits 458
Massage Therapy and Chronic Pain 459
Best Application of Massage Therapy........ 459
Summary................................... 460
Study Guide Questions 460
References and Resources.................. 460

24 **T'ai Chi Ch'uan** **464**
Historical Perspective 465
Philosophy of T'ai Chi Ch'uan 465
Physiological and Psychological Benefits 466
T'ai Chi Ch'uan and Chronic Pain 467
T'ai Chi Ch'uan as a Relaxation Technique.... 468
T'ai Chi Ch'uan Movements 468
Additional Comments on T'ai Chi Ch'uan 471
Best Application of T'ai Chi Ch'uan......... 472
Summary................................... 473
Study Guide Questions 473
References and Resources.................. 473

25 **Progressive Muscular Relaxation** **475**
Historical Perspective 476
Physiological Benefits 476
Steps to Initiate Progressive Muscular
     Relaxation............................ 477
Best Application of Progressive Muscular
     Relaxation............................ 481
Summary................................... 483
Study Guide Questions 483
References and Resources.................. 483

26 **Autogenic Training and Clinical
     Biofeedback** **485**
Autogenic Training........................ 485
Historical Perspective 486
Psychological and Physiological Responses 488
Steps to Initiate Autogenic Training.......... 489
Adding Mental Imagery..................... 491
The Use of Self-Hypnosis................... 492
Best Application of Autogenic Training 492
Clinical Biofeedback 492
What Is Clinical Biofeedback? 493
Historical Perspective 494
Purpose of Biofeedback 495
Types of Biofeedback 496
Biofeedback and Chronic Pain 498

Best Application of Clinical Biofeedback...... 498
Summary................................... 500
Study Guide Questions 500
References and Resources.................. 500

27 **Physical Exercise, Nutrition, and Stress** .. **503**
Physical Exercise and Stress................. 503
Types of Physical Exercise 504
Physiological Effects of Physical Exercise 506
Theories of Athletic Conditioning 508
Physiological Effects of Physical Exercise 510
Physical Exercise and Chronic Pain 511
Steps to Initiate a Fitness Training Program....512
Best Application of Physical Exercise
     and Activity..........................514
Nutrition and Stress....................... 515
Diet for a Stressed Planet 516
A Word about Supplements...................519
Additional Stress and Nutritional Factors
     to Consider 520
A Word about Genetically Altered Foods.......522
Spiritual Nutrition.........................522
Psychological Effects of Food 524
Recommendations for Healthy Eating Habits....525
Additional Tips for Healthy Eating 527
Summary................................... 528
Study Guide Questions 529
References and Resources.................. 529

28 **Ecotherapy: The Healing Power
     of Nature** **532**
A Historical Perspective on Ecotherapy....... 533
A Nature Deficit Disorder? 533
Physiological Effects of Ecotherapy.......... 535
Entrainment: A Symphony in Natural
     Rhythms 537
Circadian (Bio) Rhythms and Physical
     Health 537
Psychological Effects of Ecotherapy 538
Nature and the Art of Solitude 539
Spiritual Moments 539
Earning "Nature Points" 540
Best Application of Ecotherapy 540
Summary................................... 541
Study Guide Questions 541
References and Resources.................. 541

*Epilogue: Creating Your Own Stress-Management
     Program* *543*
Glossary *547*
Index *567*

Foreword

"After ecstasy, the laundry!" This ancient saying can be applied to our current understanding of health and illness. During the past 50 years, we have discovered that, beyond doubt, the mind has an enormous impact on the body. Our emotions, thoughts, attitudes, and behaviors can affect us for good or ill. Now that we have glimpsed these lofty insights, it's time to get down to practicalities and apply them. It's time, in other words, to do the laundry. But the task isn't simple. How, exactly, can we bring mind and body into harmony? How can we alleviate the stressful effects of modern life? How can they be turned to our advantage? Can we learn to benefit from these changes? Can we become wiser and healthier in the process? Advice is not difficult to find, as self-proclaimed experts are everywhere. They tout the latest formulas for stress-free living and personal transformation from tabloids, talk shows, and a plethora of self-help books, giving the entire area of stress management a bad name.

It is refreshing, amid all this blather, to discover Dr. Brian Luke Seaward's *Managing Stress: Principles and Strategies for Health and Well-Being*. In clear, uncluttered language, he takes us on a gentle walk through the territory of mind–body interaction. From cover to cover you will find that he is a very wise guide and possesses a quality almost always missing in stress management manuals: humor. Dr. Seaward knows the field well—he has taught it and lived it—and he provides scientific documentation at every step. But perhaps most importantly, Dr. Seaward daringly goes beyond the usual approach to the subject to speak of the soul and of human spirituality. He realizes that stress management and maximal health are impossible to attain unless the questions of life's meaning are addressed.

Since *Managing Stress* first came out in 1994, the pace of life has certainly quickened. With this change, Americans have begun to embrace a host of complementary healing modalities, which underscores the importance of seeking a sense of inner peace from the winds of change.

As a physician who has long advocated the integration of mind and body for optimal health, I find it a pleasure and honor, therefore, to recommend this work. It is a fine contribution to the field of stress management and will serve as an invaluable guide to anyone seeking harmony in his or her life. A new day is dawning in medicine and health promotion, and Dr. Seaward has awoken early to watch and share the sunrise.

— **Larry Dossey, MD**
Executive Editor, *Explore: The Journal of Science and Healing*
Former Executive Editor, *Alternative Therapies in Health and Medicine*
Author of *Reinventing Medicine, One Mind,* and *Healing Words*

Preface

STRESS: THE NEW NORMAL?

Young adults today are growing up in a world that is very different from not only that of their parents, but also that of their older siblings. Since the first edition of *Managing Stress* came out two decades ago, experts agree the world has become a much more frenetic place to live. In the approximately 20 years that this book has been in print there have been cultural revolutions in daily life, including significant changes to the music industry (iTunes), the news industry, the job market, the banking industry, the communication industry, the hotel industry (Airbnb), and the cab industry (Uber), not to mention daily changes in social media and the emergence of new ways to share information. Add to this layer of complexity various health issues, including the increase in autism, the Zika virus, obesity, diabetes, teen suicide, and opioid addiction, as well as the increase in population and shifting demographics, such as increased Latino, Asian, and Muslim populations and the growing number of senior citizens. There is a great quote from Roy Blixer stating that "the only person who likes change is a wet baby." By and large, people don't like change, particularly change that they cannot control. Magazine headlines that once suggested various ways to decrease stress now tell us that stress is here to stay (so get used to it). Stress is the new normal. Despite the rapidly changing dynamics on planet Earth, what hasn't changed are the means to find your center, your sense of inner peace.

Experts from a host of disciplines have been commenting on the state of information processing today in the Wi-Fi digital age. The prognosis is not necessarily good. People are spending the vast majority of their time, perhaps all of it, in what has become known as "short-form information processing" and "short-form messaging." In simple terms, this means cherry-picking information for specific facts, without taking time to process the larger context of the facts or taking time for critical thinking, synthesis, creative thinking, and memorization. Metaphorically speaking, people today are missing the entire forest because they are staring at one or two trees.

The proliferation of iPads, smartphones, and other electronic devices, coupled with instant access to information and decreased attention spans, has begun to change (some say decrease) the intellectual capacity of the twenty-first–century citizen. What is being lost is what is now called "slow, linear thinking skills," along with intuitive-based knowledge. *Knowledge* (a domain of mental well-being) is the ability to gather, process, recall, and communicate information. *Wisdom* is the alchemy of knowledge and experience (real, not virtual) accrued over time. Time, however, is a rare commodity today, and more and more experience is viewed through a computer screen. People are opting for information rather than knowledge. As a result, wisdom becomes ever more rare.

Stated simply: There is a big difference between information gathering (for example, facts and figures) and the application of deep-seated wisdom. All-too-common examples include people who venture into national parks for a day's hike unprepared, without proper equipment or supplies. Such people often have cell phones and GPS tracking devices, which they then use to call for help when stranded on a mountaintop or when they have fallen down cliffs. Facts and figures cannot replace common sense (accrued wisdom), nor is a reliance on technology an excuse for ignorance. Stressful times, such as those in which we are living, necessitate wisdom.

Managing Stress is a synthesis of wisdom: accrued knowledge and personal experience over time. More than just a collection of facts and figures, *Managing Stress* connects the dots for nearly all aspects of stress through the ageless wisdom of the mandala template of mind, body, spirit, and emotions. *Managing Stress* is also a process of transformation, in which one moves from a motivation of fear toward a motivation of love and compassion. Mountains are a symbol of strength in times of change, which is why this symbol was chosen as the cover art for this ninth edition.

A quick glance at any headline makes it obvious that dramatic change is in the air. Global warming, energy demands, terrorism, personal bankruptcy, water shortages, advances in technology, and new diseases are a few of the many changes sweeping Earth as we speak. As planetary citizens, we are not immune to change. Moreover, with change comes stress, and humans are not immune to stress either. But with each change we encounter we have a choice to view it as a threat or an opportunity for growth. This new edition offers a unique synthesis of timeless wisdom from various world cultures, combined with new insights, research studies, and practical approaches to empower you to become resilient to stress during these times of dramatic change.

Many of the multicultural concepts in this edition are considered to be ageless wisdom, also known as *common sense*. But as the expression goes, "Common sense is not too common when people are stressed." As newly initiated members of the Wi-Fi generation, people not only expect instant information retrieval but also perfect sound bites of wisdom to accommodate their every need (rarely does a sound bite solve a life problem). As such, experts have coined the term "disposable knowledge" to describe the Internet mentality of failing to dig beyond the surface (or the first ten listings of a Google search) to really gain a handle on information content. This book digs beneath the surface to reveal an alchemy of ageless wisdom, current research, and practical tips for you to have the best skills and resources for your personal life journey. As several students have said to me, "*Managing Stress* not only connects the dots; it builds a bridge to a better life."

When *Managing Stress* was first published in 1994, it broke new ground. Never before had the focus of a college textbook presented such a holistic perspective of health and well-being under the influence of stress. Twenty years ago, you would have been hard pressed to find the word *spirituality* in a college textbook, yet today it would seem awkward not to address this aspect of health. Indeed, many of the topics and aspects that were considered at the vanguard a decade ago are now so familiar that they have become household words: t'ai chi, hatha yoga, echinacea, Pilates, meridians, and chakras, to name a few. As the global village knocks on your doorstep, insights from Asia, Africa, and Latin America offer a multicultural approach to seeking and maintaining balance in our lives. Perhaps it's no secret that as the pace of life continues to increase, so does the hunger for credible information to create and

maintain a sense of balance in these times of change. As the first edition of *Managing Stress* found its place on bookshelves across the country, it became known as the "Bible" of stress management. I am happy to say that I continually hear it described that way. I am also happy to hear so many comments on the writing style, layout, and production of the textbook: aesthetically pleasing to the eyes, easy to read and understand. A lot of work goes into the selection of photographs, cartoons, and artwork to make this book visually appealing and engaging. As with all previous editions, a conscious decision was made not to include stress-inducing photographs. The television news and the Internet are saturated with these types of images, and my intention is to maintain a positive energy between the covers of this book.

WHAT IS NEW AND IMPROVED IN THIS NINTH EDITION?

The topic of stress and stress management (now called *resiliency*) is quite dynamic, and as such there is always new information to add to the ever-growing body of knowledge. Here are some things added to place this ninth edition on the cutting edge of this colossal topic.

Chapter 1: The Nature of Stress

- Social Stress in America: New research by the American Psychological Association as well as the Harvard School of Public Health now highlights the issues of stress and health well beyond the work of Holmes and Raye. Additional studies on stress by NPR and Kaiser Health also point to what they call the burden of stress in America, from big life changes to daily hassles.

- Stress and insomnia have been linked for a long time, and now this new edition adds seven ways to improve your sleep hygiene for better sleep.

Chapter 2: The Sociology of Stress

- *Technostress* may not be new, but new research highlights the problems with repeated use of screen devices, including the outsourcing of our memory to technology. New terms in the lexicon of technostress include *digital toxicity* and *digital dementia*. This section highlights a few studies about the dangers of being distracted time and again by our screen devices, thus causing more stress.

- The environmental disconnect continues to grow as more news reveals the problems nationwide with our drinking water (e.g., Flint, Michigan) and the serious climate change flooding precautions, which add to one's stress level.

Chapter 3: Physiology of Stress

- A Closer Look at Panic Attacks—from Physiology to Treatment: Many students experience their first panic attack in college, and more and more people across the country seem to be experiencing this phenomenon. Often described as the "Stress response on steroids" this section takes you through the experience and how to deal with it.

Chapter 4: Stress and Disease

New to this chapter are several topics that beg for attention regarding stress and disease; these are topics that are likely to be in the news for quite some time.

- The Human Microbiome & Stress: The secret life of healthy gut bacteria. New research suggests that understanding the gut is essential to understanding health. With more than 70 percent of our immune system in the gut, the connections between stress and disease are overwhelming.

- Lyme Disease and Stress: New studies indicate that Lyme disease (and its co-infections) is an emerging national epidemic and the connections to stress are powerful and serious. This section takes a closer look at this debilitating autoimmune disease.

- DNA, Telomeres, Stress, and Aging: Nobel prize–winning research on the topic of telomeres and stress is now headline news, with implications for health and longevity.

- Stress and Inflammation: Inflammation seems to be tied to a great many health issues. This section reveals the connection between stress and inflammation.

Chapter 6: The Stress Emotions: Anger, Fear, and Joy

- Fear: Vulnerability and Shame (Brene Brown)

The stress emotions are complicated, yet researcher Brene Brown has made it a lot less complicated by shedding light on the aspects of vulnerability and how this can perpetuate fear rather than resolve it.

- Happiness: More ways to understand and pursue eustress. Studies on the topic of happiness reveal that we can have a positive effect on our state of mind by the choices we make and the perceptions we hold.

Chapter 10: Healthy Boundaries: Behavior Modification

- Because the term "behavior modification" sounds boring, and because so many issues with stress involve poor boundaries, the title of this chapter was updated to reveal the need to create healthy boundaries.

Chapter 12: Expressive Art Therapy

- A small section was added to include the new trend with adult coloring books, now used as an accepted coping technique for stress.

Chapter 13: Humor Therapy (Comic Relief)

- A small section was added to include the topic of Laughter yoga, a coping technique for stress that combines humor and support groups for a more powerful means to cope with stress.

Chapter 14: Creative Problem Solving

- A small section was added to the obstacles of creativity from best-selling author, Elizabeth Gilbert (*Eat, Pray, Love*) about fear as a destructive role in the creative process. A human feature story (Stress with a Human Face) was added to this chapter to show students that one of their own used the content of this chapter to resolve stress in her life.

Chapter 17: Additional Coping Techniques

- Hawaiian Forgiveness: Ho'oponopono

With so much anger in the world today, learning to resolve it is essential to finding a sense of inner peace. One of the newest takes on coping with stress is the Hawaiian modality of forgiveness called *Ho'oponopono*.

Chapter 19: Meditation and Mindfulness

- A small section was added about the executive function of the brain and how this compares to the left brain/right brain understanding of consciousness.

STRESS MANAGEMENT IN A RAPIDLY CHANGING WORLD

As with each new edition, this revision contains highlights of the latest state-of-the-art research on all aspects of stress management. This book strikes a fine balance between highlighting the landmark research on health psychology, psychoneuroimmunology, and holistic healing and the newest research studies, theories, and applications of effective stress management in our rapidly changing world.

Although it may seem like health care is in a state of flux, from a different perspective it appears to be on the cusp of a new revolution where mind, body, and spirit are seen as equal parts of the whole. Once again, *Managing Stress* stands at the vanguard as the premier resource for holistic (mind–body–spirit) stress management.

Since the creation of the Office of Alternative Medicine at the National Institutes of Health in 1993 (now called the National Center for Complementary and Integrative Health), more money and more research has been focused on a host of healing modalities that fall under the domain of complementary or "integrative" medicine.

Every technique for stress management is considered at some level to fall into the category of complementary or alternative medicine. Although at best the conclusions can only be drawn from outcomes due to the dynamics of the mind–body–spirit paradigm, the interest in this field only continues to grow. This book bears the collective fruit of this growing body of knowledge.

I urge readers to consider *Managing Stress* as an invitation to further explore all of the many topics highlighted in this book in greater depth through other books, articles, and experts in each respective field. No one book can contain all of the information on any topic, let alone this one, but it is my hope that this book sets you on a path toward a well-balanced life.

Acknowledgments

When Maureen Stapleton won her Oscar for Best Supporting Actress in 1982 for her role in the movie *Reds*, she walked up to the podium and said, "I'd like to thank everyone I ever met." At times writing this book, and working on all its many editions, I have felt much the same way. In fact, I would like to include many people I have never met but whose work and wisdom have found their way into this book. While I would like to share my gratitude with everyone—and you know who you are, including Joe Pechinski, Dave Clarke, Candace Pert, James Owen Mathews, and my invaluable mentors Elisabeth Kübler-Ross and Larry Dossey—there are simply too many friends, colleagues, scholars, and luminaries to list here. A very special thanks to Mark Ellison and Sally Cadman for their insightful feedback on Chapter 28, *Ecotherapy: The Healing Power of Nature*. Heartfelt gratitude to Randy Glasbergen and Brad Veley for the use of their wonderful cartoons. Huge thanks also to all my students, friends, and colleagues too numerous to mention, who were so kind to allow me to use their art therapy pieces or pose for countless photos used in this book. I am forever grateful. Special thanks go to Cathy Esperti, Carter McCalister, Nancy Hitchcock, and Wes DeShano at Jones & Bartlett Learning, who are simply awesome. Thanks for making this *Ninth Edition* the best ever. The phrase "it takes a village" certainly applies here, so thanks to everyone who has been and continues to be part of my "village."

How to Use This Book

Based on the concept of holistic wellness, where the whole is always greater than the sum of the parts, *Managing Stress*'s content and format uniquely offer insights on the integration, balance, and harmony of mind, body, spirit, and emotions throughout each section and in various chapters (for example, the concept of entrainment can be found in Chapter 4, *Stress and Disease*, and Chapter 22, *Music Therapy*). Like the wellness paradigm it is based on, *Managing Stress* is formatted in a mandala of four parts:

Part 1: The Nature of Stress (physiology, stress, and disease)

Part 2: The Mind and Soul (mental, emotional, and spiritual aspects as they relate to stress)

Part 3: Coping Strategies (promoting insights and resolution of stressors)

Part 4: Relaxation Techniques (promoting physical homeostasis)

This book integrates all four components of the wellness paradigm. First, because it is so visible, we will look at stress from the physical point of view, including both the dynamics involved in fight-or-flight and the most current theories attempting to explain the relationship between stress and disease. We then focus on mental and emotional factors, outlining pertinent theoretical concepts of psychology: the stress emotions, anger and fear, as well as specific personality types that are thought to be either prone or resistant to stressful perceptions. (More cognitive aspects are covered in Part 3.) The much-neglected component of spiritual well-being will round out the first half of the book, showcasing selected theories of this important human dimension and its significant relationship to stress. The remainder of the book will focus on a variety of coping strategies and relaxation techniques, and come full circle to the physical realm of wellness again, with positive adaptations to stress promoted through the use of physical exercise. As you will surely find, true to the wellness paradigm, where all components are balanced and tightly integrated, there will be much overlap among the physical, mental, emotional, and spiritual factors in these chapters, as these factors are virtually inseparable. And just as the word *stress* was adopted from the discipline of physics, you will see that some other concepts and theories from this field are equally important to your ability to relax (such as entrainment).

True to the nature of holistic stress management, there is no separation or division between mind and body, emotions and spirit, or any of these four aspects. As such, you will see cross-referencing between chapters to help you connect the dots so that your understanding of the mind–body–spirit connection is solid. You may find it best to start with Chapter 1, *The Nature of Stress,* and continue straight through to the end of Chapter 8, *Stress and Human Spirituality*, to gain the best perspective of this colossal topic. From there you can cherry-pick information on which coping techniques and relaxation techniques work best for you. Keep in mind that the best approach is to try them all to find which is most effective for you.

Each chapter of the text has a number of pedagogical devices designed to aid in the mastery of the material, including feature boxes, surveys, key terms, exercises, and checklists.

Case studies titled Stress with a Human Face illustrate how real people deal with a variety of stressful situations.

Stress with a Human Face

Courtesy of Juliet Simbo.

Society, and the culture it creates, is often described in metaphors. A common one is "the social fabric." For Juliet, a more apt metaphor might be a carpet, one that was pulled right from underneath her feet as a child. Juliet Mamie Simbo now lives in Denver, Colorado, but at the age of 13 she and her family fled from Sierra Leone, a small country on the west coast of Africa. She begins her story with a Hollywood reference:

"If you have seen the movie *Blood Diamond*, starring Leonardo DiCaprio and Jennifer Connelly, then you have witnessed a realistic portrayal of the horrors of civil war in Sierra Leone. I lived in this world. I witnessed my dad held at gunpoint on our porch on January 10th, 1999, by a rebel who told all of us that he was going to kill my father and suck his blood because of his vocal opposition to the atrocities being committed in my country. The gunman spared my father's life; however, in a defiant move, he turned and shot and killed our family dog. Because of greed and hatred amongst the people of my country, death came to many in Sierra Leone for seemingly no reason. I was changed forever by these events, knowing that my life was kept alive by the slimmest of margins."

As an immigrant to the United States, she had to adapt quickly to a whole new culture, one with superhighways, fast food, snowstorms, power shopping, abundant lifestyle opportunities, high technology, and crumbling family structures. "Initially, I felt lost and lonely as I tried to merge into the fast lane that is the American lifestyle," she explained. But over time, Juliet became less shy and more assertive, adapting successfully to a new way of life in a new culture. With college graduation months away, her eyes are now set on new sights. One day Juliet hopes to return to Africa and use her knowledge, skills, and experience to help make the world a better place, beginning with the severe hunger issues known in this part of the world.

Juliet has used her experience of cultural differences in a positive way and hopes that others will do the same. As she said in her high school graduation speech, "I say to you, open your eyes to the world beyond your country's borders. Feel the presence of humanity around the world and learn about them, even experience their culture. I hope that one day, you can be as grateful as I am for what you know about a different land and people. I thank you for being a part of my world, and I welcome you to visit mine."

Key terms are clearly defined in the text where the term first appears to help with comprehension and expand your professional vocabulary.

Walter Cannon: Twentieth-century Harvard physiologist who coined the term "fight or flight."

Fight-or-flight response: A term coined by Walter Cannon; the instinctive physiological responses preparing the body, when confronted with a threat, to either fight or flee; an evolutionary survival dynamic.

Stress reaction: The body's initial (central nervous system) reaction to a perceived threat.

Freeze response: Part of the stress response, where the individual neither fights nor flees but freezes like a deer caught in the headlights, paralyzed as if the person has forgotten to run.

Homeostasis: A physiological state of complete calmness or rest; markers include resting heart rate, blood pressure, and ventilation.

Stress response: The release of epinephrine and norepinephrine to prepare various organs and tissues for fight or flight.

End of chapter summary appears at the end of each chapter and contains a comprehensive summary of the main points in the chapter along with study guide questions and references for further study.

SUMMARY

- Physical exercise is a form of stress: the enactment of all the physiological systems that the fight-or-flight response triggers for physical survival.

- Physical exercise is classified as either anaerobic (fight) or aerobic (flight). Anaerobic (without oxygen) is a short, intense, and powerful activity, whereas aerobic exercise (with oxygen) is moderately intense activity for a prolonged period of time. Aerobic exercise is the better type to promote relaxation.

- The body adapts, either negatively or positively, to the stress placed upon it. Proper physical exercise will cause many adaptations that in the long term are thought to be effective in reducing the deleterious effects of stress by returning the body to a profound state of homeostasis. Physical exercise allows the body to use stress hormones for their intended purposes, detoxifying the body of stress hormones by utilizing them constructively.

- To get the benefits of physical exercise, four criteria must be met: intensity, duration, frequency of training, and mode of exercise. Together they are called the all-or-none principle, meaning that without meeting all four requirements few if any benefits will be gained. It takes between 6 and 8 weeks to see significant benefits in the body.

- The positive effects of physical exercise are lowering resting heart rate, resting blood pressure, and muscle tension, and a host of other functions that help maintain or regain physiological calmness.

- Exercise evokes not only physiological changes, but various psychological changes (e.g., runner's high) as well, again suggesting that mind and body act as one entity. Habitual physical exercise produces both physiological homeostasis and mental homeostasis. Individuals who engage in regular physical exercise report higher levels of self-esteem and lower incidences of depression and anxiety.

- Although the primary purpose of food is as a source of nutrients, many people use food as a means to fill an emotional void created by stress.

- Because of the global condition of soil depletion, even a healthy diet is considered deficient in the essential vitamins and minerals so that supplementation is encouraged.

- A malnourished diet—one that is deficient in essential amino acids, essential fats, vitamins, and minerals—is itself a stressor on the body.

- Research has shown that some foods actually induce a state of stress. Excess amounts of sugar, caffeine, salt, and foods poor in vitamins and minerals weaken the body's resistance to the stress response and may ultimately make a person more vulnerable to disease and illness.

- Not all supplements are created equal. Check to see that the processing does not destroy what it is intended to promote. Taken in excess, supplements can do more harm than good by inhibiting the proper digestion and absorption of essential nutrients.

- Food you eat can either boost or suppress the immune system.

- Food affects not only the physical body, but the mental, emotional, and spiritual aspects as well. The concept of spiritual nutrition suggests eating a wide variety of fruits, vegetables, and grains that nurture the health of the seven primary *chakras*. In addition, spiritual nutrition suggests ensuring a balance in all aspects of food, including the acid/base balance.

- Eating disorders are emotionally rather than physiologically based, ranging from bulimia and anorexia to overeating—all of which have serious consequences if not resolved.

- Change various aspects of your diet, including reducing or eliminating the consumption of caffeine, refined sugar, sodium, and fats, to reduce the risk of stress-related problems.

Box features throughout the chapters provide unique current and historic perspectives on key topics, questionnaires, and things to consider.

BOX 27.2 Insomnia and Physical Exercise

One of the benefits of exercise that has been touted by exercise physiologists for years is the fact that regular rhythmical (cardiovascular) exercise promotes quality sleep and decreases symptoms of insomnia. The very nature of physical exercise increases one's metabolic activity, thus increasing one's body-core temperature. As the body returns to homeostasis after a vigorous workout, body-core temperature drops. During sleep, the body-core temperature is at its lowest point as a result of decreased metabolic activity. Research shows that the drop in body-core temperature that occurs when bedtime is four to six hours after a vigorous workout promotes drowsiness and deeper (delta waves) sleep than in nonactive individuals.

For this reason, it is suggested *not* to engage in strenuous physical activity shortly before bedtime. According to *Power Sleep* author James Maas, the best time to schedule a workout is around the noon hour or late afternoon, with morning exercise having the least effect on sleep quality. The best type of exercise to ensure a good night's sleep is cardiovascular in nature, including vigorous walking, jogging, swimming, or biking that elevates the heart rate to one's specific target zone for the desired duration. All types of rhythmic exercise utilize the cocktail of stress hormones for their intended purposes and help the body metabolize what's not used in this process as waste products for elimination.

Student & Instructor Resources

NAVIGATE 2 ADVANTAGE ACCESS

Each new book comes complete with a dynamic online resource packed with instructor and student resources! Navigate 2 Advantage Access provides an interactive eBook, workbook activities, audio engagement with the author, meditation audio and video, as well as assessments, knowledge checks, learning analytics reporting tools, and more.

Relaxation Media and Audio Introductions

In his own words, the author, Brian Luke Seaward, introduces each of the four sections in the book. He provides a summary of each chapter in the section and explains why the information is so important to the understanding and management of stress. This is a great resource for students and instructors!

The author also includes four relaxation audio files as well as a relaxation video—perfect to listen to while studying, meditating, or simply relaxing.

The Art of Peace and Relaxation Workbook, Ninth Edition

The new edition of the workbook is now available only through our Navigate 2 product. Worksheets are included as printable and/or writable PDFs.

Lesson Plans

This edition includes 26 lesson plans and class exercises created specifically for students and participants in the author's holistic stress management certification workshop. The lesson plans have been adapted for instructors who use *Managing Stress* as a college textbook.

Interactive Lectures

The following 16 unique audio and closed-captioned visual interactive lectures contained in Navigate 2 provide a powerful, comprehensive exposure to the holistic (mind, body, spirit, and emotions) approach to stress management, including both cognitive (coping) skills, a host of relaxation techniques, and personal life skills for optimal health and well-being (also known as mind-body-spirit homeostasis). In each weekly lesson, these online lectures combine both theoretical and experiential learning through a series of exercises to give the user the life skills to promote peace, relaxation, and optimal health.

Lesson 1: Welcome to the Stress of Life

Stress knows no demographic boundaries. It affects everyone and is often called the "equal opportunity destroyer." We begin by looking at the nature of stress, various types of stress, and stressors, followed by some definitions of stress and some classic background from experts who first studied the concept of stress. This lesson then progresses to expand your comprehension beyond the Western "mechanistic" approach to a complete wellness dynamic, including the mental, emotional, physical, and spiritual aspects, known collectively as the *holistic perspective*. Combined with this content is an introduction to a very basic relaxation technique called *diaphragmatic breathing*.

Lesson 2: SOS: Message in a Bottle

Is the world in deep trouble? Perhaps! Stress may be a perception, but many external factors are coming together in an unprecedented way that influence these perceptions. This lesson looks at several social factors that can so greatly fan the flames of personal stress. We conclude with a time-tested coping skill: journal writing as a means to release stress-based emotions and gain clarity in one's thoughts.

Lesson 3: The Stress or Relaxation Barometer

To really know what effects stress has on the body, you must first understand the basics of stress physiology. This lesson takes a closer look at the physiology of stress (both short term and long term). It also explains a classic relaxation technique, progressive muscular relaxation, that can help you understand stress physiology.

Lesson 4: Headaches, Lupus, and Hemorrhoids, Oh My!

The association between stress and disease is colossal. From tension headaches to cancer, our thoughts and the associated emotions can directly affect our health. Is the physical body the first or last place that the symptoms of disease and illness manifest? This lesson explores two perspectives of the stress and disease dynamic through several models of the stress and disease phenomenon: a holistic and a mechanistic approach. By understanding the mind–body connection, you become empowered to maintain or return to homeostasis.

Lesson 5: Reprogramming the Software of the Mind

By and large, stress begins as a perception—an interpretation of some event that we perceive as a threat. As such, it is essential to understand the framework of the mind (thoughts, perceptions, attitudes, beliefs, opinions, and emotions) to manage stress effectively. By becoming familiar with various theories of psychology, one can better achieve this goal to turn the perceived threat into a nonthreat and move on with one's life.

This lesson begins with some basic fundamentals of psychology, through the eyes of stressful perceptions, and then highlights a formidable tool, cognitive restructuring (also known as *reframing*) to use in everyday life.

Lesson 6: Feeling the Stress, Feeling the Love

In simple terms, there are two stress emotions: anger (fight) and fear (flight). But nothing is simple about stress. There are actually hundreds of stress emotions, including joy and happiness (eustress). This lesson takes a closer look at the two primary stress emotions (anger and fear) as well as ways to deal creatively with each so that you control your emotions rather than having them control you. We also look at the emotions associated with good stress (eustress) followed by specific aspects of personality that can either promote stress or help buffer against it.

Lesson 7: Minding the Body, Mending the Mind

Art therapy is a formidable coping technique that serves as an emotional release (catharsis) for unresolved emotions. Through the use of various media, feelings and thoughts can be expressed in ways that verbal language simply cannot articulate, thus opening the door to resolution and inner peace. Muscle tension is the number one symptom of stress. Physical relaxation is also a powerful stress reducer. Hence, massage is accepted as a much-desired relaxation technique. This lesson also explores bodywork (massage therapy) as a relaxation medium.

Lesson 8: Health of the Human Spirit

Spiritual well-being is very much a part of health and wellness, but it is so often ignored in dealing effectively with stress. Left unaddressed, stress can choke the human spirit. For this reason (and many others), human spirituality is very much a part of stress and stress management. In fact, spirituality is considered by many to be the cornerstone of holistic stress management regarding relationships, values, and a meaningful purpose in life, aspects that are related to every stressor. This lesson invites you to take a closer look at this often-ignored wellness component by exploring many different perspectives from various luminaries around the world.

Lesson 9: Change This!

We all have ideas on how we can improve our lives by tweaking some habits that throw gasoline on the fire of stress. Luckily, there is help. This lesson takes a look at several types of behavior that can push one over the edge and, equally important, ways to examine and change behavior for the better by becoming more assertive, more confident, and embracing change for the better.

Lesson 10: Be the Calm in the Eye of the Storm

Today, everyone is bombarded with sensory overload, from Facebook updates and YouTube links to thousands of text messages. How does anyone stay grounded in these cyber winds of change? The answer is meditation: a simple way to calm the mind of perpetual sensory bombardment and information overload, not to mention common emotional issues. Meditation is not a religion! It is a simple technique for mental training, and every athlete does it. Speaking of athletes, many athletes do a form of meditation called T'ai Chi ch'uan, often called a "moving meditation" that is also a great means of relaxation.

Lesson 11: Imagination Is More Powerful Than Knowledge

It has been said that we have the means to solve our own problems (stressors). We just need to use our heads. If stress can be disempowering, creativity is considered very empowering. Creativity allows you to have options. Einstein said that imagination was more powerful than knowledge. It was the empowerment aspect of creativity he referred to. We begin to explore the creative process and then see how it can help us solve problems (both big and small). The mind not only has the power to create options, it also has the power to promote relaxation and healing through the use of mental imagery and visualization, very effective relaxation skills.

Lesson 12: Good Vibrations

The sound of laughter and the sound of music may not seem to have much in common, but they are both regarded as ways to ease stress and lighten the heart. From an energy perspective, they are both known as "good vibrations." Humor, that which can promote laughter, is one of the finest coping techniques known to humanity. Music has been recognized for millennia as a soothing relaxation technique.

Lesson 13: Coping and Relaxation Techniques, Part I

It has been said often that time and money (more likely the lack thereof) are the causes of tremendous stress. Perhaps we have all felt this way at one time or another. By understanding the psychology of money and time, one can better navigate the shoals of stress. Good communication skills are also very important for this navigation because many stressors involve interactions with others. This lesson focuses on refining several effective coping skills essential for personal homeostasis. One of the most common techniques to promote relaxation is called *progressive muscular relaxation* (PMR). An exploration of this technique rounds out this lesson.

Lesson 14: Coping and Relaxation Techniques, Part II

There are hundreds of ways to cope with stress, from hobbies to dream therapy, all of which help give insights to our problems and help us to work toward resolution. This lesson examines some additional coping techniques that are important to include in your toolkit of stress management. Combined with this is a closer look at Hatha yoga as an essential relaxation skill. Hatha yoga has gone mainstream in the United States. More specifically, it has gone corporate (which is really the antithesis of Hatha yoga). We explore the basics of yoga as it was originally taught several thousand years ago.

Lesson 15: The Power of Suggestion

The mind has an incredible power to heal (make whole). This has been recognized the world over in many types of relaxation efforts, including autogenic training, clinical biofeedback, and ecotherapy. This lesson takes a closer look at these methods that can help the mind work with the body to achieve a greater sense of relaxation and homeostasis.

Lesson 16: A Healthy Body: Back to Basics

Stress begins in the mind but quickly ends up in the body. Perhaps the most effective relaxation technique is an activity that engages the stress response, which is exactly what physical exercise does. Exercise is stress to the body, but a controlled stress. We cannot talk about exercise without addressing nutritional habits. Moreover, we really cannot talk about stress without addressing nutrition as well. For this reason we discuss several important factors to consider when incorporating exercise and nutrition in your overall stress management program.

Additional Instructor Resources

- Test Bank
- Slides in PowerPoint format
- Instructor's Manual
- Discussion Questions
- Lecture Outlines
- Lesson Plans
- Grading and Analytics Tools

Praise for *Managing Stress*

PROFESSIONALS

Hi Luke,

Thank you so much for talking to the classes yesterday. It truly is so generous of you to do this for the students. Your answers to their varied topics were perfect, even the more challenging questions such as the GMO inquiry. The students said that they really enjoyed the opportunity to talk with you. They liked that you were so accessible and down-to-earth friendly. Also, we appreciated the extra info on Lyme disease and your reassuring words about optimism.

Teri Harbour
Frederick Community College
Frederick, MD

Hi Luke,

Thank you so much for volunteering your time and speaking with my class yesterday. It was wonderful for the students to have the opportunity to digitally meet and talk with you and gain another perspective on stress management. I appreciate you sharing more information for the student's question and sharing the letter from an AU student. It's a beautiful letter that nicely shows the impact you have on students. Thanks again for the opportunity to share yourself and work with my students!

Best wishes,
Ethan Mereish, PhD
The American University
Washington, D.C.

"This book helps students to approach stress management in a livable, realistic, and creative way. It recognizes the premise that coping with stress is a 'total' experience and Seaward's approach to spirituality and stress really opened the minds and hearts of both myself and my students. As one of my students reflected: 'This class has not only taught me an extreme amount of useful information, but learning effective ways to deal with it, coupled with the daily practice of relaxation techniques and journal writing skills, will encourage me to continue these practices after class ends.' Personally, this book has helped me refocus on taking time to practice the skills I teach and how these skills must be a part of my daily life."

— **Jacqueline R. Benedik, MS, CHES, Health Educator**

"Dr. Seaward's book is the best resource I have found for teaching a holistic approach to coping with stress. Whether I concentrate on one hour of cognitive restructuring for unemployed professionals, one day of stress and spirituality for nurses, or a semester course for university students, it provides the material I need. It's reader friendly, rich in references, and full of humor!"

— **Paula LeVeck, RN, PhD**

"Stress is at the heart of most all diseases that society faces today. Brian Luke Seaward's book goes right to the root causes of stress and communicates cutting-edge material. My hope is that more people will put this information to practice by tapping into their inner strength so that we can combat the disease crisis, including obesity, cancer, and coronary heart disease."

— **Kelly Stobbe, MEd, Wellness Councils of America, Director of Council Affairs**

"*Managing Stress* is the perfect textbook for my graduate course in stress management for advanced practice nurses. It blends beautifully the research, clinical, and educational components of each topic—a rare find! It is sophisticated enough for advanced students, yet accessible to first-time readers on this subject."

— **Valerie Yancey, PhD, St. Louis, MO**

"*Managing Stress* is a unique textbook in that it serves as an essential guide to the exploration of the interaction of the mind, body, and spirit. Dr. Seaward brings us an extensive, current, and well-researched review of approaches to stress management in a clear and uncomplicated style. This book, with its seamless blend of theory, skill building, and coping techniques, is a gift to us all."

— **Elaine Matheson Weiner, RN, MPH, CHES, Manhattan Beach, CA**

"Brian Luke Seaward's book, *Managing Stress: Principles and Strategies for Health and Well-Being*, is the most comprehensive text on stress management I've used for teaching. What makes this book so exceptional is the weaving of science, spirit, and individual stories into an organized, holistic format conducive to personal and professional learning. I would recommend this text for any educator interested in providing the most current research on a growing field that is having such an impact on the lives of individuals yearning to find balance in their lives."

— **Jamie Damico, RN, MSN, CNS, Colorado Springs, CO**

"I highly recommend Luke's text to any college professor who teaches stress management. It is a comprehensive and holistic approach to stress management in that one fully walks away with a clear and in-depth understanding of the wide variety of causes and effects, as well as the many wonderful adoptable options for managing stress. I have reviewed many stress-management books, and I have found this book to be unequivocally the best one."

— **Susan Kennen, Professor, Health Education, Poughkeepsie, NY**

"From humor to heart disease, history to holistic, physical exercise to prayer, *Managing Stress* covers all aspects of this worldwide epidemic. With its smorgasbord of techniques to manage stress, it's the perfect book on how to improve quality of life and increase joy, vitality, and inner calm. It's informative, fun, and best of all, it inspired this reader into action. It is a must-read for anyone interested in living a healthier, happier life."

— **Conee Spano, Health Educator, Las Vegas, NV**

STUDENTS

"The information I have learned from this book is definitely something I will remember and use the rest of my life. I found the exercises on breathing, yoga, and aromatherapy most beneficial."

— **Christine S., University of Northern Colorado**

"The chapter on time management was the best. Before this class I was extremely good at wasting time. Now I realize that time is an important resource that I need to make the most of. I do this by keeping a daytimer, prioritizing, and cutting out a lot of television. Thanks!"

— **Jason A., Indiana University**

"Just from reading the first chapter, I knew this was a book I wasn't going to sell back at the end of the semester. This book has been my saving grace. Thanks!!!"

— **Bill G., Richland College, Dallas, TX**

"The most valuable thing I got out of the whole book was dealing with my anger. I never knew I was holding it in. I now know how to let it go and not let my feelings ruin my life. The chapters on music therapy and breathing were excellent."

— **Melanie B., University of Northern Colorado**

"By far the most significant aspect of this book was the chapter on human spirituality. Even though I had heard most of the information before, it has never been presented to me in such a broad yet concise manner. It refreshed my desire to continue to grow spiritually."

— **Ivette B., University of New Mexico**

"I had no idea how beneficial keeping a journal is to help ease the tension that occurs in everyday life."

— **Emily B., University of Vermont**

"It is a great comfort to know there is more than one way to deal with stress. Many times in college, I have found myself very stressed out and in need of relief. I now have many techniques to promote a less stressful lifestyle."

— **Aspen V., University of Maryland**

"Like most textbooks, I thought this one was going to be boring. Boy, was I wrong! I learned a great deal about my body, my mind, and my spirit. As an athlete, I now have skills for a lifetime. The chapter on humor therapy was the best! Keep those jokes coming."

— **Will C., University of Utah**

Introduction

During the Renaissance, a philosophy shaping the direction of medicine in the Western world started taking hold. This philosophy, promulgated by René Descartes (1596–1650), stated that the mind and body are separate entities and therefore should be examined and treated differently. This dichotomy of mind and body advanced the understanding of the true human condition. Albert Einstein's revolutionary unified field theory, which at the time was regarded as ludicrous, began to lead Western science back to the ancient premise that all points (energy and matter) connect, each significantly affecting all others, of which the human entity (mental, emotional, physical, and spiritual components) is very much a part.

Only recently has modern science taken steps to unite what Descartes separated over 360 years ago. The unity of the body, mind, and spirit is quite complex, especially as it relates to stress management. But one simple truth is emerging from the research of the late twentieth century: The physical, mental, emotional, and spiritual aspects of the human condition are all intimately connected. Mental imagery, entrainment theory, *pranayama*, divinity theory, split-brain research, Jungian psychology, and beta-endorphins all approach the same unity, each from a different vantage point, and each supporting the ancient axiom that "all points connect."

Stress is a hot topic in American culture today. Its popularity stems from the need to get a handle on this condition—to deal with stress effectively enough so as to lead a "normal" and happy life. But dealing with stress is a process, not an outcome. Many people's attitudes, influenced by their rushed lifestyles and expectations of immediate gratification, reflect the need to eradicate stress rather than to manage, reduce, or control their perceptions of it. As a result, stress never really goes away; it just reappears with a new face. The results can and do cause harm, including bodily damage. Studies now indicate that between 70 and 80 percent of all disease is strongly related to, if not directly associated with, stress. So-called lifestyle diseases, such as cancer and coronary heart disease, are leading causes of death; both seem to have direct links to the stress response. Healthcare reform having become a major national issue, the ability of and the need for individuals to accept responsibility for their own health is increasing. But knowledge of the concepts of stress management alone is not enough. Continual application of this knowledge through both self-awareness and the practice of effective coping skills and relaxation techniques is essential for total well-being.

Thus, this book was written to acquaint you with the fundamental theories and applications of the mind–body–spirit phenomenon. More specifically, it offers more than sixteen coping strategies you can use as tools to deal more effectively with the causes of your stress, and twelve relaxation techniques to help you reduce or eliminate potential or actual symptoms associated with the stress response. It is my intention that collectively they may help you to reach and maintain your optimal level of physical, mental, emotional, and spiritual well-being in the years to come. For this reason, I would like to suggest that you revisit the book again and again as time goes by. What may appear today to be "some theory" to memorize for a final exam could one day take on great relevance in your life.

PART ONE

The Nature of Stress

Life is either a daring adventure or nothing at all.

– Helen Keller

CHAPTER 1

The Nature of Stress

I cannot and should not be cured of my stress, but merely taught to enjoy it.

—Hans Selye

Are you stressed? If the answer is yes, then consider yourself to be in good company. Several recent Harris and Gallup polls have noted an alarming trend in the psyche of the American public and beyond—to nearly all citizens of the global village. Across the board, without exception, people admit to having an increasing sense of anxiety, frustration, unease, and discontent in nearly every aspect of their lives. From the lingering effects of the Great Recession and subsequent job market challenges to fracking issues, genetically modified food allergies, increases in autism, overpopulation, climate change weather incidents (e.g., Hurricane Sandy and severe droughts), world banking issues, and gun violence and terrorist attacks (from Sandy Hook Elementary to the Boston Marathon), the symptoms of global **stress** can be found everywhere. Ironically, in a country where the standard of living is considered to be one of the highest anywhere in the world, the Centers for Disease Control and Prevention estimates that nearly one-quarter of the American population is reported to be on antidepressants, and current estimates suggest that one in three people suffers from a chronic disease, ranging from cancer and coronary heart disease to rheumatoid arthritis, diabetes, and lupus. Something is very wrong with this picture!

Furthermore, since the start of the Great Recession, a blanket of fear and anger has covered much of the country, if not the world, keeping people in a perpetual state of frustration and anxiety. Global problems only seem to intensify our personal stressors. It doesn't make a difference if you're a college student or a CEO of a multinational corporation, where you live, or how much money is in your checking account; stress is the equal opportunity destroyer! But it doesn't have to be this way. Even as personal issues collide with social and planetary problems, creating a "perfect storm" of stress, we all have choices—in both our attitude and behaviors. This text will help you connect the dots between mind, body, and spirit to create positive choices that empower you to navigate your life through the turbulent waters of the human journey in the twenty-first century.

Times of Change and Uncertainty

Today, the words *stress* and *change* have become synonymous and the winds of change are in the air. Changes in the economy, technology, communications, information

Stress: The experience of a perceived threat (real or imagined) to one's mental, physical, or spiritual well-being, resulting from a series of physiological responses and adaptations.

retrieval, health care, and dramatic changes in the weather are just some of the gale forces blowing in our collective faces. By and large, the average person doesn't like change because change tends to disrupt one's comfort zones. It appears that the "known," no matter how bad, feels like a safer bet than the unknown. Change, it should be noted (particularly change one cannot control), has always been part of the human landscape. However, today the rate of change has become so fast and furious, without an adequate reference point to anchor oneself, that stress holds the potential to create a perpetual sense of uneasiness in the hearts and minds of nearly everyone. Yet it doesn't have to be this way. Where there is change, there is opportunity. Where there is opportunity, there is comfort.

At one time, getting married, changing jobs, buying a house, raising children, going back to school, dealing with the death of a friend or close relative, and suffering from a chronic illness were all considered to be major life events that might shake the foundations of anyone's life. Although these major life events can and do play a significant role in personal upheaval, a new crop of social stressors has added to the critical mass of an already volatile existence, throwing things further out of balance. Consider how these factors directly influence your life: the rapid acceleration of technology (from software upgrades to Internet downloads), the use of (if not addiction to) the World Wide Web (e.g., Facebook), the proliferation of smartphones and Wi-Fi use, an accessible 24/7 society, global economic woes (e.g., unemployment, food prices), global terrorism, carbon footprints, and public health issues (e.g., the latest epidemic of bedbugs or Zika virus). Times of change and uncertainty tend to magnify our personal stress. Perhaps the biggest looming concern facing people today is the issue of personal boundaries or the lack thereof. The advances of high technology combined with a rapidly changing social structure have eroded personal boundaries. These boundaries include, but are not limited to, home and work, finances, nutritional habits, relationships, and many, many more, all of which add to the critical mass of one's personal stress. Even the ongoing war on terrorism appears to have no boundaries! Ironically, the lack of boundaries combined with factors that promote a fractured society, where people feel a lack of community and belonging, leads to a greater sense of isolation, which also intensifies our personal stress levels. Believe it or not, life wasn't always like this.

The stress phenomenon, as it is referred to today, is quite new with regard to the history of humanity. Barely a household expression when your parents were your age,

use of the word *stress* is now as common as the terms *global warming* and *smartphone apps*. In fact, however, stress in terms of physical arousal can be traced back to the Stone Age as a "survival mechanism." But what was once designed as a means of survival is now associated with the development of disease and illness that claims the lives of millions of people worldwide. The American Institute of Stress (www.stress.org) cites the following statistics:

- 43 percent of all adults suffer adverse health effects due to stress.

- 80 percent of all visits to primary care physicians are for stress-related complaints or disorders.

Stress has been linked to all the leading causes of death, including heart disease, cancer, lung ailments, accidents, cirrhosis, and suicide. Some health experts now speculate that perhaps as much as 70 to 85 percent of all diseases and illnesses are stress-related.

Government figures compiled by the National Center for Health Statistics in 2010 provide a host of indicators suggesting that human stress is indeed a health factor to be reckoned with. Prior to 1955, the leading causes of death were the sudden onset of illness by infectious diseases (e.g., polio, rubella, tuberculosis, typhoid, and encephalitis) that, in most cases, have since been eradicated or brought under control by vaccines and medications. The post–World War II era ushered in the age of high technology, which considerably altered the lifestyles of nearly all peoples of every industrialized nation. The start of the twenty-first century has seen the influence of high technology dramatically alter our lifestyles. Consumer products, such as the washer, dryer, microwave oven, television, DVD player, laptop computer, and even cell phones, were cited as luxuries to add more leisure time to the workweek. But as mass production of high-technology items increased, so too did the competitive drive to increase human effort and productivity, which in turn actually decreased leisure time, and thus created a plethora of unhealthy lifestyles, most notably obesity.

Currently, the leading causes of death are dominated by what are referred to as "lifestyle diseases," those diseases whose pathology develops over a period of several years, and perhaps even decades (**FIG. 1.1**). Whereas infectious diseases are treatable by medication, lifestyle diseases are, for the most part, preventable or correctable by altering the habits and behaviors that contribute to their etiology. Previously, it was suggested that an association existed between stress and disease. Substantial research, however, suggests that there may, indeed, be a causal factor involved

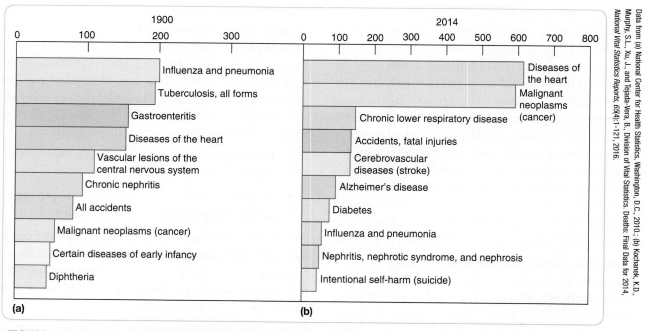

Data from (a) National Center for Health Statistics, Washington, D.C., 2010.; (b) Kochanek, K.D., Murphy, S.L., Xu, J., and Tejada-Vera, B., Division of Vital Statistics. Deaths: Final Data for 2014, *National Vital Statistics Reports, 65*(4):1-121, 2016.

FIGURE 1.1 Death rates for the ten leading causes of death per 100,000 population in the United States in (a) 1900 and (b) 2014.

with several types of diseases, particularly autoimmune diseases (Segerstrom and Miller, 2004). Regardless, it is well understood that the influence of stress weakens the body's physiological systems, thereby rapidly advancing the disease process. The most notorious lifestyle disease, coronary heart disease (CHD), continues to be one of the leading causes of death in the United States, far exceeding all other causes. The American Heart Association states that one person dies from heart disease every minute. Although the incidence of CHD has decreased over the past decade, cancer—in all its many types—continues to climb the statistical charts as the second leading cause of death. According to 2013 statistics from the American Cancer Society (www.cancer.org), cancer claims the lives of one out of every four people in the United States. Alarming increases in suicides, child and spouse abuse, self-injury, homicides, alcoholism, and drug addiction are only additional symptoms of a nation under stress. Today, research shows that many people maintain poor coping skills in the face of the personal, social, and even global changes occurring over the course of their lives.

Originally, the word *stress* was a term used in physics, primarily to describe enough tension or force placed on an object to bend or break it. Relaxation, on the other hand, was defined as any nonwork activity done during the evenings or on Sunday afternoons when all the stores were closed. On rare occasions, if one could afford it, relaxation meant a vacation or holiday at some faraway place. Conceptually, relaxation was a value, influenced by several religions and represented as a day of rest. The word *stress* as applied to the human condition was first made popular by noted physiologist Hans Selye in his book *The Stress of Life,* in which he described his research: to understand the physiological responses to chronic stress and its relationship to disease (dis-ease). Today, the word *stress* is frequently used to describe the level of tension people feel is placed on their minds and souls by the demands of their jobs, relationships, and responsibilities in their personal lives. Oddly, for some, stress seems to be a status symbol tied to self-esteem. Relaxation, meanwhile, has been transformed from an American value into a luxury many people find they just don't have enough time for. Despite the current economic crisis, some interesting insights have been observed regarding work and leisure. The average workweek has expanded from 40 to 60 hours. The U.S. Department of Labor and Statistics reports that with more service-related jobs being created, more overtime is needed to meet the demands of the customers. Not only do more people spend more time at work, they spend more time driving to and from work (which is not considered work time). Moreover, leisure time at home is often related to work activities, resulting in less time for rest and relaxation. Downtime is also compromised. Since

© Inspiration Unlimited. Used with permission.

FIGURE 1.2 With rapid economic, ecological, and technological changes, the global village appears to have become a more stressful place, which is all the more reason to learn and practice effective stress-management techniques to maintain a sense of balance in one's life despite these winds of change.

2001, Expedia has conducted an annual survey on vacations (called the Vacation Deprivation survey). The 2012 results revealed that one out of every three Americans doesn't use all of his or her vacation time. One in five respondents cited work responsibilities/pressure as the primary reason for canceling a vacation. A new word entered the American lexicon in the summer of 2010—the "staycation," in which people simply stayed home for vacation due to financial or work constraints. Those who do head for the mountains or beaches for vacation often take their work (in the form of smartphones and laptops) with them—in essence, never really leaving their job. It's no surprise that staying plugged in doesn't give the mind a chance to unwind or the body a chance to relax. By comparison with other countries, Americans take less vacation time than other global citizens (Germans, on average, take 4 to 6 weeks per year). "The stress associated with the current economy makes the need for time away from work even more important than ever, and it's unfortunate that one-third of Americans won't use all of their vacation days this year," said Tim MacDonald, general manager of Expedia.com. The "dividend" of high technology has proven to be an illusion for many that has resulted in a stressed lifestyle, which in turn creates a significant health deficit (**FIG. 1.2**).

Definitions of Stress

In contemporary times, the word *stress* has many connotations and definitions based on various perspectives of the human condition. In Eastern philosophies, stress is considered to be an absence of inner peace. In Western culture, stress can be described as a loss of emotional control. Noted healer Serge Kahili King has defined stress as any change experienced by the individual. This definition may be rather general, but it is quite correct. Psychologically speaking, stress, as defined by noted researcher Richard Lazarus, is a state of anxiety produced when events and responsibilities exceed one's coping abilities. Physiologically speaking, stress is defined as the rate of wear and tear on the body. Selye added to his definition that stress is the nonspecific response of the body to any demand placed upon it to adapt, whether that demand produces pleasure or pain. Selye observed that whether a situation was perceived as good (e.g., a job promotion) or bad (e.g., the loss of a job), the physiological response or arousal was very similar. The body, according to Selye, doesn't know the difference between good and bad stress.

However, with new psychoneuroimmunological data available showing that there are indeed some physiological differences between good and bad stress (e.g., the release of different neuropeptides), specialists in the field of **holistic medicine** have expanded Lazarus's and Selye's definitions as follows: Stress is the inability to cope with a perceived (real or imagined) threat to one's mental, physical, emotional, and spiritual well-being, which results in a series of physiological responses and adaptations (Chopra, 2000; Dossey, 2004). The important word to emphasize here is *perceived* (the interpretation), for what might seem to be a threat to one person may not even merit a second thought to another individual. For example, not long ago a raffle was held, with the winning prize being an all-expenses-paid one-week trip for two to a beach resort in Bermuda. Kelly, who won the prize, was ecstatic and already had her bags packed. Her husband, John, was mortified because he hated to fly and he couldn't swim. In his mind, this would not be a fun time. In fact, he really wished they hadn't won. Each perceived the same situation in two entirely different ways. Moreover, with the wisdom of hindsight, our perceptions often change. Many episodes that at the time seemed catastrophic later appear insignificant, as humorously stated by Mark Twain when he commented, "I'm an old man and I have known

> **Holistic medicine:** A healing approach that honors the integration, balance, and harmony of mind, body, spirit, and emotions to promote inner peace. Every technique used in stress management is considered to support the concept of holistic medicine.

a great many troubles, but most of them never happened." The holistic definition of stress points out that it is a very complex phenomenon affecting the whole person, not just the physical body, and that it involves a host of factors, some of which may not yet even be recognized by scholars and researchers. As more research is completed, it becomes increasingly evident that the responses to stress add up to more than just physical arousal; yet it is ultimately the body that remains the battlefield for the war games of the mind.

The Stress Response

In 1914, Harvard physiologist **Walter Cannon** first coined the term **fight-or-flight response** to describe the dynamics involved in the body's physiological arousal to survive a threat. In a series of animal studies, Cannon noted that the body prepares itself for one of two modes of immediate action: to attack or fight and defend oneself from the pursuing threat, or to run and escape the ensuing danger. What Cannon observed was the body's reaction to acute stress, what is now commonly called the **stress reaction**. Additional observations suggested that the fight response was triggered by anger or aggression and was usually employed to defend territorial boundaries or attack aggressors equal to or smaller in size. The fight response required physiological preparations that would recruit power and strength for a short duration, or what is now described as short but intense anaerobic work. Conversely, the flight response, he thought, was induced by fear. It was designed to fuel the body to endure prolonged movement such as running away from lions and bears. In many cases, however, it included not only fleeing, but also hiding or withdrawal. (A variation on the flight response is the **freeze response**, often noted with post-traumatic stress disorder, where a person simply freezes, like a deer staring into a car's headlights.) The human body, in all its metabolic splendor, actually prepares itself to do both (fight and flight) at the same time. In terms of evolution, it appears that this dynamic was so advantageous to survival that it developed in nearly all mammalian species, including us. (Some experts now suggest, however, that our bodies have not adapted to the stress-induced lifestyles of the twenty-first century.)

In simple terms, there are four stages of the fight-or-flight response:

Stage 1: Stimuli from one or more of the five senses are sent to the brain (e.g., a scream, the smell of fire, the taste of poison, a passing truck in *your* lane).

Stage 2: The brain deciphers the stimulus as either a threat or a nonthreat. If the stimulus is not regarded as a threat, this is the end of the response (e.g., the scream came from the television). If, however, the response is decoded as a real threat, the brain then activates the nervous and endocrine systems to quickly prepare for defense and/or escape.

Stage 3: The body stays activated, aroused, or "keyed-up" until the threat is over.

Stage 4: The body returns to **homeostasis**, a state of physiological calmness, once the threat is gone.

It is hypothesized that the fight-or-flight response developed primarily against threats of a physical nature, those that jeopardized the survival of the individual. Although clear physical threats still exist in today's culture, including possible terrorism, they are nowhere near as prevalent as those threats perceived by the mind and, more specifically, the ego. In a theory put forward by a disciple of Selye's, Simeons (1961), and repeated by Sapolsky (2009), it is suggested that, in effect, the fight-or-flight response is an antiquated mechanism that has not kept evolutionary pace with the development of the human mind. Consequently, the **stress response** becomes activated in all types of threats (mental, emotional, and spiritual), not just physical intimidations. The physiological repercussions can, and do, prove fatal. The body enters a state of physical readiness when you are about to receive your final exam grades or walk into an important meeting late, just as it does when you sense someone is following you

> **Walter Cannon:** Twentieth-century Harvard physiologist who coined the term "fight or flight."
>
> **Fight-or-flight response:** A term coined by Walter Cannon; the instinctive physiological responses preparing the body, when confronted with a threat, to either fight or flee; an evolutionary survival dynamic.
>
> **Stress reaction:** The body's initial (central nervous system) reaction to a perceived threat.
>
> **Freeze response:** Part of the stress response, where the individual neither fights nor flees but freezes like a deer caught in the headlights, paralyzed as if the person has forgotten to run.
>
> **Homeostasis:** A physiological state of complete calmness or rest; markers include resting heart rate, blood pressure, and ventilation.
>
> **Stress response:** The release of epinephrine and nor-epinephrine to prepare various organs and tissues for fight or flight.

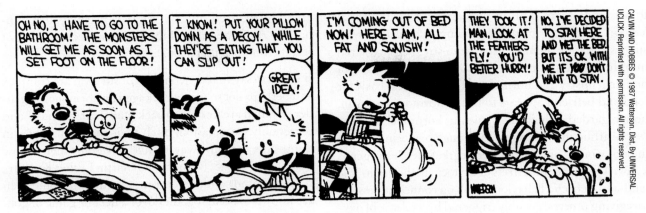

FIGURE 1.3   Some of our worst stressors are fabricated in our minds.

late at night in an unlit parking lot. Moreover, this same stress response kicks in, to the same degree and intensity, even when the threat is wholly imaginary, in reaction to everything from monsters hiding under your bed when you were 4 (**FIG. 1.3**), to the unsubstantiated idea that your boss doesn't like you anymore and is out to get you.

Cannon noted the activation of several physiological mechanisms in this fight-or-flight response, affecting nearly every physiological system in the body, for the preparation of movement and energy production. These are just a few of the reactions:

1. Increased heart rate to pump oxygenated blood to working muscles

2. Increased blood pressure to deliver blood to working muscles

3. Increased ventilation to supply working muscles with oxygen for energy metabolism

4. Vasodilation of arteries to the body's periphery (arms and legs) with the greatest muscle mass

5. Increased serum glucose for metabolic processes during muscle contractions

6. Increased free fatty acid mobilization as an energy source for prolonged activity (e.g., running)

7. Increased blood coagulation and decreased clotting time in the event of bleeding

8. Increased muscular strength

9. Decreased gastric movement and abdominal blood flow to allow blood to go to working muscles

10. Increased perspiration to cool body-core temperature

Unfortunately, the metabolic and physiological changes that are deemed essential for human movement in the event of attack, pursuit, or challenge are quite *ineffective* when dealing with events or situations that threaten the ego, such as receiving a parking ticket or standing in a long line at the grocery store, yet the body responds identically to all types of perceived threats.

Tend and Befriend

Do women respond differently to stress than men? The answer may seem obvious.

Generally speaking, men are prone to act more hostile while women have a proclivity to be more nurturing. Yet until recently every source on stress addressed the fight-or-flight response as if it were the only human default response. It was the work of Shelley Taylor and colleagues who filled in the missing piece with regard to the female response to stress. Curious about why only men were studied to formulate the basis for the fight-or-flight response, Taylor hypothesized that the stress response needed to be reexamined, this time including astute observations of the female gender. In 2000, Taylor and colleagues proposed a new theory for the female stress response that they termed **tend and befriend**. Although both men and women have a built-in dynamic for the survival of physical danger, women also have an inherent nurturing response for their offspring as well as a means

Tend and befriend: A theory presented by Shelley Taylor that states that women who experience stress don't necessarily run or fight, but rather turn to friends to cope with unpleasant events and circumstances.

to befriend others. This in turn creates a strong social support system, an invaluable coping technique. Taylor suggests that the female response to stress is hardwired into the DNA and revealed through a combination of brain chemistry and hormones. The biological basis for tend and befriend appears to be the hormone oxytocin, now regarded as both the "trusting hormone" and the "social affiliation" hormone. Although oxytocin is found in both women and (to a lesser degree) men, estrogen is known to enhance the effects of oxytocin in the brain. The tend-and-befriend behavior is built on connectedness—a caregiving process, possibly triggered by a release of oxytocin in conjunction with female reproductive hormones, that may actually override the flood of stress hormones so pronounced in women's male counterparts. Generational social factors may support the tend-and-befriend behavior pattern as well (**FIG. 1.4**).

Not only do men and women have differences in their stress physiology, but there appears to be gender-specific behaviors for discussing and solving problems as well. Whereas men tend to think their way through by looking for solutions to problems, women like to talk about problems. Women bond quickly by sharing confidences. However, although talking may be beneficial, researchers note that merely talking about stressors tends to perpetuate rather than solve one's stressors. Researchers refer to stress-based conversations as **co-rumination**. Although talking may strengthen female friendships, it is also known to increase anxiety and depression if solutions aren't introduced quickly. Experts warn against "unhealthy rumination" and the emotional contagion that results from it (Stepp, 2007).

It is fair to say that the concepts of survival are complex and perhaps not so neatly packaged by hormones or gender. Women are known to back-stab their "friends" and regrettably, on occasion, ditch their newborn babies in dumpsters and run away. Conversely, some men choose peace over violence (Gandhi and Martin Luther King, Jr., come to mind) and, when times get tough, some men are known to bond together over a beer or game of golf.

Types of Stress

To the disbelief of some, not all stress is bad for you. In fact, there are many who believe that humans need some degree of stress to stay healthy. The human body craves homeostasis, or physiological calm, yet it also requires physiological arousal to ensure the optimal functioning of several organs, including the heart and musculoskeletal system. How can stress be good? When stress serves as a positive motivation, it is considered beneficial. Beyond this optimal point, stress of any kind does more harm than good.

Actually, there are three kinds of stress: **eustress, neustress**, and **distress**. Eustress is good stress and arises in any situation or circumstance that a person finds motivating or inspiring. Falling in love might be an example of eustress; meeting a movie star or professional athlete may also be a type of eustress. Usually, situations that are classified as eustress are enjoyable and for this reason are not considered to be a threat. Neustress describes sensory stimuli that have no consequential effect; it is considered

© Liquidlibrary.

FIGURE 1.4 Fight or flight isn't the only response to stress. To cope with personal problems, women often feel the need to socialize and bond together in what is now known as the "tend and befriend" response.

Co-rumination: Stress-based conversations between women as a means of coping by finding support among friends.

Eustress: Good stress; any stressor that motivates an individual toward an optimal level of performance or health.

Neustress: Any kind of information or sensory stimulus that is perceived as unimportant or inconsequential.

Distress: The unfavorable or negative interpretation of an event (real or imagined) to be threatening that promotes continued feelings of fear or anger; more commonly known simply as stress.

neither good nor bad. News of an earthquake in a remote corner of the world might fall into this category. The third type of stress, distress, is considered bad and often is abbreviated simply as *stress*. There are two kinds of distress: **acute stress**, or that which surfaces, is quite intense, and disappears quickly; and **chronic stress**, or that which may not appear quite so intense, yet seems to linger for prolonged periods of time (e.g., hours, days, weeks, or months). An example of acute stress is the following. You are casually driving down the highway, the wind from the open sunroof is blowing through your hair, and you feel pretty good about life. With a quick glance in your rearview mirror you see flashing blue lights. Yikes! So you slow down and pull over. The police car pulls up behind you. Your heart is racing, your voice becomes scratchy, and your palms are sweating as you try to retrieve license and registration from your wallet while rolling your window down at the same time. When the officer asks you why you were speeding you can barely speak; your voice is three octaves higher than usual. After the officer runs a check on your car and license, he only gives you a warning for speeding. Whew! He gets back in his car and leaves. You give him time to get out of sight, start your engine, and signal to get back onto the highway. Within minutes your heart is calm, your palms dry, and you start singing to the song on the radio. The threat is over. The intensity of the acute stress may seem cataclysmic, but it is very short-lived.

Chronic stressors, on the other hand, are not as intense but their duration is unbearably long. Examples might include the following: being stuck for a whole semester with "the roommate from hell," a credit card bill that only seems to grow despite monthly payments, a boss who makes your job seem worse than that of a galley slave, living in a city you cannot tolerate, or maintaining a relationship with a girlfriend, boyfriend, husband, or wife that seems bad to stay in but worse to leave. For this reason, chronic stressors are thought to be the real villains. According to the American Institute of Stress (AIS), it is this type of stress that is associated with disease because the body is perpetually aroused for danger.

A concept called the **Yerkes-Dodson principle**, which is applied to athletic performance, lends itself quite nicely to explaining the relationship between eustress, distress, and health. As can be seen in **FIG. 1.5**, when stress increases, moving from eustress to distress, performance or health decreases and there is greater risk of disease and illness. The optimal stress level is the midpoint, *prior* to where eustress turns into distress.

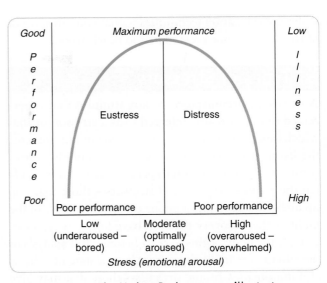

FIGURE 1.5   The Yerkes-Dodson curve illustrates that, to a point, stress or arousal can actually increase performance. Stress to the left of the midpoint is considered to be eustress. Stress beyond the midpoint, however, is believed to detract from performance and/or health status and is therefore labeled distress.

Studies indicate that stress-related hormones in optimal doses actually improve physical performance and mental-processing skills like concentration, making you more alert. Beyond that optimal level, though, all aspects of performance begin to decrease in efficiency. Physiologically speaking, your health is at serious risk. It would be simple if this optimal level was the same for all people, but it's not. Hence, the focus of any effective stress-management program is twofold: (1) to find out where this optimal level of stress is for you so that it can be used to your advantage rather than becoming a detriment to your health status, and (2) to reduce physical arousal levels using both coping

Acute stress: Stress that is intense in nature but short in duration.

Chronic stress: Stress that is not as intense as acute stress but that lingers for a prolonged period of time (e.g., financial problems).

Yerkes-Dodson principle: The theory that some stress (eustress) is necessary for health and performance but that beyond an optimal amount both will deteriorate as stress increases.

skills and relaxation techniques so that you can stay out of the danger zone created by too much stress.

Types of Stressors

A situation, circumstance, or any stimulus that is perceived to be a threat is referred to as a **stressor**, or that which causes or promotes stress. As you might imagine, the list of stressors is not only endless, but also varies considerably from person to person. Acute stress is often the result of rapid-onset stressors—those that pop up unexpectedly—like a phone call in the middle of the night or the discovery that you have lost your car keys. Usually the body begins to react before a full analysis of the situation is made, but a return to a state of calm is also imminent. Chronic stressors—those that may give some advance warning yet manage to cause physical arousal anyway, often merit more attention because their prolonged influence on the body appears to be more significant. Much research has been conducted to determine the nature of stressors, and they are currently divided into three categories: bioecological, psychointrapersonal, and social (Giradano, Everly, and Dusek, 2012).

Bioecological Influences

There are several biological and ecological factors that may trigger the stress response in varying degrees, some of which are outside our awareness. These are external influences, including sunlight, gravitational pull, solar flares, and electromagnetic fields, that affect our biological rhythms. From the field of chronobiology we learn that these factors affect three categories of biological rhythms: (1) **circadian rhythms**, fluctuations in physiological functions over the course of a 24-hour period (e.g., body temperature); (2) **ultradian rhythms**, fluctuations that occur over less than a 24-hour period (such as stomach contractions and cell divisions); and (3) **infradian rhythms**, changes that occur in periods longer than 24 hours (e.g., the menses). These biological changes are influenced by such natural phenomena as Earth's orbit and axis rotation, which give us periods of light and darkness as well as seasonal differences (**FIG. 1.6**). A prime example of a bioecological influence is **seasonal affective disorder (SAD)**, a condition affecting many people who live at or near the Arctic Circle. Many of these people become depressed when they are deprived of sunlight for prolonged periods of time. But technological changes are also included in this category, an example being jet lag as a result of airplane travel through several time zones. Electrical pollution, environmental toxins,

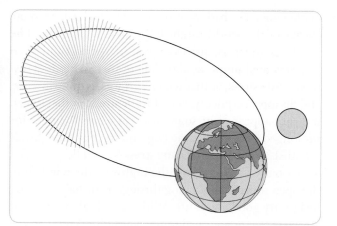

FIGURE 1.6   Because of the tilt of Earth's axis as it moves in its orbit around the sun, areas closest to the poles vary the most in the amount of daily sunlight they receive. Studies show that an inadequate amount of full-spectrum light is associated with depression, a phenomenon now known as seasonal affective disorder (SAD) or arctic winter madness.

solar radiation, and noise pollution are other potential bioecological influences. Genetically modified organisms (GMOs), petrochemicals, synthetic chemicals, and some types of nanotechnology are considered new bioecological threats. In addition, some synthetic food additives may trigger the release of various stress hormones throughout the body. Note that there is a growing opinion among some health practitioners that increased stress levels in the

Stressor: Any real or imagined situation, circumstance, or stimulus that is perceived to be a threat.

Circadian rhythms: Biological rhythms that occur or cycle within a 24-hour period (e.g., body temperature) that create the body's internal clock, also known as chronobiology. These can be affected by stress, causing a disruption that is even more stressful to the body.

Ultradian rhythms: Biological rhythms that occur many times in a 24-hour period (e.g., hunger pangs). These can be affected by stress.

Infradian rhythms: Biological rhythms that occur in periods longer than 24 hours (e.g., women's menstrual period). These can be affected by stress.

Seasonal affective disorder (SAD): The physiological response to lack of sunlight that results in feelings of depression.

twenty-first century may be a direct result of our being out of touch with the *natural* elements that so strongly influence our body's physiological systems. In any case, some of these bioecological factors can be positively influenced by lifestyle changes, including dietary habits, exercise, and the regular practice of relaxation techniques, which bring a sense of balance back into our lives.

Psychointrapersonal Influences

Our current understanding is that psychointrapersonal influences make up the greatest percentage of stressors. These are the perceptions of stimuli that we create through our own mental processes (perceptions and interpretations). Psychointrapersonal stressors involve those thoughts, values, beliefs, attitudes, opinions, and perceptions that we use to defend our identity or ego. When any of these is challenged, violated, or even changed, the ego is often threatened and the stress response is the outcome. Psychointrapersonal stressors reflect the unique constructs of our personality, and in the words of stress researcher Kenneth Pelletier, represent "the chasm between the perceived self and the ideal self-image." Because these influences are the most likely to cause stress, they are a major focus of this text. It is imperative to intercept the stress response in the mind before it cascades down as a rush of stress hormones into the body to cause potential damage.

Social Influences

Social influences have long been the subject of research to explain the plight of individuals who are unable to cope with their given environment. Most notable is the issue of overcrowding and urban sprawl. Classic studies conducted on several species have shown that when their numbers exceed the territorial boundary of each animal, despite an abundance of food and water, several seemingly healthy animals die off (Allen, 1983). This need for personal space appears to be universal in the animal kingdom. This includes humans, who likewise begin to show signs of frustration in crowded urban areas, traffic jams, long lines at checkout stands, or whenever their personal space is "invaded." The origin of this particular social influence may be instinctual in nature. Additional social causes of stress include financial insecurity, the effects of relocation, cultural assimilation issues, some technological advances, violation of human rights, and low socioeconomic status, to name but a few. New to the list of social influences are global warming concerns and water resource issues as the global population increases, taxing our very lifestyles with regard to scarcity issues.

Social Stress in America: A Twenty-first Century Look

The social influences linked to stress have been studied for decades, most notably by Holmes and Raye with the Social Readjustment Rating Scale (SRRS) and the concept of life-change units (LCUs). It was their work over 50 years ago that first highlighted the list of top life stressors, including the death of a spouse, the loss of a job, the death of a child, divorce, and high mortgage payments (even then). Although these types of stressors persist, the pace of society has moved to warp speed. With this rapid pace of change, additional stressors have reconfigured the proverbial list of stressors, as well as confirmed the deleterious impact of stress on one's health.

Comprehensive studies conducted by the American Psychological Association (APA) and the Harvard School of Public Health in 2014 and 2015 identified a host of stress indicators, suggesting that stress is indeed a health factor to be reckoned with. For the past 10 years, the APA has conducted a yearly survey titled "Stress in America: Paying with Our Health." Based on interviews with more than 3,000 people in various demographic populations (gender, income levels, generational groups, etc.), the results have not been promising. Key findings of the 2014 study, which was published in the spring of 2015, revealed the following:

- Although reported stress levels have decreased slightly over the past few years, over half of adults between the ages of 18 to 40 reported their stress level above 5 on a scale of 1–10.

- Seniors appeared to have the least stress, millennials the most.

- The top five reasons for stress were: (1) financial issues (money), (2) career responsibilities (work), (3) family responsibilities, (4) personal health issues, and (5) family health issues.

- Overall, women reported more stress than men (and the gap has been widening), and children appeared to model their stress behaviors from their parents (who are very stressed).

Effective coping skills appear to be in short supply according to this survey. The conclusions drawn from this study underscore the relationship between stress and disease/illness and highlight the need for people to harness better stress management skills.

Based on various factors, including the Black Lives Matter movement and the political aspects of sexual discrimination, the APA's 2015 survey specifically looked at the impact of discrimination on stress levels. Results revealed that perceptions of discrimination (based on race or ethnicity, age, disability, gender, sexual orientation, and gender identity) account for significant levels of personal stress, all of which impact personal health (APA, 2016).

Similar to the APA's "Stress in America" study, National Public Radio and the Kaiser Health Foundation conducted a series of surveys in 2014 and presented their findings under the title "The Burden of Stress in America." Here are some of their findings:

- Half of those questioned, more than 2,000 people, cited a major stressful experience in the past year.

- Health-related stressful experiences were the most frequently mentioned.

- Feelings of being overwhelmed with responsibilities and financial struggles topped the list of those who experienced the greatest stress.

- Additional stressors included work problems, health problems, family issues, and being unhappy with physical appearances.

The study also looked at common daily stressors/hassles. Topping the list were juggling family schedules, disillusion with government politics, watching/reading/listening to the news, household chores, running errands, car problems, commuting to work, losing cell phones, and using social media. Whether daily hassles or bigger issues, respondents reported both sleep patterns and eating behaviors as being greatly (negatively) impacted by stress.

Not all people reported having stress, and, among those who appeared to cope well, many credited their resilient personality traits, family and friends, spending time outdoors, hobbies, physical exercise, meditation, and time with pets.

Although major life events like getting married (**FIG. 1.7**) or relocating for a new job may be chronic stressors to some, renowned stress researcher **Richard Lazarus** hypothesized in 1984 that the accumulation of acute stressors or **daily life hassles**, such as locking your keys in your car, playing phone tag, or driving to work every day in traffic, are just as likely to adversely affect one's health as the death of a spouse. These hassles are often based on unmet expectations that trigger an anger response of some type, whereas stressors of a chronic nature more often than not appear to have a greater

FIGURE 1.7   Weddings are supposed to be a joyous occasion. However, they can rank near the top of one's list of stressors when planning this event, with stress lasting well after the reception when things don't always go as expected.

association with fear and anxiety. Lazarus defined hassles as "daily interactions with the environment that were essentially negative." He also hypothesized that a balance of emotional experiences—positive emotions as well as negative ones—is necessary, and that people who have no exposure to life's "highs" or emotional uplifts (eustress) are also susceptible to disease and illness. Further research by Lazarus (1983, 1984), Ornstein and Sobel (1989), and

Richard Lazarus: Renowned stress researcher credited with the concept of daily life hassles.

Daily life hassles: Occasional hassles, like locking your keys in your car; when combined with many other annoyances in the course of a day, these create a critical mass of stress.

others has proved that his hypothesis has significant merit regarding stress and disease. As might be expected, the issue of lifestyle habits, changes, and hassles as social influences has come under attack by those who argue that perception or cognition plays an important role in the impact of stressors. Suffice it to say that all stressors, regardless of classification, are connected to human well-being in a very profound way. Over the past decade, the impact of social stressors on personal stress has become dramatically significant.

The General Adaptation Syndrome

Following Cannon's lead early in the twentieth century, Hans Selye, a young endocrinologist who created a name for himself as a leading researcher in this field, studied the fight-or-flight response, specifically the physiological effects of chronic stress, using rats as subjects. In experiments designed to stress the rats, Selye noted that several physiological adaptations occurred as a result of repeated exposures to stress, adaptations that had pathological repercussions. Examples of these stress-induced changes included the following:

1. Enlargement of the adrenal cortex (a gland that produces stress hormones)

2. Constant release of stress hormones; corticosteroids released from the adrenal cortex

3. Atrophy or shrinkage of lymphatic glands (thymus gland, spleen, and lymph nodes)

4. Significant decrease in the white blood cell count

5. Bleeding ulcerations of the stomach and colon

6. Death of the organism

Many of these changes were very subtle and often went unnoticed until permanent damage had occurred. Selye referred to these collective changes as the **general adaptation syndrome** (GAS), a process in which the body tries to accommodate stress by adapting to it. From his research, Selye identified three stages of the general adaptation syndrome:

> **Stage one: Alarm reaction.** The alarm reaction describes Cannon's original fight-or-flight response. In this stage, several body systems are activated, primarily the nervous system and the endocrine system, followed by the cardiovascular, pulmonary,

and musculoskeletal systems. Like a smoke detector alarm going off at night, all senses are put on alert until the danger is over.

> **Stage two: Stage of resistance.** In the resistance stage, the body tries to revert to a state of physiological calmness, or homeostasis, by resisting the alarm. Because the perception of a threat still exists, however, complete homeostasis is never reached. Instead, the body stays activated or aroused, usually at a lesser intensity than during the alarm stage but enough to cause a higher metabolic rate in some organ tissues. One or more organs may in effect be working overtime and, as a result, enter the third and final stage.

> **Stage three: Stage of exhaustion.** Exhaustion occurs when one (or more) of the organs targeted by specific metabolic processes can no longer meet the demands placed upon it and fails to function properly. This can result in death to the organ and, depending on which organ becomes dysfunctional (e.g., the heart), possibly the death of the organism as a whole.

Selye's general adaptation syndrome outlined the parameters of the physiological dangers of stress. His research opened the doors to understanding the strong relationship between stress and disease and the mind-body-spirit equation. In addition, his work laid the foundation for the utilization of relaxation techniques that have the ability to intercept the stress response, thereby decreasing susceptibility to illness and disease. Congruent with standard medical practice of his day (and even today), initial stress-management programs were geared toward reducing or eliminating the *symptoms* of stress. Unfortunately, this approach has not always proved successful.

General adaptation syndrome: A term coined by Hans Selye; the three distinct physiological phases in reaction to chronic stress: the alarm phase, the resistance phase, and the exhaustion phase.

Alarm reaction: The first stage of Selye's general adaptation syndrome, in which a threat is perceived and the nervous system is triggered for survival.

Stage of resistance: The second stage of Selye's general adaptation syndrome, in which the body tries to recover.

Stage of exhaustion: The third and final stage of Selye's general adaptation syndrome, in which one or more target organs show signs of dysfunction.

BOX 1.1   Post-Traumatic Stress Disorder 101

There is stress and then there is STRESS! Although most people claim (even brag) to live stressful lives, the truth of the matter is that few people encounter truly horrific events of death and carnage. The repeated horrors of war, however, have notoriously ranked at the top of every list as the most unbearable of all stressors that anyone can endure psychologically—and for good reason. To quote Civil War General William T. Sherman, "War is hell." Exposure to these types of events typically include those that threaten one's life, result in serious physical injury, expose one to horrific carnage, or create intense psychological shock, all of which are so strongly influenced by the intensity and duration of the devastation either experienced or observed first hand. The result is an emotional wound embedded in the unconscious mind that is very hard to heal.

Every war seems to have its own name for this type of anxiety disorder. Somber Civil War soldiers were described as having "soldier's heart." Affected military personnel returning from World War I were described as being "shell-shocked," whereas soldiers and veterans from World War II exhibiting neurotic anxiety were described as having severe "battle fatigue" or "combat fatigue." The term *post-traumatic stress disorder*—more commonly shortened to PTSD—emerged as a result of the treatment of returning soldiers from Vietnam who seemed to lack industrial-strength coping skills to deal with the hellacious memories that haunted them both day and night. This emotional disorder was first registered in the *Diagnostic and Statistical Manual of Mental Disorders (DSM)* in 1980 and has been the topic of intense investigation ever since. Sadly, the Iraq and Afghanistan wars have provided countless case studies for this anxiety disorder today.

Although mortal combat ranks at the top of the list of hellacious experiences, one doesn't have to survive a suicide bomber in the streets of Baghdad to suffer from PTSD. Survivors and rescue workers of the World Trade Center and Pentagon catastrophes are known to still be dealing with this trauma, as are several thousands of people still displaced from the wrath of Hurricane Sandy, and the devastation of towns in the paths of class 5 tornadoes. Violent crime victims, airplane crash survivors, sexual/physical assault victims, and occasionally first responders (e.g., police officers, fire fighters, and emergency medical technicians) are also prone to this condition. Given the nature of global warming and climate change and terrorism, it is suggested that PTSD may become a common diagnosis among world citizens with the ripple effect affecting legions of friends, colleagues, and family members alike. *Secondary PTSD* is a term given to family members, friends, and colleagues who are negatively affected by the ripples of strife from loved ones (even patients) who have had direct exposure to severe trauma.

The symptoms of PTSD include the following: chronic anxiety, nightmares, flashbacks, insomnia, loss of appetite, memory loss, hypervigilance, emotional detachment, clinical depression, helplessness, restlessness, suicidal tendencies, and substance addictions (MayoClinic .com). Typically a person suffering from PTSD has several of these symptoms at one time. Whereas the symptoms for some individuals may last months, for others PTSD becomes a lifelong ordeal, particularly if treatment is avoided, neglected, or shunned. The key to working with PTSD patients is to access the power of the unconscious mind by identifying deep-seated memories so that they may be acknowledged and released in a healthy manner rather than repressed and pushed deeper in the personal unconscious mind.

Specialists who treat patients with PTSD recommend that treatment begin as soon as possible to prevent a worsening effect. Initial treatment (intervention) is referred to as critical incidence stress management (CISM). The purpose of CISM is to (1) significantly reduce the traumatic effects of the incident and (2) prevent further deep-seated PTSD occurrences. Specific treatment modalities include eye movement desensitization and reprocessing (EMDR), counseling, and group therapy as a means to promote emotional catharsis. The Trauma Recovery Institute also cites art therapy, journal writing, and hypnosis as complementary coping skills for emotional catharsis. Many patients are also prescribed medications. Although medications may help reduce anxiety, it should be noted, they do not heal emotional wounds. Whereas the nature of this book is not specifically directed toward those who suffer from PTSD, the breadth and depth of content are found in all types of counseling and therapeutic modalities.

Stress in a Changing World

All you need do is read the latest Twitter feeds, Facebook updates, or the headlines on the homepage of your Internet browser to see what you already know: These are stressful times. Our world is changing rapidly, and with this change comes potential stressors that affect nearly everyone on the planet (FIG. 1.8). Today, stress has permeated the lives of nearly every person in every corner of the planet, permeating the borders of every country, province, and locale. And because people have to work for a living to put food on the table and a roof over one's head, job stress seems to be at the top of the list of common stressors across the globe. After investigating workplace absence due to stress, *The Daily Mail*, one of England's top-selling newspapers, quoted economic experts stating that stress is the Black Death plague of the twenty-first century (Barrow, 2011). According to the Chartered Institute of Personnel and Development, stress, as a public health issue, has eclipsed heart disease, strokes, cancer, and lower back problems. Daniel L. Kirsch, President of the American Institute of Stress, also refers to stress as America's New Black Death, explaining that stress is what's killing us most right now (Perman, 2013).

Stress, it seems, knows no age, race, gender, religion, nationality, or socioeconomic class. For this reason, it is called "the equal opportunity destroyer," for when left unresolved, stress can undermine all aspects of your life. Although it may seem that stress becomes a critical mass in your life once you leave home and go to college, the truth is that the episodes and behaviors associated with stress start much earlier than the college years. Pressures in high school, even grade school, as evidenced by school shootings, cases of self-injury, Facebook issues, and insomnia, are well documented. Combined with the stress of high technology, the effects are exponential.

Which demographic group carries the most stress in the United States these days? If you said the Millennium Generation (people between the ages of 18 and 33), you would be right. Millennials are considered to be far more stressed than the baby boomer generation or even members of Generation X (ages 34–47). The backstory on this answer is a bit more complex than the daily statistics of unemployment figures and unpaid college loan debt. Experts often cite overprotective parenting styles (helicopter parents) of the millennials as a primary reason. Unlike baby boomers, typically, both parents of millennials have jobs/careers. The end result is less time with their children. Guilt kicks in, and parents overcompensate with poor boundaries. Campus counseling centers across the country see a theme among millennials walking in the door. "There is a generation of kids, now adults, who were given everything on a silver platter as they were growing up. Everything has been given to them, fostering a false sense of entitlement. These kids don't know how to fail successfully" (Neu, 2013). Millennials not only have poor coping skills when faced with adversity, but also feel that professional counseling would provide no lasting help (Ferri, 2013). In a cover story for *Time* magazine, reporter Joel Stein described the rampant impatient, narcisstic micro-celebrity status (i.e., 15 minutes of fame) as the gateway to entitlement (Stein, 2013).

Stress and Insomnia

Muscle tension may be the number one symptom of stress, but in our ever-present, demanding 24/7 society, insomnia runs a close second. **Insomnia** is best defined as poor-quality sleep, abnormal wakefulness, or the inability to sleep, and it can affect anyone. Overall, Americans get 20 percent less sleep than their nineteenth-century counterparts. According to a recent survey by the National Sleep Foundation, more than 60 percent of Americans suffer

FIGURE 1.8 Although most Americans admit to being very stressed, in comparison to half the planetary citizens who earn less than $2 per day and struggle to survive with substandard living conditions, we have it pretty darn good!

Insomnia: Poor-quality sleep, abnormal wakefulness, or the inability to sleep.

from poor sleep quality, resulting in everything from falling asleep on the job and marital problems to car accidents and lost work productivity. Does your stress level affect your sleep quality? Even if you sleep well, it is hard these days not to notice the proliferation of advertisements for sleep prescriptions, suggesting a serious public health concern.

Numerous studies have concluded that a regular good night's sleep is essential for optimal health, whereas chronic insomnia is often associated with several kinds of psychiatric problems (Maas, 2001). Emotional stress (the preoccupation with daily stressors) is thought to be a primary cause of insomnia. The result: an anxious state of mind where thoughts race around, ricocheting from brain cell to brain cell, never allowing a pause in the thought processes, let alone allowing the person to nod off.

Many other factors (sleep stealers) detract from one's **sleep hygiene**, which can affect the quality of sleep, including hormonal changes (e.g., premenstrual syndrome, menopause), excessive caffeine intake, little or no exercise, frequent urination, circadian rhythm disturbances (e.g., jet lag), shift work, medication side effects, and a host of lifestyle behaviors (e.g., social media, Internet use, bingewatching, video games, alcohol consumption, constant cell phone use) that infringe on a good night's sleep.

How much sleep is enough to feel recharged? Generally speaking, 8 hours of sleep is the norm, although some people can get as few as 6 hours of sleep and feel fully rested. Others may need as many as 10 hours. New findings suggest that adolescents, including all people up to age 22, need more than 8 hours of sleep (Dawson, 2005).

Not only can stress (mental, emotional, physical, or spiritual) affect quality and quantity of sleep, but the rebound effect of poor sleep can, in turn, affect stress levels, making the poor sleeper become more irritable, apathetic, or cynical. Left unresolved, it can become an unbroken cycle (negative feedback loop). Although many people seek medical help for insomnia and are often given a prescription, drugs should be considered as a last resort. Many (if not all) techniques for stress management have proven to be effective in promoting a good night's sleep, ranging from cardiovascular exercise to meditation.

The field of sleep research began in earnest more than 60 years ago. Yet, despite numerous studies, the reason why we spend approximately one-third of our lives in slumber still baffles scientists. From all appearances, sleep promotes physical restoration. However, when researchers observe sleep-deprived subjects, it's the mind—not the body—that

"If you have trouble falling asleep, lick your feet for a few minutes. It works for my cat!"

is most affected, with symptoms of poor concentration, poor retention, and poor problem-solving skills.

Insomnia is categorized in three ways: transient (short term with one or two weeks affected), intermittent (occurs on and off over a prolonged period), and chronic (the inability to achieve a restful night of sleep over many, many months). Although each of these categories is problematic, chronic insomnia is considered the worst.

All-nighters, exam crams, late-night parties, and midnight movies are common in the lives of college undergraduates, but the cost of these behaviors often proves unproductive. Unfortunately, the population of people who seem to need the most sleep, but often gets the least amount, are adolescents younger than age 20.

Although sleep may be relaxing, it is important to remember that sleeping is not a relaxation technique. Studies show that heart rate, blood pressure, and muscle tension can rise significantly during the dream state of sleep. What we do know is that effective coping and relaxation techniques greatly enhance one's quality of sleep.

Given the high rate of insomnia among Americans (including college students), here are a few suggestions to improve your sleep quality:

1. Avoid drinking any beverages with caffeine after 6:00 p.m., as the effects of caffeine on the nervous system promote a stress response rather than a relaxation effect.

> **Sleep hygiene:** Factors that affect one's quality of sleep, from hormonal changes and shift work to excessive caffeine intake.

2. Daily physical exertion (cardiovascular exercise) is a great way to ensure a good night's sleep.

3. Keep a regular sleep cycle. Make a habit of going to bed at the same time every night (within 15 minutes) and waking up about the same time each morning (even on weekends).

4. Enhance your sleep hygiene. Create a sleep-friendly environment where bright light and noise are minimized or completely eliminated and sheets, pillows, and comforters easily lull you to slumberland.

5. Avoid screentime right before you go to bed. Instead, try reading.

6. Honor a media curfew by not using your screen devices after 8:00 p.m. to allow your pineal gland to make the sleep hormone melatonin.

7. Make your bedroom a tech-free zone. Avoid using your smartphone and/or tablet in the bedroom, even as an alarm clock, and turn off your Wi-Fi router before you crawl under the covers.

College Stress

What makes the college experience a significant departure from the first 18 years of life is the realization that with the freedom of lifestyle choices comes the responsibility that goes with it. Unless you live at home while attending school, the college experience is one in which you transition from a period of dependence (on your parents) to independence. As you move from the known into the unknown, the list of stressors a college student experiences is rather startling. Here is a sample of some of the more common stressors that college students encounter.

- ■ *Roommate dynamics:* Finding someone who is compatible is not always easy, especially if you had your own room in your parents' house. As we all know or will quickly learn, best friends do not make the best roommates, yet roommates can become good friends over time. Through it all, roommate dynamics involve the skills of compromise and diplomacy under the best and worst conditions. And should you find yourself in an untenable situation, remember, campus housing does its best to accommodate students and resolve problems. However, their time schedule and yours may not always be the same. For those college students who don't leave home, living as an adult in a home in which your parents and siblings are now roommates can become its own form of stress.

- ■ *Professional pursuits:* What major should I choose? Perhaps one of the most common soul-searching questions to be asked in the college years is, "What do I want to do the rest of my life?" It is a well-known fact that college students can change majors several times in their college careers and many do. The problem is compounded when there is parental pressure to move toward a specific career path (e.g., law or medicine) or the desire to please your parents by picking a major that they like but you don't.

- ■ *Academic deadlines (exams, papers, and projects):* Academics means taking midterms and finals, writing research papers, and completing projects. This is, after all, the hallmark of measuring what you have learned. With a typical semester load of fifteen to twenty credits, many course deadlines can fall on the same day, and there is the ever-present danger that not meeting expectations can result in poor grades or academic probation.

- ■ *Financial aid and school loans:* If you have ever stood in the financial aid office during the first week of school, you could write a book on the topic of stress. The cost of a college education is skyrocketing, and the pressure to pay off school loans after graduation can make you feel like an indentured servant. Assuming you qualify for financial aid, you should know that receiving the money in time to pay your bills can be challenging. Problems are compounded when your course schedule gets expunged from computer records because your financial aid check was two weeks late. These are just some of the problems associated with financial aid.

- ■ *Budgeting your money:* It's one thing to ask your parents to buy you some new clothes or have them pick up the check at a restaurant. It's quite another when you start paying all your own bills. Learning to budget your money is a skill that takes practice. And learning not to overextend yourself is not only a skill, but also an art. At some time or other, everyone bounces a check. The trick to avoid doing it is not to spend money you do not have and to live within your means.

- ■ *Lifestyle behaviors:* The freedom to stay up until 2 a.m. on a weekday, skip a class, eat nothing but junk food, or take an impromptu road trip carries with it the responsibilities of these actions. Independence from parental control means balancing

Stress with a Human Face

Joseph Ramos has just started his first year at the University of Colorado-Boulder. Like nearly every other freshman, a million thoughts filter through his mind daily regarding this stage of his life: the right college major, new friends, finding a girlfriend, grades, a tendency to procrastinate, roommate dynamics, budgeting his money, volunteer work, and time to do all the things that he loves when not studying. With a physique and body composition that most college men would envy, Joseph is already worried about packing on the "freshman 15" (undesired weight gain) and he is determined not to let that happen. In high school, Joseph played football, track, and cross-country. He also was involved in student government and was a member of the National Honor Society. He is well aware that being voted senior prom king probably won't carry much weight in college. For better or worse, the college years are a time to prove, if not reinvent, yourself all over again. Joseph welcomes this challenge. Currently, Joseph's strategy to cope with his stress levels includes running and lifting weights. He also has a passion for the martial arts. These activities have helped him get through high school and a few family crises, but he realizes that he will need a few more stress-management strategies to support his study habits in college if he is to achieve the desired grades to get into medical school so that he can achieve his lifelong dream of becoming a physician.

freedom with responsibility. Stress enters your life with a vengeance when freedom and responsibility are not balanced.

- *Peer groups and peer pressure (drugs and alcohol):* There is a great need to feel accepted by new acquaintances in college, and this need often leads to succumbing to peer pressure—and in new environments with new acquaintances, peer pressure can be very strong. Stress arises when the actions of the group are incongruent with your own philosophies and values. The desire to conform to the group is often stronger than your willpower to hold your own ground.

- *Exploring sexuality:* While high school is the time when some people explore their sexuality, this behavior occurs with greater frequency during the college years, when you are away from the confines of parental control and more assertive with your self-expression. With the issue of sexual exploration come questions of values, contraception, pregnancy, sexual orientation, AIDS/STDs, abortion, acceptance, and impotence, all of which can be very stressful.

- *Friendships:* The friendships made in college take on a special quality. As you grow, mature, and redefine your values, your friends, like you, will change, and so will the quality of each friendship. Cultivating a quality relationship takes time, meaning you cannot be good friends with everyone you like. In addition, tensions can quickly mount as the dynamics between you and those in your close circle of friends come under pressure from all the other college stressors.

- *Intimate relationships:* Spending time with one special person with whom you can grow in love is special indeed. But the demands of an intimate relationship are strong, and in the presence of a college environment, intimate relationships are under a lot of pressure. If and when the relationship ends, the aftershock can be traumatic for one or both parties, leaving little desire for one's academic pursuits.

- *Starting a professional career path:* It's a myth that you can start a job making the same salary that your parents make, but many college students believe this to be true. With this myth comes the pressure to equal the lifestyle of one's parents the day after graduation. (This may explain why so many college graduates return home to live after graduation.) The perceived pressures of the real world can become so overwhelming that seniors procrastinate on drafting a resume or initiating the job search until the week of graduation.

For the nontraditional college student, the problem can be summarized in one word: *balance*! Trying to balance a job, family, and schoolwork becomes a juggling act extraordinaire. In attempting to satisfy the needs of your supervisor, colleagues, friends, spouse, children, and parents (and perhaps even pets), what usually is squeezed out is time for yourself. In the end, everything seems to suffer. Often schoolwork is given a lower priority when addressing survival needs, and typically this leads to feelings of frustration over the inadequacy of time and effort available for assignments or exams. Of course, there are other stressors that cross the boundaries between work, home, and school, all of which tend to throw things off balance as well.

A Holistic Approach to Stress Management

When the stress response was first recognized, much attention was given to the physical aspects of the dynamics involved with fight-or-flight, specifically the symptoms of stress. As this field of study expanded to explore the relationship between stress and disease, it began to overlap, and to some extent even merge, with the fields of psychology, sociology, theology, anthropology, physics, health, and clinical medicine. What was once thought to be a physical response, and then referred to as a mind-body phenomenon, is now suggested to be a complex, multifaceted, or holistic phenomenon involving the mental, physical, emotional, and spiritual components of well-being. Looking at stress from these four different perspectives may explain why there are so many definitions of it. Ironically, this new insight continues to produce some tension within the community of health care professionals.

Medical science is slowly experiencing a **paradigm shift**. A paradigm is a conceptual model used to understand a common reality. A shift is a change in the perception of that reality. For the past 375 years or so, Western culture has adopted a mechanistic model of reality, influenced in large part by the philosophy of **René Descartes** that the mind and body are separate, and by the laws of physics created by **Isaac Newton**, some of which are believed to have been inspired by Descartes. The mechanistic paradigm compares the universe and all its components to a large mechanical clock, where everything operates in a sequential and predictable form. When it was first developed, the **mechanistic model**, also called the reductionist model, seemed to logically explain nearly every phenomenon.

The field of medicine, strongly influenced by Newtonian physics, applied the mechanistic model to the human organism, comparing the body to a clock as well. This applied paradigm, during what Dr. Larry Dossey called

Era I medicine, focused on symptoms of dysfunction, and like a watch repairman, physicians were trained to fix or repair any parts that were broken. Drugs and surgery became the two primary tools forged in the discipline of clinical medicine. Prime examples of the fix-or-replace method include the prescription of penicillin and organ transplants, respectively. To no one's surprise, the application of this mechanistic model in medicine virtually stripped the responsibility of healing from the patient and placed it completely into the hands of the attending physician(s). There is no denying that many advances in clinical medicine have been nothing less than astonishing. Take, for example, heart and liver transplants and total hip replacements. Yet along with these magnificent achievements are significant limitations and hazardous side effects. Today, medicine is aptly referred to as an art as well as a science, but in the mechanistic model of reality, anything that cannot be measured or quantified is still virtually ignored. Moreover, anything that cannot be scientifically explained by cause and effect is dismissed as superstition and regarded as invalid. What this medical paradigm failed to include was the dimension of the human spirit, an unmeasurable source of energy with a potential healing power all its own. The human spirit is now considered so important by the World Health Organization (WHO) that it issued a statement saying, "The existing definition of health should include the spiritual aspect, and that health care should be in the hands of those who are fully aware of and sympathetic to the spiritual dimension."

However, the Newtonian paradigm was viewed as the ultimate truth until the turn of the twentieth century,

> **Paradigm shift:** Moving from one perspective of reality to another.
>
> **René Descartes:** A seventeenth-century scientist and philosopher credited with the reductionistic method of Western science (also known as the Cartesian principle). He is equally renowned for his influential philosophy of the separation of mind and body as well as the statement, "I think, therefore I am."
>
> **Isaac Newton:** An eighteenth-century physicist who advocated the mechanistic paradigm of the universe, which was then adapted to the human body.
>
> **Mechanistic model:** A health model based on the concept that the body is a machine with parts that can be repaired or replaced.

FIGURE 1.9   Sir Isaac Newton (along with René Descartes) is credited with what is now referred to as the mechanistic approach to scientific thinking, which is based on the idea that the universe operates like a large mechanical clock. Albert Einstein supported a different theory, called unified field theory, suggesting that the universe is a living web and validating the ancient whole systems theory in which everything is connected together and the whole is greater than the sum of the parts.

when a young physicist named **Albert Einstein** introduced his theory of relativity in 1905 (**FIG. 1.9**). In simple terms, Einstein said that all matter is energy, and furthermore, all matter is connected at the subatomic level. No single entity can be affected without all connecting parts similarly being affected. From Einstein's view, the universe isn't a giant clock but a living web. New ideas are often laughed at, and old ideas die hard. But as new truths unfold, they gather curious followers who test and elaborate on the original idea. Initially mocked, the complexities of Einstein's theory have gained appreciation among physicists today, leading to the frontiers of the new field of quantum physics and a whole new understanding of our universe in what is now called the *whole systems theory*. In his attempt to understand the big picture, one of Einstein's more colorful quotes states, "Gravity is not responsible for people falling in love."

Although current medical technology is incredibly sophisticated, physicians for the most part still view the human body as a clock with fixable or replaceable parts. In other words, the basic approach to modern medicine in the Western world has not changed in more than 375 years. Furthermore, the mind and body, so completely separate in the theory of Descartes, are still treated separately, not as one living system. The idea of a mind-body connection (which in rare cases appears powerful enough to make cancers go into spontaneous remission) is still as foreign a concept to many physicians today as the idea of a smartphone would have been to the founders of the United States more than 230 years ago. But new discoveries in the field of medicine have not fit so nicely into the concept of mechanical clock

Albert Einstein: A world-renowned theoretical physicist who revolutionized perceptions of reality with the equation $E = mc^2$, suggesting that everything is energy. His later years focused on a spiritual philosophy including pacifism.

or reductionist theory. Instead, they mirror Einstein's concept of an intricate network of connecting systems. As a result, standard concepts regarding health and disease are slowly beginning to give way to a more inclusive reality or paradigm. As an example, recently, medical researchers have learned that emotions can suppress the immune system, an idea thought to be inconceivable and ludicrous not long ago. The body-as-machine mentality no longer seems to answer all the questions posed about the human organism; and thus some issues, like subtle energy systems and the placebo effect, are being completely reexamined.

But old paradigms are not abandoned until new conceptual models are created and established. Ironically, some new paradigms are actually old concepts that have been dusted off and resurrected. Such is the case with a very old but newly rediscovered health paradigm strongly paralleling Einstein's theory and called the holistic **wellness paradigm**. This model suggests that total wellness is the balance, integration, and harmony of the physical, intellectual, emotional, and spiritual aspects of the human condition. These four components of total well-being are so closely connected and interwoven that it is virtually impossible to divide them. Although for the purposes of academic study these areas are best understood separately, in reality they all act as one interconnected living system, just as Einstein hypothesized about the universe.

The word *health* is derived from the Anglo word *hal*, meaning "to heal, to be made whole, or to be holy"; throughout the ages, wholeness has been symbolized by a circle. The wellness philosophy states that the whole is always greater than the sum of the parts and all parts must be looked at as one system (FIG. 1.10). When applied to clinical medicine, this philosophy indicates that all aspects of the individual must be treated *equally* and each considered part of the whole. Although advances have been made to integrate a host of mind-body-spirit healing modalities into Western health care, by and large, conventional medical practice still treats the physical component—the symptoms of stress—with drugs and surgery, often disregarding how the physical body connects with the mental, emotional, and spiritual aspects of well-being. Although the paradigm is slowly shifting, some physicians (because of their medical training) still refuse to fully acknowledge the link between stress and disease. Nontraditional approaches (of which stress management is a part), specifically biofeedback, meditation, massage therapy, and mental imagery, are commonly referred to as **alternative medicine** by the American Medical Association. Because the word *alternative* has a

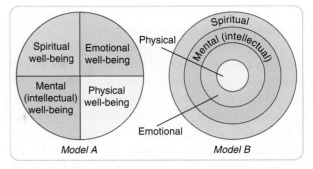

FIGURE 1.10   Two different approaches to the wellness paradigm. In Model A, expounded by Elisabeth Kübler-Ross, all components are present in the human organism, but each holds specific dominance at different phases of the individual's growth cycle. The emotional aspect is the first to develop; the spiritual aspect is the last. In Model B, each component is superimposed on the others in a holographic form, yet it is the spiritual component in which they are all contained.

negative connotation to many practitioners in the field of holistic wellness, the words *complementary* and *integrative medicine* also are used to refer to additional healing modalities. Every technique for stress management falls within the domain of complementary medicine.

Please note that healing and curing are two different concepts. Typically, the word *curing* means that the symptoms of a disease or illness are eradicated. Although in some cases healing techniques may cure a person of disease or illness, the concept of healing really means bringing a sense of inner peace to someone's life, even in the face of death. From this vantage point you can see that a person can be healed and yet still be ill. In the age of high technology and instant gratification, expectations are often placed on the curing aspects—eradicating the symptomatic problems—rather than the essence of true healing. This in itself has caused tension in the allied health fields because

Wellness paradigm: The integration, balance, and harmony of mental, physical, emotional, and spiritual well-being through taking responsibility for one's own health; posits that the whole is greater than the sum of the parts.

Alternative medicine: Modalities of healing (homeostasis) that include nearly all forms of stress-management techniques. Also known as complementary or integrative medicine.

many healthcare professionals trained in the mechanistic paradigm use both terms interchangeably. But the tension doesn't stop there. In 1993, a landmark study by David Eisenberg and colleagues published in the *New England Journal of Medicine* announced that more than one-third of the American population seeks methods of healing outside those accepted by traditional medicine because they are unsatisfied with the Western approach to health care. What makes this matter even more astounding is that most healing methods are not covered by medical insurance, meaning that people are paying for these services out of their own pockets. In the highly acclaimed PBS television series entitled *Healing and the Mind*, creator and host Bill Moyers distilled the trend in this way: "There is a deep yearning for a human (whole) approach to medicine." Stress-management techniques, which attempt to deal with the causes as well as the symptoms of stress, support and contribute to this holistic approach.

Statistics released by the National Center for Alternative and Complementary Medicine in 2008 indicate that as many as 50 percent (adults and children) of the U.S. population use various forms of integrative medicine. Many of these people pay out-of-pocket expenses (totaling in the billions of dollars) as only a few holistic modalities, such as acupuncture and some forms of bodywork, are reimbursable by insurance companies. Today, alternative healing practices have gone mainstream with acupuncture, hatha yoga, T'ai Chi ch'uan, aromatherapy, and many other modalities as common healthcare practices (Comarow, 2008).

Let us take a closer look at the components of the wellness paradigm and the effects that stress has on them. **Mental** (intellectual) **well-being** is regarded as the ability to gather, process, recall, and exchange (communicate) information. Exposure to stress tends to overload the cognitive "circuits," decreasing the processing and recall abilities needed to make sound decisions as well as the ability to communicate them. **Physical well-being** is described as the optimal functioning of the body's major physiological systems (e.g., cardiovascular, digestive, reproductive). From the observations documented in Selye's research, as explained in his book *The Stress of Life*, the inability to return to homeostasis can prove fatal to various organ tissues and eventually to the host organism. **Emotional well-being** is defined as the ability to feel and express the full range of human emotions and to control them rather than be controlled by them. Anger and fear act as "umbrella" emotions that can collectively overload emotional circuits, resulting in mental paralysis and often leading to states of depression. **Spiritual well-being** is

described as the maturation of higher consciousness through strong nurturing relationships with both the self and others; the development of a strong personal value system; and a meaningful purpose in life. Stress can create a series of obstacles on the road to spiritual development, making the path to one's higher self difficult, if not entirely inaccessible. Over the past few decades, scholars (including Bill Hetler and John Travis) have included social well-being and environmental well-being as additional components of the wellness paradigm. Actually, what they have done is tease these aspects out of the mental, emotional, physical, or spiritual factors involved. If you take a closer look at the original four components, you will see that social well-being is a large factor of spiritual well-being. And environmental well-being demonstrates how interwoven these four components really are, integrating aspects of physical and spiritual well-being. Although the major focus of this book is self-reliance—working from within to achieve inner peace—remember that our ability to harmonize with people within our collective environments is paramount to total well-being. Thus, from a holistic perspective, to effectively deal with stress, all areas of the wellness paradigm must be addressed and nurtured equally; the whole is always greater than the sum of the parts.

Not long ago (and in some cases today), many stress-management programs were based on the mechanistic model and focused solely on physical well-being. Upon initial recognition of the association between stress and disease, courses designed to intervene in this process emphasized techniques to decrease the physical symptoms of stress. These classes consisted primarily of teaching one or two relaxation techniques to help decrease the most obvious stress symptom: muscle tension. These techniques, addressing merely the symptoms (the physical component), did nothing to relieve the causes of stress

---

Mental well-being: The ability to gather, process, recall, and communicate information.

Physical well-being: The optimal functioning of the body's eight physiological systems (e.g., respiratory, skeletal).

Emotional well-being: The ability to feel and express the full range of human emotions and to control these feelings, not be controlled by them.

Spiritual well-being: The state of mature higher consciousness deriving from insightful relationships with oneself and others, a strong value system, and a meaningful purpose in life.

"It's been a difficult year. Would you like your annual bonus in cash or Prozac?"

FIGURE 1.11

(the mental, emotional, or spiritual components). As a result, people often experienced a rebound effect; their symptoms recurred. On a different front, coping skills (e.g., cognitive restructuring, time management, and journal writing) were taught by psychologists in private therapy sessions, and these coping strategies soon made their way into public awareness as well (**FIG. 1.11**).

Through the efforts of advocates of the wellness paradigm, attempts have been made to unite the practice of both relaxation skills and coping skills for a unique holistic approach to stress management. This implies viewing each person as more than just a physical body and dealing with the causes of stress as well as the physical symptoms. The primary focuses in the application of the wellness model are on the prevention of disease and illness and the enhancement of health. Furthermore, the underlying current of this empowering philosophy is to place the responsibility of healing back in the hands of the individual. Successful stress-management therapy programs have now begun to adopt the wellness philosophy and holistic approach, supporting the concept that the whole is indeed greater than the sum of the parts. A sound stress-management program does not attempt to merely reduce (fix or repair) stress, but rather to manage it efficiently. This management process attempts to focus on all aspects of one's well-being. This philosophy is implemented by attempting to both resolve the causes *and* reduce or eliminate the symptoms of stress. It is imperative to remember that, as an intervention modality, the wellness paradigm does not preclude the use of medications or surgery. Rather, it strongly suggests that there be a collaborative integration of several therapeutic techniques to produce the most effective healing process (e.g., chemotherapy and visualization). Equally important as preventive measures, coping skills and relaxation techniques are also advocated to *maintain* inner peace.

Stated simply, effective holistic stress management includes the following:

1. Sound knowledge of the body's reaction to perceived stress

2. Sound knowledge of mental, physical, emotional, and spiritual factors associated with stress

3. Utilization of several effective coping techniques to work toward a resolution of the causes of stress

4. Regular practice of relaxation techniques to maintain homeostatic balance of the body

5. Periodic evaluation of the effectiveness of coping skills and relaxation techniques

SUMMARY

- The advancement of technology, which promised more leisure time, has actually increased the pace of life so that many people feel stressed to keep up with this pace.

- Lifestyles based on new technological conveniences are now thought to be associated with several diseases, including coronary heart disease and cancer.

- *Stress* is a term from the field of physics, meaning physical force or tension placed on an object. It was adopted after World War II to signify psychological tension.

- There are many definitions of stress from both Eastern and Western philosophies as well as several academic disciplines, including psychology and physiology. The mind-body separation is now giving way to a holistic philosophy involving the mental, physical, emotional, and spiritual components of well-being.

- Cannon coined the term *fight-or-flight response* to describe the immediate effects of physical stress. This response is now considered by many to be inappropriate for nonphysical stressors.

- There are three types of stress: eustress (good), neustress (neutral), and distress (bad). There are two types of distress: acute (short-term) and chronic (long-term), the latter of which is thought to be the more detrimental because the body does not return to a state of complete homeostasis.

- Stressors have been categorized into three groups: (1) bioecological influences, (2) psychointrapersonal influences, and (3) social influences.

- Holmes and Rahe created the Social Readjustment Rating Scale to identify major life stressors. They found that the incidence of stressors correlated with health status.

- Selye coined the term *general adaptation syndrome* to explain the body's ability to adapt negatively to chronic stress.

- Females are not only wired for fight-or-flight, but also have a survival dynamic called "tend and befriend," a specific nurturing aspect that promotes social support in stressful times.

- Stress can appear at any time in our lives, but the college years offer their own types of stressors because it is at this time that one assumes more (if not complete) responsibility for one's lifestyle behaviors.

- The association between stress and insomnia is undeniable. The United States is said to be a sleep-deprived society, but techniques for stress management are proven effective to help promote a good night's sleep, including physical exercise, biofeedback, yoga, and diaphragmatic breathing.

- Previous approaches to stress management have been based on the mechanistic model, which divided the mind and body into two separate entities. The paradigm on which this model was based is now shifting toward a holistic paradigm, in which the whole is greater than the sum of the parts, and the whole person must be treated by working on the causes as well as the symptoms of stress.

- Effective stress-management programming must address issues related to mental (intellectual), physical, emotional, and spiritual well-being.

STUDY GUIDE QUESTIONS

1. How could you best define stress?

2. How does acute stress differ from chronic stress?

3. What is the general adaptation syndrome? List the stages.

4. Do men and women respond to stress in the same way? If not, how do their responses differ?

5. How does stress affect sleep? List as many ways as possible.

6. What is post-traumatic stress disorder (PTSD) and what is secondary post-traumatic stress disorder?

7. What is holistic stress management?

REFERENCES AND RESOURCES

Allen, R. *Human Stress: Its Nature and Control*. Burgess Press, Minneapolis, MN, 1983.

Alter, A. *Irresistible: The Rise of Addictive Technology and the Business of Keeping Us Hooked*. Penguin Press, New York, 2017.

American Cancer Society. *Cancer Facts & Figures 2007*. www.cancer.org/downloads/STT/CAFF2007PWSecured.pdf.

American Institute of Stress (AIS). *Homepage*. www.stress.org.

American Psychological Association. Stress in America: Paying with Our Health. February 4, 2015. http://www.apa.org/news/press/releases/stress/2014/stress-report.pdf.

American Psychological Association. Stress in America: The Impact of Discrimination. March 10, 2016. http://www.apa.org/news/press/releases/stress/2015/impact-of-discrimination.pdf.

Anxiety Disorders Association of America (ADAA). *2007 Stress & Anxiety Disorders Study*. www.adaa.org/stressOutWeek/study.asp.

Austin, J. Why Patients Use Alternative Medicine, *JAMA* 279:1548–1553, 1998.

Barrow, B. Stress Is Top Cause of Workplace Sickness and So Widespread It's Dubbed the Black Death of the 21st Century. Mail Online. October 5, 2011. www.dailymail.co.uk/health/article-2045309/Stress-Top-cause-workplace-sickness-dubbed-Black-Death-21st-century.html.

Becker, D. *One Nation Under Stress*. Oxford University Press, New York, 2013.

Beckford, M. Working Nine to Five Is Becoming a Thing of the Past, *Daily Telegraph*, May 4, 2007.

Cannon, W. *The Wisdom of the Body*. W. W. Norton, New York, 1963.

Carpi, J. Stress . . . It's Worse Than You Think, *Psychology Today* 29(1):34–41, 74–76, 1996.

Chopra, D. Personal conversation, June 22, 2000.

Comarow, A. Embracing Alternative Care, *U.S. News & World Report,* 31–40, January 2008.

Condon, G. Futurists Say World Is at Turning Point. *Chicago Tribune* (Section 5), April 9, 2003.

Cryer, B., McCraty, R., and Childre, D. Pulling the Plug on Stress. *Harvard Business Review* 81(7):102–107, 2003.

Damasio, A. *Descartes' Error*. HarperCollins, New York, 2006.

Dawson, P. *Sleep and Adolescents*. 2005. www.nasponline.org/resources/principals/Sleep%20Disorders%20WEB.pdf.

Dossey, L. Personal conversation, July 30, 2004.

Dossey, L. *Reinventing Medicine*. Harper, New York, 1999.

Dossey, L. *Space, Time, and Medicine*. Bantam New Age Books, New York, 1982.

Eisenberg, D., et al. Unconventional Medicine in the United States, *New England Journal of Medicine* 328:246–252, 1993.

Eisenberg, D., et al. Trends in Alternative Medicine Use in the United States, 1990–1997: Results of a Follow-up National Survey, *JAMA*, 280:1569–1575, 1998.

Expedia.com. *2012 International Vacation Deprivation Survey Results*. 2012. http://www.expedia.com/p/info-other/vacation_deprivation.htm.

Ferri, J. Millennials: The Most Stressed-Out Generation in America. Yahoo! February 8, 2013. http://shine.yahoo.com/work-money/millennials-are-the-most-stressed-out-americans-184318812.html.

Gerber, R. *Vibrational Medicine*, 3rd ed. Bear and Company, Inner Traditions, 2001.

Giradano, D., Everly, G., and Dusek, D. *Controlling Stress and Tension, A Holistic Approach*, 9th ed. Addison-Wesley, Boston, 2012.

Greenberg, J. *Comprehensive Stress Management*, 13th ed. McGraw-Hill Humanities, New York, 2012.

Hettler, W. *The Six Dimensional Wellness Model*. The National Wellness Institute. www.nationalwellness.org/index.php?id=391&id_tier=381.

Holmes, T. H., and Rahe, R. The Social Readjustment Rating Scale, *Journal of Psychosomatic Research* 11:213–218, 1967.

Huffington, A. *The Sleep Revolution*. Harmony Books. New York, 2016.

Kanner, A., et al. Comparison of Two Modes of Stress Management: Daily Hassles and Uplifts versus Major Life Events, *Journal of Behavioral Medicine* 4(1):1–37, 1981.

Kaplan, A., ed. *Health Promotion and Chronic Illness*. World Health Organization, Geneva, 1992.

King, S. K. Removing Distress to Reveal Health. In R. Carlson and B. Shield (eds.), *Healers on Healing*, Jeremy Tarcher Inc., Los Angeles, 1989.

Krugman, M. *The Insomnia Solution*. Grand Central Publishing, New York, 2005.

Kübler-Ross, E. Keynote Address, American Holistic Health Association Annual Conference, Lacrosse, WI, 1981.

Kuhn, T. *The Structure of Scientific Revolutions*. University of Chicago Press, Chicago, 2012.

Lazarus, R. Puzzles in the Study of Daily Hassles, *Journal of Behavioral Medicine* 7:375–389, 1984.

Lazarus, R., and DeLongis, A. Psychological Stress, and Coping in Aging, *American Psychologist* 38:245–254, 1983.

Levine, P. A. *Waking the Tiger: Healing Trauma*. North Atlantic Books, Berkeley, CA, 1997.

Levy, S. Facebook Grows Up, *Newsweek*, August 20, 2007: 41–46.

Lippmann, S., Mazour, I., and Shahab, H. Insomnia: Therapeutic Approach, *Southern Medical Journal* 94:866–873, 2001.

Luskin, F., and Pelletier, K. *Stress Free for Good: 10 Scientifically Proven Life Skills for Health and Happiness.* HarperOne, New York, 2005.

Maas, J. *Power Sleep.* Quill Books, New York, 2001.

Manning, G., Curtis, K., and McMillian, S. *Stress: Living and Working in a Changing World.* Whole Persons Associates, Duluth, MN, 2011.

Markes, J. Time Out, *U.S. News and World Report* 119 (23): 84–96, 1995.

Mayo Clinic. *Post-traumatic Stress Disorder.* www.mayoclinic.com/health/post-traumatic-stress-disorder/DS00246.

McGonigal, K. *The Upside of Stress: Why Stress Is Good for You, and How to Get Good at It.* Penguin Random House, New York, 2013.

Meyer, A. *The Common Sense Psychiatry of Dr. Adolf Meyer: Fifty-Two Selected Papers.* Ayer, Salem, NH, 1948.

Mitchum Report on Stress in the '90s. Research and Forecast Inc., New York, 1990.

Moyers, B. *Healing and the Mind.* Doubleday, New York, 1993.

Moyers, B. *Healing and the Mind.* Public Broadcasting System, 1993.

National Public Radio. Stressed-Out. 2014. http://www.npr.org/series/327816692/stressed-out.

Neu, S. Warderburg Health Center. University of Colorado, Boulder, CO. Personal conversation, March 2, 2013.

Ornstein, R., and Sobel, D. *Healthy Pleasures.* Addison-Wesley, Reading, MA, 1990.

Pelletier, K. *Mind as Healer, Mind as Slayer,* 2nd ed. Dell, New York, 2011.

Perman, C. Argggh! American Workers are at a breaking point. April 9, 2013. Business on NBCnews.com. http://www.cnbc.com/id/100624671.

Rahe, R., et al. Simplified Scaling for Life Events, *Journal of Human Stress* 6:22–27, 1980.

Rothschild, B. *The Body Remembers: The Psychophysiology of Trauma and Trauma Treatment.* W. W. Norton, New York, 2000.

Sapolsky, R. *Why Zebras Don't Get Ulcers,* 4th ed. W. H. Freeman & Company, New York, 2009.

Sateia, M. J., and Nowell, P. D. Insomnia, *Lancet* 364:1959–1973, 2004. www.sleepfoundation.org.

Seaward, B. L. *National Safety Council's Stress Management.* Jones & Bartlett, Boston, MA, 1994.

Seaward, B. L. *A Good Night's Sleep: Stress Insomnia and Digital Toxicity.* WELCOA, Omaha, NE, 2015.

Segerstreom, S. C., and Miller, G. E. Psychological Stress and the Human Immune System: A Meta-analytic Study of 30 Years of Inquiry, *Psychological Bulletin* 130(4):601–630, 2004.

Selye, H. *The Stress of Life.* McGraw-Hill, New York, 1976.

Selye, H. *Stress without Distress.* Lippincott, New York, 1974.

Shapiro, D. *Your Body Speaks Your Mind.* Sounds True Books, Boulder, CO, 2006.

Simeons, A. T.W. *Man's Presumptuous Brain: An Evolutionary Interpretation of Psychosomatic Diseases.* E. P. Dutton, New York, 1961.

Stein, J. The New Greatest Generation, *Time,* 28–34, May 20, 2013.

Stein, J. Tyranny of the Mob (Why We Are Losing the Internet to the Culture of Hate). *Time.* August 29, 2016.

Stepp, L. S. Enough Talk Already, *Washington Post,* August 21, 2007. www.washingtonpost.com/wpdyn/content/article/2007/08/17/AR2007081702267.html.

Taylor, S. *Health Psychology,* 9th ed. McGraw-Hill, New York, 2014.

Taylor, S. *The Tending Instinct.* Owl Books, New York, 2003.

Taylor, S., et al. Biobehavioral Responses to Stress in Females: Tend and Befriend, Not Fight or Flight, *Psychological Review* 107(3):411–429, 2000.

Travis, J., and Ryan, R. *Wellness Workbook,* 3rd ed. Celestial Arts, Berkeley, CA, 2004.

Wong, M. Vacationing Americans Have Given New Meaning to the Advertising Slogan, Don't Leave Home Without It, *Associated Press,* Sept. 1, 2000.

Zarski, J. J. Hassles and Health: A Replication, *Health Psychology* 3:243–251, 1984.

CHAPTER 2

The Sociology of Stress

Americans are the most entertained and least informed people on the planet.

—Robert F. Kennedy, Jr.

Today's world is a very different place from the one that existed when Walter Cannon coined the term "fight-or-flight response" and Hans Selye first uttered the words "general adaptation syndrome." Little did they know just how much stress would become a part of the social fabric of everyday life in the twenty-first century. Some experts argue that our collective stress is a result of our inability to keep up with all the changes that influence the many aspects of our lives. Simply stated, our physiology has not evolved at a comparable rate to the social changes of the last half-century. Perhaps it never will.

Futurist Alvin Toffler warned of these changes decades ago in his best-selling book *Future Shock*. In a 2010 National Public Radio (NPR) interview celebrating the fortieth anniversary of his book, Toffler stated that the "future shock" he described then is here now. *Future Shock* describes the stress that accompanies a proliferation of technology, urban sprawl, and a glut of information on the Internet.

Douglas Rushkoff is a social media theorist and author of the book *Present Shock*, a timely sequel to Toffler's *Future Shock*. Whereas Toffler described that rapid change was coming, Rushkoff states the whirlwind of change is here. Our society, he states, has become reoriented to the present moment with the likes of Twitter, Facebook, Tumblr, and Instagram. In Rushkoff's words, "Everything is live, real time, and always-on." Citizens with cell phones now post

current events on YouTube quicker than CNN can get a camera crew to report the headline news (as was evident in the Boston Marathon bombing event in 2013). Emails have lost favor to instant messaging, blogs have given way to Twitter feeds, and the search engine Google includes the Google Now option. Linear time has become compressed into a collection of single moments, each forgotten as we become immersed in the next now moment. As someone with his finger on the pulse of social media, Rushkoff sees a new series of stressors and problems with the syndrome he calls present shock. They include the following:

1. *Narrative collapse:* Because so much attention is on the present moment, people cannot get a clear perspective on their lives (e.g., addressing problems of global warming or saving for retirement). Life events are reduced to myopic 140-character tweets or quick Facebook status updates, losing the bigger context of one's life.

2. *Digiphrenia:* The tacit permission to be in more than one place at a time with a variety of social media.

3. *Overwinding:* The ability to reduce big-time scales into small ones (as a result, getting less done).

4. *Fractalnoia:* The anxiety associated with rapid media grazing and jumping to conclusions with incomplete information in the absence of cause and effect perspective.

Moreover, the need for instant gratification mixed with voyeurism and ego grooming becomes a recipe for stress. People's eyes may have adapted to viewing multiple screens and fingers may adapt to smaller keypads finding multiple search engines, but the human nervous system interprets the bombardment of sensory stimulation as overload and adapts through the general adaptation system (GAS).

Author and physician Roberta Lee has a new name for this intense state of stress: "superstress." As a practitioner on the front lines of health care, she sees the result of superstress in patients who live a hectic and demanding lifestyle, in whom chronic stress ultimately translates into chronic disease. She predicts that this association will only increase if people don't take time to integrate effective stress-management skills—specifically meditation, exercise, and healthy eating habits—into their daily lives.

Holmes and Rahe, the creators of the Social Readjustment Rating Scale, were dead-on regarding various social aspects of life that can destabilize one's personal equilibrium, even with the best coping skills employed. Yet no matter what corner of the global village you live in, the stresses of moving to a new city or losing a job are now compounded by significant twenty-first-century issues. We are a product of our society, and societal stress is dramatically on the rise. A quick look at current headlines provides a window on the impact of societal stress on the individual:

- Pedestrians Killed by Texting Driver
- Florida Family Gets Micro-Chipped: Are You Next?
- Bedbug Epidemic Spreads to University Campuses
- Consumers Addicted to Smartphones
- Impact of the Great Recession to Last for Years to Come
- Obesity Epidemic Related to Artificial Sweeteners?

Experts who keep a finger on the pulse of humanity suggest that as rapid as these changes are now, the rate and number of changes are only going to increase.

It's not just the changes we encounter that affect our stress levels, but also how we engage with these new changes. Increasingly, this engagement is online. Unfortunately, the stress that is provoked is real, not virtual. The majority of interactive Web sites are littered with negative comments, frustrations, expletives, and rants, all of which suggest a malaise in the general public combined with an unparalleled freedom to honestly express oneself anonymously. While it's true that Facebook, Twitter, and YouTube played a significant role in the social changes of Arab countries, from Tunisia and Egypt to Libya, Yemen, Syria, and even Turkey, many people found themselves persecuted for expressing these freedoms publicly.

Being overwhelmed with choices in communication technology for staying in touch with friends, colleagues, and employees leads to a whole new meaning of "burnout." Being tied to smartphones and tablets after work hours is bringing about a rash of lawsuits regarding unpaid overtime (Simon, 2010). And then there is the stress associated with the creative freedom gained or lost in cyberspace. True, freedom and creativity have been elevated to new heights by the Internet; however, in today's narcissistic and exhibitionist society, anybody can publish a book, release a single, be a critic, star in their own YouTube video, comment on any blog, and claim their full 15 minutes of fame. The rest of the world looks on in what is often described as "e-voyeurism."

The world is rapidly changing, and with it, the culture in which we live—all of which holds the potential to add layers upon layers of stress weighing on each individual. Simply stated, one cannot examine personal stress levels without looking at intertwining social mores and cultural trends, because whether we know it or not, we are greatly influenced by them all. As the expression goes, "Each of us is a product of our culture." As much as we might like, we cannot renounce the world and move to the nearest monastery or Amish community. En masse, we would only take all our cultural tendencies with us. In the words of John Donne, "No man is an island." The social fabric connects us all. There are, however, those who make a serious effort to change the fabric of the social culture, living examples of how to reduce the collective stress level. These, too, make the headlines, but mostly as curiosities:

- Organic Food Purchases on the Sharp Increase
- Man Escapes the Black Hole of his Smartphone
- Biking to Work Increases 60% in Past Decade
- Drop in Teen Suicide Linked to Legalization of Same-sex Marriage
- Pursuit of Happiness Still a Strong American Pastime

Physiology, psychology, anthropology, theology—the topic of stress is so colossal that it is studied by researchers in a great many disciplines, not the least of which is sociology. **Sociology** is often described as the study

> **Sociology:** The study of human social behavior within families, organizations, and institutions; the study of the individual in relationship to society as a whole.

of human social behavior within families, organizations, and institutions: The study of the individual in relationship to society as a whole. Because everybody is born into a family and most people work for a living, no one is exempt from the sociology of stress. Revising John Donne's observation for the modern era, "No man or woman is an island." Whether we like it or not, we are all connected to each other.

What if it is not we who are stressed per se, but the society and culture we live in (or have created)? Poorly designed urban sprawl with no consideration of sidewalks or nature paths for exercise. Food deserts in our nation's cities. Poorly drafted legislation regarding working mothers. Perpetual issues of gender and race inequality that are so woven into the fabric of society that they are often hidden to those fortunate enough to even know what stress management is. This is the argument made by Dana Becker in her book *One Nation Under Stress*, which discusses what she calls stress and the biopolitics of American life. In an overview of the past several decades, Becker, a professor of social work at Bryn Mawr College in Pennsylvania, cites many examples of societal stress that contribute to personal strife, particularly affecting women, minorities, and the poor. She contends that for stress to be addressed fully, it must be reconciled from a societal perspective or what she calls the "wear and tear of society."

Perhaps the sociology of stress can best be acknowledged through the buzzword "social networking," which describes the likes of Facebook, Twitter, Facetime/Skype, YouTube, Snapchat, Instagram, and new social media and networking outlets looming on the horizon. Technology has even changed how people converse at a dinner party (e.g., one person asks a question and five people pull out their cell phones and Google the answer). Technology, the economy, and the environment have become significant threads of the social fabric. This chapter examines some of the most current issues and trends in the global society and their potential to increase stress for each of us personally.

■ Technostress

The tsunami of cyber information has been building for years, yet the first devastating wave seems to have hit the shores of the human mind in earnest at about the same time Facebook reached over half a billion users in 2010 (**FIG. 2.1**), which was the same year that the Swiss army knife included a USB drive as a necessary tool for "survival." The deluge of tweets, Facebook updates,

FIGURE 2.1   In 2013, the popular social networking site Facebook reached over 1 billion users. What was originally created as a means for college-aged students to meet each other is now cited by some as promoting loneliness and increasing social alienation.

Skype messages, text messages, and emails has led to annoyance and addiction for a great many people who are fed up with giving their lives over to technology. The growing dependence on technology has even inspired a term: "screen addiction." If it's not computer screens and smartphones, it's iPads, google glasses, and Bluetooth technology, none of which is bad, but all of which can become problematic if your life is completely centered around being plugged in all the time.

Technology is meant to serve us, yet many people have turned the roles upside down and have become slaves to technology, hence the technostress phenomenon.

The perfect storm of stress related to the information age comes from the overwhelming amount of information available, the distractive nature of being plugged in 24/7, a sense of alienation, and the poor boundaries people maintain to regulate the information available. Examples of poor boundaries include college students who text during classroom lectures (Rubinkam, 2010) and the scores of people who bring all their technology with them on vacation, thus never separating work from leisure and possibly compromising both (**FIG. 2.2**). For example, it is not uncommon to find people plugged in to Wi-Fi technology at or near National Park campgrounds, a place people once went to get away from the trappings of modern civilization (Seigler, 2010). Similarly, fewer than half of all employees nationwide leave their desk or workstation during lunch hour, according to a Manpower survey, leading to higher stress levels and fatigue (Marquardt, 2010).

FIGURE 2.2 Copper Mountain Ski Resort in Colorado has some of the best slopes in the world to ski, but these days many people ski or snowboard one run and then check their emails and text messages. Vacations were once a way to escape from work, but now people bring their work with them via smartphones and laptops. People now say they cannot live without these accessories.

Many terms have been created for all the problems associated with this tsunami of information and the convenience of accessing it, but the one term that sums it all up is **technostress**, which is the feeling of being overwhelmed by technology. Factors contributing to techno-stress include, but are not limited to, privacy issues, identity theft, cell phone radiation, sensory bombardment, Internet scams, addiction to Internet gambling and pornography, and the problem of children having access to adult content. The Kaiser Family Foundation data suggest that 8–18-year-olds spend over 7 hours per day with entertainment media (video games, TV, apps, etc.).

> **Technostress:** A term used to define the result of a fast-paced life dependent on various means of technology, including computers, cell phones and smartphones, personal digital assistants, texting, and email—all of which were supposed to give people more leisure time. Instead, people have become slaves, addicted to the constant use of these devices and technologies.

Perhaps the most widespread stress from technology that most people experience is the perpetual distraction of email and the replacement of face-to-face conversation with digital communications (**FIG. 2.3**). In one of a series of articles in 2010 for the *New York Times*, technology investigative reporter Matt Richtel noted that people check email up to 37 times an hour on average. Furthermore, some people feel an urge to respond to emails immediately and feel guilty if they don't. How many emails can push one over the edge, past the threshold of exhaustion? According to a Harris Interactive poll, respondents said that more than 50 emails per day caused stress, many using the phrase "email stress" to explain their frustrations. According to Pingdom, a Web-monitoring firm, over 90 trillion emails were sent over the Internet in 2009, with an average of 247 billion emails per day (Swartz, 2010).

In the age of digital anxiety, what impact does repeated interfacing with Wi-Fi technology have on our brains? Given the recent discovery that our brain tissue has the ability to adapt to a host of cognitive challenges and stimuli (a phenomenon known as *neuroplasticity*), the implications are significant. Susan Greenfield (2008, 2009), a professor of synaptic pharmacology at Oxford University, is concerned regarding how six to eight hours a day of computer interfacing will affect neuronal connectivity. Research from the University of California at Irvine reveals that the constant interruption of emails triggers the stress response, with the subsequent release of stress hormones affecting short-term memory (Richtel, 2010). And if you ever wondered why people, perhaps even yourself, seem addicted to checking emails, voice mails, or tweets, consider this fact: Research shows that the receipt of emails and tweets is accompanied by a release of dopamine. Dopamine, a "feel-good" neurotransmitter, is associated with chemical addictions. In the absence of dopamine release, boredom ensues, until the next fix (Richtel, 2010).

Whereas Greenfield and others are alarmed regarding sensory input and brain physiology, others are concerned with people's emotional maturity, intuition, psychological reasoning, memory processing, and moral compass (Dossey, 2009). Clay Shirky, author of the best-selling book *Cognitive Surplus*, cites a dramatic shift in society's relationship to technology, from primarily watching television to using online media. With this shift lies both promise and peril. The promise is the collective effort (sometimes called "digital consciousness" or "wiki efforts") to solve world problems. The peril is becoming self-absorbed in cyberspace with screen-addiction or being drowned out by the sheer amount of cyber noise (Alter, 2017).

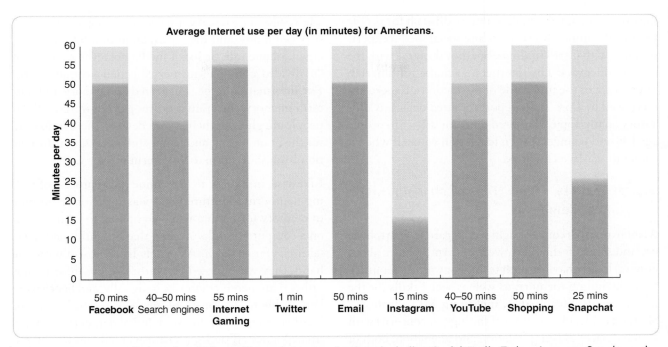

Average Internet use per day (in minutes) for Americans.

| 50 mins | 40–50 mins | 55 mins | 1 min | 50 mins | 15 mins | 40–50 mins | 50 mins | 25 mins |
| Facebook | Search engines | Internet Gaming | Twitter | Email | Instagram | YouTube | Shopping | Snapchat |

FIGURE 2.3   According to data collected by various organizations including Social Media Today, Amazon, Google, and the Entertainment Software Association for 2016, on average, people spend 8 hours per day on their screen devices, from gaming, shopping, and search engines to all kinds of social media posting. Teens (ages 12–18) spend as much as 9 hours per day. One billion hours of YouTube is watched every day. The impact of screen use and Internet interaction on society cannot be understated.

Every abrupt shift in the history of societies has had its associated stressors; for example, the shift from agrarian to industrial society was correlated with a dramatic increase in alcoholism, regarded as the "social disease" of its time. In today's abrupt shift to online technology and social media, the online technology is itself the addiction. This addiction is easy to observe: Check people's behavior inside an airplane cabin the moment the plane touches down, or in a movie theater once the credits appear on the screen—everybody reaches for their cell phone to check messages. Young people today who never knew life without a cell phone or iPad don't understand why older adults seem so concerned about their addictive tech habits, whereas adults notice that children and teens raised with screen technology may be well versed in cyber communications skills but are socially immature regarding face-to-face communication skills, including eye contact. Harvard psychologist Sherry Turkle notes these and other growing stressors in her book *Alone Together*, stating that people's social skills diminish with technology and artificial intelligence.

Another problem associated with constantly being "on" with technology is what experts describe as the **shallow effect**. According to Nicholas Carr, author of the book

The Shallows: What the Internet Is Doing to Our Brains, information grazing is not the same thing as cultivating a synthesis of wisdom, yet superficial information grazing has become the norm, resulting in a shallow understanding of complicated issues. Not long ago, there was a clear line between information and entertainment. That line is quite blurry, if not non-existent, now—so much so that many people view these two aspects as one and the same, as illustrated by Jon Stewart's *Daily Show*, Huffingtonpost.com, and DailyBeast.com. Moreover, jumping from site to site and cherry-picking information seems to "rewire" the brain to deleterious effect; specifically, it compromises one's ability to concentrate or focus on something long enough to fully understand all its implications. Carr states that this rewiring of the brain not only weakens one's ability to cultivate one's memory (by always being reliant on an outside source of

Shallow effect: A shallow understanding of complicated issues that is caused by information grazing. Jumping from site to site and cherry-picking information compromises one's ability to concentrate or focus on something long enough to fully understand all its implications.

information), but also makes it more difficult for people to calm the mind and relax. Many social media experts disagree with Carr's findings, but they do agree with the obvious dilemma: The Internet may make you smarter, but beware of the multitude of distractions. Experts interviewed by *USA Today* reporter Marco della Cava for a story on this topic all offered the same advice to people aged 30 and younger: Learn to restrain yourself when it comes to Wi-Fi technology.

Digital Toxicity, FOMO (Fear of Missing Out), and Digital Dementia

As more research comes to light with regard to smartphone use and screen technology, we are learning more about how various behaviors with technology affect cognitive skills, including memory, as well as social skills (or the lack thereof). Sociologists, including MIT Professor Sherry Turkle, identify two of the biggest concerns with screen devices as being isolation and alienation, both of which lead to or perpetuate stress.

What effect does digital overload have on memory? Research conducted by Bill Thornton at the University of Southern Maine and published in the journal *Social Psychology* revealed that people who had their cell phones within easy reach were less efficient with a given task than those who did the same task without the presence of their cell phone (Freidman, 2014). Smartphones not only distract one's attention, but the constant anticipation of social media messages derails memory processing and perhaps other cognitive functions, keeping the brain in an alert state, one that is hard to turn off when preparing for sleep.

With the world of information at our fingertips, can having access to so much information be a hindrance to memory rather than an asset? The answer appears to be a definitive YES! In an article titled "A Smart Thing That Makes You Stupid," investigative reporter Ron Friedman cites a series of studies that reveals the problem with being online with a smartphone all the time. In the first study, two groups of people were given a task: one group was allowed to have their cell phones within arm's reach (on the table where they were working) and the second group had no access to their smartphones. When the results were tabulated, the group of people with access to their smartphones did 20 percent worse on the task than the control group. In a similar study, people were asked to participate in a face-to-face conversation. Those who had a smartphone within reach found the person they were in conversation with boring, whereas those without a smartphone did not.

The results showed that when one's focus is split (distracted) between a task and the anticipation of a text message, email, phone call, or social media post (the opposite of "undivided attention") memory function is compromised. For information to be transferred from short- to long-term memory, the brain requires periods of rest. When people are glued to their screen devices, there is no time for the brain to rest, and hence shift necessary information from short-term to long-term memory.

Likewise, in a study to determine if the process of taking handwritten lecture notes was superior or inferior to memory formation, when compared to taking notes on a computer, results showed that old fashioned note-taking is far superior. As people listened and wrote by hand, they were forced to synthesize the information rather than merely transcribe it digitally, and hence were better able to demonstrate memory recall. Freidman has these suggestions to avoid digital dementia: (1) keep smartphones off desks, (2) banish email and text alerts, and (3) schedule distraction-free periods each day.

The boom in the telecommunications industry and computer industry, pillars of the information age, has led to an overnight conversion of lifestyle in both American and global society. In their book *Technostress*, authors Weil and Rosen suggest that the rapid pace of technology will only continue with greater speed in the coming years, giving a whole new meaning to the expression "24/7." They predict, as do others, that the majority of people will not deal well with this change. The result will be more stress, more illness and disease, more addictions, more dysfunction, and a greater imbalance in people's lives (Alter, 2017). There is general consensus that the rate of change of technology has far outpaced the level of responsibility and moral codes that typically accompany the creative process. The following are some aspects of technostress as they currently affect our lives:

- *Information overload:* Given the flood of Facebook updates, text messages, emails, pop-up ads, smartphone apps, Web sites, and Pinterest posts, it is easy to become inundated by information. Reviewing and responding to a slew of text messages, emails, tweets, and voice mails, not to mention deleting spam and closing pop-up ads, can eat up several hours of one's time each day. Research reveals that too much information, coupled with all the means of accessing it, results in what is now called "brain freeze," "information paralysis," and "infostress," leading to indecisiveness, inability to focus, and poor memory recall (Begley, 2011).

- *Cyber bullying:* Bullying may be a perpetual pastime, but taking this behavior online to a global audience with online harassments, accusations, slurs, and rumors can destroy one's personal integrity. (Several people have committed suicide over cyber-bullying.)

- *Identify theft:* Well beyond bank account numbers and credit card access codes, identify theft now includes imposter Facebook and Twitter accounts. One's identity can be stolen in seconds, yet it may take months to recover.

- *Cyber hacking:* It's one thing to have someone hack into your online accounts (and this is stressful), but the stakes have been raised with international hacking, most notably overseas nationals infiltrating everything from online banking systems and news outlets to power companies that connect to the power grids that service the Internet.

- *Bandwidth and cloud issues:* If you have ever tried to download and watch a movie only to find out that there are issues with bandwidth, you know the meaning of technostress. And as more and more apps and software become available only through the cloud, stress looms when there are issues with cloud accessibility.

- *Boundaries:* Less than twenty years ago, there were clear-cut boundaries between one's personal and professional lives. Today the boundaries have dissolved to a point where it's hard to tell where one ends and the next begins. With smartphones, and tablets, a person can be accessed every minute of the day. People feel compelled to take these devices to movie theaters, plays, restaurants, vacations, and even to bed. Although the expression "24/7" was first coined to refer to retail shopping, it now conveys nonstop accessibility.

- *Privacy:* With constant accessibility, one forfeits privacy. Furthermore, with many purchases made on the Internet, each person develops a consumer profile, which then is sold to a host of other vendors. From cookies to bookmarks to cyber-bullying to identity theft, privacy has become a serious if not stressful issue in the information age. With advances in reducing the microchip to the size of a molecule, information storage is predicted to go from the smart card to biotech implants.

- *Ethics:* With the completion of the Human Genome Project, scientists may be able to identify persons likely to inherit genetic-based diseases. Although this information may provide insight into cures, fear arises at the prospect of this information falling into the hands of insurance companies that revoke policies based on genetic profiling. Scientific breakthroughs in genetic research raise other moral and ethical concerns, too, such as those surrounding genetic cloning and genetically modified foods.

- *Less family time:* Unlike television watching, which can be done as a family, surfing the Internet is a solitary activity. Thus, people are spending more virtual time on their computers and cell phones and less real time with each other.

- *Online dating:* As people spend more and more time plugged into their computers, they find less time for social activities. Many people are enlisting the help of Facebook, Match.com, and eHarmony for finding relationships. Although many are happy to have this new way to meet people and have great luck with it, some find their expectations unfulfilled by people who falsely represent themselves online.

- *Wi-Fi stress:* If you were to eavesdrop on conversations or scroll through social tweets, you would be quick to notice that issues such as net neutrality, cloud distortion, and bandwidth access are producing a great deal of stress for nearly everyone tied to the Internet. As more content becomes accessible online, these issues will result in higher service fees, stretching tight budgets even tighter.

- *Technology and the generational divide:* Are you constantly being asked by your parents to assist them with all things digital, such as helping to program their iPod and digital cameras, download music files, install software packages, upgrade operating systems, download apps, or set up Wi-Fi in the house? It's not an uncommon hassle among the younger generation, who feel as if they are constantly on call for "parental tech support."

A Decline in Civility

Have you noticed that people today seem quick-tempered, impatient, cynical, self-centered, and perhaps even rude at times? If you have, you are not alone. Once again, a review of some disturbing national headlines suggests a high level of restlessness in the American culture:

- Why We're Losing the Internet to the Culture of Hate

- Responsible Gun Owner Shoots, Kills Brother in Fight over Cheeseburger

- Churchgoer Killed in Fight over Seat at Sunday Service

- Internet Harassment Is Now the Norm

- Man Shoots Woman After He Runs Red Light

- Majority of College Students Text During Classroom Lectures

Civility, as expressed through social etiquette, refers to the practice of good manners and appropriate behavior. Many consider the basic rules of civility to be sorely lacking in today's culture. Nitsa Lallas, who authored the book *Renewing Values in America*, attributes the lack of civility to an alchemy of narcissism and a national lack of values, contributing not only to social unease, but also to the economic mess that created the Great Recession of 2008–2009.

Moreover, a revolution in the way people communicate with each other over the past few years has dramatically changed the social fabric of our culture, particularly how we relate, or fail to relate, to each other in face-to-face situations, as discussed earlier. Instant accessibility has sown the seeds for impatience. Politeness has given way to rudeness. The type of behavior used in Internet rants and talk radio phone calls carries over into face-to-face shouting matches at sporting events and political rallies. Social manners (e.g., appropriate behavior and thinking of others first) have become minimal, if not obsolete, for many people, particularly when bursts of anger perpetuate feelings of victimization.

Today's self-centered, narcissistic indulgences have hit an all-time high, many of which are directly related to political incivility (**BOX 2.1**). How did things go so wrong? Some people blame poor parenting skills. Many cite talk radio and various news media outlets that broadcast incivility. Others point their finger at the proliferation of technology and the constant self-promotion that seems to go along with it (Meyer, 2008). Many say the perfect storm of "uncivil Americans" is a combination of all these factors. Noting the serious issue of American incivility, Rutgers University has initiated a one-credit course called Project Civility for students, with topics ranging from cell phone etiquette and cyberbullying to civil sportsmanship and social responsibility

Civility: The practice of good manners and appropriate behavior.

BOX 2.1   Political Incivility

Political incivility reached new heights (or lows) with the 2016 U.S. presidential election, and experts suggest that this is the new normal. It was not uncommon to see fights breaking out at political rallies and candidates name-calling (e.g., "nasty woman") during the presidential debates. The political climate was so polarized that feuds broke out among friends and family members across the country. People seem to have less tolerance for those with differing opinions. Social media rants and bullying have reached an all-time high. Many blame candidates, social media, and the Internet for the rise of political incivility. Political incivility, in turn, can lead to other antisocial behaviors in various aspects of people's lives, adding to already increased stress levels (Richards, 2016).

(**BOX 2.2**). It is likely that other colleges will follow this trend (Lanman, 2010).

According to a study by the *New York Times*, the average young American now spends every waking minute (with the possible exception of school classes) using a smartphone, computer, television, or other electronic device. Adults appear to be no different. It is not uncommon to see people texting while at movie theaters, talking on cell phones in restaurants (despite signs prohibiting their use), and texting while driving (despite the growing number of state laws banning this behavior). In 2006, researchers at the University of Utah were curious to see whether the distraction of cell phone use while driving was similar to driving while under the influence of alcohol. Using driving simulators, it was revealed that people on cell phones show a driving impairment rate similar to a blood alcohol level of 0.08%, the demarcation of drunk driving in the majority of U.S. states. Although many people may recognize the dangers of talking and driving, few offer to give up this social faux-pas mode of multitasking (Dossey, 2009).

Many people use technology to avoid stressful situations, which adds to a general lack of civility in society. Examples include quitting a job with a tweet, breaking up with a girlfriend or boyfriend via Facebook, or sending a derogatory email and blind-copying everyone in one's address book (**FIG. 2.4**). The modern lack of civility cannot be blamed entirely on technology, yet the

BOX 2.2   Civility 101

(Things Your Parents Should Have Taught You)

The following is a short list of commonly accepted polite manners that promote civil behavior. The premise of civility, as expressed through etiquette, is respect for your fellow human being (also known as the Golden Rule).

1. Always say "please" and "thank you."

2. Always look a person in the eye when addressing them.

3. Never interrupt when someone is talking; wait until they finish speaking.

4. Refrain from rude or vulgar language in public.

5. Stand when someone enters a room and greet people politely upon meeting them.

6. Shake hands when you are introduced to someone new.

7. Hold the door open for people upon entering or exiting through it.

8. Cover your mouth when you sneeze, cough, yawn, and/or chew food.

9. Wait for everyone to be served before eating.

10. Don't take cuts (e.g., airport gates, movie theaters, etc.).

11. Don't bring your cell phone to the dinner table.

12. Don't end a relationship with a text message, Facebook post, or email. Do it in person.

FIGURE 2.4   People spend less face-to-face time with each other and more screen time talking to others, leading many experts to suggest that social skills and face-to-face communication skills are on the decline in America.

dramatic rise in the use of communication devices has played its part. How would you rate your current level of social etiquette?

Americans may be lacking in the social graces, but they are renowned the world over for giving generously to the needy (e.g., the Boston Marathon bombing victims, New York and New Jersey residents affected by Hurricane Sandy, and the victims of countless devastating tornadoes in the midwest). However, texting a donation for earthquake relief while watching the Super Bowl or The Voice is far different from face-to-face contact and polite social interactions. It's the direct social contact skills that are sorely lacking in American culture today.

■ Environmental Disconnect

Even if you don't listen to the news regularly, it's hard to ignore the impact humanity is having on the state of the planet. The word "sustainable" has entered the American lexicon, even if the concept is largely ignored in practice by most people. From a sociological perspective, the earth may not be your family, an organization, or institute, but it is your home, and as such your relationship to it and with it is paramount. Modern society can be said to suffer from an **environmental disconnect**, a state in which people have distanced themselves so much from the natural environment that they cannot fathom the magnitude of their impact on it. The term **nature deficit disorder** was coined by award-winning author Richard Louv in his book *Last Child in the Woods* to describe the growing abyss between people and the outdoor world. Kids, as it turns out, would rather play

Environmental disconnect: A state in which people have distanced themselves so much from the natural environment that they cannot fathom the magnitude of their impact on it.

Nature deficit disorder: A term coined by Richard Louv to describe a now-common behavior (affliction) where people (particularly children) simply don't get outside enough, hence losing touch with the natural world and all of its wonder.

video games or surf online than play outside—where there are no outlets. A great many experts and luminaries have predicted over the years that as humanity distances itself from nature, people will suffer the consequences, primarily in terms of compromised health status.

Continuing our theme of current news headlines, consider these:

- 2016 Hottest Year on Record
- Children Spend Less Time Outdoors Than Prison Inmates
- Fracking Now Linked to Hundreds of Earthquakes
- Earth Just Passed the 400 PPM Climate Threshold
- Dangerous Depletion of the World's Aquifers
- Climate Change Puts 1.3 Billion People and $158 Billion at Risk, Says World Bank

An age-old question asks, "How many angels can dance on the head of a pin?" Today that imponderable question has become "How many humans can sustainably live on planet Earth?" It's interesting to note that some of the earliest studies on stress physiology involved placing an abnormally high number of mice in a cage. As their environment, personal space, food availability, and quality of life decreased with each additional occupant, tension significantly increased. The parallels between the environment and behavior of those mice and humans today are unavoidable, giving credence to the axiom, "As population increases, behavior decreases."

To support this premise, scientists recently reviewed over 60 studies regarding the relationship between increased global temperatures and increased violence. They concluded that as global temperatures increase, there is a corresponding increase in violence, hostility, and conflict (Kirwood, 2013).

Even if you think your drinking water is safe, you may be mistaken. Residents of Flint, Michigan, have been forced to drink bottled water for several years due to lead contamination. Lead, leaching into the drinking water from old pipes, is a well-known toxin associated with brain dysfunction, and the drinking water of Flint is full of it. Not only is the inconvenient lack of tap water stressful, so is the realization that many children may suffer the long-term effects of brain damage. People in Flint have been forced to drink bottled water for years, currently with no signs of improvement due to political squabbling. Residents of Flint may get the most headlines about toxic drinking water, but they are hardly alone with this concern. Residents from several cities and communities

around the country have similar issues, not the least of whom are the Navajo Indians in Arizona.

In other water news, rising waters due to global warming are already having an effect in Miami, where city officials have begun to elevate highways in and around the city in an effort to deal with the loss of land due to flooding from global warming. Rising sea levels have also swallowed up land in Louisiana. In fact, it is estimated that the Bayou State is losing several hundred acres a year to climate change. Once shaped like a shoe, the map of Louisiana is a much smaller land mass now than it was even a decade ago.

By now everyone has not only heard of the issues on global warming, but also has experienced the preliminary effects first hand: violent storms, hotter summers, more intense droughts, and severe weather patterns. The problems of our dependence on oil were highlighted by the massive 2010 oil spill in the Gulf of Mexico. What has yet to become clear to the average person, however, are the looming problems of water shortages, an issue that will greatly affect everyone. Former United Nations Secretary General Ban Ki-Moon has repeatedly stated that wars will most likely be fought over water sources in our lifetime. So significant is this stressor that *National Geographic* dedicated its April 2010 issue entirely to the topic of water and our thirsty world. Environmentalist Lester Brown of the Earth Policy Institute states that when valuable drinking water is used for such things as fracking, and laws make collecting rainwater illegal, tension rises. Moreover, the variables of rapid population growth, increased energy demands, farming irrigation demands, depleted aquifers, and limited water supplies make water a dramatically stressful topic for a great many global citizens, including Americans. Here are some facts concerning water that will affect you now and in the years to come:

- 97.5 percent of the earth's water is salty, with only 2.5 percent of earth's water considered fresh.
- Two-thirds of all fresh water is frozen.
- Many Western states (e.g., Texas, Arizona, and California) are draining underground aquifers quicker than they can be naturally restored.
- Many freshwater streams contain hormones and antibiotics from prescription drugs flushed down toilets and petrochemical fertilizers from agricultural run-off.
- Americans use approximately 100 gallons of water at home each day, compared with 5 gallons per day in developing nations.

Stress with a Human Face

Society, and the culture it creates, is often described in metaphors. A common one is "the social fabric." For Juliet, a more apt metaphor might be a carpet, one that was pulled right from underneath her feet as a child. Juliet Mamie Simbo now lives in Denver, Colorado, but at the age of 13 she and her family fled from Sierra Leone, a small country on the west coast of Africa. She begins her story with a Hollywood reference:

"If you have seen the movie *Blood Diamond*, starring Leonardo DiCaprio and Jennifer Connelly, then you have witnessed a realistic portrayal of the horrors of civil war in Sierra Leone. I lived in this world. I witnessed my dad held at gunpoint on our porch on January 10th, 1999, by a rebel who told all of us that he was going to kill my father and suck his blood because of his vocal opposition to the atrocities being committed in my country. The gunman spared my father's life; however, in a defiant move, he turned and shot and killed our family dog. Because of greed and hatred amongst the people of my country, death came to many in Sierra Leone for seemingly no reason. I was changed forever by these events, knowing that my life was kept alive by the slimmest of margins."

As an immigrant to the United States, she had to adapt quickly to a whole new culture, one with superhighways, fast food, snowstorms, power shopping, abundant lifestyle opportunities, high technology, and crumbling family structures. "Initially, I felt lost and lonely as I tried to merge into the fast lane that is the American lifestyle," she explained. But over time, Juliet became less shy and more assertive, adapting successfully to a new way of life in a new culture. With college graduation months away, her eyes are now set on new sights. One day Juliet hopes to return to Africa and use her knowledge, skills, and experience to help make the world a better place, beginning with the severe hunger issues known in this part of the world.

Juliet has used her experience of cultural differences in a positive way and hopes that others will do the same. As she said in her high school graduation speech, "I say to you, open your eyes to the world beyond your country's borders. Feel the presence of humanity around the world and learn about them, even experience their culture. I hope that one day, you can be as grateful as I am for what you know about a different land and people. I thank you for being a part of my world, and I welcome you to visit mine."

- It takes 2,500 gallons of water to make 1 pound of beef and 1,800 gallons to grow enough cotton for a pair of blue jeans (**TABLE 2.1**).

- Clean water is a huge issue in China, so much so that the country tried (and failed) to license and export fresh water from the Great Lakes Region in the United States and Canada.

- The Three Gorges Dam in central China caused the earth's axis to tilt by nearly an inch.

TABLE 2.1   The Real Cost of Water

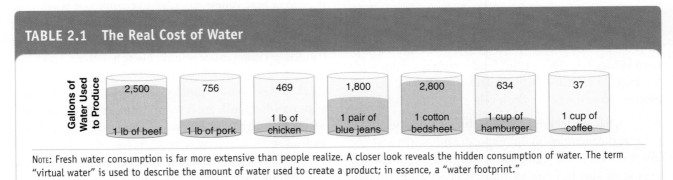

Gallons of Water Used to Produce						
2,500	756	469	1,800	2,800	634	37
1 lb of beef	1 lb of pork	1 lb of chicken	1 pair of blue jeans	1 cotton bedsheet	1 cup of hamburger	1 cup of coffee

NOTE: Fresh water consumption is far more extensive than people realize. A closer look reveals the hidden consumption of water. The term "virtual water" is used to describe the amount of water used to create a product; in essence, a "water footprint."

Data from National Geographic Society. *Water: Our Thirsty World* [special issue], *National Geographic*, April 2010; and Water Footprint Network (www.waterfootprint.org). Accessed February 16, 2011.

FIGURE 2.5 People, including children, are spending less time outside and in nature. Many children prefer to be inside playing video games or surfing the Internet. Being disconnected from nature may be harmful to one's health, including inadequate exposure to natural sunlight for vitamin D absorption.

FIGURE 2.6 In every generation, there are people who predict humanity's demise. The world is not coming to an end, but our future will certainly depend on how we act now.

Perhaps the most subtle warning of a disconnect from our environment is the news that for the first time it has been noted that Americans are not getting enough vitamin D, as explained by nutritionist and *New York Times* reporter Jane Brody. Vitamin D deficiency is due to lack of exposure to sunlight and poor dietary habits. Sunlight is often referred to as the "sunshine vitamin" because, as sunlight reaches the skin, it reacts to help form vitamin D. Today, people spend little time outdoors, denying themselves exposure to adequate amounts of sunlight (**FIG. 2.5**).

Vitamin D isn't the only nutritional/environmental problem. People who saw the documentary film *Food, Inc.* (or who read the book by Karl Weber) are acutely aware that the move away from family farms to industrial farms in the last few decades has greatly compromised the quality of food, primarily chicken and beef, and encouraged the proliferation of products that use high-fructose corn syrup. Changes in the food industry, along with inadequate exercise, help explain the recent dramatic increase in national obesity levels.

Sadly, what we lack in the sunshine vitamin, we compensate for plenty with our exposure to plastic, and not just water bottles clogging our landfills. In her acclaimed expose on this ubiquitous substance, Susan Freinkel's book, *Plastic: A Toxic Love Story*, highlights a frightening bio-ecological stressor: many plastics (derived from petroleum and natural gas) once thought to be inert are now known to leak synthetic estrogens into the fluids and foods they contain to interfere with the hormones of our endocrine system that orchestrate growth, development, and the immune system, with phthalates being one of the biggest concerns to one's health.

Some of the world's leading scientists are not optimistic about the future of humanity, given the stresses we have put on our environment and, in turn, ourselves (**FIG. 2.6**). Physicist Stephen Hawking's outlook for humanity is grim at best, unless we learn to change our ways, and quickly. In a 2010 interview with the Huffington Post blog (Stuart, 2010), he stated, "We are entering an increasingly dangerous period in our history. There have been a number of times in the past when survival has been a question of touch and go. We are rapidly depleting the finite natural resources that Earth provides, and our genetic code carries selfish and aggressive instincts." Harvard biologist E. O. Wilson and others now refer to the loss of biodiversity in our modern era as the "sixth mass extinction" on Earth, with hunting and fishing, loss of natural habitat, and pollution as the primary causes (Eldredge, 2001). Meanwhile, sociologist Jared Diamond warns that if positive changes are not made with regard to our use of resources and our relationship to our natural environment, we too will face extinction.

Not all views of the future of humanity are so dire or fatalistic. Several, in fact, are quite optimistic—with the caveat that we must act now. Consider the viewpoint of cell biologist and philosopher Bruce Lipton. In his book *Spontaneous Evolution*, he states: "Society is beginning to realize that our current beliefs are detrimental and that our world is in a very precarious position. The new science (the nexus of quantum physics, psychology, and biology) paves a way into a hopeful story of humanity's potential future, one that promotes planetary healing." Lipton uses the model of holism (in which all parts are respected and come together for a greater purpose) as the template for his optimism. Lipton is among a growing group of social luminaries, including Barbara Marx-Hubbard, Jean Houston, Christine Page, Edgar Mitchell, Elizabeth Sartoris, and Gregg Braden, who share this optimistic paradigm of humanity's shifting consciousness (Schlitz, 2010). In the words of the rock musician Sting, "Yes we are in an appalling environmental crisis, but I think as a species, we evolve through crises. That's the only glimmer of hope, really" (Richter, 2010).

Another ray of hope shone brightly on November 5, 2016, when the Paris Agreement on Climate Change became official, instituting restrictions on CO_2 emissions, as well as other strategies to halt global warming.

When technostress, incivility (mixed with political instability), and environmental disconnect combine, they form a "perfect storm of stress." How do these aspects of the sociology of stress affect you directly? Consider this: As climate changes create more droughts, food prices will increase. As chemicals from discarded technology (smartphones, flat screen TVs, etc.) pollute water supplies, environmental stressors increase. As oil reserves decrease, increasing the price of a barrel of oil, all things tied to gasoline (food distribution, travel, consumer products) will increase in price, adding to an ever-growing sense of economic anxiety. The importance of learning and using effective stress management skills becomes even more essential in the twenty-first century.

Occupational Stress

Sociologists suggest that one's family is the first and often the most important social structure, providing social support, but also stress. Coming in a close second in both aspects is one's work environment. While ideally providing professional fulfillment, a creative outlet,

FIGURE 2.7 Worker burnout has reached epic proportions as people strive to personify the Puritan work ethic that deems that work equals worth.

and a path to wealth, work is also cited as a source of significant stress by a great many employees. Paul Rosch, M.D., director of the American Institute of Stress, notes that in American society today, **occupational stress**, or job stress, is at an all-time high (**FIG. 2.7**). He defines job stress as coming from "occupational duties in which the individual perceives having a great deal of responsibility, yet little or no authority or decision-making latitude" (Rosch, 1991).

According to a 2013 Harris survey, 83 percent of American workers claim to be stressed out, a 10 percent rise from 2012. Reasons for the rise in stress are attributed to low pay, unreasonable workloads, annoying co-workers, poor work-life balance, and the fear of being laid off or fired (Perman, 2013). Few of these people take advantage of employee assistance programs offered at the worksite (Scott, 2007). One of the first signs of stress at the workplace is burnout, followed by absenteeism. The term *presenteeism* was coined to describe the related problem of going to work but being unproductive and unmotivated, there in body but not in mind.

The cost of stress is not insignificant in terms of work productivity or the bottom line of corporate profits. Rosch noted that the fiscal consequences of occupational stress cost an average of $200 billion each year. Moreover, between 60 and 80 percent of all industrial accidents are stress induced,

> **Occupational stress:** Job-related stress, which often comes from occupational duties for which people perceive themselves as having a great deal of responsibility, yet little or no authority or decision-making latitude.

"You're spending the best years of your life doing a job that you hate so you can buy stuff you don't need to support a lifestyle you don't enjoy. Sounds crazy to me!"

FIGURE 2.8

as are over 80 percent of all office visits to primary care physicians. Perhaps most striking is that workers' compensation claims associated with stress are skyrocketing, with 90 percent of claims being awarded in settlements.

What are some reasons for job stress? (**FIG. 2.8**) Although perceptions will vary from person to person, the following is a list compiled by the National Safety Council (2011):

- Lack of job security
- Too much responsibility with little or no authority
- Unrealistic expectations, deadlines, and quotas
- Corporate downsizing, restructuring, or job relocation
- Inadequate training
- Lack of appreciation
- Inadequate time to complete job responsibilities
- Inability to voice concerns
- Lack of creativity and autonomy
- Too much to do with too few resources
- Lack of clear job descriptions
- Commuting and traffic difficulties
- Keeping pace with technology
- Inadequate child care
- Poor working conditions (lighting, ventilation, noise)
- Sexual harassment and racial discrimination
- Workplace violence

Rosch noted that the Public Health Service placed stress-management courses as its top priority in order to improve health standards at the worksite. However, Rosch, who surveyed several hundred existing stress-management programs in cooperation with the Office of Occupational Safety and Health, came to the conclusion that few stress-management programs currently taught in the corporate or industrial setting offer enough substance to make a positive influential change in lifestyle behaviors, because they are either too narrowly focused or too brief, or both. Those programs he did find to be effective showed reduced illness and absenteeism, higher morale, and increased productivity.

Unfortunately, stress in the workplace is not likely to decrease any time soon. In the next decade, more companies will merge, meaning more corporate restructuring. Companies looking to appease stockholders will look for ways to trim budgets, especially by letting go of senior employees and replacing them with a young and eager workforce, or by outsourcing jobs.

Race and Gender Stress

Several national events between 2014 and 2016 brought the issues of racial and gender stress to the forefront, including the Black Lives Matter movement and the 2016 U.S. presidential campaign.

The United States, a nation of immigrants, has often been described as a melting pot, but recently another metaphor has been used to describe the make-up of her citizens: a tossed salad, where assimilation meets head on with cultural diversity. Race and ethnic issues currently make headline news, such as illegal alien issues nationwide, disenfranchised black voters in Florida, poverty in New Orleans, and Muslim Americans facing episodes of discrimination, to name a few issues. Race and gender tensions, however, are not new. It could be argued that they are as old as humanity itself. Since time began, people have felt threatened by other people of different skin color, ethnicity, gender, religion, or sexual preference. The 2008 election of the first African American president has helped jump-start a national discussion on race, but it hasn't resolved intolerance.

Stress, you will remember, is defined as a perceived threat, a threat generated by the ego. These threats manifest in a variety of ways, including stereotyping, prejudice, discrimination, harassment, and even physical harm. Race and gender stress may begin early in life; many children can attest to being bullied in grade school or excluded and teased by social cliques because of their race or gender. The emotional stress associated with this type of angst includes low self-esteem, alienation, and anxiety. Everybody wants to be accepted.

How can society help alleviate race and gender stress? Anti-bullying programs are being implemented in many schools nationwide, helping raise awareness among kids and parents of the dangers of bullying and cyber-bullying. On television, many shows have tried to better reflect the demographics of American society with casts of various ethnicities and gender identity issues (e.g., *Glee*, *Transparent*, and *Sense*). The Women's March on Washington in January 2017 also made a strong statement regarding gender inequity issues. Although these are steps in the right direction, school curricula marches on Washington D.C., and television shows alone cannot change the world overnight. They are a start, however. Remember that when people demonstrate a bias toward your race, gender, ethnic background, or anything related to these concepts, they are projecting their fears onto you. A common reaction is to meet stress with stress, but the best answer is to rise above it and take the high road.

Experts remind us that the cultural fabric of society is in a tremendous transition, one unparalleled in recorded human history. Indeed, we are products of our society, and society is in a state of rapid flux regarding demographics, technology, economics, global warming, and several other factors that lead to an increasingly dynamic landscape. In the end, everyone will be affected. The best strategy for coping with these changes is to adapt to them.

SUMMARY

- Sociology is described as the study of human social behavior within families, organizations, and institutions. Societal stress is a force to be reckoned with in today's culture. Once called *future shock*, the tsunami of social issues is now referred to as *superstress*—the inability to cope with an overwhelming amount of change.

- No one is exempt from the sociology of stress.

- *Technostress* is a term used to describe the overwhelming frustrations of sensory bombardment and poor boundaries that result from the plethora of technological gadgets. Technostress began with personal computers but has evolved with the advent of and addiction to social networking. The body's physiology wasn't designed to be "on" all the time. The result is burnout and physical health issues.

- Social stress includes a decline in social etiquette. A lack of civility (demonstrated by rude, impatient behavior) is on the rise.

- Experts suggest that one aspect of societal stress is an environmental disconnect: a growing disregard of the environment by humanity, such that dramatic changes, from dwindling supplies of fresh water to declining food quality to environmental pollution, will have a significant impact on each individual's lifestyle and health.

- *Nature deficit disorder* is a term describing people's absence from the natural world. One result is inadequate amounts of sunlight exposure, which produces a vitamin D deficiency.

- Most people garner their self-worth from their jobs or careers, yet many Americans cite their job as being stressful, thus impacting self-worth, self-esteem, family relationships, and many other aspects of their lives in negative ways.

- Race and gender issues have always been part of the social fabric and continue to contribute largely to stress, especially as people express themselves with reckless abandon in the digital age.

STUDY GUIDE QUESTIONS

1. How would you define the term *sociology*? How would you describe the concept of the sociology of stress?

2. How would you best explain the concept of technostress?

3. What factors are associated with technostress?

4. What explains the attraction of (or addiction to) being plugged in all the time?

5. What effect does information overload and sensory bombardment have on brain function and cognitive abilities?

6. How does stress affect our relationships with others, in terms of social etiquette?

7. What factors are associated with environmental disconnect?

8. Give examples of ways in which society can help alleviate race and gender stress.

REFERENCES AND RESOURCES

Alter, A. *Irresistible: The Rise of Addictive Technology and the Business of Keeping Us Hooked*. Penguin Press, New York, 2017.

Becker, D. *One Nation Under Stress: The Trouble With Stress as an Idea*. New York, Oxford University Press, 2013.

Begley, S. I Can't Think, *Newsweek*, March 7, 2011: 28–33.

Brody, J. What Do You Lack? Probably Vitamin D, *New York Times*, July 26, 2010. www.nytimes.com/2010/07/27/health/27brod.html?_r=1&partner=rss&emc=rss.

Brown, L. "The Real Threat to Our Future Is Peak Water." *The Guardian*. July 6, 2013. http://www.theguardian.com/global-development/2013/jul/06/water-supplies-shrinking-threat-to-food.

Carr, N. *The Shallows: What the Internet Is Doing to Our Brains*. W. W. Norton, New York, 2010.

Davis, D. *Disconnect*. Dutton Book, New York, 2010.

Della Cava, M. Attention Spans Get Rewired, *USA Today*, August 4, 2010.

Diamond, J. *Collapse: How Societies Choose to Fail or Succeed*. Penguin Books, New York, 2011.

Dossey, L. Plugged In: At What Price? The Perils and Promise of Electrical Communications, *Explore* 5:5, 2009.

Eldredge, N. The Sixth Extinction, *ActionBioscience.org*, June 2001, www.actionbioscience.org/.

Freinkel, S. *Plastic: A Toxic Love Story*. Houghton Mifflin Harcourt, New York, 2011.

Garrett, T. Lack of Civility in America Brought to Light, *Canyon News*, September 19, 2009.

Glei, J. *Unsubscribe: How to Kill Email Anxiety, Avoid Distractions, and Get Real Work Done*. Public Affairs Books, New York, 2016.

Greenfield, S. *ID: The Quest for Meaning in the 21st Century*, London, Sceptre, 2009.

Greenfield, S. Perspectives: Reinventing Human Identity, *New Scientist*, May 21, 2008:48–49.

Kirwood, S. Climate Change and Conflict. Living On Earth. August 2, 2013. http://www.loe.org/shows/segments .html?programID=13-P13-00031&segmentID=1.

Lallas, N. *Renewing Values in America: Are You Ready to Do Your Part?* Mill Valley, CA, ArtisPress, 2009.

Lanman, S. Choosing Civility in the Face of Rudeness, *Rutgers Focus*, March 2010. http://news.rutgers.edu/focus /issue.2010-03-02.2969546649/article.2010-03-30.3504010889.

Lee, R. *The Superstress Solution*. Random House, New York, 2010.

Lewin, T. If Your Kids Are Awake, They're Probably Online. *New York Times*, January 20, 2010, www.nytimes.com /2010/01/20/education/20wired.html.

Lipton, B., and Bhaerman, S. *Spontaneous Evolution*. Carlsbad, CA, HayHouse, 3rd ed. 2010.

Louv, R. *Last Child in the Woods*. Algonquin Books, Chapel Hill, NC, 2008.

Marquardt, K. The Value of a True Lunch Break, *US News and World Report*, November 23, 2010. http://money .usnews.com/money/careers/articles/2010/11/23/the-value -of-a-true-lunch-break.

National Geographic Society. Water: Our Thirsty World [special issue], *National Geographic*, April 2010.

National Public Radio. Digital Overload: Your Brain on Gadgets, *Fresh Air*, August 24, 2010, www.npr.org /templates/transcript/transcript.php?storyId=129384107.

National Safety Council. March 31, 2011, http://www.nsc.org /safety_work/Pages/Home.aspx.

Page, S. Poll: USA Fed Up with Political Incivility, *USA Today*, April 4, 2010. http://www.usatoday.com/news /washington/2010-04-21-civility-poll_N.htm.

Perman, C. Argggh! American Workers Are at a Breaking Point. April 9, 2013. Business on NBCnews.com. www .cnbc.com/id/100624671.

Richards, M. D. How Much Incivility Will American Voters Tolerate in the Race to the White House? February 2, 2016. http://www.krcresearch.com/how-much-incivility-will -american-voters-tolerate-in-the-race-to-the-white-house/.

Richtel, M. Your Brain on Computers: Attached to Technology and Paying a Price, *New York Times*, June 6, 2010.

Richter, A. Sting, the Yogi Behind the Music, *Energy Times*, October 2010, www.energytimes.com/pages /features/1010/sting.html.

Rosch, P. Is Job Stress America's Leading Adult Health Problem? A Commentary, *Business Insights*, 7(1):4, 7, 1991.

Rubinkam, M. During Boring Classes, Texting Is the New Doodling, *Netscape Gadgets & Tech*, November 26, 2010, http://webcenters.netscape.compuserve.com/tech /story.jsp?floc=DC-headline&sc=f&idq=/ff/story /1001/20101126/5255.htm.

Rushkoff, D. *Present Shock: When Everything Happens Now*. Current Books/Penguin., New York, 2013.

Schlitz, M. Keynote Address, Healing Touch International, St. Louis, MO, September 12, 2010.

Scott, E. New Research on Employee Burnout, *About. com Stress Management Blog*, May 22, 2016. http://stress .about.com/b/2007/10/15/new-research-on-employee -burnout.htm.

Seaward, B.L. Sleep Wellness, Digital Detox, and Mindfulness. White paper. WELCOA, Omaha, NE, May 13, 2015.

Seigler, K. Tweeting with the Birds: Pitch Tent, Switch to Wi-Fi, *NPR*, August 3, 2010, www.npr.org/templates /story/story.php?storyId=128697566.

Shirky, C. *Cognitive Surplus: Creativity and Generosity in a Connected Age*. Penguin Press, New York, 2010.

Shirkey, C. *Cognitive Surplus: How Technology Makes Consumers into Collaborators*. Penguin Books, New York. 2011.

Simon, S. Using Your BlackBerry Off-Hours Could Be Overtime, *NPR*, August 14, 2010, www.npr.org/templates /transcript/transcript.php?storyId=129184907.

Smith, R., and Lourie, B. *Slow Death by Rubber Duck: The Secret Danger of Everyday Things*. Counterpoint, Berkeley, CA, 2011.

Stuart, H. Stephen Hawking to Human Race: Move to Outer Space or Face Extinction, *Huffington Post*, www .huffingtonpost.com/2010/08/06/stephen-hawking-to -human_n_673387.html.

Swartz, J. Survey Warns of E-mail Stress, *USA Today Technology Live*, July 16, 2010, http://content.usatoday .com/communities/technologylive/post/2010/07/e-mail -stress-when-is-too-much-e-mail-too-much/1?loc =interstitialskip.

Temple, J. All those tweets, apps, updates may drain the brain. Sunday, April 17, 2011. http://www.sfgate.com/cgibin /article.cgi?f=/c/a/2011/04/17/BUTO1J0S2P.DTL.

Tugend, A. Incivility Can Have Costs Beyond Hurting People. *The New York Times*. Nov. 19, 2010. http://www .nytimes.com/2010/11/20/yourmoney/20shortcuts .html?pagewanted=all&_r=0.

Turkle, S. *Alone Together*. Basic Books, New York, 2011.

Weber, K. (ed.). *Food, Inc.: How Industrial Food Is Making Us Sicker, Fatter and Poorer—And What You Can Do About It*. Public Affairs, New York, 2009.

Weil, M., and Rosen, L. *Technostress: Coping with Technology @work @home @play*. John Wiley and Sons, New York, 1998.

CHAPTER 3

Physiology of Stress

To understand the stress response, we must possess a fundamental knowledge not only of psychology but of physiology as well.

—George Everly

Hans Selye's discovery of a direct relationship between chronic stress and the excessive wear and tear throughout the body laid the foundation for a clearer understanding of how physiological systems work in an extremely complex and integrative way. Perhaps because of this discovery and the fact that physical deterioration is so noticeable, much attention has been directed toward the physiology of stress. This chapter will take you through some basic concepts that explain the physiological dynamics involved with the stress response—specifically, the immediate, intermediate, and prolonged effects on the body. These processes will be explained in terms of "pathways," which set in action the systematic and integrative steps of the stress response. Because physiology involves specific nomenclature outside the realm of your everyday vocabulary, you may find the nature of this chapter to be very specific and its contents very detailed. Most likely it will merit more than one reading to fully grasp, understand, and appreciate how the body responds to stress. The importance of a strong familiarity with human physiology as influenced by stressful stimuli becomes

evident when the necessary steps are taken to effectively deal with the symptoms they produce, especially when using relaxation techniques. For example, it is important to know how the body functions when using specific imagery, visualization, music therapy, autogenic training, progressive muscular relaxation, and biofeedback.

In many circles, this topic of study is referred to as *psychophysiology*. This term reflects the fact that a sensory stimulus (perceived threat) that prompts the stress response must be processed at the mental level before it can cascade down one or more physiological pathways. In other words, the term **psychophysiology** suggests that there is a mind-body relationship and supports the theory that many diseases and illnesses are psychosomatic, meaning that their origins lie in the mind through the higher brain centers. Although the mind-body dualism suggested by Descartes is no longer a viable model for a complete understanding of human physiology, to hold an appreciation of the "whole person" we must first

> **Psychophysiology:** A field of study based on the principle that the mind and body are one, where thoughts and perceptions affect potentially all aspects of physiology.

Quotation reproduced from Everly Jr., G.S., and Rosenfeld, R. *The Nature and Treatment of the Stress Response*. Plenum Press, New York, 1981. With permission of Springer Nature.

examine the parts to understand how they connect to that whole.

Three systems are directly involved with the physiology of stress: the nervous system, the endocrine system, and the immune system, all of which can be triggered by perceived threats.

The Central Nervous System

The nervous system can be divided into two parts: the **central nervous system (CNS)**, which consists of the brain and spinal cord, and the peripheral nervous system (PNS), comprising all neural pathways to the extremities. The human brain is further divided into three levels: the vegetative level, the limbic system, and the neocortical level (**FIG. 3.1**).

The Vegetative Level

The lowest level of the brain consists of both the reticular formation and the brain stem. The reticular formation, or more specifically the fibers that make up the **reticular activating system (RAS)**, is the link connecting the brain to the spinal cord. Several stress physiologists believe that it is the bridge joining the mind (brain) and the body as one; this organ functions as a communications link between the mind and the body (**FIG. 3.2**). The brain stem, consisting of the pons, medulla oblongata, and mesencephalon, is responsible for involuntary functions of the human body, such as heartbeat, respiration, and vasomotor activity. It is considered the automatic-pilot control center of the brain, which assumes responsibility for keeping the vital organs and vegetative processes functioning at all times. This level is thought to be the most primitive section of the human brain because this portion is similar to those of all other mammals.

> **Central nervous system (CNS):** Consists of the brain and spinal column, while the peripheral nervous system (PNS) comprises all neural pathways to the extremities.
>
> **Reticular activating system (RAS):** The neural fibers that link the brain to the spinal column.
>
> **Limbic system:** The midlevel of the brain, including the hypothalamus and amygdala, which is thought to be responsible for emotional processing.

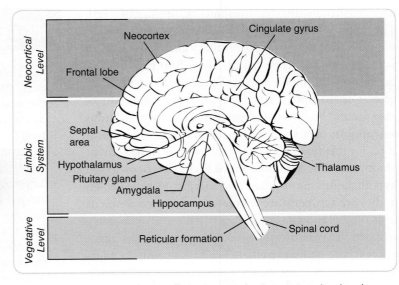

FIGURE 3.1   Three levels of the human brain: vegetative level, limbic system, and neocortical level.

FIGURE 3.2   Brain physiology at work.

The Limbic System

The second or midlevel portion of the brain is called the **limbic system**. The limbic system is the emotional control center. Several tissue centers in this level are directly responsible for the biochemical chain of events that constitutes the stress response Cannon observed. The limbic system consists of the thalamus, the hypothalamus, the amygdala, and the pituitary gland, also known as the master endocrine gland. These four glands work in unison to maintain a level of homeostasis within the body. For example, it is the hypothalamus that controls appetite and body-core temperature. The hypothalamus also appears to be the center that registers pain and pleasure; for this reason it is often referred to as the "seat of emotions." The combination of these functions in the hypothalamus may explain why hunger decreases when body-core temperature increases in extreme ambient heat, or why appetite diminishes when you are extremely worried. This also explains why tempers (and violent crimes) flare up on extremely hot days during the summer months, as crime statistics prove each year. Research evidence is clear that fear is first registered in the amygdala. When a threat is encountered, the hypothalamus carries out four specific functions: (1) it activates the autonomic nervous system; (2) it stimulates the secretion of adrenocorticotropic hormone (ACTH); (3) it produces antidiuretic hormone (ADH) or vasopressin; and (4) it stimulates the thyroid gland to produce thyroxine. All of these will be discussed in greater detail later.

The Neocortical Level

The neocortex is the highest and most sophisticated level of the brain. It is at this level that sensory information is processed (decoded) as a threat or a nonthreat and where cognition (thought processes) takes place. Housed within the neocortex are the neural mechanisms allowing one to employ analysis, imagination, creativity, intuition, logic, memory, and organization. It is this highly developed area of brain tissue that is thought to separate humans from all other species.

As Figure 3.1 illustrates, the positions of these structures are such that a higher level can override a lower level of the brain. Thus, conscious thought can influence emotional response, just as conscious thought can intercede in the involuntary control of the vegetative functions to control heart rate, ventilation, and even the flow of

Autonomic nervous system (ANS): Often referred to as the automatic nervous system, the ANS consists of the sympathetic (arousal) and parasympathetic (relaxed) nervous systems. This part of the central nervous system requires no conscious thought; actions such as breathing and heart rate are programmed to function automatically.

BOX 3.1   The Amygdala Revisited

The brain has many regions involved with consciousness, stress, and behavior. In the past several years, the small almond-shaped portion of the brain known as the amygdala, a key structure in the limbic system, has proven to be of great interest with regard to functional magnetic resonance imaging (fMRI) research and stress. For decades scientists knew the amygdala was associated with aggressive behavior (anger) as well as feelings and behavior associated with fear and anxiety. Additionally, studies have found that the amygdala is responsible for the formation and consolidation of memories associated with events that provoked a strong emotional response (including anger and fear). It is suggested that these memories are imprinted via the neural synapses, perhaps as an ancestral survival dynamic (e.g., beware of the rattlesnake). Through a complicated dynamic between the amygdala and the hippocampus, specific memories of past events can reprise the fight-or-flight response, merely by thinking about them. More recent studies have also linked the amygdala to binge drinking, most likely associated with stress.

blood. This fact will become important to recognize when learning coping skills and relaxation techniques designed to override the stress response and facilitate physiological homeostasis.

Separate from the CNS is a network of neural fibers that feed into the CNS and work in close collaboration with it. This neural tract, the peripheral nervous system (PNS), comprises two individual networks. The first is the somatic network, a bidirectional circuit responsible for transmitting sensory messages along the neural pathways between the five senses and the higher brain centers. These are called the efferent (toward periphery) and afferent (toward brain) neural pathways. The second branch of the PNS is called the **autonomic nervous system (ANS)**. The ANS regulates visceral activities and vital organs, including circulation, digestion, respiration, and temperature regulation. It received the name *autonomic* because this system can function without conscious thought or voluntary control, and does so most, if not all, of the time.

Research conducted by endocrinologist Bruce McEwen indicates that initially a stressful encounter is etched into the memory bank (so as to avoid it down the road), but that

---

BOX 3.2   A Closer Look at Panic Attacks

ABC's *Nightline* co-anchor Dan Harris didn't plan on starting a daily meditation practice. In fact, it was the furthest thing from his mind, until he experienced a series of on-air panic attacks. In his search for peace of mind (and as a way to keep his career intact) he stumbled upon mindfulness meditation. In his best-selling book *10% Happier*, he not only tells his story, but uses his position of national notoriety to explain that meditation is a skill that everyone should include in their list of daily habits. For Dan Harris, it was a panic attack, but everyone today is riding a wave of adrenaline-based information overload.

Anyone can have a rush of fear come over them, but some people are prone to a more severe experience, often called a "panic attack." A panic attack is often described as "the stress response on steroids." In short, it is the response of the sympathetic nervous system. Panic attacks can occur in any place, at any time, and often out of the blue. Physical symptoms of a panic attack include hyperventilation, a racing heart, sweating, chest pain, a choking feeling, nausea, chills, dizziness or feeling faint, tingling sensations, and muscle tremors or shaking. Some people describe it as feeling like they are having a heart attack. Other symptoms include a feeling of impending death, loss of sanity, or having a "nervous breakdown." Panic attacks are most common in early adulthood, but can occur at any age. Women are more prone to this condition than men (Smith and Segal, 2016).

Panic attacks occur abruptly. They may seem like they last forever to those who experience them, but the duration is typically about 10 to 20 minutes (in rare cases over an hour). What is the cause of a panic attack? Although they seem to come out of the blue, every panic attack is triggered by some decoded sensory stimuli (or memory) that creates an intense fear or apprehension about some future event. Ironically, some panic attacks are brought on by fearing another panic attack (Baker, 2011).

While some experts suggest that panic attacks may be hereditary, others suggest that they may be due to abnormalities (hypersensitivity) in the amygdala and/or hypothalamus that control the fight-or-flight response. Some panic attacks are associated with substance abuse, but the vast majority are caused by stress (the interpretation of an exaggerated threat).

What is the best way to cope with a panic attack? The best strategy is to bring yourself back into the present moment and ground yourself. Experts suggest to sit on the floor with your back up against the wall. Place your hands and your feet firmly on the ground and take several deep breaths. If you wish, repeat to yourself the phrase, "My hands and feet are firmly on the ground." If a panic attack occurs while driving, pull over, stop the car, place your hands down by your waist, and repeat the phrase, "My hands and feet are fully grounded." You can train yourself to avoid or minimize the effects of panic attacks by engaging in both effective coping skills and relaxation techniques (McDonagh, 2015).

---

repeated episodes of stress decrease memory by weakening hippocampal brain cells. Chronic stress is thought to wither the fragile connection between neurons in this part of the brain, resulting in "brain shrinkage."

Until recently it was believed that, unlike the voluntary somatic system involved in muscle movement, the ANS could not be intercepted by conscious thought, but now it is recognized that both systems can be influenced by higher mental processes. The ANS works in close coordination with the CNS to maintain a favorable homeostatic condition throughout the body. There are two branches of the ANS that act to maintain this homeostatic balance, the **sympathetic** and **parasympathetic** nervous systems, and these are activated by the hypothalamus. Most organs are innervated (stimulated) by nerve fibers of both the sympathetic and parasympathetic systems.

■ The Autonomic Nervous System

The Sympathetic and Parasympathetic Nervous Systems

The sympathetic nervous system is responsible for the responses associated with the fight-or-flight response (FIG. 3.3). Through the release of substances called

> **Sympathetic:** The branch of the central nervous system that triggers the fight-or-flight response when some element of threat is present.
>
> **Parasympathetic:** The branch of the central nervous system that specifically calms the body through the parasympathetic response.

Stress with a Human Face

George is 19 years old, yet the stress he has experienced in his first year serving as a Marine in Iraq makes him seem at least 10 years older—from the lines on his face to the tenor of his voice. I met George in Honolulu International Airport. We were both waiting to fly home to Colorado: me from vacation, George from the war. A delay in our scheduled departure allowed a friendly conversation at the gate's lounge, but for the most part, I just listened.

"You don't know what stress is until you are smack in the middle of a war. Your body is on alert 24 hours a day. You are constantly aroused even when you're trying to relax. You can never fully relax in a war zone. You can feel your heart pounding in your chest nearly all the time; a 24/7 adrenaline rush! I guess you just get used to it. All of your senses are heightened—never knowing what to expect, but always ready for something. This is my second visit home and I am on guard right now as we speak. When I go into a restaurant back home, the first thing I do is scout out all the exits. It's survival mode. You can never be relaxed completely in a war zone. Sadly, this mentality stays with you outside the war zone, like right now.

"The stress of war is incredible. It only gets worse when your patrol has encountered an IED [improvised explosive device]. I have lost several buddies to these. You go right into reaction mode: Stop the bleeding! They train us all in emergency first aid and you just pray you never have to use it. When one of these goes off you don't have time to be afraid. You just react. Stop the bleeding, whoever's bleeding, whatever's bleeding. Usually it's an arm or a leg blown off. I've seen stuff that would curl your hair. No matter what they tell you in basic training, there is nothing that can prepare you for war. I know several guys with PTSD (post-traumatic stress disorder). I didn't believe in PTSD until I got to Iraq. I have crazy dreams at night. They say having nightmares is part of PTSD, but how can you not? After all it is a war zone . . . your mind is processing all that's gone on in the course of the previous day. War is not the normal course of a typical day for most people, and definitely not Americans.

"Yes, they [the military leaders] hand out psychotropic drugs to keep soldiers up. Exponential Adrenaline Rush! I don't take 'em. I need all my wits about me when I am out there, outside the Green Zone . . . even inside the Green Zone. . . . Believe me . . . war is the ultimate stress zone."

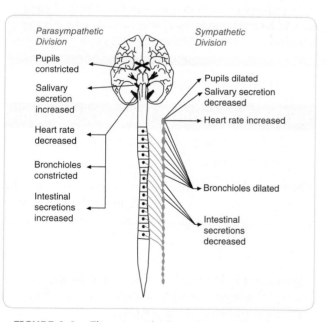

FIGURE 3.3 The sympathetic and parasympathetic systems. Internal organs are typically innervated by neural fibers from both sympathetic and parasympathetic divisions.

catecholamines, specifically **epinephrine** (adrenaline) and **norepinephrine** (noradrenaline), at various neural synapses, a series of events occurs in several organ tissues to prepare the body for rapid metabolic change and physical movement. Sympathetic drive is associated with energy expenditure (e.g., jogging), a process known as **catabolic functioning**, where various metabolites are

Epinephrine: A special neurochemical referred to as a catecholamine that is responsible for immediate physical readiness for stress including increased heart rate and blood pressure. It works in unison with norepinephrine.

Norepinephrine: A special neurochemical referred to as a catecholamine that is responsible for immediate physical readiness to stress including increased heart rate and blood pressure. It works in unison with epinephrine.

Catabolic functioning: A metabolic process in which metabolites are broken down for energy in preparation for, or in the process of, exercise (fight or flight).

BOX 3.3   Hormonal Imbalance

The endocrine system is an amazing yet delicate system of chemical properties aligned to ensure physiological homeostasis. The stress hormone dehydroepiandrosterone (DHEA), for example, is secreted from the adrenal gland. DHEA is also known as a precursor sex hormone that decreases in both production and secretion throughout the aging process. Speculation suggests that supplementation of DHEA might increase stamina and memory, and may decrease the aging process in much the same way as the antioxidants beta-carotene, vitamin C, vitamin E, and selenium. Results of a host of studies revealed that no significant changes in these aspects occurred in either animals or humans. Data published by the American Cancer Society reveals that increased amounts of DHEA, above what the body normally produces, might actually promote cancer. Supplementation is recommended only on the advice of your physician.

Serotonin and **melatonin** are not stress hormones, yet they do seem to have an effect on mood. Decreases in both serotonin and melatonin are thought to be related to bouts of depression. Many things affect serotonin levels in the brain—from the natural and synthetic chemicals in the foods you eat, to the amount of sunlight you receive in the course of a day, to perhaps things we still don't know. Research is inconclusive about how serotonin affects mood. Most likely, stress affects serotonin levels as well.

broken down for energy in preparation for movement. It is the release of epinephrine and norepinephrine that causes the acceleration of heart rate, the increase in the force of myocardial contraction, vasodilation of arteries throughout working muscles, vasoconstriction of arteries to nonworking muscles, dilation of pupils and bronchi, increased ventilation, reduction of digestive activity, released glucose from the liver, and several other functions that prepare the body to fight or flee. It is the sympathetic system that is responsible for supplying skeletal muscles with oxygenated, nutrient-rich blood for energy metabolism. Currently it is thought that norepinephrine serves primarily to assist epinephrine, as the ratio of these two chemical substances released at neural synapses is 5:1 epinephrine to norepinephrine during the stress response. The effects of epinephrine and norepinephrine are very short, lasting only seconds. Because of their rapid release from neural endings, as well as their rapid influence on targeted organ tissue, the effects of the sympathetic nervous system are categorized as **immediate**.

Just as the sympathetic neural drive is associated with energy expenditure, the parasympathetic drive is responsible for energy conservation and relaxation. This is referred to as **anabolic functioning**, during which body cells are allowed to regenerate. The parasympathetic nervous system is dominated by the tenth cranial, or vagus, nerve, which in turn is influenced by the brain stem. When activated, the parasympathetic nervous system releases **acetylcholine** (ACh), a neurological agent that decreases metabolic activity and returns the body to homeostasis. The influence of the parasympathetic drive is associated with a reduction in heart rate, ventilation, blood pressure, muscle tension, and several other functions. Both systems are partially active at all times; however, the sympathetic and parasympathetic systems are mutually exclusive in that they cannot dominate visceral activity simultaneously. These two systems allow for the precise regulation of visceral organ activity, much like the use of the accelerator and brake when driving. Sympathetic arousal, like a gas pedal pushed to the car floor, becomes the dominant force during stress, and parasympathetic tone holds influence over the body at all other times to promote homeostasis. In other words, you cannot be physically aroused and relaxed at the same time.

Serotonin: A neurotransmitter that is associated with mood. A decrease in serotonin levels is thought to be related to depression. Serotonin levels are affected by many factors including stress hormones and the foods you consume.

Melatonin: A hormone secreted in the brain that is related to sleep, mood, and perhaps several other aspects of physiology and consciousness.

Immediate (effects of stress): A neural response to cognitive processing in which epinephrine and norepinephrine are released, lasting only seconds.

Anabolic functioning: A physiological process in which various body cells (e.g., muscle tissue) regenerate or grow.

Acetylcholine: A chemical substance released by the parasympathetic nervous system to help the body return to homeostasis from the stress response.

But there are exceptions to the dynamics of these biochemical reactions. For example, it is sympathetic nerves, not parasympathetic nerves, that release ACh in the sweat glands to decrease body-core temperature during arousal. And sympathetic and parasympathetic stimulation of salivary glands is not antagonistic; both influence the secretion of saliva. In addition, all blood vessels are influenced by sympathetic dominance, with the exception of the vasculature of the penis and clitoris, which is activated by parasympathetic innervation.

The Endocrine System

The endocrine system consists of a series of glands located throughout the body that regulate metabolic functions requiring endurance rather than speed. The endocrine system is a network of four components: glands, hormones, circulation, and target organs. Endocrine glands manufacture and release biochemical substances called hormones. Hormones are "chemical messengers" made up of protein compounds that are programmed to attach to specific cell receptor sites to alter (increase or decrease) cell metabolism. Hormones are transported through the bloodstream from the glands that produced them to the target organs they are called upon to influence. The heart, skeletal muscle, and arteries are among the organs most targeted by hormones for metabolic change.

The glands that are most closely involved with the stress response are the pituitary, thyroid, and adrenal glands. The **pituitary gland** is called "the master gland" because it manufactures several important hormones, which then trigger hormone release in other organs. The

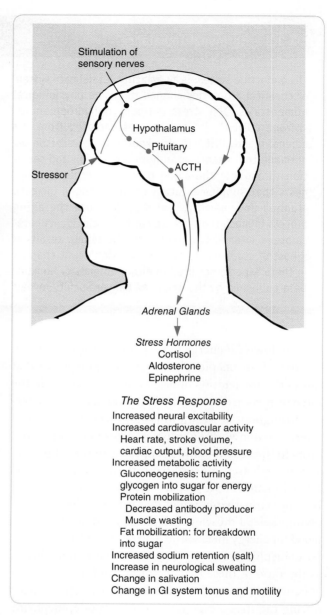

The Stress Response
Increased neural excitability
Increased cardiovascular activity
    Heart rate, stroke volume,
    cardiac output, blood pressure
Increased metabolic activity
    Gluconeogenesis: turning
    glycogen into sugar for energy
    Protein mobilization
        Decreased antibody producer
        Muscle wasting
    Fat mobilization: for breakdown
    into sugar
Increased sodium retention (salt)
Increase in neurological sweating
Change in salivation
Change in GI system tonus and motility

FIGURE 3.4   The physiological response to stress.

> **Pituitary gland:** An endocrine gland ("master gland") located below the hypothalamus that, upon command from the hypothalamus, releases ACTH and then commands the adrenal glands to secrete their stress hormones.
>
> **Hypothalamus:** Often called the "seat of the emotions," the hypothalamus is involved with emotional processing. When a thought is perceived as a threat, the hypothalamus secretes a substance called corticotropin-releasing factor (CRF) to the pituitary gland to activate the fight-or-flight response.
>
> **Adrenal gland:** The endocrine glands that are located on top of each kidney that house and release several stress hormones including cortisol and the catecholamines epinephrine and norepinephrine. The adrenal gland is known as "the stress gland."

hypothalamus, however, appears to have direct influence over the pituitary gland (**FIG. 3.4**). The thyroid gland increases the general metabolic rate. Perhaps the gland that has the most direct impact on the stress response, however, is the **adrenal gland** (**FIG. 3.5**). The adrenal gland, a cone-shaped mass of tissue about the size of a small grapefruit, sits on top of each kidney. The adrenal gland (known as "the stress gland") has two distinct parts, each of which produces hormones with very different functions. The exterior of the adrenal gland is called the adrenal cortex, and it manufactures and releases hormones called corticosteroids. There are two types of

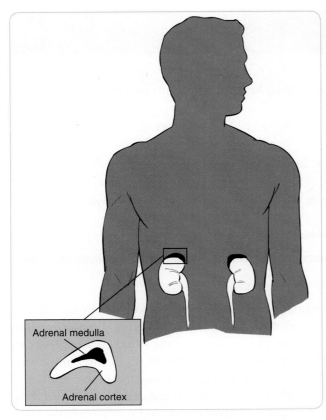

Adrenal medulla

Adrenal cortex

FIGURE 3.5   The adrenal gland, made up of the adrenal cortex and medulla, sits upon the top of each kidney and is cone-shaped in appearance.

corticosteroids: glucocorticoids and mineralocorticoids. **Glucocorticoids** are a family of biochemical agents that includes cortisol and cortisone, with cortisol being the primary one. Its function is to help to generate glucose, through the degradation of proteins (amino acids) during a process called gluconeogenesis in the liver, as an energy source for both the central nervous system (the brain) and skeletal muscles during physical exercise. A metaphor to illustrate this process is the situation in which you resort to burning the furniture to keep warm once you exhaust your supply of firewood. **Cortisol** is also involved in the process of lipolysis, or the mobilization and breakdown of fats (fatty acids) for energy. Clinical studies have linked increased levels of cortisol with suppression of the immune system. It appears that cortisol metabolizes (degrades) white blood cells. As the number of white blood cells decreases, the efficiency of the immune system decreases, setting the stage for illness and disease. It has also come to light that increased cortisol

can direct excess amounts of cholesterol into the blood, thereby adding to associated artery plaque buildup and leading to hypertension and coronary heart disease. **Mineralocorticoids**, specifically aldosterone, are secreted to maintain plasma volume and electrolyte (sodium and potassium) balance, two essential functions in the regulation of circulation. (The exact mechanisms will be discussed later in this chapter.)

Corticosteroids: Stress hormones released by the adrenal cortex, such as cortisol and cortisone.

Glucocorticoids: A family of biochemical agents that includes cortisol and cortisone, produced and released from the adrenal gland.

Cortisol: A stress hormone released by the adrenal glands that helps the body prepare for fight or flight by promoting the release of glucose and lipids in the blood for energy metabolism.

Mineralocorticoids: A class of hormones that maintain plasma volume and electrolyte balance, such as aldosterone.

TABLE 3.1 Pathways of Stress Response

Effects	Reaction	Time
The body has several backup dynamics to help ensure physical survival. Here, these dynamics are broken down into categories based on the duration of their metabolic reactions.		
Immediate effects	Epinephrine and norepinephrine from the sympathetic nervous system	2–3 seconds
Intermediate effects	Epinephrine and norepinephrine from the adrenal medulla	20–30 seconds, possibly minutes
Prolonged effects	ACTH, vasopressin, and thyroxine neuroendocrine pathways	Minutes, hours, days, or weeks

Modified from Allen, R. *Human Stress: Its Nature and Control*. Burgess, Minneapolis, 1983.

The inside of the adrenal gland is called the **adrenal medulla**. This portion of the gland secretes catecholamines (epinephrine and norepinephrine), which act in a similar fashion as those secreted at the endings of sympathetic nerves. The adrenal medulla releases 80 percent epinephrine and 20 percent norepinephrine. Under the influences of stress, up to three hundred times the amount of epinephrine can be found in the blood compared to the amount in samples taken at rest.

The Neuroendocrine Pathways

Evolutionary adaptations have provided several backup systems to ensure the survival of the human organism. Not all pathways act at the same speed, yet the ultimate goal is the same: physical survival. First, not only does the hypothalamus initiate activation of the sympathetic nervous system to cause an immediate effect (**TABLE 3.1**), but the posterior hypothalamus also has a direct neural pathway, called the sympathetic preganglionic neuron, that links it to the adrenal medulla.

Adrenal medulla: The portion of the adrenal gland responsible for secreting epinephrine and norepinephrine.

Intermediate stress effects: The hormonal response triggered by the neural aspects of the adrenal medulla that are released directly into the blood, lasting minutes to hours.

Prolonged effect of stress: Hormonal effects that may take days or perhaps more than a week to be fully realized from the initial stress response.

Next, upon stimulation by the posterior hypothalamus, the adrenal medulla secretes both epinephrine and norepinephrine. Once in the bloodstream, these catecholamines reinforce the efforts of the sympathetic drive, which has already released these same substances through sympathetic neural endings throughout the body. The release of epinephrine and norepinephrine from the adrenal medulla acts as a backup system for these biochemical agents to ensure the most efficient means of physical survival. The hormonal influences brought about by the adrenal medulla are called **intermediate stress effects**. Because their release is via the bloodstream rather than neural endings, travel time is longer (approximately 20 to 30 seconds), and unlike the release of these substances from sympathetic neural endings, the effects of catecholamines from the adrenal medulla can last as long as 2 hours when high levels of secretions are circulating in the bloodstream. These, along with hormones secreted from the adrenal gland, become a "toxic chemical cocktail" if they persist in the body for prolonged periods of time without being flushed out, primarily through exercise.

In addition, there is a third and potentially more potent system joining the efforts of the nervous and endocrine systems to prepare the body for real or perceived danger if the perceived threat continues beyond several minutes. Neural impulses received by the hypothalamus as potential threats create a chain of biochemical messages, which like a line of falling dominos cascade through the endocrine-system glands. Because the half-life of these hormones and the speed of their metabolic reactions vary in length from hours to weeks in some cases, this chain of reactions is referred to as the **prolonged effect of stress**.

BOX 3.5 *Multitasking:* **Wired For Stress**

The multitasking generation, the age of high technology, certainly has its merits, but less recognizable are its long-range pitfalls. Sociologists grow increasingly alarmed by people of all age groups' obsession with and addiction to smartphones, text messages, email, podcasts, and the Web. Sociologists and psychologists see dangers with a hyperkinetic mind that doesn't know how to unplug, turn off, and relax: Stress! Habitual multitasking may condition the brain to an overexcited state, making it difficult for people to focus even when they want or need to. Add a dearth of patience to the mix with this "Wi-Fi generation," and the stress response is compounded dramatically. As people begin to lose concentration skills, the end result is "chronic mental antsyness" (frustration).

The Myth of Multitasking

Sending a text message while watching (and voting for contestants on) *American Idol* and at the same time doing a Google search for research report content may seem like the height of organizational skills, but don't be fooled. Quantity is not quality. With the use of MRI technology, researchers, including Jordan Grafman, have identified one specific area of the brain's cortex, Brodmann's area 10, as the site specific for alternating attention from one task to another. The prefrontal cortex, which houses Brodmann's area 10, is one of the last regions of the brain to mature and the first to decline as a result of the aging process. As such, youngsters up to age 22 and those over the age of 60 do not multitask well. Research studies reveal that when young adults perform two or more tasks simultaneously, the amount of errors increases dramatically. Although there may be many causes for

poor attention span (from the TV remote control to the abundance of toxic food chemicals), the combination of short attention span and the increased use of electronic devices becomes dangerous. The take-home message is that multitasking decreases efficiency.

Although students may excel at locating and manipulating information via the Internet, their reach may be broad but ultimately quite shallow. Moreover, their ability to process the information in a deeper context is considered poor by most educational standards, states Claudia Koonzt of Duke University. "It's like they have too many windows open on their hard drive. In order to have a taste for sifting through different layers of truth, you have to stay with the topic and pursue it deeply rather than go across the surface with your toolbar" (Wallis, 2006). What are the social implications of being wired for stress? Virtual conversations will never replace the nuances of face-to-face expressions and body language that humans have developed over thousands of years of cohabitation and community building. Experts have also noticed a decrease in interaction among family members with a rise in household electronic gadgets, further eroding the family structure. Furthermore, addiction to cell phone use is fast becoming a reason for marriage counseling and breakups (University of Florida, 2007). Studies on the topic of Alzheimer's support the theory that the brain needs stimulation to promote mental acuity. Stress research, however, validates the need for quiet time for the brain. When the brain is constantly stimulated (and overstimulated) these neurological impulses rewire the brain for perpetual stress.

The ACTH Axis

Physiologically speaking, a biochemical pathway is referred to as an axis. In this section, we will discuss the ACTH axis. The other two axes, the **vasopressin axis** and the **thyroxine axis**, are covered in the following sections.

The **ACTH axis**, also known as the hypothalamic-pituitary-adrenal **(HPA) axis** (**FIG. 3.6**), begins with the release of corticotropin-releasing factor (CRF) from the anterior hypothalamus. This substance activates the pituitary gland to release ACTH, which travels via the bloodstream to in turn activate the **adrenal cortex**. Upon stimulation by ACTH, the adrenal cortex releases a set of corticosteroids (cortisol and aldosterone), which act to increase metabolism and alter body fluids, and thus blood

Vasopressin axis: A chain of physiological events stemming from the release of vasopressin or antidiuretic hormone (ADH).

Thyroxine axis: A chain of physiological events stemming from the release of thyroxine.

ACTH axis: A physiological pathway whereby a message is sent from the hypothalamus to the pituitary, then on to the adrenal gland to release a flood of stress hormones for fight or flight.

HPA axis: The hypothalamic-pituitary-adrenal axis, a term synonymous with the ACTH axis.

Adrenal cortex: The portion of the adrenal gland that produces and secretes a host of corticosteroids (e.g., cortisol and aldosterone).

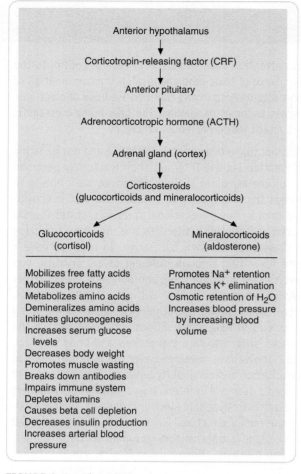

Anterior hypothalamus

↓

Corticotropin-releasing factor (CRF)

↓

Anterior pituitary

↓

Adrenocorticotropic hormone (ACTH)

↓

Adrenal gland (cortex)

↓

Corticosteroids
(glucocorticoids and mineralocorticoids)

Glucocorticoids
(cortisol)

Mineralocorticoids
(aldosterone)

Glucocorticoids (cortisol)	Mineralocorticoids (aldosterone)
Mobilizes free fatty acids	Promotes Na$^+$ retention
Mobilizes proteins	Enhances K$^+$ elimination
Metabolizes amino acids	Osmotic retention of H$_2$O
Demineralizes amino acids	Increases blood pressure
Initiates gluconeogenesis	by increasing blood
Increases serum glucose	volume
levels	
Decreases body weight	
Promotes muscle wasting	
Breaks down antibodies	
Impairs immune system	
Depletes vitamins	
Causes beta cell depletion	
Decreases insulin production	
Increases arterial blood	
pressure	

FIGURE 3.6   The ACTH axis.

pressure, respectively. The effects of hormones released by the adrenal cortex are considered to be prolonged because they activate their functions for minutes to hours. Note that increased secretions of cortisol in the blood act primarily to ensure adequate supplies of blood glucose for energy metabolism. However, when increasingly high levels of cortisol are observed because of chronic stress, this hormone compromises the integrity of several physiological systems.

The Vasopressin Axis

Vasopressin or antidiuretic hormone (ADH) is synthesized in the hypothalamus but is released by the pituitary through a special portal system. The primary purpose of vasopressin is to regulate fluid loss through the urinary tract. It does this in a number of ways, including water reabsorption and decreased perspiration. By altering blood volume, however, it also has a pronounced effect on stroke volume, or the amount of blood that is pumped through the left ventricle of the heart with each contraction.

BOX 3.6   Insomnia and Brain Physiology

Brain chemistry is a complicated subject and our understanding of it is embryonic at best, but some facts are clear with regard to how brain physiology works. Not only does an "active" mind release epinephrine and norepinephrine in the brain, compromising the ability to fall sleep, but other neurotransmitters—specifically, melatonin and serotonin—are affected by a host of daily rituals and behaviors, ranging from nutritional habits, caffeine intake, and sunlight exposure to cell phone use. Melatonin is a hormone secreted in the pituitary of the brain. This neurotransmitter is affected by real and artificial light and is thought to be associated with both sleep patterns and skin pigmentation. As daylight decreases, the melatonin level increases, giving rise to the belief that increases in melatonin help promote sleep.

The brain neurotransmitter serotonin is partially affected by light. Decreases in light decrease serotonin levels, a factor associated with seasonal affective disorder (SAD) and depression.

While the use of artificial evening light can alter serotonin levels, it can decrease melatonin levels, thus affecting natural sleep patterns (sleep patterns have changed dramatically since the turn of the twentieth century with the use of electricity). Cell phone use is thought to decrease melatonin with similar results. Increased consumption of carbohydrates (late-night snacks) can increase serotonin levels, which may, in turn, affect melatonin levels. Medications for depression include selective serotonin reuptake inhibitors (SSRIs), which act to increase serotonin levels. This activity may, in fact, act to decrease melatonin levels, thus affecting a full night's sleep.

Consequently, ADH has a pronounced effect on blood pressure. Under normal circumstances, ADH regulates blood pressure by either increasing blood volume (changing the concentration of water in the blood) should it be too low, or decreasing blood volume when it becomes too high. Under the influence of chronic stress, however, many regulatory mechanisms in the body lose their ability to maintain physiological homeostasis. Consequently, the increased secretions of vasopressin produced under duress will increase blood pressure even when someone already has elevated resting values; this is known as hypertension. The purpose of vasopressin as well as aldosterone, epinephrine, and norepinephrine is to increase blood pressure

---

BOX 3.7   Physiology of Stress: The Take-Home Message

There is no doubt that the details of the physiology of stress can be overwhelming. Here is the take-home message: The stress response involves a cascade of chemicals/hormones in the body, most notably epinephrine and norepinephrine released from the neural endings of the sympathetic nervous system. Additionally, the stress hormone, cortisol (secreted from the adrenal glands), plays a huge role in preparing the body for fight-or-flight. If stress persists, additional hormones are called into play. The strength of this stress hormone cocktail depends on the intensity and duration of the stressor(s), yet the effects can last far longer than the initial exposure/interpretation of the stressor. One notable effect of stress is that repeated stress tends to shrink brain cells. Medical science's love affair with functional magnetic resonance imaging continues to explore the brain under stress.

---

to ensure that active muscles receive oxygenated blood, but under chronic stress in a resting state this hormonal response—the abundance of stress hormones—is literally overkill, leading to hypertension and ultimately death caused by Coronary Heart Disease (CHD).

The Thyroxine Axis

Stimulation in the hypothalamus triggers the release of thyrotropic hormone–releasing factor (TRF). TRF is transported through a special portal system to the anterior portion of the pituitary, where it stimulates the secretion of thyrotropic hormone (TTH). Once in the bloodstream, TTH follows a path to the thyroid gland, which stimulates the release of two more hormones: thyroxine and triiodothyronine. The purpose of these two hormones is to increase overall metabolism, or basal metabolic rate (BMR). Thyroxine is powerful enough to double one's rate of metabolism. Note that the effects of this pathway are very prolonged. Because the production of thyroxine takes several days, it may be 10 days to 2 weeks before visible signs manifest as significant symptoms through this pathway. This explains why you may come down with a cold or flu a week after a very stressful encounter rather than the day after. The metabolic effects of thyroxine released through this pathway are increased workload on the heart muscle, increased gastrointestinal activity (e.g., gastritis), and, in some cases, a condition called **cerebration** or cerebral excitivity, which is associated with anxiety attacks and/or insomnia.

■ A Parable of Psychophysiology

A metaphor can be used to illustrate the three pathways discussed earlier (**FIG. 3.7**). Let us say that your life is in danger because of a classified CIA document you inadvertently stumbled across, and you now pose a threat to

Immediate effects	Intermediate effects	Prolonged effects
Text message or phone call	Email	Overnight delivery
Flushed face Rapid heart rate	Nauseous feeling in stomach Muscle tension	Suppressed immune system

FIGURE 3.7   Like communication networks that send and receive messages, the human body has several complex messenger systems, which not only see that the information gets through but also ensure that the body will survive the perceived threat after the message is received.

national security. You want to deliver a message and a copy of this document to your family, who live a few hundred miles away, to let them know your life is in danger. This message is, of course, very important and you want to make sure your family gets it, so you use a couple of methods to ensure its delivery. First you immediately text message your parents because it is the quickest way to deliver the message, and the message is received instantaneously. This is like the action of the sympathetic nervous system. As a backup, you send an email in case no one responds to the text. This form of communication is fairly quick, taking perhaps minutes, and is equivalent to the preganglionic nerve to the adrenal medulla. And because you also need to send a copy of the document to further explain the contents

Cerebration: A term used to describe the neurological excitability of the brain, associated with anxiety attacks and insomnia.

of your message, you ship a package via overnight delivery. This means of communication allows more comprehensive information to be sent, but it takes much longer. It is like the neuroendocrine pathways. Similarly, our bodies are composed of several communication systems, each with its own time element and function, the overall purpose being to prepare the body for physical survival. As illustrated by this story, there are many backup systems, fast and slow, to get the message through.

In the short term, the combination of these various neural and hormonal pathways serves a very important purpose: physical survival. However, when these same pathways are employed continuously as a result of the influence of chronic stressors, the effects can be devastating to the body. In light of the fact that the body prepares physically for threats, whether they are of a physical, mental, emotional, or spiritual nature, repeated physical arousal suggests that the activation of the stress response is an obsolete mechanism for dealing with stressors that do not pertain to physical survival. The inability of the body to return to homeostasis can have significant effects on the cardiovascular system, the digestive system, the musculoskeletal system, and, research now indicates, the immune system. Organs locked into a pattern of overactive metabolic activity will eventually show signs of dysfunction. For instance, constant pressure and repeated wear and tear on the arteries and blood vessels can cause tissue damage to the inner lining of these organs. Numerous changes can also occur throughout the digestive system, including constipation, gastritis, diarrhea, and hemorrhoids. As was observed by Selye, the inability of the body to return to homeostasis can set the stage for signs and symptoms of disease and illness.

Three Decades of Brain Imaging Research

Prior to the start of each decade, the medical profession selects one area of human physiology to study in-depth. In 1990, the brain was chosen as the target of this research. This area proved so fascinating that many researchers added a second decade to the data collection, despite the fact that the medical community deemed the decade 2000–2010 the

> **Allostatic load:** A term coined by stress researcher Bruce McEwen to replace the expression "stressed out"; the damage to the body when the allostatic (stress) response functions improperly or for prolonged states, causing physical damage to the body.

bone and joint decade. With the advancement of electromagnetic technology and magnetic resonance imaging (neuroimaging), thousands of studies have been conducted to determine which aspects of the brain are active in a variety of mental states and thought processes (Anderson, 2015). Despite recent news in 2016 that a bug was found in the computer program that analyzes fMRI data, suggesting that many of the findings were invalid, scientists continue to advocate the importance of brain research in unlocking one of the greatest mysteries known to humanity (Anderson, 2015). So enchanted have researchers become with brain physiology, as depicted through MRI technology, a multitude of studies have dominated non-disease-related brain physiology research and most likely will for some time to come. Although MRIs can help determine brain structure and specific physiology, it is the electroencephalagraph (EEG) that is currently needed to best understand brain function. Only recently have the dots been connected to provide a more accurate understanding of this most complex human organ. Bruce McEwen is one researcher working in this area. In his book *The End of Stress as We Know It*, McEwen synthesizes much of this information, including the work of his protégé Robert Sapolsky, author of the acclaimed book *Why Zebras Don't Get Ulcers*. Here are some highlights from McEwen's research:

- The hippocampus and the amygdala together form conscious memories of emotional events.

- The hippocampus is highly sensitive to the stress hormone cortisol, which aids in memory formation of stress.

- The hippocampus region is rich in receptor sites for glucocorticoids.

- The amygdala is responsible for the emotional content of memory, particularly fear.

- Repeated excessive exposure to cortisol accelerates the aging process of the hippocampus and may, in fact, damage or shrink brain cells. Moreover, chronic stress may affect memory and learning processes. (In Vietnam vets with post-traumatic stress disorder [PTSD], this region of the brain was 26 percent smaller than in their peers without PTSD.)

- Research by Sapolsky reveals that damage to brain cells (in animals) caused by chronic stress appears to be irreversible.

McEwen concludes that the human brain is, indeed, wired for stress, or "**allostatic load**" as he calls it.

Neuroscientists have also discovered that the brain is far more "plastic" than previously thought, giving rise to a new term: *neuroplasticity*. We now know that the brain can generate new connections to various brain cells, recruit various brain tissue for a host of functions, and generate new cell growth (which was previously thought to be impossible) (Powell, 2007).

Based on the success of President Clinton's federally funded Genome DNA Project, President Obama launched the Brain Initiative Project in 2013. The purpose of this initiative is to help scientists explore the dynamics of the brain as a means to create a comprehensive understanding of everything from, the creation of conscious thought and memory to the disease pathology of Alzheimer's, autism, Parkinson's, and several other disorders.

SUMMARY

- *Psychophysiology* is a term to describe the body's physiological reaction to perceived stressors, suggesting that the stress response is a mind-body phenomenon.

- There are three physiological systems that are directly involved in the stress response: the nervous system, the endocrine system, and the immune system.

- The nervous system comprises two parts: the central nervous system (CNS) and the peripheral nervous system (PNS). The CNS includes three levels: the vegetative, the limbic, and the neocortical.

- The limbic system houses the hypothalamus, which controls many functions, including appetite and emotions. The neocortical level processes and decodes all stimuli.

- The most important part of the PNS regarding the stress response is the autonomic nervous system, which activates sympathetic and parasympathetic neural drives. Sympathetic drive causes physical arousal (e.g., increased heart rate) through the secretion of epinephrine and norepinephrine, whereas parasympathetic drive maintains homeostasis through the release of ACh. The two neural drives are mutually exclusive, meaning that you cannot be aroused and relaxed at the same time.

- The endocrine system consists of a series of glands that secrete hormones that travel through the circulatory system and act on target organs. The major stress gland is the adrenal gland.

- The adrenal gland has two parts, each performing different functions. The cortex (outside) secretes cortisol and aldosterone, while the medulla (inside) secretes epinephrine and norepinephrine.

- The nervous system and endocrine system join together to form metabolic pathways or axes. There are three pathways: the ACTH axis, the vasopressin axis, and the thyroxine axis.

- The body has several backup mechanisms to ensure physical survival. These systems are classified as immediate, lasting seconds (sympathetic drive); intermediate, lasting minutes (adrenal medulla); and prolonged, lasting hours if not weeks (neuroendocrine pathways). Each system is involved in several metabolic pathways.

- Stress is considered one of the primary factors associated with insomnia. Good sleep hygiene consists of behaviors that help promote a good night's sleep rather than detract from it, including decreased caffeine consumption, consistent bedtimes, and a host of effective relaxation techniques that enhance sleep quality.

- A decade of brain research reveals that humans are hard-wired for stress through an intricate pattern of neural pathways designed for the fight-or-flight response. Research also suggests that chronic stress appears to atrophy brain tissue, specifically the hippocampus.

STUDY GUIDE QUESTIONS

1. What role does the nervous system play in the stress response?

2. What role does the endocrine system play in the stress response?

3. Name and explain the three pathways (axes) of stress physiology.

4. What role does the amygdala play in the stress response?

5. What are panic attacks?

6. What does new brain imaging tell us about stress physiology?

7. Explain the concept of neuroplasticity.

8. Describe which part of the brain is associated with multitasking.

REFERENCES AND RESOURCES

Allen, R. *Human Stress: Its Nature and Control.* Burgess Press, Minneapolis, MN, 1983.

Allen, R. *Psychophysiology of the Human Stress Response.* University of Maryland, College Park, 1990.

Amen, D. *Change Your Brain, Change Your Life* (Revised Expanded Ed.). Three Rivers Press, New York, 2015.

American Cancer Society. *Making Treatment Decisions: DHEA.* www.cancer.org/docroot/ETO/content/ETO_5_3X_Dhea.asp?sitearea=ETO.

Anderson, S. David Eagleman's New TC Show, "The Brain," Gets Inside Your Head. *Newsweek*, October 15, 2015. http://www.newsweek.com/2015/10/30/david-eaglemans-new-tv-show-brain-gets-inside-your-head-383843.html.

Baker, R. *Understanding Panic Attacks and Overcoming Fear* (3rd ed.). Lion Hudson Books, New York, 2011.

Bar-Tal, Y., Cohen-Mansfield, J., and Golander, H. Which Stress Matters? The Examination of Temporal Aspects of Stress, *Journal of Psychology* 132(5):569–576, 1998.

Bremner, J. D. *Does Stress Damage the Brain? Understanding Trauma-Related Disorders from a Mind-Body Perspective.* W. W. Norton, New York, 2005.

CFIDS Association of America. *Symptoms: Chronic Fatigue Syndrome.* www.cfids.org/about-cfids/symptoms.asp. Accessed February 26, 2008.

Childre, D. L. *Cut-Thru.* Planetary Publications, Boulder Creek, CA, 1996.

Daniel, J., et al. Mental and Endocrine Factors in Repeated Stress in Man, *Studia Psychologica* 15(3):273–281, 1973.

Depression and the Birth and Death of Brain Cells. www.biopsychiatry.com/newbraincell.

Dispenza, J. *Evolve Your Brain: The Science of Changing Your Mind.* Health Communications, Inc., Deerfield Beach, FL, 2007.

Dreinhofer, K. *The Bone and Joint Decade 2000–2010: How Far Have We Come?* www.touchbriefings.com/pdf/2263/Dreinhofer.pdf.

Everly, G. *A Clinical Guide to the Treatment of the Human Stress Response.* 3rd ed. Kluwer Academic Press, New York, 2013.

Everly, G., and Rosenfeld, R. *The Nature and Treatment of the Stress Response.* Plenum Press, New York, 1981.

Greenfield, N. S., and Sternback, R. A. *Handbook of Psychophysiology.* Holt, Rinehart, & Winston, New York, 4th ed. 2017. Cacioppo, J., Tassinary, L., and Berntson, G.

Guyton, A. C., and Hall, J. *Textbook of Medical Physiology,* 13th ed. Saunders, Philadelphia, 2015.

Harris, D. *10% Happier.* Dey Street Books, New York, 2014.

Johnson, S. Emotions and the Brain: Fear, *Discover* 24(3): 32–39, 2003.

Lacey, J. I. Somatic Response Patterning and Stress: Some Revisions of Activating Theory. Reprinted in H. H. Appley, and R. Trumbell, *Psychological Stress: Issues in Research.* Appleton-Century-Crofts, East Norwalk, CT, 1976.

LeDoux, J. *The Emotional Brain.* Simon & Schuster, New York, 1996.

Maas, J. *Power Sleep.* Quill Books, New York, 2001.

Makara, G., Palkovits, M., and Szentagothal, J. The Endocrine Hypothalamus and Hormonal Response to Stress. In H. Selye (ed.), *Selye's Guide to Stress Research,* Van Nostrand Rinehold, New York: 280–337, 1983.

McDonagh, B. *DARE: The New Way to End Anxiety and Stop Panic Attacks.* Beaverton, OR, BMD Publishing, 2015.

McEwen, B. *The End of Stress as We Know It.* Joseph Henry Press, Washington, D.C., 2002.

McEwen, B. S., de Leon, M. J., Lupien, S. J., and Meaney, M. J. Corticosteroids, the Aging Brain and Cognition, *Trends in Endocrinology and Metabolism,* 10:92–96, 1999.

National sleep foundation. www.sleepfoundation.org.

Nemeroff, C. The Neurobiology of Depression, *Scientific American,* June 1998.

Newberg, A., D'Aquili, E., and Rause, V. *Why God Won't Go Away.* Ballantine Books, New York, 2002.

Oatley, K. *Brain Mechanisms and Mind.* Dutton, New York, 1972.

O'Leary, A. Stress, Emotion, and Human Immune Function, *Psychological Bulletin* 108(3):363–382, 1990.

Ornstein, R., and Sobel, D. *The Healing Brain,* 2nd ed. Malor Books, San Francisco, 1999.

Peak Performance Training. New studies of human brains show stress may shrink neurons. www.peakperformancetraining.org/sitefiles/articles/stress.htm.

Pelletier, K. *Mind as Healer, Mind as Slayer.* Dell, New York, 1977.

Pittman, C., and Karle, W. *Rewire Your Anxious Brain.* Oakland, CA, New Harbinger Publications, 2015.

Powell, D., and the Institute of Noetic Sciences. *The 2007 Shift Report: Evidence of a World Transforming.* Institute of Noetic Sciences, Petaluma, CA, 2007:28–36.

Sapolsky, R. Why Stress Is Bad for You, *Science* 273:749–750, 1996.

Sapolsky, R. Stress and Your Shrinking Brain, *Discover,* March, 1999:116–122.

Sapolsky, R. *Why Zebras Don't Get Ulcers.* W. H. Freeman & Company, New York, 3rd ed. 2004.

Schnirring, L. DHEA: Hype, Hope Not Matched by Facts, *Physician and Sports Medicine,* May 17, 1998.

Sherwood, L. *Human Physiology,* 9th ed. Brooks Cole, 2015.

Shreve, J. Beyond the Brain: What's in Your Mind, *National Geographic,* March 2005.

Smith, M., and Segal, J. *Panic Attacks and Panic Disorder.* Healthguide.org. 2016. http://www.helpguide.org/articles /anxiety/panic-attacks-and-panic-disorders.htm.

Stranon, B. *The Primal Teen.* Doubleday Books, New York, 2004.

University of Florida. Addicted to Phones? Cell Phone Use Becoming a Major Problem for Some, Experts Say, *Physorg.com*, January 18, 2007. www.physorg.com /news88356303.html.

Usdin, E., et al. *Catecholamines and Stress.* Pergamon Press, Oxford, 1976.

Vgontazas, A. N., and Kales, A. Sleep and Its Disorders, *Annual Review of Medicine* 50:387–400, 1999.

Wallis, C. The Multi-Tasking Generation. *Time*, March 27, 2006.

William, D. Modernization, Stress and Blood Pressure: New Directions in Research, *Human Biology* 71(4):583–605, 1999.

Zimmer, C. Peering into the Brain, *Newsweek,* June 9, 2003.

CHAPTER 4

Stress and Disease

*By comprehending that human beings are energy,
one can begin to comprehend new ways of viewing
health and illness.*

—Richard Gerber, M.D.

An argument started more than 100 years ago about the specific cause of disease, and despite all the recent medical advances, the debate over "nature versus nurture" continues to this day. It was the French chemist Louis Pasteur who postulated that when we make contact with a pathogenic microbe (some virus or bacterium), our immune system is alerted immediately and goes on the defensive. In Pasteur's mind, the state of health or disease was not a measure of the integrity of the immune system, but rather of the strength of the invading microbe. Pasteur's idea took a while to catch on, but once it did, it soon carried considerable weight in the medical community. The acceptance of Pasteur's "germ theory" propelled medical science (with the financial backing of John D. Rockefeller) toward the direction of immunizations, antibiotics, and the pharmaceutical industry as we know it today. But Pasteur also had his critics, not the least of whom was Claude Bernard, a brilliant French physiologist and philosopher who disagreed vehemently with the idea that tiny microbes were the sole reason for imminent illness and death.

Image © Oleinikova Olga/Shutterstock.

Quotation reproduced from Gerber, R. *Vibrational Medicine* (3rd ed.), Bear & Company, Rochester, 2001.

Bernard, who coined the term *homeostasis*, marveled at the complexity of human physiology. He suggested that it wasn't the germs that did the damage, but rather the condition of the body and its state of health that either destroyed the germ or was destroyed by it. Using a metaphor of seeds and soil, he insisted that if the soil is fertile (poor health) enough for a seed (microbe) to germinate, it will. Bernard suggested that good living practices, including one's attitude and sound nutrition, were essential to keep the body at its optimal level of health, thereby creating an infertile and inhospitable place for the seeds of microorganisms to germinate. At the time, Bernard's theory fell on deaf ears. Pasteur remained adamant: Microbes were nondiscriminatory. Their effects would be felt by all those who were exposed to them, regardless of the individuals' state of physical or mental health.

Decades later, Pasteur's germ theory was termed the "theory of specific etiology," according to which every disease is believed to be caused by a specific microorganism. Today, this theory has evolved to suggest that diseases not caused by microorganisms can be reduced to a single genetic flaw in human DNA. As more research findings are revealed through the work of the Human Genome Project, news headlines will continue to promote the link between disease and one's genetic makeup. Despite efforts to shift the paradigm, Descartes's mechanistic philosophy of health is still alive in the Western world!

Etiology, the study of disease, is not an easy science. Some people who are exposed to microbes may carry—and spread—a disease but, in fact, never contract the disease itself. Typhoid Mary is the classic example of this phenomenon, as were people who spread, but never caught, SARS in 2003. In fact, toward the end of his life, Pasteur had a change of mind about his germ theory. On his deathbed, he said, "Bernard is right, [it's not the seed] it's the soil."

At roughly the same time that the germ theory was accepted as fact by Western medicine, another theory was proposed by a Chicago-based physician, Franz Alexander. He observed quite astutely that there appeared to be a profound connection between one's mental/emotional state and one's physical health. He coined the term *organ neurosis*, later called **psychosomatic**, to describe this precarious mind-body relationship. Although the word *psychosomatic* caught on quickly in the American vernacular, 50 years would pass before medical science took Alexander's theory seriously. It would be another two decades before the medical community would acknowledge the highly sophisticated intricacies of mind, body, spirit, and emotions that can produce not just a detrimental effect, but a healing effect as well.

The current focus on the stress-and-disease phenomenon is directed toward the interactions of the immune system, the CNS, and human consciousness. Recently, threads of evidence scattered far and wide throughout the literature of the many allied health disciplines have finally begun to lend credence to the ageless intuition of holism. When looked at from the traditional scientific (biomedical) point of view, however, these traces continue to raise more questions than they answer.

Perhaps because of these complexities, we still can merely speculate about the exact nature of the relationship between stress and disease. All the while, scientists continue

to take sides on the nature versus nurture debate. Despite world-class health care, improved living conditions, and abundant food choices, chronic diseases continue to plague the planet. As noted in the acclaimed book *Why Zebras Don't Get Ulcers*, researcher Richard Sapolsky states that there is a colossal link between stress and disease. Current estimates provided by the American Institute of Stress suggest that as many as 80 percent of all doctor's office visits are the result of stress. Moreover, what was once considered to be an association between stress and disease is now understood to be a direct causal link, acne, migraines, and gastrointestinal problems being prime examples (Segerstrom and Miller, 2004). Experts estimate that between 75 and 85 percent of all health-related problems are either precipitated or aggravated by stress. The list of such stress-affected disorders is nearly endless, ranging from herpes and hemorrhoids to the common cold and cancer.

To understand the relationship between stress and disease, you first must recognize that several factors act in unison to create a pathological outcome. These include the cognitive perceptions of threatening stimuli and the consequent activation of the nervous system, the endocrine system, and the immune system. In the past, these three physiological dynamics were studied separately because they were thought to be independent systems. Today they are viewed as one network, and it is this current understanding that has given rise to the new interdisciplinary field of **psychoneuroimmunology** (PNI). As defined by Pelletier (1988), psychoneuroimmunology is "the study of the intricate interaction of consciousness (psycho), brain and central nervous system (neuro), and the body's defense against external infection and internal aberrant cell division (immunology)."

There is a consensus among leaders in the field of psychoneuroimmunology that the expression "mind-body medicine" is rather limited in its scope, leading people such as Joan Borysenko, Deepak Chopra, Andy Weil, Gladys Taylor McGary, James Gordon, Larry Dossey, and others to call the approach to healing "mind-body-spirit healing."

> **Psychosomatic:** A term coined from Franz Alexander's term *organ neurosis*, used to describe a host of physical illnesses or diseases caused by the mind and unresolved emotional issues.
>
> **Psychoneuroimmunology:** The study of the effects of stress on disease; treats the mind, central nervous system, and immune system as one interrelated unit.

■ Theoretical Models

There have been several research efforts that seek to explain the relationship between stress and disease. At best, this relationship is still in the speculation stage, with no clear-cut understanding of the complexities involved. After an attempt to synthesize a definitive model, based on his own work as well as on an exhaustive survey of more than 300 research articles, Pelletier admitted that there is still not enough scientific information at the present time to create a substantiated stress and disease model, and certainly not from the current biomedical model. Nevertheless, some of the promising theories described in this section may in time provide medical science with the building blocks to create such a comprehensive model. Once this model is in place, the possibility of preventing and intercepting several disease processes will certainly take precedence over the current medical practice of relieving symptoms and fixing and replacing broken parts. The following are some of the most prominent theories regarding the mind-body-spirit relationship.

The Borysenko Model

In what is currently recognized as the most accurate description of the immune system, former Tufts University immunologist Myrin Borysenko (1987) outlined both a dichotomy of stress-induced dysregulation and a matrix describing the "immune balance" regarding four classifications of disease. The dichotomy broadly divides disease and illness into either **autonomic dysregulation** (overresponsive autonomic nervous system) or **immune dysregulation** (TABLE 4.1).

Borysenko suggests that when the autonomic nervous system releases an abundance of stress hormones, several physiological repercussions can result—among them, migraines, ulcers, and hypertension. The notion that the nervous system is responsible for several symptoms of illness and disease through the release of stress hormones

(epinephrine, norepinephrine, cortisol, and aldosterone) was first postulated by Cannon, and then established through the pioneering research of Selye.

No less important, however, are the repercussions of a dysfunctional immune system, which can precipitate infection, allergies, and perhaps cancer. To understand how the immune system can become dysfunctional or suppressed, let us first take a look at the current perception of this unique physiological system. The purpose of the immune system is to protect the body from pathogens, either externally generated (e.g., bacteria) or internally manufactured (e.g., mutant cells), which impede the proper functioning of the body's regulatory dynamics. Pathogens are composed of certain molecules (antigens) that have the capacity to interact at various receptor sites on several types of immune system cells, which in turn attempt to detoxify them. Metaphorically speaking, the immune system acts like the collective branches of the armed services to ensure national security by protecting the country from both invading forces and internal insurrection. Like all other physiological systems, the immune system begins to develop in the fetus and matures at about the time of birth, when the body becomes vulnerable to external pathogens.

The immune system is a network of several organs. These include bone marrow, which throughout life supplies the lymph tissue with stem cells (the precursors to various lymphoid cells), and eventually become B-lymphocytes (B-cells); the thymus, a gland below the throat that allows stem cells to mature into T-lymphocytes (T-cells); and the lymph nodes, spleen, and gut-associated lymphoid tissue into which T-cells and B-cells migrate and are occasionally housed. Upon completion of their maturation process, both T-cells and B-cells migrate throughout the body, ready to encounter their respective targets known as antigens. Other aspects of the immune system include the tonsils, and unique lymphoid tissue associated with the bronchioles, genitals, and skin. It is interesting to note that only 2 percent of

TABLE 4.1 Borysenko's Stress and Disease Dichotomy

Autonomic Dysregulation (Overresponsive ANS)	Immune Dysregulation
Migraines	Infection (virus)
Peptic ulcers	Allergies
Irritable bowel syndrome	AIDS
Hypertension	Cancer
Coronary heart disease	Lupus
Asthma	Arthritis

Autonomic dysregulation: Increased sensitivity to perceived threats resulting from heightened neural (sympathetic) responses speeding up the metabolic rate of one or more organs.

Immune dysregulation: An immune system wherein various functions are suppressed; now believed to be affected by emotional negativity.

lymphocytes are in circulation at any one time. The remaining 98 percent constitute a dynamic defense system, housed and circulated through various organs of the lymphatic system.

The lymphocytes are one of five types of **leukocytes** in the family of cells in the immune system and the major component of the immune system. They are produced in the bone marrow where they eventually migrate to the peripheral organs of the lymphatic system. The other members of the leukocyte family include granulocytes, macrophages (which seem to collaborate with T-cells and B-cells to help identify antigens for destruction), and eosinophils and basophils, which have a lesser role with altered immune function.

T-cells and B-cells may appear morphologically similar, but their function is different. T-lymphocytes are primarily responsible for cell-mediated immunity—that is, the elimination of internally manufactured antigens (e.g., mutinous cells) in organ tissue. It is currently believed that the human body produces one mutant cell approximately every couple of hours. In an action similar to scanning a grocery store product for its bar code, each T-cell travels throughout the body to scan all other cells for a match between their DNA structure and its own. If a cell's structure doesn't match, the T-cell considers it a foreign substance and proceeds to destroy it. Examples are a cancerous cell and transplanted tissue (i.e., organ transplant). In the laboratory where T-cells were observed performing this function, they were called "killer cells" for their search-and-destroy missions. Although the role of T-cells is more global, they have been observed to destroy mutant cells through direct attack in which they release nonspecific substances called cytokines, which assist in the elimination process. B-cells,

FIGURE 4.1   The family of T-lymphocytes includes three types of cells: T-cytotoxic cells, T-helpers (CD4), and T-suppressors (CD8). The natural killer cells collaborate with the T-cytotoxic cells.

in contrast, are responsible for humoral immunity. This means the antibodies they discharge circulate throughout various body fluids, primarily blood, and combine with foreign antigens to deactivate the agents that make them a threat. Antibodies are a special type of protein, called globulins, found in the plasma and are typically referred to as gamma globulins or immunoglobulins (Ig). The function of B-cells is primarily the elimination of pathogenic microorganisms that contribute to infectious diseases, including viruses and bacteria. Although T-cells and B-cells have their own specific functions, they often work together. In fact, in some cases, B-cells depend on T-cells for their function.

A closer examination of T-cells indicates that there are three subgroups of this crucial leukocyte, plus one additional immune cell (the NK cell) that collaborates with the T-cytotoxic cells to do its function (**FIG. 4.1**). Each leukocyte cell has a unique molecular configuration and function:

1. **T-cytotoxic cells:** The basic T-cells release cytokines, which then allow the cells to become sensitized to identify endogenous antigens on the cell membrane for destruction. In addition, with the help of macrophages, they attack and destroy tumorous cells.

2. **T-helpers:** Clinically labeled as CD4, these cells appear to increase the production of antibodies released by T-cells. T-helpers and T-suppressors (see Fig. 4.1) are referred to as immunoregulatory cells because they regulate cell-mediated immunity and humoral antibody response.

3. **T-suppressors:** Clinically labeled as CD8, these cells appear to decrease the production of antibodies necessary to assist T-cells in attacking and killing endogenous antigens. A reduction in CD8 is believed to keep cytotoxic T-cells in check so that they do not attack self-proteins and thereby cause degeneration of healthy tissue. A reduction in CD8 is thought to be associated with arthritis

---

Lymphocytes: Immune system cells that are housed throughout the lymphatic system, with 2 percent in circulation at any one time.

Leukocytes: The family of cells that constitute the major component of the immune system.

T-cytotoxic cells: Best known as the cells that attack and destroy tumorous cells by releasing cytokines.

T-helpers: Also known as CD4, these cells help in the production of antibodies released by T-cells.

T-suppressors: Also known as CD8, these cells decrease the production of antibodies, thus keeping a healthy balance of T-cells.

BOX 4.1 The Human Microbiome: A Look at Health Through the Gut

What if I were to tell you that one of the newest theories of disease and illness begins not in the secrets deep inside your DNA, but within the millions upon millions of bacteria that reside in your stomach and small intestine? In what has been called the new "medical landscape of the century," some of the most exciting discoveries in the past decade have been insights into what is going on in our gastrointestinal (GI) tract. The twentieth century may well be known for the emergence of the germ theory of disease, which ushered in the age of antibiotics and vaccinations, and the Genome Project, which sought to link every disease to a defective gene in our DNA, but today a revolution is taking place in medical science about stress and disease right in the gut. While many great things have come about based on the two perspectives of disease—germs and DNA—experts now suggest they have led to a misguided understanding of health. Twenty-first-century medicine may become known for a focus on maintaining healthy gut bacteria to ensure optimal wellness (DeSalle and Perkins, 2015).

Researchers now call the intestinal flora, which is composed of trillions of healthy bacteria, the "microbiome." The premise of the microbiome is that each human being is actually a multispecies superorganism. Each of us hosts a vast and diverse living ecological system. When this ecological system is healthy, so are we. When it is compromised, so are we. Recent evidence suggests that the typical human body hosts over 10,000 microbial species; bacterial cells alone range from 57 to 90 percent of the total number of cells in the human body. The skin,

which is the body's largest organ, itself has billions of microbes, many of which are actually essential to our well-being. The twentieth-century approach of wiping out "bugs" via antibiotics has led to a "deforestation" of essential bacteria. The end result sets the stage for many kinds of chronic illness. Maintaining the integrity of the microbiome, however, is far more complicated than eating yogurt or consuming probiotics to reseed the forest of your intestinal flora.

In his book *The Human Superorganism*, Cornell University professor and immunotoxicologist Rodney Dietert explains the delicate balance between the bacteria in our gut and our immune system. When this balance is disrupted the stage is set for a number of noncommunicable diseases, also known as "diseases of civilization." It is now known that 70 percent of our immune system resides in our gut, yet the gut is often ignored in the treatment of many chronic diseases, from asthma, obesity, and arthritis to multiple sclerosis, psoriasis, and attention deficit/hyperactivity disorder (ADHD). Perhaps the biggest take-home message about a compromised microbiome is its association with inflammation. Inflammation (excessive oxidation of tissues) is associated with many chronic diseases, and stress seems to be a major trigger for inflammation (Vida, 2014). Moreover, abysmal eating habits perpetuate a compromised microbiome, leaving one quite vulnerable to chronic disease. Dietert goes so far as to say that we have a whole generation (or more) of kids born with a compromised microbiome, and as such, this qualifies as an epidemic of birth defects.

---

and lupus. (Borysenko notes that clinical tests show a 2:1 ratio of CD4:CD8 to be normal, whereas a ratio less than this is a signal that this aspect of the immune system is deficient.)

4. **Natural killer (NK) cells:** Unlike cytotoxic T-cells, these immune cells (large lymphocytes) appear to have an innate ability to detect endogenous antigens without the help of any neuropeptides to sensitize them or previous memory experience. NK cells collaborate with cytotoxic T-cells to destroy mutant cells, virus-infected cells, and transplanted grafts. NK cells have a unique role in immune surveillance to detect malignant cell changes. Among immunologists, NK cells are known as "psychosocial friendly cells" because they mirror emotional states (ups and downs) of the mind.

Current research on the relationship between the stress response and immunofunction is now considered definitive by researchers at the Institute for Behavioral Medicine at Ohio State University: Stress increases neuroendocrine hormones, which suppress immune function. In an article reviewing the data over the past two decades, Webster Marketon (2008) states, "Such effects on the immune system have severe consequences on health, which include, but are not limited to, delayed wound healing, impaired responses to vaccination, and development and progression of cancer." Specifically, studies investigating

Natural killer (NK) cells: Large lymphocytes that can detect endogenous antigens, thus helping to destroy mutant cells.

the effect of catecholamines and stress-related hormones have reported questionable integrity of the immune system when excess levels of these substances were found in the blood. Increases in epinephrine and norepinephrine have been observed to promote the release and redistribution of lymphocytes, yet at the same time decrease their efficiency (Calcagni and Elenkov, 2006). Some types of stress (e.g., exercise) cause the release of neuropeptides (endorphins), which not only enhance immunofunction, but also produce an almost euphoric state of mind (the runner's high). Injections of norepinephrine in mice have been shown to enhance NK cell activity. During chronic stress, however, the increase of cortisol and other glucocorticoids has been linked to a marked decrease in T-cells, reducing their ability to locate and destroy mutant cells. The effects of acute and chronic stress on B-cells are still under investigation, but are speculated to be similar to those on T-cells. What all this means is that the integrity of the immune system is thought to be greatly influenced and quite literally compromised by emotional stress.

In Borysenko's model, when the immune system is operating normally, it is said to be "precisely regulated." However, when the immune system is not working as homeostatically intended, the result is immunological overreaction, underreaction, or perhaps both. In any case, disease and/or illness are certain (TABLE 4.2). The causes of overreactions can be exogenous, as in an allergic reaction created by a foreign substance, or endogenous, as when lymphocytes begin to attack and destroy healthy body tissue. Similarly, in an exogenous underreaction, foreign substances outmaneuver and undermine the ability of the B-cells to prevent infection; in endogenous underreactions, antigens are left undisturbed by T-cells, which may then develop into **neoplasms** (cancerous tumors). Similar findings are reported by Biondi (2001).

The concepts of immunity to disease, both exogenous and endogenous, are constantly being rewritten and updated as new studies reveal the nuances and complexities of the lymphatic system and its dynamic interrelationship to all other aspects of human physiology, particularly in light of an increase in lifestyle **autoimmune diseases**

Neoplasms: Another term for cancerous tumors.

Autoimmune diseases: Diseases that occur because of an overactive immune system, which "attacks the body." Examples include lupus and rheumatoid arthritis.

	Over-reactions	Under-reactions
Exogenous activity	Allergies	Infections (colds and flu)
		Herpes
Endogenous activity	Arthritis Lupus	Cancer

TABLE 4.2 Borysenko's Immune Activity Matrix

and the acknowledgment that stress plays a role in this relationship (Kemeny and Gruenewald, 1999; Kiecolt-Glaser et al., 2002).

In Borysenko's opinion, it is psychological stress that throws this precisely regulated mechanism out of balance. Stress is the catalyst that exaggerates the direction in which your immune system is headed, precipitating an over- or underreaction. Note that you can have an allergic reaction (overreaction) and a cold (underreaction) at the same time because they are produced by different dynamics. Borysenko adds that despite the differences among these aspects, the same relaxation techniques work to reinstate precise regulation of the immune system. In other words, regular practice of a relaxation technique, such as meditation or mental imagery, can bring the entire immune system back into homeostatic balance.

Although Borysenko (1991b) believes that "stress alters the vulnerability of the immune system to both exogenous and endogenous antigens," the connection between the mind's ability to perceive situations as stressful and the consequent changes in the integrity of the immune system he left to speculation (FIG. 4.2).

In support of Borysenko's model, ongoing research to understand this link between stress and the immune system suggests that acute psychological stress decreases NK cell activity through a profound effect on cytokine production. Chronic stress is observed to suppress NK cell activity, thereby increasing one's susceptibility to infections and cancer (Herberman, 2002). Moreover, stress-related changes in the immune system have been observed in secondary lymphoid tissue (spleen, lymph nodes) where T-cells are produced. Lymphoid tissues, bathed in a "hormonal milieu," appear to be significantly affected by emotions and thought processing (Rabin, 2002).

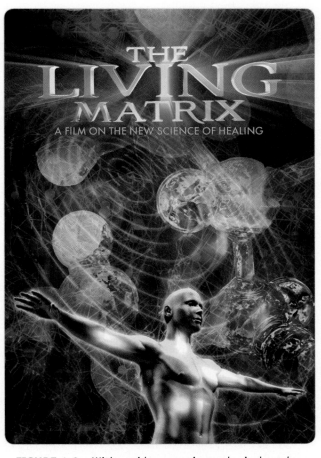

FIGURE 4.2 With rapid economic, ecological, and technological changes, the global village appears to have become a more stressful place, which is all the more reason to learn and practice effective stress-management techniques to maintain a sense of balance in one's life despite these winds of change.

New discoveries indicate that the physiological systems are more complex than was once believed. For example, formerly described as specialized lymphocytes, T-helpers and T-suppressors may, in fact, be "double agents" working for the CNS as well.

The Pert Model

Until recently, it was thought that there was no direct link between the nervous system and the immune system; virtually all physiologists believed that these two systems acted independently. But researchers have now isolated neural endings connecting the CNS to the thymus, lymph nodes, spleen, and bone marrow. In addition, the tonsils, adenoids, and some cells of the small intestine have been found to be innervated by sympathetic nerve fibers.

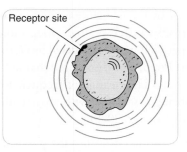

Receptor site

FIGURE 4.3 Pert's early observations were that all known neuropeptides appear to have a single molecular structure. The subtle differences among them may be the rate at which each molecule oscillates.

A second and perhaps more important link indicates that **neuropeptides** (messenger hormones) produced in the brain are able to fit into receptor sites of lymphocytes, much like keys fit into a lock, thus altering their metabolic function. This communication system is altogether different from the efferent/afferent system observed between neuromuscular tissue and the brain. The codes of neuropeptide information are "spoken" through receptor sites of various lymphocyte cells located throughout the body, and their language is apparently influenced by emotional responses.

It was Candace Pert, former Chief of Brain Chemistry at the National Institute for Mental Health, who discovered that immune cells have built-in receptor sites for neuropeptides (1985, 1986, 1987), with similar findings being reported by Edwin Blalock (1985). The identification of neuropeptides themselves is a recent discovery. In trying to uncover the dynamics in the brain associated with chemical addictions, scientists were surprised to find that the brain produces its own (endogenous) opiates, neurotransmitters that have a similar effect to those manufactured externally, such as morphine. The most publicized neuropeptide is beta-endorphin, but so far several hundred neuropeptides have been identified. They are thought to be associated with everything from mood changes to immune regulation. Pert further suggested that there may actually be only one neuropeptide molecule that, like a chameleon, changes its configuration as a result of emotional influences (FIG. 4.3). Pert hypothesized that this spontaneous change may be

Neuropeptides: Unique messenger hormones produced in the brain (and other organs of the body) that fit into the receptor sites of lymphocytes.

accounted for by the wavelike oscillations or vibrations of the electrons in each neuropeptide molecule. Pert's hypothesis parallels work conducted by German physicist Fritz-Albert Popp, who discovered that DNA is capable of sending out a large range of frequencies, with each frequency being associated with a particular metabolic function (McTaggart, 2008).

Because the hypothalamus has the greatest preponderance of neuropeptide receptors, it was first believed that these substances, which are produced by the brain, were involved in the biochemical mediation of emotional responses. Pert discovered, however, that neuropeptides are not produced solely by the brain. Her research revealed that throughout the body immune cells not only have receptors for neuropeptides, but also can manufacture them independently. Furthermore, immune cells seem to have a kind of memory that enables them to adapt to specific emotional responses. Thus neuropeptides are believed to be the means of communication between the brain and T- and B-cells, and it is a bidirectional pathway: Immune cells speak to the brain, and vice versa. Pert's discovery has given credence to the supposition that some emotions may suppress the function of lymphocytes while others may act as immunoenhancers.

Today, the scientific literature is loaded with studies that clearly document the association between the stress response, emotional regulation, and their respective influences on the immune system (Koenig and Cohen, 2002). The following are some of the landmark studies that gave PNI an established foundation of validity in the medical community.

Jermott et al. (1983) looked at the influence of academic stress on the rate of secretory immunoglobulin (S-IgA) in Tufts University dental students. S-IgA is thought to be the first line of defense against upper respiratory diseases. Subjects were administered a personality profile to identify a specific personality trait called power motivation (control), and based on this trait they were divided into two groups. Saliva samples, used to measure S-IgA, were taken five times during the academic year. The results were that mean S-IgA values were significantly reduced during stressful periods, particularly in the students who demonstrated high power motivation.

> **Immunoenhancement:** A term used to describe various stress management techniques that appear to boost the immune system.

Janice Kiecolt-Glaser and her husband, Ron Glaser, both pioneers in the field of PNI, have conducted several landmark studies that linked stress to the suppression of the immune system. Most noteworthy was a classic study that found a decrease in the number of lymphocytes in Ohio State University medical students during their first day of exams, as compared with samples taken prior to and after the exam period (1984). A 1996 paper revealed how stress retards wound healing. Kiecolt-Glaser's research (2003) suggests that chronic stress accelerates the aging process (which entails many diseases) through the overproduction of a specific proinflammatory cytokine.

Studies investigating the relationship between emotional stress and immunosuppression have also been conducted using animals as subjects (Bovbjerg et al., 1984). For example, when rats were subjected to foot shocks they could not control, a significant reduction in immune function (i.e., decreased lymphocyte proliferation) was detected (Laudenslanger et al., 1983). The suppression of the immune system was considered a *conditioned* response. The researchers concluded that a helpless-hopeless attitude, initiated by an inability to control factors of the environment, can pave a path toward illness.

Immunosuppression has also been observed in individuals during bereavement. A study by Bartrop et al. (1977) indicated that people manifested lower lymphocyte proliferation within 8 weeks of the loss of a spouse. Similar findings were observed by Schleifer et al. (1983) in men whose wives had died of breast cancer, with results showing a significant reduction in lymphocyte proliferation. These studies have led some to suggest that humans, like rats, can be conditioned to suppress their immune systems by means of emotions and/or thought processes.

One of the most interesting studies regarding the effects of relaxation and coping techniques on **immunoenhancement** was conducted by Esterling et al. (1994). In this study, the effect of various stress-management skills on NK cell activity was investigated among nursing home patients. Subjects were divided into three groups: (1) those who were taught relaxation techniques, (2) those who were provided with abundant social contact, and (3) those who received no special techniques or contact. Results revealed that after a 1-month period, the NK cell count was significantly higher in those subjects who received stress-management therapy than in the controls. Other studies, inspired by the work of Norman Cousins, have also been conducted to determine the relationship between positive emotions and changes in the immune system.

In her acclaimed book *Molecules of Emotion*, Pert highlights the journey of discovery that brought her to the realization that the body is not a machine. "What is this energy that is referred to by so many alternative healers, who associate it with the release of emotion and the restoration of health? According to Western medical terms, energy is produced strictly by various cellular metabolic processes, and the idea that energy could be connected to emotional release is totally foreign to the scientific mind. . . . It is my belief that this mysterious energy is actually the free flow of information carried by the biochemicals of emotion—the neuropeptides and their receptors." Although the focus of her current research involves peptide T for AIDS treatment, Pert (2004) sees the frontiers of subtle-energy medicine research as the most exciting paradigm of the stress and disease model.

What all these studies seem to indicate is that there is a strong relationship between emotional responses and the biochemical changes they produce, specifically with regard to constituents of the immune system. Whereas before Pert's findings it was believed that cortisol played the crucial role in immunosuppression, it is now thought that structural changes in neuropeptides, influenced by emotional thought, play the most significant role in immunoincompetence. Currently, the search is under way for other neurotransmitters produced and secreted by the brain that may be responsible for producing the emotional thoughts, which in turn synthesize specific neuropeptides to influence the immune system. Pert is of the opinion that this type of search is fruitless. In *Noetic Sciences Review* (1987), she writes, "I think it is possible now to conceive of mind and consciousness as an emanation of emotional information processing, and as such, mind and consciousness would appear to be independent from brain and body." It is this point of view that has led her and others (e.g., Joan Borysenko, Larry Dossey, Deepak Chopra, and Bernie Siegel) to look beyond the physical to the fields of parapsychology and metaphysics for answers to the puzzling relationship between stress and disease. Blazing a trail to this doorstep is cell biologist Bruce Lipton and radiologist Richard Gerber.

The Lipton Model

In tandem with the research of Candace Pert is the work of Bruce Lipton. Lipton is a cell biologist and former faculty member of both the University of Wisconsin's School of Medicine and Stanford University's School of Medicine. He also is the author of the popular book *The Biology of Belief*. For the past three decades, Lipton has researched and explored the nature of human health from the smallest unit: the cell. As one explores the nature of cell physiology, one cannot avoid the structure of the cell nucleus and its contents, specifically the DNA. While Lipton's colleagues were focused on the role of DNA (genetics) in terms of disease causality, he took a different approach: the cell's environment. An outside passion in the field of physics led Lipton to connect dots where others only saw one dot.

Lipton is a proponent of the "epigenetic theory": the study of molecular mechanisms in which environment controls gene activity of the DNA. Lipton goes one step further to suggest that the cell's brain is its cell wall, the cell membrane. The cell membrane holds a complexity of knowledge that allows your body to translate environmental signals into behavior. Understanding that at the molecular level, electromagnetic particles of energy play a significant role in the integrity of the cell's health, Lipton began to explore the significance of electromagnetic properties of the cell membrane.

Lipton's research at Stanford revealed that cells have the ability to promote growth as well as protection of their own integrity. They cannot, however, do both functions at once. The more time that is spent in the protection mode negates time and energy for growth, and thus impedes not only the health of the cell, but the organ it is a part of (and because everything connects energetically, the health of the individual). A state of constant stress can ultimately compromise the health of the cell and hence its vitality. As each cell goes, so goes the organ or system that contains it. Lipton says being scared to death is no mere metaphor. For example, take the effect of the nervous system on the gastrointestinal (GI) tract. Typically, the cells in the lining of your stomach are replaced every 72 hours. This naturally occurring growth process is suspended in the fight-or-flight response of chronic stress with more energy being provided for protection rather than growth. Over time, the functioning of the stomach and small intestine will be impaired significantly.

From cell to physiological systems, Lipton notes that stress hormones greatly affect the vitality of the immune system, so much so that patients undergoing an organ transplant are often given high doses of these hormones (e.g., cortisol) to suppress the immune system so that the new organ won't be rejected.

Over the years, Lipton has observed the relationship of thoughts and beliefs as expressed from both the conscious and unconscious minds. He notes that it is the programmed stress-prone beliefs stored in the unconscious mind that will negatively affect one's health. His research is complemented by studies that reveal that telomeres (a DNA protein) involved with cell division are greatly compromised by chronic psychological stress, hence revealing a credible link between stress and the aging process. Stated simply: Chronic stress shortens the life of cells, specifically immune cells.

Lipton supports the tenet that our learned perceptions have become more powerful than the set programming of our DNA such that our emotions can override our genetically programmed instincts. One needs to look no further than yogis who can control various aspects of human physiology, a feat once thought impossible.

Further research has led Lipton to the connection between one's attitude (belief) and one's health status. He states: "Your beliefs act like filters on a camera lens, changing how you see the world. And your biology adapts to those beliefs" (Lipton, 2008). Lipton calls his work the new biology because he says it goes well beyond the structure of the DNA to the consciousness of each cell and the programming of this consciousness from our unconscious minds. Only when a shift occurs in the belief structure of the subconscious mind will the cell biology itself change.

Lipton also discusses the electromagnetic frequencies of cells and the often unseen electromagnetic spectrum. "Hundreds upon hundreds of scientific studies over the last fifty years have consistently revealed invisible forces of the electromagnetic spectrum profoundly impact every facet of biology regulation" (Lipton, 2008). Lipton is astonished about how these findings are well noted in mainstream medical journals but have yet to be fully incorporated into the medical school curriculum. One person who has made great efforts to change the way medical schools view illness and disease is radiologist Richard Gerber, M.D.

> **Human energy field:** Subtle human anatomy that goes by many names, from the electromagnetic field around an object to a colorful aura. The human energy field is thought to be composed of layers of consciousness that surround and permeate the physical body.

The Gerber Model

Until now, clinical researchers, influenced by the reductionist theory, have designed studies based on the assumption that the mind and the brain are one, in that all thoughts are merely the result of biochemical reactions occurring within the neurons and synapses of the brain's gray matter. Yet, in many clinical circles, human consciousness is referred to as "the ghost in the machine," an intangible entity. In his books *Vibrational Medicine* and *Vibrational Medicine for the 21st Century*, Dr. Richard Gerber reviews hundreds of studies and takes an empirical look at the alternative hypothesis—a holistic or systems-theory approach—that mind as conscious and unconscious thoughts exists as energy that surrounds and permeates the body, influencing a host of corporal biochemical reactions. From this perspective, stress-related symptoms that appear in the physical body are the manifestation of "problems" that have occurred earlier as a result of a disturbance at a "higher energy level."

What at one time sounded like science fiction is now regarded as solid fact as scientists at the vanguard of medicine collaborate with quantum physicists in the search to better understand the energy called consciousness. Paul Rosch, M.D., president of the American Institute of Stress (2003), believes that subtle bioelectric energy modalities will soon replace pharmacological drugs as a means to treat stress-related disease and illness.

Gerber also cites several new studies that have begun to scientifically measure and validate the existence of what is now called the **human energy field**. While these efforts are embryonic at best, Gerber is confident that the end result will be findings that consciousness is indeed composed of subtle energy—a frequency band of oscillations that surrounds and permeates the body—and like Pert suggested, will show that human consciousness is independent yet tightly integrated with the physical body. Gerber describes the human energy field of subtle matter as consisting of several layers of consciousness (**FIG. 4.4**): the etheric, that closest to the body; the astral, which is associated with emotional thought; the mental, three tiers of consciousness including instinct, intellect, and intuition; and the outermost layer, the causal, which is associated with the soul. Each of these layers of the energy field is associated with a specific vibrational frequency and state of consciousness. Gerber points out that in a state of optimal health all frequencies are in harmony like a finely tuned piano. A disruption in the harmony of frequencies is said to eventually lead to illness and disease. According to this model, a specific thought

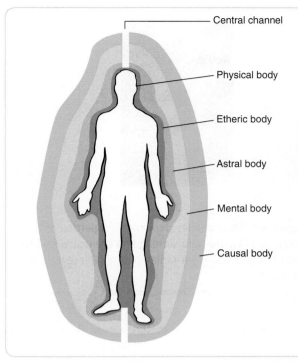

FIGURE 4.4   The human energy field, also called the electromagnetic field and the auric field, is hypothesized to have many layers, each representing a state of consciousness. Each may also have a subtle vibrational frequency associated with it.

FIGURE 4.5   Each layer of subtle energy around the body vibrates as a specific oscillation. If one layer is "out of tune," like a guitar string, then the entire energy field is affected.

(e.g., "This grade will put me on academic probation") coupled with an emotion (e.g., fear) cascades through the energy levels, resulting in an effect on some aspect of the body (e.g., a suppressed immune system). Based on Einstein's theory of relativity, which asserts, among other things, that matter and energy are interchangeable, Gerber builds a convincing argument that the mind and the brain are two distinct yet tightly intertwined elements of the human condition. In support of the Gerber model is a synthesis of information collected by Lynne McTaggart in her book *The Field*, which cites numerous studies by preeminent scholars in a host of disciplines to substantiate the quantum properties of the human energy field.

Since the beginning of recorded healing powers, shamans and medicine men have alluded to a multilayered body of energy that surrounds the physical body (**FIG. 4.5**). This energy has gone by several names, including *chi*, *prana*, *breath*, and *spirit*. In academic circles today, this has come to be referred to as **subtle energy**, with the layer closest to the body termed the **etheric energy** level or **bioplasma**. Because subtle energy is composed of matter

that appears different (less dense) than that of the physical body, it is often associated in the esoteric literature with the spiritual nature or higher consciousness. Although some people claim to actually see this energy field, which they may describe as an aura, it remains virtually invisible to the naked eye. The human energy field remained undocumented until 1940, when an ingenious photographic technique created by Russian researcher Semyon Kirlian detected traces of this energy field. Using a high-frequency, high-voltage, low-amperage electrical field, electrophotography, or **Kirlian photography** as it is now known, measured the electromagnetic field—the etheric layer—around small living objects. What was revealed through this process appeared very similar to the corona around the sun during an eclipse.

Subtle energy: A series of layers of energy that surround and permeate the body; thought to be associated with layers of consciousness constituting the human energy field.

Etheric energy: The layer of energy closest to the physical body (also known as the etheric body).

Bioplasma: Another term for the etheric layer of energy closest to the physical body.

Kirlian photography: A technique developed by Russian Semyon Kirlian enabling the viewer to see the electromagnetic energy given off by an object such as the leaf of a tree or human hand. This technique is one of several technologies that substantiates the human energy field.

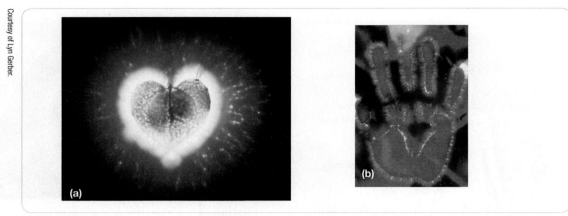

Courtesy of Lyn Gerber.

FIGURE 4.6   (a) A Kirlian photograph revealing the aura of an aspen leaf. Some studies show that if a portion of the leaf is torn away, the aura of the complete leaf remains (Gerber, 2001, p. 111). The aura surrounding the leaf is said to consist of tiny light particles observable through the electromagnetic film process. (b) A Kirlian photograph revealing the human energy field (aura) of the hand of renowned healer Olga Worell.

In simple terms, when Kirlian placed a photographic plate between an object—a leaf, say—and a specially designed electrode emitting a specific frequency (Hz), the movement of billions of charged electrons radiating from the object was captured on the film (**FIG. 4.6**). When the film was processed, brilliant colors and "spark patterns" became evident, creating an electromagnetic image similar to the leaf that was photographed. Surprisingly, if a partial (torn) leaf was photographed, an aura representing the entire leaf still appeared on film. In repeated experiments photographing human hands,

Kirlian observed marked differences in the colors and spark patterns between those of healthy people and those diagnosed with cancer.

Among Asian cultures, thoughts and feelings are believed to pass through the many layers of the human energy field through two unique systems constituting what is referred to as our **subtle anatomy**. The first system is a series of energy vortices that align themselves vertically down the front of the body. These "doors" of energy, called **chakras** (Sanskrit for spinning wheel, pronounced "shock-ra"), interface with the physical body at various points corresponding to specific organs of the endocrine and, to a lesser extent, central nervous systems. Invisible to the naked eye, these chakras act as transducers between the various layers of subtle energy.

Currently, there is much interest in the human energy field in consciousness and its relationship to the chakras. Moreover, the study of subtle energy and energy medicine has led to a new field of study called **energy psychology** (Feinstein, 2003), which attempts to unite quantum physics and subtle anatomy with psychology to better understand and treat stress-related diseases at a psychospiritual level. In her collaborative book with Norm Shealy, *The Creation of Health*, author Caroline Myss states that the chakras are the vital link to understanding the dynamics between health and disease. Myss, a clinical intuitive who can see the initial stages of disease in the auric field with a 93 percent accuracy rate, believes that illness does not happen randomly. Rather, she is convinced that the majority of disease and illness results from an overload of unresolved emotional, psychological, and spiritual crises.

> **Subtle anatomy:** Also called energy anatomy, subtle anatomy comprises the human energy field (aura), the chakra system, and the meridian system of energetic pathways that supply energy (also known as *chi* or *prana*) to the organs and physiological systems with which they connect.
>
> **Chakras:** Chakra (pronounced "shock-ra") is a Sanskrit word for spinning wheel. Chakras are part of the subtle anatomy. The seven major chakras align from the crown of the head to the base of the spine and connect to various endocrine glands. Each major chakra is directly associated with various aspects of the mind-body-spirit dynamic. When a specific chakra is closed, distorted, or congested, the perception of stress, disease, or illness may ensue.
>
> **Energy psychology:** A term used to describe the collaboration of subtle energy (chakras, meridians, and the human energy field) with psychological issues and trauma involving certain aspects of stress.

Gifted with the ability to see the human energy field and the chakras themselves, Myss has teamed up with several physicians, most notably the founder of the American Holistic Medical Association, Norm Shealy, to explore the mind-body connection with the use of intuitive skills. Myss's work, which substantiates the Gerber model of stress and disease, has proven quite remarkable as the healthcare paradigm slowly shifts from a mechanistic to a holistic approach. Myss is not alone. Physician Christiane Northrup, author of *Women's Bodies, Women's Wisdom* and former president of the American Holistic Medical Association, discusses the relationship between chakras and various disease states. In Northrup's words, "When we have unresolved chronic emotional stress in a particular area of our life, this stress registers in our energy field as a disturbance that can manifest in physical illness." As part of the subtle anatomy, the chakras are a multidimensional network that influences behavior at both the organ and cellular levels. The concept of the chakras may begin to explain why two people with the exact same stressor manifest different symptoms of disease as their thoughts and emotions are processed energetically through the layers of subtle energy and the chakra system.

The following is a synthesis of interpretations from the works of Gerber, Myss, and renowned healer Donna Eden regarding the chakra network system.

First Chakra. The first chakra is commonly known as the root chakra and is located at the base of the spine. The root chakra is associated with issues of safety and security. There is also a relationship with our connectedness to the earth and feelings of groundedness. The root chakra is tied energetically to some organs of the reproductive system, as well as the hip joints, lower back, and pelvic area. Health problems in these areas, including lower-back pain, sciatica, rectal difficulties, and some cancers (e.g., prostate) are thought to correspond to disturbances with the root chakra. The root chakra is also known as the seat of the Kundalini energy, a spiritually based concept yet to be understood in Western culture.

Second Chakra. The second chakra, also known as the sacral chakra, is recognized as being associated with the sex organs, as well as personal power in terms of business and social relationships. The second chakra deals with emotional feelings associated with issues of sexuality and self-worth. When self-worth is viewed through external means such as money, job, or sexuality, this causes an energy distortion in this region. Obsessiveness with material gain is thought to be a means to compensate for low self-worth, and hence a distortion to this chakra. Common symptoms

associated with this chakra region may include menstrual difficulties, infertility, vaginal infections, ovarian cysts, impotency, lower-back pain, sexual dysfunction, slipped disks, and bladder and urinary infections.

Third Chakra. Located in the upper stomach region, the third chakra is also known as the solar plexus chakra. Energetically, this chakra feeds into the organs of the gastrointestinal tract, including the abdomen, small intestine, colon, gallbladder, kidneys, liver, pancreas, adrenal glands, and spleen. Not to be confused with self-worth, the region of the third chakra is associated with self-confidence, self-respect, and empowerment. The wisdom of the solar plexus chakra is more commonly known as a gut feeling, an intuitive sense closely tied to our level of personal power, as exemplified in the expression, "This doesn't feel right." Blockages to this chakra are thought to be related to ulcers, cancerous tumors, diabetes, hepatitis, anorexia, bulimia, and all stomach-related problems. Gerber points out that many illnesses related to this chakra region are the result of what he calls "faulty data of old memory tapes" that have been recorded and programmed into the unconscious mind during early portions of the individual's life. Myss adds that the enculturation of fears and issues of unresolved anger are deeply connected to organic dysfunction in this body region.

Fourth Chakra. The fourth chakra is affectionately known as the heart chakra and it is considered to be one of the most important energy centers of the body. The heart chakra represents the ability to express love. Like a symbolic heart placed over the organic heart, feelings of unresolved anger or expressions of conditional love work to congest the heart chakra, which in turn has a corresponding effect on the organic heart.

Anathema to the Western mind so firmly grounded in the mechanistic model of reality, anatomical symbolism may seem to have no place in health and health care. But the ties between a symbolic and organic heart became abundantly clear through the research of cardiologist Dean Ornish. To date, Ornish is the only one known to have scientifically proven the reversal of atherosclerotic plaque. Although diet, exercise, and support groups are factors in Ornish's regime, it is the practice of meditation (what Ornish calls the "open heart meditation" to resolve anger and open the heart chakra) that seems to be the critical factor in the reversal of coronary heart disease.

The heart, however, is not the only organ closely tied to the heart chakra. Other organs include the lungs, breasts, and esophagus. Symptoms of a blocked heart chakra can include heart attacks, enlarged heart, asthma, allergies, lung cancer, bronchial difficulties, circulation problems, and problems associated with the upper back and shoulders. Also, an important association exists between the heart chakra and the thymus gland. The thymus gland, so instrumental in the making of T-cells, shrinks with age. Gerber notes that this may not be so much an age factor, but rather a reflection of the state of the heart chakra.

Fifth Chakra. The fifth chakra lies above and is connected to the throat. Organs associated with the throat chakra are the thyroid, parathyroid glands, mouth, vocal chords, and trachea. As a symbol of communication, the throat chakra represents the development of personal expression, creativity, purpose in life, and willpower. The inability to express oneself in feelings or creativity, or to freely exercise one's will inevitably distorts the flow of energy to the throat chakra, and is thought to result in chronic sore throat problems, temporomandibular joint dysfunction (TMJD), throat and mouth cancers, stiffness in the neck area, thyroid dysfunction, migraines, and cancerous tumors in this region. In *The Creation of Health*, Myss points out that self-expression and creativity are essential to one's health status. She adds that the inability to express one's feelings, whether they be joy, sorrow, anger, or love, is similar to pouring concrete down your throat, thus closing off the energy needed to sustain the health of this region.

Sixth Chakra. The sixth chakra is more commonly known as the brow chakra or the third eye. This chakra is associated with intuition and the ability to access the ageless wisdom or bank of knowledge in the depths of universal consciousness. As energy moves through the dimension of universal wisdom into this chakra it promotes the development of intelligence and reasoning skills. Directly tied to the pituitary and pineal gland, this chakra feeds energy to the brain for information processing. Unlike the solar plexus chakra, which is responsible for a gut level of intuition with personal matters, the wisdom channeled through the brow chakra is more universal in nature with implications for the spiritual aspect of life. Gerber suggests that diseases caused by dysfunction of the brow chakra (e.g., brain tumors, hemorrhages, blood clots, blindness, comas, depression, and schizophrenia) may be caused by an individual's not wanting to see something that is extremely important to his or her soul growth.

> **Meridian:** A river of energy with hundreds of interconnected points throughout the body, used in the practice of acupuncture and shiatsu massage.

FIGURE 4.7   The word *chakra* means spinning wheel. Of the seven major subtle energy chakras, Western culture recognizes only the crown chakra, known in the Judeo-Christian culture as the halo.

Seventh Chakra. If the concept of chakras is foreign to the Western mind, then the seventh chakra may hold promise to bridge East and West. Featured most predominantly in the Judeo-Christian culture through paintings and sculptures as the halo over saintly beings, the seventh chakra, also known as the crown chakra (**FIG. 4.7**), is associated with matters of the soul and the spiritual quest. When the crown chakra is open and fully functioning, it is known to access the highest level of consciousness. Although no specific disease or illness may be associated with the crown chakra, in truth, every disease has a spiritual significance. And you don't have to be a saint to have a halo—we all have one.

According to Elliot Dacher, M.D., author of *PNI: The New Mind-Body Healing Program*, the insight of chakras can be found in many cultures and disciplines, most notably in the Western culture through the field of psychology with Maslow's hierarchy of needs. Beverly Rubik, president of the Institute of Frontier Sciences in Oakland, California, states that although clinical research findings exist regarding various aspects of subtle anatomy and subtle energies, they remain outside the mainstream of Western medicine because they challenge the dominant biomedical model by defying conventional scientific theory. But she notes that just as Einstein opened the doors of thought that challenged Newtonian physics, the principles of energy and information exchanged through energy will gain validity and acceptance in Western science through the doors of quantum physics.

Similar to the chakras is the **meridian** system: a network of hundreds of interconnected points throughout the

STRESS TAKES ITS TOLL.

FIGURE 4.8

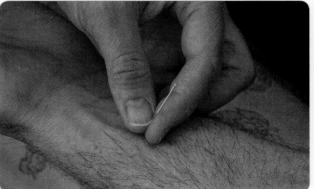

FIGURE 4.9   Acupuncture is an ancient Chinese technique that uses tiny, bulb-shaped needles to unblock congestion at specific energy gates along the paths of subtle energy known as meridians. Classical acupuncture (based on the concept of five elements) treats individuals holistically through the integration of mind, body, and spirit.

body, which allows for the passage of energy between the physical and subtle bodies of the energy field. The meridian system of energy is used in the practice of *shiatsu* massage and Chinese acupuncture.

To most Western physicians, the theoretical concepts behind Chinese acupuncture may seem completely unrelated to the dynamics responsible for the immune system, but to Gerber they are all very much related. If these subtle energy pathways are blocked or congested, the organs they supply may go into a state of dysfunction (**FIG. 4.8**). Acupuncture is a healing practice that attempts to unblock congested energy pathways, thus allowing a freely flowing current of energy (**FIG. 4.9**). This healing technique first gained national recognition during President Nixon's trip to China in 1974 (Prensky, 1995). At that time, one of his press corps, James Reston, was stricken with acute appendicitis. Rushed to the nearest hospital, he was successfully treated, without anesthesia, to the amazement of White House officials. Scientists and physicians trained in the Western tradition were quick to ridicule this healing practice, but now studies show that there appears to be a connection, albeit small, between the points designated as meridian gates (acupuncture points) and neuroimmunological crossroads.

The most clinically sound studies to determine the anatomic link between the etheric and physical bodies have been performed by Dr. Kim Han, of Korea, as reported by Rose-Neil in 1967. By injecting a radioactive isotope of phosphorus (P-32) through acupuncture needles at traditional points of insertion, he discovered that traces of the isotope followed a fine ductlike tubule system not related to the circulatory, lymphatic, or nervous systems; rather, they paralleled the acupuncture meridian system. Han's work was validated by Dr. Pierre de Vernejoul in 1985, who used radioactive technetium (^{99m}Tc) to follow the lines of the ancient acupuncture meridians. When samples of the isotope were injected randomly into the skin, no particular pathways were reproduced.

The human energy field has also been studied with regard to the healing power of touch. Several studies by Bernard Grad and Dolores Krieger, involving both plants (to avoid the placebo effect) and people, have demonstrated that "healing thoughts" in the form of energy produce statistically significant changes in chlorophyll and red blood cells, respectively. Similar studies by Drs. Leonard Laskow and Glen Rein have shown that conscious thoughts can decrease the growth rate of cancer cells in the laboratory. This conscious energy transfer is said to show properties similar to those observed with electromagnetic fields. Investigations into the subtle anatomy of the chakras have also been initiated by a handful of other researchers, including Dr. Elmer Green at the Menninger Clinic in Topeka, Kansas; Valerie Hunt at UCLA; Dr. Hiroshi Motoyama at the California Institute for Human Science; and researchers at the renowned HeartMath Institute.

To date, Hunt shows the most promise in detecting electromagnetic frequencies associated with the chakras. Her work began with biofeedback studies of muscle tension, but soon shifted to electrical activity in the seven regions associated with the primary chakras, where she noted a difference in frequency many times higher (1,600 cps) than could possibly be explained by electrochemical tissue of the heart and brain (0–250 cps). So inspired was Green by the concept of the human energy field that he co-created the International Society for the Study of Subtle Energy and Energy Medicine (ISSSEEM), which now publishes its own research journal, *Subtle Energies and Energy Medicine.*

How does the mind-body relationship lose its harmonic equilibrium? Two possibilities have been suggested. The first faults bioecological influences—that is, repeated exposure to those energy frequencies, natural (ultraviolet rays) or human-made (high-tension power lines), with a rhythm greater than 7.8 Hz, which distort some aspect of the human energy field.

To understand this relationship from Gerber's perspective, we need to first understand some additional concepts of the physical world elucidated by Einstein. First, the smallest particle within an atom is composed of energy, and energy and mass are interchangeable; thus, each object gives off a unified rhythm or series of oscillations. These oscillations are depicted in units of measurement called hertz (Hz), or oscillations per second. In turn, objects that oscillate, including the human body, create a magnetic energy field. Through processes known as **sympathetic resonance** and sonic **entrainment**, a vibration can resonate from one object to another, as observed with tuning forks. An object with a lower or weaker frequency of oscillations will alter its own frequency to entrain with (match) that of an object emitting a higher or stronger frequency of oscillations. In humans, the result over time if several organs are influenced to entrain at a higher than normal frequency is a decreased ability to return to homeostasis, resulting in metabolic dysfunction or possibly irregular cell division in those organs.

> **Sympathetic resonance:** A resonating vibration given off by one object that is picked up by another object in close proximity. Tuning forks provide a classic example.
>
> **Entrainment:** In physics, the mutual phase locking of like oscillations; in human physiology, organs or organisms giving off strong vibrations influencing organs or organisms with weaker vibrations to match the stronger rate of oscillation; thought to conserve energy.

In support of this hypothesis is the work of Dr. Robert Becker. Becker, twice nominated for the Nobel Prize in medicine, researched the relationship between the incidence of cancer and radiation emitted from various electrical sources, including power lines, microwave ovens, electric blankets, and video display terminals (VDTs). He concluded that an unequivocal relationship exists between extremely low frequencies (ELF)—the range in which electrical current oscillates (60 Hz)—and the development of diseases in people who are repeatedly exposed to them. Becker is of the opinion that oscillations of a higher frequency are somehow absorbed through the human energy field (what he calls the human electromagnetic field), resulting in alterations to the genetic makeup of cells at the atomic level.

That the human body had magnetic properties that could be enlisted as a healing mechanism was first suggested by Austrian physician Anton Mesmer in the late 1800s; it was dismissed as nonsense. But in 1992, geobiologist Joseph Kirschvink discovered that human brain cells do, indeed, synthesize a magnetic-like substance called magnetite. Like Becker, Kirschvink speculated that exposure to various electrical impulses can alter the integrity of magnetite and affect the cells' health or rate of activity. Disturbances produced by electrical interference can result in mutations at the cellular level, which may then become cancerous tumors.

Compounding the problem is the fact that T-lymphocytes are also affected by ELFs. Becker cited a study by Dr. Daniel B. Lyle of Pettis Memorial Hospital in Loma Linda, California, in which in vitro T-lymphocytes exposed to a 60-Hz energy field significantly reduced their cytotoxic ability against foreign antigens over a 48-hour period. Becker also suggested that energy currents may affect mood and emotions, which are thought to be associated with the astral and mental layers of the human energy field.

In his ground-breaking book *Cross Currents*, Becker concludes:

> At this time, the scientific evidence is absolutely conclusive: 60-Hz magnetic fields cause human cancer cells to permanently increase their rate of growth by as much as 1600 percent and to develop more malignant characteristics. These results indicate that power frequency fields are cancer promoters. Cancer promoters, however, have major implications for the incidence of cancer because they increase the number of cases of causing agents in our environment,

ranging from carcinogenic chemicals to cosmic rays. As a result, we are always developing small cancer cells that are recognized by our immune system and destroyed. Any factor that increases the growth rate of these small cancers gives them an advantage over the immune system, and as a result more people develop clinical cancers that require treatment. (Becker, 1990)

Although the hazards of high-tension power lines have fallen off the radar screen of national attention, the dangers of prolific cell phone use have surfaced as a new health care risk as reported in the *Washington Post* and the *International Journal of Radiation Biology and Environmental Health Perspectives.* Several reports highlight incidences of headaches, memory loss, and brain tumors with excessive use resulting from the close proximity of the microwaves (ELFs) to the head. A study conducted at the Cleveland Clinic by Agarwal and colleagues (2008) revealed that cell phone usage is linked to a lower sperm count. Despite the growing popularity of cell phones, the potential dangers of cell phone radiation are now well documented (Davis, 2010; Ketcham, 2010). However, it should be noted that studies regarding the microwave effects of cell phone use are certainly controversial. Excessive exposure to ELFs is considered by many health experts to be harmful. What are your thoughts on cell phone use and its impact on your long-term health status?

Regrettably, Becker's findings have largely been either ignored or denounced by the medical community and federal government. For many reasons, Becker's research, and the research of those who have followed in his footsteps, is still very controversial. For one thing, many people find the idea of electrical pollution hard to believe because it cannot be detected through the five senses. If you find this concept difficult to grasp, think of the classic Memorex TV commercial (now on YouTube) in which the vibrations of Ella Fitzgerald's voice shatter a crystal goblet. Neither a nervous system nor an immune system is necessary to feel the effects of vibrational energy (**FIG. 4.10**).

The second explanation for the loss of mind-body equilibrium is that *self-produced* emotional disturbances congest the energy field at the astral (emotional) layer and precipitate a host of physical maladies. Toxic thoughts that go unresolved, often referred to as emotional baggage, may translate into physical ailments that serve as a reminder of these issues. Gerber believes that, in essence, that which constitutes our human energy field can be thought of as a sixth (and in his opinion underdeveloped) sense. As

Courtesy of Vibe Technologies LLC.

FIGURE 4.10 Scientific studies into the use of healing vibrations are currently under way, exploring technology like the V.I.B.E. machine, created by Gene Koonce. This device creates a slight DC charge of −70 to −90 millivolts to entrain the cells of the body to hold a transmembrane potential and DC difference in potential, thus causing them to function at their optimal level. When a person sits near the V.I.B.E. machine for a specified duration, the body's cells entrain to this vibration of homeostasis.

examples, he suggests that people who have the power of clairvoyance (clear vision) are able to access various levels of the human energy field in themselves and others; out-of-body experiences and near-death experiences may be explained in the same way.

Thoughts, perceptions, and emotions, according to Gerber's theory, originate in the various layers of subtle energy, cascade through the mind-body interface, and are decoded at the molecular level to cause biochemical changes in the body. He states, "Thoughts are particles of energy. [Negative] thoughts are accompanied by emotions which also begin at the energy levels. As these particles of energy filter through from the etheric level to the physical level, the end result is immunoincompetence" (Gerber, 2001).

It is fair to say that human consciousness is the part of psychoneuroimmunology that is the least understood. As specialists examine the mind-body relationship more and more, though, they are beginning to look beyond the conventional scientific wisdom of a mind within a body and consider the alternative idea, a body within a mind. Gerber's theory may test the limits of your credibility. However, given his careful documentation and the support of a growing body of empirical research from members of ISSSEEM, the HeartMath Institute, and the Institute of Noetic Sciences, the possibility of this phenomenon is gaining ground every day. Gerber reminds us that Nobel laureates Lister and Pasteur, who were once mocked for their theories of "invisible bacteria" as causes of infectious disease, were vindicated after years of research. Ironically, practitioners in Western medicine are quick to use electromagnetic resonance imaging to diagnose disease, but are still reluctant to use energy medicine (e.g., acupuncture, homeopathy, Reiki, Healing Touch) as a bona fide treatment despite the fact that the National Institutes of Health's Center for Complementary and Alternative Medicine has identified subtle energy as one of five modality areas. Ultimately, what Gerber is saying is that the medical community is beginning to experience a paradigm shift in its approach to health, and this change is being met with much resistance.

The Pelletier Premodel

As mentioned earlier, Pelletier is yet to be convinced that sufficient medical evidence has been collected to substantiate a definitive stress-disease model. Nevertheless, his comprehensive research article entitled "Psychoneuroimmunology Toward a Mind-Body Model" and other research (e.g., Achterberg et al., 2005; Schlitz and Amorok, 2005) bring to the attention of the allied health professions some valid points he believes must be considered and understood before such a comprehensive model can be constructed. In the years since Pelletier's article was first published, significant medical advances have been made, and the National Institutes of Health's Center for Complementary and Alternative Medicine

now allocates funding for areas of research involving prayer and energy medicine. Despite these efforts, many pieces of the stress and disease puzzle remain missing, suggesting that a complete model has yet to be fully realized.

Some intriguing findings in the medical literature approach the fringes of parapsychology and metaphysics, areas that Pelletier hints should be taken a little more seriously and investigated empirically to develop a comprehensive stress-disease model. The following highlight some of these findings:

1. *Multiple personality disorder:* Braun (1983) cites people diagnosed as having multiple personality disorder (MPD) whose different personalities manifest different illnesses. For instance, a patient may be a diabetic under the influence of one personality, yet show no signs of this disease in the presence of another. Similarly, one personality may require prescription glasses or have asthma or severe allergies, whereas the remaining personalities show no traces of these symptoms. These disease states disappear within the individual when another personality becomes dominant. In most cases of MPD, the patient experienced some incredibly traumatic event as a child. Stress is thought to be strongly associated with the etiology of disease, yet its appearance and disappearance from personality to personality have medical experts baffled.

2. *Spontaneous remission:* Perhaps even more baffling to the medical community is the notion of **spontaneous remission**—the sudden disappearance of diseased tissue—most often observed with cancerous tumors but acknowledged with other diseases as well. What makes these reports so remarkable is that many people who were spontaneously cured were originally diagnosed as terminally ill. There are now even several documented cases of HIV remission (Health News, 2005). Typically, the first reaction of members of the medical community is denial, with the standard explanation that the patient was misdiagnosed. But a closer look into the matter reveals that in documented cases, some people who were given weeks to live seemed to go through an "about-face attitude" resulting in a "spontaneous cure." These people end up living years, if not decades, beyond their estimated time of departure.

> **Spontaneous remission:** The sudden (sometimes gradual) disappearance of a nonmedically treated disease, most often observed with cancerous tumors, but other diseases as well.

Stress with a Human Face

Spontaneous remission is still considered to be an anomaly in Western medicine. What should be a celebration when malignant tumors disappear is instead looked upon as a peculiarity—another unexplained ghost in the machine. But Jim Gill will tell you, it's no ghost. Rather, he says, it's a dynamic alchemy of divinity and humanity—one he now welcomes with open arms.

On September 1, 1994, Jim was diagnosed with oat cell cancer, one of the deadliest forms of cancer. Test results revealed two large tumors in his chest, one of which was wrapped around his vena cava, disrupting the flow of blood back to his heart. So discouraged were his team of physicians with the test results that they gave him at most 2 weeks to live with no treatment, and as long as 4 months with treatment consisting of radiation and chemotherapy. "Basically, they told me I wouldn't see Christmas," he said. Although Jim was scheduled for the usual routine of chemotherapy, the prognosis looked anything but promising. Knowing the odds were against him, Jim decided to call in reinforcements. He contacted Mary Linda Landauer, a therapist who was trained in mind-body-spirit healing, who taught him meditation, visualization, and guided mental imagery. She also encouraged him to explore all possible options of healing, with the most important being the power of faith. And that he did! Jim quit working for 7 months and, as he said, "I became the captain of my ship."

Jim's curiosity led him to several modalities of healing, including a trip to Tijuana, Mexico, where he stayed at a medical facility for 4 weeks to boost his immune system. His healing regime included diet supplements and herbs, but he takes delight in describing his spiritual awakening as well. When he returned to the Arthur James Cancer Center in Columbus, Ohio, one tumor had completely disappeared; the other, originally the size of a baseball, was now the size of a walnut. Fifteen years later, Jim is the picture of health.

"The medical experts were baffled, but I wasn't. Ever since then I get four to five phone calls a week from people with cancer. Most are looking for the magical silver bullet. But let me tell you something. It wasn't Mexico, or the herbs or the chemo that did it," Jim explains. "It was my reconnection to spirituality that did it. Although it was a lot of work, so many positive things have come out of that darkness. I wouldn't have traded this growth experience for anything!"

The Institute of Noetic Sciences began to document cases of spontaneous remission in the mid-1980s. It found more than 3,000 cases of spontaneous remission in the medical literature, 15 percent of which occurred with no clinical intervention (e.g., radiation or chemotherapy).

In a review of these findings, Jaylene Kent et al. (1989) noted several cases that today are still unexplained. For instance, they examined the results of the International Medical Commission of Lourdes (CMIL), a body of medical professionals that investigates the clinical cases of people who visit the shrine of St. Bernadette at Lourdes, France. Of 38 cases of "cures" examined by the commission since 1954, 19 were found to be medically and scientifically inexplicable. Kent and her colleagues are quick to point out that evidence of spontaneous remission is rare, yet its existence cannot be ignored. To date, however, it *has* been ignored, in part because the findings are "anecdotal" and cannot be replicated in controlled laboratory studies.

3. *Hypnosis:* When the powers of the unconscious mind are accessed through hypnosis, documented physiological changes have been observed that also prove baffling. Hypnosis can create a state of increased suggestibility that appears able to influence the biochemical mechanisms responsible for healing. According to Pelletier, the following illnesses have been shown to be cured by hypnosis: warts, asthma, hay fever, contact dermatitis, and some animal allergies. Case studies of ichthyosis, a congenital skin disease, have also been successfully treated with hypnosis (Dossey, 1999). Pelletier notes

FIGURE 4.11   Canadian energy healer Ilan Bendelman demonstrates his energy healing technique at the Psy-Tek Subtle Energy Laboratory in Encinitas, California, in which he is able to sense the human energy field and recalibrates frequencies (e.g., thoughts and emotions) that are no longer conducive to/compatible with one's health, or do not resonate a positive frequency.

that although hypnosis can produce a very relaxed state in which the stress hormone ACTH may be suppressed, enhancement of immune responses alone cannot account for these hormonal changes.

4. *Placebos and nocebos:* **Placebos** fall within the realm of faith healing, where a person so strongly believes that the medication he or she received will cure the illness that a healing effect occurs even when what was ingested is no "real" medication at all. The fact that a person suffering from an illness can be cured by taking a sugar pill may sound ludicrous, but indeed this is often the case. In fact, the Food and Drug Administration (FDA) insists that new medicines must produce a cure rate of greater than 35 percent—the demarcation of the placebo effect—in clinical studies before they can be approved. But some placebos have a cure rate of 70 percent (Brody, 2000). In his book *Love, Medicine, and Miracles*, Dr. Bernie Siegel cites several examples

Placebos: A nonmedicine (e.g., sugar pill) that can prove to be as effective as the medicine it is supposed to represent. Healing occurs as a matter of belief.

Nocebos: A bona fide, effective medicine that does *not* work because the patient doesn't believe that it will.

of patients who were healed by their "faith" in medicine even when it wasn't really "medicine," particularly when their attending physicians were very supportive. This type of faith healing is an aspect of clinical medicine not fully understood. What was once thought of as a fluke in modern medicine, however, is now considered a part of the mystery of the stress-disease phenomenon.

Nocebos is a name given to explain the phenomenon when a medication that has been proven to be extremely effective is given to a patient who is told that it is experimental and most likely it won't work. In many cases, the result is that the medication does nothing despite its proven effectiveness.

5. *Cell memory:* With the development of medical technology that has made organ transplants possible, a critical mass of case histories has revealed that cells of various organ tissues hold an energetic memory pattern that transfers to the next recipient. In the book *The Heart's Code*, author Paul Pearsall cites several case studies where people with transplanted organs began to have memories of events in which they took no part (yet the organ donor did). One remarkable story is that of Claire Sylvia, who, upon having a heart transplant, began to have dreams of a young blond-haired man named Tim, wearing a motorcycle jacket. Although a vegetarian and a connoisseur of wine, Claire had cravings for KFC and beer—the last food Tim had before he died in a motorcycle accident. These and other stories like them suggest that cells retain some level of consciousness that is then passed on to the recipient of the organ. Similarly, some people, who, while in therapy, recount memories of childhood physical abuse, begin to manifest bruises in the places where they were beaten decades earlier.

6. *Subtle energy:* Another area of scientific investigation that merits attention is the concept of subtle energy. Pelletier (1988, 2000) states, "Mind-body interaction clearly involves subtle energy or subtle information exchange. . . . Given that mind-body interactions involve an exchange of subtle energy, principles of physics may be appropriately applied to issues of health and disease." Pelletier advocates the use of magnetic resonance imaging (MRI) and the superconducting quantum interference device (SQUID), which are based on the concept of subtle energy, for clinical diagnosis of disease and illness. He also suggests that researchers in the

field of psychoneuroimmunology try to understand and apply the principles of quantum theory and astrophysics.

7. *Immunoenhancement:* Pelletier points out that if a suppressed immune system can, by way of conscious thought, influence the progression of tumors and other disease processes, psychological factors (e.g., mental imagery, meditation, and cognitive restructuring) may also be able to *enhance* the immune system to create an environment conducive to spontaneous remission and other healing effects. Pelletier cites two studies opening the door to this possibility. In addition to the study by Kiecolt-Glaser et al. (1999) with nursing home residents discussed earlier, he points to the findings of McClelland and Kirshnit (1989) in which subjects watched an inspirational movie about Mother Teresa. Salivary IgA samples were collected before and after viewing the film, and it was observed that values increased afterward, regardless of the subject's opinions of Mother Teresa's work.

In his review of the medical literature, Pelletier has found that most of the evidence collected so far has been anecdotal, meaning that, in his opinion, controlled studies cannot yet prove that positive emotions can enhance immune function. But he suggests that this is a prime area for research. In particular, Pelletier raises the following questions:

1. Is immunoenhancement merely a return to existing baseline levels of the constituents of this precisely regulated system?

2. Are some constituents of the immune system suppressed (e.g., T8) to create an *illusion* that the entire system is enhanced?

3. Could stressors produce a rebound effect, causing elements of the immune system to increase above baseline levels once the stressor is removed?

4. Can the immunological responses actually be increased above baseline?

These are questions he feels need to be answered to better understand what immunoenhancement really is. Pelletier's scientifically trained, analytical side is skeptical about the probability of the healing powers of the mind, but his intuitive side allows for the possibility of immunoenhancement. He writes, "Speculations concerning the ultimate role of beliefs, positive emotions, and spiritual values in organizing and transcending biological determinism might seem like philosophical speculation

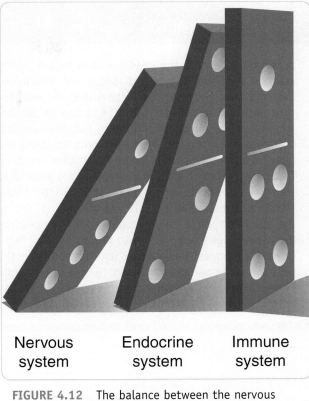

Nervous system   Endocrine system   Immune system

FIGURE 4.12 The balance between the nervous system, endocrine system, and immune system is quite delicate when repeatedly affected by chronic stress.

if the answers to these questions were not so critical to our survival as a species balanced between health and illness, life and death."

Pelletier does not specifically use the word *spirituality* with regard to stress and disease, but we can infer that he believes spiritual well-being has been largely ignored by clinical medicine, which leaves the stress-disease model incomplete. He suggests that the only logical approach to understanding the stress-disease/mind-body phenomenon is to take the whole systems approach, in which the individual is greater than the sum of its physiological parts. Until a viable model explaining the relationship between stress and disease is complete, we must work with the information we have. And what is known through the current medical model is that physical symptoms arising from stress can wreak havoc on physical health in specific regions of the body. Two decades later, Pelletier has not changed the premise of his stress and disease premodel. However, his interest has taken him further into the exploration of mind-body healing—specifically, in the realm of complementary medicine (Pelletier, 2000a).

BOX 4.2   Stress and Type 2 Diabetes

It is hard to escape the headline news regarding the dramatic increases in type 2 diabetes, not only in the United States, but also around the world. The relationship between stress and diabetes is one to neither ignore nor take lightly. According to European medical literature, the association between emotional stress and type 2 diabetes dates back to the seventeenth century. Today, many chronic emotional problems are associated with this disease etiology (Pouwer et al., 2010). Stress affects this disease in two distinct ways. First, during the stress response, blood sugar levels increase, as the demand for energy increases during fight or flight (even if one doesn't engage in it). The ability of the cells to take in and use the blood glucose (via the role of insulin) is greatly compromised among people with type 2 diabetes, thus keeping blood sugar levels high.

Secondly, emotional problems associated with chronic stress serve as a distraction to self-care behaviors (e.g., poor monitoring of sugar levels, no time for exercise, poor eating habits, more alcohol consumption, etc.). As a result, blood sugar levels remain elevated, paving the way for serious health complications (e.g., poor circulation, macular degeneration, etc.). The American Diabetes Association recommends effective stress management behaviors for all people with type 2 diabetes, including a combination of effective coping skills (e.g., cognitive restructuring, creative problem solving, even hobbies) and effective relaxation techniques (e.g., breathing exercises, progressive muscular relaxation, meditation, healthy nutrition, and physical exercise). Learning to relax is an essential skill for everyone with type 2 diabetes.

DNA, Telomeres, Stress, and Aging

At the end of each DNA strand is a region of repetitive sequences, called a telomere, that serves to protect the end of the chromosome from deterioration. Simply stated, telomeres are associated with DNA replication and become shorter each time the process is repeated. The enzyme telomerase is used to protect the telomeres by ensuring their stability. If the telomeres shorten without restoration, then cell replication becomes compromised. When cell replication is compromised, the health of the tissue is compromised, as seen in the aging process. In 2009, the Nobel Prize in Physiology or Medicine was awarded to researchers whose work substantiated the importance of telomeres and how they are influenced by stress and aging. Research now substantiates the fact that oxidative stress (the presence of free radicals) shortens telomeres. This shortening affects health in a number of ways, including compromising the cell division process and the integrity of our DNA. Speculation is that chronic stress may have the same effect. Physical exercise is suggested as a means to enhance the integrity of telomeres. Could other relaxation techniques lead you to the fountain of youth? Perhaps! While more research is needed, all evidence points in this direction. Stress not only kills, it speeds up the aging process.

■ Target Organs and Their Disorders

Looking back at Borysenko's model, we can begin to see how disease and illness can arise from either an over-responsive autonomic nervous system (elevated stress hormones) or a dysfunctional (suppressed) immune system. The importance of understanding how these physiological systems work, as well as the pathways leading to disease, is considered by Borysenko, Pert, Gerber, and Pelletier to be the first step in the healing process. Borysenko, Gerber, and Pelletier also advocate the use of relaxation techniques, including meditation and mental imagery, as supplemental aids in any recovery process. In fact, some healing methods now take a multimodal approach, combining standard Western medical practices with healing methods that employ the powers of the mind. Although this approach is now entering the mainstream of the American healthcare system, many physicians still remain "doubting Thomases," in part because they have received no formal training in these areas; others perceive the multimodal approach as a threat. Although there has been no predictive correlation between a specific stressor (e.g., divorce) and a physical outcome (e.g., ulcers), several studies have shown relationships between the inability to express emotions, the personalities most closely associated

BOX 4.3   Lyme Disease and Stress

It may have started out as a tick bite. There was no telltale "bulls-eye marking," as described in the medical literature, but then again, new research about the epidemic of Lyme disease reveals that this diagnostic sign only occurs 20 percent of the time. Molly isn't even sure when she first contracted Lyme disease, but it may have been during her college years. Nearly everyone in her extended family in western Pennsylvania has it. Her symptoms began years ago with a condition called "restless leg syndrome" characterized by spasmatic muscle tremors in the legs (and arms). What began as an occasional tremor late at night exploded into a full-blown, debilitating disease during the course of her husband's illness and his subsequent death a few years later. Looking back, Molly can identify the perfect storm of stress, from the caretaking of her young husband coupled with coastal property flooding and several other monumental stressors, all of which lowered her resistance and set the stage for her own chronic health issues. Stress, it turns out, is the catalyst for chronic Lyme disease, because when the immune system is suppressed from a repeated flood of cortisol, the bacteria that cause Lyme disease are given the opportunity to take over.

It wasn't until a few months ago that Molly was correctly diagnosed with Lyme disease (many tests are false negatives, which only compounds the difficulty of diagnosis and treatment). By all accounts, Lyme is an insidious disease that seems to be related to (or perhaps the cause of) chronic fatigue syndrome, multiple sclerosis, fibromyalgia, and even Alzheimer's/dementia, as recently noted with news headlines of beloved singer/songwriter Kris Kristofferson (Libov, 2016). Experts call Lyme disease the "great mimicker" because it mimics the symptoms of so many other diseases. Unfortunately, most physicians are not educated about what experts now call an epidemic, with some suggesting that perhaps as many as 50 percent of Americans have Lyme disease. Dr. Zubcevik, a Harvard Medical School professor and co-director of the Dean Center for Tick Borne Illness, states that a compromised immune system sets the stage for chronic Lyme disease to reveal associated symptoms, and she states that many people younger than age 50 and everyone older than age 50 has a compromised immune system (Stringfellow, 2016).

Like several diseases that are named from their place of origin, the name for the disease comes from the town of Lyme, Connecticut, where, decades ago, several people were first diagnosed with identical chronic health problems. The source of the disease is the bacteria *Borrelia burgdorferi*, which is carried by a tiny deer tick. New research from New York, Europe, and Australia, where the disease also exists, suggests that mosquitos, fleas, and mice can also carry the bacteria that cause Lyme disease. Infection with these bacteria can cause serious problems with the nervous, cardiovascular, and digestive systems. Because of its molecular make-up, Lyme is now considered to be a sexually transmitted disease, further increasing the number of people carrying it, often unknowingly (Howenstine, 2004).

Headaches and general fatigue are some of the first symptoms, but left untreated the acute problems become chronic to the point where they kidnap one's life. Sixty-nine percent of people with Lyme go untreated, and as many as 20 percent of patients suffer long-term symptoms.

Antibiotics are the first course of treatment when the disease is detected. Long-term antibiotic use is one form of treatment for chronic Lyme, yet this method can create its own series of health problems in the gut. Current research suggests that there are 10 different strains of the Lyme disease in the United States. In addition, antibiotics (e.g., doxycycline) only stop the bacteria from replicating, it doesn't kill them, hence complicating the healing process (Buhner, 2015).

Lyme disease is also a very political disease, as well documented in the acclaimed film *Under Our Skin*. Many insurance companies and pharmaceutical companies—who stand to profit by maintaining the status quo—claim that there is no such thing as chronic Lyme disease. Their efforts have led to many physicians losing their licenses for treating chronic Lyme disease (Wilson, 2009). The state of Connecticut has now passed legislation protecting all physicians who treat this disease.

The newest treatment for chronic Lyme disease is low-dose immunotherapy (LDI), a type of homeopathy, and it has been met with great success by some people. Additional therapies include relaxation techniques to help boost the immune system to keep Lyme disease in check (Vincent and Elder, 2016).

with this characteristic, and the incidence of some illness and disease. For instance, the expression of hostility is a behavioral trait of the Type A personality and is commonly associated with coronary heart disease.

For some unexplained reason, during various stages of acute and chronic stress, certain regions of the body seem more susceptible to excessive metabolic activity than others. The organs that are singled out or targeted by increased metabolic activity are called **target organs**. Any organ can be a target organ: hair, skin, blood vessels, joints, muscles, stomach, colon, and so on. In some people one organ may be singled out, while in others several organs may be targeted. Genetics, emotions, personality, and environmental factors have all been speculated as possible explanations for target organs, without conclusive evidence to support any of them. In fact, it is likely that they may all contribute to the disease process. The following are some of the more common disorders and their respective target organs, which are now known to be influenced by the stress response. Using Borysenko's model, they have been divided into two categories: nervous system–related disorders and immune system–related disorders.

Nervous System–Related Disorders

In the event of perceived stress, organs that are innervated by neural tissue or acted upon by the excessive secretion of stress hormones increase their metabolic rates. When denied the ability to rest, organs may begin to dysfunction, much like a car engine that overheats on a very hot day. Several states of disease and illness first appear as stress-related symptoms that, if undetected or untreated, may result in serious health problems. The following are descriptions of the more common ones.

1. *Bronchial asthma:* Bronchial asthma is an illness in which a pronounced secretion of bronchial fluids causes a swelling of the smooth-muscle tissue of the large air passageways (bronchi). The constriction of these passages produces a choking effect, where the individual feels as if he or she cannot breathe. Asthmatic attacks can be severe enough to send someone to the hospital and, in some cases, are even fatal. Several

---

Target organs: Any organ or tissue receiving excess neural or hormonal stimulation that increases metabolic function or abnormal cell growth; results in eventual dysfunction of the organ.

---

studies have linked the onset of asthmatic attacks with anxiety; others have linked it with an overprotective childhood (Hatfield, 2007). Currently, drugs (e.g., prednisone) are the first method of treatment. However, relaxation techniques, including mental imagery, autogenic training, and meditation, may be just as effective in both delaying the onset and reducing the severity of these attacks.

2. *Tension headaches:* Tension headaches are produced by sympathetic-mediated contractions of muscles of the forehead, eyes, neck, and jaw. Tension usually builds as the parasympathetic inhibition of muscular contraction gives way to sympathetic drive, increasing the state of muscular contraction. Increased pain results from increased contraction of these muscles. Lower-back pain can also result from the same process. Although pain relievers such as aspirin are the most common source of relief, tension headaches have also been shown to dissipate with the use of meditation, mental imagery, and biofeedback.

3. *Migraine headaches:* Unlike a tension headache, which is produced by nervous tension in the facial muscles, a migraine headache is a vascular headache. The word *migraine* literally means "half a skull," and usually when a migraine occurs, the sensation of pain occupies either the right or left side of the head but not both. Migraines are thought to be the result of a sympathetic response to the baroreceptors of the carotid artery, which undergo a rapid constriction (prodrome) followed by a rapid dilation. During the dilation phase, blood quickly moves in from the periphery to flood the cerebral vasculature. The change in vascular pressure combined with humoral secretions is considered the cause of the intense pain so often associated with migraines. Symptoms can include a flash of light followed by intense throbbing, dizziness, and nausea. It is interesting to note that migraines do not occur in the midst of a stressor, but rather hours later. Migraines are thought to be related to the inability to express anger and frustration. Although several medications are prescribed for migraines, current research indicates that biofeedback and mental imagery can be equally effective, with fewer side effects.

4. *Temporomandibular joint dysfunction:* Excessive contraction of the jaw muscles can lead to a phenomenon called temporomandibular joint

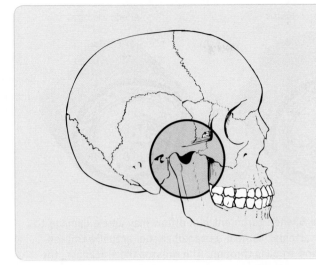

FIGURE 4.13 There are many forms of TMJD, including clicking of the jaw and grinding one's teeth during sleep. Experts suggest that 20 percent of the American population has some form of TMJD.

dysfunction, or TMJD (**FIG. 4.13**). In many cases, people are unaware that they have this illness because the behavioral damage occurs during sleep. But when they make a trip to the dentist, they find that they are showing signs of clenching and grinding their teeth (bruxism). Other symptoms include muscle pain and clicking or popping sounds when chewing, as well as tension headaches and earaches. Like migraines, TMJD is often associated with the inability to express feelings of anger. However, other behaviors are also associated with this symptom, including excessive gum chewing, resting one's chin on a hand, and even nail biting. Severe cases require that a mouth brace be worn at night. Relaxation techniques, including biofeedback and progressive muscular relaxation, have been shown to be effective in decreasing the muscular tension associated with TMJD.

5. *Irritable bowel syndrome:* IBS is characterized by repeated bouts of abdominal pain or tenderness, cramps, diarrhea, nausea, constipation, and excessive flatulence. It is often considered a result of excessive sympathetic neural stimulation to one or more areas of the gastrointestinal (GI) tract. Although symptoms may vary from person to person, this stress-related disorder is most commonly associated with anxiety and depression. One reason IBS is considered so closely related to stress

is that the hypothalamus, which controls appetite regulation (hunger and satiety), is closely associated with emotional regulation as well. Various diets and medications may be prescribed, depending on the nature of the symptoms. Several recent studies have employed various types of relaxation and cognitive skills, including thermal biofeedback, progressive muscular relaxation, mental imagery, cognitive reappraisal, and behavior-modification techniques to reduce existing levels of anxiety. All had promising results.

6. *Coronary heart disease:* There are two major links between the stress response and the development of coronary heart disease, which the American Heart Association now estimates kills one person every 32 seconds. The first link is elevated blood pressure, or hypertension. In an effort to shunt blood from the body's core to the peripheral muscles in the event of physical movement during the fight-or-flight response, several stress-related hormones are released into the bloodstream. Sympathetic arousal releases epinephrine and norepinephrine from neural endings as well as from the adrenal medulla. These agents increase heart rate and myocardial contractility and cause the heart to pump a greater supply of oxygenated blood to the body's muscles for energy production. These catecholamines are also responsible for constricting blood vessels of the gastrointestinal tract while at the same time dilating vessels to the body's periphery, causing an overall change in total peripheral resistance. Aldosterone, secreted from the adrenal cortex, increases blood volume by increasing water retention. Vasopressin, or ADH, also acts to increase blood volume. The net effect of these stress hormones is to "jack up" blood pressure far above resting levels so as to transport blood to areas where it is needed. Ironically, stress provokes the same physiological response, even when there is no conscious attempt to physically move.

When pressure is increased in a closed system, the risk of damage to vascular tissue caused by increased turbulence is significantly increased. This damage to the vessel walls appears as small microtears, particularly in the intima lining of the coronary heart vessels, which supply the heart muscle (myocardium) itself with oxygen. As a way of healing these tears, several constituents floating in the blood bind with the damaged vascular cell

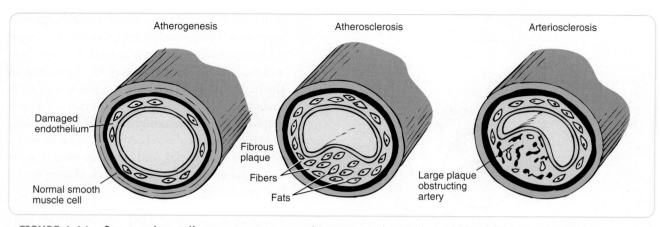

FIGURE 4.14   Coronary heart disease can start as early as age 5 when turbulent blood flow may cause damage to the inner lining of the artery wall. Cholesterol deposits, which attempt to heal damaged tissue, actually thicken the passage, thus decreasing the diameter of the vessel for blood to pass through. The greater the thickness, the greater the chance for an occlusion to that vessel—and an ensuing heart attack.

tissue. Paradoxically, the primary "healing" agent is a sticky substance found floating in the blood serum called cholesterol.

The second link between coronary heart disease and the stress response is the release of cortisol from the adrenal medulla. One of the many functions this stress hormone performs is to increase the level of free fatty acids carried by lipoproteins from the adipose (fat) tissue sites into the blood, to be used by the working muscles for energy production. An abundance of cholesterol in the blood makes it readily available for use in the attempt to repair damaged vascular cell tissue. However, what may seem like a protective mechanism actually becomes a major hindrance to the efficiency of the heart muscle, causing coronary heart disease.

The three stages of coronary heart disease are atherogenesis, atherosclerosis, and arteriosclerosis

Atherogenesis: The first stage of coronary heart disease, wherein a fat streak appears on the inner lining of artery walls.

Atherosclerosis: The second stage of coronary heart disease, wherein artery walls slowly become occluded by cholesterol-plaque buildup.

Arteriosclerosis: The third and final stage of coronary heart disease, wherein the arteries become hardened by cholesterol buildup, calcium deposits, and loss of elasticity.

(**FIG. 4.14**). With **atherogenesis**, the initial stage, a fatty streak appears on the inner lining of the artery wall. Some evidence suggests that this can occur as early as age 5. As this fatty streak continues to circumnavigate the perimeter of the artery as well as travel its length, it creates a buildup of plaque, which narrows the inside of the artery. The stage at which the passage narrows because of thickening of plaque is referred to as **atherosclerosis**. As this fatty plaque accumulates, it attracts other constituents in the blood, including calcium, causing increased resistance to blood flow and increased blood pressure. With age, plaque hardens, making the artery walls like lead pipes that are no longer able to constrict or dilate. This compounds the effect of high blood pressure, which is one reason resting blood pressure increases with age. At the third stage, **arteriosclerosis**, the arteries themselves become hard, and possibly occluded from the flow of blood. If blood flow is impeded, the heart muscle may show signs of oxygen deprivation (ischemia), resulting in either angina (chest pain) or death of myocardial cell tissue. The end result is a heart attack, or myocardial infarction (MI). The degree of coronary artery blockage determines the severity of the heart attack, with the most extreme result being death. Similar etiology may occur with tears in the carotid arteries (located on either side of the vocal cords) that supply oxygenated blood to the brain. Strokes, like coronary heart disease, are

> **BOX 4.4 Stress and Inflammation**
>
> Researchers in the field of PNI have discovered that chronic stress is associated with the body's inability to regulate the inflammatory response. This inability, due, in part, to the impact cortisol has on the immune system, appears to be a strong factor in the stress and chronic disease equation. Researcher Sheldon Cohen at Carnegie Mellon University found that people with high levels of inflammation (chronic inflammation) were more susceptible to colds and flu (Cohen et al., 2012). Further research from the Oral Biology lab at The Ohio State University reveals that chronic stress, due to its impact on the sympathetic nervous system, appears to change the gene activity of immune cells before they enter the bloodstream (Huffington Post, 2013). Inflammation, now confirmed to be a result of stress, is associated with many chronic diseases and the acceleration of the aging process and is tied to both the nervous and the immune systems.

the result of blocked arteries creating an inadequate oxygenated blood supply, in this case to the brain.

The abyss between the emotions and physiology narrowed in 2005, when Western researchers discovered that emotional stress can, indeed, produce symptoms of a heart attack. Although the research team headed by Ilan Wittstein concluded that the mechanism underlying reversible left ventricular dysfunction precipitated by emotional stress remains unknown, it was suggested that stress hormones might temporarily overwhelm heart cells. Nicknamed the **broken heart syndrome**, the cause might best be described as "adrenaline poisoning."

Immune System–Related Disorders

As mentioned previously, emotional stress appears both to alter the molecular structure of biochemical agents or neuropeptides and to suppress the number and functions of various key leukocytes. Stress hormones (cortisol) may also decrease the effectiveness of leukocytes. With this process under way, protective mechanisms are less efficient and the body becomes more vulnerable to exogenous and endogenous antigens. As previously discussed, diseases that are the result of immune dysfunction can be classified as (1) **exogenous-underreactive**, (2) **exogenous-overreactive**, (3) **endogenous-overreactive**, and (4) **endogenous-underreactive**. The following are examples of some diseases in each of these categories:

1. *The common cold and influenza (exogenous underreaction):* In 1991, a study (Cohen, Tyrrell, and Smith) published by the prestigious *New England Journal of Medicine* supported the hypothesis that colds are unequivocally related to undue stress. The results made headlines across the country. From Borysenko's model of the immune system,

we can see that as the number of B-lymphocytes decreases, the body becomes more vulnerable to the influences of the viruses that produce the common cold. Colds and influenza fall into the category of exogenous underreaction in Borysenko's immune activity matrix because there are insufficient B-lymphocytes to combat the exogenous antigen.

2. *Allergies (exogenous overreaction)* (**FIG. 4.15**): An allergic reaction is initiated when a foreign substance, or antigen (e.g., pollen, bee venom, dust spores), enters the body. In response to this intrusion, granulocytes secrete antibodies called histamines. When histamines encounter the antigens they form inactive complexes, in essence neutralizing their toxic effect. In an overreactive immune response to exogenous antigens, the excess of histamines causes swelling of mucous membrane tissue, in the case of inhaled antigens, or of skin tissue, in the

> **Broken heart syndrome:** A name given to the condition where symptoms of a heart attack occur as a result of emotional stress; when stress hormones temporarily overwhelm heart tissue cells.
>
> **Exogenous-underreactive:** An underreactive immune system affected by external pathogens (e.g., colds and flu).
>
> **Exogenous-overreactive:** An overreactive immune system affected by external pathogens (e.g., allergies).
>
> **Endogenous-overreactive:** An overreactive immune system affected by internal pathogens (e.g., rheumatoid arthritis and ulcers).
>
> **Endogenous-underreactive:** An underreactive immune system affected by internal pathogens (e.g., cancer).

FIGURE 4.15 The list of allergy-producing substances is nearly endless. Pollen and dust are two of the most common ones.

case of infection. Some studies have shown that the introduction of foreign antigens isn't necessary to trigger an allergic reaction. Borysenko suggests that B-lymphocytes have the capacity of memory that may induce the production of histamines and other antibodies (immunoglobulins) without direct contact with an antigen. In some people, allergic reactions can occur just by thinking about the stimulus that provoked a previous attack. Several studies have also shown that allergic reactions are more prevalent and severe in subjects prone to anxiety (Lehrer et al., 1993). Over-the-counter medications containing antihistamines and allergy shots are the most common approaches to dealing with allergies. New data suggest that relaxation techniques also minimize the effects of external antigens (Wright, 2003).

3. *Rheumatoid arthritis and lupus (endogenous overreaction):* Tissue swelling may also occur from inflammation produced by an overreactive immune system responding to cells perceived to be (endogenous) antigens. In this case, constituents of the immune system begin to attack apparently healthy tissue, mistaking it for a foreign substance. Rheumatoid arthritis, a joint and connective tissue disease, occurs when synovial membrane tissue swells, causing the joint to become inflamed. Over time, synovial fluid may enter cartilage and bone tissue, causing further deterioration of a joint. Severe cases of rheumatoid arthritis are most evident in deformed finger joints. A substance identified as rheumatoid

factor, a protein found in the blood, is thought to be associated with this disease. There is speculation that rheumatoid arthritis has a genetic link. It also has an association with stress, because it has been noted that the severity of arthritic pain is often related to episodes of stress, particularly suppressed anger. The treatment for this disease varies from pain relievers (e.g., aspirin) to steroid injections (e.g., cortisone), depending on the severity of pain and rate of joint deterioration. Relaxation techniques are now being recommended as a complementary treatment to help reduce symptoms. Similarly, lupus is an autoimmune disease in which the body's tissues are attacked by its own immune system, leading to chronic inflammation anywhere in the body. Primarily, inflammation affects the skin, heart, lungs, kidneys, and joints.

4. *Ulcers and colitis (endogenous overreaction):* Ulcers are often described as a hole in the stomach, and this depiction is not far from the truth. The series of events that lead to the destruction of this organ tissue begins with an excessive sympathetic neural drive. Increased secretions of norepinephrine are thought to cause a constriction of the vasculature in the lining of the stomach. This in turn is believed to decrease mucous secretions produced by the inner lining of the stomach wall. The purpose of mucus is to protect against the strong digestive enzymes that break down foodstuffs in the stomach. If the balance of mucosal fluid and digestive enzymes (hydrochloric acid) is thrown off, the inner lining becomes susceptible to these enzymes. The stomach may actually begin to digest itself, producing a hole in the stomach wall. Ulcers were one of the first diseases associated with undue stress; Selye noted this in his earliest studies with rats. Similarly, physicians immediately noticed an association between anxiety and the symptoms of ulcers in their patients, most notably sharp pains in the stomach.

The colon, situated below the stomach along the gastrointestinal tract, is also prone to ulceration, with a similar etiology producing colitis, or inflammation of the inner lining of the colon. Stress in the form of anxiety is thought to be strongly associated with colitis as well. Relaxation techniques are usually recommended, in conjunction with a special diet, to minimize the symptoms of this disease. Some techniques, including mental imagery, have even helped to heal ulcerations in the stomach wall.

For years, if not decades, it was thought that stress was the primary reason for ulcers. But in 1981, Barry Marshall, M.D., of Perth, Australia, proved that more than 75 percent of ulcers are caused by a bacterium known as *Helicobacter*, a carcinogen (Ubell, 1995). Clinical studies showed that these bacteria can settle in the lining of the stomach, creating an open wound that stomach acids then worsen, resulting in moderate to severe ulceration. Previously, it was thought that microbes such as *Helicobacter* could not survive in an acid-rich environment, but Marshall discovered this not to be the case. Treatment with antibiotics is now shown to be highly effective for a large percentage of people who have ulcers, yet two questions remain: What makes some people more vulnerable to the *Helicobacter* bacterium than others? and Why are antibiotics effective in only 75 percent of the cases of people with ulcers?

5. *Cancer (endogenous underreaction)*: Cancer has proved to be one of the most perplexing diseases of our time, affecting one out of every four Americans according to the American Cancer Society (ACS). To date, there is still no cure short of prevention and early detection. The ACS defines cancer as "a large group of diseases all characterized by uncontrolled growth and spread of abnormal cells." In other words, there are many types of cancers and the specific etiologies are still not completely understood. There are also many theories that attempt to explain the development of cancer. The two most prominent theories include the following: the first, falling back on the germ theory, suggests that all cancers are the result of an invading microbe or pathogen. The second theory suggests that there is a gene (called an **oncogene**) somewhere in the DNA structure that produces an abnormal or mutant cell (McClean, 1997). There is even a medical journal dedicated to this vein of research called *Oncogene*. Whether this gene can be inherited or is somehow externally triggered is yet to be determined; there are arguments both ways. The production of an abnormal cell in the body by itself is not uncommon. Some research suggests that the body produces about six mutant cells per day. In a precisely regulated immune system, T-cells and NK cells keep such endogenous antigens in check.

When a cell does mutate (that is, its genetic structure deviates from that of normal cells), it is regarded as an endogenous antigen and becomes subject to destruction by the cytotoxic T-lymphocytes, or T-cells. T-lymphocytes have a commando mission to search for and destroy malignant cells. If for some reason their ability is suppressed, the likelihood of a cancerous tumor is increased. Although the life span of a mutated cell is markedly shorter than that of normal cells (this process is called *relative inviability*), if undetected, it proliferates much more quickly than a normal cell, producing a tumor. Because of their structural inability to manufacture various enzymes necessary to perform normal cellular functions, cancerous tumors rob healthy cells of their nutrients. Unlike normal organ tissue, cancer cells are not self-contained and thus are able to detach from their original site and move to other areas throughout the body. This spread of cancerous tumors is referred to as metastasis, and at this advanced stage prognosis for recovery is not good.

Explanations for the manifestation of oncogenes are still speculative. Research has shown that external factors called carcinogens (e.g., ultraviolet rays, benzopyrene in cigarettes, asbestos) produce tumorous growths in both laboratory rats and humans. Medical researchers are still looking for endogenous factors that may also play a role in this disease process. At the same time, attention has been given to personality characteristics, and some traits have been found to be common among those who develop cancer. Although it is hard to put one-quarter of the American population into the same personality category, some studies show that the incidence of cancer appears higher among people who have a hard time expressing their emotions, have low self-esteem, and experience feelings of rejection (Brodie, 2008). By no coincidence, these same traits are said to characterize the codependent or addictive personality.

Oncogene: A gene in the DNA double-helix strand thought to be responsible for producing a mutant (cancerous) cell.

The treatments for cancer include drugs, radiation, and surgery. However, thanks to the work of O. Carl Simonton, Elisabeth Kübler-Ross, Bernie Siegel, Joan Borysenko, and Jeanne Achterberg, coping skills involving cognitive restructuring, art therapy, and relaxation techniques including mental imagery and meditation are being used as complementary healing methods. Although these methods are not a cure for cancer in themselves, in some cases they seem to have a pronounced effect when used in combination with traditional medicine.

Much attention is currently being given to the relationship between stress and disease in America. As lifestyles appear to become more stressful, the incidence of several illnesses that appear to be closely linked with stress is also increasing. Although stress may not seem like a direct cause of disease and illness, the association between them is too significant to be considered a mere coincidence. With the continued work of people like Borysenko, Pert, Gerber, Pelletier, and many others, some answers may be uncovered shortly.

SUMMARY

- There has been an intuitive association between stress and disease for centuries, but the link has come to be accepted scientifically only in the last decade or so. Scientists from several disciplines have come together to form a whole new field of study called psychoneuroimmunology.

- Recently, the immune system has been discovered to be greatly affected by prolonged bouts of stress.

- Pelletier states that there are still not enough data to substantiate a definitive stress-disease model that would help us to understand the relationship between the two. The focus of the stress-disease model appears to be divided between two areas: genetic predisposition, and energy medicine and subtle energy anatomy.

- Borysenko's model outlines both a dichotomy of autonomic dysregulation and immune dysregulation, and an immune activity matrix, which classifies diseases in one of four categories: (1) exogenous overreaction, (2) endogenous overreaction, (3) exogenous underreaction, and (4) endogenous underreaction.

- Pert's model cites research findings linking the nervous system with the immune system. Various cell tissues in the immune system can synthesize neuropeptides just as the brain can. Pert believes that all neuropeptides are really one molecule that undergoes a change at the atomic level brought about by various emotional states or energy thought forms.

- Lipton suggests that it is the cell membrane that is the brain of each cell. As a gatekeeper, it not only guards what goes in and out but does so by environmental programming, including the programming from our subconscious mind.

- Gerber's model states that the mind consists of energy (bioplasma) surrounding and permeating the body. Disease, then, is disturbance in the human energy field, which cascades through the levels of the subtle energy to the body via chakras and meridians.

- Pelletier's premodel states that a number of issues must be addressed and understood before a stress-disease model can be developed. These issues include disease states in people with dissociative identity disorders, spontaneous remissions, hypnosis, placebos, subtle energy, and immunoenhancement.

- Based on Borysenko's model, stress-related diseases were placed into one of two categories: those related to an overresponsive autonomic nervous system (e.g., migraines, ulcers, and coronary heart disease) and those associated with a dysfunctional immune system (e.g., colds and cancer).

- Research shows that several relaxation techniques are effective as complementary strategies in decreasing the symptoms of stress-related illness.

STUDY GUIDE QUESTIONS

1. Describe Borysenko's (immune system) stress and disease model.

2. What is the microbiome?

3. Describe Pert's (brain neurophysiology) stress and disease model.

4. Describe Lipton's (epigenetics) stress and new biology model.

5. Describe Gerber's (energy system) stress and disease model.

6. Describe Pelletier's stress and disease premodel.

7. List five diseases that occur when the nervous system is affected by stress.

8. List five diseases that occur when the immune system is affected by stress.

9. How does stress affect Lyme disease?

10. How does stress affect DNA strands?

11. How does stress affect inflammation?

REFERENCES AND RESOURCES

Achterberg, J. Imagery and Medicine: Psychophysiological Speculations, *Journal of Mental Imagery* 8(4):1–14, 1984.

Achterberg, J., et al. Evidence for Correlations Between Distant Intentionality and Brain Functions of Recipients, *Journal of Alternative and Complementary Medicine* 11(6):956–971, 2005.

Ader, R. Developmental Psychoneuroimmunology, *Developmental Psychobiology* 10:251–267, 1983.

Agarwal, A., Deepinder, F., et al. Effect of Cell Phone Usage on Semen Analysis in Men Attending Infertility Clinic: An Observational Study, *Fertility and Sterility* 89(1):124–128, 2008.

American Cancer Society. *Homepage*. www.cancer.org/docroot /home/index.asp.

American Diabetes Association. How Stress Affects Diabetes. December 6, 2013. http://www.diabetes.org/living-with -diabetes/complications/mental-health/stress.html.

American Diabetes Association. Living with Diabetes: Stress. www.diabetes.org/living-with-diabetes/complications /stress.html.

American Heart Association. *1991 Heart and Stroke Facts*, National Center, Dallas, TX, 1991.

American Heart Association. *Homepage*. www.Heart.org

American Psychological Association. Stress Affects Immunity in Ways Related to Stress Type and Duration, as Shown by Nearly 300 Studies. July 4, 2004. http://www.apa.org/news /press/releases/2004/07/stress-immune.aspx.

American Psychological Association. Stress Affects Immunity in Ways Related to Stress Type and Duration, as Shown by Nearly 300 Studies, *APA Online*, July 4, 2004. www.apa .org/releases/stress_immune.html.

Arntz, W., Chasse, B., and Vincente, M. *What the Bleep Do We Know!?* Health Communications, Inc. Deerfield Beach, FL, 2007.

Austin, J. A., et al. Complementary and Alternative Medicine Use Among Elderly Persons: One Year Analysis of a Blue Shield Medicare Supplement, *Journal of Gerontology* 55(1):M4–9, 2000.

Barrows, K., and Jacobs, B. Mind-Body Medicine, *Complementary and Alternative Medicine* 86(1):11–31, 2002.

Bartrop, R. W., et al. Depressed Lymphocyte Function after Bereavement, *Lancet* 1:834–836, 1977.

Becker, W. *Cross Currents*. Tarcher Press, Los Angeles, 1990.

BioInitiative 2012. A Rationale for Biologically Based Exposure Standards for Low-Intensity Electromagnetic Radiation. *Cell Phone Radiation Study Confirms Cancer Risk*. May 31, 2016. http://www.bioinitiative.org /cell-phone-radiation-study-confirms-cancer-risk/.

BioInitiative Report: A Rationale for a Biologically Based Public Exposure Standard for Electromagnetic Fields (ELF and RF). *Serious Public Health Concerns Raised Over Exposure to Electromagnetic Fields (EMF) from Powerlines and Cell Phones.* www.bioinitiative.org/press_release/index.htm.

Biondi, M. Effects of Stress on Immune Functions: An Overview. In R. Ader, D. L. Felten, and N. Cohen (eds.), *Psychoneuroimmunology*, 3rd ed., Academic Press Inc., San Diego, CA, 2001.

Blalock, J. E., Harbour-McMenamin, D., and Smith, E. Peptide Hormones Shared by the Neuroendocrine and Immunologic Systems, *Journal of Immunology* 135(2): 858s–861s, 1985.

Blanchard, E. B., et al. Biofeedback and Relaxation Treatments for Headaches in the Elderly: A Caution and a Challenge, *Biofeedback and Self-Regulation* 10(1):69–73, 1985.

Borysenko, M. Personal communication, December 10, 1991a.

Borysenko, M. Psychoneuroimmunology, *Annals of Behavioral Medicine* 9:3–10, 1987.

Borysenko, M. *Stress and the Immune System*, paper presented at the Sheraton Hotel, Washington, DC, October 25–26, 1991b.

Bovbjerg, D., Ader, R., and Cohen, N. Acquisition and Extinction of Conditioned Suppression of Graft-vs.-Host Responses in the Rat, *Journal of Immunology*, 132:111–113, 1984.

Braun, B. Psychophysiological Phenomena in Multiple Personality and Hypnosis, *American Journal of Clinical Hypnosis* 26(2):124–137, 1983.

Brennen, B. A. *Hands of Light: A Guide to Healing Through the Human Energy Field*. Bantam, New York, 1987.

Brodie, W. D. *The Cancer Personality*. Puna Wai Ora Mind–Body Center. 2008. www.alternative-cancer-care.com /The_Cancer_Personality.html.

Brody, H. (with Daralyn Brody). *The Placebo Response*. Cliff Street Books, New York, 2000.

Brotman, D., Golden, S., and Wittstein, I. The Cardiovascular Toll of Stress, *Lancet* 370:1089–1100, 2007.

Buhner, S. H. *Healing Lyme*. Raven Press, Silver City, NM, 2015.

Calcagni E., and Elenkov, I. Stress System Activity, Innate and T Helper Cytokines, and Susceptibility to Immune-Related Disease, *Annals of the New York Academy of Sciences* 1069:62–76, 2006.

Cawthon, R. M., Kin, J., Dhahhar, F. S., Adler, N. E., and Morrow, J. D. U.S. Study Suggests Link Between Psychological Stress, Aging, *U.S. Department of State*, November 30, 2004.

Clark, W. *The Experimental Foundations of Modern Immunology*, 4th ed. Wiley, New York, 1991.

Cohen, S., et al. Chronic Stress, Glucocorticoid Receptor Resistance, Inflammation, and Disease Risk. *Proceedings of the National Academy of Science USA*, 109(16):5995–5999, April 2, 2012.

Cohen, S., and Herbert, T. B. Health Psychology: Psychological Factors and Physical Disease from the Perspective of Human Psychoneuroimmunology, *Annual Review of Psychology* 47:113–142, 1996.

Cohen, S., Tyrrell, D., and Smith, A. P. Psychological Stress and Susceptibility to the Common Cold, *New England Journal of Medicine*, 325:606–612, 1991.

Cohen, S., and Williamson, G. M. Stress and Infectious Disease in Humans, *Psychological Bulletin* 109:5–24, 1991.

Collinge, W. *Subtle Energy: Awakening to the Unseen Forces in Our Lives*. Warner Books, New York, 1998.

Dacher, E. A Challenge to Healers: An Integrated Healing Model, Fifth Annual ISSSEEM Conference, Boulder, CO, June 26, 1995.

Dacher, E. *PNI: The New Mind-Body Healing Program*. Marlowe & Company, New York, 1992.

Davis, D. *Disconnect: The Truth About Cell Phone Radiation* Dutton. New York, 2010.

DeSalle, R., and Perkins, S. *Welcome to the Microbiome*. Yale University Press, New Haven, CT, 2015.

de Vernejoul, P., et al. Etude des Meridiens, D'Accupuncture par les Traceurs Radioactifs, *Bulletin de l'Académie Nationale de Médecine* 169(Oct):1071–1075, 1985.

Dietert, R. *The Human Superorganism*. Dutton, New York, 2016.

Dossey, L. *Reinventing Medicine*. Harper-San Francisco, San Francisco, 1999.

Dowdell, K., and Whitacre, C. Regulation of Inflammatory Autoimmune Diseases. In D. S. McEwen (ed.), *Coping with Environment: Neural and Endocrine Mechanism*, Oxford University Press, New York, 2000.

Eden, D. *Energy Medicine*. Tarcher/Putnam Books, New York, 2008.

Emoto, M. *The Message from Water*. Hado Books, Japan, 2004.

Eskola, S., Ylipaavalniemi, P., and Turtola, L. TMJ-Dysfunction Symptoms Among Finnish University Students, *Journal of American College Health* 33(4):172–174, 1985.

Esterling, B. A., Kiecolt-Glaser, J. K., Bodnar, J. C., and Glaser, R. Chronic Stress, Social Support, and Persistent Alterations in the Natural Killer Cell Response to Cytokines in Older Adults, *Health Psychology* 13:291–299, 1994.

Feinstein, D. Subtle Energy: Psychology's Missing Link, *Noetic Science Review* 64:18–23, 35, 2003.

Ferguson, M. Electronic Evidence of Aura, *Chakras* in UCLA Study, *Brain/Mind Bulletin* 3(9), 1978.

Gerber, R. Personal communication, November 25, 1991.

Gerber, R. *Vibrational Medicine*, 3rd ed. Inner Traditions, Rochester, VT, 2001.

Gerber, R. *Vibrational Medicine for the 21st Century*. Eagle Brook, New York, 2000.

Glasser, R., and Kiecolt-Glaser, J. (eds.), *Handbook of Human Stress and Immunity*. Academic Press, San Diego, CA, 1994.

Glasser, R., and Kiecolt-Glaser, J. Stress-Associated Immune Modulation, *American Journal of Medicine* 105(3A):35s–42s, 1998.

Gordon, J. *Manifesto for a New Medicine*. Addison-Wesley, Reading, MA, 1996.

Grad, B. Healing by the Laying on of Hands: A Review of Experiments. In D. Sobel (ed.), *Ways of Health: Holistic Approaches to Ancient and Contemporary Medicine*. Harcourt Brace Jovanovich, New York, 1979.

Green, E. Presidential Address, Second International ISSSEEM Annual Conference, Boulder, CO, June 26–28, 1992.

Greenberg, J. *Comprehensive Stress Management*, 13th ed. McGraw-Hill, New York, 2012.

Harman, W., and Clarke, J. *New Metaphysical Foundations of Modern Science*. Institute of Noetic Sciences, Sausalito, CA, 1994.

Hatfield, H. Stress and Asthma, *WebMD*, March 1, 2007. www.webmd.com/asthma/features/asthma-and-anxiety.

Health News. *First Case of HIV Cure Reported*, Daily News Central, November 13, 2005.

Henri-Benitez, M., et al. Autogenic Psychotherapy for Bronchial Asthma, *Psychology Psychosomatica* 11(6):11–16, 1990.

Herberman, R. Stress, Natural Killer Cells and Cancer. In H. Koenig and H. Cohen (eds.), *The Link Between Religion and Health. Psychoneuroimmunology and the Faith Factor*. Oxford Press, New York, 2002.

Hirshberg, C., and Barasch, M. *Remarkable Recovery*. Riverhead Books, New York, 1995.

Horrigan, B., and Ornish, D. Healing the Heart, Reversing the Disease, *Alternative Therapies* 1(5):84–92, 1995.

Horrigan, B., and Pert, C. Neuropeptides, AIDS, and the Science of Mind-Body Healing, *Alternative Therapies* 1(3):70–76, 1995.

Howenstine, J. New Ideas about the Cause, Spread and Therapy of Lyme Disease. Townsend Letter for Doctors and Patients, July 2004. http://www.samento.com.ec/sciencelib/4lyme/Townsendhowens.html.

Huffington Post. Chronic Stress Changes Immune Cell Genes, Leading to Inflammation Study. November 7, 2013. http://www.huffingtonpost.com/2013/11/07/chronic-stress-health-inflammation-genes_n_4226420.html.

Hunt, V. *Infinite Mind: Science of the Human Vibrations of Consciousness*. Malibu Publishing, Malibu, CA, 1996.

Hunt, V., et al. A Study of Structural Integration from Neuromuscular, Energy Field, and Emotional Approaches, paper presented at the University of California at Los Angeles, 1977.

Iliades, C. How Stress Affects Type 2 Diabetes. Everyday Health. www.everydayhealth.com/health-report/type-2-diabetes-lifestyle/stress-management-helps-type-2-diabetes.aspx.

Jermott, J. B. Psychoneuroimmunology: The New Frontier, *American Behavioral Scientist* 28(4):497–509, 1985.

Jermott, J. B., et al. Academic Stress: Power Motivation and Decrease in Saliva Immunoglobulin-A Secretion Rate, *Lancet* 1:1400–1402, 1983.

Johnston, V. *Why We Feel: Science of Human Emotions*. Perseus Books, New York, 1999.

Justice, B. *A Different Kind of Health: Finding Well-being Despite Illness*. Peak Press, Houston, TX, 1998.

Kemeny, M. E., and Gruenewald, T. L. Psychoneuroimmunology Update. *Seminars in Gastrointestinal Disease* 10:20–29, 1999.

Kent, J., et al. Unexpected Recoveries: Spontaneous Remission and Immune Functioning, *Advances* 6(2):66–73, 1989.

Kerns Geer, K. Is Stress the Source of Your Blood Sugar Swing? August 8, 2015. http://www.everydayhealth.com/hs/type-2-diabetes-management/stress-blood-sugar-swing/.

Ketcham, C. Warning: Your Cell Phone May Be Dangerous to Your Health. *Gentleman's Quarterly*, February 2010.

Kiecolt-Glaser, J. K. Slowing of Wound Healing by Psychological Stress, *Lancet* 346(8984):1194–1196, 1996.

Kiecolt-Glaser, J. K. Stress, Personal Relationships and Immune Function: Health Implications, *Brain, Behavior, and Immunity*. 13:61–72, 1999.

Kiecolt-Glaser, J., et al. Chronic Stress and Age-Related Increases in the Proinflammatory Cytokine IL-6. www.pnas.org/cgi/doi/10.1073/pnas.1531903100.

Kiecolt-Glaser, J., et al. Marital Stress: Immunological, Neuroendocrine, and Autonomic Correlates. *Annals of the New York Academy of Sciences* 840:656–663, 1998.

Kiecolt-Glaser, J., et al. Psychosocial Modifiers of Immunocompetence in Medical Students, *Psychosomatic Medicine* 46(1):7–14, 1984.

Kiecolt-Glaser, J., and Glaser, R. Chronic Stress and Mortality among Older Adults. *Journal of American Medical Association* 282(23), 2215–2219, 1999.

Kiecolt-Glaser, J. K., McGuire, L., Robles, T. F., and Glaser, R. Psychoneuroimmunology: Psychological Influences on Immune Function and Health. *Journal of Consulting and Clinical Psychology* 70:537–547, 2002.

Kiecolt-Glaser J. K., Preacher, K. J., MacCallum, R. C., Atkinson, C., Malarkey, W. B., and Glaser, R. Chronic Stress and Age-Related Increases in the Proinflammatory Cytokine IL-6. *Proceedings of the National Academy of Sciences* (US), 22; 100(15):9090–9095, 2003.

Kirlian, S., and Kirlian, V. Photography and Visual Observations by Means of High-Frequency Currents, *Journal of Scientific and Applied Photography* 6:145–148, 1961.

Kirschvink, J., et al. Magnetite in Human Tissues: A Mechanism for the Biological Effects of Weak ELF Magnetic Fields, *Bioelectronics Supplement* 1:101–114, 1992.

Koenig, H., and Cohen, H. (eds.). *The Link Between Religion and Health: Psychoneuroimmunology and the Faith Factor*. Oxford Press, New York, 2002.

Kopp, M. S., and Rethelyi, J. Where Psychology Meets Physiology: Chronic Stress and Premature Mortality—The Central-Eastern Health Paradox, *Brain Research Bulletin* 62:351–367, 2004.

Krieger, D. Healing by the Laying on of Hands as a Facilitator of Bioenergetic Change: The Response of In-Vivo Hemoglobin, *International Journal of Psychoenergetic Systems* 1:121, 1976.

Krieger, D. The Response of In-Vivo Human Hemoglobin to an Active Healing Therapy by Direct Laying on of Hands, *Human Dimensions* 1 (Autumn):12–15, 1972.

Krieger, D. Therapeutic Touch: The Imprimatur of Nursing, *American Journal of Nursing* 75:784–787, 1975.

Laskow, L. *Healing with Love*. HarperCollins, San Francisco, CA, 2008.

Laudenslanger, M. L., et al. Coping and Immunosuppression: Inescapable Shock Suppresses Lymphocyte Proliferation, *Science* 221:568–570, 1983.

Learner, M. *Choices in Healing*. MIT Press, Cambridge, MA, 1996.

Lehrer, P. M., Isenberg, S., and Hochron, S. M. Asthma and Emotion: A Review, *Journal of Asthma* 30:5–21, 1993.

Levenson, J. L., and Bemis, C. The Role of Psychological Factors in Cancer Onset and Progression, *Psychosomatics* 32(2):124–132, 1991.

Libov, C. Kris Kristofferson Has Lyme Disease, Not Alzheimer's. Newsmax Health, June 9, 2016. http://www.newsmax.com/Health/Headline/Kris-Kristofferson-Lyme-Disease/2016/06/09/id/733155/.

Lipton, B. *The Biology of Belief*. Sounds True CD set, 2006.

Lipton, B. *The Biology of Belief: Unleashing the Power of Consciousness, Matter, and Miracles*. Hay House, 2016.

Lipton, B. *The New Biology: Where Mind and Matter Meet*. DVD, Jean Meyers Productions, 2001.

Lipton, B. Epigenetics; The New Science of Human Empowerment. The Institute of Noetic Sciences 15th Conference. Indian Wells, CA, July 20, 2013

Lipton, B. *The Honeymoon Effect*. Hayhouse Books. Carlsbad, CA, 2013.

Lipton, B. Personal conversation, September 17, 2007.

McClean, P. *How Oncogenes Cause Cancer*. 1997. www.ndsu.edu/instruct/mcclean/plsc431/cellcycle/cellcycl5.htm.

McClelland, D. C., and Kirshnit, C. The Effect of Motivation Arousal Through Films on Salivary Immunoglobulin A, *Psychology and Health* 2:31–52, 1989.

McEwen, B. *The End of Stress as We Know It*. Joseph Henry Press, Washington, DC, 2002.

McTaggart, L. *The Field: The Quest for the Secret Force of the Universe*, 2nd ed. HarperCollins, New York, 2008.

Miller, G. E., Cohen, S., and Ritchey, K. Chronic Psychological Stress and the Regulation of Pro Inflammatory Cytokines: A Glucocorticoid-Resistance Model, *Health Psychology* 21(6):531–541, 2002.

Miller, R. Bridging the Gap: An Interview with Valerie Hunt, *Science of Mind*, October 12, 1983.

Mitchell, M. C., and Drossman, D. A. Irritable Bowel Syndrome: Understanding and Treating a Biopsychosocial Disorder, *Annals of Behavioral Medicine* 9(3):13–18, 1987.

Moran, M. Psychological Factors Affecting Pulmonary and Rheumatological Diseases: A Review, *Psychosomatics* 32(1):14–23, 1991.

Moriyama, Y., Kishimoto, A., and Mastushita, T. The Relationship Between Stress and the Onset of Gastrointestinal Diseases: Questionnaire Survey of Patients with Gastric Cancer and Gastric Ulcers, *Kyushu Neuropsychiatry* 34(3–4):282–288, 1988.

Motoyama, H., and Brown, R. *Science and the Evolution of Consciousness*. Autumn Press, Brookline, MA, 1978.

Motz, J. *Hands of Life*. 2nd ed. Bantam Books, New York, 2000.

Myss, C. *Anatomy of the Spirit*. Harmony Books, New York, 1996.

Nature Communications. Oncogene. www.nature.com/onc/index.html.

Nordqvist, C. Cell Phone Usage Linked to Lower Sperm Count, *Medical News Today*, October 23, 2006. www.medicalnewstoday.com/articles/54866.php.

Northrup, C. *Women's Bodies, Women's Wisdom*. Bantam Books, New York, 2010.

O'Leary, A. Stress, Emotion, and Human Immune Function, *Psychological Bulletin* 108(3):363–382, 1990.

Ornish, D. *Dr. Dean Ornish's Program for Reversing Heart Disease*. Random House, New York, 1990.

Pare, W. P. Stress Ulcer Susceptibility and Depression in Wistar Kyoto (WKY) Rats, *Physiology and Behavior* 46(6):993–998, 1989.

Pearsall, P. *The Heart's Code*. Broadway Books, New York, 1998.

Pelletier, K. *The Best Alternative Medicine: What Works? What Does Not?* Simon & Schuster, New York, 2000a.

Pelletier, K. Between Mind and Body, Stress, Emotions and Health. In D. Goleman (ed.), *Mind Body Medicine*, Consumer Reports Books, Yonkers, NY, 1993.

Pelletier, K. Life with a New Roommate: Alternative Medicine Moves in with Conventional Medicine. *Healthcare Forum Journal*, November/December: 35–37, 41, 1998.

Pelletier, K. *Mind as Healer, Mind as Slayer*. Dell, New York, 1977.

Pelletier, K. Personal communication, September 20, 2000b.

Pelletier, K. *Toward a Science of Consciousness*. Celestial Arts, Berkeley, CA, 1985.

Pelletier, K., and Herzing, D. Psychoneuroimmunology: Toward a Mind-Body Model, *Advances* 5(1):27–56, 1988.

Pert, C. B. *Everything You Need to Know to Feel Go(o)d*. Hay House Books, Carlsbad, CA, 2007.

Pert, C. B. *Molecules of Emotion: Why You Feel the Way You Feel*. Scribner, New York, 1997.

Pert, C. B. Neuropeptides: The Emotions and Bodymind, *Noetic Sciences Review* 2:13–18, 1987.

Pert, C. B. Personal communication, December 18, 1991.

Pert, C. B. Personal communication (phone), July 30, 2003.

Pert, C. B. Personal communication (phone), August 18, 2004.

Pert, C. B. The Wisdom of the Receptors: Neuropeptides, The Emotions, and Bodymind, *Advances* 3(3):8–16, 1986.

Pert, C. B., et al. Neuropeptides and Their Receptors: A Psychosomatic Network, *Journal of Immunology* 135 (2 suppl.):820s–826s, 1985.

Pert, C. B., Dreher, H., and Ruff, M. The Psychosomatic Network: Foundations of Mind-Body Medicine, *Alternative Therapies in Health and Medicine* 4(4):30–40, 1998.

Pfaffenrath, V., Wermuth, A., and Pollmann, W. Tension Headache: A Review, *Fortschritte der Neurologie Psychiatrie* 56(12):407–422, 1988.

Pouwer, F., Kupper, N., and Adriaanse, M. Does Emotional Stress Cause Type II Diabetes Mellitus? *Discovery Magazine*. February 11, 2010. www.discoverymedicine.com/Frans-Pouwer/2010/02/11/does-emotional-stress-cause-type-2-diabetes-mellitus-a-review-from-the-european-depression-in-diabetes-edid-research-consortium/.

Powell, D., and the Institute of Noetic Sciences. *The 2007 Shift Report: Evidence of a World Transforming*. Institute of Noetic Sciences, Petaluma, CA, 2007.

Prensky, W. L. Reston Helped Open a Door to Acupuncture, Letter to the Editor, *The New York Times*, December 9, 1995. http://query.nytimes.com/gst/fullpage.html?res=9E0DE5DE1739F937A25751C1A963958260.

Rabin, B. Understanding How Stress Affects the Physical Body. In H. Koenig and H. Cohen (eds.), *The Link Between Religion and Health. Psychoneuroimmunology and the Faith Factor,* Oxford Press, New York, 2002.

Rabin, B., et al. Bidirectional Interaction Between the Central Nervous System and the Immune System, *Critical Reviews in Immunology* 9:279–312, 1989.

Radin, D. *The Conscious Universe*. HarperSanFrancisco, New York, 2009.

Rayhorn, N. Understanding Inflammatory Bowel Disease, *Nursing* 29:57–68, 1999.

Rein, G. As reported in *Vibrational Medicine for the 21st Century* by Richard Gerber. Eagle Brook, New York, 2000:375.

Rosch, P. Personal communication, American Institute of Stress, August 11, 2003.

Rose-Neil, S. The Work of Professor Kim Bong Han, *Acupuncturist* 1:15, 1967.

Roundtree, R., with Carol Coleman. *Immunotics*. Putnam Books, New York, 2000.

Rubik, B. Energy Medicine and the Unifying Concept of Information, *Alternative Therapies* 1(1):34–39, 1995.

Rubik, B. Personal communication, July 30, 2003.

Saibil, F. *Crohn's Disease and Ulcerative Colitis*. Firefly Books, New York, 3rd ed. 2011.

Sapolsky, R. *Why Zebras Don't Get Ulcers* (4th ed). Holt Paperback Books, New York, 2009.

Schleifer, S., et al. Suppression of Lymphocyte Stimulation Following Bereavement, *JAMA* 250(3):374–377, 1983.

Schlitz, M., and Amorok, T. *Consciousness and Healing*. Elsevier Press, St. Louis, MO, 2005.

Schwartz, J. Cell Phones May Have Cancer Link, *Washington Post*, Saturday, May 22, 1999.

Seaward, B. L. Alternative Medicine Complements Standard, *Health Progress* 75(7):52–57, 1994.

Segerstrom, S. C., and Miller, G. E. Psychological Stress and the Human Immune System: A Meta-Analytical Study of 30 Years of Inquiry, *Psychological Bulletin* 130(4):601–630, 2004.

Shavit, Y., et al. Stress, Opioid Peptides, the Immune System and Cancer, *Journal of Immunology* 135:834–837, 1994.

Shealy, C. N., and Myss, C. *The Creation of Health*. Stillpoint Press, Walpole, NH, 1998.

Siegel, B. *Love, Medicine, and Miracles*. Perennial Library, New York, 1986.

Smith, E. M., Harbour-McMenamin, D., and Blalock, J. E. Lymphocyte Production of Endorphins and Endorphin-Mediated Immunoregulatory Activity, *Journal of Immunology* 135:779s–782s, 1985.

Smith, M., et. al., Outcomes of Touch Therapies During Bone Marrow Transplant, *Alternative Therapies* 9(1):40–49, 2003.

Spiegel, D. Healing Words: Emotional Expression and Disease Outcome, *JAMA* 281(14):1328, 1999.

Sternberg E. *The Balance Within: The Science Connecting Health & Emotions*. W. H. Freeman, New York, 2000.

Straley, C. Is Stress Hurting Your Skin? *Parents Magazine*, November: 1999:193.

Stringfellow, B. Visiting Physician Sheds New Light on Lyme Disease. *Martha's Vineyard Times*, July 13, 2016.

Talbot, M. *The Holographic Universe*. HarperCollins, New York, Reprinted 2011.

Tasner, M. *TMJ*, *Medical Self-Care*, November/December: 47–50, 1986.

Tecoma, E., and Huey, L. Psychic Distress and the Immune Response, *Life Sciences* 36(19):1799–1812, 1985.

Temoshok, L. Personality, Coping Style, Emotion, and Cancer: Towards an Integrative Model, *Cancer Surveys* 6:545–567, 1987.

Trieschmann, R. Spirituality and Energy Medicine, *Journal of Rehabilitation* 67(1):26–38, 2001.

Tucker, L., Cole, G., and Freidman, G. Stress and Serum Cholesterol: A Study of 7000 Adult Males, *Health Values* 11:34–39, 1987.

Ubell, E. Soon, We Won't Have to Worry About Ulcers, *Parade Magazine*, April 2: 18–19, 1995.

University of Maryland Medical Center. *Acupuncture*. www.umm.edu/altmed/articles/acupuncture-000345.htm.

Vida, C., Gonzalez, E. M., and De la Fuenta, M. Increase of Oxidation and Inflammation in Nervous and Immune Systems with Aging and Anxiety. *Current Pharmaceutical Design*, 20(29):4656–4678, 2014.

Vincent, T., and Elder, A. Low Dose Immunotherapy (LDI) and Lyme Disease. Personal communication. June 10, 2016.

Webster Marketon, J. I., and Glaser, R. Stress hormones and immune function. *Cell Immunology*. Mar–Apr;252(1–2):16–26, 2008.

Wilson, A. *Under Our Skin: The Untold Story of Lyme Disease*. Documentary Film, July 19, 2009. http://underourskin.com/film/.

Wittstein, L. Neurohumoral Features of Myocardial Stunning Due to Sudden Emotional Stress, *New England Journal of Medicine* 352(6):539–548, 2005.

Wright, R. J. Alternative Modalities for Asthma that Reduce Stress and Modify Mood States: Evidence for Underlying Psychobiological Mechanisms, *Annals of Allergy, Asthma, and Immunology* 92:1–6, 2003.

Wright, R. J., and Cohen, S. Stress and Allergy. May 19, 2005. http://www.thedoctorwillseeyounow.com/content/stress/art2431.html.

Wright, R. J., and Cohen, S. News: Stress and Allergy. www.thedoctorwillseeyounow.com/news/behavior/0505/allergies.shtml.

Young, E. *I Contain Multitudes: The Microbes Within Us and a Grander View of Life*. Ecco/Harper Collins Books, New York, 2016.

PART TWO

The Mind and Soul

To thine own self be true.

—William Shakespeare

CHAPTER 5

Toward a Psychology of Stress

Modern man is sick because he is not whole.

—Carl Gustav Jung

For centuries, scientists have debated the relationship between the mind and the brain. Is the mind a function of the brain, a series of biochemical reactions, or is the mind a complex dynamic of consciousness, a separate entity unto itself that uses the brain as its primary organ of choice? This question has polarized researchers to believe either that all thoughts and feelings can be explained as neurochemical messages transmitted from brain cell to brain cell or that the mind exists separately from the brain yet somehow is housed and fused with it. This one question, perhaps more than any other, initiated the discipline of psychology at the turn of the twentieth century. As the mind-body connection is more closely examined with regard to the stress response, it becomes increasingly clear that the mind is a very complex phenomenon, and not merely a by-product of neurochemical interactions. The interactions of thoughts, emotions, behaviors, and personality traits—the mind is held accountable for all of them and a bit more (Baruss, 2017). In this chapter, we will look at how the mind perceives stress so that the "antiquated" stress response can be updated or recircuited, highlighting some specific aspects of the psychology of stress.

Since the advent of the discipline of psychology, many notable figures have made significant contributions to the understanding of the mind—specifically, those regarding personality, emotions, perceptions, and a whole realm of human behaviors. From these individuals have come a host of theories attempting to interpret the complexities of emotional well-being on which stress has so great an influence. These theories have been inspired by such questions as, Why does the mind perceive some events as threatening? and What cognitive dynamics are used to deal with psychological stress? The list of those people who have contributed to the body of knowledge of human consciousness would comprise a book itself, not the least of which includes Albert Ellis (Rational Emotive Behavior Therapy), Richard Lazarus (Daily Hassles), and countless others. Although no one theorist seems to explain the psychological aspects of stress in its totality, together the following theories at least begin to address several significant issues involved. The following psychiatrists, psychologists, and therapists offer a glimpse of some of the greatest insights into the mind's role in the psychology of stress.

Freud and the Egg

Because of his profound influence on the field of psychology (perhaps more than any other individual), the work of Sigmund Freud (**FIG. 5.1**) is chosen by many scholars as the reference point from which all other psychological theories emanate. Most recognized for his concepts of conscious and unconscious thought and their associations to sexual drive, Freud established the groundwork for understanding human behavior. Specifically, he made tangible the abstract concepts of emotional thought processes and the constructs of personality. From Freud's perspective, humans operate from an instinctual nature, or those biological and physiological impulses he referred to as the id. These impulses aim to satisfy the body's immediate needs. In Freud's opinion, there is a constant **instinctual tension** between body and mind as the mind attempts to cater to these impulses in socially acceptable ways. This internal tension can be decreased, but because of the power of human instincts, it is never fully extinguished. Consequently, Freud believed that humans have some degree of *innate* stress.

Freud developed a wonderful metaphor to illustrate the intangible complexities of the human psyche. He

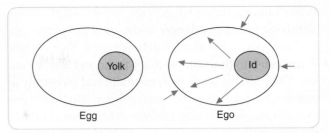

FIGURE 5.2 Freud compared the abstract human psyche to an egg. Instinctual tension is always present, Freud believed, because the id constantly releases impulses. These, along with external stimuli, threaten the integrity of the ego, which must protect itself with what Freud termed defense mechanisms.

compared the mind's innermost thoughts, memories, and feelings, components that make up one's identity, to an egg (**FIG. 5.2**). Like the contents of an egg, the human psyche is extremely delicate and fragile. And like an egg it is enclosed and protected by a sturdy yet quite vulnerable shell. According to Freud, the primary purpose of the **ego** is to seek pleasure and to avoid pain with regard to our biological impulses (a function now thought to be similar to that of the hypothalamus). That is, the ego is primarily responsible for controlling the flood of impulses from the id. The ego is also vulnerable to perceptions of outside stimuli, which constantly threaten the stability of the contents within. This, too, he observed, produces tension.

The metaphor of the egg and Freud's theory of the function of the ego have been useful to comprehend the environmental balance of the mind, specifically in terms of cognitive stress-management strategies. Understanding that stress or anxiety is aroused simultaneously by internal impulses and perceived outside stimulation (threats) means that the protection of identity (ego) is critical to survival. As if a missile were headed for the

FIGURE 5.1 Sigmund Freud.

© Hans Casparius/Stringer/Hulton Archive/Getty.

Instinctual tension: A Freudian term used to highlight the tension between the mind's impulses and the body's response, suggesting that stress is humanly inherent.

Ego: A term coined by Freud naming the part of the psyche that not only triggers the stress response when threatened, but also defends against all enemies, including thoughts and feelings generated from within.

White House, anxiety triggers the mind's alarm system, signifying imminent danger to the existence of the ego. Defense systems are immediately activated. Should these defenses fail to function properly, panic and disaster ensue. Through his work with mentally and physically ill patients, Freud observed enough stress-related behaviors to credit excessive anxiety (unknown fears that penetrate the ego's shell and produce pain) and inadequate defenses with the primary roles in the development of neurotic and psychotic behavior.

According to Freud, the mind's defense system consists of a host of thought processes, or **defense mechanisms**, to aid in the protection of the ego's fragile contents. They act to shield the contents from harm by minimizing the impact of perceived threats. From his perspective, defense mechanisms are a collection of coping strategies to deal with stress. Because of both constant inner tension produced by instinctual impulses and stressfully perceived external stimuli, Freud believed that defense mechanisms must always be in operation to some extent. Thus, he was convinced that all behavior is defensive in nature. Freud theorized that all defense mechanisms share two characteristics: (1) they are denials or distortions of reality, and (2) they operate unconsciously. Furthermore, an individual rarely uses just one defense mechanism. Rather, each person employs a variety of ego-protecting mechanisms overall, and usually several at the same time. Freud postulated a number of defense mechanisms, including denial, repression, projection, rationalization, reaction formation, regression, displacement, sublimation, and humor. The following are most commonly used in the defense of stress-produced anxiety:

> **Defense mechanisms:** Described by Sigmund Freud; unconscious thinking patterns of the ego to either decrease pain or increase pleasure.
>
> **Denial:** One of the primary defense mechanisms noted by Freud in which one disbelieves what occurred when personally threatened.
>
> **Repression:** The involuntary removal of thoughts, memories, and feelings from the conscious mind so they are less threatening to the ego.
>
> **Projection:** The act of attributing one's thoughts and feelings to other people so that they are less threatening to the ego.
>
> **Rationalization:** The reinterpretation of the current reality to match one's liking: a reinterpretation of the truth.

1. **Denial:** When people are confronted with circumstances they find to be a threat, they often deny association or involvement with any aspect of the situation. Young children are often caught in the act of lying (denial) when they are accused of eating cookies right before dinner or making a mess in the bathroom. Examples in adulthood include denying a drinking or gambling problem. Any stimulus perceived to be a threat to the integrity of one's identity can push the button to deny involvement or knowledge. At a conscious level, the person truly believes he or she is innocent and sees nothing wrong with the behavior.

2. **Repression:** Repression is the involuntary removal of thoughts, memories, or feelings from the conscious mind. It differs from suppression, wherein painful experiences are intentionally forgotten, in that the conscious mind is unaware of this process. Freud referred to repression as an unconscious denial of something that brings emotional discomfort or pain. Examples are memories of unpleasant family holidays, child abuse, or embarrassing moments you cannot seem to recall even when friends and family tell you in fine detail what you did.

3. **Projection:** Projection is a process in which an individual defends the ego by attributing unacceptable feelings, impulses, and behaviors to other people—or objects such as dogs, tennis racquets, swim goggles, or the weather. In this way, when an impulse or emotion is manifested, it is now less threatening because its source appears to be generated externally rather than from within. Ownership of painful feelings is minimized. According to Freud, projection is most prevalent in response to feelings of sexual desire, insecurities, and aggression. An example of projection is oversleeping, getting a late start for work, getting caught in traffic, and then blaming every dumb driver for your lateness.

4. **Rationalization:** Rationalization is the reinterpretation of the reality of one's behavior or circumstances. It's a manipulation of the truth. Rationalization can be described as a filtered lens that makes emotional pain more acceptable, even appealing, to one's emotional vision. Actions or thoughts that are perceived to be threatening are quickly reinterpreted in terms of another, more acceptable, rational explanation. For example, someone who has been fired from a job he loved might rationalize this outcome by saying, "It was

an awful job and I'm glad to be done with it." Another example would be when your boyfriend breaks up with you and you tell friends you wanted to break it off because the relationship was too great a time commitment.

5. ***Displacement:*** When something that causes pain to the ego is inaccessible or otherwise cannot be responded to directly, the painful feelings can be transferred to an unrelated person or object. This is what Freud called displacement. Displacement involves transferring emotional pain and its related behavior from an unacceptable object (e.g., an authority figure) to a nonthreatening object (usually children and pets). For example, your boss is a jerk and you would love to choke him, but instead you go home and shoo away the cat who begs for attention. Even though feelings of anger and aggression are most commonly cited as those that are displaced, it is also possible to displace feelings and behaviors associated with joy and love to those you perceive to be most receptive to them, rather than those you believe would not respond favorably.

6. ***Humor:*** Later in his career, Freud began to study the psychology of humor and jokes. Reviewing the works of several humorists, he was at first perplexed at the phenomenon but soon saw it as a device for the body to release sexually repressed thoughts through laughter. This is the rationale he proposed to explain the popularity of "dirty" jokes. Humor, remarked Freud, is a unique defense mechanism unlike the others. It simultaneously decreases pain and increases pleasure, making it the most advanced of all the defense mechanisms.

These are but six of the many defense mechanisms Freud believed are most commonly used in response to anger and fear. Each mechanism, used to protect our identity, is a camouflage of reality (**FIG. 5.3**). The ego perceives uncamouflaged threatening stimuli as attacks on the existence of our innermost feelings, perceptions, values, beliefs, and attitudes, so protection is often necessary, especially for children in the early stages of growth and development. However, over-protection of the ego can ultimately be as dangerous to the maturation process as lack of adequate protection. Overprotection usually results in the inhibition of emotional growth and maturation of the individual's mental and emotional boundaries, a situation analogous to a houseplant rootbound by too small a pot. When anxiety or a perceived threat enters the walls of the

FIGURE 5.3

ego, emotional pain results. With a less defensive attitude, however, this pain can enable the individual to expand his or her self-awareness and personal growth. In this case, the result is an expansion of the ego. Each time this "space" grows, therein lies an opportunity to expand one's capabilities and enhance one's human potential. It may not seem that stress always involves the ego, but in truth, it really does. Our ego is *our identity*, and whether it is fear or anger that triggers the stress response, things that cause stress typically attack the integrity of our identity and perceptions of self-worth. Freud's coping mechanisms are the front-line defense. The degree to which defense mechanisms are innate or learned behavior has yet to be decided. Perhaps because Freud understood anxiety to be an inseparable part of the individual, he left no substantial advice on minimizing it, short of psychoanalysis. Despite varying opinions of his work, Freud's theories of personality have become so well acknowledged, if not respected, it is not uncommon to find strong parallels in the concepts of other theorists.

> **Displacement:** The transference of emotional pain (usually anger) from a threatening source (one's boss) to a nonthreatening source (one's cat).
>
> **Humor:** The defense mechanism noted by Freud that both decreases pain and increases pleasure.

Jung and the Iceberg

The theories of Freud inspired many physicians to investigate the new clinical field of the psyche and human behavior. One such physician was Carl Gustav Jung (FIG. 5.4) of Switzerland, who was hand-picked by Freud to be his "heir apparent" and champion his theories. During the close collaboration of the two, Jung began to voice disagreement with some of Freud's theoretical concepts. As a result, their professional (as well as personal) relationship quickly eroded. Although Jung and Freud parted company in their opinions of the mysteries of the mind, Jung has become respected as the second greatest influence on modern psychological thought. His theories involving introverts and extroverts, personality types (inspiring the Myers-Briggs Type Inventory), midlife crisis, synchronicity, anima-animus, archetypes, the shadow, and the spiritual nature of humankind sowed many seeds in the human potential movement, and his following continues to grow both within and outside the field of psychology.

Unlike Freud, who postulated that humans act by instincts, biological forces, and childhood experiences, Jung theorized human personality as a process of self-discovery and realization, a concept he referred to as **individuation**. Individuation involves not only the culmination of childhood experiences, but also a spiritual life force that shapes one's being and life direction. Jung was convinced that self-awareness and a quest for a greater understanding of the self enhance the process of individuation, helping one navigate through the difficult passages of life. This ability to soul-search, to wrestle with personal issues, and to further the understanding of one's life purpose, he believed, augmented psychological health. On the other hand, reluctance, avoidance, and indolence contribute to self-ignorance and perpetuate the stress associated with underutilized inner resources. Jung also disagreed with Freud's notion that human behavior is driven primarily by sexual impulses. And although Freud placed less importance on aspects of the unconscious

FIGURE 5.4   Carl Gustav Jung.

mind, Jung focused his life's work on this construct, particularly in his empirical research on dreams as a means to enhance the individuation process.

Jung likened the human mind to an iceberg (FIG. 5.5). Metaphorically speaking, the conscious mind is represented by the tip above the water, while the unconscious, the greatest percentage of the mind, lies below the water. The conscious mind, with its limited awareness, focuses on specific thoughts, which compete for attention (e.g., What should I have for dinner tonight? How will I be able to afford a new car? What time is it? Will he ask me to the formal?). The unconscious mind is the receptacle for ideas, images, and concepts the conscious mind has no room to hold, as well as repressed thoughts, memories, and a host of undiscovered thoughts of enlightenment. Jung divided the unconscious mind into two levels. The first layer, the level he referred to as the **personal unconscious**, is the repository of the thoughts, perceptions, feelings, and memories of the individual—everything dropped from the attention of the conscious mind. However obscure these ideas, feelings, and perceptions may be, they do not cease to exist, and in fact continue to influence conscious thought and behaviors. The second level Jung called

Individuation: A term coined by Carl Jung to describe self-realization, a process leading to wholeness.

Personal unconscious: A repository of personal thoughts, perceptions, feelings, and memories.

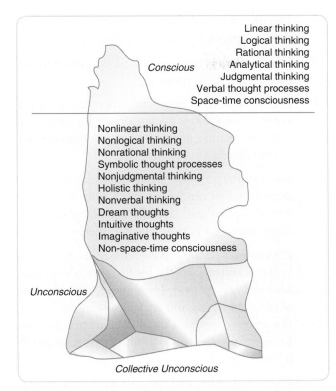

Linear thinking
Logical thinking
Rational thinking
Analytical thinking
Conscious
Judgmental thinking
Verbal thought processes
Space-time consciousness

Nonlinear thinking
Nonlogical thinking
Nonrational thinking
Symbolic thought processes
Nonjudgmental thinking
Holistic thinking
Nonverbal thinking
Dream thoughts
Intuitive thoughts
Imaginative thoughts
Non-space-time consciousness

Unconscious

Collective Unconscious

FIGURE 5.5 Jung compared the mind to an iceberg. That which is above the water represents the conscious mind, while that below represents all unconscious thought processes. Despite the fact that the unconscious mind may appear dormant at the conscious level, Jung theorized that it is perpetually active.

the **collective unconscious**, a profound and potentially inexhaustible reservoir of human thoughts and ideas integrated with ancient wisdom, which he claimed is essentially passed down from generation to generation, not unlike physical characteristics genetically passed down through generations of humanity. Jung believed that although this level was more difficult to access, the resources in this reservoir were invaluable in aiding the self-discovery process.

Jung believed that the passage of thoughts from the conscious to the unconscious mind is quite easy when compared to the difficult migration of intuitive or suppressed thoughts and dream images trying to surface to conscious attention. From Jung's viewpoint, consciousness naturally rejects anything unknown and unfamiliar. Consequently, the threshold of consciousness, like the membrane of a cell, acts as a barrier, censoring material from the unconscious mind that seems irrelevant, incoherent, inane, or ego-bruising.

From the analysis and interpretation of his own dreams as well as thousands of dreams of his patients, Jung discovered that the conscious and unconscious minds speak two different languages. The conscious mind communicates through very linear, rational, analytical, and verbal processes. Conversely, the processes of the unconscious mind are nonlinear, irrational, intuitive, and non-time-oriented processes represented through dreams in symbols and vivid colors. (It is interesting to note that Nobel Prize–winning research by Roger Sperry et al. has documented a similar division of cognitive functions in the left brain and right brain, respectively.) If you reflect on some of your own dreams, you may recall images that seem absurd—flying, swimming in red air, a herd of elk grazing in the attic, or a conversation with a college buddy and a high school sweetheart who in real life are thousands of miles apart and have never even met.

In Jung's view, daily stress is compounded by internal tension between the seemingly incompatible thought processes of the two minds. Although we are not typically aware of our unconscious minds' activities during the waking hours of the day (unlike the dream state during sleep), the unconscious mind is constantly open to sensory stimulation and countless thought processes, whereas the conscious mind only functions this way while we are awake. Moreover, the unconscious mind acts as a navigator for the driver of the conscious mind. Yet in many cases, the two are worlds apart in the front seat of the same car, with the conscious mind in a dominant role, charting its own course. In the dream state, however, the unconscious mind both navigates and drives, working to resolve issues raised in the course of the day. Confusion arises when the unconscious presents resolutions in dream symbols that the conscious mind passes off as ludicrous or unimportant. To the conscious mind, dreams hold little significance if there is no overt understanding, yet in Jung's opinion they continually offer impeccable insight into the problem-solving process.

To understand the concept of the unconscious better, imagine that while driving in a foreign country you become lost and stop to ask directions from people who speak no English. You do not speak a word of their native tongue either. They try to warn you that the road you are

> **Collective unconscious:** A term coined by psychologist Carl Jung; the deepest level of unconsciousness, which connects all people together as one; divine consciousness.

on is unsafe, but even their pantomimes are unclear. You proceed and encounter the same situation with more natives a mile down the road. Baffled and discouraged, you shake your head, ignoring the warnings and continuing to drive on into potential danger.

Similarly, Jung proposed that internal tension develops at the interface of the conscious and unconscious minds because of the inability of these two entities to communicate effectively. In an attempt to minimize this tension, Jung explained that the conscious mind acts as a censoring mechanism that limits access to unconscious thought processes trying to bubble up from below. This explains why many people initially cannot recall their dreams or make sense of them if they do remember them. Although the censoring process may seem effective in the short term, the inability to decipher the language of the unconscious perpetuates internal stress in the long run.

New languages may be difficult to master at first, but with practice comes fluency. According to Jung, the conscious mind can be trained to interpret the dream symbols created by the unconscious mind by manipulating and playing with these images. Based on five decades of dream analysis, Jung made the following observations about dreams:

1. Dreams should be treated as fact, not as fabrications of the mind.

> **Psychic equilibrium:** A term coined by Carl Jung to describe the balance of thought (and subsequent health-wholeness) between the conscious and unconscious minds, by having the conscious mind become multilingual to the many languages of the unconscious mind (e.g., dream interpretation).

2. Dreams have a definite and purposeful idea or theme expressed in unique symbols.

3. Dreams make sense when time is devoted to understanding their meaning.

4. Recurring dreams may represent a traumatic life event, be an attempt to compensate for a personal defect in attitude, or signal an event of importance in the future.

5. Dream interpretation is individualistic in that no dream symbol can be separated from the person who dreams it (e.g., the meaning of a plane crash is specific to the person who dreamed it).

6. Dream interpretation is essential to the resolution of stress and anxiety. In his last published book, *Man and His Symbols*, Jung wrote, "For the sake of mental stability and even physiological health, the unconscious and the conscious minds must be integrally connected and thus move in parallel lines."

Jung's concept of individuation emphasized the importance of self-reflection: quality time spent in solitude dedicated to expanding one's conscious awareness as well as learning the language and wisdom of the unconscious mind. His travels to Asia, during which he studied the concepts behind meditation, reinforced his belief that self-reflection was essential to mental health. Jung was convinced that when you take the time to examine the depths of your own mind, a unity of conscious and unconscious thought processes occurs, which helps you to resolve personal issues and leads to a greater sense of inner peace. This unity he called **psychic equilibrium**.

FIGURE 5.6 Dreams offer a source of insight and information that we often don't get any other way. For this reason it is important to pay attention to our dreams.

Stress with a Human Face

Pattie is a middle-school teacher who is currently working on her master's degree in psychology at the University of Northern Colorado. One day, after hearing a lecture on dreams and dream therapy, she became very intrigued with the notion of accessing the wisdom of the unconscious mind through dream interpretation. It didn't take long for her to decide the focus of her term paper for this course. It would be on the study of dreams and dream therapy.

Like most people, Pattie confides that she doesn't remember her dreams, yet knowing that all people have dreams, she was curious to learn more about herself and what wisdom would be revealed to her by making a more concerted effort to remember her dreams. The research paper became a catalyst for self-exploration.

Based on information she researched, Pattie knew that it was possible to train the conscious mind to remember dreams and uncode the language of dream symbols. She bought a notebook specifically to record her dreams and made a habit of practicing a relaxation technique before she went to bed, a technique she noted as an important step in the dream therapy process. Just as one would learn any skill, the first few attempts to record dreams were fruitless, but Pattie persisted.

One night, after listening to a relaxation tape, Pattie fell asleep. When she awoke, she recalled having a dream so vivid, so real, that she remembered the entire dream sequence. Taking pen in hand, Pattie recorded the dream in her notebook.

"I dreamt I was in my classroom and a student came by and popped her head in the door and smiled. She was much older than my typical students and, although I didn't recognize her, I knew her. In analyzing the dream, I came to understand that she was actually a composite of several former students, and her appearance in my door was a message. She had come back to tell me that my teaching had had a positive influence on her life, and her smile to me was an acknowledgment of her gratitude. I interpreted her visit as a vote of confidence in my teaching skills and the dream served as a reminder that my job is worthwhile, and my work is having a positive impact on my students.

"Through my research I really learned how valuable dream therapy is to people with post-traumatic stress disorder (PTSD), and through my own experience I learned how valuable dream interpretation is. It has had a positive impact on my life."

In describing her dream experience, she added, "I would like to pass along a quote from Carl Jung: 'No dream symbol can be separated from the individual who dreams it, and there is no definite or straightforward interpretation of any dream.'"

To assist his patients toward the goal of psychic balance, Jung employed what he called **active imagination**. This is a process where, in a conscious yet relaxed state, an individual uses creativity to manipulate dream fragments and complete the dream experience. This technique is most useful with recurring dreams, where the dreamer gives a desired ending to the neglected issues represented in these unfinished stories. Active imagination has been adapted to many coping and relaxation techniques alike, including mental imagery, journal writing, and art therapy. Jung was of the firm opinion that sickness, both mental and physical, was the result of the inability to bridge the gap between conscious and unconscious minds as a way to share knowledge to resolve inner tensions. In fact, he was once quoted as saying, "Modern man is sick because he is not whole," with wholeness being a peaceful union of the conscious and unconscious minds.

Jung suggested that each individual become introspective and dive below the waters of the conscious mind to gain insight into the causes of specific anxiety and stress. Once this awareness is gained, the source of anxiety can be confronted and handled at the conscious level, where it can lead to resolution and strength of the spirit. Throughout his life, Jung was devoted to the development of human potential, which begins with self-awareness. Many of Jung's followers have augmented and developed his concepts for application to psychotherapy, specifically

> **Active imagination:** A term coined by Carl Jung describing a mental imagery process where, in a lucid dream state or relaxed state, you consciously imagine (and resolve) the end of a recurring dream. Active imagination is a form of visualization.

dream therapy. All in all, Jung's theories are quite profound, and they invite us to continue the exploration of the mysteries of the mind.

With the groundwork established by Freud and Jung, other theories were added throughout the twentieth and twenty-first centuries to the collective body of psychological knowledge. With each new insight we gain a stronger grasp of the psyche, particularly the influence that stress has on it. The following theories only begin to touch on aspects of emotions, behavior, and personality. Yet when combined with those of Freud and Jung, they give a wider perspective on the factors associated with the psychology of stress.

■ Elisabeth Kübler-Ross: The Death of Unmet Expectations

When the Social Readjustment Rating Scale was designed, it became obvious to its creators that the death of a spouse is the most stressful event a person can experience. The death and dying process, be it your own or that of someone you are close to, is very traumatic. Similarly, the death (grieving) of any unmet expectation is stressful and hence relates to this theory. One person who brought the issue of death to the forefront of human consciousness is Elisabeth Kübler-Ross (**FIG. 5.7**). A Swiss psychiatrist, Kübler-Ross stepped onto the global stage in 1969 with her pioneering work studying and counseling terminally ill cancer patients. Through her work she taught the world about the emotions and mental processes associated with death. Her work was inspired by her experiences as a teenager assisting in first-aid stations in Poland and Russia after World War II with survivors of Nazi concentration camps. From the carnage of the war and the concentration camps, Kübler-Ross realized that humankind had a great need to understand and cope with the problems of death and dying. She soon learned that the fear of death is universal, and that the death and dying process brings with it an abundance of emotional baggage. Not only grief, but guilt, shame, fear, and anger are all associated with the death experience.

Relocating to the United States after earning her degree in psychiatry, she was asked to join a group of physicians

FIGURE 5.7   Elisabeth Kübler-Ross.

conducting a research seminar involving interviews and counseling sessions with terminally ill cancer patients. In the course of this work, she noted similarities in the patterns of emotional behaviors among the patients, which led her to outline a process of mental preparation for death applicable to everyone. In her most acclaimed book, *On Death and Dying*, Kübler-Ross refers to these stages as the psychological **stages of grieving**. Although these stages were observed among dying cancer patients, the same stages apply to any type of loss, including the death of unmet expectations. The following is a description of the five stages with examples she observed among her cancer patients. Also included are examples of how each stage applies to the death of an unmet expectation—a more common stressor—the discovery that one's wallet has been stolen.

> **Stages of grieving:** A process outlined by Elisabeth Kübler-Ross regarding the mental preparation for death, including denial, anger, bargaining, depression, and acceptance.

1. *Denial:* The refusal to accept the truth of a situation—a rejection of the truth. Kübler-Ross observed denial in her patients who, upon learning of their diagnosis, were often heard to exclaim, "I don't have cancer. This isn't happening to me.

It cannot happen to me. I'm too young to die. I won't let it happen." Denial is also described as shock. In the case of a stolen wallet, the comparable reaction would be observed, "My wallet must be at home. I couldn't have misplaced it. Perhaps it's in my other pants (purse)."

2. *Anger:* The anger stage is a fit of rage that may include yelling, pounding, crying, and/or deep frustration manifested in a physical and emotional way. In this stage, anger is the physical expression of hostile feelings. Kübler-Ross typically saw anger directed not only at clinicians and family members but also toward a "higher power," even in those people who claimed not to believe in one. Similarly, a stolen wallet can provoke an outward expression of anger, where everyone becomes a suspect in its disappearance.

3. *Bargaining:* Kübler-Ross described this phase as a very brief but important one. Bargaining is an agreement between the conscious mind and the soul involving an exchange of offerings—primarily, a negotiation for more time to live. With cancer patients it may be expressed as, "If you let me live, I'll never smoke again." In the case of the stolen wallet, the negotiations would be something along the lines of, "Go ahead and take the money—but please don't use my credit cards."

4. *Depression:* Kübler-Ross divides the depression stage into two categories: reactive depression, when a patient grieves for a specific anatomical loss resulting from surgery (as with breast or bone cancer), and preparatory loss, feelings of impending losses related to the cancer, including personal freedom, time, family, and perhaps one's own life. Preparatory-loss depression is best described as a quiet or passive mood of uneasiness while feeling overwhelmed with thoughts and responsibilities at the same time. With depression there is very little, if any, perceived hope. In the case of the wallet, not only is there depression over the missing article, but also a feeling of being overwhelmed by having to arrange the replacement of its contents.

5. *Acceptance:* If and when a person has moved through the previous stages of the grieving process, then and only then can he or she arrive at the final stage, acceptance. Acceptance is an approval of existing conditions, a receptivity to things that cannot be changed. Acceptance is *not* giving in or giving up. It is *not* a surrender to the circumstance. Rather, it

is acknowledgment of the particular situation in which you find yourself. Acceptance allows you to move on with your life. With acceptance comes hope. For those cancer patients who arrive at this stage, their frame of mind can be described as, "Okay. So this is the way it is. I'm going to keep living my life as best I can. I'm going to put up a good fight." In the case of the stolen wallet, "So I lost my wallet. I'll get a new license, credit cards, ATM card, and a new wallet." In the acceptance stage there is no trace of anger or pity. Kübler-Ross indicates that this stage is very difficult to arrive at; in fact, many people never reach this stage in the course of their grieving. A significant component of the stage of acceptance is **adaptation**—consciously adapting to the new situation with thoughts and actions.

Kübler-Ross states that these stages are experienced by virtually every terminally ill patient. By no coincidence, these same stages are observed, to a greater or lesser degree, among people who go through other losses, including relationships (the end of a romantic relationship, divorce, or separation), identity (unemployment, retirement, new location, or new job), possessions (a lost/stolen wallet, damaged car, or fire-damaged house), as well as less tangible items (a failed exam, poor athletic performance). Actually, it could be the loss of anything significant. This mental-preparation-for-death process happens hundreds of times in one's lifetime. As Kübler-Ross explains, the stress associated with the mental stages is a catalyst to provide a greater mental awareness of several or all unresolved emotions. As an individual passes from one stage to the next, he or she enters a deeper level of mental awareness. In later years, Kübler-Ross amended her original theory to suggest that, in some cases, one of the first four stages may be skipped. She has devoted her whole life to assisting people so that they may complete the final stage peacefully.

To paraphrase Kübler-Ross, acceptance is your ability to acknowledge the emotional chains that bind you to your primary cause of stress, and acceptance allows you to free yourself from their bondage. Complete, unconditional acceptance, a full resolution without any resentment, animosity, or pity associated with these emotional potholes,

> **Adaptation:** A behavior and attitude considered the epitome of the acceptance stage of grieving, where a person adapts to the new situation and no longer views him- or herself as a victim.

leads to what Kübler-Ross calls essential inner peace. The process of acceptance, resolving pent-up feelings or frustrations, is not an easy one. In fact, it can be quite emotionally painful. In her work, she observed some people with a stubborn streak who would rather leave matters unresolved than face the fear of this process. Others were unsure how best to resolve these emotions and eventually became hostage to them.

Typically, individuals repress or rationalize painful feelings that are perceived to be a threat to their inner self. As Kübler-Ross notes, the defense mechanisms of the ego serve, function, and manipulate well on a short-term basis but cause utter chaos in the long run. Through repression and rationalization, unresolved feelings, like phases of the moon, come full circle and ultimately resurface to haunt the conscious mind. To leave these emotional debts unresolved is what she refers to as the unfinished business of the soul. Kübler-Ross suggests that the process of addressing and completing unresolved feelings should not be delayed; rather, it should take top priority on a daily basis. The best way to initiate this resolution process, she says, is to grant yourself some quality "alone-time" to learn to recognize unresolved feelings between yourself and others, and perhaps most importantly within yourself, and then attempt to resolve them. There may be several strategies for resolution, including accepting a situation that is unchangeable and continuing to live with this fact. In any case, without a doubt, unconditional acceptance promotes inner peace.

Viktor Frankl: A Search for Life's Meaning

Stressors come in all shapes and sizes. Little problems, like small potholes on a dirt road, are easily avoided, but major stressors obstruct your progress in the journey of life and can stop you dead in your tracks. Whatever the events in your life you perceive as stressful, few, if any, can match the intensity of the suffering experienced by psychiatrist Viktor Frankl (**FIG. 5.8**) as a Nazi concentration camp prisoner and survivor. Frankl's experiences prior to and during his 3 years in Auschwitz led him to the development of a form of psychoanalysis he refers to as **logotherapy**, an existential analysis simply defined as a search for the meaning of life.

> **Logotherapy:** A term coined by psychiatrist Viktor Frankl describing the search for meaning in one's life.

FIGURE 5.8   Viktor Frankl.

In his most acclaimed book, *Man's Search for Meaning*, Frankl illustrates the depth of human suffering in the Nazi concentration camps. From this basis of personal experience and observation, he augmented his understanding of the human quest for the meaning of existence. Having been stripped of every possible possession including clothes, jewelry, and even hair, camp prisoners were left with what Frankl calls the last human freedom: "the ability to choose one's attitude in a given set of circumstances." Of the prisoners who were fortunate enough to avoid the gas chambers and crematoriums, Frankl noted that it was largely the ability to choose one's attitude that ultimately distinguished those who lived from those who later perished from disease and illness in the concentration camps. Those who found and held onto a reason to live were able to survive the ghastly conditions, while those who saw no substantial meaning for living became physically and spiritually weak and succumbed to death.

Many of Frankl's psychological theories center on the concept of human pain and the meaning of suffering. Unequivocally, suffering is a direct consequence of profound stress. One does not have to experience the horrors of Auschwitz to feel suffering. Any experience that promotes feelings of emotional trauma, according to Frankl, contains the essence of a purposeful meaning.

The death of a child, severe illness, major debt, retirement, a change of jobs—these are all candidates for inducing personal suffering. Frankl was convinced that suffering is as much a part of life as happiness and love, and that like love, suffering has a purpose in the larger scheme of things. From his own observations, Frankl realized that suffering is a universal experience. Therefore, he reasoned, it must have some significant value to the advancement of one's human potential or spiritual evolution. In *Man's Search for Meaning* he writes, "If there's meaning in life then there must be meaning in suffering. Suffering is an ineradicable part of life, and death. Without suffering and death, human life would not be complete." Frankl did not advocate avoiding suffering, but rather suggested that the cause of emotional pain be examined to try to make some rational sense out of it—to find a meaningful purpose in suffering. This search for meaning is not a defense mechanism, a rationalization of pain, but the search for a truthful understanding. In fact, writes Frankl, meaning is not a fabrication of the mind, but a truth uncovered by the soul.

A tool to augment the search for meaning, as defined by Frankl, is **tragic optimism**. Tragic optimism he defined as the ability to turn suffering into a meaningful experience, and to learn from this experience with a positive perspective on life's events. The history of humanity is filled with inspiring examples of people who completed their grieving by finding meaning in their stressful suffering. One such person was Candy Lightner, who after losing her young daughter to the recklessness of a drunk driver, assembled her creative energies and formed the national organization Mothers Against Drunk Driving (MADD). Another example is Bethany Hamilton, who in 2003 overcame the emotional anguish of losing her left arm in a shark attack while surfing. She continues to compete and win professional surf competitions. In fact, many contemporary heroes and role models are individuals who overcame obstacles of biblical proportions, and soon became the epitome of human potential in action for others to emulate.

Finding meaning in a painful experience is not easy. Frankl notes that many people in contemporary society look upon victimization as more prestigious than personal achievement. Quite often people tend to wallow in self-pity beyond the point where it serves any beneficial purpose. So how does one begin a quest for the meaning of one's own life? Frankl suggests that the best time for this to occur is when you feel mental anguish or emotional suffering of any kind. When these conditions surface, you must journey into the garden of your soul and examine your conscious mind. A mental examination quite often leads to questioning your ideals and values, and testing your will to fulfill or abandon them. Frankl notes that the will to find meaning in most people is *supported* by something or someone, not based on faith alone. It is also important to note that each person must find his or her own unique meaning, not a universal one, and that one cannot be borrowed or adopted from others. In fact, as people age there will be many different meanings to be searched for and recognized in their lifetimes. And suffering awaits in between the periods of life's meanings.

Frankl was convinced that, to an extent, stress plays an important role in mental health. Like Freud and Jung, Frankl believed that internal tension is inevitable among humans, but he held that mental health is dependent on the tension that exists between past accomplishments and future endeavors. A sense of boredom is what he called an existential vacuum, a state of tension where the current meaning to life is as yet undiscovered. In his experience, this reason outnumbered all other reasons combined for bringing people to psychotherapy and counseling. Frankl coined the term **noo-dynamics** to describe a process to resolve this existential vacuum by using the tension of boredom to search for life's meaning. Whereas Freud placed emphasis on childhood experiences, Frankl was concerned with the present and future as if to say, "So, what happened, happened. What are you going to do with your life now? Where are you headed from here? What new contribution can you make to humanity?" In logotherapy, Frankl advocates the concept of goal-setting to aid in the search for personal meaning in one's life. Setting and accomplishing goals involve creativity, to visualize where you are going, and stamina, the energy to get you there. The fundamental purpose of personal goals, Frankl states, is to enhance one's human potential. Furthermore, pleasure should be a consequence of meaning, not a purpose in and of itself. Frankl also suggests that a quest for true meaning has a spiritual quality to it. (*Logos* in Greek translates not only as "meaning" but also as "spirit.") In this case, however, the term *spirituality*

> **Tragic optimism:** A term coined by psychiatrist Viktor Frankl to explain the mindset of someone who can find value and meaning in the worst situation.
>
> **Noo-dynamics:** A term coined by Viktor Frankl describing a state of tension, a spiritual dynamic, that motivates one to find meaning in life. The absence of noo-dynamics is an existential vacuum.

has less of a formal religious connotation; rather, it refers to the human dimension of inner balance between faith in self-reliance and individual will. Spiritual health is imperative in the search for one's own meaning in life and in dealing with the suffering brought about by various life experiences, regardless of their cause. In his autobiography, Frankl spoke of those who, in the midst of a crisis, lost their belief in the future, in themselves, and their spiritual hold. Without spiritual health they were subject to mental and physical deterioration and eventual premature death.

Although Frankl's theories may seem rather abstract, the fundamental messages are clear: (1) one must continually search from within for life's meaning to achieve inner peace, and (2) in the absence of everything but one's body, mind, and soul, one has the ability to choose one's attitudes; in so doing one either perpetuates or resolves each circumstance. He writes, "We had to learn from ourselves and we had to teach despairing men that it did not matter what we expected from life, but rather what life expected from us."

Wayne Dyer: Guilt and Worry

Relaxation is said to be achieved when the present moment is fully experienced and appreciated; this belief has been passed down for more than 2,000 years by wise people of all cultures (**FIG. 5.9**). Yet for many people, the present moment is a scary and insecure place to be. Feelings of discomfort, boredom, and inadequacy arise. In the earliest years, all a child knows is the present moment. But as the child matures into adulthood, the ability to enjoy the present moment seems to become ever more elusive. Instead, the mind becomes willingly preoccupied (often paralyzed) with either past or future events. The fact that many people spend their conscious thought processes in either the past or the future has not gone unnoticed. Psychotherapist Wayne Dyer (**FIG. 5.10**) observed this phenomenon in virtually all his clients. His most present works integrate the mind and the soul, but his earliest work is as solid today as it was decades ago.

In his best-selling book *Your Erroneous Zones*, Dyer states that to be occupied with the past or future can diminish, even extinguish, our appreciation of the present moment, thus robbing us of the ability to relax and be at peace with ourselves. The zones Dyer describes highlight certain stress-prone emotional responses—those unhealthy defensive processes learned very early in life as cognitive survival skills. In his theory of unproductive emotions and their related behaviors, Dyer states that one of two

FIGURE 5.9   Learning to live in the present moment.

FIGURE 5.10   Wayne Dyer.

emotions, guilt or worry, is associated with virtually every stressor perceived by people in America. Guilt is an expression of self-anger; worry, a manifestation of fear. When these emotional responses are triggered, they tend to immobilize rational thought processes, resulting in clouded thinking, delayed reactions, and poor decision making. Dyer goes as far as to say that guilt and worry are in fact the most ineffective coping techniques for stress management because they perpetuate the avoidance of stress-related issues needing resolution.

The Sin of Guilt

Dyer defines guilt as the conscious preoccupation with undesirable past thoughts and behaviors. Guilt feelings surface in our internal but conscious dialogue in the form of "should haves." Guilt feelings can easily be produced by thinking about something you said or did just as easily as by something you didn't say or do but feel you should have. Dyer is of the opinion that guilt contains a perplexing element of cultural respect, like that recorded by those who fled religious persecution in Europe to become this nation's earliest settlers. Three hundred years later, guilt, he observes, is still a socially acceptable way to express the responsibility of caring. Yet true, productive caring, Dyer believes, should never be confused with this immobilizing emotion. When guilt is the overriding emotion, all thoughts and behaviors are influenced by it. Guilt is so powerful an emotion that it can have a paralyzing effect on all other thoughts and feelings and prevent a positive behavior or action from taking place. According to Dyer, guilt experienced to any extent can result in mild to severe depression. He states that, for the most part, guilt is fruitless because no amount of it can change the past. Although guilt appears to be a "natural" human emotion, Dyer is convinced that it serves no functional purpose beyond fostering recognition of important lessons to be learned and issues to be resolved. If and when these lessons are learned, guilt disappears.

From observations he made counseling his clients, Dyer created a dichotomy of guilt. **Leftover guilt** he describes as remnant thought patterns originating in early childhood, primarily through parental disciplinary tactics as, for example, shame imposed by an authority figure for naughty or unapproved behaviors. What worked as an inspirational force during childhood (approval seeking to avoid guilt), however, produces significant stress when carried into adulthood, yet the same unhealthy behaviors are usually continued. By contrast, **self-imposed guilt** is described as the guilt placed on oneself when an adult

FIGURE 5.11   Freud's analysis of guilt.

moral or ethical behavior, based on the constructs of one's personal value system, has been violated. Examples are missing church on Sunday or saying yes to something because it seemed like the right thing to say, then later regretting having agreed to it because you were never committed to it. Dyer notes that guilt is also used as a conventional tool for manipulating other people's thoughts, feelings, and actions, a behavior that inappropriately transfers stress to others. He advocates avoiding using guilt and shame on others, and most important, avoiding using it on yourself.

The Art of Worrying

While guilt, like Dickens's Ghost of Christmas Past, is associated with keeping the mind hostage with thoughts and behaviors from the past, worry infiltrates the mind to immobilize thought processes regarding events yet to

---

Leftover guilt: A term coined by psychologist Wayne Dyer explaining the ill effects of unresolved guilt left over from an early childhood experience.

Self-imposed guilt: A term coined by psychologist Wayne Dyer to describe the guilt one places on oneself when a personal value has been compromised or violated.

come. Dyer defines worry as the immobilization of thinking in the present moment as a result of preoccupation with things that may, or may not, occur in the future. Like guilt, Dyer notes that worry is looked on by many as an act of compassion. In reality, it too immobilizes cognition, clouds rational thought processes, and cultivates stress. The practice of worrying, like guilt, can lead to severe depression. Corrie ten Boom, a Dutch Christian who helped Jews escape from the Nazis during the Holocaust, said that "Worry does not empty tomorrow of its sorrow, it empties today of its strength." The bottom line is that worry is a misuse of your imagination.

Dyer believes it is essential for everyone to distinguish the difference between worrying about the future and planning for the future. Worrying paralyzes and overrides present-moment thought processes and dilutes self-control. Then the imagination goes wild, creating a series of worst-case scenarios, all of which can seem very real and threatening. Dyer is convinced that worrying tends to produce a rebound effect, first resulting in a less effective means to deal with a given situation, which then produces more worry. Ironically, Dyer notes that people typically worry about matters over which they have no control. In addition, many seemingly insurmountable worries are later regarded as quite trivial (the making-a-mountain-out-of-a-molehill syndrome). Unfortunately, the knowledge of hindsight is ignored when worrying thoughts surface again. Unlike the worrying process, the constructive thought process of planning contributes to a more effective and productive future, minimizing potential stressors. Planning for the future, for example, by setting goals, making a strategy, and evaluating progress, provides a sense of empowerment.

To illustrate this difference, consider a person who worries about finding a job after graduation: He sits and stews about not finding a job and the hazards of being unemployed. Conversely, planning involves drafting a résumé, making phone calls, writing cover letters, networking, following up with contacts, and making appointments. Although planning a strategy of options for future events does not guarantee a "smooth ride," it does provide a base of security, whereas worrying leaves one in the driver's seat with no keys, gas, or tires.

> **Love:** The emotion studied and advocated by Leo Buscaglia as being the cornerstone to self-esteem and ultimately altruism.

As mentioned earlier, Dyer suggests that American culture breeds the emotion of worry by equating it with caring and love. He discovered that many of his clients emphatically prove their love by demonstrating the worry process. Several other psychotherapists note a similarity between this characteristic and the stress-prone codependent personality.

What the emotions of guilt and worry share is the *distraction* of one's present mental processes. Both guilt and worry are what Dyer calls negative or nonproductive emotional states of cognition, and he confirms that these emotions are a waste of energy. As a therapist, Dyer counsels that the first step to removing these two erroneous zones is the awareness that they are used as ineffective coping techniques. When the practice of employing guilt or worry enters your awareness as a result of perceived stress, Dyer suggests removing guilt or worry by reframing your perception either to find the lessons to be learned from the past or to start planning strategically for future events that are occupying your attention. Like other leading psychologists, Dyer advocates acceptance of past events as an important stress-management strategy to enable you to move on with your life. Dyer is in the company of several prominent psychologists and scholars who concur with his theories of guilt and worry, two emotions responsible for more visits to psychologists' offices than all others combined.

Since his first book, *Your Erroneous Zones*, Dyer has written several other best-selling books that focus on the theme of moving from a motivation of fear to a motivation of love. In his book *Your Sacred Self*, Dyer continues the theme of erroneous zones, with guilt and worry both manifestations of fear. Ultimately, Dyer says, the ego is the cause of these two "erroneous zones," and the sooner the ego is tamed, the sooner we move to a place of love.

■ Leo Buscaglia: The Lessons of Self-Love

Of all the psychological theories developed over the past century, most, if not all, have been influenced by anxiety as the primary force of human motivation. This narrow focus has eclipsed several equally motivating emotions, particularly love. Until the start of the twenty-first century, science had remained reticent on this subject. To paraphrase the words of psychologist Abraham Maslow, "It's amazing how little time the empirical sciences have to offer on the subject of love." One might assume that the concept of **love** has been perceived to be either unimportant or too complex an emotion to adequately define and study. Both assumptions hold elements of truth. In the past, love was left to poets, philosophers, actors, and songwriters to be explored, explained, and elaborated; psychology maintained a hands-off approach. Although this approach continues today, love as a viable motivational force and healing tool has recently moved out of the anthologies of poetry and Hollywood cinema and into classrooms, corporate boardrooms, and operating rooms. Upon taking a closer look at the theory and application of this enigmatic emotion, love is now recognized as a powerful inner resource much too important to ignore (Johnson, 2003). In simple terms, love is the epitome of eustress; its absence, distress. In recognition of the importance of love and health, the Institute for Research on Unlimited Love was created in 2000 as a joint collaboration between the Fetzer Institute and Sir John Templeton so that the merits of love, expressed as altruism, could be studied.

One man to bring the theoretical concept of love into the respectable forum of academia was Dr. Leo Buscaglia (**FIG. 5.12**). Buscaglia developed an experimental undergraduate course at the University of Southern California in the late 1960s called the "love class." Through his

FIGURE 5.12   Leo Buscaglia.

investigations, he brought forth some simple yet profound concepts of this elusive emotion, with many implications for both eustress and distress. Furthermore, he gave credibility to a component of emotional well-being that had been long overlooked.

Buscaglia is quick to admit that love is very difficult to define. First and foremost, he states, "Love is a response to a learned group of stimuli and behaviors." An infant learns to love primarily through contact with his or her parents in the home environment. Love—specifically, self-love—is not innate, but taught. Yet, unlike many other subjects, it is taught neither in school nor in church. Buscaglia notes that as children we are taught to control our emotions (e.g., don't cry, stop laughing, wipe that smile off your face). As a result, the ability to express our emotions fully is denied, including the emotion of love. The emotional pain of rejection, or denied love, only compounds this inability. That is, ego defenses strengthen to prevent or minimize recurrences. As a child matures to adulthood, love often diminishes to the point of dormancy. Sadly enough, Buscaglia indicates, most of us never really learn to love at all. This, he believes, can have dangerous repercussions later in the growth process, when one forms lifelong relationships. And this may be the reason, he explains, why the divorce rate is hovering around 50 percent.

One reason why love is so hard to define, Buscaglia admits, is that so many people equate it with related concepts: sex, romance, attraction, needs, security, and attention. Love is also perceived to comprise a wide spectrum of feelings, including ecstasy, joy, irrationality, dissatisfaction, jealousy, and pain. In Buscaglia's opinion, however, there may be many degrees of love, from joy to grace, but there is only one love, that which leads to the positive growth process of self-discovery. Love is love, he proclaims. In his best-seller, *Love*, he writes, "for love and the self are one, and the discovery of either is the realization of both." Love brings with it change, and change requires adaptation, which like other types of stress can produce either pleasure or pain. Despite fairy-tale endings in which love conquers all with relative ease, Buscaglia repeatedly states that love takes much work, continuous work. There is much responsibility with love. Left unattended and unnurtured, it will evaporate and disappear. Buscaglia also compares love to knowledge, which you must have before you can teach it. Likewise, you must feel and experience love before you can share it. There are no exceptions.

In Buscaglia's words, "To love others, you must first love yourself," and this is no small feat. As youngsters, we experience some degree of love from our parents, yet self-love is rarely taught and thus remains a foreign concept to many people. In fact, self-love is misrepresented as egotistical selfishness and is strongly discouraged. Humbleness *is* advocated, but often at the risk of sacrificing self-love. The Christian ethic commands that you "love your neighbor as yourself"; however, Buscaglia observes that this equation is rarely balanced. Through his research, Buscaglia has found that most people are deficient in their capacity to love themselves unconditionally, and that they are restrained from expressing self-love by their low self-esteem. Moreover, he cites several deterrents to self-love. The greatest of these are the conditions we place on ourselves for self-acceptance, primarily physical appearance and capabilities—in short, everything that prevents perfection. A recurring pattern of "not completely liking myself because . . ." creates a negative-feedback system that perpetuates a lifetime of unhappiness. This phenomenon is more descriptively referred to as chronic stress, and it is associated with low **self-esteem**.

Buscaglia offers an alternative to this self-defeating attitude. He suggests that you take an honest look at yourself from within. Be prepared to openly accept all that there is to see, for better or worse, and exclude nothing. From this honest look, begin to accept yourself as you really are. This means accepting all those qualities you cannot change (e.g., height, eye color, parents) while pushing the limits of those qualities that allow room for growth (e.g., creativity, humor, intellect, love). Then, take the initiative to enhance those qualities that will help you reach your highest potential. In addition, Buscaglia emphasizes the need for each individual to focus on his or her individuality rather than aiming for conformity by comparing oneself to others. He coined the term the **X-factor** to symbolize a prized quality that makes each person special and unique. People need to focus on this quality to move toward unconditional self-acceptance and unconditional self-love.

In Buscaglia's quest for love, he has searched for every color of love's rainbow to comprehend and share his understanding of this often misused, misunderstood, and misacknowledged emotion. His attempts to understand the fundamental concepts of love have taken him to the shores of nearly every continent. Unlike the approach of Western culture, which is geared toward the achievement of happiness through external pleasures, Buscaglia has turned toward the East, adopting a philosophy that supports unconditional self-love. The philosophy of many Eastern cultures is one in which the individual focuses inward to understand him- or herself; the continuous journey toward self-understanding yields inner peace. Inner peace, in turn, creates universal harmony. Harmony, in turn, promotes happiness. And happiness nurtures love. Buscaglia illustrates this concept with the Hindu greeting *namaste*, which literally translated means, "I honor the place in you where, if you are at peace with yourself, and I am at peace with myself, then there is only one of us."

Buscaglia argues that for love to be an inner resource it cannot lay dormant. It must be acted out and acted on continually. And for love to exist there must be a will or desire to love. The will to love is an attitude of choice. Poets, film directors, and songwriters often make love seem too dynamic, distant, or elusive, sometimes even unattractive. But love of the self begins and grows with positive feelings toward the self, which each person is capable of creating. Buscaglia's message of self-love is directly tied to self-esteem, for we value only those things we love and feel positively about. When we do not love ourselves completely, or place conditions on our self-love, our self-esteem is compromised and thus deflated. And low self-esteem makes us vulnerable to, and almost defenseless against, the perceptions of stress.

From all his research, Buscaglia has developed six hypotheses regarding love as a motivating influence:

1. One cannot give what one does not possess. To give love you must possess love.

2. One cannot teach what one does not understand. To teach love you must comprehend love.

3. One cannot know what one does not study. To study love you must live in love.

4. One cannot appreciate what one does not recognize. To recognize love you must be receptive to love.

5. One cannot admit what one does not yield to. To yield to love you must be vulnerable to love.

6. One cannot live what one does not dedicate oneself to. To dedicate yourself to love you must be forever growing in love.

Self-esteem: The sense of underpinning self-values, self-acceptance, and self-love; thought to be a powerful buffer against perceived threats.

X-factor: A term coined by psychologist Leo Buscaglia to describe that special quality that makes each one of us unique. By focusing on our X-factor and not our faults and foibles, we enhance our self-esteem.

Buscaglia's attempt to validate love as a crucial component of human motivation has been met with both enthusiasm and apathy. His work is accepted by many professionals who implement his concepts in counseling and therapy with their clients, but for the most part, the topic today remains ignored by researchers. Be that as it may, the focus on love in psychology is slowly gaining momentum as the field of psychospirituality begins to unfold.

Abraham Maslow: The Art of Self-Actualization

Perhaps the most optimistic of all psychologists who have made contributions to modern psychology is Dr. Abraham Maslow (FIG. 5.13). While his predecessors and contemporaries studied mentally ill, emotionally disturbed, and maladjusted individuals to form the basis of their theories of human behavior, Maslow chose to study examples of men and women who epitomized the height of human potential, individuals exhibiting the unique combination of creativity, love, self-reliance, confidence, and independence. Despite the atrocities of World War II, Maslow was convinced of the existence of a brighter side of human nature, and he became committed to the development of a theoretical construct to

support this hypothesis of a humanistic approach to psychology. Maslow's faith in humankind led him to believe that by understanding individuals with positive personality characteristics and admirable traits, he could devise a framework to serve as a model for others to follow in their pursuit of self-improvement. Unlike other psychologists, who attempted to describe how personality and behavior are affected by stress, Maslow placed emphasis on personality traits, those reflections of inner resources that seem to help people cope with stress and achieve psychological health. In other words, certain personality traits he observed in this special collection of people combine to act as a buffer in personal confrontations with stress.

Maslow's concept of behavior and personality is referred to as the **theory of motivation** for the nature of the characteristics he studied. This theory suggests that human beings operate on a **hierarchy of needs** that influence behavior. When the needs at one level are met, then needs at higher levels can be addressed in a linear, stair-step approach. In this hierarchy, the more advanced needs will not appear until lower needs have been acknowledged and addressed. In addition, when lower needs, such as hunger, reappear, all higher needs momentarily vanish.

This hierarchy of needs consists of six tiers or levels (similar in many ways to the chakras). Once described in terms of climbing a ladder, it is now usually illustrated as a series of steps (FIG. 5.14). The first tier comprises the most basic physiological needs to ensure survival of the human organism. These include food, sleep, and sex (and, in some cases, the need for drugs or alcohol when chemical dependency is involved). The second tier, safety needs, also contributes to survival and includes those factors that provide security, order, and stability, including clothing, money, and housing. Maslow called these first two tiers lower, or deficit, needs, while the remaining levels of the hierarchy he referred to as growth needs. Affection and strong bonding relationships constitute the third stage, belongingness and love needs. The fourth tier he called personal esteem needs, or the need and

Courtesy of the Robert D. Farber University Archives & Special Collections Department, Brandeis University.

FIGURE 5.13   Abraham Maslow.

Theory of motivation: Maslow's theory associated with personality and behavior, based on his theory of the hierarchy of needs.

Hierarchy of needs: Maslow's concept of a stair-step approach of consciousness (thoughts and behaviors), ranging from physiological needs to self-transcendence.

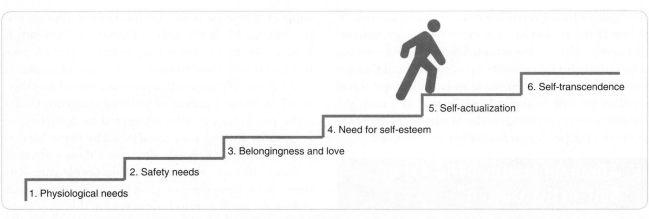

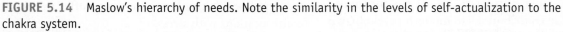

FIGURE 5.14   Maslow's hierarchy of needs. Note the similarity in the levels of self-actualization to the chakra system.

desire to seek or prove self-worth. The fifth level Maslow called the need for **self-actualization**, a stage of personal fulfillment in which ego boundaries and attachments are virtually eliminated, and a feeling of oneness with the universe is experienced, thus allowing one to maximize one's human potential. Ideally, self-actualization is the fulfillment of one's highest human potential and capabilities. Maslow writes in *Religions, Values, and Peak Experiences*, "Self-actualization is the point where one is ultimately at peace with oneself." In later years, Maslow added a sixth stage, which he referred to as the highest stage: **self-transcendence**, where one offers oneself to the service of others or dedicates oneself to a bigger cause for pure altruistic purposes.

According to Maslow, to progress from one level to the next, each area or need must be fulfilled and satisfied. What is important to note is that there is often fluctuation between levels when needs in the lower levels reappear. Even a person who has reached the level of self-actualization does not stay there indefinitely. What makes the level of self-actualization so challenging to attain is the requirement that one lower the walls of the ego and explore the unknown with anticipation, not fear. In fact, Maslow

---

Self-actualization: The fifth level of Maslow's hierarchy of needs where one experiences a sense of personal fulfillment.

Self-transcendence: The sixth and highest stage of Maslow's hierarchy of needs, where one offers oneself altruistically to the service of others. Mother Teresa, Jane Goodall, Jimmy Carter, and Desmond Tutu serve as examples of this stage.

---

states that the need to know (curiosity), and a desire to take risks and actively pursue an understanding of oneself are essential to reaching self-actualization.

In his quest to understand this highest level of needs, self-actualization, Maslow studied the lives of thousands of people, including students, acquaintances, public figures (Albert Einstein, Eleanor Roosevelt, and Albert Schweitzer), and historical figures (Thomas Jefferson, Jane Addams, and Abraham Lincoln), finding a number he considered both healthy and prime examples of quality human beings. From his research, cited in *Motivation and Personality*, Maslow noticed many characteristics common to people he identified as being self-actualized. It is this collection of characteristics that appears to contribute to the resilient nature of people who possess psychological health. To the untrained eye, these people appear to have no stress in their lives, but upon closer scrutiny of the makeup of their personalities, they do in fact have stress but know how to deal with it effectively. According to Maslow, self-actualized people display the following characteristics (or coping techniques):

1. *A highly efficient perception of reality:* Self-actualizers are individuals who are able to maintain a clear and objective perspective on themselves and others. Their perceptions are not clouded or disturbed by egotistical influences; rather, they are unbiased by prejudice and supposition. Maslow found that these people had a strong sense of qualitative judgment.

2. *Acceptance:* People in this class of individuals are aware of not only their strengths, but their weaknesses as well. Like everyone else, they have faults

and imperfections. But they harbor no guilt, animosity, or shame about the failings or shortcomings in themselves or others. These people accept their shortcomings and do not victimize themselves with their less-than-desirable traits. They work to move beyond them.

3. *Naturalness and spontaneity:* Self-actualizers are themselves, and they feel very comfortable with themselves. They display no false facade, nor are they rigid in their mannerisms. They are open, frank, and present natural, unfiltered behavior in most, if not all, situations and circumstances. Most important, they go with the flow and are unthreatened and unfrightened by the unknown. They can think on their feet and react favorably to changes in a spontaneous fashion. They are not easily stressed when plans or circumstances change abruptly.

4. *Problem centering:* People who exhibit the traits of self-actualizers have a strong sense of commitment and dedication to their jobs and other responsibilities. They see themselves as part of the whole, not the whole. When problems arise, these people do not get bogged down in petty personal issues. They confront issues, not people. Because of this strong sense of commitment and purpose in life, self-actualizers work very hard, yet they derive much pleasure from their work. Maslow was once quoted as saying, "If the only tool you have is a hammer, you tend to see every problem as a nail." Self-actualizers have many tools for problem solving.

5. *Solitude and independence:* Self-actualized people can find as much pleasure in being by themselves as in the company of friends, without feeling lonely. They like their moments of privacy and make time for them. Solitude is considered a blessing, often a time to recharge. Satisfaction is derived from within, as opposed to being dependent on others. Alone-time is often a time of reflection and a time to draw on inner strengths. There is a strong element of autonomy and free-spiritness.

6. *A continual freshness of appreciation:* Grasshoppers, falling leaves, the Big Dipper—these people "stop and smell the roses" along the way. Not only do self-actualizers continually find unexpected wonder and awe in the simplest of surroundings, but like children they typically face daily living with freshness and a bigger-than-life attitude. These

people know how to live in the present moment, minimizing feelings of guilt and worry. Rarely do they take anything for granted, and they count their blessings regularly.

7. *Creativity:* Self-actualizers are highly creative individuals who bring imagination, inventiveness, originality, and energy to the thought process. They are able to conceive an idea, visualize it, and then implement it. They are inquisitive and open to new possibilities in their thinking. They are not afraid to fail because they know that failure leads to success. In his book *The Farther Reaches of Human Nature,* Maslow writes, "My feeling is that the concept of creativeness and the concept of the healthy, self-actualized, fully human person seem to be coming closer and closer together, and may perhaps turn out to be the same thing."

8. *Interpersonal relationships:* To be self-actualized does not mean one has hundreds of friends. Rather, the circle of friends is small, but those in this circle are very similar in interests and compatible. Self-actualizers develop closeness to individuals who stimulate them and who contribute to their own growth and human potential. Relationships are selective and based on the ability to inspire rather than influence.

9. *Human kinship:* Self-actualizers appear compelled to assist in social and moral causes, and they are willing to help all levels of humanity. According to Maslow, they take on a brother or sister role toward other people. Above all, these people have a genuinely unselfish desire to help the human race.

10. *A democratic character:* People who display this characteristic find they have something to learn from everyone. They do not come across as condescending or "uppity." These people have the ability to relate to people from all walks of life.

11. *Strong sense of ethical values:* Maslow found that people he considered self-actualized consistently demonstrated knowledge of right and wrong in their own terms. "These people," wrote Maslow, in the book *Motivation and Personality*, "rarely show the confusion and inconsistency, or the conflict that are so common in the average person's ethical dealings."

12. *Resistance to enculturalization:* Self-actualizers are their own people. They are not likely to conform to or follow trends of fashion or politics. Although

they may greatly appreciate aspects of other cultures, they do not adopt them as their own. They are directed more by their own nature rather than by the influences of cultural tides.

13. *A sense of humor:* Self-actualizers possess the ability to appreciate the flood of incongruities and ironies in life as well as laugh at their own foibles and mistakes. A light and happy heart is a common trait; these people do not employ sarcasm or hostility in their repertoire of humor. There is a strong spontaneous and playful nature to their sense of mirth.

14. *Mystical or peak sensations:* A peak experience is considered by Maslow to be the climax of self-actualization. A peak experience is any experience of real excellence, real perfection, or of moving toward a perfect justice or perfect values. He found that people who described a peak experience often analogized it to spiritual orgasm. A **mystical (peak) sensation** is a very spiritual moment when you feel one with the world and very much at peace with yourself.

If all of this sounds like the Wonderful World of Disney, it is, because there are very few people who completely fit this description. Maslow estimated from his research that approximately 1 percent of the human population has ever reached this level with any great frequency. And even then, people who do fulfill this need don't tend to stay at this level for their entire lives. Most of the people he classified as self-actualizers were over 30 years old. Teenagers, he found, were too busy polishing their identity to reach this level in high school, or even college. What Maslow came to realize is that individuals are not born self-actualizers. Instead, they must evolve through a multitude of human experiences, smooth the rough edges, and polish the surface of their personal existence. Those who succeed have developed a remarkable human potential and, in the process, a healthy example for others to follow. Yet, to be sure, people who show the traits of self-actualization don't *always* exhibit these characteristics. Maslow noted that, on occasion, they get angry, bored,

depressed, selfish, and perhaps, on occasion, even rude. They, too, have ups and downs, and must address the other needs of their existence as well. Overall, though, it is their desire to be all they can be that puts them in this select group of individuals. Self-actualizers are not angels, messiahs, or prophets. They have imperfections and flaws like the rest of Earth's inhabitants. But unlike other people, they don't dwell on them. Basically, self-actualizers are people with a strong positive outlook on themselves and life in general. They hold a tremendous amount of faith in themselves and their work. They live life with a passion, not a grudge. They know themselves inside and out, and without a doubt, they are their own best friends.

It is interesting to note that Maslow often talked about the relationship between emotional states and disease. In a presentation to a group of people at the Esalen retreat center in California, he spoke of the concept of **meta-disease**, where disease and illness are the results of unresolved emotional states of consciousness.

The exciting aspect of Maslow's theory of self-actualization is that we all have this potential. We all have the ability to access our inner resources, and we are all capable of becoming self-actualized. Unfortunately, Maslow states, we limit our capabilities, and these limits stifle our evolution to self-actualization. We place barriers (defense mechanisms) around ourselves for emotional protection. But the barriers around emotional security often cause us to stagnate and eventually inhibit the growth of this remarkable human potential. Self-actualizers have learned to collapse the barriers, lower the walls of the ego, and welcome the opportunity for growth. In a society where stress is becoming more and more apparent, Maslow's theory is an illuminating torch in the field of psychology, so much so that several psychologists have taken his lead and advocated his "hardy" characteristics as being among those conferring the ability to resist the effects of stress.

■ Martin Seligman: Optimism and the Art of Being Happy

For the past several decades, the field of psychology has been greatly influenced (some say co-opted) by the pharmaceutical industry, with a proliferation of medications for depression, anxiety, bipolar disorder, and so on. At the same time, however, several people championed a different perspective of psychology. In the wake of Maslow's theory of self-actualization and human potentials, comes

---

Mystical (peak) sensation: A euphoric experience during which one feels a divine or spiritual connection with all life.

Meta-disease: A concept by Maslow that depicts origins of physical disease as being based in unresolved emotional issues.

FIGURE 5.15   Martin Seligman.

Martin Seligman, Ph.D. (**FIG. 5.15**), a renowned psychologist, who, like Maslow, opted to look at the brighter side of human potential rather than its darker side. Seligman first gained notoriety for his work on the topic of learned helplessness and the traits associated with the helpless-hopeless personality. It was this work that created the platform for his landmark theories of **positive psychology** and launched two best-selling books, *Learned Optimism* and *Authentic Happiness*. Seligman was so well respected by his colleagues for his work that he was elected president of the American Psychological Association (APA) by the widest margin in its history. It was in this position as president of the APA where he began to shift the focus of the field of psychology to include positive aspects of the human psyche. In doing so, many colleges across the country now offer courses and degree programs in this specialty.

Seligman writes in his book *Authentic Happiness*, "For the last half century, psychology has been consumed with a single topic only—mental illness." He explains further that psychosis and neurosis are rooted in rotten-to-the-core religious dogma and that over the years the field of psychology, so greatly influenced by pharmacology, became derailed in its efforts to nurture people's highest potential. By focusing on the negative aspects of human psychology, little if any limelight has been placed on those aspects that make life worth living. In an effort to move beyond a theory of happiness to a documented science that supports this theory, or what Aristotle called the "Good Life," Seligman set out to prove that positive thoughts and emotions are an inherent part of the human condition and a birthright for everyone. Moreover, it is these traits we need to cultivate, nurture, and enhance during times of stress.

According to Seligman, the field of positive psychology is based on three aspects: (1) the study of positive emotions (e.g., happiness, joy, trust, gratitude, forgiveness); (2) positive personality traits (what Seligman calls strengths and virtues); and (3) the study of positive institutions (e.g., democracy, strong families, free inquiry). Seligman believes that the time has finally arrived for a science and paradigm that seeks to understand positive emotions, build strength and nurture the virtues for optimal living, and provide a workable structure to help people achieve a balanced life. Positive psychology reveals the pathway to live in what he calls "the upper reaches of your set-point of happiness." The events of September 11, 2001, only reinforced his belief that the suffering during troubled times does not trump the understanding and building of happiness. In the preface to his book *Authentic Happiness*, Seligman shares what Hans Selye discovered in the last decade of his life: "Experiences that induce positive emotion cause negative emotions to dissipate rapidly."

One concept that Seligman expounds upon is the "happiness thermostat," an abstract emotional control made tangible through real thoughts, perceptions, memories, and personal experiences. This thermostat is one that can be programmed through our thoughts and intentions. It also can be programmed through our inherent strengths and virtues, which include wisdom and knowledge, courage, love and humanity, justice, temperance, and spirituality and transcendence.

As president of the APA, and well beyond his term in this position, Seligman has devoted much time to shifting the paradigm of Western psychology from a disease-based model to a more holistic model that includes the

Positive psychology: A field of modern psychology that focuses on three aspects: (1) positive emotions, (2) positive personality traits, and (3) positive institutions.

Courtesy of Martin Seligman.

prevention of mental illness and a greater understanding and application of authentic happiness. Seligman's talk on positive psychology isn't just fluff. He backs up his words with research, whether it's the landmark happiness and longevity study on 180 Catholic nuns, or countless research studies on optimism. His work has also inspired others (Emmons, 2007) to explore the topic of gratitude as a pathway toward authentic happiness. Suggesting that his happiness theory has fallen short of positive psychology's potential, Seligman has revised his theory to include five measurable constructs that he describes in his new book, *Flourish*: positive emotions, engagement, relationships, a purposeful life meaning, and achievements/accomplishments. Augmenting the base of the human potential movement, Seligman now dedicates his life work to teaching others how to amplify their strengths and virtues; human assets in times of strife pay an immeasurable dividend, allowing people to enjoy the good times even more. In the words of Benjamin Franklin, whom Seligman quotes often: "The constitution only gives you the right to pursue happiness. Ultimately, you have to catch it yourself."

◼ A Tibetan Perspective of Mind and Stress

Long before Freud coined the terms *ego* and *id*, millennia before Jung realized the importance of synchronicity, and eons before anyone ever dreamed of drugs like Prozac and Ritalin, the concept of mind (and the stress associated with it) was examined by a young man who tried to understand the nature of human existence, particularly human suffering. Today that man is referred to as the Buddha (the enlightened one), and his introspection of the human mind is studied extensively throughout the world. It is believed that the philosophy of Buddhism arrived in Tibet more than one thousand years ago. When Tibet was invaded by China in 1959, however, not only did its citizens flee to all corners of the world, but they took with them the ancient wisdom of inner peace they

> **Desires:** In the Buddhist perspective of stress, desires are conditions and expectations that are associated with goals. Desires with attachments cause stress.
>
> **Self, the (two versions, Tibetan psychology):** The *Self* is the higher self or the true self; the *self* is identified as the false self or the ego-driven self.

had practiced for hundreds of years and have now begun to share it with the world.

In the past decade, many Tibetan lamas, including the Dalai Lama, have spoken and written extensively on the topic of stress as viewed through the perspective of the mind. Based on the concept of the four noble truths, suffering (stress) is believed to be a consequence of **desires** with strong attachments. In the words of the Dalai Lama, "I think there are two kinds of desire. Certain desires are positive, a desire for happiness. It's absolutely right. The desire for peace. The desire for a more harmonious world, a friendlier world. But at some point, desires can become unreasonable." Expectations, conditions, and fears associated with desires become negative, as a result of the ploys of the ego. Initially, these teachers didn't make reference to the ego. Instead, this concept was referred to as the **self** (lowercase). Over the years, however, Western vernacular has been adopted to share this message in a context that can be more easily understood.

In the acclaimed book *The Art of Happiness*, the Dalai Lama writes, "Hatred, jealousy, anger, and so on are harmful. We consider them negative states of mind because they destroy our mental happiness."

Sakyong Mipham is a Tibetan lama who was raised in India and educated in the United States. In his book *Turning the Mind into an Ally*, Mipham describes the nature and complexities of the mind and the training it takes to find a place of balance (mental stability). Laziness, procrastination, and desire are the strengths of the ego, which Mipham suggests needs taming so that the smaller mind can connect with the higher mind to reach one's full potential. Meditation is advocated as a means to "domesticate the ego" and cultivate the mind's potential.

A tamed mind, detachment from desire, and a connection to the higher mind (higher self) set the stage for healing and inner peace. Tulku Thondup is a Tibetan rimpoche (teacher) who describes stress as the mind's grasping for things that it cannot own, but merely enjoy. With a dualistic perspective, the mind creates judgments and anxiety as one differentiates between oneself and others—good from bad, rich from poor, and so on. As the mind clears itself from the limitations of ownership (attachment) and sees the oneness of everything, however, inner conflict ceases. Happiness begins, and the true nature of the collective mind is revealed.

Some Theoretical Common Ground

From these theories, we can see that the mind creates several strategies to deal with stressful stimuli. Many of these strategies fall in the realm of defenses used to protect the mind from the threat of painful or dangerous events in our lives. Whether these defenses are as specific as those described by Freud and Jung, or more general, like those described by Kübler-Ross, Frankl, Dyer, and Buscaglia, they appear to be a very real, if primitive, part of the coping process to deal with stress. When one looks at these theories, it becomes evident that self-awareness is a critical process to move beyond defensive action and into the realm of resolution (FIG. 5.16). In fact, the premise of psychotherapy is to put the client back on track through the process of self-awareness, as painful as it may be. Moving from a stance of defensive thoughts and actions toward more positive coping styles based on the strength of our inner resources is thought to be the most effective strategy to deal with stress. It is these inner resources that Maslow began to identify with his theory of self-actualization. His theory indicates that we all have the potential to move beyond the primitive defense mechanisms outlined by Freud, which stunt our human potential.

A. Identifying My Stressor(s)
What bothers me?

B. Why Do I Feel Stressed?
If you are having a hard time pinpointing this reason, or have let your stressors go unresolved, then follow this list of questions based on the concepts presented by these theorists.

(1) Am I defensive?—*S. Freud*
(Why does my ego feel threatened? Am I using one or more defense mechanisms to cope?)

(2) Do I lack psychic equilibrium between the conscious and unconscious minds?—*C. Jung*

(3) Do I have unresolved grief?—*E. Kübler-Ross*
(What stage of the grieving process am I in: denial, anger, bargaining, withdrawal, acceptance?)

(4) Is there an absence of purpose or meaning in my life?—*V. Frankl*

(5) Do I feel guilty? Am I worried?—*W. Dyer*

(6) Do I lack self-acceptance and self-love?—*L. Buscaglia* (What is my level of self-esteem?)

(7) Am I lacking in the traits necessary to be self-actualized?—*A. Maslow*

(8) Am I stuck in an emotional rut missing out on the happiness in my life?—*M. Seligman*

(9) Is my stress a result of desires combined with attached expectations?—*Tibetan philosophy*

FIGURE 5.16   Stress awareness chart. Select a problem you are confronted with and ask yourself the questions suggested by each theorist.

SUMMARY

- Many theories attempt to explain the psychological nature of stress or, more specifically, how humans attempt to deal with the problems they face. These theories are based on the many aspects of psychology, including personality, emotional responses, perceptions, and a wide range of human behaviors.

- Freud believed that humans maintain a level of (instinctual) tension that arises from both internal sources (instinctual impulses) and external sources that attack our ego or identity. The ego copes with stress through the use of a host of defense mechanisms, including denial, repression, projection, rationalization, displacement, and humor.

- Jung suggested that there is a certain level of innate tension, psychic tension, which exists because of the language barrier between the conscious and unconscious minds. This tension can be reduced through the process of individuation, a continual soul searching that builds a bridge of understanding between the conscious and unconscious minds. Jung advocated self-awareness through dream analysis because he believed that the unconscious mind works to resolve issues and problems, but the conscious mind, which does not understand the language of symbols presented in dreams, tends to ignore them.

- Stress can also be aroused through the death of unmet expectations, which produces a series of mental processes described by Kübler-Ross. These are denial, anger, bargaining, depression, and acceptance. Resolution of emotional baggage leads one to the final stage, acceptance, which in turn enhances inner peace.

- Viktor Frankl's logotherapy was founded on the belief that for life to be complete there must be suffering, but that there must also be a search for the meaning of the suffering to resolve the issues of emotional stress.

- Stressors fall into two categories, according to psychologist Wayne Dyer: guilt and worry, which are two emotional states that immobilize the thought processes, distract one from the present moment, and thus make one unable to conquer stress and attain inner peace.

- Self-love is the critical inner resource described by Leo Buscaglia to cope with life's hardships. Self-love is unattainable, however, without unconditional acceptance of who you are (self-acceptance). To share love, you must first possess love.

- People who are able to achieve self-acceptance and self-love are what Abraham Maslow called self-actualized people. They are well centered, balanced, and enjoy an unparalleled appreciation of life, proving self-acceptance and self-love to be sound tools to deal effectively with stress. This chapter listed fourteen characteristics Maslow found to be common among self-actualized people. These characteristics seem to allow them to interpret situations in a nonstressful manner and buffer themselves against undue stress.

- Authentic happiness is not a gift but a birthright for all humans. Increasing one's level of happiness to balance the scale of emotions is not only possible but encouraged in this stress-filled world, according to Martin Seligman.

- Eastern philosophy (Tibetan Buddhism) explains stress as the tension between the self (ego) and the greater mind (higher self), with desired expectations and outcomes pointed to as the specific cause of this tension.

- Common themes among the theories are the concepts of self-awareness and self-acceptance, two inner resources that become the most important coping skills to manage personal stress effectively.

STUDY GUIDE QUESTIONS

1. According to Freud, what does the mind do to defend against stress?

2. According to Jung, what should the mind do to resolve stress?

3. According to Kübler-Ross, what process does the mind use to cope with stress?

4. According to Frankl, what aspect needs to be addressed in coping with stress?

5. According to Dyer, which two aspects perpetuate emotional stress?

6. According to Buscaglia, what is essential to cope with and resolve personal stress?

7. According to Maslow, what inner resources can be used to cope with stress?

8. According to Seligman, what aspect constitutes positive psychology?

9. What can be learned from the Tibetan culture about the mind and stress?

10. What do the views espoused by these theorists have in common?

REFERENCES AND RESOURCES

Baruss, I., and Mossbridge, J. *Transcendent Mind: Rethinking the Science of Consciousness*. American Psychological Association, Washington, D.C., 2017.

Briggs Myers, I. *Gifts Differing*. Consulting Psychologists Press, Palo Alto, CA, Reprint 1995.

Buscaglia, L. *Born for Love: Reflections on Loving*. Fawcett Columbine, New York, 1994.

Buscaglia, L. *Living, Loving, and Learning*. Fawcett Books, New York, 1982.

Buscaglia, L. *Love*. Fawcett Crest, New York, 1996.

Campbell, J. (ed.). *The Portable Jung*. Viking Press, New York, 1976.

Dalai Lama, H. H., and Cutler, H. *The Art of Happiness*. Riverhead Books, New York, 10th ANP ed. 2009.

Dyer, W. *Pulling Your Own Strings*. HarperCollins, New York, Reprint 2001.

Dyer, W. *Wisdom of the Ages*. Harper, New York, 1998.

Dyer, W. *Your Erroneous Zones*. 1st Harper Perennial, New York, 2001.

Dyer, W. *Your Sacred Self Make the Decision to Be Free*. HarperPaperback Books, New York, 2001.

Emmons, R. *Thanks: How the Science of Gratitude Can Make You Happier*. Houghton Mifflin, New York, 2007.

Ewen, R. *An Introduction to Theories of Personality*. Lawrence Erlbaum Associates. Mahwah, NJ, 8th ed., 2010.

Feinstein, D. Subtle Energy, Psychology's Missing Link, *Noetic Sciences Review* 64:18–23, 35, 2003.

Fetzer Institute, Scientific Research on Altruistic Love and Compassionate Love. www.fetzer.org/Programs/programs_altrusic_comp_love.htm. www.unlimitedloveinstitute.org/grant/request_proposal.html.

Frankl, V. *The Doctor and the Soul*. Knopf, New York, 1986.

Frankl, V. *Man's Search for Meaning*, Beacon Press, New York, 2006.

Freud, S. *Jokes and Their Relation to the Unconscious*. Norton, New York, 1960.

Freud, S. *Standard Edition of the Complete Psychological Works of Sigmund Freud*. Hogarth Press, London, 1986.

Gedo, J. The Enduring Scientific Contributions of Sigmund Freud, *Perspectives in Biology and Medicine* 45(2):200–212, 2002.

Hall, C. *A Primer of Freudian Psychology*. Mentor Books, Harper & Row, New York, 1999.

Johnson, S. *Research on Altruism and Love*. Temple Foundation, 2003.

Jung, C. G. *Man and His Symbols*. Anchor Press, New York, 1964.

Jung, C. G. *Memories, Dreams, Reflections*. Vintage Books, New York, 1963.

Jung, C. G. *Modern Man in Search of a Soul*. Harvest Books, New York, 1933.

Jung, C. G. *The Undiscovered Self*. Mentor Books, New York, 1958.

Kübler-Ross, E. Death Does Not Exist. In E. Brown et al., eds. *The Holistic Health Handbook*, And/Or Press, Berkeley, CA, 1981.

Kübler-Ross, E. *Death, the Final Stage of Growth*. Simon & Schuster, New York, 1988.

Kübler-Ross, E. *On Death and Dying*. Touchstone, New York, 1997.

Kübler-Ross, E. *On Life after Death*. Scribner Arts, Berkeley, CA, 2014.

Kübler-Ross, E. Personal communication. Scottsdale, AZ, January 14, 2000.

Kübler-Ross, E. *The Wheel of Life: A Memoir of Living and Dying*. Scribner, New York, 1997.

Kübler-Ross, E., and Kessler, D. *Life Lessons*. Scribner, New York, 2nd ed. 2014.

Maslow, A. H. *The Farther Reaches of Human Nature*. Penguin Books, New York, 1976.

Maslow, A. H. *Motivation and Personality,* 3rd ed. Harper & Row, New York, 1997.

Maslow, A. H. *Religions, Values, and Peak Experiences*. Penguin Books, New York, 1976.

Maslow, A. *Self-Actualization,* Esalen Lecture Series, Big Sur Tapes, Tiburon, CA, 1966 and 1972.

Maslow, A. H. Self-Actualization and Beyond. In J. F. T. Bugental (ed.), *Challenges of Humanistic Psychology*. McGraw-Hill, New York, 1967.

Maslow, A. H. *Toward a Psychology of Being,* 3rd ed. Van Nostrand Reinhold, New York, 1999.

Mipham, S. *Turning the Mind into an Ally*. Riverhead Books, New York, 2003.

Positive Psychology Center. www.ppc.sas.upenn.edu.

Restak, R. *The Brain: The Last Frontier*. Grand Central Press, New York, 2004.

Schultz, D. *Theories of Personality,* 7th ed. Wadsworth, Belmont, CA, 2013.

Scully, M. Victor Frankl at Ninety: An Interview. www .firsthings.com/ftissues/ft9504/scully.html.

Scully, M. Victor Frankl at Ninety: An Interview. *First Things*, April 1995. https://www.firstthings.com/article /1995/04/004-viktor-frankl-at-ninety-an-interview.

Seligman, M. *Authentic Happiness: Using the New Positive Psychology to Realize Your Potential for Lasting Fulfillment*. Free Press, New York, 2002.

Seligman, M. *Flourish: A Visionary New Understanding of Happiness and Well-Being*. Atria Books, New York, 2012.

Seligman, M. *Learned Optimism*. Pocket Books, New York, 2006.

Seligman, M. *Optimism and Positive Psychology*. National Wellness Institute Conference, Stevens Point, WI, 1999.

Seligman, M. *The Optimistic Child*. Mariner Books, New York, 2007.

Seligman, M. *What You Can Change and What You Can't: The Complete Guide to Successful Self-Improvement*. Vintage Books, New York, 2007.

Sperry, R. The Great Cerebral Commissure, *Scientific American* 174:42, 1964.

Thondup, T. *The Healing Power of Mind*. Shambhala Books, Boston, 1996.

Ursin, H., Baade, E., and Levine, S. *Psychobiology of Stress*. Academic Press, London, 1978.

CHAPTER 6

The Stress Emotions: Anger, Fear, and Joy

"As I walked out the door toward the gate that would lead to my freedom, I knew if I didn't leave my bitterness and hatred behind, I'd still be in prison."

—Nelson Mandela

Sandy Hook Elementary School, Virginia Tech, Ft. Hood, the Aurora, Colorado, movie theater, and Columbine High School are more than locations on a map. These places, and several others like them, have become synonymous with episodes of uncontrolled rage, senseless violence, and carnage. Though we may never know the full rationale behind these acts of violence, experts remind us that as stress continues to escalate on the national stage, this renowned list of locations across the country will likely grow to include many others.

Human nature may be slow to change, but the horror of senseless violence is never diminished. Sadly, with memories of the Great Depression and the hardship of two World Wars retreating into the background, there is a cost to forgetting the past. Sociologists have observed that the Western lifestyle has become a little too comfortable for the "Millennials." In this age of abundance, the "Entitlement Generation" has arrived for whom expectations are high, and unmet expectations generate a wellspring of unbridled stress emotions: anger and fear.

Emotional well-being, as defined in the wellness paradigm, is the ability to feel and express the entire range of human emotions and to control them, not be controlled by them. This sounds like a tall order, yet it is not impossible. It takes some unlearning, relearning, and implementation. At an early age, we are socialized to behave in a certain way. We are told to calm down, chill out, never talk back, not cry, and wipe that smile off our face. The implied message that we receive is that it is not socially acceptable to exhibit various emotions. Consequently, as adults we carry a lot of unresolved emotional baggage with us. Many health-related problems are thought to

Courtesy of Sabrina Neu.

FIGURE 6.1 Stressful situations can promote feelings of either anger or fear, or in some cases both.

be directly tied to our inability to recognize and appropriately express our emotions. There are two primary emotions especially associated with the stress response: anger, which produces the urge to fight, and fear, which promotes the urge to run and hide (**FIG. 6.1**). Each of these emotions has many shades and layers, which often overlap each other and allow them to coexist in the same situation. This chapter will look at both anger and fear, the dangers that await those who do not recognize these emotions consciously, the problems associated with mismanaging or being controlled by these emotions, their relationship to depression, and some helpful strategies to gain control of them.

The Anatomy of Anger

As the story goes, Cain killed his brother Abel in a fit of jealous rage. Since this early case of blatant, hostile aggression, the expression of anger has haunted men and women alike as perhaps the most uncomfortable of all human emotions. It is uncomfortable because the feelings are powerfully real, yet at the same time the hazards of expressing them can be very serious. Anger is equally uncomfortable, perhaps, because mixed messages abound

> **Rage reflex:** A concept coined by Darwin that reflects the aggressive (fight) nature of all animals as a means of survival.
>
> **Seville Statement:** A statement drafted in Seville, Spain, endorsing the belief that aggression is neither genetically nor biologically determined in human beings.

as religious dogma and society's ethic advocate turning the other cheek in the face of aggression, while recent voices in the field of psychology advocate the benefits of ventilating it. Only in the past two decades have researchers begun to uncover the importance of this dark and powerful emotion and its potential relationship to coronary heart disease, as well as other serious maladies. And only recently have new behaviors been suggested as effective ways to creatively ventilate anger and thus bring about a clear resolution of frustrations to promote inner peace. This is a good thing because anger has escalated to become a national issue, including the likes of road rage, air rage, phone rage, desk rage, and sports rage.

In its most basic form, anger is a survival emotion common to all animals. Darwin referred to this as the **rage reflex**. He believed that this aggressive nature was essential to the survival of all species. While animals act instinctually to defend and protect themselves, their territory, or their young, humans have engineered the ability to combine conscious thought with the rage reflex to produce a hybrid of anger unparalleled in the animal kingdom. In that sense, human anger is a unique phenomenon. Humans are the only species that can process anger into delayed revenge and behave aggressively for seemingly inexplicable reasons. Freud, in his study of the human psyche, wrote off the rage reflex as an immutable instinct. Although he and his protégés studied acts of human aggression, Freud focused most of his attention on anxiety, an emotional state he believed could be more greatly influenced by psychotherapy. For the better part of a century, caused in large part by Freud's influence, anger was considered to be uncontrollable by conscious thought. Hence, little research was conducted in this area. Even today, in the *Diagnostic and Statistical Manual of Mental Disorders* (DSM-5), the diagnostic bible for psychiatrists and psychologists, there are few diagnoses specifically addressing anger or aggression.

In the last two decades, researchers have uncovered some myths and simple truths about this baffling emotion. One of the first myths to be revealed is that although anger is apparently a universal emotion, aggressive behavior is not instinctual in nature; that is, it is not a part of the genetic makeup of humans. For example, the Semai people of Malaysia are reported to show no aggressive behavior toward one another, rather, they display passive behavioral responses thought to be a result of resolving issues through informal group dream analysis. From this and other research reports the so-called **Seville Statement** was drafted in Seville, Spain, in 1986 by twenty prominent researchers from twelve countries, and endorsed by the American Psychological Association. This document proclaimed that aggression is neither genetically nor biologically determined in humans. A second myth about anger regards a theory presented by Dollard et al. in 1939, which stated that aggression is a direct result of frustration. Contrary to this hypothesis, two cultures in the South Pacific—the Kwoma of Papua New Guinea and the Balinese of Bali—demonstrate withdrawal, avoidance, and fasting, not aggression, in the face of frustration. These findings reveal that aggressive behavior is only one of several possible responses to feelings of frustration.

About thirty years ago, *Psychology Today* published an article on anger, titled "The Hostile Heart," citing that the average person experiences approximately 15 situations each day that provoke an anger response. All of these episodes were found to be based on violations of unmet expectations, such as long lines at the checkout stand, car problems, a game of phone tag, or a rude driver on the way to work. Although data on the number of anger episodes per day have not been measured since, experts suggest that the number is closer to 20 to 25 per day, given the rapid acceleration of the pace of life for members of what some call the "entitlement generation" who complain repeatedly about unmet expectations (Svitil, 2006). When one considers the many emotions related to anger, including rage, hostility, frustration, jealousy, prejudice, resentment, guilt, impatience, and even fear, it becomes clear that this number of anger episodes per day is not high. It was also revealed that the expression of anger is influenced by the source of provocation, with a predominantly passive style toward figures of higher authority, and a more active style with people of equal or lower status.

Perhaps it's no coinsidence that one of the most popular video games today is Angry Birds. Typically, the manifestation of the anger response reveals the dark underside of civilization rather than the height of human achievement. Newspaper headlines and newscast sound bites are repeatedly filled with stories pointing a finger at the dangers of uncontrolled aggression. Yet despite its negative reputation, anger has a place in human interactions. First and foremost, anger is a form of communication. It reveals information about one's values and personal constructs of importance. Like other species of animals, humans communicate territorial boundaries through the expression of anger. But with humans, these territorial boundaries represent the ownership of the ideas, perceptions, values, and beliefs that constitute one's identity or ego, as well as the ownership of material

possessions. In addition, the expression of anger is used to assert authority as well as to strengthen or terminate relationships. Anger also provides an incredible source of energy and physical strength that remains unparalleled when compared to the influences of other emotions. The hormonal and other metabolic processes that occur during feelings of aggression have spared several lives in the face of death, and reportedly even fueled the performance of many athletes to Olympic medals (in which case it is called "controlled aggression").

Jane Middelton-Moz is a nationally recognized therapist and author of the book *Boiling Point*. She explains that anger is a force to be reckoned with in the American culture. Road rage, sky rage (disgruntled airline passengers), and teenagers who shoot teenagers are just the tip of the iceberg of the anger phenomenon. It is her contention that the primary reason for the heightened level of anger is the loss of connection, a result of technology, poor community relations, and the illusion of the American dream.

Raising Cain is an expression to connote making trouble, but it's also the title of a book that explores the emotional life of boys. Authors Kindlon and Thompson suggest that because of social pressures, boys are not encouraged to get in touch with their emotions. Episodes of violence, which typically involve men (and sadly young boys and teenagers, too), are traced back to a series of episodes where boys learn to mask and hide their true feelings. Although boys may transfer their aggression in sports activities, not all boys take up sports. In their research, Kindlon and Thompson have found that a growing number of boys are hurt, sad, afraid, angry, and silent—not because of protective mothers, male programming, or testosterone, but rather because of the emotional miseducation of boys. Like many others, Kindlon and Thompson are advocates of **emotional literacy**, a term used to describe the awareness of emotional well-being: the ability to feel and safely express the entire range of human emotions and to control them, rather than be controlled by them.

Gender Differences

In her landmark book *The Dance of Anger*, Harriet Lerner discusses the gender differences and inequities between male and female anger styles (FIG. 6.2).

> **Emotional literacy:** A term used in reference to one's ability to express oneself in an emotionally healthy way. Someone who routinely goes ballistic would be said to lack emotional literacy.

FIGURE 6.2 Anger knows no gender difference, yet women have been socialized not to display anger because it contradicts the image of femininity.

From her research, Lerner concluded that social mores allow men to express their anger openly and freely in public, and even encourage them to express aggression in some sports (e.g., ice hockey and football). Women, on the other hand, have been denied the same opportunity. The inability of women to express their feelings of anger has fueled much personal frustration and depression over the decades, if not centuries. According to social mores, women are supposed to be pleasant and happy, not angry, aggressive, or violent. When "temperament" is displayed by a woman, it is perceived by men (and some women) to be unfeminine, unladylike, sexually unattractive, and symbolic of evil. As a result of such cultural influences, women are less likely to express their anger. The ramifications can be dangerous to their health. In addition to the more obvious anger-related symptoms (e.g., ulcers, migraines), a study by Greer and Morris (1975) found that breast cancer is related to unresolved anger. Similar findings were cited by Mate (2011). In other surveys and questionnaires designed to study the phenomenon, virtually all women said that they feel uncomfortable, and even guilty and afraid, when anger feelings surface. Lerner also points out that even when men are cursed for their bad behavior with names such as "son of a bitch" or "bastard," it is the female gender that ultimately takes the blame, as these names indicate. Observations made by psychologist Mary Kay Biaggio (1988) indicate that men feel more comfortable with aggressiveness and tend to project their feelings onto the person who provoked them. Women, she noted, are more likely to feel shame, or direct their anger inward, which often manifests itself in physiological symptoms.

Lerner states that the greatest problem for many women is to recognize feelings of anger because these feelings are often ignored, avoided, or suppressed. Until anger can be recognized and validated, she adds, it cannot be expressed correctly.

Is there an advantage to feeling angry? Deborah Cox and colleagues (2003) think so, when one approaches anger consciously rather than irrationally. Cox picked up where Lerner's *The Dance of Anger* ends by starting the Women's Anger Project with a mission to study women's anger. She and her colleagues studied and interviewed more than one thousand women from a broad range of populations to better understand the baggage associated with unresolved anger. The conclusion: Ingrained thoughts and behavior patterns associated with dysfunctional anger must be unlearned and the energies of this emotion must be reharnessed for self-improvement. In their acclaimed book *The Anger Advantage*, Cox, Bruckner, and Stabb write, "When women attempt to get around their anger without fully acknowledging it, they lose a lot of valuable information and experiences that keep them from evolving into their full selves. When we attend to our anger, give it a place of respect in our consciousness, allow it to take shape and become spoken aloud, we increase the odds of our learning from it, growing through it, making important things happen in our lives because of it."

A significant finding by Kessler and McLeod presented in 1984 revealed not only that men and women respond to the same types of stressors differently, but also that the two genders have different stressors. It was observed that women, for example, carry an additional burden of responsibilities—and stress—in their roles as mothers and wives. The Framingham study investigated various aspects of anger in both women and men. Using a specially designed questionnaire, the Framingham Anger Scales Inventory, researchers measured anger-in (anger withheld and internalized), anger-out (the physical expression of anger toward others), anger discussed (confiding to a friend about anger), and anger-related symptoms (physical symptoms possibly brought on by anger episodes). The results were that women scored higher than men in both anger-in and anger-related symptoms.

In a similar study conducted in 1991, Thomas and Donnellan observed that the manifestation of anger-related symptoms in middle-aged women was strongly associated with a high number of daily hassles and a less-than-adequate social support system. Paradoxically, they also reported that, like women who suppress their feelings of hostility, women who habitually expressed their anger did not escape anger-related physical symptoms, specifically breast cancer. Several other empirical studies designed to uncover variations in the expression of anger between men and women show no overt differences, yet there is still a consensus that differences exist as a result of strong cultural influences. Whatever is the case, the topic of inequities in anger expression between men and women is now gaining attention as a major focus with regard to women's health issues. Just how these emotions influence the body's physiological systems and pave the path toward dysfunction is also under clinical investigation.

Physiological Responses

As might be expected, sensory stimuli that are interpreted as aggressive threats produce physiological arousal, or the stress response. Research into the physiology of anger first suggested that it triggered the release of norepinephrine because large amounts were once found in the blood during moments of intense aggression. More recent studies, however, show that norepinephrine in urine and blood samples appears in conjunction with several emotional states, not solely anger. Past attention was also focused on the role of the hypothalamus, which was thought to control emotional responses. But again, recent studies have revealed that the hypothalamus is not solely responsible for the feelings and responses associated with anger; indeed, there are several interactions involved between the hypothalamus and the higher cognitive centers of the brain.

Early studies by Albert Ax in 1953 showed that although most of the physical responses to anger and fear are similar, some are different—specifically, peripheral vasodilation. Anger produces a flushed face—a greater percentage of blood flow to the skin of the face and neck. Fear produces the opposite effect, causing the face to become pale. Studies designed to investigate the relationship between stress and disease—more specifically, emotional response and manifestations of the stress response—found that migraine headaches, ulcers, colitis, arthritis, and hypertension were a few of the ailments significantly associated with anger. But the most startling finding, presented by Friedman (1988) and Rosenman (1985), was that hostility was directly linked to the development of coronary heart disease, making this the most prominent disease-related behavioral trait.

Even though perceptions that arouse sensations of anger may bend the limits of reality, the feelings produced by those perceptions are very real. The current focus of anger research and therapy suggests that anger is within the normal range of human emotions and that feelings of anger should be recognized and validated as legitimate. Along with this validation, however, comes the responsibility to diffuse anger sensations in a healthy fashion. Problems arise when feelings of anger are either suppressed or expressed violently. Anger is considered by many psychologists to be healthy only when expressed or ventilated correctly. Yet it is now documented to be unhealthy, perhaps fatal, when improperly expressed. Herein lies the myth of anger ventilation.

The Myth of Catharsis

In perhaps the most comprehensive review of the subject of anger, social psychologist Carol Tavris described the difference between effective and noneffective catharsis, dispelling yet another myth about anger. To ventilate anger randomly is no longer thought to be therapeutic. The term **catharsis**, used by Freud to mean "purification," is a concept to describe the emptying of emotional reservoirs, such as by crying, laughing, yelling, and, in some cases, exercise. Citing several studies in which subjects were encouraged to ventilate anger as a therapeutic catharsis, Tavris concluded that randomly released feelings of anger and ventilated frustrations did not produce a healthy catharsis. To the contrary, not only did the random release of pent-up emotions not relieve feelings of aggression, but it also validated them, in effect reinforcing anger and causing even greater emotional arousal. In a study by Ebbesen, Duncan, and Konecni (1975), 100 aerospace engineers were interviewed after losing their jobs prior to the end of their 3-year contract. Their responses were compared to those of engineers who left voluntarily with no apparent grievances. Results showed that both responses to questionnaires and the chance to ventilate during interviews by those who were laid off proved to be an ineffective catharsis, resulting in greater hostility toward management (**FIG. 6.3**). To the surprise of many psychologists, these and similar findings by psychologist Edward Murray (1985) indicate that random, hostile expression of anger is not a suitable means of achieving emotional composure, despite popular belief to this effect.

As someone who has spent a great deal of time studying the connections among anger, Type A behavior, and health, Dr. Redford Williams cautions against feelings of unresolved anger. Williams predicts that at least

> **Catharsis:** Emotional release through crying, yelling, laughing, and the like.

FIGURE 6.3 Recognizing one's anger is the first step toward resolving it.

20 percent of the American population has levels of hostile anger that can produce serious health problems, with another 10 to 20 percent teetering on the edge of anger-health-related issues. In his book *Anger Kills*, Williams underscores the significance of the connection between unreconciled anger and a plethora of symptoms associated with it, from ulcers to coronary heart disease. Williams notes that hostile people, as a rule, tend to be loners or lack a strong social support network, thus making their plight even more difficult. Many thoughts and feelings can surface as sarcasm, cynicism, and pessimism, and the use of these behaviors is a sure sign of unresolved issues. One way Williams recommends to deal with anger is to first make yourself aware of your thoughts, feelings, and behaviors through journaling, including the time and date of the anger episode, the thought, feeling, action, and involvement, so that patterns of behavior can be tracked and modified.

Taking note of the strong association between anger and heart disease, Joseph Sundram and colleagues at the Institute of HeartMath in Boulder Creek, California, have designed several studies to develop an understanding of the effect on the heart of the connection between stress and disease. Their findings, many of which can be found in the book *Cut-Thru* by Doc Lew Childre, speak to the importance of love, compassion, and empathy as the most effective means to defuse the anger response and reverse the physiological parameters maladapted by a closed heart.

To generate a healthy catharsis of anger, certain criteria must be met. In her book *Anger—The Misunderstood Emotion*, Tavris made the following recommendations regarding effective catharsis, all of which should be used simultaneously to resolve anger conflicts:

1. *The expression of anger must be cast in the direction of the provocation.* Tavris observed that for anger feelings to be resolved, they must be vented directly at the person or object that is perceived to violate personal space, values, or identity, not randomly. The ventilation of anger at third parties or at unrelated inanimate objects provides temporary relief but no lasting resolution.

2. *The expression of anger must restore a sense of self-control.* For anger to feel resolved, there must be a sense of justice, a vindication of the personal violation you felt, whether this means just explaining your side of the story or seeing that someone is tried in a court of law for his or her misconduct. Self-esteem must be reinstated, but not at the expense of the person you feel did you an injustice. In other words, revenge is not a viable option in anger resolution.

3. *The expression of anger must change the behavior of the provoker or provide insight to create personal resolution.* When feelings of anger are verbalized, drawn, or written out in a journal, new insights are often revealed, which can explain and give a wider perspective on the problem. Conversation with friends who act as sounding boards is also beneficial when this means of communication invites objective viewpoints. The most beneficial conversations, however, are with the person(s) with whom you share a grievance and ultimately influence toward a common understanding. In the words of Tavris, "such repeated expressions, without illumination, are not cathartic." Insight provides understanding, and understanding cultivates forgiveness (resolution).

4. *Anger must be expressed in understandable language.* When animals communicate anger there is no doubt about it; their language is direct. Humans, however, can be less than direct in their expressions of anger.

Frustrations can be candy-coated and passed over, exaggerated, or masked in deceptive retaliation, none of which is beneficial. The ventilation of anger verbally causes an immediate defensive reaction in those who are nearby. For this reason, anger must be communicated clearly but diplomatically. Psychologists suggest the use of "I" statements (e.g., I am angry because I . . .) rather than "you" statements (e.g., You really made me mad when you . . .), which are less effective in bringing about resolution. In situations where verbal communication is not possible (as with a deceased parent), some type of communication (e.g., an unsent letter) is advocated.

5. *The expression of anger must not provoke retaliation.* For a catharsis to be beneficial, it must put an end to feelings of anger on all sides. Retaliation to one or more outbursts of anger will result in ongoing battles that only perpetuate the anger cycle, making the problem(s) more difficult to resolve.

A review of the literature regarding the expression of anger shows that holding anger in is not the answer, yet neither is yelling to the wind. The expression of anger, like love, requires direct and diplomatic contact, two elements that seem rather distant if not absent when most people get angry. Rarely is anger managed correctly.

Anger Mismanagement Styles

What has become obvious from research on anger is that those who mismanage their feelings of aggression far outnumber those who express it effectively. In his acclaimed book, *Make Anger Your Ally*, describing the expression of anger, Neil Warren categorizes people into four classic anger-mismanagement types based on the behaviors they typically employ: somatizers, self-punishers, exploders, and underhanders. As you read through these four styles, see if you can recognize yourself doing these behaviors.

1. **Somatizers:** Somatizers, as the name implies (*soma* = body), present a passive behavior style that takes its toll on the body. Somatizers are individuals who choose not to express their feelings of anger overtly, but rather suppress them for fear of rejection or loss of approval by those who have caused a grievance. This management style promotes the role of martyr for those who choose it. Somatizers can also be distinguished from those employing other mismanagement styles by the fact that their suppressed anger may soon manifest as physical symptoms such as migraine headaches, ulcers,

colitis, arthritis, and temporomandibular joint dysfunction (TMJD).

2. **Self-punishers:** A second passive mismanaged-anger style involves those who channel their anger into guilt. These people often get angry with themselves for getting angry at others. As a result, they deny themselves the proper outlet or catharsis of their anger. Instead, they punish themselves with control measures that, in effect, lower self-esteem. For example, overeating or deliberate starvation, excessive drinking, and sleeping and shopping can all deflate self-esteem and are displayed by self-punishers. Sadly, self-mutilation and cutting are examples of this style.

3. **Exploders:** Exploders represent the stereotype of uncontrolled aggression. These people express their anger in a hostile manner, either verbally or physically, and like a volcano they erupt, spreading their hot lava in a path of destruction toward anyone around them. These people make headline news, as was evidenced by the Virginia Tech massacre in the spring of 2007. Exploders hold in their feelings of anger and then often erupt at people or objects that have nothing to do with the cause of their frustration. Explosive behavior is sometimes displaced onto others, as when feelings of anger toward the provoker are suppressed, then released onto innocent bystanders such as employees, spouses, and children. In many cases, explosive anger is used as a form of intimidation (e.g., swearing, yelling) to maintain control over a situation or other people's emotions. Road rage is explosive behavior. It is this behavior that is considered by psychologists to be indicative of Type A personality, and the factor most closely associated with coronary heart disease.

Somatizers: People exhibiting an anger style by suppressing rather than expressing feelings of anger. *Soma* means body, and when anger is suppressed, unresolved anger issues appear as symptoms of disease and illness.

Self-punishers: People exhibiting a mismanaged-anger style by denying a proper outlet of anger, replacing it with guilt. Self-punishers punish themselves by excessive eating, exercise, sleeping, cutting, or even shopping.

Exploders: People exhibiting a mismanaged-anger style by exploding and intimidating others as a means to control them.

Stress with a Human Face

Brian had just completed his sophomore year and, like every other college student, he was looking forward to summer vacation. The Boston waterfront is the place to be on hot summer nights, and there were many that year. But this particular summer was hot in another way, too, the likes of which Brian had never experienced. Things just seemed to get out of control. First, his summer job working construction fell through. Second, and more important, his father, to whom he was very close, was diagnosed with terminal cancer. He was given 2 months to live, a prognosis that turned out to be right on the button. Brian got angry that his summer plans, and for that matter his life plans, didn't go as expected.

To Brian, this just wasn't how it was supposed to turn out. The whole dynamics of his life changed, and there was resentment in every corner of his heart. When I saw Brian the first day of school I barely recognized him, for he seemed to have doubled his body weight in muscle mass, and his typical smile was absent. Right away he told me

how difficult it can be to lose a father and become the head of a household while still a teenager. Brian was in a lot of pain. After a few minutes I thought I would change the subject and inquire about his new and improved physique. But Brian didn't want to change the subject.

"Well," he said, "I started lifting weights to take out my aggression. I'd go down to the gym every night and try to release it somehow."

"It must have worked," I replied, "Just look at you."
"Yeah!" he answered. "I was really pissed." Then he paused for a moment and added, "You know, it didn't solve my problems, but it did help me work through them."

Brian had directed his feelings of anger in a way that literally augmented his strength to deal with the situation in which he found himself.

---

4. **Underhanders**: Like the exploder, the underhander exhibits an active style of mismanaged anger that inflicts mild abuse on individuals in his or her proximity. What separates underhanded behavior from the explosive style is that underhanders usually target their aggression toward the cause of the threat, but indirectly—in what they perceive to be socially acceptable ways (**passive-aggressive** behavior). Underhanders seek revenge for injustices to their egos and try to sabotage their "enemy" with little acts of aggression that are somewhat socially acceptable. Underhanded behavior is the most common style at the worksite. Examples include Facebook jabs, walking into a staff meeting late, and making sarcastic comments (verbal sabotage) that demonstrate the need to gain control of the aggressor. Underhanders see themselves as life's victims, and although their anger is often directed at the proper cause, resolution is rarely accomplished.

Warren points out that we each tend to employ all of these mismanagement styles at some time, depending on the situation and people involved. One style, however, becomes the dominant behavior in our personality and is used most extensively in daily interactions. It should be pointed out that none of these four behavior patterns is healthy; that is, to switch from being a somatizer to an exploder is not recommended. Warren suggests that we begin to recognize our feelings of anger, and then channel them into more creative outlets.

Creative Anger Strategies

Human anger is thought to consist of conscious thought, physiological changes, and some form of consequent behavior. Therefore, the most successful strategies to deal with anger involve cognitive coping strategies, relaxation techniques, and behavior modification to deal with these three components. Anger *should* be dealt with and reconciled. But there are both effective and

---

Underhanders: People exhibiting a mismanaged-anger style by seeking revenge and retaliation. This passive-aggressive anger style is a means to control others, but in a very subtle way.

Passive-aggressive: A mismanaged-anger style (see Underhanders) in which people seek revenge, while at the same time fronting a smile.

noneffective ways to deal with the various shades of this emotion. The best approach is to learn a variety of ways so that one or more are available when various situations trigger the anger response in you. Based on the works of Tavris (1989), Weisinger (1985), Fleeman (2003), and Cox, Bruckner, and Stabb (2003), and in the spirit of twelve-step self-help programs to modify behaviors, the following suggestions are provided to help you learn to manage your anger more creatively:

1. *Know your anger style.* Is your anger style predominantly passive or active? Are you the type of person who holds anger in, or are you the kind of person who explodes? Are you a somatizer, exploder, self-punisher, or underhander? Become aware of what your current style of anger is. Take mental notes of what ticks you off and how you react when you get angry.

2. *Learn to monitor your anger.* Keep track of your anger in a journal, or even on a calendar. Write down the times that you get angry and what precipitates it. Are there predictable trends to your anger feelings? Ask yourself why. After several entries, look for patterns of circumstances or behaviors that lead to the "critical mass" or "boiling point" of your anger.

3. *Learn to deescalate your anger.* Rather than show an immediate response, count to ten, take a walk around the block, get a drink of water, try some deep breaths, use some mental imagery to relax—but calm down. Research shows that the anger response is initially quick, then followed by a long simmering process. Give yourself 10 to 20 seconds to diffuse, to collect and regroup your mental faculties. A great way to begin to deescalate your anger is to take a deep breath (and continue abdominal breathing for several cycles). No rational conversation can take place while you are shouting in anger. So, take a "time-out" by removing yourself from the scene momentarily to cool off. Time-outs are very helpful to validate your feelings, and at the same time get a full perspective on the circumstances. Remember, though, that a time-out must be immediately followed by a "time-in."

4. *Learn to out-think your anger.* What are some ways to resolve this feeling in a constructive way so that you and everyone involved feel better? Anger carries with it much energy. How can you best utilize this energy? Learn to construct rather than destruct.

5. *Get comfortable with all your feelings, and learn to express them constructively.* People who are most vulnerable to stress-related disease and illness are those who are unable to express their feelings openly and directly. In other words, don't ignore, avoid, or repress your feelings. Anger, especially, is like acid; it needs to be neutralized. And it is neutralized by creative (constructive) expression.

6. *Plan ahead.* Some situations can be foreseen as potential anger provocations. Identify what these situations are, and then create viable options to minimize your exposure to them. Interactions with people (e.g., family get-togethers, traffic, long lines at the post office) are especially likely to trigger anger. Try to plan your time wisely and work around situations you think will light your fuse.

7. *Develop a support system.* Find a few close friends you can confide in or vent your frustrations to. Don't force a person to become an ally; rather, allow him or her to listen and perhaps offer an insight or objective perspective your anger blinds you to. By expressing yourself to others, you can begin to process bits of information, and a clearer understanding of the situation will usually surface.

8. *Develop realistic expectations of yourself and others.* Many moments of anger surface because the expectations we place on ourselves are too high. Anger also arises when we place high expectations on others and these are not met. Learn to reappraise your expectations and validate your feelings before your top blows off. Learning to assess a situation by fine-tuning your perceptions is essential to minimizing anger episodes.

9. *Learn problem-solving techniques.* Don't paint yourself into a corner. Implement alternatives to situations by creating viable options for yourself. To do this you must be willing to trust your imagination and creativity. You must also take risks with the options you have created and trust the choices you have made. But remember that problem-solving techniques do not include retaliation.

10. *Stay in shape.* Staying in shape means balancing your mental, emotional, physical, and spiritual components of well-being. Studies show that people who are in good physical shape bounce back from anger episodes more quickly than those who are not. Exercise has been proven to be beneficial as

one step in the catharsis process, to validate feelings of anger. Eat well, exercise on a regular basis, give yourself alone-time or solitude, and learn to laugh more. Laughter is a great form of stress reduction, and it gives you a better perspective on the situation at hand. Remember, though, that although laughter is the best form of medicine, anger vented in sarcasm is neither creative nor healthy for anyone.

11. *Turn complaints into requests.* Pessimists tend to complain, whine, and moan. Anyone can complain. Complaining is a sign of victimization. When frustrated with a co-worker or family member, rework the problem into a request for change with the person(s) involved. Seek opportunities rather than problems. Take a more optimistic outlook on how you perceive situations. This will most likely aid in the request process.

12. *Forgiveness: Make past anger pass.* Learn to resolve issues that have caused pain, frustration, or stress. Resolution involves an internal dialogue to work things out within, and an external dialogue to work things out with others, done of course in a diplomatic way. Most important, learn to forgive both yourself and others. Forgiveness is an essential part of anger management. Set a "statute of limitations" on your anger, and hold to it.

There are some who say that anger and fear are two very different sides of the same coin. There are others who believe that anger is really just another shade of fear, inspired by that which generates a sense of uneasiness inside of us. Whether they are two entirely different emotions, or derived from the same source but expressed differently, they are both very real. Left unresolved, they perpetuate stress.

The Anatomy of Fear

Like anger, fear is an element of survival. In its most primitive form, fear stimulates a physical response to flee and hide from threats that are intimidating, overwhelming, and sometimes fatal. In some cases, it produces a period of inactivity known as "freezing"—or

> **Conditioned response:** A response learned over time to a particular (negative) situation, such as displaying caution or apprehension about something perceived as stressful.

"I spend a lot of time at the airport, trying to lose my emotional baggage."

FIGURE 6.4

the "deer in the headlights" moment. Often described as a state of anxiety, fear comes in many shades, including embarrassment, prejudice, anxiety, despair, worry, arrogance, doubt, intimidation, and paranoia, to name a few. This aspect of human behavior spurred extensive inquiry long before Freud recognized it as a purpose for therapy. Perceptions of what is intimidating or fatal are extremely individual to the person who experiences them. A large black dog, for example, can be perceived as either friendly or dangerous. Freud's theories substantiated the need to deal with human fears, and his work has paved the way for a host of anxiety-reduction therapies (**FIG. 6.4**). According to Freud, anxiety is an unknown fear, meaning that the individual is unaware of his or her reason for feeling anxious. More recently, many psychologists and other health professionals have used the terms *fear* and *anxiety* interchangeably, which is how they are used in this chapter as well. Like anger, chronic anxiety produces physiological adaptations created by the stress response, with a strong involvement of the immune system. Repeated episodes of fear are thought to be associated with colds, flus, warts, impotence, and, according to some research, cancer.

The current school of thought suggests that fears are not instinctual. Rather, they are a learned response from one or more exposures to an event (e.g., a third-degree burn, the death of a loved one, a poor exam grade, being jilted) that resulted in some amount of physical or emotional pain. Exposures can be either direct, as in getting stung by a wasp, or indirect, by learning through another's experiences, as in listening to horror stories or even watching TV. These exposures create a **conditioned response**, ranging from caution and apprehension to paralysis in the presence of the event that initiated it. After one or more experiences, fear can be manufactured and replicated by the imagination, and it can seem as real as any face-to-face confrontation. For this reason, anxiety is categorized as either **rational** (useful) or **irrational** (useless). Useful fears are stimulated by real events that are life-threatening and require a response to survive or avoid the threat. Conversely, irrational or useless fears are imagined, exaggerated, or distorted threats that override cognitive processes in the higher brain centers, resulting in some degree of mental, emotional, physical, or spiritual paralysis. Useless fears are illusions created by the ego. Over time, irrational fears can produce a dangerous habit of negative self-talk that feeds upon itself, creating a whirlpool of negativity that is hard to escape from. Illusory fear is the target of therapy and treatment in stress management.

In his groundbreaking books *Emotional Intelligence* and *Destructive Emotions*, author Daniel Goleman synthesizes a plethora of research and information about the emotional aspect of the human condition. As Goleman explains, whereas mental intelligence (as measured in IQ) is praised and rewarded, our emotional intelligence, the ability to feel and express the full range of human emotions, suggests a higher level of intellect than that measured by mere brain power alone. Emotions offer a different, if not superior, level of intelligence, and our ability to use our emotional skills to our greatest advantage will separate those who live a healthy life from those who are prone to disease.

As one of the basic human emotions, fear tends to dominate the emotional palette; Goleman refers to this as "emotional hijacking." Neuroscientists now indicate that one portion of the brain, the amygdala, is responsible for registering and acknowledging any fear-based stimulus. In a complicated network, neural transmissions quickly travel from one or more sensory ports (e.g., eyes) to the thalamus and on to a specific area of the cerebral cortex. Yet another impulse goes from the thalamus directly to the amygdala, which itself can arouse the stress response before the cortex can even decipher the cause of fear.

Whereas with anger there is a rush of adrenaline and with it a surge of energy, fear is a very draining emotion. The urge to hide serves as a metaphor for pulling in one's energy rather than radiating it, for whatever purpose. Worries that become chronic in nature tend to become self-defeating, says Goleman. In other words, problems, issues, and concerns do not get resolved through worry or fear. Rather, they are perpetuated by the emotional energy put into them. And Goleman is one of many people who are convinced of the stress and disease connection. He is convinced that learning to identify, empathize, and resolve our feelings (e.g., anger, anxiety, depression, pessimism, and loneliness) is in itself a necessary form of disease prevention.

In an age of terrorism, is there a good side to fear? Gavin De Becker thinks so. In fact, he calls fear "a gift." Fear, he suggests, is part of the survival dynamic, a necessary aspect of life in times of true danger. The problem arises when people get stuck in the fear mode or what he calls **unwarranted fear**. De Becker, one of the country's leading authorities on fear and violence, states that real fear is a momentary signal from the brain based on a combination of sensory information and intuition (a gut feeling) for the sole purpose of physical survival. Any sensation of fear that lasts longer than the initial signal can cause serious problems. Perpetual fear, a condition that affects millions of Americans, deafens the signal of real fear when real danger is imminent. Given the potential for terrorism in today's world and the fear associated with it, De Becker is concerned about a blanket of unwarranted fear covering the country.

Although anger is a problem in our society, so is fear, and much of our nation's fear is fueled by the media. In the Academy Award–winning documentary *Bowling for Columbine*, director Michael Moore concludes that changes approved by the Federal Communications Commission shifted the focus of news and entertainment entirely to viewer ratings. Fear brings big advertising dollars, and the reverberations of fear-based programming are reflected throughout society on a daily basis, as perhaps you've noticed.

Basic Human Fears

Virtually anything can trigger fear. However, events or situations that elicit anxiety tend to fall into one of six categories: (1) failure, (2) rejection, (3) the unknown,

---

Rational: A term to mean useful, as in rational fear of poisonous snakes.

Irrational: An overwhelming feeling of anxiety based on a false perception.

Unwarranted fear: Similar to an irrational fear, an instance when anxiety overcomes one's thoughts based on a nonphysical threat to one's existence.

(4) death, (5) isolation, and (6) loss of self-dominance. The complexity of anxiety, as Freud and his followers discovered, lies in the fact that many of these basic fears tend to overlap and intertwine, making the origin of some stressors difficult to isolate. But if attention is paid to identifying stressors that trigger anxiety, one basic fear will usually become evident. That is, typically one basic fear tends to dominate our perceptions of specific threats. The six categories of fears are all associated with the inability to access and utilize inner resources, resulting in low self-esteem. The following provides a description and some examples of each category:

1. **Fear of failure**: Fear of failure is associated with low self-esteem or the potential loss of self-esteem. People are more apprehensive about and less likely to try new ventures or repeat their efforts at a previously defeating task when their self-value is low. Fear of failure is a conditioned response from a past experience wherein one's performance did not meet one's own expectations. When people perceive that they have failed at something, their confidence, and thus their self-value and self-acceptance, decrease. This can become a cyclical process, paving the way for repeated failures. A bad experience in the past inhibits a person from attempting an identical or similar task again. Examples include public speaking, using a computer, taking an exam, even marriage. Maslow called this the **Jonah complex**, and it means that one is afraid to maximize one's potential. Fear of failure sets the stage for the self-fulfilling prophecy: If a person thinks he or she will not succeed at a given task, chances are he or she will not. If for some reason someone does succeed, chance and fate are given credit, not his or her own resources and talents. Failure is often associated with lack of achievement, when in reality it is caused by lack of

---

Fear of failure: Anxious feelings of not meeting your own expectations.

Jonah complex: A term coined by Abraham Maslow to illustrate the fear of not maximizing one's potential.

Fear of rejection: Anxious feelings of not meeting the expectations of others.

Fear of the unknown: Anxious feelings about uncertainty and future events.

Misoneism: A term coined by Carl Jung to explain the fear or hatred of anything new (fear of the unknown).

---

effort—not giving something your all when called upon to do so. The flip side of fear of failure is fear of success. This occurs when people achieve success and then become frightened of "defending the title," fearing they cannot match their previous success.

2. **Fear of rejection**: Fear of rejection is also associated with low self-worth, but this fear involves your perception of how others perceive and accept you, whereas fear of failure is based solely on self-acceptance. The seeds of this fear are sown early in life, when a child seeks the approval and love of parents and figures of authority. At a young age, however, children cannot distinguish between disapproval for acts for which they are responsible (e.g., breaking a lamp) and nonrelated incidents (a parent's bad day at the office); rejection appears identical in both cases. As one matures, fear of rejection manifests itself during daily interactions with family, friends, bosses, co-workers, and acquaintances in one's environment. Circumstances in which fear of rejection may surface include negotiating a raise, asking a woman or man for a date, applying for a job, pursuing an intimate relationship, exchanging presents, submitting manuscripts to publishers, and remarrying into families with stepparents and/or stepchildren. Fear of rejection also goes by other names, including fear of intimacy and fear of commitment. Rejection becomes anxiety only when lack of approval or acceptance supports one's inner feelings of low self-esteem. Dyer associated fear of rejection with feelings of guilt and worry.

3. **Fear of the unknown**: There is great comfort in the familiar, and there can be tremendous apprehension of and intimidation by the unknown. This is one reason why many battered women stay in bad relationships and why many people stay in jobs they hate. It may seem paradoxical, but there is some degree of comfort and security even with the undesirable, while there appears to be intolerable tension with the unknown. Jung called this **misoneism**, the fear or hatred of anything new. At its worst, fear of the unknown is paralyzing. With all other basic fears, there are "known quantities" to work with and manipulate; this fear produces shades of panic caused by a lack of information. Other fears give you a visible "enemy"; fear of the unknown makes you feel defenseless. When details and sources are unavailable, security of

the ego begins to evaporate. Examples of this fear include vacationing in new corners of the globe, graduating from college, getting married, becoming pregnant, or getting lost while driving. In the case of a battered wife, fear of the unknown entails how to survive financially without the support of a husband. Fear of the unknown is a black hole in the wall of the ego. It may appear difficult to create a comfortable strategy for dealing with situations unknown, but it is not impossible. Methods include gaining information about the situation, and employing the inner resources of faith and self-reliance.

4. **Fear of death**: Fear of death falls into the domain of useful fears when danger is present and survival is jeopardized. But this fear becomes a useless fear when the danger is exaggerated or "fabricated out of whole cloth." The fear of death includes many phobias where death seems imminent, such as acrophobia (heights), claustrophobia (small spaces), and hydrophobia (water). In a more general sense, this fear is coupled with fear of the unknown when one contemplates the existence of an afterlife and reaches no comfortable answers. The conscious mind can't fathom life without itself, and the thought of nonexistence is less than comforting. Psychologists indicate that many people who demonstrate fear of death are excessively cautious, typically have many unresolved issues in their lives, and have many personal regrets. They may also acquire many possessions as a base of security, and feel naked without them. This fear inhibits the ability to take calculated risks. Kübler-Ross felt that fear of death was universal, but also conquerable.

5. **Fear of isolation**: Fear of isolation is the fear of being left alone, and may very well be the first fear developed in life. From the moment we enter this world, we are nurtured in the company of caregivers who address all our needs. In a baby, the absence of this nurturing presence elicits crying. Later, in adulthood, lack of quality social contact through support systems results in anxiety and depression. Just as people need quality alone-time for self-reflection, they also require human interaction and support to feel connected to other members of their community. Buscaglia notes that the absence of love does not produce fear of rejection so much as it cultivates fear of loneliness. Moreover, Harold Benjamin, founder of the Wellness Community,

in his book *From Victim to Victor*, states that this fear and fear of the loss of self-dominance are the two significant fears of cancer patients.

6. **Fear of the loss of self-dominance**: This fear is exhibited when one feels the loss of control over major events and circumstances in one's life. In other words, this is a fear of loss of personal freedom. This is a predominant fear of people with substance addictions, battered wives and children, nursing home patients, and even the nation's homeless. It also surfaces when individuals contract prolonged illnesses such as cancer or AIDS. This fear is also prevalent in people whose personality type is described as learned helpless-hopeless, people who feel they have little control of their lives.

Fear, Vulnerability, and Shame

Fear takes many forms, but what is the foundation of fear? If you were to ask Professor Brené Brown, Ph.D., at the University of Houston, you would hear the word "shame." Dr. Brown has spent years doing research on the topics of vulnerability, fear, shame, empathy, and courage, but she gained national recognition when her TED Talk, "The Power of Vulnerability," went viral, with over 26 million views (and counting). In her book *Daring Greatly*, Brown explains that fear has deep roots in feelings of shame (the fear of disconnection) with thoughts, feelings, and actions. From her observations in the corporate world, where shame (the absence of connection) is as prevalent as at home and the early school years, she describes stress as the following: the fear of staying relevant in a rapidly changing world and the desire for clarity of purpose. She states, "When shame becomes a management style, engagement dies. When failure is not an option, we can forget about learning, creativity, and innovation." The opposite of shame is the alchemy of whole-heartedness and vulnerability, where self-worth and the courage to be imperfect allows complete authenticity, and fear does not exist. When vulnerability and shame are numbed, so is the ability to experience joy, happiness, and purpose in life (Brown, 2010, 2012).

Fear of death: Anxious feelings about death and the dying process.

Fear of isolation: Anxious feelings of being left alone.

Fear of the loss of self-dominance: Anxious feelings of losing control of your life.

Strategies to Overcome Fear

Because of the complexity of anxiety, several types of therapies exist to help people overcome specific fears and phobias. Although no therapy holds dominance over another, what they all have in common is the premise that the fear must be confronted at some level. Using a pure psychoanalytical approach (Freud's approach), attention is focused on uncovering childhood experiences (e.g., child molestation) that have been suppressed or repressed in the unconscious mind and are thought to be the cause of the anxiety. The length of this type of therapy is dependent on the type and severity of the anxiety. A second option is called **behavioral therapy**, based on the work of behavioral psychologist John B. Watson, where an individual engages in coping (cognitive reappraisal) and relaxation (mental imagery) techniques to desensitize himself or herself to the stressor(s) (Wolpe, 1988). Additional work by Joseph Wolpe (1992) helped clients to create a mindset that would be conducive to modifying behaviors. In **systematic desensitization** and **exposure desensitization**, clients are repeatedly exposed to their stressors, first at small and tolerable levels, and then with a systematic progression toward face-to-face confrontation with the stressor. In essence, people are taught to overcome their fears by piecemeal steps in which they always feel in control of their tolerance level.

Lufthansa Airlines offered a very successful program based on this technique for potential passengers who have a fear of flying. Such people take a course in airflight anxiety reduction, which includes visiting an airport terminal and waiting for a plane; boarding a mock plane, sitting for a short duration, and deplaning without flying; and then progressing to very short flights (Kindelbacher, 2007). Another type of behavior therapy is assertiveness training,

---

Behavioral therapy: A therapy based on the work of John B. Watson, in which coping and relaxation techniques are used to desensitize oneself to stress.

Systematic desensitization: A process of learning to destress from something in small, manageable stages.

Exposure desensitization: A process of learning to destress from something by brief, yet safe, encounters with the stressor.

Depression: A state of mind where thoughts are clouded by feelings of despair. Physiologists suggest that depression is caused by a chemical imbalance; psychologists suggest that depression is the result of unresolved stress emotions (anger turned inward).

---

the goal being to increase self-esteem. The greatest success with these therapies comes from awareness of the fear(s) and the stressors that produce them, proficiency in applicable coping and relaxation techniques, and the ability to confront stressors peacefully, emerging the victor, not the victim.

The HeartMath Institute provides a series of instructional biofeedback training programs in which clients are taught to control and reframe not only their thoughts, but also their emotions (both anger and anxiety), which often govern their thought processes. Based on years of well-documented research, an interactive PC software package, titled EmWave PC Stress Relief System, guides the user through a series of activities that, in essence, opens the heart to resolve anxiety- and anger-related issues that affect the mind, body, and spirit (www.HeartMath.org).

Here is a closing thought on fear from the celebrated Sufi poet Hafiz: "Fear is the cheapest room in the house. I would much prefer to see you living under better conditions."

Depression: A By-Product of Anger or Fear?

It would be erroneous to assume that anger and fear are the only two emotions associated with stress. There are, in fact, many others, but they all appear to be linked, either directly or indirectly, to anger and/or fear. One emotion that surfaces as a result of unresolved stress is depression.

Overwhelming sadness. The blues. Eternal darkness. Shuffling underwater. Prolonged grieving. Deep heaviness. Melancholy. Just like anger and fear, **depression** goes by several names and descriptions. With estimates from the Centers for Disease Control and Prevention that more than one-quarter of the American public is on medication for depression, this topic certainly merits more attention than a passing comment. Depression is the silent face of stress. And depending on who you talk to, there seem to be many causes of mood swings, from high-carbohydrate diets and traumatic childbirth to hormonal imbalances and poor brain chemistry. What is often overlooked are stressful events that precede each bout of depression.

Although it's true that no one word seems to adequately describe this emotional state, many of the following symptoms are common to those who share this feeling:

- Persistent sadness or empty moods
- A loss of interest or pleasure in activities
- Lethargic moods with decreased productivity

- Loss of appetite and weight loss or overeating and weight gain

- Difficulty concentrating, remembering, or making decisions

- Pervading hopelessness in personal and professional lives

- Alcohol and drug use to cope with problems

- Thoughts of death and suicide to "resolve" issues

Depression is a lot more than just brain chemistry. And although Prozac, Paxil, and Zoloft may work to alleviate the imbalance in serotonin, norepinephrine, and dopamine levels in the brain, in the words of author Susan Skog, "a chemical cure cannot heal emotional wounds." For many people, pharmacological aids have worked wonders; however, given the complexity of depression, the best approach is a holistic one.

Those who have studied this emotion describe depression as "anger turned inward." Experts now agree that unresolved anger issues, however long they have been lingering in the psyche, are essential to resolve for the clouds of depression to lift and clear.

Although it is common to feel down in the dumps at times, to be locked into this emotion for prolonged periods, to the exclusion of all others, is neither normal nor healthy. Some type of intervention is needed to reestablish a balance between the positive and negative feelings generated by daily life so as to regain emotional well-being. Psychotherapeutic intervention to treat depression includes many coping and relaxation techniques. For example, several studies have shown that physical exercise results in a less depressed state of mind. In a literature review on the topic of exercise and depression, authors Gill, Womack, and Sanfranek (2010) reported that, indeed, exercise decreases patient-perceived symptoms of depression, with a combination of high-frequency, light-resistance exercise and aerobic exercise offering the best results. T'ai Chi and yoga were also noted to decrease symptoms of depression. In an article titled "Exercise Against Depression" (1998), authors Artal and Sherman state that exercise plays a significant role in the treatment of depression. Similar results have been observed following the use of St. John's wort, nutrition therapy (decreasing simple sugars), music therapy, art therapy, and humor therapy. These same techniques are equally effective for individuals who find themselves occasionally "under the weather" after a stressful day, and may in fact help move them toward a peaceful resolution of their stress.

Joy, Eustress, and the Art of Happiness

Fear and anger may be the most recognized, if not most common, stress emotions, but let us not forget that there is another emotion associated with stress: joy and happiness, also known in stress circles as eustress. The emerging field of positive psychology has placed joy and happiness as a big X on the psychological treasure map. The search for happiness has begun in earnest in all corners of the globe. A quick look at the titles in the self-help section of any bookstore or on Amazon.com, from authors including the Dalai Lama, Harvard professors, and HBO comedians, reveals that the pursuit of happiness is a hot commodity in the age of twenty-first-century stress.

Simply stated, joy is the antithesis of distress. Although some researchers in the field of positive psychology insist that joy is the anticipation of an event, spiritual luminaries suggest that happiness is a state of living in the present moment. Happiness, however, isn't just a psychological issue. It appears to be a leading economic indicator as well, which may explain why experts in the field of economics also contribute significant amounts of research to the happiness data collection. Interestingly, the Asian country of Bhutan measures its country's growth not just in GDP (gross domestic product) but GDH (gross domestic happiness). Other countries, such as England and France, are considering similar measures. There is even a world database of happiness in Rotterdam, the Netherlands (http://worlddatabaseof happiness.eur.nl/).

Is happiness a function of nature or nurture? Experts suggest that it's a combination of both, but that each of us has the ability to nurture the nature of our happiness, hence bringing a sense of emotional balance to our lives (**FIG. 6.5**).

What do scientific studies tell us about happiness? Researchers have looked at all kinds of indices, such as stress hormones, neuropeptides, cardiac activity, facial coding (smiles per day), creative pursuits, nutritional diets, and spending habits. The following are some conclusions from the current research on joy and happiness, known in research circles as "subjective social well-being."

- Until people's basic needs are met (food, clothing, shelter, income), happiness is elusive (Graham, 2010).

- There is a strong correlation between happiness and trust. If trust is lacking, happiness is non-existent. Trust is a prerequisite for happiness (Robinson, 2008).

FIGURE 6.5 The search for happiness and joy begins inside, cultivating and focusing on pleasant thoughts and perceptions. Creating a pleasurable environment and surrounding yourself with happy people and friends also helps to cultivate feelings of eustress.

- Serotonin, a neurotransmitter, seems to be a chemical by-product of feeling happy. (A lack of serotonin is associated with depression, hence the name the "happiness hormone" given to serotonin.) Carbohydrates may increase serotonin levels, but carbohydrates do not necessarily make one happy (Sommers, 1999).

- Having choices (freedom) makes people happy to a point, after which too many choices make people feel overwhelmed and eventually stressed (Nauert, 2006).

- Money does not equate with happiness, but poverty can promote stress (Deaton, 2008).

- There is a strong correlation between happiness and the ability to be creative, according to findings by Harvard researcher Teresa Amabile (2005).

- Fulfilling relationships are the cornerstone to lifelong happiness (Buettner, 2010).

- The happiest people aren't always found living on tropical islands. Eric Weiner, the author of the best-seller *The Geography of Bliss*, states that people in Iceland, Denmark, Sweden, Holland, and Switzerland rank as some of the happiest people on the planet (the people of Moldova ranked last).

- There may be a genetic component to happiness, yet one's environment can either increase or decrease one's general disposition. Cultural distractions and ego (i.e., technology, emails, text messages, Facebook posts) where one can easily compare his or her life with others may reduce happiness (Kluger, 2013).

Happiness may be many things to many people, and there may be many things that cause one to be happy, including wealth, a quality standard of living, and great relationships, but research suggests that trust, more than income, fame, or even health, is the biggest factor in determining happiness (Weiner, 2008). Happiness has proven to be quite popular as a field of study, though rather than referring to happiness the scientific term is "psychological wealth." According to many sources, creativity is also a significant factor of happiness; when people are busy creating art, apps, gardens, music, film, or any other creative work, the act of creation promotes true happiness. Conversely, one of the greatest sources of unhappiness is isolation (a common occurrence in the cyber-filled world we live in).

Health is also an essential criteria for happiness, and we now have data to prove it. In 1938, researchers at Harvard University designed and ran a longitudinal health study, which continues to this day. It has become known as the Harvard Happiness Study. Initially, 724 men were enrolled in the study, including Harvard students and various people from the Boston area. Initial data were drawn from personal interviews, medical records, and conversations with wives. About 60 of the initial participants are still alive. In a popular TED Talk, researcher Robert Waldinger explains that the study's findings, although not necessarily groundbreaking, nevertheless prove quite validating with regard to happiness and longevity and health. Simply stated: Happiness is love and love reveals itself in social connections, whereas isolation becomes toxic and kills.

In the continual debate between nature and nurture on the human condition, research indicates that both play a vital role in one's state of happiness, yet a third factor—consciousness—also plays a pivotal role (Nichols, 2014). In what is now being referred to as "happiness baselines," current research suggests that the alchemy of happiness is composed of three aspects: genetics, circumstances, and one's choices. Genetics (nature) is responsible for 50 percent of one's happiness. Circumstances (nurture) are associated with 10 percent, and the remaining 40 percent is greatly influenced by the choices we make and the actual practice of being happy (Nichols, 2014). This suggests that happiness, as a perception, is greatly influenced by our choice of thoughts. Ryan Howell, an assistant professor at the San Francisco State University, advocates the philosophy of Aristotle, noting that there are two kinds of happiness.

The first is commonly referred to as "Hedonistic happiness" (short-term happiness based on short-term pleasures). The second type of happiness is referred to as "eudemonic happiness," and is derived from working toward a greater life purpose (Chopra, 2014; Nichols, 2014).

Finally, March 20 is International Happiness Day, but don't relegate it to one day, try to celebrate good stress every day.

First and foremost, happiness is a perception—a thought combined with an emotion generated from within. Money, cars, clothing, food, or vacations in Tahiti may seem to promote happiness, but the real measure of happiness is your attitude—your ability to appreciate these things. In the words of Abraham Lincoln, "People are about as happy as they make their minds up to be."

SUMMARY

- Anger and fear are two sides of the same coin. Both emotions are triggered by stimuli perceived to be a threat at a physical, mental, emotional, or spiritual level, or perhaps a combination of these.

- Feelings of anger initiate the fight response to defend oneself and the components that constitute one's identity.

- Fear triggers the flight response, which makes one want to run and hide.

- Both anger and fear are thought to be survival emotions, yet when conscious thoughts are combined with these innate reflexes, feelings are magnified rather than resolved, leading to an unbroken cycle of stress.

- Social factors may play a significant role in the different anger-management styles of men and women. Women are often flooded with feelings of guilt after tempers flare; men demonstrate anger in more overt ways.

- There are several myths regarding the emotion of anger, the most common being that any type of ventilation producing a catharsis is healthy. However, research reveals that undirected ventilation only validates and perpetuates feelings of anger.

- People who do not ventilate anger correctly are categorized as one of four mismanaged-anger types: somatizer, self-punisher, exploder, or underhander.

- Current stress-management programs are introducing courses in creative anger management to change anger-generated thoughts and feelings into constructive energies that work toward peaceful resolution.

- Fear is based on an actual or vicarious exposure to physical or emotional pain. Those fears that enable a person to avoid life-threatening situations are called useful fears, while those that are exaggerated and immobilize the individual are deemed useless fears. It is the latter, irrational fears that are targeted for change.

- Fear is now recognized as a gut feeling that occurs seconds before physical danger. Anything after that is unwarranted fear.

- Basic human fears include failure, rejection, the unknown, death, isolation, and loss of self-control. Most anxieties can be placed in one of these categories.

- The most effective way to dissolve fear is to confront it. One way to do so is through a technique called systematic desensitization, where the stressor is confronted piecemeal to build a psychological immunity to it.

- The road to resolution for both anger and fear is not difficult, yet it is often avoided, resulting in mismanaged styles of anger and fear and consequent physical ailments.

- Left unresolved, both anger and fear can sow the seeds of depression, an emotional state that may require therapy.

- Several strategies, involving both coping and relaxation techniques, are recommended to express anger and fear in a healthy fashion and to control these emotions for optimal well-being.

- Joy and happiness are the eustress emotions. The field of positive psychology has illuminated these two emotions as vital aspects of life, necessary for emotional balance.

STUDY GUIDE QUESTIONS

1. Describe the emotion of anger (the fight response).

2. In what ways is anger mismanaged?

3. What are ways to help cope with, manage, and resolve anger feelings?

4. Describe the emotion of fear (the flight response).

5. In what ways does fear become manifested as stress?

6. Describe one or more ways to cope with, manage, and resolve fear or anxiety.

7. Explain eustress as a means to achieve emotional balance.

8. Describe the two kinds of happiness.

REFERENCES AND RESOURCES

Agentur Texter-Millott. *Seminars for Relaxed Flying*. www
.flugangst.de/en/prim00/00.php3.

Amabile, T., et al. Affect and Creativity at Work, *Administrative
Science Quarterly* 50:367–403, 2005.

Amen, D. G., and Routh, L. *Healing Anxiety and Depression*.
Putnam, New York, 2003.

Archer, J. *The Behavioral Biology of Aggression*. Cambridge
University Press, Cambridge, 2009.

Artal, M., and Sherman, C. Exercise Against Depression,
Physician and Sports Medicine October: 55–60, 1998.

Ax, A. F. The Physiological Differences Between Fear and Anger
in Humans, *Psychosomatic Medicine* 15:433–442, 1953.

Baumeister, R., Smart, L., and Boden, J. Relation of Threatened
Egotism to Violence and Aggression: *The Dark Side of Self-
Esteem, Psychological Review* 103(1):5–33, 1996.

Benjamin, H. *From Victim to Victor*. Dell Publishing, New
York, 1989.

Biaggio, M. *Sex Differences in Anger: Are They Real?* Paper
presented to the American Psychological Association,
Atlanta, Georgia, 1988.

Bramson, R. *Coping with Difficult People*. Dell, New York, 1988.

Breakey, P. The Entitlement Generation Expects All. *DailyStar*,
July 2, 2005. www.thedailystar.com/news/stories/2005/07/02
/gen1.html.

Britten, R. *Fearless Living*. Perigee Books, Berkeley, CA, 2002.

Brown, B. *Daring Greatly*. Avery Books, New York, 2012.

Brown, B. The Power of Vulnerability. TED Talk, June 2010.
https://www.ted.com/talks/brene_brown_on_vulnerability?
language=en.

Buettner, D. *Thrive: Finding Happiness the Blue Zone Way*.
National Geographic Society, Washington, DC, 2010.

Buscaglia, L. *Love*. First Ballantine Books, New York, 1996.

Childre, D., and Rozman, D. *Transforming Anger*. New
Harbinger Publications, Oakland, CA, 2003.

Childre, D. L. *Cut-Thru*. Planetary Publishing, Boulder
Creek, CA, 1996.

Chopra, D. Two Kinds of Happiness (One Is Bad for You).
October 3, 2014. https://www.linkedin.com/pulse/20141003223344
-75054000-two-kinds-of-happiness-one-is-bad-for-you.

Cox, D., Bruckner, K., and Stabb, S. *The Anger Advantage*.
Broadway Books, New York, 2003.

Dalai Lama. *The Art of Happiness*, 10th anniversary ed. Riverhead Press, New York, 2009.

Dalai Lama. *Healing Anger—The Power of Patience from a Buddhist
Perspective*. Snow Lion Publishers, New York, 1997.

Deaton, A. Income, Health, and Well-Being Around the
World: Evidence from the Gallup World Poll, *Journal of
Economic Perspectives* 22:2, 2008.

De Becker, G. *The Gift of Fear*. Dell Books, New York, 1999.

Dentan, R. K. *The Semai—A Nonviolent People of Malaysia*.
Thompson Custom Publishing, New York, 2002.

Dollard, J. R., et al. *Frustration and Aggression*. Praeger, West-
port, CT, 1980.

DuPont, R. *Phobia*. Brunner/Mazel, New York, 1982.

Ebbesen, E., Duncan, B., and Konecni, V. Effects of Content
of Verbal Aggression on Future Verbal Aggression: A Field
Experiment, *Journal of Experimental Social Psychology* 11:
192–204, 1975.

Engel, B. *Honor Your Anger*. John Wiley & Sons, New York, 2004.

Esler, G. *United States of Anger: The People and the American
Dream*. Penguin Books, New York, 1997.

Fleeman, W. *Pathways to Peace: Anger Management Workbook*.
Hunter House, Alameda, CA, 2003.

Friedman, M. *Overcoming the Fear of Success*. Warner Books,
New York, 1988.

Gilbert, D. *Stumbling on Happiness*. Vintage Press, New York,
2007.

Gill, A., Womack, R., and Safranek, S. Clinical Inquiries:
Does Exercise Alleviate Symptoms of Depression? *Journal
of Family Practice* 59(9):530–531, 2010.

Glassner, B. *The Culture of Fear: Why Americans Are Afraid of
the Wrong Things*. Basic Books, New York, 2009.

Goldstein, A. *Agress-less: How to Turn Anger and Aggression into
Positive Action*. Prentice-Hall, New York, 1982.

Goleman, D. *Destructive Emotions: A Scientific Dialogue with
the Dalai Lama*. Bantam Books, New York, 2003.

Goleman, D. *Emotional Intelligence: Why It Can Matter More
Than I.Q.* Bantam Books, New York, 1997.

Goodwin, D. *Anxiety*. Oxford University Press, New York, 1986.

Graham, C. *Happiness Around the World: The Paradox of Happy
Peasants and Miserable Millionaires*. Oxford University Press,
Oxford, England, 2010.

Greer, S., and Morris, T. Psychological Attributes of Women
Who Develop Breast Cancer: A Controlled Study, *Journal
of Psychosomatic Research* 19:147–153, 1975.

Handly, R., and Neff, P. *Beyond Fear*. Fawcett Crest, New
York, 1991.

Harbin, T. J. *Beyond Anger: A Guide for Men: How to Free
Yourself from the Grip of Anger and Get More Out of Life*.
Marlow & Company, New York, 2000.

Haynes, S., et al. The Relationship of Psychosocial Factors
to Coronary Heart Disease in the Framingham Study, I.
Methods and Risk Factors, *American Journal of Epidemiology*
107:362–383, 1978.

Howell, R. T. Train Your Brain to Spend Smarter. Beyond the
Purchase, August 1, 2014. www.beyondthepurchase.org/blog/.

Institute of HeartMath. *Homepage*. www.heartmath.org.
Accessed February 26, 2008.

Jung, C. G. *Man and His Symbols.* Dell Press, New York, 1968.

Kessler, R., and McLeod, J. Sex Differences in Vulnerability to Understand Life Events, *American Sociological Review* 46:443–452, 1984.

Kindelbacher, B. Personal conversation, November 10, 2012.

Kindlon, D., and Thompson, M. *Raising Cain: Protecting the Emotional Life of Boys.* Ballantine Books, New York, 2000.

Kluger. J. The Happiness of Pursuit. *Time.* 24-32. July 8, 2013.

Kübler-Ross, E. *Death: The Final Stage of Growth.* Touchstone Books, New York, 1988.

Lazarus, R. *Stress and Emotions.* Springer, New York, 1999.

Lerner, H. G. *The Dance of Anger.* 1st Perennial Currents, New York, 2005.

Lyon, L. Taking a Bite Out of Anger, *U.S. News and World Report*, December 17, 2007:66.

Martinsen, E. W. Benefits of Exercise for the Treatment of Depression, *Sports Medicine* 9(6):219–231, 1985.

Maslow, A. H. *The Farther Reaches of Human Nature.* Arkana, New York, 1993.

Mate, G. *When the Body Says No: Understanding the Stress–Disease Connection.* John Wiley & Sons, New York, 2011.

McEwen, B. *The End of Stress as We Know It.* Dana Press, Washington, DC, 2002.

McKay, M., Rogers, P., and McKay, J. *When Anger Hurts: Quieting the Storm Within.* New Harbinger Publications, Oakland, CA, 2003.

Middelton-Moz, J. *Boiling Point: The High Cost of Healthy Anger to Individuals and Society.* Health Communications, Deerfield Beach, FL, 1999.

Middelton-Moz, J. *Boiling Point: The Workbook.* Health Communications, Deerfield Beach, FL, 2000.

Mogg, G. *Creative Anger Management.* American University, Washington, DC, 1992.

Moore, M. *Bowling for Columbine.* Michael Moore Productions, 2002.

Murray, E. Coping and Anger. In T. Field, P. McCabe, and N. Schneiderman (eds.), *Stress and Coping,* Erlbaum, Hillsdale, NJ, 1985.

Naiman, L. Happiness, *Creativity at Work Newsletter*, May 2007. www.creativityatwork.com/blog/2007/05/28/creativity-at-work-newsletter-happiness/.

Nauert, R. Does Freedom of Choice Ensure Happiness? *PsychCentral*, July 18, 2006. http://psychcentral.com/news/2006/07/18/does-freedom-of-choice-ensure-happiness/101.html.

Neale, R. E. *The Art of Dying.* Harper & Row, New York, 1977.

Nichols, W. *Blue Mind.* Bantam Books, New York, 2014.

Nuckols, C., and Chickering, B. *Healing an Angry Heart: Finding Solace in a Hostile World.* Health Communications, Deerfield Beach, FL, 1998.

Prinzivalli, S. How Not to Be Offended. The Unbounded Spirit, 2016. http://theunboundedspirit.com/how-not-to-be-offended/.

Reed, G. L., and Enright, R. D. The Effects of Forgiveness Therapy on Depression, Anxiety and Posttraumatic Stress for Women After Spousal Emotional Abuse, *Journal of Consulting and Clinical Psychology* 74(5): 920–929, 2006.

Reich, J. The Epidemiology of Anxiety, *Journal of Nervous and Mental Disease* 174(3):129–136, 1986.

Robinson, J. Happiness Flows from Trust, *National Post*, October 24, 2008. www.nationalpost.com/story.html?id=906300.

Rosenman, R. H. Health Consequences of Anger and Implications for Treatment. In M. A. Chesney and R. H. Rosenman (eds.), *Anger and Hostility in Cardiovascular and Behavioral Disorders,* Hemisphere, Washington, DC, 1985.

Santella, A. All the Rage. *Utne Reader*, November 2007: 36–41.

Schimelpfening, N. Depressed Women at Greater Risk for Breast Cancer. http://depression.about.com/health/depression/library/weekly/aa100300.htm.

Schwartz, G. E., Weinberger, D. A., and Singer, J. A. Cardiovascular Differentiation of Happy, Sad, Anger, and Fear Following Imagery and Exercise, *Psychosomatic Medicine* 43:343–364, 1981.

Segal, J. *Living without Fear.* Ballantine Books, New York, 1989.

Serotonin—The Molecule of Happiness, *HubPages.* http://hubpages.com/hub/Serotonin-The-Molecule-of-Happiness.

Shekelle, R., et al. Hostility and Risk of CHD, and Mortality, *Psychosomatic Medicine* 45:109–114, 1983.

Skog, S. *Depression: What Your Body's Trying to Tell You.* Avon, Whole Care Books, New York, 1999.

Snyder, C. R., and Heinze, L. S. Forgiveness as a Mediator of the Relationship Between PTSD and Hostility in Survivors of Childhood Abuse. *Cognition and Emotion*, 19(3):413–431, 2005.

Sommers, E. *Food and Mood.* Henry Holt, New York, 1999.

Sundram, J. *Re-engineering the Human System: The Physiology of Conscious Evolution.* Institute of Noetic Sciences, 5th Annual Conference, Boca Raton, FL, July 18–21, 1996.

Sussman, V. To Win, First You Must Lose, *U.S. News and World Report,* January 15, 1990.

Svitil, K. *Psychology Today: Calming the Anger Storm.* Alpha/Penguin Books, New York, 2006.

Tavris, C. *Anger–The Misunderstood Emotion.* Touchstone, New York, 1989.

Thomas, S., and Jefferson, C. *Use Your Anger: A Woman's Guide to Empowerment.* Pocket, New York, 1996.

Thomas, S. P., and Donnellan, M. M. Correlates of Anger Symptoms in Women in Middle Adulthood, *American Journal of Health Promotion* 5(4):266–272, 1991.

Warren, N. *Make Anger Your Ally: Harnessing Our Most Baffling Emotion.* Living Books, New York, 1999.

Weiner, E. *The Geography of Bliss.* 12 Books, New York, 2008.

Weisinger, H. *Weisinger's Anger Work-Out Book*. William Morrow, New York, 1985.

Williams, R., and Williams, V. *Anger Kills*. Harper-Perennial, New York, 1994.

Williams, R. B., et al. Type A Behavior, Hostility, and Coronary Atherosclerosis, *Psychosomatic Medicine* 42: 539–549, 1980.

Witvliet, C. Surprised by Happiness, *Huffington Post*, November 25, 2010. www.huffingtonpost.com/charlotte-vanoyen-witvliet-phd/surprised-by-happiness-wh_b_787126.html.

Wolpe, J. *The Practice of Behavior Therapy*. 4th ed., Allyn: Bacon, New York, 1992.

Wolpe, J., and Wolpe, D. *Life without Fear*. New Harbinger Publications, Oakland, CA, 1988.

Wood, C. The Hostile Heart, *Psychology Today* 20:9, 1986.

World Database of Happiness. http://worlddatabaseof happiness.eur.nl/.

Worthington, E. L., Jr., and Scherer, M. Forgiveness Is an Emotion-Focused Coping Strategy That Can Reduce Health Risks and Promote Health Resilience: Theory, Review and Hypotheses. *Psychology and Health* 19(3): 385–405, 2004.

Zane, M., and Milt, H. *Your Phobia*. American Psychiatric Press, Washington, DC, 1984.

CHAPTER 7

Stress-Prone and Stress-Resistant Personality Traits

Happiness is a decision. . . . Optimism is a cure for many things.

—Michael J. Fox

In the summer of 1966, at the age of 55, Nien Cheng (**FIG. 7.1**) was placed under house arrest in her private home in Shanghai. It was the dawn of the Cultural Revolution in Mao Tse-Tung's communist China. Thousands of innocent people found themselves incarcerated, political prisoners accused of being enemies of the state. Educated in London, employed by Shell Oil as a management advisor, and widow of a former official of Chiang Kai-shek, Nien Cheng quickly became the target of several communist indictments. She was soon moved from house arrest to solitary confinement, in a cell no bigger than a walk-in closet, at the Number 1 Detention House for political prisoners. Convinced she had committed no crime, she defended her innocence despite hunger, disease, intimidation, terror, and humiliation. Many innocent prisoners perished from the torture of the communist Red Guards, yet Nien Cheng was determined not merely to survive but to prove her innocence. Upon her release in 1972, after six and a half years in solitary confinement, she was declared a victim of false arrest.

At this time, she frantically sought the whereabouts of her only daughter. What she discovered about the fate of Meiping Cheng made it impossible for her to remain in her homeland. In 1980, Nien Cheng emigrated to North America, whereupon she wrote of how she prevailed over this tumultuous experience in her stirring autobiography, *Life and Death in Shanghai*. As a guest speaker in my Strategies for Stress Reduction class, Mrs. Cheng was asked what it was that allowed her to survive such a harrowing ordeal. Gracefully, she answered, "I saw my stay at the detention house as a challenge, and with the grace of God, I was committed to proving my innocence." She left no doubt that she demonstrated a special personality in surviving her ordeal.

Until her death in 2009 at age 94, Nien Cheng practiced T'ai Chi ch'uan daily and stayed current with world events. In my last conversation with her, in which she reflected back on that time in prison as well as present-day events, she said, "Patience is an important aspect of survival, as is faith. The pace of the world has become quite fast today.

FIGURE 7.1 Mrs. Nien Cheng was falsely imprisoned at age 56 for six and a half years during the rule of Mao Tse-Tung. She credited her survival to many factors, including commitment to her innocence and patience, which helped her cope with a grueling ordeal.

Please tell your students how important it is to employ these inner resources."

Many words can be used to describe the likes of Nien Cheng and others who express the epitome of the triumph of the human spirit—Nelson Mandela, Rosa Parks, and the scores of unsung heroes, who grace the Facebook feeds, have overcome great adversity to declare victory and move on with their lives. That word is resiliency. Resiliency is the new catchphrase in corporate stress management circles. It is also the new buzzword in military training, where soldiers and military officers are being taught skills to cope with stress both on the battlefield and in the transition back to civilian life. The most common definition of resiliency is to bounce back from crisis. The people we call heroes share a common personality trait: resiliency. For some it's innate, for most it's learned.

Although almost everyone has a concept of what personality is, scholars in the field of psychology have yet to agree on a definition of the term. The word originally derives from the Latin word *persona*, meaning mask, as in the masks used by actors in ancient Greek plays. In more contemporary times, personality has come to mean a conglomeration of several characteristics—behaviors, expressions, moods, and feelings—that are perceived by others. The complexity of one's personality is thought to be shaped by genetic factors, family dynamics, social influences, and a wealth of personal experiences. Just as there are many definitions, so there are also many theories of personality that attempt to explain the differences in the psychological make-up from one person to another. The basis of many of these theories centers on whether these traits and behaviors are primarily innate or learned—the nature versus nurture question. No clear-cut answers have emerged, and whether personality can actually be changed is still being argued. The research findings are fascinating but quite inconclusive. Can you change your personality? Like the ability to improve your IQ, the answer seems to be yes! Pessimists can become optimists. Curmudgeons can learn to laugh regularly. Introverts can abandon shyness. Addicts can remain drug free. Currently, a growing body of opinions suggests that the most likely components of one's personality to be alterable are behaviors and traits associated with these behaviors. By changing various personality traits, one can change one's personality. It is this consensus that has led to the formation of, and emphasis on, behavior modification, counseling, and classes in health promotion programming, including stress management.

The story of Nien Cheng is a remarkable testimony to the strength of the human spirit. It is this characteristic, as well as many others, that psychologists and psychiatrists have attempted to study to determine which personality types are prone to suffering the effects of stress, and which seem to be immune or resistant to it. Although the search has not been easy, researchers have identified specific personality traits and behaviors, classified as personality types, that have begun to shed some light on the relationship between personality and disease. They include Type A behavior, codependent personality, helpless-hopeless personality, hardy personality, survivor personality, and sensation seeker or Type R personality. As people strive to learn more about themselves, these labels have now become household words in North America. What follows is a look at these personality types and the factors that separate stress-prone from stress-resistant traits and behaviors.

Type A Behavior

In the late 1950s, coronary heart disease emerged as the number one killer in the country, claiming the lives of many men and women, including several politicians, physicians, and executives of the nation's leading corporations. Unlike infectious diseases initiated by viruses and bacteria, this disease was attributed to factors associated with specific lifestyle behaviors and, therefore, was recognized as being potentially preventable. During the Eisenhower and Kennedy administrations this "epidemic" was given national attention, and federal funds were appropriated for research to understand the nature of this disease. Like detectives at the scene of a murder, federally funded researchers searched for potential clues that might lead to the development of this killer disease. Studies conducted at Harvard University and the Framingham Study in Massachusetts revealed several factors that were believed to place an individual at risk for coronary heart disease, including cigarette smoking, hypertension, elevated levels of cholesterol and triglycerides, inactivity, diabetes, obesity, and family history of heart disease. Surprisingly, data also revealed that several heart attack victims had few, if any, of these risk factors. So the search went on.

Although assumptions had previously been made about the seemingly obvious relationship between emotional responses and health status, it was the initial work of cardiologists Meyer Friedman and Ray Rosenman whose research in 1964 added one more significant risk factor to the list: **Type A personality**, or a rushed or hurried lifestyle. As the story goes, they stumbled upon this insight while having their office furniture reupholstered, during which they discovered that their patients literally sat on the edge of the chairs while waiting to be seen. This tip led them to look at the psychological profiles of their patients, as well as the usual physical assessments. From their research, they developed an assessment tool to diagnose Type A behavior, called the Structured Interview. This interview process between the trained physician and patient was designed to measure the intensity, frequency, and duration of several criteria associated with Type A behavior. Later, a second assessment questionnaire, based on Friedman and Rosenman's work, was developed by psychologist David Jenkins and called the Jenkins Activity Questionnaire (JAQ). Because of its simplicity—individuals can fill it out on their own—the JAQ has been used more often than the Structured Interview to assess Type A behavior.

Initially, Friedman and Rosenman referred to Type A behavior as the "hurried sickness." In several research studies, the behavioral traits of "tense" individuals were compared to others who were regarded as "laid back" and called Type B individuals. Striking evidence was observed by Rosenman et al. (1964) in the landmark Western Collaborative Groups Study, which examined more than 3,500 subjects over an 8-year period. Results revealed that Type A behavior was a greater predictor of heart disease than all other risk factors combined. Physiologically speaking, research shows that Type A individuals are more prone to sympathetic arousal (i.e., increased secretion of catecholamines), hypertension, and elevated levels of cholesterol and triglycerides, placing these people at greater risk for several stress-related disorders, but especially coronary heart disease (Rice, 1992). Based on years of research by Rosenman, Friedman, and others, the following personality traits may identify Type A behavior. As you will see, many of these traits are interrelated. Friedman and Rosenman felt that it took only one of these traits to be classified as Type A, though in truth Type A's have been found to share many of these characteristics.

1. *Time urgency (impatience):* Type A people were found to be preoccupied, if not obsessed, with the passage of time and appeared very impatient. Typically these individuals hate to wait in lines, honk at the car in front when the light turns green, and show incredible impatience with others who are too slow with tasks that threaten their own work schedule or personal responsibilities. Type A's feel uncomfortable or guilty about relaxing when there is no set agenda. They rarely take vacations. Everything in the course of a working day—eating, walking, talking—is done with speed. Time itself becomes a major stressor in **time urgency**.

2. *Polyphasia:* **Polyphasia** is engaging in more than one thought or activity at one time. Today, it's called

---

Type A personality: This personality, once associated with time urgency, is now associated with unresolved anger issues.

Time urgency: A characteristic or behavior of someone who displays Type A personality, someone who is constantly time conscious.

Polyphasia: A trait of thinking or doing many activities at once, also known as multitasking. This is also a trait of the Type A personality.

multitasking. It can lead to sensory overload as the mind juggles thoughts competing for attention. An example of polyphasia is the following: driving to work, talking on a cell phone, putting on make-up or shaving, and listening to the radio, all at the same time. Polyphasia is related to the sense of time urgency in that these people feel that they must do many things at once because their time is so limited.

3. *Ultra-competitiveness:* Type A's are very self-conscious in that they compare themselves with others of similar social status. This trait is exhibited by working extra hours, working on several projects at one time, and vying for top recognition at work. All colleagues or peers at the same status level are perceived as personal threats. Type A's may also appear to be egocentric, perceiving that they are more important than others with regard to their work. Moreover, Type A's are found to be more concerned with quantity of work than quality of work, despite what they may say. The ultra-competitiveness may carry over into non-work-related events, such as sporting activities. This manifests itself when Type A's are in the presence of other people who exhibit a similar competitive drive.

4. *Rapid speech patterns:* Type A people are found to raise their voices in normal conversations, and use explosive words to influence, control, or intimidate others. During conversations, Type A's often finish sentences for people who take their time expressing or articulating their thoughts.

5. *Manipulative control:* Manipulative control is a trait symbolic of a person who is very ego driven. This behavior results from a desire to influence, and even intimidate, co-workers, family members, and acquaintances. Control is achieved through either direct intimidation or circuitously, in a passive-aggressive way. As one might expect, this attitude of dominant control is maintained to promote feelings of one-upmanship. Type A's assert control when they feel threatened.

6. *Hyperaggressiveness and free-floating hostility:* Type A's have a need to dominate other people. They not only strive for high goals, but walk over people to get to the top, showing little or no compassion. These people are very aggressive and may even come across as abrasive. Type A's are also noted to have what is now called free-floating hostility, which is permanently in-dwelling anger that erupts at trivial occurrences like traffic lights, long lines at the supermarket, or broken photocopy machines. At closer range, Type A's seem to have an inability to express anger in a creative fashion. In many cases, they momentarily suppress feelings of anger and then later explode. Hostility of this nature is also observed to be unfocused, free-floating, and often unresolved. Type A's typically display annoyance with circumstances that would seem barely noticeable to Type B's.

One factor that all these traits share is low self-esteem, here meaning the perception of self-worth based on both how one perceives oneself and how one perceives others' perceptions of oneself. People classified as Type A are also preoccupied with how they are perceived by others regarding material possessions and social status. (The issue of self-esteem will be explained in more detail at the end of this chapter.)

Hostility: The Lethal Trait of Type A's

Originally, time urgency was considered the most critical factor associated with Type A and heart disease, and it was this trait that was thought to be directly related to hypertension. Upon closer examination, several people classified as Type A exhibited neither hypertension nor coronary heart disease, leaving doubt as to whether this criterion merited further research. Investigations by Rosenman (1990) and others suggest that the most important, even dangerous, component of Type A behavior is hostile aggression. Work in this area now supports the idea that this factor alone is more responsible for the strong correlation to coronary heart disease than are all the other traits classified as Type A behavior.

With the suspicion that hostile aggression was the most important predictor of CHD, new ways to assess aggressive behavior were considered. To date, the most popular method is the Cook-Medley Hostility Index, also referred to as the Ho Scale (Cook and Medley, 1954). This index was developed from questions on the Minnesota Multiphasic Personality Inventory (MMPI) to measure hostility. Using this and other assessment tools (e.g., Potential for Hostility Scale, or PoHo),

> **Multitasking:** Acting on many responsibilities at one time (driving and talking on a cell phone) to save time, yet potentially compromising the integrity of both outcomes.

several studies have begun to show a strong correlation between hostility and the development of CHD. In one study by Williams et al. (1980), for example, it was found that hostility was correlated with coronary blockage, suggesting that hostile aggression could be used as a predictor for CHD. Studies by Barefoot et al. (1983, 1987) also indicated a strong correlation between hostility and increased risk of heart disease. Using the Ho Scale, Barefoot and colleagues studied a group of physicians over a 25-year period. Those who scored high on the aggression index showed a fourfold greater incidence of CHD than those who scored low.

Hostility is an expression of anger, and anger can surface in many ways, including cynicism, sarcasm, intimidation, and various other aggressive behaviors. It should be noted that impatience is also a form of anger, and although it may not seem as potent as hostility, Friedman and Rosenman were not far off when they cited time-consciousness as the cornerstone of the Type A personality and its relationship to CHD. It may be that impatience festers into what they referred to as free-floating hostility, which in turn snowballs into mismanaged anger. Whatever the case, hostility and aggression are thought to be the most important factors with regard to heart disease, rather than the collection of Type A behaviors as a whole.

Behavior Modification for Type A Behavior

Since the identification of the Type A personality, much research has been conducted to determine if its traits and behaviors can be changed or modified to reduce the risk of coronary heart disease. Friedman et al. (1984), for example, placed more than 500 post–heart attack patients in an education/behavior modification program, including 29 counseling sessions, for a 3-year period. Those who participated in this program showed a 44 percent decrease in Type A behaviors as measured by questionnaires and personal interviews. Many individuals also reduced the incidence of recurring heart attacks. The findings of this and other studies have led many health specialists to develop intervention programs that can alter negative health behaviors and improve health status. The same study also indicated that although the totality of personality will not change, components of it can be favorably influenced and altered to improve one's health status. Currently, behavior modification programs focus on the creative release of anger. It is the findings of Friedman and associates that led to current behavior modification programs in anger management.

Social Influences on Type A Behavior

Several researchers have speculated on the origins of Type A behavior, and the nature (genetics) versus nurture (environment) issue surfaces again. It is well accepted that children model their behavior on that of parents and other figures of authority, including aggressive behaviors. But researchers seem to agree that Type A behavior is a product of broader social and cultural factors as well, including the corporate culture, which breeds employee burnout through long hours, 24/7 accessibility, multitasking, and guilt associated with taking vacation time. Many of the behaviors associated with Type A are often rewarded in our society as positive attributes leading toward success in one's career. Based on the work of Friedman and Rosenman, Schafer (1992) lists these as the following:

1. *Material wealth:* Part of the American dream is to have the freedom to own a house, car, and a number of consumer goods. In a free-market economy, people seem caught up in the accumulation of material goods. This fact became most evident in the 1980s, when sociologists noted a veritable obsession with material possessions.

2. *Immediate gratification:* The ability to drive up to a window and receive service immediately, whether for food, liquor, money, or videos, has had a big impact on our expectations for virtually all goods and services. In general, the pace of life has quickened in tandem with the pace of technology. In keeping pace with technological advancements, people have come to expect immediacy in everything.

3. *Competitiveness:* Competition for grades, salary increases, and sales are just three examples of the ways people feel pressured to become successful and get ahead. There is constant pressure to keep up with the Joneses. Friedman and Rosenman referred to this as "the excess of the competitive spirit," where more never seems to be enough.

4. *People as numbers:* Bureaucratic policies and procedures often make one feel like a number rather than a person. To be identified by your Social Security number for class registration, auto insurance, or taxes decreases the personal aspect of human interaction. This lack of personal attention is thought to contribute to an overall sense of alienation from oneself and others.

5. *Secularization:* As people become less and less involved with spiritual issues and growth, a vacuum

is created, leading to a decline in self-reliance, self-esteem, and social connectedness.

6. *Atrophy of the body and right brain:* Reliance on technology to carry out functions humans used to do can make us physically sedentary. Moreover, there is a general consensus that our society encourages left-brain thinking processes, such as analysis and judgment skills, over right-brain thinking processes, which in excess can lead to increased tension and frustration.

7. *Television watching:* Studies show that the average person watches between 20 and 40 hours of television per week. Many of the qualities and behaviors observed in Type A's are the same ones depicted in television programming. The rise in violent crimes, for example, is thought to be significantly correlated to the preponderance of violence seen on TV. The sheer number of violent acts on television programs implies condoning of this behavior.

It should come as no surprise that the behavioral traits associated with Type A personality precipitate the stress response. When left unmanaged, these create a vicious cycle of perceived stress-related problems spiraling into physiological responses. The pressures of time, threats of competition, and unresolved anger generate a modus operandi of perpetual stress.

Did Someone Say Type D Personality?

Research is now shifting its focus from Type A (aggression) to what some call Type D (depression) and others call "psychocardiology" or "behavioral cardiology": the relationship between emotional stress (specifically, anxiety and depression) and cardiac function. The idea that personality traits associated with anxiety and depression affect the course of heart disease is now supported by clinical data. It is now noted that the words *anger* and *angina* share a common root.

Dr. Johan Denollet, intrigued by the personality differences among heart attack patients, devised a 14-question survey (DS-14) to help determine a person's cardiovascular health based on a proclivity to depression, what he calls negative affectivity (BOX 7.1). Questions attempt to identify personality traits such as worry, irritability, gloom, social inhibition, and depression (e.g., "I am often down in the dumps"). With an estimated

one-quarter of the American population on antidepressants, the Type D personality is taking on greater relevance in the medical community with regard to many chronic illnesses.

Given the connection between anger and depression (anger turned inward), perhaps Type A and Type D personalities share some common ground: Stress! The association between stress and heart disease appears so strong that *Newsweek* magazine dedicated nearly a whole issue to the topic in the fall of 2005 with a feature article by renowned cardiologist Dr. Dean Ornish, the first person to prove the reversal of plaque buildup in the arteries. Ornish states that love, expressed through compassion, is often the missing component in people prone to heart disease. Love and compassion, it should be noted, are not traits commonly expressed in either the Type A or Type D personalities.

Codependent Personality Traits

The concept of **codependency** was introduced by psychologists in the 1980s to describe individuals who, in simple terms, are dependent on making other people dependent on them as a means of self-validation. In layman's terms, this label has been used to describe people who "love (conditionally) too much." Codependency is also referred to as an addictive personality because the behaviors associated with it are similar to those observed with other process addictions ("addictions" to behaviors rather than substances). The term *codependency* was first coined by a handful of counselors and therapists who were themselves recovering from chemical and process addictions. It evolved primarily from the study of individuals participating in alcohol rehabilitation programs. Originally, these programs focused solely on the addict. Over time, however, it was found to be imperative to include the spouses and children for greater success of the recovery process of the addict. When family members were introduced into the therapy process, it was learned that many of these individuals "enabled" the alcoholic to continue his or her addictive habits by covering up for

> **Codependency:** A stress-prone personality with many traits and behaviors that seem to increase the likelihood of perceived stress and the inability to cope effectively with it; addictive in nature; based on the need to make others dependent to receive self-validation.

BOX 7.1   Type D Personality Inventory

The following questionnaire is adapted from Johan Denollet's Type D (Depression) Personality Questionnaire, which connects the dots between personality (negativity and social inhibition) to the predictability of coronary heart disease. Please read each question and answer as you are (not how you wish to be), circling the most appropriate answer. Then check your answers with the key below.

	Never	Somewhat	Maybe	Often	Always
1. More often than not, I feel "blue" or unhappy.	0	1	2	3	4
2. I tend to make mountains out of molehills.	0	1	2	3	4
3. I am shy and reserved with people I meet.	0	1	2	3	4
4. I tend to get overwhelmed with responsibilities.	0	1	2	3	4
5. I am not a very sociable person.	0	1	2	3	4
6. I tend to get frustrated easily.	0	1	2	3	4
7. I find social interactions rather awkward.	0	1	2	3	4
8. I tend to be a loner.	0	1	2	3	4
9. The word "moody" describes me well.	0	1	2	3	4
10. In the company of others, I tend to be reserved.	0	1	2	3	4
11. It's a bother to maintain relationships.	0	1	2	3	4
12. I tend to worry a lot about most things.	0	1	2	3	4
13. No one can relate to me and my problems.	0	1	2	3	4
14. I would best describe my tendencies as pessimistic.	0	1	2	3	4

Negativity Index:
Add scores for questions 1, 2, 4, 6, 9, 12, 14   _____

Social Inhibition Index:
Add scores for questions 3, 5, 7, 8, 10, 11, 13   _____

Scores of 10 or higher for both Negativity and Social Inhibition suggest one is very likely classified as a Type D and possibly prone to coronary heart health issues.

Data from Denollet, J. Standard Assessment of Negative Affectivity, Social Inhibition, and Type D Personality. *Psychosomatic Medicine*, 67(6), 2005.

---

them, allegedly out of concern, loyalty, and love, but in fact to act out their need to be needed. Thus, these individuals were labeled **enablers**, and strangely enough, it was observed that many of their own personality traits and related behaviors were of an addictive nature as well.

> **Enablers:** A term coined in the alcohol recovery movement, referring to a person who enables a spouse, parent, or child to continue either a substance or process addiction.

Further studies on this group of people, many of whom were adult children of alcoholics (ACOA), led researchers to redefine the parameters of the enabler personality type and the traits associated with it.

Codependency, as defined by Melodie Beattie in her book *Codependent No More* (a book that continues to sell millions of copies each year), is "an addiction to another person(s) and their problems or to a relationship and its problems." This personality first became evident among children of alcoholics, but now, three criteria have been established as precursors to the development of this personality: having alcoholic parents or guardians, having divorced parents, or having emotionally repressive parents. A fourth criterion suggests that codependent traits are simply a product of American social mores. Regardless of one's background, codependent traits and their related behaviors are thought to develop early in childhood, in a lifestyle or environment that is chaotic, unpredictable, or threatening. Children are believed to unknowingly adopt various codependent behaviors as **survival skills** in their developmental years, usually to win approval and love from the parents and elders who most influence their lives, as well as to cope with family stress on a day-to-day basis. In many cases, these children assume adult responsibilities long before they reach high school. As they mature, they carry these survival skills—many inappropriate—into adult relationships as excess baggage. Nevertheless, these skills remain the first line of defense in their attempt to deal effectively with others and themselves, yet the nature of these characteristics only perpetuates the stress cycle of threatening perceptions and consequent physical arousal.

Psychologist Ann Wilson Schaef (1986) describes codependency as a **process addiction** because each behavior is like a "fix" to acquire self-validation. But like the effects of a chemical addiction, the "high" is only short-lived so these behaviors are continually repeated. New process addictions include constant checking of email and voice mail and constant cell phone use. The traits associated with this personality type are many and have been criticized by some (Katz and Lieu, 1991) as being so widespread that they include nearly everyone living in the United States. Perhaps because the identification of this personality style emerged from psychotherapy and not clinical medicine, it has not been researched to the same extent as Type A personality. Regardless, there are several key traits that stand out as indicative of individuals who validate their own existence through the approval and manipulation of others. It should be pointed out, first, that codependent people are extremely nice and very well liked because they like to please others. (Many gravitate to the health-care industry; Schaef points out that many nurses are first-born children of alcoholics.) Either individually or collectively, the traits associated with codependency are not considered bad; in fact, many of them are looked on as being quite admirable. However, it is the habitual exhibition of these traits, in an obsessive-compulsive manner, that defines the codependent personality. These traits include the following:

1. *Ardent approval seekers:* Codependent people know how to say the right things, wear the right clothes, and do the right things to draw other people to them and to avoid rocking the boat. Often they ask for an opinion or feedback on their performance and appearance, looking for approval from others.

2. *Perfectionists:* These people are extremely well organized and are in the habit of going beyond a quality job every time. They do, however, get caught up in details, spending extra time on every project or activity to make everything just right. They get very stressed (either annoyed or worried) when things aren't perfect.

3. *Super-overachievers:* This trait means being involved in an abundance of activities and obligations—school, sports, social functions—and receiving stupendous recognition for all of these (**FIG. 7.2**). These people do it all, and they do it all extremely well.

4. *Crisis managers:* Perhaps because of the environment in which they were raised, codependents thrive on crisis. They constantly try to make order out of chaos and, for the most part, are successful at it. They rush to take control in time of crisis and show that they can be counted on to be there and steer the ship back to a safe harbor.

5. *Devoted loyalists:* Codependents are extremely loyal to friends and family, despite their addictions and abusive behavior. It has been suggested that extreme loyalty may be shown for fear of rejection and abandonment.

6. *Self-sacrificing martyrs:* People who express this personality put everyone else first, before their own needs, to the point of sacrificing their own time, values, property, and even life goals.

7. *Manipulators:* Unlike Type A's, who use intimidation and dominance to manipulate others, codependents manipulate others through acts of generosity and "favors." They feel that the ability to express their own emotions and control their own lives is nowhere

> **Survival skills:** A term associated with codependency in which certain behaviors are adopted in adolescence to "survive" demanding, alcoholic, or abusive parents.
>
> **Process addiction:** The addiction to a behavioral process such as shopping, intercourse, gambling, television watching, cutting, and codependent behaviors.

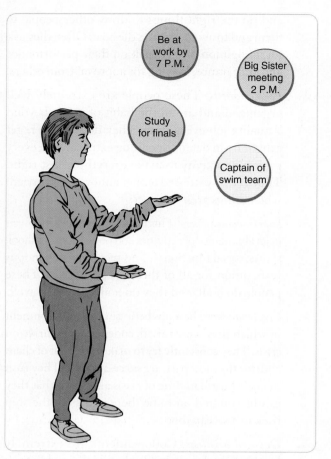

Be at work by 7 P.M.

Big Sister meeting 2 P.M.

Study for finals

Captain of swim team

FIGURE 7.2 People with a codependent personality are typically super-overachievers. They take on many responsibilities and do them all extremely well.

as easy as doing these for other people. Control and manipulation are performed in a humbling fashion. Codependents adopt what Schaef calls the **illusion of control**, wherein they try to control others and their environment to compensate for the fact that they cannot maintain self-control (e.g., of emotions or perceptions).

8. *Victims:* In tandem with repeated acts of martyrdom, these people perceive that they never receive enough gratitude or credit for self-sacrifice. These people find it impossible to say no but feel taken advantage of

Illusion of control: A term used in association with codependent behavior, thinking that one can control (manipulate) things/others that one really cannot.

Reactionaries: A term associated with the codependent personality illustrating a behavior of reacting, rather than responding, to stress.

after the fact when feeling used sets in. Both crisis management and simple charitable tasks are unconsciously described by the codependent individual as "I've been wronged."

9. *Feelings of inadequacy:* Simply stated, codependents have a black cloud of inferiority over their heads, despite the fact that they are overachievers. (Remember, every action is a "fix" of self-validation.) They feel that the quality and quantity of work done are never to their satisfaction, that more is always expected of them. By being dependent on others for approval, they forfeit self-reliance, the ability to turn inward for strength, faith, and confidence. Self-reliance is the ability to be inspired from within, not motivated solely by external factors. And feelings of inadequacy dissolve self-reliance.

10. *Reactionaries:* Codependent individuals tend to overreact rather than respond to situations. At a young age, these **reactionaries'** expressions of concern and worry were perceived as expressions of love. But worrying is an immobilizing emotion that inhibits the ability to respond adequately to a given situation. When small problems arise, overreacting makes them appear catastrophic, which in turn makes them all the more important to address.

Schaef elaborates on several behaviors that appear to be hallmarks of the codependent personality in her book *Codependence: Misunderstood, Mistreated.* The manifestation of codependent traits includes the following behaviors:

1. *External referencing:* This is a process whereby an individual gains feelings of importance from external sources. Codependents often doubt their own intrinsic value, so the greatest percentage of their self-validation is derived externally. An example of this behavior is trying to live up to other people's expectations.

2. *Lack of emotional boundaries:* This means that an individual takes on other people's emotional feelings—sadness, happiness, fear, or whatever people around them are feeling or thinking. Codependents often cannot delineate where their feelings end and where the feelings of others begin.

3. *Impression management:* Codependents are always trying to be good people, and they believe they can control the perceptions of others by their good deeds. Their main goal in life is to try and figure out what others want and then deliver it to them. They develop amazing abilities to learn about

the likes and dislikes of other people. They truly believe that if they can just become what others want, they will be safe and accepted. When things go unexpectedly wrong, they often use the words, "I'm sorry," to win sympathy and approval.

4. *Mistrust of one's own perceptions:* Codependents tend to ignore their own perceptions of situations unless or until they are verified externally by others. Even though they might have a very clear impression of a person or a situation, they often dismiss it as being crazy or mistaken. They have learned not to trust their own intuition.

5. *Martyr syndrome:* There is a difference between helping people in need and living their lives for them. Codependents will help anyone (most often their immediate families), and they help them with everything. They say yes because they don't know how to say no. They are afraid that saying no will mean permanent rejection. Martyrs actually perpetuate chaotic situations by accepting responsibility for spouses, parents, and other family members to keep the household together, rather than blowing the whistle on inappropriate behavior.

6. *Lack of spiritual health:* Codependents adopt a mode of dishonest behavior (lying) to survive. The habit of lying begins as white lies to appease people. In this process, they also lie to themselves, hiding their own feelings. In the opinion of Schaef, "Lying does not keep with our deepest spiritual self. Lying to ourselves is always destructive to the self, and it is always destructive to others." According to Schaef, this is a form of spiritual destruction. The mental, emotional, and often physical imbalances spill over into a spiritual imbalance as well.

Estimates by Larsen (1983), Wegscheider-Cruse (1984, 2008), and Schaef (1987) suggest that the codependent personality is so prevalent in the United States that it has become "the American personality," with over 96 percent of Americans exhibiting traits of codependency (and leading to what Schaef calls "an addictive society" as a whole). This number is quite likely inflated, but according to data provided by the National Association for Children of Alcoholics (NACoA) for 2007, one out of every eight Americans (approximately 12.5 percent) is an alcoholic. Also, data show that 76 million Americans (approximately one out of every four children) are directly affected by the behavior of an alcoholic—this does not include other family members or co-workers.

A spokesperson for the NACoA stated that the terms *enabling* and *codependency* are the primary focus of intervention. (Some estimates are that each alcoholic negatively affects between 10 and 12 people, thus surpassing the country's population.) In many families where one or both parents are alcoholics, children often assume the role of an adult, handling many parental responsibilities. These children learn to react to family crises by taking charge in hopes of winning love and approval. Like Type A behavior, codependency is not gender specific, and both personality types include the inability to recognize and express emotions. But unlike Type A individuals, who operate on the energy of misdirected and unresolved anger, codependents are motivated by fear—most notably, fear of rejection, fear of the unknown, and fear of failure. The codependent personality has many similarities to what medical researchers have identified as the cancer-prone personality (Type C personality), which is described as a people-pleasing and emotionally repressed personality.

Helpless-Hopeless Personality

The **helpless-hopeless personality**, while less defined by various traits than the Type A or codependent personality, nevertheless is a stress-prone personality based on low self-esteem. Seligman (1975) was the first to study this personality and to derive the theory of what he called learned helplessness. Seligman described people with this personality as those who have encountered repeated bouts of failure, to the point where they give up on themselves in situations where they clearly have control. That is, repeated failure becomes a learned response. Seligman noted that the signatures of learned helplessness are (1) poor self-motivation, where no attempt is made at self-improvement; (2) cognitive distortion, where perceptions of failure repeatedly eclipse prospects of success; and (3) emotional dysfunction, where repeated failures result in chronic depression. Dr. Arthur Schmale (Locke and Colligan, 1986) also has studied individuals whom he classifies as the helpless-hopeless personality. These individuals, he found, perceive that their problems are beyond the range of their own resources and ultimately give up. Schmale defines the helpless-hopeless personality as "Feelings

> **Helpless-hopeless personality:** Describes a person who has given up on life, or aspects of it, as a result of repeated failure.

of frustration, despair, or futility perceived as coming from a loss of satisfaction for which the individual himself assumed complete and final responsibility by a sense of frustration that one has failed miserably at accomplishing anything in life." In a study reported by Locke and Colligan (1986), Schmale and Iker surveyed the personalities of 51 women using psychological tests and personal interviews to detect an intrinsic state of hopelessness. Based on the analysis of these tests and interviews, eighteen women were predicted to contract cancer, and these predictions held true.

Perhaps the characteristic that best identifies the helpless-hopeless personality is referred to as an external **locus of control**. This concept was developed by psychologist Julian Rotter in the early 1960s. Rotter theorized that behavior is normally influenced by both internal and external sources. A preponderance of external factors reinforcing behavior constitutes what Rotter defined as an external locus of control. Examples of external factors might include other people, luck, the weather, chance, or even astrological influences. Conversely, people who demonstrate an internal locus of control feel responsible for their own actions as derived by the internal resources of self-confidence, faith, intuition, and willpower.

Rotter observed that those individuals identified as having an internal locus of control were, on the whole, healthier and more productive individuals. They were observed to be information seekers and goal directed, and to obtain a sense of mastery to cope with problems. Individuals who were identified as having an external locus of control often showed signs of apathy and complacency. The helpless-hopeless personality is the epitome of an external locus of control. Such attitudes and behaviors appear to have been learned early in life, when failure with tasks was a common occurrence. The lack of success, coupled with less-than-desirable environmental factors, shapes the individual's personality to feel helpless in stressful situations and give up productive attempts to overcome the circumstances perceived as stressful. Rotter believed

that although many features of personality were fixed entities, locus of control was not an absolute; it could be changed to the advantage of the individual. This is the premise of many drug- and alcohol-treatment programs, wherein patients are taught to capitalize on aspects of their lives they do in fact have control over so as to beat the chemical dependency.

Extreme examples of individuals with the helpless-hopeless personality type include alcoholics, drug addicts, abused children, abused wives, some elderly, and some of the nation's homeless. Although these examples may seem distant from the average person, everyone experiences moments of hopelessness. However, repeated bouts of failure at any time in one's life could allow shades of this personality to manifest. Because of the failure-control issues involved, the helpless-hopeless personality is considered synonymous with an ongoing stress response.

Resiliency: The Hardy Personality

Using the framework of the mechanistic medical model, many researchers in the 1960s and 1970s were trying to find a relationship between personality traits and the leading killers in the country, coronary heart disease and cancer. Growing evidence suggested a link between mind (negative thoughts) and body (physical symptoms), and this in turn spurred the pessimistic suggestion that the greater the stress level, the greater the chance of disease and illness.

But one group of researchers, headed by Dr. Suzanne Kobasa and Salvatore Maddi, became interested in individuals who despite stressful circumstances appeared *resistant* to the psychophysiological effects of stress. Kobasa et al. (1979, 1981, 1982, 1983) studied several hundred AT&T employees during the period of federal deregulation when scores of executives were laid off or transferred to other positions. In this study, more than 700 executives were given a version of the Holmes and Rahe stress inventory and a checklist of physical symptoms and illnesses. Although hundreds of executives showed physical symptoms of stress, under the same circumstances several did not. When this smaller group of individuals was studied further, it became quite obvious that what distinguished them from those who succumbed to the stress were specific personality traits enabling them to cope with their perceptions of stress. Kobasa et al. found

> **Locus of control:** A sense of who or what is in control of one's life; people with an internal locus of control take responsibility for their actions; those with an external locus of control place responsibility on external factors like luck or the weather; the latter is associated with the helpless-hopeless personality, a stress-prone personality.

BOX 7.2   Hardy Personality Profile: Test Your Hardiness

This questionnaire is adapted from the work of Suzanne Kobasa, co-creator of the hardy personality. This inventory is based on 12 questions. In the words of Kobasa, "Evaluating hardiness requires more than a quick test, but this survey will give you an idea of your degree of hardiness." Using a scale of 0–3, estimate your answer for each question. Please answer how you are, not how you would like to be. Then score your answers for Control, Commitment, and Challenge.

0 = strongly disagree, 1 = mildly disagree, 2 = mildly agree, 3 = strongly agree

_____   1.   My best efforts at work/school make a difference.

_____   2.   Trusting to fate/universe is sometimes all I can do in a relationship.

_____   3.   I often wake up each day eager to start, work on, or complete a project.

_____   4.   Viewing myself as a free person tends to promote stress and frustration.

_____   5.   I would be willing to sacrifice financial security in my work if something really challenging came along.

_____   6.   I get stressed when my plans go awry and my schedule is disrupted.

_____   7.   Anybody, from any social demographic, can have an influence on politics.

_____   8.   Without the right breaks, it is difficult to be successful in my field.

_____   9.   I know what I am doing and why I am doing it at work/school.

_____ 10.   Becoming close to people makes me feel a sense of obligation to them.

_____ 11.   I relish the chance to encounter new situations as an important part of life.

_____ 12.   I really don't mind when I have lots of free time with nothing to do.

Score: To estimate your level of hardiness, calculate the scores for each component (by adding and subtracting where indicated). A total score of 10–18 indicates a hardy personality, 0–9 suggests moderate hardiness, and a score less than 0 indicates low hardiness.

Control Score = _____	Commitment Score = _____	Challenge Score = _____
1 _____ + 7 _____	3 _____ + 9 _____	5 _____ + 11 _____
subtract	subtract	subtract
2 _____ + 8 _____	4 _____ + 10 _____	6 _____ + 12 _____
		Total Hardiness Score _____

---

three specific personality traits that collectively acted as a buffer to stress and contributed to what Kobasa called the **hardy personality** (BOX 7.2):

1.   *Commitment:* The dedication to oneself, one's work, and one's family that gives the individual a sense of belonging. Commitment involves an investment of one's values and life purpose to the growth of one's human potential and is a direct reflection of one's willpower.

2.   *Control:* In this case, control means a sense of personal control, a sense of causing the events in one's life rather than a feeling of helplessness. Self-control, or empowerment, helps one overcome

> **Hardy personality:** A term coined by Maddi and Kobasa; personality characteristics that, in combination, seem to buffer against stress: control, commitment, and challenge.

factors and elements in one's environment so that one does not feel victimized.

3. *Challenge:* The ability to see change and even problems as opportunities for growth, rather than threats to one's existence. Challenge, in Kobasa's mind, symbolized a hunger of the heart that serves as an inspiration. Challenge can also be viewed as a sense of adventure.

The results of this and similar studies with lawyers, housewives, and other groups revealed that the traits of the hardy personality were not limited to white, upper-middle-class, executive males employed by AT&T, but were found in people from both genders and all races and religions. In addition, Kobasa concluded the following:

■ A hardy personality may override a genetic disposition to illness.

■ A person can exhibit several Type A traits without risk of heart disease.

■ Inner resources are more important than strong family support during high-pressure jobs.

■ Some people observed as hardy showed signs of Type A personality minus feelings of hostility. These people enjoyed life so much they would often hurry with some tasks to enjoy others.

Kobasa and a colleague, Sal Maddi (1982, 1999, 2002), are of the opinion that although the hardy personality appears to be innate, the traits of commitment, control, and challenge can be learned as well. In a study to determine the efficacy of teaching hardiness skills to Illinois Bell executives over an 8-week period, sixteen executives experiencing stress-related health problems were divided into two groups: a treatment group to learn hardiness skills, and a control group. The skills taught to the treatment group were (1) **focusing**, or recognizing the body

signals of stress (e.g., muscle tension); (2) **reconstruction**, reinterpretation of a stressor, and viable options to resolve it; and (3) **compensation**, turning control of personal talents into abilities that accent strengths rather than foster helplessness. After exposure to the new behavior skills, the treatment group scored higher on the hardiness scale, and even demonstrated a decrease in resting blood pressure, while the control group showed no change. The research findings of Kobasa et al., which closely parallel the theories of Abraham Maslow and his concept of self-actualization, led them to believe that commitment, control, and challenge were necessary traits to maintain a buffer against the effects of stress, and that a hardy personality contributed to overall good health. Today, Maddi continues his research of the hardy personality at the University of California at Irvine where he calls hardiness a type of "existential courage" (Maddi, 2004). His research adds to the body of knowledge in the discipline of positive psychology. Maddi's faculty Web site states that he is especially interested in stress management and creativity. Through deepening the attitudes of commitment, control, and challenge and marking hardiness, persons can simultaneously develop, reach their highest potentials, and cope with any stress encountered on the way.

Reivich (2003) and Al Siebert (2005) have taken the premise of the hardy personality and renamed it for the twenty-first century. Each calls it "resiliency." Resiliency can best be defined as the ability to pick yourself up after being knocked down in the face of adversity from life-changing events (**BOX 7.3**).

■ Survivor Personality Traits

Aron Ralston is a survivor—perhaps the epitome of it. While rock climbing in the southwest corner of Utah's desert in spring 2003, Ralston got caught. An 800-pound boulder wedged itself over his right arm, pinning him against the side of a mountain. Unable to free himself, Ralston did the unthinkable. After days of deliberating about his situation, he pulled out his pocket knife and proceeded to amputate his own arm. Once liberated from the boulder, he was still a long way from safety. He rappelled 80 feet down the rock face and then hiked several miles in the direction of his car to reach help. Although Ralston's story, portrayed by Academy Award–nominated actor James Franco in the biopic *127 Hours*, is unfathomable, he stands in good company among those who survive, even thrive, in the face of unbeatable odds

Focusing: The ability to recognize the body signals of oncoming stress (e.g., muscle tension, increased breathing, sweating).

Reconstruction: The reinterpretation (from negative to neutral or positive) of a stressor (also known as reframing).

Compensation: The ability to cultivate and utilize one's strengths in times of need, rather than claim victimization.

BOX 7.3   Resiliency 101

The newest buzzword in stress management is the term "resiliency," a twenty-first-century makeover of the hardy personality. More than just the ability to bounce back from personal setbacks, resiliency is the ability to overcome the tremendous stress of trauma, loss, and tragedy. In the words of philosopher Friedrich Nietzsche, "That which doesn't kill us, makes us stronger." Moreover, the traits of resiliency are now considered to be those that enrich our lives—an attitude of *can do*. The alchemy of resiliency includes optimism, courage, flexibility, humor, compassion, and the ability to adapt to change (rather than be a victim of circumstance). Al Siebert, author of *The Resiliency Advantage* and *The Survivor Personality*, explains that resilient people have the ability to create good luck out of circumstances that many others see as bad luck. Others describe resiliency as our capacity to not only deal with discomfort and adversity, but also thrive in the face of chaos. Professional dancer Adrianne Haslet-Davis is one such example. Nearing the finish line at the 2013 Boston Marathon, she was thrown off her feet during the second bomb explosion. Her husband (an Air Force captain who served in Afghanistan) quickly put a tourniquet on her leg. She was rushed to the hospital, where doctors did all they could to save her foot, but to no avail. She ended up losing her foot and lower leg. This event has not deterred her from her passions. Adrianne is committed to continuing her career as a dancer and vows to complete her next Boston Marathon, even if she has to crawl across the finish line.

For some people resiliency comes naturally, yet many believe that it is a life skill that can be learned and practiced by everyone. Resiliency training is available for people from all walks of life, including returning soldiers from Iraq and Afghanistan, first responders (police and EMTs), corporate executives, and Olympic athletes. Courses in resiliency, from those taught at the Mayo Clinic to nearly all branches of the U.S. military,

include some or all of these aspects to strengthen the resolve of those moving through life's transitions:

1. *Positivity:* Carrying a positive attitude about life and your role in it
2. *Creative problem-solving:* Focusing on the solution to a problem rather than the problem itself
3. *Compassion and gratitude:* Being grateful for what you have rather than what you don't have; seeing yourself as a victor, not a victim; and honoring the connectedness of life through service to others
4. *Self-care:* Honoring yourself to engage in personal wellness activities
5. *Humor:* Having the ability to laugh at yourself without sacrificing self-esteem
6. *Purpose in life:* Being able to cultivate a meaningful purpose in one's life through change

The topic of resiliency is being studied from a great many perspectives, including brain activity scans (fMRIs) during the practice of resiliency skills to the inclusion of mindfulness meditation as a resiliency-based activity. These and other topics were the subject of discussion at the 2013 Harvard Medical Schools conference on resiliency, under the direction of Herbert Benson, M.D.

In a quiet corner of the second floor of the Claude Moore Nursing Education Building at the University of Virginia is the Resiliency Room. This room is used for yoga classes, mindfulness meditation, and personal solitude for students and faculty alike. As professionals on the front lines of health care who help others cope with the spectrum of issues from disease to death, resiliency is considered a necessary skill in nursing. Students, faculty, and staff are all encouraged to make good and frequent use of the room. The University of Virginia is not alone with this strategy. *Fortune* 500 corporations and the U.S. Army are exploring ways to create resiliency centers for their employees as the rapid pace of life quickens.

(and making a mockery of all reality TV shows). Moreover, anyone who has heard the story of Ernest Shackleton and the crew of the *Endurance*, for example, knows the story of incredible and grueling survival in the world's most inhospitable climate, Antarctica.

Al Siebert, the author of *The Survivor Personality*, has studied the likes of Ralston and Shackleton—that is, people who have kept a cool head in the face of danger and come out alive from their ordeal. Siebert defines this type of personality as someone who responds rather than reacts to danger. The traits of a **survivor personality** include acceptance (of the situation), optimism, and creative problem solving. Beyond the classic will to survive, this personality type integrates the right-brain abilities of intuition, acceptance, and faith with the left-brain skills of judgment and organization. Siebert suggests that the survivor personality has mastered an integrative problem-solving ability with the use of **biphasic** (left and right brain) **personality traits**: proud yet humble, selfish yet altruistic, rebellious yet cooperative, spiritual yet irreverent. Perhaps the most important trait is mental flexibility, according to both Siebert and Peter Suedfeld (Jenkins, 2003). Beyond the will to survive, the foremost character trait of a survivor is intellectual flexibility. As the expression goes, there are three ways to cope in times of crisis: leave the environment, change the environment, or change your attitude. The survivor personality isn't determined by genetic make-up. Instead, those who study the survivor personality agree that these traits can be learned and practiced by anyone, whether it's Nien Cheng, Aron Ralston, or someone with a flat tire on a highway in the middle of nowhere.

Sensation Seekers

If you are familiar with extreme sports, the X Games, or even the reality shows that depict extreme survival challenges, then no doubt you are familiar with whom psychologists refer to as **sensation seekers** or Type R (risk taker) personalities, a term coined by Zuckerman (1971) to describe people whose personalities appear to be dominated by an adventurous spirit (**FIG. 7.3**). For these people, adrenaline is their drug of choice. Studies by both Zuckerman (1971) and Johnson, Sarason, and

> **Survivor personality:** The traits that comprise a unique winning attitude to overcome adversity and challenges, no matter what the odds may be, so that one comes out the victor, not the victim.
>
> **Biphasic:** Survivor personality traits; the ability to use both right-brain and left-brain thinking processes to successfully deal with a problem or stressors.
>
> **Personality traits:** Thoughts and behaviors that combine to form or color one's personality; in this case, cognitive traits associated with survival.
>
> **Sensation seeker:** Also known as Type R personality, these courageous people confront stress by calculating their risks in extreme situations and then proceeding with gusto.

FIGURE 7.3   Calculated risk taking is what separates sensation seekers from those who choose to sit on the sidelines watching the world go by. To accomplish a goal under these conditions is thought to augment self-esteem, which in turn enables one to deal more effectively with stress.

Siegel (1979) found that people who are inclined toward "extreme" activities providing intense sensation, like rock climbing, skydiving, windsurfing, hang gliding, and exotic travel, are better able to cope with life events than those who are more inclined to avoid taking risks. It is hypothesized that in their intentional exposure to "approachable stress," or sensation activities, they calculate the risks involved. This prepares them for unexpected stressful events, which they also approach in a calculated manner. In other words, sensation seekers think through their strategies rather than reacting impetuously. They are spontaneous, yet calculating. An additional hypothesis suggests that the inner resources required to perform sensation activities (e.g., confidence, self-efficacy, courage, optimism, and creativity) are the same qualities used as coping skills to deal effectively with stress. These hypotheses do not imply that sensation seekers do not have stress; rather, they try to meet it head on and aim to overcome it. Examples might include athletes who participate in extreme sports.

In a questionnaire designed to assess this characteristic, Zuckerman focused on four specific traits—adventure seeking, experience seeking, disinhibition, and susceptibility to boredom—to define the parameters of sensation seeking. Results suggested that individuals who had a low stimulation threshold are more vulnerable to stressful life events. Perhaps for that very reason, many outdoor education programs, including Outward Bound, Project

Adventure, and National Outdoor Leadership School (NOLS), use the concept and application of calculated risk taking in their activities to build "survival skills" that will carry over into the everyday lives of adolescents and corporate executives alike.

Self-Esteem: The Bottom-Line Defense

There are many traits common to all individuals, which makes distinguishing among personality types and their related behaviors difficult at times. Level of **self-esteem**, however, appears to be a critical factor in how people respond to stress, regardless of personality type. Low self-esteem is the common denominator in stress-prone personalities, as can be seen in Type A, codependent, and helpless-hopeless types. High self-esteem is a prerequisite for creating stress-resistant personalities because it is directly linked to the accessibility of one's internal resources. Self-esteem is often described as self-value, self-respect, even self-love. It is reflected in the things we say, in the clothes we wear, and perhaps most evidently in our behaviors. Self-esteem has also been described as the harmony or discrepancy between actual self-image and ideal self-image, where high self-esteem is harmony between the actual and ideal, and low self-esteem is the distance between the two.

When we place little or no value on our self, we become quite vulnerable to the perceptions of stress. Conversely, with high self-esteem, problems and worries tend to roll off one's back and might even go unnoticed. Self-esteem is continually fed by the thoughts, feelings, actions, and even memories that contribute to our identity. Self-esteem, however, is a variable entity; it rises and falls, like ambient temperature, over the course of a day. But these variations remain within a specific range where the core of one's self-value resides. Individuals with stress-resistant personalities typically have a high level of self-esteem. For this reason, it is the construction and maintenance of high self-esteem that is the goal of many behavior modification programs involving recovering addicts, battered wives and children, and juvenile delinquents.

In his classic book *The Six Pillars of Self-Esteem*, Nathaniel Branden calls self-esteem the immune system of the consciousness. The author of several books on the topic of self-esteem, Branden highlights what he calls the six pillars (practices) of self-esteem, the internal resources that guide us on the human journey:

- *The practice of living consciously:* Living in the present moment, rather than confining yourself to past or future events, and being mindful of each activity you are engaged in.

- *The practice of self-acceptance:* The refusal to be in an adversarial relationship with yourself.

- *The practice of self-responsibility:* Choosing to acknowledge responsibility for one's feelings, such as saying, "I am responsible for my own happiness," rather than surrendering your feelings to the whims of those you are in a relationship with.

- *The practice of self-assertiveness:* Honoring one's wants, needs, and values, and seeking appropriate ways in which to satisfy these.

- *The practice of living purposefully:* Getting out of the thought processes of hoping and wishing, and instead doing what you need to do to make your goals happen.

- *The practice of personal integrity:* Working to achieve congruence between your values and actions.

Researchers are now placing a greater focus on ways to raise self-esteem as the primary goal in stress management therapy programs. As might be expected, prevention is more effective than rehabilitation, and for this reason, a special task force was created in California to incorporate self-esteem lesson plans into classroom curricula at the primary- and secondary-education levels. It is too early to know any results from this curriculum change, but it is hoped that, by giving attention to this crucial element of human potential, significantly fewer problems with **substance addiction**, divorce, and homelessness will result in the coming decades. According to child psychologists Harris Clemes et al. (1990), the seeds for self-esteem are planted early in childhood and comprise four basic elements: connectedness, uniqueness, power, and models. All four of these factors need to be present, and cultivated continuously, to ensure a high sense of self-esteem. And these four characteristics are essential for self-esteem not only in early childhood development, but also in all

Self-esteem: The sense of underpinning self-values, self-acceptance, and self-love; thought to be a powerful buffer against perceived threats.

Substance addiction: The addiction to a host of substances, from nicotine and caffeine to alcohol and various drugs.

developmental stages throughout one's life. They are defined as follows:

1. *Connectedness:* A feeling of satisfaction that associations and relationships are significant, nurturing, and affirmed by others.

2. *Uniqueness:* A feeling that the individual possesses qualities that make him or her special and different, and that these qualities are respected and admired by others as well as oneself.

3. *Power:* A sense that one can access inner resources as well as use these resources and capabilities to influence circumstances in one's life, and not give one's power away to other people or things.

4. *Models:* A mentoring process by which reference points are established to guide the individual on his or her life journey by sharing goals, values, ideals, and personal standards.

Individuals with low self-esteem often feel powerless, are easily influenced by others, express a narrow range of emotions, become easily defensive and frustrated, and tend to blame others for their own weaknesses (**FIG. 7.4**). Individuals with high self-esteem promote their independence, assume given responsibilities, approach new challenges with enthusiasm, exhibit a broad range of emotions, are proud of accomplishments,

and tolerate frustration well. Because high self-esteem is central to the stress-resistant personality, much attention is now placed on ways to increase self-esteem in people of all ages. Among the many ways to raise and maintain self-esteem, Clemes gives the following suggestions:

1. Disarm the negative critic. Challenge the voice inside that feeds the conscious mind with put-downs and negative comments. A critic taking only one side is unbalanced and dangerous to your self-esteem.

2. Give yourself positive reinforcements and affirmations to remind yourself of your good qualities. Write these down, and look at the list when you're feeling down.

3. Avoid "should haves," where you place a guilt trip on yourself for unmet expectations. Learn from the past, but don't dwell on it. Look for new opportunities for growth.

4. Focus on who you really are, your own identity, and your role models or mentors (**BOX 7.4**).

5. Avoid comparisons with others. Respect your own uniqueness, and learn to cultivate it.

6. Diversify your interests. Don't put all your eggs in one basket. Diversify so that if one aspect of your life becomes impaired, other areas can compensate to keep you afloat. (For instance, if you see yourself solely as a student and you do badly on an exam, this will pull down your self-esteem like a rock.)

7. Improve your connectedness. Widen your network of friends, and find special places in your environment that recharge your energy and strengthen your social bonds.

8. Avoid self-victimization. Martyrs may be admired, but begging for pity and sympathy gets old and the effects are short-lived.

9. Reassert yourself and your value before and during a stressful event.

Is there a difference between self-esteem and self-image? Yes! Self-image, how you perceive yourself, and self-esteem, how you value yourself, are related, yet two different concepts. Self-image is recognized as being a by-product of one's level of self-esteem. This difference between self-esteem and self-image became quite clear in the early 1960s through the work of Maxwell Maltz, author of the book *Psycho-Cybernetics*. In his work as a plastic surgeon, Maltz was intrigued to learn that after

FIGURE 7.4

BOX 7.4 Technology and Personality

The Internet has opened a whole new avenue to explore personality traits. Take a glance at any page from Facebook, Twitter, Match.com, or the domains that include personal avatars and Internet video games, and you are likely to see more than simple lifestyle preferences. Similar to a Halloween costume, what appears on the computer screen is likely to be different than what meets the eye during a face-to-face exchange. Internet games give a whole new meaning to the term *role playing*. However, changes to or magnifications of one's personality are not new to the Internet generation. Long ago, psychologists noticed that people behave differently behind the wheel of a car than they might in an aisle of a grocery store. With two tons of metal behind one's persona, aggressive behaviors are more common. Before caller ID, people could also hide anonymously behind the voice piece of a telephone. In each of these cases, Freud would say the alter ego has taken center stage. Has the Internet expanded the bandwidth of the alter ego? That's the opinion of Robbie Cooper and Tracy Spaight (2007), co-authors of the book *Alter Ego: Avatars and Their Creators*.

Things have come a long way since the days of Dungeons and Dragons. In a piece aired on National Public Radio, commentator Ketzel Levine reported that online games such as Everquest and Star Wars Galaxies include players who use avatars with different genders, races, and physical attributes. Personalities are certainly more complex than what we reveal to others on a day-to-day basis. In a unique way, the Internet not only allows us to try on different personalities or magnify our best characteristics, but also levels the playing field regarding race, ethnicity, gender, and many disabilities. In this regard, virtual personalities open the potential to augment one's sense of confidence and perhaps even courage, traits associated with a stress-resistant personality. There is also concern regarding the transfer effect of war-based video games and how this may trigger neural responses during episodes of anger. Perhaps the real question is, what beneficial transfer effect, if any, occurs from the virtual world to the actual world we live in? The jury appears to be out on this issue. Across the country, however, it is not uncommon to hear conversations in middle school and high school staff lounges bemoaning the negative change in students' interpersonal communication skills in tandem with the proliferation of Internet activity, where comfort level with one's online persona does not transfer to face-to-face encounters. This, unlike the virtual world, is where the greatest percentage of stressors exists.

Omar is a recent graduate of Metro State University in Denver, Colorado. He believes there are pros and cons to online video games. He is no stranger to spending time playing X-Box 360, poker on Full Tilt, and first-person shooter games such as his favorite, Team Death Match.

"There certainly can be an addictive quality to these games. I lost a semester of school due to my [Everquest] video habit. I kept putting off my homework to a point where I had to drop all my classes for a semester. On the plus side, I ended up meeting some neat people from Florida and Las Vegas."

---

performing scores of nose jobs and facelifts, his clients didn't seem all that much happier with their new appearance. (Similar results have been observed with participants in the television reality shows *Extreme Makeover*, *Dr. 90210*, and *The Swan*.) After scores of interviews with patients, he came to the realization that before any external changes take place, the real change first has to take place inside. In other words, if people change their physical image but their self-image remains poor, no amount of surgery will change how one feels about oneself. The changes have to come from within first, changes that nurture and cultivate our inner resources such as confidence, courage, love, compassion, and willpower. If your level of self-esteem is low, so, too, will be your self-image. Through his principles of psycho-cybernetics, Maltz suggests that we first work within before changing external features. Working within means focusing on our positive aspects; shedding old beliefs, attitudes, and perceptions that trap us in the mindset of low self-esteem; and learning to use our inner resources to move out of crisis into creative opportunity.

High self-esteem is considered the best defense against stress; strategies used to combat stress are useless without a strong feeling of self-worth or self-value. Although an abstract concept, your self-esteem should be attended to regularly, every day, like brushing your teeth and eating. It is that important.

SUMMARY

- Personality comprises several traits, characteristics, behaviors, expressions, moods, and feelings as perceived by others.

- Personality is thought to be molded at an early age by genetic factors, family dynamics, social influences, and personal experiences.

- Personality is thought to be a fixed entity, not subject to significant changes; however, the most likely part of personality to change is behavior.

- Personalities can be classified as either stress prone (seeming to attract stress) or stress resistant (providing a buffer against various stressors).

- Type A, codependency, and helpless-hopeless are three personalities that have been associated with both acute and chronic stress. They have one common factor: low self-esteem.

- Type A personality, "the hurried sickness," was first observed by cardiologists Rosenman and Friedman as a major risk factor for heart disease. Later studies revealed that the trait of hostility is most closely linked with hypertension and coronary heart disease.

- Type A behavior is not gender specific; as many females demonstrate Type A behavior as males. However, desire for higher social status is thought to be strongly correlated with Type A behavior.

- Codependency, first observed in the spouses and children of alcoholics when recovery programs began to include family members, is now thought to apply as well to children of broken homes and those with emotionally repressive parents. Codependents are

people who validate their existence by serving others at their own expense. Codependents typically operate from fear of rejection, failure, and the unknown.

- The helpless-hopeless personality develops as a result of repeated bouts of failure over time, to the point where individuals no longer feel competent to try things they really do have control over. Low self-esteem and an external locus of control appear to be significant factors in this type of personality.

- The hardy personality and the sensation seeker are two personalities currently believed to be stress resistant. The commonality between the two is high self-esteem.

- The hardy personality was identified by Kobasa and Maddi, who observed that some people under severe stress did not succumb to stress-related ailments while others did. People who showed a strong sense of commitment, control, and challenge were labeled hardy personalities.

- The survivor personality uses biphasic personality traits to endure danger with a level head. Everyone has the ability to access these traits.

- Zuckerman identified the sensation-seeking personality as those people who seek thrills and sensations but take calculated risks in their endeavors.

- Self-esteem is a crucial cornerstone of personality. Low self-esteem attracts stress; high self-esteem seems to repel it. Clemes states that self-esteem consists of four components: connectedness, uniqueness, power (control), and models. The strength or weakness of these components is highly correlated with level of self-esteem.

STUDY GUIDE QUESTIONS

1. List the stress-prone personalities and give an example of each.

2. List the stress-resistant personalities and give an example of each.

3. Define resiliency.

4. Describe self-esteem and explain what role it plays in promoting and resolving stress.

5. List several ways to help promote self-esteem.

REFERENCES AND RESOURCES

Associated Press. Attention-Deficit Drug OK'd, *Denver Post,* August 2, 2000.

Baker, L. J., Dearborn, M., Hastings, J. E., and Hamberger, K. Type A Behavior in Women: A Review, *Health Psychology* 3:477–497, 1984.

Barefoot, J. C., Dahlstrom, W. G., and Williams, R. B., Jr. Hostility, CHD Incidence, and Total Mortality: A 25-Year Follow-Up Study of 255 Physicians, *Psychosomatic Medicine* 45:59–63, 1983.

Barefoot, J. C., et al. Predicting Mortality from Scores on the Cook-Medley Scale: A Follow-Up Study of 118 Lawyers, *Psychosomatic Medicine* 49:210 (abstract), 1987.

Barry, C. R. *When Helping You Is Hurting Me: Escaping the Messiah Trap.* HarperCollins, New York, 2003.

Beattie, M. *Beyond Codependency.* Harper/Hazelton Press, New York, 1989.

Beattie, M. *Codependent No More.* Harper/Hazelton Press, New York, 1987.

Branden, N. *The Power of Self-Esteem.* Health Communications, Deerfield Beach, FL, 1992.

Branden, N. *The Six Pillars of Self-Esteem.* Bantam Books, New York, 1994.

Cheng, N. *Life and Death in Shanghai.* Penguin Books, New York, 1986.

Cheng, N. Personal communication, June 26, 2003.

Clemes, H., Bean, R., and Clark, A. *How to Raise Teenagers' Self-Esteem.* Price Stern Sloan, Los Angeles, 1990.

Cook, W., and Medley, D. Proposed Hostility and Pharisaic-Virtues Scale for the MMPI, *Journal of Applied Psychology* 38:414–418, 1954.

Cooper, R., and Spaight, T. *Alter Ego: Avatars and Their Creators.* Chris Boot Books, London, 2007.

Degennaro, G., Personal conversation and tour. School of Nursing, University of Virginia, Charlottesville, VA. April 25, 2013.

Friedman, M. Type A Behavior Pattern, *Bulletin of the New York Academy of Medicine* 53:593–603, 1977.

Friedman, M., and Rosenman, R. H. *Type A Behavior and Your Heart.* Knopf, New York, 1974.

Friedman, M., and Ulmer, D. *Type A Behavior and Your Heart,* 2nd ed. Knopf, New York, 1984.

Friedman, M., et al. Alteration of Type A Behavior and Reduction in Cardiac Recurrences in Post-myocardial Infarction Patients, *American Heart Journal* 108:237–248, 1984.

Galloway, J. Coordinator Affiliate Services. Personal conversation, February 21, 2008.

Gonzales, L. *Deep Survival.* Norton Books, New York, 2003.

Holmes, T. H., and Rahe, R. H. The Social Readjustment Rating Scale, *Journal of Psychosomatic Research* 11:213–218, 1967.

Jenkins, D., et al. Development of an Objective Test for the Determination of the Coronary Score Behavior Pattern in Employed Men, *Journal of Chronic Diseases* 20:371–379, 1967.

Jenkins, M. The Hard Way: Between a Rock and a Hard Place, *Outside Magazine* August: 51–54, 2003.

Johnson, J. H., Sarason, I. G., and Siegel, J. M. Arousal Seeking as a Moderator of Life Stress, *Perceptual and Motor Skills* 49:665–666, 1979.

Katz, S., and Lieu, A. *The Codependency Conspiracy.* Warner Books, New York, 1991.

Kobasa, S. Commitment and Coping in Stress Resistance among Lawyers, *Journal of Personality and Social Psychology* 42:707–717, 1982.

Kobasa, S. Stressful Life Events, Personality, and Health: An Inquiry into Hardiness, *Journal of Personality and Social Psychology* 37:1–11, 1979.

Kobasa, S., Maddi, S., and Courington, S. Personality and Constitution as Mediators in the Stress-Illness Relationship, *Journal of Health and Social Behavior* 22:368–378, 1981.

Kobasa, S., Maddi, S., and Kahn, S. Hardiness and Health: A Prospective Study, *Journal of Personality and Social Psychology* 42(1):168–177, 1982.

Kobasa, S., and Puccetti, M. Personality and Social Resources in Stress Resistance, *Journal of Personality and Social Psychology* 45(4):839–850, 1983.

Kristol, E. Declarations of Codependence, *American Spectator,* June 20–23, 1990.

Larsen, E. *Basics of Codependency.* E. Larsen Enterprises, Brooklyn Park, MN, 1983.

Leftcourt, H. M. *Locus of Control: Current Trends in Theory and Research.* Hillsdale, NJ, Earlbaum, 1976.

Levine, K. Alter Egos in a Virtual World, *National Public Radio,* July 31, 2007. www.npr.org/templates/story/story.php?storyId=12263532.

Locke, S., and Colligan, D. *The Healer Within.* Mentor Books, New York, 1986.

Maddi, S. Hardiness: An Operationalization of Existential Courage, *Journal of Humanistic Psychology,* 44(3):279–298, 2004.

Maddi, S. Salvatore R. Maddi. http://socialecology.uci.edu/faculty/srmaddi.

Maddi, S., et al. The Personality Construct of Hardiness, *Journal of Research in Personality,* 36(1):72–85, 2002.

Maddi, S. R. Hardiness and Optimism as Expressed in Coping Patterns, *Consulting Psychology Journal* 51:95–105, 1999.

Maddi, S. R. *Personality Theories: A Comparative Analysis,* 6th ed. Waveland Press, Prospective Heights, IL, 2002.

Maltz, M. *Psycho-Cybernetics.* PocketBooks, New York, 1960.

McKay, M. *Self-Esteem.* New Harbinger Publications, Oakland, CA, 4th ed. 2016.

Miller, M. C. The Dangers of Chronic Distress, *Newsweek,* October 3, 2005: 58–59.

Minchinton, J. *Maximum Self-Esteem: The Handbook for Reclaiming Your Sense of Self-Worth.* Arnford House Publishers, Vanzant, MO, 1993.

Monte, C. *Beneath the Mask: An Introduction to Theories of Personality.* Wiley, NY, 8th ed. 2008.

National Association for Children of Alcoholics. Homepage. www.nacoa.org.

Ornish, D. Love Is Real Medicine, *Newsweek,* October 3, 2005: 56.

Ragland, D., and Brand, R. J. Type A Behavior and Mortality from Coronary Disease, *New England Journal of Medicine* 318:65–69, 1986.

Reivich, K. *The Resilience Factor.* Broadway Books, New York, 2003.

Rice, P. *Stress and Health,* 2nd ed. Brooks/Cole, Pacific Grove, CA, 3rd ed. 1998.

Rosenman, R. H. Type A Behavior Pattern: A Personal Overview, *Journal of Social Behavior and Personality* 5:1–24, 1990.

Rosenman, R. H., and Friedman, M. Modifying Type A Behavior Pattern, *Journal of Psychosomatic Research* 21: 323–331, 1977.

Rosenman, R. H., et al. A Predictive Study of Coronary Heart Disease: The Western Collaborative Groups Study, *Journal of the American Medical Association* 189:15–22, 1964.

Rotter, J. B. Generalized Expectancies for Internal versus External Control of Reinforcement, *Psychological Monographs* 609:80, 1966.

Schaef, A. W. *Codependence–Misunderstood, Mistreated.* Harper & Row, San Francisco, 1986.

Schaef, A. W. *When Society Becomes an Addict.* Harper & Row, San Francisco, 1987.

Schafer, W. *Stress Management for Wellness,* 2nd ed. Harcourt Brace Jovanovich, Fort Worth, TX, 1992.

Schmale, A., and Iker, H. Hopelessness as a Predictor of Cervical Cancer, *Social Science and Medicine* 5:95–100, 1971.

Schultz, D. *Theories of Personality,* 10th ed. Cengage Learning, 2012.

Seligman, M. *Authentic Happiness.* Free Press, New York, 2002.

Seligman, M. Happy Days (Positive Psychological Movement), *Psychology Today* 33(3):32, 2000.

Seligman, M. *Learned Optimism: How to Change Your Minds and Life.* PocketBooks, New York, 2006.

Seligman, M. E. *Helplessness: On Depression, Development, and Death.* Freeman, San Francisco, 1975.

Shackleton, E. *South: The Last Antarctic Expedition of Shackleton and the Endurance.* Lyons Press, New York, 1919.

Shiraldi, G., and Kerr, M. H. *The Anger Management Sourcebook.* Contemporary Books, New York, 2002.

Shekelle, R. B., Schoenberger, J. A., and Stamler, J. Correlates of the JAS Type A Behavior Pattern Score, *Journal of Chronic Disease* 29:381–394, 1976.

Siebert, A. *The Resiliency Advantage.* Berrett-Koehler Publishers, San Francisco, 2005.

Siebert, A. *The Survivor Personality.* Perigee Books, New York, 2010.

Smith, E. Fighting Cancerous Feelings, *Psychology Today* 22(5):22–23, 1988.

Sorenson, G., et al. Relationships among Type A Behavior, Employment Experiences, and Gender: The Minnesota Heart Survey, *Journal of Behavioral Medicine* 10:323–336, 1987.

Steffenhagen, R. *Self-Esteem Therapy.* Praeger, New York, 1990.

Steffenhagen, R. *The Social Dynamics of Self-Esteem: Theory to Therapy.* Praeger, New York, 1987.

Taylor, S. E. *Health Psychology,* 9th ed. McGraw-Hill, New York, 2014.

Turnipseed, D. L. An Exploratory Study of the Hardy Personality at Work in the Health Care Industry, *Psychological Reports* 85(3, pt 2):1199–1217, 1999.

Underwood, A. The Good Heart, *Newsweek,* October 3, 2005: 49–55.

Wegscheider-Cruse, S. Codependency: The Therapeutic Void. In *Codependency: An Emerging Issue.* Health Communications, Pompano Beach, FL, 1984.

Wegscheider-Cruse, S. Personal conversation, February 20, 2008.

Whitfield, C. *Co-dependence.* Health Communications, Deerfield Beach, FL, 1991.

Williams, R. B., et al. Type A Behavior Hostility and Coro-nary Atherosclerosis, *Psychosomatic Medicine* 42:539–549, 1980.

Zuckerman, M. Dimensions of Sensation Seeking, *Journal of Consulting and Clinical Psychology* 36:45–52, 1971.

CHAPTER 8

Stress and Human Spirituality

The winds of grace are blowing perpetually.
We only need raise our sails.

—Sri Ramakrishna

Laura Wellington was less than a half a mile from the finish line when she heard a loud explosion. Stunned, she stopped to ask someone what had happened and learned that the location where her family was waiting in downtown Boston was bombed. She was quickly diverted away from the marathon route. Once she made contact with her brother, Bryan, via cell phone and learned everyone in her family was safe, she sat down and cried. At that moment a married couple walking by stopped to comfort her. The man asked if she had finished the race. Laura shook her head no, whereupon he took his coveted Boston Marathon medal, placed it around her neck, and said, "You are a finisher in my eyes." In between her tears and sobs, she said thanks. Laura never learned this stranger's name, but will forever be indebted to his random act of kindness. That afternoon, hundreds of similar acts were performed for total strangers across the city, all in the name of compassion. Equally amazing were the scores of runners who crossed the finish line after running 26-plus

miles only to continue running a few more miles to the nearest hospital to donate blood. In the words of Mother Teresa, "We can do no great things, only small things with great love." Times of stress may seem anything but spiritual, yet there is always a choice; the ego reacts, the soul responds.

To write a book about stress without addressing the concept of human spirituality would be a gross injustice to both topics. In my quest for understanding and personal journey of enlightenment, I have met these two at the junction of many a crossroad. I know I am not alone. Human spirituality and stress seem to be as inseparable as the Taoist yin and yang, earth and sky, and, quite literally, mind and soul. I became aware of this relationship in my first year of teaching stress management in 1984. Many of the topics I taught, and several of the issues I was asked to address by students, had strong parallels with the cornerstones of several (if not all) religions: relationships, values, the meaning of life, and a sense of connectedness—the common denominator of these four being a unique level of human consciousness known as human spirituality. British author Aldous Huxley called this the **perennial philosophy**, or a transcendent reality beyond the limitations of cultures, politics, religions, and egos.

The association between eustress (those moments of exhilaration and ecstasy) and spirituality, those cosmic moments Maslow called "peak experiences," is so profound that it is often taken for granted or overlooked. The converse, distress, is quite another matter. I have learned that, in many cases, stress (specifically, unresolved anger and fear) can be a roadblock to spiritual well-being, and that a strong human spirit can be a vital asset to dismantling roadblocks, resolving stress, and promoting a greater sense of inner peace. In turn, the resolution of life's stressors can actually enhance the strength and health of the human spirit if we choose to learn from our experiences. Although stress and the human spirit appear, on the surface, to be at opposite poles, they are quite literally partners in the dance of life (**FIG. 8.1**).

It is no coincidence that as the topic of stress grabs headlines across the nation, Americans seem to be on the verge of a new spiritual awareness. In fact, in the past decade alone, the word *spirituality* has begun to take on a greater

> **Perennial philosophy:** A term used by Aldous Huxley to describe human spirituality, a transcendent reality beyond cultures, religions, politics, and egos.

© Inspiration Unlimited. Used with permission.

FIGURE 8.1 In times of stress, people often search for answers to life's most difficult problems. This search is known as a spiritual hunger and often leads to a deeper search for life's meaning. A spiritual hunger can progress to a spiritual exploration, thus allowing for a deeper soul growth learning process.

level of comfort in the vocabulary of the media and the population in general. This new awareness of human spirituality, promoted by a nucleus of individuals with grass-roots inspiration, goes by several names—the human potential movement, the consciousness movement, and the New Age movement, among others—all of which imply both spiritual bankruptcy and spiritual awakening in humankind, at least in the Western hemisphere. In his classic book *As Above, So Below*, Ronald Miller describes a collective search for new forms of spirituality with which to make our lives more meaningful and relevant in a world of global social upheaval. With an appetite greater than that which can be satisfied by their existing institutions, people have begun to look beyond their own backyards to answer questions about how they fit into the bigger picture. As indicated by the title of Miller's book (which is an axiom from ancient Egypt), there is a growing appreciation and understanding that no separation exists between the two worlds. Rather, the divine essence "above" resides within ourselves, making the two one.

The speed of this movement has also been fueled by a growing concern about ecology and the protection of the environment—a wake-up call of sorts. For example, the 2010 oil disaster in the Gulf of Mexico, the dramatic effects of global warming, and the rapid depletion of our natural resources, including the tropical rainforests—all issues on the discussion table at the 2012 United Nations "Earth Summit" in Rio de Janeiro—are fire alarms beckoning us to set aside our cultural and political differences and work together as one people. This was most clearly stated by 2007 Nobel Laureate Al Gore in his best-selling book *Earth in the Balance: Ecology and the Human Spirit*, in which he wrote, "The ecological perspective begins with a view of the whole, an understanding of how the various parts of nature interact in patterns that tend toward balance and persist over time. But this perspective cannot treat the earth as something separate from human civilization; we are a part of the whole too." This message was echoed once again as a moral imperative in his best-selling book *An Inconvenient Truth* based on his Academy Award–winning documentary. His message is as pertinent today as it was when it was originally written in 1993—perhaps even more so.

■ A Spiritual Hunger?

Genetic engineering. Global terrorism. Cloning. Global warming. Stem cell research. Extraterrestrial life. In times of crises and uncertainty, people of every generation and every culture have been known to seek help from a divine source. In the past, people took spiritual refuge in their religious traditions, and to a large extent this remains true today. However, at the beginning of the twenty-first century, new questions have emerged that are not so easily addressed by ancient texts, particularly as humans start to play God. Although the fear associated with the terrorist attacks on September 11, 2001, coupled with a perceived moral decay of the American culture, has sent many people running back to their religious roots, others seem a little disenchanted with the standard religious practices because they do not seem to provide adequate answers to the problems looming on the horizon of humanity. According to a 2012 Pew Research Center (PRC) study, the fastest growing religious group in the United States is made up of people who say they are not religious. Referred to as the "nones" (because when asked about their religious affiliation they reply "none"), the PRC estimates this group to be 46 million people and growing. Nones come from all walks of life, but are primarily under the age of 30. A PRC spokesperson noted that although some nones identify themselves as atheists or agnostics, the majority often describe themselves as "spiritual, but not religious," suggesting a shifting demographic within the United States (Glenn, 2013).

In what is being referred to by some as the post-denominational age, many people do not feel a loyalty to one particular religion; rather people seek a host of sacred traditions, blending various practices to form their own spiritual path. There are Catholics who practice Buddhist meditation, Jews who participate in American Indian sweatlodges, and Methodists, Lutherans, and Protestants who participate in Sufi dancing. Even hell has gotten a makeover: The biblical conception of the most dreaded place in the universe has moved from a literal to a figurative interpretation. Once described as eternal flames of death, the Vatican currently describes hell as "a state of those who freely and definitively separate themselves from God." Many of those who claim to have already been to hell (on earth, that is), as well as those who have come close, are seeking a better understanding of God.

The expression used today is **spiritual hunger**, a term that describes a searching or longing for that which cannot be attained by traditional religious practices. Another term used in conjunction with spiritual hunger is **spiritual bankruptcy**, a concept that suggests a sense of moral decay, perhaps caused by an emptiness that cannot be filled with material possessions. Yet a

strong element of human nature (the ego) encourages us to try anyway. One only need reflect on the shootings on several college campuses, or other similar horrific events, to see that something is terribly amiss.

A third phrase commonly heard today is **spiritual dormancy**. It refers to people who for one reason or another choose not to recognize the importance of the spiritual dimension of health and well-being at both an individual and a societal level. The result of such inaction often leads to a state of dysfunction (a term many now call the "national adjective"). Like a person who hits the snooze button on the alarm clock, falling asleep on the spiritual path can have real consequences because one is ill equipped to deal not only with the problems at hand, but also with potential problems down the road.

A Turning Point in Consciousness

A number of factors have come together to raise human consciousness to today's current level of awareness. They include but are not limited to the following:

- Vatican II, which in the 1960s changed the Catholic mass from Latin to various indigenous languages around the world, thereby opening the doors to a wealth of knowledge of Christianity (which had pretty much remained known only to a chosen few because Latin is not a contemporary language).

- The invasion of Tibet by China in 1959, which not only forced thousands of Tibetans into exile around the world, but ultimately allowed for the sharing of their sacred knowledge, which had been largely inaccessible for thousands of years.

- The Apollo Space Project, with its mission to land Americans on the moon in 1969, allowed us for the first time to see planet Earth as a whole,

> **Spiritual hunger:** A term to illustrate the quest for understanding of life's biggest questions, the bigger picture, and how each of us fits into it.
>
> **Spiritual bankruptcy:** A term to convey the lack of spiritual direction, values, or less than desirable behaviors, suggesting moral decay.
>
> **Spiritual dormancy:** A state in which someone chooses not to recognize the importance of the spiritual dimension of life, individually and socially.

suspended in space, a planet without borders. This view altered many minds with regard to the future of the planet and her many inhabitants.

- The proliferation of self-help groups that use variations of the twelve-step program, as outlined by Alcoholics Anonymous, that provide for relinquishing control of addiction to a higher power. Self-help membership is nondenominational.

- The American Indians, particularly the Lakota and Hopi, who for decades have been told by their elders not to share various aspects of their cultural heritage and spirituality because of lack of trust, have now been told this is the time to reveal their sacred knowledge, and they have done so. The Lakota Sioux prophecy foretold of the age of the white buffalo, when a shift in consciousness would appear. A white buffalo named Miracle was born in Janesville, Wisconsin, on August 20, 1994.

- The Hebrew Kabalah, the sect of Jewish mysticism held only by a chosen few for the past several millennia, has recently been made available to anyone who has an interest in this topic.

- A growing interest in Sufism, a mystical sect of Islam (often symbolized by the photographs of whirling dervishes) with republished and retranslated works of Rumi, Hafiz, and several others.

- Since the early 1970s, near-death experiences (NDEs) have been studied in earnest to learn more about the survivor's recollection. Research compiled by critical care physician Sam Parnia reveals that advances in modern medicine over the past several decades have resulted in a new phenomenon in which millions of documented NDEs have been reported by people from all religious denominations (Parnia, 2013). Those who recall their experience describe a new mission of compassion and inner peace. Children, many of whom have not been exposed to various spiritual matters, come back to consistently describe experiences of a divine mystical nature.

- In the 1990s, South American shamans for the first time shared their wisdom of healing with "their younger brothers" in the Northern hemisphere.

- The Telecommunications Revolution opened the door of information to anyone with access to the Internet. Knowledge from around the world in all its many sources suddenly has become accessible without the censorship of intellectuals, religious leaders, or politicians, who for centuries have played a major role in keeping people in the dark about a great many issues and facts. Access to information has become a major stepping stone toward higher consciousness.

- The official acceptance of global warming and climate change (Engel, 2002) has become a new wake-up call for planetary citizens to unite in a global effort to reduce greenhouse gases or face potentially catastrophic consequences due to dramatic shifts in population and utilization of natural resources.

- The collaboration between media giant Oprah Winfrey and best-selling author Eckhart Tolle in spreading the message of higher consciousness through his book, *A New Earth*, via her television show, Web site, online chat rooms, and podcasts to millions of people around the world.

Unthinkable right after September 11, 2001, today it is not uncommon to see universities and corporate health-promotion programs including courses on spiritual well-being as well as more traditional programs on physical well-being. Today, as the information age of the twenty-first century unfolds, concepts from all cultures, religions, and corners of the globe are now accessible to us. As the pieces of this jigsaw puzzle called the human spirit are assembled, it becomes increasingly obvious that despite subtle nuances and obvious differences, there are common denominators that tie and bind the integrity of the human spirit. First and foremost is a desire to learn, a personal quest of self-exploration. Be it instinctual or a learned trait, human behavior is often inspired by self-improvement, and herein lies the first step of the journey. In the words repeated by many Zen masters in the spirit of Chinese philosopher Lao Tzu, "There are many paths to enlightenment. The journey of each path begins with the first step."

The material in this chapter is a synthesis of several different perspectives on human spirituality. Some of these ideas may resonate with your way of thinking, whereas others may seem foreign, perhaps even intimidating, to your attitudes, beliefs, and values. The purpose of this chapter is not to intimidate you, but to show that despite our varied backgrounds and religious differences, there are elements common to all of us. I ask you to focus on these common elements, not the differences, as you read. It would serve you best to respect and be receptive to all ideas different from your own because, as you will see, an open attitude will ultimately strengthen your own beliefs and the integrity of your spiritual well-being.

Definition of Spirituality

It would be fair to say that human spirituality has been the focus of countless conversations dating back to antiquity. Yet, despite the millions of words and hundreds of philosophies exploring this concept, human spirituality is still a phenomenon for which no one definition seems adequate. Undoubtedly, it includes the aspects of higher consciousness, **transcendence**, self-reliance, self-efficacy, self-actualization, love, faith, enlightenment, mysticism, self-assertiveness, community, and bonding, as well as *God*, *Allah*, *Jesus*, *Buddha*, and a multitude of other concepts. Yet no aspect alone is sufficient to describe the essence of human spirituality. In various sources, the human spirit has been described as a gift to accompany one through life, an inner drive housed in the soul, and even a living consciousness of a divine-like presence within us and around us. These descriptions are poetic and profound, but they don't bring us any closer to a concrete understanding of what human spirituality really is. In many cultures, the word *spirit* means "first breath": that which enters our physical being with our first inhalation at birth. The Hebrews called this *ruah*, and even as the word is spoken, you can hear the rush of wind pass through your lips. Among some Eastern cultures, *pranayama*, or diaphragmatic breathing, is thought to have a spiritual essence that enhances physical calmness by uniting the body and mind as one, by breathing the universal energy. The ancient Greeks used the words *pneuma* to connote spirit and *psyche* to describe the human soul, the latter of which is now commonly associated with the study of human behavior, psychology. More recently, the World Health Organization (WHO) defined human spirituality as "that which is in total harmony with the perceptual and nonperceptual environment."

Sometimes defining what a concept is *not* becomes a type of definition in itself. For instance, human spirituality is neither a religion nor the practice of a religion (**FIG. 8.2**). Religions are based on a specific dogma: an active application of a specific set of organized rules based on an ideology of the human spirit. Being actively involved in a religion is considered enhancing of one's spirituality. This is one of religion's primary goals, and on the whole, religions are very effective in this. But now and again it has been noted by several psychologists that, like too much of anything at

FIGURE 8.2 When people hear the word *spirituality*, many think of religion. Although spirituality and religion share common ground, they are not the same thing. Spirituality is inclusive whereas religions are exclusive.

one time, too much religion can impede the growth of the human spirit for some people, leading to what psychologists Anne Wilson Schaef (1987) and Leo Booth (1991) call an addiction to religion. By the same token, elements of spirituality pushed to the extreme are considered unhealthy, too. Comedian Steven Wright jokingly states, "My girlfriend and I had conflicting attitudes. I wasn't into meditation and she wasn't into being alive." There is no doubt that religion can promote spiritual evolution; the two are very compatible. But individuals can be very spiritual, and not "religious" (in the sense of attending services), just as they can be very religious but have poor awareness of their spirituality. It is often said that where religion separates, spirituality unites. In the words of psychiatrist Viktor Frankl, "Spirituality does not have a religious connotation, but refers specifically to the human dimension." Spirituality, like water, and religions, like the various containers that attempt to hold it, are related yet separate concepts (**FIG. 8.3**). Like a Venn diagram (**FIG. 8.4**), spirituality and religion share common ground, but they are not the same thing.

To define a term or concept is to separate and distinguish it enough from everything else to gain a clear focus and understanding of what it really is. All nonrelated aspects must be factored out to reach a clear and undiluted meaning.

> **Transcendence:** A means to rise above the mundane existence to see a higher order to things, often used to describe human spirituality.

© Inspiration Unlimited. Used with permission.

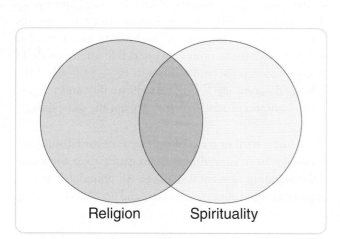

FIGURE 8.3 Although no language can adequately describe the concept of spirituality, the language of metaphor works the best. Spirituality is often described as being like water. Religions are similar to containers (some beautiful, some questionable) that hold water.

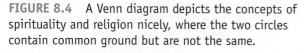

Religion   Spirituality

FIGURE 8.4 A Venn diagram depicts the concepts of spirituality and religion nicely, where the two circles contain common ground but are not the same.

This is where the difficulty lies when one attempts to formulate an adequate definition of the word *spirituality*. It appears that human spirituality encompasses so many factors, possibly everything, that to separate anything out denies a full understanding of the phenomenon. On the other hand, perhaps at this time, we just don't possess the vocabulary to express it to our complete comprehension. Sometimes, to understand a concept, you just have to experience it, and experiences will certainly vary, as will their interpretation. Typically, people tend to describe their collective spiritual experiences as a journey or path. Most important, for a path to enhance the maturation or evolution of the soul, it must be creative, not destructive; progressive, not regressive. It must stimulate and enhance, not stifle, spiritual well-being. Given this premise, remember, too, that there are many paths to enlightenment. No one path is superior to the others, so it doesn't matter which path you take, but only that you keep moving forward (growing) on the path you have chosen. To quote Carlos Castaneda in *The Teachings of Don Juan*, "Look at every path closely and deliberately. Try it as many times as you think is necessary. Then ask yourself, and yourself alone, one question. Does this path have a heart? If it does, the path is good; if it doesn't, it is of no use."

Theories of Human Spirituality

Human spirituality has been studied by several academic disciplines—most notably, philosophy, theology, sociology, and psychology. More recently, this topic has begun to be investigated in the fields of physics, nursing, and clinical medicine as well. Thus, human spirituality will be described henceforth in terms of the various theories devised to provide a better understanding of this concept in several different disciplines.

In the scientific disciplines, theories give rise to operational (working) definitions. From these definitions come conceptual models. From models come tools to assess and measure, and from measurements come a holistic picture of understanding. More often than not, the synthesis of a number of theories offers a mosaic that, up close, may look confusing, and even incomprehensible, but from a distant perspective, it closely approaches a representation of this mystical phenomenon. If human spirituality were compared to a huge mountain, then the individuals who created these theories are the ones who have bushwhacked a path to the top by articulating their own perspectives. Metaphorically speaking, what follows is an aerial view of this mountain, capturing but a few of the many paths reaching toward the summit. The paths described here are by individuals who have encountered and studied matters of the soul with various prophets, sages, and masters. Their personal perspectives, which arise from a range of disciplines and cultures, contribute pieces of the mosaic we call human spirituality. But they only begin to illustrate the nature of this unique human characteristic.

The Path of Carl Jung

Typically, when individuals first consider the source of the human spirit, their search leads them to external things, like nature and the heavens above. It was the work of psychiatrist **Carl Jung** who, as a pioneer in psychology, turned the search inward to explore the depths of the mind, as a means to understand the spiritual nature of humanity. Jung was fascinated with the human psyche, especially the relationship between the conscious mind and the unconscious mind. He spent much time learning about intuition, clairvoyance (dreams foretelling events that later actually happened), seemingly bizarre coincidences, and supernatural occurrences. His fascination led him to explore the mystical side of the mind, and for this reason he was ridiculed by many of his contemporaries. Yet, with time, perceptions have changed. Although Jung is still considered ahead of his time by many, today his theories are recognized as the cornerstones of not only mental and emotional well-being, but also spiritual well-being. And although Jung did not advocate any particular religion, his work is studied, taught, and cited by psychologists, theologians, and spiritual leaders around the world. Moreover, his work has given impetus to a new discipline of healing called **transpersonal psychology** or **psychospirituality**, the study of the relationship between the mind and the soul.

Unlike his mentor, Freud, an atheist who hypothesized that humans functioned at an instinctual level, Jung proposed that there was a spiritual element to human nature, a spiritual drive located in the realm of the unconscious mind, which manifests itself when it bubbles to the conscious level. As a man who studied the myths and belief systems of many cultures on virtually every continent, Jung observed similarities in the symbols in dreams and art by various races of people who had no possible way of communicating them to one another. From research conducted during his professional experiences as well as intensive self-reflection, Jung theorized that these similarities were often represented in symbolic forms he called **archetypes**. Archetypes are primordial images or concepts originating in the unconscious mind at a level so profound that they appear to be common elements, or elements of unity, among all humankind.

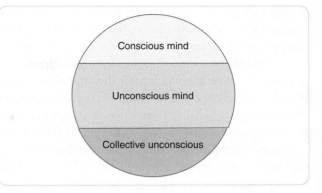

FIGURE 8.5 A symbolic representation of Jung's view of the mind with the collective unconscious residing in the depths of the unconscious mind. This aspect of the mind surfaces to consciousness through intuition, creativity, and dreams.

Jung proposed a dichotomy of levels constituting the unconscious mind: the personal unconscious and the collective unconscious (**FIG. 8.5**). The latter he described as universal consciousness: a unifying force within all individuals, or the collective soul. He believed that the collective unconscious was divine in its nature, the essence of God within all of us. According to Jung, this divine essence manifests in the conscious mind through several cognitive functions, including intuition, creativity, and the interpretation of dreams.

In his exploration of dreams, Jung discovered several people who dreamed of events they could have no possible knowledge of at a conscious level, only to discover that their dreams emerged as crystal-clear predictions of circumstances yet to come. In addition, sometimes during

Carl Jung: A twentieth-century psychiatrist who, under the initial tutelage of Sigmund Freud, forged a new premise of psychology honoring the importance of the human spirit. He became the second greatest influence in the field of psychology.

Transpersonal psychology: A discipline in the field of psychology that recognizes the spiritual dimension of the human condition.

Psychospirituality: A focus in the field of psychology, influenced by Carl Jung, to acknowledge the spiritual dimension of the psyche.

Archetypes: A Jungian term to describe primordial images that become symbolic forms with an inherent understanding among all people.

his counseling sessions, Jung would find himself in awe of coincidences that unfolded right in front of him. One example was listening to a client's dream about spotting a fox while the two were walking along a dirt road, only to have a fox appear seconds after the animal was mentioned. Studying the phenomenon of coincidences more closely, Jung concluded that when two seemingly unrelated events happen at once, there is a reason and purpose for it, whether significant or banal, a purpose that cannot be explained rationally by cause and effect. He coined the term **synchronicity** to explain this phenomenon. He also hypothesized that in reality there is no such thing as coincidence; rather, everything is connected, and events unfold simultaneously for a reason. His study of Taoism and the *I Ching* led him to believe that there is a connectedness extending beyond the individual throughout the entire universe, a concept not well accepted in the West during his lifetime (**FIG. 8.6**).

> **Synchronicity:** A term coined by Carl Jung to explain the significance of two seemingly unrelated events that, when brought together, have a significant meaning.

© Bradford Veley, Marquette, MI.

"Look, I've got a really busy day planned. I don't have TIME for a complete shakedown of my belief system!"

FIGURE 8.6

Jung was once quoted as saying that "every crisis a person experiences over the age of 30 is spiritual in nature." While some only credit Jung with addressing the midlife-crisis phenomenon, Jungian psychologists have maintained the importance of spirituality to the individual, especially at midlife. With regard to this spiritual crisis, Jung further believed that modern men's and women's inability to get in touch with their inner selves provided fertile ground for life's stressors. He added that sickness is a result of not being whole—that is, never connecting with the divine qualities of the unconscious mind to clarify values and gain sharp focus on one's life's meaning.

Another of Jung's theories is that there are characteristics of the personality called the shadow that individuals keep hidden, even from themselves, but which they usually project onto other people. Confronting the shadow of the soul, or attaining profound self-awareness, allows individuals to come to terms with several issues that form the undercurrents for stress in their own lives so that they may become whole.

In a story recounted in his autobiography, *Memories, Dreams, Reflections*, Jung tells of a young boy who asked an old wise man why no one in this day and age ever sees the face or hears the voice of God. The wise old sage replied that man no longer lowers himself enough to God's level. Jung tells this story to reinforce the idea that people in "civilized" cultures have become distant from the wisdom and knowledge seated in the fathoms of the unconscious mind. Instead, they see God primarily as an external force or supreme being in the clouds. By contrast, Jung suggested that God is a unifying force that resides in all of us, in the depths of the unconscious mind. Like the ancient Asian mystics he studied, who practiced meditation to attain spiritual enlightenment, Jung advocated personal responsibility to examine the conscious and unconscious mind in an effort to find what he called psychic equilibrium. In *Modern Man in Search of a Soul*, he further warned that the advancement of technology and materialism, now accepted by many to be stressors, would further widen the gap between the conscious and unconscious minds. Jung believed that as technology and materialism increased, people would spend less and less time cultivating their inner selves. This observation, made in 1933, has come to pass at the beginning of the twenty-first century. It is interesting to note that Jung advised one of his clients that psychoanalysis alone would not cure him of his chronic alcoholism. In a letter to this client, Jung suggested that his best chance for cure was a "spiritual conversion." After Roland H.'s recovery, which he attributed to spiritual enlightenment, he and a friend, Bill W., started the now well-known organization for problem drinkers called Alcoholics Anonymous. Although this program is not tied to any particular religion, it is based on a very strong sense of spirituality.

Shortly before his death in 1961, Jung was interviewed by John Freeman of the British Broadcasting Corporation. When asked if he believed in God, Jung replied, "No." Then he paused for a moment, and stated, "I know."

The Path of M. Scott Peck

In 1978, **M. Scott Peck** ushered in a new age of spiritual awareness in American culture with a seminal book entitled *The Road Less Traveled*, now considered to be a classic. As a psychiatrist who spent many years counseling clients with neurotic and psychotic disorders, Peck became aware of a commonality among virtually all of them: either an absence or immaturity of spiritual development. He also noted that not all people were at the same level of spirituality, which made it a challenge to treat his clients.

Upon intense reflection on his own spiritual beliefs, coupled with what he observed in his clients, Peck developed a framework he called the road to spiritual development. This framework consists of four systematic, hierarchical stages of spiritual growth and development (**FIG. 8.7**): **chaotic antisocial, formal-institutional, skeptical,** and **mystic-communal.** (These stages are similar to James Fowler's stages of faith.) Admittedly, as Peck states in his book *The Different Drum*, not everyone falls neatly into one of these four categories. Some people hover between stages, and others migrate back and forth from one stage to another. Despite its shortcomings, which Peck admits to, this model provides a basis from which we can begin to understand the maturation of the human spirit. The stages are described as follows:

> **Stage 1:** *The chaotic antisocial individual.* The first stage of Peck's road to spiritual development is an undeveloped spirituality or, in some cases, a spiritual absence or bankruptcy. As a rule, young children fall into this category because of their immaturity, but among adults, the chaotic antisocial individual is someone whose life is in utter chaos. This chaos can be represented by various attitudes and behaviors, including drug or alcohol addiction, codependency, or a helpless-hopeless attitude. Chaotic antisocial individuals can be very manipulative and unprincipled, and they often find that controlling others is easier than

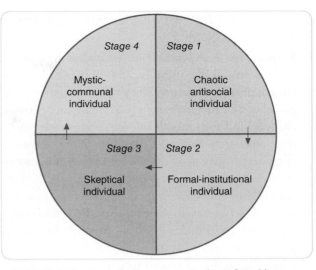

FIGURE 8.7 A symbolic representation of Peck's conception of human spirituality as a maturation process with four hierarchical stages.

taking responsibility for their own lives. Individuals at this stage have a poor self-relationship; completely avoid self-awareness; maintain poor relationships with family, friends, and co-workers; hold a weak value system with many unresolved conflicts; and show an absence of a meaningful purpose in their lives. Some people remain at this stage their whole lives. A life-threatening situation, however, can act as a catalyst to move to the next stage. In preparation to leave this stage, the chaotic antisocial individual looks for some kind of structure to make order out of the chaos, and to

M. Scott Peck: A contemporary psychiatrist who reintroduced the aspect of human spirituality and psychology with his classic book, *The Road Less Traveled*.

Chaotic antisocial: The first stage of Peck's hierarchy of spiritual growth in which one's spiritual essence is lacking (spiritual bankruptcy).

Formal-institutional: The second stage of Peck's hierarchy of spiritual growth where one tends to find comfort in the guidelines of religious institutions.

Skeptical: The third stage of Peck's spiritual hierarchy where one shuns all religious dogma.

Mystic-communal: The fourth stage of Peck's spiritual hierarchy in which one perpetually and joyfully seeks life's answers in the mystical divine universe.

help slay some personal dragons masking themselves as chronic stressors.

Stage 2: *The formal-institutional individual.* Institutions such as prisons, the military, and, in many cases, the church provide structure. They offer rules, structured guidelines, and dogma to help individuals leave personal chaos behind and rebuild their lives. People who make the transition to this stage from the chaotic antisocial stage desperately need rules, dogma, and guidance to survive. Although many young people enter this stage through the influence of their families (e.g., going to religious services with their parents), Peck found that adults enter it by making an almost overnight conversion, a "born-again" transformation. In essence, they adopt the dogma of an institution as a means of personal survival. Peck observed that when an individual advances to this stage, it may be not only very sudden but also perhaps unconscious. A relationship with God parallels the parent–child relationship, where God is a loving but punitive God. In the words of Peck, "God becomes an 'Irish cop' in the sky." A supreme being is personified in human terms, and perhaps most important, God is purely an external figure who rewards and punishes one's behavior. People who advance to this stage come looking for personal needs to be met and for life's answers. Quite often they find what they are looking for. Comfortable with this stage, many people stay at this level for the rest of their lives. Some, however, may slip back into the first stage, and then oscillate between the two. Others eventually leave this stage because of unmet needs. They become skeptical of (perhaps) all institutions, yet remain spiritually stable enough to avoid slipping back to stage 1. At this point, such people begin a free-floating process, unanchored to anything.

Stage 3: *The skeptical individual.* When a person questions the dogma and rules necessary to maintain membership in a church or other organization that has provided some security, and becomes skeptical about the answers (or lack of answers) received, he or she may eventually leave the safety the organization once provided. Peck said that this is a crucial stage of spiritual development, when one begins to question the understanding the institution represents. This is also a very risky stage because there are no guaranteed answers elsewhere. Tongue in cheek, Peck calls people in this stage born-again atheists. People become skeptical when they find that the institution they joined does not fulfill or answer all their needs or expectations. Frustration turns into

distrust, and they often leave the institution they once joined for refuge, becoming very cynical about it and perhaps about life in general. The skeptical individual is looking for truth, and according to Peck, is more spiritually developed than many devoted churchgoers. Some college students, and even more college graduates, reach this stage after years of following their parents' religious lead, and then finding that the beliefs on which they were raised no longer seem adequate for the situations in which they currently find themselves. The skeptical individual finds him- or herself in a very tenuous position, however, because everyone needs sure footing or an anchor eventually. Two outcomes are possible at this stage. Either one samples other church institutions and makes a half-hearted compromise along the way, or the individual progresses to the next and final stage of spiritual development.

Stage 4: *The mystic-communal individual.* In the continual search for answers to life's questions, some people eventually come to the realization that there are questions that have no answers. Unlike the skeptical individual who fights this premise, the mystic-communal individual takes delight in life's paradoxes. These people find comfort in the unanswerable, yet like sleuths, they seek out the continuing challenge, ever hungry for clues and possible answers. People in this stage of spiritual development love a good mystery, and they love to explore. Mystic-communals begin to depersonify God and come to the realization that God is an internal source (the power of love, faith, and will) as much as an external source (an unexplained energy or consciousness). Mystic-communals begin to see an outline of the whole picture even though several pieces are missing. These people see spirituality as a living process, not merely an outcome or heaven-oriented goal. Perhaps as important, they see the need to build and maintain a sense of community by developing quality relationships built on acceptance, love, and respect. They see and feel the need to be connected. Upon arrival at this stage, individuals realize that it is only the beginning of a very long but fruitful journey.

Like Jung, Peck hints that the continued inability to deal with psychological crises often manifests itself as spiritual immaturity, or not progressing through these stages of spiritual growth. And, similar to Maslow's hierarchy of needs, Peck agrees that individuals regress when stressful situations cause them to lose their footing on this road. For example, a person in the mystic-communal stage who experiences the death of a loved one may feel anger or guilt if the death is perceived as a form of punishment (Why me?). Many stressful situations cause individuals to focus on the external side of "God" (or lack thereof), often causing them to slip back into stage 2 or 3. Although the road to spiritual development is an independent one, Peck suggests that we are not alone on this journey. Love and grace are the guides that lead the way, when we choose to listen.

The Path of Hildegard von Bingen

The word *spirit* often conjures up the expression *mystic* for many, and in the case of **Hildegard von Bingen** this adjective is most accurate. However, the word *mystic* alone is not enough to describe this unique woman who lived in Germany at the turn of the twelfth century (1098–1179). *Visionary*, *poet*, *composer*, *healer*, *artist*, and *saint* are also words used to describe her, yet even these seem inadequate to capture the essence of Hildegard von Bingen. Born of a noble family near the town of Mainz, Hildegard was 8 years old when she first experienced a vision of light, followed by a period of intense illness. At first not familiar with the meaning of her experience, she soon understood that this vision was in some way a message from God. Not long after her first vision, she acquired a remarkable psychic ability, which left her family rather puzzled. As was the custom of her day, Hildegard, the tenth child in her family, was brought to a monastery to be looked after and raised in the hope that her work and accomplishments would please the church.

The first vision was actually one of many to occur throughout her life. Hildegard was encouraged by members of her order to write what she saw in these visions.

> What I write is what I see and hear in the vision. I compose no other words than those I hear, and I set them forth in unpolished Latin just as I hear them in the vision, for I am not taught in this vision to write as philosophers do. And the words of the vision are not like words uttered by the mouth of many but like a shimmering flame, or a cloud floating in a clear sky.

In what is considered to be her most impressive writing, *Scivias*, she describes a series of visions illustrating the story of creation, the dynamic tension between light and darkness, the work of the holy spirit, and several words of encouragement to ponder and savor as we each journey on the human path. Her writings didn't go unnoticed. Word soon traveled to Pope Eugenius III, who sent for copies of these writings. So impressed was he that he not only gave

his blessings, but also sent words of support to Hildegard to continue her writings, thus making her a celebrity.

In the time of the Dark Ages, the vision Hildegard saw wasn't just a ray of light in the shadows—it became a philosophy that breathed life into a people with a spiritual hunger. And in a time when women took a back seat to the dominance of male authority, Hildegard's presence and renown demonstrated a higher order of humanity.

Her message was simple: There is a holistic nature to the universe, just as there is a holistic nature to humanity. And just as man and woman are essential parts of the universe, so too is the universe an essential part to be found within each individual. In other words, this message is similar to the axiom, "As above, so below," or "As the microcosm, so the macrocosm." As if extending an invitation into nature, she encouraged the "greening" of the soul, a process whereby one engages with the natural world as a part of it, instead of shutting oneself off from it. Hildegard also spoke to the principle of each soul. She routinely emphasized that our soul is not to be found in our body; rather, it is our body that resides in our soul. The body, she said, is the instrument of the soul, a means by which our divine essence can function in the material world. The soul, a unique aspect of our divine nature, is boundless and contains our dreams, hopes, wishes, and desires. Can all things be spiritual? This, indeed, was the message of Hildegard von Bingen. From her visions described in *Scivias* she learned that all things are sacred, "Every creature is a glittering, glistening mirror of divinity."

In times of spiritual hunger, people often look back to those in earlier times who were able to hold the light of divine essence and in turn share it. Perhaps this is why today, after nearly 1,000 years, the music composed by Hildegard von Bingen has been recorded in a popular CD entitled *Vision*, along with a similar best-selling recording of Benedictine monks entitled *Chant*.

The Path of Black Elk

American Indians in the United States number some several hundred tribes. Although cultural differences abound among them, from the Algonquins in the Northeast to the Navajo in the Southwest, their spirituality is fairly

> **Hildegard von Bingen:** An early Christian mystic who added a feminine voice to a male-dominated Christian theology.

consistent regardless of tribe. One voice that ascended the heights of consciousness in American Indian culture was that of **Black Elk**, a medicine man of the Ogalala Sioux (Lakota) nation. His mystical visions, recorded by John G. Neihardt in the book *Black Elk Speaks*, have galvanized the understanding and appreciation of American Indian spirituality, also referred to as **Mother Earth spirituality**. Despite the devastation of his culture by European traditions and values, Black Elk's vision was quite profound and elaborate with respect to the essence and integrity of the human spirit and the bonding relationship between the two-legged (man) and his natural environment.

Perhaps the features that most distinguish American Indian spirituality from that of other cultures are its set of values demonstrating respect for and connectedness to Mother Earth. Black Elk is not alone in voicing this philosophy; it has been expressed by a great many American Indians. In the words of Shoshone shaman Rolling Thunder, who describes the earth as a living organism, "Too many people don't know that when they harm the earth they harm themselves" (Boyd, 1974). In his book, *Mother Earth Spirituality*, Ed McGaa (Eagle Man) both expounds on Black Elk's vision and augments this knowledge with additional insights of the American Indian culture to provide a more profound understanding of Black Elk's enlightenment. The following is a brief synopsis of Black Elk's influence on spiritual healing.

First, despite the conviction of Christian missionaries that Indians were pagans, American Indians had established a very profound relationship with a divine essence. Unlike Europeans, who personified this higher power, American Indians accepted divine power as the Great Mystery, with no need to define or conceptualize God in human terms. In the words of Chief Seattle, transcribed for a letter to President Franklin Pierce in 1855, "One thing we know, our God is the same God. You may think you own Him

as you wish to own land, but you cannot. He is the God of man; and his compassion is equal for the red man and the white. The earth is precious to Him, and to harm the earth is to heap contempt on its creator. Our God is the same God. This earth is precious to Him" (Gore, 1993) (BOX 8.1). This preciousness was and continues to be represented in the bonding relationship between each American Indian and the earth's creatures, the wind, the rain, and the mountains.

North American indigenous peoples see Mother Earth as a symbol of wholeness and represent it with a medicine wheel. Just as the seasons are divided into quarters, so too are many concepts of American Indian spirituality. Some, for example, identify four elements: earth, fire, water, and air; four earth colors: red, yellow, black, and white; four directions: east, west, north, and south; and four cardinal principles or values of the Red Way: to show respect for Wankan Tanka (the Great Mystery or Great Spirit), to demonstrate respect for Mother Earth, to show respect for each fellow man and woman, and to show respect for individual freedoms. The American Indian medicine wheel is a symbol of Mother Earth spirituality from which the lessons of nature are used to better understand oneself (FIG. 8.8). To people of these cultures, each quadrant of the wheel represents a specific aspect of spiritual growth and various lessons to learn. The eastern quarter represents the Path of the Sun, where respect is shown for ourselves, others, and the environment. The southern quarter is the Path of Peace and is characterized by the traits of youth, innocence, and wonder. The western quarter is referred to as the Path of Introspection, where time is allocated for the soul-searching process and striving for a balance between physical substance and spiritual essence within oneself. The northern quarter represents the Path of Quiet, which symbolizes the importance of mental health, in which the intellect is stimulated by the lessons of nature.

Although there are several ceremonies to celebrate American Indian spirituality—the most famous being a feast of Thanksgiving taught to European settlers nearly 400 years ago—one practice, called the **vision quest**, exemplifies the strong bond with Mother Earth especially well. The vision quest is recognized as a time of self-reflection, which helps one to understand one's purpose in life, to become grounded in the earth and centered with the Great Spirit, and to reach a clearer understanding of one's contribution to the community. During a vision quest, an individual isolates him- or herself in the wilderness, on a hilltop, a large meadow, or any area that provides privacy. The vision quest creates an opportunity for emptying the mind (meditation) and body

Black Elk: An early twentieth century Native American elder whose perspective of spirituality is often cited as the clarion vision of our relationship with Mother Earth.

Mother Earth spirituality: The expression used to describe the American Indian philosophy with the divine through all of nature.

Vision quest: An American Indian custom of a retreat in nature where one begins or continues to search for life's answers.

BOX 8.1   A Letter from Chief Seattle (1855)

The president in Washington sends word that he wishes to buy our land. But how can you buy or sell the sky? the land? The idea is strange to us. If we do not own the freshness of the air, and the spark of the water, how can you buy them? Every part of this earth is sacred to my people. Every shining pine needle, every sandy shore, every mist in the dark woods. All are holy in the memory and experience of my people. We know the sap that courses through the trees as we know the blood that courses through our veins. We are part of the earth and it is part of us. Perfumed flowers are our sisters. The bear, the deer, the great eagle; these are our brothers. The body heat of the pony and man belong to the same family. The shining water that moves through the streams and rivers is not just water, but the blood of our ancestors. If we sell you our land, you must remember it is sacred.

Each ghostly reflection in the clear water of the lakes tells of the event and the memory in the life of my people. The water's murmur is the voice of my father's father. The rivers are my brothers. They quench our thirst, they carry our canoes and feed our children. So you must give to the river the kindness that you would give any brother. If we sell you our land, remember that the air is precious to us. The air shares its spirit with all life which it supports. The wind that gave our grandfather his first breath also receives his last sigh. The wind also gives our children the spirit of life.

So if we sell you our land, you must keep it apart and sacred as a place where man can go to taste the wind that is sweetened by the meadow's flowers. Will you teach your children what we have taught our children; that the earth is our Mother? What befalls the earth, befalls all the sons of the earth. This we know: the earth does not belong to man, man belongs to the earth. All things connect, like the blood that unites us all. Man did not weave the web of life, he is merely a strand in it. Whatever he does to the web, he does to himself. One thing we know: our God is your God. The earth is precious to him and to harm the earth is to heap contempt on the creator.

Your destiny is a mystery to us. What will happen when the buffalo are all slaughtered, the wild horses tamed? What will happen when the secret corners of the forest are heavy with the scent of many men and the view of the ripe hills is blotted with talking wires? Where will the thicket be? Gone! Where will the eagle be? Gone! And what is it to say good-bye to the swift pony and the hunt—the end of living and the beginning of survival. When the last red man has vanished in his wilderness, and his memory is only the shadow of a cloud moving across the prairie, will these shores and forests still be here? Will there be any spirit of my people left? We love the earth as a newborn loves his mother's heartbeat. So if we sell you our land, love it as we love it. Care for it as we have cared for it. Hold in your mind the memory of the land as you received it. Preserve the land for all children, and love it as God loves us all. As we are part of the land, you too are part of the land. It is precious to us, it is also precious to you. One thing we know: there is only one God. No man, be he red man or white, can be apart. We are brothers after all.

Modified by Ted Perry, loosely based on Chief Seattle's 1854 oration, "The Great Ecology" as it appeared in the *Seattle Sunday Star*, Oct. 29, 1887.

(fasting). The emptying process allows the human spirit to be filled with energy from the Great Spirit, leading the individual toward a path of self-enlightenment and self-improvement. Typically performed as a rite of passage from adolescence into adulthood, a vision quest can also be taken any time there is a need for spiritual growth or guidance.

Nearly extinguished by Christian missionaries a century or more ago, many elements of American Indian spirituality are now beginning to be recognized and respected, particularly in light of concerns about the poor "health status" of the planet (the environment). Ironically, it is now the "white man" who is adopting this value from the American Indian.

The Path of Matthew Fox

Matthew Fox is a former Roman Catholic theologian who, much like American Indians in the centuries before, was silenced by the Vatican in 1989 for his "progressive" views on human spirituality and has since been excommunicated from the church. The premise of Fox's theory is that the

> **Matthew Fox:** A Christian theologian renowned for his theory of creation spirituality and many other concepts. He was silenced by the Vatican in 1989 for one year followed by excommunication in 1999. He is now an Episcopal minister in California.

FIGURE 8.8   The Native American medicine wheel, which honors the four directions and the four seasons (Mother Earth spirituality).

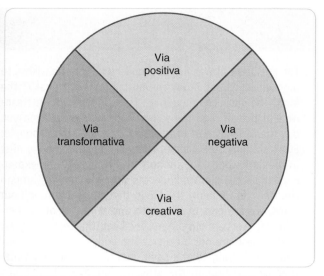

FIGURE 8.9   A symbolic representation of Fox's creation spirituality.

Judeo-Christian concept of spirituality, formulated when it was believed that the earth was the center of the universe, has not kept pace with scientific discoveries of the earth as but a piece of the whole universe and by no means its center. Fox has attempted to unite many concepts of theology with the laws and theories of physics in what he terms **creation spirituality**. Creation spirituality suggests that divinity can be found in any act of creation, from the atom to the far reaches of the cosmos, and every particle in between. The seed of creativity is energy, an element that binds all things together. And, as stated in the first law of thermodynamics, energy is neither created nor destroyed.

Fox was inspired by the work of the thirteenth-century German theologian Meister Eckhart, many American Indians, Albert Einstein, and a divine presence he terms the cosmic Christ. Through these influences, he has developed four paths or attitudes of creation spirituality (FIG. 8.9), which in his opinion raise individual

consciousness and thus the spiritual level of humankind as a whole. These paths are as follows:

Path 1: *Via positiva*. A sense of awe and wonder at the design and creation of all that surrounds us. Like the wonder of a young child, via positiva is a continual awareness and appreciation of all things, from the simplicity of a blade of grass to the mechanical complexity of the space shuttle. All creation should be celebrated, not feared or shamed.

Path 2: *Via negativa*. The process of emptying or letting go of thoughts, feelings, values, even possessions that weigh down, enclose, and smother the soul, depriving it of nutrients for growth. Via negativa is a period of darkness, silence, even fasting of the soul, for only when emptiness occurs is there room for new growth. This stage also goes by a less favorable name, "the dark night of the soul." This process may be emotionally painful at times, yet it is necessary for the maturation of the human spirit.

Path 3: *Via creativa*. A breakthrough or explosion of enlightenment, which fills the space vacated through the cleansing process of via negativa. This enlightenment may come in the form of divine inspiration, intuitive thoughts, or imagination. Via creativa is human creativity, which increases the quantity and quality of awe in the universe.

Path 4: *Via transformativa*. Fox calls via transformativa the path of struggle, compassion, and celebration. With this path comes the responsibility to act on the

Creation spirituality: A term coined by theologian Matthew Fox to describe the paths of human spirituality blending the laws of physics and theology.

Via positiva: Fox's term to describe a sense of awe and wonder of creation.

Via negativa: Fox's term to describe the act of emptying and letting go of unnecessary thoughts and feelings.

Via creativa: Fox's term to describe a breakthrough or moment of enlightenment.

Via transformativa: Fox's term to describe the euphoria from the realization of insights and the responsibility to share these with others.

enlightenment and inspiration from via creativa by channeling divine energy into personal acts of creation, and using this positive creative energy for the betterment of humankind.

Fox suggests that all people see themselves as acts of creation, deserving of awe and wonder. In turn, the ability to use one's imagination and creativity will add to the awe of the universe. These four paths align themselves in what Fox calls a sacred hoop, or a circle symbolizing wholeness, with each path nourishing the others to their full potential. The connection between each element of this hoop is compassion. Compassion, as defined by Fox, is a continual celebration of life and includes the fulfillment of love, forgiveness, and a personal as well as public display of one's spirituality. Thus, human spirituality involves the integration of all four paths into one road, or what Fox refers to as a "**personal cosmology**'—a relationship to the divine presence that dwells in us." When asked how to cultivate this divine relationship, Fox in turn asks these questions: What poets do you read? What music moves you? What acts of creation are you involved with? What social issues are your passion? What work do you most love doing? What pain is in your emptiness? When do you feel a connection to the universe? From Fox's perspective, the fulfillment of these answers nurtures the growth of the human spirit.

The Path of Joan Borysenko

New to the emerging discipline of psychoneuroimmunology, **Joan Borysenko** hit the ground running as cofounder, therapist, and director of the Mind/Body Clinic affiliated with the Harvard Medical School in Boston, Massachusetts. Through working with her mentor, stress physiologist Dr. Herbert Benson, her patients, and her personal journey of self-enlightenment, Borysenko began to synthesize an understanding of the connections among the body, mind, and soul. One observation inspiring her journey was that some of her clients' personal faith seemed to be stronger than any clinical medicine—faith that caused cancerous tumors to go into spontaneous remission, healed several illnesses, or simply brought inner peace in the last moments of life.

But just as faith can heal, so its absence can quicken the pace of physical illness and even death. Borysenko is among a growing number of clinical specialists who believe that the mechanistic approach to medicine is very much outdated. As explained in *Guilt Is the Teacher, Love Is the Lesson*, the mind and spirit play a crucial role in the health and healing process of the body. For example,

for a new medicine to be proven clinically effective, it must cure more than 35 percent of the people who use it. Below this point of demarcation, cures are considered the result of the placebo effect, or healing by faith alone (Brody, 2000). That is, sugar water and sugar pills have a healing rate of 35 percent (and in some cases up to 70 percent) among people who believe they will cure them of their disease. In addition, in a now-famous study cited by Borysenko, patients who had a view of nature outdoors from their rooms were released from the hospital sooner, indicating a significantly faster recovery rate, than those patients who had either no view or a view of adjacent brick buildings (Ulrich, 1984). These facts and several others indicated to Borysenko that a significant factor in the human equation has been ignored regarding the treatment of illness and disease—the factor of human spirituality.

In her campaign of health promotion, which has included several books, interviews, and national presentations, Borysenko advocates healing the human spirit as an integral part of physical healing and emphasizes the important role of spirituality in the self-healing process. Spirituality is defined by Borysenko (1990) as "a reconnection (remembrance) of our eternal connection with a lifeforce or power that we are a part of." Strongly influenced by the works of Jung, Larry Dossey, and others, Borysenko advocates the importance of building a relationship with the inner self and taking the time to get to know the real self. The distance that people keep from this self-center—distance created by shame, guilt, and the expectations of who we should be rather than who we really are—is fertile ground upon which to sow the seeds of stress. She also believes that through the ability to know the self we strengthen the bonds with higher consciousness as well as with the people within our community. In her original definition, influenced by Richard Lazarus, she believed stress to be the inability to cope, but she now proposes that stress is a lack of connectedness.

Personal cosmology: Fox's term to explain one's personal relationship with the divine that dwells in each of us.

Joan Borysenko: An early pioneer in the field of psychoneuroimmunology who emphasized the importance of spirituality as part of the mind-body concept.

Borysenko (1990) describes two possible attitudes relating to the development of the human spirit: **spiritual optimism** and **spiritual pessimism**. She defines spiritual optimism as "an intuitive knowledge that love is the universal energy and the human condition is ripe for learning experiences in which love manifests." Conversely, spiritual pessimism she describes as an attitude that nurtures low self-esteem, guilt, and all that impedes the way of love. Borysenko adds that spiritual pessimism is directly tied to low self-esteem, which produces psychological helplessness. In her work, she has observed many emotional roadblocks that not only impede spiritual development, but also appear to wreak havoc on the physiological systems of the body, leading to the onset of disease and illness. These emotions are commonly seen in the stress response: fear, anger, worry, and guilt, with guilt (in her opinion) as one of the largest obstacles to spiritual growth. Like Fox, Borysenko emphasizes the importance of compassion: "the flower of psychospiritual growth." To access this and other spiritual components of human nature, Borysenko advocates the practice of meditation to calm the mind and find peace in the soul. Stress, she says, is an obstacle to the spiritual nature of humankind. Meditation, like a warm wind that clears the sky of clouds to allow a view of the heavens, clears the mind of the taxing and toxic thoughts that obstruct the pathway of nutrients to the soul. Meditation, she believes, is a process for emptying the mind and making way for new insight into the real self, an insight that can guide one around the obstacles of life.

In her book *A Woman's Journey to God*, Borysenko notes that women constitute the greatest percentage of Americans she labels as "religious drop-outs"—those women who leave the institution of their religious upbringing to wander, drift, and possibly reconnect to another affiliation with more acceptance. One reason for this apathy can be found in the language of several religions where male pronouns describing God exclude the female gender—a big issue to many women in an age of equal rights. She states that the white-male hierarchy has become a huge roadblock on the spiritual path to women of the baby-boomer generation and their children.

Borysenko describes each woman's quest for a relationship to the divine as a spiritual pilgrimage. Although not outlining a systematic progression of steps on this pilgrimage, Borysenko shares her insights on how a woman might journey through various stages of the feminine quest. Borysenko suggests that each woman connect to the creative aspect of the divine and not see God entirely as a male entity. She cites menses and childbirth as examples of the creative process. Next she conveys the importance of resolving anger issues that develop (some as early as childhood) in what she terms as the first step to healing. Borysenko then speaks of the practice of rituals as a means to remember the divine connection. Rituals may include baby showers, candle ceremonies, retreats—anything to place one in the conscious recognition of God or Goddess. A final aspect of the feminine path Borysenko talks about is the connection to other women through support groups, prayer circles, or other venues where women can share their stories. For generations upon generations, stories have been the vehicle by which women have passed on spiritual truths to each other and their children.

In *A Woman's Journey to God*, Borysenko writes, "A quiet awakening is under way as women are coming together to worship, to tell stories, and find their place spiritually, if not always religiously, in the household of God. Women's spirituality groups are popping up everywhere. . . . Women often report a deep sense of connection to God as part of friendship, or mothering. We see God in others." It is this aspect of the feminine path that Borysenko shares in the hopes of inclusiveness and healing of the human spirit.

The Path of Deepak Chopra

One might think that spirituality and medicine would go hand in hand because both honor the essence of life, but that is not how Dr. **Deepak Chopra** or any of his physician colleagues and peers were introduced to the science of medicine. An endocrinologist by training, Chopra came to the United States from India and landed a job in New Jersey in 1970. With his sights set on a bigger hospital, he soon ended up outside of Boston, working as chief of staff at New England Memorial Hospital. Frustrated at the limitations of Western medicine, Chopra returned to his Indian roots and began to explore Ayurvedic medicine,

---

Spiritual optimism: Joan Borysenko's description of an intuitive knowledge that love is *the* universal energy.

Spiritual pessimism: Joan Borysenko's description of an attitude that nurtures low self-esteem, guilt, and other less-than-becoming behaviors.

Deepak Chopra: A contemporary physician and metaphysician originally from India, he presents and integrates the ageless wisdom of spirituality, quantum physics, and medicine.

an ancient form of holistic health care, which, when translated, means the Science of Life where mind, body, and spirit connect as one. On a path that led him from allopathic to holistic medicine, Chopra soon discovered that mind-body medicine, or psychoneuroimmunology as it is referred to clinically, is really mind-body-spirit medicine, in which the human spirit plays an integral role in the healing process. His search into psychoneuroimmunology and the essence of spirituality led him to study with the founder of Transcendental Meditation (TM), Maharishi Mahesh Yogi, where he began to understand the concepts of mind and consciousness. This exposure to consciousness began to galvanize his understanding of the intricacies of the human condition in states of disease and health and matters of the soul.

But Chopra didn't rest there. An avid reader, he, like a child with a crayon, began to connect the dots of wisdom from all corners of the earth, including the writings of Einstein, Blake, Rumi, the *Bhagavad Gita*, the Bible, the Koran, Lao Tzu, Tagore, and others to synthesize a comprehensive if not universal understanding of the nature of God and the laws that govern all creation.

The author of several books, including *Quantum Healing*, *Perfect Health*, and *Ageless Body, Timeless Mind*, Chopra has now focused his attention on the matters of the soul. In his book *The Seven Spiritual Laws of Success*, Chopra presents a simple guideline of seven principles for embracing the spirit of life in everyday living.

The Law of Pure Potentiality. Understanding that at the core of our essence is pure consciousness, the law of pure potentiality reminds us to enter in silence the core of our being and tap the universal wisdom in which to create and reach our potential. In the Western culture, it is common to seek validation through external objects. The law of pure potentiality reminds us that we only need look inside to find our divine essence. Once this source is accessed, we become co-creators and active participants, rather than passive victims on the human journey.

The Law of Giving. According to this law, the universe is a dynamic cornucopia. Nothing is static. Energy flows freely. In support of the axiom, "As you give, so shall you receive," the law of giving reminds us to keep open the channels of our heart, for when the heart is closed, the energy becomes blocked and the stagnation of universal energy leads to an atrophy of the spirit. Chopra points out that the derivation of the words *affluence* and *currency* has nothing to do with money. Rather, it means to flow, a lesson the law of giving teaches. Nature abhors

a vacuum; however, she is not fond of gluttony either. The law of giving reminds us to walk in balance.

The Law of Karma (or Cause and Effect). As if taken from a law of physics stating that every action has an equal and opposite reaction, the law of karma invites us to become more responsible for our thoughts and actions. The law of karma, similar to the Christian expression, "As you sow, so shall you reap," invites us to shed the habits that inhibit our growth, break the bonds of conditioned thoughts, and become responsible (the ability to respond) for our every action.

The Law of Least Effort. Nature teaches us that water finds its own level. The universe unfolds in its own time and place. If we try to rush it, we only tire ourselves. The law of least effort invites us to go with the flow, not resist what we cannot change or influence. Chopra writes that nature's intelligence functions effortlessly. To be in harmony with nature means to go with the flow. One aspect of least effort is to accept those things we cannot change. A second aspect of least effort is to initiate self-responsibility rather than cast blame on others. The law of least effort asks us to travel the human path lightly, discarding those opinions, beliefs, and attitudes that are defensive in nature, for when we carry these, the human journey becomes a struggle, rather than a delightful sojourn.

The Law of Intention and Desire. We attract what we submit to the universal consciousness through intention. "Intention," writes Chopra, "grounded in the detached freedom of the present, serves as the catalyst for the right mix of matter, energy, and space-time events to create whatever it is that you desire." The Buddha once said that all suffering comes from desire. What is implied in the teachings of the Buddha is that the partner of desire is

---

The Law of Pure Potentiality: A reminder to be silent and look within for guidance and insights rather than validation through external means.

The Law of Giving: A reminder to live life with an open heart to give and receive freely.

The Law of Karma (or Cause and Effect): A reminder that we reap what we sow.

The Law of Least Effort: A reminder to go with the flow with things that we cannot control as well as to live in harmony with nature.

The Law of Intention and Desire: A reminder to set our intentions for both big and small goals, yet not become encumbered by the ego's desires.

detachment or letting go. Attachment to our desires most likely will create suffering when our intentions are not fully realized. As you intend, so must you detach, and let the universe take care of the details.

The Law of Detachment. The law of detachment is an invitation to let go of our desires, wishes, and dreams. It's not that we don't want the desired outcome, but detachment allows the desire to stand on its own two feet. This law serves as a reminder that we are co-creators in the universe of our lives, but not codependent on it. Detachment means to let go of the emotions that align with our desires—fear and anger, if our desires go unfulfilled. The law of detachment is one of the hardest laws to honor because we often place our security in those things we keep near us. Implicit in the law of detachment is the concept of trust. When we let go of thoughts, wishes, and desires, we are trusting that whatever the outcome, it is in our best interest. So if we apply for a job (intention) and we don't get it, we must realize that at a higher level of consciousness, this was in our best interest. Those things in our best interest will come back to us as intended.

The Law of Dharma or Life Purpose. Each of us has a unique gift and talent to share with the community of humanity. This law invites us to realize what our life purpose or mission is, and to act on it, so that we help raise consciousness for one and all. *Dharma* is the ancient Sanskrit word for purpose or mission. The acceptance of life on Earth requires that we not only realize our purpose, but also act to fulfill it so that all may benefit from it.

In his acclaimed book *How to Know God*, Chopra uses the template of the seven chakras as a way to expand one's level of awareness to a higher level of consciousness. It is Chopra's thesis (and he is not alone in this thought) that each person must journey back to the divine source by cultivating a relationship through mind and heart.

> **The Law of Detachment:** A reminder to release and let go of all thoughts that hold back our human potential.
>
> **The Law of Dharma or Life Purpose:** This law invites contemplation of one's purpose in life.
>
> **Jesus of Nazareth:** A remarkable spiritual leader with a timeless message of compassion, forgiveness, and integrity.
>
> **Unconditional love:** An altruistic love expressed by Jesus of Nazareth, where nothing is expected in return.

In doing so, we come to realize that we partner with God in the creation process of our own lives.

Chopra has become a bridge that unites not just spirituality and medicine, but many facets of humanity that have become divided through ego and fear. If asked, he and others like him will tell you that we, the human species, stand on the precipice of great change. For us to weather this change and become self-realized, we must work to evolve our soul growth, and this can be done by honoring and practicing the seven universal laws of spirituality.

The Path of Jesus of Nazareth

More than 2,000 years ago, a unique man appeared in the Middle East, and his presence has since left an indelible mark on humanity. His teachings were profound, his healings miraculous, and his death a mystery. Some people called him a prophet, others called him the Messiah, and still others called him a heretic. Little is known about **Jesus of Nazareth** other than that he was born in a barn, worked as a carpenter, shared his philosophies with others, and died a cruel death. He never wrote down any of his teachings; rather, he shared his simple yet profound wisdom with followers who yearned to understand his enlightenment, and they in turn created a community years later called Christianity. Decades after his death, in an effort to remember those teachings, his followers recorded his wisdom, stories, and healing practices in a collection of manuscripts now known as the New Testament of the Holy Bible. Scholars and theologians continue to study and interpret his words of wisdom today. It may be difficult, if not impossible, to separate the messenger from the message, but if we focus on the fundamental principle taught by Jesus, we find that his basic premise is the power of **unconditional love** (**FIG. 8.10**). What follows is a small sampling of insights and reflections on this theme (Borg, 2008).

When Jesus began teaching in the Middle East, there was much civil conflict and strife. The Hebrews in Jerusalem were oppressed by the Romans and in essence were treated as second-class citizens in their own country. Many were searching for a political leader to save them and return them to a life of undisturbed peace. In this time of ambivalence and hatred, Jesus preached and practiced the power of unconditional love. He was charismatic, his style was uniquely humble, and he attracted many followers who in their hearts believed he possessed the qualities of a great political leader. But Jesus of Nazareth regarded himself as a spiritual leader only. By his example and teachings, he showed men and women

FIGURE 8.10 A symbolic representation of human spirituality from the perspective of Jesus of Nazareth.

how to restore and maintain inner peace through a loving relationship with God. Beyond all else, he believed that through love all things were possible.

Based on the inspirational words of Jesus and his followers, many people have since attempted to illustrate the concept of love on the canvas of their own hearts. Scottish theologian Henry Drummond described love as a spectrum of several attributes, including patience, kindness, generosity, humility, unselfishness, and sincerity. Theologian Thomas Merton wrote in his book *The Ascent to Truth* that love is the source of one's merit, and as such, it is in love that God resides. Psychiatrist Gerald Jampolsky defines love as an experience absent from fear and the recognition of complete union with all life. To Jesus, the expression of love was like a passageway. For love to be effective as a channel of communication or healing energy, there must be no obstructions and no conflicting thoughts to pollute it. In other words, there must be no conditions or expectations placed on the expression of love. Like a child who acts spontaneously, the expression of love must be uninhibited, not filtered by conscious (ego) thought. As Jesus elaborated, people under oppression, whether by foreign rulers or the perceptions of their own minds, begin to close and harden their hearts. Their ability to feel and express love is overridden by critical, judgmental, and conditional thinking, thought processes often rooted in fear. But as described by Ken Carey in the book *Starseed*, these two concepts are mutually exclusive: You cannot experience love and fear

at the same time. From the writings of Jesus' followers, we see that it is fear, expressed in terms of hatred, greed, and guilt, that is the greatest obstacle to love.

Love has an inherent healing power all its own, and it was this power that Jesus demonstrated in performing his miracles of giving sight to the blind and health to the infirm. Inspired by the book *A Course in Miracles*, Jampolsky cites love as a divine energy that knows no bounds. In his own book, *Teach Only Love*, Jampolsky explains that when love is undiluted it becomes the most powerful source of healing energy. When there is a conscious shift from the motivation of fear to the motivation of love, then nothing real is impossible.

Once while teaching, Jesus was asked about the greatest rule to live by. His reply was to love unconditionally—specifically, to love God and to extend this love to each human being as you would to yourself. Jesus further explained that God resides in each and every one of us: "The Kingdom of God is within you." These words, although not new, were novel in their meaning. Given the hatred and fear in the hearts of the Hebrews at the time, it seemed incongruous to love one's enemy as Jesus suggested. His message here was that forgiveness is a crucial element of unconditional love. To elaborate on this theme, he shared the story of the prodigal son, a young man who wasted his inheritance on foolish pleasures and then came crawling back home destitute. Yet his father welcomed him back and forgave him completely. This was an example of the depth of God's unconditional love for all people.

Jesus also spoke about faith and its relationship to love. Faith, a confident belief and conviction in the power of God's love, is the intent or desire to express love. Jesus explained the concept of faith through metaphors and parables. In one such case, he compared faith to a tiny mustard seed, implying that a small seed of faith could expand to phenomenal proportions and overcome the trials of human experience. To paraphrase the words of theologian C. S. Lewis, faith is a necessary virtue to complete the will of God. And in the words of President John F. Kennedy, "God's work must truly be our own."

Paul, one of Jesus' earliest followers, in a letter to friends in the city of Corinth (which has since been recited at many weddings), described love this way:

Love is patient and kind, never jealous or envious, never boastful or proud, never haughty or selfish or rude. Love does not demand its own way. It is not irritable or touchy. It does not hold grudges and will hardly ever notice when others do it wrong. It is never glad about injustice, but rejoices whenever truth wins out. Above all there are three things that remain, faith, hope, and love. The greatest of these is love. Let love be your greatest aim.

The Path of Joseph Campbell

The word *myth* comes from an ancient Sanskrit word, meaning the source of truth. Today the word *myth* has become synonymous with the word *fallacy*, but it is fair to say that every myth is based on a source of truth, perhaps exaggerated to make a point, but truth nevertheless. **Joseph Campbell** is the most respected scholar in the study of mythology. For more than 60 years, he studied myths, legends, and stories from all cultures, from the ancient Hindus to several American Indian tribes. Campbell left no stone unturned when it came to looking behind the message of each story. What he found was not only astonishing parallels (e.g., virgin births, resurrections, healings), but remarkable patterns, regardless of the story's origin, which speak to the nature of the human spirit. His own quest brought him to the front door of psychologist Carl Jung, mystic Jiddu Krishnamurti, poet Robert Bly, and scores of luminaries over the world, all of whom added to his collective wisdom.

Campbell's work went largely unrecognized outside of academic circles during the twentieth century until PBS television host Bill Moyers aired a six-part special, titled *The Power of Myth*, with Joseph Campbell in the spring of 1987. Campbell died soon thereafter on October 30. Despite his death, his work grows increasingly popular as people discover the links between mythology and spirituality—a legacy for all to share.

In the first episode with Bill Moyers, Campbell explained the connection between mythology and human spirituality like this:

> Myths are clues to the spiritual potentialities of the human life. Our problem today is that we are not well acquainted with the literature of the spirit.

Joseph Campbell: Renowned for his wisdom about human mythology gathered from all cultures over time, Campbell's greatest work illustrates the human experience as the hero's journey as exemplified in the template of every great story.

Hero's journey: Mythologist Joseph Campbell's classic template of the human journey with three stages: departure, initiation, and return.

Having studied the myths and legends of every culture throughout the ages, from Zeus to *Star Wars* (George Lucas was a student of Campbell's), Campbell noticed an interesting trend. In each myth there is a hero, and although the face of the hero may change over time, the story line remains consistent. In his book *The Hero with a Thousand Faces*, Campbell highlights the progression of the **hero's journey**, which, as it turns out, mirrors our own life sojourn. The stages include departure, initiation, and return. Let's take a closer look at each one.

- *Departure:* The first step in any adventure is to leave your place of origin. Whether one travels like Ulysses on a ship or like Luke Skywalker on a spacecraft, every hero must leave home to go and find him- or herself. The departure stage is also referred to as severance or separation, where the reluctant hero is forced into a situation unwillingly. Campbell cites Adam and Eve as examples of reluctant departure. Stepping outside of the classic myth tale, departure may begin with the first year in college away from home, the death of a parent, or the end of a marriage. Departures can occur in a great many ways. With the first step out the door and across the threshold, the journey has begun.

- *Initiation:* Traveling down the road far away from home, the hero is put to the test. Campbell calls this stage "the road of trials." It can be observed in nearly every story from Frodo Baggins in *Lord of the Rings* to each Harry Potter book. For some heroes, the test may be dragons (the symbol of fear); for others, it may be a symbolic river to cross (the River Styx). For still others, it may be an evil witch, a wicked stepmother, a rescue, or the betrayal of a close friend. In the legend of King Arthur, it began with the apprenticeship with Merlin. In the life of a college student, initiation can manifest itself in thousands of ways, including the roommate from hell or the abusive alcoholic parent. In every mythological story, the hero must demonstrate strength, courage, patience, and willpower. If she fails the first test, another will appear until she is strong enough to conquer it and move on.

- *Return:* At some point in the journey, usually upon success with the initiation process, the hero must return home. Upon crossing the threshold of return, the hero shares the wealth of riches acquired on the road. Symbolically, the return home is accompanied with a trophy of sorts: magical runes, the golden fleece, a broomstick, or Medusa's head. Campbell

Stress with a Human Face

In 1960, at the invitation of renowned anthropologist Louis Leakey and the government of Tanzania, a young British woman named Jane Goodall ventured into the forests of Africa, known then as the "Dark Continent." Her assignment was to observe and study the behaviors of the chimpanzee, one of the great apes whose behavior in the wild was virtually unknown at the time. Today, Goodall is recognized not just for her discovery that humans are not the only species to make and use tools, but also for her tireless efforts as an environmental activist to save wildlife habitats around the globe. In her autobiography *Reason for Hope*, she shares both her life's work and her spiritual insights, for Goodall is a very spiritual person.

Every once in a great while a person enters the world stage and makes an indelible mark in the minds of the entire world. Even rarer is the person who touches our hearts in a way that leaves us inspired to reach our highest potential. Goodall is one such person. Through her unyielding inspiration, compassion, humility, vision, and unceasing effort to make the world a better place, she has been compared to such luminaries as Gandhi, Einstein, the Dalai Lama, and Mother Teresa. In recognition of her achievement and world influence, former United Nations Secretary General Kofi Annan appointed her a UN Messenger of Peace in 2002, a title balanced with honor and responsibility. By all counts, Goodall demonstrates the traits of a leader, hero, and role model. She embodies the expression "Live simply, so that others (including all of God's creatures) may simply live." In doing so, she reminds us that we, too, must do the same.

Through a wonderful path of serendipity, I found myself having breakfast with Goodall in spring 2004 to collaborate on a project. Despite the clouds of uncertainty, she shared with me her conviction to make planet Earth a better world in which to live and her reasons for hope in achieving this result—symbols of achievement that transcend the limitations of ego. The first was a California condor feather given to Goodall by those who were responsible for bringing this magnificent bird back from the brink of extinction—a symbol of what is possible. The second was a piece of rock from the prison quarry where Nelson Mandela was confined for more than 26 years under the rule of apartheid. Goodall carries it with her as a sign of both forgiveness and powerful, peaceful transformation. The third reason for hope was a mystical experience in Nebraska watching the migration of the sandhill cranes—the same day war broke out in Iraq in 2003. Goodall viewed the experience as a sign that in a world of chaos, there is still beauty, and that beauty is worth saving.

To sit in the presence of Jane Goodall is to experience grace firsthand. She is a very spiritual individual. Moreover, to see her work take root around the world through her youth-based programs like "Roots & Shoots" is proof that one person can, indeed, make a difference. In Goodall's words, "Each of us has a role to play. Each one of us must take responsibility for our lives and, above all, show respect and love for living things around us, especially each other. Together we must reestablish our connection with the natural world and with the spiritual power that is around us. Despite signs of imbalance, I believe in the power of the human spirit, but we must act now," she says.

---

points out that there may be a reluctance to go home, caused either by feelings of shame or the lust for additional conquests. But return we must to complete the story. The stage of return is also called incorporation, where the returning hero is accepted by his family and peers as an equal, and everyone benefits from his wisdom as a master of two worlds: the one he conquered and the one he has returned home to. The return phase offers a promise that all ends well.

There was a time when the sharing of myths was passed down from parent to child, not merely for entertainment purposes but as wisdom to guide the child on his or her own life journey. Stories from the Bible, the *Bhagavad Gita*, and other sacred scriptures as well as scores of legends, fairy tales, and folklore all serve the same purpose. However, for the most part the tradition of finding wisdom from these stories has vanished in the American culture. In his discussion in *The Power of Myth*, Campbell drew a connection between the rising state of spiritual hunger and the absence of our connection to mythological stories. As he explained, when a society forgoes the power of myth, instead replacing it with information, technology, or perhaps nothing, the society becomes less civilized and more destructive.

Knowing the power of myth himself, Campbell had ever the optimistic outlook on the journey of humanity itself, for he knew the end of the story: "We are at this moment participating in one of the very greatest leaps of the human spirit—to a knowledge not only of outside nature, but also our own deep inward mystery—the greatest leap ever!"

The Path of Lao Tzu

Around 500 B.C., the writings of China's most famous philosopher, **Lao Tzu**, were first published under the title of *Tao Teh Ching*. Originally written primarily for the leaders of his country, this collection of 5,000 words soon became the doctrine of Chinese living, outlining the path to spiritual enlightenment through inner peace. Lao Tzu used the word *Tao* to describe the movement, path, or way of universal energy. The literal translation of the title of Tzu's book is "the path that leads straight from the heart," and the Chinese character for this title symbolizes "walking wisdom." Tzu's writings speak of building a peaceful world through inner peace. Only when peace is created within yourself can you move in tandem with the energies that circulate within and around you and to establish world peace.

The concept of Taoism suggests that all things connect with a flow of energy called *chi*. To move along with the patterns of flow allows a peaceful coexistence with both oneself and the environment. Movement against the flow causes internal as well as external disturbances, often with far-reaching consequences. This movement of life energy goes in cycles, like the ebb and flow of the ocean tide. One of the many concepts the *Tao Teh Ching* teaches is balance between the opposing forces of yin and yang, which provides harmony, patience, and timing of the events of life. That is, to move with rather than against the flow promotes and maintains inner peace. Tzu's *Tao* invites the individual to look inward, beyond the superficial facade of humanness, and sense the inner rhythms that move in

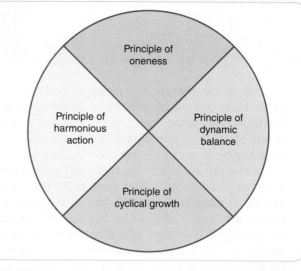

FIGURE 8.11   A symbolic representation of the four principles of Taoism created by Lao Tzu.

harmony with the universal rhythms. By doing this, not only is inner peace achieved, but also harmony with nature and all relationships. Tzu also spoke of the importance of self-reliance: "Wise people seek solutions, the ignorant only cast blame." Although initially Taoism may seem like a foreign concept, it can be found in many Western writings as well. Perhaps the best example of it is the Taoist mannerisms and character of Winnie the Pooh, described by Benjamin Hoff in the renowned best-seller, *The Tao of Pooh*. In fact, with a closer look, Taoist principles can be found virtually everywhere.

In her book *The Tao of Inner Peace*, Diane Dreher explains that Tzu outlined four "great disciplines" to help achieve inner peace through the way of the *Tao*: oneness, dynamic balance, cyclical growth, and harmonious action (**FIG. 8.11**).

The Principle of Oneness. The principle of oneness suggests that we are part of the whole, connected to a dynamic network of universal energy. Oneness means to be one with, or a part of, nature, not above or apart from it. When we see ourselves as separate from the whole, we distance ourselves from other people and the natural elements. This distance weakens our spiritual strength. Just as there is strength in numbers, there is also strength in oneness.

The Principle of Dynamic Balance. Taoist philosophy speaks of the composition of all creation as two complementary opposites: yin and yang. In simple terms, yin comprises the quiet, feminine, receptive elements of

---

Lao Tzu: An ancient Chinese philosopher and writer. He is the author of the acclaimed book *Tao Teh Ching*, a manifesto for human spirituality based on the concept of balance with nature. Lao Tzu is believed to be the creator of the concept of Taoism.

The Principle of Oneness: A Taoist concept of oneness with nature serving as a reminder of our oneness with it.

The Principle of Dynamic Balance: A Taoist concept revealing the opposites that make up the balance of life.

nature, while yang is seen as active, dynamic, and masculine. Alone, each side is overbearing. The union of yin and yang within the individual provides a perpetual movement that strives for balance and harmony. After rain comes sunshine. After disaster comes calm. To live in dynamic balance in the world, one must move with the flow through the mountains and valleys of life. To stay always static or always dynamic goes against the laws of nature of which both men and women are very much a part.

The Principle of Cyclical Growth. The natural world consists of many cycles: day and night, birth and death, winter and summer. Each human life is also filled with cycles, from the life cycle of a red blood cell to the highs and lows of our emotions. The wisdom of the *Tao* advocates that these cycles be recognized and appreciated. Too often, impatience blinds human vision to the natural cycles of which we are a part. The universe is not still. The *Tao* encourages patience.

The Principle of Harmonious Action. As a part of nature, we must work in cooperation with it and not try to dominate, monopolize, or destroy it. The wisdom of the *Tao* advises individuals to live in harmony with nature, respecting her many components, including the lives of others. To live in harmony means to live in moderation, not excess; to live with simplicity, not complexity; and to slow down, know oneself, and make wise choices. One concept of harmonious action is called the *wu wei*, which means knowing when to wait for the right moment, and knowing when to be spontaneous, moving with the rhythms of life.

There are many ways to reinforce the attitudes of Taoist philosophy behaviorally. The most commonly known techniques are yoga, meditation, and T'ai Chi ch'uan.

The characteristics of a *Tao* person are very similar to those of the self-actualized individuals described by Maslow, and those of the hardy personality described by Kobasa and Maddi. These characteristics include self-acceptance, humor, creativity, commitment, challenge, and self-control, and they serve as buffers against the perceptions of stress. *Tao* individuals have faith in themselves and what they do. They carry no illusions about who they are. They embrace life joyously. This is what it means to be "one with the *Tao*."

The Path of Albert Einstein

It may seem rather strange to include a physicist among the several people noted here who have speculated on the nature of human spirituality, yet at the same time it would be a gross oversight to omit this perspective. The fields of physics and theology, which were so bitterly divided more than 300 years ago, are finding they have more commonalities than differences today. These commonalities were first brought to scientific light about 100 years ago by a physicist named **Albert Einstein**, who took it upon himself to challenge the accepted principles of natural physics developed by Isaac Newton. Like an earthquake, Einstein's concepts of the physical laws of nature rocked the foundations of the scientific community. But as can be seen today, the ramifications of this challenge actually parallel, and may eventually validate, the concept of a higher power, albeit somewhat differently from the way that many people currently perceive it. In 1999, *Time* magazine named Einstein "Man of the Century," not solely for his scientific theories or Nobel Prize, but rather for changing the paradigm of thought of humanity in a nonthreatening way.

Curious about the nature of the universe and the laws that govern it, Einstein was convinced that all matter is made up of energy, and that time and space are not locked into a continuum as previously thought, giving way to his famous theory of relativity: $E = mc^2$. Very simply put, this suggests that all matter is energy that is not confined to the "local" concept involving space and time. Although the complexities of this theory are beyond the scope of this book, the premise of Einstein's theory, once rejected by his peers, is now completely accepted by the scientific community, as well as those mystically inclined individuals who see Einstein's theory as a stepping stone toward higher consciousness. Moreover, the impact of Einstein's work has reached far beyond science to the fields of poetry, art, and even psychology. (It was Einstein's theory of relativity that

---

The Principle of Cyclical Growth: A Taoist concept that suggests that everything is cyclic: the moon, tides, seasons, and all aspects of human life.

The Principle of Harmonious Action: A Taoist concept that reminds us to work in harmony with nature, not in opposition to it or control over it.

Albert Einstein: A world-renowned theoretical physicist who revolutionized perceptions of reality with the equation $E = mc^2$, suggesting that everything is energy. His later years focused on a spiritual philosophy including pacifism.

gave Jung the idea for the collective unconscious.) With energy being the word that opened the door to understanding, theologians also gravitated toward Einstein's theories, making the concept of light a solid foundation from which to explore the divine nature of the universe. Compare, for example, the concept of universal energy with the following description (Dreher, 1991):

> We Look at it and we do not see it;
> Its name is The Invisible.
> We Listen to it and we do not hear it;
> Its name is The Inaudible.
> We Touch it and don't find it;
> Its name is The Subtle.

> —Lao Tzu, *Tao Teh Ching*, 14

Stepping out of the scientific box that Newton had created centuries earlier, Einstein paved the way for others to follow. With the initial theoretical basis constructed, other physicists (Heisenberg and Chew) quickly added corollaries to Einstein's theory, leading the way to the field of quantum physics. Today, pioneers in the field of energy medicine credit Einstein with building a conceptual model from which to understand the human energy field and even human consciousness (**FIG. 8.12**). Biophysicist Itzhak Bentov expounded on Einstein's concept that "energy equals matter" in his widely acclaimed book, *Stalking the Wild Pendulum*. From his added insight we begin to see that consciousness is actually a form of energy that surrounds, permeates, and connects all living

FIGURE 8.12   A glimpse of the universe depicting Einstein's perspective where everything is energy and the universe is indeed a friendly place.

objects. Like the atom's electrons, which vibrate to give off an energy field, so too does the human body produce an oscillation and energy field, which Bentov refers to as subtle energy. He hypothesized that this *subtle energy* comprises many layers or "frequencies," which he suggests constitute various layers of human consciousness (and the soul itself).

Since the introduction of the theory of relativity, physicists have discovered that subatomic particles called photons appear to travel at or greater than the speed of light. Renowned quantum physicist Dave Bohm has combined this knowledge with that of emotional thought, neuropeptide activity, and coherence. He too postulates that thoughts are a form of energy: Negative thoughts (e.g., fear and anger) are expressed by electrons, and positive thoughts (e.g., love and peace) are conveyed through the movement of photons. This idea has gained momentum among those who have taken a scientific look at the power of prayer and clairvoyant "coincidences" (McTaggart, 2008). For instance, in the landmark double-blind study designed by cardiologist Randolph Byrd (1986), more than 300 hospital patients were randomly assigned to either a "prayed for" group or control group. Results demonstrated a statistically significant difference on various health parameters between those who received prayer and those who did not, suggesting that there may actually be a healing power in prayer. Even more significant, the people doing the praying lived hundreds if not thousands of miles away from the hospital where the patients were located. Additional studies of prayer have been conducted by the Spindrift Organization in Lansdale, Pennsylvania, using both direct and indirect prayer on the metabolic rate of plants. These studies have produced results similar to those found by Byrd. An analysis of case studies by psychiatrist Jean Bolen in her book *The Tao of Psychology* indicates that distance (time and space) was not a factor among people who experienced a clairvoyant "coincidence," but that love (a positive emotion) was.

Dr. Larry Dossey—author of the books *Space, Time, and Medicine*; *Recovering the Soul*; and *Healing Words*—applauds Einstein for his "quantum leap" of new understanding regarding both the universe and its relevance to human consciousness. Dossey, a former internist at the Dallas Diagnostic Association, synthesized the theories of quantum physics and medicine in an attempt to validate that human spirituality is a vital element in the healing process. Borrowing a term from the field of physics, Dossey refers to the spiritual-healing nature of humankind as the **nonlocal mind**, meaning thoughts that are not bound by time or space. Dossey also explains that there is a connectedness to all things in the universe and that this connectedness has a spiritual quality to it. It is this same spiritual quality that Pelletier referred to as the "missing piece" of the stress and disease model, and why he suggested that the principles of quantum physics be included in the study of psychoneuroimmunology. In the words of Dr. Richard Gerber, "With respect to his theory of relativity, Einstein was more right than even he imagined."

With a greater understanding of the theory of relativity, several physicists have noted connections between the world of physics and the spiritual nature of the universe. In his book *The Tao of Physics*, Fritjof Capra outlined many similarities and parallels between the disciplines of physics and the Eastern mystical philosophies of Buddhism, Hinduism, and Taoism, suggesting that there is an incredible linkage between them and that whether it is called "energy," the "Tao," or the "Holy Spirit," its essence appears to be very similar. Capra writes, "Physicists and mystics deal with different aspects of reality. Physicists explore levels of matter, mystics levels of mind. What their explorations have in common is that these levels, in both cases, lie beyond ordinary sensory perception." Capra suggests that these two disciplines, in effect, are looking at the same mountain, but from different vantage points and through different binoculars. To Capra, the paradigm shift that occurred in physics with Einstein's theory of relativity is currently rippling through other Western disciplines, including clinical medicine and psychology. In his autobiography *Memories, Dreams, Reflections*, Jung wrote, "There are indications that at least part of the psyche is not subject to the laws of space and time." The collective unconscious and subtle energy in which all things connect may, in fact, be the same component of human spirituality. As science continues to explore the realm of human energy and consciousness, the fields of physics and theology may not only connect but someday become one and the same (Radin, 2006).

Those who knew him and studied his works say that Einstein was a spiritual man but not a religious one. Yet these same people note that he appeared to be driven by a spiritual quest to understand the nature of the universe. One of Einstein's most famous quotes speaks to this fact: "I want to know the thoughts of God, the rest are just details." And although some people infer from his theory of relativity that his view of the cosmos is impersonal at best (with the order of the universe simply calculated by mathematical equations), Einstein retorted, "God does not play dice with the universe." From his own writings it becomes very obvious that he was not only a scientific genius, but a world-class philosopher as well. A person who spent much time in deep personal reflection, he once wrote,

> A human being is part of the whole, called by us "universe," a part limited in time and space. He experiences his thoughts and feelings as something separate from the rest, a kind of optical delusion of his consciousness. This delusion is a kind of prison for us, restricting us to our personal decisions and to affection for a few persons nearest us. Our task must be to free ourselves from this prison by widening our circle of compassion to embrace all living creatures and the whole of nature in its beauty.

Einstein spent the better part of his later years conceiving his unified field theory (a thesis to explain the relationship of gravity and electromagnetic energy), as well as playing a more subtle role as pacifist for world peace—a moral position in which he took great pride. Yet through it all, it was light, symbolically and literally, that fascinated Einstein.

"For the rest of my life, I want to reflect on what light is," he said.

■ Common Bonds of Human Spirituality

Although no one path seems to offer complete insight into the mystery of the human spirit, some common themes run through the various paths. Specifically, these common themes are four processes that collectively nurture the growth of the human spirit: **centering**, **emptying**, **grounding**,

---

Nonlocal mind: A term given to consciousness that resides outside the brain (possibly outside the human energy field), which may explain premonitions, distant healing, and prayer.

Centering: A time for soul searching, cultivating one's internal relationship.

Emptying: Also known as the "dark night of the soul" and the winter of discontent. The emptying process is a time to release, detach, and let go of thoughts, attitudes, perceptions, and beliefs that no longer serve you.

Grounding: The point at which new insights may be revealed to assist a person to move from point A to point B.

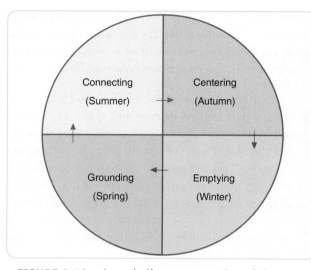

FIGURE 8.13 A symbolic representation of the common themes among approaches to human spirituality referred to as "seasons of the soul."

FIGURE 8.14 The centering process (like the autumn season) is a time to go inside and explore the landscape of the soul.

and **connecting** (FIG. 8.13). These processes provide a nurturing enlightenment to our own spiritual growth. And some or all of these processes are found in virtually every form of relaxation and several coping techniques used to deal with stress.

In its simplest terms, the common bonds of human spirituality can be viewed as a cycle of seasons (seasons of the soul): centering (autumn), where one goes inside to do some soul searching; emptying (winter), a process of letting go of thoughts, perceptions, and frustrations to make room for new insights; grounding (spring), where new insights are sought and received; and connecting (summer), a time of sharing and celebration. Let's take a closer look.

Centering Process (Autumn)

The centering process involves deep reflection on one's real self: who we are and what our purpose in life is. Jung devoted much of his professional as well as personal life to understanding the centering process. He was deeply committed to the idea that centering our thoughts—or more specifically, accessing the powers of the unconscious mind—was imperative to mental, emotional, spiritual, and even physical well-being. The American Indian vision

> **Connecting:** A realization that we are all connected, and the connection is made and nurtured through love.

quest is also an exercise in centering. It is uninterrupted time devoted to addressing those questions that can only be answered by the soul in the midst of deep solitude. Likewise, Lao Tzu was an advocate of the centering process: "Be still, and discover your center of peace. Returning to the center is peace." Fox's creation spirituality theory also extolls the virtue of centering: the ability to appreciate the creative process within and to initiate the emptying process, which plants the seeds of personal transformation. Borysenko advocates centering to unite the body, mind, and soul as one. She suggests many ways this can be done, including journal writing, yoga, and meditation (FIG. 8.14). As Borysenko points out, the purpose of virtually every relaxation technique is to create an opportunity for centering.

Emptying Process (Winter)

It appears that for spiritual growth to continue there must be a continual process of emptying, or cleansing, of our consciousness. Some people refer to this as entering the void. Emptiness typically occurs as a result of sustained centering, where the individual discovers and makes peace with the real self by an act similar to spring cleaning: getting rid of old ways of thinking, toxic thoughts, and perceptions and feelings that inhibit spiritual growth. Jung referred to this process as confronting the shadow of our unconscious mind. Peck's stage 3 is an emptying process, where one tosses out the old concept of an authoritarian

God, the "Irish cop in the sky," and questions any divine existence at all. The American Indian vision quest is a time of fasting and removing oneself from the community to find a deep sense of self-awareness and self-purpose. Via negativa, as Fox stated, is also a period of emptiness, when one edits out of one's life the thoughts, feelings, and even possessions that obstruct the path of spiritual growth. Darkness symbolizes this emptiness. The wisdom of the Tao also advises emptying oneself. To quote Lao Tzu, "Close your mouth, shut your doors and live close to the Tao. Open your mouth, be busy all day and live in confusion." Borysenko, as well as many others, cites the practice of meditation (clearing the mind of thoughts) as a vehicle for the emptying process. Journal writing also serves this purpose.

This emptying process can be painful. Peck compares it to a walk in the desert. Fasting will make one's stomach growl just as Jung's shadow and Fox's darkness will promote their respective growls. Chopra reminds us that detachment is the cornerstone of the emptying process. Regardless of how it is done, this emptying must be a conscious process. It is not a process you fall into by chance, but rather one that is intentionally created.

A Zen story illustrates the concept of emptiness. Years ago, an American professor toured Asia. One day he came upon a Buddhist monk and sat down to talk with him over a cup of tea. The professor graciously held out his cup while the Zen monk poured—and continued to pour, until the cup was overflowing. The professor, baffled, asked, "Why do you keep pouring?" The monk smiled kindly and replied, "Your mind is like this cup. It is so full of concepts that there is no room for new wisdom." The emptying process is a cleansing of the spirit (**FIG. 8.15**). Just as the body needs exercise to rid itself of chemical waste, and the mind exhibits laughter and tears as emotional catharsis, so too the soul needs to empty and cleanse itself.

Grounding Process (Spring)
The grounding process quickly follows the emptying process. In this stage, the soul or spirit is filled with new insight and knowledge made possible by the "space" made available during emptying. This insight may occur immediately, as an intuitive thought, or it may be synthesized over a short period of time and unfold right in front of you (**FIG. 8.16**). If the emptying process is like plowing a field, the grounding process is planting and harvesting. During grounding comes the vision of the vision quest, answers to life's most difficult questions, and light to replace the darkness of the emptiness stage.

FIGURE 8.15 The emptying process (winter) is a time of cleansing, releasing, and letting go to make room for new insights. Of all the four seasons, this can be the most painful. Like a cold waterfall, it feels refreshing once you are out.

FIGURE 8.16 The grounding process (spring) is the "eureka" moment. An epiphany, a streak of intuition, or some insight helps you get from where you are to where you need to go.

It is a time of revelation and resolution with regard to life purpose and value conflicts, respectively. In Eastern cultures (from India to Tibet), the grounding process is referred to as enlightenment. To be grounded also means to feel secure with the insight received during this process. In a literal sense, groundedness means being connected to the earth and feeling a part of nature. In a figurative sense, grounding is the ability to feel comfortable in your surroundings, in your own environment. Grounding also means establishing clear paths of communication between the conscious and unconscious mind, thereby giving focus to one's life. From a Taoist perspective, to be grounded

© Inspiration Unlimited. Used with permission.

FIGURE 8.17 The connecting process (summer) is a celebration with friends, family, and colleagues in the realization that we truly are all connected to something much bigger and more powerful than ourselves.

means to be in touch with the cycles of nature (the phases of the moon, the seasons of the earth) and to move in rhythm with these cycles. In the vision quest, a new name (e.g., Walking Rainbow) is chosen to symbolize the vision and is "worn" proudly upon return to the community.

Connecting Process (Summer)

In the Taoist philosophy, all things connect; nothing is separate. This is the premise of the principle of oneness. Quantum physics, likewise, has reached this conclusion. Jung proposed that we are all connected by a universal soul he called the collective unconscious. Peck cites connectedness as a crucial element in the development of both inner and world peace (**FIG. 8.17**). In a process described as community building, he explains that bonding with others in one's environment builds a community of oneness and is the manifestation of the spiritual nature of humankind. This connecting process is what some people refer to as social well-being, and it is best manifested by participation in formal or informal support-group activities. Originally, a vision quest was completed only when the individual returned to the community, reunited with friends and family, and shared insight gained from his or her unique vision. But American Indians believe in connecting not only with other people, but with all creations on Mother Earth, from trees and lakes to animals, birds, and fish. Chief Seattle wrote, "What is man without beasts? If all the beasts were gone, men would die from great loneliness of spirit, for whatever happens to beasts, soon happens to man. All things are connected." Thus, connecting

is based on respect for all creation. Borysenko also cites the importance of the connecting process as the foundation of support groups for individuals overcoming addictions. The strength of the connecting process is related to the power of centering, emptying, and grounding oneself. Finally, the work of Jesus of Nazareth was about building bonds of love between persons so that all may become one people.

Clearly, the order of the four steps is important to the effectiveness of the process as a whole. Each step alone confers strength, but the dynamics of the four steps in sequence is an unparalleled strategy to nurture inner strength and enhance spiritual well-being.

A Model of Spirituality for Stress Management

In my efforts to integrate spiritual well-being into the wellness paradigm of total well-being for corporate health promotion, I created an integrative theoretical model to emphasize the dynamic relationship between stress and human spirituality. I synthesized this spiritual well-being model from the psychological theories of Jung, Maslow, Frankl, Peck, Fox, Selye, Schaef, and Borysenko, as well as several other influences from American Indian and Asian cultures. In this model, human spirituality is defined as the maturation process of our higher consciousness as developed through the integration of three facets: an insightful, nurturing relationship with oneself and others; the development of a strong personal value system; and a meaningful purpose in one's life. These facets, each tightly integrated with the other two, constitute a dynamic configuration that, when attended to and nurtured, will advance human consciousness to a higher level of understanding—that is, seeing oneself as a part of a larger whole.

Let us take a closer look at the three facets.

Internal and External Relationships

Internal and external relationships involve a twofold process whereby one explores, confronts, and resolves one's inner thoughts, feelings, and perceptions, as well as strengthens ties or connectedness with others in one's environment. In some ways, human spirituality can be thought of as a form of self-government. It consists of both a domestic policy, or a personal philosophy and behavioral guidelines for the relationship with oneself, or the self, and a foreign policy concerning relationships with all other people in one's environment. A weak domestic policy will carry over into a weak foreign policy. Human spirituality works the same way: A poor internal relationship carries over into weak relationships with family, friends, co-workers, and other people with whom you come in contact. For optimal spiritual well-being, there must be a healthy balance between internal and external relationships. In other words, love your neighbor as yourself.

An Insightful Internal Relationship. The internal relationship begins with the practice of centering, or discovering and nurturing your real self. Some ancient mystics referred to the centering process as "entering the heart." According to Lao Tzu, "The way of inner peace begins with self-acceptance, to seek peace outside is to leave it behind." This process of centering involves dedicating quality alone-time to self-discovery, and separating who you are from what you do, as well as from your relationships with other people. Centering means coming to terms with the constituents of your identity and going beyond asking "What?" during the process of internal dialogue to ask "Why?" Similarly, in the process known as individuation, Jung emphasized the importance of self-reflection to bridge the gap between the conscious and the unconscious mind, thereby accessing the divine power within to help resolve spiritual crises. Jung was convinced that continual soul searching strengthened one's internal resources, including intuition, creativity, willpower, faith, patience, optimism, and humbleness. A strong internal relationship is characterized by improving and maintaining honesty in your inner thoughts, feelings, and even dreams, through introspection and exploration of your conscious and unconscious mind. The quest for self-knowledge is a soul-searching effort that leads to awareness of inner wisdom from the unconscious mind. It is this quest that develops the strength of your human spirit. In both accepting your fixed personal limitations and expanding your conscious barriers, you are led to new heights of spiritual development and consciousness, or what Jung referred to as spiritual evolution. The result of increased self-awareness, and ultimately the most powerful of inner resources, is the ability to accept and love yourself.

Divine Personification. Consensus among leaders in the emerging field of psychospirituality suggests that as you develop your own internal relationship, you also strengthen the bond to a higher power residing both within and beyond your physical domain. This, in fact, is a necessary part of the internal relationship: to see yourself as whole, yet a part of a bigger whole. In the words of Fox, this bond is "a personal cosmology—a relationship to the divine presence that dwells in us." Thus, a strong internal relationship also includes a comfortable and nurturing relationship with a higher power, however you might perceive that to be. Perceptions, however, need to be refocused, perhaps even changed, as this relationship matures. At a young age, our first introduction to a higher power is often through personification. A higher power of consciousness is given a name (e.g., God, Yahweh, Allah, Supreme Being) and described with human features, which are easy for children to identify, understand, and find comfort in. More often than not, however, this image does not develop or keep pace with a person's physical, emotional, and intellectual maturation into adulthood. In fact, Fox notes that many adults still envision God as a wise old man in a white robe resting on a cloud.

A comparable example is the American personification of the spirit of Christmas, in which the concept of loving kindness is symbolized by the human figure of Santa Claus. For those children who were introduced to the jolly fat man in a red suit, a new reality seeps in somewhere between the ages of 6 and 10 years. With the death of the personification, so wither away other elements of the essence of Christmas, and sometimes these elements are lost forever. Likewise, many adults experiencing a painful emptiness choose not to find their "God," but rather elect to leave this relationship underdeveloped. In theology circles, the phrase "killing off the old gods" is used to describe the depersonification process at this stage of maturation, as individuals are counseled to strengthen their internal relationship. Sometimes even the word *God* can be too limiting to conceptualize this mystical phenomenon. In fact, for many people, the word *God* carries with it a lot of baggage. Be that as it may, a strong and maturing relationship with a higher power is the anchor of the soul in the rough seas of crises. It provides a means of connectedness on a very personal and special level. Internal relationships are augmented by activities of solitude, meditation, reflection or prayer, and vision quests, where quality alone-time is allocated

> **An insightful internal relationship:** How well do you know and love yourself? What is your relationship with your higher self?
>
> **Divine personification:** A term signifying one's evolving perception or image of the divine, whatever this happens to be.

for the purpose of strengthening this relationship with the real self. Many relaxation techniques and coping skills are rooted in the premise of centering to nurture this relationship.

External Relationships. External relationships constitute a healthy bonding with anyone or anything outside the relationship with the inner self, including family, friends, acquaintances, and the creations of Mother Earth such as animals, trees, lakes, and the planet itself. External relationships are improved and maintained through your expression of acceptance, peace, compassion, communication, and respect for all individuals in your environment as well as your sense of connectedness with nature on the planet Earth. More specifically, strong external relationships include open tolerance, acceptance, and respect for other people's opinions, beliefs, and values, even when they don't agree with your own. This aspect of spirituality includes a forgiving (accepting) attitude toward others when their behavior is different from or inconsistent with your own ideals. Remember the saying espoused by all major religions: Do unto others as you would have them do unto you.

To Peck, this element of human spirituality also involves building community. Community is defined as the bonding and belongingness of supportive individuals in your collective environments. Building community means reaching out to other people to raise the level of human consciousness and human potential, for in the face of stress there is strength in numbers. Some scholars have designated social well-being as a fifth and separate component of well-being. However, a sound understanding of spirituality includes this social aspect in the framework of external relationships and community building. Finally, healthy external relationships necessitate the continual nurturing of the spiritual growth and love of other individuals in your environment through behaviors that will raise your human consciousness and human potential to new heights.

Both internal and external relationships require continuous work to further your spiritual evolution. Relationships are living organisms that, like plants and animals, need nutrients to survive. Neglect leads to starvation, atrophy,

root rot, and eventual death of the human spirit. A loss of connectedness is detrimental to the health of the human spirit. Peck once remarked that true evil is masked as laziness and apathy. With regard to human spirituality, there is a consensus among his colleagues that he is right.

Personal Value System

The identification, clarification, and implementation of a personal value system is tantamount to spiritual well-being. Values, as described by Lewis (1990), are constructs of importance: personal beliefs based on the concepts of goodness, justice, and beauty that give meaning and depth to our thoughts, attitudes, and behaviors. Values, including love, honesty, self-esteem, independence, leisure, education, privacy, forgiveness, and respect for Mother Earth, to name a few, typically dictate our attitudes and behaviors. As suggested by the research of Milton Rokeach (1972), values—both basic or core, such as love and honesty, and supporting, or those that support the core values, including trust and creativity—constitute a collection of ideals, or hierarchy of values, specific to each person. Individuals adopt many values unconsciously throughout their lives; however, most values are acquired in early childhood. Values such as acceptance, love, respect, and trust are learned from our parents, teachers, and respected individuals when there is strong interaction and the development of emotional bonds with them. These and other values are adopted as a means of acquiring approval from role models, or figures of importance, whom one chooses to emulate in the development of one's own identity.

Values that are adopted consciously or unconsciously lay the developmental groundwork for personality traits and behaviors. In addition, they construct a framework for self-validation and development of moral judgment of right and wrong, good and bad, and pain and pleasure. Values are abstract in nature, yet are often symbolized by material objects or possessions that represent a specific thing. For example, a diploma is a symbol of the value of education, and a television set is a symbol of leisure. As we mature, our value system also changes, but it continues to account for the way we think and behave. Like earthquakes caused by movements of the earth's tectonic plates, our values shift in importance as we mature, causing our own earth to quake. These shifts are called value conflicts, and they can result in a great deal of stress. Jung referred to this type of stress as a spiritual crisis, because these conflicts rock the foundations of the soul. Examples of value conflicts abound, ranging from those on the personal level all the way up to the governmental

---

External relationships: One's relationships with others (e.g., family, friends, and colleagues) as well as the earth, water, and air we breathe.

level. The abortion controversy is an example of a values conflict at the governmental level. Another example is the preservation of national wetlands versus the push for housing and industrial development. Both of these issues have caused much stress in the national consciousness. On a more personal level, leisure versus work, integrity versus wealth, and fame versus privacy are just a few examples of value conflicts causing stress at a spiritual level.

According to psychiatrist Viktor Frankl, "We are our values." Frankl observed that stress arises when values conflict with each other, leading to an arousal of inner tension, thus disturbing the homeostasis of the mind. But Frankl saw opportunity where others saw disaster, believing that resolution of value conflicts brings with it incredible strength of inner resources. The challenge is to assume responsibility for bringing these conflicts to resolution. Maslow (1976) considered the ultimate disease of our time to be "valuelessness," the condition wherein society's traditional value systems have proven ineffective and value conflicts at all levels go unresolved. He believed that a new valid, usable system of human values must be created, initially by the individual, and then adopted by society. This new value system, he argued, must be based on trust rather than on the false hopes and ignorance inspired by laziness, greed, and inability to know oneself.

Conflicts in values can be helpful in our own maturation process if we work through the conflict to a full resolution. But this takes work, which many people would rather avoid. However, a strong personal value system is one in which the hierarchy of basic and supporting values is regularly assessed and reorganized, allowing conflicts of values to be resolved so as to promote inner peace.

Meaningful Purpose in Life

A major facet of the spiritual well-being model is represented by one's meaningful purpose in life. According to Frankl (1984), a life mission can be accomplished through the design and achievement of a series of life goals, and through the experience of a value conflict or emotional suffering. Frankl asserted that the health of the human spirit rapidly declines with the loss of meaning in one's life, while a continual search for and fulfillment of one's aim in life are essential to spiritual development. He was convinced that the search for meaning was a primary force, instinctual in nature, and not merely a rationalization by humans, for humans (FIG. 8.18).

In my work with Olympic athletes, I was introduced to the concept of the "Olympic blues," a period of time directly after the Olympic Games when non–medal winners lost

FIGURE 8.18

all sense of meaning in their lives. The rebound time could be months or even years. Similarly, mothers suffer the empty-nest syndrome when their last child leaves home, creating a vacuum of life purpose. Men and women who retire after 30 to 40 years of employment may also suffer from feelings of lack of purpose. Frankl suggested that there is no ordained life purpose for each person; rather, a series of progressive life goals culminates in a life mission. He believed that emotional suffering at the completion of a goal is an essential part of the process of moving to the next ambition and continuing with one's purposeful meaning. The premise behind his logotherapy was to help people move beyond the suffering and thereby find a new meaning on which to focus. Finding a new life purpose in the ashes of suffering is not impossible, but this, too, takes work. One must create new goals and ambitions to aim for and accomplish.

Hans Selye, renowned for his work in stress physiology, later turned his attention to matters of the spirit as well. In his book *Stress Without Distress*, he stated that one's health status is dependent on the ability to maintain a purpose in life that commands self-respect and pride. As a result of his research on the effects of perceived stress and the physiological manifestations of the stress response, Selye theorized that the most significant strategy for conquering stress is to pursue what he called the aim of life. This aim, or meaningful purpose, of one's life is the foundation of health, and is built on both short-term and long-term attainable goals. The process of pursuing and completing the aim of life is initiated by self-reflection, giving strength to the individual's internal relationship.

In this model of spiritual well-being, all components are so tightly integrated they are difficult to separate. Each facet—nurturing, insightful, and bonding relationships; a strong personal value system; and an assessment of progress in one's meaningful purpose in life—is mutually inclusive of the other two. Moments of solitude and self-reflection lend themselves to the assessment of personal values and steps toward conflict resolution, as well as toward refinement of one's purpose in life. Values influence the direction of life's meaningful purpose. For example, the expression of love, perhaps the strongest spiritual value, not only nurtures self-growth, but also influences the strength of external relationships and inspires the direction of one's life mission. This integration of components is exemplified by the works of Nobel Peace Prize winners Martin Luther King, Jr., Mother Teresa, and the Dalai Lama, as well as thousands of lesser known but equally inspiring individuals (**FIG. 8.19**).

FIGURE 8.19 Dr. Martin Luther King, Jr., Mother Teresa, and the Dalai Lama are among the recipients of the Nobel Peace Prize, the highest possible honor for humanitarian achievement in the world.

The Divine Mystery

There is a fourth pillar of human spirituality that is often neglected in the discussion of psychology and theology—the mystical aspect. If for no other reason than looking foolish (another type of stress), many people rarely talk about the mystical side of spirituality. Yet this pillar is equally important to the full understanding and appreciation of the divine aspect in which we are all connected. Jung was so impressed by the mysteries of the divine that he spent many years devoted to their study, and for this reason was shunned and ridiculed by many of his colleagues. Under the cloud of Descartes's reductionistic paradigm, things that cannot be explained are often ignored. Yet the mystical side of life begs our attention, if only to better appreciate the complexity of life in the universe. Peck addressed the mystical side of the spiritual path as a yearning to understand the bigger picture of life, even though several pieces will be missing. The mystery begins where science fails to explain any or all dynamics of the unexplainable.

Spontaneous remissions are not merely miracles, but qualify as mystical experiences. Synchronistic moments, divine apparitions, premonitionistic dreams, and perhaps some crop-circle formations qualify as mystical moments. The popularity of this topic, as depicted by Oprah Winfrey on her TV specials, Coast to Coast AM radio show, and many national conferences, supports the concept that spiritual hunger is very real in terms of trying to understand the bigger picture of which each of us is a part. The lack of scientific evidence does not invalidate the divine mystery. Rather, it supports the idea that the human mind will never understand everything in the universe by using just the five senses. Furthermore, to be a good mystic doesn't mean to be able to rationally explain the supernatural; it merely means to appreciate the fact that we will never fully understand all aspects of the cosmos. In essence, to be a good mystic means to see the supernatural as natural and the ordinary as extraordinary.

Spiritual Potential and Spiritual Health

This spiritual well-being model suggests that the configuration of the four components to promote higher consciousness yields a host of personality traits specific to the integrity of the human spirit. I call these traits or inner resources **spiritual potential**, and they can be either dormant or active parts of one's personality. Creativity, will, intuition, faith, patience, courage, love, humility, and optimism are examples of these human spiritual traits. The manifestation of spiritual potential, which I label **spiritual health**, is expressed as specific emotional responses and behaviors that often expand the limits of human potential as a whole. Employing faith or an optimistic attitude in the face of diversity exemplifies spiritual health. In addition, Maslow might have considered creative acts or peak experiences to be examples of spiritual health; Peck cites community building, while Schaef would describe it as a "living process." Spiritual *potential* is like a group of instruments (e.g., violin, cello, and piano), and spiritual health is the music created by the individual with the instrument in hand. With practice, we are all capable of making beautiful music.

Roadblocks and Interventions

In Eastern philosophies, the division between the conscious and unconscious mind is considered the major obstacle to spiritual enlightenment. In Western philosophies, the walls of the ego, serving to protect one's thoughts, feelings, and identity, can hinder one's spiritual growth and human potential (**FIG. 8.20**). Although the ego wall is an abstract concept, elements that constitute its bricks and mortar are more easily recognized. These obstacles, some specific and concrete, others quite general and abstract, might include the following: laziness, greed, despair, anger, fear, low self-esteem, unresolved loss, substance addictions, and codependency. **Roadblocks**, both specific characteristics and/or related behaviors, undermine the maturation process of human spirituality to the detriment of spiritual health and total well-being. Roadblocks actually perpetuate the stress response rather than minimize it. Whereas roadblocks impede the progress

Spiritual potential: A term coined by the author to describe the potential we all have as humans to cope with stress through the use of our inner resources (e.g., humor, compassion, patience, tolerance, imagination, and creativity).

Spiritual health: A term to describe the use of our inner resources to help us cope with stress and dismantle the roadblocks on the path of life.

Roadblocks: A metaphor to explain how stressors act as obstructions on the human journey or spiritual path, yet these are not meant to be avoided—rather they are meant to be dismantled, circumnavigated, or transcended so that one can move on with one's life.

Photo courtesy of Mietek and Margaret Wirkus, www.mietekwirkus.com.

FIGURE 8.20   Divine mysteries are best defined as those unexplained happenings that often reveal a bigger picture of life than that observed through the five senses. This photograph of the Virgin Mary, taken in Medjugorje, Bosnia, emerged on a roll of film by a visitor to the shrine where her apparition appeared only to three teenagers.

of our spiritual journey, **distractions** actually pull you off the path, sometimes indefinitely. Distractions begin as attractions. A beer is an attraction; alcoholism is a distraction. Campbell indicates that each story depicting the hero's journey is loaded with distractions disguised as temptations that the hero must learn to overcome. Like the story of Rip Van Winkle, many people fall asleep on the spiritual path because of distractions. Like behavioral changes to influence physical well-being

Distractions: Material possessions (greed or wealth) and/or behaviors (addictions) that distract one from making progress on the spiritual path. Distractions begin as attractions, pulling one off the spiritual path indefinitely.

(e.g., aerobics, smoking cessation, balanced diet), intervention techniques can be utilized to enhance the development of inner resources and behaviors associated with spiritual health. The most common technique mentioned as an intervention is meditation. Meditation includes many styles of increasing self-awareness. In line with the idea that all things are connected, you will see that most, if not all, of the coping skills and relaxation techniques described in this book have some tie to the concepts discussed in this chapter. Art therapy, music therapy, humor therapy, communication skills, and several others include many aspects of spiritual well-being that integrate the concepts of centering, emptying, grounding, and connecting. They reinforce the importance of internal and external relationships, value systems, and the search for a meaningful purpose in life. In many Eastern cultures, relaxation techniques and coping skills were originally created as vehicles to enhance spiritual enlightenment and inner peace. Western cultures adopted several of these techniques and even created a few more, but lost in the translation were their true meaning and purpose. Slowly, this purpose is being rediscovered and recognized as an essential factor in these techniques, integrating the spiritual component with total well-being.

As we begin to understand the dynamics of human nature, it becomes increasingly obvious how important spiritual well-being is to total well-being. Spirituality involves many academic disciplines, including theology, psychology, and quantum physics. The theories presented here are only a handful of concepts describing personal insights into the elements associated with human spirituality and the soul. Because of the sensitive relationship between spirituality and religion, this area of health promotion, particularly as it applies to stress management, has often been neglected altogether, or not incorporated fully, as a significant aspect of the wellness paradigm. As researchers continue to explore and measure human consciousness, they may reveal that the mind and the soul play integral roles in both the understanding of human stress and the most effective ways to deal with it (**BOX 8.2**).

Current Research on Spirituality and Health

What was once a taboo subject in academia (**FIG. 8.21**) has now become a hot topic of study, particularly with regard to prayer, faith, and the outcomes for healing (Levin, 2001; Koenig and Cohen, 2002; Miller and Thoresen, 2003). In large part because of the synthesis of work presented by Dr. Larry Dossey, prayer has become a bona fide field of study in medicine. Moreover, several medical schools

---

BOX 8.2   Stress and Human Spirituality

Here is a series of questions based on the work of several luminaries in the field of human spirituality. Take a moment to proceed through each question as a means to help resolve one or more issues in your life.

Are you aware of coincidences that go beyond chance?
—Carl Jung

What stage of spiritual growth are you at now?
—M. S. Peck

Are you open to questions that have no earthly answers?
—Hildegard von Bingen

What is your relationship with Mother Earth?
—Black Elk

Are you stuck in the dark night of the soul?
—Matthew Fox

Do you employ the skills of spiritual optimism?
—Joan Borysenko

Do you live within the seven laws of spirituality?
—Deepak Chopra

Do you approach situations from a place of fear or love?
—Jesus of Nazareth

Where are you on your hero's journey?
—Joseph Campbell

What aspect of your life is out of balance?
—Lao Tzu

Do you see yourself as a single entity or connected to all of life?
—Albert Einstein

What "season of the soul" do you avoid?
—*Common Bonds of Human Spirituality*

What stressors in your life involve relationships, values (value conflicts), and a meaningful purpose in life?
—*Three Pillars of Human Spirituality*

© Ron Russell. Reprinted with permission.

FIGURE 8.21   To some, authentic crop circles suggest a divine mystery.

now offer lectures, seminars, and courses on the topic of spiritual health and healing. Unfortunately, because the concept of spirituality is difficult to define and perhaps impossible to measure, many researchers have opted instead to measure the relationship between religiosity (going to church) and several health parameters, adding to confusion about the distinction between the concepts of spirituality and religion. Nevertheless, spirituality and health continue to be a topic of academic inquiry (Vaillant

et al., 2008; Blumenthal et al., 2007). Although faith or church attendance may or may not be associated with health and healing, community support within church groups (connectedness) appears to be a significant factor in one's health status. What is interesting to note is that the abyss between science and spirituality, which formed during the Renaissance period, is narrowing, particularly as a greater appreciation of quantum physics unfolds to reveal aspects of ageless wisdom shared by spiritual luminaries over the past 2,000 years (McTaggart, 2008). So important is the spiritual aspect of health that the governing body that provides accreditation for hospitals across the country, the Joint Commission, has now mandated that each person who is admitted to any hospital be given a "spiritual assessment" as part of the admission process (Goliath, 2006).

The timeless insights of the perennial wisdom-keepers remind us that stress and human spirituality are partners in the dance of life. The following is a letter from one of my college students who asked me to share it with others:

Dear Professor Seaward,

Ahoy from the peaceful shores of Seattle! This is a long overdue letter from one of your American University students, class of '93, your last semester I believe. I should have written much sooner, there's been something I've been meaning to tell you.

Remember when you told us that the things you were teaching might take on greater significance as we aged and matured (or failed to mature)? That was a major understatement! In fact, you may have saved my life. This is my story:

I'm an alcoholic. I've been one since I was in my teens, and I was headed for more advanced stages when we crossed paths. I had a DWI and was charged with another misdemeanor before I reached twenty. And that's when they caught me. But my legal difficulties were the least of my problems. I was becoming a vicious, animalistic monster, the very antithesis of who I really was. I was alienating everyone I loved and lost all self-respect. But try to tell me that back then and you would've been treated to the work of a master manipulator with true genius toward rationalization and self-deceit.

And then, I had the beginnings of what I now see to be a spiritual awakening. It was suggested that I go to Alcoholics Anonymous. I went and my first instinct was to run out the door. They used words like God and spirituality. What the hell did God and spirituality have to do with my problems? I am sure you know the answer to this question better than I. But of course my ego told me that these people were freaks thinking that spirituality was the answer for them.

When was the last time I heard of talk like this? It was from you. And you certainly weren't a freak. You possessed a sincere inner calm. You helped people and I believed you were behind the concepts you taught. I remembered how impressive some of your presentations were. How you could get a group of students to open their minds and try meditation. I remember when you had a Native American shaman visit the class and how impressed I was with what he shared. I remembered when you told us that drugs and alcohol did not enhance spiritual development, they put up walls. I did feel a spiritual link back then for all my faults and I saw some of the things you covered in the Twelve Steps. So maybe there was something to this spiritual angle they talked about in AA, I thought. And I stayed.

I celebrated four years of sobriety on December 10th, 1999, and am still sober as I write this letter. I have gained a deep and very personal appreciation for the concepts you introduced me to and promised would become important further down the road. Thank you.

Sincerely,

Steven M.

SUMMARY

- The term *spirituality* is becoming a more comfortable one in the Western world. Although stress seems to be omnipresent in American lifestyles, there also appears to be a spiritual awakening taking place, from seeds planted by the human consciousness movements of the late 1960s. The World Health Organization cites spiritual well-being as critical to overall well-being.

- Spirituality has proved elusive to define because its essence seems to permeate everything. Harmony with self, others, earth, and a higher power is often considered a description of this concept. Spirituality and religion are related, but separate, concepts.

- Several viewpoints of human spirituality by intellectuals from Eastern and Western cultures representing several disciplines, including psychology, theology, philosophy, physics, and medicine, were described.

- Jung postulated that there is a profound, divine level of unconsciousness, the collective unconscious, which unites all people. Poor spiritual health results from the inability to access this source within us.

- Peck outlined the road to spiritual development, a systematic path consisting of four stages: chaotic antisocial, formal-institutional, skeptical, and mystic-communal.

- Hildegard von Bingen was a mystic who reminds us of the mystical side of human nature and highlights that every aspect of creation is spiritual and sacred in its own way.

- American Indian spirituality, called Mother Earth spirituality, was described to Anglo-Americans by Black Elk. It includes four cardinal principles: respect for the Great Spirit, respect for Mother Earth, respect for fellow men and women, and respect for individual freedoms. The vision quest, a soul-searching retreat, is one of the most profound experiences of Mother Earth spirituality.

- Fox synthesized several concepts of theology and physics into creation spirituality, which consists of four phases: via positiva, via negativa, via creativa, and via transformativa.

- Borysenko outlines a categorical difference between spiritual optimism and spiritual pessimism: the

former, an asset to total well-being; the latter, a significant contributing factor to the stress-and-disease relationship.

- Deepak Chopra reminds us to continually explore our consciousness and live in harmony with the spiritual laws of the universe. These include the laws of pure potentiality, giving and receiving, karma, least effort, intention and desire, detachment, and Dharma or life purpose.

- Jesus spoke of love as a divine source that resides in every one of us. It is this source that longs to bond with all others. His message was to love ourselves and then share this love with each member of humanity.

- Campbell stated that the hero's journey involves three distinct phases: (1) departure, (2) initiation, and (3) return.

- Lao Tzu described spirituality as the *Tao*. He outlined four principles of the *Tao* that help to clarify human interaction with the universe: oneness, dynamic balance, cyclical growth, and harmonious action. Many of the traits associated with these principles can be seen as parallels to Maslow's characteristics of self-actualization.

- Einstein's theory of relativity brought new light to the concept of energy and mass and properties of the nonlocal mind. His theory bears a remarkable resemblance to Jung's theory of the collective unconscious.

- Four common themes among theories of human spirituality constitute a systematic series of processes to strengthen the human spirit: centering, emptying, grounding, and connecting.

- Human spirituality can be defined operationally as the maturation process of higher consciousness as developed through the integration of three facets: an insightful, nurturing relationship with oneself and others; the development of a strong personal value system; and a meaningful purpose in life.

- A fourth but often unmentioned aspect of human spirituality is the mystical aspect of life—that which can be experienced but cannot be measured scientifically, and perhaps not completely understood in rational terms.

- The explosion in research regarding spirituality and health actually measures religious factors, not spirituality. Nevertheless, the connectedness of religiosity appears to be a major factor in optimal well-being.

- There are many roadblocks to spiritual evolution, perhaps the most significant being the stress emotion, fear.

- Many coping and relaxation techniques share characteristics that foster the spiritual process of centering, emptying, grounding, and connecting.

STUDY GUIDE QUESTIONS

1. Define human spirituality (as best you can).

2. Select four theories of human spirituality and explain each (e.g., the theory of Jung, Peck, Black Elk, Campbell, or Jesus of Nazareth).

3. Define and explain the common bonds (seasons) of human spirituality.

4. Explain how relationships, values, and a meaningful purpose in life are affected by stress.

5. Define spiritual potential and spiritual health.

6. Describe roadblocks and distractions in terms of stressors of spiritual health.

REFERENCES AND RESOURCES

Bellingham, R., et al. Connectedness: Some Skills for Spiritual Health, *American Journal of Health Promotion* 4:18–31, 1989.

Benedictine Monks. *Chant.* Angel Records, 1993.

Bentov, I. *Stalking the Wild Pendulum.* Destiny Books, Rochester, VT, 1988.

Blumenthal, J. A., et al. Spirituality, Religion, and Clinical Outcomes in Patients Recovering from an Acute Myocardial Infarction, *Psychosomatic Medicine* 69(6):501–508, 2007.

Bobko, J. *Vision: The Life and Music of Hildegard von Bingen.* Penguin Studio Books, New York, 1995.

Bohm, D. Toward a New Theory of the Relationship of Mind and Matter, *Frontier Perspectives* 1(9), 1990.

Bolen, J. S. *The Tao of Psychology.* Harper & Row, San Francisco, 25th Anniversary ed. 2005.

Bonham, T. *Humor: God's Gift.* Broadman Press, Nashville, TN, 1988.

Booth, L. *When God Becomes a Drug.* Tarcher Press, Los Angeles, 1991.

Bopp, I., et al. *The Sacred Tree: Reflections on Native American Spirituality.* Four Worlds Development Press, Wilmot, WI, 1985.

Borg, M. *Jesus: Uncovering the Life, Teachings, and Relevance of a Religious Revolutionary.* Harper One, New York, 2008.

Borysenko, J. *Fire in the Soul: A New Psychology of Spiritual Optimism.* Warner Books, New York, 1993.

Borysenko, J. *Guilt Is the Teacher, Love Is the Lesson.* Warner, New York, 1990.

Borysenko, J. *The Ways of the Mystic: Seven Paths to God.* HayHouse, Carlsbad, CA, 1997.

Borysenko, J. *A Woman's Journey to God.* Riverhead Books, New York, 1999.

Borysenko, J., and Dveirin, G. *Your Soul's Compass.* HayHouse, Carlsbad, CA, 2008.

Boyd, D. *Rolling Thunder.* Delta, New York, 1974.

Brody, H. *The Placebo Response.* Cliff Street Books, New York, 2000.

Byrd, R. C. Cardiologist Studies Effect of Prayer on Patients, *Brain/Mind Bulletin*, March 7, 1986.

Byrd, R. C. Positive Therapeutic Effects of Intercessory Prayer in a Coronary Care Unit Population, *Southern Medical Journal* 81(7):826–829, 1988.

Cousineau, P. *The Hero's Journey.* Element, Shaftsbury, UK, 1999.

Campbell, J. *The Hero with a Thousand Faces*, 3rd ed. Princeton Bollinger, Princeton, NJ, 2008.

Campbell, J. *The Power of Myth* (with Bill Moyers). Doubleday Books, New York, 1988.

Campbell, J. Radio interview on New Dimension Radio. San Francisco, CA, 1988.

Capra, F. *The Tao of Physics*, 4th ed. Shambhala Publications, Berkeley, CA, 2010.

Carey, K. *Starseed: The Third Millennium.* HarperCollins, San Francisco, 1991.

Carlson, R., and Shield, B. (eds.). *Handbook for the Soul.* Little, Brown, Boston, 1995.

Carlson, R., and Shield, B. *Healers on Healing*. Tarcher, Los Angeles, 1989.

Castaneda, C. *The Teachings of Don Juan: A Yaqui Way of Knowledge*. Pocket Books, New York, 1968.

Catford, L., and Ray, M. *The Path of the Everyday Hero: Strategies for Finding Your Creative Spirit*. Tarcher, Los Angeles, 1991.

Chapman, L. Developing a Useful Perspective on Spiritual Health: Wellbeing, Spiritual Potential, and the Search for Meaning, *American Journal of Health Promotion* 1: 31–39, 1987.

Chapman, L. Spiritual Health: A Component Missing from Health Promotion, *American Journal of Health Promotion* 1(1):38–41, 1986.

Chopra, D. *The Higher Self*. Nightengale-Conant, Chicago, 1996.

Chopra, D. *How to Know God: The Soul's Journey into the Mystery of Mysteries*. Harmony Books, New York, 2000.

Chopra, D. Personal communication, October 14 & 15, 1996.

Chopra, D. *The Seven Spiritual Laws of Success*. New World Library, San Rafael, CA, 1995.

Cimino, R., and Lattin, D. Choosing My Religion, *American Demographics,* April 1999: 60–65.

Clark, R. W. *Einstein: The Life and Times*. Avon Books, New York, 1971.

Cochran, T., and Zalenski, J. *Transformations: Awakening to the Sacred in Ourselves*. Bell Tower, New York, 1995.

Course in Miracles (3rd ed.). Foundation for Inner Peace, Farmingdale, NY, 2008.

Coutuier, L. Speaking in Silence, *New Women Magazine,* March 1992:58–61.

Crow-Dog, M., and Erdoes, R. *Lakota Woman*. Harper Perennial Books, New York, 1990.

Dossey, L. *Healing Words*. HarperCollins, San Francisco, 1993.

Dossey, L. *Recovering the Soul: A Scientific and Spiritual Search*. Bantam New Age Books, New York, 1989.

Dossey, L. *Reinventing Medicine*. HarperSanFrancisco, San Francisco, 1999.

Dossey, L. *Space, Time, and Medicine*. Bantam New Age Books, New York, 1982.

Dreher, D. *The Tao of Inner Peace*. (Revised ed.) Harper Perennial Books, New York, 2000.

Drummond, H. *Drummond's Address*. Henry Altemus Company, Philadelphia, 1891.

Einstein, A. *Ideas and Opinions*. Crown, New York, 1954.

Eley, G., and Seaward, B. L. *Health Enhancement of the Human Spirit*. National Center for Health and Fitness, Spiritual Well-Being Symposium, Washington, DC, April 16–17, 1989.

Elliot, W. *Tying Rocks to Clouds*. Image Books–Doubleday, New York, 1996.

Engel, M. It's Official, Global Warming Does Exist, Says Bush. *The Guardian*, June 4, 2002. www.guardian.co.uk /environment/2002/jun/04/usnews.globalwarming.

Fahlberg, L. L., and Fahlberg, L. A. Exploring Spirituality and Consciousness with an Expanded Science: Beyond the Ego with Empiricism, Phenomenology, and Contemplation, *American Journal of Health Promotion* 5:273–281, 1991.

Fields, R., et al. *Chop Wood, Carry Water: A Guide to Finding Spiritual Fulfillment in Everyday Life*. Tarcher Books, Los Angeles, 1984.

Foster, S., with Little, M. *Vision Quest: Personal Transformations in the Wilderness*. Prentice-Hall, New York, 1988.

Fowler, K. *Stages of Faith: The Psychology of Human Development and the Quest for Meaning*. Revised ed. HarperSanFrancisco, San Francisco, 1995.

Fox, M. *Creation Spirituality*. Harper, San Francisco, 1991.

Fox, M. *Illuminations of Hildegard von Bingen*. 2nd ed. Bear and Company, Santa Fe, NM, 2003.

Fox, M. *One River, Many Wells*. Tarcher Books, New York, 2000.

Fox, M. *A Spirituality Named Compassion*. Winston Press, Minneapolis, MN, 1999.

Frankl, V. *Man's Search for Meaning*. Pocket Books, New York, 1984.

Freeman, J. *Interview with Carl Jung*. British Broadcasting Corporation, 1959. Film.

Galanter, M. Healing Through Social and Spiritual Affiliation, *Psychiatric Services* 53(9):1072–1074, 2002.

Gerber, R. Personal communication, November 25, 1991.

Glenn, H. Losing Our Religion: The Growth of the "Nones." NPR, January 13, 2013. www.npr.org/blogs/thetwo-way /2013/01/14/169164840/losing-our-religion-the-growth-of -the-nones.

Gore, A. *An Inconvenient Truth*. Rodale Press, Emmaus, PA, 2006.

Gore, A. *Earth in the Balance: Forging A New Common Purpose* (Revised ed.). Plume Press, New York, 2007.

Grof, C. *The Thirst for Wholeness: Attachment, Addiction and the Spiritual Path*. HarperCollins, New York, 1993.

Hammerschlag, C. *The Theft of the Spirit: A Journey to Spiritual Healing*. Fireside Books, New York, 1994.

Hand, F. *Learning Journey in the Red Road*. Learning Journey Communications, Toronto, 1998.

Hodges, S., et al. Effect of Spirituality on Successful Recovery from Spinal Surgery, *Southern Medical Journal* 95(12):1381–1385, 2000.

Hoff, B. *The Tao of Pooh*. Penguin Books, New York, 1982.

Hoyman, H. The Spiritual Dimension of Man's Health in Today's World, *Journal of School Health,* February 1966.

Hunt, S. Spring Cleaning, Spiritual Healing, *Black Issues Book Review* 4(3):51–53, 2002.

Huxley, A. *The Perennial Philosophy.* Perennial Library, New York, 1945.

Jampolsky, G. *Teach Only Love.* (Expanded ed.) Bantam Books, New York, 2000.

Jung, C. G. *Man and His Symbols.* Anchor Books, New York, 1964.

Jung, C. G. *Memories, Dreams, Reflections.* Vantage Press, New York, 1964.

Jung, C. G. *Modern Man in Search of a Soul.* Harvest/HBJ Books, San Diego, CA, 1933.

Jung, C. G. *The Undiscovered Self.* Mentor Books, New York, 1958.

Kennedy, J. F. Inaugural Address, January 20, 1961, *Department of State Bulletin,* February 6, 1961.

Klivington, K., et al. Does Spirit Matter? Four Commentaries, *Advances* 8(1):31–48, 1992.

Koenig, H., and Cohen, H. (eds.). *The Link Between Religion and Health: Psychoneuroimmunology and the Faith Factor.* Oxford Press, New York, 2002.

Koerner, B., and Rich, J. Is There Life After Death? *U.S. News & World Report*, February 23, 1997.

Krebs, K. The Spiritual Aspect of Caring—An Integral Part of Health and Healing, *Nursing Administration Quarterly* 25(3):55, Spring 2001.

Krishnamurti, J. *On God.* HarperSanFrancisco, San Francisco, 1992.

Lao Tzu. *Tao Teh Ching,* trans. J. C. H. Wu. Shambhala, Boston, 1990.

Larson, D. B. *The Faith Factor.* National Institute for Healthcare Research, Bethesda, MD, December 1993.

Leichtman, R. *Einstein Returns.* Ariel Press, Columbus, OH, 1982.

Lerner, M. *Spirit Matters.* Walsh Books, Charlottesville, VA, 2000.

Leskowitz, E. The Relationship of Spirituality to Coronary Heart Disease, *Alternative Therapies* 7(5):96–98, 2001.

Lesser, L. *The New American Spirituality.* Random House, New York, 1999.

Levin, J. *God, Faith and Health: Exploring the Spirituality–Healing Connection.* John Wiley & Sons, New York, 2001.

Lewis, C. S. *Mere Christianity.* Collier Books, New York, Revised 2015.

Lewis, H. *A Question of Values.* Harper & Row, San Francisco, Revised 2007.

Maslow, A. H. *The Farther Reaches of Human Nature.* Penguin Books, New York, 1976.

Maslow, A. H. *Religion, Values, and Peak Experiences.* Penguin Books, New York, 1964.

McFadden, S. *Profiles in Wisdom: Native Elders Speak about the Earth.* Bear and Company, Santa Fe, NM, 1991.

McGaa, E. (Eagle Man). *Mother Earth Spirituality: Native American Paths to Healing Ourselves and the World.* HarperCollins, San Francisco, 1990.

McGaa, E. *Nature's Way: Native Wisdom for Living in Balance with the Earth.* Harper, San Francisco, 2004.

McTaggart, L. *The Field: The Quest for the Secret Force of the Universe,* 2nd ed. HarperCollins, New York, 2008.

Merton, T. *The Ascent to Truth.* Harcourt Brace Jovanovich, San Diego, CA, 1951.

Miller, W., and Thoresen, C. Spirituality, Religion, and Health: An Emerging Research Field, *American Psychologist* 58(1):24–36, 2003.

Millman, D. *The Laws of Spirit.* H. J. Kramer, Tiburon, CA, 1995.

Moore, T. *Care of the Soul.* HarperCollins, New York, 1992.

Muller, W. *Sabbath: Restoring the Sacred Rhythm of Rest.* Bantam Books, New York, 1999.

Naranjo, C., and Ornstein, R. *On the Psychology of Meditation.* Esalen Books, New York, 1971.

Neihardt, J. G. *Black Elk Speaks.* University of Nebraska Press, Lincoln, Complete ed. 2014.

O'Murchu, D. *Quantum Theology.* Crossroad, New York, Updated ed. 2004.

O'Murchu, D. *Reclaiming Spirituality.* Crossroad, New York, 1998.

Parnia, S. *Erasing Death.* Harper One, New York, 2013.

Peck, M. S. *The Different Drum: Community Making and Peace.* Simon & Schuster, New York, 2nd ed. 1998.

Peck, M. S. *The Road Less Traveled.* Simon & Schuster, New York, 1978.

The Pew Forum on Religion and Public Life. U.S. Religious Landscape Survey. http://religions.pewforum.org/reports.

Piedmont, R. Spiritual Transcendence and the Scientific Study of Spirituality, *Journal of Rehabilitation* 67(1):4–14, 2001.

Pilch, J. Wellness Spirituality, *Health Values* 12(3):28–31, 1988.

Powell, L., et al. Religion and Spirituality: Linkages to Physical Health, *American Psychologist* 58(1):36–53, 2003.

Radin, D. *Entangled Minds.* Paraview Pocket Books, New York, 2006.

Redwood, D. Rediscovering the Soul: A Scientific and Spiritual Search (interview with Larry Dossey), *Pathways,* Spring 1992:19–29.

Remen, R. N. On Defining Spirit, *Noetic Sciences Review* 8:7, 1988.

Remen, R. N. Spirit: Resource for Healing, *Noetic Sciences Review* 8: 4–9, 1988.

Rifkin, I., ed. *Spiritual Innovators.* Starlight Paths, Woodstock, VT, 2002.

Rokeach, M. *Beliefs, Attitudes, and Values.* Jossey-Bass, San Francisco, 1972.

Roman, S. *Spiritual Growth: Being Your Higher Self.* H. J. Kramer, Tiburon, CA, 1989.

Rosewall, A. Drawing Out the Spirit, *EAP Association Exchange* 31(3):14, 2001.

Schaef, A. W. *When Society Becomes an Addict.* Harper & Row, New York, 1987.

Seaward, B. L. From Corporate Fitness to Corporate Wellness, *Fitness in Business* 2:182–186, 1988.

Seaward, B. L. Giving Wellness a Spiritual Workout, *Health Progress* 70:50–52, 1989.

Seaward, B. L. *Health of the Human Spirit,* (2nd ed.) Jones & Barlett, Burlington, 2012.

Seaward, B. L. *Quiet Mind, Fearless Heart.* John Wiley & Sons, New York, 2005.

Seaward, B. L. Reflections on Human Spirituality at the Worksite, *American Journal of Health Promotion* 9(3):165–168, 1995.

Seaward, B. L. Spiritual Wellbeing, a Health Education Model, *Journal of Health Education* 22(3):166–169, 1991.

Seaward, B. L. *Stand like Mountain, Move like Water.* Health Communications, Deerfield Beach, FL, Revised ed., 2007.

Seaward, B. L., Meholick, B., and Campanelli, L. Introducing Spiritual Wellbeing in the Workplace: A Working Model for Corporations, Wellness in the Workplace National Conference, Baltimore, MD, March 21, 1990.

Seaward, B. L., Meholick, B., and Campanelli, L. A Program in Spiritual Wellbeing at the United States Postal Service, *Wellness Perspectives* 8(4):16–30, 1992.

Selye, H. *Stress without Distress.* Signet Books, New York, 1974.

Schmidt, L. E. *Restless Souls.* 2nd ed. Harper, San Francisco, 2012.

Shield, B., and Carlson, R., eds. *For the Love of God: New Writings by Spiritual and Psychological Leaders.* New World Library, San Rafael, CA, 1990.

Siegel, B. *Peace, Love, and Healing.* Walker, New York, 1990.

Spindrift Inc. Century Plaza Bldg., 100 W. Main St, Suite 408, Lansdale, PA 19446, (215) 361–8499.

Spirituality, Happiness, and Health. *Christian News Notes.* New York, 1991.

Storr, A. *Solitude: A Return to the Self.* Ballantine Books, New York, 1988.

Sweeting, R. *A Values Approach to Health Behavior.* Human Kinetics, Champaign, IL, 1990.

Tatsumura, Y., et al. Religious and Spiritual Resources, CAM and Conventional Treatment in the Lives of Cancer Patients, *Alternative Therapies* 9(3):64–71, 2003.

Taylor, E. Desperately Seeking Spirituality, *Psychology Today,* Nov/Dec 1994:54.

Taylor, K. *Living Bible.* Tyndale, Wheaton, IL, 1971.

Thompson, I. Mental Health and Spiritual Care, *Nursing Standard* 17(9):33–39, 2002.

Thorton, L., Gold, J., and Watkins, M. The Art and Science of Whole-Person Caring: An Interdisciplinary Model for Health Care Practice, *International Journal of Human Caring* 6(2):38–47, 2002.

Ulrich, R. L. View Through a Window May Influence Recovery from Surgery, *Science* 224:420–421, 1984.

Vaillant, G., Templeton, J., Ardelt, M., and Meyer, S. E. The Natural History of Male Mental Health: Health and Religious Involvement, *Social Science Medicine* 66(2):221–231, 2008.

von Bingen, H. *Scivias,* Bruce Hozeski, trans. Bean & Company, Santa Fe, NM, 1986.

von Bingen, H. *Vision. The Music of Hildegard von Bingen.* Angel Capitol Records, Los Angeles, CA, 1995.

Walsh, R. The Practice of Essential Spirituality, *Noetic Science Review* 58:8–15, 2002.

Williams, R. Social Ties and Health, *Harvard Mental Health Letter,* April 1999: 4–5.

World Health Organization, as quoted in "Spirituality, Happiness and Health." *Christian News Notes.* New York, 1991.

Young-Sowers, M. *Spiritual Crisis: What's Really Behind Loss, Disease, and Life's Major Hurts.* Stillpoint Publishing, Walpole, NH, 1993.

Zeckhausen, W. Spirituality and Your Practice, *Family Practice Management* 8(5):60, 2001.

PART THREE

Coping Strategies

There is no such thing as a problem without a gift for you in its hands. You seek problems because you need their gifts.

—Richard Bach

When we encounter a situation or event we perceive as a stressor, some part of us feels very vulnerable and threatened. To survive the threat, whether minimal or colossal, some type of coping strategy is created to deal with it. Each stressor necessitates its own coping strategy. Some coping strategies are second nature to most people when the stressor is minimal, and a course of action is taken with little or no conscious thought involved. But as the number and intensity of stressors increases and a critical mass of tension manifests, then routine coping strategies may fail to do an effective job. The result can be feelings of immobilization, mental paralysis, and emotional fatigue until a more effective coping technique, or combination of techniques, is employed. For the most part, the expression **coping responses**, unlike defense mechanisms, has a positive connotation, suggesting that a positive outcome is likely. However, this is not always the case, because some coping behaviors perpetuate stress rather than promote inner peace.

The word *coping*, as defined by stress scholar Richard Lazarus (1981), is "the process of managing demands that are appraised as taxing or exceeding the individual's resources." He went on to add that coping consists of both cognitive and action-oriented (behavioral) efforts. According to Lazarus, this managing process involves several important criteria, including some or all of the following: an increased awareness process of oneself, the situation, and the environment; an emotional regulation process he referred to as **palliative coping**; and quite often, a series of behavioral changes, referred to as **instrumental coping**, which accompany this awareness and cognitive process. Lazarus also believed that coping isn't the employment of several techniques so much as it is a specific frame of mind. Part of this mind frame is a personality trait, **self-efficacy**, a term coined by psychologist Albert Bandura to describe an inner sense of faith culminating in a "can-do" attitude. Self-efficacy describes access to several inner resources including self-confidence, faith, willpower, and self-reliance. The possession and implementation of this trait tend to divide those who choose effective coping strategies from those who elect noneffective ones. In other words, your dominant coping style may be a function of your personality.

To date, the best and most comprehensive conceptual model to understand the coping process is that created by Lazarus and colleagues. According to Lazarus, every stressor undergoes primary appraisal to determine the extent of damage. It is then reprocessed in a secondary appraisal.

At this point, a series of coping responses are lined up with the stressor to see which is the best course of action. These coping responses fall into one of two categories: action-oriented, such as time management or assertive behavior, or intrapsychic (acceptance). The responses used to cope with stress can be derived internally (from inner resources) and/or externally. Inner resources include, among other things, willpower, sense of humor, creativity, sense of reason, self-efficacy, faith, and optimism. External resources would include time, money, and social support from friends and family. Lazarus cites the purposes of coping skills as the following:

1. To reduce harmful environmental conditions
2. To tolerate or adjust to negative events or realities
3. To maintain a positive self-image
4. To maintain emotional equilibrium
5. To continue satisfying relationships with others

Coping responses can elicit three outcomes: (1) to regain the emotional status quo, (2) to resume normal activities interrupted by the stressor, or (3) to feel psychologically overwhelmed.

Other researchers have noted a dichotomy of coping styles: **avoidance versus confrontation** (Holahan and Moos, 1987) and **combative versus preventive** (Matheny et al., 1986). From the first perspective, both have positive and negative aspects. When avoidance is used to minimize exposure to a stressor (e.g., staying clear of a bee's nest), this is considered effective. When avoidance perpetuates the stressor (e.g., not talking to your boss about his sexual advances), then this is considered ineffective. Likewise, to confront a stressor takes courage, but there is a world

---

Coping responses: Positive skills to cope with stress.

Palliative coping: A positive emotional regulation process during a stressful encounter (e.g., responding, not reacting).

Instrumental coping: The implementation of a series of effective coping skills to alter one's behavior to stress.

Self-efficacy: A term coined by Albert Bandura to describe a sense of faith that produces a "can-do" attitude.

Avoidance versus confrontation: A dichotomy to describe how some people deal with stress.

Combative versus preventive: Another dichotomy to describe how some people deal with stress.

of difference between diplomacy and vigilantism. Again, coping styles seem to be closely tied to personality. Matheny's dichotomy highlights the positive aspects of each style. The combative style, like confrontation, is considered to be a physical reaction or response, whereas preventive coping, initially, is more cognitive in nature, with the intent to buffer oneself against the impending stress. Taylor (2011) notes that coping styles may be a direct result of the strength of available resources. For instance, a wealthy person with many social contacts may rely more on external resources, whereas a person without these is going to have to access inner resources to deal with his or problems, or suffer the consequences. As is typical with research, once a concept is well tested, studies then begin to investigate these models with specific populations of people, such as the elderly and coping (Krause, 2007), medical students and coping (Dunn et al., 2008), and fourth-graders' coping skills with anger (Rice et al., 2008).

Successful coping strategies to deal with the cause of perceived stressors involve four basic components. The first is an **increased awareness** of the problem: a clear focus and full perspective on the situation at hand. By their very nature, stressors tend to encourage a myopic view, distorting both focus and perspective. A good coping strategy will begin to remove the blinders to the true nature of the problem and open your view to a host of possibilities. Second, effective coping strategies involve some aspect of **information processing**. The dynamics of information processing include adding, subtracting, changing, and manipulating sensory input to deactivate the perception of the stressor before physical damage occurs. Lazarus referred to this as secondary appraisal. Information processing also includes assessing all available resources that could be used in *peaceful confrontation*. Third, the result of information processing will most likely include a new series of actions, or **modified behaviors**, which, combined with the new cognitive approach, ambush the stressor from all sides. The fourth and perhaps most important component is **peaceful resolution**. For a coping strategy to be effective, it must work toward a satisfactory resolution. If closure is not successfully brought to the stressor at hand, then the coping technique is less than effective. The following equation highlights the concepts of effective coping strategies:

Effective coping strategies = Increased awareness + Information processing + Modified behavior + Peaceful resolution

Although some coping strategies may seem appropriate for a particular situation, they might fail to achieve a peaceful resolution, in which case a new strategy should be chosen. Coping strategies can be either positive or negative. Positive coping techniques are those that prove effective in satisfactorily dealing with stress, based on the accomplishment of a peaceful resolution. This is the goal of all effective coping strategies: not merely to survive, but to thrive in the face of adversity. Negative coping strategies, on the other hand, provide no enlightened resolution. Instead, they perpetuate perceptions of stress and further ineffective responses in a vicious circle that may never be broken or intercepted. Some examples of negative coping strategies are avoidance of the problem or inhibition of action, victimization, emotional immobility (worrying), hostile aggression, and self-destructive addictive behaviors (e.g., drinking, drugs, food binging).

Is there a relationship between the use of effective coping strategies and personality? Some researchers think so. People who exhibit Type A behaviors, codependent behaviors, and helpless-hopeless behaviors are more likely to employ a negative coping style and claim victimization by their stressors. People who exhibit components of a hardy personality, self-actualization, or sensation seeking (Type R) are more likely to take calculated risks, confront rather than avoid problems, and see their stressors through to peaceful resolution. More recently, as the secrets of split-brain functions have been revealed, scholars and practitioners in the field of stress management and psychotherapy are recognizing the importance of unifying the efforts of the right and left brains to effectively deal with stress. This means that some coping techniques that access different cognitive functions are most effective when employed together, such as creative problem solving combined with communication skills.

Increased awareness: The first step of an effective coping technique when one becomes more aware of the situation.

Information processing: The second step of an effective coping technique when one works toward resolution of the problem.

Modified behaviors: The third step of an effective coping technique when one works toward a sense of resolution.

Peaceful resolution: The ultimate goal of any effective coping technique allowing one to move on with life.

Researchers agree there are literally hundreds of coping strategies. Each coping strategy can be used alone, but quite often several are used together for a stronger defense against the effects of perceived stress. And there is a host of positive coping techniques from which to choose. Those strategies that emphasize increased awareness and information processing include journal writing, art therapy, cognitive restructuring, humor therapy, dream therapy, and creative problem solving. Coping skills emphasizing a course of action or behavior change include time management, assertiveness training, social orchestration, and communication skills. Like learning to use a computer or improving your tennis game, coping techniques are skills, and their effectiveness increases with practice. It is important to remember that no coping technique will work as a defense against all perceived stress. This is why it is important to have as wide an assortment to choose from as possible; it will make the path of resolution easier to travel. You may notice that some coping techniques, as well as relaxation techniques, have the word *therapy* attached to them. This word may connote clinical treatment for a physical or emotional problem to you, but the term is used here as an encouragement, and a reminder that each person must take an active role in his or her own well-being.

Expecting the Unexpected

Amid the countless tragedies and deaths caused by the rash of tornadoes and floods in the Midwest (and other calamities equally intense), there have been remarkable, heroic survival stories and wonderful examples of calm bravery and clever ingenuity, all of which underscore the importance of putting effective coping strategies to work under the most horrific of conditions. In essence, these essential coping skills are nothing less than survival skills: ones we must learn to adopt and employ to deal with the mundane as well as the most inconceivable events that await us. Information seeking, assertiveness (in the form of leadership), creative problem solving, reframing, prayer, social orchestration, communication skills, acceptance, and, where appropriate, comic relief are used time and time again, proving themselves worthy of their merits. It behooves us to not only learn these coping skills, but also practice them so that we can rise to our highest human potential no matter the circumstances we encounter.

Lessons learned in the aftermath of recent natural disasters such as the devastation from Hurricane Sandy, the Sandy Hook Elementary School shootings, the Boston Marathon bombings, and the Class 5 tornados that ripped through Oklahoma reveal that change can happen to anyone—at any time. Recent catastrophic hurricanes, tornadoes, wildfires, earthquakes, and floods—all of biblical proportions—that resulted in the evacuation of millions of people have brought this message home repeatedly (**FIG. 1**). Whether it's a personal crisis or a global disaster of biblical proportions, there are two ways to deal with stress: The first is to see yourself as a victim. The second is to see yourself as the victor. Those who claim victimization tend to act out with a host of stress-prone personality traits to reinforce feelings and attitudes of victim consciousness. Conversely, those who take the high road with a conscious choice to rise above the problems they face tend to use effective coping techniques to become the victor over their stress rather than the victim of it. Homeowners interviewed after the devastating 2013 tornadoes often showed the epitome of hardiness by stating that they would return to the rubble and start rebuilding their lives and their homes.

If history is any indication of the future, this we surely know: There will be more floods, fires, hurricanes, droughts, earthquakes, and senseless acts of violence in the coming years. In each case there will be one of two ways to turn: victim or victor. We, too, can learn from the experience of those who weathered through the

FIGURE 1 The catastrophic floods that ripped through Boulder and many mountain communities of northern Colorado destroyed scores of houses, flooded thousands of basements, and washed out countless roads and bridges, making life difficult for residents of the region. Disasters like this require an array of essential coping skills to help deal successfully with these life-changing events.

turbulent times of scores of natural disasters and other equally devastating life transitions that happen nearly each and every day. The choice is ours.

Conclusion

It would be impossible to cover all of the positive coping techniques in this book. But the following chapters cover some of the more common and effective strategies offering assistance to the monumental stressors and daily hassles we encounter. The format of the chapters is the same throughout Part 3. First, the elements of the specific coping technique are introduced and defined, followed by a brief historical account where applicable. Then, a description of positive psychological (and physiological) effects are highlighted, and each chapter concludes with a list of steps on how to initiate the coping mechanism as a viable technique in your own strategy for stress reduction. (An exception is Chapter 14, "Creative Problem Solving," which deviates a bit from this format in a creative style all its own.)

You may notice a crossover effect with some coping strategies; that is, some designed specifically to deal with the causes of stress also seem to promote the relaxation response. Conversely, some relaxation techniques can augment or even become coping mechanisms in their own right. This is no coincidence because the mind and body can no longer be viewed as two separate entities. Humor therapy and laughter, once thought to be defense mechanisms, are now proven to produce a physiological homeostatic effect that strengthens the integrity of the immune system (as explained in Chapter 13). In some people, habitual practice of endurance exercise triggers a switch to include right-brain cognitive functions, thus augmenting awareness and information-processing abilities. In fact, there can be many crossover effects. In the organization of this book, however, I designated each technique as either primarily a coping skill or primarily a relaxation technique and placed it according to its greatest influence on either resolving the cause of stress or intercepting the stress response.

I recommend that you try all the following coping techniques when and where appropriate. Each technique has its particular strength. You may find many of these suitable to your own current management style. As time moves on and the effectiveness of some techniques diminishes, you may want to reread some of the chapters to reacquaint yourself with other coping techniques that may become more suitable later on in your journey through life.

REFERENCES AND RESOURCES

Bach, R. *Illusions: The Adventures of a Reluctant Messiah.* Dell, New York, 1981.

Dunn, L. B., Iglewicz, A., and Moutier, C. A Conceptual Model of Medical Student Well-Being: Promoting Resilience and Preventing Burnout, *Academy of Psychiatry* 32(1):44–53, 2008.

Holahan, C. J., and Moos, R. H. Personal and Contextual Determinants of Coping Strategies, *Journal of Personality and Social Psychology* 52:946–955, 1987.

Kaplan, A. (ed.). *Health Promotion and Chronic Illness.* World Health Organization, Geneva, 1992.

Krause, N. Evaluating the Stress-Buffering Function of Meaning in Life Among Older People, *Journal of Aging Health* 19(5):792–812, 2007.

Lazarus, R. *Stress and Emotions: A New Synthesis.* Springer, New York, 1999.

Lazarus, R. S. The Stress and Coping Paradigm. In C. Eisdorfer and A. Kleinman (eds.), *Conceptual Models for Psychopathology.* Spectrum, New York, 1981.

Lazarus, R. S., and Folkman, S. Coping and Adaptation. In W. D. Gentry (ed.), *Handbook of Behavioral Medicine.* Guilford Press, New York, 1984.

Lazarus, R. S., and Folkman, S. *Stress, Appraisal, and Coping.* Springer, New York, 1984.

Matheny, K., et al. Stress Coping: A Qualitative and Quantitative Synthesis with Implications for Treatment, *Counseling Psychologist* 14:499–549, 1986.

Rice, M., Kang, D. H., Weaver, M., and Howell, C. C. Relationship of Anger, Stress, and Coping with School Connectedness in Fourth-Grade Children, *Journal of School Health* 78(3):149–156, 2008.

Rice, P. R. *Stress and Health,* 2nd ed. Brooks/Cole, Pacific Grove, CA, 1992.

Taylor, S. *Health Psychology,* 8th ed. McGraw-Hill, New York, 2011.

CHAPTER 9

Cognitive Restructuring: Reframing

Everything can be taken away from man but one thing—the last human freedom, to choose one's attitude in any given set of circumstances.

—Viktor Frankl

A bounced check. The roommate from hell. A flat tire. Alcoholic parents. Stressors come in all shapes, sizes, and degrees of intensity. Scholars concur that it is not the circumstance that is stressful, but the *perception* or interpretation of the circumstance. We now know that if the perception is negative, it can become both a mental and physical liability. Whatever the event, perceptions can become distorted and magnified entirely out of proportion to their seriousness. This is referred to as **cognitive distortion** (mole hills into mountains), and it turns everyday problems into gigantic monsters. Attempts have been made to deal with the "stress monster" from all angles,

including decreasing or manipulating sensory information and teaching people to control the stress response by employing various relaxation techniques. Perhaps the coping skill most advocated—which goes right to the heart of the matter but is initially very difficult to employ—is favorably altering the stressful perception of the circumstance that has precipitated feelings of anger and/or fear. This alteration in perception is made through changes in cognition. Cognition is the mental process that includes an assortment of thinking and reasoning skills. Across the country, this coping technique goes by several names: cognitive restructuring, cognitive

> **Cognitive distortion:** Distorting a situation beyond how bad it actually is.

reappraisal, cognitive relabeling, cognitive reframing, cognitive therapy, and attitude adjustment. Despite the variations, they all suggest the same approach: to favorably alter the current mind frame to a less threatening perception, from a negative, self-defeating attitude to a positive one, which may then allow the initiation of the steps toward a peaceful resolution.

The seeds of cognitive therapy took root in 1962 with the work of Albert Ellis in what he referred to as **rational emotive behavior therapy (REBT)**. The premise of Ellis's work was that stress-related behaviors are initiated by perceptions and that these self-defeating *perceptions* can be changed. He explained that all stimuli sent to the brain go through a process of interpretation. When enough stimulation is interpreted as threatening, it becomes a critical mass of negative thought. Ellis was of the opinion that once a critical mass of perceived stress arises, it dims the ability to think rationally. As a result, a self-defeating attitude becomes reinforced day after day, year after year, through internal dialogue that is scripted by the tone of these irrational thought processes. Ellis became convinced that people could be educated and trained to favorably alter negative or stress-related perceptions (irrational thoughts) into positive attitudes, which in turn would decrease the intensity of perceived stress. In a 2008 news briefing, author J.K. Rowling of the *Harry Potter* series shared publicly her experience with depression and thoughts of suicide, and she credited the use of REBT as what pulled her though her darkest hour. The term **cognitive restructuring** was coined by Meichenbaum in 1975 to describe a coping technique for patients diagnosed with stress-related disorders. This coping style aimed to modify internal self-dialogue by tuning into the conversation within the mind. The practice of cognitive restructuring was an important step in what Meichenbaum referred to as stress inoculation, a process to build up positive thoughts when negatively perceived events are encountered. Work by Bandura in 1977 and Beck in 1976 also supported the concept of cognitive change of perceptions as a means to effectively deal with stress. To understand how stimuli are interpreted and how interpreted thoughts are structured from stimuli, let us take a closer look at how the human thought process works.

A Thinking-Process Model

The human mind is an extremely complex phenomenon, and one that we are just beginning to comprehend. Scholars in the discipline of cognitive science have created a theory, the **information-processing model**, to attempt

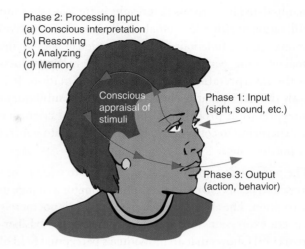

Phase 2: Processing Input
(a) Conscious interpretation
(b) Reasoning
(c) Analyzing
(d) Memory

Conscious appraisal of stimuli

Phase 1: Input (sight, sound, etc.)

Phase 3: Output (action, behavior)

FIGURE 9.1   The information-processing model of human thought.

to explain exactly how the mind processes information (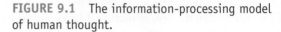 **FIG. 9.1**). This theory suggests that sensory input (e.g., a flashing blue light in your rearview mirror), sensory manipulation (e.g., danger, speeding violation, slow down, court hearing), and cognitive/behavioral output (e.g., foot on the brake, pull over to the side of the road, pray), as well as a feedback system to correct or refine this mechanism (e.g., several officers going to the scene of an accident, calm down), are synthesized to produce a linear progression of mental processes. Each cognitive deciphering process begins with an *interpretation* of the stimulus that comes into any of the five (possibly six) senses to determine its threat potential. In simple terms, stimuli can be interpreted as either threats or nonthreats. Resulting attitudes can be labeled in one of three ways: (1) defensive (negative), (2) neutral (innocuous), or (3) offensive (positive). Fragments of information, as well as memories of previous similar experiences, are then

---

Rational emotive behavior therapy (REBT): Developed by Albert Ellis as a means to help people cope with anxiety by changing the perceptions associated with the stressor.

Cognitive restructuring: A coping technique; substituting negative, self-defeating thoughts with positive, affirming thoughts that change perceptions of stressors from threatening to nonthreatening.

Information-processing model: A model that reveals how we potentially perceive sensory information, for better or worse.

manipulated in a process that results in the accessing and utilization of either left- (analytical) or right- (receptive) brain cognitive functions, or a combination of both. In the final outcome, perceptions and attitudes are by-products of the interpretation of all sensory information. It is both the manipulation of stimuli and the subsequent interpretation process that are targeted in cognitive restructuring to convert negative thoughts into neutral or positive ones.

The purpose of cognitive restructuring is to widen one's conscious perspective and thus allow room for a change in perception. The ability to expand perception is not merely a poetic expression. Research by optometrist Jacob Liberman (1991) shows that an individual's perceptual field of vision actually constricts (myopia) under stress. Thus, one literally sees less than the whole picture. Data analysis by Anderson and Williams (1989) corroborates this evidence, showing a causal relationship between perceived stress and loss of peripheral field of vision. As Liberman points out, stress forces one to see through a small hole rather than view the entire field of vision or whole picture.

Unconsciously, many people use a nonproductive coping technique called rationalization that they think is one and the same as cognitive restructuring. Cognitive restructuring should not be confused with this defense mechanism. Rationalization is making excuses, blaming, and shifting responsibility away from oneself toward someone or something else. Freud referred to this as denial of reality. Cognitive restructuring, on the other hand, involves assuming responsibility, facing the reality of a situation, and taking the offensive to resolve the issues causing stress. Creating and adopting a positive mind frame take some work. People often find it simpler to avoid this responsibility and be consumed by their own negative thinking styles, which produce a preponderance of toxic thoughts.

Two Minds Are Better Than One

A documentary video called *The Secret* made international headlines on the *Oprah* show and *Larry King Live*. Using the Power of Attraction as its premise, several popular self-help gurus spoke to the nature of achieving ultimate goals of wealth and relationships merely by thinking positive about these ideals. Countless examples were reenacted to illustrate the abundance of the universe and the power of intention. If they could do it, surely you could, too! The problem is . . . it's not this simple.

What the makers of the video failed to include (although this may be revealed in subsequent sequels) is the power

FIGURE 9.2 Silent film actor Buster Keaton was famous for his "kick the hat" routine, in which he would accidentally drop his hat and try to pick it up with his hand, only to repeatedly kick it out of reach before he could grab it. This routine is the perfect metaphor for how the conscious mind and one's subsequent behavior (the hand) are greatly influenced by the unconscious mind (the foot kicking the hat). To change behavior, one has to unite the powers of both the conscious and unconscious minds.

of ego-driven thoughts from the subconscious mind (a portion of the unconscious mind). So much of our behavior (some experts think all of it) is directed by our unconscious minds. Perhaps this concept is best illustrated by the famous actor Buster Keaton (and imitated by Johnny Depp in the movie *Benny and Joon*) who tries in vain to pick up his hat but repeatedly seems to kick it out of his reach before he can grab it (**FIG. 9.2**). If the conscious mind and the unconscious mind are not acting together, all the intentions and reframing in the world aren't going to help. In the field of psychology this is known as the "unconscious resistance," a self-sabotaging effect that undermines the conscious mind's best efforts to make (positive) things happen. It is the foundation of the negative self-fulfilling prophecy. Coaches see this all the time with promising athletes. Physicians see this in many of their patients too, specifically with patients who say they want to be healed, yet have too much of their identity wrapped up in the disease to leave it behind. Here is another common example: Consciously, you want to find that perfect person to go out with (or marry) and you set your intention. Consciously, you believe you are attracting your soul mate. But nothing happens. Perhaps the reason why is because unconsciously you like your carefree lifestyle and really don't want to change. Perhaps unconsciously, you still believe that you are not worthy of a quality relationship. Regardless of the reason, some belief system (usually an ego, fear-based one) hidden in the depths of the unconscious mind is holding on to old ways, thus negating the law of attraction to its highest potential. This is the real secret: The unconscious mind governs 80 to 90 percent of human behavior (Lipton, 2009; Mlodinow, 2012).

Experts suggest that these old beliefs and perceptions are learned and adopted early in life (ages 2–6) when the child's brain, like a sponge, soaks up sensory stimuli from the child's environment (e.g., parents, teachers, siblings). As the child matures into adulthood, behavior is directed by these ingrained, subconscious thought patterns and beliefs. Until they are erased and replaced with new beliefs and perceptions, not much will change.

To use an apt metaphor, the mind is like a radio playing music from two stations (the conscious and the unconscious), but the station you want to hear is being drowned out by the one you don't want to hear. In the case of the radio, fine-tuning is in order. In the case of the mind, it is coming to terms with old, fear-based thought patterns that tend to hold us back from reaching our highest potential. If you have doubts as to the power of the unconscious mind's influence, listen to the choice of your words spoken. More than just Freudian slips, our choice of words often reveals the ego's hidden agenda.

Experts in the field of psychology suggest that the secret to harnessing the strength of your thoughts is to combine the powers of the conscious and subconscious mind to achieve one's goals and aspirations (Taylor, 2013; Mlodinow, 2012; Murphy, 2008; Hari, 2005). Bruce Lipton speaks of this with regard to the health and healing process in which we need to erase the subconscious messages and rerecord new thoughts to help navigate the intended direction of our lives. Some people erase and rewrite these messages through hypnosis. Others do reprogram themselves by listening to subliminal CDs. Consciously, it can be done through neurolinguistic programming (NLP). Still others do it in a relaxed state through meditation and guided mental imagery or hypnotherapy. So, here is a question for you: What goals and aspirations do you have that are sabotaged by early childhood programming (e.g., trust issues, self-esteem issues, confidence, perceptions of leisure, money, or relationships)? How can you reprogram new (positive) thoughts, beliefs, and perceptions of yourself

that can steer you in the direction and to the destination you wish to go? When you can answer these questions you have really discovered "the secret."

Toxic Thoughts

Negative perceptions are often the result of low self-esteem. They also perpetuate it by suppressing or obliterating feelings of self-worth and self-acceptance. It has been suggested (Canfield, 1988; Ingerman, 2007) that toxic thoughts originate from repeated exposure to feelings of shame and guilt in early childhood. Canfield cites a study conducted at the University of Iowa where parent–child interactions were observed over a period of several days. Results revealed that, on average, there were 400 negative comments for every positive one spoken to the child. It was concluded that negative thoughts are actually a conditioned (learned) response that is then carried into adulthood. Catastrophic thoughts are also reinforced in the messages we receive from the headlines—rarely does a human interest story beat a cataclysmic event on the six o'clock news. Disasters, world problems, and crimes permeate the news, which tends to condition our thinking toward the negative side of things. Many counselors, therapists, and psychologists suggest that negative thinking has an addictive quality to it.

The term **toxic thoughts** was coined in the early 1980s by several psychologists to educate their clients about the dangers of negative thinking. Pessimism, a personality trait heavily grounded in negativism, promotes toxic thoughts. To demonstrate just how destructive they could be, Dr. Leslie Kaymen conducted a study at the University of Pennsylvania in 1989 to determine the physiological responses to stress between individuals who identified themselves (through a psychological survey) as either optimists or pessimists. All subjects were exposed to minute doses of pathogens (tetanus, mumps, and yeast), which, when placed on the skin, would indicate their stress-tolerance levels. Subjects were then divided by attitude into two groups, and both groups were given an impossible task to complete in a brief time period. While the pessimists quickly gave up, the optimists continued until the last possible moment. Days later, the PNI response (skin rashes) of the pessimists was significantly greater than that of the optimists. These results revealed

---

Toxic thoughts: Repeated negative thought processing that tends to pollute our view of our lives and ourselves.

Stress with a Human Face

Courtesy of Allison E. Fisher Memorial Fund, Inc./Pat and Ron Fisher.

A tribute to Allison Fisher: In the spring of 1991, I had a remarkable student named Allison Fisher. Allison was bright, energetic, and beaming with success. At the midpoint of each semester, I invite my students to do an exercise called "Confrontation of a Stressor." I believe that the concepts of stress management remain only concepts if they are not practiced outside the classroom. In other words, to know and not to do is not to know. In this exercise, students are asked to pick one of their top three stressors and are given two weeks to resolve it—with the condition that they must enter the classroom with no bruises or broken bones. Although students are asked to write up this assignment, on the day it's due we all sit in a circle with the lights down low and, one by one, under an agreement of confidentiality, we share our stories. This particular semester Allison went first.

"My stressor is breast cancer; it runs in the family," she explained. "My mother has had it—my aunt and my grandmother, too. For many years I have been scared of breast cancer, because I know I am at risk. Upon hearing this assignment, I decided it was time to go for a mammogram. I was extremely nervous, but last week I made an appointment with my physician."

The class was silent, all eyes fixed on Allison. With an air of confidence, she concluded her story with a smile: "I am happy to say that the test was negative!"

As a graduating senior with a major in broadcast journalism, Allison was looking forward to a promising broadcasting career. Less than a month after her graduation, she found herself working for a PBS affiliate. Within a year's time, she took a job with Voice of America and then moved to Los Angeles to start a highly coveted job as an anchor/reporter for *Channel One*, a cable program for high school youth. Several years later our paths would cross again, when I found myself in Los Angeles for a book signing. We agreed to meet for lunch the next day. At that time, Allison confided in me that she was a cancer survivor.

To be a cancer survivor means you confront death face to face. You challenge it with a mindset rather than run from it with a defeatist attitude. Being a survivor means you adopt an attitude of realistic optimism. You acknowledge the problems at hand, but you focus on the positive. You live life in the present moment rather than reliving the past or worrying about what the future may hold. You break through the fear of dying, the fear of the unknown, and the fear of isolation, and you come through on the other side as a victor, not a victim—what Joseph Campbell called the hero of the hero's journey.

"I had my first mastectomy over a year ago, my second one several months ago. The bad news is that the cancer is back and this time it has spread to my lungs. I'm okay, though," Allison said confidently. Then Allison shared with me theories and concepts that I had taught her as a student—but now she was teaching me insights and wisdom known only from the perspective of a survivor.

"It's all about attitude. I'm not sure how much time I have to live now, but I don't have time for toxic thoughts, or the fear of what might happen. I chose to look at the bright side of life, because I discovered long ago that that's all that really matters. I don't know if I will be cured of my cancer, but I can tell you right now, I am healed of my disease, because I am at peace, and there is no greater feeling than this."

Allison Fisher crossed the threshold of heaven on March 9, 1998 (www.allisonfisherfund.org).

that an optimistic attitude was associated with sound physical health, whereas a negative attitude perpetuated the mental and physical stress response. In short, negative thoughts can have a toxic effect on the body. Kaymen's data analysis confirms the hypothesis that negative thinking can suppress the immune system.

In an updated version of Kaymen's work, Andrew Steptoe and colleagues (2008) designed a study with nearly 3,000 subjects to examine the biological links of positive thoughts (mood). Results revealed that both men and women who reported experiencing a happy mood had lower cortisol levels, suggesting that happiness and optimism reduce biological vulnerability. Moreover, female subjects indicated significant decreased amounts of two proteins (C-reactive protein and interleukin 6) that are associated with inflammation, a factor linked with heart disease and cancer. Steptoe concluded that mood states are not merely hereditary, but depend on social relationships and life purpose.

Dr. Lissa Rankin is a physician who has studied the effect that positive and negative thoughts have on health. In her book, *Mind over Medicine*, she cites several studies including one that investigated the early deaths of Chinese

Americans who considered themselves ill-fated by being born under less than auspicious astrological signs. The results revealed that the more closely they believed in the power of astrology, the earlier they died—deaths that could not be explained by genetic factors, lifestyle choices, lifestyle behaviors, or any other variables. Stated simply, the negative thoughts they associated with their fate impacted their health. Rankin states that disease is not just a consequence of our genetic make-up, pathogens, or even bad luck. For better or worse, our health is greatly influenced by our mindset (attitude). Negative thoughts can compromise one's level of well-being. Barbara Frederickson agrees. As one of the leaders in the positive psychology movement, Frederickson coined the term "positivity" to express the power of optimism, as expressed through love. "The new science illuminates for the first time how love, and its absences, fundamentally alters the biochemicals in which your body is steeped" (Frederickson, 2013).

What is your PQ? PQ stands for Positive Intelligence, a term created by Stanford University lecturer, author, and CEO of one of the largest coach training programs in the world, Shirzad Chamine. The premise of Positive Intelligence is to reclaim the power of your mind by disarming the saboteur (the voice of the ego that offers a steady stream of negative thoughts). Chamine states that the reason why only 20 percent of people reach their true potential is because the mind is held hostage by negative thinking. Positive Intelligence is a program to learn to reframe one's thoughts and harness one's highest potential.

Is it really possible to change the programming in our minds to break the habit of negative thinking? According to Richard Bandler and John Grinder (Andreas and Faulkven, 1994), the answer is a definitive yes! Years ago, Bandler, a psychologist, and Grinder, a linguist, combined their efforts to create and teach the theory and application of changing our mental language. They called it **neurolinguistic programming (NLP)**. The premise of NLP is based on the concept of uncovering hidden grammar woven in the unconscious and conscious thoughts of our vernacular, systematically removing these expressions as we think or speak, and learning to develop a language of affirmative thoughts to positively change the direction of our lives. NLP is an empowering skill to reprogram the software of human linguistics so that our human energies can be focused in the direction of our highest human potential or human excellence. Part selective awareness, part self-hypnosis, the dynamics of NLP work to eliminate the self-defeating thoughts that inhibit our energies and

keep us from reaching our goals. Over the years, NLP has proven quite successful and is used by athletes, actors, executives, business associates, lawyers, and professionals from all walks of life. By encouraging reprogramming and eliminating from daily vernacular words, phrases, and thoughts that reinforce stress-prone behaviors, NLP helps one to unlearn old thoughts and learn a new approach toward optimal excellence. NLP Comprehensive, based in Boulder, Colorado, offers seminars and workshops in the dynamics of NLP. Understanding that one cannot change behaviors quickly as a result of a one- or two-day workshop, the NLP training coaches participants through a 21-day Achievement Program to help decondition and reprogram the human thought process.

Far more than lauding creative and optimistic thinking styles, Western culture rewards and praises critical thinking, the ability to judge and analyze situations, breaking them down into smaller, more manageable parts. In theory, when problems are dismantled into smaller pieces, they are easier to understand. Under stress, an emotional side effect of critical thinking is that smaller pieces of stressful stimuli may be considered less threatening to the ego and thus help to minimize emotional pain. In practice, though, when critical thought processes are directed toward the self, judgmental and analytical thoughts often nurture a negative perspective about yourself, making you more vulnerable to the perceptions of stress (**BOX 9.1**). When threatened, critical thought can become a defensive weapon to protect the components of your identity. In addition to critical thinking, a common mental attitude seen in American culture is **victimization**. Victimization is a perceptual attitude wherein one feels specifically targeted by events or circumstances and has no choice but to suffer the consequences. Individuals who see themselves as victims often seek pity and sympathy from their friends as a means of coping with the stressors at hand. Through the sympathy of others, they validate their own perceptions of personal violation. People who express feelings of victimization apply what psychologists refer to as attribution theory, blaming other people or factors for perceived injustices (Taylor, 2011).

The concept of victimization is closely associated with Rotter's concept of locus of control, where people who

---

Neurolinguistic programming (NLP): A program designed to look at how our thoughts control our language and how our language influences our behavior.

Victimization: A mindset of continually seeing yourself as a victim.

BOX 9.1 Cognitive Distortions: Stop the Insanity!

The human mind can be our greatest asset or our worst liability. Under the influence of the ego, the mind becomes misguided and heads down a path of self-sabotage. All of this is exacerbated in times of stress. This behavior in psychological circles is known as *cognitive distortion*. It can be said that cognitive distortions are spin-offs of Freud's defense mechanisms. More than the ego's intent to decrease pain or increase pleasure, over time these distortions become a habitual mindset that can sabotage our best efforts. David Burns writes in great detail about this phenomenon in *The Feeling Good Handbook* where he describes the ten distinct styles of cognitive distortion that perpetuate perceptions of stress. Mental thought processes and the behaviors they elicit cannot be changed until they can first be identified. (It should be noted that the benefit of meditation is to become the observer of your thoughts.) As you read through this list, ask yourself if one or more styles sound all too familiar to your way of stress-based thinking. If you don't see these in yourself, ask a trusted friend to give you feedback.

1. *All-or-none thinking:* There is only good or bad, black or white, no middle ground (e.g., there is only *one way* to solve this problem).

2. *Overgeneralization:* One single negative circumstance manifests into a life pattern (e.g., A flat tire elicits the comment, "This always happens to me!").

3. *Mental filter:* A solitary negative detail becomes the focus of your attention, obscuring the bigger picture (e.g., an hour drive is tainted by one driver early on who cut you off).

4. *Disqualifying the positive:* A negative belief pattern that eclipses positive circumstances, reducing any that surface as insignificant all the while focusing on the negative.

5. *Jumping to conclusions:* Affirming a negative interpretation without supporting facts often by insisting on a strong intuitive feel, which is little more than projection of one's own feelings.

6. *Magnification:* The classic story of making a mountain out of a mole hill, by exaggerating facts with the end result in a myopic vision of the situation and thus missing the big picture.

7. *Emotional reasoning:* Living the assumption that one's negative emotions are a true reflection of how things really are.

8. *Should statements:* A thought process influenced by a "rewards and punishment" mentality in which one motivates oneself with the words *should, must, ought*. This behavior often results in feelings of guilt or resentment toward others.

9. *Labeling and mislabeling:* Considered an extreme form of overgeneralization, statements such as "I'm a loser," or "He's always a jerk," are examples in which mislabeling involves words that are highly charged or emotionally loaded.

10. *Personalization:* Taking credit or blame for events that you had little or nothing to do with.

---

feel violated by stressors are more greatly influenced by external sources than by internal strength and inspiration. Here is a simple test to detect use of the victimization attitude: During the next casual conversation you encounter, listen objectively to what is said and notice how often people appear to fall victim to their bosses, spouses, roommates, kids, traffic, the weather, or any other circumstance in the vicinity. Next, listen objectively to how you present your perceptions to others when you describe your own levels of stress. Do you consciously or unconsciously label yourself as a victim? Many people take great comfort in being a victim because it fulfills an immediate need to feel needed, as well as the instant gratification of sympathy and pity. People who take on the role of one of

life's victims (a characteristic of codependency) often see themselves as martyrs. This is a socially rewarding role, so they find it difficult to change their perceptions.

Can optimism be learned? According to Martin Seligman the answer is yes! In his much-acclaimed book *Learned Optimism*, Seligman states that we are most likely to learn the traits of optimism or pessimism from our parents, but even if the environment in which we were raised was a negative one, we can cultivate the aspect of optimistic thinking and gravitate toward a positive approach to life. Seligman studied several nationally ranked swimmers prior to the 1988 Olympics and soon realized that optimism is not only an inherent trait, but one that can be augmented or learned. Using a term he coined,

Copyright 2001 by Randy Glasbergen.
www.glasbergen.com

"No, I don't think you're crazy. Like most of us,
you're just a victim of bad programming."

FIGURE 9.3

petals, some people sense the pain of the thorns. Cognitive restructuring is a way to focus on the rose petals. Here is the lesson: Every situation has a good side and a bad side. Each moment . . . you decide! During World War II, a song by Johnny Mercer and Harold Arlen hit the air waves and quickly became a national hit. It was called "Accentuate the Positive, Eliminate the Negative," and this song was one of many credited with helping the nation deal with the consequences of war (**FIG. 9.4**).

■ The Choice to Choose Our Thoughts

In his book *Man's Search for Meaning*, Frankl credited his survival in Auschwitz to his ability to find meaning in his suffering, a meaning that strengthened his willpower and choice of attitude. Frankl noted that despite the fact that prisoners were stripped of all their material possessions and many essential human rights, the one thing concentration camp officials could not take away was the ability of prisoners to choose their perceptions of their circumstances.

flexible optimism, Seligman states that although the trait of optimism is not a panacea for the bumps in the road of life, we can harness the power of positive thinking to help us achieve our goals and promote a greater state of health and well-being (**FIG. 9.3**).

The dialogue mentioned earlier that seems to run nonstop in our minds is referred to as **self-talk**, and it has been observed that the preponderance of this is negative self-thoughts. Schafer (1999) has identified several types of negative self-talk thinking patterns that produce and/or perpetuate the toxic-thought process. He lists them in the following categories: **pessimism**, or looking at the worst of almost every situation; **catastrophizing**, making the worst of a situation; **blaming**, shifting the responsibility for circumstances to someone other than yourself; **perfectionism**, imposing above-human standards on yourself; **polarized thinking**, where everything is seen as an extreme (good versus bad) and there is no middle ground; **should-ing**, reprimanding yourself for things you should have done; and **magnifying**, blowing problems out of proportion.

One technique to convert negative thoughts to neutral thoughts, similar to Ellis's REBT, is called **thought stopping**. When you catch yourself thinking negatively, you interrupt the flow of consciousness and say to yourself, "Stop this thought." With practice, thought stopping can help to disarm your negative critic and give balance to your emotional thoughts.

As you can see, toxic thoughts are very real. Over time, these can have consequential effects on the body as well. But stimulation received by the brain is open to reinterpretation, and perceptions can change. Metaphorically speaking, some people appreciate the beauty of the rose

---

Flexible optimism: A term coined by Seligman to convey that we can all harness the power of optimism into positive thinking.

Self-talk: The perpetual conversation heard in the mind, usually negative and coming from the critical (ego), which rarely has anything good to say.

Pessimism: Looking at the worst of every situation.

Catastrophizing: Making the worst out of every situation.

Blaming: Shifting the responsibility of a problem away from yourself.

Perfectionism: Perpetually imposing above-human standards on oneself.

Polarized thinking: A condition where things are always viewed in extremes, either extremely good or horribly bad.

Should-ing: Reprimanding yourself for things you "should" have done.

Magnifying: A term to describe blowing things out of proportion.

Thought stopping: A coping technique where one consciously stops the run of negative thoughts going through one's head.

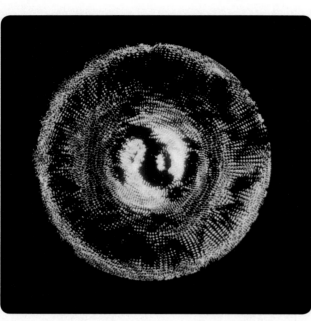

FIGURE 9.4 In this photo, a recording of opera singer Luciano Pavarotti is projected into a small sample of water. The wave trains in the water reveal the delicate harmonic pattern of the audio frequencies of his voice. From this, and many similar images, one can begin to appreciate the impact (either harmonious or discordant) that spoken words and even our thoughts—which are more subtle forms of vibration—can have on our bodies, which are composed mostly of water.

One concept that evolved from Frankl's theory of logotherapy is **brief grief**, which means acknowledging and mourning an unmet expectation but not prolonging the grieving process beyond a reasonable period of time. Death-education experts suggest there are three basic stages of grief: shock (denial), anger (depression), and understanding (acceptance). The time for each stage will vary depending on the person as well as the magnitude of loss. Feelings of loss, sadness, anger, pain, and fear are all natural, but not for prolonged periods of time. To deny these feelings is unhealthy, just as it is abnormal to prolong these feelings beyond their purpose. Brief grief is a strategy to allocate the correct amount of time to the grieving process (finding

Brief grief: A concept that suggests that some grieving is appropriate and healthy, versus unhealthy, prolonged grieving.

Awfulizing: A mindset where one tends to see (or hope for) the bad in every situation.

meaning in the suffering) and then move on to personal resolution and growth. When many people are introduced to the concept of cognitive restructuring, they incorrectly sense they must adopt a "Pollyanna" or cheerful attitude and that grief is not an appropriate sensation to acknowledge. As a result, they reject the entire idea of looking at the "brighter side" of a situation. Until feelings of suffering, no matter how big or small, are brought to awareness, it will be difficult to adopt a new frame of mind. Frankl wrote that even in suffering there can be tragic optimism; the discovery of light-hearted moments and personal meaning in the saddest of times. Even in the death-grip of the concentration camp, Frankl found it possible to laugh at many of life's absurdities. Moments like these helped him get through his ordeal.

Comparisons between war and sports are not uncommon. A winning attitude is everything. Tennis champion Andre Agassi explained his reframing style from an athlete's perspective in his best-selling book *Open:* "I've won 869 matches in my career, fifth on the all time list, and many were won during the afternoon shower."

In her classic book *Minding the Body, Mending the Mind,* Borysenko refers to the preponderance of negative thoughts as **awfulizing**. The process of awfulizing consists of judgmental and analytical thoughts that greatly narrow one's perspective and put our mental processes into a shallow, one-track mode. The result is what Borysenko calls regressive coping, a nonproductive coping skill. Awfulizing creates worst-case scenarios for every situation. Although it is good to prepare for all possibilities, a worst-case scenario is only one in a wide spectrum of possibilities.

Psychologists use the term *self-fulfilling prophecy* to describe the link between perceptions/beliefs and their related behaviors. The self-fulfilling prophecy can work to one's advantage as well as one's disadvantage. Sports events are filled with stories of athletes who believed they were winners and proved that indeed they were. In highly competitive events like the Olympics, the difference between a gold medal and a silver or bronze is not only a superlative athletic body, but an accompanying winning attitude. Many an athlete has lost an event, and thus failed to meet an expectation, because a seed of self-doubt took root somewhere between the starting block and the finish line. Individuals who harbor negative thoughts about themselves or the situations they encounter promote behaviors generated by these perceptions. The result can be a negative cycle that sets the stage for recurring stressful perceptions and what appears to be a stagnant black cloud over one's head; this is the fulfillment of the self-fulfilling prophecy.

An example of this concept occurred in the 1990 hit movie *Pretty Woman*, when actress Julia Roberts, in the role of a Hollywood hooker, described to actor Richard Gere how she fell into her "career rut." She stated that while growing up she received a lot of negative feedback from her parents and peers, and that these were so much easier to believe, eroding her self-esteem. Another example is John Travolta's character, Edna Turnblad, in the movie *Hairspray*; he plays an overweight woman who refuses to leave the house for many years because of her struggle with obesity. This "underdog" trait in both Roberts's and Travolta's characters was one many audience members could identify with and relate to, perhaps because this attitude is so prevalent in American society.

To break this self-defeating thought cycle, Borysenko suggests employing the concept of **reframing**. Reframing involves looking at the same situation from a new reference or vantage point and finding some good aspect in it. Quite often, stubbornness and the comfort of our own opinions become obstacles to the reframing process. Tools to initiate the process and dismantle the obstacles include the use of humor, positive affirmations, and creativity. Positive affirmations are designed to bolster self-esteem. Confidence building through self-praise in the form of positive feedback tends to counterbalance the voice of the inner critic constantly telling us we're not up to standards when we compare ourselves with others.

For example, as a health promotion and stress-management consultant, I meet many people from all parts of the country and all walks of life. During one workshop in 2007, I met a remarkable woman from New Orleans who shared her story of the terrible devastating experience she endured (and continues to endure). My interactions with her and others from New Orleans have allowed me to experience first-hand the expression of the hardy personality, which scholars Kobassa and Maddi describe as the stress-resistant personality. Here is Chris's story:

> Chris is a native New Orleanian. It is a city she loves with a passion. From the Dixieland jazz and Mardi Gras to Cajun cooking, New Orleans is loaded with a unique culture all its own. Living on the Gulf Coast, however, has its perils. Louisiana is no stranger to hurricanes. They are as much a given, Chris said, as snow storms are in New England. When Katrina was forming in the Gulf of Mexico, Chris and her husband boarded up the house, packed up the car, and headed north to Baton Rouge. With gale forces up to 150 miles per hour, they expected some wind damage to the house, but no one expected the levees to break

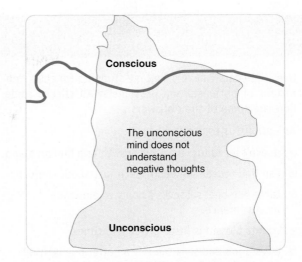

FIGURE 9.5 According to some experts, the unconscious mind does not acknowledge negative thoughts. Thoughts such as "I won't get nervous," are interpreted as "I will get nervous," which then often results in nervous behavior. Thinking positively allows the conscious and unconscious minds to work together.

and cause massive flooding. When they were allowed to go back to their home weeks later, they found water damage clear up to the second floor. Chris lost priceless heirlooms, family portraits, computers, and a manuscript of a book she had been working on for 5 years—practically everything she owned.

To lose everything in a flood can be devastating. How do you rebuild your life at the age 35? Chris said it would have been easy to play the role of victim, but what good would that serve? "You take stock of what you do have and build from there. I may have lost my house and my belongings, but I have my health and my wits. I am resilient. I will get through this, and I am determined not to give up, but to rise above the situation and move on." And that she has. Rebuilding her life and rebuilding her house move on parallel tracks, but within a year's time she regained her sense of balance. She says, "Losing everything is both devastating and liberating. I chose to focus on the positive and that is what has gotten me through the tough times."

One final thought about reframing (**FIG. 9.5**). Borysenko recounts the story of an Australian friend, Ian

Reframing: The name given to the thought process where a negative perception is substituted for a neutral or positive one, without denying the situation.

BOX 9.2   Optimism and Pessimism

Over the years I have asked my students for their definitions of optimists and pessimists. All clichés aside, here are some of their answers:

An optimist is someone who:

- doesn't let failure limit his growth as a human being.
- can find redeeming qualities in just about everyone.
- takes personal setbacks as only a temporary inconvenience.
- counts blessings instead of misfortunes.
- loses a job and says there is a better one waiting.
- has the ability to reevaluate her expectations so as not to become depressed when she falls short.
- describes a pessimist as a person with potential.
- continually explores new areas of life and can accept others who are different as unique.
- has enough faith in herself to see her through a crisis.
- on his deathbed, says, "I have no regrets."

A pessimist is someone who:

- cannot accept opposing viewpoints or thoughts as valid.
- enjoys nothing more than finding out that his negative view is right.
- typically prejudges and pigeonholes others before getting to know them.
- delights in Murphy's law that anything can and will go wrong, at the worst possible moment.
- constantly sees obstacles in her way, which are usually put there by herself.
- gains energy by drawing on a negative perspective.
- claims to be a realist, but he's not fooling anybody.
- describes an optimist as being out of touch with reality.
- not only has a black cloud of negativity over her head, but created the thunderhead as well.

Gawlen, who was diagnosed with bone cancer and given 2 weeks to live. This man adopted the attitude that if he had 2 weeks to live, he was going to make the best of it. So, he proposed to his girlfriend, got married, and went off on a honeymoon to the South Pacific. Twenty years later, telling of his experiences to Borysenko, he explained why he was still alive. He discovered for himself that the unconscious mind does not respond to negative thoughts such as "cannot," "won't," and "don't." Therefore, rather than telling himself, "I cannot die," which the unconscious mind would understand as "I can die," he fed himself a flood of positive thoughts, such as "I will live," and he has (BOX 9.2).

■ Acceptance: An Alternative Choice

Many times we encounter situations we have no ability to control: a manipulative boss, an obnoxious

Acceptance: Often the final outcome of reframing a situation: Accepting that which you cannot change and moving on with your life.

Serenity Prayer: A popular short prayer encouraging acceptance and wisdom, attributed to Reinhold Niebuhr.

roommate, or a significant personal loss. The reality of the situation is not pleasant in the best of moments. A common theme found among the theories of many psychologists in these cases is **acceptance**. The acceptance of situations we have no control over is thought to be paramount as a stress-management strategy, yet it is perhaps the hardest frame of mind to adopt. There is a fine line between control and acceptance. This is the essence of Reinhold Niebuhr's **Serenity Prayer** for Alcoholics Anonymous: "Lord, grant me the serenity to accept the things I cannot change, the courage to change the things I can, and the wisdom to know the difference." Acceptance is not an "overnight sensation," but rather an attitude that may take several days, weeks, or months to adopt and implement. Often, acceptance involves some aspect of forgiveness. The concept of acceptance is very similar to one described by Lao Tzu in the *Tao Teh Ching*. Lao suggested that we move in rhythm with the universal energy, not against it. Denial and manipulation, like spinning car wheels in the dirt, prove fruitless because they go against the rhythm of natural energy. Swimming against the tide can prove exhausting, and sometimes fatal. As the saying goes, sometimes it takes more strength to let go than to hang on. Finally, the use of acceptance or forgiveness appears to be a greater tool in the face of anger than of fear.

There have been thousands of empirical studies to determine the effectiveness of cognitive restructuring on health-related problems associated with stress. These studies have focused on both mismanaged anger (coping skills for men who battered their wives and children) and anxiety disturbances, most notably substance abuse and eating disorders. The results of these studies indicate that thought processes can be changed to produce a better state of health, although this is not effective in all cases.

Steps to Initiate Cognitive Restructuring

A simple, four-stage process introduced by the field of behavioral medicine is a model for implementing changes in lifestyle behaviors through cognition to promote health. The following model explains how cognitive restructuring can be implemented as a coping technique to reduce stress. Initially, this process does not appear to take a lot of time. Thoughts last less than seconds, yet they may resurface often in the course of a day. And the feelings these perceptions generate can last for days and weeks. A closer look suggests that cognitive restructuring is a refinement of the continuous dialogue of the mind, and as a result is, for the most part, an ongoing process. The stages are as follows:

1. *Awareness:* The awareness process has three steps. In the first, stressors are identified and acknowledged. This may include writing down what is on your mind, including all frustrations and worries. The second step of the awareness process is to identify why these situations and events are stressors and, more specifically, what emotional attitudes are associated with each. In the last step, a primary appraisal is given to the main stressor and acknowledgment of the feelings associated with it. If the original perception appears to be defensive or negative, and inhibits you from resolving this issue, then the next stage is reappraisal.

2. *Reappraisal of the situation:* A secondary appraisal, or reappraisal, is a "second opinion" you generate in your mind to offer a different (objective) viewpoint. A reappraisal is a new assembly or restructuring of the factors involved, and the openness to accept a new frame of mind (**FIG. 9.6**). At this stage, a second or third opinion involves choosing a neutral, or preferably positive, stance to favorably

"It's a special hearing aid. It filters out criticism and amplifies compliments."

FIGURE 9.6

deal with the issues at hand. Remember, a new appraisal isn't a rationalization process, nor is it a suppression of emotions. Also, remember exactly what factors you can control and what you must accept as out of your control.

3. *Adoption and substitution:* The most difficult part of any attitudinal change is its implementation. Once a new frame of mind is created, it must then be adopted and implemented. Humans tend to be creatures of habit, finding comfort in known entities even if the "known" is less than desirable. Pessimism is a defense mechanism, and although it is not seen as enhancing human potential, there is comfort in the familiarity of old ways, and change does not come easily. There are risks involved in change. Substituting a positive attitude for a negative perception may make you feel vulnerable at first, but like other skills that improve with practice, a new comfort will emerge. With cognitive restructuring, the new mind frame must often be substituted when the stress is encountered, and repeated again and again.

4. *Evaluation:* The test of any new venture is to measure its effectiveness. Did this new attitude work? Initially, it may not. The first attempt to shoot a basket through the hoop may result in an embarrassing miss. Evaluate the new attitude and decide how beneficial it was. If it turns out that the new mind frame was a complete failure, return to stage 2 and create a new reappraisal. If the new mind frame worked, repeat this process with stressors that demand a change in attitude to resolve and bring closure.

■ Some Additional Tips for Cognitive Restructuring

1. *Initiate a relaxation technique to calm your mind.* When a relaxation technique is employed, the mind begins to unwind and consciousness shifts from an analytical mode to one of receptivity. In this unwinding process, unimportant thoughts begging the conscious mind for attention are dismissed, allowing greater receptivity to a wider perspective on the issue at hand. A wider perspective in turn fosters personal enlightenment and opens up room for positive thoughts.

2. *Take responsibility for your own thoughts.* In times of stress we may feel victimized. We may also feel that things are out of our control. A way to gain temporary control is to blame others for the personal injustice of the perceived stressor. Blame is associated with guilt and guilt can be a toxic thought. If you find yourself blaming others for events that make you feel victimized, ask yourself how you can turn this blame into personal responsibility for your own thoughts and feelings *without* feeling guilty.

3. *Fine-tune expectations.* It is believed to be easier to refine expectations prior to meeting a stressor than to reframe an attitude after the fact. Many times we walk into situations with preconceived expectations. When these expectations are not met to our satisfaction, then negative feelings are generated. Fine-tuning expectations doesn't mean abandoning ideals or lowering self-esteem. Rather, it means running your perceptions through a reality check, questioning their validity, and allowing them to match the given situation.

4. *Give yourself positive affirmations.* The constant internal conversation going on within the conscious mind tends to be dominated by negative thoughts generated by the ego to defend itself. Although created with good intentions, a preponderance of negative self-feedback erodes self-esteem. Positive affirmations balance this internal conversation with good thoughts to enhance self-confidence and self-esteem. Repeat a phrase to yourself that boosts your self-esteem (e.g., "I am a lovable person" or "I am a winner").

5. *Accentuate the positive.* There is a difference between positive thinking and focusing on the positive. Positive thinking is an expression of hope concerning future events. It is often characterized by setting goals, wishful thinking, and dreaming. Although positive thinking can be healthy, done to excess it can be a form of denial. Focusing on the positive is reframing the current situation. It is an appreciation of the present moment. Acknowledge the negative. Learn from it, but don't dwell on it. Focus on the positive aspects and build on them.

Best Application of Reframing

When you find yourself stressed out and are perhaps entertaining toxic thoughts, first identify what makes you stressed, and then ask yourself why you feel this way. Get in the habit of then asking yourself, "What good can come from this situation?" In other words, what positive aspect can you learn from that which stresses you out? Recognize what feelings of anger and fear surface, and then shift your thinking to a proactive stance so you do not become the victim of your own thoughts and perceptions.

SUMMARY

- All stimuli received by the brain are processed through interpretation and classified as negative, neutral, or positive; this process is called perception.

- When the interpretation is exaggerated, it is referred to as cognitive distortion.

- Cognitive restructuring means changing a perception from a negative interpretation to a neutral or positive one, making it less stressful. This process is also called reappraisal, relabeling, reframing, and attitude adjustment.

- The seeds of this coping technique were planted by Ellis in rational emotive behavior therapy (REBT); the term cognitive restructuring was coined by Meichenbaum in 1975.

- The information-processing model describing how stimuli are interpreted consists of four components: sensory input, sensory manipulation, cognitive/behavioral output, and a feedback system.

- Negative thoughts are often called toxic thoughts. Research has now substantiated the hypothesis that negative thoughts can suppress the immune system.

- Negative thoughts are a conditioned response, starting as early as childhood, to negative feedback given by parents, which is transformed into guilt and shame.

- Toxic thoughts come in various styles, including pessimism, catastrophizing, blaming, perfectionism, polarized thinking, should-ing, magnifying, and self-victimizing.

- Frankl brought to light the fact that we have the ability to choose our own thoughts, to alter our thinking process and adopt new perspectives.

- Borysenko calls creating negative thoughts "awfulizing," and explains that the way to change these thoughts is through reframing, wherein the stressful event is reframed in a positive light.

- Positive psychology is an emerging field that focuses on using human attributes to cope with stress.

- When there seems to be no positive light available, acceptance of the situation (not to be confused with giving in) is suggested. Acceptance means to go with, rather than against, the flow that you cannot control.

- A four-point plan to reconstruct negative thoughts includes the following: (1) awareness, (2) reappraisal of the situation, (3) adoption of a new frame of mind, and (4) evaluation of the new mind frame.

- Additional hints for cognitive restructuring include meditation to clear your mind, taking responsibility for your own thoughts, fine-tuning expectations, giving yourself positive affirmations, and accentuating the positive aspects of any situation.

STUDY GUIDE QUESTIONS

1. What is the thinking process model?

2. What role does the unconscious mind play in changing behavior?

3. How can you best describe toxic thoughts?

4. List the steps to initiate cognitive restructuring.

5. What is cognitive restructuring?

6. What role does the unconscious mind play in the process of restructuring?

7. What effect does attitude have on human physiology?

REFERENCES AND RESOURCES

Agassi, A. *Open*. Vintage Books, New York, 2010.

Albom, M. *Tuesdays with Morrie*. Broadway Books, New York, 2002.

Allen, R. J. *Human Stress: Its Nature and Control*. Burgess Press, Minneapolis, MN, 1983.

Anderson, M. D., and Williams, J. M. Seeing Too Straight: Stress and Vision, *Longevity,* August 1989.

Andreas, C., with Andreas, T. *Core Transformation: Reaching the Wellspring Within*. Real People, Moab, UT, 1994.

Andreas, S., and Faulkven, C. (eds.). *NLP: The New Technology of Achievement*. Quill Books, New York, 1994.

Bandura, A. *Self-Efficacy: The Exercise of Control*. W. H. Freeman, New York, 1997.

Beck, A. T. *Cognitive Therapy and Emotional Disorders*. International Universities Press, Ann Arbor, MI, 1976.

Borysenko, J. *Minding the Body, Mending the Mind*. Bantam Books, New York, 2007.

Burns, D. *The Feeling Good Handbook*. William Morrow and Co., New York, 1989.

Canfield, J. *Self-Esteem and Peak Performance*. Vantage Communications, Nyack, NY, 1988.

Chamine, S. *Positive Intelligence*. Greenleaf Book Group Press. Austin, TX, 2012.

Danner, D., et al. Positive Emotions in Early Life and Longevity: Findings from the Nun Study, *Journal of Personality and Social Psychology* 80:804–813, 2001.

Ellis, A. *Reason and Emotion in Psychotherapy*. Carol Publishing, New York, 1996.

Frankl, V. *Man's Search for Meaning*. Pocket Books, New York, 1974.

Frederickson, B. *Love 2.0*. Penguin Books. New York. 2013.

Frederickson, B. The Science of Love. Aeon Magazine. March 15, 2013. http://www.aeonmagazine.com/oceanic-feeling/barbara-fredrickson-biology-of-love/.

Frederickson, B. The Science of Love. *Aeon*. March 15, 2013. https://aeon.co/essays/love-works-its-magic-in-mysterious-biochemical-ways.

Hari, G. *The Conscious, Unconscious and Super-Conscious Mind*. Jasmin Publishing House, Downy, CA, 2005.

Ingerman, S. *How to Heal Toxic Thoughts*. Sterling Books, New York, 2012.

Janis, I. L. *Stress, Attitudes, and Decisions*. Praeger, New York, 1982.

Katz, S., and Liu, A. *The Codependency Conspiracy*. Warner Books, New York, 1991.

Kaymen, L. P. Learned Helplessness, Cognitive Dissonance, and Cell-Mediated Immunity. Doctoral dissertation, University of Pennsylvania, 1989.

Kleinke, C. *Coping with Life Challenges*. Waveland Press, Prospect Heights, IL, 2003.

Kobasa, S., Maddi, S., and Kahn, S. Hardiness and Health: A Prospective Study, *Journal of Personality and Social Psychology* 42(1):168–177, 1982.

Lazarus, R. *Stress and Emotions*. Springer, New York, 1999.

Liberman, J. *Light: Medicine of the Future*. Bear & Company, Santa Fe, NM, 1991.

Lipton, B., and Bhaerman, S. *Spontaneous Evolution*. Hay House Books, Carlsbad, CA, 2009.

Meichenbaum, D. H. *Cognitive-Behavior Modification*. Plenum Press, New York, 1977.

Meichenbaum, D. H. A Self-Instructional Approach to Stress Management: A Proposal for Stress Inoculation. In C. D. Spielberger and I. Sarsason (eds.). *Stress and Anxiety,* vol. 2. Wiley, New York, 1975.

Mlodinow, L. *Subliminal: How Your Unconscious Mind Rules Your Behavior*. Pantheon Books, New York, 2012.

Murphy, J. *The Power of Your Subconscious Mind*. Wilder Publications, New York, 2008.

Neisser, U. *Cognition and Reality: Principles and Implications of Cognitive Psychology*. Freedom Press, New York, 1976.

Ornstein, R., and Sobel, D. *Healthy Pleasures*. Addison-Wesley, Reading, MA, 1989.

Peale, N. V. *The Power of Positive Thinking*. Prentice-Hall, New York, 1987.

Pettingale, K. W., et al. Mental Attitudes to Cancer: An Additional Prognostic Factor, *Lancet* March 30: 750, 1985.

Positive Psychology Center at the University of Pennsylvania. Homepage. www.ppc.sas.upenn.edu.

Pretty Woman. Orion Pictures, Los Angeles, CA, 1991. Film.

Rankin, L. *Mind Over Medicine: Scientific Proof That You Can Heal Yourself*. Hay House, Carlsbad, CA, 2013.

Rankin, L. Scientific Proof That Negative Beliefs Harm Your Health, 2013. www.mindbodygreen.com/0-9690/scientific-proof-that-negative-beliefs-harm-your-health.html.

Rasmussen, L. *Reinhold Niebuhr: Theologian of Public Life*. Augsberg Fortress Press, Minneapolis, MN, 1991.

Schafer, W. *Stress Management for Wellness,* 4th ed. Wadsworth, Belmont, CA, 1999.

Seligman, M. *Authentic Happiness*. Free Press, New York, 2002.

Seligman, M. *Learned Optimism*. Knopf, New York, 1991.

Siegel, B. *Love, Medicine, and Miracles*. Perennial Press, New York, 1987.

Steptoe, A., O'Donnell, K., Badrick, E., Kumari, M., and Marmot, M. Neuroendocrine and Inflammatory Factors Associated with Positive Affect in Healthy Men and Women, *American Journal of Epidemiology* 167(1):96–102, 2008.

Taylor, S. *Health Psychology,* 9th ed. McGraw-Hill, New York, 2014.

Taylor, E. *I Believe: When What You Believe Matters*. Hay House, Carlsbad, CA, 2013.

Whacker, W. *The Visionary's Handbook*. HarperBusiness, New York, 2001.

Wright, J. *There Must Be More Than This*. Broadway Books, New York, 2003.

CHAPTER 10

Healthy Boundaries: Behavior Modification

How many psychiatrists does it take to change a light bulb? One, but the light bulb has really got to want to change.

—Anonymous

Good parents give their children healthy boundaries, essential rules to live by, such as "Eat your vegetables," "No phone calls after 9:00 p.m.," "Dessert comes after dinner, not before," and so on. Simply stated, healthy boundaries are codes of appropriate and responsible behavior that one should follow to live a healthy and productive life. We learn these boundaries from our parents and/or loved ones as we grow up. But as we mature into adults we must create and maintain our own adult behaviors. Consider basic cell physiology as a metaphor for healthy boundaries: Each cell has a cell membrane, a gatekeeper to keep things in that must stay in (e.g., nucleus, DNA) and keep those things out that do not belong inside the cell, while regulating what comes in (oxygen) and what leaves (waste products). Healthy cells have great cell membranes. Cells with impaired cell membranes have all kinds of problems. Human beings are no different.

Healthy boundaries promote great health; a lack of such boundaries sets the stage for poor health and well-being.

Take a look around today and you will notice that there are flagrant violations of healthy boundaries everywhere: poor eating habits, rude technology habits, questionable drinking habits, abysmal financial habits, and dysfunctional relationships. The list goes on and on. Poor boundaries often lead to a sense of victimization. At some point everyone trips and falls. Some people stay face down and dig a hole, hit rock bottom, and keep on digging. Others hit rock bottom and decided to make a course correction, get out of the hole, stand up, and start walking again. Healthy boundaries are guidelines for healthy living, and behavior modification is the strategy to keep you on the road, rather than driving off a cliff. The key to life is structure and flexibility, that is, healthy boundaries and behavior modification.

■ Behavior as a Component of Personality

One school of thought in psychology states that personality is made up of three factors: values, abstract constructs of importance; attitudes, perceptions derived from values; and behaviors, conscious and unconscious actions based on attitudes and perceptions.

Values are those aspects that give meaning to our lives. Values are abstract constructs we adopt early in life by emulating figures of authority, including our parents, grandparents, and older brothers and sisters, as well as schoolteachers and other influential people from whom we seek love and acceptance. They are intangible concepts such as love, honesty, freedom, joy, wealth, pleasure, education, privacy, and creativity, to name a few. They are often made tangible through objects that symbolize their value. For example, education is a value, and it is symbolized by books and a diploma. Creativity may be symbolized by a musical instrument. Values may consist of morals and ethics, but they include more than these. Research by Milton Rokeach in 1972 suggests that each person has a hierarchy of approximately two dozen values. This hierarchy consists of two levels. The first tier Rokeach described as instrumental values, a handful of values that are "core" to the meaning of the individual. The second level he called terminal values, those important constructs that lend support to the core values. A personal value system is not static. Values can change in order of importance, moving up and down the continuum, to be replaced by or even exchanged for others. When values shift or are deleted, this may represent a conflict in values, and stress may ensue.

Attitudes are beliefs based on our values. Although the number of values in our personal value system is limited, Rokeach states that each value may carry with it hundreds of attitudes. Attitudes are beliefs, perceptions, and feelings based on a specific value. Attitudes can be positive or negative in nature. Negative attitudes are associated with perceived stress.

Behaviors are considered to be any action, direct or indirect, that is based on a conscious or unconscious thought. Behaviors are thought to be physical manifestations of an attitude based on a specific value. For example, clapping your hands at the end of a concert is a behavior influenced by your perception that the music you heard sounded pleasant. The music, in turn, can symbolize a value of freedom, or creativity. In terms of well-being, behaviors can be considered either health promoting or health impeding. The behaviors deleterious to one's health are often targeted for change.

Personalities are difficult, if not impossible, to change. Of the three components making up personality, psychologists suggest that values are the most difficult to influence. Attempts to change attitudes have met with some success (e.g., through cognitive restructuring); however, attitudinal changes may not last without significant attention being devoted to their associated responses. Behaviors, on the other hand, have been shown to be the most likely modified or favorably altered factor to improve health status. Millions of dollars and years of research have been spent to understand the concepts involved in behavior, particularly with respect to those lifestyle diseases resulting in astronomical healthcare costs. Results from these studies indicate that changes are possible when several factors (biological, psychological, and sociological) are collectively taken into consideration. For example, in the treatment of alcoholism, the factors taken into account include genetics, stress levels, and social contacts.

As complex as human behavior is, there is no shortage of theories as to why we behave the way we do. Whether our behaviors are learned or innate, we are creatures of habit. Here are some of the more well-recognized theories of human behavior as applied to the practice of behavior modification. Understanding the nature of these theories may help you to modify your behavior.

Classical Conditioning. The concept of **classical conditioning** was first described by Russian physiologist Ivan Pavlov in the late 1920s. Pavlov's theory, based on his research with dogs, suggests that animals become conditioned to specific stimuli to act in a specific way. What Pavlov observed was that his dogs began to salivate when they heard a bell that they associated with food. People, like dogs, can also become conditioned to behave in a

---

Values: Abstract, intangible concepts of importance or meaning, such as time, health, honesty, and creativity, that are symbolized by material possessions.

Attitudes: These are beliefs about our values, often expressed as opinions.

Behaviors: Actions (direct or indirect) that are based on conscious (sometimes unconscious) thoughts.

Classical conditioning: A learned behavior to a stimulus with regard to involuntary functions, such as becoming hungry when the clock strikes 12 noon.

certain way. In this regard, when a stimulus is coupled with a physiological reflex, the result can be a behavior with some pretty deep roots, one that can take years to unlearn. I am reminded of a student of mine who, upon listening to a relaxation CD with the natural sound of a brook, felt the undeniable urge to go to the bathroom. Slightly embarrassed, she approached me after class and told me that she felt very uncomfortable with the CD track. When she was a young child, she told me, her mother, who often was in a hurry to do shopping or errands, would run the water in the bathroom to get her to urinate quickly. Now whenever she hears running water, she gets the urge to go to the bathroom.

Operant Conditioning. Unlike classical conditioning, in which the behavior is specific to physiological autonomic functions, operant conditioning speaks to the nature of voluntary behaviors—those that we make a conscious decision about. Although the concept of **operant conditioning** dates back to the late eighteenth century, this approach to human behavior became the primary focus of psychologist B. F. Skinner, whose significant work spanned from 1930 to 1970. In simple terms, operant conditioning is based on the concepts of rewards and punishments, in which good behavior is reinforced and bad behavior is disciplined. The logic to operant conditioning is that when behavior is positively reinforced, the behavior is likely to be repeated, whereas punishment is used to deter unbecoming behavior. Most likely your parents raised you under the influence of operant conditioning, because child rearing typically uses this style of behavior modification. But it doesn't stop in childhood; motivational techniques such as incentives are used with great frequency in the business world to boost profit margins and work productivity. Variations of operant conditioning are used in a host of recovery programs as well.

Modeling. Little children aren't parrots, but if you were to listen to how closely a child imitates his or her mom or dad, you would be amazed at the degree of accuracy in both language and body postures. **Modeling** is a name given to the concept of imitation—that is, a behavior learned through imitation. Modeling differs from operant conditioning in that usually no direct reinforcement is involved. Out of sheer will, a person is motivated to copy one or several aspects of someone with whom they are closely bonded or to whom they find some degree of attraction (Pescuric and Byham, 1996). It may be parents, but in the age of multimedia exposure, it could be any public figure with whom the individual wishes to identify.

As might be expected, negative as well as positive behavior can be imitated, and often is. More often than not, the expression "Life imitates art" comes to mind when individuals are seen to model negative behavior viewed on television or in the movies. Although children often model themselves after those people they see as heroes, we never outgrow the capacity to model our behavior after someone we admire. During the aging process, the word *hero* changes to *role model*, or *mentor*. Modeling is typically used as a crucial component in the practice of building self-esteem.

There are several types of *behavior modification* programs currently conducted in the United States that focus on negative health habits. Most of these programs center on substance addictions (alcoholism, eating disorders, smoking cessation, and drug addictions) and behavioral addictions (workaholism, shopping, sexual habits). Additional programs target lifestyle improvement changes, including time management and assertiveness. Regardless of focus, the bottom line in all positive behavioral-change programs is building and maintaining self-esteem. The focus of this chapter will be assertiveness skills, which are considered paramount in the development and maintenance of self-esteem. But before we look at the skills highlighted in assertiveness training workshops, let's examine the dynamics involved in behavioral change.

The Behavior Modification Model

In learning about their stress-prone personality traits, individuals often see themselves, or parts of themselves, as less than flattering. Acknowledgment of these traits may in fact contribute to their stress. Whereas some individuals recognize these traits and behaviors and make corresponding changes to fine-tune their personalities, others have difficulty overcoming the obstacles to change. Thousands of investigations have been conducted to determine the effectiveness of changes in behaviors to promote health. The topics of these studies include everything from substance abuse and wife beating to eating disorders and insomnia. The majority show that it is far

> **Operant conditioning:** A learned behavior that stems from a voluntary function or something we make a conscious decision about.
>
> **Modeling:** The ability to emulate or imitate our behaviors from the observation of others we respect (e.g., parents, schoolteachers, and peers).

easier to *initiate* a new behavior than it is to *maintain* it over a prolonged period of time. Motivation, it appears, is strong at the start of any desired behavior change but fades fast (in about 1 to 2 weeks) when immediate effects are not observed. Recent studies reveal that before and after functional magnetic resonance imaging (fMRI) brain images of people who have undergone a behavior change (e.g., quitting smoking) reveal that neural activity can be detected in the frontal cortex, which is associated with behavior inhibition and self-discipline. Like a dirt road that becomes a paved highway, the neural activity becomes more pronounced each time the new behavior is acted upon (Duhigg, 2012). Perhaps no one is better suited to know behavior and subsequent behavior changes than scores of marketing executives whose sole purpose in life is to get you to buy their products. In his book, *The Power of Habit*, author and New York Times investigative reporter Charles Duhigg examines many case studies in which advertising executives try to convince consumers to make specific purchases, from Pepsodent toothpaste to Febreeze deodorizer. Reducing behavior to its simplest terms, Duhigg first reviews the basics of behavioral habit, all of which occur in three simple steps: (1) cue (something that triggers an action), (2) routine (the action), and (3) reward (gratification). Behavior modification, he states, comes down to changing one or more of these aspects. And this is what advertisers do, quite successfully, to get customers to try or even switch to a new product. The same can be done to shift from a stress-prone behavior to a stress-resistant behavior. Buying a product is one thing. Moving from a fear- or anger-based behavior takes a little more effort. To first understand and then favorably alter factors associated with unhealthy behaviors, psychologists in the field of behavioral medicine have devised a model based on observational research. All successful programs contain this progression of steps to change behavior. When applied to lifestyle and behavior changes, these steps may lead toward improved health status and quality of life. This **behavior modification model** has one precursory phase (denial) and five distinct systematic stages.

Behavior modification model: A model that illustrates the steps taken to change a negative behavior into a positive one.

Denial: In some cases, this is the first step of changing a negative behavior.

Awareness: Learning to become aware of a specific behavior in the effort to change it.

Several behavioral psychologists and therapists agree that **denial** is actually the initial stage of or a precursor to a behavioral change. For example, Freud described denial as a defense mechanism employed to soften the blow of perceived threats to the ego. In the denial stage, people refuse to admit either that they practice an unhealthy behavior or that a specific behavioral practice they engage in is unhealthy. A prime example is someone with a chronic drinking problem who refuses to admit he or she is unable to control his or her drinking. Although not everyone starts with this stage, many people do. It is often this difficult stage therapists and counselors help their clients to work beyond, to get to what many people agree is the primary stage of behavior modification: **awareness**.

1. *Awareness:* In the awareness stage, you realize that you actually think or behave in a certain way that is unhealthy or less than ideal. In the context of this text, these behaviors are stress-producing habits. Awareness may come about as a result of some educational experience (e.g., a class, public service advertising, a newspaper article, journal writing, or the advice of a close friend) wherein your consciousness is raised about a certain behavior. Awareness can also occur when you simply admit that one (or more) of your current behaviors is no longer desirable. Once you see this undesirable behavior in yourself (e.g., codependent tendencies such as ardent approval seeking and victimization, or Type A behaviors including hostile aggression), the process of change can begin.

2. *Desire to change:* Many people recognize they practice a negative health behavior, yet they are not inspired to change it. Without the desire to alter behavior, even when it becomes obvious how damaging it might be, no change will occur. Many people are aware that consuming foods with cholesterol is related to heart disease and that cigarette smoking causes cancer, yet these behaviors remain intact because the will to change is less than the immediate desire to hang on to whatever benefits the behaviors provide. Desire to change usually comes about when the behavior no longer provides the ability to cope, and in fact places one square on the path to either disaster or death. The expression "hit bottom" is often used to describe the ultimate low point experienced by people, who then generate a desire and become quite motivated to make a behavioral change.

3. *Cognitive restructuring:* In this stage, you actually catch yourself in the act of the undesirable behavior and think of a new and suitable alternative.

For example, rather than ask someone a closed-ended, approval-seeking question such as, "Did you like my performance last night?" you ask an open-ended question like, "What did you think of the performance last night?" This gives the responder a chance to answer freely and takes the focus off you. Cognitive restructuring is really self-dialogue recognizing both current and pending behavior, as well as the option to favorably change it.

4. *Behavioral substitution:* In the substitution stage, an undesirable behavior is consciously replaced with a healthy or stress-reducing behavior. Sometimes this **behavioral substitution** process is thought out or rehearsed in the form of mental imagery before it is acted out. In a case where you have become aware of the habit of self-victimization (in the way that stressors are described to others), you change the description of this circumstance to friends or relatives, thus shifting the emphasis off yourself and onto the real problem. Not all changes are substitutions. Some modifications may be additions to the repertoire of your behaviors. For example, the initiation of one or more coping skills and relaxation techniques may be an example of additions to your behavior. Usually, however, when a new behavior is adopted, because of time limitations, something else in one's daily schedule gets pushed out of the way. This is a reflection of one's priorities and values.

5. *Evaluation:* After a substitution has been made, during **evaluation** you should figuratively "step back" to analyze whether the new behavior worked, ask yourself why or why not, and decide what can be done to fine-tune this process when the occasion arises again.

A Second Behavior Modification Model: Stages of Change

By some estimates, there are more than 300 strategies to changing one's behavior from less desirable actions to more desirable ones, from going "cold turkey" and hypnosis to 30-day recovery programs and much in between. As a child of alcoholic parents, James Prochaska became fascinated with behavior change and studied the topic extensively. In 1982, his efforts resulted in what has become regarded as one of the premier models of behavior modification, called the "Stages of Change." Prochaska and his colleague, Carlo DiClemente, observed that by and large behavior change (particularly for behavior of an addictive nature) is not a singular event but a process, if not a skill (much like an athletic skill), that may take months or longer to master. What makes his approach unique is that he acknowledges the aspect of relapse as a common part of the process and not failure unto itself.

This model contains six steps and includes the following:

1. *Precontemplation stage:* A stage that might also be called denial of the problem or unconvinced that a behavior problem exists (**FIG. 10.1**).

2. *Contemplative stage:* A point at which a crucial mass of information is acknowledged to consider that change might be a worthy choice to make.

3. *Determination stage:* A period where willpower is called into play to put the thought process of behavior change into action.

> **Behavioral substitution:** Substituting a new (positive) behavior for a less desirable one.
>
> **Evaluation:** The process of observing and analyzing a newly adopted behavior, to see if the new behavior works.

Cornered by Mike Baldwin

7-26 © 2003 Mike Baldwin / Dist. by Universal Press Syndicate www.cornered.com

"But I do exercise. I exercise discretion."

FIGURE 10.1

4. *Action stage:* A stage when, indeed, action is taken, yet like an athletic skill, it may take several tries to get it right.

5. *Maintenance stage:* The stage where the person steps into the flow of making this change a part of his or her regular routine. This stage could also be called "second nature."

6. *Relapse stage:* A period where the old behavior is resumed for a while, until the newer (healthier) behavior is readopted.

Although Prochaska's model doesn't involve a stage for self-examination per se, this model has been adopted by many groups and organizations geared toward positive behavioral change from substance addictions to personal growth programs. It also has been used for health promotion programming with regard to weight loss and exercise programming. Whereas some programs tend to focus on strengthening the internal locus of control, others include external incentives or rewards (e.g., T-shirts, tote bags, coffee mugs) as a means of behavioral modification motivation, often with mixed results. This use of external rewards is one area of criticism of Prochaska's behavior model (Robison and Carrier, 2004). As the saying goes, "Real change has got to begin from within."

Is Stress a Trigger for Relapse?

What role does emotional stress play in behavior modification? The research in behavior change is conclusive: Stress (threatening perceptions of an event) is the most likely catalyst of unhealthy behavior. In the field of psychology, the term used to describe this is *antecedent*, and it means that various events or situations perceived as stressful act as a means to adopt stress-prone behaviors or revert to old behavior patterns such as smoking, drinking, binge watching (and screen addictions) (**FIG. 10.2**). Outside the field of psychology, they are referred to as buttons (e.g., "He really pushed my buttons"). Does emotional stress affect your behavior? What are your buttons (antecedents) that, when pushed, steer you in the direction of less than healthy behaviors? Becoming aware of these is also part of any behavior modification process.

As the field of life coaching gains acceptance in American society, motivational interviewing has become a cornerstone to behavior modification in this profession. Motivational interviewing grew out of efforts of William Miller and Stephan Rollnick (1991) to help alcoholics identify and change their addictive behaviors. Motivational interviewing is defined as "a directive, client-centered

FIGURE 10.2   Changing behaviors is not always easy if they have been lifelong habits. Some behaviorists suggest that change will take place only when there is sufficient desire.

counseling style for eliciting behavior change by helping clients to explore and resolve ambivalence. Compared with nondirective counseling, it is more focused and goal-directed." Today, this approach is used by many life coaches for all types of behavior changes, from credit card shopping and career goals to fitness training and various health behaviors.

Note that when people desire to change or improve their lifestyles they are typically eager to change all their undesirable behaviors at once, almost to become new individuals altogether. This approach, though most admirable, is often doomed to failure. Behavioral psychologists suggest altering one undesirable behavior at a time as the best method.

Many behavior theories, including self-monitoring, classical conditioning, operant conditioning, and modeling, suggest that behaviors can indeed be changed. From the nature of these theories and the research that led to them, it can be seen that there is no one best way to change behavior. The current school of thought is that the best approach to behavioral change is a multimodal approach (also called the biopsychosocial or holistic model) wherein many theories and their related techniques are combined in an attempt to produce a lasting effect. One major focus of all these theories is self-esteem. It appears that low self-esteem is associated with virtually every stress-related behavior. Therefore, it has taken on major importance with regard to behavior modification, particularly as it relates to assertiveness and assertiveness skills.

Assertiveness

Assertiveness is described as the ability to be comfortably strong-willed about one's thoughts, feelings, and actions, and neither inhibited nor aggressive in actions for the betterment of oneself in the surrounding environment. Andrew Salter is credited with introducing the term **assertiveness**, in 1949, to mean an inner resource to deal peacefully with confrontations. The term was reintroduced by Arnold Lazarus, who defined it as "expressing personal rights and feelings." Since its introduction, it has become the major focus in changing stress-related behaviors.

Psychologist Dennis Jaffe (Jaffe and Scott, 1984) developed a continuum of behavior styles employed by people in their relationships with others. Behavior styles at either end of the continuum are conducive to stress:

Passive	Assertive	Aggressive
behavior	behavior	behavior

Stress often produces many needs. Specifically, it produces the need to express one's feelings; other needs are often an offshoot of these expressions. The need to be assertive exists when situations arise that involve contact with other people. The assertive style, rather than the passive or aggressive, is advocated to minimize feelings of anger or fear associated with stressful encounters, and to work toward a peaceful resolution. The following is a more detailed explanation of these three dominant personality styles:

1. **Passive behavior style:** The passive style is where one is too intimidated to express thoughts and feelings. As a result, the person usually forfeits his or her rights and freedoms. A person employing this style comes across as shy and gives in to other people's demands so he or she will be more easily accepted. A passive style avoids confrontations at any cost. Consequently, this style makes one feel used and taken advantage of. The passive style is thought to be anxiety driven, yet the enactment of passive behavior results in feelings of resentment and victimization. The passive style is often employed by the codependent personality.

2. **Aggressive behavior style:** The aggressive style is where one acts to intimidate others and gain control of their thoughts and actions. Aggressive behavior includes manipulation, intimidation, accusations, and perhaps fighting. There is little or no regard for other people's feelings. Aggressive behavior may result in personal gain, but also breeds loss of respect and trust in those who were walked over and bruised on the way. The aggressive style is thought to be anger driven. It is often used by people who exhibit Type A behaviors.

3. **Assertive behavior style:** This is the preferable style, in which a person focuses on specific issues and problems, neither belittling him- or herself nor attacking others in the process of problem solving (McKay and Fanning, 2000). An assertive person recognizes his or her individual rights and stands up to protect those rights. Assertiveness includes expressing your opinion and being able to defend your rights, but not at the expense of violating others' rights. The assertive style minimizes opportunities to be taken advantage of by others. Assertive individuals are open, tolerant, and considerate of other people's feelings. To be assertive means to be able to overcome feelings of fear and to confront issues that demand resolution as well as communicate feelings of anger diplomatically, without putting others on the defensive.

Assertiveness carries with it the recognition of legitimate personal rights. These have been described by several

Assertiveness: The term given to a behavior that is neither passive nor aggressive, but proactively diplomatic.

Passive behavior style: A behavior influenced by intimidation that can often lead to feelings of resentment and victimization.

Aggressive behavior style: An aggression-based behavior that employs intimidation and manipulation.

Assertive behavior style: A behavior style that is neither passive nor aggressive, but one that is tolerant and considerate in the quest for individual rights.

Stress with a Human Face

If you could see Patty's face today, you would notice a glow about her. She radiates self-reliance and love. As brilliant as her smile is now, it wasn't always like this. In Patty's case, the road to inner peace began with a side trip to hell. At the age of 16, she looked to all the world like a normal teenager. But the allure of Fifth Avenue beauty in a weight-conscious society soon found Patty with an obsession to control her eating habits. Anorexic behaviors gave way to bingeing and purging, and the pattern remained an addictive ritual well into her 23rd year.

Reflecting back on her earlier years, Patty confided, "I was a perfectionist. I was obsessed with my weight. Food became a way to escape from my own feelings. Until I was 19, I denied I really had a problem, then I tried several methods to stop. Nothing worked."

In the fall of 1992, Patty pulled out the white flag and checked into a hospital. As she put it, "I hit rock bottom. It was this or die." The recovery program she started, well grounded in the twelve-step approach, led Patty to become fully aware of her behaviors and then slowly allowed her to substitute positive thoughts and actions for existing negative ones.

"Oh, I still get the urge now and then," she admitted during a quick visit to my office one day. "But I have never been happier in my life than I am now. I am at peace with myself and my higher power. I am very grateful," she sighed. The gratitude showed; the sparkle in her eyes said it all.

therapists, including Davis, Eshelman, and McKay (2002), and involve the following:

1. To say no and not feel guilty

2. To change your mind about anything

3. To take your time to form a response to a comment or question

4. To ask for assistance with instructions or directions

5. To ask for what you want

6. To experience and express your feelings

7. To feel positive about yourself under any conditions

8. To make mistakes without feeling embarrassed or guilty

9. To own your own opinions and convictions

10. To protest unfair treatment or criticism

11. To be recognized for your significant achievements and contributions

Typically, there are some people toward whom we are less than assertive in our manner. Usually these are people of higher authority, such as bosses and parents. Being unassertive, however, can occur with anyone by whom we feel intimidated, including members of the opposite sex, people perceived to be more attractive than ourselves, and all strangers.

Assertiveness Skills

To change one's behavior, there must first be recognition that current behavior is undesirable and may in fact be stress promoting. Once awareness and the will to change occur, then alternative behaviors can be devised and implemented. From workshops on assertiveness training come a host of skills that may be included in one's behavioral approach to potentially stressful encounters. The following are advocated to help improve assertiveness:

1. *Learn to say no.* We are often asked to assist friends, family, and co-workers with their responsibilities. There are, in fact, times when we cannot complete a task alone. An American ethic has evolved suggesting that we must work together and help each other in times of need. Over time, this ethic has become warped so that individuals put other people's needs before their own (e.g., codependent personality). Saying no is mistakenly equated with rudeness, and doing so results in feelings of rejection in the other person. But saying yes when it is inconvenient or impossible results in resentment and victimization in oneself. Assertiveness training teaches people to

FIGURE 10.3   In the 1980s, First Lady Nancy Reagan started a campaign to stop drug use with the now-famous slogan "Just say no!" This same degree of assertiveness can be used in all types of situations, including taking on additional responsibilities you simply do not have time for.

say no without feeling guilty about hurting someone else's feelings. People have the right to refuse a request without harboring feelings of guilt. Remember that other people's problems are no more or less important than your own, and that you are not required to solve all the world's problems. If you have personal obligations that conflict with requests by others, then diplomatically refuse to offer your support at that time. Do not let other people's comments generate feelings of guilt (**FIG. 10.3**).

2. *Learn to use "I" statements.* When one examines stress-prone personalities, it is evident that the inability to feel and express emotions is common among the various types. Assertiveness training teaches people to feel comfortable expressing themselves by using "I" statements (e.g., "I feel angry about . . ." or "I perceive what you said to me as incorrect"). This skill also teaches people to be more spontaneous with their expressions, rather than suppressing their feelings. The use of "I" statements encourages a person to claim ownership of thoughts, feelings, opinions, perceptions, and beliefs. Assertiveness training programs teach that opinion statements

may take time to formulate. Don't feel compelled to say the first thought that comes to mind. Rather, take a moment to consolidate your thoughts into a concise and direct response.

Nonassertive people often avoid describing their feelings for fear that others will disagree. Fearing rejection, they also tend to agree with other people's thoughts and take a middle-of-the-road position rather than risk expressing their own feelings. The use of "I" statements strengthens ego boundaries. Although strong ego boundaries might seem more indicative of an aggressive behavior style than an assertive one, the constituents of one's identity must first be recognized before they can be adjusted or exchanged in the ego development process.

3. *Use eye contact.* Body language is a very important communication skill. Nonverbal communication is more readily believed than the spoken word. Lack of eye contact during self-expression is perceived by others as either dishonesty or feeling insecure about what you are saying. Eye contact is often most difficult when you express your feelings toward someone else, for fear of rejection. Assertiveness training involves increasing eye contact while expressing various thoughts, feelings, and opinions. Learning this skill starts with a short time interval (1 or 2 seconds) and progresses up to 8- to 10-second periods. When pauses in eye contact are taken, people are advised to direct their eyes neither down nor up, but in a lateral direction momentarily, and then return again to direct eye contact. Just as poor eye contact communicates lack of confidence, staring (prolonged eye contact) is perceived as a violation of personal space and should be avoided.

4. *Use assertive body language.* An assertive tone of voice with a wimpy posture sends a mixed message to the person with whom you are communicating. The message is interpreted as either insincere or unsure. Postures, the ways in which you carry your body, either reinforce your message or detract from it. In addition to eye contact and tone of voice, your spinal posture and head position reveal at an unconscious level how you really feel about the messages you are communicating. It is suggested that your posture be erect, with your body weight equally distributed between both legs and your center of gravity directly above your feet.

5. *Practice peaceful disagreement*. When opinions and facts are voiced peacefully so that all perspectives can be viewed during a decision-making process, then disagreement is considered healthy. This assertiveness skill allows the individual to become comfortable with peaceful confrontation. It is employed when you feel the need to express an opposing view and want it to be acknowledged.

6. *Avoid manipulation*. In the course of asserting yourself, you may find that others may consciously or unconsciously try to block your efforts to accomplish resolution. The following are some roadblocks of manipulation to be aware of, as well as some suggested strategies that may help to dismantle them:

    a. *Intimidation*. Asserting yourself may intimidate others who are in the habit of using manipulation and control to get their way. They in turn may raise their voices and display their tempers. When you recognize this behavior, you can defuse it by saying that you want to hold off further discussion of this issue until the other person calms down. For example, "I can see that you are quite angry; let's talk about this after lunch."

    b. *Content substitution*. Sometimes people will draw peripheral issues into a discussion to derail the issue at hand. If you become aware that the concern you brought up has become lost in tangential issues, quickly shift focus back to the original topic until your issue has been put to rest.

    c. *Personal attacks (character assassination)*. You may find that in an attempt to resolve an issue, the person you are talking to comes back at you with a character flaw. One way to get back on track is to agree, in part, about the character flaw and ignore the rest. Davis calls this response clouding, the attempt to deflect an attack by concurring with some part of it. When employing this technique, rephrase the attack in your best interest, and get back to the issue at hand.

    d. *Avoidance*. Often people deny there is a problem by avoiding specific issues or their feelings about certain concerns. This roadblock can be confronted with a bold inquiry—a direct question—to unlock their perceptions. For example, "Is there something I did to make you angry?"

7. *Respond rather than react*. A reaction is a type of reflex, almost instinctual in nature, and a very natural part of human behavior. Here, a reaction deals with spontaneous emotional thoughts. Although spontaneity is an admirable trait where creativity is concerned, following through on emotional reactions can lead to some regrets. A response, on the other hand, is a thought-out plan for a situation. Many times our response is the same as our reaction, and this is when we are likely to wish we had thought before we spoke or acted. Responding to a situation means acknowledging your initial reaction, then thinking of a reasonable response to the situation at hand. Not every response will seem adequate, but as you practice this skill, you will find that it will help you deal with your perceptions of stress.

These are just a few of the recommended behaviors taught in assertiveness-training workshops. The purpose of all these skills is to build and maintain self-esteem.

■ Steps to Initiate Behavior Modification

To begin to change an undesired behavior, like smoking, biting your fingernails, or worrying about issues you seem to have no control over, you must first become aware of what this behavior is. Using the behavior modification model, select a behavior that you wish to change or modify.

It is a good idea to regularly monitor the thoughts and actions that seem to surface during stressful episodes and issues that disrupt your sense of inner peace. Then, using the behavior modification model, take yourself through the remaining steps. Remember, it is important not to change all target behaviors at once. Try to modify one behavior at a time.

SUMMARY

- People are constantly trying to change, improve, and manipulate their behaviors. Behaviors associated with poor health are those most often targeted for change.

- Personality is thought to be made up primarily of values, those abstract qualities that give meaning to our lives; attitudes, perceptions derived from these values; and behaviors, any actions based on one or more attitudes. Of the three, behaviors are thought to be the most easily influenced.

- Many variables affect behaviors, including biopsychosocial influences. To positively affect behaviors, a multimodal approach is advocated, where biological, psychological, and social factors are all considered to provide a holistic approach to well-being.

- There are many ways to change behavior, all having a common format called the behavior modification model. This progression of stages includes denial that a behavior contributes to poor health, or that one practices an undesirable behavior; then (1) awareness of the undesirable behavior; (2) desire to change; (3) cognitive restructuring, a conscious attempt to change; (4) behavioral substitution; and (5) evaluation of the results.

- The Stages of Change behavior modification model acknowledges that falling back on old (less desirable) behaviors (relapsing) is part of the process of refining the skill or new intended behavior.

- Although any conscious change in behavior can be referred to as behavior modification, in terms of stress management, behavior modification generally includes assertiveness training. The three styles of social behavior are passive, assertive, and aggressive, with assertive being the most effective.

- The purpose of every behavior modification program is to foster assertiveness. Such programs educate participants to practice several types of assertiveness skills, on the premise that assertiveness increases self-esteem.

- The best results occur when an individual tries to favorably alter one behavior at a time until it becomes part of his or her regular routine. If several behaviors are targeted at once, the person often feels overwhelmed and within a short time reverts back to old habits.

STUDY GUIDE QUESTIONS

1. Explain the difference between values, attitudes, and beliefs.

2. List and explain three behavior models.

3. Describe the behavior modification model.

4. Describe Prochaska's Stages of Change model.

5. What is an antecedent to behavior change?

6. Explain the concept of assertiveness and list three assertiveness skills.

REFERENCES AND RESOURCES

Alberti, R. E., and Emmons, M. *Your Perfect Right*, Revised ed. Impact Press, San Luis Obispo, CA, 1974.

Baldwin, J. D., and Baldwin, J. I. *Behavior Principles in Everyday Life*. Prentice-Hall, Englewood Cliffs, NJ, 1998.

Bandura, A. *Principles of Behavior Modification*. Holt, Rinehart, & Winston, New York, 1969.

Beech, H. R., Burns, L. E., and Scheffeld, B. F. *A Behavioral Approach to the Management of Stress*. Wiley, Chichester, UK, 1982.

Beighle, D. G. *Dancing with Yesterday's Shadows*. Gospel Films, Nashville, TN, 1998.

Bloom, L. Z., Coburn, K., and Pearlman, J. *The New Assertive Woman*. Dell, New York, 1975.

Bower, S. A., and Bower, G. H. *Asserting Your Self*. Addison-Wesley, Reading, MA, 1976.

Chapman-Novakofski, K., and Karduck. J. Improvement in Knowledge, Social Cognitive Theory Variables, and Movement through Stages of Change after a Community-Based Diabetes Education Program, *Journal of the American Dietetic Association* 105(10):1613–1616, 2005.

Chiriboga, D. A. Social Stressors as Antecedents of Change, *Journal of Gerontology* 39(4):468–477, 1984.

Davis, M., Eshelman, E. R., and McKay, M. *The Relaxation and Stress Reduction Workbook*, 6th ed. MJF Books, New York, 2002.

DiClemente, C. C., and Prochaska, J. O. Self Change and Therapy Change of Smoking Behavior: A Comparison of Processes of Change in Cessation and Maintenance, *Addictive Behavior* 47(9):133–142, 1982.

Duhigg, C. *The Power of Habit*. Random House, New York. 2012.

Dyer, W. *Pulling Your Own Strings*. Avon Books, New York, 1978.

Hawkins, D. *Power vs. Force: The Hidden Determinants of Human Behavior*. Hay House Books, Carlsbad, CA, 2002.

Hellman, E. A. Use of the Stages of Change in Exercise Adherence Model among Older Adults with a Cardiac Diagnosis, *Journal of Cardiopulmonary Rehabilitation* 17:145–155, 1997.

Jaffe, D. T., and Scott, C. D. *Self-Renewal*. Fireside Books, New York, 1984.

LeVert S. *The Complete Idiot's Guide to Breaking Bad Habits*, 2nd ed. Indianapolis, IN, Alpha Books, 2001.

Marlatt, G. A. Cognitive Factors in the Relapse Process. In G. A. Marital and J. R. Gordon, eds., *Relapse Prevention*. Guilford Publications, New York, 1985.

Martin, G., and Pear, J. *Behavior Modification: What It Is and How to Do It*, 8th ed. Upper Saddle River, NJ, Prentice Hall, 2007.

McKay, M., Davis, M., and Fanning, P. *Messages: The Communication Skills Book*. New Harbinger Press, Oakland, CA, 1995.

McKay, M., and Fanning, P. *Self-Esteem*. New Harbinger Publications, Oakland, CA, 2000.

Miller, W. R. What Really Drives Change? *Addiction* 88: 1479–1480, 1993.

Miller, W. R., and Rollnick, S. *Motivational Interviewing: Preparing People to Change Addictive Behavior*. Guilford Publications, New York, 1991.

Pavlov, I. *Conditioned Reflexes*. Dover, New York, 1927.

Peck, M. S. Journeys along the Road Less Traveled, Life Cycle Learning Workshops, Arlington, VA, Dec. 2, 1989.

Pescuric, A., and Byham, W. The New Look of Behavior Modeling, *Training and Development* 50:25–30, 1996.

Prochaska, J. O., and DiClemente, C. C. Transtheoretical Therapy: Toward a more Integrative Model of Change, *Psychotherapy: Theory, Research, Practice, Training* 19: 276–288, 1982.

Prochaska, J. O., DiClemente, C. C., and Norcross, J. C. In Search of How People Change, *American Psychology* 47:1102–1104, 1992.

Prochaska, J. O., Velicer, W. F., Rossi, J. S., Goldstein, M. G., Marcus, B. H., Rakowski, W., et al. Stages of Change and Decisional Balance for 12 Problem Behaviors, *Health Psychology* 13:39–46, 1994.

Robison, J., and Carrier, K. *The Spirit of Science of Holistic Health*. Author House, Bloomington, IN, 2004.

Rokeach, M. *Beliefs, Attitudes, and Values*. Jossey-Bass, San Francisco, 1972.

Salter, A. *Conditioned Reflex Therapy: The Direct Approach to Reconstruction of Personality*. Allen & Unwin, London, 1952.

Sarafino, E. *Behavior Modification: Understanding Principles of Behavior Change*. McGraw-Hill, New York, 2000.

Skinner, B. F. *The Behavior of Organisms*. Appleton, New York, 1938.

Smith, D. E., Heckemeyer, C. M., Kratt, P. P., and Mason, D. A. Motivational Interviewing to Improve Adherence to a Behavioral Weight-Control Program for Older Obese Women with NIDDM: A Pilot Study, *Diabetes Care* 20: 52–54, 1997.

Smith, M. J. *When I Say No I Feel Guilty*. Dial, New York, 1975.

Taylor, S. E. *Health Psychology*, 8th ed. McGraw-Hill, Englewood, NJ, 2014.

Tubesing, D. A. *Kicking Your Stress Habits: Y's Way to Stress Management*. Whole Person Associates, Duluth, MN, 1981.

CHAPTER 11

Journal Writing

All sorrows can be borne, if you put them in a story.

—Isak Dinesen

The way that J. Ivy tells it, "There were no therapists in the section of Chicago where I grew up. We just didn't do that kind of thing." J. Ivy is a Grammy-award winning spoken word artist and hip hop poet whose work appeared on Kanye West's debut album, *College Dropout*. It was in high school that one of J. Ivy's English teachers encouraged him to put his creativity, emotions, and feelings onto paper. So he did. It was cathartic just to get it out of his head. When his teacher passed back the assignment, she asked him to read it aloud to the class. Though J. Ivy was hesitant and nervous, he did. Not long after, this same teacher entered him into a spoken word event. Soon this teenager from the South Side of the Windy City found a voice in his pain and a way to release it, rather than keeping it inside. The passion of his words combined with the dramatic intensity of his narrative became more than rap, it became his unique alchemy of healing. One of J. Ivy's most poignant works, "Dear Father," describes the turbulent relationship with his estranged dad, who left the family when J. Ivy was quite young. To hear him recite this poem on stage in a live performance is to know the meaning of making order out of chaos. "When I write, I write to cleanse my soul. I find words that create a tapestry of my feelings and weave these thoughts into rhyme to help me cope with the loss, the stress, the challenges I have faced. I have learned that in sharing these words, it helps others too." And they have. While attending Illinois State University he honed his journal writing/poetry skills and became known as "The Poet" among his friends and peers. Like many others who have found their voice in their personal writings and soul-searching efforts, J. Ivy's collection of words can now be found in his book, *Here I Am: Then and Now*. A few of J. Ivy's favorite words, which he repeats with passion, are these: "Dreams don't come true. They are true."

To open up and disclose feelings, perceptions, opinions, and memories has always been found to be therapeutic (**FIG. 11.1**). Confessions of the mind lighten the burden of the soul. Many religions have adapted this concept for spiritual healing. This is also the cornerstone on which modern psychology is based. Although conversation is the most common method of disclosure, writing down thoughts occupying the mind is extremely therapeutic as well, as was revealed by countless American soldiers fighting in Iraq and Afghanistan through their blogs. Therapeutic **journal writing** can be defined as a series of written passages that document the personal events, thoughts, feelings, memories, and perceptions in one's journey throughout life leading to wholeness. The practice

> **Journal writing:** A coping technique; expression of thoughts, feelings, memories, and ideas in written form, either prose or poetry, to increase self-awareness.

27 pens, 15 notebooks and a dozen epiphanies later, Ellen was ready to admit she may have gone a bit overboard on her first try at journaling…

FIGURE 11.1

of journal writing has proven a formidable coping technique to deal with stress. For years, it has been used by psychologists, life coaches, and health educators alike as a tool for self-exploration, soul searching, and the enhancement of personal development.

Historical Perspective

For centuries, people have felt the need to keep personal records or logs of important information, from celestial navigation to the rise and fall of the Nile River's water levels. Written records served as a basis of comparison for annual events, lunar eclipses, famines of epic proportion, and changes of world leaders. In Europe's Age of Exploration, when men were inspired to explore and travel the globe, written records were of paramount importance. To this very day, world leaders, including the president of the United States, those serving in global conflicts (e.g., Afghanistan, Iraq), soldiers, and space station astronauts keep daily journals.

The word *journal* comes from the French word *journée*, meaning from sunrise to sunset. Journals originally started as a means of guidance on long trips, or as a record of orientation for a safe return passage. Long before there

were newspapers, most news was written by people who were describing events contributing to their own life journeys. Even today, much of what we call world history is based on the journal writings of travelers and explorers, including Columbus, Lewis and Clark, Admiral Perry, and even today's astronauts. Journals were kept to record the passage of time as well as distance. Throughout history, many people have kept journals or diaries to record their everyday experiences. Many important historical perspectives have been gained from the written passages of Vermont farm wives, homesteaders on the Oregon Trail, schoolteachers in the Southeast, and panners in Alaska's Klondike gold rush. Originally, journal writing was something men did because women were not educated to read or write. But when women adopted this idea as their own, the word *diary* became associated with women who kept journals. Today, the words *diary* and *journal* are used synonymously, yet there still appears to be a feminine association with the word *diary*. The distinction appears to be that diary writing is a listing of personal events, while journal writing expands personal awareness, emotional thought processing, and creativity, and offers seeds of resolution in personal struggles.

One of the first psychologists to study the use of journal writing was Dr. Ira Progoff in 1975. Trained in Jungian psychology, Progoff discovered that his own journal writing allowed direct access to a higher consciousness or spiritual awareness, which encouraged the search for meaning in his own life. The fruits of these efforts led him to share this coping technique with others who might benefit from it. Journal writing, Progoff suggested, allows for the synthesis of personal thoughts, feelings, perceptions, attitudes, and insights toward spiritual growth. In 1966, he established a seminar, called the Intensive Journal Workshop, in which he trained participants in the art of journal writing for self-improvement. Progoff's method of journal writing, with its use of a three-ringed notebook divided into twenty-one sections separating various components of one's thoughts, sought to open doors in the mind through various themes or springboards to self-exploration. His sections included Daily Log, Stepping Stones, Time Stretching, Dialogue Dimension, Imagery Extensions, A Personal Autobiography, and Dream Interpretation, as well as a series of personal dialogues on a host of topics, from body awareness to societal expectations. Collectively, these topics provided lessons in making order out of chaos from the glut of sensory information that is continually processed in the mind. Journal writing, Progoff said, allows the writer to initiate a positive confrontation with several issues that contribute to the understanding of one's personal existence.

In an experiment to examine the effects of journal writing on personal growth, 300 people were recruited from New York City's welfare and unemployment programs and introduced to the practice through Progoff's workshop, in conjunction with a job training program. Within a 12-month period, more than 90 percent of those enrolled in the workshop improved their job status and housing conditions. Credit for these improvements was given to the enhanced state of self-reliance attained through journal writing. As Progoff states in his book *At a Journal Workshop*, journal writing "plays an active role in reconstructing a life, but it does so without imposing any external categories or interpretations or theories of the individual's experience. It remains neutral and open-ended so as to maintain the integrity of each person's development, while drawing him further along the road of his own life process." He refers to journal writing as **transpsychological**, a word describing the therapeutic effects of self-discovery through active awareness, which allows the individual to access personal resources and promotes wholeness.

The Intensive Journal Workshop offered a very organized method to journal writing, yet some people felt it lacked the spontaneity and freedom that make self-expression through journal writing unique. The current approach to journal writing, advocated by renowned journal therapist Kathleen Adams, is called humanistic journal therapy, where journal writing is a vehicle for the development and maintenance of the transpersonal self or the bonding between oneself and one's enlightened self. In Jungian psychology, the transpersonal self would be described as a union of the conscious and unconscious minds through communication of words, symbols, and dreams to enhance human potential.

In the past 20 to 30 years, journal writing has often been combined with other coping techniques for personal growth. In the Outward Bound program, for example, which is loosely based on an American Indian rite-of-passage custom, risk-taking skills are taught. At the culmination of this weeklong experience, where survival skills are put to the test, participants are given journals to write down their feelings to enhance the soul-searching and soul-strengthening processes. In a similar type of program conducted in the Sierra Nevada, author Steven Foster writes in his book *Vision Quest* of journal writing as a supplemental tool for self-exploration in a 3-day soul-searching rite of passage. Portions of his book are painfully revealing, with candid descriptions written by those who shared their experiences of inner growth and spiritual development.

Once a privilege of the upper class, reading and writing have now become birthrights of people in almost every nation. Yet, although journal writing was once a popular pastime, the evolution of the high-technology age, which, in effect, has placed a barrier between humans and the natural environment, has also undermined the impetus for self-exploration, with the exception of blogs. Since the increase in popularity of Facebook and Twitter, however, the number of blogs has decreased dramatically. In previous generations, clergy filled the role of sounding boards to hear confessions of guilt, the sorrow of loneliness, depression, and emotional suffering. Today that role has been largely filled by psychologists, who act much the same way. As more research, greatly inspired by the pioneer work of James Pennebaker, on the topic of journal writing is conducted, a critical mass of evidence suggests what was known intuitively all along: Expressing oneself through journal writing is a highly effective means to help cope with stress. It is a practice strongly encouraged in the allied health professions. In the field of psychology, too, journal writing has surfaced as a viable tool in the journey to the self.

■ Journal Writing as a Coping Technique

Journal writing is perhaps the most effective coping skill available to provide profound internal vision and enhance the self-awareness process in times of stress (**FIG. 11.2**). Journal writing initiates the communication of self-reflection between the mind and the soul, the necessary first step in the resolution and closure of perceived stress. Journaling, in its own way, is a vehicle for meditation. As a technique to clear the mind of thoughts (by either focusing on one particular theme or jotting down random thoughts as they surface and circulate through the conscious mind), a calming effect takes place as thoughts and feelings are transferred from the mind to the written page.

Research suggests that journal writing is not only good for the soul, as a mode of catharsis to express the full

Transpsychological: A term used to describe the therapeutic effects of self-discovery through active awareness in journaling.

© SW Productions/Photodisc/Getty.

FIGURE 11.2   Journal writing is a means of self-exploration of thoughts and feelings.

range of emotions, but has proven to be good for the body as well. In a series of studies conducted by psychology professor James Pennebaker (2004; Pennebaker and Chung, 2007), students at Southern Methodist University were asked to write about a traumatic experience for 15 minutes on 4 consecutive days. Although the immediate response to these journal entries was often tears, even unpleasant dreams, Pennebaker observed that the subjects subsequently frequented the campus health center for "illness visits" less often than the control subjects who wrote about superficial topics. When this experiment was repeated in collaboration with J. Kiecolt-Glaser, with blood samples taken before and after the writing episodes, it was noted that those people who searched their souls to uncover latent, unresolved feelings associated with personal traumas showed "heightened immune function" of T-lymphocyte cells, when compared to those who addressed superficial topics in their journals.

Pennebaker's work has influenced many others to research the effects of journal writing on both emotional and physical health. Here are some highlights:

- Expressive writing has been shown to decrease elevated blood pressure (Beckwith, Greenberg, and Gevirtz, 2005).

- Affectionate writing has been shown to decrease cholesterol levels (Floyd, Mikkelson, Hesse, and Pauley, 2007).

> **Poetry therapy:** A therapeutic tool; a modality of writing poetry to enhance both increased awareness and emotional catharsis of a variety of issues.

- Expressive writing has been shown to decrease stress levels in college students (Opre, Coman, Kallay, Rotaru, and Manier, 2005).

- Expressive writing has shown beneficial health aspects for people suffering from fibromyalgia (Broderick, Junghaenel, and Schwartz, 2005).

- Expressive writing is revealed to help people grieving a romantic breakup (Lepore and Greenberg, 2002).

- Emotional expression helps to cope with stressful life events (Ullrich and Lutgendorf, 2002; Baikie and Wilhelm, 2005).

- Expressive writing has proven to be a major cathartic release for wives of American soldiers serving in the Iraq war (Hightower and Sherer, 2007).

- In a 2013 interview with the BBC, Pennebaker stated that although he is an advocate of the writing process, he is not a fan of people who keep daily diaries. From his perspective, people who keep hashing and rehashing their problems in a diary only spin their emotional wheels, reinforcing what is wrong rather than working to release and resolve the issues of stress, trauma, and pain.

As demonstrated by poet and spoken word artist J. Ivy, prose is not the only style that is thought to be therapeutic for journal entries. Poetry is strongly suggested as a proven means to foster emotional catharsis as well. Although not all poems employ rhyme, the use of rhyme in writing poetry allows the author to make "order out of chaos," thus giving a feeling or sense of control. In addition, poetic license to use metaphors and similes describing personal feelings allows a deeper sense of emotional expression. Emily Dickinson credited her poetry with the ability to gain a better perspective on the expression of her own feelings. The healing process of self-expression through poetry described by Morris Morrison in his book *Poetry as Therapy* incorporates imagination, intuition, and the development of personal insight—three characteristics essential in the healing process. The poems, in turn, augment the self-awareness process because each poem is first written and then read in its entirety. As with other journal entries, poems can address a whole host of issues and emotions. For this reason, **poetry therapy** is currently used as a therapeutic tool in the treatment of emotional disorders. Thus, this method of writing is encouraged as a complementary journal-writing style. It could even be suggested that some rap songs are a form of poetry therapy.

As a coping technique, journal writing seems to offer both immediate and long-term effects (**FIG. 11.3**).

FIGURE 11.3   The art of journal writing goes back eons. When taking the time to put your thoughts on paper, you begin to process not only *what* you are thinking and feeling, but also *why* you may be thinking and feeling this way. Some suggest that writing, rather than typing, allows the mind better quality of time to process these thoughts and feelings to come to a sense of resolution (catharsis).

Immediate Effects. For a host of reasons, people naturally tend to have an inability to fully express the entire range of human emotions. This conscious inhibition of emotional expression, coupled with the unconscious suppression of perceptions, attitudes, and feelings, may eventually result in neurotic (worrisome) behavior or the manifestation of physical symptoms. The results can be devastating, perhaps leading one to several visits to a psychologist. One of the primary goals of psychotherapy is to nurture self-awareness and honest self-expression.

In the short term, self-expression through journal writing may serve as an emotional catharsis by getting out on paper the toxic thoughts roaming through one's head. Journal writing allows the release of thoughts, feelings, and perceptions that liberates the mind and softens or expands the walls of the ego. Journal writing has often been called a writing meditation because as old thoughts are permitted to leave, the empty space they once occupied allows for expanded awareness of one's internal landscape as well as expanded depth of thought. This expanded awareness is analogous to a panoramic view from a mountaintop compared to an obstructed view from the base. Increased awareness opens the door for increased understanding of ourselves in our many environments. Writing down personal thoughts gives one permission to let them go, no longer thinking about them with the intensity that may have cluttered the mind and drained energy. Release of thoughts and

feelings may also act as a personal confession, an honest confrontation of one's behaviors. And this is an initial step toward healing both one's internal relationship and personal relationships with others. In addition, unlike conversation or internal dialogue, use of writing as a channel of self-expression makes the writer accountable for, or allows the writer to take solid ownership of, feelings as abstract thoughts become tangible on paper (**BOX. 11.1**).

Long-Term Effects. Lewis and Clark made daily journal entries during their expedition to the Northwest coast, and they often referred back to them to orient themselves for a safe return to St. Louis. Similarly, on a day-to-day basis it may prove difficult to observe changes in personal perceptions and attitudes toward events and circumstances perceived to be stressful. All of this increased awareness is paramount to making desired behavioral changes. But by periodically retracing one's steps, by rereading previous journal entries with a degree of objectivity, an awareness of patterns begins to emerge regarding values, attitudes, and even behaviors that inoculate against, precipitate, or perpetuate the stress response. Clues from reading between the lines may shed light on the precursors to stress: elements of anger and fear, and levels of self-esteem that make oneself vulnerable to stressors. This new awareness becomes extremely valuable when efforts are made to change these factors. Perhaps the best phrase to sum up the long-term effects of journal writing is "personal resolution." When thoughts are transferred to paper, the writer can begin to detach him- or herself from the scribed contents and begin to look at these as an impartial outsider would.

As a component of stress-management courses I have taught, I ask my students to keep a stress-management journal. At the end of the course, each person is asked to reread all entries over the duration of the course (typically 16 weeks) and write a summary. A journal summary is not a recapitulation of 4 months of stressors, but rather what the individual learned from him- or herself by rereading the entries and noticing trends or patterns in thoughts and behaviors, primarily trends that promote anger and/or anxiety, as well as conflicts in values and factors promoting or deflating self-esteem. Sometimes, first-hand accounts of the benefits of journal writing are more influential than the theories on which they are based. In (**BOX. 11.2**) are selected passages from summaries written to describe what some students learned from this coping-technique experience.

BOX 11.1   Reflections: A Journal Summary

by Jason Alvine, University of Northern Colorado

Having never kept a journal or even thought of writing down my feelings, this was a new experiment for me. Although I wasn't fond of the idea in the beginning, I learned many things from these exercises. From thinking of myself as an optimist to thinking of what makes me angry, I enjoyed writing my thoughts and feelings in a journal. This activity definitely taught me a lot about myself, how I view others, and what makes me tick. The main thing this journal taught me was that I care about others' feelings more than I let on. I think that I have more of a sensitive side than most guys would admit to, but this is by no means a bad thing. I looked at my values, which is something that I hadn't done in a long while, and realized I needed to focus more on the values that I was raised with than the values of my friends. I also looked back and saw that I have a great distaste for violence against another human being. I strongly believe that violence is a way for people who don't know how to deal with their stress properly to relieve themselves of this perceived negativity.

These exercises really made me examine myself and look at how I was, and how I want to strive to be. These entries made me look at my future and think about what I want to do with my life. I feel that the exercises reinforced that the best way to a successful future is to have success in the present. I do this by keeping up in my classes and trying to work as much as possible. Working gives me a sense of what I want to do with my life, and what I don't want to do. With my jobs in the past I have seen the effects of not having a college degree and where you can end up without it. The journal also made me think of continuing to write my thoughts down. Because it is a new technique, I learned to vent my frustrations and reveal my thoughts without telling anybody. This was a most beneficial activity and it made me think about finding new ways to let go of my stress.

Courtesy of Jason Alvine

BOX 11.2   More Journal Summary Excerpts

"For a long time now, I've known what stresses me the most. It has been a long time since I've been able to confide in or let anyone get really close to me. I've been so wrapped up in school for the past eight years of my life, and it's really getting lonely. As time goes on, it gets harder and harder to express myself. In a sense, I'm scared of situations because I don't know how I'll react. In this aspect, I don't know myself very well and I'm afraid to find out. This journal has really helped me get in touch with myself."

—A. C.

"This stress-reduction journal offered no cure-all for my problems, but it gave me valuable help. It helped me understand and see what I thought. By knowing what was going through my mind, I began to realize things about myself, some things I might have never known. A common phrase I saw in my journal was 'good enough.' The paper was 'good enough,' the letter I wrote home was 'good enough,' I was doing things so they would be 'good enough,' and in doing so, not achieving my potential. I was striving for mediocrity. I'm trying to break this bad habit and I think I have made a little headway. Creativity is now more clear and interesting to me than ever before. I found myself writing short stories in my journal or just creating ideas for work or pleasure."

—J. S.

"When I divorced my husband of seven years I cried on everyone's shoulder for months. That was a year ago. But people get tired of the same old complaints, even from best friends. So I took refuge in writing in my journal. It served as a great sounding board. It certainly helped me heal some very deep wounds. I've learned that there are some thoughts that are best left between my mind and the pages of a journal notebook."

—B. T.

■ Steps to Initiate Journal Writing

Only three essential elements are needed for effective journal writing: (1) a notebook dedicated solely to the journal, (2) a pen or pencil, and, perhaps most important, (3) a quiet, uninterrupted environment to collect your thoughts and then put them down on paper. There appears to be no best time of day to write; it varies from person to person. The end of the day may seem ideal, but perhaps not convenient. Although the time of day to write may vary, the suggested frequency of entries is more established. It is recommended that a good goal to start with is a minimum of 15 to 20 minutes for each entry, and three entries per week, to realize the benefits of this technique. Typically, people start out writing a couple of paragraphs mainly emphasizing events of the day rather than perceptions of these events. If continued, however, entries become longer, with more elements of the author's personality.

The current school of thought suggests that there really are no rules for keeping a journal. However, as an effective coping technique, there are some things to keep in mind. A journal should include descriptions of both stressful events *and* positive experiences. Life is full of highs and lows, and over the course of time, your journal should reflect both sides of the emotional teeter-totter. In addition, journal writing is not limited to thoughts and feelings expressed solely in words. Drawings serve as a wonderful expression of feelings, thoughts, and memories that words often cannot fully describe. Sketches also help augment recollections of images to complement the written text. It is important for you to remember that you write for yourself and not for the pleasure or intent of others. In fact, the best journal entries are those that are completely confidential. The premise of journal writing is to strengthen the bond of honesty from your mind to your soul. The contents of a stress-reduction journal aren't for publication; thus they are and should remain confidential. Thoughts should be articulated, yet unedited. When this premise is acted on, thoughts and feelings become easier to articulate and the rewards of inner peace are more substantial.

Although there is no specific formula for successful journal writing, some criteria may aid the writer to use this coping strategy to deal more effectively with perceived stress. These include the following:

1. *Try to identify those concerns and problems that cause the most frustration, grief, and tension*. Identification and prioritization of stressors are essential in the self-awareness process. For the first two to three weeks, this may be all you choose to include in each journal entry. Journal entries often can best be started by answering one or two questions, such as, How was my day today? or, What thoughts are occupying my mind right now?

2. *Ask yourself what emotions are elicited when these stressors are encountered*. The two major stress emotions are anger and fear; however, there are many shades of these emotions, including impatience, jealousy, frustration, sadness, grief, guilt, and worry. After identifying your current emotional state, the question Why? should be pondered to identify the origins of your emotions (e.g., Why do I feel frustrated? Why do I feel victimized?).

3. *Allow the writing process to augment your creative process to further resolution*. When you have begun to feel comfortable with identifying stressors and the respective emotions they produce, the next phase is to create a process of resolution for the concerns and problems. This includes searching for viable options and employing them to bring satisfying closure to the circumstances that promoted stress.

Perhaps in an effort to address the needs of people searching to use journaling as a coping technique, several books have appeared on the market in the past decade providing guidelines to the art of journal writing. The following is a compilation of tips, hints, and suggestions that appear to have the consensus of therapists who advocate this coping technique:

1. *Centering:* Before you begin to write, take a moment to relax. Close your eyes, take a few deep breaths, and try to unwind. Centering means to be well grounded or well connected to the here and now. Sometimes playing soft music or sipping hot tea can help foster the centering process.

2. *Labeling your journal entries:* Identify each entry with day, date, and year. On occasion you will want to review your past entries and it is much easier to recall the events surrounding the journal entry when this information is at the top of the page.

3. *Uncensorship:* Write whatever comes to mind without editing your thoughts before you put

---

BOX 11.3   To Blog or Not to Blog

The proliferation of laptops and Web pages has put a new face on personal writing in the twenty-first century. Although most emails contain no more than a few sentences (with a postcard writing style), many people have taken up the art of writing their personal thoughts in diary form and posting these writings on their personal Web pages in what is now called a **blog**. (The word *blog* is an adaptation of the words *Web log*.)

What's the difference between a personal journal and a blog, you ask? For starters, a personal journal is just that—personal. It's a private relationship between you and your thoughts and emotions. Journals are meant to be confidential. On rare occasions passages or pages may be shared—but this is the exception, not the rule. The Internet (including all Web pages) is considered public; hence, blogs are anything but confidential. Although most blogs do, in fact, contain personal thoughts and feelings, they can best be described as personal editorials.

So, blog if you wish (it definitely improves your writing skills), but remember that blogging isn't the same thing as keeping a journal.

---

them on paper. Don't censor your thoughts as they travel from your mind to the tip of your pen. Let them flow naturally. Journaling is transcribing your conscious dialogue. Don't be inhibited about expressing how you really feel. Also, don't worry how your writing style appears. Neat or sloppy, it makes no difference as long as you can read it; that is all that matters.

4. *Spontaneity:* Let your thoughts be free-flowing. You don't have to write in sentences and paragraphs all the time. Often, in trying to phrase a thought just the right way, the essence of the thought becomes diluted or lost. Get whatever thoughts you have down on paper and then sort them out however you choose. If you get a mental block when in front of a blank piece of paper, draw lines and store your ideas in separate boxes, or make lists of your thoughts. It is good to have variety in your journal entries, or the routine of writing becomes a boring chore. If words fail you, make a sketch or perhaps try writing a poem.

5. *A private place:* In theory, journal entries can be written anywhere, but having a designated place of solitude lends depth to self-disclosure. Find a place you can call your own. Open spaces also provide the opportunity for mind expansion. If the weather is conducive to sitting outdoors for a while, find a tree, beach, mountaintop, or grassy knoll, and make this spot your own as well. Sometimes combining this technique with music therapy allows the mind to wander more freely and emotions to surface to a greater level of consciousness.

6. *A private journal:* Experts agree that, unlike a blog, your journal is for your eyes only. If you make it a habit to share entries frequently, then the vow of honesty with yourself is compromised. If you live with other people (i.e., roommates, girlfriend/boyfriend, spouse, parents), then it would be a good idea to keep your journal away from wandering eyes. A journal is like Pandora's box to anyone but the author. You may choose to make it known that you keep a journal and specifically ask that no one invade your privacy. If someone does, it is at his or her own risk (**BOX 11.3**).

7. *Overcoming writer's block:* One reason people find writing in a journal challenging is that there is the risk of pain from confronting one's innermost thoughts. People become afraid of learning what is below the surface of immediate thoughts. Pain arises when the premise of our thoughts and perceptions doesn't match the ideals or expectations we set for ourselves. Fears surface with the realization of unmet expectations or a change in our current reality of ourselves. These conflicts can be painful to the ego. But with pain comes the opportunity for learning, and learning sows the seeds of personal growth and development. Remember that Frankl believed suffering to be an essential part of the personal-growth process.

> **Blog:** A term depicting someone's Internet journaling practice. Unlike a personal journal that is kept confidential, a blog is a public document to express opinions, beliefs, and newsworthy items of the author.

At the novice stage of journal writing, a blank piece of paper, not to mention an empty notebook, can look mighty intimidating. Some people are reluctant to write because of the unrealistic expectation that something profound must be written on every page. A journal serves as a catalyst to begin and strengthen your relationship with yourself. Relationships begin with introductions, background information, and questions. Journal entries can begin the same way. **Writer's block** happens to everyone at some point. Many people go in cycles, where they write religiously for months at a time, get a block, and then abandon their journals for a stretch. Sometime later, they come back to this coping style after a hiatus of a few weeks to a month. Writer's block can be overcome by trying a new approach or theme to journal entries, including creative writing or entries in the form of letters. For example, the book *The Color Purple* was written as a series of letters by author Alice Walker to a fictitious sister in Africa. If you find yourself with writer's block, try a new format of writing.

In his book *Opening Up: The Healing Power of Confiding in Others*, author Jamie Pennebaker advocates journal writing as a means of self-expression. Just as there can be benefits to journal writing, however, it can also be used incorrectly, negating the potential personal gains to be made. The following are suggestions to keep in mind when using journal writing as a positive coping technique:

1. *Journal writing should not be used to replace a more viable coping technique.* Journals can be great sounding boards. The echoes from these passages should be a strong personal invitation to find solutions to the problem at hand. Remember, for a coping technique to be effective, it must work toward a peaceful resolution. When journal writing is employed in place of more appropriate coping techniques, such as effective communication with other people or social engineering of factors for the betterment of your environment, resolution is compromised, if not completely prevented, and full closure on stressors never comes.

2. *Journal writing should encourage, not discourage, honest feelings.* As a coping technique, journal writing invites the writer to soul-search and turn thoughts inward. Although many writing themes, concepts, and philosophies can be used as vehicles to explore and augment the soul-searching process, these should not be the specific focus of one's writing. The primary theme is the writer. Ideally, journals should be kept confidential, though often people choose to share parts of journal entries, sometimes entire passages. However, if journal entries are written for an audience other than yourself, then the likelihood of honesty is greatly compromised.

3. *Paralysis by analysis.* Sometimes, when people get too absorbed in the expression of their thoughts and feelings, awareness gets fogged in and the effectiveness of self-expression and self-reflection is stifled. Cognitive paralysis sets in, which deters rather than augments the coping process. Be careful not to get caught in this trap. Journal writing is meant to give a wide perspective on yourself in your environment. Make sure you are able to see the forest as well as the trees.

Pennebaker reached some interesting conclusions about subjects he observed keeping journals. First, only a handful of people (3 percent) wrote every day in their journals, and while more women than men kept journals, the difference was not significant. Second, journal entries were centered less on emotions than on facts to describe specific events, a style that may not have been as beneficial an experience as perceived by the journal writer. Last, he found that journal writers seemed to fall into two distinct categories. The first group tended to write only during periods of mental frustration and monumental stress. The journal became a sounding board and tended to carry the burden of anxieties. The second group wrote nearly every day; however, when a major stressor arose (e.g., death of a spouse, career stress), a time when writing might be the most help, a safe distance was kept from the journal and no writing took place. Pennebaker noted a third group of people, though, who instead of keeping a journal, wrote letters. Although this may seem similar to journal entries, letters are often less than candid about internal feelings about oneself to oneself. In my work with clients, I have also noticed a fourth group: people who do not necessarily write frequently, perhaps once or twice a week, but whose journal entries tend to be balanced between positive and negative experiences. The positive experiences are more factual, and perhaps even integrated into a creative story. The narratives of negative experiences include inner feelings to describe the reasons for these emotions.

> **Writer's block:** The inability to write down one's thoughts and feelings, usually attributed to fear (e.g., fear of failure).

Journal Writing Styles, Themes, and Ideas

Whereas journal entries can consist of a daily report on personal events, they can also be inspired by specific themes that surface and merit exploration to give the writer a new vantage point on him- or herself. Examples include dreams, rites of passage, values assessment and clarification, unwritten letters, self-esteem issues, free thought relationships, things to do, wish lists, creative story writing, poems, or any topic the writer chooses to expound upon. Themes can also be conveyed in many styles of writing, including linear (left to right), circular (rotating the paper as you write), in boxes, and free-form. Three of these are as follows:

1. *The Buzan style:* The **Buzan writing style** for journal entries, developed by Tony Buzan (1983), involves words in a pictorial fashion that accesses both right- and left-brain cognitive functions. In this technique (**FIG. 11.4**), you draw a vertical line to the left of center on the page. Everything to the left of this line is reserved for thoughts or perceptions. Examples might include "I have to feed the dog tonight before I go out" or "My boss was a jerk today." In the center of the remaining two-thirds, draw a circle, and in the middle write the words, "I feel." Every time you feel an emotion, draw a line from the circle out. On each line, describe how you feel in three words. (Buzan suggests the use of a different colored pen or pencil for each feeling.) Whatever comes into your mind, write it down as either a thought or feeling; do this for about 15 to 20 minutes. You may want to listen to some soft, relaxing instrumental music at the same time. This type of journal entry

serves as an eraser to clean the blackboard of your mind. Once the thoughts are on paper, the mind becomes uncluttered and achieves a state of mental homeostasis.

2. *The proprioceptive method:* Linda Metcalf, author of the book *Writing the Mind Alive*, has been teaching journaling for decades and it was early in her career that she discovered a way for people to really get in touch with their inner selves. She calls it the proprioceptive writing method, and it consists of synthesizing one's emotions and imagination into a culmination of one's own authentic voice. The term *proprioceptive* means a sense of body awareness, but in this case, Metcalf expands the definition to include your mind. In essence, why do you have the thoughts you have? Metcalf suggests for the best response to play some Baroque music, light a candle, and have a pad (unlined paper works best) and pen ready at hand. She also suggests setting dedicated writing time several times a week for no less than half an hour each time. With the focus on writing from one's heart space, one writes with focused awareness to dissolve one's inhibitions (fears) and builds a foundation to build trust from within. Metcalf's style is to frequently have the writer ask him- or herself the question: What do I mean by _____? By answering this question one delves deeper into the soul-searching process of awareness.

3. *A dream journal:* Dreams make fascinating material for journal entries. Jung, remember, believed attempting to understand the symbolism of one's dreams would lead to psychic equilibrium, a balance of the conscious and unconscious minds promoting personal wholeness. Often the loose ends of perceptions and emotions associated with stress materialize in the dream state as the unconscious mind works on its own analysis and resolution process of thoughts and sensory information received in the conscious state. The unconscious mind is rich in color and symbols, yet poor in its ability to express these symbols as words. Thus, the collaboration of the conscious and unconscious minds is a dynamic one to deal with stressors. It should be noted that with the massive proliferation of television, DVDs,

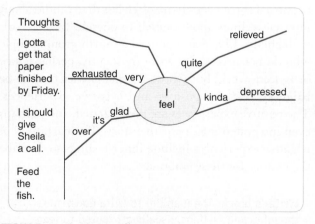

FIGURE 11.4   Buzan diagram.

> **Buzan writing style:** A specific journal approach to access the powers of both the right and left hemispheres of the brain through words and images.

and other media entertainment, dreams may be less a function of our own thoughts and more a function of making sense or relating to that which we are consuming from these venues. Regardless, dreams should not be discounted! Although we often do not remember all our dreams, everyone does dream. But many times, dreams seem to fade into thin air the second we wake up and enter the conscious world. Researchers who study dreams have come up with the following list of ways to help people remember their dreams:

a. Before you go to sleep, write a review of the day's events and your feelings about them.

b. As you drift off to sleep, remind yourself, silently or out loud, that you want to remember your dreams.

c. Reserve a few quiet moments, with your eyes closed, when you wake up to recall your dreams. Linger in a semi-dream state to observe dream thoughts.

d. Keep your journal and a pen/pencil handy by your bedside to record your dream thoughts or fragments when you wake up.

e. Dream thoughts can surface to the conscious state when triggered by some event in the course of your day. Write down any dream fragments.

Return to the passages describing your dream images and ponder what their symbolism can reveal to you. Jung believed that every dream was a source of information. Prompt recording of your dreams can help prevent distortions created by the conscious mind. Journal writing can also be a good outlet to draft a written closure or final scene of a recurring dream. Recurring dreams often represent serious unresolved issues that need to be addressed. Although writing a final scene to a recurring dream may not fully resolve each stressful issue, it does initiate increased awareness that may aid in the resolution of the stressor that causes this type of dream.

4. *Unsent letters:* Another topic common to journal writers is called "unsent letters." One type of resolution people tend to avoid like the plague is rifts occurring in relationships of any kind. The hardest rift to resolve occurs when a friend or loved one dies without your getting the chance to say goodbye. Kathleen Adams (2000) states that unsent letters provide the opportunity for "the three C's": catharsis, clarity, and completion. As a cathartic tool, the drafting of an unsent letter allows release of suppressed emotions including grief, anger, or guilt. For this journal technique to prove effective, it is a given that the letter does *not* go in the mail so that emotions can bubble up freely and surface without fear of self-censorship or reprisal. We all carry excess emotional baggage from unresolved relationships. The drafting of unsent letters allows us to lighten our emotional load. Clarity becomes evident when the writer realizes there is no chance for rebuttal from the addressee. Under this circumstance, you can be as direct as you wish and state exactly how you feel and why you feel this way. Although writing a letter to someone you need to communicate with does not resolve all issues, it does *begin* to bring the unresolved issues to closure. A variation on this journal technique is to write down thoughts of anger and hostility and then crumple up the paper and throw it away. The crumpling adds to the emotional catharsis.

Best Tips for Journal Writing as a Coping Technique

Here are some additional tips on getting started on this most valuable coping technique:

1. Buy a nice notebook (leather-bound journals are great) to call your own. Investing in a nice journal deepens your commitment to the journal-writing process.

2. Sometimes making a list of things going through your head is a great way to start a journal entry. Once you get these ideas down, then begin to expound on them.

3. Consider playing some relaxing background music (instrumental music works best) to relax the mind and let the thoughts and emotions flow.

4. Consider holding a centering device (such as a seashell or tumble stone) as a means to start the soul-searching process.

5. If prose isn't your thing, consider writing in a rap style. Remember that putting things to rhyme can help you make order out of the chaos in your life.

6. Consider keeping a section of your journal for creative ideas, doodling, and photo collages.

■ Best Application of Journal Writing

Good-quality journal writing has several purposes. The first is to act as a personal sounding board—to cleanse the mind overloaded with perceptions, emotions, and toxic thoughts. Journal writing is a great way to vent anger. In moments of rage, a verbal description helps pinpoint how and why these feelings are surfacing. Sometimes writing how you feel, and perhaps what you should have said or would like to say, becomes a draft script to resolve issues between you and the person(s) involved in your perceived stress. Writing down feelings of anxiety and apprehension is a good release of emotions that can drain your energy. Effective coping involves the ability to access and employ both internal and external resources.

The second purpose is to map out strategies for resolution, both attitudinal perceptions and behavioral changes. Depending on the situation, these two purposes can be used as an offensive tactic in the face of stress, or in strategic planning when in momentary retreat. As an offensive tactic, journal writing can be used to cope with an immediate problem. Just by pulling out a pad of paper and pen and writing down what is on your mind, thoughts become organized and order begins to emerge from chaos. In many stressful events, however, this option is not possible. Then journal writing can be used as a postponed coping response, perhaps at the end of the day, to collect your thoughts and process major events—those chronic stressors—that need attention. Last, a periodic review of journal entries serves to increase awareness of trends and patterns in your thoughts and behaviors. Recognition of trends is the first step in changing undesired or negative thoughts and actions in an effort to reach your highest human potential and enjoy inner peace. Although the primary resource needed for journal writing is a single notebook, you might consider having two: one very private one to be used exclusively at home, and a second one, perhaps less structured, to be used at work.

Personal computers have added a whole new dimension to journal writing that was inconceivable just two decades ago. Many people have found that using a word processor actually allows them to write as fast as they think, thereby enabling them to capture the essence of several thoughts simultaneously, rather than fighting to retrieve some. If you find it easier to type entries in a personal computer file than in a notebook, give it a try.

SUMMARY

- Journal writing has been used as a form of self-expression and soul searching for centuries. Psychologists and health educators have advocated journal writing for decades as a means to increase self-awareness on issues that need attention.

- Journal writing is said to promote emotional catharsis when thoughts, perceptions, attitudes, values, beliefs, and the tensions these create are allowed to work themselves out on paper.

- Use of soul searching is no coincidence as a stress-management technique because this activity is the epitome of the emptying process.

- There are short-term and long-term effects of habitual journal writing. Short-term benefits include releasing pent-up feelings of anger and anxiety. When a series of journal entries is reread, long-term effects include seeing patterns and habits of thought, perceptions, and behaviors that are not detectable on an entry-to-entry basis. Putting thoughts down on paper also widens one's perspective to become more receptive to solutions and resolutions to stressors.

- An additional benefit, demonstrated by Pennebaker, is that writing about personal experiences in a journal increases the integrity of the immune system. Expressive writing has also proved to benefit fibromyalgia patients and wives of U.S. servicemen, as well as to decrease resting blood pressure and cholesterol levels.

- Not all journal entries have to be written in prose form. Poetry therapy is likened to making order out of personal chaos. This coping style is used in many settings, including prisons, nursing homes, hospitals, and counseling centers.

- There is no wrong way to write a journal, save writing too infrequently. This chapter gave a number of guidelines for effective journal writing, including several themes (Buzan, dreams, and unsent letters) that can add variety to your repertoire of entry styles.

STUDY GUIDE QUESTIONS

1. Explain how journaling is used as an effective coping technique.

2. Differentiate between the immediate effects and the long-term effects of journal writing.

3. List several steps that help promote the journal-writing process.

REFERENCES AND RESOURCES

Abercrombie, B. *Keeping a Journal*. McKelderry Books, New York, 1987.

Adams, K. *The Write Way to Wellness*. Center for Journal Therapy, Denver, CO, 2000.

Baikie, K. A., and Wilhelm, K. Emotional and Physical Health Benefits of Expressive Writing, *Advances in Psychiatric Treatment* 11:338–346, 2005.

Baldwin, C. *One to One: Self-Understanding through Journal Writing*. Evans & Company, New York, 1977.

Beckwith, K. M., Greenberg, M. A., and Gevirtz, R. Autonomic Effects of Expressive Writing in Individuals with Elevated Blood Pressure, *Journal of Health Psychology*, 10:197–209, 2005.

Blair, E. "More Than 50 Years of Putting Kids' Creativity to the Test." *NPR All Things Considered*, April 17, 2013.

Broderick, J. E., Junghaenel, D. U., and Schwartz, J. E. Written Emotional Expression Produces Health Benefits in Fibromyalgia Patients, *Psychosomatic Medicine*, 67:326–334, 2005.

Brophy, B. Dear Diary: A History, *U.S. News and World Report*, October 23:89, 1995.

Buzan, T. *Use Both Sides of Your Brain*. E. P. Dutton, New York, 1983.

Cappachione, L. *The Creative Journal*. Swallow Press, Athens, GA, 1979.

DeSalvo, L. *Writing as a Way of Healing: How Telling Our Stories Transforms Our Lives*. Beacon Press, New York, 2000.

DeVota, B. (ed.). *The Journals of Lewis and Clark*. Houghton Mifflin, Boston, 1953.

Dickinson, E. *Selected Poems and Letters of Emily Dickinson*. Doubleday, New York, 1959.

Dinesen, I. *Out of Africa*. Random House, New York, 1983.

Floyd, K., Mikkelson, A. C., Hesse, C., and Pauley, P. M. Affectionate Writing Reduces Total Cholesterol: Two Randomized Controlled Trials, *Human Communication Research*, 33:119–142, 2007.

Foster, S., with Little, M. *Vision Quest: Personal Transformations in the Wilderness*. Prentice-Hall, New York, 1989.

Goldberg, N. *Writing Down the Bones*. Shambhala, Boston, 1986.

Hagan, K. L. *Internal Affairs: A Journal-Keeping Workbook for Self-Intimacy*. Escapadia Press, Atlanta, GA, 1988.

Hightower, K., and Sherer, H. Tell It to Your Journal, 2007. www.armytimes.com/community/family/military_married_journaling_070212/.

Holly, M. L. *Writing to Grow: Keeping a Personal Profession Journal*. Heinemann Educational Books, Portsmouth, NH, 1989.

Ivy, J. Personal conversation. July 19, 2013, 15th Annual Institute of Noetic Sciences Conference, Indian Wells, CA.

Ivy, J. Spoken Word (Keynote Address). July 19, 2013, 15th Annual Institute of Noetic Sciences Conference, Indian Wells, CA.

Jacobs, B. *Writing for Emotional Balance*. New Harbinger Press, Oakland, CA, 2005.

Kaiser, R. B. The Way of the Journal, *Psychology Today* 15:64–65, 1981.

Leedy, J. L. *Poetry Therapy: The Use of Poetry in the Treatment of Emotional Disorders*. Lippincott, Philadelphia, 1969.

Lepore, S. J., and Greenberg, M. A. Mending Broken Hearts: Effects of Expressive Writing on Mood, Cognitive Processing, Social Adjustment and Health Following a Relationship Breakup, *Psychology and Health*, 17:547–560, 2002.

Mallon, T. *A Book of One's Own: People and Their Diaries*. Tickner and Fields, New York, 1984.

Mayer, H., Lester, N., and Pradl, G. *Learning to Write, Writing to Learn*. Boynton/Cook, Portsmouth, NH, 1983.

Metcalf, L., and Tobin, S. *Writing the Mind Alive: The Proprioceptive Method for Finding Your Authentic Voice*. Ballantine Books, New York, 2002.

Metzger, S. *Writing for Your Life: A Guide and Companion to Inner Worlds*. Harper, San Francisco, 1992.

Meyers, L. J. *Becoming Whole: Writing Your Healing Story*, 2nd ed. Iaso Books, New York, 2007.

Meyn, S. *Journal Magic! Lessons in Therapeutic Writing*. JournalMagic, Scottsdale, AZ, 2007.

Morrison, M. R. *Poetry as Therapy*. Human Sciences Press, New York, 1987.

Opre, A., Coman, A., Kallay, E., Rotaru, D., and Manier, D. Reducing Distress in College Students through Expressive Writing: A Pilot Study on a Romanian Sample, *Cognitie, Creier, and Comportament* [*Cognition, Brain, and Behavior*] 10:53–64, 2005.

Pennebaker, J. W. Mind Changers: Expressive Writing and Pain. *BBC Radio*, July 2013. http://www.bbc.co.uk/programmes/b01rrc11.

Pennebaker, J. W. Confession, Inhibition, and Disease, *Advances in Experimental Social Psychology* 22:211–244, 1989.

Pennebaker, J. W. *Opening Up: The Healing Power of Confiding in Others*. William Morrow, New York, 1990.

Pennebaker, J. W. *Writing to Heal: A Guided Journal for Recovering from Trauma and Emotional Upheaval*. New Harbinger Press, Oakland, CA, 2004.

Pennebaker, J. W., and Chung, C. K. Expressive Writing, Emotional Upheavals, and Health. In H. Friedman and R. Silver (eds.), *Handbook of Health Psychology*. Oxford University Press, New York, 2007:263–284.

Pennebaker, J. W., Colder, M., and Sharp, L. Accelerating the Coping Process, *Journal of Personality and Social Psychology* 58:528–537, 1990.

Pennebaker, J. W., and Francis, M. E. Putting Stress into Words: The Impact of Writing on Physiological, Absentee, and Self-Reported Emotional Wellbeing Measures, *American Journal of Health Promotion* 6(4):280–287, 1992.

Plaut, T. F. Symptom Reduction after Writing about Stressful Experiences, *JAMA* 282(19):1811–1812, 1999.

Progoff, I. *At a Journal Workshop*. Dialogue House Library, New York, 1975.

Progoff, I. *The Practice of Process Meditation*. Dialogue House Library, New York, 1980.

Rainer, T. *The New Diary*. J. P. Tarcher, Los Angeles, CA, 1978.

Rico, G. L. *Writing the Natural Way*. J. P. Tarcher, Los Angeles, CA, 1983.

Seaward, B. L. Effects of a Comprehensive Stress-Management Program on Self-Reported Physiological Manifestations of the Stress Response, *Psychophysiological Monographs* 5(3):1–7, 1988.

Senn, L. *The Many Faces of Journaling: Topics and Techniques for Personal Journal Writing*. Penn Central Press, New York, 2001.

Siegel, A. Dreams: The Mystery That Heals. In E. Bauman (ed.), *The Holistic Health Handbook*. And/Or Press, Berkeley, CA, 1972.

Simons, G. F. *Keeping Your Personal Journal*. Ballantine/Epiphany, New York, 1978.

Ullrich, P. A. and Lutgendorf, S. L. Journaling about Stressful Events: Effects of Cognitive Processing and Emotional Expression, *Annals of Behavioral Medicine* 24:244–250, 2002.

Walker, A. *The Color Purple*. Harcourt Brace, New York, 1992.

Woodward, P. *Journal Jumpstarts; Tips for Journal Writing*. Cottonwood Press, Fort Collins, CO, 1991. www.journalforyou.com/.

Zakowski, S. G., Ramati, A., Morton, C., Johnson, P., and Flanigan, R. Written Emotional Disclosure Buffers the Effects of Social Constraints on Distress in Cancer Patients, *Health Psychology*, 23:555–563, 2004.

CHAPTER 12

Expressive Art Therapy

Draw me how you feel.

—Brian Luke Seaward

When the children of Sandy Hook elementary school in Newtown, Connecticut, returned to classes about a week after the massacre, teachers and therapists skipped the prepared lesson plans and instead had the children draw their feelings about what had happened on December 14, 2012. So much of what they experienced was not only beyond their comprehension, it was beyond their ability to describe in words. Where words fail, pictures deliver. It is well understood that many thoughts and feelings about tragedy and stress are nonverbal. It is also well recognized that holding these feelings inside can become toxic. Drawing as a form of therapy isn't just for kids. The visual arts are now known to be an effective coping tool for people of all ages.

With the advent of the Internet, where people can and do add their two cents to any Web site, send hourly Facebook updates, text message until their thumbs go numb, and send hundreds of 140-character tweets all over the planet, we have entered what is now being called the age of self-expression. Words, however, only represent a small fraction of true self-expression. The unconscious mind, which governs behavior, uses symbols, images, and pictures as a far more efficient means to communicate and express itself. Expression of oneself through art goes back ages (FIG. 12.1). In fact, art, as a mode of self-expression, dates back several thousands of years to the cave drawings in Lascaux, France, and perhaps much earlier. But just recently in the development of modern civilization has art become a recognized effective coping technique in the field of stress management. **Art therapy** is based on the premise that many thoughts, feelings, and insights are verbally inexpressible. Several abstract constructs of the human mind lack the necessary vocabulary to adequately describe the focus, intensity, and understanding of daily encounters that the mind tries to process and grasp. This is only exacerbated in times of stress. Self-expression through visual artistic media offers a balance to verbal expression in the search for wholeness through the understanding of our personal thoughts, feelings, perceptions, and attitudes.

Art therapy has been described by the American Art Therapy Association as "the use of art in a creative process to provide the opportunity for a nonverbal expression

> **Art therapy:** A coping technique of self-expression and self-awareness employing various media to describe feelings and thoughts in ways that verbal language cannot.

FIGURE 12.1 Art, as a personal expression, dates back thousands of years, as shown in these photos of rock art petroglyphs drawn by ancient American Indians, discovered at Three Rivers, New Mexico, and believed to be more than 2,000 years old.

and communication in which to reconcile and foster self-awareness and personal growth." Art therapy is centered on exploration of the individual's internal landscape, carved and shaped by one's collective experiences and delivered through a visual, artistic sense. Art therapy can strengthen the bonds of self-communication, thereby promoting greater self-awareness and self-comfort. Art therapy can also be described as a voyage of self-discovery, with process and product uniting to promote self-realization and self-healing. For this reason, art therapy is considered a coping technique in the strategic plan to deal with stress because awareness of problems must occur before steps to resolve perceived stress can be taken.

If you consider that your thoughts and behaviors are a product of your unconscious mind, and the unconscious mind communicates in symbols, colors, and images, rather than words, then tapping into the wealth and power of the unconscious mind as a means to cope with stress is advantageous, if not essential, for everyone. Art therapy is a proven way to do just this.

Origins of Art Therapy

The seeds of this discipline took root as early as the field of professional psychology itself. At the turn of the twentieth century, Freud and Jung engaged several of their patients in drawing to better understand several psychological disorders through the visual expression of their emotions. But it was the work of Margaret Naumburg, an American art teacher and director of Walden Art School, who found the use of art a powerful form of therapeutic communication for several

children she taught. Naumburg observed that self-expression through spontaneous art became a psycho-therapeutic treatment in its own right. With the backing and assistance of her colleague, Dr. Nolan Lewis, she conducted research involving children classified with problem or troublesome behaviors at the New York State Psychiatric Unit. Her first findings were published in 1947; however, it took several more years for her theory to take root. Naumburg's theory dealt primarily with the unconscious expression of nonverbal thoughts as an important tool in psychoanalysis. She proposed that with the interpretive help of a therapist, the patients' artwork would aid in their own treatment and recovery.

A second theory, developed by art teacher Edith Kramer in 1971, suggested that the process of drawing itself was therapeutic, and that more attention should be given to the creative, cathartic process than to the final product, the illustration. Since its inception as a discipline, many theories have been added to the study of art therapy, based on the foundation by Naumberg and Kramer. The role of the art therapist has also matured in this evolution. Originally seen as the primary vehicle for interpretation of the artist's work, the art therapist is now viewed as a blend of artist, therapist, and teacher. The art therapist serves as a catalyst to help the artist uncover his or her own meaningful interpretation and to use that interpretation as an awareness tool to further personal growth and development. According to art therapist Eleanor Ulman (1961), the role of an art therapist is "to help people bring out from within themselves a source of motivation—the wish to organize the experience of their inner and outer worlds into a coherent form."

Not until the 1960s did art therapy emerge as its own discipline, with specialists becoming trained and certified in the theoretical basis and application of this type of therapy. In 1969, the American Art Therapy Association was established. Originally, in its most clinical form, art therapy was designed as a diagnostic tool used by art therapists and psychologists to understand personality development and self-expression of patients with clinical disorders. In the late 1970s and early 1980s, however, art therapy became recognized and accepted as a coping technique for all individuals to increase self-awareness as well as act as an outlet for emotional expression. Currently, the benefits of visual expression through various art media are acknowledged for everyone. To date, research in the field of art therapy consists mostly of clinical case studies—that is, individuals, who, in their recovery process, have attained a breakthrough in self-discovery through creative art. Conventional wisdom indicates that art therapy initiates a stronger partnership between the nonverbal, artistic, and spatial right-brain functions and the analytical, logical, and verbal left-brain functions. With the evidence gathered from split-brain research, it has now become obvious that the optimal human potential involves balance and integration of the right and left cognitive functions of the brain. As the discipline of art therapy continues to expand beyond the clinical setting, a greater understanding of its benefits will be realized.

You may think that coloring books are just for kids, but art therapy has gone mainstream with the popularity of coloring books designed specifically for adults. What was once considered a trend in the mid-2000s has now become a fixture in offices where employees are striving for work–life balance and detoxing from staring at computer screens all day. The most popular coloring books include mandalas, and people are encouraged to go "outside the lines." Although art therapy experts claim that coloring books are a watered-down version of art therapy ("art therapy lite"), their relaxation effects are well recognized, including reduced anxiety levels (Fitzpatrick, 2016) (**FIG. 12.2**).

Today, art therapy is recognized for its many therapeutic effects on aspects of mental, physical, spiritual, and, most notably, emotional well-being. Art therapists agree that there are several goals associated with this technique to enhance the healing process and well-being. As described by art therapist Myra Levick (1983), these include:

1. *To provide a means for strengthening the ego:* To allow a better sense of identity through discovery of personal interests and growth issues

2. *To provide a cathartic experience:* To let emotions that have an immobilizing effect be released in the physical act of creating personal expression through art

3. *To provide a means to uncover anger:* To employ the use of colors and shapes to express and detect feelings of aggression

4. *To offer an avenue to reduce guilt:* By conveying inner thoughts of past feelings and behavior associated with the guilt process

5. *To facilitate impulse control:* To allow freedom of self-expression, rather than its repression, through a positive behavior

6. *To help patients/clients use art as a new outlet during incapacitating illness:* To use art as a tool to strengthen the mind-body connection by using various art media to augment the imagery aspect of self-healing

Clinical Use of Art Therapy

Art therapy, primarily drawing and illustration, has been employed in many settings, including drug rehabilitation centers, eating-disorder clinics, veterans' hospitals, clinics for the emotionally disturbed, prisons, and oncology (cancer) hospital wards. Often, the manifestations of physical and emotional problems inhibit people in the verbal expression of their feelings. Yet, without some type of communication or self-expression, the progress of healing is stifled. Art therapy serves to break through this barrier. The dichotomy of hemispheric cognitive functions, revealed through split-brain research, has validated the concept that verbal communication is only one way to express our innermost thoughts. Feelings of anger, depression, fear, grief, guilt, and worry, when expressed in graphic form, begin to release residual toxins of these thoughts from the depths of the unconscious mind. In guided art therapy, drawings are either directed—themes or guidelines are suggested by the art therapist—or spontaneous, with the freedom to draw whatever comes to mind, to help release suppressed or toxic feelings.

FIGURE 12.2   Adults are rediscovering what young kids have known all along; coloring books can be stress relievers. Adult coloring books, particularly mandalas, are more than a passing trend, they have become a popular coping technique for stress.

FIGURE 12.3 A simple drawing of a tree can indicate a great many things about someone and his or her level of self-esteem.

Every mark, every spot, and every line drawn, painted, or sketched is considered an extension of the individual's mind. Through repeated analysis and interpretation of the works created by a host of patients from every conceivable background and with every health-related problem, some recurring archetypal images appear to represent specific parts of one's personality. For example, trees (FIG. 12.3) are thought to represent energy levels or a perspective on one's life. A full, leafy tree with a broad trunk is indicative of vibrant energy and strong-willed nature, while a barren, skinny tree suggests frailty, lack of hope, perhaps even death. Houses may represent either security or imprisonment, depending on the size of windows, doors, and the location of people in the setting. All images have importance, just as all aspects of each image convey a special meaning to the person who drew the picture (Asperheim, 1982). The recognition of this importance reveals various aspects of one's psychic landscape. And, as much can be revealed by what is not drawn as by what is pictorially represented. For instance, in self-portraits, people who draw faces with no mouths or ears suggest an inability to express their feelings verbally. Long arms may express a desire to reach out for help or affection. Short arms may signify feelings of withdrawal. Short necks indicate stubbornness. Boxed shoulders hint of the inability to let matters roll off the back.

Nonverbal expression: Many thoughts and feelings cannot be expressed verbally, giving rise to art therapy as a means of nonverbal expression.

According to art therapist Evelyn Virshup (1978), the importance of art therapy is in the process, not necessarily the outcome. The expression of oneself through art far exceeds the aesthetic quality to the viewer: "Someone who is asked to draw how they feel, and is then measured by the yardstick of aesthetics will feel betrayed, and will repress further feelings. Creativity of expression is stifled by judgmental evaluation." A crucial factor in the practice of art therapy is the collaborative verbal description of the picture once it has been drawn. The role of the art therapist is to guide the artist through his or her understanding of each work. This is done by asking open-ended questions such as, What does the picture mean? In many cases, the artist may not overtly recognize the emotional significance of the work (e.g., missing features, significant color selection, or disproportional figures) or may not be quite ready to accept verbally what has been depicted graphically. Art therapists suggest that, upon completion of the drawing, the artist try to explain what the figure represents, perhaps even to write it down on the corner of the drawing. This serves to balance the **nonverbal expression** with the verbal expression and further the communication process of the conscious and unconscious minds. This combination leads to better awareness and comprehension of the situation at hand and the emotions associated with it (FIG. 12.4).

In 1971, a radiation oncologist named Carl Simonton formulated a concept for cancer patients involving, among other things, the integration of mental imagery and art therapy. In a pioneer program to teach cancer patients to take an active role in their own recovery, Simonton and his then-wife Stephanie designed a strategic approach to attack cancer from all sides—mentally, physically, emotionally, and spiritually—with a host of progressive coping and relaxation techniques. In perhaps the most significant plank to bridge the fields of alternative and modern medicine, mental imagery and art therapy were employed as complementary tools to fight cancer cells and help rejuvenate the body (Simonton, 1978).

On the premise that people must take active responsibility for their own health, Simonton asked his patients to imagine a flood of white blood cells attacking and devastating the cancer cells in their bodies. In the creative minds of his patients, the white blood cells took on metaphorical images of armies of white knights in shining armor or schools of great white sharks in confrontation with their prey. Simonton had several patients draw pictures of these images to reinforce the power of visualization. Additional pictures were drawn at various stages of their

FIGURE 12.4 The artist drew a picture of herself with some health issues (sore neck and hands) explaining that she was "experiencing some physical limitations yet I plan to do some more activities such as hiking and swimming" (left). Her second illustration (right), drawn weeks later, reveals a new direction and energy in her life, with good things on the horizon.

illnesses. The progression of visual images gave striking evidence of the patients' attitudes toward their disease and their willingness to attempt to either augment the healing process through enhanced willpower and positive attitudes (with some cases of "terminal" cancer going into remission) or remain passive, even helpless, victims.

In her pioneering work, Kübler-Ross (1981) also used art as a therapeutic tool with children who had cancer. Those with a limited vocabulary but total lack of inhibition about drawing were able to express a multitude of feelings surrounding the many progressions of the death process. Kübler-Ross found that the utilization of illustrations and sketches by terminally ill children served as a phenomenal coping technique toward the resolution of the emotional and spiritual stress associated with this traumatic experience. She believes that self-expression through art has the potential to become a vehicle to promote wholeness in the individual.

Using an approach similar to Simonton's and Kübler-Ross's, physician Bernie Siegel (1986) also employed art therapy among his cancer patients. Whereas most physicians have their patients first fill out medical-history questionnaires, Siegel handed out blank sheets of white paper and boxes of crayons and asked individuals to draw themselves in their current state of health or disease. According to Siegel, mental imagery in the form of art therapy is more useful than a battery of laboratory tests to assess a patient's disease state and prospects for recovery (**FIG. 12.5**). He adds that the analysis of these illustrations is one of the most accurate tools in determining the prognosis of disease and, potentially, the development of other health-related problems.

As a general surgeon with a speciality in oncology, Siegel was struck by several factors hinting at which patients would succumb to their disease and which would defy the odds of terminal cancer. Those who seemed to grab the bull by the horns and took responsibility for their recovery he referred to as exceptional cancer patients (ECaP). More specifically, critical factors included willpower, humor, hope, and love, all of which were

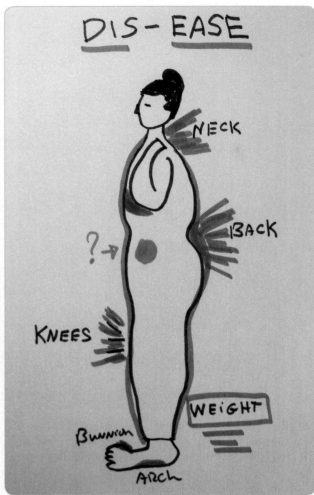

FIGURE 12.5 Choosing the theme of illness (stress and disease), this woman made an immediate connection between her emotions and various physical ailments, even labeling her illustration "Dis-Ease."

represented in some aspect of the patients' illustrations. Not all of his patients had this exceptional ability, and their drawings often foreshadowed imminent death. In the spirit of Jung, Siegel soon came upon the realization that messages from the unconscious mind manifest in symbolic images and characteristics. These images accentuate the patient's fears, anger, levels of self-esteem, grief, guilt, and the intensity of the personal problems

Post-traumatic stress disorder (PTSD): The mental, emotional, and physical repercussions experienced after an extremely stressful experience (e.g., war combat, natural disasters, rape and sexual abuse, car accidents).

and conflicts that ultimately pave the path to disease. In one illustration, a patient drew herself at the extreme right-hand, bottom corner of the page, leaving the rest of the paper blank. This was interpreted to suggest low self-esteem, which was later confirmed by the artist. In a similar episode, a young boy drew only the top half of his body over the entire page, leaving the physician curious and frightened. The young boy then turned the page over to reveal the bottom half, hinting that recovery was well on its way—and putting a huge smile on Siegel's face.

Although there are exceptions, there is a consensus among art therapists that regardless of gender, nationality, or ethnic upbringing, each color in art therapy represents an archetypal meaning. Typically, the color selection as well as the objects drawn (e.g., house, tree) parallel emotional expressions of one's mental health. The following list suggests associations between colors and their archetypal meanings:

Red: passionate emotional peaks (from pleasure to pain); can represent either compassion or anger

Orange: life change (big or small)

Yellow: energy (usually a positive message)

Blue and green: happiness and joy (blue may even mean creativity)

Purple/violet: highly spiritual nature; unconditional love

Brown (and earth-tone colors): a sense of groundedness and stability

Black: (1) grief, despair, or fear or (2) a sense of personal empowerment

White: (1) fear, avoidance, or coverup or (2) hope

Gray: ambiguity or uncertainty

Although cancer patients have received the most publicity from their use of art therapy as a coping technique, art therapists have also used this tool in the awareness and recovery process of other stress-related problems, including migraine headaches (**FIG. 12.6**), gastrointestinal problems, anorexia, and post-traumatic stress disorders of patients surviving the atrocities of war. The creation of sketches and sculptures has been a significant tool in the treatment of Vietnam veterans with **post-traumatic stress disorder (PTSD)** as described by J. Horgan (1988) in *Scientific American*. Horgan reported that many former soldiers were still held prisoner by the haunting memories of death and carnage, leaving them emotionally immobilized after returning home. But through the introduction of this type of therapy,

FIGURE 12.6   An example of art therapy used to treat migraine headache. Notice no mouth is drawn in this illustration (supporting the concept of the somatizer).

veterans found a tremendous sense of relief through transferring their destructive images from the depths of their minds onto paper, canvas, or clay. Although not particularly anxious to talk about their war experiences, the vets used their illustrations and sculptures as an outlet to help vanquish the emotions associated with their traumatic experiences and to initiate one facet of the healing and growth process. Art therapy for Vietnam veterans has proved so successful that in 1981 an art museum in Chicago was established for Vietnam vets to exhibit their work. Efforts have been made with similar art therapy programs involving Iraq war veterans, as noted by *Washington Post* reporter Jackie Spinner (2007).

The treatment of self-mutilation and eating disorders, particularly anorexia nervosa, has also included art therapy as a part of the process. In these conditions, the patient often feels helpless to control his or her existing environment and identity. Perceptions of stress are turned inward and manifested through a process of slow physical self-destruction. Inner conflicts regarding control issues are manifested through significant weight loss, which is paralleled by a distorted body image. In

a study conducted at Goldsmiths College employing art therapy with anorexics (Levick, 1983), it was noted that the subjects rarely drew human figures. When they were drawn, however, they showed adolescent characteristics suggesting a denial of adult responsibilities and physical maturation. Paintings and sketches by patients often depicted images of isolation and loneliness; in one case, a subject drew herself as a cactus. Progress was noted when subjects began to represent their true physical conditions—that is, they drew themselves in human form. Art as a means of self-expression by anorexic patients was perceived to help increase self-awareness by opening the lines of communication within the individual, thus acknowledging strengths and weaknesses, and an increased comfort with both.

In the immediate aftermath of September 11, 2001, when schools reopened in New York City (and even other districts nationwide), students were invited to express and share their level of stress by drawing their thoughts, feelings, and images on paper as a cathartic exercise to relieve emotional suffering, much of which could not be articulated by words alone (Flatow, 2002). Schoolteachers in and around military bases are known to often use art therapy with grade-school and middle-school children during military conflicts and natural disasters such as the 2010 earthquake that devastated Haiti. Students are asked to draw their feelings regarding the respective wars and their parents' involvement. Typically, the drawings reveal fears of abandonment, detachment, sorrow, and loneliness. The bottom line is that everyone, regardless of their personal experiences, can benefit from art therapy.

Just as much can be revealed by a picture, much can also be revealed by casual doodles, the kind that accompany lecture notes, decorate grocery lists, or are scribbled on paper napkins (**FIG. 12.7**). Psychologist Robert Burns has researched the meanings of doodles only to find that they are another form of art therapy. Doodles are nonverbal messages that surface from the unconscious mind, each doodle or mark important in its own right. Often, doodles are symbols of thoughts, feelings, and perceptions in visual form. Although the understanding of "doodling" is in its infancy, several observations have been made by Burns (Jaret, 1991). Aggression is often expressed in dark, heavy, jagged lines with arrows or points. Horizontal lines convey inner peace. Happiness is typically represented by soft, curvy lines. Burns discovered that men typically draw geometric shapes—squares, triangles,

FIGURE 12.7 Doodles may not seem like a form of therapy, but they, too, reveal what cannot be expressed verbally.

FIGURE 12.8 This illustration was drawn by a student who saw herself as having high self-esteem. The fish represents beauty and freedom. The color orange represents a major life change (the artist was a graduating senior) and the green plant (stability) with four leaves represented four job offers she had received.

circles—whereas women tend to sketch faces. Like the conscious effort to draw a graphic representation of our feelings, unconscious doodling also conveys important messages about the internal landscape (**FIG. 12.8**).

> **Artistic roadblocks:** The perceived inability to express oneself though creative expression (often based on fear).

■ Steps to Initiate Art Therapy

The beauty of art therapy is that anyone can participate and its significant therapeutic effect benefits not only cancer patients, but anyone experiencing the signs and symptoms of perceived stress. In this case, as with other coping and relaxation techniques, the word *therapy* does not reflect weakness or needing help. Rather, art therapy serves to augment understanding of the personal awareness and resolution process. Art therapy appears to trigger a progression of two responses. The first is a cathartic effect, whereby you can release pent-up emotions and thoughts from your mind onto paper (or clay). The second is a greater sense of personal awareness based on an objective look at or interpretation of the artwork—that is, the message it suggests or implies. This interpretation or awareness is often a communication from the unconscious mind regarding less-than-obvious symbolic images. Although an interpretation can be helpful in the self-awareness process, without some prior knowledge or assistance, meaning could also be overlooked, mistaken, or misconstrued. Thus, there are several factors to consider to ensure the effectiveness of this technique, including **artistic roadblocks**, materials, illustrative themes, and interpretation.

Artistic Roadblocks

The most common reaction people have to art therapy is, "I can't draw!" The truth is, everyone can draw, in a way specific to their own talents and abilities. A case in point is Irishman Christie Brown. A paraplegic without use of his hands because of cerebral palsy, he painted with his left foot. Many people are hesitant to draw out of embarrassment. But in art therapy it doesn't matter what your abilities are. Whether your creative talents are best described as third-grade stick figures or are undisputed re-creations of Monet and Rembrandt, it makes no difference. Abstract images, fine-detailed sketches, simple lines, colors, and shapes are all equally important. Art therapy is noncompetitive. There is no right or wrong. With this obstacle out of the way, you're ready to give it a try.

Materials

Opinions vary greatly on the choice of medium recommended for art therapy. The one factor agreed upon is that there should be a wide assortment of colors to allow full expression. Art therapists generally agree that the best medium is colored pastels, as they are the easiest to work with for both broad strokes and fine lines. Siegel, on the other hand, advocates crayons. Crayons not only come in all colors of the rainbow, says Siegel, but they bring out the child in the artist, a characteristic that promotes familiar receptivity to this medium. While pastels and crayons are preferred, colored pencils can also be used. Virshup advocates the availability of all media, including string dipped in paint and dragged across the paper. The purpose behind all these media is to have as wide a variety of colors as possible, so pen and pencil are not advocated but in a pinch will suffice. Finger paints have been used with children, and modeling clay has also been shown to be effective for this technique. Paper selection is a less problematic decision. Art therapists highly recommend the economical blank newsprint (18" × 24"); Siegel suggests a white sheet of paper; however, any type of paper in most any size will suffice. Once you have these materials, all you need is an idea and some inspiration to put pastel or crayon in your hand and draw.

Illustrative Themes

When art therapy is used as a coping technique to deal with stress, there is a host of themes and concepts providing inspiration to choose from. One approach is just to start drawing (anything) until you achieve some level of comfort with this technique. Other themes are more specific to events, feelings, or situations that words seem inadequate to describe. I have tried (with much success) the following themes in my classes:

1. *Art therapy images:* Introductory art therapy sessions are typically initiated with two or three themes such as:

   a. *Draw something that represents you.* This could be a symbol of yourself; a picture of something you identify yourself with, such as your profession, family, hobbies, home; or something that gives you inner strength.

   b. *Draw two fantasy animals.* Draw whichever two animals come to mind, even creations of animals that do not exist on the planet. Then, describe the animals you have drawn in a few words (approximately three adjectives) on the back of the paper (from Virshup's art therapy workshop).

   c. *Close your eyes and draw a line on the paper.* Make the line any shape—straight, curved, jagged, fuzzy, or thin, whatever strikes your fancy, but keep your eyes closed while you draw. Next, open your eyes and take a look at

FIGURE 12.9 This illustration was drawn by a student who chose the theme in which one closes one's eyes, draws a line, and then opens the eyes and turns the paper around slowly until an image comes to mind. In this case, the student completed the illustration by drawing a Santa Fe fresco in the likeness of the Virgin Mary.

what you see. You can rotate the paper around slowly until something strikes the fancy of your creative eye. Then, complete the drawing (FIG. 12.9). Make something out of the line you drew. Give the line meaning. Do with it whatever comes to mind (FIG. 12.10).

2. *Healing images:* Although art therapy has been used extensively with cancer patients, many other diseases and symptoms can be represented on paper. The following themes are ideas to enhance positive internal image, body awareness, and mental imagery.

   a. *Draw yourself.* Sketch an image of yourself in a state of perfect health.

A

B

FIGURE 12.10   (A) Up from the unconscious comes a message of planetary healing as the earth is cradled by an external force. "The image that initially appeared was the classic figure of a young woman, as I let loose with quick orange strokes. As she emerged, the earth image felt needed—the blue circle/drum, then the need to offer healing, the desire to put in the breath and the Scandinavian herbal bundle as well. As I drew this, I started to cry." (B) Angered by all the cyber-noise (cacophony), this person drew himself "in the age of TRON," frustrated by the brave new, noisy world he finds himself in. "These days I cannot think for myself," he added.

b. *Draw a picture of a part of your body you feel needs special attention.* Draw an area that you feel is perhaps a target organ of stress, one that shows signs of excessive wear and tear, or a part of your body that does not feel completely whole—for example, a headache, sore back, stomach cramps, clenched teeth. On another sheet of paper (or the back side), draw an image of this same body region fully healed. Use your imagination to restore this image to health through metaphor (e.g., a sock completely darned to represent a healed stomach ulcer).

3. *Mental images:* Art therapy can be a vehicle for mental imagery also. The images drawn provoke the mind to wander. For example:

a. *Draw a peaceful image.* Draw an image that makes you feel relaxed just by thinking about it. It can be a place you have been to that you would like to return to, if only on paper. It can also be a place you have never been to but have always wanted to go.

b. *Draw how you feel right now.* What emotion(s) are you feeling now? Anger, fear, guilt, worry, love, joy, peace? What does your anger look

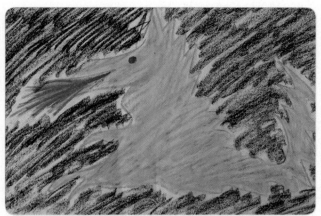

FIGURE 12.11 I created the dragon image first as an image that represented fear. (Workbook p. 111, #1. "Draw an expression of how you feel when you are either angry or afraid.") Then I chose "draw anything" and a beautiful flower emerged. (Workbook p. 111, #10 "Draw whatever you wish!"). When I looked at them together, to me the flower represented love overcoming fear (dragon).

like to you? How would you illustrate your feelings of love? Try to visualize your emotions on paper (**FIG. 12.11**).

c. *Draw a dream image.* Try to include whatever fragments of a particular dream you can recall. Include the use of colors.

Interpretations

Interpretations are the hardest component of art therapy. They are difficult because there is wide latitude for impressions and understanding the figures, colors, shapes, and sizes that have made their way onto paper. Jung once said that the most important factor in dream analysis is the patient's impressions because dreams are the creation of the dreamer. Drawings and sketches are no different when it comes to interpretation. As a cathartic experience, interpretations of drawings are secondary to simply getting feelings down on paper.

Art therapists, and even psychologists who now use art therapy in their practices, engage in a fair amount of training to understand the commonalities, expressions of colors, and a host of other components of drawings (www.arttherapy.org). When interpreting the colors you have chosen, be careful to keep in mind both the context of the illustration and mood you were in when you drew the picture. For example, black is often used to represent death or grief, but for an African American, the color may also symbolize pride.

Interpretation is the search for understanding as the unconscious mind communicates to the conscious mind thoughts and feelings best described through a visual medium. In all art therapy sessions, patients are encouraged to explain their drawings to members of their group. Members, in turn, ask questions that may aid the artist in understanding his or her drawing. If done alone, a written description of the work helps with this process. But caution should be used when trying to interpret the meaning of your own artwork. First, go for the obvious. In the words of Freud, "Sometimes a cigar is just a cigar."

■ Best Application of Art Therapy

Art is a nonverbal expression of one's thoughts and feelings—expression that is not only necessary, but also therapeutic. There are many circumstances, in times of both ecstasy and torment, in which words do not adequately describe the full extent of our emotions. These are the times to employ art therapy. Remember that emotional well-being is defined as the ability to feel and positively express the full range of human emotions. Everyone, regardless of their levels of stress or chaotic life situations, can benefit from the use and practice of art therapy. As crazy as it may sound, keeping a box of crayons or colored pencils in your desk drawer is as important as having an address book or weekly planner (**FIG. 12.12**). If you don't have art supplies, it might be a good idea to obtain them (**FIG. 12.13**). And remember, pictures don't have to be masterpieces. They can start off as doodles.

FIGURE 12.12 Selecting the theme: Close your eyes and draw a line, then open your eyes and finish the drawing, this person saw vitality and energy in the form of a dancer, expressing a freedom of movement, a feeling reinforced with color selection.

FIGURE 12.13 You don't have to be an artist to do art therapy. It's not about talent; it's about allowing the unconscious mind to speak through colors and images.

SUMMARY

- Art as a means of self-expression dates back to antiquity. Art therapy has its roots in Freudian and Jungian psychology, where illustrations were used to aid in understanding unconscious thoughts.

- In 1969, the American Art Therapy Association was established to educate and certify people in the skills of art therapy. Art therapy has since been introduced into a variety of settings, including counseling centers, hospitals, and addiction treatment centers, as well as nontraditional settings such as corporate wellness centers. It has proved an effective coping technique for all types of people to get in touch with their emotions in a nonverbal way.

- Art therapy is described as the creative use of art to provide for nonverbal expression and communication through which to foster self-awareness and personal growth.

- Every stroke, every color, every detail has some relevant meaning at the unconscious level.

- There are varying opinions on the use of materials for art therapy, meaning that there is no preferred method. Crayons, pastels, colored pencils, finger paint, and clay are all possibilities. Art therapists do suggest that a wide variety of colors be available. Colors provide specific meaning to thoughts and unconscious messages.

- Art therapists offer a series of themes to explore in this type of nonverbal communication, including a picture of yourself, a fantasy animal, and a house with trees.

STUDY GUIDE QUESTIONS

1. Explain how art therapy is used as an effective coping technique.

2. What archetypal meanings do colors represent or symbolize in art therapy?

3. List several steps that help promote art therapy as a coping technique.

REFERENCES AND RESOURCES

Adamson, E. *Art as Healing*. Coventure, London, 1990.

American Art Therapy Association, 1202 Allanson Road, Mundelein, IL 60060, (708) 949–6064.

Asperheim, J. T. Art Cure: Colors, Shapes, and Images Can Say as Much as Words, *Health* March 1982: 31–32.

The Big Book of Mandalas: Coloring for Everyone. Skyhorse Publishing, New York, 2016.

Boschen, T. Art Therapy Program Will Be Offered to Victim's Kin, *News Transcript*, November 14, 2001. http://news transcript.gmnews.com/News/2001/1114/Front_Page /004.html.

Capacchione, L. *The Creative Journal: The Art of Finding Yourself*. Swallow Press, Athens, GA, 1979.

Cornell, J. *Mandala*. Quest Books, Wheaton, IL, 1994.

Crane, R. R. An Experiment Dealing with Color and Emotion. In C. Levy and E. Ulman (eds.), *Art Therapy Viewpoints*. Schocken Books, New York, 1980.

Dalley, T. (ed.). *Art as Therapy*. Tavistock, New York, 1984.

Farrelly-Hansen, M. *Spirituality and Art Therapy: Living the Connection*. Jessica Kingsley, London, 2001.

Fink, P. J. Art as a Language, *Journal of Albert Einstein Medical Center* 15:143–150, 1967.

Fitzpatrick, K. Why Adult Coloring Books Are Good for You. CNN Health, January 6, 2016. http://www.cnn .com/2016/01/06/health/adult-coloring-books-popularity -mental-health/.

Flatow, I. Talk of the Nation: Science Friday: Psychological Effects of 9-11, *National Public Radio*, September 6, 2002. www.npr .org/templates/story/story. php?storyId=1149527.

Franklin, M. Becoming a Student of Oneself: Activating the Witness in Meditation, Art, and Super-vision, *American Journal of Art Therapy* 38(1):2–13, 1999.

Ganim, B. *Art and Healing: Using Expressive Art to Heal Your Body, Mind, and Spirit*. Three Rivers Press, New York, 1999.

Gin, S. Draw Me How You Feel, paper presented at the American University, Washington, DC, Nov. 20, 1992.

Harms, E. The Development of Modern Art Therapy, *Leonardo* 8:241–244, 1975.

Horgan, J. Rx: Art; Drawing or Sculpturing Can Help Traumatized Vietnam Veterans, *Scientific American* June 1988:38.

Jaret, P. How Do You Doodle? *Health* 5(2):34–37, 1991.

Jung, C. G. *Man and His Symbols*. Anchor Press, New York, 1963.

Kramer, E. S. *Art as Therapy with Children*. Schocken Books, New York, 1971.

Kramer, E. S. The History of Art Therapy in a Large Mental Hospital, *American Journal of Art Therapy* 21:75–84, 1982.

Kramer, E. On Quality in Art and Art Therapy, *American Journal of Art Therapy* 40:218–222, 2002.

Kübler-Ross, E. Keynote Address, American Holistic Medicine Association Conference, LaCrosse, WI, 1981.

Levick, M. *They Could Not Talk So They Drew*. Charles C. Thomas, Springfield, IL, 1983.

Levy, C., and Ulman, E. (eds.). *Art Therapy Viewpoints*. Shocken Books, New York, 1980.

Lusebrink, V. B. Art Therapy and the Brain, *Journal of the American Art Therapy Association* 21(3):125–135, 2004.

Malchiodi, C. *Art Therapy Sourcebook*, 2nd ed. McGraw-Hill, New York, 2006.

Malchiodi, C. *The Soul's Palette: Drawing on Art's Transformative Powers*. Shambhala Press, Boston, 2002.

McKim, R. *Experiences in Visual Thinking*. Brooks/Cole, Pacific Grove, CA, 1972.

McNiff, S. *Art Heals: How Creativity Cures the Soul*. Shambhala Press, Boston, 2004.

Mills, J. C., and Crowley, R. J. *Therapeutic Metaphors for Children and the Children Within*. Brunner/Mazel, New York, 1986.

Moon, C. H. *Studio Art Therapy*. Jessica Kingsley, Philadelphia, 2002.

National Vietnam Veterans Art Museum. About Us. www.nvvam.org/aboutus/index.htm.

Naumburg, M. *Dynamically Oriented Art Therapy: Its Principles and Practice*. Grune and Stratton, New York, 1966.

Rhyne, J. *The Gestalt Art Experience*. Brooks/Cole, Monterey, CA, 1973.

Robbins, A. (ed.). *The Artist as Therapist*. Human Sciences Press, New York, 1987.

Rubin, J. *Child Art Therapy*. Van Nostrand Reinhold, New York, 1978.

Searle, Y., and Steng, I. *Where Analysis Meets the Arts*. Karnac Books, New York, 2001.

Shovlin, K. J. Discovering a Narrative Voice through Play and Art Therapy: A Case Study, *Guidance and Counseling* 14(4):7–11, 1999.

Siegel, B. *Love, Medicine, and Miracles*. Harper & Row, New York, 1986.

Simonton, O. C., Mathews-Simonton, S., and Creighton, J. *Getting Well Again*. Bantam Books, New York, 1978.

Spinner, J. War's Pain, Softened With a Brush Stroke: VA's Art Therapy Eases Battle Stresses, *Washington Post*, Sunday, April 15, 2007, page C01. www.washingtonpost.com/wp-dyn/content/article/2007/04/14/AR2007041401246.html.

Stepney, S. *Art Therapy with Students at Risk*. Charles C. Thomas Publisher, Springfield, IL, 2001.

Sutherland, J. I. Art Therapy with a Woman Who Has Multiple Medical Conditions, *American Journal of Art Therapy* 37(3):84–98, 1999.

Swenson, A. Relationships, Art Education, Art Therapy, and Special Education, *Perceptual and Motor Skills* 72:40–42, 1991.

Taylor, P. Art as Psychotherapy, *American Journal of Psychotherapy* February 1950:599–605.

Ulman, E. Art Therapy: Problems of Definition, *Bulletin of Art Therapy* 1:10–12, 1961.

Virshup, E. *Right-Brain People in a Left-Brain World*. Guild of Tutors Press, Los Angeles, 1978.

CHAPTER 13

Humor Therapy (Comic Relief)

A good laugh and a long nap are the two best cures for anything.

—Irish Proverb

In 1964, a man admitted himself to a hospital for severe pain throughout his entire body. After a series of tests, he was diagnosed with a rare rheumatoid disease called ankylosing spondylitis, a progressive deterioration of the body's connective tissue. Chances for recovery were predicted to be roughly one in five hundred; the disease was quite advanced. Like most people, **Norman Cousins** decided to learn all he could about the etiology of his disease. He soon discovered that there is a strong correlation between stress, particularly negative perceptions and emotions, and his specific disease. So, the question occurred to him: If negative emotions such as guilt, worry, and anxiety are thought to be related to, and perhaps even promote, disease, is it possible for positive emotions to maintain health, or even restore one's health? He came to the conclusion that to increase his chances of recovery, he had to assume responsibility for his treatment. And that he did. He had nothing to lose.

With a defiant determination to recover and the support of his personal physician, Cousins checked out of the hospital and into a nearby hotel. He acquired copies

of humorous movies and TV shows, including those of Laurel and Hardy and the Marx Brothers. One of his friends, Alan Funt, even sent some classic clips from his hit TV show *Candid Camera*. Cousins later wrote in his now-famous book *Anatomy of an Illness* that "ten minutes of laughter allowed two hours of pain-free sleep." After a time, he checked out of the hotel and went home; his disease had gone into remission. On the advice of his doctor, Cousins (1978) wrote up his story as a case history for the *New England Journal of Medicine*. Although he attributed his successful healing process to several factors, including large doses of vitamin C, the interpretation by those who read the article was

Norman Cousins (1915–1990): An author of the classic book *Anatomy of an Illness* (1976), he used humor to help heal himself from a serious disease and brought the importance of humor to the national consciousness in terms of mind-body-spirit healing, paving the way for the field of psychoneuroimmunology.

that Cousins literally laughed himself back to health. The man who is credited with revealing the positive side of psychosomatic medicine and validating the psychoneuroimmunology (PNI) movement often closed his speaking events on the healing power of humor with these words: "The more serious the illness, the more important it is for you to fight back, mobilizing all your resources—spiritual, emotional, intellectual, physical."

Norman Cousins's story is now just one of many supporting the idea that positive emotions do indeed have healing effects on health. However, it was this single case study of comic relief, perhaps more than any other, that paved the road to a whole new field of study called PNI, and Cousins will always be remembered for his generous contribution to it. What has been learned since his hospital discharge is that positive emotions play an incredible role in maintaining the health of the human body. Humor therapy, or comic relief, is the use of humor to promote well-being through positive thoughts, attitudes, and emotions by counterbalancing the deleterious effects of negative thoughts, perceptions, and emotions on one's health. Humor as a coping technique is not a panacea for all ills, but it does provide benefits in a bad situation, whether in a hospital bed or outside a locked car, with your keys still in the ignition. Upon the death of legendary comic Bob Hope, who lived to be 100, his daughter, interviewed on the former talk show *Larry King Live*, noted that comedians and musical composers tend to live longer than most, most likely because of having a positive attitude.

Historical Perspective

Humor is a human magnet: It attracts all ears and minds. And laughter is a universal language, breaking through cultural barriers when words cannot. Cousins certainly was not the first person to use humor as a coping technique. Comic relief has been pondered since men and women first tickled their funny bones. The ancient Greeks held humor as a virtue. The philosopher Plato, for instance, believed humor nurtured the soul, and he advocated its use as a healing practice (Shelley, 2003). From the ancient Greeks came the formulas for theater, including comedy, still used today. And as

far back as Old Testament times, people in the Middle East believed "A merry heart doeth good like a medicine, but a broken spirit drieth the bones" (Proverbs 17:22). In fact, humor as a "healing medicine" can be found at the root of virtually every culture on the globe, from the earliest practices of the native peoples of Africa to those of the Americas. It seems that humor and the viruses it helps to fight are equally contagious.

The word **humor** comes from a Latin word of the same spelling that means "fluid" or "moisture." According to the physiology of the medieval period in Europe (the age of alchemy and potions), there were four basic body fluids, with each "humor" associated with a specific mood or general disposition. Choler, the yellow bile produced by the gallbladder, allegedly made one melancholy and depressed. Similarly, black bile, produced by the kidneys or spleen, was responsible for anger and hostility. A happy, cheerful spirit was associated with blood; while phlegm, produced by the respiratory system, was the reason behind apathy and sluggishness. If any one humor was produced in excess, it was thought to change mood, which put the individual at risk of social ridicule—ergo, the first comedians. If all body fluids were balanced, however, a person was said to be "in good humor." Note, too, that the practice of blood letting, or draining the body of fluids to relieve symptoms and causes of these ailments, was a common practice in the United States as well as Europe until 1850. Sad to say, many a person died from melancholy, and a career as a physician was not looked upon with favor as it is today.

Intrigued with the use of humor as a healing agent, Dr. Raymond Moody surveyed several history books in 1978 to discover the following. In the year 1260, a progressive French physician, Henri de Moundeville, saw the important relationship between positive emotions and sound health, and made a practice of allowing family and friends to cheer and joke with their sick relatives. He wrote, "Let the surgeon take care to regulate the whole regimen of the patient's life for joy and happiness." European monarchs also saw the importance of laughter, and often employed court jesters (those guys with funny shoes) to add mirth to their castle courts. Perhaps the most renowned court jester was Richard Tarlton, who was credited with keeping British Queen Elizabeth I (1533–1603) in better health than did her team of physicians.

But laughter has not always been looked upon with favor. Europeans in the Middle Ages and Puritans on the eastern shores of North America, among others,

> **Humor:** A perception of something funny or comical; not a mood, but a perception that can trigger a feeling or mood of joy and happiness.

perceived laughter to be the work of the devil. People caught laughing out loud were often denounced as witches or believed to be possessed by Satan. The expression of humor was considered a sin in many Christian denominations. Other comments from those days about laughter (Moody, 1978):

> Laughter on any occasion is immoral and indecent.
> Laughter obscures truth, hardens the heart, and stupefies understanding.
> A man of parts of fashion is therefore only seen to smile, but never heard to laugh.
>
> —Lord Chesterfield, 1748

And if you look at the portraits of European nobility commissioned over a period of several hundred years, you are hard-pressed to find anyone smiling (except perhaps the Mona Lisa).

The words "say cheese" were not coined for use with the first camera in the nineteenth century, either; people were afraid of being caught sinning in public (**FIG. 13.1**). In fact, according to Allen Klein (1989), it was not until the twentieth century that people would risk a smile in a photograph.

Social norms are often influenced by figures of authority, so humor scholars have turned to the American presidency, a high-stress job, to observe the use of humor in the Oval Office. Lincoln was reported to use humorous stories in his political speeches and even read jokes to his cabinet during the Civil War period. Jimmy Carter once said to reporters at a press-conference dinner, "I'm not going to say anything important, so you can put your crayons away." When Ronald Reagan, a politician known for his sense of humor, was brought to George Washington University Medical Center hospital after the assassination attempt on his life, he turned to the assembled medical team and said, "I hope you're all Republicans." And when Dan Quayle's father said that his son studied only "booze and broads" in college, presidential candidate George H. W. Bush was heard to reply, "Not many students had a double major." President Clinton's jokes we cannot print in this book. And George W. Bush readily admits that it takes him 2 hours to watch *60 Minutes*. It appears that humor helps in the stressful role as president, too. Even President Obama has a sense of humor. When asked about the interest his teen daughters had in the former boy band the Jonas Brothers, he said, "I have two words for the Jonas Brothers: Predator drones."

Times have changed since the days of Victorian prudery. With the help of the American and European

FIGURE 13.1 Because laughing and smiling were thought to be sins at the turn of the last century, no one did so in front of a camera for fear of being blackmailed with the proof.

entertainment industries, from vaudeville to Hollywood to television, the use of humor has gained wide acceptance throughout the world as a prominent factor in enhancing positive emotions. Slow to join this opinion until it had undisputable proof, the medical community now also accepts humor as a viable technique for health promotion and wellness. And it is Norman Cousins we have to thank for validating the use of humor as an authentic therapy in its own right.

Humor and comic relief are no less important now than when Cousins first checked into the hospital decades ago. Some would say that given the state of the world today, the need for comic relief is at an all-time high. Perhaps for this reason, a study was conducted in England in 2002 to determine the funniest joke—ever! A multitude of submissions were sent via email from around the world and screened by a group of "experts." The following joke was selected as one of the winners:

> Famed fictional detective Sherlock Holmes and his gruff assistant Dr. Watson pitch their tent while on a camping trip. In the middle of the night, Holmes nudges Watson to wake him up.
>
> **Holmes**: Watson, look up at the stars and tell me what you deduce.
>
> **Watson**: I see millions of stars. And if there are millions of stars, even if a few of those have planets, it is quite likely there are some planets like earth. And if there are a few planets like earth, then indeed, there might be intelligent life, much like our own, Sir.
>
> **Holmes**: Watson, you idiot, someone stole the tent!

Theories of Humor

For ages, perhaps longer, humankind has tried to understand just what it is that makes somebody laugh. As might be expected, no one answer appeared. To date, there are four major theories to explain the lighter side of human nature, as described by humor scholars Ziv (1984), Goldstein and McGhee (1972), and Bonham (1988). First, according to Steve Allen, Jr. (1990), "Humor is a physical release, one of four, actually. These include crying, yawning, orgasm, and laughter. You can do them in succession, just get the order right." Where appropriate, I have included anonymously credited jokes from Novak and Waldok's *Big Book of American Humor* (1990) to illustrate these theories.

Superiority Theory

Superiority theory, thought to be originated by Plato during the fourth century B.C., is the oldest theory attempting to explain people's affinity for the ridiculous. When laughter occurs at the expense of someone else, as in mockery or ridicule, so that the end result is that the jokester feels better than the object of ridicule, then the reason for laughter illustrates superiority theory (BOX 13.1). To laugh at someone else's misfortunes gives slight, and temporary, comfort to our own condition. Typically, the greater the dignity of the object—for

> **Superiority theory:** First coined by Plato describing the reason why people laugh is at other people's expense.

BOX 13.1   Life in the Fast Lane: American Graffiti

- Just say NO to negativity!
- Money is the root of all evil. (For more information, send $20 to me.)
- Never believe generalizations.
- Be different . . . like everybody else.
- Talk is cheap . . . until you hire a lawyer.
- If pro is the opposite of con, what is the opposite of progress?
- When life hands you gators . . . make Gatorade.
- Vegetarian: American Indian word for "lousy hunter."
- Always try to be modest, and be proud of it!
- Warning: Dates on calendar are closer than they appear.
- Gravity—It's not just a good idea, it's the LAW!
- Duct tape is like the Force. There is a light side and a dark side and it holds the universe together.
- Never knock on Death's door. Ring the bell and run, he hates that.

---

example, Tiger Woods and his sexual escapades, Queen Elizabeth picking her nose in public, and former President George W. Bush reading books upside down to preschoolers—the greater the laugh.

Superiority theory is also said to be the reason for negative and offensive humor. According to Goldstein and McGhee (1972), superiority theory explains aggression-based humor used to define and maintain ego boundaries. It is often used to boost or lower self-esteem, depending on which end of the joke you are on. At the extreme in this category are sarcasm and ethnic, sexist, racist, and even blonde jokes.

Incongruity (Surprise) Theory

On *Saturday Night Live*, parodies of commercials are a part of the format, and sometimes it takes a devoted fan to distinguish the real ads from the fake ones. A classic SNL commercial aired for a "Moms on Facebook" filter; a software program that, in the event your mother "friends" you, converts things you don't want your

BOX 13.2   Comic Relief

A gentleman walks into a bank in New York City and asks for the loan officer. He says he is going to Europe on business for 2 weeks and needs to borrow $5,000.

The bank officer says the bank will need some kind of security for such a loan. So, the gentleman hands over the keys to a new Rolls Royce parked on the street in front of the bank. Everything checks out, and the bank agrees to accept the car as collateral for the loan. An employee drives the Rolls into the bank's underground garage and parks it there.

Two weeks later, the gentleman returns, repays the $5,000 and the interest, which comes to $15.41. The loan officer says, "We are very happy to have had your business, and this transaction has worked out very nicely, but we are a little puzzled. While you were away, we checked you out and found that you are a multimillionaire. What puzzles us is why you would bother to borrow $5,000." The gentleman replies, "Where else in New York can I park my car for 2 weeks for 15 bucks?"

mother to see into bland updates. It even converts the contents of uploaded photos.

Incongruity theory concerns two unrelated thoughts joined for a surprisingly comic effect (BOX 13.2). Humor arises because the mind just doesn't expect the outcome. As eighteenth-century philosopher Immanuel Kant once said, "Laughter is the affliction arising from the sudden transformation of a strained expectation into nothing" (Robinson, 1991).

Ziv (1984) maintains that a surprise in the processing of information can best be described as incongruous, the juxtaposition of two strikingly different concepts (e.g., a Norwegian mariachi player). Oxymorons fall into this category. Humor and creativity are lifetime partners in incongruity theory. Koestler (1964) described this creative thought process as **bisociation**, the catalyst of humor, especially incongruous humor.

There are said to be two types of incongruities: ascending, or "ah ha," which produces wonder and awe, and descending, or "ha ha," which produces humor.

Thus, the incongruity theory is a cognitive-based theory necessitating the intellectual processing of information.

The formation of thoughts that do not fit the mold of pattern recognition trigger either a light-bulb effect or a smile.

Split-brain research on subjects who suffered cerebral strokes indicates that humor is most likely a right-brain function. In a study reported by Vera Robinson (1991), stroke patients with right-brain damage showed no sign of amusement at the punch lines of a series of hundreds of jokes. Incongruity theory suggests that the left brain tries to analyze the joke's contents. When the punch line is revealed, the left brain is stumped and the right brain picks up the meaning, resulting in a laugh. But as Confucius said, "He who laughs last didn't get the joke."

Release/Relief Theory

Release/relief theory suggests that people laugh because they need to release nervous energy built up from repressed thoughts. This theory is credited to Freud. In his study of the psychology of humor, which included works by Mark Twain, Freud asserted that the act of laughter is a physical release or expression of sexual and hostile impulses suppressed by the conscious mind. He believed that the greater the suppression of these thoughts, the greater the laughter in response (BOX 13.3). Thus, humor, Freud postulated, is a reflection of underlying anxieties. Release/relief theory is applied to taboo humor, those subjects that are not socially acceptable in mixed company or professional settings. Freud's theory

BOX 13.3   Comic Relief

Overheard in an airport men's room—a guy talking on his cell phone in a bathroom stall: "Listen, I'm in the middle of some really busy paperwork that can't wait. I'll call you back in a bit. Bye!"

Incongruity theory: A theory that states the reason we laugh is because when two concepts come together in our head and they don't make sense, we get a chuckle.

Bisociation: The ability to perceive two aspects to a situation, in this case, resulting in a laugh.

Release/relief theory: Freud's theory of laughter is based on his concept that all laughter is the result of suppressed sexual tension, thus relieving it through humor.

attempted to explain the popularity of these jokes. Taboo subjects that include sexual references are "dirty jokes," but jokes can come from other social taboos such as illegal drugs and questionable behavior, as shown on the bumper sticker "Cocaine addiction is God's way of saying you make too much money." Freud believed that humor was a "rare and precious gift," and he called it the most advanced defense mechanism. (By the way, Twain was not impressed with this or many other of Freud's theories.)

Divinity Theory

Although recognized intuitively for quite some time, the newest theory of the humor phenomenon is that it strengthens the spiritual nature of humanity. The **divinity theory** suggests that humor is a gift from God. In his book *Humor: God's Gift*, author Tal Bonham supports his theory with a host of anecdotes, from stories in the Bible to well-researched case studies. The same theory is espoused by Cal Samra in his book *The Joyful Christ*. Humor, they believe, makes order out of chaos by dissolving threats (both anger and anxieties) to the ego (FIG. 13.2). Humor can also reveal the naked truth about topics people are often unable to address any other way; in the words of Chaucer, "Many a truth be told in jest." Perhaps most important, humor has an adhesive quality that connects and bonds people together, if only for the duration of a joke, and connectedness is a component of spiritual well-being. This theory is also shared by the Dalai Lama, who advocates laughing and smiling as means to cleanse the spirit.

Humor, as Bonham explains, is God's way of telling us we're not perfect. Laughter and giggling are natural responses by children as they explore life. It is ironic that in a child's first year, parents are elated when the baby smiles and giggles; in fact, these behaviors are strongly encouraged. But as children mature, they are told to wipe the smile off their faces, act their age, and stop laughing. A strong message may be received that the expression of humor isn't appropriate or appreciated, to the detriment of their spiritual development.

There is also a connection between clowns and a divine presence in many cultures spanning the globe. Medicine men and shamans have dressed in funny outfits and

FIGURE 13.2 The divinity theory of humor becomes evident in cartoons like Bizarro.

acted in outrageous ways, which has been, and continues to be, regarded as clownlike in their respective cultures. A similar concept was adopted in Europe with the introduction of clowns in circuses as a form of entertainment. With an androgynous face mask or make-up that was neither male nor female, these people held the mystical power to heal. To this day, clowns still have this appeal and are used in hospital wards, especially in children's hospitals throughout the United States (Miller and Blerkom, 1995). There is even a story that, years ago, in Sunday services held for employees of the Barnum and Bailey Circus, the altar boys were always the circus clowns. Does God have a sense of humor? Most theologians think (and hope) so.

It is quite possible for some of these theories to blend or combine together to explain the laughter response. For example, if the Queen of England were to tell a Polish joke (which she hasn't done), it could be interpreted as an argument for superiority theory. However, laughter could also arise from the incongruity of this sense of humor among royalty, or even the release of anxiety from the perception of ethnic jokes as taboo. Despite the different theories as to why we laugh, one idea is agreed upon: Humor helps us cope with the stress of everyday life.

Divinity theory: The belief that humor is a gift from God.

Types and Senses of Humor

For all the philosophical studies on the topic of humor—and there have been many—there has yet to be consensus on what humor really is. It encompasses so many facets and seems so profoundly complex that it has proved quite difficult to define succinctly. Most experts agree that humor is not itself a positive emotion, but that it can elicit positive emotions, including happiness, joy, love, faith, hope, and willpower. Humor is not a behavior, although it can produce actions (laughter and smiling) that are specific to its nature. Humor is best described as a perception, for as we all know and have experienced, what one person finds funny someone else does not. The following are two definitions to illustrate this elusive perception (McGhee, 1979):

1. Humor is "the mental experience of discovering and appreciating ludicrous or absurd ideas, events, or situations that bring pleasure or enjoyment to the individual."

2. Humor is "the quality of being funny or appreciating funny thoughts or acts of behavior; the ability to perceive/enjoy what is funny or comical, a state of mind, feeling, or mood."

It appears from the definitions that humor has two fundamental aspects. Simply stated, these are give and take. First, humor can be absorbed like a sponge, or experienced by internalizing this perception cognitively. Second, humor can be expressed externally through an action in an effort to share it with others. It is accepted that everyone has a sense of humor, although from your personal experience, you may think you have proof to deny this statement. Among those who have studied humor, McGhee (1979) cites three factors that must be present for humor to exist:

1. Sources that act as potential stimuli (e.g., a pie thrown in someone's face)

2. A cognitive and intellectual activity involved with the perception and evaluation of these sources (perceiving a faceful of whipped cream to be amusing)

3. Behavioral responses that are the expressions of humor (i.e., smiling or laughing)

Types of Humor

Perhaps the reason humor has been so difficult to define is that there are so many shades of it that can be internalized or expressed. Furthermore, types of humor overlap and integrate with each other so that it is hard to separate them out sometimes. Although there are several theories of how humor can be categorized, I list them here in a particular order—parody first and sarcasm last—according to their efficacy at coping with stress. Everything between parody and sarcasm is fairly equal, and powerful in its own way, as either a subtle means to dissolve anger and fear, or to distract attention away from stress long enough for the body to return to homeostasis.

1. *Parody:* **Parody** is a work of humor that closely imitates something, or someone, for comical effect. Parody is typically a verbal or physical expression of humor bringing imperfections to light. This type of humor is considered to be one of the best, if not the best, types of humor to deal with stress, as long as it doesn't sacrifice self-esteem. Exaggerating behaviors and personality traits are examples. Good-natured parody, however, should not be mistaken for self-criticism expressed as an appeal for sympathy. When individuals can begin to parody and laugh at their own shortcomings, in their own minds, it will have the wonderful effect of reducing perceptions of stress. Celebrity "roasts" are probably the best-known parodies. *The Onion*, a national paper, and the former television show *Parks and Recreation* with Amy Poehler are also prime examples of parody.

2. *Satire:* Although satire and parody have many commonalities, **satire** is most often thought of as a written or dramatic expression of personal and social flaws. In the use of satire, many personal, political, and cultural quirks are described and exaggerated for humorous effect. America's most celebrated humorists, Art Buchwald, Erma Bombeck, Tom Robbins, P. J. O'Rourke, Molly Ivins, and Dave Barry, are well known for their styles of satire. Trevor Noah and Stephen Colbert are the epitome of late night political satire. *Saturday Night Live* skits are prime examples of satire, as are the movies *The Circle*, starring

---

Parody: A style of humor where something or someone is made fun of. Self-parody is thought to be the best type of humor to reduce stress.

Satire: A written or dramatic form of parody. Examples include the works of Bill Maher or Louis C.K., and the movie *Zootopia*.

Tom Hanks and Emma Watson, *Get Out*, and *Zootopia*.

3. *Slapstick comedy:* In the early days of American vaudeville, many actors used physical farce to generate laughs (**FIG. 13.3**). Slipping on a banana peel, getting a pie in the face, or reeling from a slap on the cheek was sure to get a rise out of the audience. While banana peels and cream pies were real, face slaps were faked. Behind the curtain stood a person making the sound effects. Originating in the French theater, the slap stick was a piece of leather nailed to a flat board. At the appropriate moment on stage, use of the slap stick would also produce laughs. The Marx Brothers, Laurel and Hardy, Abbott and Costello, the Three Stooges, and Lucille Ball all had their professional roots in American vaudeville. Steve Carrell, Jim Carrey, and Amy Schumer are also well known for their slapstick comedy. Scholars note that **slapstick** comedy is an aggression-based humor through which audience members can release latent anger in a cathartic way (laughing) by watching someone else give and receive physical, yet harmless, blows.

4. *Absurd/nonsense humor:* **Absurd or nonsense humor** is described as two or more concepts that unite to result in a stupid, ludicrous, or ridiculous perception. Cartoonist Gary Larson's cartoon strip *The Far Side* depicting cows driving cars, sharks wearing horn-rimmed glasses, and cheetahs using vending machines on the Serengeti plain are all absurd. John McPherson's *Close to Home* strip conveys the same humor (**FIG. 13.4**). Steven Wright is to stand-up comedy as Gary Larson and Dan Piraro (*Bizarro*)

FIGURE 13.3 Many types of humor (irony, dry humor, even slapstick and bathroom humor) are written into the scripts of the hit show *Modern Family* (with some of the best scenes written for Ty Burrell's character), making the show a widespread hit. Jordan Peele (bottom photo above, left) and Keegan-Michael Key starred in the Comedy Central series *Key & Peele* for five seasons from 2012 to 2015 and continue to add comic relief to popular shows and movies.

Slapstick: Originating from vaudeville, a physical farce such as getting a pie thrown in the face or slipping on a banana peel.

Absurd or nonsense humor: This type of humor is best exemplified by the works of Gary Larson's *The Far Side*. The comedian Steven Wright is also a prime example.

Double entendre: A joke that has two meanings.

are to cartoons, with a brand of absurd humor that has to be heard to be believed. Absurd or nonsense humor is also thought to be a good brand of humor to reduce stress because it acts as a diversion from the inundation of daily stressors. Take Monty Python, for example. Both styles put a gentle chaos back into the order of everyday thinking, making one realize that life shouldn't be taken too seriously.

5. *The double entendre:* The **double entendre** is a type of wordplay where the expression has two meanings (usually of a sexual nature). James Bond movies are filled with these verbal gags. Bumper stickers are

FIGURE 13.4

notorious for these wordplays as well. Even Disney cartoons are written at two levels—for both kids and parents—where each laughs, but for what appears to be different reasons. Double entendres abound in everything from cartoons to political commentaries on Comedy Central. For example, Chris Rock notes that in determining legislation about the legalization of medical marijuana, both houses of Congress went into a joint session. Here is another example, in honor of Earth Day 2011: Clean up the Earth, it's not Uranus!

6. *Black humor:* **Black humor** is not a type of ethnic humor as some people are led to believe. Black, or "gallows," humor is based on the fear of death. It is sometimes described as a "flirtatious brush with death." Death is a common fear among human beings, and one way the human mind has devised to deal with this fear is to poke fun at it, attempting to become more comfortable with the concept, if only momentarily. Typically, during national tragedies, black-humor jokes surface as a way to cope with the gruesome reality of death, as was the case when jokes circulated immediately after the *Columbia* space shuttle explosion in 2003. Some of the best examples of black humor can be found in films and videos like the infamous

Harold and Maude and the more recent *Bad Santa 2, Horrible Bosses 2*, and *Bad Moms*. Much of the comic relief used in the television shows *Scream Queens* and *Fargo* express various shades of black humor. Cartoonists also make light of this phenomenon in their illustrations.

The dead as well as the living seem to have the last laugh, as expressed in the last words of American humorist Dorothy Parker (etched on her tombstone), "Pardon my dust." In a survey of gravestone epitaphs, Louis Schafer (1990) discovered that cemeteries are not devoid of tongue-in-cheek black humor either, as illustrated in the following examples:

John Strange
Here lies an honest lawyer.
This is Strange.

Here lieth the body of Martha Dias
Always noisy, not very pious,
Who lived to the age of three score and ten
And gave to worms what she refused to men.

Here lies John Bun, He was killed by a gun,
His name is not Bun, but Wood,
But Wood would not rhyme with gun, but Bun would.

William Reese
This is what I expected, but not so soon.

Here lies the body of Susan Louder,
who died while drinking a seltzer powder.
Now she's gone to her heavenly rest,
She should have waited till it effervesced.

7. *Irony:* **Irony** is described as two concepts or events, which when paired together, come to mean or expose the opposite of the expected outcome (e.g., "Honk if you love peace and quiet") (FIG. 13.5). Life is full of ironies: receiving a surprise check for one hundred dollars in the mail only to find a credit card bill for one hundred dollars the same day. Bumper stickers, such as "My other car is a broom," often use irony. Irony can also be seen in everyday occurrences such as

Black humor: Humor about death and dying; thought to decrease fear of death.

Irony: A type of humor where the opposite from what was originally expected occurs.

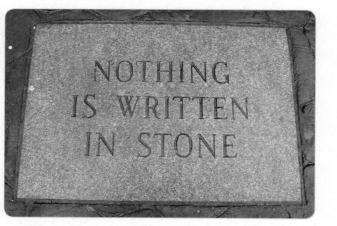

FIGURE 13.5 Humor in the form of irony is abundant in our lives. Keep your eyes open and you will see it everywhere.

buying four candy bars—and a Diet Coke. Oxymorons (two opposite concepts) provide yet another type of irony. Examples are working vacation, honest politicians, and jumbo shrimp. One of the best examples of irony I have ever heard, though, went like this (Klein, 1989): Charlie Chaplin once entered a Charlie Chaplin Lookalike Contest, and won third prize! Many stand-up comics, including George Lopez, Sarah Silverman, Louis C.K., Dave

> **Dry humor:** Often found in storytelling (e.g., Garrison Keillor, Mark Twain), where the humor is subtle and clever.
>
> **Quick-witted humor:** A style of humor that is based on quick wit without using sarcasm. Quick-witted humor often involves clever wording or phrasing that catches you off guard and leaves you impressed. Examples include the works of Mark Twain and NPR's "Car Talk" radio show.
>
> **Puns:** A type of wordplay that may leave people sighing rather than laughing.
>
> **Bathroom humor:** A form of humor often described as vulgar, crude, and tasteless, it derives its name from the use of various bodily functions known to occur in the bathroom.
>
> **Sarcasm:** Thought to be the lowest form of humor, the word *sarcasm* means to tear flesh. Because sarcasm is a latent form of anger, it promotes rather than reduces stress.

Chapelle, and Aziz Ansari, use this type of humor in their acts, and playwright Neil Simon uses ironic twists in his films and Broadway plays. Native American humor includes a number of humor styles, particularly irony, including the works of Sherman Alexie, Gary Farmer, and Chris Eyre.

8. *Dry humor, quick wit, and puns:* **Dry humor** can be described as clever, esoteric wit. It often involves double entendres, words with more than one meaning or connotation (e.g., a Jewish zydeco band called So How's Bayou), frequently with sexual innuendo. Mark Twain, Will Rogers, Groucho Marx, Winston Churchill, the cast of Britain's *Monty Python's Flying Circus*, and, more recently, Garrison Keillor of *Prairie Home Companion* are fine examples of creators of esoteric wit. Click and Clack of NPR's "Car Talk" fame are examples of **quick-witted humor**, as is comedian Stephen Colbert. **Puns**, or plays on words, also fall into this category. It has often been said that puns are the lowest form of humor because, unlike clever wit, they border on the silly or inane. Actually, puns have no malicious intent and therefore are not the lowest form of humor. Some examples of puns follow:

   - A pessimist's blood type is always B-negative.
   - I fired my masseuse today. She just rubbed me the wrong way.
   - A Freudian slip is when you say one thing but mean your mother.
   - I used to work in a blanket factory, but it folded.

   You may find it takes effort to laugh at puns, however, whereas other types of humor provoke laughter more spontaneously. Here's one: You can pick your friends and you can pick your nose, but you cannot pick your friend's nose.

9. *Bathroom humor:* If you have seen *American Pie*, *South Park*, *Spy* with Melissa McCarthy, or *Trainwreck* with Amy Schumer, then you know what **bathroom humor** is. If you haven't, the words *vulgar*, *ruthless*, *crude*, and *irreverent* come close to describing the topics of every body function imaginable chosen for cheap (and in some cases, hilarious) laughs.

10. *Sarcasm:* The word **sarcasm** means "to tear flesh," and if you have ever borne the brunt of sarcasm, then you know all too well that this is a figurative yet accurate description. Although sarcasm may share

elements with clever wit, it reveals latent anger. It is an attempt to get verbal revenge. Sarcasm is perceived by its users to be a socially acceptable way to express hostile feelings through words rather than physical aggression, but words can hurt as much, if not more, than physical abuse, and the memory of it far exceeds that of physical pain. A sarcastic remark is typically followed by the punch line, "I'm just kidding," to take the sharp edge off the potential pain inflicted. Sarcasm is the lowest form of humor. Although sarcastic remarks may seem funny, they actually induce stress rather than relieve it in the person toward whom they are aimed. For this reason, sarcasm is not advocated as a vehicle for expressing humor. Almost everyone employs it to some extent, but its use should be minimized if not altogether abandoned.

Although types of humor have been compartmentalized into various categories here, for the most part, in practice they mix and blend together to form a score of permutations. Examples would be a sarcastic joke about death, or a parody of slapstick. It is equally difficult to neatly categorize senses of humor, or why individuals laugh at what they do.

Senses of Humor

Just as there is more than one type of humor, experts of humor research have identified several **senses of humor**. Senses of humor appear to be a function of one's upbringing and collective environments. Quite possibly, each individual has the makings for all the senses of humor, but one type tends to dominate in each personality. For this reason, it is complicated to give general advice on ways to improve one's sense of humor. In his book *Laugh after Laugh*, Dr. Raymond Moody identifies four categories describing most people's senses of humor:

1. *Conventional:* In the **conventional sense of humor,** two or more people find common ground by sharing a similar humorous perception and laughing at the same thing. Laughter occurs with someone, not at someone. There is a mutual appreciation for things that appear universally funny. Jay Leno's former sidekick, Kevin Eubanks, who laughed at nearly everything, might be an example of the conventional sense of humor.

2. *Life of the party:* While some people soak up humorous episodes like a sponge, others have the ability to provide laughable moments for the amusement of everyone else. People with **life-of-the-party sense of humor** are the ones who wear the lamp shades at parties, recite numerous jokes and always remember the punch lines, and can tell any story and make it funny. These people love an audience and may have played the role of class clown in school in younger days. They are spontaneous, creative, and quick-witted. They have the ability to make everyone laugh, or at least smile. This is the kind of person you want to call up when you're feeling down and need to lift your spirits. Someone who pulls up alongside you at a red light, rolls down the window, and asks if you have any Grey Poupon mustard has this sense of humor.

3. *Creative:* The **creative sense of humor** is best observed in those whose professional career is joke writing. They are extremely quick-witted, very imaginative, and creative. These are people who can find humor in just about anything. People with the creative sense of humor frequently laugh to themselves, and if you ask them, "What's so funny?" they might tell you, or they might just say, "It was nothing." They are easily entertained. Although creative in their joke making, they often prefer to let someone else make the delivery. Anonymous graffitists also fall into this category.

4. *Good sport:* A **good-sport sense of humor** is demonstrated by those who can laugh at their own foibles and mistakes and enjoy being human. These people know how to employ self-parody and make good use of it. With this style, laughter is used to cope with personal imperfections rather than rationalize pitfalls. These people can take a practical joke without calling

---

Senses of humor: A frame of mind as part of one's personality in how one uses humor and laughter in one's life.

Conventional sense of humor: A term to describe more than one person laughing at the same thing, all agreeing to its humor.

Life-of-the-party sense of humor: The class clown, the person who gets all the laughs.

Creative sense of humor: This describes a person who thinks of jokes or funny things, but may be shy to share them.

Good-sport sense of humor: This describes someone who can take a practical joke without suing.

a lawyer afterward. In the sense of good sportsman-ship, the walls of the ego are low if not completely dissolved after a practical joke.

Group Laughter = Laughter Yoga

In 1995, a small group of people gathered together in a park in Mumbai, India, under the direction of a physician named Mandin Kataria. They came to laugh, and then laugh some more. Dr. Kataria named this activity "laughter yoga," and it spread like wildfire all over the globe, as described in his book *Laugh for No Reason*. What is laughter yoga? The simple explanation is that laughter yoga is prolonged voluntary laugher. In a typical session, people face each other, make eye contact, and engage in childlike behavior, causing smiles followed by laughter, and more laughter. Instructors begin sessions with stretching, clapping, and other body movements so participants will loosen up, and feel less self-conscious. Due to laughter's infectious nature, people in the group continue laughing for quite some time (as can be seen in the YouTube video "Contagious subway laughter"). In formal laughter yoga sessions, the laughter usually lasts for about 20 minutes. Sessions often end with laughter meditation where participants lie down and contemplate something funny (Briar, 2016).

Humor Therapy as a Coping Technique

In simplest terms, the use of humor is a defense mechanism. Yet, unlike other conscious or unconscious defense strategies to protect the ego, such as rationalization and projection, humor seems to dissolve the walls of the ego rather than intensify them. Humor is the one defense mechanism that can increase pleasure and reduce pain at the same moment; it gives two effects for the price of one. Theorists agree that humor is an adaptive coping mechanism liberating the ego. A 1978 article in *Psychology Today* asserted that the average person laughs about fifteen times per day. Although this study has not been updated, one might infer, given the state of the world today, that the quota of fifteen laughs per day is not being met. Humor's greatest asset is to balance the emotional scale between positive and negative perceptions. Although the study of psychology has maintained a particular bent toward the darker side of the human psyche, even this is beginning to change, in both the focus of research and the application of psychotherapy. Many psychologists argue that the expression of laughter and smiling is nothing less than a catharsis of emotions, a physical release tied to emotional thoughts. Overall, a well-intended catharsis can be quite healthy to the mind and body. But the complexity of humor hints of something more than just catharsis. In any event, mirth serves as a catalyst to unite mind, body, and spirit for total well-being.

It may seem intuitively obvious that humor can be used to diffuse stress, which is proven by the effectiveness of humor therapy. Over the years, a handful of studies have been conducted to measure the effects of humor (laughter) on stress, all with positive results. Miller and Fry (2009) studied the effect of mirthful laugher on the cardiovascular system and found that the release of beta-endorphins has a beneficial effect on the heart and vascular system. Bennett et al. (2003) investigated the effect of mirthful laughter on stress and natural killer cell activity. They concluded that positive emotions derived from laughter likely have a positive effect on the immune system and that laughter is a recommended cognitive-behavioral intervention. In a study to determine the efficacy of clown therapy (humor) on children undergoing surgery, Fernandes and Arriaga (2010) found that this type of humor not only helped the children cope better with anxiety, but also helped the parents.

Viktor Frankl, an Auschwitz survivor, noted in his book *Man's Search for Meaning* that humor was a saving grace among fellow prisoners in the shadows of death. Frankl wrote, "Humor was another of the soul's weapons in the fight for self-preservation." Fear of death even has its own brand of mirth: black humor. People often joke about death and dying in an effort to ease their tension and perhaps better understand their own mortal plight. Hollywood often uses comic relief in horror movies (e.g., *28 Days Later* and *Scary Movie*) so that the audience isn't so emotionally spent that they miss the film's climactic scene. It is virtually impossible to be both angry and happy at the same time. Thus, if you can separate yourself from your aggression for a moment and see how silly and out of character prolonged anger really is, feelings of hostility dissipate, succumbing to a crescendo of mirth. For this reason, self-parody is thought to be the type of humor best suited to dispel anger.

In the book *The Healing Power of Humor*, Klein states that the use of humor gives a sense of power in the midst of chaos. Being able to make light of a stressful circumstance allows people to feel they have control over a situation. Humor becomes a weapon to disarm the cause of the stress response. Whereas some consider humor as a catalyst to tap the power of intelligence and emotional fortitude, others see it as a diversion tactic. In this case, humor allows for an intermission in the cognitive war against stressors and a "cease-fire" of the stress response. The use of **humor therapy** in several hospital settings, as noted by Norman Cousins (1989) in his book *Head First*, helps to alleviate the sterile atmosphere these institutions are known for by allowing cancer patients to momentarily forget intravenous tubes, chemotherapy, radiation treatments, and bedpans.

In an attempt to better understand humor appreciation, *Psychology Today* conducted a survey of its readers in 1978. Thirty jokes were printed along with a questionnaire to gauge readers' opinions of the jokes' quality and laughability. More than 14,000 questionnaires were returned, and responses varied as much as the styles of jokes printed. Humor, like beauty, is a relative concept. The study concluded that sexual humor was the most popular topic of jest, with ethnic humor running a close second. Humor scholar Avner Ziv (1984) offers two reasons why sexual humor remains so popular. First, the craving for sexual humor compensates for the continuous desire to physically satisfy this basic human drive. Second, sexual humor may compensate for the disappointment of unmet sexual expectations.

Comic relief is currently used as a mode of therapy in many rehabilitation programs, including the treatment of physical trauma, alcoholism, and drug addiction. Psychologists who recognize the effectiveness of humor and utilize comic relief with their patients identify it as both an assessment tool, to indicate values, inner feelings, and meaning in life, and a therapeutic tool, to encourage a cathartic release of emotions. In psychotherapy, it is the patient's own use of humor that is nurtured and encouraged; it is not initiated by the therapist. When patients begin to joke about their conditions or predicaments, it is acknowledged as a breakthrough in the emotional self-healing process. Once manifested, the practice of comic relief is encouraged during laughable moments. Humor has been found to be very effective in aiding patients through the transitions of the many stages of recovery.

Just like other coping techniques that can prove ineffective for resolution, the power of humor can be abused. Negative and offensive humor such as racial, ethnic, and sexist humor, as well as sarcasm in both its delivery and reception, do not lend themselves to satisfaction as coping mechanisms. Negative humor may inflate self-esteem, but it is a false inflation with no lasting value. Humor can also be used as a means of seeking approval by controlling other people's attitudes and making them feel good. Used in this manner, humor takes on an addictive quality, where each laugh becomes a "fix" leading to the next laugh. Thus, humor employed to win the approval of others takes on the quality of codependent behavior. In a study by Fisher and Fisher (1983) investigating the personalities of comedians, it was observed that many professional comedians and humorists were raised in less-than-enviable environments, including homes with alcoholic parents (Carol Burnett), orphanages (Charlie Chaplin, Art Buchwald), or broken families. In these cases, the use of humor often brought recognition, approval, and a feeling of self-validation. In her book *It's Always Something*, comedian Gilda Radner described her use of comedy as an occasionally negative behavior: "Comedy is very controlling— you are making people laugh. You feel completely in control when you hear a wave of laughter coming back that you have caused. Probably that's why people in comedy can be so neurotic and have so many problems. Sometimes we talk about it as a need to be loved, but I think that with me it was also a need to control."

Comedian Ricky Gervais said it best when he said, "Humor guides you through the uncomfortable places. That is what humor is for—it gets us through the bad stuff." As a coping technique, humor therapy has the immediate effect of increasing awareness of the cause of stress, which may then lead to the path of resolution. The greater the quantity of laughs and the quality of humor, the greater the sensation of pleasure. The long-term effects of comic relief as a coping mechanism at best remain a mystery, particularly because these have not been investigated to any great degree.

The Physiology of Laughter

Norman Cousins was right: Positive emotions augment the mind-body relationship. Laughter indeed influences the body's physiology, resulting in restoration and possibly healing. In his own clinical tests, Cousins noted that several hours of laughter produced a small but significant decrease in the sedimentation rate of his blood, a predictor of inflammation or infection. In *Anatomy of an Illness*, Cousins (1976) wrote, "The drop itself (five points) was not substantial, but it was cumulative." Once thought of

---

Humor therapy: A coping technique; the use of humor and comic relief as a means to relieve and reduce emotional stress by focusing on the funny, humorous, and positive apects of life.

as only a coping technique, humor therapy now qualifies as a relaxation technique as well because of its physiological effects. Since this discovery, scientists have investigated the mysteries of the immune system and its relationship to the experience and expression of various emotions.

Dr. William Fry has devoted his life to the investigation of this mind-body relationship, and his work has yielded some fascinating results. Laughter appears to have both short-term and long-term effects on the body's major physiological systems. In the short term, a bout of laughter appears to initiate the stress response, with a slight increase in heart rate, blood pressure, muscle tension, and ventilations. But this is quickly followed by a rebound effect, where these parameters decrease to below previous resting levels. The overall effect is a profound level of homeostasis, much like that seen when progressive muscular relaxation is practiced. In the short term, laughter is credited with stabilizing blood pressure, "massaging" vital organs, stimulating circulation, facilitating digestion, and increasing oxygenated blood throughout the body. As Fry (1986) stated, "Laughter is clearly related to the reduction of stress and the physical symptoms related to stress."

Fry also conducted a series of studies on the composition of tears, those shed from pain and laughter as well as those artificially induced (e.g., from cutting onions). His research revealed that the constituents of emotional teardrops include a greater percentage of proteins and toxins than those produced artificially. Fry concluded that tears resulting from emotional responses serve to rid the body of stress-related toxins. Once again, this suggests that physical expressions—both laughter and crying—are natural and healthy to the well-being of the individual. As author Kurt Vonnegut once quipped (Klein, 1989), "Laughter and tears are both responses to frustration and exhaustion. I myself prefer to laugh, since there is less cleaning up to do afterward."

Perhaps more impressive than the short-term effects of laughter are its long-term effects. Through the new multidiscipline of PNI, researchers are now finding that the immune system plays an ever-increasing role in the mind-body relationship. In the words of Bernie Siegel (1986), "Thoughts are chemicals; they can either kill or cure." It appears that thoughts and perceptions are quickly transformed in the brain into chemical reactions that have impact throughout the body. Negative thoughts actually trigger the neural release of the stress hormones and suppress the immune system. Positive thoughts strengthen the integrity of the immune system

by inducing the release of special neuropeptides from the pituitary gland and other tissues located throughout the body. Neuropeptides—endorphins, interleukins, and interferons, to name a few—act as messenger molecules to various organs throughout the body.

Recent research has revealed that neuropeptides are also manufactured and released by the lymph nodes and other components of the immune systems. Although several hundred neuropeptides have been discovered to date, scientists believe there may be many more acting in the interest of the body's immune system. In effect, laughter causes the body to produce its own painkillers. A study by David McClelland (McClelland and Kirshnit, 1989) measured changes in secretory immunoglobulin A (S-IgA), a salivary immune-defense agent, as a result of three emotional responses (humor, cynicism, and trust) elicited by three types of movies. Films of W. C. Fields and Mother Teresa produced a significant rise in S-IgA, while a Nazi propaganda film corresponded with a decrease. The long-term effects of humor and the positive emotions it produces may serve as one of the most beneficial health practices currently known to humanity. It would be unwise to suggest that humor-induced laughter can cure all ailments; this simply isn't true. But humor can "lighten the load," making the pain of some diseases more bearable. In some remarkable incidences, such as that reported by Norman Cousins, there may also be a true healing effect. There are currently too many missing pieces to complete the mind-body model to our full comprehension. But in the short time that humor therapy has been employed as a therapeutic agent in cancer wards, many patients have been given the opportunity to die with a smile instead of a lonely frown. And their loved ones have that fond memory to look back on.

■ Steps to Initiate Humor Therapy

Years ago, I designed and taught an experimental course entitled Humor and Health. At least once a week, students asked me how they could improve their sense of humor. From the volumes of resources I read in preparation for this course, I gleaned a number of ways to incorporate humor therapy into your arsenal of stress-management coping techniques. The best suggestions are as follows.

1. *Learn not to take life too seriously.* Chris Flanagan, R.N., is the former head nurse on the oncology unit at Shady Grove Adventist Hospital in Rockville,

Stress with a Human Face

It was a hot summer day, and the pool looked so inviting. Andrew was a bright, good-looking, athletic kid about to enter high school. That day, he and his younger brother were making the most of their summer freedom. The odds of what was about to happen were about as great as winning $20 million in the lottery, except Andrew wasn't that lucky. For some reason no one seems able to explain, the angle at which he entered the deep water was just enough to snap his second vertebra and paralyze him from the neck down. Within the blink of an eye, *freedom* became a word he would cry over. And cry he did. In his therapy, he withdrew into his own world of darkness.

But one of his nurses had a natural funny bone that reverberated in its enthusiasm, and in time it became infectious. Soon Andrew asked to have some cartoon books brought in to him, as well as some comedy videos. His bouts of depression became fewer and fewer. It seemed that with his change in attitude came a desire to leave the hospital and get back to as normal a life as could be expected.

If you could see Andrew today, you would be drawn immediately toward his smile, an attribute he cherishes. Oh, he still has his downtimes like the rest of us, but he will be the first to tell you of the healing power of humor and how it enabled him to cope with a stressor he would have never imagined facing that fine summer day. Currently, he is a self-proclaimed ambassador of humor therapy for the disabled, traveling around the country to share his stories of comic relief. The newest joys in his life are his wife, Lauren, and their daughter, Alexis.

Maryland. Chris was awarded a grant from the Hyatt Foundation to start a Humor Cart on her cancer ward. Describing her work, Chris said, "We have a policy on my floor: Take your work seriously, but take yourself lightly." Most oncology wards have high turnover rates among nursing staff, but this philosophy has kept the nursing staff at Shady Grove intact for several years now. In a nutshell, this attitude means seeing yourself as more than your work. Many times we place all our eggs in the career basket, and if we have a bad day at work, then our self-esteem withers away. See yourself as a whole person, with many aspects and talents, not just as a student, spouse, or professional. People who are able to laugh at their mistakes are considered more emotionally sound than those who fret at the slightest hint of imperfection. We start out in life as a square block. Through a multitude of life's experiences, we polish the rough edges and, by the end, finish up a gem.

2. *Find one humorous thing a day.* Humorous events and concepts are around us all the time. Life is full of ironies, incongruencies, and just plain funny stuff. One's frame of mind is either receptive to these or simply dismisses them. If humor is a perception, as is currently believed, then the way to adopt comic relief as a coping mechanism is to adopt this humorous frame of mind and make it your own (cognitive restructuring). It is commonly understood that if you make yourself consciously aware of and receptive to an idea, you will attract things to reinforce this perception many times over. Take planning a holiday, for example. You decide that this summer you want to go on a safari in Kenya. Once you commit yourself to the trip, you discover all kinds of people who have gone on safari with the same touring company, you start noticing ads in magazines and TV specials, and your mind becomes a magnet for news and ideas about Africa. The same can be done with humor, if you make yourself receptive to the lighter side of life. Tell yourself that you want to find one funny thing each day. You will find that instead of just one little tickle, you will discover a wealth of humorous experiences each and every day (**BOX 13.4**). In addition, allocate some fun time for each day, whether this means watching a funny YouTube video, reading comics, or going to your nearest comedy club.

It is important to remember, however, that there are times when it is inappropriate to laugh. People can interpret laughter as rude during serious moments, so use caution and judgment. On the other hand, life is full of *laughable moments*, when it is

A bunch of inmates gathered together every Friday afternoon after basketball practice to tell jokes and lift their spirits. Because they had been together so many years, rather than telling the actual joke, they assigned a number to each joke. Some guy would call out a number and the group would laugh, sometimes uncontrollably. One day a new inmate joined the group and after observing the process of joke telling, yelled out the number 9. No one laughed! After a few moments, one inmate muttered under his breath, "Jeez, some people just can't tell a joke."

Comedian's lament: "I don't have health insurance. Too expensive . . . and I was told I have a pre-existing condition. But I do have a good car insurance policy. It's the law! So whenever I come down with the flu or start to bleed, I get in my car and drive around looking for an accident."

Three elderly men are at the doctor's office for a memory test. The doctor asks the first man, "What is three times three?" "274," came the reply. The doctor rolls his eyes and looks up at the ceiling, then says to the second man, "It's your turn. What is three times three?" "Tuesday," replies the second man. The doctor shakes his head sadly, then asks the third man, "Okay, your turn. What's three times three?" "Nine," says the third man. "That's great!" says the doctor. "How did you get that?" "Simple," he says, "just subtract 274 from Tuesday."

quite acceptable to laugh and smile. When these times arise, capitalize on them and give yourself permission to let go and enjoy.

3. *Work to improve your imagination and creativity.* Creativity and humor are virtually inseparable. One has only to read headlines in supermarket tabloids to be reminded of this: "Termite Baby Eats Newlyweds' House," "Bigfoot Seen Boarding a UFO," "Ski Mask Found on Surface of Mars," "Teenager Swallows Seed, Grows Palm Tree in Stomach." Lately, the creative "muscle" of many an American has atrophied as the adrenal glands have hypertrophied. Remember, the funny bone is just as susceptible to the general adaptation syndrome as is your adrenal gland. Start placing more emphasis on this target organ. It is commonly thought (and currently under study) that the use of one right-brain cognitive function enhances other functions of the same hemisphere. Imagination is a right-brain function. So is humor. They tend to feed off each other. So how does one augment imagination skills? Here are a few suggestions:

   a. *Read more books (fiction and nonfiction) and watch less television.*

   b. *Write a story, fable, or poem every now and then.*

   c. *Play with children.* Kids have wonderful imaginations. Maybe some of theirs will transfer to you by osmosis. Get closer to the earth. Observe the world from the eye level of a young child.

   d. *Go exploring.* Do something completely new and outrageous. Spend an afternoon in a hardware store, a museum of fine art, or a greenhouse. Get out of the comfortable rut you take refuge in and discover the world all over again.

   e. *Create something.* Pull out a cookbook and play "Wolfgang Puck." Make your own holiday presents this year. Invent something. Plant a garden. Bonsai a tree. Plan a trip around the world. Start a new hobby. Make your world a better place to live in.

4. *Start a joke/cartoon-of-the-week swap with a friend.* Use either Twitter, Facebook, or email so that you have something to look forward to, as well as making someone else's day with a chuckle.

5. *Learn to hyperexaggerate when describing a situation or story.* A comedian begins his monologue, "I knew a guy so ugly . . . ," and a call comes back from the audience, "How *ugly* was he?" The comedian continues, "He was so ugly that if you were to look up the word *ugly* in the dictionary, you'd find his picture beside the definition." Exaggeration is a staple in virtually all comedians' joke repertoires. Comparisons are hilarious when they are exaggerated, and they can lighten up the description of the most stressful event. Ways to employ exaggeration include substitution of familiar words with others (e.g., since your last communiqué . . .) and use of figurative versus literal meanings (e.g., Why do

we drive on a parkway, and park on a driveway?). Creative use of metaphor is also a component of exaggeration for a good laugh, as in "My final in economics was worse than the Spanish Inquisition."

6. *Build a humor library*. One of the essentials of coping is the use of available resources, which can include anything and everything. For humor therapy, resources involve the collection and use of books, CDs, and DVDs, and even hand buzzers and water guns. Designate a small corner of your home for a humor library and start to fill the shelves with a collection of every conceivable resource. Online streaming services have designated comedy sections; bookstores have humor sections. No matter how often you have heard favorite CDs or read favorite books, they will still trigger a laugh. Don't let these resources collect dust, either. Make a habit of using them frequently.

Here is another idea: Start a **tickler notebook**. Buy a notebook and fill it with anything that puts a smile on your face (**BOX 13.5**). It can include, among other things, cartoons, favorite jokes, letters, funny photographs with your captions attached, favorite newspaper columns, love poems, and a host of personal items (e.g., JPEGs/photographs, birthday cards, postcards) that make you feel good inside. When I assign the tickler notebook to my Humor and Health students, I give these instructions: "Imagine that one day you are diagnosed with a major illness (e.g., cancer). What humor time capsule can you assemble that upon review is bound to jack up your white blood cell count and put you on the road to recovery?" We all have down moments; this is perfectly natural. But an extended period of negative emotions is neither natural nor healthy. A tickler notebook is your personal humor prescription. And it is a growing organism; keep feeding and looking after it. Treat it well, and it will repay you a hundred times over.

7. *Find a host of varied humor venues*. Telling jokes is only a pebble of the mountain we call humor,

> **Tickler notebook:** A personal collection of humorous items (e.g., cards, letters, JPEGs, jokes) to lighten your spirits.

BOX 13.5　Classic Jokes for Your Tickler Notebook

The Good Son

An old man lived alone in Idaho. He wanted to spade his potato garden, but it was very hard work. His only son, Bubba, who always helped him, was in prison for armed robbery. The old man wrote a letter to his son and mentioned his predicament:

> Dear Bubba, I'm feeling pretty low because it looks like I won't be able to plant my potato garden this year. I've gotten too old to be digging up a garden plot. If you were here, my troubles would be over. I know you would dig the plot for me. Love, Dad.

A few days later, the old man received a letter from his son:

> Dear Dad, For HEAVEN'S SAKE, don't dig up the GARDEN! That's where I buried the GUNS and the MONEY! Love, Bubba.

At 4:00 A.M. the next day, a dozen FBI agents and local police officers showed up at the old man's house and dug up the entire area. After finding nothing, they apologized to the old man and left. That same afternoon the old man received another letter from his son:

> Dear Dad, Go ahead and plant the potatoes now. It's the best I could do under the circumstances. Love, Bubba.

The Conversation

God is sitting in Heaven when a scientist says to Him, "Lord, we don't need you anymore. Science has finally figured out a way to create life out of nothing. In other words, we can now do what you did in the beginning."

"Is that so? Tell me about it," replies God.

"Well," says the scientist, "we can take dirt and form it into the likeness of You and breathe life into it, thus creating man."

"Well, that's interesting. Show me."

So the scientist bends down to the earth and starts to mold the soil.

"No, no, no," interrupts God. "Get your own dirt."

Courtesy of Patch Adams, M.D.

FIGURE 13.6   Patch Adams, M.D., has dedicated his career in the healing profession to making health care free and nonhierarchical for all people in a loving playful hospital. So to use humor as both a context for medical practice and for living life, he sees clowning as a trick to bring love close. Sharing humor seems to multiply the effects of laughter on well-being. Here Adams is with refugee children from the former Yugoslavia.

yet it is often the first thing we think of when we hear the word. But humor can be found in a multitude of venues, and the greater the access to a wide variety of humor media, the more advantageous this coping skill will be to deal with stress (**FIG. 13.6**). Humor venues include (but are not limited to) movies, theater, books, music, television, and live stand-up comedy. Humor and entertainment are also very compatible, if not always the same. The human mind likes to be entertained. Be on the lookout for ways to incorporate a wide variety of humor venues into your lifestyle.

8. *Improve your self-esteem*. It is hard to laugh when your self-esteem is deflated. At times, we all think we are fat, ugly, or stupid, and these characteristics constitute the punch line of many a joke. Low self-esteem derives from negative feedback we create in our own minds and come to believe. Remember Einstein's theory: Everything is relative. Separate fact from fiction. Give yourself positive affirmations every day, accentuate your good qualities, and learn to accept and love yourself and all your human potential.

9. *Access your humor network*. Every now and then, there are bound to be times when you find yourself on the bottom rung of the emotional ladder. These moments should be recognized and, perhaps for a short time, even appreciated. But if, after an allocated period of "emotional downtime," you need some help getting up again, don't be afraid to call for help. We all know someone who can make us smile at the mere thought of his or her name. Call this person and ask for a "humor lift." It's the next best thing to being there. Conversely, it would be a good habit to minimize time spent with people who seem to live with black clouds over their heads; their pessimism is not conducive to enhancing your positive emotions. You don't have to go down with their ship.

Best Application of Comic Relief

Humor therapy integrates a little cognitive reappraisal, a little behavior modification, and a lot of fun. Employing comic relief as a coping style involves a conscious effort to live life on the lighter side. Humor therapy does not try to eclipse the emotions associated with anger, fear, or sadness; it only attempts to neutralize them so that there is balance to your emotional responses. To best apply the use of humor in your life, take note of what sense of humor you best identify with and see if you can sharpen this edge a little. Also note which type of humor you find most gratifying and make a habit of employing more of it in the course of each day. In addition, monitor your high and low moods and their durations. If you find that the majority of your thoughts are negative, jaded, or laced with pessimism, try to balance these out with a greater number of positive, even humorous, thoughts. No one who advocates humor therapy suggests that everybody should always be smiling. This is neither realistic nor healthy. Emotional well-being is the ability to feel and express the *full* range of human emotions, both positive and negative. The danger lies in the imbalance of positive and negative emotions because a preponderance of the latter will ultimately inflict bodily damage. Cousins highlighted humor as a symbol of all the positive emotions that can lend themselves to emotional well-being. Use humor therapy to find and maintain that balance of human emotions in your life.

SUMMARY

- Cousins legitimized the use of humor therapy when he treated himself with hours of funny films, which contributed to the remission of his potentially fatal disease. The premise of the therapy was that if negative thoughts can result in illness and disease, positive thoughts should enhance health. Cousins also believed that for his health to return he had to take personal responsibility for it.

- Greeks advocated humor therapy more than 2,000 years ago, as did ancient Africans, American Indians, and medieval European kings and queens. However, laughter was declared by the Puritans to be the work of the devil, and to laugh or smile was considered a sin.

- Humor is not a positive emotion, but it can elicit several positive emotions. Humor, like stress, is a perception.

- Humor is a very complex phenomenon. There are many types of humor, including parody, satire, slapstick, absurd/nonsense, black, irony, dry, and sarcasm. Self-parody is thought to be the best type

of humor to reduce stress, whereas sarcasm is the worst.

- Just as there are different types of personalities, there are also several senses of humor, including conventional, life of the party, creative, and good sport.

- There is no one accepted reason why we laugh. Four theories attempt to explain the nature of the funny bone: superiority theory, incongruity (surprise) theory, release/relief theory, and divinity theory.

- Research investigating the psychoneuroimmunological effects of laughter have found that there is a strong relationship between good health and good humor. In essence, laughter helps restore physiological homeostasis.

- Studies also show that humor promotes mental, emotional, physical, and spiritual well-being.

- There are many ways to tickle your funny bone and augment your sense of humor, but like anything that is worth having, you have to work at it.

STUDY GUIDE QUESTIONS

1. How is humor best defined?

2. List five different types of humor.

3. List the four theories of humor (why we smile/laugh). Each humor theory can be associated with one component of the wellness paradigm (mind, body, spirit, emotions). Which goes with which?

4. How do humor and laughter work together as a coping technique for stress?

5. List four ways to incorporate more humor and laughter into your life.

REFERENCES AND RESOURCES

Allen, S., Jr. Humor and Creativity Conference, Saratoga, NY, April 21, 1990.

Anthony, J., and Hurley, J. Humor Therapy: To Heal Is to Make Happy, *Nursing Clinical Currents*. Shady Grove Adventist Hospital, Rockville, MD 2(1):1–4, 1989.

Apte, M. *Humor and Laughter*. Cornell University Press, Ithaca, New York, 1985.

Balick, M. The Role of Laughter in Traditional Medicine and Its Relevance to the Clinical Setting: Healing with Ha! *Alternative Therapies* 9(4):88–91, 2003.

Bennett, M., et al. The Effect of Mirthful Laughter on Stress and Natural Killer Cell Activity, *Alternative Therapies* 9(2):38–45, 2003.

Bennett, M. P., and Lengacher, C. Humor and Laughter May Influence Health. *Evidence Based Complementary Alternative Medicine* 3:61–63, 2006.

Bennett, M. O., Zeller, J. M., Rosenberg, L., and McCann, J. The Effect of Mirthful Laughter on Stress and Natural Killer Cell Activity. *Alternative Therapies in Health and Medicine*. 9(2): 38–45, 2003.

Berk, L. S., Felten, D., Tan, S. A., et al. Modulation of Immune Parameters during the Eustress of Humor Associated Mirthful Laughter, *Alternative Therapies* 7(2):62–67, 2001.

Berk, L. S., Tan, S., Fry, W., et al. Neuroendocrine and Stress Hormone Changes during Mirthful Laughter, *American Journal of Medical Science* 298(6):390–396, 1989.

Black, D. Laughter, *Journal of the American Medical Association* 252:2995–2998, 1984.

Blalock, J. The Immune System as a Sensory Organ, *Journal of Immunology* 132:1067–1069, 1984.

Blumenfeld, E., and Alpern, L. *The Smile Connection: How to Use Humor in Dealing with People*. Prentice-Hall, New York, 1986.

Bombeck, E. *I Want to Grow Hair, I Want to Grow Up, I Want to Go to Boise*. Harper & Row, New York, 1989.

Bonham, T. *Humor: God's Gift*. Broadman Press, Nashville, TN, 1988.

Borge, V. International Humor Treasure, *Humor Matters* 7:127–139, 1991.

Boston, R. *An Anatomy of Laughter*. Collins Press, London, 1974.

Briar, J. *The Laughter Yoga Book*. North Charleston, SC, CreateSpace, 2016.

Chapman, A., and Foot, H. *Humor and Laughter*. Wiley, New York, 1976.

Clark, A., Seider, A., and Miller, M. Inverse Association between Sense of Humor and Coronary Artery Disease, *International Journal of Cardiology* 80(1):87–88, 2001.

Cousins, N. *Anatomy of an Illness*. Norton, New York, 1976.

Cousins, N. Anatomy of the Illness (as Perceived by the Patient), *New England Journal of Medicine* 295(26):1458–1463, 1978.

Cousins, N. Beware of Those Who Can't Stand Good News, *Christian Science Monitor*, December 27, 1988.

Cousins, N. *Head First*. Penguin Books, New York, 1989.

Dossey, L. Now You Are Fit to Live: Humor and Health, *Alternative Therapies in Health and Medicine* 2(5):8–13, 98, 1996.

Ed, F. *God Grant Me the Laughter: A Treasury of Twelve-Step Humor*. CompCare Publishers, Minneapolis, MN, 1989.

Fernandes, S. C., and Arriaga, P. The Effects of Clown Intervention on Worries and Emotional Responses in Children Undergoing Surgery. *Journal of Health Psychology*. 15(3): 405–415, 2010.

Fisher, S., and Fisher, R. Personality and Psychopathology in the Comic. In P. McGhee and J. Goldstein, (eds.), *Handbook of Human Research*. Springer-Verlag, New York, 1983.

Frankl, V. *Man's Search for Meaning*. Pocket Books, New York, 1956.

Freud, S. *Jokes and Their Relation to the Unconscious*. Norton, New York, 1960.

Fry, W., and Rader, C. The Respiratory Component of Mirthful Laughter, *Journal of Biological Psychology* 24:38–50, 1977.

Fry, W., and Salameh, W. (eds.). *Handbook of Humor and Psychotherapy*. Professional Resource Exchange, Sarasota, FL, 1986.

Goldstein, J., and McGhee, P. *The Psychology of Humor*. Academic Press, New York, 1972.

Graham, B. The Healing Power of Humor, *Mind-Body Health Digest* 4(2):1–6, 1990.

Hageseth, C. *Positive Humor 101*. Berwick, Fort Collins, CO, 1989.

Hassett, J., and Houlihan, J. Different Jokes for Different Folks, *Psychology Today* 12:64–71, 1979.

Hassett, J., and Houlihan, J. What's So Funny? *Psychology Today* 12:101–113, 1978.

Hillard, N. *Laughing: A Psychology of Humor*. Cornell University Press, Ithaca, NY, 1982.

Johnson, P. The Use of Humor and Its Influences on Spirituality and Coping in Breast Cancer Survivors, *Oncology Nursing Forum* 29:691–695, 2002.

Joshua, A. M., Controneo, A., and Clarke, S. Humor and Oncology, *Journal of Clinical Oncology* 23(3):645–648, 2005.

Kant, I. *Critique of Pure Reason*, ed. K. Norman. St. Martin's, New York, 1969.

Keller, D. *Humor as Therapy*. Pine Mountain Press, Wauwatosa, WI, 1984.

Klein, A. *The Healing Power of Humor*. Tarcher Press, Los Angeles, 1989.

Koestler, A. *The Act of Creation*. Hutchinson, London, 1964.

Koller, M. *Humor and Society: Expectations in the Sociology of Humor*. Cap and Gown Press, Houston, TX, 1988.

Krieger, D. Brain Peptides: What, Where, and Why, *Science* 222:975–984, 1983.

Kuhlman, T. *Humor and Psychology*. Dow Jones-Irwin, Homewood, IL, 1984.

Ljungdahl, L. Laugh If This Is a Joke, *Journal of the American Medical Association* 261(4):558, 1989.

Long, P. Laugh and Be Well, *Psychology Today* 21:28–29, 1987.

Lynn, K. S. *The Comic Tradition in America*. Norton, New York, 1958.

Martin, R., and Leftcourt, H. Sense of Humor as a Moderator of the Relations between Stress and Moods, *Journal of Personality and Social Psychology* 45:1313–1324, 1983.

McClelland, D. C., and Kirshnit, C. The Effect of Motivation Arousal through Films on Salivary Immunoglobulin A, *Psychology and Health* 2:31–52, 1989.

McGhee, P. *Humor: Its Origin and Development*. Freeman, San Francisco, 1979.

McGhee, P., and Goldstein, J. *Handbook of Humor Research, Applied Studies*, vols. I & II. Springer-Verlag, New York, 1983.

Miller, L., and Blerkom, V. Clown Doctors: Shaman Healers of Western Medicine, *Medical Anthropology Quarterly* 9(4): 462–475, 1995.

Miller, M., and Fry, W. F. The Effect of Mirthful Laughter on the Human Cardiovascular System. *Medical Hypotheses*. 73(5): 636–639, 2009. www.ncbi.nlm.nih.gov/pubmed/19477604.

Minders, H. *Laughter and Liberation: Developing Your Sense of Humor*. Nash Publications, New York, 1971.

Moody, R. *Laugh after Laugh: The Healing Power of Humor*. Headwaters Press, Jacksonville, FL, 1978.

Morreal, J. *The Philosophy of Laughter and Humor*. SUNY Press, Albany, NY, 1987.

Morreal, J. *Taking Laughter Seriously*. SUNY Press, Albany, NY, 1983.

Nahemow, L. *Humor and Aging*. Academic Press, Orlando, FL, 1986.

Novak, W., and Waldoks, M. (eds.). *Big Book of American Humor*. Harper, New York, 1990.

Pasero, C., and McCaffery, M. Is Laughter the Best Medicine? *American Journal of Nursing* 98(12):12–13, 1998.

Peters, L., and Dana, B. *The Laughter Prescription*. Ballantine Books, New York, 1982.

Polivka, J. Cartoon Humor as an Aid in Therapy, *Clinical Gerontology*, Fall 1987:63–67.

Porterfield, A. Does Sense of Humor Moderate the Impact of Life Stress on Psychological and Physiological Wellbeing? *Journal of Research and Personality* 21:306–317, 1987.

Provine, R. *Laughter: A Scientific Investigation*. Viking, New York, 2000.

Radner, G. *It's Always Something*. Simon & Schuster, New York, 1989.

Rickler, M. *The Best of Modern Humor*. Knopf, New York, 1983.

Robinson, V. *Humor and the Health Professions*, 2nd ed. C. S. Slack, Thorofare, NJ, 1991.

Samra, C. *The Joyful Christ: The Healing Power of Humor*. HarperCollins, New York, 1986.

Sanfranek, R., and Schill, T. Coping with Stress: Does Humor Help? *Psychological Reports* 51:222, 1982.

Schafer, L. S. *The Best of Gravestone Humor*. Sterling, New York, 1990.

Schill, T., and O'Laughlin, S. Humor Preference and Coping with Stress, *Psychological Reports* 55:309–310, 1984.

Science Daily. Humor Can Increase Hope, Research Shows, April 11, 2005. www.sciencedaily.com/releases/2005/04/050413091232.htm.

Seaward, B. L. Good Vibrations: The Healing Power of Humor, *Bridges. ISSSEEM Magazine* 6(3):5–7, 16, 1995.

Seaward, B. L. Humor's Healing Potential, *Health Progress* April:66–70, 1992.

Shaeffer, N. *The Art of Laughter*. Columbia University Press, Baltimore, 1981.

Shelley, C. Plato on the Psychology of Humor, *Humor* 16(4): 351–367, 2003.

Siegel, B. *Love, Medicine and Miracles*. Perennial Books, New York, 1986.

Silberman, I. Humor and Health: An Epidemiological Study, *American Behavioral Scientist* 30:100–112, 1987.

Weisenberg, M., Tepper, I., and Schwarzwald, J. Humor as a Cognitive Technique for Increasing Pain Tolerance, *Pain* 63(2):207–212, 1995.

Wooten, P. Humor: An Antidote for Stress, *Holistic Nurses Practice* 10(2):49–56, 1996.

Wright, S. *I Still Have a Pony*. Warner Brothers Records, Los Angeles, 2007.

Yoshino, S., et al. Effects of Mirthful Laughter on Neuroendocrine and Immune Systems in Patients with Rheumatoid Arthritis, *Journal of Rheumatology* 23(4):793–794, 1996.

Ziv, A. *Personality and Sense of Humor*. Springer, New York, 1984.

CHAPTER 14

Creative Problem Solving

Make it a practice to keep on the lookout for novel and interesting ideas that others have used successfully. Your idea only has to be original in its adaptation to the problem you are working on.

—Thomas Alva Edison

Light bulb. Bicycle. Printing press. Airplane. Cotton gin. Telephone. Laptop. iPad. Smartphone. Airbnb. Uber. Snapchat. Each one has become an item of necessity. Necessity, it is said, is the mother of invention, and the human mind has risen to the occasion to create some fantastic inventions. There is no better time for necessity to bear the fruits of creativity than during times of frustration or crisis, when one needs to get from point A to point B. If you have been following any of the news headlines recently then you are well aware that the world has no shortage of problems today. Problem solving requires both a personal and planetary effort, giving credence to the expression, if you are not part of the solution, you are part of the problem (Meng, 2016).

At one time, the United States took pride in its American ingenuity. Young in age and pregnant with possibilities, early generations of Americans made more improvements to the proverbial mouse trap than there are stars in the sky. Before the turn of the twentieth century, the United States was a productive society, the vast majority of its citizens making more than 70 percent of their household items themselves. As the country became a consumer society, however, more and more items were bought rather than made at home. The availability of several new inventions, like the washer and dryer, provided more leisure time. But with some of these inventions, lifestyles became very comfortable, and our collective creative skills became dull (Bronson and Merryman, 2010). With the advent of television, it is said, the creative American mind began showing signs of atrophy. People now take a passive role in the creative process, letting other people do the important creative problem solving.

You may have heard of the IQ test, but have you heard of the CQ test? CQ stands for creative intelligence. The test was designed by Paul Torrance in the 1950s and is still used today. Experts have noted that while IQ scores have increased, as a whole, over the years, CQ scores in America have decreased, leading many experts to suggest that American ingenuity is in dramatic decline. The blame seems to lie with too many hours in front of the television and video games and too much emphasis on school testing. Creativity is a skill, however, and skills can be learned and cultivated. Mark Runco, who directs the Torrance Center for Creativity and Talent Development at the University of Georgia, found that people who utilize their creative muscles with regard to problem solving have better relationships and, through the empowerment of creativity, are better able to handle stress when problems, big or small, arise (Bronson and Merryman, 2010; Blair, 2013).

Experts agree that a happy mind is a creative mind. The inability to deal with many problems is directly related to the inability to tap into and utilize creativity. It would be unfair to point the finger of blame solely at television or video games. Many critics believe that the American educational system continues to play a role in the decline of creative skills as well, by stifling the limits of imagination with conformity and critical-thinking skills (**FIG. 14.1**). Moreover, American companies are now looking to hire Asians who are deemed more creative. The dominant style of thinking in the Western hemisphere is considered left-brained: linear, logical and rational, analytical, and judgmental. Left-brain modes of thinking are those most rewarded in both school and work environments. And this style of thinking has devalued recreational and play time.

Music. Poetry. Architecture. Fiction. Art. Pottery. Photography. If necessity is the mother of invention, then play can be said to assume the paternal role in this relationship. Creativity definitely has a playful, relaxed side to it. Playing is as much a part of human nature as is work, although playful behavior often atrophies as individuals make the transition from childhood to adulthood. But play, like the creativity it stimulates, can be nurtured. It has been said that more good ideas have arisen from play in garage and basement workshops than anywhere else, including the genesis of Xerox Corporation, Hewlett-Packard, and Apple Computers. Why is creativity so important? Why do corporate executives currently pay big bucks to bring in creative consultants to conduct workshops for their employees? The answer can be summed up in one word: change.

Change is inevitable. There is comfort in familiar routines, even if they are boring or stressful. Change meets resistance. Someone once said that the only person who likes change is a wet baby. But we live on a planet that travels at a rate of 66,000 miles per hour in its ellipse around the sun, with a population approaching 7 billion people. Given these dynamics alone, change is inevitable. In 1970, Alvin Toffler wrote a book, *Future Shock*, describing the rapid changes the human race would encounter in the age of high technology by the end of the twentieth century and beyond. The book might have been titled *Future Stress* because, as Toffler indicated, the shock from rapid change can be very difficult to handle, and even more difficult to adapt to. Resistance to change seems to be a basic part of human nature. Change is often equated with chaos, and chaos spells stress. This is where the importance of creativity comes in. Futurists

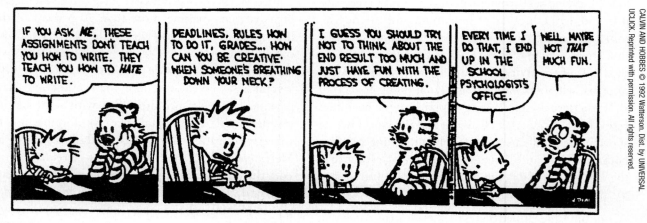

FIGURE 14.1

© 360b/Shutterstock.

FIGURE 14.2 Creativity isn't a gift for a chosen few. It is a birthright for everyone. The renowned Blue Man Group show has been described as a visual and sensory extravaganza, just one example of people who have put their creative talents to use. You can, too, in a way that empowers you.

agree that, given the state of the world today and the direction in which it appears to be headed, the inner resource of creativity and the skills of creative problem solving will be the most important coping strategy in the coming decade.

Creativity can help make order out of chaos. It has the ability to make change palatable, even enjoyable. But to be creative takes the right attitude and a workable strategy. The ability to be creative resides within each and every one of us. Creativity is not a gift—it is a human birthright (**FIG. 14.2**). But like muscles that atrophy with disuse, creativity must be exercised to be effective. For those of you who have let your creative abilities slip into hibernation, here is a refresher course in the basics (**FIG. 14.3**).

Think Like da Vinci!

When lists are compiled of the world's most brilliant, creative minds, Leonardo da Vinci is found at the top of many lists. A painter, inventor, scientist, and philosopher, and a man many consider ahead of his time, da Vinci is revered as a genius by everyone, including Michael Gelb. So impressed was Gelb with da Vinci's creative genius that he pooled da Vinci's talents into a book, *How to Think Like da Vinci*, so that the rest of the world could rise a few steps in creative consciousness by emulating the Italian. Among the many tips in Gelb's book are the following:

1. Be curious about how things work; don't take everything for granted; ask questions.

© Justin Sullivan/Getty Images News/Getty.

FIGURE 14.3 If you think you're not creative, you'll prove yourself right. You may not be a Steve Jobs, but everyone has the makings of a creative person, including you!

2. Make a habit of using all five of your senses to explore the world.

3. Be willing to embrace ambiguity, paradox, and uncertainty.

4. Be willing to make mistakes and learn from them.

The Creative Process

The creative process is not complex, but it is wonderfully profound because there are so many possible ways to get from point A to point B. During the 1980s, intense interest in the human creative process developed. And like the goose that was cut open to find out how she laid the golden egg, the creative process has since been examined from every side, angle, and perspective and has been dissected and inspected. Unlike the goose, though, the process wasn't killed; instead, it has become well understood so that the creative muscle could flex with strength, power, and agility for the whim and benefit of those anxious to use it.

The creative process has two parts, which by no coincidence match the functions of the right and left hemispheres of the human brain. Torrance described the creative process as a combination of both divergent (expansive possibilities, right-brain) and convergent (collective synthesis, left-brain) thinking processes.

The best creativity comes from using both sets of cognitive skills, both sides of your brain. Maslow observed a number of characteristics contributing to total well-being, or as he called it, self-actualization. Creativity was among these characteristics. In his later work on self-actualization, Maslow concluded that the creative process and the path to self-actualization were one and the same. He called the creative process the "art of being happily lost in the present moment." He divided the creative process into *primary* and *secondary* parts. **Primary creativity** is the origin of ideas: the playground of the mind where ideas are generated and hatched. **Secondary creativity** describes the strategic plan to bring to fruition the ideas brought forth in primary creativity. Secondary creativity is like the mind's workshop: a place to saw, chisel, glue, hammer, and polish ideas.

Players on the Creativity Team

Creative consultant Roger von Oech took Maslow's idea one step further, dividing primary and secondary creativity each into two phases in what is considered the best description of the creative process. In his celebrated book, *A Kick in the Seat of the Pants*, von Oech's model of creative thinking includes a team of four players—the **explorer**, **artist**, **judge**, and **warrior**. The explorer and artist provide primary creativity, and the judge and warrior provide secondary creativity. The explorer and artist team together for what von Oech calls the germination phase of

creativity. In this phase, inspiration and imagination are used to their fullest potential. The germination phase involves soft, pliable, right-brain thinking. Examples of this thinking style include irrationality, nonlinear perceptions, synthesis, metaphor, dreams, humor, and global awareness. The judge and warrior join forces in the harvesting of the creative crops sowed in the depths of imagination. The harvest phase of creativity involves hard, critical, left-brain thinking. Examples include logic, rationality, linear analysis, and factual thinking. Each type of thinking style has an equal responsibility in the creative process. The key is to let each player do its job without interference from the other three. In the footsteps of von Oech, Charles M. Johnson, founder of the Institute for Creative Development, delineates the creative process as a combination of creative differentiation and creative integration. Like von Oech, he divides the creative process into four stages: (1) incubation, (2) inspiration, (3) perspiration, and (4) administration (Johnson, 2005).

The overall goal of creative thought is to sharpen the skills of all four team players so that one or two aspects don't overpower the others, cause them to atrophy, and stifle the entire process. Let us take a more detailed look at the members of the creative team.

The Explorer. Although some ideas may actually bubble to the surface of consciousness, the human mind generally needs to be stimulated. If the mind is like a field, it needs frequent fertilization for robust growth of ideas. In the words of Nobel Prize winner Linus Pauling, "The best way to get a good idea is to get a lot of ideas," and to get a lot of ideas you need to look around. Whether abstract or concrete, the construction of almost everything requires raw materials. The explorer searches for raw materials with which to create ideas. People tend to get into cognitive ruts. We become prisoners of familiarity, unwilling to leave our turf, and the consequence is boredom and burnout. The walls of security can become the bars of imprisonment. As a result, our ability to create becomes obstructed. Where should you explore? Anywhere and everywhere; the possibilities are limitless. Bookstores, national parks, museums, magazines, rock concerts, libraries. Leave your territory and go explore a new environment. Make an adventure out of it. In the spirit of *Star Trek*, "Go where no one has ever gone before."

Singer/surfer Jack Johnson goes exploring by reading books by Kurt Vonnegut and Joseph Campbell. In an interview in *Rolling Stone* magazine, Johnson said, "A lot of artists fall into a thing where they're constantly trying to create art. But I think you can forget to take

---

Primary creativity: Maslow's term for the first stage of the creative process in which ideas are conceived.

Secondary creativity: Maslow's term for the last stage of the creative process in which a strategy is played out to have the selected idea come to fruition.

Explorer: Von Oech's term to identify the first stage of the creative process in which one begins to look for new ideas by venturing outside one's comfort level.

Artist: Von Oech's term to identify the second stage of the creative process, in which one plays with or incubates ideas that the explorer has brought back.

Judge: Von Oech's term to identify the third stage of the creative process, in which one selects the best idea and prepares it for manifestation.

Warrior: The last stage in von Oech's creative process template, in which the idea is taken to the street and campaigned to the rest of the world for its merits.

things in. You've got to fill up your mind" (Scaggs, 2008). Rock singer Sting shared that, when looking for inspiration for his albums, he turned to several volumes of Shakespeare and other notable classics in his beloved library and, using poetic license, exploited them to come up with new lyrics to his songs. Examples like this abound in the arts and humanities. The most important equipment the explorer needs, then, is an open mind: a container in which to put the raw materials. If you explore with a closed mind, there will be no room to transport the makings of ideas to your mental workshop. Negative thoughts, too, close a mind watertight. An open mind employs several attitudes to act as fertilizer; among these are curiosity, optimism, and enthusiasm. Curiosity is permission to get lost. In fact, many explorers do get lost. And when they emerge from the "woods," often they have discovered something far different, and more important, than what they had set out to find. Columbus was looking for spices in the Far East and "discovered" a whole new hemisphere. Roger Sperry was looking for a cure for epilepsy and discovered how the left and right hemispheres of the brain process information. Chef "Crusty" George Crumb was looking for a faster way to cook French fries (to please his customers), and he ended up with the potato chip. Alexander Graham Bell set out to create a hearing aid for his girlfriend and invented the telephone instead. Facebook creator Mark Zuckerberg wanted to design a dating Web site for Harvard students and instead created the most popular social networking site on the Internet. Exploration should be fun. Fun is generated from optimism, a positive outlook, and enthusiasm, the application of optimism. When doubt or fear is introduced, fun disappears and the mind closes up like a steel trap. Another important piece of equipment for the explorer is a notebook or pad of paper. Good ideas are like butterflies: They may land, but they soon take off again. Write them down!

The Artist. Poet William Blake once said that every individual is "an artist, a child, a poet, and an animal." Although you may not consider yourself the likes of Picasso or Rembrandt, every individual has what it takes to be an artist. In the role of the artist, you cultivate, manipulate, and sometimes incubate the raw materials gathered for ideas until they are molded into functional use. The role of the artist is perhaps the most challenging. It also takes some dedication and persistence. If the explorer asks Where? then the artist asks How? and What? How can I adapt other ideas for my own use? What can I do to make this idea my own?

A creativity course was introduced into the College of Business at Stanford University years ago in response to the criticism that American business lacked creativity. In their 1986 best-selling book *Creativity in Business*, Michael Ray and Rochelle Myers highlight this aspect of the creative process by including a chapter entitled "Ask Dumb Questions." To the artist, questions are the paintbrush and canvas; to the architect, questions are the pencil and tape measure. Questions probe for the seeds of solution. You can begin by asking "What if?" questions (and not all of these have turned out to be dumb!). Consider these examples: What if we made a music video with musicians dancing on treadmills? What if you could store and play music from 5,000 CDs in one small handheld device? What if a car ran on solar power rather than gas? What might seem like a dumb question now may hold the answer to a nagging problem down the road. Regarding the creative process, there is no such thing as a dumb question. "Dumb" questions shift the train of thought from the left (analytical) to the right (receptive) hemisphere of the brain, and receptivity is needed to play with the raw materials of thought. What if? questions are as valuable a tool to the artist as the compass and map are to the explorer. Asking What if? questions gives permission to manipulate and tailor ideas. Sometimes being an artist means being ridiculous, turning thoughts upside down or inside out. To an artist, paint, clay, plaster, and bronze are some of the media with which to create. In the creative process, there are many cognitive media as well. Thinking styles to manipulate ideas include reversing the perspective on concepts (e.g., throwing a barbecue for Christmas), connecting ideas together (a squirt gun and toothpaste), or comparisons (life is like a tea bag—you don't know your strength until you're put in hot water). And here is some food for thought: Picasso once said that "every act of creation first involves an act of destruction." Ideas that worked well in one situation may not be applicable to other circumstances; however, they can be adapted to the situation at hand.

The Judge. When the role of the judge comes into play, a shift from soft to hard thinking takes place. The crops are ready to be harvested. The judge decides thumbs up or thumbs down for each idea, with the good ideas becoming reality. The role of judge is crucial, for it can just as easily destroy good ideas as bring them to fruition. In American culture, the judge is usually the strongest player on the creative team. More often than not, in fact, the strength of the judge overwhelms and destroys the team. Rational thought and overanalysis used at the wrong time are a waste of both time and resources. To kill or use an idea before it has been manipulated by the artist's hands is like walking out of the middle of the best movie you ever saw. You wouldn't do that. Neither would you make a habit of eating unripe fruit. As a rule, Americans are "top-heavy" in judgment to the detriment of the other necessary aspects of the creative process. In the Stanford creativity course mentioned previously, one of the first concepts students were taught was to "unlearn" judgment skills. Judgment in the germination stage of creativity is unhealthy. Later on, in the secondary phase of creativity, judgment skills are reassembled and strengthened. The skill of intuition is also emphasized. Although intuition is regarded as a right-brain function, it serves as a bridge to left-brain thinking. Intuition is the quarterback in the football game of creativity.

The role of judge involves taking risks. As inventor Grace Hopper once said, "A ship in a port is safe, but that's not what ships are built for." To that we can add this advice from business executive Harry Gray: "No one ever achieved greatness by playing it safe" (von Oech, 1986). Risk taking can seem like a dangerous proposition because there is always the possibility of failure. Failure, of course, can prove painful, a sensation the ego would rather avoid. With failure is the chance of rejection, and rejection tends to lower self-esteem. This may sound incongruous, but failure is the first step to success. Edison tried 1,800 different types of filaments before he found one that worked in the light bulb. Author Mario Puzo approached nineteen different publishers before he found one that would accept his manuscript entitled *The Godfather*. Contrary to popular opinion, failure isn't lack of achievement—it is lack of effort. In the words of comedian and film producer/director Woody Allen, "If you're not failing every now and again, it's a sign that you're not trying anything innovative."

Risks can be classified as either good or bad. With a little bit of intelligence, a calculation can be made regarding the strength of an idea. A good judge weighs the positive aspects against the negative ones. A good judge isn't biased by assumptions that preclude future possibilities. In the event of a calculated risk that sours, failure can still be a great teacher. Use your intuition and go with the good risks.

The Warrior. Giving the green light to go ahead with a good idea doesn't signify the end of the creative process. As von Oech explains, the role of the warrior is to campaign for the idea. It tries the idea out and markets it. The warrior is the anchor leg of the creative relay team,

and it doesn't take any coaching experience to figure out that the anchor leg has got to be strong. Many good ideas sit around collecting dust because the warrior never finished the race. The role of the warrior, in tandem with the judge, is to take creative ideas to completion. The warrior devises a strategy, a winning game plan. On Wall Street, the importance of strategy and campaigning is summed up as follows: To know and not to do is not to know. Warrior skills include good organization and administration abilities. The warrior also takes risks, but good risks. To be a good warrior, you need strength and endurance—strength to carry the idea to reality, and endurance to carry it far, if need be. A good warrior is an optimist. A good warrior has confidence. And a good warrior is persistent (**FIG. 14.4**).

A quick review of books on creativity reveals that although women are just as creative as men, they rarely receive any acknowledgments. Madame Curie, Fanny Mendelssohn, and Georgia O'Keeffe notwithstanding, women receive little if any credit for their creative efforts. In her book *The 12 Secrets of Highly Creative Women*, author Gail McMeekin not only highlights scores of creative women and their achievements over the past few centuries, but also notes the trends that got them to success. Like von Oech, McMeekin sees the creative process in distinct stages. Some of the twelve secrets include acknowledging your creative self, following your fascinations, conquering your saboteurs, and selecting empowering alliances.

Author Jonah Lehrer has a different take on the creative process through his examination of companies on the vanguard of creativity, from 3M and Google to Apple. Many companies recognize the importance of the creative thought process and encourage this in their employees both on and off the clock. (Despite the fact that Lehrer was too creative with the first chapter turning fact to fiction, *Imagine: How Creativity Works* offers a unique look at how the corporate world values the creative process.)

The Myths of Creativity

In the cut-throat global marketplace where good ideas equate with big bucks, corporate America lauds the flexing of the creative muscle. In an effort to better understand the creative process in corporate America, Harvard MBA professor Teresa Amabile (2005) shattered some common myths about creativity by reading 12,000 journal entries of 238 corporate employees across

Stress with a Human Face

Sometimes what you learn in the classroom has immediate implications for life once outside it. Such was the case of one of my students, Deb, who came to Colorado to participate in a holistic stress management instructor workshop. Among the topics covered was creative problem solving a skill that came in handy only a day later. Rather than flying to Colorado from Indiana for the event, she and her husband opted to take the train. When she arrived at the Amtrak station in Denver for her return trip back home, she discovered (after hours and hours of waiting) that the delay was the result of mechanical problems. Once the train left the tracks there were more delays. Any other trip back home might have been different, but Deb's husband, (an organ transplant patient) had a physician's appointment the following morning that simply could not be rescheduled.

With all the delays, they were not going to make it. Rather than getting stressed, Deb reflected on her assets, including her new creative problems-solving skills to cope with the predicament. After coming up with lots of viable options (and a few crazy ones) to get home in time, the plan she selected was to rent a car and drive from Galesburg, Illinois, to Indianapolis, Indiana. It worked! They got home in time for her husband's appointment. According to Deb, "Instead of complaining about this situation, I jumped right into solution mode. Here is the epilogue to this story. Amtrak did not issue me a $136.13 refund, but they did give me a $200 travel voucher to use within the next year toward my next Amtrak travel. We'll see."

FIGURE 14.4 Several decades after his death, Thomas Alva Edison is still considered to be one of the most creative Americans with more than 1,093 patents. Here is his desk in his Florida studio where much of his creative process—from artist to warrior—took place.

the country. She summarized her findings of her diary study as the "Six Myths of Creativity":

1. *Creativity comes from creative people.* Amabile found that everybody with normal intelligence has the potential to be very creative, not just those in research and design.

2. *Money is a creativity motivator.* Not true! People who spent gobs of time thinking about bonuses did very little creative thinking.

3. *Time pressure fuels creativity.* In truth, people are the least creative when they are under the pressure of deadlines. Creativity requires an incubation

BOX 14.1   Creativity in the Twenty-First Century Job Market

It's no secret that America's once thriving economy has undergone massive changes in the past decade. More changes are on the way. Not only have manufacturing jobs gone overseas, but also jobs in research and design, all to increase quarterly profits for stockholders. According to experts, no longer do we have high-wage, middle-skilled jobs. Instead, we have low-wage/low-skilled jobs and high-wage, high-skilled jobs. According to *New York Times* columnist Thomas Friedman, today's college graduate will have to learn to be innovative. "Because knowledge is available on every Internet-connected device, what you know matters far less than what you can do with what you know. The capacity to innovate—the capacity to solve problems creatively or bring new possibilities to life, and skills like critical thinking, communication, and collaboration are far more important than academic knowledge," he said. Friedman goes on to say that today's graduates need to learn how to think, something not currently taught in our education system (Friedman, 2013).

Educational experts question whether high school students are being adequately prepared for college, while many professionals question whether college student are being adequately prepared for the workforce. Like Friedman, several op-ed columnists writing for the online news site *The Huffington Post* suggest that today's college graduates need to consider creating their own jobs. The expert advice: invent yourself. Make yourself necessary! To do this, you will need to sharpen and utilize your own creativity skills.

Take, for example, Nick D'Aloisio. In 2011 at the age of 14, he purchased an inexpensive instructional software package to design mobile apps. Then, using his imagination (and some sweat equity), he created a popular app that soon got the attention of Yahoo!, who two years later (in 2013) bought the rights for $30 million. Or consider Sara Blakely. She was frustrated by how the clothing available made women's derrieres look less than flattering. So in her search for better options she created a nylon underwear product that women found they couldn't live without. She marketed it to some local stores (including Neiman Marus) and called it Spanx. In 2013, *Forbes* magazine listed her as one of the top billionaires in the United States. Not all creative people are billionaires like Sara, but they are equally happy.

For example, Sherri knew she had great organizational skills. She also found out that many others don't. Putting a few ideas together and combining these with some assertiveness, she created a high-paying position for herself as a personal assistant to several high-profile people (e.g., authors, musicians, actors). She earns a great salary and loves the excitement. Passion comes in many ways. Mark, an avid photographer, took a free weekend Photoshop course and saw that he could make a good living cleaning up other people's images.

How important is creativity in the workforce? One of my students went for a job interview and was offered the job on the spot. Here's how it happened: When asked what was the most significant thing he learned in college, Ira mentioned he had just finished a creativity project in his stress management course. After describing his project, the interviewer offered him the job immediately, saying that creativity was an essential aspect of every twenty-first century position. Ira smiled ear to ear.

Job market experts insist that creating your own position puts you at an advantage of empowerment, but getting started isn't easy. You have to be extremely self-directed. You have to be hungry! Experience helps. Making mistakes is part of the learning process. Not only do you need to have great networking skills, but you have to know your resources (including inner resources) and you have to know how to collaborate with others. These days, simply writing a blog, posting a YouTube video, organizing a flashmob dance, or baking designer cupcakes isn't enough to launch a career. Here are some time-honored questions necessary to ask yourself:

1. What is your passion? If money wasn't an issue, what would you love to do?

2. What are your resources? (Don't forget your inner resources.)

3. How can you turn your passion into a viable (desirable) product?

4. How can you use your networking skills to promote yourself?

5. How can you invent (reinvent) yourself and make yourself relevant in a world where nearly everyone else is doing the same?

period; without this, the creative process suffers. Google now gives one day a week to employees to explore their creativity outside of their work responsibilities. Google executives figured out quickly that unstressed employees are more creative, which then benefits the company.

4. *Fear forces breakthroughs.* Although there is a common belief that depressed people have a greater artistic flair, this wasn't borne out in this study. Rather, happiness, not anxiety, was a key factor in the creative process.

5. *Competition beats collaboration.* Actually, creativity suffers when competition overrides the collaboration process. Once again, stress stifles the creative process and prevents it from reaching its highest potential.

6. *A streamlined organization is a creative organization.* Not true! Downsizing and restructuring inhibit the creative process. Unsurprisingly, rumors of downsizing seem to inhibit the creative process even more.

The bottom line, notes Amabile: When people do the work they love, creativity flourishes, even in tough economic (stressful) times.

Obstacles to the Creative Process

The act of creation can be most pleasant. Roger von Oech called it "mental sex." Maslow (1987) called the feelings associated with it "peak experiences," describing exhilaration or euphoria. If creativity is so much fun, why do so many people shy away from it? Lately, researchers have directed much attention to the reasons people shun the creative process as a whole, as well as its constituents.

What is the biggest roadblock to creativity? Celebrated author Elizabeth Gilbert (*Eat, Pray, Love*) says that without a doubt it is fear. She describes the creative process as amplifying one's existence—a creative, empowering existence that is driven more by curiosity than by anxiety. A fear-based existence is toxic to the creative process. Relying on the word "no" when it comes to being assertive with boundaries may be appropriate most of the time, but not during the creative process. Fear-based actions (such as saying no) become a cage that can imprison us. To set yourself free, you must accept the challenge of being creative. You have to give yourself permission and be persistent to reverse the mind-set of fear-based thinking (Gilbert, 2015).

Contrary to what you might think, creativity is not solely a right-brain function. Rather, it is a partnership between the right brain, the house of the imagination, and the left brain, the source of organization. There are many reasons why the creative process becomes stifled. Most of these have to do with the inability to access the functional powers of the right brain, the overbearing powers of the left brain, or a combination of the two. What is needed is a balance of right- and left-brain cognitive skills. Lack of balance is induced by attitudes and other obstacles that block the creative process. These attitudes are called mental blocks, or in von Oech's terms, mental locks. Von Oech describes ten mental blocks in his book *A Whack on the Side of the Head*, each an attitude debilitating to the creative process. Four of the most common pertaining to stress management are The Right Answer (explorer), I'm Not Creative (artist), Don't Be Foolish (judge), and To Err Is Wrong (warrior). According to von Oech, "We all need a whack on the side of the head to shake us out of routines and force us to rethink our problems." With each following description of a "lock" is an exercise to "whack" the side of your head so that you become more creative.

The Right Answer

Is it possible there is more than one right answer to any problem? More than likely, yes! (See FIG. 14.5 .) But people generally look for just one answer, call it right, and then stop looking. Years ago, singer/songwriter Harry Chapin wrote a song called "Flowers Are Red." The song was inspired by a note sent home with his preschool-aged daughter that said that she had not colored the flower assignment correctly. "Flowers are red, not black," the note said. "My flower died," his daughter explained. Chapin's daughter symbolizes just one of many millions of such experiences. From day one we seemed to be educated that there is a "right" way and a "wrong" way to everything. In the germination phase of the creative process, there are many possibilities. If you are in search of one right answer, you will surely stop once you have found it (FIG. 14.6). Nothing could be more dangerous.

FIGURE 14.5 Slice a pie into eight pieces using only three cuts. There is more than one right answer.

BSAINXLEATNTEARS

FIGURE 14.6   The creative word game. In the letters above, cross out letters so that the remaining six letters, without altering their sequence, will spell a familiar English word.

FIGURE 14.7   Learning to think outside the box.

I'm Not Creative

In one of my courses, I assign students a creativity project on the first night, to be completed by the end of the semester. The moans can be heard from one coast to the other: "I'm not creative" (**FIG. 14.7**). But in the words of author Richard Bach (*Illusions*), "Argue for your limitations, and sure enough, they're yours." Creativity isn't a perception, it is a process. When it is thought of as a perception, it can be very stifling. Everyone is creative—it just takes work. What separates Pablo Picasso, Georgia O'Keeffe, and Paul McCartney from those who say they are not creative is belief in their own creativity. The inspiration from this belief is phenomenal. At the end of each semester, I am told repeatedly by students that the creativity exercise was the best thing they ever did because it taught them they really could be creative.

Don't Be Foolish

Have you ever dropped your tray in the cafeteria, walked around all day with your fly open, made a presentation with food stuck in your teeth, or locked your keys in the car? The embarrassment resulting from such episodes is painful to the ego. Being foolish is thought of as being stupid, and stupidity earns no points in the game of life. We are so cautious about making mistakes for fear of how we will look in public that we constantly keep our guard up. But guarded behavior promotes conformity, and conformity breeds staleness. In the creative process, this mentality can lead to a concept called groupthink, where everyone conforms, goes along with the crowd. Groupthink is dangerous; it stifles creativity. Sometimes it is necessary to be foolish. A giddy outlook gives a new perspective on a situation. Playing the fool can augment the role of the judge to determine the worth of ideas. Being foolish can also mean having a sense of humor, and humor and creativity make wonderful partners.

To Err Is Wrong

There are times when making a mistake is not a good idea. It may cost you your job, marriage, or life. Then again, there are times when making a mistake may result in the most appropriate course of action. Mistakes offer invaluable learning experiences. In the creative process, mistakes are necessary (**FIG. 14.8**). Each mistake bushwhacks a clearer path to a more viable answer. Errors are stepping stones to the next workable possibility. Fear of failure can immobilize the creative process. To the mind of Thomas J. Watson, founder of IBM, "The way to success is to double your rate of failure."

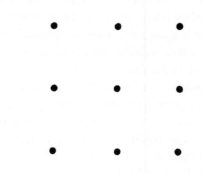

FIGURE 14.8   Connect all nine dots with four straight lines. Go through each dot only once. Do not lift your pencil from the paper. (And don't be afraid to make a mistake or two.)

From a different vantage point, Arthur VanGundy discusses several types of obstacles or roadblocks to the creative process in his book *Training Your Creative Mind*. They include the following:

1. **Perceptual roadblocks:** Perceptual obstacles involve the inability to separate yourself from the problem. Ego attachment blurs creative vision. Perceptual problems occur when left-brain cognitive skills overrule the primary creative processes. Analysis, judgment, and negative perceptions place plaster casts around the creative muscle and cause it to atrophy. There is a time to open up, and a time to narrow your vision. Creativity is like humor: Timing is everything.

2. **Emotional roadblocks:** The primary emotion acting as an obstacle to creativity is fear—fear of making a mistake, fear of the unknown, and fear of rejection, once others find out about past mistakes. When people say they are not creative, many times what they are really saying is, "I am afraid of failure." Fear of failure can paralyze the creative thought process. Fears are natural, but with a little work they can be alleviated or resolved to enhance creativity. Conversely, sometimes we fall so deeply "in love" with an idea we have given birth to that we become blind to its true value or contribution. In these cases it is often best to "sit on" the ideas, and give them time to hatch and prove their merit. But don't sit on an idea too long, or someone else might come along with the same idea and leave you bobbing in the wake of their creativity.

3. **Intellectual/expressive roadblocks:** Humans rely very heavily on vision and hearing, sometimes to the exclusion of other senses. The consequence can be poor receptivity to additional information that could be employed in the gathering and processing of creative ideas. Language can also be a real barrier. Words have specific but different connotations to the people who hear them. For example, a doorway to one person is a passageway to someone else. Each word represents a different image and a different result. Don't let language become a barrier to your creative thoughts.

4. **Cultural roadblocks:** We become socialized to certain thinking patterns. Western culture is now widely recognized as encouraging left-brain-dominant thinkers. That is, the critical styles of thinking associated with the left brain are praised, while the cognitive thinking styles of the right brain are ridiculed or ignored. The net result is asymmetrical thinking. How can this barrier be dismantled? One way is to access your right-brain thinking styles through meditation, yoga, or recreation. Sidney Parnes, a creative consultant to the Disney Corporation, advocates listening to instrumental music to set the imagination free and get creative juices flowing.

5. **Environmental roadblocks:** Environmental factors include personal constraints such as time, noncreative influences (i.e., your friends, spouse, or boss), and resources such as a support network of other people. Have you ever had what you thought was a really good idea and then received feedback that was less than favorable? Negative feedback invariably has a toxic effect on creativity. Be on the lookout for toxic influences and learn to avoid them.

Roadblocks are seldom dead ends. They are merely influences impeding the fruits of creative labor. Several of these roadblocks are self-defeating attitudes, but attitudes can change. If you want to move beyond a roadblock, surrender the attitude. Other roadblocks may involve people, places, or things. In these cases, a roadblock just means that you have to travel a longer distance to get to your final destination. The removal or diversion of roadblocks takes a little time. Sometimes you have to be creative even in the dismantling of obstacles. But in the end, much strength will result from the effort.

Perceptual roadblocks: Obstacles to the creative process, placed by the ego, in the role of the judge.

Emotional roadblocks: Obstacles to the creative process, in the guise of fear, such as the fear of making a mistake (failure), rejection, or the unknown.

Intellectual/expressive roadblocks: Obstacles to the creative process, in this case, created by the language we use that gives bias to our way of thinking (e.g., doorway vs. entrance).

Cultural roadblocks: Cultural thinking patterns that limit our ability to take in new ideas, leading to asymmetrical thinking.

Environmental roadblocks: Personal constraints such as time, money, or a host of responsibilities that impede the creative process.

From Creativity to Creative Problem Solving

Creativity is perhaps one of the most valuable coping techniques to use in your personal battle against stress. If the mechanics involved in creative problem solving—awareness, new ideas, new courses of action, and evaluation—seem familiar, it is because they are the cornerstones of many other coping techniques. In addition, several coping techniques can be included in the creative strategic plan (e.g., cognitive restructuring, social engineering, and communication skills). At first glance, creative problem solving might appear to be a linear sequential process. Linear thinking, however, is a left-brain skill. Without a trip through the corpus callosum for a visit to the right side of the brain, your chances of bringing troublesome situations to closure are about as good as an ice cube's in hell. It makes sense, then, that use of creative skills in the problem-solving process may be circuitous rather than a straight line. Creativity may be used to make order out of chaos, but no one ever said that orderly is synonymous with linear. This is all right because many problems are nonlinear, too. Some are like amoebas, amorphously stretching about.

To illustrate nonlinear thinking (**FIG. 14.9**), let us say that you start out gathering ideas to solve a problem, which is the most logical way to begin. So, you put on your pith helmet and go exploring to collect ideas. When you have a lot of raw materials, you pull out your artbox, toolbox, or whatever toys you need to play with, and hammer away. But in the course of playing, you find you need a few more ideas. So, you change hats and explore some more, and then return to hammering away again. Soon the hammer becomes a gavel as the judge steps in to review the progress so far. The judge approves. "Hmm, not bad," says the warrior. "Let's take this baby out and see if it flies." In flight, the artist says, "Wait! Let's add this to make it stronger." So, there are a few more trips back to the workshop before the product is finished. As you can see, the process, in practice, is anything but a straight line.

> **Creative problem solving:** A coping technique; utilizing creative abilities to describe a problem, generate ideas, select and refine a solution, implement the solution, and evaluate its effectiveness.

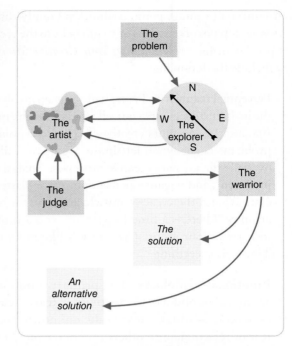

FIGURE 14.9   Creative problem solving is rarely a linear process.

Steps to Initiate Creative Problem Solving

Just as there are many paths to enlightenment, there are many solutions to each problem. Granted, some may be more viable than others, but rarely, if ever, is there only one way out. This is perhaps the most important concept in **creative problem solving**. Among the several theories of creative problem solving, some common concepts do emerge (**FIG. 14.10**), yet the paths to and from these concepts vary significantly depending on the person using them. The first step in creative problem solving is to write everything down on paper. This will make the other steps easier.

Description of the Problem

Before you can attack a problem successfully, you have to understand it. This means looking at the problem from all sides. Objectively state the problem. Define it. Give it some history. Give it someone else's perspective. Project its future influence. Then, subjectively state how you feel about it, the depth of your involvement, and the impact or influence it has had on you. Next, analyze the problem. Dissect it. Look at its components. What are its strengths and weaknesses? What is its face

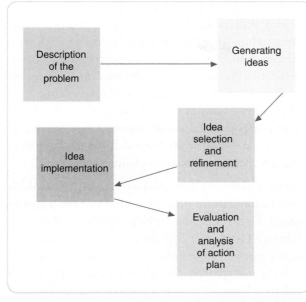

FIGURE 14.10 The map of creative problem solving. Creative problem solving is rarely a linear process because what appears to be a good idea at the start may result in heading back to the drawing board and starting all over again until success is achieved.

value and what is the bottom line? Once you have a handle on the nature of the problem, then you can move on. Remember, though, that throughout the creative process, you will want to revisit this description because over time you will gather more information about it. Any subsequent changes to it may, in turn, alter the final approach you select to handle the problem.

Generating Ideas

Generating ideas is fun; it is also challenging. So, where do ideas come from? Memory is a good place to start—previous experience is always a good teacher. But memory alone isn't enough. Ideas should come from any available resource, both internal and external, from books to people, movies, museums, and you name it. This is where the explorer role comes in. The more ideas you can come up with, the better your chances of solving the problem effectively. When searching for ideas, leave mental censorship behind. Take in every conceivable idea, even if it seems ridiculous. If you start to censor ideas before you gather them, you will come up empty-handed.

Idea Selection and Refinement

Not all of your ideas will be good or usable. But you won't know that until you spread them all out and look at them collectively. Play with the ideas. Order them. Circle them. Line them up like an army of troops. Once your ideas are out on the table, one or two are likely to jump out at you. You might also want to rank-order (judge) your ideas by degree of feasibility (plan A, plan B, plan C, and so on) because not every idea will work, and the idea that looks best now might flop the hardest. Now bring in the artist again and manipulate your idea of choice. Manipulation means adapting the idea to "best fit" the problem. You may need to streamline the idea or to otherwise change it a little to suit your specific needs. Once you have selected your first choice, play it out in your mind. Visualize the idea. What are the pros and cons? Explore hypotheticals and look for potential weaknesses that could be corrected to avoid major pitfalls. Expect the unexpected. Now remember plan B and plan C. A person without options is a person in trouble, so you will want to have some backups. Give some thought to your second and third choices because there is a good chance you will someday use them. Once you have narrowed your ideas down to one choice, it is a good practice to do a quick inventory to see what resources it may require. Not all ideas require additional resources, but many do. Remember that resources may include people as well as material goods, and don't overlook those intangible resources, the hidden talents within each individual.

Idea Implementation

Implementation takes bravery—perhaps not much, but in the face of stress, maybe a lot. Implementation involves a game plan, a strategy. This means thinking about how the idea can be put into effect and end in resolution. It means trying the idea out. In addition to bravery, implementation requires faith.

Evaluation and Analysis of Action

A good inventor observes his or her invention to see how well it works. When the tests are through, either a bottle of champagne is opened or there is a trip back to the proverbial drawing board. Problem solving works the same way. The final lesson a problem has to offer is if and how well it has been resolved. This takes a bit of analysis, so once again call the judge back in to declare a verdict. But there is no verdict of guilty or not guilty. There is either a hard pat on the back or a soft kick in the seat of the pants. In life's journey, you will do well to have an equal number of each, as all of our rough edges need to be polished.

◼ Best Application of Creative Problem Solving

We all have the skills to be creative; the issue is whether we choose to use them. With this coping technique, there really is no choice if you want to deal effectively with stress. How good are your exploring skills? Do you have a curious nature? When was the last time you ventured someplace you have never been before to shop around for ideas? How good are your artistic talents? When is the last time you played in the garage or basement? For that matter, when is the last time you just plain played? Is your artist's hammer a judge's gavel in disguise, ready to smash an idea before it is ripe? These are some questions to ask yourself to find out your strengths and weaknesses in the creative process. Once you identify these areas, you are ready to sharpen these skills.

Psychologist Abraham Maslow said that creativity is a necessary skill to deal with the stress of change. As the understanding of right- and left-brain cognitive skills continues to unfold, it is becoming increasingly obvious that the mind is capable of much more intelligence than was thought before. Creative problem-solving skills are life skills—skills to not only survive but also thrive through the potential chaos of change. Once refined, these skills can and should be used repeatedly as the foundation of every strategy used to confront and resolve stress.

Here is an idea for you to enhance your creativity skills. Be on the lookout for great ideas that you can adapt for yourself. Begin this adventure by finding a three-ring notebook. Then, start collecting images, ads, anything that inspires you to be creative. What you are doing is collecting raw materials to adapt for future projects or problem-solving solutions. This notebook will become a very valuable resource. Know that the most brilliant minds have one of these (and refer to it regularly).

SUMMARY

- Necessity is the mother of invention. When problems arise, solutions come from creative thinking. However, in American culture, critical rather than creative thinking is rewarded.

- In troubled times, people look to the epitome of genius for guidance. Da Vinci's creativity offers insights on how we, too, can be creative.

- Maslow found two stages to the creative process: primary creativity, where ideas are generated in a playful mode; and secondary creativity, where these ideas are refined and implemented.

- Von Oech outlined four phases of creative thinking: the explorer, the artist, the judge, and the warrior. The first two roles are responsible for searching out and generating ideas, whereas the second two refine and implement the selected idea.

- There are many myths about creativity, including that anxiety fosters more creativity. Happiness, it turns out, is creativity's best ally.

- Roadblocks to the creative process can occur at any stage; however, most occur at the explorer and artist phases. Four roadblocks were described in this chapter: The Right Answer, I'm Not Creative, Don't Be Foolish, and To Err Is Wrong.

- VanGundy categorizes obstacles to creativity as roadblocks—emotional, intellectual/expressive, cultural, and environmental.

- The creative problem-solving strategy has five phases: describing the problem, generating ideas, idea selection and refinement, idea implementation, and evaluation and analysis of action.

- Creativity is a large component of mental well-being. The right and left hemispheres of the brain work together as a team to overcome problems resulting in acute or chronic stress.

STUDY GUIDE QUESTIONS

1. Why is creativity thought to be such an important coping technique?

2. Describe the four stages of von Oech's creative-thinking process model.

3. What are four common roadblocks to the creative process?

4. List the five steps in the creative problem-solving process.

APPENDIX: ANSWERS TO CREATIVE PROBLEMS

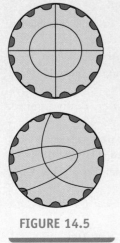

FIGURE 14.5

BANANA and/or LETTER

FIGURE 14.6

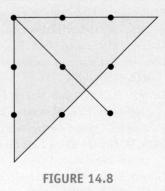

FIGURE 14.8

REFERENCES AND RESOURCES

Allen, W. *The Complete Prose of Woody Allen*. Outlet Books, Avenal, NJ, 1991.

Amabile, T., et al. Affect and Creativity at Work, *Administrative Science Quarterly* 50:367–403, 2005.

Bach, R. *Illusions: The Adventures of a Reluctant Messiah*. Dell, New York, 1977.

Barrett, D. *The Committee of Sleep: How Artists, Scientists, and Athletes Use Dreams for Creative Problem Solving, and How You Can Too*. Crown Publishers, New York, 2001.

Bartlett, J. *Familiar Quotations*, 6th ed. J. Kaplin, ed. Little Brown, Boston, 1992.

Blair, E. More Than 50 Years of Putting Kids' Creativity to the Test. *All Things Considered*, April 17, 2013. www.npr.org/2013/04/17/177040995/more-than-50-years-of-putting-kids-creativity-to-the-test.

Brightman, H. J. *Problem Solving: A Logical and Creative Approach*. College of Business Administration, Georgia State University, Atlanta, 1980.

Bronson, P., and Merryman, A. The Creativity Crisis, *Newsweek*, July 19, 2010.

Buzan, T. *Use Both Sides of Your Brain*, 2nd ed. Dutton, New York, 1983.

Cameron, J. *The Artist's Way*. Jeremy Tarcher/Putnam Books, Los Angeles, CA, 1992.

Clark. R. Why Jonah Lehrer's Imagine Is Worth Reading Despite Its Problems. Poynter.org, September 12, 2012. www.poynter.org/how-tos/newsgathering-storytelling/writing-tools/188506/why-jonah-lehrers-imagine-is-worth-reading-despite-the-problems/.

Crandall, R. (ed.). *Break-Out Creativity: Bringing Creativity to the Workplace*. Select Press, Corte Madera, CA, 1998.

Dossey, L. Creativity: On Intelligence, Insight, and the Cosmic Soup, *Alternative Therapies in Health and Medicine* 6(1): 12–17, 1999.

Elijah, A. M. *Thinking Unlimited*. Institute of Creative Development, Pune, Delhi, India, 1980.

Friedman, T. Need a Job? Invent It. *New York Times Sunday Review*, March 30, 2013. www.nytimes.com/2013/03/31/opinion/sunday/friedman-need-a-job-invent-it.html.

Gardner, H. *Creative Minds*. Basic Books, New York, 1993.

Gawain, S. *Creative Visualization*. New World Library, San Rafael, CA, 1978.

George, B., Don't Just Search for a Job: Create Your Own. *Huffington Post*, November 2, 2011. www.huffingtonpost.com/bill-george/job-creation_b_1070463.html.

Gelb, M. *How to Think Like Leonardo da Vinci*. Dell/Random House, New York, 1998.

Gilbert, E. *Big Magic: Creative Living Beyond Fear*. River Press, New York, 2015.

Gorman, C. K. *Creativity in Business: A Practical Guide for Creative Thinking*. Crisp Publications, Los Altos, CA, 1989.

Harman, W., and Rheingold, H. *Higher Creativity*. Tarcher Press, Los Angeles, 1984.

Jackson, H. Research on the Effects of Television, *Labour of Love*, May 30, 2004. www.labouroflove.org/tv-toys-&-technology/television/research-on-the-effects-of-television.

Johnson, C. H. Stages of Creativity, *Shift* 6:14–15, 2005.

Kelly, T., et al. *The Art of Innovation: Lessons in Creativity from IDEO*. Doubleday, New York, 2001.

Knapp, L. Brazen Life, 6 Simple Steps to Create a Badass Career. *Huffington Post*, March 12, 2013. www.huffingtonpost.com/brazen-life/6-simple-steps-to-create-_b_2860340.html.

Lehrer, J. Imagine: How Creativity Works. Houghton Mifflin, New York, 2012.

Mander, J. *Four Arguments for the Elimination of Television*. Harper Books, New York, 1978.

Maslow, A. *The Farther Reaches of Human Nature*. Esalen/Penguin Books, New York, 1971.

Maslow, A. H. *Motivation and Personality*, 3rd ed. Harper & Row, New York, 1987.

McMeekin, G. *The 12 Secrets of Highly Creative Women*. Conari Press, Berkeley, CA, 2000.

Meng, T. K. Everyone Is Born Creative, but It Is Educated out of Us at School. *The Guardian*, May 18, 2016. https://www.theguardian.com/media-network/2016/may/18/born-creative-educated-out-of-us-school-business.

Moyers, B. *A World of Ideas*. Doubleday, New York, 1989.

O'Connor, C. Undercover Billionaire Sara Blakely Joins the Rich List Thanks to Spanx. *Forbes*, March 7, 2013.

Olson, R. W. *The Art of Creative Thinking*. HarperCollins, New York, 1986.

Parnes, S. J. *Visionizing*. D. O. K. Publishers, East Aurora, NY, 1988.

Ray, M., and Myers, R. *Creativity in Business*. Doubleday, New York, 1986.

Scaggs, A. Jack Johnson—The Dude Abides, *Rolling Stone*, March 6, 2008. www.rollingstone.com/news/story/18684236/jack_johnson.

Shallcross, D. J. *Teaching Creative Behavior*. Bearly Limited, Buffalo, NY, 1985.

Sicchy, I. What Happened When the Bard Questions Music: Interview with Sting, *Interview* August, 2003: 134–135.

Stok, G. *The Book of Questions*. Workman Press, New York, 1987.

Tharp, T. *The Creative Habit: Learn It and Use It For Life*. Simon & Schuster, New York, 2003.

Toffler, A. *Future Shock*. Bantam Books, New York, 1970.

VanGundy, A. B. *Techniques of Structured Problem Solving*. Van Nostrand Reinhold, New York, 1981.

VanGundy, A. B. *Training Your Creative Mind*. Prentice-Hall, Englewood Cliffs, NJ, 1982.

von Oech, R. Creative Think. http://blog.creativethink.com. Accessed March 14, 2008.

von Oech, R. *A Kick in the Seat of the Pants*. Harper & Row, New York, 1986.

von Oech, R. A *Whack on the Side of the Head* (revised edition). Business Plus, New York, 2008.

von Oech, R., and Willett, G. *Expect the Unexpected*. Berrett-Koehler Publishers, San Francisco, 2002.

Wynett, C. B., and Harris, G. Yes, You are a Creative Genius! *Spirituality & Health* 5(4):40–43, 2003.

CHAPTER 15

Communication Skills in the Information Age

The three most important words for any successful relationship are: Communication, Communication, Communication.

—Anonymous

John is a partner in a *Fortune* 500 telecommunications firm. Just a few years out of college, he is the epitome of success: a great job; a beautiful wife, Sherry; two children (twins); a 4,000-square-foot house; and a six-figure salary. What began as a fascination with software programs in high school quickly led to a management position with the biggest phone company in the country. But the cell phone technology that launched his career nearly became his downfall. One day his wife game him an ultimatum: the smartphone or her.

John, it turns out, had quite the addiction to his smartphone. During conversations with Sherry, he would constantly check text messages, his Twitter feed, Facebook updates, video links, Google+, emails, Skype, and voicemail messages. These communications were not only John's business links to the outside world, but also an incessant ego-driven fix, at the expense of his marriage. At first Sherry was upset that John interrupted every conversation with what she called "the other woman." Then she became indignant. She couldn't even have a decent conversation with her husband unless she called or texted him first. Finally, she gave him an ultimatum: If the smartphone wasn't turned off at home, she was leaving—with the twins! John knew she was right. The smartphone now stays in his car when he pulls into the driveway each night.

Experts find that John's troubles are common in this age (Winch, 2011; Alleyne, 2012). Moreover, people, particularly young adults, are changing their communication styles about as quickly as the devices and apps that they communicate with. Ironically, young people (from middle-school to graduate school) often text message, tweet, and email in close proximity of the person with whom they are communicating (FIG. 15.1). For some, it's a whole new language (e.g., LOL, 4EAE, and TTYL). For many, it has become the preferred way to communicate, mostly out of convenience (but avoidance of direct face-to-face communication also plays a role). Despite expectations, instant messaging doesn't mean an instant reply. Unmet expectations often cause frustration (stress!). If young people are not text messaging or tweeting, they are sharing information through their Facebook, Pinterest, or Google+ accounts. In fact, so new are the changes in technology that few studies have been done to understand the ramifications of how communication skills affect relationships when convenience is a higher priority than content. But this we do know: Emails don't convey voice intonation. Text messages don't convey body language (an important part of communication), and voicemail can't replace eye contact. Even Skype has limitations. All this means that much is lost in translation. Consequently, the potential for stress in interpersonal relationships increases dramatically when people use incomplete forms of communication. Moreover, experts note that people under the age of 30 might have savvy, if not annoying, text messaging habits, yet their

interpersonal (face-to-face) communication skills are deplorable—little or no eye contact, awkwardness, and so on. Companies that interview college graduates express frustration with the growing number of interviewees who demonstrate poor interpersonal communication skills leading to interpersonal difficulties and miscommunications in today's workplace (Compton, 2001, Education-Portal.com). Poor communication of one's thoughts and feelings affects more than just roommates, spouses, children, or colleagues; the ripple effect goes beyond the family or worksite to the entire community. Despite the rapid advances in technology and how we employ these means to express ourselves, the basics of communication skills remain the same. Because of the rapid changes in technology and communication, this chapter is now divided into two sections: High-Tech Communication and Face-to-Face Communication.

High-Tech Communication: Welcome to Information and Communication Overload

It's no exaggeration to say that there is an explosive mass of information and cyber-noise in the world today. This tsunami of bits, bytes, words, photos, tweets, and YouTube video clips brings about the need to assimilate, digest, and share this information with others. Many people call this age we are living in the "information age," but a more apt description is the "communication age." Ironically, face-to-face communication is becoming a rare event, if not a thing of the past for some as our global society progresses further into this social networking labyrinth. Middle school and high school teachers as well as college professors bemoan the fact that kids today don't know how to make proper eye contact when speaking face to face. Convenience has come at a price of a greatly diminished quality of interpersonal communications, adding a whole new layer of stress to the human condition. Without a doubt, communication stress affects the relationships between college roommates, friends, acquaintances, spouses, co-workers—indeed, nearly everyone!

Despite the multitude of communication options we have (and the number grows daily), our skills at conveying information, specifically in terms of our own thoughts and feelings, are considered to be poor at best, and diminishing. This fact has not gone unnoticed in the corporate world, where the competition for jobs is fierce and poor communication plays a significant role in who gets hired. This chapter invites you to examine (or perhaps re-examine) your assets and liabilities in terms of your ability to communicate,

FIGURE 15.1

and then work to improve these skills so that you may minimize this aspect of stress in your life.

High-Tech Miscommunication

Perhaps the biggest problem that arises when two or more people communicate is that the message is not received as it was intended. As the expression goes, "Something was lost in translation." This issue is known as miscommunication. This stressor can become an intense whirlpool of negativity, as stress increases among all parties involved, thereby magnifying feelings of anger and fear, many of which are left unresolved until the next communication episode, or perhaps indefinitely.

Miscommunication can be cited as an underlying cause for everything from divorce to wars and a multitude of arguments and conflicts in between. Repeated miscommunication fans the flames of anger (frustrations and annoyances) and fear (anxiety, doubt, and insecurity). Although it might seem that advances in technology would decrease the frequency of miscommunication, we all know this not to be true. The vast majority of text messages and emails have no emotional intonation, often creating an air of doubt (Is she or he mad at me?). Furthermore, dishonesty (a defense mechanism of the ego) arises when people claim to have an urgent phone call for a quick exit to avoid issues and people.

Although technology has changed dramatically over the years, the ego's influence on human nature has remained the same. Hence, age-old problems with communication persist, yet are now greatly magnified under a multifaceted communications network. Excellent communication skills as an effective coping technique in the age of high-technology are not only important, but essential.

■ The Technology Gap

Decades ago, the term "generation gap" was used to describe the communication chasm between parents and their teen children. Today, the expression "technology gap" is used to explain the technology preferences of people over and under 30 years of age. Generally speaking, people over 30 have a preference for phone calls over text messages and emails, whereas people under 30 favor texting as their primary method of communication (**FIG. 15.2**). Tension arises when these generational communication preferences conflict, often with a little arrogance (from sarcasm to indifference) thrown in on both sides of the divide. For example, people under age 30 who have grown up in a world of immediate gratification tend to be more impatient when responses are less than instantaneous. On the other hand, people over the

FIGURE 15.2   People under the age of 30 prefer to text rather than email or talk face-to-face, often placing convenience over quality when it comes to communication.

age of 30 take offense at emailed thank you notes, finding them less genuine than a handwritten card.

■ Anger and Fear Influences with High-Tech Communication

Both fear and anger can cloud our ability to communicate effectively. Under the influence of anger, thoughts and feelings that might have been consciously filtered before leaving the mouth (or keypad) become verbal projectiles, often offending others, hurting some and ultimately leaving a mess to clean up afterward. Conversely, fear can add multiple layers of filters to one's thoughts and feelings. The result is that people often don't say what they really think or feel. For example, you might not like the new corporate organizational structure due to lost work hours, but directly conveying your thoughts and/or feelings may result in losing your job altogether. Simply stated, poor communication skills—the inability to express one's thoughts and feelings—amplifies one's stress levels.

Smartphones, Dumb Messages

Before exploring some of the basics of good communication skills, it would be wise to give this topic more perspective with regard to the use of technology today and much of the stress it produces. The following are some of the more prevalent issues with regard to communication and miscommunication in the age of high-tech information gadgets:

1. *Communication without emotions:* How many times have you received a text message or email and

wondered if the sender was mad, upset, or less than ecstatic about something? Not having emotional cues to match the message can leave one in a cloud of doubt. Compelling word choice, punctuation, and the craft of an engaging writing style are what makes reading a novel so enthralling. Rarely, if ever, are text messages and emails enthralling. When the emotional flavor is missing, the mind tends to fill in the blanks, often creating more stress, usually turning molehills into mountains.

2. *Hiding behind technology:* Technology has made avoiding some face-to-face situations quite easy, such as quitting your job with a text message, dumping a girlfriend or boyfriend with a public tweet or email, or even inadvertently humiliating a friend on Facebook with an unflattering photo. Although people have always found ways to avoid others they don't wish to talk to, technology (through the use of caller ID) has made it much easier to avoid direct communication.

3. *Covering up the truth:* How many times have you said, "This call is urgent," when it really wasn't? Just like avoidance, lying has always been a part of the human condition, but technology allows people to add a whole new layer of deceit by, for example, denying they received phone calls, voice messages, or text messages via dropped calls. As we all know, lying is a poor communication skill, and compromises the integrity of any relationship.

4. *Absence of body language:* Well before language was ever used as a form of communication, humans used body language as the primary means of personal expression. Body language, it is said, is hardwired into our DNA and often expressed unconsciously. By and large, people will trust body language much more than the spoken word, particularly when there is a mixed message. As the expression goes, the body doesn't lie. Things are different now. Unless you're on Skype (and even then this is limiting), body language is basically irrelevant with the use of smartphones. Although some people may use emoticons (e.g., ☺) at the end of a text, there is little to go on beyond the typed word or abbreviation (IMHO). Trust issues, wrapped in anxiety and frustrations, often ensue without the ability to fall back on body language.

5. *Privacy issues:* Conversations using technology are no longer just between two people. Like it or not, our privacy is not what it used to be. Many employers are now asking employees for their Facebook passwords, and even if you think your Facebook settings are private with postings to just your friends, most likely they are not.

6. *Communication/information overload:* Years ago, people had healthy boundaries with the use of the home telephone (e.g., the no phone calls after 9:00 P.M. rule). Now that people carry their cell phones everywhere (including to bed), accessibility is constant. The fact that people can now access you 24/7 can lead to communication overload. Add to this the constant trolling for information on Facebook, Twitter, Pinterest, Instagram, Snapchat, Tumblr, or other means, and information overload becomes quite common.

7. *Brevity vs. integrity:* The convenience of communicating with technology is nothing short of amazing (e.g., 140 characters on Twitter or a brief text message), but convenience can carry with it carelessness and brashness, a bad combination. Carelessness in brief communication, from typos (or even auto-correction) to poor word choices, can lead to abundant miscommunication (as anyone who has seen the Twitter bloopers circulating on Facebook can attest). Moreover, the spoken word has many intonations and nuances that are simply not there with text messages and emails (with the prevalent use of all caps and exclamation points to make a point). Although it may be true that attention spans have decreased dramatically, brevity in the expression of thoughts and feelings can promote misunderstanding to others and frustration for the recipient of these messages. Stated simply, brevity can compromise one's communication integrity. Short text messages and tweets cannot possibly convey the depth of one's consciousness.

8. *Screen time vs. direct eye contact:* Admit it: It is hard to take your eyes off of a smartphone screen, tablet screen, or for that matter even a flat screen TV. The allure of the screen can be very addicting, particularly with high-resolution features. When speaking to someone face to face, the eyes are the most compelling feature. To paraphrase an expression, the eyes are the screen of the soul. So why has it become hard to make eye contact in the digital age? It is more difficult to lie to someone while making eye contact. In some Asian cultures, prolonged eye contact is considered rude, yet in the majority of American cultures, the lack of

eye contact conveys not only rudeness, but also dishonesty. Is abundant screen time changing the culture of face-to-face communication regarding eye contact? The answer appears to be yes, but not without an added stress component for many.

How to Incorporate Effective Communication Skills into Your Life Routine

1. *Establish healthy boundaries.* Contrary to popular belief, you do not have to be accessible 24 hours a day, 7 days a week. Create blocks of time when you are free of the electronic leash of your smartphone and computer and stick to this schedule (e.g., no emails or text messages after 9:00 P.M., or no smartphones in the bedroom). Technology is supposed to serve you, not enslave you. If you feel like you are always accessible, you need better boundaries. Additionally, communicate to others these boundaries so they know when you are available and when you are not. This will help them avoid feeling frustrated.

2. *Honor the "touch it once" rule.* If you open emails and read them but plan to respond later, most likely later will never come. The "touch it once" rule suggests that once you open an email or text, you need to respond in some way, even if it's a short message. Remember to honor your healthy boundaries as well.

3. *Be courteous.* When you are talking to someone, no matter who it is, turn off your cell phone. Interrupting a face-to-face conversation to answer a phone call is simply rude. No exceptions. Being courteous also means being honest. This includes not indicating that every phone call or text message is important when it's really not.

4. *Maintain polite eye contact.* When addressing someone face to face, make it a point to maintain polite eye contact. If you find your eyes glancing down, gently remind yourself to redirect your focus toward the eyes of the person with whom you are speaking.

5. *Keep personal issues private.* Privacy is certainly an issue these days, but making a private argument public through various social media is simply immature. Avoid airing dirty laundry through social networking. It not only makes you look bad, it's inappropriate behavior.

6. *Attack issues, not people.* When you find yourself in the midst of a conflict, step back and look at the issues at hand. Rather than resorting to mud-slinging (attacking people), address the issues. For example, rather than saying to some, "You lie!" say, "I sense the issue here is honesty. Can we address this issue?"

7. *Avoid putting others on the defensive.* When people are stressed, they tend to take things personally. Taking things personally is code for being on the defensive. When people are on the defensive, they don't hear words as they are meant to be expressed; rather, they hear through the filter of ego, which tends to exaggerate one's insecurities. Two people who are stressed compound the degree of defensiveness, resulting in much miscommunication. Learn to disarm others by learning to avoid putting them on the defense. Equally important, learn to let down your defensive guard as well.

8. *Learn to be technology multilingual.* If you are like most people, most likely you have a preference in your communication styles (e.g., texting rather than phone calls). Remember that not everyone has the same preference. Some people prefer phone calls. Others prefer emails. Still others prefer live, face-to-face contact whenever possible. Learn to know what the preferred style is for the people with whom you communicate. If you are unsure, ask! Honor their preference when at all possible.

9. *Avoid information overload.* When the mind is flooded with information, mental processes are compromised, from concentration skills and memory to communication skills. The mind's ability to absorb and process information (both consciously and unconsciously) is extraordinary, but not without limits. Too much information, also known as sensory overload, is also called burnout. Burnout is a code word for stress. How do you control the amount of information you take in through your eyes and ears? Once again, healthy boundaries are suggested.

10. *Resolve communication problems when they arise.* It's a given that episodes of miscommunication and conflict will arise among people with whom you are connected. Avoidance (the flight response) may seem like an easy course of action, but ageless wisdom reminds us that ignoring problems only tends to make them worse down the road. When you find yourself in the midst of a communication meltdown, take time to resolve problems as soon as possible. Face-to-face communication is always the best way.

The Basics of Face-to-Face Communication Skills

When Marissa Mayer took over the helm of Yahoo! in 2013 as the new CEO, the first thing she did was require everyone to work on-site at the company headquarters in Sunnyvale, California, rather than telecommute from their homes (or the nearest Starbucks). As Mayer and many other CEOs have learned, face-to-face contact and interpersonal communication have become essential for the cutting-edge creative process in the high-tech business world. To improve communication among employees, several CEOs of high-tech companies have mandated no-email Fridays as a way for people to get out of their cubicles and have direct human contact with their fellow employees. High-tech communication has its benefits, but for many reasons including trust, spontaneity, creativity, honesty, and integrity, it simply cannot and should not replace face-to-face communication.

If you were to make a list of your top ten stressors, you would probably find that at least half of these involve relationships with family, friends, and co-workers. Strong relationships necessitate good communication skills. To paraphrase poet John Donne, "No man is an island entire of itself. Each is a piece of the continent, a part of the main." As such, our lives are filled with much interaction. Like molecules ricocheting around a glass jar, we are bound to come in contact with a number of people over the course of any day. These "contacts" often prove stressful because of the nature of our communicative interactions. Experts indicate that the average person spends approximately three-quarters of his or her waking day communicating with others. Included under the rubric of communication are phone calls, emails, text messaging, blogging, lectures, staff meetings, dinner conversations, listening to radio and television, and simply talking with friends and acquaintances. The degree of perception and interpretation required for communication, and the many layers of meaning in even common words, leaves much room for misunderstanding—and hence stress. This is why the practice of good communication skills is so important to help minimize and resolve misunderstandings. Good communication skills are *essential* as a coping technique.

To be a good communicator, one must not only express thoughts and feelings in understandable words, but also listen, clarify, and process information as it is intended.

BOX 15.1   The Art of Gender: Decoding the Spoken Language

Both men and women code their choice of words. Here are some of the most common words and phrases, and what they really mean if each gender actually said what was on their mind.

Women (talking to men):

1. *Fine:* This is the word women use to end an argument. It does not mean fine as in good or "fine dining," it means the conversation is over and you lost. If you are married and you hear the word "fine," most likely you will be sleeping in a different room that night.

2. *Nothing:* This is the answer to the question, "What's wrong?" Nothing really means something is *very* wrong. Her side of the conversation will begin with the word "nothing" and will usually end with the word "fine."

3. *Don't worry about it:* This phrase is used after a woman asks a man to do something and months later decides instead to do it herself. This will eventually end with the man asking, "What's wrong?"

4. *Go ahead:* This phrase translates to a dare. It does not, repeat, does not mean you have permission. If you do go ahead, most likely you will hear the word "fine" later in the day.

Men (talking to women):

1. *Really?:* This is not a question. This is a ploy men use to get more information because they weren't paying attention the first time you spoke.

2. *I'll do it later:* The operative word here is "later." It could mean next week, it could mean in a few years. If it can be postponed long enough, all the better. At some point, he might hear her say, "Don't worry about it" (see "Women").

3. *Go ahead:* This phrase really means "Do whatever you want for several hours, while I get caught up on my video games."

4. *You sure?:* This really means, "We don't have enough money in our savings account to cover this purchase, can you find something else?" If she explains why she has to have it, answer, "Really?"

Communication skills are so important in the business world that workshops and seminars are given regularly on this topic; poor communication skills are simply not cost-effective. As you will see in this chapter, almost every theory and accompanying skill is based on common sense. Yet common sense is often bound and gagged when the ego is threatened. When people are defensive, their ability to gather, process, and even exchange information becomes greatly impaired. The result is miscommunication and the stress that miscommunication produces.

Conversational Styles

Each person has his or her own distinct style of communication. According to linguistics expert Dr. Deborah Tannen of George Washington University (2001), not only do the interpretations of words cause misunderstandings in relationships, but so do the styles in which people speak. Both, she notes, are a major reason for marital problems and, in some cases, divorce. Moreover, Tannen indicates that people from different regions of the country have specific communication styles (e.g., New York City versus Texas). And, perhaps to no surprise, men typically display a different communication style than women do. Communication styles include, among others, dominant, interruptive, manipulative, polite, creative, sarcastic, and passive means. It is friction caused by differing conversational styles that causes or adds to conflict. In our attempts to communicate under stress, styles become exaggerated, which Tannen terms **schismogenesis**, thus further widening the gap of misunderstanding.

A particular conversational style is a type of behavior, which in some situations may need to be refined, adapted, or changed to resolve issues between two people. Take, for example, the case of a woman from Texas who moved to Washington, D.C., as an assistant director of human

resources management for a large company. Within weeks her communication style and demeanor were perceived as unassertive, whereas in Texas she had been praised for being appropriately polite.

In her much-acclaimed book *That's Not What I Meant*, Tannen also describes the serious problem of misinterpretation of the spoken message. Tannen calls the underlying intent of communications **metamessages**, or the meanings of the messages that are clear to the speaker but masked by a particular vernacular and style construed as polite or nonoffensive. Misunderstanding is compounded by the interpretation of the listener as well. For instance, upon learning that his sister Sheila is pregnant, Mark may ask, "Did you quit smoking yet?" The metamessage expresses concern for the health of the baby. But Sheila's interpretation may be that Mark is passing judgment on her health habits, making her quite angry. From Tannen's research, she has come to the conclusion that people—or Americans, at least—tend to be indirect rather than direct in the messages they communicate, whether out of politeness, fear, or manipulation. This indirectness is a precursor to perceived stress, and greatly compromises the effectiveness of communication, leading to further misunderstanding and potential conflict. Verbal communication is one way to get a message across, but by no means the only way. Metamessages also are stated indirectly through postures, clothes, and facial expressions. Thus, communication is basically categorized as verbal and nonverbal.

Verbal Communication

Verbal language is a series of expressive thoughts and perceptions described through word symbols. Linguistic experts divide verbal communication into two components: encoding and decoding. **Encoding** is the process wherein a speaker attempts to frame thoughts and perceptions into words (e.g., someone saying to the person next to her, "Boy, it's stuffy in here"). **Decoding** is the process wherein the message is translated, dissected, analyzed, and interpreted by the listener (e.g., the person hearing this thinks, "Yeah, the room does smell rather gamey"). Misunderstanding, confusion, and stress can arise anywhere in this process.

Although it may seem that two people who speak English would have a common understanding of all English words, in fact, variations in the meanings given to words can lead to much confusion as well. Anyone who has traveled to Great Britain, Australia, or New Zealand

> **Schismogenesis:** A term coined by Deborah Tannen suggesting that exaggerated conversation styles become intensified under stress, thus adding to miscommunication.
>
> **Metamessages:** The underlying intention of verbal communication when people are indirect with their comments, thus adding to miscommunication.
>
> **Encoding:** The process in which the speaker attempts to frame his or her thoughts and perceptions into words.
>
> **Decoding:** A process in which the listener attempts to understand what the speaker has encoded in his or her verbal message.

has discovered that even in English-speaking countries, language barriers exist. For example, a jumper is a dress in the States, whereas it is a sweater Down Under. And don't use the words "fanny pack" in England or you'll get strange looks. Moreover, you don't have to leave America to experience this phenomenon; vernacular differences can be found all across the country. For example, the words *tonic*, *soda*, and *pop* are all used colloquially to describe soft drinks. But in the Boston area a tonic is considered a cola, whereas in Denver it denotes seltzer. Additionally, cultural vernacular gives rise to new meanings for words, often representing the opposites of their dictionary definitions. For example, the word *bad* may have negative connotations to you, but currently many people employ this adjective to describe something emphatically good, as in "That's a bad hat." Quite often, the meanings of words are arbitrary. And possessing both literal and figurative meanings, words and expressions can also be ambiguous. FBI chief J. Edgar Hoover once corrected a memo his secretary typed with a note to "watch the borders" (margins). Misunderstanding, she added his comment to the memo and sent it out nationwide. Immediately all FBI agents on the Canadian and Mexican borders were placed on alert. Verbal and written communication is more complex than meets the ear or eye.

The key to interpersonal communication can be summed up as: Say what you mean, and mean what you say. In other words, be direct. Implementing this rule in our conversational style, however, is extremely difficult. One reason confusion arises is that there are many concepts, ideas, and particularly feelings that are difficult to articulate within the limits of vocabulary. Thoughts, like color photographs, can often be described only in black-and-white terms, leaving many details to assumption, interpretation, and imagination. Some thoughts cannot be expressed in words at all, and the words we choose to describe the contents of our conscious minds can limit our own understanding of what we wish to express as well.

The **Sapir-Whorf hypothesis**, created to explain the use of words, suggests that our perception of reality is largely based on the depth of the vocabulary in which we express ourselves. In other words, our vocabulary limits our understanding of our current reality. So, someone with a limited vocabulary will have a more difficult time expressing him- or herself, as is easily illustrated when learning a new language. Even when vocabulary does appear to describe thoughts adequately, words are often used to camouflage true feelings in an attempt to avoid hurting others or even ourselves. The inability to express how we really feel can also promote unacknowledged anxiety.

Communicating Ideas and Feelings

Sharing personal ideas and feelings is referred to as **self-disclosure**, opening up and revealing a part of you that is not obvious from external appearances. Self-disclosure is based on mutual trust. It is believed by those who study communication skills that all verbal communication involves some element of self-disclosure. It can be a double-edged sword, for there is risk in divulging personal insights and feelings. When individuals sense that sharing feelings will promote a closer relationship or bonding, then the risk is assessed as minimal and opening up is worth it. If rejection or alienation may ensue, however, then the degree of openness will be greatly limited. Likewise, when trust has been violated in the past, the ability to self-disclose is greatly compromised. One might think that the closer two people are, the greater the depth of self-disclosure there is, and initially this may be true. But in many cases, once the parameters of a relationship are established, laziness sets in and styles are taken for granted, thus leaving many perceptions and assumptions that may or may not represent true feelings.

Describing feelings differs from expressing feelings, in that description involves the use of words, whereas expression may include physical responses such as crying, laughing, touching, or some other physical action. Although there are many ways to express emotions, verbal communication is deemed essential when they involve other people. When feelings are not put into words, assumptions occur in the minds of those with whom you interact, and assumptions can be dangerous. These guessing games often lead to confusion about the intentions and thoughts of everyone involved. Again, the result is frustration and emotional pain.

> **Sapir-Whorf hypothesis:** The idea that our perception of reality is based largely on the words we use to communicate or express ourselves.
>
> **Self-disclosure:** The process in which a person reveals various aspects of him- or herself that are not readily apparent.

Stress with a Human Face

Photo courtesy of Gianni Scozzarro.

Swimming was Gianni's passion, and you could tell just by listening to him talk about it. He was a freestyle sprinter, and proud of it. Training and competition are not without their stressful moments, nor is the transition from high school to college swimming an easy one. In a visit to my office one day, Gianni confided that he was having some problems, specifically communication and attitude problems, with the coach. "I'm a sprinter, not a distance swimmer," he exclaimed. "And I thrive on positive reinforcement. All I seem to get is negative talk. I can tell he really doesn't like me."

"Gianni, have you made it a point to sit down and talk with the coach?" I asked. "Does he even know you feel this way?" The answer was No! "I know this guy," I continued, "and he's a lousy psychic. He can't read your mind. You've got to talk to him. Make an appointment to see him, tell him how you feel, and give it to him straight. Tell him exactly what you've told me."

It didn't take much for Gianni to agree this was the only reasonable course of action. Although I saw him at several home swim meets after that, the subject never came up and I never thought to ask about it. But about 6 months later, when I was at a basketball game talking with the swimming coach and he mentioned Gianni's name, I inquired about the rapport between the two.

"Oh, we get along great," the coach replied. "Less than a month into the season, he came to see me and presented his perception of our relationship, his need for lots of positive feedback, negotiating some sprinting events with distance events, and a few other aspects of training." I just nodded and smiled. I know someday Gianni will be not only a fine swimmer but a wonderful coach himself.

Nonverbal Communication

Nonverbal communication is described as any communication that does not involve words. It may include postures, facial expressions, touch, and even style of clothing. Nonverbal communication differs from verbal communication in that it is multichanneled—addressing all senses—not merely stimuli received through the sense of hearing. Nonverbal communication is not only indirect, but often unconscious. Conversely, verbal communication is typically dominated by conscious thought. Ideally, nonverbal messages support verbal communication, reinforcing words with gestures to promote a clearer understanding of the intended message. However, a spoken message can also be contradicted by nonverbal gestures. The result is a series of mixed messages and the feelings these incongruencies generate.

Research shows that when a contradiction occurs between verbal and nonverbal messages, people are more inclined to believe nonverbal cues ("the body doesn't lie") (Barker and Collins, 1970). Several factors have been identified as elements of nonverbal communication, any of which can either reinforce or contradict spoken messages. These are categorized as either physical or nonphysical elements.

Physical Elements

Research shows that there are many styles of nonverbal communication, involving a number of physical movements:

1. *Touch:* Touch is thought to be a universal form of communication. Handshakes, pats on the back, and hugs are the most common forms of touch. As a rule, Americans tend to be less contact oriented than other cultures (Stoeltge, 2003; Field, 1999), although comfort levels vary greatly from one person to another. Depending on the style of touch, the individual, and the circumstances, this nonverbal form of communication can be perceived as either threatening or reassuring.

2. *Emblems and illustrators:* **Emblems** are defined as physical gestures that replace words, such as the "OK" symbol and the thumbs-up sign. Many emblems have been incorporated into American Sign

> **Nonverbal communication:** All types of communication that do not involve words, including body language and facial expressions.
>
> **Emblems:** Physical gestures that tend to replace words, such as the thumbs-up signal.

Language, used by those with hearing impairment. **Illustrators**, on the other hand, are movements that augment verbal communication, such as waving your hand by your face to show how hot you are. Emblems are often used when speech is prohibited (in a church or lecture hall), while illustrators typically accompany a verbal narrative.

3. *Affect displays:* Facial expressions, or **affect displays**, are often used to express a point also made through the spoken word. Banging your thumb with a hammer hurts, and the facial contortion usually following afterward suggests the intensity of the pain.

4. *Regulators:* **Regulators** are nonverbal messages used to regulate or manipulate a conversation. Eye movements, slight head movements, and shifting weight from foot to foot can send a message for the speaker to speed up, slow down, repeat, or hurry up and finish a sentence. Although regulators are sometimes important to communication, they can also be construed as rude, depending on their nature.

5. *Adaptors:* **Adaptors** are often called body language, and they are important (FIG. 15.3). Adaptors are believed to be among the most difficult physical elements to decode in nonverbal communication. Folding your arms across your chest or crossing

your legs away from the speaker may, or may not, indicate boredom, defensiveness, or aggression.

6. *Paralanguage:* **Paralanguage** consists of the elements of speaking that color the use of words. Pitch, volume, and rate all convey inferences that influence the listener.

Nonphysical Elements

Many additional factors sensed by speakers and listeners communicate a host of impressions, from values to feelings:

1. *Territorial space:* Each individual maintains an area of comfortable personal space or territory around him- or herself. When personal space is invaded, it causes feelings of discomfort. Too great a distance between people may also cause uneasiness or feelings of rejection.

2. *Clothing:* Styles of clothing send very strong messages about personal values, attitudes, and behaviors, and may or may not meet the expectations of other individuals in one's environments. Professional settings, for example, call for a particular style of clothing. That which deviates from the expected or normal dress code can communicate anything from ignorance, to disrespect, to a rebellious attitude.

Knowing that communication involves both verbal and nonverbal messages, it is important to recognize and utilize elements of both to make your style of communication as effective as possible. Recognition and utilization of effective verbal and nonverbal skills require, specifically, listening, attending, and responding skills.

FIGURE 15.3   Body language can be more revealing than the spoken word. Studies show that people trust body language more than verbal communication.

Illustrators: Movements or postures used in combination with verbal conversation, such as various hand motions.

Affect displays: Facial expressions used to express a particular emotion (e.g., amazement).

Regulators: Nonverbal messages used to regulate or even manipulate a conversation, including eye movements and other types of body language.

Adaptors: The most difficult type of nonverbal communication to decode, such as the folding of one's arms across the chest or the crossing of one's legs.

Paralanguage: A term used to describe speaking aspects such as volume, tone, and pitch, that actually color verbal language.

Listening, Attending, and Responding Skills

The process of communication is like the two sides of a coin. The first side represents self-expression; the second, listening. You have probably heard someone say, "He heard me, but he didn't listen to what I said!" Hearing is the *reception* of auditory sensations, whereas listening is the *understanding* of these auditory sensations. Research shows that in a typical day more than 50 percent of communication involves listening (Burley-Allen, 1995). Under closer observation, however, individuals show a general complacency about listening and attending skills; they may hear, but they do not listen very well. In the words of Tannen (2001), "Communication is a system. Everything that is said is simultaneously an instigation and reaction, a reaction and an instigation. Most of us tend to focus on the first part of that process while ignoring or downplaying the second." Typically, in conversation, when people finish expressing a thought or feeling, they almost immediately begin to prepare their next statement, listening only to the first couple of words of response. The most common example occurs during introductions, when a new person states his or her name while you prepare to say yours. Seconds later, you cannot remember what the person's name is. As a rule, the concentration required for listening is very tiring.

The key elements involved in effective listening, attending, and responding are the following:

1. *Assume the role of listener*. Listening requires that all attention be paid to what the speaker is saying. Your mind should be clear of all thoughts that direct attention away from the speaker. Attention to your own thoughts, rather than the message directed to you, is the primary reason for poor listening habits. Although the role of speaker and listener shifts back and forth several times in the course of a conversation, don't prepare comments or rebuttals while you are in the role of listener.

2. *Maintain eye contact*. Good eye contact is considered essential to effective listening. Wandering eyes suggest wandering thoughts. Lack of eye contact can also convey disinterest in the subject or the person. Good eye contact does not mean continual staring, as this can be construed as an invasion of personal space. Good eye contact conveys respect for the person to whom you are listening.

3. *Avoid word prejudice*. Some words elicit obvious emotional responses, which then lead to disinterest or surprise. Words such as *feminist*, *gay*, *Jew*, or *liberal* can press buttons and set emotional wheels spinning, resulting in raised eyebrows, frowns, and side glances. Recognition of these types of words and the responses they elicit will enable the listener to prepare to be objective. The listener's objectivity is believed to enhance the communication process.

4. *Use "minimal encouragers" to indicate that you are on the same wavelength as the person speaking to you*. Minimal encouragers include short-word questions such as "oh?" and "uh-huh?" and repeating key words to encourage the speaker to give you more detailed information. These should be used genuinely, not mechanically.

5. *Paraphrase what was said to ensure understanding*. Paraphrasing is a more elaborate style of minimal encouragement. In addition to repeating key words, paraphrasing includes the use of personal observations to ensure understanding of the content of the message intended.

6. *Ask questions to improve clarity of statements*. When you are at a loss to understand facts, concepts, or feelings expressed to you, questions become imperative. But beware. Questions can sometimes put the speaker on the defensive. Use questions to clarify your understanding, not to confuse the person you are listening to.

7. *Use empathy to reflect and share feelings*. Empathy is thought to be an important attending skill that galvanizes the listening experience. Empathy refers to attention to the speaker's feelings as well as thoughts. This does not imply that you must adopt these feelings as your own. Rather, you should recognize the feelings in the individual with whom you are conversing.

8. *Provide feedback*. Responding to the speaker often requires feedback from the listener. Before you offer feedback, however, inquire whether it is desired. Sometimes people speak as a means to increase self-awareness using you, the listener, as a sounding board. The speaker may not want feedback. If your viewpoint is wanted, offer comments and criticism in a constructive way. Feedback should be specific, combining feelings and reasons for or details of your opinions. If and when criticism is

elicited, balance positive and negative perceptions, and be specific. To be effective, criticism should offer insights.

9. *Summarize the content of what was said*. Summarization is similar to paraphrasing thoughts, but it requires more concentration on and synthesis of the speaker's thoughts and feelings into an integrated understanding.

These are just a few elements that can be used to enhance your listening skills. They can also increase the effectiveness of delivery and interpretation of your thoughts and perceptions. Regardless of how effective you think your communication skills are, even under the best circumstances there is still room for misunderstanding and conflict as, for example, in the interpretation of a mixed message.

Conflict Resolution

Conflicts often arise because of misunderstanding both verbal and nonverbal messages that are sent and received. Although conflicts can occur within yourself as well as between you and other individuals, it is the latter type of conflict this section will address. Typically, conflicts between individuals involve emotions associated with anger and fear. Left unresolved, they can generate many toxic thoughts, including resentment and hostility. Ideally, conflicts should be resolved right away; however, not every situation allows for this. A roommate who goes away for the weekend leaving the apartment a shambles, or a boss who sends an email at 4 P.M. asking you to hand in a report by 5 P.M. are two instances that necessitate a postponement of **conflict resolution**. People often need some time to organize their thoughts for conflict resolution. In any case, the sooner a plan of resolution is implemented, the better. Although conflicts tend to be multidimensional, scholars divide them into three categories:

1. *Content conflict:* Content conflicts arise from the misunderstanding of factual information, definition of terms or concepts, goals, or elements of strategies used in a cooperative effort. Disagreement occurs over the perception of information available. In this type of conflict, the problem is not in dispute; rather, it is the solution to the problem that generates conflict. Examples include how to finance a house, where the best place to go on vacation is, or what time the movie starts at the cineplex.

2. *Value conflict:* When a person has conflicting values within his or her own value system, value clarification

FIGURE 15.4 Communication skills are paramount in resolving conflicts, but each person must have a chance to share thoughts and feelings to make this skill effective in reducing stress.

is needed. But when values between people collide, resolution is much harder. Value conflicts can often be seen on the political scene, as when forces lobbying for the environment (clean drinkable water) oppose economic forces (hydraulic fracturing energy companies). The result is often a compromise, with neither side obtaining a complete (or satisfactory) victory.

3. *Ego conflict:* Ego conflict is based on a win-lose mentality. Conflicts of this nature involve manipulation and control to support one's identity, and to prove one is right. Ego conflicts are based on power, competency, identity, and emotional attachment. They are thought to be the hardest type to resolve (**FIG. 15.4**).

> **Conflict resolution:** The resolution of arguments displayed as three styles: content conflict, value conflict, and ego conflict.

Conflict-Management Styles

Several management styles deal with conflict. Not all styles are beneficial and, in fact, some may actually perpetuate conflict. The following offers descriptions of both negative and positive **conflict-management styles**:

1. *Withdrawal:* When a conflict seems overwhelming, the first reaction is usually avoidance. Withdrawal can be defined as either a physical or a psychological removal from the problem. Walking out of a room, taking a circuitous route to your office or dorm room, or merely remaining silent are examples of avoidance. Many people fear confrontation beacuse of previous conflict experiences that left deep emotional scars. Withdrawal is seen as a coping style, albeit regressive, when conflicts involve figures of authority, such as bosses or parents, or when a person feels outnumbered by colleagues or peers. On the positive side, withdrawal can be beneficial when it is used as a time-out to cool off, as long as a "time-in" follows shortly thereafter. Withdrawal is typically regarded as immature behavior, and thus a negative conflict-management style, because physical or verbal absence prevents resolution.

2. *Surrender:* To habitually give in to a situation or problem is also construed as a negative conflict-management style. Like withdrawal, surrender is a type of avoidance people use to appease fellow workers, family, peers, and especially close friends and spouses for fear of rejection and damaging relationships. But surrendering to the will of others deflates self-esteem. What might look like a noble act actually inhibits complete resolution. Resolution of conflicts involves decisions by all parties involved. When one person holds back, merely expressing dissatisfied agreement, the merits of a solution are unbalanced. This style of conflict management generates feelings of victimization.

3. *Hostile aggression:* The words *conflict* and *confrontation* often bring to mind visions of yelling, fists pounding, and objects flying across the room. Indeed, this is how some conflicts are handled. Aggression is often used as a form of intimidation to manipulate others into submissive agreement.

> **Conflict-management styles:** There are five conflict-management styles: withdrawal, surrender, hostile aggression, persuasion, and dialogue.

Verbal aggression is more common than physical aggression, with the use of harsh words and increased speaking volume to win points. Rarely does aggressive behavior result in the resolution of any conflict and, in fact, it often perpetuates resentment. Unbroken, this cycle can repeat itself forever.

4. *Persuasion:* Persuasion is defined as an attempt to alter another person's attitude or behavior. It is believed by some scholars that all verbal expression is rooted in persuasion. When persuasion is used to win a conflict at the expense of others, it is viewed as negative. But persuasion can be a positive style as well. In the initial stage of the conflict-resolution process, all voices need to be heard. Persuasion may include the use of reason, emotional awareness, or motivation to get a point across. When used tactfully, persuasion opens new lines of thinking, which can then be tools to resolve issues and promote mutual agreement.

5. *Dialogue:* Dialogue is a verbal exchange of opinions, attitudes, facts, and perceptions that opens the doors to greater understanding of the nature of the problem. During the dialogue process, discussions center on the costs and benefits of solving a problem. Dialogue involves the same steps as those employed for creative problem solving. In dialogue, negotiations are a means to a solution to which all parties feel they have made a contribution. Compromise plays an important role in the dialogue process because the intent is to reach a decision that is agreeable to everyone.

Steps to Enhance Face-to-Face Communication Skills

The following are additional suggestions to strengthen your communication skills and help promote conflict resolution (**FIG. 15.5**). They may look like common sense, but they bear listing because under stress the walls of the ego are thick. The more we remind ourselves of these skills, the more likely we will be to use them.

1. *Speak with precision and directness.* To express yourself clearly, select words that accurately describe your thoughts and feelings. Be direct about your thoughts and perceptions by verbalizing the intent of your message as clearly as possible.

2. *Enhance your vocabulary.* Vocabulary affects the effectiveness of verbal communication. A small

UN Photo/Eskinder Debebe.

FIGURE 15.5 Conflict resolution requires adept communication skills, such as those demonstrated by former UN Secretary General Ban Ki-moon during a world summit on climate change and global warming. All conflicts, large or small, require these same diplomatic skills.

vocabulary decreases the ability to express yourself, whereas a greater number of words to choose from provides you with greater flexibility to say what you want to say.

3. *Use language appropriate for your listening audience.* The manner in which you speak to a child probably differs from that which you use with an adult. Assess which words, expressions, and gestures are most conducive to getting your point across.

4. *Attack issues, not people.* When trying to resolve conflicts with others, focus on the problem, not the people involved. In other words, avoid character assassination. Attacking people clouds the issue and makes it harder, if not impossible, to resolve issues.

5. *Avoid putting others on the defensive.* When initiating self-disclosure or a dialogue to resolve conflicts, begin your statements with "I perceive. . . ." Placing the responsibility of understanding on yourself rather than blaming others minimizes defensiveness.

6. *Avoid asking someone else to pass on your thoughts and feelings to a third party.* The most effective communication involves talking with someone face to face. Involving a third party (e.g., "Please tell my roommate to call John") not only increases the chances of miscommunication, but not making personal contact also sends one or more nonverbal messages.

7. *Avoid information overload.* Attention span is limited, as is the amount of information that can be received and processed. The greater amount of information given, the greater the chances some

---

BOX 15.2   Pillow Talk

A chapter on communication skills would be incomplete without some mention of the dialogue that takes place between sexual partners. In light of the facts that more than 1 million people in the United States are now infected with HIV or have AIDS, and that the incidence of date rape is so high, this aspect of human behavior can no longer be left to assumptions. Tannen was right that men and women have different styles of communication, and nowhere is this more evident than in sexual relations. Because of American social mores, the issues surrounding sexual relations are still considered taboo in normal conversation. Ironically, it may be these very mores that have nurtured an environment of hostility and anxiety with regard to sexual issues. At a time when trust is paramount, sexual desire and arousal seem to short-circuit the self-disclosure so vital to one's health.

There are many issues involving sexual intercourse that are stressors behind closed doors. These include contraception, birth control, the risk of pregnancy, infertility, sexually transmitted diseases, vaginismus, molestation, celibacy, guilt, rape, self-respect, abortion, impotency, premature ejaculation, intimacy, the ability to reach orgasm, homosexuality, and sexual satisfaction. As you can see, this (incomplete) list is quite long, and each topic weighs heavily as a stressor for those who experience it. Problems of a sexual nature do not go away once a couple has initiated sexual relations, either. To the contrary, if communications are poor at the start of a relationship, they tend to get worse as the relationship continues. Sex counselors advise that *before*, *during*, and *after* every act of sexual intimacy there should be a thorough conversation airing problematic sexual issues. As any AIDS patient or woman with an unwanted pregnancy can tell you, the short-term pleasures of sex are surely not worth the risks involved. And days, months, or years of agony may ensue when other sexual matters go unresolved. Make a point to include a healthy conversation as part of your sexual habits.

of it will get lost. Be careful to pace your conversation, allowing ample time to process the messages that have been expressed.

8. *Validate your assumptions.* Confirm what you think to be true with those who have given you this impression.

9. *Resolve problems when they arise.* If you feel there is a misunderstanding, there probably is. Avoiding it, or giving it too much time to fester, allows the conscious mind to validate feelings of victimization, anger, or fear. Try to deal with issues as they surface by talking them out with those involved. In the short term, this may seem confrontational and threatening, but in the long term, it relieves the pressure of undue stress and promotes inner peace.

■ Best Benefits of Effective High-Tech Communication Skills

Welcome to the full force of the information age, where the greater your communication skills are, the greater your chances are of reducing your stress levels, and most likely the stress levels of those people around you. By establishing healthy boundaries with technology, learning to be multilingual with the various forms of technology, and being present when involved with face-to-face interactions you will decrease miscommunication dramatically. Remember, communication skills are just that, skills. They require practice. Take time to practice the art of great communication skills; they'll be useful no matter what advances in technology await us.

SUMMARY

- The abundance of vehicles for communication (text messaging, Twitter, Facebook, email, etc.) has not improved the quality of communication and, in fact, has added to the stress of miscommunication.

- Various forms of technology offer many means of communication, yet people often communicate using short messages and spend more time with a screen than with face-to-face interpersonal communication.

- All forms of communication can lead to information overload, which compromises one's ability to communicate.

- People often use technology as an excuse for poor behavior (avoidance) or the urgency to answer a call or text message.

- Three-quarters of our waking day is spent in some form of communication. Typically, stressors involving other people are caused by miscommunication.

- There are many conversation styles. Miscommunication may result when two or more styles are incompatible.

- Schismogenesis refers to the process wherein people become more deeply entrenched in their own communication style, widening the gap of misunderstanding.

- Tannen believes that one reason for misunderstandings between people is that they tend to speak in metamessages, or indirect expressions of thoughts. Indirectness can result from many different intentions.

- Communication is divided into verbal and nonverbal forms. Verbal communication involves both encoding our thoughts into words and decoding other peoples' words through the sifter of our perceptions. During the encoding and decoding process, some thoughts can get lost in translation.

- Verbal communication involves some level of self-disclosure. The degree of disclosure depends on the level of trust among those involved.

- Nonverbal communication involves a host of gestures and postures, as well as intonation. Handshakes, hugs, finger gestures, clothing, and territorial space are examples of how we communicate nonverbally.

- Communication also involves listening and attending skills: the ability to receive and interpret information as it is intended.

- Miscommunication can lead to conflicts, which are broken down into three types: content conflicts, value conflicts, and ego conflicts. The last are the hardest to resolve.

- There are effective and noneffective conflict-management styles. To withdraw, surrender, or act aggressively is not effective. Persuasion and dialogue are advocated as effective ways to negotiate, compromise, and come to a peaceful resolution.

- Sexual intimacy without dialogue is an open invitation to acute and chronic stress. Sex counselors advocate a healthy dialogue before and after every act of sexual intimacy.

- Several suggestions, based on common sense, were listed to improve your communications skills. For these skills to be effective, they must be practiced regularly.

STUDY GUIDE QUESTIONS

1. How does technology compromise good communication skills?

2. Why do many stress-related problems involve poor communication?

3. List three aspects of verbal communication.

4. List three aspects of nonverbal communication.

5. List the five conflict-management styles and highlight the most effective one.

6. What are five ways to improve your communication style?

REFERENCES AND RESOURCES

Alleyne, R. Mobile Phone Addiction Ruining Relationships. *The Telegraph*, November 30, 2012. www.telegraph.co.uk /technology/news/9714616/Mobile-phone-addiction-ruining -relationships.html.

Barker, L. L., and Collins, N. Nonverbal and Kinesic Research. In P. Emmert and W. D. Brooks (eds.), *Methods of Research in Communication*. Houghton Mifflin, Boston, 1970.

Bartlett, L. Personal conversation. Sunset Middle School. Longmont, CO. March 2012.

Bennie, B. *101 Ways to Improve Your Communication Skills Instantly*, 4th ed. Goldminds, Inc., Springfield, MO, 2005.

Burley-Allen, M. *Listening: The Forgotten Skill*. John Wiley & Sons, New York, 1995.

Compton, J. Future IT Workforce Has Poor Communication Skills, *CIO*, November 1, 2001.

Dana, D. *Conflict Resolution*. McGraw Hill, New York, 2000.

Davis, L. *I Thought We'd Never Speak Again*. Quill Books/ HarperCollins, New York, 2002.

Davis, M., Paleg. K., and Fanning, P. *The Messages Workbook: Powerful Strategies for Effective Communication at Work and Home*. New Harbinger, Oakland, CA, 2004.

Education-Portal.com. Poor Communication Skills Hurt Students in Recruiting Process. http://education-portal.com /articles/Poor_Communication_Skills_Hurt_Students_in _Recruiting_Process.html.

Field, T. Preschoolers in America Are Touched Less and Are More Aggressive than Preschoolers in France, *Earth Childhood Development and Care* 151:11–17, 1999.

Flemming, C. *It's the Way You Say It*. IUniverse, Bloomington, IN, 2010.

Good Morning America. Can You Live Without a Cell Phone? Self-Professed Cell Phone Junkies Try to Curb Their Addictions, *ABC News*, January 10, 2008. http://abcnews.go.com /GMA/OnCall/story?id=2665376&page=1.

Gordon, L. *Passage to Intimacy*. Fireside Books, New York, 1993.

Gray, J. *Men Are from Mars, Women Are from Venus: A Practical Guide for Improving Communication and Getting What You Want in Your Relationships*. HarperCollins, New York, 1992.

HR In-Motion. Interview Body Language, March 8, 2008. http://hrinmotion.wordpress.com/2008/03/08/interview -body-language.

Ivey, A., and Gluckstern, N. *Basic Attending Skills*. Microtraining Associates, North Amherst, MA, 1982.

Koprowski, G. Many "Addicted" to Cell Phone Use, *TechNewsWorld*, April 13, 2006. www.technewsworld.com/story /49849.html.

Lickerman, A. The Effect of Technology on Relationships: The Risks of Internet Addiction. *Psychology Today*. June 8, 2010.

www.psychologytoday.com/blog/happiness-in-world /201006/the-effect-technology-relationships.

Maggio, R. *The Art of Talking to Anyone: Essential People Skills for Success in Any Situation*. McGraw-Hill, New York, 2005.

McKay, M., Davis, M., and Fanning, P. *Messages: The Communication Skills Book*, 2nd ed. New Harbinger Press, Oakland, CA, 1995.

Satir, V. *Making Contact*. Celestial Arts, Berkeley, CA, 1976.

Scott, G. G. *Resolving Conflict with Others and within Yourself*. New Harbinger Press, Oakland, CA, 2006.

Silberman, M. PeopleSmart: Developing Your Interpersonal Intelligence. Berrett-Koehler, San Francisco, CA, 2000.

Snelling, A., Meholick, B., and Seaward, B. L. Communication Skills, *Fitness Management* 6:40–41, 1990.

South, A. Technology's Influence on Interpersonal Communication. March 9, 2009. www.helium.com/items/1369744 -technology-interpersonal-communication.

Stoeltje, M. F. Other Cultures Touch More, *EhMac.ca*, August 30, 2003. www.ehmac.ca/everything-else-eh/19893-truth -out-americans-out-touch.html.

Stone, D. *Difficult Conversations*. Penguin Books, New York, 2000.

Tannen, D. *Talking From 9–5*. Avon Publishing, New York, 1995.

Tannen, D. *That's Not What I Meant: How Conversational Style Makes or Breaks Relationships*. Ballantine Books, New York, 1991.

Tannen, D. *You Just Don't Understand: Women and Men in Conversation*. Quill, New York, 2001.

The New Conversations Initiative. Home page. www .newconversations.net.

Thomas, M. The Impacts of Technology on Communication— Mapping the Limits of Online Discussion Forums. University of Adelaide. http://online.adelaide.edu.au/LearnIT.nsf /URLs/technology_and_communication.

Ury, W. *The Power of a Positive No*. Bantam Books, New York, 2007.

Verderber, R., and Verderber, K. *Inter-Act: Using Interpersonal Communication Skills*, 3rd ed. Wadsworth, Belmont, CA, 1983.

Williams, F. *Executive Communication Power*. Prentice-Hall, Englewood Cliffs, NJ, 1983.

Wilmot, W. W. *Dyadic Communication*, 3rd ed. McGraw-Hill, New York, 1987.

Winch, G. Is Your Partner Addicted to Their Phone or Blackberry? *Psychology Today*, January 15, 2011. www.psychology today.com/blog/the-squeaky-wheel/201101/is-your-partner -addicted-their-phone-or-blackberry.

CHAPTER 16

Resource Management: Managing Time and Money

The best way to save your money is to fold it in half and put it back in your wallet.

—Anonymous

Time and money. Time and money. For most people, it seems as if every stressor involves time and money because these two resources are constantly in high demand and often squandered. Would you agree? If so, you are in good company. A great many people think that most of their problems would simply vanish if they had a few more hours in the day and a few extra thousand dollars tucked away in a private bank account. The sad truth is that old habits die hard. Unless a change of attitude is adopted, more time and more money will merely result in more responsibilities and more purchases (and possible debt). The year 2008 will be forever known as the start of the Great Recession, when *subprime loans*, *derivatives*, *credit default swaps*, *foreclosures*, and *toxic assets* became household words. When people's spending habits far exceed their income levels and credit is overextended, economic stability will certainly collapse. You didn't need to be a Nobel Prize–winning economist to realize it was only a matter of time before the economy imploded. Add a healthy dose of greed into the mix and you had the makings of a global financial crisis that has affected everyone on the planet. Since the economic crash of 2008, Americans have dramatically cut back on their spending and deposited more money into their savings accounts. Foreclosures, job losses, and job furloughs have also forced people to carefully reexamine their finances. Add to this lifestyle picture the dramatic changes that social networking has made to our lives in terms of how we spend our time and the result for many people is stress with a capital *S*. Despite the waves of economic and societal changes that reach our shores, the wisdom of how to manage both personal finances and time remains constant, which is why we need to revisit the timeless lessons of resource management.

This chapter first looks at the topic of finances. It then examines the essentials of budgeting your time so that you can begin to utilize these two precious resources for your best interest.

Money Matters

You might think that maintaining one's personal finances, including keeping a checkbook balanced, would seem rather simple with these four simple rules:

1. Make a budget and follow it.

2. Don't spend what you don't have.

3. Pay all your bills on time.

4. Put away at least 10 percent of your monthly income into a savings account (and don't touch it).

If only it were this easy. Giving in to life's many temptations, big and small, can add up significantly over a short period of time. For example, the cost of a high-end cup of coffee priced at $4.00 each day adds up to approximately $1,400 per year—enough for a spring-break vacation or a dent in your school loans. It is good to live in the present moment, but don't squander it! The key to managing your money is to maintain a healthy balance. On the one hand, you don't want to be a neurotic, penny-pinching Scrooge; on the other hand, you cannot afford to be fiscally flamboyant. People never get rich throwing their money away. Prudent fiscal habits promote less stress.

The relationship between finances and stress has always been a dubious one, ever since the first coin was exchanged for goods millennia ago. However, with the advent of credit cards, it became all too easy to spend what you don't have, making financial debt a very common stressor, and for most a way of life. Although it's true that buying

> **Retail therapy:** The behavior attributed to people who go shopping to alleviate their stress. The consequence is buying things they don't really need on a budget they cannot always afford.

now and paying later with a credit card provides a sense of power, the truth is that it's an illusion of power. Remember, the ego (whose purpose is to decrease pain and increase pleasure) also loves power, even if it's a delusion.

Mass Marketing to Your Ego

Are you one of the countless Americans who lives outside your means? Do you spend your money eating at restaurants and buying lots of nice brand-name clothes? Do you purchase expensive coffee and entertain yourself with a huge plasma TV screen? Does shopping give you a sense of power? Do you purchase material possessions to fill a spiritual emptiness? Do your mood swings mirror the daily stock report? Are you swayed by instant gratification? Do you make purchases (**retail therapy**) to allay your anxieties and frustrations? Do you buy items that your friends have, like iPods, iPads, or satellite radio? Keeping up with the Joneses is a full-time job, and sadly one that never pays a dividend. Rather, it takes hard-earned money away.

The next time you watch TV, pay close attention to the lifestyles of the characters. Few, if any, shows deal with poverty—it doesn't make good viewing! Actors in TV sitcoms and crime shows alike portray upper-middle-class people striving to become upper-class people. According to researchers, the subtle advertising in TV programming is akin to an intravenous tube delivering a desirable lifestyle that most people cannot afford (and this doesn't even include the commercials) (Taylor, 2010). The ego, looking for pleasure (and a quick fix), is easily manipulated by slick corporate marketers eager to sell you anything and everything (remember P. T. Barnum's philosophy, "There's a sucker born every minute!").

Take a quick look around you at the clothes people are wearing. How many people do you see walking around as unpaid billboards for corporate America? Take a look around your house or apartment. How many purchases have you made on impulse that are now collecting dust? Marketing to the insecurities of the ego has become an art form in corporate America (Schlosser, 2001). With the proliferation of magnetic resonance imaging (MRI) studies to determine the brain's neural code for each thought and behavior, scientists have now teamed up with marketing experts to unlock the code for greater purchasing power, which may soon allow marketers to bypass the ego altogether. The term for this strategy is "neuromarketing." Harvard marketing professor Gerald Zaltman has filed a patent (#5,436,830) for his technique to market goods and services to your unconscious mind using Jung's theory of archetypal images (Szegedy-Maszak, 2005).

The Psychology of Poverty

A theory, often attributed to 1998 Nobel Prize winner Amartya Sen, suggests that if you took all the money in the world from the wealthiest people and distributed it evenly among all the planet's inhabitants, in less than 2 years it would all be back in the hands of the people who initially held it. Why? Because human nature is prone to act on fear (and laziness). As such, people's attitudes are very hard to change. Most people would quickly spend their portion, some would simply lose theirs, gamblers would gamble their money away, and very few people would save or invest their funds. As odd as it might sound, many people have a fear of money, or simply stated, a fear of the lack of money, often called **poverty consciousness** (Twist, 2003). Unfortunately, the fear of poverty becomes a self-fulfilling prophecy that repels money rather than attracts it, and this thought process becomes a never-ending cycle played out in daily behaviors, according to Joe Dominguez and Vicki Robin, authors of the best-selling book *Your Money or Your Life*.

Money Problems? Try This . . .

Perhaps the causes of money problems are as varied as the amounts of money found in each person's checking account. Stated in simple economic terms, the demand for goods and services always exceeds the supply of cash in hand. Regardless of what the expenses are, the result begins with fiscal hemorrhaging and ends up with undeniable debt. Catastrophic medical bills and huge car repair bills are one thing, but frivolous spending is another—and currently in this country it's reaching epidemic levels. There is no shortage of suggestions on how to pull in the reins of one's financial spending. Here are some time-tested tips to consider.

Tips for Financial Freedom

1. *Make and follow a budget.* If you don't already have a budget, now is the time to create one. If you do have one, when was the last time you fine-tuned it? You should know, within a few dollars, how much you have each month to spend as discretionary income.

2. *Live a sustainable lifestyle.* Life isn't a sprint, but rather an ultra-marathon. As such, spending money should be well paced, yet some people spend like there is no tomorrow. A sustainable lifestyle means living a conscious lifestyle, in which purchases are made consciously rather than frivolously. It also means enjoying the present moment, while keeping a wary eye on the future. A sustainable lifestyle also means buying only what you will use and not wasting precious natural resources. Behaviors include using reusable cloth grocery bags; carpooling when possible, library DVD rentals, and driving a hybrid car.

3. *Freeze your credit cards.* Credit cards are nothing more than expensive loans. Every time you pull out a credit card, you are borrowing money and paying a high interest rate (13 to 23 percent). Get in the habit of going cold turkey with your credit cards. One suggestion is to cut up all but one card, stick the remaining card in a glass of water, and then place the glass in the freezer. This tactic ensures that you will use it only for emergencies.

4. *Keep a spending journal.* If your money or debit card burns a hole in your pocket, and you are not sure where it really goes, start a spending journal to see where your money is wasted. (Quicken is a recommended accounting software program that allows you to keep track of your spending habits.) You may be quite surprised at how quickly frivolous spending adds up and reflects a habit of hard-earned money going down the drain.

5. *See each purchase as an investment.* What are your assets? Your house, your car, your stock portfolio? Every purchase you make is an investment, yet most of these items depreciate to nothing quickly, including clothes. Here is a question to ask yourself: Will I want or use this item a year from now? If the answer is no, then walk away.

6. *Consolidate your debt.* Do you have several credit card bills and other loans? Talk to your bank manager about consolidating your debt into one loan, and pay it off as soon as possible.

7. *Consider opening a 401(k) or a Roth IRA as soon as possible* (Kranz, 2005). As a college student, retirement may seem like a long way off, but when it comes

Poverty consciousness: A term used to describe an attitude or perception held by a person reinforcing the idea that he or she never has enough money, which in turn becomes a self-fulfilling prophecy.

to investing in your retirement, it's right around the corner. Tuck a small amount into a retirement plan each year (even if you think you cannot afford it) so that you can live a comfortable life in your golden years.

Michelle Singletary is a syndicated columnist for the *Washington Post* and the author of *Spend Well, Live Right.* Following are some of her tips for achieving financial stability:

1. *Remove yourself from temptation.* If you don't have money to spend (or waste), then don't hang around people who go shopping and spend lots of money because this can become a trap. Also, before you go shopping, make a list of what you really need and maintain the willpower to buy only what's on your list.

2. *Ask "why" before you buy.* Do you really need the item you're about to purchase? Underwear and toothpaste are necessities. Lattes, appetizers, weekly DVD rentals, and new shoes are not.

3. *Don't buy on impulse.* If you find something you like, hold off from buying it that day. Sleep on it. If it's still something you think you need, go back the next day.

4. *Be wary of bargains.* You may save money on sales, but many people end up spending more money than they expected by purchasing more items than they need. Rather than saving money, they spend money they don't have.

5. *Clean your house.* One of the best incentives to curtail uncontrolled spending is realized by taking stock of what you already have. There is no need to buy something, only to find out you already own it. And follow the two-year rule: If you haven't used an item or article of clothing in two years, donate it to a charity before it collects more dust.

6. *Learn to say no to your kids, spouse, friends, and marketers.* Don't allow other people to spend your money for you. Identify good boundaries with your money and be assertive with these boundaries.

Suze Orman is a best-selling author and talk show host on the topic of financial planning and a syndicated television financial expert. Her tips for financial freedom include the following:

1. *Adopt a healthy attitude toward money.* What is your relationship with money? Do you have poverty consciousness? Do you waste money? Do you repel money? Do you maintain the fiscal poverty attitude of your parents? Your attitude toward money has a lot to do with how little or how much you have, and will have over time.

2. *Make sound financial goals.* Do you intend to work for the rest of your life? Do you have a retirement account? Can you see beyond your next paycheck? Do you want to take a yearly vacation? Financial goals are guidelines to help you achieve financial security. What are your goals? What is your long-term strategic plan for financial security?

3. *Put your money to work for you.* Even if you think you have no money to invest, you really do, even if it's only $100 per year. There are mutual funds, IRAs, shares of stock, Treasury bills, and savings accounts available for investment. Talk to a financial advisor (usually the first consultation is free) to discuss your options and make a plan to have your money make money for you.

4. *The best financial advisor is you.* Having a financial advisor is good, but remember that advisors are making money off of your money. Get sound advice, and then do your homework by reading books on this topic. Check out information on the Internet. Learn how to budget your money, how to invest your money, and how to make your money work for you.

Money management is a skill that takes practice. Now is the time to put these skills into practice. Your wallet, your marriage, and all aspects of your life will thank you.

The Hands of Time

There is a joke that states time is nature's way of making sure everything doesn't happen at once. That joke has lost it's relevance in the warp speed of the twenty-first century lifestyle where time is flying by even if you are not having fun and everything seems to be happening at once. It is a well-known fact that there are only 24 hours in each day, and no matter how sophisticated our technology becomes, no app in the world can ever change this. Despite the constraints on the 24-hour cycle, people try in vain to squeeze in a few more hours by shaving off precious and essential time needed for quality sleep. There is a consensus among people all over the country that time is speeding up. The reason time seems to be flying is often attributed to a combination of increased responsibilities and increased technology (toys to play with). Douglas Rushkoff, author of *Present Shock: When Everything Happens Now*, says that if you feel like you are being compressed in the vice of time, you're in good company. Time compression is an unintended consequence of the digital age of social networking, information overload, and increased social demands. He reminds us that with the dizzying pace of constant information updates coupled with instant gratification and an abundance of choices to keep one's mind occupied, time management becomes all the more important to keep one's head above the metaphorical waters of rapid change. With this in mind, humankind's attempts to organize and manipulate time merit a closer review.

The constructs of seconds, hours, days, months, and years are creations of the human mind. It is believed that the concept of time was originally created to master the natural environment, particularly the position of the sun over the earth and the change of seasons. The Babylonians are credited with the first 360-day calendar, composed of 12 lunar months, each with 30 days. In due time, 5 days were added to the year by the Egyptians to compensate for rotational differences between the earth and moon. Additional changes were made by the early Romans, and again by Pope Gregory XIII in 1582, who devised the contemporary, or Gregorian, calendar. On a smaller but no less important scale, the first mechanical clock is credited to an eleventh-century Chinese man, Su Song. Two more centuries would pass before a similar machine would appear in the Western world, a clock constructed of iron gears and weights built for an English monastery. The pendulum clock arrived 300 years later, through the creativity of a Dutch scientist, Christian Huygens. Pocket watches were in vogue at the turn of the twentieth century until the invention of the wristwatch. With the advent of high technology, time is now measured in nanoseconds through the use of quartz crystals and digital displays (O'Connor and Robertson, 2002).

As civilizations developed and technology was shared among cultures, awareness and utilization of time contributed to the organization and advancement of the human race, and hence became accepted ways to make order out of chaos. Time became a tool used by various societies to unite and synchronize the efforts of individuals in their communities. American time zones (Eastern, Central, Mountain, and Pacific), for example, were created by railroad companies to synchronize their schedules over various parts of the country, and were eventually adopted by the United States government in 1883. Global time zones followed suit in 1884 (Boslough, 1990).

Once conceived, time has been manipulated constantly. The international dateline, daylight savings time, and leap year are three examples of attempts to refine and manipulate the basic constructs of time. The 8-hour workday is another. In an attempt to harness time and manipulate it for gain and pleasure, however, citizens of the industrialized world have often found themselves to be slaves to the concept rather than masters of it. The result: Time, or the lack thereof, is now considered to be a premier stressor in the lives of many people. And although time is not considered a precursor to disease and illness in itself, a rushed lifestyle, or as psychologist Robert Levine (1989) calls it, "clockwork blues," which constantly disrupts the body's biological clock, is now associated with the incidence of coronary heart disease, ulcers, and other stress-related illnesses. Perhaps not surprisingly, more people have heart attacks on Monday mornings than on any other day of the week.

Looking busy might be considered a status symbol to some people, but not to Stephan Rechtschaffen, M.D. In his highly acclaimed book *Time Shifting*, Rechtschaffen explains that being overproductive is an index of stress, a fast-paced rhythm that leads to dysfunction. Rechtschaffen says that the rhythm of society itself is increasing, and many people are unaware they are caught up in it. People are entrained by the rhythm of their working environment in what he calls *hyperproductivity*. The short-term gains may seem impressive. The long-term results are devastating to one's health. Rechtschaffen, who founded the Omega Institute for Holistic Studies in Rhinebeck, New York, suggests that we need to learn to time shift—that is, to decelerate from the fast-paced lifestyle by consciously changing the rhythm of our activity to live in the present moment.

He's not alone. With daily quantum leaps in technology and continual access to information at one's fingertips, experts agree that good time management means getting back to the basics of simple organization (Morgenstern, 2000; Allen, 2003).

Classic research into leisure habits suggests that the two limiting factors (stressors) on recreation and leisure are time and money (Allen, 2015). Many people who have come to the conclusion that time equals money compound the effects of this stressor. With advances in technology and perceived increases in responsibility, time, or the mismanagement of it, has often become an enemy—and a major stressor unto itself. In light of time as a stressor in today's culture, this chapter places special emphasis on changing negative perceptions of this construct as well as manipulating it to allow individuals to make order out of their personal chaos.

FIGURE 16.1 Taking time to balance your checkbook (either electronically or on paper) is essential for managing your money. In an age of credit card debt, make a habit of only spending what you have, and make sure you know where you stand financially.

Time management is actually a part of a larger coping skill referred to as social orchestration (**FIG. 16.1**). Social orchestration is a cognitive strategy employed to help minimize stressors without avoiding them. This technique is a reorganization process where you manipulate factors and elements (not people) in your environment to your best advantage so as to travel the path of least resistance. Social orchestration involves analyzing a problem, creating a series of viable options, and then choosing the best option to clear stress-prone obstacles out of the way. To manipulate time in a well-organized fashion so that it can bear the fruit of productivity is the essence of time management.

According to time-management expert Robert Roesch, despite the fact that the pace of life is speeding up with the rush of technological advancements, from cell phones to palm computers, the age-tested means to manage time remain the same. However, with the impending invasion of technology in our personal lives, maintaining proper boundaries is paramount to one's sanity and overall health. To paraphrase Roesch (1998), unless you are a physician on call, you do not need to be accessible 24 hours a day through cell phones. Finally, technology is marketed to

> **Time management:** The prioritization, scheduling, and execution of daily responsibilities to a level of personal satisfaction. Effective time management does not mean you have more time; it means you make better use of the time you have.

be time saving, all in the name of increased productivity. As we all know, this is not always the case. Use technology to simplify, not complicate, your life.

In attempting to be more efficient, the human mind tends to break down and compartmentalize entities, such as time, into smaller parts to better comprehend and manipulate them. Neurophysiologists who have studied right- and left-brain cognitive functions have observed that the right hemisphere has no concept of time, and they therefore agree that time awareness is clearly a left-brain function. Yet imagination and spatial awareness have been found to be crucial factors in the effective utilization of time. So, it would be wise to assume that the effective management of time involves the cognitive functions of both cerebral hemispheres.

Time management can be defined as the ability to prioritize, schedule, and execute personal responsibilities to personal satisfaction. Time management is a relatively new concept in both personal and professional development. Corporations that desire greater productivity invest their own time and money in creative consultants to train and educate their employees to manage time more efficiently. The following are some of the lessons they teach.

Roadblocks to Effective Time Management

Without a doubt, technology such as smartphones and iPads has added to the efficiency of life. It has also added to increased procrastination. Taking a few moments to do a Google search on one topic can end up as a trip down the proverbial rabbit hole of curiosity, only to emerge hours later wondering where the time went. When you combine curiosity, voyeurism, ego, and instant gratification—all via the Internet—you end up with one incredible roadblock to time efficiency (**FIG. 16.2**).

Before one can begin to employ strategies for the more efficient use of time, several roadblocks must be overcome. With a greater awareness of pertinent attitudes, issues, and concerns, the ability to employ time-management skills, without becoming stressed in the process, will become a strong coping strategy when needed. There are many reasons for mismanaged time, including attitudes about oneself and one's working environment or organization, personality styles, values, and lack of knowledge about time-management skills.

The most prevalent of these are attitudes and their associated behaviors. In her book *How to Put More Time in Your Life*, Dru Scott addresses some of these attitudes.

FIGURE 16.2

behaviors that influence one's personality as a whole. Seven distinct personality behaviors have become evident. These are Type A's, workaholics, technophiles, time jugglers, procrastinators, perfectionists, and those who fall into lifestyle traps. These behaviors are labeled "time robbers," or time wasters, because they steal valuable time rather than promote effective time usage. Although these behaviors are listed separately, it should be noted that the personalities of some people include many of these behaviors, making effective time management even more elusive.

1. *Type A personality:* Type A personality is thought to comprise several dominating behaviors: time urgency (a rush to meet deadlines), anger/hostility (explosive aggression), lack of planning (poor organization skills), and polyphasia (preoccupation with many thoughts at one time). Although time urgency might seem to be the target behavior for efficient time management, the combination of all four factors contributes to inefficient use of time. People who exhibit traits of Type A behavior may appear to be organized and productive, but studies indicate that Type A individuals are less organized and complete no more work than their Type B counterparts, and their work is often of lower quality.

2. *Workaholism:* Workaholics spend grossly excessive amounts of time working (**FIG. 16.3**). Workaholism is considered a process addiction wherein self-validation is received from prolonged working hours to maintain a sense of importance or self-esteem (Robinson, 2007). Whereas the average person may spend 8 hours a day at work, the workaholic spends 10 to 14 hours. Workaholics spend time doing many little tasks between 9 and 5, then feel the need to stay longer to get the big projects completed. They tend to shy away from time-saving techniques and productivity measures because these threaten the security of their self-confidence-building strategy. Workaholics may complain about the excessive

Scott refers to these as "secret pleasures" because the human ego can actually derive pleasure from them; they ultimately act as defense mechanisms.

Scott also cites several myths people harbor with respect to the feasibility of effective time-management skills. One myth is the illusion that time is an adjustable, rather than fixed, variable and that there are more than 24 hours in a day. This perception suggests that there will always be "more time" to get a job done. A second myth, perhaps based on one's prior experience, is that time-management techniques just don't work. This perception arises when specific time-management skills are used individually instead of collectively and then fail to meet expectations. Another common perception is that a methodical strategy to organize oneself is unexciting and even boring, compared to the stimulation of a crisis orientation. In other words, some people (e.g., codependents) thrive on crisis management.

Personality Styles and Behaviors

To try to understand the attitudes that become obstacles to efficient time management, scholars have also targeted

Type A personality: A time-conscious (aggressive) personality that, in terms of time management, rushes to meet deadlines.

Workaholism: A personality style that inhibits good time-management skills with excessive hours devoted to work, often at the expense of other responsibilities.

FIGURE 16.3 Putting in extra time after hours does not always indicate increased productivity. It may, in fact, be a sign of wasted time during the working day.

time they spend on work, but the simple truth is, long hours give them great pleasure.

3. *Technophile:* Cell phones, iPads, Wi-Fi, laptops, text messaging, Facebook, the Internet, Twitter, and new technologies that have yet to come on the market are great and can certainly save time, but they can also rob you blind when it comes to time management. What is a device of convenience for some is an addiction for many. Technophiles spend countless hours with their computers, and although they may give the impression of high efficiency,

Time juggler: Someone who multitasks, overbooks, and double-books oneself and bargains for time, often dropping responsibilities in the process.

Procrastinator: Someone who employs diversions and avoidance techniques rather than tackling a host of responsibilities.

Straightforward procrastinator: A person who knowingly avoids completing a task.

Deceptive procrastinator: Someone who attempts to work on projects, but only scratches the surface, stalling on the completion of tasks.

Time-trap procrastinator: A person who does other tasks, such as laundry, thus keeping busy while still avoiding the more important responsibilities.

Perfectionist: A person who is obsessed with the details of every task, aiming for quality, yet who ends up getting caught up with the details and missing the whole picture.

don't be fooled. The clock is ticking and time often runs out for other important responsibilities including spouses, families, and sleep.

4. *Time juggler:* A time juggler is someone who tries to do more than one thing at a time. An example might be someone who shaves or puts on make-up with one hand while making a call on the cell phone with the other hand, leaving the knees to handle the steering wheel. Time jugglers also schedule themselves to be at more than one place at a time and make cameo appearances at both or skip one altogether with an award-winning excuse. Time jugglers overbook and double-book appointments in hopes that something might be canceled. In any case, a time juggler is someone who bargains for time and quite often loses: Many responsibilities get dropped in the juggling process.

5. *Procrastinator:* Procrastination is a diversion tactic. Procrastinators avoid responsibilities and put off until tomorrow what should have been done today. There are three factors associated with procrastination: laziness or apathy, fear of failure, and need for instant gratification. Scholars of time management classify procrastinators as follows:

   a. *Straightforward procrastinator:* Someone who knowingly does something other than the job at hand, like going to a ball game or movie rather than studying for an exam.

   b. *Deceptive procrastinator:* Someone who takes a stab at a task (e.g., filing taxes or creating a résumé), but finds excuses to drift away from completion of it until the last minute. On the surface, it looks like progress is being made, but it is a deception.

   c. *Time-trap procrastinator:* Doing the less difficult tasks rather than required ones (e.g., cleaning, washing the car, or walking the dog before completing homework or term papers). The result here is that there is not enough time for a quality job, and these procrastinators then feel like they are painted into a corner with the clock ticking. In addition, other responsibilities are neglected while completing the required task at the last minute.

6. *Perfectionist:* A perfectionist is someone who is obsessed with carrying out every task and responsibility to perfection. Although aiming for quality

Stress with a Human Face

The train schedules are so precise in Germany, it is said that you can set your watch by them. Bernhard not only sets his watch by the trains when he returns home to Frankfurt, but also keeps his eye on the plane schedule. Bernhard, you see, is an executive at Lufthansa Airlines, which itself has a pretty good eye on the time departure schedule. Bernhard came to the United States to obtain his MBA. While in graduate school, he learned to master a precise time schedule that included his studies, family time with his baby boy Philip, and his arduous triathlon training, which in itself could be a full-time job. Bernhard's dream was to qualify and compete in the Hawaiian Ironman competition, a goal he accomplished in 1998. After returning home to Germany and taking a job with Lufthansa, he was soon transferred back to the United States to head up the company's North American regional headquarters.

New York City is a far cry from Frankfurt, and it's fair to say that no one sets their watches by the New York subway schedule. In fact, there are constant jokes about what "a New York minute" really is.

Despite the culture shock, traffic, typical congestion, and repeated terrorism alerts you would expect to find in the Big Apple, Bernhard has adapted quite well. He organizes his affairs for the next day each night before he goes to bed. He uses technology—cell phones and email—to serve him rather than become a slave to them. He creates healthy boundaries between work and his personal life. He also carves out quality time with his wife Netti and his two children, Philip and Sophie, and makes time to do his cardio workouts as well. Equally important, Bernhard sets aside dedicated vacation time so that his hard work is balanced by his hard play time. Bernhard will tell you that Germans as a rule are indeed punctual, a trait he finds very beneficial in a rapidly changing world—and a survival skill necessary for all people.

is an admirable attribute, the perfectionist gets too caught up in the details and never sees the whole picture. Thus, projects (or other aspects of life) are compromised. Evidence shows that about 20 percent of all human acts are mistakes. Total perfection is an illusion; it does not exist. But the perfectionist deceives him- or herself by thinking it is possible.

7. *Lifestyle behavior trap:* People who fall into this category are individuals who have a hard or impossible time saying no. These individuals, who show many codependent traits, are extremely nice people. They receive validation of their self-worth by helping other people, often at the expense of their own needs. These people take on inappropriate responsibilities (e.g., house sitting, feeding the neighbor's cat, driving someone to the airport), often for approval or acceptance to build self-esteem. They may even volunteer for responsibilities they have not been asked to do. But feelings of victimization may result after the task is completed, when just a thank-you is not enough and self-esteem is not enhanced.

■ Distractions: Roadblocks on the Time Management Highway

The biggest issues people have today in terms of effective time management is the ability to navigate the multitude of distractions, both internal (anxiety and fear-based thoughts and feelings about getting specific things done) and external (social media, texting, Netflix shows, video games, friends, family, etc.). Good time management skills require effectively handing both types of distractions. Keeping well-motivated during challenging tasks takes practice. External distractions have become so prevalent in today's society that it requires willpower and setting healthy boundaries in key aspects of your life to get things done and done well. One of the best suggestions for eliminating external distractions is clearing your workspace so only that which you are working on is in your field of vision. This includes setting aside your smartphone.

> **Lifestyle behavior trap:** A behavior in which people have a hard time saying no and end up overwhelmed with multiple responsibilities.

Make a habit of clearing your workspace, as clutter of any kind can lead to feelings of being overwhelmed.

Estimated Time of Completion

When starting a project, many people fail to take into consideration a realistic completion date or deadline. While many deadlines are pre-established (e.g., term paper deadlines), the completion dates for many nonacademic responsibilities, from household chores to countless personal life tasks, are more nebulous. The suggested rule of thumb for estimating completion time of a project is one and a half times what you consider it will take, which builds in time to accommodate the inevitable interruptions (Kondo, 2014; Lissard, 2016).

■ Steps to Initiate Good Time-Management Techniques

Effective time management can be broken down into three skills: prioritization, scheduling, and execution.

1. *Prioritization:* **Prioritization** means ranking responsibilities and tasks in their order of importance. Before this can be done, however, a list of all current responsibilities must be made. List making is an invaluable skill in one's time-management strategy. The following three methods are advocated:

   a. The **ABC rank-order method** involves assigning the letters A, B, or C to various responsibilities: A for the highest-priority activities (must do immediately), B for second-priority activities (anything that is not A or C but you should do soon), and C for low-priority tasks or things you would like to do (can wait to do). In this method of prioritization, once a list of responsibilities has been made and a letter assigned to each item, rewrite the list in this new order and complete the tasks in the same order.

   b. The **Pareto principle** states that 20 percent of the tasks we do give 80 percent of the rewards or satisfaction (Reh, 2008). Also referred to as the 80/20 rule, this principle suggests that individuals should focus on one or two significant tasks that are worth the time invested in them. According to this principle, out of every ten responsibilities listed, only two will produce recognizable gains. These tasks should be given attention and time. (These two tasks will most likely fall in the A category, suggesting that completion of C, and even B, items may prove unfruitful in the long run.)

   c. Sometimes it is difficult to differentiate among responsibilities, all of which seem important, to decide what to do first. One answer is to employ Stephen Covey's **important-versus-urgent method** (BOX 16.1) as highlighted in his best-selling book *The 7 Habits of Highly Effective People*. Divide your responsibilities for the day (or week) into four boxes. Note that people tend to direct their energies toward box IV (Not urgent, Not important) because these responsibilities look quick, easy, and perhaps enjoyable. Covey suggests that one's overriding attention should go to the box labeled II (Important but not Urgent) because this will yield the highest results. Box I (Important and Urgent) needs adequate time, but this is not where the majority of your attention should be placed, for it will only lead to a reactionary lifestyle. Covey suggests that it's not time that needs to be managed but ourselves that need attention. Quadrant II is the key to effective personal management.

2. *Scheduling* (BOX 16.2): **Scheduling** is time allocation for prioritized responsibilities, or the skill of matching a specific task or responsibility with a designated time period in which to accomplish

---

Prioritization: The first of three aspects necessary in effective time management, for which tasks are given priority for completion.

ABC rank-order method: A time-management technique for which things are prioritized by order of importance.

Pareto principle: Also known as the 80/20 rule, this time-management technique prioritizes tasks by the satisfaction factor.

Important-versus-urgent method: A prioritization time-management technique in which tasks are categorized.

Scheduling: The second of three aspects necessary in effective time management, for which prioritized tasks are scheduled for completion.

BOX 16.1   The Important-Versus-Urgent Matrix

		Importance	
		Low Importance	High Importance
High Urgency		III. A. B. C.	I. A. B. C.
Urgency			
Low Urgency		IV. A. B. C.	II. A. B. C.

BOX 16.2   Time-Management Skills

Scheduling

Once you have a solid idea of what needs to get done, there are several choices you can make about scheduling your responsibilities. If you have a few major projects to do, try the boxing method.

Boxing

Divide your day into five parts: morning, noon hour, afternoon, dinner hour, and evening. Then, write down the significant tasks and assign them a block of time that is most suited to your schedule.

8–12 noon _____

12–1 _____ Lunch _____ (perhaps

do some small errands) _____

1–6 _____

6–7 _____ Dinner _____ (exercise)

_____

7–10 _____

Remember: To be effective you will want to take small breaks during these large blocks of time.

---

and completion times/dates of designated goals and responsibilities. The three-P's method is planning, implementing a schedule of tasks; prioritizing doing a regular check on the relative importance of tasks; and perhaps most important, pacing, or the rate at which each task is performed. The following scheduling techniques are advocated. Remember, though, that flexibility in scheduling is essential, or these time-management techniques will cause stress rather than reduce it.

a. *Boxing:* The concept of **boxing** involves breaking down your daily waking hours into 3- to 5-hour chunks or boxes of time such as morning, afternoon, and evening. In each time box, you designate a specific responsibility. Boxing is primarily geared toward big projects that necessitate large blocks of time (e.g., yard work, term papers, and other major projects). Example:

8–9 A.M.	Term
9–10 A.M.	paper
10–11 A.M.	research
11–12 noon	at library
12–1 P.M.	Lunch/exercise
1–2 P.M.	Write paper
2–3 P.M.	
3–4 P.M.	

it. Time-management experts use the three-C's method and the three-P's method for scheduling. The three-C's method consists of clocks, the designation of time periods for short-term time management; calendars, for weekly, monthly, and even yearly forecasts of goals and responsibilities;

Boxing: A scheduling technique used in time management for which the day is divided into 3- to 5-hour chunks of time devoted to accomplishing big projects.

b. *Time mapping:* **Time mapping** is similar to boxing, but with this strategy, the day is broken down into very small blocks of time, usually about quarter- to half-hour segments. Specific tasks (e.g., drafting a letter, making a phone call, running a quick errand) are designated for specific times:

9 A.M.—Meet with boss, pass in budget report
9:15 A.M.—Mail letters
9:30 A.M.—Phone Atlanta
9:45 A.M.—Pick up book at library
10:00 A.M.—Pick up résumés at printer

c. *Clustering:* When you orchestrate your own responsibilities, it's known as **clustering**. Clustering is a scheduling technique for the completion of errands outside the house or office. Responsibilities are listed and then clustered or mapped out by location. Clustering is a time-saving device allowing the individual to complete errands in close proximity to one another rather than ricochet around town.

As you can see, prioritization and scheduling are partners. At the end of each day, look at your list to see which tasks weren't finished and then reprioritize your responsibilities for the next day.

3. *Execution:* The **execution** of responsibilities is a systematic progression of steps taken toward the satisfactory completion of each task. More specifically, execution can be described as the implementation of an established schedule. A prioritized schedule is like a blueprint or military strategy. The most effective method of execution

is the establishment of goals. Here are some tips to improve execution:

a. Assign a deadline (goal) for each task or project.

b. Break large projects down into smaller tasks, and assign a deadline for each task.

c. Work on one section or task at a time. Work on it until it is complete. Experts indicate that it is better to have one or two completed tasks than a handful of unfinished ones.

d. Reward your accomplishments with small pleasures to motivate yourself to accomplish designated goals. Avoid immediate gratification, though. In other words, reward yourself after satisfactory completion of each job, not before.

■ Additional Time-Management Ideas

The following are some additional ideas that don't fall into any specific category but are nevertheless helpful in managing your time effectively:

1. *Use technology to your advantage.* Technology acumen and social networking skills are essential assets in today's world. Learn to use them wisely, from making job contacts and organizing social events to utilizing apps to navigate your day more easily. Today you have the world at your fingertips...learn to make good use of it. Losing your smartphone (your second brain) can be very stressful. Make a habit of backing up the most important information on your smartphone or tablet. Learn to make smart choices in the use of your technology.

2. *Establish healthy boundaries with technology.* Without a doubt, the biggest time robber today is time spent on the Internet. What starts as a quick Google search or Facebook update ends up being a 2-hour surfing expedition. Time, like ice, melts in front of a computer screen. The Internet is a great tool, but too much of anything can be problematic (and this doesn't even include online gambling, porn, or other types of screen addictions). Learn to establish healthy boundaries with the Internet via set time limits. Practice saying the mantra "Healthy boundaries," and then honor these healthy boundaries by knowing when to turn off the computer, smartphone, and iPad.

Time mapping: A time-management technique; breaking down the day into 15- to 30-minute segments and assigning a task or responsibility to each segment.

Clustering: A scheduling technique used in time management for which errands are grouped by location (e.g., dry cleaners, post office, pharmacy).

Execution: The third of three aspects essential for effective time management, in which tasks are actually completed.

3. *Schedule personal time in each day.* Experts agree that a day filled to the brim with career and family responsibilities, leaving no time for oneself, results in burnout and possibly disease and illness. Your health should be a high priority. Time allocated for a walk, jog, or meditation alone is crucial to the effectiveness of carrying out personal responsibilities. But health is often taken for granted until illness occurs. So, keep your health a top priority. As Ben Franklin once said, "An ounce of prevention is worth a pound of cure."

4. *Edit your life.* This journalistic phrase is used here as a personal house-cleaning technique. (It is also known as the emptying process of spiritual well-being.) Despite the fact that civilization has progressed light-years since the days when people lived in caves, we have not lost the Neanderthal trait of hunting and gathering possessions. Whether material in nature or not, we tend to carry around a lot of excess baggage. In the editing process, a regular assessment of physical, mental, emotional, and spiritual needs is conducted. This includes an objective evaluation of relationships, values, and personal needs. Once you have listed your various needs, decide which factors in your life are essential or core to your life, and which factors are peripheral ones draining your energy. Then, let go of the ones you feel are draining off valuable time and energy. The editing process, then, is a technique by which you reduce your life to its simplest terms. In the book *The Dove*, a true story of a teenager who sailed around the world by himself, author Robin Lee Graham said, "It's not how much I need to survive, it's how little I need to survive."

5. *Schedule interruptions.* One time-management technique advocated by experts is to be flexible with your work schedule. Office visits, phone calls, meetings, and 2-hour "power lunches" can become distractions and interrupt your work when they are not expected. Resulting feelings of frustration, impatience, and anger can contribute to the pressures of task completion. If you allow for a small number of interruptions in your day, however (**FIG. 16.4**), anger and hurriedness can be minimized. Experts suggest that interruptions should actually be scheduled into your daily activities by allotting them 7 to 10 minutes per hour. Conversely, interruptions should also be prevented during crucial time periods when continuity of

FIGURE 16.4 Good time management requires you to balance your life between work and leisure. Remember that balance is essential for optimal well-being.

work flow is paramount. Taking the phone off the hook, closing the office door, or leaving the worksite when distractions are unavoidable may be necessary.

6. *Delegate.* The old adage "If you want something done right, you have to do it yourself" can lend itself to stress if you feel you have to do everything yourself. Many people dislike delegating responsibilities; it is equated with loss of control and personal identity. **Delegation** involves trusting yourself to relinquish control, as well as trusting the individuals to whom you delegate the responsibilities. In many cases, items marked as B or C on your To Do list can be delegated to or shared with other people. When you delegate responsibilities, explain instructions clearly and assign a completion time or date to each task. Avoid delegating responsibilities for which the time to explain the task exceeds the time to complete it. Follow-up is a crucial component of delegation to prevent reverse delegation, wherein the task comes back to you unfinished.

7. *Develop organizational skills:* Although some people think that organizational skills are innate, the truth is that, with practice, anybody can learn strong organizational skills to increase personal

Delegation: Relinquishing control of a responsibility by turning it over to someone else.

productivity. The following tips will help to sharpen your organizational skills:

a. Some people receive up to 100 text messages a day. Reading and responding to these can become a full-time job. Here is a tip: If emails and text messages are a stressor in your life, delete all the forwarded emails to save time for those that are really important. Second tip: Answer emails and text messages when you first open them, not days or weeks later (Glie, 2016).

b. Once used in cars for emergencies, cell phones can now be found attached to anyone's ear practically anywhere rather than just for emergencies. Make it a habit to limit cell phone use to practical hours and turn off the phone while at the movies, restaurants, classrooms, bedroom, and other inappropriate places.

c. Much time is wasted looking for items that seem to have fallen in a black hole. Precious time can be saved by designating a place for bills, assignments, budget sheets, car keys, and so forth. Make it a habit to put items in the same place every time.

d. Learn what resources are available to help you complete what you need to get done, including fellow students as study partners.

e. Learn where these resources are, and when you can use them.

f. Make a master chart including a list of deadlines, or coursework responsibilities with a time limit attached to them. Update the list regularly.

g. Buy a master calendar, daily planner, or calendar app, and write down all your deadlines to get a comprehensive picture of the events in your life. Learn to look at the entire week, and then the entire month to get a wider perspective. Then, zoom in and focus on immediate as well as long-term needs.

h. Learn to make outlines of projects, papers, lectures, and proposals—introduction, development, conclusions.

i. Learn when people you need to contact are available. Learn/remember to tell others where you are or when you can be reached.

j. Learn/recognize your physical/mental limitations. Learn *how* to say no to people who plead for time you don't have (e.g., I'm sorry, but I simply don't have time). Be gentle but firm! Learn *when* to say no to people who plead for time you don't have.

k. A lot of time can be spent on the Internet (this might actually be a great time to practice diaphragmatic breathing). Addiction to the Internet is no laughing matter. Monitor your computer usage time and if it exceeds 2 to 3 hours a day (outside of work), consider limiting it to a respectable amount.

8. *Find balance:* All work and no play means poor work quality. Balance your life between work and play. Don't place all your self-esteem eggs in one basket.

True to the Puritan ethic that "worth equals work," Americans, by and large, spend an inordinate amount of time at their jobs. According to the International Labour Organization, the additional hours that Americans work each week amounts to an extra week of work each year (Moyers, 2003). Experts detect a cultural shift with professionals working longer hours and taking less vacation time out of fear for job security (Kinsman, 2006). Because of corporate downsizing and restructuring, people are more inclined not to use their entire vacation time, for fear that if they take time off from their job, they might be next in line to leave permanently. Time-management expert Jeff Davidson notes that not only do more people spend more time at work, but they also tend to sleep fewer hours, resulting in feelings of fatigue and irritability while on the job. Davidson also notes that as we continue to wallow in the throes of the information age, we tend to become suffocated in information, from junk mail to the Internet. The following are some additional tips on managing your time more effectively:

1. *Watch less television.* Television (this includes Hulu and Netflix) is definitely a time robber. People say they watch TV to relax, but what is really happening is that they are substituting one form of sensory stimulus for another. And because of the addictive nature of television watching, even though you may plan to watch only one half-hour show, you may end up sitting in front of the television for the entire evening, wasting the night away.

2. *Change your Internet home page to Google.* High-tech gadgets are great, but they can certainly become huge distractions and result in getting little

done. One distraction is the home page of Internet service providers, chock full of ads and attention-grabbing news headlines. Consider changing your home page to Google to minimize distractions and focus your mind on what really needs to get done. Once again, set healthy boundaries for time spent surfing the Web.

3. *Clean your office, room, desk, or work space once a week.* Things tend to accumulate rather quickly in the course of a week. Mail, books, papers, and odds and ends all take up space. They also compete for your attention. Using what Davidson calls the "urge to purge," don't be afraid to throw away those things you know no longer serve you. By making a habit of clearing off your desk and work space, you will not only spend less time searching for things throughout the week, but at the same time start the cleansing process in your mind to focus on your work.

4. *Get a good night's sleep every night.* The average recommended time for sleep is between 7 and 8 hours a night. When we get pressed for time, the allocation of time for sleeping is often the first thing cut. In the short term, what may seem like a clever idea to cram for an exam, write a paper, or finish a project is in the long run an invitation to disaster. Although scientists who study sleep do not agree why adequate sleep is necessary, they all agree that sleep is essential to our health and well-being (Huffington, 2016). Denying ourselves adequate sleep not only affects the quality of the work we do the next day, but it also affects the quality of our health. The more tired you are, what might normally take 1 hour to complete could take 3 hours with poor quality to show for it.

5. *Create personal boundaries, and honor them.* Boundaries are those invisible lines we draw around ourselves to keep our identity and give structure to our lives. Just as it is important to be flexible and go with the flow when working with the element of time, it is equally important to honor personal boundaries, both yours and those of other people in your life. Honoring boundaries includes knowing when to leave the library, office, worksite, or friend's house, or turn off the smartphone and call it a day. By honoring your boundaries, you maintain a sense of personal integrity. When boundaries are not honored, feelings of victimization surface, and these too can have a negative impact on the quality and quantity of the work you do.

6. *Do one activity at a time.* Multitasking is a myth. Research studies show that you cannot do more than one thing at the same time and do them both well (e.g., driving and texting). In this day and age, it is easy to get caught up doing many things at once, like scrolling through Facebook updates while writing a term paper, while watching March Madness basketball or *Game of Thrones.* Dividing your attention between two or more activities results in less quality in the work actually done. It wastes time as well. Learn to focus yourself by doing one task at a time.

7. *Learn and practice the art of decision making.* We are constantly faced with choices in both our personal and professional lives—where to eat, what movie to see, what topic to present, or what job to take. Decision making requires a good sense of judgment, coupled with a sense of compassion. Some decisions can be made rather quickly, whereas those with long-term implications need more time to survey and process. When we have big decisions to make, we tend to drag our feet and, in the information age, it is not hard to become overwhelmed with tidbits of facts and figures. In the words of Davidson, more choices mean more decisions. He suggests that we avoid being overwhelmed by learning to limit our choices and, hence, the decisions that come from too many choices.

■ Best Application of Time-Management Skills

Time-management skills can appear overwhelming and stress producing if they are seen as dogmatic and rigid. Use of time-management skills should be proportional to the number of responsibilities one assumes. In all likelihood, you are already fairly adept at these time-management techniques and may even use some of them in your normal working schedule. It is during periods when responsibilities accumulate beyond normal that these techniques may assist in your overall coping strategy. Before you begin to apply these techniques, first inventory your attitudes and behavior styles for the roadblocks listed earlier in the chapter. See if you can relate to any factors that sabotage efforts to get tasks accomplished on time. Then experiment with the techniques to find out which work best for you. After employing these techniques, evaluate their effectiveness. It is fair to say that virtually all other stress-management skills hinge on time management, for without adequate time allocated to rethink strategies to deal with stress or practice relaxation techniques, learning them serves no lasting purpose.

SUMMARY

- Time and money are considered the two primary resources necessary to navigate the shoals of a stressful life, but people tend to waste both, resulting in a personal shipwreck.

- Financial responsibility means making a budget and following it rather than spending money you don't have and accruing a mass of credit card debt. There are many ways to incorporate fiscal management into your life that can reduce personal stress.

- Time is a human-made concept. Calendars and time zones were created to bring organization to cultures and civilizations that needed to coordinate activities.

- Although the concept of time was created to help organize, people often find themselves becoming slaves to the clock, and hence become stressed by it.

- Time management is defined as the ability to prioritize, schedule, and execute responsibilities to personal satisfaction. Time-management skills are now taught to people to help them gain a sense of control over personal responsibilities.

- There are several roadblocks to effective time management, which impede productivity and, in essence, rob us of valuable time. They include Type A personality, workaholism, time juggling, procrastination, and lifestyle behavior trapping.

- Three methods of prioritization are the ABC rank-order method, the Pareto principle, and the important-versus-urgent method.

- Recommended scheduling techniques are boxing, time mapping, and clustering.

- The execution of personal responsibilities is the last step of time management. Setting goals and providing rewards can be powerful incentives to finishing the task at hand.

- Additional tips to help manage time better are delegating responsibilities, scheduling interruptions and personal time each day, editing your life to the bare essentials, and using strong organizational skills.

STUDY GUIDE QUESTIONS

1. List the four rules for financial stability.

2. Describe the psychology of money.

3. What personality styles undermine one's time-management skills?

4. Explain the following time-management concepts: the Pareto principle, boxing, time mapping, and clustering.

5. List five strategies for effective time management to decrease stress.

REFERENCES AND RESOURCES

Allen, D. *Getting Things Done*. Penguin Books, New York, 2003.

Allen, D. *Getting Things Done: The Art of Stress-Free Productivity*. Penguin Books, New York, 2015.

Beech, H. R., Burns, L. E., and Sheffield, B. F. *A Behavioral Approach to the Management of Stress*. Wiley, Chichester, UK, 1982.

Bliss, E. *Getting Things Done: The ABCs of Time Management*. Scribner's, New York, 1976.

Boslough, J. The Enigma of Time, *National Geographic* 177(3): 109–132, 1990.

Charlesworth, E. A., and Nathan, R. G. *Stress Management: A Comprehensive Guide to Wellness*. Ballantine Books, New York, 1984.

Covey, S. *First Things First*. Fireside Books, New York, 1996.

Covey, S. *Seven Habits of Highly Effective People*, 15th ed. Free Press, New York, 2004.

Davidson, J. *The Complete Idiot's Guide to Managing Your Time*. Alpha Books, New York, 1995.

Dominguez, J., and Robin, V. *Your Money or Your Life*. Penguin Books, New York, 1999.

Edginton, C. R., DeGraaf, D., Dieser, R. B., and Edginton, S. R. *Leisure and Life Satisfaction: Foundational Perspectives*, 4th ed. McGraw Hill, New York, 2005.

Girdano, D., Everly, G., and Dusek, D. *Controlling Stress and Tension: A Holistic Approach*. Prentice-Hall, Englewood Cliffs, NJ, 1990.

Glei, J. *Unsubscribe: How to Kill Email Anxiety, Avoid Distractions, and Get Real Work Done*. Public Affairs Books, New York, 2016.

Goodman, B. A. Field Guide to the Workaholic, *Psychology Today*, December 22, 2006. www.revolutionhealth.com/healthy-living/relationships/time/work-life-balance/workaholic?s_kwcid=ContentNetwork|953541294.

Graham, R. L. *The Dove*. Bantam Books, New York, 1972.

Hout, T. M., and Stalk, G. *Competing against Time*. Free Press, New York, 1990.

Huffington, A. *The Sleep Revolution*. Harmony Books, New York, 2016.

Jasper, J. *Take Back Your Time: How to Regain Control of Work, Information and Technology*. St. Martin, New York, 1999.

Kinsman, M. What 40-hour Work Week? *The San Diego Union-Tribune*, September 3, 2006. www.signonsandiego.com/uniontrib/20060903/news_1z1b3what.html.

Knaus, W. *The Procrastination Workbook*. New Harbinger Publications, Oakland, CA, 2002.

Koch, R. *The 80/20 Principle: The Secret of Achieving More with Less*. Bantam Doubleday Dell, New York, 1998.

Kondo, M. *The Life-Changing Magic of Tidying Up: The Japanese Art of Decluttering and Organizing*. Ten Speed Press, Berkeley, CA, 2014.

Kranzt, M. Roth IRA vs. 401(k): A Guide for the Perplexed, *USA Today*, November 25, 2005. www.usatoday.com/money/perfi/columnist/krantz/2005-11-25-retirement-accounts_x.htm.

Lee, M. D. *Management of Work and Personal Life*. Praeger, New York, 1984.

Levine, R. The Pace of Life, *Psychology Today* 20:42–46, 1989.

Lissard, C. Synchronicity Life Coaching. Personal communication. November 1, 2016.

Maas, J. Power Sleep. *Quill Books*, New York, 2001.

Mackenzie, A. *The Time Trap*. AMACOM, New York, 1990.

Mayer, J. *Time Management for Dummies*. IDG Books, Indianapolis, IN, 1995.

McPeak, M. Living It Up, Paying It Down—ZipUSA: 19886, *National Geographic* February 2005. http://ngm.nationalgeographic.com/ngm/0502/feature7/index.html.

Morgenstern, J. *Time Management from the Inside Out*. Henry Holt, New York, 2000.

Moyers, B. Working Overtime, *PBS*, April 18, 2003. www.pbs.org/now/politics/workhours.html.

O'Connor, J. J., and Robertson, E. F. A History of Time: Classical Time, August 2002. www-history.mcs.st-andrews.ac.uk/HistTopics/Time_1.html.

Oldenburg, D. Fast Forward: Living in Artificial Time, *Health* 20:52–56, 80–81, 1988.

Orman, S. *Suze Orman's Financial Guidebook*. Three Rivers Press, New York, 2002.

Peterson, K. *The Tomorrow Trap*. Health Communications, Deerfield Beach, FL, 1996.

Quirk, T. J. The Art of Time Management, *Training* 26(1): 59–61, 1989.

Rechtschaffen, S. *Time Shifting*. Doubleday, New York, 1996.

Reh, J. Pareto's Principle: The 80/20 Rule, *About.com: Management*, 2008. http://management.about.com/cs/generalmanagement/a/Pareto081202.htm.

Robinson. B. *Chained to the Desk*, 2nd ed. NYU Press, New York, 2007.

Roesch, R. *Time Management for Busy People*. McGraw-Hill, New York, 1998.

Rushkoff, D. *Present Shock: When Everything Happens Now*. Current/Penguin Books, New York, 2013.

Rutherford, R. D. *Just in Time: Immediate Help for the Time-Pressured*. Wiley, New York, 1981.

Schlosser, E. *Fast Food Nation*. Houghton Mifflin, Boston, 2001.

Scott, D. *How to Put More Time in Your Life*. Rawson, Wade, New York, 1980.

Singletary, M. *Spend Well, Live Right*. Ballantine Books, New York, 2004.

Szegedy-Maszak, M. Mysteries of the Mind, *U.S. News and World Report* February 28, 2005.

Taylor, E. *Mind Programming*. Hay House, Carlsbad, CA, 2010.

Tucker, M. *It's Your Time—Use It or Lose It*. Exposition Press, New York, 1980.

Twist, L. *The Soul of Money*. W. W. Norton, New York, 2003.

Yates, B. *Applications in Self-Management*. Wadsworth, Belmont, CA, 1986.

Yates, B. *Self-Management*. Wadsworth, Belmont, CA, 1985.

CHAPTER 17

Additional Coping Techniques

One cannot collect all the beautiful shells on the beach, one can collect only a few.

—Anne Morrow Lindbergh

According to several psychologists, just as there are many shells on the beach, there are hundreds of coping techniques. Some fall nicely into well-defined categories; others do not, but are every bit as important in their function and outcome. Much like acquiring a personal collection of seashells, chances are you will choose a handful of coping strategies for your own stress-management program and leave the rest behind. And just as a return to the beach may inspire you to pick up a new shell, which at another time seemed unattractive or banal, a new encounter with stress may entice you to select a new method of coping. This chapter outlines some additional coping techniques that are often used to deal with stress effectively. Although they may not serve as your first line of defense in every case, at some point in your life you may find them very helpful (**FIG. 17.1**).

> **Information seeking:** A common coping technique; searching for detailed information to increase awareness about a situation that has become a perceived threat.

Information Seeking

Fear of the unknown accompanies many formidable stressors, from job interviews to cancer diagnoses. Several circumstances we encounter are perceived as threats because of our lack of information about the event. Lack of information allows the mind to fill in missing pieces with hypothetical facts or worst-case scenarios, which often perpetuates the stress response. To conquer fear of the unknown, gathering information about a specific circumstance becomes one of the best defenses against stressors. **Information seeking** involves collecting and processing facts about a stressful event or situation, which can then be used to help solve the problem and regain emotional stability. As suggested by psychologist Shelly Taylor (2011), the gathering and processing of information also allows mastery of control because knowledge can become a powerful tool with which to confront and dismantle a stressor.

Information seeking has been found to be an essential skill following diagnosis of terminal illness, in the recovery process of alcoholics and drug abusers, during

FIGURE 17.1 Never underestimate the power of support groups.

pregnancy, and for any other stressor that makes an unpredictable change in your life, however big or small. When encountering stress, people pose many questions in an attempt to gain a handle on the unknown. When an individual contracts a disease such as cancer, multiple sclerosis, or atherosclerosis, all attention becomes focused on gathering answers to a host of questions. What is the nature of this disease? How did I contract it? What is the best method to manage it? Similarly, when your car breaks down, a set of questions runs through your mind. What's wrong with the engine or transmission? How long will it take to fix? How much will it cost? Can I afford this? Or academic stressors: How many exams are there in this course? What types of questions are on the exams? How much is the term paper worth toward the final grade? Like a large jigsaw puzzle, small pieces of information become crucial to the ability to cope with the cause of the stress so as to assemble a wider perspective on the whole problem as well as potential solutions.

In times of distress, questions need answers, and there are many resources typically accessed to provide these answers. The three most common sources are the Internet, people, and books, magazines, and journals. Perhaps because the Internet is so easily accessible, it has become the first avenue for information seeking, rather than direct contact with people. In a short amount of time, the Internet has become the world library of information. But beware: Surfing the Internet for answers is like drinking water from a fire hydrant. Ironically, although there are vast amounts of information available, many

people never surf past the first ten links. Moreover, not all the information in the world is posted on the Internet! Ask any investigative reporter and he or she will tell you to validate your sources. Although surfing topics on any search engine is a good place to start to seek insights on various issues, your search shouldn't end there.

A lot of valuable information in the form of first-hand knowledge (wisdom) can be found only by talking directly to people who are "in the know." For this reason, conversing with others who have experienced a similar situation (or stressor) is highly recommended in the skill set of information seeking. Sometimes, however, when information is disseminated through people, facts can be intertwined with emotional perceptions. As a result, the objectivity of this information must be assessed very carefully.

Finally, don't abandon the use of books, journals, and magazines as important sources of information. The use of these references to cope with stress even has its own name: bibliotherapy. Like the creative solving process, information seeking is not a linear process, but rather a circuitous route until answers are found and a sense of resolution is reached (Foster, 2005).

Like other coping techniques, though, information seeking can be a liability as well as an asset. Too much information can be as detrimental as too little because it can feed the imagination to create worst-case scenarios, which are then adopted as reality. Nevertheless, when you are confronted with a stressor that promotes fear of the unknown, information seeking can be your best strategy to begin to cope with this problem.

Social Orchestration

Perhaps the most common response to events or circumstances that elicit the stress response is avoidance—the most ineffective coping mechanism. Whereas avoidance of life-threatening events such as fire is wise, avoidance of mental, emotional, and spiritual threats is not a viable option. Avoidance is a defense mechanism deeply rooted in the ancient flight response. It is popularly believed that if we avoid situations that cause fear or frustration, our lives will become simple and stress free. But what may seem like a quick fix offers no permanent resolution, only further problems down the road. Avoidance is a negative coping style, especially when the stressors involve relationships and human confrontation.

Can you make educated choices about how to minimize stressful situations? Yes! The answer is **social orchestration** (formerly called *social engineering*, a term that has now been adopted by political and technological fields to mean "mass societal influence" or "obtaining confidential information by manipulating people"). Social orchestration is a positive coping style designed to help minimize stress by following a path of least resistance, but not avoidance. Social orchestration involves analyzing a problem, creating a series of viable options, and then choosing the best option to resolve feelings and perceptions of stress. It is also described as a reorganization process wherein individuals manipulate factors and elements (not people) in their environment to their best advantage.

There are two approaches to the social orchestration process. The first is to change factors in your environment that can cause stress. If this is not a viable option, your health status is at risk, and attempts at cognitive reappraisal prove fruitless, then the second approach is to change your environment. Changing factors in your environment might include driving a different route to work or blocking out time periods throughout the day during which you do not answer the phone so as to get a major task completed. In situations where you change specific factors, you attempt to manipulate or control your environment so that your encounters with potential stressors are minimal. To change your environment means relocating from unhealthy or intolerable living conditions to a new setting that is conducive to better health status. Because changing one's environment is both costly and time consuming, this approach is often used as a last resort. Keep in mind that if you choose to change your environment so as to avoid people or run away, then this coping technique is being used improperly and no resolution is guaranteed. Also, Holmes and Rahe found that relocating to a new environment is a stressful experience in itself.

On a larger scale, social orchestration can be seen in many political grass-roots efforts—lobbying Congress to pass legislation favoring particular issues and concerns, for example. In fact, social orchestration is the coping skill of choice at both local and national governmental levels for issues such as landfills and recycling. On a smaller scale, social orchestration is a strategy we employ regularly with personal chores and responsibilities, but it is an effective one in the management of major life stressors.

A prime example of social orchestration where factors in the environment were changed for all Americans was the fallout from the terrorist attacks on September 11, 2001. In Manhattan, commuter train routes were disrupted for months, as were some roads and highways leading into the city, which changed going to and coming home from work into a challenge. Many people learned to telecommute and actually found they preferred this style of work. Many businesses whose locations were either devastated in the collapse of the World Trade Center buildings or closed because of smoke and falling ash needed to open temporary offices in outlying areas. Perhaps one of the biggest changes that affected the U.S. population was related to air travel, when new security checks required additional hours of time before take-off, readjusting time schedules for everyone involved. Additional examples include changes made by those who lost their homes to the 2011 Mississippi River floods or devastating tornadoes. Whether it's reorchestrating your life because of a change in the family (e.g., new baby or aging parents) or some world event that landed on your doorstep, social orchestration offers a way to gain an upper hand in the situation.

Although social orchestration is often the coping skill of choice for large-scale issues like earthquakes and human-made disasters, the ability to change factors in the environment can be done at a personal level as well. Many coping skills are used at the same time to deal with a stressor; there is strength in numbers. Thus, social orchestration may incorporate the use of other coping skills, including assertiveness, cognitive restructuring, creative problem solving, and time management. Cognitive restructuring is essential to create a new frame of mind in which to manipulate factors in the environment. The following is a step-by-step process for social orchestration:

1. *Define your stressors.* Write down what is bothering you by trying to describe what this stressor really is (e.g., an obnoxious roommate, a bad marriage, car repair problems).

2. *Identify your initial response.* Do you feel angry, frustrated, afraid, impatient, or resentful? Does this stressor cause you to worry or feel guilty? What emotions are running through your mind? Write these down. Next, describe what your first reaction

Social orchestration: A coping technique; either (1) changing stress-producing factors in the environment or (2) changing the entire stress-producing environment; the path of least resistance (as distinguished from avoidance).

or course of action to this stressor is (or was). Do you feel the urge to avoid a certain person? Do the words *retaliation* or *avoidance* come to mind? How would you describe your first course of action?

3. *Generate alternatives.* This is the creative stage, where you write down any and all possible solutions. Let us say, for example, that the route you drive to work is under construction and now it takes you an extra 25 minutes to get there. You find yourself feeling pretty irritated with the traffic and the fact that you are wasting so much time. What are some viable alternatives? Perhaps carpooling, taking a bus or subway, leaving for work 20 minutes earlier, finding a new route to work, working at home on a computer with high-speed Internet access, or walking.

4. *Choose the best alternative.* Once you have a handful of ideas that are plausible, pick the one that seems most suited to your circumstances and do it. Regarding the preceding example, assume that the walk is too far, and that there is no mass transit or potential carpool members readily available. Working at home with high-speed Internet access sounds attractive, and you decide to go with this plan of action. To your surprise, your plan is approved by your boss for 3 out of 5 work days until the road construction is done. So, you work at home, while miles away road construction takes place.

5. *Evaluate the outcome of your choice.* In this last step, you take a moment to analyze the option you have chosen to measure its effectiveness. If the option is a good one, you keep it. If not, you pick a new option and give it a try. In the case of the road-construction problem, it turns out that working at home seems to require much more discipline than you realized. It actually takes more time to get your work done because of distractions from the refrigerator and the television. After evaluating this option, you decide to return to your office, leaving 30 minutes earlier than before, and this second option works fine.

The key to social orchestration is to provide yourself with many viable options from which to choose. Options are like cushions that soften the blow when a stressor disrupts your center of gravity, causing you to fall. People with only one option—or worse, no options—begin to feel that a stressor is beyond control and that they are victims of their environment. By creating and choosing one of several options, you strengthen your internal locus of control and get an early start on resolving the issues at hand.

Friends: Social-Support Groups

You can never have enough friends—really good, supportive friends (not just in your Facebook directory)—especially in times of stress. Talking to, hanging out with, or confiding in a close friend or two dissipates emotional tension, which is why building strong social support in each phase of our lives is considered paramount to one's health. The word "friend" has taken on a new aspect with the popularity of Facebook. Virtual friends are nice, yet in terms of social support, real friends who drop whatever they are doing and come over to be there for you are the only ones you can really count on. This is what is meant by strong social-support groups: friends who have shared a meaningful experience and who are there for you in times of personal need.

There is an old proverb suggesting that misery loves company. This does not mean that we wish our troubles on others, nor does it mean that we are happy to see others encounter the same problems we faced ourselves. Rather, it means that when two or more people experience a problem of daunting magnitude, the emotional burden seems to be shared, is more bearable, and is consequently not as heavy a load as a solo attempt at working against the odds. This is the premise that has given rise to the recommendation of regular social contact and the plethora of support groups across America.

The first support group to gain a foothold of respect in the American culture was Alcoholics Anonymous (AA Services, 2002). Since its inception more than 50 years ago, this group has helped millions of people cope with the problems of alcohol addiction through the care and love shared by its members. Because of its tremendous success, the philosophy, format, traditions, and twelve-step recovery process have been borrowed by virtually every support group for all substance and process addictions.

Research has also shown that feelings of connectedness, belongingness, and bonding arising from social contact contribute to one's health (Ornish, 1998; Pelletier, 2000) (**FIG. 17.2**). This is the social well-being aspect of spiritual well-being. The desire to belong is considered a basic human need, as was first suggested by Maslow in 1943. There are several theories as to why **social support**

> **Social support:** A coping technique; those groups of friends, family members, and others whose company acts to buffer against and dissipate the negative effects of stress.

FIGURE 17.2 More and more, evidence points to the idea that strong social support from friends may act to buffer against the ill effects of stress and add to both the quality and quantity of life.

is considered an aid in the coping process. The **buffer theory**, proposed by Cassel (1976), suggests that social support acts as a buffer against stress, in that social ties tend to filter out the deleterious effects of both ordinary hassles and devastating life events. This theory is shared by several researchers in the field of health psychology, but the exact dynamics of this buffering action are still uncertain. Connell and D'Augelli (1990) hypothesized that when individuals express fondness for others and make themselves available to both receive help (succor) and give help (nurturance), perceptions of stress are significantly decreased. In the **compensation theory**, social support

is thought to act as a compensation for those who are at an emotional loss because of life's stressors. Perhaps the landmark study of the power of support groups was one designed by Spiegel and colleagues (1989). This study showed that metastatic breast cancer patients who were involved with a support group lived statistically significantly longer than those who did not belong to such a group. Spiegel called this coping technique **supportive-expressive group therapy**. Connectedness, through the loving support of friends, family, and colleagues, appears to be an essential factor for optimal health (Ornish, 1998). The **direct-effect theory**, suggested by Andrews and Tennant (1982), indicates that social contact only provides positive exposure to the individual and that these positive stimuli are pleasing to the ego. Finally, the **cognitive-dissonance theory** states that when individuals are engaged in social contact where values and attitudes are similar, the collective energy far exceeds the negative feelings experienced by any one person individually.

Research investigating the role of social support as an effective coping skill has found that having a small group of individuals whom you can relate to, bond with, trust, and confide in not only improves one's quality of life, but most likely extends the duration of one's life. Whether these studies include breast cancer patients, alcoholics, teen anorexics, war veterans, low-income pregnant women, or any other demographic group, this has been proven true (Byrd-Craven 2013). From these and other studies,

Buffer theory: A theory that suggests that people invited to a support group act to buffer the participants from stress to lessen the impact.

Compensation theory: A theory suggesting that support groups compensate for various emotional losses one experiences during stress.

Supportive-expressive group therapy: A term coined by Dr. David Spiegel for women with breast cancer to share their experiences, grief, and healing with others going through the same experience.

Direct-effect theory: A theory suggesting that social contact serves to provide uplifting aspects to the individual, and thus pleasure to the ego.

Cognitive-dissonance theory: A theory suggesting that the collective energy of one's support group supersedes any individual's negative experience of stress.

BOX 17.1 Virtual Friends in Need?

The term "social support group" has taken on a whole new meaning because of new arenas of social networking, including Facebook, Myspace.com, text messaging, Twitter, and other forums not yet created. In an age where the world is at your fingertips (through a keypad), friends are as close as the farthest corner of the globe. But what constitutes a real friend? Is it merely interfacing with a name and photo on a Web site, or is it receiving several emails or text messages a day from acquaintances? Nothing can replace the empathy of eye-to-eye contact and a familiar human voice, yet emails, text messages, and the newest virtual contacts can serve as a powerful supplement to the human connection and evaporate feelings of loneliness. How strong is your support group, and is there a balance between your real and virtual worlds?

it seems that companionship is truly a basic human need. When this need is filled through the demonstration of caring, love, and moral support, the intensity of stress is alleviated.

It should be mentioned that since the advent of Facebook, social researchers have noted that the number of close friends people actually confide in has decreased. The reason suggested appears not to be related to social networking per se, but rather the time constraints preventing people from fostering and nurturing quality friendships (Cohen, 2011).

Hobbies

Is there such a thing as a therapeutic escape? Perhaps. Whereas psychologists and stress-management counselors caution against the hazards of avoidance, the practice of diversions has often been advocated as a bona fide coping strategy. Healthy diversions are any activities that offer a temporary escape from the sensory overload that can produce or perpetuate the stress response. Diversions offer the conscious mind a "change of venue" to promote clear thinking. Taking your mind off a problem, or removing an issue from conscious attention for a designated period of time, and diverting attention to an unrelated subject focuses the mind and enables it to deal better with these issues upon return. As with most strategies, diversions offer either positive or negative repercussions. Positive diversions are those in which the individual takes an *active role* in the escape process. (An example of a passive escape is watching television or sleeping.) Active escapes are those that contribute to one's identity, character, and self-esteem. With this in mind, the best temporary active escape is said to be a **hobby** (**FIG. 17.3**), the pursuit of a leisure interest that provides pleasure (Kaplin, 1960). Most hobbies, such as needlepoint, photography, and many others, involve some degree of creativity as well as the ability to make order out of chaos on a very small and manageable scale. The latter factor tends to give a person a sense of control over life, which in turn augments self-esteem. And high self-esteem transfers from outside interests to areas of one's life where factors contribute to personal stress. Moreover, the ability to bring order to a small-scale operation, like haute cuisine cooking or bonsai gardening, also has a carry-over effect in dealing with larger problems. In fact, many people find that their time spent in the pursuit of hobbies transfers to solutions for major life problems.

However, not all experts agree that hobbies are stress relieving. Relaxation therapist Edmond Jacobson in his

FIGURE 17.3 Involvement in hobbies allows people to make order out of chaos on a small scale, which often transfers to larger-scale problems. Any activity that boosts self-esteem is thought to be worthwhile.

book *You Must Relax* warned of drawbacks of hobbies, indicating that they produce tension and frustration when expectations are not met. Jacobson believed that for relaxation to be most effective, the individual must be doing absolutely nothing. In his opinion, leisure activities—and hobbies in particular—actually compound the accumulation of stress. His point is valid when people focus on perfectionism rather than leisure. When pleasure is absent from leisure activities, it is definitely time to stop and do something else.

> **Hobby:** A pleasurable pursuit or interest outside one's daily work responsibilities through which one begins to make order out of chaos (e.g., botanical gardening).

One reason why hobbies are advocated as self-esteem builders is that they allow you to invest yourself in several areas. If you have a bad day at the office or school, hobbies can neutralize the negative feelings and bolster self-esteem. In essence, self-esteem remains intact when not all eggs are placed in one basket.

Forgiveness

Every stressor generated by anger that results in feelings of victimization is a prime candidate for **forgiveness**. Forgiveness is a cognitive process, and although it might seem to fall in the domain of cognitive restructuring, its significance as a process merits separate recognition. In their book *Forgiveness*, authors Sidney Simon and Suzanne Simon describe acts of pardon as an essential step in the resolution of major life stressors. When many people hear the word *forgiveness*, they associate the process with condonement, absolution, and self-sacrifice, which, in the opinion of some, perpetuates feelings of victimization. Consequently, because of the emotional pain involved, forgiveness is not initially looked upon as a viable option to reduce personal stress. Strange as it may seem, holding a grudge or feelings of resentment appears to be a form of control over the person or circumstance involved. But these feelings are an illusion of control. The toxicity of these thoughts sours one's outlook on life and eventually seeps into other aspects of one's personality, causing defensiveness and even more vulnerability to stressors, perpetuating the cycle of self-victimization.

Simon and Simon paint a different picture of forgiveness as a coping style. They describe it as an internal healing process where self-esteem is restored through devictimization, where toxic thoughts and emotions are diluted and released, and where one can begin to move on with one's life, not by just forgetting the past, but by coming to terms with stressful issues to find peace. As directors of several workshops for adults who were sexually abused, adult children of alcoholics, and people who were divorced, Simon and Simon teach that forgiveness is not an easy process. Based on their research, they propose six emotional steps to work through in

> **Forgiveness:** A coping technique for anger-related stressors for which a shift in attitude is adopted toward those against whom a grudge was previously held.

the process from victim to survivor. These steps are very similar to those outlined in the grieving process by Elisabeth Kübler-Ross: the denial stage, or refusal to admit you have been wronged or taken advantage of; the self-blame stage, or directing hurt inward and accepting other people's responsibility as your own; the victimization stage, or realization that you have indeed been violated; the indignation stage, or anger toward those you feel have violated your personal rights; the survivor stage, or reassessing your self-worth and beginning to feel whole again; and finally, the integration stage, or forgiving and getting on with your life. Simon and Simon agree that the major hurdle to jump to get to the last stage is the ability to demonstrate unconditional love toward yourself and others.

Some of the original research on the topic of forgiveness comes from the work of Fred Luskin (2003, 2009), the director of the Stanford University Forgiveness Project. Luskin's work, based on subjects from war-torn northern Ireland, has become the hallmark of forgiveness therapy and his HEAL method is now being used by survivors of other war-torn countries. Current trends in the science of forgiveness parallel similar research in mindfulness meditation where acts of forgiveness are central to achieving inner peace (Menahem and Love, 2013). An interesting study by Friedberg, Suchday, and Shelor (2007) supports the work of Luskin with regard to forgiveness and heart physiology.

Ho'oponopono: Forgiveness Hawaiian Style

The practice of forgiveness is a part of every culture on the planet, yet a style known as ho'oponopono, derived from Polynesian culture and practiced in Hawaii, has gained popularity in various regions of the United States. Because a strong family structure is essential for group cohesion, violations of this cohesion tear the fabric of society, affecting everyone. This principle can be applied to family members, the worksite, local communities, and the world at large. The underlying concept behind ho'oponopono is that when a violation has occurred toward another person, it affects everyone, and there needs to be resolution. Metaphorically speaking, a violation is a tear in the tapestry of the group (e.g., family, work environment, etc.). The resolution process (repairing the tapestry) begins with a group meeting, where the offender seeks forgiveness. A Hawaiian healer named Morrnah Simeona adapted this Hawaiian practice, from one of a societal ritual to a soul-searching practice of self-forgiveness, via a stronger connection to the Divine (whatever one perceives that to be). The premise being that by looking inward the offender can arrive at a deeper level of peace and resolution. The offender does this by repeating four sentences aloud: "I am sorry. Please forgive me. I love you. Thank You." With the understanding that we all have done or said something to disturb others, it becomes necessary to consciously "rewrite" our past history and make peace within ourselves and the universe. Other people serve as a mirror for us to correct our own faults and misgivings. This is what ho'oponopono does (Bodin, 2012).

Dream Therapy

Since ancient times, dreams have been espoused as a vehicle of divine communication. They have also been valued as a tool to unravel the complexities of life in the waking state. Although for centuries dreams have been regarded as an intriguing aspect of human nature, their importance to mental and emotional stability has been neglected for quite some time. It was not until the work of Freud that these nocturnal images produced by the unconscious mind were considered worthy of scientific investigation. Like Hippocrates in ancient Greece, Freud discovered that dreams were closely related to the physical symptoms many of his patients demonstrated. It was this insight that led Freud into the study of dreams and dream analysis.

Calling dreams "the royal road to the unconscious," Freud became convinced that they act to disguise sexual desires and thought. It was his exploration in the field of dreams that paved the way to a greater scientific understanding of the unconscious mind. But, whereas Freud viewed dreams as a means to *conceal* conscious thoughts, his protégé, Jung, regarded dreams as a means to *reveal* a whole new language to understand human consciousness and restore psychic balance. The work of these two men gave birth to the modern practice of **dream therapy**. Today, this work continues with dream researchers Gayle Delaney (1988), Patrick Garfield (1995), and Robert Van de Castle (1995).

The popularity of dream interpretation with the American public waxed and waned throughout the twentieth century in tandem with that expressed in clinical research. But from research in this area, it has become clear that dream analysis and the therapeutic effects of dreams are powerful means to increase awareness of personal issues as well as viable tools to help resolve them (**FIG. 17.4**). The following is a collection of

FIGURE 17.4 Dream therapy experts believe that the more we try to remember our dreams, the better we are able to deal with problems in our waking state.

observations about the dream process reported by several experts in the field:

- Everyone dreams, though not everyone remembers their dreams.

- For the average person, the dreams that stand out are those that are perceived as utterly bizarre, terrifying, or triggered by something in the course of a day.

- The majority of dreams consist of information received in the waking state during the previous day or two.

- Recurring dreams represent significant unresolved issues.

- Dreams were once thought to occur only during rapid-eye-movement (REM) periods, but are now thought to occur during several other times in the course of a night's sleep.

- Opinions vary on the issue of categorical dream symbols (e.g., water signifying the spirit of life), but virtually all experts agree that interpretation ultimately resides with the person who created the dream.

Dream therapy is a cognitive process that includes dream interpretation, dream incubation, and lucid dreaming.

> **Dream therapy:** A coping technique in which dreams, including recurring dreams, are explored and deciphered to help understand acute or chronic stressors.

The purpose of dream therapy, which can be done either with the assistance of a therapist who specializes in dream therapy or by yourself, is to access a greater share of consciousness through dream images and symbols to clarify and resolve personal issues (Taylor, 2005; Flanagan, 2000).

Dream interpretation involves three phases. After writing down the actual dream images, the first step is to find any possible associations between these images and those that take place during the waking state. The best method is to write down brief descriptions of a dream and then list as many associations with the symbolic images that come to mind. For example, viewing a plane crash from a farmer's field could be associated with one's career, a relationship, driving a car, or a new diet. The more associations that can be made, the greater the chance for a solid connection.

Dream therapist Robert Johnson, in his book *Inner Work*, states that the second phase is to draw parallels with these associations by asking yourself a series of questions. For example, What do I have in common with that image? Have I seen this image in my waking state? What behavior(s) do I have that is like that portrayed in this image? What emotional response does this dream image elicit, and what circumstances in everyday life elicit this same emotional response?

The third phase of the interpretation process is to select the interpretation that seems to be most relevant to your life at that moment. The best choice can also be made by asking questions such as the following: What is the central message of the dream? Did the dream have any advice or moral to it? When choosing a dream interpretation, consider each possibility a viable one because the ego-controlled conscious mind tends to protect itself from that which is unflattering or potentially harmful to itself. Dream expert Ann Faraday advises looking at the dream from someone else's perspective to allow a greater expansion of possibilities to choose from. Then, make a selection with your heart, not solely with your analytical mind.

Dream interpretation is still an art form, not a science, and the true interpretation rests solely with the dreamer.

> **Dream incubation:** A process in which an idea to be used as dream material is consciously seeded to prompt the unconscious mind during sleep; a technique effective to help resolve stressors.

However, Johnson's advice to get the best results is, first, to consider as an interpretation something you don't already know; second, to avoid interpretations that inflate the ego; and third, to disregard dream interpretations that pass blame from you to someone or something else. Also, be careful to consider only the obvious because dream symbols look different from various perspectives. Finally, Johnson says, dream interpretation is useless if it is not acted upon. Each dream, no matter how obvious its relevance, is a message—and messages that are ignored may prolong the stress associated with them. It is up to the dreamer to grasp the message and resolve the issue that inspired it.

Just as dreams reveal messages to the conscious mind, they can also be used as drills to tap the wealth of knowledge hidden beneath consciousness for advice when dealing with problems, a practice dating back to ancient Greece. This process, called **dream incubation**, has been explored by researcher Gayle Delaney. To incubate a dream, a person ponders a specific concern or issue by asking a question and perhaps even writing it down before going to sleep. Upon awaking, he or she writes down whatever images come to mind, and then follows the process of dream analysis to determine what information the unconscious mind has suggested. From her research, Delaney has found this technique to be very effective in the resolution of stressful issues. It can be combined with journal writing to augment the awareness process.

Lucid dreaming is the ability to enter the dream state while still conscious. As in the practice of Jung's active imagination or creative visualization, in lucid dreaming you consciously choose to add aspects of your dream while in the waking state. In essence, you direct the script of your dream. Lucid dreaming is often practiced to finish dream fragments or to provide an ending to a recurring dream.

When utilized effectively, dreams offer a wealth of knowledge that begs to be addressed during the hours of conscious thought. To ignore the advice, to waste this resource, to leave inaccessible the knowledge of the unconscious mind only perpetuates the perceptions, emotions, and behaviors associated with stress. The importance of dreams cannot be overstated; they have proved many times over to provide a means of mental stability. Or, as Jung stated in his book *Man and His Symbols*, "One cannot afford to be naive about dreams."

Prayer and Faith

Prayer, the greatest wireless network in the universe, is one of the oldest and most commonly used coping mechanisms known to humankind (**FIG. 17.5**). In its simplest form, prayer is thought: a desire of the heart, and often a call for help in what can best be described as a plea for divine intervention. Although prayer is not synonymous with meditation, these two processes share many similarities in that they both initiate a process of centering, increased concentration, and connectedness. They differ in that as a coping technique, prayer specifically elicits the element of divine intervention. It is a request, whereas meditation can encompass many modes of thinking and is not specifically limited to divine thought. Studies by Manfredi and Pickett (1987) and Koenig (1988) report that prayer is the most common coping style used by the elderly, especially when dealing with issues related to death. Schafer (1992) writes that prayer can lower anxiety, increase optimism, and instill hope in the individual. Yet when abused, prayer can promote dependency, escape, and even doubt.

Although there are many definitions of stress, one that comes to mind with regard to spiritual well-being is this: "Stress is a 'perceived' disconnection or separation from our divine source." The operative word is *perceived*, for in the words of sages and wisdom keepers the world over, we are never disconnected from our divine source. It is unresolved fear and anger that creates the illusion of separation. The premise of prayer as a coping technique rests on **faith**: the belief that each person is connected to a divine source (however this is named or perceived). Faith in a higher power, the ultimate source, can certainly be tested in times of stress.

Types of Prayer

When it comes to prayer, the styles are countless. Perhaps most common to many people is a recited prayer (much like a poem) that draws our attention from the self to the higher self. American Indians dance their prayers so as to reinforce their connection to the earth. South Africans have an expression: When you sing, you pray twice. There are prayers of gratitude and prayers of forgiveness. The type of prayer most commonly associated with stress is called **intercessory prayer** (Dossey, 1993). Basically, this is a call for help, in which one seeks divine guidance or, more likely, divine intervention. Intercessory prayer is most common in two situations. The first is when you need help yourself; the second is when you offer a prayer for the assistance of others. Those who study the nuances of prayer describe it as a form of energetic consciousness. In simple truth, all thoughts are prayers.

Of Prayer and Meditation

There is a joke by comedian Lily Tomlin that goes like this: How come when we talk to God, it's called praying, but when God talks to us, it's called schizophrenia? To some, prayer and meditation may be the same activity, but in the strictest sense, they are not. Meditation is a clearing of the mind to gain insight and wisdom. Praying, specifically intercessory prayer, is more of a soliloquy. As the expression goes, praying is when we talk to God, meditation is when God talks to us. Indeed, there are times when prayer and meditation may seem the same, and this is all right. However, to those who study the art and science of meditation, there are significant differences, and the two should never be considered to be the same.

© Inspiration Unlimited. Used with permission.

FIGURE 17.5 Prayer (from any denomination of faith) is viewed as a tremendous coping technique, particularly for fear and anxiety.

Faith: An optimistic attitude adopted to cope with stress for which one perceives a connection to something bigger than oneself (e.g., a divine source).

Intercessory prayer: One style of prayer for which the individual seeks assistance from a higher (divine) source to intervene or assist with his or her problems.

Stress with a Human Face

The first signs of stress began with Matt Pfenninger telling his father Jack, a physician, that he woke up with double vision. The last thing anyone suspected was a brain tumor. But in 1994 Matt, a high school sophomore, was diagnosed with exactly that. Actually, the diagnosis wasn't immediate. In fact, Matt spent a fair amount of time in and out of hospitals. If you were to ask him, he would tell you that he has seen more than his share of magnetic resonance imaging (MRI) machines. Matt's mother has a standing joke: "The only specialists we didn't consult were those in obstetrics." Eventually the diagnosis did reveal a brain tumor, a pineal germinoma—a rare form of brain cancer. It also revealed cancer cells isolated in the fluid of Matt's brain and spinal cord.

Matt began to receive the typical treatment: surgery followed by radiation. At first, things looked great. Ten months later, however, a follow-up MRI showed three golf-ball-sized metastases in the brain and one in the spine. This time Matt was given a round of chemotherapy. Although often effective, chemotherapy is not infallible. It can not only kill cancer cells, but also destroy healthy cells. And it doesn't always work. In Matt's case, the overall situation simply worsened.

Both Jack and his wife Kay have a strong faith in God, and they believe in the power of prayer. One day the couple had an idea. They invited members of their local community in Midland, Michigan, to come to a healing prayer service for Matt at the hospital. Jack was delighted to see about 60 of his fellow physicians attend and participate. What happened next can only be described as a miracle.

"Ten days later there were no tumors," Jack said. "I went to the neuroradiologist and asked him if he could recheck the films to be sure that they were, indeed, Matt's. The shunt tube was there. The dye had been injected. They were Matthew's films. The tumors were gone! I asked him how this could happen, since even an abscess would

not be totally resolved in just 10 days. He said he could not explain it." In sharing the good news, Jack sent a letter to all the physicians and the medical staff thanking them for their help. This is how he explained the healing power of prayer to his colleagues: "For those who do believe in prayer, no explanation is necessary. For those who don't believe in prayer, no explanation will do."

In Matt's words: "I think I'm the luckiest guy in the world. I can walk. I can talk. I can see. I have good friends. I'm playing my four musical instruments. I'm taking electrical engineering courses and I'm doing well. I have my family to take care of me and a lot of people said, if my dad wasn't a doctor, I would have died."

In Jack's words: "I don't wear my religion on my shirt sleeve, and I still do not pray with my patients. However, I am being forced, not only from my own experiences, but from the science of prayer, to encourage more patients to pray. I am a fan of Larry Dossey's work on prayer. Did I tell you that in 2004, Matt graduated with a master's in electrical engineering from the University of Michigan just before Christmas and took a job with General Electric in Cincinnati? Not bad for a kid with ten major operations who was told five times he wouldn't make it through the night, spent 1.5 years out of 3 in the hospital, and had a tracheostomy for 3 years and a feeding tube in his stomach for 1.5 years! Truly, a miracle.

My advice to your students: Attitudes, beliefs, friends, and strangers (all unknowingly) play a role in survival and recovery. Be positive. Do not dwell on the negative. Ask for and focus on recovery. It will be given to you. Life can change in a mere instant. Don't look forward and don't look back. Enjoy what you have and be thankful for everything. See the sunrise. Smell a rose. Experience a hug, and ask God for help when you need it."

Research on Prayer and Faith

With regard to scientific inquiry, there is no lack of studies on the healing power of prayer, particularly in the past two decades. The most famous study on prayer was conducted by Randolph Byrd involving prayers for cardiac patients. Shying away from the word *pray*, researchers have coined the more scientific term "intercessory distant healing." To date, Byrd's study has been replicated several

times (Sicher and Targ, 1998; Harris et al., 1999), showing statistical significance beyond pure chance.

An investigation into the efficacy of prayer by Herbert Benson and colleagues (2006) at Harvard Medical Center found that intercessory prayer had no effect on cardiac bypass patients. Conversely, David Hodge from Arizona State University compiled empirical data from more than 17 recent studies on intercessory prayer. Based on

FIGURE 17.6

By permission of John L. Hart FLP and Creators Syndicate, Inc.

12 criteria, he concluded that as an experimental intervention, prayer indeed had a small but significant effect. Prayer as a mode of compassionate intentionality is now being studied by several researchers including Marilyn Schlitz of the Institute of Noetic Sciences and Lynn McTaggart, author of the book *The Intention Experiment* (2007). You can visit McTaggart's Web site and participate in this worldwide study by going to www.theintention-experiment.com.

Some scientists remark that if divine intervention is scientifically valid some of the time, why not all of the time? Perhaps the answer is found in the standard joke: When you pray to God and your prayer isn't answered, it isn't that God didn't hear you. It's just that the answer was "No!"

Are people who pray more healthy? As usual with research studies, there is proof that lines up on both sides of the argument. A 2008 study conducted by Gonnerman and colleagues at the University of Northern Iowa found that people who attended church services were more likely to be healthy (e.g., not suffering from loneliness, depression, or insomnia) than those who did not. A study by Pressman and colleagues found similar results nearly two decades earlier in 1990. Keeping in mind that science and religion have been at odds for several hundred years, these findings came under much scrutiny. In his book *The Faith Factor*, Matthews cites habitual attendance at church or synagogue as a factor that promotes health. Although these findings suggest that a strong relationship with the divine is certainly healthy, skeptics argue that religious behavior (attendance) itself and not belief per se, as well as the support of friends in church and marital status, are the true health factors. Religious practices are easy to measure, but spirituality is not. There are those who are spiritual but not religious, and there are those who are religious but not spiritual.

Prayers for Non-Believers

Are people who are less than sure about a higher power, or who perhaps don't believe in a divine source, divinely disadvantaged in times of stress? Perhaps not (**FIG. 17.6**). There is no research that suggests that **agnostics** (those who don't know) and **atheists** (those who don't believe in a higher source) fall dead at an earlier age or are prone to lifelong chronic illnesses. More than likely the conversation in their heads resembles a style of nonscripted prayer that might be heard in the heads and hearts of believers in a higher power. Just as no religion has a monopoly on *the* style of prayer that gets the best results, people of strong faith are not necessarily at an advantage. Remember that coping with stress involves changing perceptions that are threatening. Prayer (in whatever form, whether it be a Hail Mary or a positive affirmation) is a way in which to allay the fear involved. Similarly, faith for believers is trust in the unknown, whereas faith for non-believers may be viewed as an internal locus of control. Like prayer, faith is subjective, meaning that it comes from a personal experience, not something learned in a book. Intention is paramount.

Agnostics: Individuals who do not know if there is a higher source.

Atheists: Individuals who do not believe in a higher source.

Ways to Pray

Is there a right way to pray? Perhaps! You may ponder this very question should you feel at times that your prayers have not been answered. Author Sophie Burnham (*The Path of Prayer*) states that the style of communication is very important in the process of prayer. Burnham hypothesizes that people are rarely taught to pray correctly, and she offers the following guidelines to practice this coping skill most effectively so that these thoughts may be received as intended.

1. *Clear transmission* of prayer thoughts is crucial to delivery of the message. A mind cluttered with several thoughts is analogous to a radio tuned to static. Clearing your mind of all thoughts save that which necessitates attention is imperative to the prayer process. There is no sacred place to pray. It may help to find a quiet spot, but temples, churches, and mosques are no better a conduit for this form of communication than your bedroom, shower, or car.

2. Prayers, Burnham explains, must be expressed in the *present tense*. With divine energy, as expressed by Jung as the collective unconscious, by Einstein as the cosmos, or by whatever term you wish to use, time does not exist. It is a human-made concept, a fabrication of the human mind. Therefore, past tense and future tense are not understood. Prayers as thought forms must be expressed in the present moment.

3. Burnham writes that prayers must be phrased in a *positive context* and not a negative one. The universe, she states, does not understand the words *not*, *can't*, and *don't*. When a prayer such as "Don't let me do badly on this exam" is expressed in negative terms, it is interpreted as "let me do badly on this exam."

Similarly, the unconscious mind does not recognize negative words. Stress therapist Joan Borysenko tells a story of an Australian friend who lost a leg to bone cancer and who was subsequently given a few months to live. Twenty years later this gentleman is enjoying life to the fullest. She explained that his coping mechanism focused on positive rather than on negative thoughts; instead of thinking, "I can't die," he thought, "I must live." Like Burnham, Borysenko insists that the unconscious mind does not recognize negative verbs.

Burnham adds to this list that special attention be made to notice the response. She says that in many cases people ignore or deny the response because the prayer or the timing of it was not answered to one's liking.

One's style of prayer may be a function of one's personality type. Research by the Spindrift Organization in Salem, Oregon, suggests that introverts and extroverts tend to organize their prayer thoughts in different ways (Sweet, 2007). The prayer style of extroverts tends to be more goal oriented, whereas introverts are noted as being more general (e.g., Thy will be done, or go with the flow), with both styles showing effectiveness.

There are those who hesitate to include prayer as a viable coping strategy because they believe that it nurtures false (negative) hope and perhaps even encourages an external locus of control, both of which are thought to negate the premise of positive coping techniques. However, it is held by those who do believe in prayer as a viable coping strategy that it can draw upon those inner resources that contribute to dealing with stress successfully. In the words of Jackson H. Brown, "Do not pray for things, but rather pray for wisdom and courage." When prayer is used as a means to strengthen faith and provide hope, it can be an effective coping mechanism; in the words of John F. Kennedy, "*God's work must truly be our own.*"

SUMMARY

- No one strategy works for all people in all situations to cope effectively with the causes of stress. In many cases, several coping techniques should be used together.

- For a coping technique to be effective, it must do one or all of the following: increase awareness of the cause of stress, help process information about the stressor, and adjust attitude and possibly behavior to work toward a peaceful resolution.

- Information seeking is a coping technique that helps to increase awareness of facts regarding the problem at hand.

- Social orchestration is called the path of least resistance. The purpose of this technique is to favorably alter specific factors in your environment to minimize stress, or change environments completely if current conditions are deleterious to your health.

- When people bond together in friendship in times of trouble, they are better able to cope with the problems at hand. There is mental, emotional, physical, and spiritual strength in numbers. Social-support groups provide coping that individuals cannot generate themselves.

- Avoidance is considered a negative coping technique; however, to step outside your problems for a short while to gain a better perspective on them is thought to be quite healthy. Hobbies can be used as positive diversion tactics that allow for a healthy release from daily stressors. When approached in this way, hobbies can contribute to self-esteem, which then transfers to other areas of one's life.

- Stress can induce a sense of personal violation. Harboring feelings of resentment and anger is a means of maintaining control over someone we feel has unjustly attacked us. But when feelings of anger are not released correctly, they become toxic. Forgiveness allows these feelings to be released so that a peaceful resolution is the final outcome.

- Dream therapy—the practice of dream seeding and dream interpretation to find answers to problems and decode the meaning of dream symbols and images, respectively—is a cognitive technique that has been employed since ancient times. The use of dreams to resolve problems with the help of the unconscious mind continues to be used and explored in the field of psychology as a means to deal with stress.

- Prayer, the original chat room, is one of the oldest coping techniques known to humankind.

- Although there are many different ways to pray, intercessory prayer is the most common type in times of crisis.

- Prayer and meditation are not the same thing.

- Several research studies on the topic of prayer reveal a statistical significance with intention, particularly relative to aspects of health and healing.

- Although there is no one way to pray, suggestions for intercessory prayer are similar if not identical to mental imagery.

- The relationship between stress and spirituality is gaining more and more attention in the allied health fields. Prayer is defined as a thought form directed toward divine consciousness. In more subtle terms, prayer is a request to nurture our self-reliance.

STUDY GUIDE QUESTIONS

1. How does information seeking both reduce and promote stress?

2. Why are support groups thought to enhance coping skills?

3. How do hobbies help one to reduce stress?

4. Why is forgiveness considered an effective coping skill?

5. How can dream therapy help one reduce stress?

6. Why is prayer considered an effective coping technique?

REFERENCES AND RESOURCES

AA Services. *The Big Book: The Story of How Many Thousands of Men and Women Have Recovered from Alcoholism*, 4th ed. Alcoholics Anonymous World Services, New York, 2002.

Ai, A. L., et al. The Role of Private Prayer in Psychological Recovery among Midlife and Aged Patients Following Cardiac Surgery, *The Gerontologist* 38(5):591–601, 1998.

Allen, R. J. *Human Stress: Its Nature and Control*. Burgess, Minneapolis, MN, 1983.

Allen, R. J., and Hyde, D. H. *Investigations in Stress Control*. Burgess, Minneapolis, MN, 1983.

Anderson, N. *Work and Leisure*. Free Press, New York, 1961.

Andrews, G., and Tennant, C. Life-Event Stress, Social-Support Coping Style, and the Risk of Psychological Impairment, *Journal of Nervous and Mental Disorders* 166(7):605–612, 1982.

Ashby, J. S., and Lenhard, R. S. Prayer as a Coping Strategy for Chronic Pain Patients, *Rehabilitation Psychology* 39(3):205–209, 1994.

Austin, J. The Efficacy of "Distant Healing": A Systematic Review of Randomized Trials, *Annals of Internal Medicine* 131(11):903–910, 2000.

Begley, S. The Stuff That Dreams Are Made Of, *Newsweek*, August 14, 1989:41–44.

Benson, H. Spirituality and Healing in Medicine Conference. Denver, CO, March 19–21, 2000.

Benson, H., et. al. Study of the Therapeutic Effects of Intercessory Prayer (STEP) in Cardiac Bypass Patients: A Multicenter Randomized Trial of Uncertainty and Certainty of Receiving Intercessory Prayer, *American Heart Journal* 151(4):934–942, 2006.

Berkman, L. F. Social Networks, Support, and Health: Taking the Next Step Forward, *American Journal of Epidemiology* 123:559–562, 1986.

Berkman, L. F., and Syme, S. L. Social Networks, Host Resistance, and Mortality: A Nine-Year Follow-up Study of Alameda County Residents, *American Journal of Epidemiology* 109:186–204, 1979.

Bien, J. Color Dream Therapy, Sleep on It . . . And in the Morning You'll Have the Answer, *Awareness Magazine*, January/February 2000. www.awarenessmag.com/janfeb0.html/jf0_color_dream_therapy.htm.

Bodin, L. *The Book of Ho'oponopono: The Hawaiian Practice of Forgiveness and Healing*. Destiny Books, New York, 2016.

Borysenko, J. Personal communication, Oct. 25, 1991.

Bower, B. Dreams May Be Gone But Not Forgotten, *Science News*, September 15, 1984:173.

Brannon, L., and Feist, J. *Health Psychology: An Introduction to Behavior and Health*, 6th ed. Wadsworth, Belmont, CA, 2006.

Brown, J. H. *Life's Little Instruction Booklet*. Rutledge Hill Press, Nashville, TN, 1991.

Burnham, S. *A Book of Angels*. Ballantine Books, New York, 1990.

Burnham, S. *The Path of Prayer*. Compass Books, New York, 2002.

Butler, M. H., et al. Not Just Time-Out: Change Dynamics of Prayer for Religious Couples in Conflict Situations, *Family Process* 37(4):451–474, 1998.

Byrd-Craven, J., and Massey, A. R. Lean on Me: Effects of Social Support on Low Socioeconomic-Status Pregnant Women. *Nursing Health Science* 15(3):374–378, 2013.

Can Prayer Lower High Blood Pressure? *Jet* 94(14):14–17, 1998.

Capel, I., and Gurnsey, J. *Managing Stress*. Constable, London, 1987.

Cartwright, R. D. Happy Endings for Our Dreams, *Psychology Today*, December, 1978:66–76.

Casarjian, R. *Forgiveness: A Bold Choice for a Peaceful Heart*. Bantam Books, New York, 1992.

Cassel, J. The Contribution of the Social Environment to Host Resistance, *American Journal of Epidemiology* 104:107–123, 1976.

Cassidy, T. *Stress, Cognition, and Health*. Routledge, New York, 1999.

Childre, D. *Forgiveness: A Real Stress Buster*. HeartMath, Boulder Creek, CA, 2001.

Chollar, S. Dreamchasers, *Psychology Today*, April, 1989: 60–61.

Clift, J., and Cliff, W. *Symbols of Transformation in Dreams*. Crossroad, New York, 1986.

Cohen, H. The Number of Real Friends Declining. Baseline for Health Foundation, December 10, 2011. www.jonbarron.org/article/number-real-friends-declining.

Connell, C. M., and D'Augelli, A. R. The Contribution of Personality Characteristics to the Relationship between Social Support and Perceived Physical Health, *Health Psychology* 9:192–207, 1990.

Craig, K. T. *The Fabric of Dreams*. Dutton, New York, 1918.

Davis, J. Can Prayer Heal? Scientists Have Some Surprising Evidence That Prayers Help in Some Amazing Ways, *Saturday Evening Post* 273(6):14–17, 2001.

Dayton, T. *The Magic of Forgiveness*. Health Communications, Deerfield Beach, FL, 2003.

Delaney, G. *All about Dreams: Everything You Need to Know about Why We Have Them, What They Mean, and How to Put Them to Work for You*. HarperCollins, New York, 1998.

Delaney, G. *Living Your Dreams*. HarperCollins, New York, 1988.

Diemer, R. A., et al. Comparison of Dream Interpretation, Event Interpretation and Unstructured Sessions in Brief Therapy, *Journal of Counseling Psychology* 43:99–112, 1996.

Dossey, L. *Be Careful What You Pray For: You Might Just Get It*. Harper SanFrancisco, San Francisco, 1997.

Dossey, L. *Healing Words*. Harper Collins, New York, 1993.

Dossey, L. *Prayer Is Good Medicine*. HarperCollins, San Francisco, 1996.

Dossey, L. *Reinventing Medicine*. Harper SanFrancisco, San Francisco, 1999.

Dowrick, S. *Forgiveness and Other Acts of Love*. Viking Books, New York, 1997.

Duke Study, *Journal of Gerontology and Biology Medical Science* 54(M370–376), 1999.

Evans, C. *Landscapes of the Night*. Viking, New York, 1984.

Faraday, A. *Dream Power*. Berkley, New York, 1972.

Flanagan, O. *Dreaming Souls, Sleep, Dreams, and the Evolution of the Conscious Mind*. Oxford University Press, New York, 2000.

Foster, A. A Non-linear Model of Information Seeking Behaviour, *Information Research* 10(2), paper 222, 2005. http://informationr.net/ir/10-2/paper222.html.

Freud, S. *The Interpretation of Dreams*. Modern Library, New York, 1950.

Friedberg, J., Suchday, S., and Shelov, D. V. The Impact of Forgiveness on Cardiovascular Reactivity and Recovery, *International Journal of Pscyhophysiology* 65(2):87–94, 2007.

Gachenbach, J., and Bosveld, J. Take Control of Your Dreams, *Psychology Today* October, 1989:27–32.

Garfield, P. L. *Creative Dreaming: Plan and Control Your Dreams to Overcome Fears, Solve Problems and Create a Better Self*. Fireside, New York, 1995.

Gonnerman, M. E., Lutz, G. M., Yehieli, M., and Meisinger, B. K. Religion and Health Connection: A Study of African-American, Protestant Christians, *Journal of Health Care for the Poor and Underserved* 19(1):193–199, 2008.

Gundersen, L. Faith and Healing, *Annals of Internal Medicine*, January 2000.

Hadfield, J. A. *Dreams and Nightmares*. Pelican Books, New York, 1973.

Hall, J. A. *Clinical Use of Dreams*. Grune and Stratton, New York, 1977.

Harris, W. S., et al. A Randomized Controlled Trial of the Effects of Remote, Intercessory Prayer on Outcomes in Patients Admitted to the Coronary Care Unit, *Archives of Internal Medicine* 159:2273–2278, 1999.

Hawley, G., and Irurita, V. Seeking Comfort through Prayer, *International Journal of Nursing Practices* 4:9–18, 1998.

Hill, C., et al. Structured Brief Therapy with a Focus on Dreams or Loss for Clients with Troubling Dreams and Recent Loss, *Journal of Counseling Psychology* 47(1): 90–101, 2000.

Hodge, D. R. A Systematic Review of the Empirical Literature on Intercessory Prayer, *Research on Social Work Practice* 17(2):174–187, 2007.

House, J. S., Robbins, C., and Metzner, H. L. The Association of Social Relationships and Activities with Mortality: Prospective Evidence from the Tecumseh Community Health Study, *American Journal of Epidemiology* 116:123–140, 1982.

Jacobson, E. *You Must Relax*. McGraw-Hill, New York, 1987.

Johnson, R. A. *Inner Work: Using Dreams and Active Imagination for Personal Growth*. Harper & Row, San Francisco, 1986.

Jung, C. G. *Man and His Symbols*. Anchor Press, New York, 1964.

Jung, C. G. *Memories, Dreams, Reflections*. Vintage Press, New York, 1964.

Jung, C. G. *The Wisdom of a Dream*, vols. 1–3 (videos). RM Associates, 1989.

Kaplan, G. A., et al. Social Connections and Mortality from All Causes and from Cardiovascular Disease: Prospective Evidence from Eastern Finland, *American Journal of Epidemiology* 128:370–380, 1988.

Kaplin, M. *Leisure in America: A Social Inquiry*. Wiley, New York, 1960.

Katra, J., and Targ, R. *The Heart of the Mind*. New World Library, Novatno, CA, 1999.

Kelsey, M. *Dreams: A Way to Listen to God*. Paulist Press, New York, 1978.

King, D. Beyond Traditional Means: Ho'oponopono: An Interview with Morrnah Simeona and Dr. Stan Hew Len. IZI LLC. http://www.self-i-dentity-through-hooponopono.com/article1.htm.

Koenig, H. Religious Behaviors and Death Anxiety in Later Life, *Hospice Journal* 4:3–24, 1988.

Krippner, S., et al. *Extraordinary Dreams and How to Work with Them*. State University of New York Press, Albany, NY, 2002.

Laberge, S. *Lucid Dreaming*. Tarcher, Los Angeles, 1979.

Langs, R. *Decoding Your Dreams*. Ballantine Books, New York, 1988.

Levine, A. *Love Canal: Science, Politics, and People*. Lexington Books, Lexington, MA, 1982.

Lindbergh, A. M. *Gift from the Sea*. Pantheon Books, New York, 1975.

Lowenthal, M. F., and Harven, C. Interaction and Adaptation: Intimacy as a Critical Variable. In B. Neugarten (ed.), *Middle Age and Aging*. University of Chicago Press, 1968.

Luskin, F. *Forgive for Good*. Harper San Francisco, 2003.

Luskin, F. *Forgive for Love*. HarperOne San Francisco, 2009.

Mahoney, M. *The Meaning of Dreams and Dreaming*. Citadel Press, New York, 1970.

Manfredi, C., and Pickett, M. Perceived Stressful Situations and Coping Strategies Utilized by the Elderly, *Journal of Community Health Nurses* 4(2):99–110, 1987.

Maslow, A. Dynamics of Personality Organization, *Psychological Review* 50:514–518, 1943.

Matthews, D. A. *The Faith Factor*. Penguin Books, New York, 1998.

McTaggart, L. *The Intention Experiment*. Free Press, New York, 2007.

Menahem, S., and Love, M. Forgiveness in Psychotherapy: The Key to Healing. *Journal of Clinical Psychology* 69(8):829–835, 2013.

Milstein, J. Invoking Spirituality in Medical Care, *Alternative Therapies* 6(6):120–122, 2000.

Oman, M. *Prayers for Healing*. Conari Press, Berkeley, CA, 1997.

Ornish, D. *Love and Survival*. HarperCollins, New York, 1998.

Pearsall, P. *Wishing Well*. Hyperion, New York, 2000.

Pelletier, K. *Alternative Medicine: What Works and What Doesn't*. Simon & Schuster, New York, 2000.

Pelletier, K., and Herzing, D. Psychoneuroimmunology: Toward a Mind-Body Model, *Advances* 5(1):27–56, 1988.

Pilisuk, M., and Parks, S. H. *The Healing Web: Social Networks and Human Survival*. University Press of New England, Hanover, NH, 1986.

Pressman, P., et al. Religious Belief, Depression and Ambulation Status in Elderly Women with Broken Hips, *American Journal of Psychiatry* 147:758–760, 1990.

Raphael, B. Preventive Intervention with the Recently Bereaved, *Archives of General Psychiatry* 34:1450–1457, 1977.

Rathbone, J. *Teach Yourself to Relax*. Prentice-Hall, Englewood Cliffs, NJ, 1957.

Roth, R. *The Healing Path of Prayer*. Harmony Books, New York, 1997.

Rycroft, C. *The Innocence of Dreams*. Pantheon Books, New York, 1913.

Savary, L. M., Berne, P. H., and Williams, S. K. *Dreams and Spiritual Growth: A Christian Approach to Dreamwork*. Paulist Press, New York, 1984.

Schafer, W. *Stress Management for Wellness*. Harcourt Brace Jovanovich, Fort Worth, TX, 1992.

Schlitz, M., and Braud, W. Distant Intentionality and Healing: Accessing the Evidence, *Alternative Therapies in Health and Medicine* 3(6):62–73, 1997.

Sicher, F., and Targ, E. A Randomized Double-Blind Study of the Effect of Distant Healing in a Population with Advanced AIDS: Report of a Small-Scale Study, *Western Journal of Medicine* 169(6):356–363, 1998.

Siegel, A. Dreams: The Mystery That Heals. In E. Bauman (ed.), *The Holistic Health Handbook*. Stephen Press, Greene, Berkeley, CA, 1984.

Simon, S. B., and Simon, S. *Forgiveness: How to Make Peace with Your Past and Get on with Your Life*. Warner Books, New York, 1990.

Spiegel, D., et al. Effect of Psychosocial Treatment of Patients with Metastatic Breast Cancer, *Lancet* ii:888–891, 1989.

Stauth, C. Adventures in Dreamland, *New Age Journal*, 79–83, 145–149, 1995.

Stewart, W. A., and Freeman, L. *The Secret of Dreams*. Macmillan, New York, 1972.

Sweet, B. *A Journey Into Prayer: Pioneers of Prayer in the Laboratory*. Xlibris Corporation, New York, 2007.

Targ, E. Evaluating Distant Healing: A Research Review, *Alternative Therapies in Health and Medicine* 3(6):74–78, 1997.

Targ, R., and Katra, J. *Miracles of Mind*. New World Library, Novatno, CA, 1998.

Taylor, J. *The Wisdom of Your Dreams*. Teacher Books, New York, 2009.

Taylor, S. *Health Psychology*, 8th ed. McGraw-Hill, New York, 2011.

Tipping, C. *Radical Forgiveness*. Global 12 Publications, Inc., Marietta, GA, 2002.

Ullman, M., and Limmer, C. *The Variety of Dream Experience*. Continuum, New York, 1987.

Van de Castle, R. *Our Dreaming Mind*. Ballantine Books, New York, 1995.

Weiss, L. *Dream Analysis in Psychotherapy*. Pergamon Press, New York, 1986.

Weiss, M. What Your Dreams Really Mean: What Dreams Can Do for You, *Reader's Digest*, February 2006. www.rd.com/health/mind-and-body/sleep/dare-to-dream----what-your-dreams-really-mean/article24427-2.html.

PART FOUR

Relaxation Techniques

*That the birds fly overhead, this you
cannot stop. That they build a nest
in your hair, this you can prevent.*

—Ancient Chinese Proverb

We process information from the five senses: vision, hearing, smell, taste, and touch. Stimuli picked up through one or more of these senses are then delivered to the cerebral cortex and deciphered, and then processed by the subcortex of the brain. Each piece of information tracked by the senses is labeled with a perception, which is interpreted as either a threat or a nonthreat. If a stimulus is perceived to be a threat, then an alarm is sounded and the body is activated as a means of survival.

To relax the body from a heightened state of physical arousal to homeostasis, action must be taken to alter both the quality and the quantity of stimuli taken in by the five senses. In other words, the five senses must be deactivated or reprogrammed, temporarily, to allow the body to calm down. The purpose of relaxation techniques is to do just that: to deactivate the body's sensory system, decrease stimuli and their associated perceptions, and replace these with nonthreatening sensations that promote the relaxation response. In effect, the primary purpose of relaxation techniques is to *intercept* the stress response, specifically at the neurological and hormonal levels, and return the body to physiological homeostasis.

Of the five senses, two are paramount in the acquisition of sensory information for processing: vision and hearing. By no coincidence, these same two senses are targeted for deactivation during relaxation, through various relaxation techniques such as mental imagery and music therapy, to name two. In addition, because muscle tension is considered the most common symptom of stress, touch is targeted through techniques such as progressive muscular relaxation, massage, and physical exercise.

When the field of stress management unfolded in the early 1970s, the emphasis of attention and instruction was placed solely on relaxation techniques because of the apparently strong association between stress-related symptoms and ensuing diseases. As mentioned in Chapter 1, this is still the common medical approach to the treatment of disease and illness: to first treat the symptoms of the problems. Originally, relaxation techniques were used in both prevention of and intervention for stress-related health problems. What was discovered through this approach, however, was that relaxation techniques alone offered only temporary solutions to long-term problems or chronic stressors. Moreover, if the relaxation techniques were practiced irregularly or discontinued, then stress-related symptoms returned. Thus, by themselves, relaxation techniques are only half the solution. To effectively deal with stress in a preventive or interventive manner, techniques for relaxation must be integrated with positive coping techniques.

Unfortunately, relaxation techniques are not magic. What may provide a calming effect for one person may offer nothing but added frustration for others. The ability to relax (even heal) is largely dependent on the individual. So experts in the field of stress management suggest that you become acquainted with several different techniques and add these to your arsenal of stress defense. As you might expect, some techniques and their intended reactions are less suited to certain situations than others are. For example, you cannot easily plug yourself into a biofeedback machine during a traffic pile-up on the highway, but you can try some mental imagery and diaphragmatic breathing. Ultimately, the choice is up to you and your experience as to how you should employ relaxation techniques. In addition, relaxation techniques, such as playing the piano or shooting hoops, are skills; skills require regular practice to achieve proficiency. Experts agree that regardless of which technique is chosen (and many may be used in combination), you must practice some form of relaxation every day, usually for 20 minutes. Done effectively, these skills will serve your goal to achieve inner peace.

Because the mind-body connection is so strong, relaxation techniques promote not only physical calming, but also rebound to calm mental processes, creating mental homeostasis. This allows for greater self-awareness. For this reason, several relaxation techniques provide fertile ground for the seeds of several coping strategies. When Jim Fixx wrote the best-seller *The Complete Book of Running*, he thought he would address the physiological relationship between cardiovascular fitness and coronary heart disease. However, with virtually every runner interviewed by Fixx, the first topic mentioned was not the physiological effects of running, but the mental and emotional effects—the runner's high. Renowned runner and 1968 Boston Marathon winner Amby Burfoot, editor of *Running World* magazine and author, is no stranger to the mental well-being aspects of running either (Burfoot, 2004). At first, researchers dismissed runner's high as an extraneous effect. Now, a more serious approach has been adopted to understand the mysteries of this profound connection between mind and body. As you will see in Chapter 29, there is a strong crossover between the two, and we have only scratched the surface of the wealth of knowledge to be learned about this unique relationship.

The origins of relaxation techniques span many continents and cultures over many centuries. In Part 4,

East meets West as techniques from the Orient dating back thousands of years are paired with contemporary techniques from the New World. Over the past 20 years, some components of the older techniques have begun to merge with the newer techniques, lending them depth and strength. Some methods are best suited as intervention techniques, to be done right on the spot in the face of stress. Others are more appropriate when postponed to later in the day. Yet all the techniques are preventive in nature. So, read through these techniques and try them. See what you think. Chances are, there are some you will take an immediate liking to, while others won't do much for you. Once you have tried them all, select one or two that seem very effective and begin to incorporate these into your daily routine. With regular practice, you will be amazed at how your body responds, not only in terms of immediate effects but over time as well. Should there come a time that your favorite relaxation technique seems to lose its ability to bring calmness, then select an alternative technique. There are many to choose from.

Like Part 3, most chapters in this section include a historical introduction to each relaxation technique, as well as a full description of the technique, specific physiological (and psychological) effects induced by the technique, and best steps to take to incorporate the technique into your personal strategy for stress management. Because of the association between stress and chronic pain, a section on this topic is also included in appropriate chapters.

REFERENCES AND RESOURCES

Burfoot, A. *Runner's World Complete Book of Running: Everything You Need to Run for Fun, Fitness, and Competition*. Rodale Books, New York, 2004.

Fixx, J. *The Complete Book of Running*. Random House, New York, 1977.

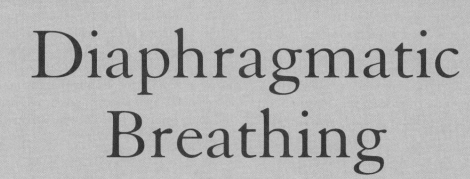

CHAPTER 18

Diaphragmatic Breathing

Let the air breathe for you.

—Emmett Miller, M.D.

Diaphragmatic breathing is unequivocally the easiest method of relaxation to practice. It is easy because breathing is an action that we do normally without thought or hesitation. In its simplest form, **diaphragmatic breathing** is controlled deep breathing. It is symbolic of a deep sigh, or a big breath taken when one is about to regroup one's thoughts, gain composure, or direct one's energies for a challenging task. What makes normal breathing different from diaphragmatic breathing is its emphasis on expansion of the chest.

Diaphragmatic breathing involves the movement of the lower abdomen. In the practice of yoga, this technique is called **pranayama**, or the restoration of one's energy or life force, the breath behind the breath.

Most Americans breathe emphasizing upper chest and thoracic cavity movement while deemphasizing abdominal movement. This is thought to be a learned behavior influenced by cultural preferences for a large chest and small waist. As children mature, they shift from abdominal to thoracic breathing. When fast asleep, however, without the influence of the conscious mind, all individuals revert back to breathing by distending the stomach as the diaphragm is allowed to expand and contract without inhibition.

Over the past two decades, the use of diaphragmatic breathing has become well accepted in childbirth (Nakahata, 1993). A major tenet of the Lamaze childbirth method is controlled **belly breathing**. In Lamaze classes, expectant mothers (and fathers) are taught to place the emphasis of their breathing on the lower stomach. Then, during the several hours of labor and delivery, this breathing skill is employed to ease pain. And what is taught and practiced for the stressful event of childbirth is now taught and practiced for several other stressful situations as well.

> **Diaphragmatic breathing:** The most basic relaxation technique; breathing from the lower stomach or diaphragm rather than the thoracic area.
>
> **Pranayama:** A Sanskrit term to describe diaphragmatic breathing that restores one's vital life force of energy.
>
> **Belly breathing:** The most common form of relaxation by means of placing the emphasis of one's breathing on the lower stomach area (belly or diaphragm) rather than the upper chest (thoracic area), thereby decreasing sympathetic response and inducing a greater sense of relaxation.

The Mystery of Breathing

Under normal resting conditions, the average person breathes approximately fourteen to sixteen times per minute. In a state of arousal, breathing is fast-paced and shallow, with pronounced muscular contractions of the chest cavity (**BOX 18.1**). During heavy exercise, ventilations per minute can increase to as many as 60 as the body tries to meet the increased demand for oxygen (Sherwood, 2006). In a relaxed state, the body's metabolism is significantly decreased, allowing for a slower and deeper breathing cycle. Physiologically speaking, when pressure resulting from the expansion of the chest wall and muscular contraction is taken off the thoracic cavity, sympathetic drive decreases. Parasympathetic drive overrides the sympathetic system, and homeostasis results. Itzhak Bentov (1988) offers a second explanation for the pacifying effect of diaphragmatic breathing, which he relates to vibrations emitted from the heart. The force of contractions of the left ventricle and the blood that it ejects sends a vibration through the aorta, which then reverberates throughout the body. A pause in the breathing cycle causes the reverberation to cease. Breathing from the diaphragm, which accents long pauses, decreases this resonance, creating a calming effect. Some Himalayan yogis, in a state of complete relaxation, are reported to take in as few as one or two breaths per minute (Green, 2003). As you can imagine, this requires much concentration and practice. Typically, when people learn to modify their breathing from thoracic to diaphragmatic breathing, they can comfortably reduce the number of breaths to between four and six per minute.

Diaphragmatic breathing is as old as the ancient exercises of yoga and T'ai chi ch'uan, and it is a fundamental component of these practices. The therapeutic power of breathing is often associated with higher consciousness or spirituality. In fact, the word *spirit* in many cultures is described as "the first breath." Currently, diaphragmatic breathing is itself a form of relaxation, but because of its simplicity and compatibility, it is often incorporated into other techniques, including progressive muscular relaxation, autogenic training, and mental imagery, for a combined relaxation effect (**BOX 18.2**). Many people consider diaphragmatic breathing to be the first recognized mantra; a singular repetitive thought or motion to cleanse the mind. Among those who practice yoga and T'ai chi ch'uan, diaphragmatic breathing is thought to be more effective when inhalation and exhalation occur through the nasal passages because there is a greater ability to regulate air flow that way. Respiratory and sinus problems, however, invite use of both mouth and nose for this style of breathing. In any case, diaphragmatic breathing promotes concentration on one body sensation to the exclusion of all other sensory stimuli: feeling air slowly pass through the nose or mouth, down into the lungs, and then return via the same pathway.

© 1998 Randy Glasbergen.   www.glasbergen.com

"I can't work next to Phil anymore.
I'm tired of inhaling secondhand stress!"

FIGURE 18.1

BOX 18.2   Insomnia and Diaphragmatic Breathing

When you stop and think about it, counting sheep is merely a simple form of guided visualization to promote sleep, but it's not always effective. The problem is that most people's minds start wandering off with the sheep. If you are having trouble sleeping, here is a suggestion: Try counting your breath cycles instead. Before you start counting, lie comfortably on your back. Then, take the emphasis of your breathing off your upper chest (this tends to increase the stress response) and place it instead on your lower stomach. Try to make each breath comfortably slow and comfortably deep. Counting backward from 100 also seems to help tire the mind, as the body relaxes. Diaphragmatic breathing is perhaps the simplest way to initiate the relaxation response. If you find your mind wandering, redirect your thoughts back to your breathing, and release each wandering thought with each exhalation.

Scientists have observed that over the course of a single day, barring colds or sinus problems, one nostril dominates the breathing cycle for several hours before allowing the other nostril to take over (Searleman et al., 2005). Several studies now suggest that these changes in breathing patterns can actually enhance brain lateralization and their respective modes of thinking (Neimark, 1985). The right side of the brain controls and is influenced by actions of the left side of the body. Scientists suggest that allowing air to enter and exit through your left nostril will access right-brain functions more readily. Thus, when right-brain thinking is preferred, as in the use of imagination, this style of breathing is advocated.

Breathing and Chronic Pain

An expression in China states there are more than 40 different ways to breathe. Whereas most Westerners think there are only two (inhale and exhale), Asians have studied and worked with breathing as a healing modality for thousands of years, primarily combining mental imagery with diaphragmatic breath work. Although few, if any, studies have investigated the relationship between diaphragmatic breathing and the treatment of chronic pain, energy healers who treat patients with a host of diseases use breath work as the core of their energy work (Rosen, 2002; Swayzee, 1998). Rosen describes a concept called **Bandha**, a series of respiratory contractions to unlock the cause of pain. It is also suggested by healers that clients not merely practice diaphragmatic breathing, but combine imagery with their breath work and visualize inhaling and exhaling "through" that specific area for pain relief.

Steps to Initiate Diaphragmatic Breathing

1. Assume a Comfortable Position

The beauty of this technique is its simplicity. It can be done anywhere, at any time. To benefit most, first learn and then practice diaphragmatic breathing in a comfortable position, either sitting or, preferably, lying down on your back with your eyes closed (**FIG. 18.2**). To enhance this position, loosen constrictive clothing around the neck and waist. When first learning this technique, it is suggested that you place your hands over your stomach and feel the rise and fall of your abdomen with each breath. Once the technique is practiced with proficiency, it can be performed just about anywhere, under any circumstances, including while driving in heavy traffic, waiting in line at the post office, giving a public speech, or taking a final exam.

2. Concentration

As with all relaxation techniques that offer respite to the body, diaphragmatic breathing requires focused concentration. Concentration can easily be interrupted

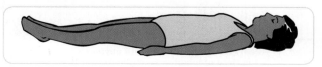

FIGURE 18.2   Lie on a carpeted floor with arms by your sides, back straight, and eyes closed.

Bandha: A series of breathing exercises to unlock chronic pain.

Stress with a Human Face

"You know, I really thought all this breathing stuff was a crock," said Tom, a lieutenant in the Navy. "Yup! You could say I have a stressful life right about now." Tom was about to graduate from college, start flight school in Florida, and become a father.

All three events converged about 2 weeks later. Whatever mental toughness Tom had attained in boot camp melted away when the first labor pain arrived. What otherwise seemed like a short drive to the hospital became a comedy of errors as Tom faced traffic of biblical proportions on the Capital Beltway. And it only got worse when the right front tire was punctured by some glass by the side of the road. "I just kept telling Kathy, 'Take a deep breath, keep breathing, it will be all right.' I was breathing right along with her. I'm not sure who it helped more, me or her. You know, you always hear about babies being born in the back seat of a car, but I never thought mine would be one of those."

by both external noises and internal thoughts. Whenever possible, take steps to minimize external interruptions by finding a nice quiet place to practice this technique. When first learning this and other techniques that require total concentration, you will notice that on occasion your mind begins to wander. This is common. When you notice competing thoughts, allow them to dissipate and refocus your attention on your breathing. One suggestion is to allow these interrupting thoughts to metaphorically escape your body as you exhale.

Normal breathing is for the most part an involuntary, unconscious act. It is regulated by the medulla oblongata of the brain, allowing the conscious mind to focus on other aspects of functional survival. Diaphragmatic breathing, though, necessitates a conscious decision to redirect your attention to this basic physiologic function and turn off the autonomic influence that normally controls it. One approach to deeper awareness is to mentally follow the flow of air as it enters the body and travels to its destination in the lower lobes of the lungs and back out again. Sometimes a mental suggestion can help: "Feel the air come into my nose (or mouth), down into my lungs, and feel my stomach rise and then descend as I exhale the air, feeling it leave my lungs, throat, and nasal cavity." Repeat this with each breath.

Concentration can be augmented further by focusing on the components of each breath. Each ventilation is said to be composed of four distinct phases:

Phase I: Inspiration, or taking the air into your lungs through the nose or mouth

Phase II: A very slight pause before exhaling

Phase III: Exhalation, or releasing the air from your lungs through the passage it entered

Phase IV: Another very slight pause after exhalation before the next inhalation is initiated

These phases can be experienced to a greater extent by exaggerating the breathing cycle, taking a very slow and comfortable deep breath. When trying this technique, try to isolate and recognize the four phases as they occur. Remember not to hold your breath at any time during each phase. Rather, learn to regulate your breathing by controlling the pace of each phase in the breathing cycle. Diaphragmatic breathing is not the same as hyperventilation; this style of breathing is slow, relaxed, and as deep as feels comfortable. It is commonly agreed that the most relaxing phase of diaphragmatic breathing is the third phase, exhalation. At this phase, the chest and abdominal areas relax, sending the relaxing effect throughout the whole body. It requires no effort whatsoever. So, when focusing on your breathing, feel how relaxed your whole body becomes during this phase, especially your chest, shoulders, and abdominal region.

In addition to acknowledging the four phases of each breath, become aware of your capacity to breathe. In the tradition of yoga, there are said to be three regions of the lungs: the upper, middle, and lower lobes. During normal breathing, we typically use only the upper lobes. During the initial stages of relaxed breathing, both the upper and middle lobes are filled with air. But in deep breathing, all three lobes of the lungs are used. As you monitor your breathing, become conscious of filling each layer or region of your lungs.

3. Visualization

Breathing and imagery are dynamic partners in the art of relaxation. Many images can be combined with this breathing technique. The following are two common ones accompanied by suggestions often used in Asian relaxation practices.

Visualization Exercise 1: Breathing Clouds. This technique can be traced back to the origins of yoga in Asia and Zen meditation in Japan. It was introduced as a cleansing process for the mind and body (Shiamora, 1992). To begin (**FIG. 18.3**), close your eyes and focus all your attention on your breathing. Visualize the air that you take into your lungs as being clean, fresh air; pure and energized air; clean air with the power to cleanse and heal your body. As you breathe in this clean, fresh air, visualize and feel air enter your nose (or mouth), travel up through the sinus cavities to the top of your head, and down your spinal column to circulate throughout your body. Now, as you exhale, visualize that the air leaving your body is dirty air—dark, cloudy smoke that symbolizes all the stressors, frustrations, and toxins throughout your mind and body. With each breath you take, allow the clean, fresh air to enter, circulate, and rejuvenate your body, and expel the dirty air to help rid your body of its stress and tension. Repeat this breathing cycle for 5 to 10 minutes. As you repeat the breathing clouds exercise, you may notice that, as the body becomes more relaxed through the release of stress and tension, the color of the exhaled air begins to change from gray to an off-white, symbolic of complete relaxation and cleansing.

Visualization Exercise 2: Alternate Nostril Breathing. This technique dates back to the origins of yoga and is

FIGURE 18.4 Alternate nostril breathing exercise.

also called *nadi shadhanam*. It may seem very difficult if not impossible at first, but with repeated practice it will enhance the relaxation response. To begin, close your eyes and focus all your attention on your breathing. Feel the air enter your mouth or nose and travel down into your lungs. Feel your stomach rise as the air enters, and then slowly descend as you exhale. After becoming relaxed from the sensations of your breathing, take a slow, deep breath. Exhale, allowing the air to leave exclusively through your left nostril (**FIG. 18.4**). When your lungs feel completely empty, begin your next breath by inhaling air exclusively through your right nostril. Repeat this cycle for the next fifteen to twenty breaths by continuing to exhale air through your left nostril and draw air in through your right nostril.

When you feel completely comfortable with this air flow, take a very slow but comfortably deep breath through the right nostril again, but change the direction of the air flow: exhale through the right nostril and inhale through the left. Repeat this cycle for the next fifteen to twenty breaths. Throughout the whole process, try to visualize the flow of air as you breathe. You may want to hold a finger to your nose to feel the effectiveness of this visualization. Even if you don't feel a difference, keep trying. Although it may take a while, the nasal passages will begin to open up as a result of these suggestions. Although normally the two nostrils take turns dominating the breathing cycle, you can learn to control this as a relaxation technique.

Visualization Exercise 3: Energy Breathing. Energy breathing is a way to vitalize your body, by not only

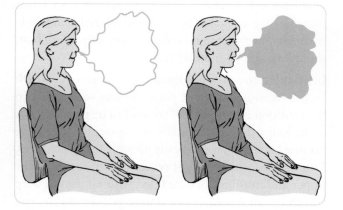

FIGURE 18.3 Breathing clouds exercise.

FIGURE 18.5 Energy breathing exercise.

taking in air through your nose or mouth but, in effect, breathing through your whole body as well. In essence, your body becomes one big lung, taking in air and circulating it throughout. You can do this technique either sitting or lying down. There are three phases to this exercise. First, get comfortable and allow your shoulders to relax. If you choose to sit, try to keep your legs straight. Now, imagine that there is a circular hole at the top (crown) of your head. As you breathe in, visualize energy in the form of a beam of light entering the top of your head (FIG. 18.5). Bring the energy down from the crown of your head to your abdomen as you inhale. As you exhale, allow the energy to leave through the top of your head. Repeat this five to ten times, coordinating your breathing with the visual flow of energy. As you continue to bring the energy down to your stomach, allow the light to reach all the inner parts of your upper body.

When you feel comfortable with this first phase, you are ready to move on to the second phase. Imagine that there is a circular hole in the center of each foot. Again think of energy as a beam of light. Concentrate only on your lower extremities, and allow the flow of energy to move up from your feet into your abdomen as you inhale with your diaphragm. Repeat this five to ten times, coordinating your breathing with the flow of energy. As you continue to bring the energy up into your stomach area, allow the light to reach all the inner parts of your lower body (FIG. 18.6).

Once you feel you are coordinating your breathing and the visual flow of energy to your lower extremities, combine the movement of energy from both the top of your head and your feet, and bring it to the center of your body as you inhale with your diaphragm. Then, as you exhale, allow the flow of energy to reverse direction, leaving the way it came. Repeat this ten to twenty

FIGURE 18.6 Take time for belly breathing exercises each day.

BOX 18.3 Benefits of Breathing

1. Decreases resting heart rate
2. Promotes feelings of relaxation
3. Decreases muscle tension
4. Improves mental clarity
5. Increases oxygen capacity in lungs
6. Helps deal with stress overload

---

times. Each time you move the energy through your body, feel each body region, each muscle and organ, and each cell become energized. At first it may be difficult to visually coordinate the movement of energy coming from opposite ends of your body, but with practice this will come more easily (BOX 18.3).

SUMMARY

- Diaphragmatic breathing is thought to be the easiest method of relaxation. When the emphasis of breathing is centered in the lower abdomen rather than the thoracic cavity, a less sympathetic neural activity is generated, causing a greater relaxation effect.

- Diaphragmatic breathing, or belly breathing, is the basic relaxation technique taught in childbirth classes.

- In a normal state of consciousness, the average number of breaths is twelve to sixteen per minute. In a relaxed state, this number can be reduced to as few as three to four breaths very comfortably.

- Breathing is thought to be paramount to relaxation in nearly every culture, especially Asian cultures, where breath (*prana* or *chi*) is thought to give the body energy. Diaphragmatic breathing is incorporated into nearly every relaxation technique.

- Diaphragmatic breathing takes little more than a comfortable position, focused concentration, and a little mental imagery.

- Diaphragmatic breathing is known to decrease episodes of chronic pain.

- Diaphragmatic breathing can be done anywhere, under any condition where stress arises. For this reason alone, diaphragmatic breathing is said to be the most accessible (and perhaps effective) technique to initiate the relaxation response.

STUDY GUIDE QUESTIONS

1. What is diaphragmatic breathing?

2. Why is diaphragmatic breathing thought to be an effective relaxation technique?

3. What are the four phases of each breath cycle?

4. What three steps are important to engage in this technique?

REFERENCES AND RESOURCES

Bentov, I. *Stalking the Wild Pendulum: On the Mechanics of Consciousness.* Destiny Books, Rochester, VT, 1988.

Birkel, D. *Hatha Yoga: Developing the Body, Mind, and Inner Self.* Eddie Bowers, Dubuque, IA, 1991.

Borysenko, J. *Minding the Body, Mending the Mind.* Bantam Books, New York, 1987.

Brown, R. P., and Gerbarg, P. L. *The Healing Power of the Breath.* Shambhala Publications, Boston, 2012.

Calihan, L., et al. Efficacy of Diaphragmatic Breathing in Persons with Chronic Obstructive Pulmonary Disease, *Journal of Cardiopulmonary Rehabilitation* 22:7–21, 2002.

Caponigro, A. Healing with the Breath of Life, *Body Mind Spirit* 15(1):6–11, 1996.

Courtney, R. Breathe Easy Eucapnic Breathing: A Powerful Tool for the Somatic Therapist, *Massage & Bodywork* 15(4):12–16, 2000.

Davis, M., McKay, M., and Eshelman, R. *The Relaxation and Stress-Reduction Workbook,* 3rd ed. New Harbinger Press, Oakland, CA, 1988.

Engle, B. T., and Chism, R. A. Effects of Increases and Decreases in Breathing Rate on Heart Rate and Finger-Pulse Volume, *Psychophysiology* 4:83–89, 1967.

Farhi, D. *The Breathing Book: Good Health and Vitality through Essential Breathwork.* Owl Books, New York, 1996.

Fixx, J. *The Complete Book of Running.* Random House, New York, 1977.

Funderburk, J. *Science Studies Yoga: A Review of Physiological Data.* Himalayan International Institute of Yoga Science and Philosophy, Honesdale, PA, 1977.

Green, E. Personal conversation (Stress Physiology of Swami Rama). June 22, 1992. ISSSEEM Conference, Boulder, CO.

Hendricks, G. *Conscious Breathing.* Bantam Books, New York, 1995.

Iyengar, B. K. *Light on Pranayama.* Crossroad, New York, 1981.

Iyengar, B. K. *Light on Pranayama: The Yogic Art of Breathing.* Crossroad/Herder & Herder, New York, 1995.

Kabat-Zinn, J. *Full Catastrophe Living.* Delta Books, New York, 1990.

Miller, R. Working with Breathing, *Yoga Journal,* September/October, 1989:67–75.

Nakahata, A. K. Mastering Lamaze Skills: Discover Breathing and Relaxation Skills to Help You through Labor and the Years to Follow, *Lamaze Parents Magazine* 12:36–37, 1993.

Neimark, J. Brain Rhythms: What the Nose Knows, *American Health,* May 1985.

Peper, E. *Effortless Diaphragmatic Breathing.* www.bfe.org/protocol/pro10eng.htm.

Rama, S., Ballentine, R., and Hymes, A. *The Science of Breath.* Himalayan Institute Press, Honesdale, PA, 1998.

Rosen, R. *The Yoga of Breathing: A Step by Step Guide to Pranayama.* Shambhala Books, Boston, 2002.

Searleman, A., Hornung, D., Stein, E., and Brzuszkiewicz, L. Nostril Dominance, *Laterality: Asymmetries of Body, Brain, and Cognition* 10(2):111–112, 2005.

Seaward, B. L. Breathing Clouds Meditation. *A Change of Heart: Meditations and Visualizations* (audio CD). Inspiration Unlimited, Boulder, CO, 2002.

Seaward, B. L. Dolphin Breath Meditation. *A Wing and a Prayer: Meditations and Visualizations* (audio CD). Inspiration Unlimited, Boulder, CO, 2004.

Shannohoff-Khalsa, D. Breathing for the Brain, *American Health* 5:16–18, 1986.

Sherwood, L. *Fundamentals of Physiology: A Human Perspective.* Thomson Brooks/Cole, 2006.

Shiamora, S. Personal conversation. January 25, 1992. The American University, Washington, DC.

Spreads, C. *Breathing: The ABCs.* Harper & Row, New York, 1978.

Stern, R. M., and Anschel, C. Deep Inspirations as Stimuli for Responses of the Autonomic Nervous System, *Psychophysiology* 5:132–141, 1968.

Straub, W. The Effects of Diaphragmatic Breathing and Sleep Training on Sleep, Jet Lag, and Swimming Performance, *The Sports Journal,* 2003. www.thesportsjournal.org/2003Journal/vol6-No1/swedish.htm.

Stringer, H. Breathing Lessons: Yoga Helps Busy Nurses Find Physical Freedom, Maximize Relaxation, *Nurseweek* 6(1):17–18, 2001.

Swami Rama, et al. *Science of Breath.* Himalayan International Institute of Yoga Science and Philosophy, Honesdale, PA, 1979.

Swayzee, N. *Breathworks: Strengthening Your Back from the Inside Out.* Avon Books, New York, 1998.

Taylor, K. *Exploring Holotropic Breathwork.* Hanford Mead Publishers, 2003. www.hanfordmead.com.

Weil, A. *Breathing: The Master to Self-Healing.* Sounds True, Boulder, CO, 1999.

CHAPTER 19

Meditation and Mindfulness

When the pupil is ready, the teacher will come.

—Ancient Chinese Proverb

I n case no one has officially said this to you yet, "Welcome to the digital-WiFi-YouTube-GPS information age." Today more than ever before, the human mind is barraged with bits and bytes every waking hour, practically nonstop. The once humorous cries of "too much information" are not quite so funny anymore as we become deluged in information, with nonstop access to the Internet, cell phones, text messages, tablets, and information technology that is being invented as I write this, but that will be commonplace by the time you read these words. Although the ability to access information is wonderful, the inundation of information is deafening to the mind. The term is **sensory overload**.

If you were to listen to people talk about the negative aspects of technology (cell phones, email, text messages, podcasts, Twitter and Facebook updates, and such) you surely would hear the word *distraction* used repeatedly.

> **Sensory overload:** An inundation of information and distractions that overwhelm the mind.
>
> **Meditation:** A practice of increased concentration that leads to increased awareness; a solitary practice of reflection on internal rather than external stimuli.

It is hard to focus your mind when there are countless constant distractions begging for your attention during every waking moment. Distractions have always been part of the human condition, primarily fear-based thoughts created by the ego. In the twenty-first century, however, the number of distractions has grown exponentially, due in part to the cyberworld. The result is that today people are less focused, less mindful, less patient, and more cynical. Meditation isn't a cure for the world's ills, but the purpose of meditation is to train the mind to minimize distractions, both internal (ego-based thoughts) and external, so that one becomes more focused, more mindful, more patient, and reports a higher degree of happiness and well-being. Simply stated, meditation is a way to detoxify the mind from sensory bombardment, sensory overload, and the multitude of daily distractions that interfere with clear thinking.

In every age of humanity, the mind has always needed a respite from thoughts, worries, and external stimuli. **Meditation** is the quintessential respite to calm the mind from sensory overload (**FIG. 19.1**). Today, meditation is rapidly gaining recognition in the West as a powerfully effective relaxation technique. What at one time may have been considered a fringe behavior by "new agers"

FIGURE 19.1 We are guided by our inner wisdom only when we take the time to stop and listen.

is now considered an American mainstream habit. So declared *Time* magazine in a cover story, with nearly 30 million people citing meditation as a formal practice of relaxation. In that same month, *Business Week* magazine highlighted several CEOs of *Fortune* 500 companies who meditate regularly. The surge in corporate meditation practice correlates with a rise in occupational stress, yet CEOs see meditation as a means to gain not only mental clarity, but also a sharper creative edge in the business world. Those who follow basketball know that former Los Angeles Lakers coach Phil Jackson is a big advocate of meditation as well. Actor Richard Gere, Sting, and former President Jimmy Carter also meditate regularly. With a rise in the number of people practicing yoga, this practice, too, has had an impact.

By all confirmed reports, meditation is not a religion. Rather, it is a solitary practice of reflection on internal rather than external stimuli. Technically speaking, meditation is an increased concentration and awareness—a process of living in the present moment to produce and enjoy a tranquil state of mind. The practice of meditation is the oldest recognized relaxation technique known. So accepted are several components of meditation that they have become tightly integrated into virtually every relaxation technique known and practiced today.

Shakespeare once said, "The eyes are the windows to your soul." By consciously closing the eyes now and again, the soul is given a chance to pause and cleanse itself. Indeed,

all the body's senses are ports of entry bringing in stimuli from outside for the mind to interpret and censor. Human beings are visually oriented animals; we take in more than two-thirds of our sensory information through vision alone. Stimulation from any sensory organ bombards the conscious mind, and under the influence of stress, the mind juggles many thoughts produced both externally and internally, as they compete for attention. Quite often, the result of this abundance of sensory stimulation is sensory overload. You have probably experienced this at the end of a long day of classes or work, or perhaps during a visit to an art museum, where after 2 hours every painting looks about the same. Sensory overload is like a blackboard filled to capacity with notes and scribbles that are quite difficult to organize and assimilate into use. When our minds are overloaded with information, concentration is compromised. The term *polyphasia* (also known as multitasking) is used to describe an abundance of simultaneous thoughts cluttering the mind, and there is a strong association between a cluttered mind and a stressful mind.

To use a simile, meditation is like an eraser that cleans the mind's blackboard. In fact, some would say, meditation gets rid of the blackboard as well. Meditation is a tool to unclutter the mind and bring about mental homeostasis (**FIG. 19.2**). In the language of information technology (IT), meditation increases the bandwidth of human consciousness. When the mind is clear of thought, it is more receptive to new information, new perspectives, and new ways of dealing with unresolved problems. In the acclaimed book *The Prophet*, Kahlil Gibran writes, "No man can reveal to you aught but that which lies half asleep in the dawning of your knowledge." In other words, the student is also the teacher. But before lessons can be taught, the proper learning environment must be created. This is the primary purpose of meditation: concentration promoting self-awareness. Thus, as expressed in the ancient Chinese proverb, when the student is ready, the teacher will come.

Historical Perspective

Although it is likely that the practice existed much earlier, the roots of meditation can be traced back to Asia in the sixth century B.C., when several individuals traveling separate paths to enlightenment took refuge and solace in contemplative and reflective thought. The fruits of this thought became the cornerstones of several philosophies, which gathered many followers eager to learn and share them. These followers in turn established rules and guidelines to live by, which evolved into several prominent religious philosophies: namely, Hinduism, Buddhism, Taoism, Confucianism, and the Essenes. Meditation, or self-reflective thought, was integrated into the practices of these religions as a means to cleanse and purify the soul. From this perspective, we can see that although meditation has been adopted by nearly every religion, it is not a religion in itself (Allen, 1983).

Self-reflection is considered essential to the maturation process. Every culture and every religious sect has some element of meditation or self-reflective practice, including Judaism, Catholicism, Protestantism, Islam, and the worship of several American Indian tribes. There are subtle but significant differences between Eastern and Western cultures in their approach to meditation. Western views promote a search for inner peace through external means, whereas Eastern philosophies direct thoughts inward for harmony and atonement. This dichotomy of approaches has resulted in a high degree of perceived mysticism, and perhaps misunderstanding, in the West. In simple terms, like the mind it affects, meditation appears to have several layers. Initially, meditation has a calming effect on the mind's basic thought processes. Once this layer is peeled away, a deeper series of layers is unveiled to reveal insights of the soul, intuition, or enlightenment (Levey and Levey, 1999).

Eastern cultures have accepted the essence of meditation and all its many principles. Western cultures, more skeptical by nature, have only recently begun to appreciate meditation as a means to calm the mind and all its thought processes to achieve inner peace. Meditation became popular in the United States during the 1960s by way of the Beatles, whose music and lifestyles included meditation, thus influencing many people (Woo, 2008). Meditation gained additional momentum from the counter-culture movements of the 1960s, specifically the human potential movement, which sought to elevate all humanity to a higher level of consciousness. The materialism of the 1980s and 1990s, however, nearly derailed this movement. With the dawning of the twenty-first century, a revival of interest in the advancement of human potential and a quest for spiritual growth and development have emerged. Meditation has again become a major component of this movement, particularly in various self-help workshops, motivational retreats, and corporate seminars. In essence, meditation is now a mainstream practice in America, with more than 30 million people claiming to practice it on a regular basis (Stein, 2003). One researcher, José Silva, has taken the concept of meditation one step further, integrating it

COSMIC BREADCRUMBS

After several attempts, Jason finally gets the hang of meditation.

FIGURE 19.2

into a technique to enhance what he calls personal mind control. In the Silva Method, meditation is used to access great thinking power and memory function (Silva and Miele, 1975). The premise of meditation has also been adapted to a concept called alpha thinking, named for the state of mind physiologically represented by alpha waves, in which specific meditation concepts are integrated with other relaxation techniques, including breathing, biofeedback, and mental imagery, to promote deep relaxation and improved memory.

The medical profession has now adopted meditation as its own behavior-modification technique to combat rising morbidity and mortality from stress-related heart disease. Originally doubtful of claims that meditation promotes physical calmness as well as inner peace, the American Heart Association now advocates it as a preventive health measure in conjunction with proper diet and aerobic exercise to reduce modifiable risk factors for coronary heart disease. In fact, Dr. Dean Ornish (1998) has proven that coronary heart disease is reversible, in some cases, in people who combine meditation with changes in diet and exercise. The National Institutes of Health advocates meditation for the mental and emotional relief of cancer.

Slowly, as Eastern and Western cultures become more closely integrated, the basic concepts of meditation as a relaxation technique will become even more readily accepted for achieving both mental and physical homeostasis.

Although some see meditation as a means only for personal enlightenment, others value it for its greater potential—to raise the collective human consciousness. According to Lyall Watson's Hundredth Monkey theory (Keys, 1987) and Rupert Sheldrake's morphogenic field theory (1995), once a critical mass of conscious thought is reached, the direction of human evolution will shift to a higher (stress-free) level. Moreover, it is believed that when a critical mass of people engage in meditation for world peace and ecological harmony, more and more people will eventually resonate with this mind frame to the point of significant positive influence (Hagelin, 2007). Can a collective think tank (or non–think tank, as the case may be) of meditators make a difference? Many practitioners of Transcendental Meditation are known to travel collectively to various cities for weeks on end and use meditation as a means to decrease violent crime; the results of their efforts appear promising. As ironic as it sounds, some groups of Pentagon employees meditate for world peace using a practice known as "human peace shields" for the moral protection of humanity (Winchester, 2007). Although they have not claimed responsibility for the demise of Soviet communism, the fall of the Berlin Wall, or the reduction of nuclear armaments, they do feel that their efforts were partially influential in these events.

Types of Meditation

From the seeds of Eastern philosophy grew two distinct branches of meditation: exclusive or **restrictive meditation**, and inclusive or **opening-up meditation**. Although the two vary in style and format, the processes of concentration and awareness are paramount to the benefits of both of them. The end result is the same: a cleansing of the mind that leads to inner peace. Once the conscious mind is calm and without ego chatter and clear of distracting thoughts, new insights bubble up from the unconscious mind to the surface of the conscious mind; these insights often give subtle direction for the next step of our human journey (the "ah ha" moment of meditation). Whether one practices a form of exclusive or inclusive meditation, people often refer to these modalities as **insightful meditation** because of the nature of the intuitive thought processes that follow when the mind is disciplined to listen.

Exclusive Meditation

Consider this metaphor: The mind is a sky full of clouds, with several layers superimposed on one another above the earth. Each cloud layer represents a multitude of thoughts that compete for conscious attention. **Exclusive meditation** (also known as concentration meditation) involves the restriction of consciousness to focus on a single thought. This single thought becomes a device to wipe all other thoughts from the conscious slate. A single thought is like a gentle wind that blows the clouds away, leaving a clear blue sky. The power of this single thought is repetition, which continually breaks the surface of attention to the exclusion of all other thoughts. Restrictive meditation advocates a closed awareness to the external senses and all outside stimulation, and directs the focus of one's thoughts inward. In most cases, exclusive meditation is practiced with the eyes closed to prevent visual distractions. There are five actions used to refine one's attention on a single focused thought: mental repetition, visual concentration, repeated sounds, physical repetition, and tactile repetition.

1.　*Mental repetition:* Mental repetition means a thought is produced over and over again. Mental repetition is most commonly done by use of a **mantra**, which is a one-syllable word (e.g., *Om*, *one*, *peace*, or *love*) and should be done in conjunction with exhaling.

Restrictive meditation: A form of meditation wherein concentration is focused on one object (e.g., *mantra*, *tratak*) to the exclusion of all other thoughts, to increase self-awareness and promote relaxation.

Opening-up meditation: *See* Inclusive meditation.

Insightful meditation: An expression given to any type of meditation (inclusive or exclusive) whereby a person, once clearing the mind of interrupting thoughts and ego chit-chat, begins to expand his or her awareness to the intuition, or the deep-seated wisdom of the collective unconscious, thus giving insight into the person's life.

Exclusive meditation: A form of meditation wherein concentration is focused on one object (e.g., *mantra*, *tratak*) to the exclusion of all other thoughts, to increase self-awareness and promote relaxation.

Mantra: Typically a one-syllable word (e.g., *om*, *peace*, *love*) or a short phrase that acts like a broom to sweep the mind of nonessential (ego-based) thoughts.

A mantra can also be a short positive phrase (e.g., *I feel good*, *I am worthy of love*, or *My body is calm and relaxed*) to reinforce positive self-esteem. In some cases, prayers are also considered a type of mantra. In cultures where yoga meditation is practiced, it is believed that certain sounds (audible energy) have the power to heal. Thus, chanting in a soft whisper or silently repeating the word *Om* is believed to access the highest level of concentration, that which represents the essence of truth, love, and peace. This and other yoga mantras are created of special sounds that are thought to help release "blocked energy" impeding mental homeostasis. Chanting the word *Om* is thought to produce a vibration that draws the body's rhythm into synchrony with the earth's magnetic field, thus evoking a feeling of oneness with nature. Western philosophy suggests that the vibrations from any one word can have a calming effect. Regardless of philosophical bent, it is commonly accepted that when practiced regularly, the repetition of a one-word mantra will clear all other thoughts from the conscious mind.

2. *Visual concentration:* Visual concentration involves visually focusing on or staring at an object or image. In yoga meditation, this is called steady gazing or **tratak**. Visual concentration is like a visual mantra. The practice of *tratak* involves staring at an object about 3 to 5 feet away, without blinking, until it is etched on the mind's blackboard to the exclusion of all other thoughts. The suggested duration is about 60 seconds. Then, close your eyes and visualize the object. If the mental image fades or vanishes, open your eyes and repeat this again. Common visual mantras include a candle flame, flower, seashell, beautiful scene, or **mandala** (**FIG. 19.3**)—a circular object that is intricately

FIGURE 19.3 A mandala is a circular object symbolizing wholeness that can be used as a visual mantra. (This is the famous stained glass window design of Notre Dame Cathedral in Paris, France.)

designed, intense in color, and often divided into four quarters.

3. *Repeated sounds:* In some forms of meditation, a sound is repeated continually to help focus the mind's attention. The term for this is **nadam**. Examples of sounds are a beating drum, chimes, Tibetan bells, or Gregorian chants. Natural sounds such as the rush of a waterfall, ocean waves on the shore of a beach, or rolling thunder are also examples of *nadams*. In Western culture, some types of repetitive New Age music may be considered *nadams*.

4. *Physical repetition:* This is repetitive motion such as the sensation of breathing, or some forms of rhythmic aerobic exercise (e.g., running, swimming, or walking) that are believed by many to produce a meditative state (runner's high), either from the sound of breathing or rhythmic motions of feet and arms. Physical repetition is thought to shift the mind to an altered state of consciousness or relaxed thinking mode. Several people say their most creative thoughts come during this type of exercise. In Sufi religious practice, the whirling dervish dance is said to induce a trance-like state through the repetitive circular motion. Pranayama or diaphragmatic breathing is also used extensively as a physical repetitive mantra in virtually every relaxation course. This approach,

Tratak: A visual type of mantra, such as a seashell, a colorfully designed mandala, or any object that is used by the eyes to focus attention and ignore distracting thoughts.

Mandala: A circular-shaped object used as a visual mantra for the purpose of clearing the mind of unnecessary (ego-based) thoughts.

Nadam: An auditory mantra for which a repetitive sound is used to help clear the mind of unnecessary (ego-based) thoughts.

where there is repetitive motion, is also called **active meditation**.

5. *Tactile repetition:* Holding a small object, such as a tumble stone or seashell, also brings focus to the mind. Hindu yogis use a strand of beads called a *mala* (108 small beads and one large *meru* bead), holding it in their right hand, and rolling the beads one by one between the thumb and third finger as they meditate. In Western culture, rosary beads offer a similar focus of concentration.

Meditation Position. In all forms of meditation, but particularly in restrictive meditation, correct body position is essential. Perhaps the most recognized posture is the lotus position. In the lotus position, an individual sits with his or her legs crossed and folded, each foot resting on the alternate thigh. A more comfortable position for beginners is the half-lotus position (**FIG. 19.4**), with the legs simply crossed in a comfortable manner. In this passive position, one sits with the back (spinal column) completely aligned from the crown of the head to the tail bone. This alignment minimizes neural firing to the muscles and thus allows for increased

© Thinkstock/Index Stock Imagery.

FIGURE 19.4 A meditation posture based on the lotus position.

(active) concentration on the mental focus. The hands can be placed on the thighs either with the palms down (to center oneself with the earth's energy) or facing up with thumb and index finger joined (to receive energy). Breathing is regulated by placing emphasis on the expansion of the stomach area, rather than the chest, during inhalation. The position should be comfortable enough to maintain for approximately 30 minutes or more without interfering with your ability to concentrate. You may notice some pain in the muscles and joints of your hips and knees. If this occurs, stretch your legs to find a more comfortable position. Pain is not conducive to meditation.

There are several types of restrictive meditation. Transcendental Meditation and the relaxation response are two examples.

Transcendental Meditation

Transcendental Meditation (TM) is a classic example of exclusive meditation. TM was developed by the Hindu Maharishi Mahesh Yogi (2001). The story of the development of TM reads like an ancient fable. A young Hindu gentleman named Mahesh Prasad Varma yearned to become a scientist, and in 1942 he received a degree in physics. But the winds of change soon brought him to study with the famed religious leader Swami Brahmanada Saraswati, with whom he spent the next 13 years in divine worship. In this calling, he accepted the challenge to create a simple version of Hindu meditation, one that "anyone" could learn and practice. His life mission became to sow the seeds of world peace through the trained, tranquil soul of each individual. Off he went to the Himalaya mountains, taking refuge in an abandoned cave. After a 2-year retreat, he returned to India with the new technique we know today as TM. This technique, a simplified version of yoga meditation stripped of its spiritual dogma, was introduced into the United States in the late 1960s as a secular practice and gained instant popularity. It was the favorite alternative for those whose recreational drug habits produced nasty side effects, as well as those

> **Active meditation:** A term given to a physical activity (e.g., walking, swimming) that promotes a cleansing of the mind through repetitive motion.
>
> **Transcendental Meditation:** This meditation is the epitome of exclusive meditation in which all thoughts are eliminated save the mantra itself.

who were seeking inner peace during the tumultuous and rocky years of the Vietnam War. In the practice of TM, individuals are given a "special mantra" and taught to focus their thoughts on that one word. The mantra, the Maharishi and his teachers instructed, must remain secret to be effective, a statement later proved unfounded (Russell, 2001).

Within 10 years' time, more than a million Americans had learned this technique. People reported that it indeed brought inner peace and harmony to their lives when practiced with regularity. TM became the object of scientific curiosity, and inner peace soon became measured by significant decreases in resting blood pressure as well as the absence of many disease symptoms associated with stress. Intrigued by the possibility that TM could be a new relaxation technique, a team of medical researchers headed by Robert Keith Wallace and Herbert Benson (1972) investigated the effects of TM. To their surprise, they found that it proved quite effective as a mediating factor for chronic stress. In a Harvard laboratory, Wallace asked 36 subjects well trained in TM to practice this technique for three 20- to 30-minute sessions. Before, during, and after meditation sessions, oxygen consumption (VO_2), blood lactate, electrical skin conduction (sweating), and alpha brain waves were measured. Results revealed that TM did, in fact, induce a profound state of physiologic homeostasis. Perplexed at the incongruity between its simplicity and the expensive price tag to learn TM (currently priced at $2,500), Benson Americanized the technique and called it the **relaxation response**.

The Relaxation Response

In his book *The Relaxation Response*, Benson describes four basic steps to follow to promote physiological homeostasis. These same four components can be found in virtually every relaxation technique, from mental imagery to progressive muscular relaxation. These simple components are as follows:

1. *A quiet environment:* A quiet environment can be any room with minimal distractions. It should be a room or area in which you feel completely comfortable. The premise of meditation is to reduce all sensory stimuli, including external stimuli such as ringing phones and doorbells, blaring televisions or radios, and outside street noise. A quiet environment also is interpreted to mean a reduction of internal stimuli, such as tense muscles and physical discomfort.

2. *A mental device:* A mental device is any object or tool used to replace all other thoughts. It is a focal point to direct all attention. A mental device can include repetition of a mantra, concentrated breathing, or a *tratak* or *nadam*. Benson suggests the word *one* for a mantra. He also suggests that if your mind wanders, use the word *no* to discontinue the free association.

3. *A passive attitude:* A passive attitude is a receptive attitude. A passive attitude is a frame of mind in which you are open to thoughts rather than blocking them out. At first this may sound contradictory to the exclusive nature of restrictive meditation. But without this frame of mind, the walls of the ego censor any effort to relax completely.

4. *A comfortable position:* The earliest meditation advocates stated that to relax the mind, one must first relax the body. So, you must first find a comfortable position. Benson advocates a sitting position with most of the body weight supported. The body should be relaxed, with no sign of muscular tension. Positions conducive to sleep should be avoided (BOX 19.1).

Inclusive Meditation

The second type of meditation is called **inclusive meditation**. It is also referred to as access meditation, insightful meditation, and **mindfulness**. Inclusive meditation appears to be very similar to free association, where the mind wanders aimlessly. In the practice of inclusive meditation, the mind is free to accept all thoughts; no attempt is made to control the mind's content. The conscious mind simply accepts spontaneous thoughts that make themselves available from the unconscious mind. There is one condition to this receptivity, however: All thoughts

Relaxation response: A term coined by Dr. Herbert Benson, who Americanized TM to make it more accessible to the Western world.

Inclusive meditation: A form of meditation where all thoughts are invited into awareness without emotional evaluation, judgment, or analysis. Zen meditation is an example.

Mindfulness: A type of meditation where all senses concentrate on the activity being performed during the present moment, like eating an apple or washing the dishes.

BOX 19.1   Insomnia and Meditation

It has been long recognized that meditation is a viable antidote for insomnia. Given that meditation is a vehicle for mental discipline, perhaps it should come as no surprise that people who meditate on a regular basis admit to sleeping soundly. By training the mind to release thoughts and feelings that constantly compete for attention, a deep sense of peace is achieved in an awakened state, a skill that carries over to presleep conditions. In essence, the ability to elicit mental clarity appears similar, if not identical, to the presleep state of consciousness. Studies reveal that people who meditate on a regular basis achieve the theta (brain wave) state of consciousness, which is closest to the delta wave pattern observed when sleeping. Sleep/insomnia studies reveal that subjects who lay awake at night or who repeatedly wake up show an alpha or beta wave pattern indicative of a busy mind. Given the chance, the effects of meditation groom the mind's ability to decrease mental activity for a good night's sleep.

---

that enter the conscious mind must do so objectively and without judgment or emotional directive. This process is called **detached observation**. No emotional reaction can be connected with these thoughts. In effect, the mind becomes a movie screen with thoughts projected as images, and the individual observes without judgment or analysis. By detaching yourself from your emotions, the process of inclusive meditation allows barriers of the ego to dissolve. In this type of meditation the eyes are usually open, but you may find that this style can best be learned with the eyes closed.

The goal of inclusive meditation is to observe the observer, meaning that you learn to step outside yourself to observe your own thought processes. In doing so, you retrain your mind to keep an even keel during times of stress in a manner that is called "domesticating the ego," not overreacting. Mindfulness is really just a name for being mindful of the present moment. Eckhart Tolle, author of the best-seller *The Power of Now*, states, "The moment you start watching the thinker, a higher level of consciousness becomes activated. You then begin to realize that there is a vast realm of intelligence beyond thought, that thought is only a tiny aspect of intelligence. You also realize that all the things that truly matter—beauty, love, creativity, joy, inner peace—arise from beyond the mind. You begin to awaken."

Zen Meditation

Zen (Zazen) meditation, or some aspects of it, can be considered inclusive meditation. Zen meditation comes from Zen Buddhism. Around 590 B.C., a young man named Prince Gautama Siddhartha left his family, wealth, and life of foolish pleasures to become a monk, or "wanderer," living a simple life on the Ganges Plain.

He became known as Sakyamuni (Prince of the Sakyas) and later on in life, the Buddha (the Awakened One). Sakyamuni began a journey of profound soul searching, pondering the meaning of life and death, leading to his own enlightenment. He soon became a recognized and respected teacher with a great many followers. What separates Zen from other similar philosophies is the abandonment of the concept of dualities (good versus bad, right versus wrong, male versus female), which are thought to separate rather than unite one with the universe. Thoughts expressed in either-or terms tend to be of an analytical or judgmental nature. Pure Zen thought is devoid of judgment, thus connecting rather than separating one from the world. When the word *Zen* is heard, it is often associated with deep, pensive, intellectual thought. The purpose of Zen meditation is to reach the highest level of consciousness to achieve divine enlightenment. It is believed in Eastern cultures that truth and knowledge come from within and are housed in the soul. One must be patient to receive this gift of enlightenment, however, for it will not come if one is hurried in thought or strong in emotional attachment (Dumoulin, 1981).

Zen meditation has many styles. Some have a restrictive nature to them (e.g., counting your breaths from ten

---

Detached observation: A term derived from inclusive meditation during which the individual observes himor herself meditating, in essence detaching from the ego's desire.

Zen (Zazen) meditation: A form of meditation wherein one learns to detach from one's emotional thoughts by becoming the observer of those thoughts.

Stress with a Human Face

When Adam graduated with his degree in childhood education, he was ready to change the world, and he had every intention of doing so. An excellent student with excellent student-teaching evaluations from his supervisors, Adam believed he had everything he needed to start his teaching career. Like most college graduates, Adam believed he would take the summer off, go to Europe with a friend, and then start work in the fall. As things happened, his plans changed when he ended up graduating in January. Adam found himself looking for a teaching job immediately. His prayers were answered when he landed a job in the Southeast section of the District of Columbia—or so he thought.

"You can learn all the theory you want in school, and you can do your practicum in the nicest schools around, but when it comes to working in a city school, I had to learn everything all over again. These kids need a lot of discipline and a lot more love, before they are ready to learn," he said in frustration.

As one of my former students in a stress-management class, Adam took an immediate liking to meditation, and from the second semester of his sophomore year, he practiced meditation regularly every morning. He mentioned to me several times that, as a varsity soccer player (now semi-professional), meditation was what kept him grounded before, during, and after his games. He reminded me regularly how valuable meditation had become in his life. Now entering the real world, meditation took on a whole new meaning.

"I come home from work exhausted, more so than after any soccer practice. Every day, those kids zap all my energy until I am completely drained. Do you realize how attentive you have to be with kids like these?" he said one day over lunch. "And let me tell you something else," he added, "If I didn't meditate every morning before I go to work, I wouldn't have lasted the first week in that school. I can't tell you how important meditation is in my life. It's essential."

Adam proceeded to explain his daily meditation routine: a half hour of breathing exercises followed by some mental imagery. "Sometimes I even do it on the subway ride to school. In college, I used to do it for the mystical experience, which was pretty powerful in its own right, and to increase my concentration skills for soccer. I still do it for those reasons, but now more than ever, I do it to clear my mind." Meditation. It's not what you think!

down to one), while others lend themselves to opening the mind (Austin, 2000). Zen meditation is a very difficult and disciplined practice, often requiring several hours of motionless contemplative thought in one sitting. Moreover, Zen meditation includes the mind asking an unanswerable question, or **koan**, such as, What is the sound of one hand clapping? Or, What did your face look like before you were conceived? Or this riddle: An egg is placed through the narrow opening of a glass bottle. In less than one day the egg hatches, yet the chick is too big to escape through the opening. How do you remove the chick from the glass bottle without harming the chick or destroying the bottle? Each koan invites profound contemplation. Because there are no answers, the mind acquiesces to the riddle. This submission through mental frustration is said to open the mind's door to new thought or sudden insight leading to greater awareness. The ultimate purpose of koans is to lead one up the path of enlightenment by learning, questioning, and accepting one's purpose in life. In Zen, meditation is only one step in the preparation for enlightenment.

Inclusive meditation is very difficult to practice at first. It is extremely challenging to try to divorce your emotions from your thoughts. But it is the walls of the ego that are believed to separate the mind from the soul. It is the ego (the keeper of our identity) that is vulnerable to the perceptions of stress. Initially, opening up to uncensored thoughts can be a very difficult strategy to deal with stress. Perhaps for this reason, restrictive meditation is preferred over inclusive meditation, and it is the former that is most commonly thought of when meditation is mentioned.

> **Koan:** An unsolvable riddle that aims to shift one's consciousness from analytical thoughts to profound contemplation.

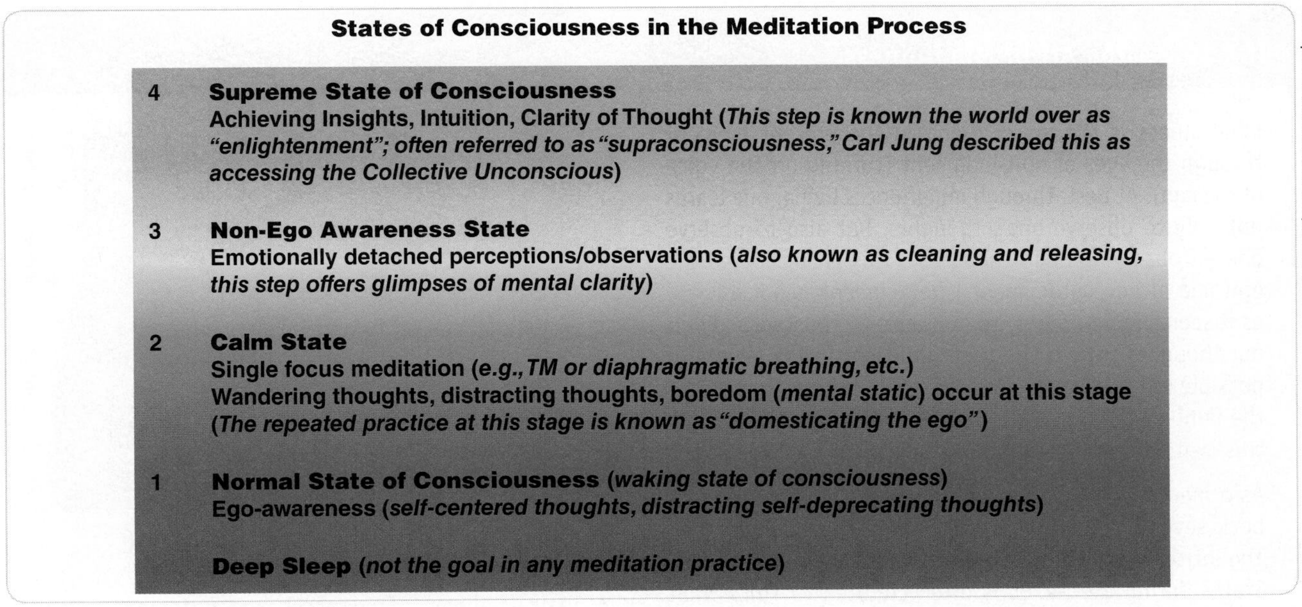

States of Consciousness in the Meditation Process

4   Supreme State of Consciousness
Achieving Insights, Intuition, Clarity of Thought (*This step is known the world over as "enlightenment"; often referred to as "supraconsciousness," Carl Jung described this as accessing the Collective Unconscious*)

3   Non-Ego Awareness State
Emotionally detached perceptions/observations (*also known as cleaning and releasing, this step offers glimpses of mental clarity*)

2   Calm State
Single focus meditation (*e.g., TM or diaphragmatic breathing, etc.*)
Wandering thoughts, distracting thoughts, boredom (*mental static*) occur at this stage (*The repeated practice at this stage is known as "domesticating the ego"*)

1   Normal State of Consciousness (*waking state of consciousness*)
Ego-awareness (*self-centered thoughts, distracting self-deprecating thoughts*)

Deep Sleep (*not the goal in any meditation practice*)

FIGURE 19.5   The meditation process, steps 1–4, is known as "raising awareness." As a skill, one learns to "train" the mind to increase attention, hence awareness without emotional attachment.

Everly and Rosenfeld (2002) created a meditation continuum highlighting the entire range of mental consciousness during the meditative process (**FIG. 19.5**). When one begins a meditation session, the first minute is devoted to preparation: getting comfortable, closing the eyes, perhaps even taking a few deep breaths, followed by more focused concentration. After this time, boredom may set in as the conscious mind fights the mental directive to block out all thoughts and their emotional attachments. (In many cases, people stop here in their first few encounters.) The conscious mind may then become distracted by any thoughts that will relieve the boredom. But once distracting thoughts are removed, the mind begins to enter a state of deep relaxation. In this state, a shift in dominance is said to occur from the left to the right hemisphere of the brain. This shift can be measured by a decrease in beta waves coupled with an increase in alpha waves on an electroencephalogram (EEG). With continued deep relaxation, any thoughts that appear on the mind's screen are observed objectively rather than given any emotional meaning. No judgment or analysis is associated with any thoughts (**BOX 19.2**). As the mind continues to observe, a state of supraconsciousness in which there is increased awareness of one's inner self begins to manifest. At this stage of meditation, the individual may feel almost euphoric, with sensations of enlightenment and connectedness with incorporeal surroundings—in essence, feeling one with the universe.

Split-Brain Theory

The idea that there is a distinct dichotomy of human thought processes (e.g., sequential versus nonlinear) is not new; it has, in fact, been suggested for centuries. Anatomical studies even seemed to support this idea when it was discovered that the human brain is an organ consisting of two hemispheres. But these theories became reality when an attempt was made to find a cure for epilepsy. In the mid-1950s, researcher Roger Sperry and his colleagues conducted a series of experiments designed to alleviate the intensity of grand mal epileptic seizures in monkeys. It was hypothesized that the intensity could be halved if a seizure could be contained to only one hemisphere of the brain. To their surprise, they found that by severing the corpus callosum, the neural isthmus uniting the right and left hemispheres, seizures significantly decreased in both frequency and severity. Curious to see if similar results would occur in humans, a new series of studies was conducted on four patients who volunteered to undergo this surgical procedure. Remarkably, this operation revealed neither damaging side effects nor noticeable changes in the patient's personality or intelligence. Some minor changes in cognitive thought processes were noticed, however, and it was these subtle differences in cognition and everyday behavior that soon gave rise to a new paradigm of human consciousness (Gazzaniga, 1967).

BOX 19.2 The Art of Mindfulness

Mindfulness is the art of living in the present moment through the eyes of non-judgment (turning off the voice of the ego). At best, through mindfulness living, one learns not only to observe one's thoughts, but also to observe oneself observing one's thoughts. (This is considered the epitome of ego detachment.) Detachment is not as easy as it seems, given the ego's influence to constantly direct our thoughts toward the past (guilt) or future events or possible events (worry). Remember, it is the ego that trips the fight-or-flight response. Mindfulness helps deactivate this switch in non-threatening times.

As a meditation practice, the roots of mindfulness date back several millennia to the beginnings of Buddhism. The introduction of mindfulness meditation in the United States during the 1970s is often credited to Thick Nhat Hanh, a Vietnamese Buddhist monk. Today mindfulness is taught and practiced by thousands of people in various demographic groups, and has become very popular in the corporate business world, all with one purpose in mind: to reduce stress through the achievement of inner peace.

Several decades ago the concept of mindfulness meditation gained a more rudimentary Western approach as a simple, non-sectarian relaxation technique for pain management through the efforts of Jon Kabat-Zinn, at the University of Massachusetts Medical School, who taught mindfulness meditation to patients with chronic pain. His success with pain management quickly spread throughout the field of mind-body practitioners. This eventually led Kabat-Zinn, the author of the highly acclaimed book *Full Catastrophe Living*, to create a structured, systematic program to teach other instructors his method of success. He calls it Mindfulness-Based Stress Reduction, or MBSR. Anyone who has ever taken a mindfulness meditation workshop with Kabat-Zinn knows the raisin exercise: For what seems like hours, you hold, smell, study, gaze at, and then finally taste and chew a raisin, all with the utmost awareness. (Some people use chocolate.) The underlying premise of this mindfulness exercise is that as you become more aware of your thoughts and actions, you can control your thoughts (through detached observation) to the point where you are less stressed. Many instructors sum up mindfulness in three words: attention, intention, and attitude.

Today MBSR is taught by certified instructors in over 250 hospitals nationwide, as well as many corporate wellness programs and the U.S. Army. Mindfulness as a relaxation technique has been well researched at Harvard, UCLA, and Stanford, and perhaps is most recognized through the studies of Dr. Richard Davidson at the University of Wisconsin-Madison. Evidence-based outcomes reveal dramatic decreases in pain sensation, and through fMRI data, have led to the exploration of neuroplasticity of brain tissue. Kabat-Zinn's MBSR program is taught as a structured 10-session (31-hour) group session over an 8-week period with suggested daily home practice. Some programs like Duke Medical Center add a 2-hour orientation program. The typical cost for this program is about $500, and it is offered on a sliding scale fee. As described in the MBSR workbook, the basics of MBSR include the following:

1. *Sitting meditation:* Sitting still, back straight, eyes closed, with an undivided focus on your breathing.

2. *Body scan:* Moving your awareness from the top of your head, down to your neck, shoulders, torso, arms and hands, legs, and feet.

3. *Gentle yoga (stretching):* This aspect includes a series of simple hatha yoga asanas performed lying down.

4. *Walking meditation:* Walking (preferably outside) for a specific duration, being mindful of your foot placement, the sights, the sounds, the smells, and so on.

5. *Loving kindness meditation:* Enhancing one's sense of connection to others and the world by observing one's thoughts with an intention of loving kindness to people, events, and the like to create a more harmonious living environment. This meditation is often done by repeating an affirmation phrase such as "May you be happy."

The MBSR program offers both an informal practice and a more formal practice. The informal practice includes a free-floating awareness to be mindful in all daily activities, from breathing and eating to walking, sitting, and even

---

BOX 19.2   The Art of Mindfulness (*continued*)

washing the dishes. The formal practice invites participants to maintain a specific structure to their practice (e.g., a specific time of day) by beginning with a mindful morning check-in, followed by a five-minute mindful breathing exercise, a body scan, and a routine of mindful gentle yoga. This formal practice (a single focused effort rather than a multi-tasking approach) also encourages the participant to keep a journal of all the experiences through these activities to help guide and deepen the practice. Participants are encouraged to continue the formal practice until it becomes a second-nature routine.

Like all other forms of meditation, the benefits attributed to MBSR include an increased ability to relax, a decrease in physical pain, an enhanced ability to cope with physical pain, an increased quality of sleep, decreased self-criticism, increased self-compassion, decreased resting blood pressure and heart rate, the ability to create and sustain an improved sense of self-esteem, and an increased ability to respond, rather than react, to stressful situations. Mindfulness is taught as an essential life skill, rather than a specific means to achieve a single result or goal.

FIGURE 19.6   To test the split-brain cognitive functions of a subject, a word or object is projected onto a translucent screen. The subject is asked to retrieve the object, which is hidden from view and identifiable only by touch.

Under close observation after surgery, first it was noticed that the patient's right side of the body was controlled by the left hemisphere. Conversely, the left side was influenced by the right brain. Later these patients were asked to identify an object that was hidden from sight, placed alternately in each hand. In one study, when a pencil was placed in the right hand, it was correctly described as a pencil (**FIG. 19.6**). When the pencil was placed in the left hand, however, no description could be given at all, suggesting the absence of verbal capacity in the right hemisphere. Additional experiments were then designed to combine visual and tactile objects. In one

test, a picture of a spoon was shown to the left field of vision (right hemisphere), and subjects were asked to feel around with their left hand for an object resembling the picture. Patients had no difficulty identifying the spoon but again could not describe the item they retrieved. Thus, it was concluded that the right brain seemed to have poor verbal acuity but was extremely proficient in spatial perception.

From these and several other studies, it was concluded that each hemisphere appears to be responsible for specific types of thinking processes. Moreover, each hemisphere can function independently as a whole brain. Additional research with stroke victims seemed to confirm these findings. As a result, we now understand that each hemisphere is responsible for different information gathering and processing functions and yet they work together as one unit at the same time. It should be noted that most, if not all, of the research regarding left- and right-brain lateralization has involved epilepsy and stroke patients. Whether the brain works the same way in healthy people is still left to speculation. The work of Sperry and his colleagues has prompted many other studies on the dichotomy of cognitive functions. (**TABLE 19.1**) provides a partial list of these distinct hemispheric functions (Gazzaniga, 1972).

Sperry's colleague and fellow researcher Robert Ornstein explains in his book, *The Psychology of Consciousness*, that right-brain cognitive functions are a foundation of intelligence yet to be explored. Intelligence is currently measured verbally; there is no standard method to evaluate nonverbal intelligence. This single approach to the duality of cognitive processes has limited the potential

TABLE 19.1 Cognitive Functions of the Left and Right Hemispheres of the Brain

Left-Brain Functions	Right-Brain Functions
Analytical skills	Synthesis skills
Judgmental skills	Accepting, receptive nature
Time consciousness	Non-time consciousness
Verbal acuity	Symbolic imagery
Linear thought progression	Nonlinear thought progression
Rational thought process	Irrational thought process
Math acuity	Intuition
Sequential thought process	Imagination
Facts and detail orientation	Music appreciation
Logical thought process	Humor
	Spatial orientation

for human consciousness. Perhaps it has even contributed to perceptions of stress. In the words of Ornstein, "The problem is not that our technology is leading us to a path of destruction, but that our technical innovations have outstripped our perspective and judgment. We live in a world that is often difficult for us to understand." Ornstein supports the idea that the two modes of thinking are complementary, not competitive, and that they must be integrated and balanced for the health of the mind.

Since the initial discoveries, many inferences have been drawn from split-brain research. For example, comparisons have been made between the functions of the left and right brains and dominant thinking processes of Western and Eastern cultures, respectively, and this has since been investigated with MRI brain studies (Parsons and Osherson, 2001). Western culture is considered by many to be left-hemisphere dominant (strong in analytical and judgmental skills, weak in intuitive abilities), while Eastern cultures are right-hemisphere dominant. It is also hypothesized by several sources (Schaef, 1986; Borysenko, 1987) that there is a strong association between left-brain thinking patterns and the frame of mind observed during the stress response. Although generalizations may cloud the understanding of both cultural differences and human cognition, comparisons of this kind may explain why meditation has been less readily accepted by industrialized nations in the Western hemisphere. It may also explain the role meditation plays in accessing right-brain functions to obtain a balance of hemispheric cognition.

Left Brain, Right Brain, Top Brain, Bottom Brain

The human brain is truly remarkable. For millennia scientists, artists, philosophers, and poets have marveled at the capacity of human thought. Scientific investigations to peer into the anatomy and physiology of the brain have revealed many of its secrets, but all of this research has barely scratched the surface of what lies behind consciousness, thought processes, memory, creativity, intuition, imagination, and so much more.

No one piece of research can explain the complexities of the brain (though many have tried). Roger Sperry won a Nobel Prize in 1981 for his research about right-brain and left-brain cognitive function. More recently, research has focused on understanding the "executive function" of the brain (the frontal cortex), and now with umpteen research studies using functional magnetic resonance imaging (fMRI) of the brain many more secrets are being revealed. Some researchers are now dividing thought processes into top brain (executive function) and bottom brain (the reptilian brain associated with fight or flight). Perhaps the greatest research finding in the past decade is that the brain and all of its neural wiring can be reprogrammed to a specific task. The ability of the brain to form and reorganize synaptic connections is called "neuroplasticity." People who meditate regularly train the brain to stay calm during stressful events. People who engage in repetitive use of computer screens and mobile devices, which involves rapid surfing and data grazing, train their minds to be aroused and vigilant in this particular skill. It's true that some people tend to be more judgmental (left brain) than others. Conversely, some people seem to be more intuitive (right brain) than others. It is interesting to note that the left-brain skills associated with Roger Sperry's research, when used to an extreme, tend to promote more stress-related thought processes (same with the reptilian brain). Right-brain skills are more closely associated with relaxation. No doubt, the complexities of the human brain are certainly complicated, but the answer to all of this brain research is to use your whole brain, not just a part of it.

■ Altered State of Consciousness

When the results of these and other studies by Sperry and his colleagues (1964) were made public, researchers saw strong similarities between the cognitive functions of the right hemisphere and those traits associated with the altered state of consciousness produced by meditation. Studies have since shown that the act of meditation produces a different type of brain wave than that observed in either nonmeditative waking states or sleep (**FIG. 19.7**) (Murphy and Donovan, 1997). In a "normal" state of consciousness, the predominant brain waves emitted are rapid and jagged beta waves (15–20 cycles/second). They appear to signify rapid neural conductivity. Thought processes in our typical waking state are those characteristically observed when the left hemisphere of the brain is performing its specific cognitive functions. In other words, during a normal state of consciousness, the mind leans toward censorship, analysis, judgment,

and rationality. Critics theorize that this normal state of consciousness is rewarded in academic, cultural, and social practices, and that as a result, alternative ways of thinking and processing information are frowned upon. The normal state of consciousness can be quite taxing to the brain: every now and then, for brief periods, we may catch ourselves in an altered pattern of consciousness, most likely daydreaming.

Meditation, on the other hand, tends to produce what is now called an **altered state of consciousness**. Although not advocated, alcohol and/or drugs are known to produce a similar response. An altered state of mind occurs where there is a shift in the thinking style of cognitive processes. Physiologically speaking, in an altered state the brain produces slow (7–10 cycles/second) and almost rhythmical oscillations called alpha waves, which represent a significant decrease in sensory input or a desensitization effect. (Sleep produces delta and some theta waves, with beta waves during rapid-eye-movement periods.) In many ways, an altered state of consciousness closely parallels the functions characteristically observed in the right hemisphere of the brain: The mind is open to suggestion, receptive to new ideas, and able to observe without judgment.

During meditation, some characteristics that also indicate the occurrence of an altered state of consciousness have been noted (Allen, 1983). When these sensations are experienced, then the meditative processes are believed to have induced the desired switch from left- to right-brain dominance. They are as follows:

1. **Time distortion**: Time consciousness is a left-brain function. During meditation, a distortion of time perception may result as dominant thinking shifts from the left to the right hemisphere. The usual response is a sense of time loss in which a 20-minute session appears to have been only a few minutes. The right hemisphere does not recognize the element of time; therefore, it can neither express nor judge the passage of time in the terms the left brain perceives in a normal state of consciousness.

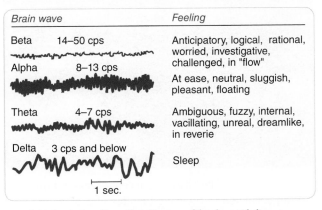

Brain wave		Feeling
Beta	14–50 cps	Anticipatory, logical, rational, worried, investigative, challenged, in "flow"
Alpha	8–13 cps	At ease, neutral, sluggish, pleasant, floating
Theta	4–7 cps	Ambiguous, fuzzy, internal, vacillating, unreal, dreamlike, in reverie
Delta	3 cps and below	Sleep

1 sec.

FIGURE 19.7 Neural patterns of brain activity are shown to be variable during different states of consciousness. Alpha waves are thought to suggest a relaxed yet fully alert consciousness.

> **Altered state of consciousness:** A shift in one's thought process, typically from left-brain to right-brain thinking, to become more aware and more receptive.
>
> **Time distortion:** As an altered state, one's perception of time is changed or distorted so that a segment of time seems either longer or shorter than it actually is.

2. **Ineffability**: Have you ever had an experience that was literally indescribable? One where you just could not find words to adequately describe the experience? Then you've experienced ineffability. The mind's verbal skills are housed in the left hemisphere. The right hemisphere "speaks" in symbols, images, and vivid colors. Many times an experience will occur during meditation that you simply will not be able to put into words. It can be appreciated in sensory (visual) form.

3. **Present-centeredness**: In a normal state of consciousness, the mind is darting at lightning speed among the past, present, and future. The past tends to be the repository for feelings of guilt, while the future harbors a wealth of worries about things that may or may not ever happen. The goal of meditation is to exist in the present moment, to be present and centered in the here and now.

4. **Perception distortion**: If you have ever felt like your arms and legs have sunk into the floor or disappeared altogether while relaxing, then you have experienced perception distortion. It is not that the mind cannot process information during an altered state of consciousness; it is just that information is processed differently by the right hemisphere of the brain. Spatial orientation is a right-brain function. When the right brain is dominant during thinking, perceptions of space

appear distorted when transferred to the left brain. Perception distortions during meditation also include what is called **synesthesia**, or sensory crossover. In synesthesia, sensory stimuli are processed by neurons usually designated for other cognitive functions, thus leading to quite different interpretations. For example, you might be able to *hear* colors and *see* sounds, which is impossible to fully explain in words.

5. **Enhanced receptivity**: In a meditative state, the walls of the ego are temporarily lowered, perhaps even dissolved altogether. When this happens, thoughts from the unconscious mind enter the conscious mind freely. As consciousness expands, the mind becomes more receptive to ideas and thoughts from the unconscious mind that it might not access in a normal state of consciousness. Thus, enlightenment is self-generated. This characteristic of an altered state is similar to hypnotic or subliminal suggestion; however, in meditation, the suggestions come from the inner self.

6. **Self-transcendence**: Meditation really does appear to have a mystical, spiritual quality to it. It is spiritual in the sense that it evokes the ability to experience expanded consciousness or enlightenment that is not manifested in normal consciousness (**FIG. 19.8**). This is the original premise of meditation as taught thousands of years ago to those seeking enlightenment: When the pupil is ready, the teacher will come. Self-transcendence

---

Ineffability: Experiences that cannot be expressed verbally; especially common during meditation.

Present-centeredness: An altered state in which one is fully aware of the present moment with no regard to past or future time periods.

Perception distortion: A sense during meditation (an altered state) in which, for example, one's arms and legs seem extremely heavy.

Synesthesia: A cross-wiring of one's senses (during an altered state) during which one smells sounds or sees noises.

Enhanced receptivity: In the practice of meditation, one's mind opens to become more receptive to ideas that are often censored by the ego during normal consciousness.

Self-transcendence: A sense of becoming one with something bigger than oneself; a mystical experience that occurs in meditation.

FIGURE 19.8 The abstract concept of meditation is often compared to the more tangible idea of water. When the mind is calm, like a pond, stream, or lake, it begins to reflect a bigger picture of deep-seated wisdom.

also consists of the essence of positive thought, inner peace. Inner peace results from the realization of unity or oneness with the universe after censorship and all other barriers are removed. When a state of supraconsciousness is achieved, the lack of ego boundaries is experienced as a connectedness to virtually all things.

Physiological and Psychological Effects of Meditation

As of 2011, more than 1,200 peer-reviewed scientific studies had been conducted and published on the topic of meditation. The vast majority of these studies observe an impressive direct influence of meditation (inclusive, exclusive, and mindfulness) on mood states (Carlson et al., 2004; Shamini, 2007), immune function (Kim et al., 2005), sleep (Bootzin and Stevens, 2005), chronic pain (Morone et al., 2007), and various aspects of mental, emotional, and physical well-being (Rausch et al., 2006). Researchers Tonya Jacobs and Clifford Saron at the University of California-Davis found that resting cortisol levels decreased in 57 subjects who participated in a three-month mindfulness meditation program, with the promise of a follow-up study with more subjects and control subjects as well (Fell, 2013). The current emphasis of research is moving from outcomes toward the actual "why" with further explorations into how meditation can change the way the brain processes information (MRI studies). This section of the chapter looks at some early landmark studies as well as the contemporary focus on brain research. In reviewing the clinical studies regarding the physiological aspects of meditation, one also crosses the paths of yoga, biofeedback, and autogenic training. They all appear to be related. The first account of clinical research to measure mind control of the body occurred in 1935, when a French woman traveled to India with a portable electrocardiogram. Her findings revealed that the yogi masters who were her subjects possessed the incredible ability to decelerate their heart rates. One yogi was observed to have virtually stopped his heart from beating altogether. Therese Brosse's (1946) pioneer research went unremarked for about two decades, perhaps because her findings contradicted all previous thought about autonomic nervous system regulation. In 1957, attempts were made to replicate Brosse's original findings with better equipment. Although no yogi meditators were observed to stop their hearts from beating, Bagchi and Wenger did observe amazing control of the autonomic nervous system

in their subjects. The Swami Ramma's cooperation as a subject in several clinical case studies at the Menninger Institute by Elmer Green and Alyce Green in the early 1970s gave much credence to the earlier studies by Brosse, and Bagchi and Wenger. Once again, mind control was exhibited to decrease heart rate and ventilation, and alter the distribution of blood flow.

With the introduction of TM in the United States, several great claims were made regarding its effectiveness as a technique for mental calmness and relaxation. Among these were the ability to control heart rate, ventilation, and blood flow. When these claims were put under the "scientific microscope" through a battery of investigations designed by Wallace and Benson (1970, 1972), they held up. More recent studies on Benson's relaxation response (Benson, 1989) revealed that meditation acts to reduce the release and responsivity of norepinephrine throughout the central nervous system. From original observations by Wallace and Benson and by Treichel et al. (1973), as well as more recent research by Michael Delmonte (1984, 1985), it now appears that the practice of meditation promotes an immediate decrease in both some physical responses and learned responses. The following physiological changes have been known to occur with regular meditation practice:

1. Decreased oxygen consumption
2. Decreased blood lactate levels
3. Increased skin resistance
4. Decreased heart rate
5. Decreased blood pressure
6. Decreased muscle tension
7. Increased alpha waves

New explorations into the efficacy of meditation have investigated the effects of mindfulness meditation on everything from jet lag to cardiovascular disease. One study looked at how mindfulness meditation affected the quality of life in breast and prostate cancer patients. Findings showed favorable results, including reduced levels of pituitary-adrenal-mediated stress (Carlson et al., 2004). Bootzin and Stevens (2005) found that adolescent substance abusers who practiced mindfulness meditation showed improved sleep function. College students at the Virginia Commonwealth University who were exposed to a single session of meditation (and progressive muscular relaxation) demonstrated a reduction in provoked anxiety levels (Rausch et al., 2006). Whereas mindfulness meditation may be the focus of many recent research studies, Zazen meditation was investigated by researchers in South Korea regarding its effects on several physiological factors associated with coronary heart disease, with favorable results (Kim et al., 2005).

Along with claims that meditation creates mental calmness, its psychological effects were also investigated with great zeal. To no one's surprise, results proved it quite effective in reducing many factors related to perceived stress and improved mental health (Baer, 2003; While, 2010).

In a comprehensive review of the studies investigating the psychological effects of meditation, Delmonte concluded that, above all else, its practice did promote a greater sense of general well-being or inner peace. As a result of these and similar findings, the technique of meditation has been integrated into the practice of psychotherapy as a major tool to promote psychological well-being.

In the most extensive review on the physical and psychological effects of meditation, Michael Murphy and Steven Donovan (1997) conclude that meditation, in all its many methods, unequivocally produces beneficial changes to both mind and body.

Neuroplasticity: The Neuroscience of Meditation

It is well accepted that the practice of meditation can promote relaxation, but can meditation actually change the neurobiology of the brain? The answer appears to be yes. When clinical research first began on the biological promise of meditation (e.g., in regulating heart rate, blood pressure, and muscle tension), the focus was on Transcendental Meditation because of the specific methodology used in this relaxation practice. A conversation between the Dalai Lama and neuroscientist Richard Davidson regarding the neurophysiology of mindfulness meditation formed a new direction of research in this area: the effects of mindfulness meditation on brain physiology. The results have shattered previous "facts" about brain science.

Previously, it was commonly accepted that with the onset of adulthood, the neural wiring of the brain remained unchanged. Clinical studies with Tibetan monks with this form of mental training have proved otherwise. Over the past decade, the use of functional magnetic resonance imaging (fMRI) has revealed a new perspective on brain physiology and the neuroscience of meditation (Davidson et al., 2003; Horrigan, 2005; Rubia, 2009), much of

this shared by the Dalai Lama himself at the Society for Neuroscience's annual meeting in 2006. Some of the findings are as follows:

- Longtime meditators who meditate on the theme of loving kindness and compassion produce a significant level (30 times stronger) of gamma brain wave activity. (This is normally so low, it cannot be detected with non-meditators.)

- There is increased activity in the left prefrontal and limbic regions of the brain with meditation, reflecting processes of sustained attention and emotion regulation (Rubia, 2009).

- Even a short program in mindfulness meditation produces measurable effects on brain physiology and the immune system.

- Portions of the brain used in meditation practice grow in size and undergo neural rewiring, now known as neuroplasticity.

- Portions of the brain associated with compassion increased in size, leading researchers to wonder whether meditation could affect the brain physiology of depression.

Meditation and Brain Imaging Research

With the advent of magnetic resonance imaging, in which the brain can be observed as it undergoes a variety of thought processes, researchers have taken a keen interest in seeing how meditation affects different parts and layers of the brain tissue (Stein, 2003). Herbert Benson and colleagues (Lazar et al., 2000) have observed that blood flow decreases to the limbic system, an area associated with stress-based emotions. Research by Richard Davidson, at the University of Wisconsin–Madison, using Tibetan monks, revealed that meditation appears to reorient the brain from a mode of stress to a sense of acceptance and contentment (Land, 2003). It appears that regular meditation causes neurons to adapt to less sensory information by activating frontal lobe brain tissue that is responsible for present-moment awareness. Newberg (2003) concludes from his research involving Tibetan monks and Franciscan nuns that, indeed, portions of the brain responsible for time and space awareness are rewired to be more receptive and less judgmental, while the hippocampus decreases neural input, thereby softening the boundaries of the self and increasing the sense of oneness. Newberg and others conducting similar research have coined the term **neurotheology** to describe the brain's circuitry for spiritual consciousness and mystical experiences. In the book *Why God Won't Go Away*, Newberg et al. suggest that the brain can be trained to decrease stressful stimuli, in essence being rewired for cerebral homeostasis. This neural reprocessing for inner peace is available to anyone who meditates.

Meditation and Chronic Pain

Many people recognize the name of Jon Kabat-Zinn as the country's greatest proponent of mindfulness meditation, but many do not know that his career in this field began by focusing on the response to pain relief through meditation (Kabat-Zinn, 1982; Kabat-Zinn et al., 1987). Through this work, Kabat-Zinn found substantial evidence for nonmedical pain relief through the Zen practice of mindfulness meditation. Since then, others have replicated his findings, most recently Morone and colleagues (2007). Although pain may seem like a physical phenomenon, the mind-body-spirit paradigm suggests that by involving the mind and spirit with pain relief, the cause of the problem as well as the symptoms (pain) may be lessened, if not eradicated altogether. Whereas Kabat-Zinn's method of mindfulness utilizes association (getting in touch and comfortable with the pain), others advocate the use of meditation (exclusive) to dissociate from pain as a means of temporary relief.

Steps to Initiate Meditation

As pointed out by Benson, the elements of meditation are quite simple. All you need is a quiet space, a comfortable position, a receptive attitude, and a mental device or "meditative broom" to sweep clean the corners of your mind. One component that Benson neglected to emphasize, however, was practice on a regular basis. Meditation is a state of mind, but to be effective it requires the habitual practice of employing concentration. Concentration, like so many other behaviors, is a skill. The more you practice this skill, the better it will serve you.

The following are two meditation practices I use when teaching this technique. The first is an example of exclusive meditation, which was passed on to me by a yogi master. The second is based on the concept of inclusive meditation. Read each exercise first to familiarize yourself with the technique. Then, give it a try. Start with a short duration of time (5 minutes), and with each session, add a few minutes until you build up to about 30 minutes.

(It may take a few weeks to feel comfortable with this length of time.)

Grand Perspective Mental Video

The grand perspective mental video is an example of inclusive meditation. In this exercise, you invite any and all thoughts to freely enter your conscious mind. During this exercise, try not to attach any emotional responses to the images that appear on your mind's screen. See the images, but detach yourself emotionally from them. Should you find that you sense some emotional attachment, simply allow that thought to fade and invite a new thought in. This exercise is often compared to free association, and you may find your mind wandering down a trail of thoughts that all seem connected; this is fine. Try this exercise for a 3- to 5-minute period. Each time you return to this exercise, add on a few more minutes. If one issue keeps appearing on the mind's screen and you find yourself unable to be objective about it, this may be an advisory to deal with it as soon as possible. You may elect to do this exercise with some soft instrumental background music; sometimes it can help.

1.   Sit or lie comfortably, keeping your back completely straight. Take a deep breath and relax.

2.   Close your eyes. Imagine that your mind's eye sees all the mind's thoughts projected onto the mind's screen. The movies that play on your mind's silver screen are produced and directed by you, but now your primary role is that of an observer or audience member.

3.   Separate yourself from directing your thoughts. Just let them roll, unedited and uncensored. Take a back seat in the mind's theater to get a grand perspective on these images. To do this effectively, look at whatever thoughts come onto your mind's screen objectively, without emotional attachment, ownership, or analysis. This may seem rather hard to do at first, but with time it will become easy. Just sit back in the audience and enjoy the show.

Mindfulness

Meditation does not have to be done in the confinement of your room. The underlying premise of meditation is to

> **Neurotheology:** A name coined to describe how the brain is hardwired to perceive metaphysical or mystical experiences of a divine nature.

BOX 19.3   Meditation and ADD

It's no secret that attention deficit disorder (ADD) has become a national epidemic in America. The inability to focus one's attention on anything for a specific period of time has become a societal norm. There are many reasons for this, ranging from poor diet (lack of omega-3's and an abundance of aspartame) to the oscillation of repeated television broadcast signals (not to mention commercial camera shots and angles). Add to this the obsession with texts, email, and instant messaging, and it's a wonder anybody gets anything done at all with the proliferation of technological distractions. Despite the push for medications, we can safely assume that people do not have a Ritalin deficiency.

Zen masters laugh at the notion of ADD. Not because it's funny, but because they are of the opinion that *everybody* with an ego has some degree of ADD. They are of the opinion that meditation is the means to train the mind to focus. More specifically, meditation is the way to domesticate the ego from wandering all over the conscious map. Meditation is the age-old tool of consciousness to increase attention and sharpen one's focus.

Many people claim that because they have been diagnosed with ADD, they cannot (and perhaps never will be able to) meditate. Nothing could be further from the truth! Although it may be difficult at first (and to be honest, initially it is hard for everyone to learn to meditate), stay with it. It will get easier. It would be a good idea to learn to minimize distractions such as cell phone use and to eat healthier, too!

FIGURE 19.9   The practice of meditation can be done anywhere, but a quiet, peaceful place is best. Sometimes the repeated sounds of nature, such as a waterfall, help to cleanse the mind of ego-based thoughts to provide clarity of one's life and purpose.

enjoy the present moment. And to paraphrase Buddhist Thich Nhat Hanh, meditation can be done anywhere (**FIG. 19.9**). This is what Eckhart Tolle means by the power of now. Mindfulness meditation means to be conscious of the present moment in all that you do, to fill your body's senses with what you are experiencing at the present moment. For example, mindfulness can be done while walking, by feeling your body's weight shift as you place each foot in front of you, and feeling every other movement of your body. Mindfulness can be done while washing dishes, by becoming aware of the feeling of the water and soap on your hands. The following exercise asks that you try to increase your awareness and concentration by eating an apple.

1. Pick an apple and hold it in your hand.

2. Sit comfortably, with your back straight. (You may choose to sit against a wall for support.)

3. Feel the weight of the apple in your hand. Feel the texture of the apple's skin. Feel the curves. Feel the stem (if there is one). Notice all the nuances of the apple with your fingers.

4. Look at the apple. What color is it? Look at it carefully. Study it. Know this apple so well that if it were put back into a barrel of apples, you could find it.

5. Now smell the apple. Close your eyes and focus your sense of smell on the apple. What does it smell like?

6. Bite into the apple. Savor its taste, both flavor and texture. Feel your tongue and jaws move as you chew. Feel your breathing pause as you swallow. Make each bite of the apple seem like the first.

7. Take note of any other observations about this experience.

Best Application of Meditation

It has been said that in our contemporary age of sensory fulfillment, seldom if ever are we in the presence of silence for any length of time. Between the sounds made by televisions, dishwashers, radios, cell phones, refrigerators, and personal computers—not to mention air and street traffic—there is hardly an uninterrupted moment of mental calmness. As a result, the human mind becomes supersaturated with sensory stimulation. To keep one's sanity, one's mind has to unload these thoughts or it will suffer the consequences. The typical consequence for many people is heightened physical arousal, which leads to deciphering these sensory stimulations as potential threats (stress). The mind craves homeostasis just as the body does. Given the cacophony of sensory bombardment found in nearly all corners of the global village, taking time to quiet the mind is no longer a luxury but a necessity to maintain a sense of mental equilibrium.

Back in the days when yoga meditation was first taught, it was practiced in the early morning, between 4 and 6 A.M., because this was the time best suited to expanded awareness. Three thousand years later, early morning is still advocated as the best time to meditate. But time of day is not as important as length of time, which should be about 20 to 30 minutes per day. If you can only sit quietly for 5 minutes a day and focus on your breathing, that is a great start. In any case, meditation necessitates a designated time period in your schedule—whatever fits into your daily routine. It is also helpful to specify a special place to meditate, any corner that you want to designate for this purpose.

However and whenever you do it, the bottom line is that we all need times of solitude to cleanse the cluttered mess from the mind. Unequivocally, meditation can be classified as a technique to help prevent the heightened, sustained arousal of stress. Rare would be the opportunity, however, to employ quality meditative skills in the face of stress, particularly during spontaneous moments of anger. It might be best used as a technique to quell the fires of fear. With practice, you will find that meditation has many layers and can create many profound effects of relaxation.

SUMMARY

- Meditation is thought to be the oldest form of relaxation. In simple terms, it is a mind-cleansing or emptying process. At a deeper level, meditation is focused concentration and increased awareness of one's being. When the mind has been emptied of conscious thought, unconscious thoughts can enter the conscious realm to bring enlightenment to our lives.

- Basically, there are two methods of mind cleansing: to exclude all thoughts from the mind save the one that is used to clear the rest out, and to include all thoughts but detach oneself emotionally from these images. Transcendental Meditation and Zen meditation are examples of exclusive and inclusive meditation, respectively.

- Benson Americanized Transcendental Meditation, calling it the relaxation response. He found that all one needs to relax are four components: a quiet environment, a mental device for concentration, a passive attitude, and a comfortable position in which to meditate.

- The practice of meditation can lead to an altered state of consciousness, where sensory perceptions are different from those in a normal waking state of consciousness. Perceptual changes include time distortion, ineffability, present-centeredness, perception distortion, enhanced receptivity, and self-transcendence.

- These changes in perception and information processing mirror those observed by Sperry, who found that when surgically separated, the left and right hemispheres of the brain demonstrate unique and separate cognitive functions, similar to those cited under normal and altered states of consciousness, respectively.

- Research also shows that habitual meditation has extensive physiological effects on the body, among which are decreased resting heart rate, decreased resting blood pressure, and decreased resting ventilation, suggesting that there is a connection between mind and body that can profoundly influence homeostasis.

- Brain imaging studies reveal that meditation appears to rewire the brain's neurons, thereby creating the perception of inner peace.

- Research studies reveal that regular meditation practice creates neuroplasticity (i.e., new growth and a rewiring of brain tissue) that promotes a deeper sense of mental well-being.

- Mindfulness meditation is known to decrease episodes of chronic pain.

- Meditation is now recommended by the American Heart Association as a means to reduce stress levels, which are thought to be a risk factor for heart disease.

- Every relaxation technique involves some aspect of meditation.

STUDY GUIDE QUESTIONS

1. Explain the difference between inclusive and exclusive meditation, and give an example of each.

2. Herbert Benson Americanized TM and called it the relaxation response. Describe his method of meditation.

3. How does the practice of meditation affect the brain?

4. What is an altered state of consciousness?

5. What effects does meditation have on the mind and the body?

6. What is neuroplasticity? How does meditation affect it?

REFERENCES AND RESOURCES

Alexander, C., et al. Transcendental Meditation, Mindfulness, and Longevity: An Experimental Study with the Elderly, *Journal of Personality and Social Psychology* 57(6):950–964, 1989.

Allen, R. J. *Human Stress: Its Nature and Control.* Burgess, Minneapolis, MN, 1983.

Anand, B. K., China, G. S., and Singh, B. Some Aspects of Electroencephalographic Studies in Yogis, *Electroencephalographology and Clinical Neurophysiology* 13:452–456, 1961.

Atwood, J. D., and Maltin, L. Putting Eastern Philosophies into Western Psychotherapies, *American Journal of Psychotherapy* 45(3):368–382, 1991.

Austin, J. Stress Reduction through Mindfulness Meditation, *Psychotherapy Psychosomatics* 66:97–106, 1997.

Austin, J. Zen and the Brain: Toward an Understanding of Meditation and Consciousness, *Philosophy East and West* 50(3):464, 2000.

Baer, R. A. Mindfulness Training as a Clinical Intervention, *Clinical Psychology: Science and Practice* 10(2):125–143, 2003.

Bagchi, B. K., and Wenger, M. A. Electrophysiological Correlates of Some Yoga Exercises, *Electroencephalography, Clinical Neurophysiology, and Epilepsy* 3: International Congress of Neurological Sciences, 1959.

Baruss, I., and Mossbridge, J. *Transcendent Mind: Rethinking the Science of Consciousness*. American Psychological Association, Washington, D.C., 2016.

Begley, S. Religion and the Brain, *Time*, May 7, 2001:50–58.

Benson, H. *Beyond the Relaxation Response*. Berkeley Publications, Berkeley, CA, 1994.

Benson, H. The Relaxation Response, *Psychiatry* 37:37–46, 1974.

Benson, H. *The Relaxation Response*. Morrow Press, New York, 1975.

Benson, H. The Relaxation Response and Norepinephrine: A New Study Illuminates Mechanisms, *Australian Journal of Clinical Hypnotherapy and Hypnosis* 10(2):91–96, 1989.

Benson, H. *Timeless Healing*. Morrow Press, New York, 1996.

Bernardi, L., et al. Effect of Rosary Prayer and Yoga Mantras on Autonomic Cardiovascular Rhythm: Comparative Study, *British Medical Journal* 323:1446–1449, 2001.

Bootzin, R., and Stevens, S. J. Adolescents, Substance Abuse, and the Treatment of Insomnia and Daytime Sleepiness, *Clinical Psychology Review* 25:5,629–644, 2005.

Borysenko, J. *Minding the Body, Mending the Mind*. Bantam Books, New York, 1987.

Brosse, T. A. Psychophysiological Study of Yoga, *Main Currents in Modern Thought* 4:77–84, 1946.

Carlson, L. E., Speca, M., Patel, K. D., and Goodey, E. Mindfulness-Based Stress Reduction in Relation to Quality of Life, Mood, Symptoms of Stress and Levels of Cortisol, Dehydroepiandrosterone Sulfate (DHEAS) and Melatonin in Breast and Prostate Cancer Outpatients, *Psychoneuroendocrinology* 29(4):448–474, 2004.

Carroll, D., and Seers, K. Relaxation for the Relief of Chronic Pain: A Systematic Review, *Journal of Advanced Nursing* 27:476–487, 1996.

Castillo, R. J. Depersonalization and Meditation, *Psychiatry* 53(2):158–168, 1990.

Cauthen, N. R., and Prymak, C. A. Meditation versus Relaxation: An Examination of the Physiological Effects of Transcendental Meditation, *Journal of Consulting and Clinical Psychology* 45:496–497, 1977.

Chalmers, D. The Puzzle of Conscious Experience, *Scientific American*, December 1995:80–86.

Davidson, R., Kabat-Zinn, J., Schumacher, J., et al. Alterations in Brain and Immune Function Produced by Mindfulness Meditation, *Psychosomatic Medicine* 65:564–570, 2003.

Delmonte, M. An Overview of the Therapeutic Effects of Meditation, *Psychologia: An International Journal of Psychology in the Orient* 28(4):189–202, 1985.

Delmonte, M. Physiological Responses during Meditation and Rest, *Biofeedback and Self-Regulation* 9(2):181–200, 1984.

Der Hovanesian, M. Zen and the Art of Corporate Productivity, *Business Week*, July 22, 2003:56.

Dumoulin, H. *Zen Enlightenment*. Weatherhill, New York, 1981.

Elson, B. D., Hauri, P., and Cunis, D. Physiological Changes in Yogi Meditation, *Psychophysiology* 14:52–57, 1977.

Everly, G. *A Clinical Guide to the Treatment of the Human Stress Response*. Plenum, New York, 2002.

Everly, G. S., and Rosenfeld, R. *The Nature and Treatment of the Stress Response: A Practical Guide for Clinicians*. Plenum Press, New York, 2002.

Fell, A. *Mindfulness from Meditation Associated with Lower Stress Hormone*. UC Davis News and Information. March 27, 2013.

Ferguson, P., and Gowan, J. TM—Some Preliminary Findings, *Journal of Humanistic Psychology* 16:51–60, 1977.

Fosshage, J. *Healing Implications for Psychotherapy*. Human Sciences Press, New York, 1978.

Gazzaniga, M. S. One Brain, Two Minds? *American Science* 60(3):311–317, 1972.

Gazzaniga, M. S. The Split Brain in Man, *Scientific American* 508:24–29, 1967.

Geirland, J. Buddha and the Brain, *Wired*, February 2006.

Gibran, K. *The Prophet*. Knopf, New York, 1981.

Goldberg, B. Slowing Down the Aging Process through the Use of Altered States of Consciousness: A Review of the Medical Literature, *Psychology, a Journal of Human Behavior* 32(2):19–21, 1995.

Goleman, D. J., and Schwartz, G. E. Meditation as an Intervention in Stress Reactivity, *Journal of Consulting and Clinical Psychology* 44:456–466, 1976.

Green, E., and Green, A. *Beyond Biofeedback*. Knoll, Topeka, KS, 1977.

Grossman, P. et. al., Mindfulness-Based Stress Reduction and Health Benefits; A Meta-analysis. Journal of Psychosomatic Research 57 (1) 35-43, 2004. http://www.sciencedirect.com/science/article/pii/S0022399903005737

Hagelin, J. Beyond Miracles—The Discovery of the Unified Field in Its Practical Applications to Prevent Crime, Terrorism and International Conflict, 17th Annual ISSSEEM Conference Keynote Address, June 22, 2007. www.istpp.org/crime_prevention/.

Holistic-Online.com. *Health Conditions That Are Bene-fited by Meditation*. http://1stholistic.com/Meditation/hol_ meditation_ benefits_health_conditions.htm.

Holistic-Online.com. *Meditation May Reduce Hardening of Arteries Without Medications*. www.yogasite.com/stroke.htm.

Horrigan, B. Meditation and Neuroplasticity: Training Your Brain, *Explore* 1(5):380–388, 2005.

Jaret, P. You Don't Have to Sweat to Reduce Your Stress, *Health*, November/December, 1995:82–88.

Johnston, W. *Silent Music: The Science of Meditation*. Harper & Row, New York, 1974.

Kabat-Zinn, J. *Full Catastrophe Living*. Delta Books, New York, 1990.

Kabat-Zinn, J. An Outpatient Program in Behavioral Medicine for Chronic Pain Patients Based on the Practice of Mindfulness Meditation, *General Hospital Psychiatry* 4:33–37, 1982.

Kabat-Zinn, J. *Wherever You Go, There You Are: Mindfulness Living in Everyday Life*. Hyperion Books, New York, 1994.

Kabat-Zinn, J., Lipworth, L., Burnery, R., and Sellers, W. Four Year Follow-up of a Meditation Based Program for the Self-Regulation of Chronic Pain, *Clinical Journal of Pain* 2:159–173, 1987.

Kabat-Zinn, J., Mindfulness For Beginners. Sounds True. Boulder, CO, 2011.

Kaplan, K., Goldenberg, D., and Galvin-Nadeau, M. The Impact of a Meditation-Based Stress Reduction Program on Fibromyalgia, *General Hospital Psychiatry* 15:284–289, 1993.

Kapleau, P. (ed.). *The Three Pillars of Zen*. Doubleday, New York, 1980.

Keys, K. *The Hundredth Monkey*. Visih Books, Coos Bay, OR, 1987.

Kim, D., et al. Effect of Zen Meditation on Serum Nitric Oxide Activity and Lipid Peroxidation, *Progress in Neuro-Psychopharmacology and Biological Psychiatry* 29(2):327–331, 2005.

King, M., and D'Cruz, C. Transcendental Meditation, Hypertension and Heart Disease, *Australian Family Physician* 31(2):164–166, 2002.

Kornfield, J. *Buddhist Meditation and Consciousness Research*. Institute of Noetic Sciences, Sausalito, CA, 1990.

Kuna, D. J. Meditation and Work, *Vocational Guidance Quarterly* 23:342–346, 1975.

Land, D. *The Dalai Lama and Scientists Unite to Study Meditation*. August 8, 2003. www.news.wisc.edu/view.html?get=6205.

Larkin, M. Meditation May Reduce Heart Attack and Stroke Risk, *Lancet* 355:206, 812, 2000.

Lazar, S., et al. Functional Brain Mapping of the Relaxation Response and Meditation. *Neuro Report*. Lippincott Williams & Wilkins, Philadelphia, 2000.

Levey, J., and Levey, M. *The Fine Arts of Relaxation, Concentration, and Meditation*. Wisdom Books, Boston, MA, 1991.

Levey, J., and Levey, M. *Simple Meditation & Relaxation*. Conari Press, Berkeley, CA, 1999.

Maas, J. *Power Sleep*. Quill Books, New York, 2001.

Meditation Really Does Reduce Stress. *New Scientist* 196(2625): 21, 2007.

Merzel, G. *The Eye Never Sleeps*. Shambhala, London, 1991.

Mipham, S. *Turning the Mind into an Ally*. Riverhead Books, New York, 2003.

Morone, N., Greco, C., and Weiner, D. Mindfulness Meditation for the Treatment of Chronic Low Back Pain in Older Adults: A Randomized Controlled Pilot Study, *Pain*, June 2007. www.sciencedirect.com.

Motoyama, H. *Toward a Superconsciousness: Meditation Theory and Practice*. Asian Humanities Press, Berkeley, CA, 1990.

Murphy, M., and Donovan, S. *The Physical and Psychological Effects on Meditation: A Review of Contemporary Research with a Comprehensive Bibliography*. Institute of Noetic Sciences, Sausalito, CA, 1997.

Naranjo, C., and Ornstein, R. E. *On the Psychology of Meditation*. Esalen Books, New York, 1971.

Newberg, A., D'Aquili, E., and Rause, V. *Why God Won't Go Away*. Ballantine Books, New York, 2002.

Newberg, A., and Iversen, J. The Neural Basis of the Complex Mental Task of Meditation: Neurotransmitters and Neurochemical Considerations, *Medical Hypotheses* 61(2):282–291, 2003.

Ornish, D. *Dr. Dean Ornish's Program for Reversing Coronary Heart Disease without Drugs or Surgery*. Ballantine Books, New York, 1992.

Ornish, D. *Love and Survival*. Harper Collins, New York, 1998.

Ornish, D., et al. Inexpensive Lifestyle Changes for Reversal of Coronary Heart Disease, *Journal of the American Medical Association* 280(3):2001–2007, 1998.

Ornstein, R. *The Psychology of Consciousness*. Penguin Books, New York, 1972.

Pagano, R. R., et al. Sleep during Transcendental Meditation, *Science* 191:308–309, 1976.

Parsons, L. M., and Osherson, D. New Evidence for Distinct Right and Left Brain Systems for Deductive versus Probabilistic Reasoning, *Cerebral Cortex* 11(10):954–965, 2001.

Pritz, A. *Pocket Guide to Meditation*. Crossing Press, Freedom, CA, 1997.

Rausch, S. M., Gramling, S. E., and Auerbach, S. M. Effects of a Single Session of Large-Group Meditation and Progressive Muscle Relaxation Training on Stress Reduction, Reactivity, and Recovery, *International Journal of Stress Management* 13(3):273–290, 2006.

Ricard, M., Lutz, A., and Davidson, R. Mind of the Meditator. *Scientific American* 311:39–45, 2014.

Roth, B., and Stanley, T. Mindfulness-Based Stress Reduction and Healthcare Utilization in the Inner City: Preliminary Findings, *Alternative Therapies* 8(1):60–67, 2002.

Rubia, K. The Neurobiology of Meditation and Its Clinical Effectiveness in Psychiatric Disorders, *Biological Psychology* 82(1):1–11, 2009.

Russell, P. *The TM Technique*. Elf Rock Productions, Las Vegas, 2001.

Schaef, A. W. *Codependence: Misunderstood, Mistreated*. Harper, New York, 1986.

Seaward, B. L. *A Change of Heart: Meditations and Visualizations* (audio CD). Inspiration Unlimited, Boulder, CO, 2002.

Seaward, B. L. *Sweet Surrender: Meditations and Visualizations* (audio CD). Inspiration Unlimited, Boulder, CO, 2002.

Seaward, B. L. *A Wing and a Prayer: Meditations and Visualizations* (audio CD). Inspiration Unlimited, Boulder, CO, 2004.

Shaffi, M. Adaptive and Therapeutic Aspects of Meditation, *International Journal of Psychoanalytic Psychotherapy* 2:364–382, 1973.

Shamini, J. A Randomized Controlled Trial of Mindfulness Meditation versus Relaxation Training: Effects on Distress, Positive States of Mind, Rumination, and Distraction, *Annals of Behavioral Medicine* 33(1):11–21, 2007.

Shapiro, D. H., and Zifferblatt, S. M. Zen Meditation and Behavioral Self-Control: Similarities, Differences, and Clinical Applications, *American Psychologist* 31:519–532, 1976.

Sheldrake, R. *A New Science of Life*. Inner Traditions, Rochester, VT, 1995.

Silva, J., and Miele, P. *The Silva Mind-Control Method*. Pocket Books, New York, 1975.

Sperry, R. The Great Cerebral Commissure, *Scientific American* 174:44–52, 1964.

Stahl, B., and Goldstein, E. A Mindfulness-Based Stress Reduction Workbook. New Harbinger Publications, Oakland, CA, 2010. http://www.sciencedaily.com/releases/2012/03/120314170647.htm.

Stein, J. Just Say OM, *Time* 162(5):48–56, 2003.

Stek, R. J., and Bass, B. A. Personal Adjustment and Perceived Locus of Control among Students Interested in Meditation, *Psychological Reports* 32:1019–1022, 1973.

Sudsuang, R., et al. Effect of Buddhist Meditation on Serum Cortisol and Total Protein Levels, Blood Pressure, Pulse Rate, Lung Volume, and Reaction Time, *Physiology and Behavior* 50(3):543–548, 1991.

Sun, T., Kuo, C., and Chiu, J. Mindfulness Meditation in the Control of Severe Headache, *Chang Gung Medical Journal* 25:538–541, 2002.

Tolle, E. *The Power of Now*. New World Publishing, Novato, CA, 1999.

Treichel, M., Clinch, N., and Cran, M. The Metabolic Effects of Transcendental Meditation, *Physiologist* 16:472, 1973.

Wallace, R. K. Physiological Effects of Transcendental Meditation, *Science* 167:1751–1754, 1970.

Wallace, R. K., and Benson, H. The Physiology of Meditation, *Scientific American* 226:85–90, 1972.

While, A. Mindfulness: Me-Time Counts, *British Journal of Community Nurses* 11:570, 2010.

Winchester, E. Pentagon Meditation Club, 2007. www.pentagonmeditationclub.org.

Woo, E. Yogi, Maharishi Mahesh. Founded Transcendental Meditation Movement, *Los Angeles Times*, February 6, 2008. www.latimes.com/news/nationworld/world/la-me-maharishi6feb06,1,6839087.story.

Yogi, M. M. *Science of Being and Art of Living: Transcendental Meditation*. Plume Publishing, New York, 2001.

Zaichkowsky, L. D., and Kamen, R. Biofeedback and Meditation: Effects on Muscle Tension and Locus of Control, *Perceptual and Motor Skills* 46:955–958, 1978.

CHAPTER 20

Hatha Yoga

Yoga is the martial art of the soul, and the opponent is the strongest you've ever faced: Your ego.

—Anonymous

In the past twenty years, hatha yoga has gone from an esoteric activity people did in the privacy of their own homes to a mainstream activity—it has become fodder for late night television jokes and parody YouTube video clips. The good news is that today hatha yoga is mainstream. The bad news is that it has gone corporate, far removed from the egoless activity it started as millennia ago. Welcome to American hatha yoga, where people brag about everything from how hot the yoga studio is during a session to correctly pronouncing the sutras or attending Yoga Bootcamp. Today it is quite common to see photos of U.S. Army soldiers on yoga mats doing downward dog stretch, or corporate executives including hatha yoga as part of their wellness retreats. Reduced to its simplest terms, hatha yoga is a metaphor for balance: a series of physical movements that promote a sense of inner peace and tranquility. At its purest form, hatha yoga is about removing the ego from this experience in an effort to achieve inner peace. Ironically, most yoga classes in America today miss the mark. Trendy yoga instructors, posh yoga studios,

Yoga: A Sanskrit word that means union, specifically the union of mind, body, and spirit.

Hatha yoga: One of five yogic paths; the path of physical balance.

expensive yoga mats, spandex yoga apparel, exclusive yoga club memberships, and high-end yoga vacations are the antithesis of this non-ego activity.

The word **yoga** comes from ancient Sanskrit. It is translated to mean "union"—specifically, the ultimate union of the mind, body, and soul. The development and practice of yoga are deeply rooted in the philosophy of spiritual enlightenment. As the practice of this technique migrated to the Western hemisphere, particularly the United States, many traditional yoga positions were assimilated into American culture. They were adopted as flexibility exercises and used both prior to and following the completion of physical activity. Currently, the *shavasana*, or Corpse Pose, is employed in many relaxation techniques, including progressive muscular relaxation and autogenic training. But many other aspects of yoga, including breathing, and the symbolism and philosophy associated with the classic positions, were abandoned. Lately, however, as Americans have acquired a thirst for additional relaxation techniques, the original concepts of yoga have not only reemerged, but also become extremely popular around the country, if not the world. They form a simple yet profound technique to promote relaxation, and to unify mind, body, and spirit (Krafsow, 1999).

There are many yoga styles, and the practice of yoga can create many levels of inner peace. The **hatha yoga** style places special emphasis on physical postures, which are integrated with ***pranayama***, or breathing control. The word *hatha* comes from two Sanskrit words, *ha*, meaning "sun," and *tha*, meaning "moon." The symbolic meaning of these words is the balance of universal life forces (Iyengar, 1981; Rosen, 2002). The more concrete meaning is the balance of mind, body, and spirit through action, emotion, and intelligence. The following is a brief introduction to several hatha yoga concepts and postures. To learn hatha yoga, you must experience it. This chapter serves only as an invitation to pursue this technique under qualified instruction.

Historical Perspective

Scholars have traced the roots of yoga as far back as the sixth century B.C., to the teachings of the Hindu philosopher Kapila. These, along with teachings attributed to the Hindu deity Krishna, laid the foundation of several concepts to promote the enhancement of life through the union of mind, body, and spirit. While ancient scriptures cite Lord Shiva, or Supreme Consciousness, as the founder of yoga, credit for its earliest postures (*raja* yoga) is given to Patanjali, who codified these *asanas* (physical postures) in a written collection called the ***Yoga Sutras*** (Allen, 1983). Patanjali is also credited with creating the whole system of raja yoga, including raja meditation, *pranayama*, and the principles for living. Originally, *asanas* were created to cleanse the body, unlock energy paths, and raise level of consciousness. Through the ages, many variations or paths have emerged, each with its own interpretation of the path to enlightenment. The renowned yogi master Swami Rama cites five yoga paths: ***karma* yoga**, the path of action; ***bhakti* yoga**, the path of devotion; ***jnana* yoga**, the path of knowledge; ***kundalini* yoga**, the path of spiritual awakening, an advanced form of meditation; and perhaps the most common style practiced in the United States, hatha yoga, the path of physical balance. Several yoga styles include a strong component of meditation to enhance the union of mind, body, and soul, and it is not uncommon for many people to use the terms *yoga* and *meditation* synonymously (Allen, 1983).

The premise of this mind-body-spirit union, as suggested by its earliest proponents, is that humanity's most salient nature is of a divine quality. The abyss that separates the corporeal and incorporeal is the wall of conscious intellect, or ego censorship. As described in the earliest teachings, divine enlightenment is made possible when this wall is dissolved through the realization of the self, transcending the limitations of consciousness. The remnants of the dissolved wall are then constructed as a bridge to greater understanding or enlightenment.

Yoga was first formally introduced into the United States when Swami Vivekananda made a presentation to the World Parliament of Religions in Chicago in 1893. His visit to America lasted well over 2 years as he traveled to several cities around the country. By the turn of the century, two *ashrams* (yoga centers) were established in California, with many more to follow throughout the nation. In 1970, Swami Rama, a yogi master from the Himalayan Institute, was invited to the Menninger Foundation in Topeka, Kansas. There, he collaborated in several clinical investigations into yoga and physiological adaptations to meditation as measured with various biofeedback modalities. It was observed that Swami Rama demonstrated nearly incredible control over several autonomic functions (e.g., respiration, heart rate, and blood flow), indicating to clinical researchers that many of the bodily functions previously thought involuntary could in fact be controlled, in a relaxed state, by conscious thought. In what can best be described as a grassroots movement, yoga has slowly become accepted in America as a proven means to relax (Swami Rama, 1979) (**FIG. 20.1**).

It is raja yoga, or the "royal path," that most closely resembles the practice of restrictive meditation, wherein the body must be relaxed to open the mind. Hatha yoga, by contrast, integrates components of muscular strength, endurance, flexibility, and muscle relaxation, as well as serving as a catalyst for meditation. According to a 2008 marketing study conducted by the *Yoga Journal* titled "Yoga in America," approximately 15.8 million Americans practice yoga. The study indicated that maintaining or improving one's health status was

---

Pranayama: A yogic term describing the concept of breath control during each of the *asanas* (yoga postures).

Yoga Sutras: The ancient yogic text attributed to Patanjali, who described each of the yoga *asanas*.

***Karma* yoga:** One of five yogic paths; the path of action.

***Bhakti* yoga:** One of five yogic paths; the path of devotion.

***Jnana* yoga:** One of five yogic paths; the path of knowledge.

***Kundalini* yoga:** One of five yogic paths; the path of spiritual awakening.

FIGURE 20.1

the primary reason for engaging in this habitual practice. "Yoga is no longer a singular pursuit but a lifestyle choice and an established part of our health and cultural landscape," said Bill Harper, publisher of *Yoga Journal* (Macy, 2008).

Physiological and Psychological Benefits

Since the start of the twenty-first century, yoga (primarily hatha yoga) has been studied extensively as a means to improve one's overall health status, suggesting that age-old claims of improved vitality are indeed quite valid (Oken et al., 2006). Proponents assert that the repeated daily series of selected *asanas* promotes longevity and facilitates homeostasis of mind, body, and spirit. Researchers have focused on the more measurable physiological outcomes. Hatha yoga certainly is proven to decrease stress levels (Smith et al., 2007). Claims regarding increased muscle strength and flexibility have been substantiated, and reports about increased aerobic capacity appear positive (Ray et al., 2001; Tran et al., 2001). Hatha yoga is now recognized as a suitable complementary healing modality for many chronic health-related issues as well as a

multimodal approach to stress management. Here is a look at some of the most recent research.

One of the upshots of the proliferation of hatha yoga as a relaxation technique are the number of studies to show its efficacy to promote health and well-being. A Norwegian study that looked at ten participants who engaged in a hatha yoga retreat found that in as little as a four-hour yoga session there was a positively changed expression of 111 genes related to the body's immune function. In contrast, music and walking-based meditation were less than half as effective. The data suggest that yoga affects the body at the molecular level and may provide long-lasting health benefits. Kiecolt-Glaser (2010) also found that the practice of hatha yoga decreased stress levels and induced a positive endocrine/immune response, suggesting that regular yoga practice contributes to substantial health benefits. Hatha yoga is not only good for the body, but also good for the mind. An article published by the American Occupational Therapy Association (2012) showed that the practice of yoga proved extremely valuable in helping soldiers returning from the Iraq war reduce anxiety and cope with post-traumatic stress disorder (PTSD). Researchers Huang and colleagues (2013) found that hatha yoga proved to be a very beneficial technique to reduce stress in middle-aged women.

Moreover, an explosion of research studies has permeated health-related journals regarding the effects of hatha yoga on premenstrual syndrome, diabetes, clinical depression, and academic test anxiety. In studies by Booth-Laforce and colleagues (2007), Khalsa (2004), and Schell (1994), hatha yoga proved to be an effective complementary modality to reduce menopausal symptoms (e.g., hot flashes, sleep disturbances, and reduced quality of life). Hatha yoga also appears to be a beneficial means to cope with breast cancer (Carson et al., 2007), depression (Uebelacker et al., 2010), and diabetes (Mercuri et al., 2000).

Without a doubt, hatha yoga improves flexibility (Ruiz, 2000). The more difficult *asanas* require muscle endurance and even strength because these postures involve lifting the body off the ground. The practice of yoga is also thought to reduce blood pressure through the relaxation effect of these postures. But perhaps the best benefit provided by yoga is a greater sense of body awareness. It is no secret that the comforts of high-technology society and their consequent sedentary lifestyles often result in poor posture, muscle tone, flexibility, strength, balance, agility, and endurance. The progression of yoga *asanas* allows for greater awareness of all these components.

Many, if not all, yoga practitioners acknowledge a sense of mental enjoyment from the habitual physical practice of *asanas*. Now science has begun to back up these claims. Michaelsen and colleagues (2005) conducted a study to determine the cognitive benefits of a 3-month intensive hatha yoga program. Results revealed that, indeed, subjects noted a dramatic decrease in anxiety levels attributed to this stress-management modality. Birkel and Edgren (2000) observed that the repeated practice of hatha yoga improved the breathing (vital) capacity, considered by many to be a significant factor for optimal health. Further empirical study of yoga in all its forms can only help to contribute to our understanding of the various paths of the mind-body connection.

Recent studies by Carneiro, Moraes, and Terra (2016) and Schuver and Lewis (2016) have confirmed previous research, finding that subjects who engaged in hatha yoga programs experienced decreased symptoms of depression and anxiety.

Hatha Yoga and Chronic Pain

Among the many videos that circulate on Facebook, one continues to be shared among all kinds of people year after year. It is the remarkable story of Arthur Boorman, a retired soldier who suffered from a disability from his years as a paratrooper. Faced with a life of severe back pain and knee problems, he was told he would never walk without the assistance of a cane or crutches and that he would never, ever run. Confronted with a bleak future of bodily decay, Arthur decided to empower himself by starting a hatha yoga practice. Over the course of several years, he not only lost weight, but now he can run without pain. Yoga has become his salvation! And he is not alone. Many people with chronic pain have found relief through the practice of yoga.

Back pain is one of the most common maladies to afflict people older than the age of 25. Poor sitting and standing posture, poor shoe support, weak stomach muscles, and athletic activities top the list of factors contributing to chronic lower-back pain (Baxter, 2003). Many people who find little or no relief from standard medical practices are turning to hatha yoga as an alternative or complementary modality, particularly with regard to sacroiliac joint problems (Lee, 1997) and lower back pain (Galantino et al., 2004; Jacobs et al., 2004). By stretching tight muscles and balancing strength and flexibility of the muscles supporting the joints where pain originates, yoga can be a positive and inexpensive means to reduce and eliminate joint pain. Yoga has also been found to be helpful for a variety of health-related problems, including carpal tunnel syndrome (Garfinkel et al., 1998).

Steps to Initiate Hatha Yoga

Chances are, you have already done some of the yoga positions before, perhaps without even knowing they were yoga postures. If you are at all familiar with hatha yoga, this will be a brief review. If you are new to these exercises, the following selection of yoga *asanas* will introduce you to the concepts and applications of hatha yoga as a relaxation technique. In the original *Yoga Sutras* text, *asanas* are described as "comfortable and steady." They are to be done slowly, and gracefully. They are designed to awaken your sense of body awareness.

There are three stages of each *asana*: (1) moving into the pose, (2) maintaining the pose, and (3) coming out of the pose. Always remember to come out of a pose as slowly as you enter it. At first, perhaps all you will be aware of is the physical experience of each *asana*. With time, though, you may begin to notice an internal (mental) calmness to equal the physical tranquility (muscular relaxation). As in any new learning experience, there are a couple of things to remember. First, pain and yoga *asanas* are incompatible. You should *not* push yourself to the point of pain. Some postures may seem quite easy, while others seem impossible. Move to the limit of your own physical ability. With practice, the more difficult *asanas* will become easier. Second, there are three concepts to remember when practicing yoga: breathing, conscious stretching, and counterpositions or balance.

The Art of Breathing

In the practice of hatha yoga, breathing plays a crucial role in the attempt to unite mind, body, and spirit. Breathing, or *pranayama*, influenced by the diaphragm, is the current that draws the flow of universal energy throughout the body. The word *prana* means "breath," and the word *yama* means "pause." Diaphragmatic breathing is the most natural style of breathing. It differs from thoracic breathing in the expansion of the stomach area as air enters the lungs (**FIG. 20.2**). The emphasis of breathing from the abdomen allows for increased relaxation throughout the body. Unlike thoracic breathing, *pranayama* invites

> **The art of breathing:** A term in hatha yoga that honors the importance of the pause of the breath (*pranayama*).

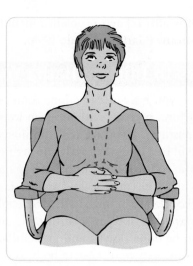

FIGURE 20.2 The art of breathing means becoming conscious of your breathing and allowing your abdominal area to expand as you inhale.

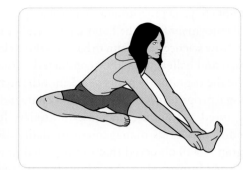

FIGURE 20.3 The art of conscious stretching means becoming aware of the flexibility of your muscles as you move a specific joint through a range of motion.

conscious effort of the entire pulmonary system, including the nose, throat, lungs, intercostal muscles, and diaphragm.

Within each yoga posture are a contraction phase and a release phase; muscles are slowly stretched and relaxed. *Pranayama* is integrated into each posture. Breaths are comfortably slow and deep, and correspond with the contraction and relaxation phases of each movement. As muscles are stretched, air is drawn into the lungs by the diaphragm. Then when the muscles relax, air is exhaled. Inhalations are usually taken when the head is lifted up and the body is going into a position or expanding. Air is exhaled when the head is down and the body is coming out of a position. Usually a breath is held for approximately 10 seconds. When first learning these positions, you may find breathing sequences difficult to coordinate with movements. Over time, coordination will become easier.

The Art of Conscious Stretching

Have you ever noticed a cat or dog stretch after taking a nap? Animals do this to prepare the body for motion. Stretching is a natural reflex. In a sleeping or fetal position, the body coils up, and several muscles, specifically those on the back of the body, contract and shorten. To

> **The art of conscious stretching:** An expression that suggests to yoga participants to be fully mindful as they assume and maintain an *asana*.

move efficiently upon awakening, these muscles must be stretched and elongated (**FIG. 20.3**). But the fetal position is not the only posture that allows muscles to constrict in this manner. Desk work, computer work, prolonged driving, even walking in high-heeled shoes cause muscles, tendons, and ligaments to shorten. Eventually, the body adapts to these positions and muscles remain contracted. The result is a significant loss in flexibility and restricted movements of certain joints. With time, loss of flexibility may result in muscular stiffness and joint pain as body alignment is slightly distorted.

Exercise physiologists have long known that chronically tight muscles are less capable of a full range of motion. Decreases in flexibility are also related to decreases in strength. Extremely tight muscles during a resting state may actually clamp off or occlude the blood supply at the microcapillary level, producing a vicious cycle of tension. Furthermore, as we mature physically (particularly after the age of 30), the body gradually loses its ability to produce elastin, a protein that gives muscle fibers stretching capabilities. Thus, the need to maintain flexibility becomes more important throughout the aging process. For these—and perhaps some cultural—reasons, the yoga postures may seem difficult at first. However, with continued practice, the body will adapt and they will become easier.

It is important to remember that in all yoga postures, one should not go to the point of pain; this may result in tears to muscle, tendon, and ligament fibers. Body awareness is a kinesthetic skill: being fully conscious of each body movement and what each body part is experiencing—specifically, the contraction and relaxation of each set of muscles. Don't push yourself. Hatha yoga is meant to be enjoyable.

BOX 20.1   Insomnia and Yoga

With its premise of promoting a union or balance between mind, body, and spirit, yoga is now touted as a skill to relieve the problems associated with repeated poor sleep quality. The spectrum of yoga styles varies from light stretching to demanding muscular endurance, all of which can groom the mind-body dynamics for a better night's sleep. Currently, the topic of hatha yoga as a bona fide treatment for insomnia is being studied through a grant from the National Institutes of Health. Conventional wisdom suggests that the combination of deep abdominal breathing and specific poses (*asanas*) evens out the mind's hemispheres to optimal consciousness (non-fear-based thinking), thereby decreasing the neural firing associated with fear-based thoughts and the subsequent fight-or-flight response. Specific poses that are used to promote a good night's sleep include the Mountain Brook Pose, Supported Child's Pose, Legs Up the Wall Pose, and *shavasana* (Corpse Pose).

The Art of Balance

The art of balance refers to counterpositions. Yoga philosophy asserts that balance is the key to life. To find harmony in life, there must be balance. Thus, the practice of *asanas* is a reminder to seek balance in all thoughts and actions, and the progression of *asanas* is a subtle lesson in its meaning. As you try the *asanas*, you will soon notice that there is a progressive pattern to the series of positions. For example, a position that stretches the lower back muscles should be followed by a posture that relaxes muscles in that same area (**FIG. 20.4**). When the body can maintain a balanced position, as well as balance the tension and relaxation of muscles through a series of postures, then greater unity will be experienced between body, mind, and soul. Regardless of the philosophical underpinnings involved, the concept of balance demonstrated in the *asanas* will provide a better range of motion and potentially reduce the risk of injury with advanced postures.

The following is a series of simple yoga *asanas*. As you try these, slowly integrate the concepts of breathing, body awareness, and balance.

Salute to the Sun (*Surya Namaskar*)

The **Salute to the Sun** is a very symbolic series of *asanas*. It is traditionally performed at the beginning and end of each yoga session. *Surya Namaskar* began as a form of meditation worship wherein one would start the day by facing east and performing the series of movements to maintain harmony throughout the day. Today it is recognized as an excellent exercise to stretch and limber muscles throughout the entire body, but particularly the spine and legs. Runners and joggers may recognize a few of these stretches because they are excellent flexibility exercises

FIGURE 20.4   The art of balance means following the natural laws of balance as the body moves into each position. Once one muscle group has been stretched, the body is balanced by performing the same posture on the opposite side.

for hamstrings and calf muscles. The Salute to the Sun should be performed slowly, and every effort should be made to maintain balance through each posture. Once the movements become more natural, the exercise can be done more rapidly. Each posture is counterbalanced in the next *asana*. A complete Salute to the Sun consists of

---

The art of balance: A term in hatha yoga that requires a balance of *asanas* on both the right and left sides of the body.

Salute to the Sun (*Surya Namaskar*): One of the most classic and symbolic series of hatha yoga postures, often performed at the beginning and/or end of each yoga session.

BOX 20.2   Desk/Cubicle Yoga Asanas

Getting away to your favorite yoga studio is a great escape from one's home office or work routine, but you don't have to head off to the nearest yoga center each day to practice hatha yoga. Several *asanas* can (and should) be adapted to one's desk or work station for ideal posture in the course of each day. Prolonged sitting (with poor posture) will cause a lot of tension in the muscles of the neck, shoulders, and back.

Keeping in mind that many of the yoga *asanas* are based on assuming correct spinal posture and balance, the adaptation of several yoga positions are ideal for those in a sitting position. Here are a few simple exercises to try and incorporate into your daily work routine.

1. *Trunk-Rotation:* Sitting in your chair, lift your hands to shoulder height and twist your body from the waist up toward your right side. Hold for 5–10 seconds. Relax and return to a straightforward sitting position. Then, with hands at shoulder height, twist toward your left side. Hold for 5–10 seconds. Repeat two to three times on each side.

2. *Lower Back Arch:* Sitting straight, head over shoulders, arch your lower back, pushing your abdominal area toward your desk. Hold for 5–10 seconds. Relax. Repeat two to three times.

3. *Shoulders to Ear Stretch:* Sitting straight up and facing your desk, slowly lower your right ear to your right shoulder without moving your shoulder. Hold for 5–10 seconds. Relax and return to resting position. Next, slowly lower your left ear to your left shoulder without moving your shoulder. Hold for 5–10 seconds. Repeat each side twice.

4. *Sitting Mountain Pose:* Sitting with your spine straight, extend your hands over your head, reaching for the ceiling. Hold for 5–10 seconds. Grasp hands and lean toward your right side (from your shoulders to your hands, keeping your torso straight). Hold for 5–10 seconds and then relax, bringing arms/hands overhead. Then reach/lean toward your left side, hold for 5–10 seconds, and then relax, arms down by your side. Repeat one to three more times.

5. *Cat Back Arch:* Push your chair away from your desk about 12 inches. Lower your chin to your chest, and then your head to your desk, stretching your arms in front of you (or off to the sides), arching your back (like a cat). Hold for 5–10 seconds. Sit back up straight. Repeat one to three times.

6. *Chest Expansion:* Sitting up straight, grasp your hands (interlocking fingers) behind your lower back. Straighten your arms and pull your shoulders back. Hold for 5–10 seconds. Relax. Repeat one to three times.

7. *Eye Yoga:* Sitting straight up, with your chin up, keep your head still, but look in the upper right corner of your field of vision and hold for 5–10 seconds. Then, keeping your head still, moving only your eyes, shift your focus to your lower left corner of your field of vision. Hold for 5–10 seconds. Next shift your field of vision to your upper left and hold for 5–10 seconds. Then shift the focus of your field of vision to the lower right. Hold/stare for 5–10 seconds. Relax and return to a forward gaze. Repeat all four corners of your field of vision in a random order, occasionally looking at the tip of your nose in between corners.

two sequences. In the first cycle, lead with the right foot in position 4; in the second, lead with the left. It makes no difference what direction you face when doing this exercise; however, facing east marks symbolic awareness of the beginning of the life of each new day.

Pre-position: Stand with your feet shoulder-width apart, spine completely aligned, and weight evenly distributed on both feet. Hold hands straight above head, palms facing out, with arms fully extended.

Position 1 (**FIGs. 20.5 and 20.6**): Raise your arms in a wide circular motion over the head and

FIGURE 20.5   **FIGURE 20.6**

then slowly down in front of the face to the midpoint of the chest. Hold palms together and exhale.

Position 2 (**FIG. 20.7**): Raise your arms directly over your head, pushing from the waist, keeping legs straight and back slightly arched. As you do this, slowly inhale and look up to the sky.

Position 3 (**FIG. 20.8**): Leading with your hands, reach to your toes, exhaling as you lower your head to your knees. Keep your back comfortably straight and knees slightly bent. (Tight hamstrings will decrease the length of your reach. Reach only as far as is comfortably possible.)

Position 4 (**FIG. 20.9**): Place your palms on the floor, and then bring your right foot between your hands. Extend the left leg behind you, and lower your knee to the floor. Inhale as you extend the leg, arch your back, and look up to the sky.

Position 5 (**FIG. 20.10**): Bring the right foot back to meet the left, and exhale. Raise your hips and buttocks high, keeping your head down and eyes

FIGURE 20.11   **FIGURE 20.12**

FIGURE 20.13   **FIGURE 20.14**

directed toward your feet. Arms should be fully extended.

Position 6 (**FIG. 20.11**): Lower your knees to the floor, followed by your chest and then your forehead. Hips should be slightly bent and raised off the floor. Breath is slowly exhaled throughout.

Position 7 (**FIG. 20.12**): Bring your hips to the floor, fully extending your legs behind you. Then, inhale while placing your hands directly beneath your shoulders and raising your chest. Look up to the sky, and arch the head and back slightly.

Position 8 (**FIG. 20.13**): Raise hips and buttocks high off the floor, keeping your palms and feet flat on the floor. As you do so, exhale. Keep your head down, eyes directed toward your feet, and your arms fully extended.

Position 9 (**FIG. 20.14**): Place your left foot between your hands, extend your right leg back, and place the knee on the floor as you inhale. Arch your back and head slightly, looking up to the sky.

Position 10 (**FIG. 20.15**): Bring your feet together, shoulder-width apart, with arms extended and hands reaching toward feet. Keep your back straight, and knees slightly bent. As you bring your head to your knees, exhale.

FIGURE 20.7   **FIGURE 20.8**

FIGURE 20.9   **FIGURE 20.10**

FIGURE 20.15

FIGURE 20.16

FIGURE 20.17

FIGURE 20.18

Position 11 (FIG. 20.16): Reach with your hands overhead, and slowly inhale. Extend your head back to look up to the sky, arching the back slightly.

Position 12 (FIG. 20.17): Lower your arms to midchest height, palms facing together, and exhale.

Now repeat the entire exercise, this time leading with the left foot in position 4. Upon completion, turn your attention inward to observe physical sensations.

Hatha Yoga *Asanas*

The following *asanas* are arranged in order from standing, to sitting, to lying down. It is important to remember, however, that every posture should be counterbalanced with one that works the opposite muscle groups. Positions should be done slowly and held for about 10 seconds. These thirteen *asanas* are but a few (the simplest) of the many hatha yoga postures. Even in hatha yoga, nuances in each position vary from instructor to instructor, so you may notice slight differences between these *asanas* and previous or future experiences. A sample workout of exercises is listed after the descriptions of the *asanas*. Remember that your yoga workout should end with the Corpse Pose

Mountain Pose (*Tadasana*): A classic yoga *asana* intended to promote balance and stability.

Head of Cow (*Gomukhasana*): A classic yoga *asana* intended to promote balance with arms and shoulders.

Fist over Head (*Araha Chakrasana*): A classic yoga *asana* intended to promote balance with arms and shoulders.

for a few minutes of quiet time. This time period can also include body awareness, with specific attention to relaxing all body parts (and self-reflection).

1. **Mountain Pose (*Tadasana*)** (FIG. 20.18): Stand with your feet about shoulder-width apart, spine completely straight, and eyes straight ahead. Raise your arms completely over your head, palms facing inward, and inhale. Hold comfortably for 10 seconds, and exhale as you return your arms slowly to your sides.

2. **Head of Cow (*Gomukhasana*)** (FIG. 20.19): Stand with feet shoulder-width apart and spine straight. Reach under and behind your back with your left arm as if to scratch between the shoulder blades. Reach over and behind with your right arm. Try to touch hands behind your shoulders, and hold for 10 seconds. (If hands cannot touch, you may use a hand towel.) Relax. Then, reverse arm positions and try to touch hands; hold for 10 seconds. Breathe normally throughout this exercise.

3. **Fist over Head (*Araha Chakrasana*)** (FIG. 20.20): Begin with the Mountain Pose. Place arms behind the waist, grasping hands (fist) together. Lean forward while slowly raising hands over head. Hold for 10 seconds, and then slowly release hands, letting them hang toward floor. Slowly straighten spine to fully erect position. Exhale as you raise fist over head, and inhale as you release and return to the Mountain Pose.

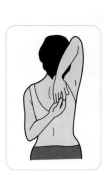

FIGURE 20.19

FIGURE 20.20

FIGURE 20.21

FIGURE 20.22

around the right calf. Hold for 10 seconds. Relax by extending the right leg back onto the floor. Then, bring the left leg to the chest and hold for 10 seconds. Exhale as each leg is brought to the chest; inhale as the leg is returned to full extension.

7. **Two Knees to Chest (*Apanasana*)** (**FIG. 20.24**): Lying on your back and keeping the back flat, bring both legs to the chest by holding the legs with your hands behind the knees. Hug the knees to the chest for 10 seconds. Breathe normally throughout.

8. **Cobra (*Bhujanghasana*)** (**FIG. 20.25**): Lie on your stomach with legs fully extended and feet curled. Placing your hands directly under your shoulders, slowly raise your chest and head off the floor by contracting the lower back muscles. Try not to push with your hands. Hold for 10 seconds, and then slowly return chest to the floor. Inhale as the chest rises off the floor, and exhale as you return to starting position.

9. **Sit and Reach (*Paschimottasana*)** (**FIG. 20.26**): In a sitting position, extend legs straight in front of

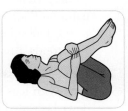

FIGURE 20.23   **FIGURE 20.24**

4. **Human Triangle (*Trikonasana*)** (**FIG. 20.21**): Beginning in the Mountain Pose, slowly move legs to 3 feet apart. Raise right arm and hand straight above head. Rotate head to look at right hand. Bend slightly at the waist and extend left arm and hand down to left ankle, palm open and facing in. As you reach down, rotate left foot out to protect knee joint. Hold for 10 seconds. Inhale as your right hand reaches up, and then exhale. Inhale as you return to the Mountain Pose. Exhale upon completion.

5. **Thigh Stretch (*Bandha Konasana*)** (**FIG. 20.22**): Sit in a comfortable position with knees bent and soles of the feet touching each other. Gently press knees toward the floor until tension is felt, and hold for 10 seconds. Allow thighs to relax, and repeat. Breathe normally throughout.

6. **One Knee to Chest (*Pawan Muktasana*)** (**FIG. 20.23**): Lying on your back and keeping the back flat, bring the right knee to the chest by clasping your hands

Human Triangle (*Trikonasana*): A classic yoga *asana* intended to promote balance with the upper torso.

Thigh Stretch (*Bandha Konasana*): A classic yoga *asana* intended to promote balance with the leg muscles.

One Knee to Chest (*Pawan Muktasana*): A classic yoga *asana* intended to promote balance with the lower back.

Two Knees to Chest (*Apanasana*): A classic yoga *asana* intended to promote balance with the lower back.

Cobra (*Bhujanghasana*): A classic yoga *asana* intended to promote balance with the lower back.

Sit and Reach (*Paschimottasana*): A classic yoga *asana* intended to promote balance with the hamstrings and lower back.

FIGURE 20.25   **FIGURE 20.26**

FIGURE 20.27

FIGURE 20.28

FIGURE 20.29

FIGURE 20.30

the hips, keeping spine straight. Lean chest comfortably toward the knees, ankles, or feet, reaching forward also with the hands. Keep back straight; hold for 10 seconds. Then, relax by slightly bending the knees and sitting upright. Exhale as you lean toward the feet, and inhale as you relax. Repeat three more times. If having both legs extended is uncomfortable, try one leg at a time.

10. **Spinal Twist (*Ardha Matsyendrasana*) (FIG. 20.27):** In a sitting position, with spine erect, place left leg over right knee and position the foot flat on the floor. Extend right arm and place hand on left ankle. Extend left arm behind waist and place the palm on floor for balance. Turn head and trunk to the left side, keeping the chin up. Hold for 10 seconds. Breathe normally throughout.

11. **Fish (*Matsyasana*) (FIG. 20.28):** Lying on your back with legs fully extended, place hands palm down beneath the lower back. Raise chest by arching lower back and neck. Hold for 10 seconds. Relax and then repeat three times. Breathe normally throughout.

12. **Bow Pose (*Dhanurasana*) (FIG. 20.29):** Lying on stomach, grab either the left or right foot with the

---

Spinal Twist (*Ardha Matsyendrasana*): A classic yoga *asana* intended to promote balance with the upper and lower back and hips.

Fish (*Matsyasana*): A classic yoga *asana* intended to promote balance with the lower back.

Bow Pose (*Dhanurasana*): A classic yoga *asana* intended to promote balance with the muscles of the lower back and stomach, as well as neck and shoulders.

Corpse Pose (*Shavasana*): This is the typical position assumed at the close of each yoga session to restore energy.

---

opposite hand. Slowly arch back by pulling feet over buttocks. Hold for 10 seconds. Relax with hands on floor by shoulders and legs fully extended. Repeat with each leg three times. Inhale as back is arched; exhale as body comes to full extension. (***Note:*** This exercise should be avoided if you have lower-back problems.)

13. **Corpse Pose (*Shavasana*) (FIG. 20.30):** Lie on your back, shifting your legs back and forth to find a comfortable position. Rotate your arms from the shoulders and rest comfortably, palms facing up. Next, rotate your spine, turning your head side to side. Then, return spine to resting alignment. Breathe from the diaphragm.

If you wish, you can start your workout with the Corpse Pose and return to this position intermittently or after each *asana*. A yoga session should always conclude with this position.

Sample Workout

1. Salute to the Sun
2. Mountain Pose
3. Head of Cow
4. Fist over Head
5. Human Triangle
6. Cobra
7. Two Knees to Chest
8. Mountain Pose
9. Salute to the Sun
10. Corpse (relaxation) Pose

Additional Thoughts on Hatha Yoga

The following guidelines may add to the enjoyment of yoga:

1. It is best not to perform *asanas* on a full stomach. Allow 1 to 2 hours between eating and yoga practice.

2. Wear loose-fitting clothing and avoid heavy jewelry. Bare feet are recommended to make better floor contact.

3. Find a quiet place to practice; a well-lit and well-ventilated room is ideal. A thin rug is also suggested to perform the positions in greater comfort.

4. Early morning is the preferred practice time for conscious awareness. But evening is the time when the body is more limber, and yoga postures tend to have a greater relaxation effect after a busy day. Find a time that is best suited to your own schedule.

5. Concentrate on the postures, sensing each move and your body's response to it.

6. There are no nutritional guidelines accompanying this relaxation technique, but if you pursue yoga further, you will find that a healthy, well-balanced diet is considered an important part of the art-of-balance concept.

7. The ultimate goal of all aspects of yoga is to lower the walls of the conscious mind—the ego. If you approach it with a competitive attitude, there is no chance for the union of mind, body, and spirit to occur. Beginning yoga students often push themselves to match the postures of the instructor or fellow classmates. This can result in physical pain as well as a deeper abyss to enlightenment. In the words of yogi master Swami Rama, "This is absolutely not the way to practice yoga."

8. Meditation is not a requirement of hatha yoga, but it is a nice complement to it. After you finish your selection of *asanas*, ending with the Corpse Pose (*shavasana*) is the perfect time to collect your thoughts and perhaps do some internal awareness or soul searching.

The popularity of hatha yoga has now fully exploded in the American culture, to the point where styles and instructors (over 70,000, according to a *Yoga Journal* survey [Hodge, 2005]) have become very territorial (e.g., certifications, trademarks, patents, precision in postures) making hatha yoga more technical (and ego-based) than it needs to be. The upshot of all this is that finding a quality yoga instructor is quite easy. However, not all hatha yoga classes are created equal (**TABLE 20.1**). If possible, it would be a good idea to sample a class (a 1-day pass) to determine if you find the instructor's teaching style and health philosophy compatible with your own. Most instructors will agree to an introductory class where you can either participate or observe. Classes are often offered at community recreation centers, yoga centers, and YMCAs and YWCAs, as well as through private instruction. One book on yoga stands far above the rest in its detailed explanations and wonderful photographs: *The Sivananda Companion to Yoga*, by Lidell et al. I recommend it for further reading on yoga as a special relaxation technique (see Table 20.1).

Best Application of Hatha Yoga

As previously mentioned, hatha yoga can be practiced at the start of each day or at the conclusion of each day. Even if you do only a few *asanas* each morning before you begin your working day, this would be a good start, and many *asanas* can be done (briefly) in the course of a day (e.g., stepping away from the computer, before or after exercise). As a relaxation technique, it is best employed to unleash the stress and frustration that for whatever reason have to be resolved. The use of individual *asanas* to stretch various muscle groups during waking hours might be the best course of action when you feel muscles

Stress with a Human Face

As the Assistant Dean of Wellness at Florida Southern College in Lakeland, Florida, Kelly Andrew's position entails administering the entire campus wellness program for over 3,000 faculty, staff, and students. Her position allows her to teach a weekly yoga class, which she embraces with great passion. She has also opened her own yoga studio, which holds weekly classes and workshops. Although Kelly had been practicing yoga on and off over the past decade, it was the heart-wrenching breakup of a serious relationship in 2000 that propelled her into making yoga a regular practice, one that allowed her to regain and maintain balance in her life. It worked! Once committed to a regular yoga practice, she decided to become certified with the Southern Institute of Yoga Instructors. Hatha yoga has provided an unparalleled stability in her life ever since.

Kelly teaches a variety of beginning and intermediate yoga sessions in her new yoga studio, The Yoga Place, but has found that over the years, more and more people are coming to her restorative yoga classes, which offer a greater emphasis on breath work, longer time with each *asana*, more rest between poses, and a special focus on renewal—all of which offer more space in the body and, hence, the mind. Simply stated: The restorative practice cultivates an environment of renewal by focusing on being as opposed to doing. "I think more people come to the restorative yoga classes because stress levels are so high these days," she explained. "Personally, I get as much out of the restorative classes as I do the basic hatha yoga class."

Like many yoga instructors, Kelly is concerned about the dogmatic approach some instructors are now taking with yoga instruction, as highlighted in a 2011 *Newsweek* article entitled "Bow Down to the Yoga Teacher" (Schwartz, 2011). "First and foremost we are there for people's health and safety. Hatha yoga is not about ego! When a teacher forgets they are also a student, it's trouble for everyone; they have lost the essence of teaching." You can visit Kelly's website at www.kellyandrewstoday.com.

TABLE 20.1 Types of Hatha Yoga

Type	Method	Advantages	Website
Ashtanga yoga	Intense classes that synchronize breath work with speed series of *asanas*	Considered a serious workout for muscles and cardio work	www.ashtanga.com
Power yoga	Hatha yoga with intense muscle power *asanas*	Americanized yoga, very demanding for muscular strength	www.power-yoga.com
Bikram yoga	Yoga practiced in 105° heat to replicate Indian climate	Heat brings its own challenge; said to provide a cleansing feeling	www.bikramyoga.com
Iyengar yoga	Focus is placed on the specifics of each *asana* with each posture held for more time	Good for beginners who are not flexible; props (blocks) are often used	www.iyengar-yoga.com

begin to tense. Research indicates that yoga helps decrease anxiety and maintain a sense of emotional balance, reinforcing the mind-body connection that the promise of yoga (union) promotes. Those who teach hatha yoga recognize that the union of mind, body, and spirit is solidified by self-acceptance, self-love, and the absence of anger and fear in one's life. The inner peace derived from practicing yoga is credited with keeping people emotionally well balanced during unexpected encounters of the stressful kind.

SUMMARY

- *Yoga* is a Sanskrit word meaning "union," which is accomplished through meditation. More specifically, it refers to the union of mind, body, and spirit. Hatha yoga is one of five types of meditation and it emphasizes physical balance. *Hatha* actually translates to (a balance of) the sun (*ha*) and the moon (*tha*). Hatha yoga is the most commonly practiced form of yoga meditation in the United States.

- Hatha yoga, first and foremost, is a non-ego-based exercise. The American culture has added layers of ego with various certifications, clothing fashions, mats, posh studios, and even a competitive nature regarding precision in the *asanas*. There is no room for ego with true hatha yoga.

- Hatha yoga is known to decrease episodes of chronic pain, particularly lower-back pain.

- Hatha yoga is built on three concepts: the art of breathing, the art of conscious stretching, and the art of balance.

- In most cases, a hatha yoga session will begin with the *Surya Namaskar* (Salute to the Sun), which is a series of movements or postures initiating integration of the mind, body, and spirit. It also serves as a warm-up for the other postures, or *asanas*.

- There are literally hundreds of *asanas*. This chapter highlighted some of the more popular ones that can easily be incorporated into a yoga session.

- Although not meant solely as a series of flexibility exercises, hatha yoga increases flexibility. It has also been shown to improve muscle tone and create inner calmness, which yoga instructors attribute to improved self-esteem.

STUDY GUIDE QUESTIONS

1. Why is hatha yoga thought to be an effective relaxation technique?

2. Explain both the physiological and the psychological effects of yoga.

3. Hatha yoga involves three aspects (arts); name and explain each.

4. How does one's ego affect one's yoga practice?

REFERENCES AND RESOURCES

Allen, R. J. *Human Stress: Its Nature and Control*. Burgess Press, Minneapolis, MN, 1983.

American Occupational Therapy Association. Iraq Study Shows Yoga Warriors Method Reduces Symptoms of Combat Stress & Potentially PTSD. January 15, 2012. http://www.aota.org/news/media/pr/2012-press-releases/yoga.aspx.

Arpita, B. Physiological Effects of Hatha Yoga: A Review of the Literature, *International Journal of Yoga Therapy* 1:1–28, 1990.

Ballantyne, J. *Sankhya Aphorisms of Kapila*. Chowkhamba Sanskrit Series, Varanasi, India, 1963.

Baxter, C. Chronic Pain Release through Yoga, *The Yoga Site*. www.yogasite.com/chronicpain.htm.

Bell, B. Insomnia and Hatha Yoga. www.couplescompany.com/Advice/Jayson/yoga/insomnia.htm.

Bender, B. Power Yoga for Better Health: More Strength and Flexibility, Less Pain and Stress, *Bottom Line/Health* 15(3):14, 2001.

Bhattacharya, S., et al. Evaluation of Effect of Yogic Breathing and Exercises on Pulmonary Function, Free Radicals and Antioxidant Status among Healthy Individuals, *Chest* 118(4):204s, 2000.

Birkel, D. *Hatha Yoga*. Eddie Bowers, Dubuque, IA, 1991.

Birkel, D. A., and Edgren, L. Hatha Yoga: Improved Vital Capacity of College Students, *Alternative Therapies* 6(6):55–63, 2000.

Booth-LaForce, C., Thurston, R., and Taylor, M. A Pilot Study of a Hatha Yoga Treatment for Menopausal Symptoms, *Maturitas* 57(3):286–295, 2007.

Carneiro, E. M., Moraes, G. V., and Terra, G. A. Effects of Isha Hatha Yoga on Core Stability and Standing Balance. *Advances in Mind Body Medicine* 30(3):4–10, 2016.

Carson, J., et al. Yoga for Women with Metastatic Breast Cancer: Results from a Pilot Study, *Journal of Pain and Symptom Management* 33(3):331–341, 2007.

Chaudhuri, H. Yoga Psychology. In C. T. Tart (ed.), *Transpersonal Psychologies*, Harper & Row, New York, 1975.

Chopra, A., and Doiphode, V. Ayurvedic Medicine: Core Concept, Therapeutic Principles and Current Relevance, *Medical Clinics of North America* 86(1):75–89, 2002.

Coulter, A. Yoga and Cancer: A Move Toward Relaxation, *Alternative and Complementary Therapies* (4)3:150–155, 1998.

Desai, Yogi Amrit. *Kripalu Yoga: Meditation in Motion*. Kripalu Publications, Lenox, MA, 1985.

Etsten, D. The Benefits of Yoga: Treating Mind and Body Helps Clients Recover from Addictions, *Journal of Addiction and Mental Health* 5(20):9, 2002.

Feuestein, G. Yoga and Stress: A Bibliography, *International Journal of Yoga Therapy* 10:11–16, 2000.

Feuestein, G. *The Yoga Tradition: Its History, Literature, Philosophy and Practice*. Holm Press, Prescott, AZ, 1998.

Folan, L. *Lilias, Yoga, & Your Life*. Macmillan, New York, 1981.

Galantino, M. L., et al. The Impact of Modified Hatha Yoga on Chronic Low Back Pain: A Pilot Study, *Alternative Therapies in Health and Medicine* 10(2):56–59, 2004.

Garfinkel, M., et al. Yoga-Based Intervention for Carpal Tunnel Syndrome, *Journal of the American Medical Association* 280(18):1601–1603, 1998.

Gregoire, C. Yoga Associated with Gene Expression in Immune Cells, Study Finds, *The Huffington Post*, April 24, 2013. www.huffingtonpost.com/2013/04/24/yoga-immune-system-genetic-_n_3141008.html.

Greuel, J. Iraq Study Shows Yoga Warriors Method Reduces Symptoms of Combat Stress and Potentially PTSD, Yoga Warriors International, January 26, 2012. http://www.yogawarriors.com/about-yoga-warriors/news/iraq-study-shows-yoga-warriors-method-reduces-symptoms-combat-stress.

Haich, E., and Yesudian, S. *Self-Healing, Yoga, and Destiny*. Aurora Press, New York, 1966.

Hodge, J. Yoga Teaching Profession Grows Along with Interests in Yoga, *Yoga Yoga*, May 5, 2005. www.yogayoga.com/press/YYTTmove.

Huang, F. J., Chien, D. K., and Chung, U. L., Effects of Hatha Yoga on Stress in Middle-Aged Women. *Journal of Nurse Research*. 21(1) 59-66, 2013.

Iyengar, B. K. *Light on Pranayama*. Crossroad, New York, 1981.

Jacobs, B. P., Mehling, W., Avins, A. L., et al. Feasibility of Conducting a Clinical Trial on Hatha Yoga for Chronic Low Back Pain: Methodological Lessons, *Alternative Therapies in Health and Medicine* 10(3):80–83, 2004.

Kelly, A. L. Team up to Fight Pain, *Yoga International* September/October, 2003:98.

Khalsa, H. K., How Yoga, Meditation, and a Yogic Lifestyle Can Help Women Meet the Challenges of Perimenopause and Menopause, *Sexuality, Reproduction and Menopause* 2(3):169–175, 2004.

Kiecolt-Glaser, J. K. Stress, Inflammation, and Yoga Practice, *Psychosomatic Medicine* 72(2):113–121, 2010.

Krafsow, G. *Yoga for Wellness with the Timeless Teachings of Viniyoga*. Penguin, New York, 1999.

Krishna, G. *The Kundalini: The Evolutionary in Man*. Shambhala, Berkeley, CA, 1971.

Lasater, J. Down in the Back: Poses for Lower Back Pain, *Alternative Therapies for Health and Medicine* 1(5):72–82, 1995.

Lasater, J. *Relax and Renew*. Rodmell Press, Berkeley, CA, 1995.

Lee, M. *Phoenix Rising*. Health Communication, Inc., Deerfield Beach, FL, 1997.

Lidell, L., with Rabinovitch, N., and Rabinovitch, G. *The Sivananda Companion to Yoga*. Simon and Schuster, New York, 1983.

Macy, D. Yoga Journal Releases 2008 "Yoga in America" Market Study, *Yoga Journal*, February 26, 2008. www.yogajournal.com/advertise/press_releases/10.

Mercuri, N., Olivera, E., et al. Yoga Practice in People with Diabetes, *Diabetes Research and Clinical Practice* 50 (suppl. 1):234–235, 2000.

Michalsen, A., Grossman, P., Acil, A., Langhorst, J., Lüdtke, R., Esch, T., Stefano, G. B., and Dobos, G. J. Rapid Stress Reduction and Anxiolysis among Distressed Women as a Consequence of a Three-Month Intensive Yoga Program, *Medical Science Monitor* 11(12):CR555–561, 2005.

Mishra, R. *Fundamentals of Yoga*. Julian Press, New York, 1959.

Oken, B. S., Zajdel, D., Kishiyama, S., et al. Randomized, Controlled, Six-Month Trial of Yoga in Healthy Seniors: Effects on Cognition and Quality of Life, *Alternative Therapies in Health and Medicine* 12(1):40–47, 2006.

Ott, M. J. Yoga as a Clinical Intervention, *Advance for Nurse Practitioners* January, 2002:81–90.

Oz, M. Say "Om" Before Surgery, *Time*, January 20, 2003:71–73.

Pettinati, P. Meditation, Yoga and Guided Imagery, *Holistic Nursing Care* 16(1):47–55, 2001.

Qu, S., et al. Rapid Gene Expression Changes in Peripheral Blood Lymphocytes upon Practice of a Comprehensive Yoga Program, *Plos One*, April 17, 2013. www.plosone.org/article/info%3Adoi%2F10.1371%2Fjournal.pone.0061910.

Ray, U. S., Sinha, B., Tomer, O. S., Pathak, A., et al. Aerobic Capacity and Perceived Exertion after Practice of Hatha Yogic Exercises, *Indian Journal of Medical Research*, December 2001.

Rosen, R. *The Yoga of Breathing: A Step by Step Guide to Pranayama*. Shambhala Books, Boston, 2002.

Ruiz, F. What Science Can Teach Us about Flexibility, *Yoga Journal*, March/April, 2000:92–101.

Schaffer, R. Calm Digestive Upset with Yoga, *Natural Health* 32:38–40, 2002.

Schell, F. J., Allolio, B., and Schonecke, O. W. Physiological and Psychological Effects of Hatha-Yoga Exercise in Healthy Women, *International Journal of Psychosomatic Medicine* 41(1–4):46–52, 1994.

Schuver, K. J., and Lewis, B. A. Mindfulness-Based Yoga Intervention for Women with Depression. *Complementary Therapies in Medicine* 26:85–79, 2016.

Schwartz, C. Bow Down to the Yoga Teacher, *Newsweek*, February 20, 2011.

Serber, E. Stress Management through Yoga, *International Journal of Yoga Therapy* 10:11–16, 2000.

Sivananda, S. *Raja Yoga*. Yoga Vendanta Forest University, Rishikesh, India, 1950.

Smith, B. *Yoga for a New Age: A Modern Approach to Hatha Yoga*. Prentice-Hall, Englewood Cliffs, NJ, 1982.

Smith, C., Hancock, H., Blake-Mortimer, J., and Eckert, K. A Randomized Comparative Trial of Yoga and Relaxation to Reduce Stress and Anxiety, *Complementary Therapies in Medicine* 15(2):77–83, 2007.

Stoller, C., et al. Effects of Sensory-Enhanced Yoga on Symptoms of Combat Stress in Deployed Military Personnel, *American Journal of Occupational Therapy*, 2012. ajot.aotapress.net/content/66/1/59.full.

Swami Karmananda. Relaxation through Yoga. In J. White and J. Fadiman (eds.), *Relax*. Dell, New York, 1976.

Swami Rama. *Lectures on Yoga*. Himalayan International Institute of Yoga Science and Philosophy, Honesdale, PA, 1979.

Swami Satyananda Saraswati. *Asana, Pranayama, Mudra, Bandha*. Bihar School of Yoga, Monghyr, Bihar, India, 1973.

Taylor, M. Good Grief: Use Yoga and Meditation to Make Sense of Loss, *Alternative Medicine*, October 2007:73–76.

Tran, M. D., Holly, R. G., Lashbrook, J., and Amsterdam, E. A. Effects of Hatha Yoga Practice on the Health-Related Aspects of Physical Fitness, *Prevention Cardiology* 4(4):165–170, 2001.

Uebelacker, L. A., et al. Hatha Yoga for Depression: Critical Review of the Evidence for Efficacy, Plausible Mechanisms of Action, and Directions for Future Research, *Journal of Psychiatric Practice* 16(1):22–33, 2010.

Weintraub, A. Yoga: It's Not Just an Exercise, *Psychology Today* 33(6):22, 2000.

CHAPTER 21

Mental Imagery and Visualization

*I saw the angel in the marble and carved until
I set him free.*

—Michelangelo

Close your eyes for a moment and listen to the gentle, rolling waves of the ocean. See the clear, aqua-blue water break as it approaches the shore. Feel the white sand between your toes, the warm sun on your hair, and the soft wind as it caresses your face and continues on to sway the branches of a Royal palm tree behind you. The salt air fills your senses, and as you exhale, you feel completely relaxed.

Imagination is a powerful gift. It is one of the characteristics that makes humans unique creatures on Earth. As a cognitive skill, imagination is the first step of the creative process. Yet imagination is a skill we do not use to our full advantage or potential. When Einstein said that imagination was more powerful than knowledge, he meant that our wealth of knowledge is based on the framework of the depths of human imagination. Knowledge without imagination is like a car without fuel: It is not functional; it won't go anywhere. Now, it would be inaccurate to say that imagination isn't used in times of stress. It is. More often than not, though, it is used in the wrong way. Our imagination creates worst-case scenarios from our frustrations and fears. We imagine the most drastic consequences of stressful situations by making mountains out of molehills. Why do we do this? Have we been socialized to think this way? Is it a defense mechanism? One can only guess the real reason. It is fair to say, however, that when imagination is used in this negative way, it feeds behaviors that somehow reward the ego, or humanity would have discontinued this mode of thinking generations ago. Stress-management therapists have concluded that in the face of stress, imagination can be an asset as well as a liability. And as the saying goes, "If it was your mind that got you into this mess, then use your mind to get you out of it." Employed in a positive way, imagination can be a very valuable asset as a tool to conquer stress. The rewards produced through positive imagery range from slain metaphorical dragons, to attained goals and answered dreams, to an improved overall state of health.

The technique of **mental imagery** goes by several names, sometimes signifying variations in the purpose and use of this technique. The word **visualization** is often used synonymously with mental imagery, but it can also mean additional aspects of mental imagery not directly related to the relaxation effect. Psychophysiologist and biofeedback specialist Patricia Norris (1992) describes visualization as "a conscious choice with intentional instructions," whereas "imagery is a spontaneous flow of thoughts originating from the unconscious mind." Mental training and mental rehearsal are also part of the mental imagery process. These terms are used primarily in sports psychology and behavioral medicine to express a more elaborate type of imagery for behavioral change. The purpose in these two disciplines is to promote positive behavioral changes such as, for example, the refinement of motor skills for improved athletic performance, or positive changes in health behaviors such as smoking cessation.

In cases where suggestions are given by an instructor, therapist, or counselor to enhance imagination, this technique is referred to as **guided mental imagery**. In his book *Visualization for Change*, Patrick Fanning defined visualization as "the conscious, volitional creation of mental sense impressions for the purpose of changing yourself." The skill of visualization involves the creation of images, scenes, or impressions by engaging one's imagination of the body's physical senses of sight, sound, feel, smell, and even taste, for an overall pleasurable desired effect.

Mental imagery goes by another name altogether in psychological circles: **predictive encoding**—a mental training strategy to utilize the unconscious mind for better performance. The relationship between mental training and personal performance continues to be studied around the world, from elite athletes to cancer patients and everyone in between.

Mental imagery and visualization, when used to promote physical calmness, involve several components of meditation—specifically, increased concentration and expanded awareness of consciousness of the scene created in the mind's eye. Perhaps the greatest strength lies in the ability to turn down the volume and intensity of information received by the five senses, and in many cases to replace threatening stimuli with pleasurable ones from the depths of the imagination. The net result is an overall calming effect and, in some cases, even a healing effect (**FIG. 21.1**).

FIGURE 21.1   Either viewing a beautiful sunrise or creating an image of one in your mind can help to relax mind, body, and spirit.

Historical Perspective

The use of mental imagery as a healing technique can be traced back to the origins of virtually every culture on nearly every continent. In one form or another, mental imagery and visualization have been used by Australian aborigines, American Indian shamans, Hindu yogis, and the ancient Greeks as a supplemental tool to fight disease and promote health. For example, in the book *Black Elk Speaks*, a semi-autobiographical account of a Sioux medicine man, Black Elk describes the use of "visions"

Mental imagery: Using the imagination to observe, in the first person, images created by the unconscious mind; falls into three categories: (1) images that replicate peaceful scenes to promote relaxation, (2) images that substitute a less desirable behavior with a more healthy one, and (3) images that help to heal damaged body tissue.

Visualization: A directed exercise in mental imagery; consciously creating images of success, healing, or relaxation for the purpose of self-improvement.

Guided mental imagery: An exercise in which one is guided through a series of suggestions provided by an instructor, therapist, or counselor to enhance one's imagination.

Predictive encoding: A mental training strategy to utilize the unconscious mind for better performance; an academic term for *mental imagery*.

in his treatment of several sick people. Other cultures have their stories as well. Too sophisticated for cures of the mystical type, Western culture abandoned such practices centuries ago. During the European Renaissance, the Cartesian principle separated the study of the mind (philosophy) and body (medicine), and weakened the authority of mental imagery as a healing practice. Although visualization in its many forms was still practiced by various cultures throughout the world, it failed to gain approval of the influential medical community in the West until the turn of the twentieth century. As the field of modern psychology began to unfold, however, the concepts of mental imagery and visualization reemerged as viable means to connect mental and physical aspects of well-being.

In the early works of Joseph Breuer, Sigmund Freud, and Carl Jung, the elements of imagination were introduced into psychoanalysis. Each therapist documented cases in which patients' ability to tap into their imagination helped cure them of specific ailments. Whereas Freud theorized that imagination was insight into basic human drives, Jung believed that it was the wealth of knowledge in the unconscious mind surfacing as images to consciousness. Jung formulated a hypothesis that many images have an "archetypal nature," a term he used to describe symbols common to all people of all races. These include trees, circular objects (*mandalas*), and winged creatures. As early as 1940, Jung encouraged his patients to use **active imagination**, a creative exercise to complete the final scenes of recurring dreams, in an effort to find a peaceful resolution. In many cases, it helped to cure them of their physical ailments.

From Jung's lead, several other psychologists, including Robert Assaglioli, Erik Peper, and Paul Eckman, demonstrated the power of imagination to influence cognitive processing as well as physiological changes produced by creative thoughts. With time, mental imagery became well accepted in the practice of clinical psychology, with the Rorschach ink-blot test becoming one of the most renowned applications of this technique. Joseph Wolpe suggested the use of imagination when he advised that systematic desensitization be employed as a coping technique when known stressors would be encountered. Systematic desensitization is a process of progressive tolerance to stress through the replacement of stressful stimuli with more comfortable images created in the mind. (This will be described in more detail later in this chapter.) In the 1970s, O. Carl Simonton and his wife, Stephanie, resurrected the use of active imagination, applying this technique to help fight cancer in patients who were terminally ill. It is largely their inspiring work that has prompted much research on the use of mental imagery in clinical settings.

One of the most respected names in the field of guided imagery today is Belleruth Naparstek. As a practicing psychotherapist, Naparstek sees three kinds of people in her practice: trauma victims, people with self-defeating behaviors, and the chronically ill. Guided imagery, she states, works for people in all three categories. "Guided imagery," she says, "is a kind of directed daydreaming, a way of using imagination very specifically to help mind and body heal, stay strong, and even perform as needed" (Naparstek, 1994). To date, her most renowned work involves trauma and she has dedicated her life work to helping scores of people suffering from trauma, including Vietnam vets, Iraq war vets, Columbine high school teachers and students, and those who survived the horrors of September 11, 2001, in New York City. The author of several books and more than 100 audio CDs, she now makes her CDs available to people who have suffered from a traumatic event, including the students at Virginia Tech (www.healthjourneys.com).

Neurophysiologists now understand that of the hundreds of billions of cells in the human brain, only a fraction (approximately 2 billion, or 10 percent) is used for conscious thought. The remaining cells may actually constitute the tangible network associated with the unconscious mind. Work inspired by Sperry to gain a greater understanding of the cognitive functions of the right and left hemispheres of the brain has deduced that imagination, like intuition, music appreciation, and spatial awareness, is a right-brain function. And the ability to access and employ right-brain functions is considered an asset in dealing with perceived stress.

Active imagination: A term coined by Carl Jung describing a mental imagery process where, in a lucid dream state or relaxed state, you consciously imagine (and resolve) the end of a recurring dream. Active imagination is a form of visualization.

■ Mental Imagery Research

The practices of mental imagery and visualization as healing modalities are relatively new to Western medicine and are not universally accepted among healthcare professionals. There are two scientific journals devoted to research in this topic: *The Journal of Mental Imagery* (Marquette University) and *Imagination, Cognition, and Personality* (Yale University). Studies can be found in several other journals as well. One focus of these journal articles involves the use of visualization as a complementary tool for improved health status in the treatment of cancer, elevated blood pressure, chronic pain, asthma, obesity, bone fractures, and headaches, to name just a few. The promising results of these studies have added sustenance to the emerging field of psychoneuroimmunology. Other studies involve positive changes in various behaviors through the use of mental imagery, including sports performance and recovery from chemical dependencies. The following are samples of the type of research that has been conducted in this field.

To examine the effects of mental imagery as a relaxation technique on various biochemical reactions, Jasnoski and Kugler (1987) measured the response of salivary immunoglobulin A (SIgA), cortisol, and mood states when under the influence of mental images specific to enhancement of the immune system. Results supported the hypothesis that when cognition is directed toward these biochemical factors, there is a subsequent change in neuroimmunomodulation. Ievleva and Orlick (1991), at Florida State University, studied the effects of mental imagery, positive self-talk, and goal setting on subjects diagnosed with knee and ankle injuries, compared to subjects with the same types of injuries who had no such treatment. Those subjects who practiced these relaxation techniques demonstrated more rapid healing of their injuries than the control subjects.

The stories emerging regarding the use of mental imagery for cancer are mostly anecdotal, but Epstein (1989) believes they must be regarded with as much validity as controlled studies. Jeanne Achterberg (1978, 1984, 1985), renowned for her use of mental imagery in the treatment of cancer, is also of the opinion that this type of treatment is as essential as radiation and chemotherapy and must not be thought of as "a last alternative." She believes that mental imagery plays both a reactive and a causative role in the biochemical healing process.

Despite claims of remission of cancerous tumors, it should be noted that mental imagery has never been touted as a panacea for all ailments and diseases. Furthermore, not all studies of mental imagery show promising results. Barrie Cassileth (1990) at the University of Pennsylvania School of Medicine, for example, found no relationship between psychosocial factors (mental imagery and sheer will) and physiological effects in 359 cancer patients. These results

confirmed her hypothesis that mental imagery falls in the realm of "fraudulent quackery." A caveat to findings such as these is explained by health psychologist Shelly Taylor (2005), who, in an attempt to explain the placebo effect, indicates that the *attitude* of the physician is sometimes more important than the medicine he or she administers. Citing several clinical studies, Taylor notes that health-care practitioners who show confidence in the treatment they administer, as well as professional bonding with the patient, always observe a stronger effect than those who are skeptical of the treatment. This occurs whether the medication is "real" (Feldman, 1956) or a placebo (Miller, 1989). Thus, Taylor considers the placebo effect neither a "medical trick" nor a purely psychological side effect, but a very real aspect of the healing process.

More recent research involving guided imagery includes the use of various suggestive images with bulimics (Tuschen-Caffier et al., 2003), clinically depressed patients (Chou and Lin, 2006), nursing home patients (Crow and Banks, 2004), kidney dialysis patients (Matthews et al., 2001), and cancer patients (Freeman and Dirks, 2006; Wyatt et al., 2007) and the use of imagery as a means to improve memory (Paddock et al., 2000), all with favorable results. This suggests that the power of the mind is a force to be reckoned with when used to promote our highest potential. If there is any doubt about how the mind can affect the body's stress physiology, research results from Japan indicate that guided imagery relaxation used by more than 150 subjects revealed a significant decrease in salivary cortisol (Watanabe et al., 2006), suggesting one more link in the mind-body equation.

The United States military brass has taken notice regarding the promising effects of mind-body skills that help regulate the autonomic nervous system, specifically for returning Army soldiers with PTSD and traumatic brain injury (TBI). In a white paper (summarized research findings) drafted by the Defense Center of Excellence for Psychological Health and Traumatic Brain Injury, mental imagery (along with diaphragmatic breathing, meditation, and biofeedback) was highlighted for its ability to positively influence nervous system regulation, specifically referred to as "balanced autonomic functioning."

The white paper stated that brain scans have indicated that imagery can stimulate the same areas of the brain and nervous system as an equivalent experience can. In terms of evidence supporting the use of guided imagery, a meta-analytic review of 46 studies suggests that guided imagery may be helpful for managing stress, anxiety, depression, and pain management (Naparstek, 2011). Simply stated, the combined power of symbolic creativity and imaginary sensory stimulation holds great promise for optimal (improved) health and performance for people of all walks of life.

As the former director of biofeedback research at the Menninger Clinic in Topeka, Kansas, Dr. Patricia Norris documented several case studies in which mental imagery and visualization were used successfully to complement traditional medical treatment. She lists eight characteristics that help to make mental imagery effective as a healing tool, especially with regard to cancer:

1. *Visualization needs to be **idiosyncratic**; that is, it must be self-generated.* Images that are created by the practitioner and not the patient appear to be ineffective in the healing process.

2. *Imagery must be **egosyntonic**.* This means that it must fit with the values and ideals of the person. If, for example, the individual has a pacifistic nature, then combative or warlike imagery will undermine the effectiveness of this type of treatment. Norris notes that typically there is emotional involvement with the imagery. Many patients actually protected their cancer in their imagery, even during disposal (e.g., in packing it out in garbage bags, or viewing cancer cells longing to be released).

3. *There must be a positive connotation to the imagery.* Imagery that is negative reinforces negative thoughts, which are not conducive to healing. As an example, Norris notes that sharks, as a healing image, are not a good idea. Imagery must be what she calls "restorative and preparative."

> **Idiosyncratic:** A term meaning self-generated, such as images used in visualization that are created by the person performing the visualization.
>
> **Egosyntonic:** A visualization expression meaning that images created/suggested in the visualization process must fit with the values and ideals that are most beneficial.
>
> **Kinesthetic:** A visualization expression meaning the actual involvement through the five senses in the practice of this technique.
>
> **Blueprint aspect:** A term to suggest that the visualization has a goal to complete or accomplish; thus, the blueprint is the template for completion (e.g., a healed wound).

4. *Imagery must be **kinesthetic** and somatic.* Rather than watch the imagery on a movie screen, you must feel the sensations of your images "in the first person." You must have a sense that what you are seeing is happening inside your body, not "out there somewhere."

5. *Imagery must be anatomically correct and accurate.* Knowing exactly what body region and physiological system is diseased and what the nature of the disease truly is should dictate the type of imagery used. In other words, you need to know whether to access the central nervous system or the immune system. Certain diseases and illnesses fall under specific categories. Norris suggests accessing your body wisdom as well as clinical data and test results. She also states that more than one image can be used in the healing process. In her work with children, she noted that kids used both a symbolic (figurative) image and a literal (representational) one.

6. *Maintain constancy and dialogue.* Constancy means regularity in your imagery. Norris suggests three 15-minute sessions per day, with brief intermittent thought messages at other times. When you feel pain in your body, your body is communicating to you. In fact, she refers to pain as a metaphorical friend. Through a dialogue of self-talk, she suggests thanking the pain for making you aware of a problem so that you may be able to fix it. Finally, she suggests destroying a tumor with its permission. Respond with love. Think of your afflicted part as a child you want to protect and nurture. Make peace with your body.

7. *Employ a blueprint aspect.* A blueprint is a strategy. Norris suggests that you always see your imagery as a mission accomplished. A blueprint visualization is like a time-lapse photograph where a flower (symbolizing a tumor) is shown to bloom within seconds and then close back up and fade away. Visualize a formula and see it through to completion. An example would be to see the construction of a building, from the hole in the ground to opening day when you are cutting the ribbon at the entrance.

8. *You must include the treatment in the imagery.* Norris has found that patients who use mental imagery incorporating chemotherapy treatment and radiation do better than those who "fight" these medical procedures. She notes that it helps

to have benevolent feelings (versus ambivalent feelings) toward the treatment. She suggests to mentally "welcome the treatment into the body." Consider the treatment a guest in your house. From her patients, she offers these examples:

a. *Chemotherapy:* A gold-colored fluid that healthy cells, acting as a bucket brigade, pass along to cancer cells, who drink it up.

b. *Radiation treatment:* A stream of silver energy aimed at the cancerous tumor(s). Ask the white blood cells to move out of the way—or shield themselves—and act like mirrors to reflect the radiation toward the cancer cells; then watch the cancer cells go belly-up.

Norris, like other researchers (Rossman, 2002; Krippner, 2000), admits that just exactly how visualization promotes healing is still a mystery and that the answers to this mystery can be learned as we further explore human consciousness and the human energy field. Similar to the theory described by Pert, Achterberg (1984) hypothesizes that the function of imagination, housed in the right brain, converts thoughts to biochemical messages and intentionally directs them toward target body regions. Although mental imagery and visualization have been hailed as wonderful adjuncts to clinical medicine, their benefits can be obtained by anyone in any state of health, especially to promote and enjoy a deep sense of relaxation.

FIGURE 21.2 A beach scene such as this, reminiscent of some vacation areas, is often used by people to promote relaxation.

Mental Imagery as a Relaxation Technique

Daydreaming may be the most common type of mental imagery used to relax (**FIG. 21.2**). Researchers have come to understand that the conscious mind needs to break away periodically and "download" sensory information for "reprocessing." (Computer software screensavers are loosely based on this concept.) Many people are aware that they daydream, yet when asked to recall the images they are hard-pressed to give an answer. Mental imagery as a form of relaxation has taken the concept of daydreaming and organized it to give it a sense of legitimacy. People rarely daydream spontaneously during a bout of stress. Instead, as mentioned previously, the mind conjures up worst-case scenarios that seem more real than the actual event. So, to alter this mind frame, the daydreaming concept has been adapted to intercept the stress response and give the body a chance to unwind. It does this by replacing negative thoughts and perceptions

with peaceful scenes. Just as real or imaginary thoughts can trigger the stress response, relaxing thoughts can promote the relaxation response. This is the primary goal and purpose of mental imagery. When imagination is used to promote relaxation, the body's five senses are in effect deactivated or desensitized to stressful stimuli. The body is allowed to recharge so that upon return to your physical environment, you can deal with perceptions of stress more effectively.

In many ways, the creation of mental imagery is like making a motion picture in which characters wear a number of hats. In this case, you take on all the roles: producer (selecting the sets and scenery), director (organizing the sensory cues), actor, and audience (experiencing the effects of the production). All the roles are equally significant to making the images as powerful as possible. With practice, the use of this technique will enhance your skills in all these roles and great satisfaction will be derived from participation in your own creation.

Over time, as the concept of mental imagery developed, it was divided into three distinct categories. As more and more people began to share this technique, many variations and combinations of these emerged. The original three are discussed here.

Tranquil Natural Scenes

The use of guided mental imagery gained popularity and clinical approval in the late 1960s and early 1970s when therapists and psychologists began to explore variations on meditative thought. In this type of visualization, patients are instructed to close their eyes and follow a series of suggested scenes during which they access and utilize the cognitive skills of imagination. In essence, through the creative process, individuals mentally place themselves in the peaceful and relaxing scenes. These **tranquil natural scenes** are selected because they simulate locations where people typically vacation to escape the stress of home or office environments. Images such as a tropical island beach, a mountain vista, or a path through an evergreen forest are often used.

Once introduced to this technique, participants who repeatedly engage in the practice of visualization find that, like actually being at a vacation site, the re-creation of these settings provides an equal if not more profound sense of relaxation. These natural scenes, full of vivid color, fresh air, natural sounds, and other elements of nature, allow participants to put their thoughts in perspective. Natural scenes, like the real ones they imitate, have the ability to place perceptions and the people who harbor them in proportion to the rest of the natural world, turning distorted perceptions back into manageable thoughts. Moreover, with repeated practice of visualization, physical changes indicating a return to homeostasis begin to occur. Consequently, to gaze at a wide ocean horizon at sunrise or sunset, to stare at a deep blue sky filled with stars close enough to touch, or to reflect before a backdrop of jagged mountain peaks covered with snow tends to momentarily dwarf any problem, no matter how big or stressful. Although the visualization of these scenes will not make personal problems go away, it appears to help shrink them down to tolerable size, which then makes them manageable to deal with and resolve. And the acknowledgment of stressors in the presence of any

one of these scenes makes the concern less threatening, if not insignificant altogether.

Of all the natural settings used to promote relaxation, the most common include water, such as ocean beaches, mountain lakes, or waterfalls and streams. It is commonly believed that scenes of water are reminiscent of the earliest sensations experienced in the womb. Any scene perceived to be relaxing, however, can have the same effect. The power of this type of imagery lies in using not just visual imagination sense but other senses as well. Seeing the image, hearing the sounds, smelling the fragrances or freshness of the air, sensing the air temperature, and feeling the wind and the sun on your skin all coalesce into a very powerful scene. By accessing the imagination of these sensations, you go from being a passive observer to an active participant in your own image. Furthermore, by acknowledging all sensations, you experience the calming effects of this technique firsthand rather than observing them from a vicarious or "third-person" viewpoint.

There is no dearth of images that can help produce the relaxation response, nor is there one image that will have the same effect on everyone. Perhaps the greatest positive influence on the visualization of natural scenes is the perception that it promotes tranquility. A disturbing association with a natural image may actually promote stress rather than decrease it. For instance, an image of a mountain vista may not be considered relaxing to someone with a fear of heights. When introducing guided mental imagery, a good instructor will suggest that participants take the liberty to augment or change the suggestions so that the tailored image promotes a personal sense of relaxation. For example, because of my Colorado roots, I often use a mountain lake as a peaceful image when I teach mental imagery. But once I had a student who had never experienced a view of a mountain lake. As a former lifeguard, he instead took the concept of a body of water and envisioned looking at reflections from an undisturbed indoor pool. It was a scene he could relate to; it worked for him.

Some guided mental imagery invites individuals to compare the visualized image with their own state of physical relaxation. Such comparison tends to promote a deeper sense of calmness throughout the body.

Behavioral Changes

For years, many psychologists have held strongly to the belief that the key to addressing negative health habits is to change behavior. This, more than values

> **Tranquil natural scenes:** One of three categories used in mental imagery (e.g., ocean beach, mountain vista, old-growth forest, lavender gardens).

BOX 21.1   Peaceful Scenes to Promote Relaxation

As a class assignment, I ask my students to create five mental images that promote a sense of deep relaxation specifically for them. Some are long, some are short, but each conveys an image that promotes calmness in the person who created it. I never cease to be amazed at what they come up with. The following is a "best-of" collection of mental imagery scenes as seen through the creative eyes of my students. Close your eyes for a moment after reading each one and decide whether it brings you a sense of tranquility.

1. Stretched between two trees is a hammock, and I am lying in that hammock swinging slowly in the breeze. There are a few trees around, and in front of me is a large meadow. The grass is lush green and spotted with hundreds of multicolored flowers that seem to stretch forever. The sky is blue and clear, with only a few small white clouds moving slowly across the sky. The breeze caresses my face in syncopation with the hammock's motion.

2. I am in the wilderness, staring into a clear, star-filled sky. There is a campfire nearby, which is slowly losing its zest, but is still throwing off intense amounts of heat. I'm lying on my sleeping bag, my face is looking straight up. The fire occasionally crackles and a spark is seen shooting in the air. As I examine the sky, a shooting star lights up the darkness and throws a brilliant white light for what appears to be miles. My body snuggles into the sleeping bag as I dream of the wish I just made.

3. With my legs I can feel the sides of my horse expand as he breathes. We have stopped in the middle of a clearing. We have been riding through a woods blanketed with snow. The snow is no longer falling, and the air is cool and crisp. The horse's breath can be seen as mist rising from his nose. We remain still for a moment, listening to the sounds of the other animals in the woods. I give my horse a nudge and he responds, moving forward through this winter wonderland.

4. The water is turquoise, even at a depth of 30 feet, with perfect visibility. I am weightless. The rays of the sun pierce through the water, but seem to soften as they reach to touch the sand below. The coral varies in shape and color; I can't begin to describe its beauty. Schools of small fish surround my body and then disappear in the blink of an eye. With each kick, my body is caressed by the warmth of the water; the bubbles tickle as they pass my face headed for the surface.

5. I am soaring through the crisp blue air. I am flying as if I have wings. I do; I am hang gliding. The sky is a deep blue with white puffy clouds. As I float through one, it is silent. I am completely alone. I see Earth below me. It is far away. I feel weightless. I hear the soft hush of the breeze. My hands make waves in the air. I can see the sun. I can almost touch it as I glide effortlessly through the air.

---

and attitudes, is the part of personality that is easiest to change. Ingestive habits such as smoking, drinking, various eating behaviors, and substance addictions are the most common health concerns targeted for behavioral changes. Process-addiction behaviors (workaholism, shopaholism, and the like) fall into this category as well. Mental imagery combined with power of suggestion was taken up as the premise of behavioral medicine to help people change negative health behaviors into positive ones. Although this technique alone will not produce changes, when used in conjunction with other behavior modification tactics and coping strategies, **behavorial changes** have proved effective for some people. What mental imagery does is reinforce a new desired behavior. Repeated use of images reinforces the desired behavior more strongly over time.

Mental imagery used to influence behavioral changes is a specific style of cognitive restructuring. As mentioned earlier, in his work to help people overcome their fears, Wolpe created a process of mental imagery called **systematic desensitization**. In this process, a person uses

Behavioral changes: One of three categories used in mental imagery (e.g., quitting smoking, improved athletic performance, weight loss programming).

Systematic desensitization: A term coined by psychologist Joseph Wolpe to describe a process of progressive tolerance to stress by gaining a greater sense of comfort with the unknown through repeated exposure and visualization.

his or her imagination to help overcome anxiety related to a specific situation by building up a tolerance to the stressor through progressive exposures to it. The first step is for the subject to create the exposures in his or her own mind while in a relaxed state. For example, let's say that you have a fear of public speaking and you are slated to give a presentation to 300 people next month. In the process of systematic desensitization, you would create a scene in your mind where you are standing at a podium in an empty auditorium giving a flawless speech. Along with this image you might also practice some diaphragmatic breathing and mental imagery of tranquil natural scenes to calm down before you start talking. After repeating this image several times, you then imagine one or two people (very close friends) in the audience who applaud vigorously when you are done. After repeating this image enough to feel comfortable, you then imagine that you give your successful speech to half an audience, followed by the same great speech to a full house, both to thunderous applause. With practice, the strength of this calm image overrides the intensity of the stressor so that your stress response is minimal, if triggered at all. The second phase of systematic desensitization would be to actually rehearse your speech at a podium while recalling the images (either relaxing scenes or your image of success) to help re-create the feeling of calmness you attained earlier. Again the stress response is minimal and disappears seconds after the speech starts.

Another example of someone who made behavioral changes through mental imagery is Allison, who tried numerous times to quit smoking. She cut down from two packs to six cigarettes per day, but still felt the need to smoke when she was driving to and from work. Attempting to quit smoking altogether, Allison practiced mental imagery wherein she visualized herself in her car driving to work. She imagined that she opened the window a little and played soft music on the radio. At traffic lights—a point of frustration and impatience—she looked for birds until the light changed. After having found a parking space, she got out of her car and imagined herself walking into the office without feeling the need for a cigarette. By taking herself through the drive to work in her imagination, Allison was able to envision herself accomplishing the goal she set. The repeated use of her image laid the groundwork—the reinforcement of the desired behavioral change—enabling her to accomplish her task when she encountered the problematic situation directly.

At about the same time that mental imagery and visualization started being used in the clinical setting to promote positive behavioral health changes, the discipline of sports psychology took root and was also introduced into the world of athletics. The sport that first received publicity from the use of mental imagery was tennis. In the book *The Inner Game of Tennis*, Timothy Gallwey (1974) described his theory that by rehearsing the game in one's mind, one could improve one's game on the court. Studies employing this technique began to show support for the theory, concluding that when the mind rehearses a motor skill, the neural tract through which impulses are sent from the brain to the muscles is better defined (Harris and Robinson, 1986). An example is imagining practicing the serve into the service box. When repeated over and over again, the result is improved coordination during actual play. Thus, the technique of mental training became very popular in amateur and professional sports when athletes were sidelined with injuries, and it was soon incorporated into rehabilitation programs. In addition, athletes began to use visualization (**FIG. 21.3**) in their mental training programs to decrease competitive anxiety and to improve motivation and self-esteem through the use of positive affirmations.

Integrated into the technique of mental imagery to influence behavioral change is the use of verbal messages (positive affirmations) to reinforce the strength of the image. Positive affirmations are positive thoughts that the conscious mind sends to itself as well as to the unconscious

FIGURE 21.3   Many athletes use mental imagery (mental training, mental rehearsal) to complement their physical training. For amateurs and professionals alike, the mental skills of competition are extremely important for peak performance.

mind to build confidence, assertiveness, and self-esteem. These positive thoughts, expressed in words, phrases, or sentences, are repeated to yourself through your inner voice while you are in a relaxed state. Often they are used in conjunction with diaphragmatic breathing, and are repeated silently during the exhalation phase, when the body is most relaxed. The mind is most receptive to the message it hears in a relaxed state. For example, the famous coffee mug slogan "Damn, I'm Good" is a wonderful positive affirmation that can be combined with an image of personal success to reinforce its message. Members of Alcoholics Anonymous also use a number of these statements as mental reminders or *mantras* in their recovery program, the most common being "One day at a time."

The rationale behind positive-affirmation statements goes something like this. Either through learned behaviors or an innate characteristic common to all humans, we tend to feed our minds a preponderance of negative thoughts. The cumulative effect of these thoughts is to erode the foundations of self-esteem. And low self-esteem makes us vulnerable to stress. The advertising industry employs this concept through ads that target our insecurities. They repeatedly suggest that we buy the products to improve our self-image. The underlying message is that we are not good enough unless we do. Research reveals that we are bombarded with an average of over 3,000 media messages per day (MortarBlog, 2006). Although not all advertisers exploit our insecurities, so many slant their messages in a negative direction that they reinforce our tendency toward negative self-feedback, making the cycle even harder to break. We become our own worst critic. The voice inside our head, the sentry guard of the ego, constantly tells us that we are doing something wrong or that we fail to meet our own expectations. By contrast, the use of positive affirmations helps to balance the emotional scales, disarm the internal critic, and reinforce the foundations of positive self-esteem. Any positive thought or phrase will do. Take a moment to think of a phrase you can say to yourself to make you feel good inside. Once you have one, repeat it to yourself when you practice your relaxation techniques. When you are feeling low or stressed out, close your eyes for a moment and try to recall the phrase. Repeat it to yourself along with a supporting mental image and feel the strength it gives you. It may take a few tries, but this technique has proved effective for a great many athletes in their games—and in the game of life. It can work for you, too!

For example, I once worked with an Olympic athlete who years previously had defected from the (then) Soviet Union. Although he enjoyed his newfound freedom, at times he felt that he had lost his "European" competitive edge. He never took hold of the idea of positive affirmations, perhaps because he didn't believe this internal feedback would work. At the 1987 World Championships in Lake Placid, he once again found himself competing face to face against his former Soviet teammates. During the final competition, in a sudden burst of energy, he pulled ahead to win. After his victory, he told me about his new positive-affirmation statement. With an undeniable accent coming through a smile, he said, "I still got the goods."

Remember, not only can positive-affirmation statements combined with mental images augment a message during a relaxed state, but this same technique can be used during stressful encounters such as traffic jams, public speeches, or staff meetings. Many times negative behaviors or stress-prone behaviors are manifestations of low self-esteem, feelings of failure or rejection we place on ourselves. Positive visualization can often be used to boost and maintain high self-esteem.

Internal Body Images

The third type of mental imagery involves direct changes in physiological functions by using imagination to see a particular body region in a healthy state. Signs and symptoms of the stress response manifested throughout the body are by far the greatest concern to people. The major question posed by health practitioners is this: If stress-related thoughts produce physical ailments, can the mind repair the body with healing thoughts? This type of mental imagery was springboarded into the realm of progressive medicine in 1971 when Simonton and Simonton taught a group of cancer patients several relaxation techniques, including the use of mental imagery. Specifically, patients were invited to imagine the white blood cells of their immune systems fighting the cancerous tumor cells. Through employing their sense of imagination and assuming responsibility for their treatment and recovery, many patients saw their tumors go into remission. The Simontons' book *Getting Well Again*,

Internal body images: One of three categories used in mental imagery for the purpose of healing disease or illness (e.g., shrinkage of cancerous tumors, mending broken bones).

which describes the protocol used to develop this landmark program, served as a catalyst for similar programs across the United States. As the co-founder and president of the Academy for Guided Imagery, Marty Rossman, M.D., is currently championing the cause of mental imagery and the healing powers of guided visualization for everything from asthma to cancer as described in his book, *Fighting Cancer from Within*.

In the past 10 years, there have been many documented cases of people using mental imagery to rejuvenate and restore their bodies to health, from spontaneous remissions of cancerous tumors and dysfunctional organs, to mended bones and connective tissue. These cases have predominantly involved cancer patients, but other illnesses have been targeted as well, including hypertension, migraines, and lower-back pain. As mentioned previously, these cases are anecdotal in nature, in that control subjects were not observed. Moreover, mental imagery was not the sole intervention, but rather one of many therapies used. However, these case studies imply that there is indeed potential benefit when mental imagery and other related therapies are used in conjunction with conventional medicine. The key is that the patient must begin to assume responsibility for his or her own health status.

As mentioned earlier, the healing mechanism of mental imagery is not fully understood scientifically. Achterberg (1984) hypothesized that the images produced in the mind, specifically the right brain, appear to send, or are converted to, biochemical messages, most likely through neuropeptides, and affix themselves to receptor sites on lymphocytes and perhaps other targeted cells to promote the healing process. This process somehow initiates a path of cancer-cell destruction or organ-cell reconstruction. Quite possibly this healing process employs the integration of several body systems, including the inhibition or suppression of the nervous and endocrine systems from secreting stress hormones. Keep in mind that mental imagery is not meant to be a replacement for standard medical practices. But the use of this technique as a complement to medical treatment appears, for some people, to be more effective than pharmacological medicine alone. The stories of those who survive their ordeals with cancer are remarkable testimonials. It would be inaccurate and misleading, however, to imply that every case of mental imagery ended in successful spontaneous remission of cancerous tumors, or healed organic tissue.

Among the group of characteristics that affect the success of mental imagery, several factors seemed crucial

to Achterberg, Simonton, Norris, and Siegel. These include willpower, or the desire to take responsibility for health status, and faith, the belief that self-generated thoughts will bear fruit and are not an exercise in futility. In addition, it has been shown that when individuals have a detailed understanding of their body's physiological functions, the nature and location of the disease, and the specific physiological mechanisms involved, suggestive imagery is more effective.

In an autobiographical case study reported in the book *Why Me?* by Garrett Porter and Dr. Patricia Norris, a young boy describes his fatal diagnosis of a malignant inoperable brain tumor and his fight to live. Through the use of mental imagery, biofeedback, and art therapy, Garrett was able to "think" or visualize the cancerous tumor away by imagining the tumor being destroyed and eaten away by friendly yet hungry white blood cells (**FIG. 21.4**). Having an incredible sense of imagination and body awareness, and knowing exactly where the tumor was located, he visualized shrinkage of the tumor successfully. Within several months a CT scan revealed that the cancerous tumor had indeed vanished.

In her acclaimed book *It's Always Something*, comedienne Gilda Radner also describes her use of mental imagery with her ovarian cancer, which eventually claimed her

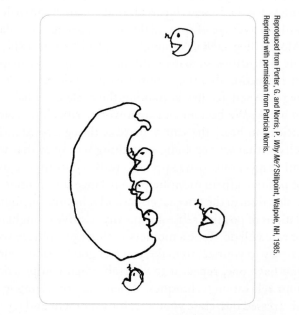

FIGURE 21.4   A sketch made by Garrett Porter to help him visualize the healing process in his body. The small "Pacman" creatures (white blood cells) are destroying and eating the tumor, which he named "planet meatball."

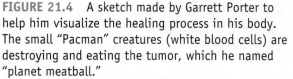

life. She created the image that her body was like a big, fluffy pink towel. Washing and drying the towel was symbolic of the chemotherapy. In her mind, Gilda saw the cancer cells as pieces of lint on the towel when it was pulled from the dryer. To rid her body of the unwanted cancer cells, she imagined that she would pull the lint off the towel and make it completely clean.

Healing images can be as specific as one ailment or illness (e.g., cancer or thyroid dysfunction) or general in scope, depending on the desired effect. It appears that images, whether direct or indirect (symbolic), can have the same effect on the healing process. Ulcers have been "healed" through images of darning the heels of socks as well as repairing spider webs. Elevated blood pressure has been decreased through images of the release of bottle-neck traffic jams as well as dilating blood vessels to reduce pressure and resistance. There are many examples of a more symbolic approach to imagery as an aid in the physical healing process. They can be adapted to a host of specific physical manifestations.

Color Therapy

Exposure to colored light and color imagery is another technique to promote relaxation. In a series of landmark studies to determine emotional and physiological responses to color stimulation, Faber Birren (1961, 1978) learned of differences between the colors red and blue. Red was associated with the heightened emotional responses of love, fear, and anger. Corresponding neural activity of the autonomic nervous system included increased heart rate, blood pressure, respiration, muscle tension, and perspiration. When subjects were in a state of emotional arousal, exposure to red light was perceived to be more "disturbing." Blue showed the opposite effect, a return to physiological homeostasis. Blue light was described as a calming color. In situations where babies are exposed to blue light, they tend to show a calm response, whereas the colors yellow and green give a neutral response. If you feel tense or frustrated, close your eyes and feel yourself surrounded by the color blue—aqua-blue, sky blue, indigo, any shade of blue you can imagine. Perhaps even imagine yourself floating in aqua-blue water. Then take a deep breath and feel your body relax all over.

Since Birren's initial work in **color therapy**, the ability to heal with colors has attracted new interest, particularly in the concept of "vibrational medicine." Light, as expressed in colors, it seems, is energy made visible. Colors are actually vibrations of energy particle waves at different rates. In his book *Light: Medicine of the Future*, Dr. Jacob Liberman points out some interesting facts about light and **light therapy**. Artificial indoor lighting (incandescent and fluorescent) is not full-spectrum lighting; it is missing some wave particles, including the color blue. People denied exposure to full-spectrum lighting (which Liberman calls malillumination) are more prone to bouts of stress and depression, more prone to dental decay, and likely to have higher levels of serum cholesterol. Studies conducted on plants grown under full-spectrum and different colors of light reveal that the health of the plant is dependent on full-spectrum lighting (Ott, 1985). According to Liberman, the same may be true for people. He suggests that when proper lighting is not available, use your imagination to see your body as a prism that captures and splinters light into the colors of the rainbow (red, orange, yellow, green, blue, indigo, and violet). Colors that are pale or hard to imagine require more attention to bring them into detail. Furthermore, some specialists (Gardner, 1990) hypothesize that light therapy and color therapy may add yet another dimension to the healing process. According to Gardner, this theory, in conjunction with the vibrations of human chakras, has been studied at MIT and UCLA.

Mental Imagery and Chronic Pain

Since the publication of Carl O. Simonton's classic book *Getting Well Again*, mental imagery and visualization have been used extensively for pain management—initially with cancer patients, but now with a wide variety of chronic pain problems from lower-back pain to fibromyalgia. Seldom are mental imagery and visualization used alone as therapies. Rather, these techniques are used in combination with diaphragmatic breathing, biofeedback, art therapy, meditation, and other modalities. Rossman (2002) states that a symptom of pain is a signal; mental imagery is used to answer the question, "What does this signal mean?" Chronic pain, resulting from causes ranging

---

Color therapy: A type of mental imagery exercise for which color is imagined as an agent for tranquility (e.g., green) or healing (e.g., blue).

Light therapy: An extension of color therapy for which full-spectrum lighting or one color from the light spectrum is used to promote homeostasis and healing.

from sports injuries and lower-back pain to gastrointestinal problems and cancer, is just one of the many types of pain that this modality is used to treat.

Steps to Initiate Mental Imagery

1. *Assume a comfortable position.* Mental imagery, like diaphragmatic breathing, can be done anywhere you can close your eyes momentarily to your current surroundings and allow your imagination to replace it with a setting more conducive to relaxation. When starting out, either sit or lie comfortably with your eyes closed and loosen any constrictive clothing around your neck and waist. You may even want to kick your shoes off. Sometimes it helps if you dedicate a special place to the practice of mental imagery.

2. *Concentrate and maintain a positive attitude.* As with other relaxation techniques, mental imagery requires sound concentration. It is important to find a quiet place and try to reduce interrupting noises that may compete with the sensory images you create (FIG. 21.5). Concentration, like imagination, is a skill, and the two are very compatible in their development. A mental image can last anywhere from seconds to minutes. Initial exposure to this technique may be short, while allowing powers of concentration to build. When employing mental imagery, tap into the imaginative powers of all your senses to place yourself at the scene you have created.

Copyright 2002 by Randy Glasbergen.
www.glasbergen.com

"There's no picture and no sound. It's the Peace and Quiet Channel."

FIGURE 21.5

Focus your attention on the vividness of colors, shapes, textures, sounds, noises, silence, smells, and the entire feel of the environment you have created. At first it is common to visualize a third-person image of yourself in a scene. But the real power of imagery is delivered when you experience the image in the first person, as you normally do in life. Focus your attention on the image in your mind's eye (the image you see with your eyes closed). Over time you will be able to focus for longer periods of time and in greater detail with each image you work with. As with all relaxation techniques, remind yourself to breathe comfortably, deep, and regularly. If your mind begins to wander to other thoughts while you initiate an image, try to steer your attention back to the details of the image and allow it to hold you captive.

A positive attitude is crucial to the effectiveness of mental imagery. The cornerstone of a positive attitude is the faith that your imagination can deliver the goods. In the experience of Siegel, Borysenko, and Simonton, *belief* in the power of the image was as important as the image itself. Whether it is called hope, faith, or confidence, this is the element that dreams, and more importantly images, are made of.

3. *Choose visual themes.* The choice of mental images is unlimited. Begin by deciding the purpose of your visualization. Is it a momentary escape to clear your thoughts? Will it help promote a healthier lifestyle through adaptations of current health behaviors? Is it a healing image to restore and rejuvenate your body? Once you have decided, build on your purpose and tailor a vision to answer it. There are several images in this chapter to start with, but eventually you may want to use these to create your own special image. The use of imagination and creativity is a skill: The more it is employed, the stronger it becomes, and the better it is as a stress-management resource. Sometimes on journeys travel guides are used to lead the way. In her therapy, Norris uses questions to help guide her patients through their mental imagery experience. For instance, with an image of a house or castle, she may ask, What does your castle look like? What is it made of? What colors are the materials? Walk up to the entrance. What does the door look like? What do the door-knob and knocker look like? Push the door open and walk inside. What do you see? Norris states

that by asking questions such as these, individuals are encouraged to create images from the depths of their own unconscious minds, the place where healing takes place.

■ Best Application of Mental Imagery

Mental imagery is very portable. Although it is best to learn mental imagery in a quiet environment, once you are proficient, the technique can be used right in the middle of a stress situation. It can be employed minutes before a public speech, at the start of an exam, waiting in line at the post office, sitting in the dentist's chair, during a boring staff meeting, or in any circumstances where you can close your eyes for a moment to regain composure. With practice, some people can even recall an image with their eyes open. Unlike other techniques, which need a minimum amount of time to be effective, mental imagery can be effective even when used for a short period. Thus, this is considered an optimal intervention technique to use in the face of stress. As a preventive technique, the art of visualization can be a powerful meditation practice for training the body to lower stress. Mental imagery is effective in both dispelling the thunderheads of fear and defusing the powder kegs of anger.

SUMMARY

- Mental imagery describes the ability of the unconscious mind to generate images that have a calming, healing effect on the body. Visualization is one aspect of mental imagery, wherein there is conscious direction of self-generated images. Guided mental imagery is a variation wherein images are suggested by another person (either live or on tape).

- Mental imagery in some form has been used for thousands of years as a means to access the power of the mind to heal the body, mind, and soul.

- Freud and Jung reintroduced mental imagery in the twentieth century. Jung coined the term *active imagination* to mean the powers of the unconscious mind to help resolve issues associated with recurring dreams.

- Several studies have been conducted using mental imagery and visualization as a complementary healing tool, specifically with cancer patients. Norris outlined several criteria necessary for mental imagery to prove effective.

- Mental imagery can be divided into three types: peaceful natural scenes, or images that place one in a natural environment; behavioral changes, or images that allow one to see and feel oneself performing a different, more health-conscious behavior; and internal body images, or images of trips inside the body to observe damaged, diseased, or dysfunctional tissue being healed or repaired.

- Systematic desensitization is a technique that breaks down a stressor into small parts and allows one to slowly gain control of feelings and perceptions about a stressor through progressive exposures to it. Mental imagery is used to augment this process.

- Color therapy and light therapy, which are loosely associated with mental imagery, are also shown to have a healing quality to them. Colors of light have specific vibrations that may augment the healing abilities of the mind. Red is said to generate feelings of arousal, whereas blue is believed to have a calming quality to it.

- Certain criteria contribute to profound experiences with mental imagery: a quiet environment, a comfortable position, and a passive attitude.

- Mental imagery is commonly used as a modality to decrease episodes of chronic pain and is often used in combination with other stress-management modalities for an optimal effect.

STUDY GUIDE QUESTIONS

1. What is mental imagery, and how does it differ from visualization?

2. List three ways that imagery and visualization can be used for relaxation.

3. What is color therapy, and how can it be used to promote relaxation?

4. List three steps that, when followed, help promote relaxation.

REFERENCES AND RESOURCES

Academy of Guided Imagery. 10780 Santa Monica Blvd., Suite 290, Los Angeles, CA 90025. (800) 726-2070. http://acadgi.com.

Achterberg, J. *Imagery and Cancer*. Institute for Personality and Ability Testing, Champaign, IL, 1978.

Achterberg, J. *Imagery in Healing: Shamanism and Modern Medicine*. Shambhala Publications, Boston, 1985.

Achterberg, J. Imagery and Medicine: Psychophysiological Speculations, *Journal of Mental Imagery* 8(4):1–14, 1984.

Araoz, D. L. Use of Hypnotic Technique with Oncology Patients, *Journal of Psychosocial Oncology* 1(4):47–54, 1983.

Arnheim, R. *Visual Thinking*. University of California Press, Berkeley, 1972.

Becker, W. *Cross Currents*. Tarcher Press, Los Angeles, 1990.

Birren, F. *Color and Human Response*. Van Nostrand Reinhold, New York, 1978.

Birren, F. *Color Psychology and Color Therapy*. Citadel Press, Secaucus, NJ, 1961.

Birren, F. *Light, Color, and Environment*. Van Nostrand Reinhold, New York, 1969.

Bry, A. *Visualization: Directing the Movies of Your Mind*. Harper, New York, 1979.

Bryant, L., and Harvy, A. G. Visual Imagery in Post-traumatic Stress Disorder, *Journal of Traumatic Stress* 9(3): 613–619, 1996.

Cassileth, B. R. Mental-Health Quackery in Cancer Treatment, *International Journal of Mental Health* 19(3): 81–84, 1990.

Chou, M. H., and Lin, M. F. Exploring the Listening Experiences during Guided Imagery and Music Therapy of Outpatients with Depression, *Journal of Nursing Research* 14(2):93–102, 2006.

Clark, L. *The Ancient Art of Color Therapy.* Devon-Adair, Old Greenwich, CT, 1974.

Coue, E. *Self-Mastery through Conscious Auto-Suggestion.* Allen & Unwin, London, 1922.

Crow, S., and Banks, D. Guided Imagery: A Tool to Guide the Way for the Nursing Home Patient, *Advances in Mind Body Medicine* 20(4):4–7, 2004.

Einstein, A. *Living Philosophies.* AMS Press, New York, 1979.

Epstein, G. *Healing Visualizations: Creating Health through Imagery.* Bantam Books, New York, 1989.

Fanning, P. *Visualization for Change.* New Harbinger Publications, Oakland, CA, 1988.

Feldman, P. E. The Personal Element in Psychiatric Research, *American Journal of Psychiatry* 113:52–54, 1956.

Fisher, S. *Body Experience in Fantasy and Behavior.* Appleton-Century-Crofts, New York, 1970.

Freeman, L., and Dirks, L. Mind-Body Imagery Practice among Alaska Breast Cancer Patients: A Case Study, *Alaska Medicine* 48(3):74–84, 2006.

Gallwey, W. T. *The Inner Game of Tennis.* Random House, New York, 1974.

Gardner, K. *Sounding the Inner Landscape.* Caduceus Publications, Stonington, ME, 1990.

Garfield, P. *Creative Daydreaming.* Simon and Schuster, 1975.

Gawain, S. *Creative Visualization.* New World Library, San Rafael, CA, 1978.

Gawain, S., with Grimshaw, D. *Reflections in the Light: Daily Thoughts and Affirmations.* Whatever Publishing, Mill Valley, CA, 1978.

Gebhardt, P. Helping Veterans Overcome Their Fears, *The Washington Post,* January 11, 2000.

George, L. Mental Imagery—Enhancement Training in Behavior Therapy: Current Status and Future Prospects, *Psychotherapy* 23:81–92, 1986.

Giusto, E., and Bond, N. Imagery and the Autonomic Nervous System: Some Methodological Issues, *Perceptual and Motor Skills* 48:427–438, 1979.

Harris, D. V., and Robinson, W. J. The Effects of Skill Level on EMG Activity during Internal and External Imagery, *Journal of Sport Psychology* 8(2):105–111, 1986.

Holt, R. Imagery, the Return of the Ostracized, *American Psychologist* 19:254–264, 1964.

Hope, A., and Walch, M. *The Color Compendium.* Van Nostrand Reinhold, New York, 1990.

Ievleva, L., and Orlick, T. Mental Links to Enhanced Healing: An Exploratory Study, *Sport Psychologist* 5(1):25–40, 1991.

Isaacs, N. Good Health Could Be All in Your Imagination. *Alternative Medicine,* October 2005:78–82.

Jasnoski, M., and Kugler, J. Relaxation, Imagery, and Neuro-immunomodulation, *Annals of the New York Academy of Sciences* 496:722–730, 1987.

Jung, C. *Man and His Symbols.* Anchor Press, New York, 1964.

Katra, J., and Tang, R. *The Heart of Mind.* New World Library, Novatno, CA, 1999.

Klisch, M. The Simonton Method of Visualization: Nursing Implications and a Patient's Perspective, *Cancer Nursing* 33:295–300, 1980.

Krippner, S. Healing and the Mind. International Conference on Science and Consciousness, Albuquerque, NM, April 28–May 3, 2000.

Krippner, S. The Role of Imagery in Health and Healing: A Review, *Saybrook Review* 5(1):32–41, 1985.

Lang, P. J. Imagery and Therapy: An Information-Processing Analysis of Fear, *Behavior Therapy* 8:862–886, 1977.

Leland, N. *Exploring Color.* North Light, Cincinnati, OH, 1985.

Liberman, J. *Light: Medicine of the Future.* Bear & Company, Santa Fe, NM, 1991.

Matthews, W. J., Conti, J. M., and Sireci, S. G. The Effects of Intercessory Prayer, Positive Visualization, and Expectancy on the Well-Being of Kidney Dialysis Patients, *Alternative Therapies in Health and Medicine* 7(5):42–52, 2001.

McKim, R. *Experiences in Visual Thinking.* Brooks/Cole, Monterey, CA, 1972.

Menzies, V., and Gill Taylor, A. The Idea of Imagination: An Analysis of "Imagery," *Advances in Mind-Body Medicine* 20(2):4–10, 2004.

Miller, N. E. Placebo Factors in Types of Treatment: View of a Psychologist. In M. Shepherd and N. Sartorious (eds.), *Nonspecific Aspects of Treatment.* Hans, Hubur, Lewiston, NY, 1989.

MortarBlog. How Many Ads Do We See Every Day? *MortarBlog,* July 27, 2006. www.mortarblog.com/2006/07/average_america.html.

Murphy, S. Models of Imagery in Sport Psychology: A Review, *Journal of Mental Imagery* 14:153–172, 1990.

Murphy, S., and Jowdy, M. Imagery and Mental Rehearsal. In T. Horn (ed.), *Advances in Sport Psychology.* Human Kinetics, Champaign, IL, 1991.

Naparstek, B. DCoE Releases "Promising Practices" White Paper. June 6, 2011. http://belleruthnaparstek.com/update-from-belleruth/promising-practices-paper-is-out-fort-sill-effort-kicks-up-a-notch.html.

Naparstek, B. Entering Our Broken Hearts: Guided Imagery for Posttraumatic Stress—An Interview with Belleruth Naparstek. Interview by Sheldon Lewis. *Advances in Mind Body Medicine* 21(1):29–32, 2005.

Naparstek, B. *Invisible Heroes*. Bantam Books, New York, 2004.

Naparstek, B. *Staying Well with Guided Imagery*. Warner Books, New York, 1995.

Naptarstek, B. *Your Sixth Sense*. Harper One, New York, 1998.

Neihardt, J. G. *Black Elk Speaks*. University of Nebraska Press, Lincoln, 1988.

Norris, P. Psychoneuroimmunology: Visualization and Imagery, paper presented to the Association for Applied Psychophysiology and Biofeedback, Colorado Springs, CO, March 19, 1992.

Ornstein, R., and Sobel, D. *The Healing Brain: Breakthrough Discoveries about How the Brain Keeps Us Healthy*. Simon and Schuster, New York, 1987.

Ott, J. N. Color and Light: Their Effects on Plants, Animals, and People, *Journal of Biosocial Research* 7:1, 1985.

Paddock J. R., Terranova, S., Kwok, R., and Halpern D. V. When Knowing Becomes Remembering: Individual Differences in Susceptibility to Suggestion, *Journal of Genetic Psychology* 161(4):453–468, 2000.

Parnes, S. *Visionizing*. D. O. K. Publishers, East Aurora, NY, 1988.

Peale, N. *The Power of Positive Thinking*. Prentice-Hall, Englewood Cliffs, NJ, 1956.

Pelletier, K. *Mind as Healer, Mind as Slayer*. Dell, New York, 1977.

Pettinati, P. Meditation, Yoga and Guided Imagery, *Holistic Nursing Care* (16)1:47–55, 2001.

Phillips, C. *Color for Life*. Ryland, Peters & Small, London, 2004.

Porter, G., and Norris, P. *Why Me? Harnessing the Healing Power of the Human Spirit*. Stillpoint, Walpole, NH, 1985.

Radner, G. *It's Always Something*. Simon and Schuster, New York, 1989.

Richardson, A. *Mental Imagery*. Springer, New York, 1969.

Richardson, M., et al. Coping, Life Attitudes and Immune Response to Imagery and Group Support after Breast Cancer Treatment, *Alternative Therapies* 3(5):62–70, 1997.

Rossman, M. *Fighting Cancer from Within*. Owl Books, New York, 2003.

Rossman, M. *Guided Imagery for Self-Healing*, 2nd ed. HJ Kramer, Tiburon, CA, 2000.

Rossman, M. Imagery: The Body's Natural Language for Healing (an interview), *Alternative Therapies* 8(1):80–89, 2002.

Samuels, M. *Seeing with the Mind's Eye*. Random House, New York, 1975.

Scarf, M. Images That Heal: A Doubtful Idea Whose Time Has Come, *Psychology Today* 14:33–46, 1980.

Seaward, B. L. *A Change of Heart: Meditations and Visualizations* (audio CD). Inspiration Unlimited, Boulder, CO, 2002. www.brianlukeseaward.net.

Seaward, B. L. *Sweet Surrender: Meditations and Visualizations* (audio CD). Inspiration Unlimited, Boulder, CO, 2002. www.brianlukeseaward.net.

Seaward, B. L. *A Wing and a Prayer: Meditations and Visualizations* (audio CD). Inspiration Unlimited, Boulder, CO, 2004. www.brianlukeseaward.net.

Simonton, O. C., Matthews-Simonton, S., and Creighton, J. L. *Getting Well Again*. Bantam Books, New York, 1980.

Singer, J. *Daydreaming*. Random House, New York, 1966.

Singer, J. *Imagery and Daydream Methods in Psychotherapy and Behavior Modification*. Academic Press, New York, 1974.

Singer, J., and Pope, K. *The Power of Human Imagination*. Plenum Press, New York, 1978.

Sokel, B., Devane, S., and Bentovim, A. Getting Better with Honor: Individualized Relaxation/Self-Hypnosis Techiques for Control of Recalcitrant Abdominal Pain in Children, *Family Systems Medicine* 9(1):83–91, 1991.

Taylor, S. *Health Psychology*, 6th ed. McGraw-Hill, Englewood, NJ, 2005.

Tuschen-Caffier, B., Vogele, C., Bracht, S., and Hilbert, A. Psychological Responses to Body Shape Exposure in Patients with Bulimia Nervosa, *Behavior Research Therapy* 41(5): 573–586, 2003.

Tusek, D., Church, J., and Fazio, V. Guided Imagery: A Significant Advance in the Care of Patients Undergoing Elective Colorectal Surgery, *Diseases of the Colon and Rectum* 40:172–178, 1997.

Vines, S. The Therapeutics of Guided Imagery, *Holistic Nursing Practice* 2:34–44, 1988.

Watanabe, E., Fukuda, S., Hara, H., Maeda, Y., Ohira, H., and Shirakawa, T. Differences in Relaxation by Means of Guided Imagery in a Healthy Community Sample, *Alternative Therapies in Health and Medicine* 12(2):60–66, 2006.

Wilkinson, J. B. Use of Hypnotherapy in Anxiety Management in the Terminally Ill, *British Journal of Experimental and Clinical Hypnosis* 7(1):34–36, 1990.

Winger, W. *Voyages of Discovery*. Psychogenics Press, Gaithersburg, MD, 1977.

Wolpe, J. *The Practice of Behavioral Therapy*. Pergamon Press, New York, 1969.

Wyatt, G., Sikorskii, A., Siddiqi, A., and Given, C. W. Feasibility of a Reflexology and Guided Imagery Intervention during Chemotherapy: Results of a Quasi-experimental Study, *Oncology Nursing Forum* 34(3):635–642, 2007.

CHAPTER 22

Music Therapy

Music acts like a magic key, to which the most tightly closed heart opens.

—Maria Von Trapp

Perhaps since the first melodic birdsong was recognized by the human ear for its beautiful sound, music has been perceived to hold a special property of subtle mystical influence. Close your eyes for a moment and think of your current favorite song. Let the music linger in your mind, consciously savor it, and then sense how your body responds to the tones and rhythm of the melody. Various sounds, as a sensory stimulus, can provoke what is known as **stimulus generalization**, a type of conditioned response. For example, the sound of a car backfiring could elicit anxiety among combat veterans who have post-traumatic stress disorder (PTSD), just as a favorite love song can immediately retrieve memories of a former courtship. Without a doubt, the auditory stimulation called music can strongly influence our physical and emotional states. Music has the ability to motivate: For centuries it was utilized in the call to war with fife and drum. More recently, it has been used for a similar purpose during sports events with pep bands. But music can equally pacify or sedate: One need only think of a lullaby to help send a crying baby off to sleep.

For this reason, music in all its many styles can be considered a way to profoundly affect the human condition and, for the purposes of this text, a positive influence on relaxation. Although this seems to have been known intuitively for ages, music is now finally being recognized scientifically as possessing a strong therapeutic quality. There are two schools of thought regarding **music therapy**. The first advocates music making through singing and/or instrumentation for a therapeutic effect. This school of thought, clinically based on and shaped by specialists in the field, defines music therapy as the systematic application of music by the music therapist to bring about helpful changes in the emotional or physical health of the client. The second approach to music therapy seeks to achieve relaxation by listening to music. In this sense, music therapy can be defined as the ability to experience an altered state of physical arousal and mood through processing a progression of musical notes of varying tone, rhythm, and instrumentation of pleasing effect. It is this approach to music therapy that receives the greater attention in this chapter.

Music is a formidable part of the American (and world) culture as evidenced by the popularity of streaming

Image © Inspiration Unlimited. Used with permission.

Quotation reprinted from *The Story of the Trapp Family Singers* by Maria Augusta Von Trapp. Copyright 1949 by Maria Augusta Von Trapp, Copyright Renewed 1977 by Maria Augusta Von Trapp. Reprinted by permission of HarperCollins Publishers.

> **Stimulus generalization:** A conditioned response to a sound.
>
> **Music therapy:** The ability to listen to, sing, or perform music as a means to promote relaxation and homeostasis.

music services such as Spotify and Apple Music. Music as a means to promote tranquility has proven itself many times over as a very popular relaxation technique for all age groups, though the types of music used certainly vary. Although music therapy is considered, for the most part, a treatment to promote relaxation, it has characteristics of a coping technique as well, the main one being to increase conscious awareness of the inner self. Listening to certain types of music is believed by several musicologists to enhance the mind's receptivity to new ideas by accessing the less dominant right-brain thought processes. More specifically, music is thought to enhance creativity through spontaneous mental imagery. In many ways, music soothes the "savage beast" of us all. Those who play video games will tell you how important music is to the experience. Although investigations of this type of relaxation technique are young, and the physiological dynamics affected are not fully understood, the benefits of music therapy are unequivocal. So popular is this relaxation technique that it has become an area of great research interest in the past several years. Today, the focus of research into the benefits of music therapy is quite wide and far-reaching, from the effects on post-operative pain (Bradt, 2010; Whitaker, 2010) to Alzheimer's patients (Zare et al., 2010) and pediatric health care (Treurnicht Naylor et al., 2010), all of which reveal the healing powers of music as a powerful agent for stress reduction. To best understand how music is currently used as a therapy, it is helpful to see how this tool has been used through the ages.

Historical Perspective

The earliest humans about which we have any knowledge believed that music could exorcise evil spirits and heal wounds. Ancient Greeks, including Aristotle, Plato, and Pythagoras, possessed an intuitive understanding of the healing power of music, suggesting that daily exposure could contribute to health. Aristotle held the notion that flute music offered a cathartic release of emotions. Plato indicated that music restored the harmony and contentment in one's soul as well as the moral welfare of the nation at large. "Music is the moral law," he wrote. "It is the essence of order and leads to all that is good, just, and beautiful, passionate and eternal form." Pythagoras credited the rhythm of music with special healing qualities. "All things are constructed of harmonic patterns. It is only when we are out of step with the natural harmonic that disharmony arises," he wrote (Merritt, 1990).

Medieval monarchs employed court minstrels, as well as jesters, to bring the comfort of peaceful melodies to their castles to relieve their melancholy, depression, and fevers. Later many classical musicians, including Bach, Pachelbel, and Mozart, were commissioned by royalty and nobility to compose pieces of music for this very reason. But the power of music was enjoyed not only by the upper classes. For centuries, long before radios, videos, and CD players, family members of all social classes gathered together regularly for words and melody. It was not uncommon for both parents and children to learn to play instruments for the purpose of soothing entertainment. The ability to play together harmoniously was a metaphor for attempts to live together in peace.

Native American medicine men or shamans often used music in their healing rituals as a powerful medicine for the sick and dying, as well as for peace and prosperity. The musical incantations and accompanying drumbeats served as a vehicle of divine communication to heal or strengthen the will of the human spirit. Likewise, across the ocean, Africans have been known for centuries to employ percussion rhythms as healing tools to lower heart rates and fever in the sick (Assagioli, 1999). Music (Gospel spirituals) was known to be a saving grace to Africans brought over as slaves, who lived under the most austere and brutal conditions. In fact, all music was a relief to those subjected to the institution of slavery, and the influence of African music and percussion on American music gave birth to jazz, delta blues, soul, and hip hop.

With the invention of the phonograph in 1877, music became more easily accessible to people in all corners of the globe. In the late nineteenth and early twentieth centuries, it became a respected therapeutic practice in Europe for the treatment of mental disorders. Not until 1926, however, was music recognized by the established medical community as a form of therapy for the treatment of several clinical disorders, most notably depression. And although music in its many forms and styles, and in nearly every culture around the world, has been accepted by the masses as a tool to promote relaxation and healing, it was not until 1946 that it was formally acknowledged in the United States as a bona fide therapy and legitimate discipline worthy of investigation. The introduction of music in several Veterans Administration hospitals serving World War II veterans with battle fatigue (now called PTSD) demonstrated that this type of stimulation could boost morale and improve patients' mental state by decreasing symptoms associated with depression. The National Association for Music Therapy (NAMT) was founded in 1950. Through the work of several pioneer researchers, by the 1970s and 1980s music therapy was advocated as a viable tool to deal with the clinical symptoms of stress.

Norman Cousins is most well known for introducing and legitimizing the healing power of humor and laughter, but in his acclaimed book, *Anatomy of an Illness*, he dedicated a whole chapter to the healing properties of music. Recounting stories of when he met cello virtuoso Pablo Casals and famed physician Albert Schweitzer, Cousins described how both men took creative refuge in playing the piano. Cousins once observed Casals, at the age of 90, get painfully out of bed, and then become youthfully transformed when he sat down at the piano to play the Brahms B-flat Quartet. Similarly, Schweitzer, in his eighth decade of life, would balance his work in medicine with a nightly rendition of Bach's Toccata in D minor. Cousins saw in both men a regeneration and restoration in their savoring of music, hinting that it may have contributed to their health and longevity. Renowned neurologist and author Oliver Sacks discovered the use of music as therapy for his patients with severe Parkinson's disease. His insights were made famous in the movie *Awakenings* starring Robin Williams. In his book *Musicophilia*, Sacks notes that today persons suffering from Alzheimer's, strokes, and severe depression can all benefit from the use of music therapy. "Music is full of mysterious powers," he states.

In the late 1970s and early 1980s, about the same time that stress entered the consciousness of the American public and became a household word, there began to emerge a new type of relaxing composition now commonly referred to as New Age music. Markedly different from rock, pop, blues, classical, and jazz, New Age music consists of a slow-tempoed instrumental, often synthesized, and occasionally acoustic collaboration of melodies and chord progressions to alter moods and increase levels of conscious awareness. Musicologists Andrew Watson and Nevill Drury trace the beginnings of New Age music to the "psychedelic" counterculture period of the 1960s, when elements of rock, jazz, folk, Indian *ragas*, and meditative music were integrated to create repeated cycles of gentle "undulating sounds" for a relaxing effect. The band Pink Floyd is given credit for making this style of music popular with its "Meddle" album in which the entire second side, "Echos," is a single instrumental composition played on a synthesizer.

The lineage of New Age musicians unfolded from Pink Floyd's inspirational work to include a collaborative effort by King Crimson's Robert Fripp and Roxy Music's Brian Eno entitled "Evening Star." Eno went on to record several albums, including "Music for Airports" and "Ambient Two," becoming a dominant force in the New Age genre (Watson and Drury, 1987). This style of music has now spread to all continents, giving rise to many other New Age and environmental musicians, including Kitaro (Japan), Andreas Vollenweider (Germany), Jean-Michel Jarre (France), Vangelis (Greece), Enya (Ireland), and Paul Horn, Philip Glass, Steven Halpern, David Lanz, and William Ackerman (North America), to name a few. Although the methods of distribution of music have changed over the years from record stores to Web site downloads, the popularity of various types of music has not changed. Perhaps this is most obvious with the plethora of music programming on satellite radio (SiriusXM) and various Web broadcasts. Although New Age music is no longer considered "new," the ambient relaxing style of this genre remains quite popular for many adults. But New Age music is just one of many styles that can promote relaxation. Classical, jazz, and acoustic folk are thought to be equally successful in effecting or enhancing the relaxation response. Today, music of all styles is used in many different clinical and professional settings as a therapeutic tool.

■ From Sound to Noise to Music

Sound is energy made audible. It is created through random or periodic vibrations that are represented as waves. Sounds can be perceived as either pleasant or unpleasant, the latter commonly referred to as "noise." Sound waves or oscillations are measured in **hertz** (Hz)—cycles or vibrations per second. These oscillations are perceived as **pitch** by the human ear (**FIG. 22.1**). The audible frequency or sonic range detectable to the human ear is 20 to 20,000 Hz, depending on the health and training of the auditory nerve tissue. Sound waves can also be detected, by means of different neural pathways, through the conduction of skin and bone tissue.

Hertz: A physics term describing the number of oscillations or vibrations produced per second.

Pitch: The human ear detects vibrations or oscillations as pitch.

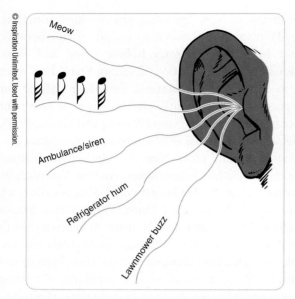
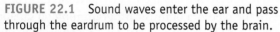

FIGURE 22.1 Sound waves enter the ear and pass through the eardrum to be processed by the brain.

FIGURE 22.2 Headphones can provide a sense of solitude when listening to music. Repeated exposure to high volumes with headsets, however, can impair hearing and result in early-onset deafness.

While vibrations are measured in hertz, or frequencies representing a number of oscillations per second, sounds are recorded in units of measurement called **decibels** (dB), in honor of inventor Alexander Graham Bell. Decibels signify the air pressure that specific sounds produce as detected by the human ear. One decibel is said to be the softest sound that can be detected by humans. In the days of horse-drawn carriages, calls for help could be yelled from windows and heard across town. With the advancement of modern technology, however, average ambient noise levels in metropolitan cities are currently measured at 122 dB, two decibels above the demarcation inducing pain. Today, a yell would not be heard over the cacophony of sounds two city blocks away. Repeated exposure to high-decibel noise can not only trigger the body's stress response, but also cause damage to the human ear (Halpern, 1985) (**FIG. 22.2**). Noise-induced hearing impairment or loss is both cumulative and permanent. **Tinnitus** is the clinical name given to constant buzzing, hissing, or ringing in the ear that can arise from repeated exposure to loud noise. A concern exists today among the

Decibels: A unit of measurement (named in honor of Alexander Graham Bell) to denote the level of sound/noise measured as pressure through air.

Tinnitus: The clinical name given to the symptom of ringing, hissing, or buzzing in the ears.

nation's audiologists that the onset of hearing impairment from ambient noise levels, combined with use of portable headphones, will occur at an increasingly younger age. It has been speculated that not only can noise be perceived as stressful, but hearing dysfunction may also become a low-intensity chronic stressor. Like hypertension, the early stages of hearing loss go undetected without a diagnostic test. (**TABLE 22.1**) is a list of outdoor locations and various noise producers and their respective decibel levels.

Perhaps in reaction to noise pollution, sound stimulation, called white noise, has been used to mask, balance, or neutralize stressful, noisy environments. Technically speaking, white noise is composed of broadband sounds that include all frequencies of the audible spectrum. This is the concept behind the noise-canceling headphones you see advertised in airports and various magazines. Although some music can serve as white noise,

TABLE 22.1	Loudness of Some Everyday Sounds

Sound	Loudness (dB)
Rustling leaves	10
Normal conversation	50
Suburban neighborhood noise	52
Vacuum cleaner	70
City noise; busy traffic	80
Inside a passenger jet (take-off)	78–83
Heavy trucks at 50 feet	76–88
Home shop tools	65–110
Subway noise	80–114
Nearby jet airplane	150
Shooting a gun	150–170

Reproduced from Alters, S., and Schiff, W. *Essential Concepts for Healthy Living,* 5th ed. update. Jones & Bartlett Learning, Sudbury, MA, 470, 2011.

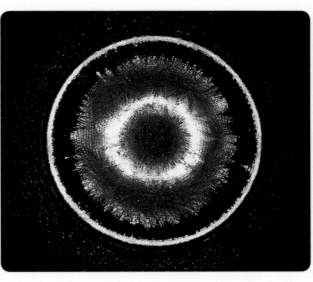

FIGURE 22.3 "Sound waves" produced by the didgeridoo, an Australian Aboriginal instrument, are captured in a small sample of water revealing this beautiful harmonic pattern and showing the entraining effect of sonic vibration on water.

its greatest potential is in enhancing tranquility. In his acclaimed book *This Is Your Brain on Music,* former rock musician turned neuroscientist Daniel Levitin explores exactly how music coordinates the hemispheres of the brain in ways previously unknown before the use of magnetic resonance imaging (MRI). From Mozart to U2, Levitin concludes that music, more so than language, is fundamental to the development of human nature.

Music in its entirety is greater than the sum of its parts. In the words of music scholar Randall McClellan (1988), "Music is a dynamic multilayered matrix of constantly shifting tonal relationships unfolding within time." It is this dynamic matrix that induces a profound sense of relaxation (**FIG. 22.3**).

Music as a Relaxation Technique

There are several schools of thought regarding the relationship between music and relaxation, developed by both the hard and soft sciences. Each can make a contribution to the understanding of music's role in the relaxation response. Regardless of the theory invoked, the frequencies transmitted as the sounds of music and received by the body significantly affect human physiology. But exactly how these frequencies are received is

still in the speculation stage. Maybe the answer is a combination of two or more theories.

Biochemical Theory

Music appears to affect human physiology directly, through the cerebral cortex and autonomic nervous system. Through the ear's complicated structure, sound stimuli are received by the brain via special nervous tissue of the ear (organ of Corti, or hair cells), where vibrations are converted to electrical nerve impulses. (It is interesting to note that these hair cells are only a membrane away from the lymph fluid of the inner ear, suggesting a link to the immune system. In addition, the eardrum appears to have a liaison with the parasympathetic nervous system via the vagus nerve.) In a very complex network of neurons, these impulses are thought to be first decoded by the cerebral cortex, then deciphered by the subcortex, and subsequently directed from the limbic system through the autonomic nervous system, potentially throughout the entire body. Elements involved with these auditory sensations include pitch, rhythm, tone, tempo, volume, and, perhaps most important, perceptual quality, or the emotional effects of deciphered sounds. Depending on interpretation (like or dislike), either the sympathetic or parasympathetic nervous system may be activated.

Music consists of many qualities that combine for an esthetic auditory experience:

Tone: An initial sound or vibration.

Pitch: The frequency of oscillations or vibrations. The higher the pitch, the more rapid the vibrations. A high pitch is thought to produce sympathetic nervous arousal, whereas a low pitch is thought to be conducive to relaxation.

Intensity: Relative loudness or amplitude of vibrations. High intensity has the effects of emotional domination and coerciveness, whereas low intensity is considered more tranquil and serene.

Timbre: "Tone color." Timbre is what makes the same notes played on different instruments sound very different.

Harmony: The ratio and relationship between tones (sounds) and their rhythmic patterns.

Interval: The units of the musical scale and the vertical distance between notes, giving rise to the structure of melodies and harmonies.

Rhythm: The most dynamic of musical qualities. Rhythm is described as the time pattern (horizontal distance) of music that seems to elicit such strong emotional responses. The bass frequencies most influence the rhythm of music.

Perceptual quality: The intellectual processing of sounds with the attachment of subjective attitudes to each sound.

Modified from A. Watson and N. Drury, *Healing Music: The Harmonic Path to Wholeness* (Dorset, UK: Prism Press, 1987).

One theory proposed by neuropsychologist and composer Dr. Manfred Clynes (1982) suggests that humans have a dominant rhythm style (DRS), a pulse indirectly controlled by the heart, directed by neural and hormonal chemical processes. This DRS, like a thermostat, has a set-point specific to these internal influences. The body's rhythm, however, can be additionally influenced

Essentic forms: Musical patterns (vibrations) that are thought to influence neuropeptide activity and thus metabolic activity in the body.

by external rhythms, from the repetitive pulsations of a jackhammer to the symphonic rhythm of Mozart's Piano Concerto in C minor. The body's DRS is thought to be subject to the influences of musical resonance or sympathetic vibrations. Clynes hypothesizes that the nervous system contains several codes capable of influencing the body's responses to musical rhythm, melody, and tone. Clynes's theory implies that these codes comprise **essentic forms** that influence neuropeptide activity and thus the metabolic functions of body organs, most notably the heart muscle.

Although many organs are involved in producing the DRS, the most obvious window to the body's rhythm is heart rate. Although there are variations from person to person, the average human heart rate has a rhythm of between 60 and 80 beats per minute. By no coincidence, music therapists have found, most Western music is paced at this same tempo, and some believe that music with this rhythm has the greatest influence on physiological homeostasis. Several studies have investigated the effects of music on electrical stimulation of the heart, with inconclusive results (Knight, 2001; Shaw, 2000). Although some suggest that slow-paced music lowers heart rate, others find no significant effect. This may be related to the perceptual quality of the music because other studies indicate the relaxation response is most pronounced when subjects select their own music.

A neurological study involving subjects connected to an electroencephalograph (EEG device) while listening to slow-tempoed music revealed that the musical rhythm quickly synchronized brain rhythms to its beat, even more so with musicians than non-musicians (Bhattacharya and Petsce, 2005).

Other physiological effects of musical stimulation, including muscle tension and corticosteroid levels, have also been researched. In these cases, music was used in conjunction with other relaxation techniques such as guided mental imagery and biofeedback. In one study conducted by Mark Rider and his colleagues at Eastern Montana College in 1985, subjects listened to audiotapes of two orchestral pieces for a 3-week period. Progressive relaxation techniques were dubbed over the music track. Results revealed decreases in cortisol levels much more pronounced than those observed when listening to relaxation techniques without a music track. Similarly, when music was integrated with biofeedback, the combined effect was even greater in reducing muscle tension than by biofeedback alone. The use of relaxing music as a sedative has also been shown to be effective in reducing stress and muscular tension associated with the process of childbirth, especially when subjects have had numerous positive exposures to a piece of music prior to delivery.

If a slow musical rhythm is conducive to relaxation, is there a rhythm or beat that is unhealthy? A theory called switching, postulated by Dr. John Diamond (1983), hints of the validity of this notion. Measuring electrical conduction and strength in muscle fibers, Diamond found that the "stop anapestic beat" common in rock music (i.e., short, short, long, pause, or da-da-DAA-pause) decreased the force of muscle contractions. Diamond hypothesized that this "weak" beat distorts or switches the communication of neural messages from the right and left hemispheres of the brain. Diamond also believes this beat decreases several cognitive functions, including judgment and perception. In addition, Diamond suggests that music with this beat has an addictive quality and that repeated exposure may, in fact, be harmful. That is, music of this kind may be associated with the inability to return to a homeostatic baseline, as measured by higher resting heart rate and blood pressure values.

Music appreciation is thought to be a right-brain function; it is the right hemisphere of the brain that recognizes and processes auditory stimulation in the form of musical note and chord progressions. This appears especially true when music is instrumental, or without lyrics. The left cerebral hemisphere, proficient in verbal acuity, is thought to intercept auditory stimulation of music *with* lyrics, if analysis of musical composition and instrumentation is initiated. For this reason, instrumentals are thought to promote a greater sense of relaxation than music combined with lyrics. (Note: Lyrics sung in a foreign language—such as Enya singing in Latin or Celtic—can be relaxing because the brain merely interprets the singer's voice as a calming instrument.) In addition, music that consists of a series of repetitive notes or beats may act much like a mantra, inducing a meditative state of relaxation. Although yet unproven, it has been speculated by some that music may release endorphins (neuropeptides and chemical opiates) from the brain and other body tissues, which create a sensation of euphoria or inspirational high. Another neurotransmitter, melanin, has been researched to determine its effects as an electrical semiconductor. According to Dr. Frank Barr, melanin is capable of converting light energy to sound energy through neurochemical messages. Further research on these and other functions of special neurotransmitters may support **biochemical theory** (Barr, 1983).

Entrainment Theory

Scientists are in agreement that cell metabolism operates on chemical energy—the breakdown of carbohydrates, fats, and proteins for energy metabolism at the biochemical level. There is also agreement that the human body is a channel for electrical energy that can be measured through various types of biofeedback, including EKGs, EEGs, and EMGs, which record the electrical impulses given off by various organ tissues. You have probably experienced this type of energy when getting a shock from walking across a carpeted floor to turn on the stereo. A new theory, which parallels and possibly integrates with biochemical theory, suggests that sounds are received through a "sixth sense," the human energy field (Campbell, 1991; Halpern, 1985).

From physics we learn that virtually all objects produce oscillations, including living organisms. Any object that produces vibrations creates its own field of energy; and the movement of subatomic particles is typically called an electromagnetic field. In terms of human beings, this may be referred to as an energy field or aura. In quantum physics, research has shown that the smallest subatomic particles create vibrations. The human body contains many organs that produce biorhythmic oscillations (e.g., brain waves, heart rate, and those produced through muscle tension). But the body as a whole, composed of jillions of atoms, also produces oscillations. As suggested by Itzhak Bentov in *Stalking the Wild Pendulum*, in a natural, relaxed state, the body itself produces a single unified series of oscillations at 7.8 Hz; this is the "frequency of human homeostasis." **Schumann's resonance** is a term used to describe the planet Earth's own vibration, which is a function of its circumference and electromagnetic radiation calculated at a frequency of approximately 7.8 cycles per second. Remarkably, this frequency is identical to both the frequency of alpha waves produced by the human brain at rest and the sounds produced by dolphins. In the words of music therapist Steve Halpern

---

Biochemical theory: A theory suggesting that music is received internally through the eardrum with sounds converted into neurochemicals that are registered by the brain, which one then finds either pleasant or unpleasant.

Schumann's resonance: A physics term given to the actual vibration of the planet Earth: 7.8 Hertz.

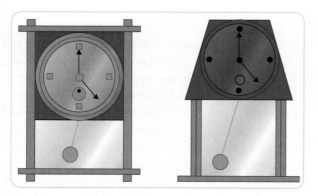

FIGURE 22.4 The concept of entrainment was first observed in the motion of two pendulum clocks. This energy pattern has since been detected in both inanimate and animate objects, such as schools of moving fish and even the synchronous flashing of fireflies (Kim, 2004).

(Halpern, with Savary, 1985), "Being in harmony with oneself and the universe is more than a poetic concept."

In 1665, a Dutch physicist named Christian Huygens discovered that when he placed two clocks side by side, eventually their pendulums would swing together in a unified rhythm (**FIG. 22.4**). This matched rhythm is called **entrainment** and is defined as the "mutual phase-locking oscillations of like frequencies in the same environment." When two or more objects produce oscillations in close proximity, the dominant frequency will prevail. Eventually, they will "entrain" together in a unified frequency. The entrainment of oscillation is thought to be nature's own attempt to conserve energy.

Like a tuning fork that begins to resonate when another tuning fork producing sound waves is brought in close proximity, entrainment theory suggests that if one organ—the heart, say—increases its oscillations as a result of heightened metabolic activity, adjacent organs will entrain to that frequency. If several body organs are influenced to entrain at a higher frequency, over time the result is a decreased ability to return to a homeostatic condition. The same phenomenon occurs in response to external

> **Entrainment:** In physics, the mutual phase locking of like oscillations; in human physiology, organs or organisms giving off strong vibrations influencing organs or organisms with weaker vibrations to match the stronger rate of oscillation; thought to conserve energy.

oscillations. Like a radio receiver, the body is a transformer; it receives (absorbs) as well as emits oscillations. If external rhythms are more dominant (i.e., greater than 7.8 Hz), then they force the body to go "out of tune" with itself by entraining to a higher vibration. The most common example of human entrainment is the female menstrual cycle. It has long been recognized, but until recently poorly understood, that in some areas when two or more women live or work together for prolonged periods of time, their menstrual cycles entrain—their menses occur on or about the same day (Weller and Weller, 1999). The same phenomenon has been observed in the blinking patterns of fireflies that land on the same bush, as well as the movement patterns of schools of fish and flocks of birds.

The entrainment theory gained support from a series of studies conducted in the early 1970s on the effects of music on the growth of plants, organisms with no known nervous system. Dr. Dorothy Retallack (1973), for example, conducted a study examining leaf growth and water absorption when corn, squash, petunias, zinnias, and marigolds were exposed to music. She found that some types of music induced a "fertilizing effect," promoting plant growth. Interestingly, she discovered that when in the presence of classical music (Bach) and Indian sitar music (Ravi Shankar), plants grew in the direction of the speakers (sometimes even around the speakers), showing a preference for these styles of music. When subjected to loud rock and roll or acid rock, though, they grew away from the speakers. In fact, many of these plants became dehydrated; some even died. Other comparable studies investigating the effects of music on animals have revealed that chickens lay more eggs and some cows produce more milk when music is piped into their living quarters. Although obviously more complex than either plants or chickens, humans are thought to be influenced in much the same way (Harrelson, 2006).

Robert Monroe, former director of the Mutual Broadcasting Network and founder/director of the Monroe Institute, experimented with various frequencies and their effects on brain waves. His findings led him to conclude that specific frequencies (0.5 to 20 Hz), not musical rhythms, were what allowed the brain to entrain to an alpha rhythm, or what he called a frequency following response. Experimenting further with various frequencies directed toward the right and left ear, he found that he could actually entrain both cerebral hemispheres—which Monroe calls "hemi-Sync"—producing a most profound state of relaxation and altered state of consciousness.

Stress with a Human Face

The sound of applause is not usually considered to be a symphony of sorts, but it is music to the ears of singer/songwriter Naomi Judd, who, with her daughter Wynonna, became one of the nation's most renowned country music acts, the Judds. Stricken with a potentially fatal case of hepatitis C, Naomi's singing career was nearly cut short in the summer of 1990. Told she could have only a few years to live, her team of physicians gave a typical forecast for a person in Naomi's condition and then sent her home. A woman of great faith, Naomi decided to listen to the voice in her heart more than the voices of her physicians, and determined that she would not be a passive victim to her condition. Instead, she would become an active participant in her healing journey.

A long-time advocate of the mind-body-spirit connection, Naomi began to apply what she knew in her heart to be true. Setting her focus on healing, she planned a strategy for her recovery. One day, after calling her husband Larry, daughters Wynonna and Ashley, and other family members to her bedside, she informed them of her game plan. In her heart Naomi knew that if she were to disconnect from her profession, her colleagues, and her music, she would die in record time. She decided to fight back. She announced to those around her that she would go back on tour—a farewell tour. But this would be no ordinary tour. Not only would she give the gift of music, this time she would receive it as well—from the audience. Knowing how powerful the energy of love was, after performing each song, she would soak up the applause, the whistles, the cheers, and direct this energy throughout her body—asking the vibrations to stimulate her immune system to heal the cells of her liver and send the virus into remission. She said, "I would turn each standing ovation, this applause into prayerful support." And it worked! More than two decades later, she is doing well, having tested "negative" 15 years in a row, and sharing the message of faith, hope, and love as essential components of the mind-body-spirit equation.

Music has always held a soft spot in Naomi's heart and that spot continues to grow as she shares her message of the healing journey that we all must take part in to nurture our souls and become whole.

Thus, the entrainment theory concludes that relaxing music can have a calming effect because elevated body rhythms entrain with a slower, more natural homeostatic rhythm produced by a musical composition. Quite literally, relaxation occurs when the body is in harmony with itself and the natural world. Proponents of this theory indicate that many people who listen to upbeat music to relax may in effect throw off their natural body rhythm. This could explain why various parameters measured by biofeedback instruments have not shown a musically induced state of relaxation with all types of music. Currently, musicians such as Steven Halpern and James Owen Matthews are experimenting with incorporating the 7.8 Hz frequency into music, including dolphin "songs" and whale "music" (**FIG. 22.5**).

Metaphysical Theory

The least scientific but perhaps the most intuitively true theory suggests that music has a divine quality. Music is a gift from God, or so Orpheus thought. Greek legend has it that Orpheus was given a lyre by Apollo (the god of music) to offer songs of praise. Although Apollo bequeathed this gift, it was the muses who taught Orpheus to play, hence the word *music*. While neurophysiologists like Oliver Sacks have looked for "substance" in the calming effects of music, students of higher consciousness such as Jonathan Goldman have searched for "essence." They theorize that music is a holy (i.e., making whole or healing) gift communicating through the soul or human spirit. Virtually every culture employs music as a vehicle for meditation, from European Gregorian chants, to Native American "sings," to African American gospels. Even classical composers such as Bach, Beethoven, and Mozart were often said to compose through divine inspiration. Bach was once quoted as saying, "The aim and final reason of all music should be nothing else but the glory of God and the refreshment of the spirit." Beethoven once said, "Music is the one incorporeal entrance into the higher world" (Merritt, 1990).

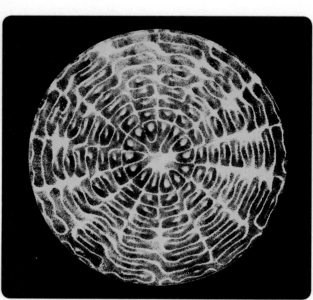

FIGURE 22.5   This mandala-shaped, sonorous figure was created by vibrating a steel plate that was covered with quartz sand, a process referred to as Cymatics. The sand collected in the areas of least vibration, along the nodal lines of the steel plate. The plate diameter is 32 cm, the thickness 0.5 mm. This pattern occurred at a frequency of 8,200 Hz.

Proponents of **metaphysical theory**, including French psychologist and audiologist Alfred Tomatis (1981), hypothesize that music and song have a transcending quality that provides a direct communications link to a higher power. This theory also gives credence to the idea that music is a universal language. Musicologist and composer Dr. Steven Halpern advocates a musical meditation that pairs musical notes with the body's seven metaphysical energy sources, or chakras. In an exercise he titles the spectrum meditation (**TABLE 22.2**), musical notes are paired with visualization of specific colors, body regions, and meditative thoughts in a particular sequence for a 20-minute period. In research conducted by Halpern (1978) to measure the relaxing effects of musical composition, it was observed that both classical and New Age—specifically Halpern's Spectrum Suite Meditation—produced a significant decrease in the stress response as measured by biofeedback (galvanic skin response).

Metaphysical theory: A theory that suggests that music is a gift from God.

Music therapist Stephanie Merritt (1990) suggests that music has the divine ability to unite or connect the human spirit of all individuals. Citing many examples of the powerful effects of classical music in her book *Mind, Music, and Imagery*, Merritt writes, "Music brings us back to the consciousness of our oneness and shows us, on a deep level, how much our progress as a human race depends on a mutual love and assistance." Integrating concepts of Jung's theory of individuation and intuition with elements of creativity and right-brain thinking, Merritt hypothesizes that music influences more than just neurons in the body. Although not every type of music can raise one's spirits, the influence of music to provide inspiration of all kinds cannot be argued.

Psychological Effects of Music

Perhaps equal to the profound physiological effects produced by music are its apparent effects on attitudes and moods, including fear and depression. Typically, the first thing people say when they hear music they like is how good it makes them feel inside. This was the desired effect when musical recordings were played for several World War II veteran patients. Exposure to selections of music appeared to decrease symptoms of despondency and in some cases altered mood into modest expressions of joy and pleasure.

The limbic system, particularly the hypothalamus (known as "the seat of the emotions"), is believed to house the neurons that, when stimulated through auditory sensations, can alter mood or emotion. While individuals often recognize at the conscious level the influence music has on mood, auditory stimuli can also penetrate the unconscious mind and promote their own changes in perception and mood. It has long been known in the world of marketing that when slow versions of familiar music, and now even golden oldies, are played in grocery stores, consumers tend to stay longer and make more purchases. This is the intent of the music—to increase sales. Mark Alpert and colleagues validated this marketing ploy in an article published in the *Journal of Business Research* (2005). Slow-tempoed music has also been introduced into settings of anxiety such as dentists' and physicians' offices. The premise of this type of music is "stimulus progression," instrumental music that is easily digested by auditory channels. It is the basis for contemporary background music produced by the Muzak Corporation.

Music in all its complexity of arrangement can produce as well as reduce stressful emotions. In the days of silent

TABLE 22.2   Spectrum Meditation

Note	Body Region (Chakra)	Color	Meditative Thought
B	Crown of head	Violet	I am connected.
A	Center of forehead	Indigo	I am balanced.
G	Throat	Blue	My life has a meaningful purpose.
F	Heart	Green	I choose to love.
E	Solar plexus	Yellow	I am loved.
D	Below navel	Orange	I am centered.
C	Base of spine	Red	I am grounded.

B Violet
A Indigo
G Blue
F Green
E Yellow
D Orange
C Red

7 keynotes of sound
7 colors
7 chakras

movies, theaters would hire piano players to compose on-site "sound tracks" to enhance the emotions of viewers during both dramatic and romantic scenes. With the advent of "talkies," Hollywood incorporated musical sound tracks into its films to highlight emotionally charged scenes and fuel the emotional roller coaster from fear to love, a practice still employed in both movies and television commercials.

Whereas music in elevators and grocery stores may appear normal these days, music in operating rooms may seem a rather novel approach to speeding the healing process. In an experiment to determine the effects of classical music on anxious hospital patients, music therapist Dr. Helen Bonny (Bonny, with Savary, 1973) created a series of tapes to be played primarily in the intensive care units at Jefferson General Hospital in Port Townsend, Washington, and St. Agnes Hospital in Baltimore, Maryland. Results revealed significant reductions in both physiological parameters, including blood pressure, heart rate, ventilations, and muscle tension, and increased ability to sleep, as well as reductions in psychological factors including anxiety and depression. Nurses even noticed increased ease in changing intravenous needles.

Music can reach and extend our deepest thoughts and feelings in a way that verbal language cannot. Music has the ability to break down strong emotional defenses and allow for the expression of feelings. Thus, controlled music-therapy sessions have been conducted for hundreds of patients as an exercise for the cathartic release of latent or suppressed emotions. Loud, rapid-tempoed music has been used by music therapists to assist in the release of latent anger. Uplifting, slow, rhythmic music has been played to both sedate and rejuvenate the body's organ tissues (**FIG. 22.6**).

© Inspiration Unlimited. Used with permission.

FIGURE 22.6   Listening to calming music can be very relaxing. Music therapy also includes playing music, which can also bring about a sense of tranquility.

There is no doubt that music has a profound effect on emotions at both the conscious and unconscious levels. Music heard for the first time often forms associations with the listener's state of mind at that time; hence, emotional attachments are often made to particular pieces of music. Thus, different types of music can be strongly correlated with physical arousal as well as relaxation. In a study to assess the relationship between type of music, musical selection, and enjoyment, and self-reported states of relaxation, Valerie Stratton and Anthony Zalanowski (1984) found no single type of music effective in enhancing relaxation for all subjects. Rather, the critical factor was the degree to which the subject *liked* the music selection. A similar study by McCraty (1998) found similar results. In another investigation, William Davis and Michael Thaut (1989) attempted to determine which

TABLE 22.3   Highly Recommended Playlists of Instrumental Music CDs for Relaxation

Artist	CD Title	Instrumentation
Eversound Collection	*One Quiet Night*	Various instruments
Jim Wilson	*Northern Seascapes*	Solo piano
Bruce Becvar	*Forever Blue Sky*	Solo guitar
Michael Hoppé	*The Poet*	Solo cello
Michael Hoppé	*The Dreamer*	Solo flute
Secret Garden	*White Stones*	Violin and piano
David Lanz	*Christophori's Dream*	Solo piano
Chris Spheeris	*Eros*	Solo guitar
Yanni	*In My Time*	Solo piano
Deuter	*Sun Spirit*	Synthesizer

types of music people considered relaxing. The music selected by subjects ranging in age from 18 to 43 included U2, Liz Story, Dan Fogelberg, Santana, Mozart, George Thorogood, Wynton Marsalis, Vangelis, William Ackerman, and Beethoven. As might be expected, it was observed that physiological homeostasis (as indicated by heart rate, muscle tension, and finger-skin temperature) was not attained through all musical selections. Subjects indicated, however, that *their* music selection was relaxing to them (TABLE 22.3).

Other musicologists have attempted to study the relationship between performing—singing (the first instrument) or playing an instrument—and well-being. In his book *The Roar of Silence*, Don Campbell suggests that singing is, in itself, a relaxation technique because it positively alters body rhythms through its changes in ventilation, heart rate, blood pressure, and brain waves. Tone rather than rhythm, however, is believed responsible for these changes. Campbell relates the story of a policy change at a Benedictine monastery in southern France suspending the practice of Gregorian chants. As a result of being denied the opportunity to sing, the Christian monks manifested several symptoms of stress, including repeated bouts of fatigue and illness. When chanting was

reinstituted, the health condition of the monks improved significantly. Interestingly, music performed in the form of chants differs markedly from both other lyrical melodies and talking. Halpern notes that singing (specifically Gregorian and Zen chanting) consists of clean vowel sounds, soft in nature, which trail off into a slight hum, creating a tranquil resonance throughout the body. Talking and pop vocals, on the other hand, emphasize consonants, which lend a less tranquil resonance.

Is it true that listening to classical music can make you smarter? Perhaps! According to one study, students who sang or played an instrument scored up to 51 points higher on their SATs than the national average (Rauscher et al., 1993). According to Raymond Bahr, M.D., classical music was proven to be as effective as Valium for some coronary care patients (Bahr, 2007). These and other findings have led music therapist Don Campbell to call this the **Mozart effect**. He explains this as music's lifelong effect on health, learning, and behavior. In his book of the same name, Campbell (1997) cites various studies supporting the premise that music not only calms the nerves, but also provides other benefits (FIG. 22.7).

Although the concept explaining why music promotes relaxation is not fully understood, this fact hasn't stopped inquiring minds from exploring additional ways to prove the efficacy of music therapy. Music as a means of inducing a deeper sense of homeostasis during grueling gastrointestinal endoscopic procedures was investigated by Rudin (2007). Findings validated the ageless wisdom that, indeed, music therapy is an effective tool for stress relief during

Mozart effect: A term coined by renowned music therapist Don Campbell to illustrate the lifelong effect of classical music on healing, learning, and behavior.

Cosmic Breadcrumbs

"No... it's not the Mozart Effect. Actually, I'm calling Tech Support in Bangalore, India."

FIGURE 22.7   Many hospitals now use music therapy as a form of relaxation for patients, including during some surgical procedures.

FIGURE 22.8   Russian composer Sergei Prokofiev combined music and imagination in his masterpiece, *Peter and the Wolf,* wherein each character is represented by a melody on a different instrument.

these medical procedures. Music also appears to promote quality of sleep for older adults (Lai and Good, 2005) and for bone marrow transplants (Sahler et al., 2003). Can music help reduce pain for kids undergoing medical procedures in a pediatric burn center? That was the research question posed by Whitehead-Pleaux and colleagues (2007). The answer proved to be a resounding yes: "Music therapy reduced pain and anxiety, and that engagement in music therapy enhanced relaxation." A Google search on the topic of current music therapy research provides enough data to boggle even Mozart's mind.

■ Visualization and Auditory Imagery

Music and imagination are wonderful partners. Perhaps the best example of this is the 1940 film *Fantasia*, in which Walt Disney and conductor Leopold Stokowski united cartoon images and several great classical music pieces in a truly inspiring achievement. Another example is the 1936 musical masterpiece by Prokofiev, *Peter and the Wolf*, a musical fable that pairs the sounds of particular musical instruments with animal and human characters (**FIG. 22.8**). Both music and imagination are right-brain capabilities, which may explain the bond between the two. Dr. Sidney Parnes (1988), a creative consultant employed by Disney in the design of Florida's Epcot Center, advocates using music to generate ideas and enhance the imagination and creative processes. In his creative workshop training sessions, Parnes often plays instrumental pieces to inspire imagination during creative exercises. Music's ability to augment imagination supports the idea that it can be a coping technique as well as a relaxation technique; imagination and creativity are essential tools in the resolution of stress. Often during relaxation-training sessions, the sounds of natural environments are used to augment participants' imagination, including thunderstorms, ocean waves, mountain streams, and bird sanctuaries.

Merritt also advocates the use of music (classical) to unleash the creative powers of the mind. In workshops conducted for all age groups across the North American continent, she plays a series of classical selections and asks participants to answer the following questions: Did the music calm you? Did it energize you? Did it put you in a dreamlike state? Did it stir up your emotions? Did it focus your mind? Merritt contends that different music styles open up a universe of thoughts and images that leads listeners on a journey of creative expression.

Just as mental imagery can be performed anywhere you have a chance to close your eyes and visualize, the familiar sounds of music can be re-created in your mind. This practice is called **auditory imagery**, or associative recall, and means that a song can be called up and played on the mind's own internal MP3 player. An example might include thinking of the first couple of notes of Beethoven's Fifth Symphony, which then triggers the mind to "play" a portion of the melody or the entire melody. With repeated exposure to and practice of auditory imagery, a desired song that promotes relaxation in an individual can be recalled and played any time, particularly when one feels the need to relax in the midst of stress.

Music Therapy and Chronic Pain

Just as several theories attempt to explain the nature of music's relaxing qualities, so various theories purport to explain music's ability to reduce pain. The most obvious one suggests that music acts as a diversion, by distracting one's thoughts from the origin of pain. This dissociation from pain offers temporary relief. With regard to healing vibrations, the entrainment theory is called upon once again to explain music's ability to decrease pain, with the healing sounds providing a stronger vibration than the energy created by neural pain. Music's healing quality likely combines these two aspects. Current research into approaches utilizing sound vibration, entrainment, and cancer continues to show promise in the search for a cancer cure and other immune system illnesses (Lynes, 1987; Roberts, 2002; Sahler et al., 2003).

In his book *The Healing Power of Sound*, Dr. Mitchell Gaynor discusses the use of music in a variety of healing parameters. Gaynor cites several studies, including research that shows a relationship between music and pain-relieving opiates. He also cites examples where music is used in maternity wards during childbirth as complementary pain management as well as in hospitals at the time of death for the chronically ill. Even though music as medicine is not considered mainstream therapy yet, Deena Spear (2002) thinks it's only a matter of time. As a violin maker and acoustic researcher, Spear has been involved with many healing sessions and has observed many amazing results of pain reduction through music.

> **Auditory imagery:** A term representing a means to imagine or recall a song or melody in one's head to promote relaxation.

Steps to Initiate Music Therapy

Because of the vast array of musical compositions, it should be recognized that individuals' tastes vary greatly with regard to this relaxation technique. Despite personal differences, however, certain factors are associated with effective music therapy as a relaxation technique (and possible coping strategy). The following suggestions will enhance its effects as a relaxation technique:

1. *Musical selection:* The type of music most conducive to relaxation and return to homeostasis satisfies two criteria.

    a. *The music should be an instrumental or acoustic selection with a slow tempo.* This can include classical, improvisational jazz, New Age, or any music that falls in this domain. There are many types of classical music of varying tempo and rhythm, just as there are many types of jazz, from improvisation to fusion. Not all types of classical or improvisational jazz are slow or relaxing. Typically, classical composers wrote three movements of varying tempos in symphonies and concertos, with the andante and adagio movements being considered by most to be calming in nature. Research conducted by Dr. Charles Schmid (1987) at the Lind Institute found that classical music sequenced in a particular composition of pitch, tempo, and instrumentation proved most conducive to relaxation. The Baroque period was renowned for its calming musical pieces. And now New Age music has begun to integrate synthesized music and sounds of nature, including ocean waves, babbling brooks, dolphins, and songbirds. Particular groups of instruments are credited with contributing to different components of wellness. According to musicologist H. A. Lingerman (1983), brass and percussion instruments parallel the strengths of physical well-being; woodwinds and strings (violins) strengthen emotional well-being; strings (cello and piano) augment mental well-being; and synthesizers and harps nurture the soul.

    b. *The selection should be enjoyable rather than disturbing.* No one piece of music will relax everyone equally. Experimentation with and an open mind to new musical compositions will lead you to a type of music that is right for you. A range of relaxation music can be found online, in special radio programs, and in friends' music libraries. Music that is grating or agitating to listen to will promote stress rather than reduce it. Find something you like and build on this style.

2. *Listening environment:* To fully enjoy the effects of music therapy, all interruptions should be minimized or eliminated so that full attention can be directed toward this special auditory stimulation, and for a sufficient length of time. In his book *Sound Health*, author/composer Steven Halpern states that listening environment is second in importance only to selection of music. He believes that music therapy is best practiced at home in a peaceful environment. Once comfortable with this skill, you can then transfer it to the office or other stress-producing environments.

3. *Postures and cognition:* There are two suggested postures for music therapy. The first and most effective one is similar to a meditative posture, where the individual either sits or reclines in a comfortable position with eyes closed to minimize distractions. In this posture, a right-hemisphere cognitive style is adopted; that is, you accept the music without analysis of composition or instrumentation. Simply surround yourself with the music and let unedited thoughts appear on the mind's screen without subjectivity or emotional attachment. The second posture is an active one where the music serves as background sound to balance other auditory stimulation in your environment, whether you are involved with housework, homework, or office work. This approach also calls for a right-hemisphere cognitive style; that is, you assume an attitude of acceptance and harmony with your environment, seeing yourself as part of the whole, not the whole.

4. *Making your own music:* A more active style of music therapy is making your own music. This can mean singing, humming or whistling a song, or playing an instrument. It can also include programming your smartphone with selections you want to play when you need or want to relax. As was illustrated by the monks who sang Gregorian chants, singing a song you like can be an uplifting experience. Try it sometime when you are down in the dumps. Playing an instrument also can be very rewarding, even if there is no audience but yourself. And at times when you can neither sing nor play an instrument, you can always carry a song in your heart.

Best Application of Music Therapy

Thanks to advances in technology (e.g., smartphones), music can be played in a host of environments—while driving a car, sitting in an office, or walking on a sidewalk—to create a more tranquil setting. In these cases, music is often used as background sound, an almost unconscious attempt to promote physiological calmness, while one's attention is directed elsewhere. Although this can certainly be effective, the ideal setting for getting the most out of music therapy is the home environment, with quality time dedicated *solely* to the enjoyment of each note. Perhaps the best application of music therapy today is to create your favorite music playlist to be used at times when you feel the need to unwind from a stressful day or merely end the day on a relaxing note. Audio imagery, like mental imagery, can be done anywhere. Music can affect any mood. Your favorite melody can dissolve anger in milliseconds. And if you have ever heard anyone whistling in the face of fear, remember that this, too, is effective at calming the body.

SUMMARY

- Music therapy is defined as "the systematic application of music by the music therapist to bring about helpful changes in the emotional or physical health of the client," and the "ability to experience an altered state of physical arousal and subsequent mood by processing a progression of musical notes of varying tone, rhythm, and instrumentation for a pleasing effect."

- Music therapy includes both listening to and creating music for a soothing effect.

- Music as therapy has been used for hundreds of generations. Music is also the most popular way to relax for Americans.

- Music is energy made audible through sound waves. These waves are measured in vibrations (oscillations) per second and in terms of decibels. A sound above 120 decibels is known to cause damage to neural tissue in the ear. Tinnitus is the clinical name for buzzing and ringing in the ear caused by repeated exposure to high-decibel noises.

- There are three explanations for how music promotes the relaxation effect. Biochemical theory states that music is a sensory stimulus that is processed through the sense of hearing. Sound vibrations are chemically changed into nervous impulses that activate either the sympathetic or the parasympathetic nervous system. Entrainment theory suggests that oscillations produced by music are received by the human energy field and various physiological systems entrain with or match the hertz (oscillation) of the music. Metaphysical theory suggests that music is divine in nature.

- Various clinical studies demonstrate that, under certain conditions, music can alter physiological parameters as well as mood; however, the exact mechanisms underlying these effects are still not completely understood.

- Music therapy can be used as a modality to decrease episodes of chronic pain.

- For music therapy to be fully effective as a relaxation technique, it is best that the music be instrumental (without lyrics). Type of music selected, listening environment, posture, and attitude also affect the quality of the relaxation response.

STUDY GUIDE QUESTIONS

1. What is music therapy?

2. List and explain the three ways (theories) that music is thought to promote relaxation.

3. Listening to music is one form of music therapy. Name two others.

REFERENCES AND RESOURCES

Abrams, B. Music, Cancer and Immunity, *Clinical Journal of Oncology Nursing* 5(5):1–3, 2001.

Allen, J., and Good, M. Music during Crisis: Music Can Be Used to Relieve Symptoms That Interfere with Healing, *American Journal of Nursing* 100(12):24AA–24FF, 2000.

Allen, K. Melodies, Mutts Reduce Stress, *Men's Fitness* 52:2001.

Alpert, M., Alpert, J. I., and Maltzc, E. N. Purchase Occasion Influence on the Role of Music in Advertising, *Journal of Business Research* 58(3):369–376, 2005.

Alvin, J. *Music Therapy.* Basic Books, New York, 1975.

American Music Therapy Association. 8455 Colesville Road, Suite 100, Silver Spring, MD 20910. www.musictherapy.org.

Andrade, P. E., and Bhattacharya, J. Brain Tuned to Music, *Journal of the Royal Society of Medicine* 96:284–287, 2003.

Assagioli, R. Music: Cause of Disease and Healing Agent. In D. Campbell, (ed.), *Music Physician for Times to Come.* Quest Book, Wheaton, IL, 1991:97–110.

Bahr, R. Personal conversation (Effects of Classical Music on Critical Care Patients: Discussion with Helen Bonny). April 9, 2008. St. Agnes Hospital, Baltimore, MD.

Barr, F. Melanin, *Medical Hypothesis* 11:1–140, 1983.

Becker, R. *Cross Currents.* Tarcher Press, Los Angeles, 1990.

Bentov, I. *Stalking the Wild Pendulum: On the Mechanics of Consciousness.* Destiny Books, Rochester, VT, 1988.

Bhattacharya, J., and Petsce, H. Phase Synchrony Analysis of EEG during Music Perception Reveals Changes in Functional Connectivity Due to Musical Expertise, *Signal Processing* 85(11):2161–2177, 2005.

Bonny, H., and Savary, L. *Music and Your Mind: Listening with a New Consciousness.* Harper & Row, New York, 1973.

Bonny, H. L. The State of the Art of Music Therapy, *The Arts in Psychotherapy* 24(1):65–73, 1997.

Borling, J., and Scartelli, J. The Effects of Sequenced versus Simultaneous EMG Biofeedback and Sedative Music on Frontalis Relaxation Training, *Journal of Music Therapy* 23:157–165, 1986.

Bradt, J. The Effects of Music Entrainment on Postoperative Pain Perception in Pediatric Patients, *Music and Medicine* 2(3):150–157, 2010.

Bryant, D. R. A Cognitive Approach to Therapy through Music, *Journal of Music Therapy* 24:27–34, 1987.

Burns, D. The Effect of the Bonny Method of Guided Imagery and Music on the Mood and Life Quality of Cancer Patients, *Journal of Music Therapy* 1:51–65, 2001.

Campbell, D. Do You Hear What I Hear? *Alternative Therapies* 7(1):34–37, 2001.

Campbell, D. *Introduction to the Musical Brain.* Magnamusic-Baton, St. Louis, MO, 1984.

Campbell, D. *The Mozart Effect.* Avon Books, New York, 1997.

Campbell, D. *Music: Physician for Times to Come.* Quest Books, Wheaton, IL, 1991.

Campbell, D. *The Roar of Silence.* Theosophical Society, Wheaton, IL, 1990.

Campbell, D. Personal conversation. June 2010. Boulder, CO.

Chance, P. Music Hath Charms to Soothe a Throbbing Head, *Psychology Today* 21(2):14, 1984.

Chou, M. H., and Lin, M. F. Exploring the Listening Experiences during Guided Imagery and Music Therapy of Outpatients with Depression, *Journal of Nursing Research* 14(2):93–102, 2006.

Clynes, M. (ed.). *Music, Mind, and Brain: The Neuropsychology of Music.* Plenum Press, New York, 1982.

Cousins, N. *Anatomy of an Illness as Perceived by the Patient.* Bantam Books, New York, 1979.

Crussi-Gonzalez, F. Hearing Pleasures, *Health* 21(3):65–71, 1989.

Darnley-Smith, R., and Patey, H. *Music Therapy.* Sage Publications, London, 2003.

Davis, W., and Thaut, M. The Influence of Preferred Relaxing Music on Measures of State Anxiety, Relaxation, and Physiological Responses, *Journal of Music Therapy* 26:168–187, 1989.

Davis, W., et al. *An Introduction to Music Therapy: Theory and Practice.* McGraw Hill, Boston, 1999.

Diamond, J. *The Life Energy in Music,* vol. I & II. Archaeus Press, New York, 1983.

Elligan, D. *Rap Therapy.* Dafina Publishing, New York, 2004.

Espring, A. *Sympathetic Vibrations: A Guide for Private Music Teachers.* Charles C. Thomas, Springfield, IL, 2000.

Evans, D. Review: Music as a Single Session Intervention Reduces Anxiety and Respiratory Rate in Patients Admitted to Hospital, *Evidence-Based Nursing* 5(3):86, 2002.

Floyd, J., Kirkpatrick, J., and Rider, M. The Effect of Music, Imagery, and Relaxation on Adrenal Corticosteroids and the Re-entrainment of Circadian Rhythms, *Journal of Music Therapy* 22:46–58, 1985.

Gardner, K. *Sounding the Inner Landscape: Music as Medicine.* Caduceus Publications, Stonington, ME, 1990.

Gaynor, M. *The Healing Power of Sound.* Shambhala Books, Boston, 1999.

Goldman, J. Sonic Entrainment. In D. Campbell (ed.), *Music Physician for Times to Come.* Quest Book, Wheaton, IL, 1991:217–233.

Goldman, J. Sound as Subtle Energy, Sound Colloquium, Loveland, CO, August 1998.

Golin, M. New Age Prescription for Sound Health, *Prevention* 40:66, 1988.

Gutheil, E. *Music and Your Emotions.* Liveright, New York, 1952.

Halpern, S. *Tuning the Human Instrument.* Spectrum Research Institute, Belmont, CA, 1978.

Halpern, S., with Savary, L. *Sound Health: The Music and Sounds That Make Us Whole.* Harper & Row, San Francisco, 1985.

Hanser, S. Music Therapy and Stress-Reduction Research, *Journal of Music Therapy* 22:193–206, 1985.

Hanser, S. B. *The New Music Therapist's Handbook.* Berklee Press Publisher, Milwaukee, 2000.

Hanser, S. B., Larson, S. C., and O'Connell, A. The Effects of Music on Relaxation of Expectant Mothers during Labor, *Journal of Music Therapy* 20:50–58, 1983.

Harrelson, J. Making an Eggs-cellent Discovery, *Palo Alto News*, October 8, 2006. www.paloaltodailynews.com/article/2006-10-7-smc-4-h.

Haun, M., et al. Effect of Music on Anxiety of Women Awaiting Breast Biopsy, *Behavioral Medicine* 27:127–132, 2001.

Heline, C. *Healing and Regeneration through Music.* New Age Press, Santa Barbara, CA, 1969.

Hodges, D. *Handbook of Music Psychology.* National Association of Music Therapy, Lawrence, KS, 1980.

Hoffman, N. *Hear the Music! A New Approach to Mental Health.* Star, Boynton Beach, FL, 1974.

Horner, C. *Music: More Than Just Entertainment.* www.wisdomnetworks.com/tvrd/healthcheck/musictherapy.asp.

International Medical News Group. Music Therapy for Parkinson's, *Family Practice News* 30(6):18, 2000.

Jenny, H. *Cymatics: A Study of Wave Phenomena.* MACRO media Publishing, Newmarket, NH, 2001. www.cymaticsource.com.

Kenny, C. B. Music, a Whole Systems Approach, *Music Therapy* 5:3–11, 1985.

Kim, D. A Spiking Neuron Model for Synchronous Flashing of Fireflies, *Biosystems* 76(1–3):7–20, 2004.

Knight, W. Relaxing Music Prevents Stress-Induced Increases in Subjective Anxiety, Systolic Blood Pressure, and Heart Rate in Healthy Males and Females, *Journal of Music Therapy* 38(4):254–272, 2001.

Kumar, A., et al. Music Therapy Increases Serum Melatonin Levels in Patients with Alzheimer's Disease, *Alternative Therapies in Health and Medicine* 5(6):49–57, 1999.

Kwekkeboom, K. Music versus Distraction for Procedural Pain and Anxiety in Patients with Cancer, *Oncology Nursing Forum Online* 30(3):433–440, 2003.

Lai, H. L., and Good, M. Music Improves Sleep Quality in Older Adults, *Journal of Advanced Nursing* 49(3):234–244, 2005.

Lai, Y. Effects of Music Listening on Depressed Women in Taiwan, *Mental Health Nursing* 20:229–246, 1999.

Larkin, M. Musical Healing, *Health* 17:12, 1985.

Lauterwasser, A. *Water Sound Images.* MACROmedia Publishing, Newmarket, NH, 2006.

Leblanc, A. An Interactive Therapy of Music Preference, *Journal of Music Therapy* 19:28–42, 1982.

Lehmann, A. C. Affective Responses to Everyday Life Events and Music Listening, *Psychology of Music* 25:84–90, 1997.

Leonard, G. *The Silent Pulse.* Bantam New Age Books, New York, 1981.

Levitin, D. *This Is Your Brain on Music.* Plume Books, New York, 2007.

Licht, S. *Music in Medicine.* New England Conservatory of Music, Boston, 1946.

Lingerman, H. *The Healing Energies of Music.* Theophysical Society, Wheaton, IL, 1983.

Llaurado, J. G., and Sances, A. *Biological and Clinical Effects of Low-Frequency Magnetic and Radiational Fields.* Charles Thomas, Springfield, IL, 1974.

Logan, T., and Roberts, A. The Effects of Different Types of Relaxation Music on Tension Levels, *Journal of Music Therapy* 21:177–183, 1984.

Lynes, B. *The Cancer Cure That Worked.* Marcus Books, Queensville, Canada, 1987.

Marwick, C. Music Therapists Chime in with Data on Medical Results, *JAMA* 283:731–734, 2000.

McClellan, R. *The Healing Forces of Music.* New House Publications, Amity, NY, 1988.

McCraty, R. The Effects of Different Types of Music on Mood, Tension and Mental Clarity, *Alternative Therapies in Health and Medicine* 4(1):75–84, 1998.

McKinney, C. H., et al. Effects of Guided Imagery and Music (GIM) Therapy on Mood and Cortisol in Healthy Adults, *Health Psychology* 16(4):390–400, 1997.

Merritt, S. *Mind, Music, and Imagery.* Plume Books, New York, 1990.

Michael, D. E. *Music Therapy.* Thomas Books, New York, 1985.

Mitchum Report on Stress. Research & Forecast, New York, NY, 1990.

Monroe, R. *Journeys Out of the Body.* Bantam Books, New York, 1993.

Nelson, N., and Weatherbs, R. Necessary Angels: Music and Healing in Psychotherapy, *Journal of Humanistic Psychology* 38:101–108, 1998.

O'Kelly, J. Music Therapy in Palliative Care: Current Perspectives, *International Journal of Palliative Nursing* 8(3):130–136, 2002.

Overy, K. The Potential of Music as an Early Learning Aid for Dyslexic Children, *Psychology of Music* 218–229, 2000.

Parnes, S. J. *Visionizing.* D. O. K. Publishers, East Aurora, NY, 1988.

President and Fellows of Harvard College. Music as Medicine, *Harvard Men's Health Watch* 7(8):5–6, 2003.

Priestly, M. *Music Therapy in Action.* St. Martin's, New York, 1975.

Rauscher, F. H., Shaw, G. L., and Ky, K. N. Music and Spatial Task Performance, *Nature* 365:611, 1993.

Retallack, D. *The Sound of Music and Plants.* DeVorss, Santa Monica, CA, 1973.

Rider, M. S., Floyd, J. W., and Kirkpatrick, J. The Effect of Music, Imagery, and Relaxation on Adrenal Corticosteroids and the Re-entrainment of Circadian Rhythms, *Journal of Music Therapy* 22(1):46–58, 1985.

Robb, S. Music Assisted Progressive Muscle Relaxation, Progressive Muscle Relaxation, Music Listening, and Silence: A Comparison of Relaxation Techniques, *Journal of Music Therapy* 37(1):2–21, 2000.

Roberts, S. Music Therapy; Pain—Treatment, *Music Therapy for Chronic Pain* 55(9):26–28, 2002.

Rosenfeld, A. Music: The Beautiful Disturber, *Psychology Today* 19:48–57, 1985.

Rudin, D. Frequently Overlooked and Rarely Listened To: Music Therapy in Gastrointestinal Endoscopic Procedures, *World Journal of Gastroenterology* 7;13(33):4533, 2007.

Sacks, O. *Musicophilia: Tales of Music and the Brain.* Knopf Books, New York, 2007.

Sahler, O. J., Hunter, B. C., and Liesveld, J. L. The Effect of Using Music Therapy with Relaxation Imagery in the Management of Patients Undergoing Bone Marrow Transplantation: A Pilot Feasibility Study, *Alternative Therapies in Health and Medicine* 9(6):70–74, 2003.

Scarletti, J. The Effect of EMG Feedback and Sedative Music, EMG Biofeedback Only, and Sedative Music Only on Frontalis Muscle Relation Ability, *Journal of Music Therapy* 21:67–78, 1984.

Scarletti, J. The Effect of Sedative Music on Electromyographic Biofeedback-Assisted Relaxation Training of Spastic Cerebral Palsied Adults, *Journal of Music Therapy* 14:210–218, 1982.

Schmid, C. *Relax with the Classics.* Lind Institute, San Francisco, CA, 1987.

Schrader, C. Modern Alchemy: Holistic High Tech, *Harper's Bazaar* 3316 (April):161, 1988.

Scofield, M., and Teich, M. Mind-Bending Music, *Health* 19:69–76, 1987.

Shaw, G. *Keeping Mozart in Mind, Listening to Mozart Sonata (k.488) Enhances Spatial-Temporal Reasoning: The "Mozart Effect."* Academic Press, San Diego, CA, 2000.

Simkin, B. Mozart (Medical and Musical Byways of Mozartiana), *Journal of the American Medical Association* 286(12):1514, 2001.

Solomon, A., and Heller, G. Historical Research in Music Therapy, *Journal of Music Therapy* 19:161–177, 1982.

Sound, Mind and Body; Music's Healing; Mozart's Healing Powers, *The Economist (US)*, January 13, 2001:8.

Spear, D. Z. *Ears of the Angels.* HayHouse, Carlsbad, CA, 2002.

Staum, M. The Effect of Music Amplitude on the Relaxation Response, *Journal of Music Therapy* 37(1):22–39, 2000.

Stratton, V., and Zalanowski, A. The Relationship between Music, Degree of Liking, and Self-Reported Relaxation, *Journal of Music Therapy* 21:184–192, 1984.

Summer, L. Imagery and Music, *Journal of Mental Imagery* 9:83–90, 1985.

Thayer, G. *Music in Therapy.* Macmillan, New York, 1968.

Tomatis, A. *La Nuit Uterine.* Editions Stock, Paris, 1981.

Trapp, M. A. *The Trapp Family Singers.* Doubleday, New York, 1949.

Treurnicht Naylor, K., Kingsnorth, S., Lamont, A., McKeever, P., and Macarthur, C. The Effectiveness of Music in Pediatric Healthcare, *Evidence Based Complement Alternative Medicine* 2011:464759, 2011. Epub 2010 Sep 30.

Waldon, E. The Effects of Group Music Therapy on Mood States and Cohesiveness in Adult Oncology Patients, *Journal of Music Therapy* 38(3):212–238, 2001.

Waldrop, M. Why Do We Like Music? *Science* 227:36, 1985.

Watson, A., and Drury, N. *Healing Music: The Harmonic Path to Wholeness.* Prism Press, Dorset, England, 1987.

Weller, L., and Weller, A. Menstrual Term Synchrony in a Sample of Working Women, *Psychoneuroendocrinology* 24(4):449–459, 1999.

Westle, M. Music Is Good Medicine, *Newsweek,* September 21, 1998:103.

Whitaker, M. H. Sounds Soothing: Music Therapy for Postoperative Pain, *Nursing* 40(12):53–54, 2010.

Whitehead-Pleaux, A. M., Zebrowski, N., Baryza, M. J., and Sheridan, R. L. Exploring the Effects of Music Therapy on Pediatric Pain: Phase 1, *Journal of Music Therapy* 44(3):217–241, 2007.

Winkelman, M. Complementary Therapy for Addiction: "Drumming out Drugs," *American Journal of Public Health* 93(4):647–652, 2003.

Zare, M., Ebrahimi, A. A., and Birashk, B. The Effects of Music Therapy on Reducing Agitation in Patients with Alzheimer's Disease, a Pre-Post Study, *International Journal of Geriatric Psychiatry* 25(12):1309–1310, 2010.

CHAPTER 23

Massage Therapy

Oh, that the water softens the rocks with time, may thy hands craft my body soft like the weathered rocks.

—Anonymous

Of all the relaxation techniques available for reducing symptoms of stress, one requires special assistance: the muscle massage. Although you can certainly rub and knead your own muscles to relieve soreness in some reachable body regions, an extra set of hands is a virtual necessity to get the full relaxation effect. Muscle tension is the premier symptom of the stress response, and massage therapy (also known as bodywork) is the best technique to diminish it. Professional muscle massage is defined as the manipulation of skin, muscles, ligaments, and connective tissue for the purposes of decreasing muscle tension and increasing physical comfort of musculature and its surrounding joints. But massage therapy has a more profound effect than manipulation of tissue. In a very "touch-conscious" society, professional physical contact can nurture a sense of connectedness otherwise missing in our lives. In its own way, muscle massage creates harmony among the body, mind, and spirit.

In the past decades, as the world has grown smaller through increased accessibility of information and travel, a greater appreciation of muscle massage has spread throughout the global village, particularly the United States. According to articles in *U.S. News and World Report*, *Time*, and *Newsweek*, **massage therapy** has now hit the mainstream as an acceptable healing modality. This technique gained acceptance in Western cultures as a result of the health and fitness boom of the 1980s, especially in health clubs and corporate settings in addition to the routine practices in professional- and amateur-sport locker rooms (**FIG. 23.1**).

Massage therapy is now a bona fide practice. Massage therapists can receive certification from accredited schools across the United States. Certification requirements vary from state to state, but most massage therapy schools require about 500 hours of classroom instruction combined with practicum experience. Since the inception of the **American Massage Therapy Association** (AMTA) in 1943, the popularity of massage as a therapeutic modality has grown exponentially over the decades, with hundreds

> **Massage therapy:** A relaxation technique; the manipulation of skin, muscles, ligaments, and connective tissue for the purpose of releasing muscle tension and increasing physical comfort of musculature and surrounding joints.
>
> **American Massage Therapy Association:** The governing body that accredits massage therapy schools and certifies graduates in massage therapy.

"Relax! That first crack is just me getting past your deductible."

FIGURE 23.1

of approved massage therapy schools and hundreds of thousands licensed massage therapists. Massage therapy was even offered to athletes at the most recent Olympic Games.

To be sure, an extra set of hands does not come cheap. Rates range from $50 to $120 per massage, depending on length of time and location involved (home visits are usually more). In some cases, corporations and insurance companies now cover the cost as a medical benefit for employees. Despite the expense, anyone who has had a professional muscle massage will testify that the benefits are well worth it. For decades, if not centuries, muscle massage was considered a luxury affordable only by the elite. With the current prolific use of desktop and laptop computers, bodywork has become a necessity for nearly everyone in the effort to maintain personal health and well-being. The recent focus of massage therapy has been on the use of warm stones (stone therapy) to heat muscle tissue to relieve soreness, stiffness, and pain. Regardless of the approach, the use of touch relieves stress.

Historical Perspective

Massage therapy has been in use for more than 3,000 years; the earliest references to it are in Chinese treatises on medicine. It was believed that touch not only relieved muscle soreness, but also contributed a profound healing quality to one's life force or spiritual energy. Greek philosopher and physician Hippocrates, the "father of modern medicine," advocated a mind-body approach to physicians' care. In one of his writings he stated, "The physician must be experienced in many things, but most assuredly in rubbing." Muscle massage was apparently practiced in several other ancient cultures as well; records of the Persians, Hindus, and Egyptians all refer to it. The practice of healing touch is not even specific to the human species: Many other members of the animal kingdom are known to use elements of therapeutic touch as well (Downing, 1972).

Although there are several types of massage therapies, they all seem to fall into two categories: those originating in the East, particularly China and India, and those deriving from Scandinavian forms. Through the influences of these cultures, massage has long flourished as a viable relaxation technique in Asia and northern Europe. By contrast, Victorian cultural influences on the United States of a century ago made this therapeutic method less than socially acceptable. Even today, physical contact (of any kind) is not a dominant behavior in America. Nevertheless, human beings in every culture need some regular form of healthy touch for their well-being.

The Need for Human Touch

In 1999, John Naisbitt, author of *Megatrends 2000*, said, "The more high technology around us, the greater the need for human touch." As he mentions in his book, high technology has been repeatedly cited as a reason for increased stress. Naisbitt's prophetic comments have proved themselves true. They also reveal the insight that as we move closer and closer to a full technology society, we distance ourselves further and further from the basic elements that used to provide physical, emotional, and spiritual sustenance. Even before the high-tech age, though, American culture was known for its habits and customs minimizing physical contact. In Naisbitt's opinion, technological advancement has only exaggerated this cultural idiosyncrasy. Naisbitt is not alone in his thinking. Several health practitioners recognize what they call a "famine of touch," or touch deprivation, in the United States. But human touch is as much a necessity as air, food, and water. Reports from orphanages assert that babies deprived of touch can actually die (Field, 2008). Tongue in cheek, but very serious about their message, health practitioners Bob Czimbal and

TABLE 23.1 Vitamin T (Touch)

Type	Level	Examples
Public touch	T7	Introductions with handshakes
Professional touch	T6	Touch dispensed by professionals
Social touch	T5	Greetings, talk touch, social dance
Friendly touch	T4	Hugging, playful touch, comforting
Family touch	T3	Cuddling, hugging, kissing
Special touch	T2	Holding, sleeping, hugging, dancing
Personal touch	T1	Massage, bathing, time in nature
Sexual touch	TS	Passionate pleasure involving consenting adults

Vitamin T Terminology

Leveling: Achieving harmony between two people with differing comfort levels regarding touch, usually by expressing the less intimate level (e.g., T7 or T6)

Intimacy: Level of friendship, familiarity, or closeness with another person, reflected by the frequency, intensity, and duration of contact

Primary deficiency: An inadequate supply of vitamin T

Space invaders: People who invade your personal space, physically or verbally

Ouch: A painful touch experience (Touch minus T = Ouch)

Stop: Refusal skills for dealing with space invaders or ouches

REPRODUCED FROM B. Czimbal and M. Zadikov, *Vitamin T: A Guide to Healthy Touch* (Portland, OR: Open Book, 1991). Used with permission from Bob Czimbal.

Maggie Zadikov explain that people need vitamin T (touch) for their well-being (**TABLE 23.1**) just like the other vitamins. So, as the mind-body-spirit relationship continues to be acknowledged in the United States, active interest in the effects of massage therapy has developed, leading also to several research studies on this topic.

Back 30 years ago, when futurist John Nesbitt suggested that massage and bodywork would become a popular part of the social fabric, even he didn't foresee the problems with spinal deformity via the use of handheld screen devices like smartphones and tablets. But such is becoming the norm today, so much so that specialists now call it "text neck." This syndrome, common among millennials, results from the 60-degree head tilt used when looking at a smartphone. This tilt puts 60 pounds of pressure on the upper vertebrae, causing curvature of the spine and contorted musculature of the head, neck, and shoulders (Bever, 2014).

Massage Therapy Research

Research in the area of massage therapy has involved several demographic populations, including premature babies, cocaine-addicted babies, college students, recovering alcoholics, and the elderly, to name just a few. Overall, the findings of these studies indicate that massage (primarily Swedish massage, described later in this chapter) is a very viable technique to promote physical relaxation as well as other health-related benefits. Dr. Tiffany Field, who heads the Touch Research Institute at the University of Miami School of Medicine, has conducted several studies on the effect of massage on infant health. In a reliability study with Scafidi and associates (1990) (designed to validate previous findings), it was revealed that three 15-minute periods of massage therapy for three consecutive hours over a 10-day period stimulate growth in premature babies. In twenty babies who received "tactile kinesthetic stimulation," a 21 percent average increase in weight gain per day was observed. Perhaps more impressive, these babies left the hospital an average of 5 days earlier than control subjects did. Thus, Field is of the opinion that touch therapy is crucial in the development of the infant into childhood. Her theory is that those infants who are "touch deprived" (receive less than adequate physical nurturing) manifest several mind-body problems throughout life.

Massage was also studied by McKechnie and colleagues (1983). They found that connective-tissue massage aided in reducing resting heart rate, skin resistance, and muscle tension (as recorded by EEG), thus indicating that this mode of relaxation was beneficial in reducing the symptoms associated with anxiety. The combined effects of exercise and muscle massage on mood in college students were examined by Weinberg et al. (1988), who discovered that when combined, these two variables produced mood enhancement exceeding that by exercise alone. Subjects maintained high levels of "vigor," while at the same time they reported noticeably decreased levels of muscle tension, fatigue, anxiety, depression, and anger. In a similar study, Channon (1986) compared massage therapy with progressive muscular relaxation. She found that as a relaxation technique, massage was far more effective in reducing muscle tension than Jacobson's relaxation technique. Using biofeedback technology, Naliboff and Tachiki (1991) looked at the effect of muscle massage on skin conductance, skin temperature, and electromyographical activity in subjects receiving a 30-minute "dermapoint massage" to forearm and trapezius muscles. This treatment resulted in a significant decrease in muscle activity and an increase in skin temperature of the forearm.

In the then–Soviet Union, Kolpakov and Rumyantseva (1987) conducted a study to determine what effect regular eye massage would have on vision and eye fatigue in factory employees. They found that this treatment was effective in decreasing visual strain and recommended massage as a viable form of medical treatment. In Japanese subjects, a daily 20-minute facial massage, as reported by Jodo and colleagues (1988), seemed to produce greater physiological homeostasis, including a greater sense of perceived relaxation, compared to controls. There have been many claims that massage influences biochemical reactions (hormones and enzymes) within the body as well as changes to peripheral body tissues. In an attempt to investigate these claims, one

study by Green and Green (1987) measured the effect of massage therapy on biochemical constituents in saliva (SIgA) and cortisol. They found that a 20-minute massage significantly increased salivary immunoglobulin, suggesting that massage may actually enhance immune function. Likewise, Day and associates (1987) found that massage therapy had a significant effect on serum levels of beta-endorphins and B-lipoproteins.

With regard to chemical dependency, a study conducted by Adcock (1987) noted that when patients combined drug or alcohol treatment with massage therapy, the detoxification period was shorter, and subjects reported a greater sense of physical relaxation and self-acceptance and self-esteem. Gauthier (1990) studied the use of massage therapy in children diagnosed as emotionally deprived as an effective part of a multi-modal-therapy approach. Massage continues to be a topic of academic interest well into the 21st century with a focus on specific populations, many with positive outcomes. The following is a sample of findings with positive outcomes: massage for cancer patients (Liu, 2008; Stringer et al., 2008), massage for patients with carpal tunnel syndrome (Moraska et al., 2008), and massage for patients who have chronic lower-back pain (Imamura et al., 2008). One study went back to examine health claims suggested decades ago: Kaye and colleagues (2008) investigated the effect of deep-tissue massage on the vital signs of heart rate and blood pressure, revealing a significant reduction of both systolic and diastolic values as well as a decrease of one's resting heart rate by 10 beats per minute. Tiffany Field's most recent research (2010) on touch involved massage for pregnant women. Subjects who received massage therapy reported not only decreased leg and back pain (common with pregnancy), but also noticeable decreases in depression and anxiety. Moreover, levels of the stress hormone cortisol decreased. Not only was labor pain reduced with massage, but also labor periods were noticeably shorter (by 3 hours) and there was less need for medication. From these and other studies, it can be concluded unequivocally that massage therapy is a viable technique to promote relaxation and several other health-related benefits.

Types of Massage

Massage can take many forms. Typically, licensed massage therapists are trained in most, if not all, of these techniques and then go on to specialize in one particular

Stress with a Human Face

If you ever happen to be traveling to, or living in, Houston and need a massage, the first person to call for an appointment is Rafael O'Neil. Why? Because he was voted the Best Massage Therapist in Houston, that's why. His clients, including several professional athletes and celebrities, say it's not only his hands that work magic, but also that the whole ambiance of his office radiates healing. Rafael has been a licensed massage therapist since 1992. His training has taken him all over the world, including Spain, Switzerland, France, and Mexico. Wherever he goes, success follows, including an enviable list of day spas often cited in the "Best of" section of the *Houston Business Journal*.

To look at Rafael you might not guess he is half Irish, yet it's his Mexican roots, passed down from his mother and grandmother, that inspired a career in healing. It's the Irish side, however, that adds an element of light-heartedness to those smiling eyes, which also offer a unique healing quality. Over the years, Rafael has perfected his alchemy of holistic healing to include Swedish massage, deep-tissue massage, detoxifying massage, stone massage, prenatal massage, and foot reflexology as well as aromatherapy, sound therapy (Tibetan bowls), and energy work.

"Every person I work on today has stress, and lots of it. Stress begins in the mind, but quickly becomes physical tension. Years ago people thought of a massage as a luxury. Today it's a necessity in this frenetic society," he explains. What does Rafael do to relax? At the top of his list is spending quality time with his son, Rafael Jr. "That, to me," he said, "is healing!"

---

style. Some integrate various types in a synthesis all their own. This chapter focuses on five major types of massage—shiatsu, Swedish, rolfing, myofascial release, and sports massage—each with its own nuances. Additional methods worth mentioning, all classified as bodywork, include Traeger, zero balancing, postural integration, cranial-sacral therapy, Reiki, Feldenkries, reflexology, and trigger-point therapy.

Although the primary benefit of massage is muscle relaxation, several therapists claim additional health effects, including increased blood and lymph flow (making one less susceptible to illnesses), and a general sense of well-being. Many people add emotional well-being, which also contributes to the overall health of the individual. Knowing that emotional well-being is so closely tied to physical health, these claims are not unfounded. The healing power of touch has long been accepted in many cultures, and is now gaining recognition in the United States, as made evident by the proliferation of massage therapy certification programs and the boom in the profession of massage therapists

nationwide. Whereas the techniques of massage are clearly directed toward physical constituents, primarily muscle, connective tissue, and bone and nerve endings, the neural, hormonal, and immune systems may unite for a healing effect yet to be clinically understood. Above all else, it is important to remember that the mind and body are one, not two separate entities, and relaxing the body through massage may certainly have a cross-over effect on other aspects of well-being. For this reason, massage therapy is now being fully integrated into medical practices, in nursing, physical therapy, and other aspects of clinical medicine. The five styles presented here are among the most popular styles of muscle-massage therapies.

Shiatsu

Shiatsu, also known as acupressure, is based on the concept of freeing blocked energy currents within the body. The term *shiatsu* translates as "finger pressure" (*shi* = finger, *atsu* = pressure). It is a distant cousin of acupuncture, and applies force through finger pressure as well as forearm, elbow, knee, and palm pressure instead of needles to unblock energy congestion (**FIG. 23.2**). In this ancient Japanese practice, based on the concept of *chi* or life force, pressure is applied to specific body locations that house the crossroads or meridians of energy. These energy paths in the body seem to parallel, yet are unrelated to,

Shiatsu: A type of massage, also known as acupressure, in which pressure is placed on various points (*tsubos*) to release blocked energy and thus promote relaxation.

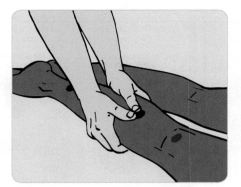

FIGURE 23.2 The practice of shiatsu is based on the premise that pressure applied to specific points on the body can release energy congested in the meridians of the body's subtle anatomy. Not all pressure points directly correspond to the area of the body that is sore or distressed.

the nervous system. The manual application of gentle pressure relieves blockage, thus allowing free-flowing energy essential to health and longevity. On the surface, shiatsu appears only to relax muscle tension. Upon closer examination, it is believed to have a healing quality through the subtle anatomy as well. The philosophy of shiatsu, derived from the concepts of yin and yang, is that interruptions in the flow of energy create an imbalance in the life force that may become manifest in a host of physical ailments. Restoration of energy through energy channels is thought to relieve ailments specific to the site of blockage, which in many cases is distant from the region of discomfort.

There are fourteen segments or major meridians in the body. Points along these meridians, where pressure is applied, are called *tsubos*. The application and release of pressure to *tsubos* is thought to remove an energy block caused by muscle tension or toxins in the muscle tissue that can cause cramps. Once a specific *tsubo* is located, about 20 pounds of pressure is applied in a brisk, circular motion for 15 to 20 seconds. This is then repeated on the equivalent pressure point on the opposite side of the body. Shiatsu uses primarily the thumbs to single out pressure points on the body with both a soft approach (the first interphalangeal joint) or a hard approach (the tip of the distal phalanx).

Although shiatsu is used specifically to reduce muscle tension, it has also been practiced to relieve sinus aches and tension headaches. Research investigating *tsubos* has found they are indeed in close proximity to neural plexuses and stretch receptors, validating the premise of this pressure-relief technique (Lundberg, 2003). Although

the effects of acupressure can be felt immediately, practitioners agree that daily applications for 7 to 10 days bring full restoration and energy balance. Shiatsu is often preferred over other types of massage for its simplicity; individuals can remain fully clothed while being treated. This type of massage is often used by individuals in the performing arts such as ballet. Other advantages of shiatsu include that (1) it has no adverse side effects, (2) it can be practiced on individuals of any age, and (3) it allows for relaxation of the entire body.

Swedish Massage

Known to Americans as the total body massage, the Swedish or Western massage, created by Swedish fencing master and gymnast Peter Heinrik Ling, emphasizes decreased muscle tension and increased circulation. It is currently the most commonly practiced massage style in the United States and Europe, as noted by the American Massage Therapy Association (AMTA). In **Swedish massage**, the individual disrobes and lies face down on the table with a sheet over the buttocks. Massage oils or lotions are used on the regions of application to nourish the skin and avoid irritating friction by the massage therapist's hands. Relaxing music is often played in the background (**FIG. 23.3**).

There are five progressive steps in Swedish massage. The first movement, called *effleurage* (**FIG. 23.4**), is a smooth, gliding stroke along the length of the muscle fibers. Both hands are used to relax soft tissue, generally in the direction of the heart. A motion to begin to limber muscles and prepare the body for the next phase, it may also include light strokes along the spine up to the base of the head. The second movement, *petrissage*

Tsubos: The specific point on the meridian that is used in acupressure to release tension.

Swedish massage: The most common and well-known type of massage in Western culture that uses a variety of hand motions (e.g., kneading, stroking, and karate-type chops) to relieve the tension for muscle tissue, often expressed as knots.

Effleurage: The first of five progressive steps/hand maneuvers in the Swedish massage that consists of long strokes along the length of the muscle tissue.

Petrissage: The second of five progressive steps/hand maneuvers in the Swedish massage, it consists of a series of rolls, rings, and squeezes made by the fingertips or palm of the hand.

FIGURE 23.3

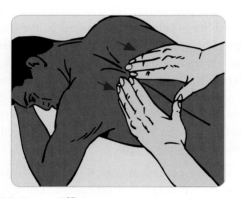

FIGURE 23.4   *Effleurage.*

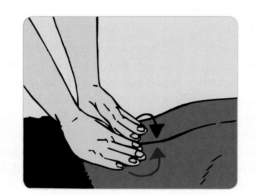

FIGURE 23.5   *Petrissage.*

(FIG. 23.5), is a series of rolls, rings, and squeezes made with either the fingertips or the palm of the hand. *Petrissage* motions include a little more pressure than is involved in the first stage. The third phase of Swedish massage is referred to as **friction** (FIG. 23.6) and involves a deep **kneading** action of muscle tissue between the fingers and thumbs. Friction can also include deep, small circular motions with the thumb,

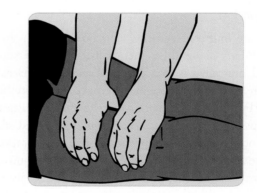

FIGURE 23.6   Friction, or kneading.

Friction: The third of five progressive steps/hand maneuvers in the Swedish massage, also known as kneading the muscle tissue.

Kneading: Also known as friction in Swedish massage, when hands knead the muscle tissue to promote relaxation.

Tapotement: The fourth of five progressive steps/hand maneuvers in the Swedish massage that looks like karate chops on the belly of the muscle.

knuckles, or finger points to extend the penetration of friction beyond the surface of the skin. The fourth movement, *tapotement* (FIG. 23.7), similar in appearance to the percussive strokes of karate chops, is performed in specific regions to activate or revive nerve cells within extremely hard muscle tissue. The last

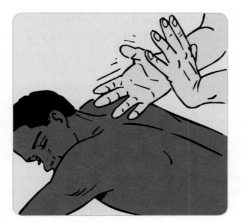

FIGURE 23.7 *Tapotement.*

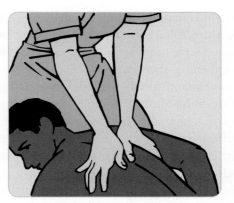

FIGURE 23.9 Rolfing is a very deep, penetrating massage used to realign muscles that have become shortened because of poor posture or maladaptive body positions such as sitting at computers or desks.

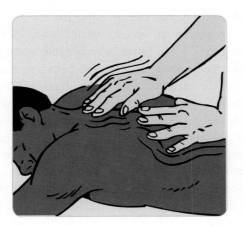

FIGURE 23.8 Vibration.

phase, **vibration** (FIG. 23.8), is described as a "trembling shaking gesture" to increase circulation throughout a desired body region.

The area targeted by Swedish massage is the posterior side of the body—calves, hamstrings, lower back, neck, and shoulders. These muscle groups are most prone to tension from sleeping, walking, standing, and sitting postures because in these positions muscles are shortened (contracted) for an extended period of time. Sleeping in a fetal position, for example, leaves the hamstrings and calf muscles contracted for 6 to 8 hours. These lifestyle postures can create imbalance and disalignment in both anterior and posterior muscles.

Rolfing

If styles of massages were classified, as are the martial arts, from softest to hardest, **rolfing** would be designated as the hardest of all the massage techniques. In fact, there are

those who would describe rolfing as physical torture because of the deep-tissue work. Rolf therapists deny that rolfing is a type of massage at all, although like massage, they define it as "a manipulation of muscle and soft connective tissue" (FIG. 23.9). The technique of rolfing was developed by Ida Rolf over a 50-year period starting in 1925. Rolf, a researcher for the Rockefeller Foundation specializing in the study of collagen and connective tissue, hypothesized that human musculature begins to lose alignment from repeated movement established in childhood and carried through to adulthood. These imbalances result from a shortening and thickening of the myofascia surrounding muscle fibers. Rolf's theory suggests that because the human skeletal structure is held in place by soft tissue (muscles, tendons, and ligaments), a muscle contracted for prolonged periods of time will pull the skeletal frame out of its natural alignment. Rolfing borrows the concept that the physical whole is greater than the sum of its muscular parts. The premise of rolfing is that deep muscular penetration can correct imbalances through slight but repeated alterations of body structure. If body segments become realigned, then the body as a whole can function more efficiently (Jones, 2004).

Vibration: The fifth of five progressive steps/hand maneuvers in the Swedish massage that resembles a type of shaking gesture to promote increased circulation.

Rolfing: Deep-tissue massage created by Ida Rolf to promote better posture by working with the soft connective tissue around and between muscles.

Whereas other massage techniques apply gentle to moderate pressure, rolfing involves deep "digging" into soft tissue, often separating layers of muscles and stretching and lengthening them with the hands, elbows, and sometimes the entire body weight of the massage therapist. This technique is not advocated for everyone. Rather, it is suggested for highly muscular individuals or those suffering from intense stress-related problems that manifest in extreme muscular tightness such as lower-back pain resulting from poor hip alignment and neck and shoulder pain. Rolfing therapists assert that changes in "pressure stretches" and muscle-fascia alignment over ten sessions can be maintained for improved health. Although the initial manipulation is considered painful, individuals who experience this technique indicate that overall the effects are quite satisfying.

Myofascial Release

Not all forms of physical therapy are created equal, especially when one considers the holistic focus of **myofascial release**. Frustrated with the mechanistic approach to health care, specifically as it applied to physical manipulation, John Barnes, a physical therapist, searched for a greater understanding of the mind–body connection as it applied to the more clinical applications of bodywork. What led Barnes on this search early in his career was the frustration he felt when, after restoring a sense of alignment and pain-free comfort in his patients, he would notice that their symptoms would reappear soon after they left his office. His search led him to all corners of the globe, to courses in acupuncture, joint mobilization, muscle energy, and bioenergy techniques. The synthesis of his experiences, well grounded in the fundamentals of physical therapy, soon became known as myofascial release. In the words of Barnes, "Myofascial release is the three-dimensional application of sustained pressure and movement into the fascial system in order to eliminate fascial restrictions and facilitate the emergence of emotional patterns and belief systems that are no longer relevant or are impeding progress."

Rather than placing the emphasis on muscular manipulation, as so many bodyworkers do, Barnes focuses on the fascial (connective) tissue itself, which in truth holds the muscles in place. When fascial strains occur

> **Myofascial release:** Deep-tissue massage created by John Barnes to release tension by working with the myofascial (soft connective) tissue.

throughout the body, as they will from vigorous movements, trauma, surgery, or the subtleties of the aging process, tightness occurs, resulting in a loss of flexibility and spontaneity of movement. Eventually, fascial tension can distort one's posture through the three-dimensional alignment of the vertebral column. Barnes notes that current estimates suggest that more than 90 percent of patients treated in physical therapy have some level of myofascial dysfunction. Unlike various forms of bodywork that are often symptom-specific (massaging the lower back for lower-back pain), the technique of myofascial release is holistic in that connections among muscles through the fascia may require distant musculature to be worked to release the tension formed through the strands of connective tissue.

How does myofascial release differ from a Swedish or sports massage? First, an assessment is made by visually analyzing the human frame, searching for symptoms of distortion and imbalance. Next, by palpating the tissue texture of the various fascial layers, the therapist evaluates symmetry, rate, quality, and intensity of craniosacral rhythm, and possible energy disturbances in the gross or subtle anatomy. Upon locating an area of fascial tension, gentle pressure is applied in the direction of the restriction. With a gentle, sustained pressure, rather than a forced manipulation, the restriction is released. As the collagenous barrier is released, the tissue length is increased. And that's not all. Barnes notes that, because of the dynamic connection between mind and body, a release of fascial tension is often accompanied by an emotional release as well. In Barnes's words, "The tissue seems to hold a consciousness all its own. As releases occurred, patients reported memories or emotions emerging that were connected to past events or traumas. As their fascial systems changed, and the memories or emotions surfaced, patients improved, even though they previously were unresponsive to all forms of traditional care." The goal of myofascial release is to eliminate fascial tension, reduce pain and headaches, restore motion, and restore the body's equilibrium. When the body reaches a state of balance or equilibrium, full health is restored, and this, says Barnes, is what life is all about: finding balance.

Sports Massage

In the pursuit of athletic excellence, individuals now train three times as long per day as their colleagues did less than a decade ago. Since the creation of ultra-endurance sports, including the triathlon (swimming, cycling, and running), Ride Across America (RAAM), and ultramarathons (50+ miles), athletes have been pushing their bodies beyond where they have ever been before (Johnson, 1995). The last thing any competitive athlete wants to encounter is damage to muscle tissue, which may result in prolonged injury. In the world of competitive athletics, any method or device to gain a competitive edge over one's opponent has merit. This edge is often found in **sports massage**, which has quickly gained acceptance throughout the athletic community. Since the 1984 Los Angeles Olympics, where sports massage was made available to all athletes at no cost, the demand for such therapists has increased dramatically for all athletic purposes, from high school and college competitions to all levels of amateur and professional sports. It is now considered one of the responsibilities of professional physical trainers.

Sports massage appears to be a hybrid of shiatsu, Swedish massage, and deep-tissue massage in its emphasis on both compressive and rhythmic pumping movements to remove the buildup of lactic acid in the muscles because of repeated contractions. Metabolic by-products of physical exercise, of which the most common is lactic acid, have fatiguing effects on muscle tissue. It is the repeated pumping motion to circulate metabolites for removal that has made sports massage so popular. In addition, however, repetitive movement often promotes micro-tears, most commonly at sites where connective tissue attaches to bone. So, another purpose of sports massage is the restoration of cell tissue by increasing circulation to stimulate new cell growth. One method often used in sports massage is **trigger point therapy**, in which pressure is placed on "hyper-irritable" points of the muscle that are causing a radiating pain in a region. Manipulation (deep-tissue work) of specific trigger points releases tension throughout the entire muscle tissue and associated areas.

Spectators at athletic events can watch sports massages being given to athletes during pre-event warm-ups, as a means to prepare muscles for activity; for postevent restoration; and occasionally during competition, between stages of coupled events. Most commonly, though, they are performed during training seasons to improve the rate of tissue regeneration after each workout. Although to date there is no scientific evidence that lactic acid is removed in this manner (Hemmings et al., 2000; Moraska, 2005)—lactic acid clears the muscles within 2 hours (Fox, Bowers, and Foss, 1989)—sports massage enjoys the greatest degree of medical acceptance for healing muscle tissue.

Other Touch Therapies

Other techniques are closely associated with the concepts and practice of muscle massage, so they have been placed in this chapter. These types of touch, although not new, have not been studied extensively, and therefore their dynamics for apparently causing relaxation effects are not completely understood. Be that as it may, they make for interesting additions to the category of therapeutic touch.

Aromatherapy. **Aromatherapy** is a technique where perfumed scents are used to promote feelings of calmness. The practice of rubbing natural essences on the body to create tranquility dates back to the age of Egyptian pharaohs, when it was commonly believed that the fragrance of flowers and herbs forged a unique bond between body and soul. The technique was revived in the New World in the late 1920s by Dr. Edward Bach, a homeopathic physician, and again in 1990 in Japan, where various fragrances (e.g., peppermint) were introduced into the workplace as a means to stimulate productivity. There appear to be two theories to explain the effectiveness of aromatherapy. The first is that it replaces threatening sensations with pleasurable ones. More specifically, aromatherapy works to desensitize conscious thought, or sensory overload of all five senses, through fragrances perceived to be appealing to the olfactory sense. Many fragrances also elicit powerful thoughts and memories (**FIG. 23.10**).

Many research studies have been conducted on the efficacy of aromatherapy, mostly in Europe and Asia. The National Association for Holistic Aromatherapy now publishes *Aromatherapy Journal* with a mission to revive the knowledge of medicinal use of aromatic plants and essential oils to its fullest extent. Essential oils have been used in the healing process of cancer patients. One study

---

Sports massage: A combination of Swedish massage, shiatsu, and some type of deep-tissue bodywork now popular among professional and amateur athletes.

Trigger point therapy: Applied pressure to and manipulation of hyper-irritable points of the muscle that are causing radiating pain in a region; used in sports massage.

Aromatherapy: The use of essential oils to promote relaxation through the sense of smell, often used in many types of bodywork as a complementary relaxation method.

"Lately, I've been experimenting with aroma therapy. Nothing soothes the soul like the smell of money."

FIGURE 23.10

revealed that cancer patients became more relaxed with Roman chamomile essential oils (Wilkinson et al., 1999). And it is well known that the Sloan Kettering Cancer Hospital uses vanilla extract as a means to relax patients who appear anxious to enter the CAT scan apparatus, just as many maternity wards use lavender to relax women ready to give birth.

It is recognized that the brain center processing olfactory sensations is in close proximity to the hypothalamus, which may explain why specific fragrances can elicit memories and their related emotions quite quickly. Furthermore, emotions are part of the right-brain domain, and it is accepted that when one part of the cerebral hemisphere is activated, in this case by positive emotions, then other hemispheric functions are enhanced. The second theoretical approach to aromatherapy involves the application of fragrance-laced oils to the skin during massage. The pores of the skin are believed to soak up the oils and circulate these essences through the body via the circulatory and lymphatic systems, cleansing the body internally and instilling a sense of physiological calmness.

The topic of aromatherapy has gained much interest in the past 20 years, in both esthetic and clinical practices. Clinical aromatherapy, as defined by Peter Holmes (1995), is a unique healing process achieved through aroma or scent by three means—physiologically, topically, and psychologically. According to Holmes, the main function of clinical aromatherapy is to affect "the specific actions for the purpose of altering human physiology (decreased stress hormone secretion), nurture the skin (through essential oils), and affect the psyche by promoting a sense of mental and emotional relaxation." Most frequently combined with massage therapy, acupuncture,

and some nursing practices, clinical aromatherapy is thought to provide a unique dynamic to the integrity of the mind-body-spirit connection in terms of relaxation.

Lavender, widely accepted for its calming effects, has been the topic of scientific interest over the past several years, perhaps more than any other aromatherapy essential oil. The results are mixed. Kiecolt-Glaser and colleagues (2008), at Ohio State University, investigated the effects of lavender and lemon on mood, and endocrine and immune function. Results revealed that fragrances had no reliable effect on salivatory cortisol levels, heart rate, blood pressure, or immune function, though subjects found the scent of lemon boosted one's mood. Conversely, Shiina and colleagues (2007) found that the scent of lavender significantly reduced serum cortisol levels and improved coronary flow in healthy men, yet blood pressure and heart rate appeared not to be affected.

The following are some popular aromatherapy essences and their biomedical applications for stress reduction:

Lavender: Lavender is known primarily as a neurocardiac sedative, triggering the nervous system to decrease neural firing, thus allowing a decrease in resting heart rate and blood pressure. Used in a state of tension, this fragrance is said to calm, uplift, and relax the mind and body.

Juniper: Best known for its muscle-relaxant qualities, juniper is recommended for muscle spasms, fibromyalgia, intestinal and uterine cramps, and peptic ulcers.

Chamomile/Moroccan Blue: A fragrance that calms, nurtures, and regenerates, chamomile is also known as a nervous sedative/relaxant with the ability to help promote decreased blood pressure, act as a bronchodilator, and be an anti-allergenic. It is used primarily for situations resulting in suppressed anger, irritability, and resentment.

Vetiver: Vetiver is known as an immunoregulator in that it is said to help boost the integrity of the immune system. It is used for immunodeficiency and autoimmune disorders. This fragrance is noted for its ability to make a person feel more grounded and centered.

Palmarosa: The palmarosa essence is used as an anti-infective agent for cases involving bacteria, viruses, or fungi, as well as sinus infections, candidiasis, and chlamydia. The healing vibration of palmarosa is thought to help boost the constituents of the immune system and bring the body back to a state of homeostasis.

Hydrotherapy. Baths, hot tubs, and **flotation tanks**, which collectively make up the category of **hydrotherapy**, are distant relatives to muscle massage. The use of hot baths can be traced back to several ancient cultures, from the Romans and Japanese to the Maori of New Zealand. When the body is immersed in hot water, peripheral blood vessels (those nearest the skin and muscles) dilate. Blood is then shunted from the body's core to the periphery to dissipate heat. This influx of blood to the muscles reduces tension by decreasing neural firing at the site of the motor end plate, and the muscles soon become pliable and incredibly relaxed. The addition of water jets to the hot bath by Candido Jacuzzi in the early 1950s increased the effects of hot tubs, and this relaxation technique remains quite popular today.

In 1980, the cult movie *Altered States* introduced flotation tanks to the American public. Whereas the movie was science fiction, flotation tanks are very real. The first such tank was created by Dr. John C. Lilly in 1954 at the National Institutes of Health. It was designed to eliminate all external stimuli, including gravity. The subject disrobed and was suspended vertically in water. All senses were basically "turned off." Earlier changes in tank design included the addition of Epsom salts, which allowed the body to float horizontally, and controlled water temperature. Today, commercial flotation tanks are similar in concept, but with the use of computer technology they feature lighting, ultraviolet water purification, underwater stereos, and even optional video screens to cater to the preference of clients who can afford the $50 to $100 per flotation hour. Without a doubt, the cessation of sensations has a profound effect on both mind and body, sometimes lasting four to five days after immersion. Research conducted at the National Institutes of Health revealed that flotation-tank therapy decreases the following: depression, insomnia, muscle tension, plasma stress hormones (cortisol and ACTH), resting heart rate, resting blood pressure, anxiety, and physical (musculoskeletal) pain (Hutchinson, 1984). As a result, overall well-being is dramatically increased. Flotation tanks, in fact, are said to provide the ultimate relaxation experience (Harby, 1988). As people around the world become more stressed with sensory bombardment, interest in flotation tanks has resurfaced for purposes of relaxation, obstetrics, and rehab therapy (Kotz, 2008; Kjellgren, 2003; Stark et al., 2008).

Pet Therapy. With the recent discovery of a special neuropeptide called beta-endorphin, a natural morphinelike

FIGURE 23.11　By and large, people who own or care for pets are less stressed and more healthy than people who do not have pets. Many pet therapy programs exist around the country, serving a spectrum of stressed people from hospital patients and quadriplegics, to members of various cancer support groups.

substance secreted by the brain, lymphocytes, and perhaps other cells, new theories quickly developed about its relationship to positive mood change as well as factors that may release it in the body. About the same time, a therapeutic practice was started in several nursing homes, clinical care settings, prisons, and some schools: **pet therapy** (**FIG. 23.11**). It was noticed that physical and psychological responses were altered favorably when people came in contact with pet animals, suggesting a link between the two discoveries. Pet therapy involves the integration of animals into clinically directed therapeutic activities, particularly through holding and petting small domestic animals, such as cats and dogs, and in some rare cases, swimming with dolphins. In the past few years, pet therapy has moved from

Flotation tanks: A moderate sensory deprivation tank in which a person floats on his or her back in warm water to calm the nervous system through decreased stimulation.

Hydrotherapy: The use of baths, hot tubs, Jacuzzis, and flotation tanks to augment the sense of touch to promote relaxation.

Pet therapy: The use of hand contact with pets to promote relaxation among hospital patients, nursing home patients, and now everyday pet owners who claim better health through decreased resting heart rate and blood pressure values.

cats and dogs making the rounds in nursing homes to riding horses in Virginia and swimming with dolphins in Florida and Hawaii. The new name given to pet therapy is pet-assisted therapy. Several years ago, a "pet partners" program was developed for burn victims through the Hope Therapy Program of the University of Texas in Houston, in conjunction with the Moody Gardens in Galveston, Texas. Pet Partners, a national pet therapy program, is now located in 45 states and four countries.

The results of pet therapy are quite remarkable: The tactile contact, combined with new companionship, seems to have a special healing quality. Although changes in muscle tension were not investigated, significant changes in resting heart rate, blood pressure, and mood have been observed with interest (Cusack and Smith, 1984; Holden, 1984; Burke, 1992). In the company of pets, resting heart rate and blood pressure showed significant decreases while perceived mood improved. In addition, pet owners felt physically better when they touched and petted their animals. Professor Erika Friedman, at Brooklyn College, notes that survival rates for coronary patients are higher among pet owners than non–pet owners, and that elderly people who own pets make fewer visits to their physicians (Burke, 1992). The conclusion from these and other findings suggests that physical contact with friendly animals promotes relaxation similar to that associated with meditation and biofeedback. Although the specific physiological factors associated with improved mood remain a mystery in the field of psycho-neuroimmunology, current conventional wisdom suggests a strong link between the release of beta-endorphins and other neuropeptides and touch, which can indeed have a healing or restorative effect on the body. Researchers may one day find that the relaxing effect is related to entrainment of the animals' energy field with that of humans.

Therapeutic Touch. Clinical medicine, which for centuries shunned the metaphysical aspects of healing through touch, is slowly beginning to acknowledge the possibility that this type of healing can augment standard medical treatment. **Therapeutic touch** (TT) was made popular by Dolores Krieger, RN, and has been taught to thousands of nurses worldwide. In her book *Hands of Light*, healer Barbara Ann Brennen discusses her collaborative efforts with prominent physicians,

> **Therapeutic touch:** An energy-based healing modality using the science of subtle energy to restore homeostasis (also similar to Reiki and healing touch).

particularly in the field of oncology. Like shiatsu, therapeutic touch and bioenergy healing involve the manipulation of blocked energy centers, thus clearing the pathways (chakras) of the human energy field. Rather than applying pressure with the thumbs or palms, however, healing occurs through the laying on of the hands, which "conducts" positive or healing energy through the body's energy field. Similarly, the ancient Japanese Reiki method integrates physical manipulation of muscle and connective tissue with universal energy (*ki*). As the disciplines of physics and clinical medicine expand and the gap of understanding narrows regarding the dynamics of human matter, a greater collaboration of all aspects of healing may unfold.

Physiological and Psychological Benefits

Perhaps the most notable effect of massage therapy is the state of complete physical relaxation one experiences during and immediately after the experience. The application of touch at the site of tense muscles first increases neural reflex receptor activity, causing a dilation of blood vessels and increased circulation. This increase in blood supply apparently decreases neural drive through the afferent neural mechanism. In effect, this desensitizes the nerve endings receiving messages from the brain, thus decreasing muscle tension. Repeated claims have been made that massage cleans the muscles of metabolic waste products through gentle pumping of the circulatory and lymphatic systems; however, no scientific evidence supports this theory. A more likely theory, yet to be proven, is that touch triggers the release of neuropeptides, including beta-endorphins, which may neutralize or diminish the effects of metabolic byproducts. Despite the fact that many claims are yet unproven scientifically, it is commonly accepted that the effects of massage therapy on the musculoskeletal and neuromuscular systems, including increased flexibility and decreased muscle tension, are unrefuted (Harrison, 1986; Moraska, 2005). In fact, physicians are increasingly referring their patients with lower-back pain, bone fractures, multiple sclerosis, structural bone disease, and arthritis to massage therapists for treatment complementary to their own prescribed medical therapy for these ailments (Bailey-Lloyd, 2007).

The physical effects of massage are only superseded by the emotional experience of relaxation. It appears the mind also benefits from the powers of touch, as described earlier. When the mind is cleared of thought, stress is minimized. The nursing community reports that massages also provide a sense of serenity and security to patients. In a study reported by Cohen (1987), where massage therapy was administered to cancer patients, questionnaires measuring mood and symptoms of distress revealed that massage promoted a greater sense of tranquility and vitality with less lethargy, compared to just "relaxing" in a prone position.

The reduction of tension headaches and other stress-related ailments suggests that there is a significant relationship between mind and body, and that both benefit from this relaxation technique. Massage therapists often comment on the ease with which their clients express themselves verbally while being massaged, suggesting the loosening of mental and emotional blocks as well as muscular knots. Note that there are times when massage is not recommended—for example, when people have skin rashes, severe bruises, and muscle strains—contraindications with which massage therapists are well acquainted.

Massage therapy can be a wonderful supplement to your collection of relaxation techniques. It is suggested, however, that you check the qualifications of the massage therapist because there are many practitioners who have no certified training. In addition to certification, many states now require that massage therapists become licensed. (The state of New York, for example, requires competence in anatomy, physiology, kinesiology, neurology, pathology, hygiene, and first aid and CPR, in addition to massage techniques.) For more information, see American Massage Therapy Association in References and Resources.

Massage Therapy and Chronic Pain

With muscle tension being the number one symptom of pain, massage therapy is often recommended as the first healing modality for acute and chronic pain, particularly muscular pain involving the neck and shoulder region, lower back, and legs. Bodywork is available in the forms of sports massage, rolfing, myofascial release, and others, all of which offer their own unique style of physical manipulation to relieve pain (**FIG. 23.12**). The literature is loaded with books and articles supporting the premise and efficacy of pain relief through a

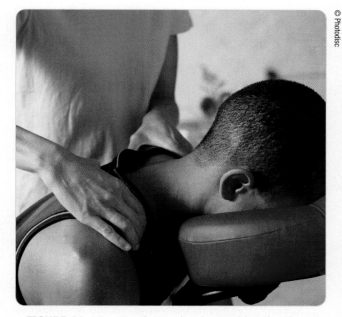

FIGURE 23.12 Muscle tension is considered to be the number one symptom of stress. Muscle massage in the form of Swedish massage is the most common type of massage. Also popular are shiatsu, sports massage, Thai massage, and myofascial release. Some types of bodywork include aspects of all of these.

host of bodywork modalities (Schatz, 2001; Imamura et al., 2008). Research also supports the use of aromatherapy for pain reduction (Buckle, 1999).

Best Application of Massage Therapy

Muscle tension is cited as the number one symptom of stress. Bodywork, in all its forms, can be used to help decrease muscle tension, lessen muscle stiffness, and help restore a sense of physical (and mental) homeostasis. People in service professions (from food servers and nurses to store clerks and shelf stockers) who stand and walk in their jobs would benefit greatly from massage therapy as a means to reduce muscle tension. As people spend less time being active and more sedentary time in front of their computer screens, muscles of the neck, shoulders, and upper back receive undue stress from a specific posture associated with screen viewing. As a result, bodywork offers a powerful means to intercept the stress response and promote relaxation in overworked, stiff, or tired muscles.

SUMMARY

- Muscle massage is the manipulation of skin, muscles, ligaments, and connective tissue for the purpose of decreasing muscle tension and increasing physical comfort in musculature and surrounding joints. This is the one relaxation technique that requires the assistance of someone else to achieve the full relaxation effect.

- Massage therapy is now a bona fide practice, with more than 56,000 practitioners certified through the American Massage Therapy Association. Massage therapists must go through formal education (500 hours of classroom instruction) as well as 3 years of practice before becoming certified.

- Massage therapy not only aids in the reduction of muscle tension, but also provides an essential human need: touch. Research indicates that human touch is vital for well-being, and that as people become more involved with technology there is less human contact, resulting in what some call touch deprivation.

- Landmark studies by Field showed that infants require human touch to thrive; speculation is that people of all ages need it as well. Other research shows that massage therapy is as effective in promoting the relaxation response as are other forms of relaxation.

- There are several different types of massage, or bodywork. Swedish massage is the most widely recognized style in the West, but shiatsu, rolfing, myofascial release, and sports massage, well known in other parts of the world, are gaining popularity.

- Aromatherapy, hydrotherapy, pet therapy, and therapeutic touch are other related touch therapies.

- Studies involving various massage therapies indicate that there is not only a physical relaxation effect, but in many cases an emotional benefit as well.

- Since the advent of the fitness boom in the late 1970s and early 1980s, massage has become a significant aspect of health maintenance. Today, several corporations offer muscle massage as part of wellness programs for employees who spend their workdays in front of a computer terminal.

- Massage therapy is used as a modality to decrease episodes of acute and chronic pain.

STUDY GUIDE QUESTIONS

1. What is massage therapy, and why is it thought to be an effective means to relax?

2. List and describe five styles of massages (bodywork).

3. What is aromatherapy, and why is this technique thought to be relaxing?

4. What is hydrotherapy, and why is this technique thought to be relaxing?

5. What is pet therapy, and why is this technique thought to be relaxing?

REFERENCES AND RESOURCES

Adcock, C. L. Massage Therapy in Alcohol/Drug Treatment, *Alcoholism Treatment Quarterly* 4(3):87–101, 1987.

Allen, K. Melodies, Mutts Reduce Stress, *Men's Fitness* 17: 52–54, 2001.

American Massage Therapy Association, 500 Davis Street, Evanston, IL 60201. 1-877-905-0577. www.amtamassage. org.

American Massage Therapy Association. *A Guide to Massage Therapy in America.* Chicago, 1989.

American Massage Therapy Association. *Sports Massage.* Chicago, 1986.

Ashton, J. Holistic Health Six: In Your Hands, *Nursing Times* 80(19):54, 1984.

Auckett, A. *Baby Massage: Parent–Child Bonding through Touching.* Newmarket Press, New York, 1981.

Bach, E. A. Clinical Comparison between the Action of Vaccines and Homeopathic Remedies, *British Homeopathic Journal* 9:21–24, 1921.

Bailey-Lloyd, C. What's All the Buzz about Massage Therapy? *The CollegeBound Network*, 2007. http://ezinearticles .com/?Whats-All-the-Buzz-about-Massage-Therapy?&id =879643.

Barber, B. *Sensual Water, A Celebration of Bathing*. Contemporary Books, Chicago, 1978.

Barker S. B., and Dawson, K. S. The Effects of Animal-Assisted Therapy on Anxiety Ratings of Hospitalized Psychiatric Patients, *Psychiatric Services* 49(6):797–801, 1998.

Barnes, J. *Myofascial Release: The Search for Excellence*. RSI-T-A, Myofascial Treatment Centers, Paoli, PA, 1990.

Barnes, J. Personal communication. Sedona, AZ, August 5, 1995.

Bentley, E. *Head, Neck, and Shoulders Massage: A Step-by-Step Guide*. St. Martins Griffin, New York, 2000.

Bever, L., "Text neck" is becoming an epidemic and could wreak your spine. Washington Post. Nov 14, 2014.

Box, D. Putting on the Pressure, *Nursing Mirror* 160:22, 1985.

Brennen, B. A. *Hands of Light*. Bantam Books, New York, 1987.

Buckle, J. The Smell of Relief, *Psychology Today* 33(1):24, 2000.

Buckle, J. Use of Aromatherapy as a Complementary Treatment for Chronic Pain, *Alternative Therapies* 5(5):42–50, 1999.

Burke, S. In the Presence of Animals, *U.S. News and World Report*, February 24, 1992:64–65.

Caddy, S. H., and Jones, G. Massage Therapy as a Workplace Intervention for Reduction of Stress, *Perceptual & Motor Skills* 84(1):157–158, 1997.

Cassar, M. *Handbook of Massage Therapy*. Butterworth-Heinemann, Woburn, MA, 1999.

Channon, L. D. Relaxation Techniques: Alternatives to Progressive Relaxation, *Australian Journal of Clinical and Experimental Hypnosis* 14(2):133–137, 1986.

Ching, M. Contemporary Therapy: Aromatherapy in the Management of Acute Pain? *Contemporary Nurse* 8(4): 146–150, 1999.

Cohen, N. Massage Is the Message, *Nursing Times* 83(19): 19–20, 1987.

Cunningham, S. *Magical Aromatherapy: The Power of Scent*. Llewellyn Publications, St. Paul, MN, 2000.

Cusack, O., and Smith E. Pets and the Elderly: The Therapeutic Bond, *Activities, Adaptations, and Aging* 4(2–3):33–49, 1984.

Cuva, L. Is Your Company at Risk? *Corporate Health Solutions* 1(1), 2000.

Czimbal, B., and Zadikov, M. *Vitamin T: A Guide to Healthy Touch*. Open Book, Portland, OR, 1991.

Day, J. A., Mason, R. R., and Chesrown, S. E. Effect of Massage on Serum Level of β-Endorphin and β-Lipoprotein in Healthy Adults, *Physical Therapy* 67:926–930, 1987.

Dion, K. Massage Therapy—What Is It? *Healthcare Review* 14(3):5, 2001.

Downing, G. *The Massage Book*. Random House, New York, 1972.

D'urso, M. A. Massage for the Masses, *Health* 19:63–67, 1987.

Edmunds, A., and Tudor, H. *Some Unrecognized Factors in Medicine*. Theosophical Society, London, 1976.

Elliott, M. Back from Hell, Healing Post-traumatic Stress Disorder, *Massage & Bodywork* December/January, 1999:13–21.

Feitis, R. *Ida Rolf Talks about Rolfing and Physical Reality*. Harper & Row, New York, 1978.

Feltman, J. (ed.). *Hands-on Healing*. Rodale Press, Emmaus, PA, 1989.

Field, T. Massage Therapy Effects, *American Psychologist*, December, 1998:1270–1281.

Field, T. Pregnancy and Labor Massage, *Expert Review of Obstetrics and Gynecology* 5(2):177–181, 2010.

Field, T. Stressors during Pregnancy and the Postnatal Period, *New Directions for Child Development* 45:19–31, 1989.

Field, T. Personal communication (email). April 3, 2008.

Field, T., et al. Massage Therapy for Infants of Depressed Mothers, *Infant Behavior and Development* 19(1):107, 1996.

Fisher-Rizzi, S. *The Complete Aromatherapy Handbook*. Sterling Publishing, New York, 1990.

Fox, E., Bowers, R., and Foss, M. *The Physiological Basis of Physical Education and Athletics*. William C. Brown, Dubuque, IA, 1989.

Friz, S. *Fundamentals of Therapeutic Massage*. Mosby, St. Louis, MO, 2000.

Gauthier, P. Development of a New Approach to Emotionally Deprived Children and Youth, *Child and Youth Services* 13(1):71–81, 1990.

Goleman, D., and Bennett, T. *The Relaxed Body Book*. Doubleday, Garden City, NY, 1986.

Green, R., and Green, M. Relaxation Increases Salivary Immunoglobulin A, *Psychological Reports* 61(2):623–629, 1987.

Gurudas, H. *Flower Essences and Vibrational Healing*. Cassandra Press, San Rafael, CA, 1983.

Harby, K. Troubles Float Away, *Psychology* 22(2):20, 1988.

Harrison, A. Therapeutic Massage: Getting the Massage, *Nursing Times* 82(48):34–35, 1986.

Havemann, J. S. Rubbing out Workday Pain: Massage Rooms Win Departmental Support, *The Washington Post*, Feb. 6, 1989.

Hemmings, B., Smith, M., Graydon, J., and Dyson, R. Effects of Massage on Physiological Restoration, Perceived Recovery, and Repeated Sports Performance, *British Journal of Sports Medicine* 34(2):109–114, 2000.

Hirsh, J. S. Doesn't Everyone Need to Be Kneaded Once in a While? *Wall Street Journal*, October 17, 1989.

Holden, C. Human–Animal Relationship under Scrutiny, *Science* 214(23):418–458, 1984.

Holmes, P. Aromatherapy: Applications for Clinical Practice, *Alternative & Complementary Therapies* 1(3):117–182, 1995.

Howdyshell, C. Complementary Therapy: Aromatherapy with Massage for Geriatric and Hospice Care—A Call for a Holistic Approach, *Hospice Journal* 13:69–75, 1998.

Hutchinson, M. *The Book of Floating: Exploring the Private Sea.* Quill Books, New York, 1984.

Imamura, M., Furlan, A. D., Dryden, T., and Irvin, E. Evidence-Informed Management of Chronic Low Back Pain with Massage, *Spine Journal* 8(1):121–133, 2008.

Jacobs, M. Massage for the Relief of Pain: Anatomical and Physical Considerations, *Physical Therapy Review* 40:93–98, 1960.

Jodo, E. R., et al. Effects of Facial Massage on the Spontaneous EEG, *Tohoku-Psychologica Folia* 47(1–4):8–15, 1988.

Johnson, J. *The Healing Art of Sports Massage.* Rodale Press, New York, 1995.

Jones, T. A. Rolfing, *Physical and Medicine Rehabilitation Clinics of North America* 15(4):799–809, 2004.

Jorgenson, J. Therapeutic Use of Companion Animals in Health Care, *Image: Journal of Nursing Scholarship* 29(3): 249–254, 1997.

Kahn, R. New Era for Massage Research, *Massage Therapy Journal* 40(3):104, 2001.

Katcher, A. H. Physiological and Behavioral Responses to Companion Animals, *Veterinary Clinics of North America: Small Animal Practices* 15:403–410, 1985.

Kaye, A. D., Kaye, A. J., Swinford, J., Baluch, A., Bawcom, B. A., Lambert, T. J., and Hoover, J. M. The Effect of Deep-Tissue Massage Therapy on Blood Pressure and Heart Rate, *Alternative Complementary Medicine* 14(2):125–128, 2008.

Kiecolt-Glaser, J. K., Graham, J. E., Malarkey, W. B., Porter, K., Lemeshow, S., and Glaser, R. Olfactory Influences on Mood and Autonomic, Endocrine, and Immune Function, *Psychoneuroendocrinology* 33(3):328–339, 2008.

Kjellgren, A. Relaxation in a Flotation Tank Brings Peace and Quiet, Increased Well-Being, and Reduced Pain, *Innovations Report*, May 11, 2003. www.innovations-report.com /html/reports/studies/report-23064.html.

Kolpakov, S., and Rumyantseva, S. Use of a Combined Method of Correcting the Human Psychophysiological State during Work and Constant Vision Strain, *Human Physiology* 13(1):36–42, 1987.

Kotz, D. Stressed Out? Try a Flotation Tank, *U.S. News & World Report*, March 12, 2008. www.usnews.com/blogs/on -women/2008/3/12/stressed-out-try-a-flotation-tank.html.

Kresge, C. Benefits of Sports Massage, *Sports Medicine, Fitness, Training, Injuries* 43–48, 1996.

Lacroix, N. *Massage for Total Stress Relief.* Random House, New York, 1990.

Lippin, R. Alternative Medicine in the Workplace, *Alternative Therapies* 2(1):47–51, 1996.

Liu, Y. The Role of Massage Therapy in the Relief of Cancer Pain, *Nursing Standards* 22(21):35–40, 2008.

Lundberg, P. *The Book of Shiatsu: A Complete Guide to Using Hand Pressure and Gentle Manipulation to Improve Your Health, Vitality, and Stamina.* Fireside Books, New York, 2003.

Mauskop, A. Alternative Therapies in Headache: Is There a Role? *Medical Clinics of North America* 85(4), 2001.

Maxwell-Hudson, C. *The Complete Book of Massages.* Random House, New York, 1988.

McKechnie, A., et al. Anxiety States: A Preliminary Report on the Value of Connective-Tissue Massage, *Journal of Psychosomatic Research* 27(2):1245–1249, 1983.

Mercati, M. *Thai Massage.* Sterling, New York, 1998.

Mochizuki, S. Japanese Chair Massage, Part I, *Massage & Bodywork* 15(1):98–100, 2000.

Moraska, A. Sports Massage: A Comprehensive Review, *Journal of Sports Medicine and Physical Fitness* 45(3):370–380, 2005.

Moraska, A., Chandler, C., Edmiston-Schaetzel, A., Franklin, G., Calenda, E. L., and Enebo, B. Comparison of a Targeted and General Massage Protocol on Strength, Function, and Symptoms Associated with Carpal Tunnel Syndrome: A Randomized Pilot Study, *Journal of Alternative and Complementary Medicine* 14(3):259–267, 2008.

Muhammad, L. Animal Therapy Spurs Human Touch, *USA Today*, May 3, 1999:10D.

Muschel, I. J. Pet Therapy with Terminally Ill Cancer Patients, *Social Casework* 65(8):451–458, 1984.

Naisbitt, J. *Megatrends 2000.* Avon, New York, 1999.

Naliboff, B. D., and Tachiki, K. H. Autonomic and Skeletal Muscle Response to Nonelectrical Cutaneous Stimulation, *Perceptual and Motor Skills* 72(2):575–584, 1991.

Namikoshi, R. *The Complete Book of Shiatsu Therapy.* Japan Publications, New York, 1981.

National Association for Holistic Aromatherapy. www.naha .org.

Nixon, T. Make Money with Massage, *Fitness Management*, September, 1989:40–42.

Okvat, H., et al. Massage Therapy for Patients Undergoing Cardiac Catheterization, *Alternative Therapies* 8(3):68–77, 2002.

Pecher, K. Pet Therapy for Heart and Soul, *Prevention*, August, 1985:80–84.

Pelletier, K. R., and Herzing, D. L. Psychoneuroimmunology: Toward a Mind-Body Model, *Advances* 5(1):27–56, 1988.

Pitcairn, R. H. Why Pets Are Good for Us, *Prevention,* February, 1985:49–51.

Price, S. *Aromatherapy Workbook.* HarperCollins, San Francisco, 1993.

Proulx, D. Animal-Assisted Therapy, *Critical Care Nurse* 18(2):80–85, 1998.

Rimmer, L. The Clinical Use of Aromatherapy in the Reduction of Stress, *Home Healthcare Nurse* 16:123–126, 1998.

Robinson, I. Pet Therapy, *Nursing Times* 95(15):33–34, 1999.

Samples, P. Does Sports Massage Have a Role in Sports Medicine? *The Physician and Sports Medicine* March, 1989:177–187.

Scafidi, F., et al. Massage Stimulates Growth in Preterm Infants: A Replication, *Infant Behavior and Development* 13(2):167–188, 1990.

Schatz, B. *Soft Tissue Massage for Pain Relief.* Hampton Roads, Charlottesville, VA, 2001.

Sheldrake, R. *Dogs That Know When Their Owners Are Coming Home.* Crown Publishers, New York, 1999.

Shiina, Y., Funabashi, N., Lee, K., et al. Relaxation Effects of Lavender Aromatherapy Improve Coronary Flow Velocity Reserve in Healthy Men Evaluated by Transthoracic Doppler Echocardiography, *International Journal of Cardiology* 129(2):193–197, 2008.

Sims, S. Slow-Stroke Back Massage for Cancer Patients, *Infant Behavior and Development* 13(2):167–188, 1990.

Smith, M., et al. Benefits of Massage Therapy for Hospital Patients: A Descriptive and Qualitative Evaluation, *Alternative Therapies in Health and Medicine* 5(4):64–71, 1999.

Stark, M. A., Rudell, B., and Haus, G. Observing Position and Movements in Hydrotherapy: A Pilot Study, *Journal of Obstetric, Gynecolologic, and Neonatal Nursing* 37(1):116–122, 2008.

Steiner, R. *The Etherisation of the Blood.* Steiner, London, 1971.

Stringer, J., Swindell, R., and Dennis, M. Massage in Patients Undergoing Intensive Chemotherapy Reduces Serum Cortisol and Prolactin, *Psycho-Oncology,* February 26, 2008.

Tignore, S. Massage Therapy Research: A Paradigm for Success, *Massage Therapy Journal* 42(2):80–89, 2003.

Toufexis, A. Massage Comes out of the Parlor, *Time,* March, 1987:17–20.

Vickers, A., et al. Massage Therapies, *Western Journal of Medicine* 175(3):202–204, 2001.

Weaver, M. R. Acupressure: An Overview of Therapy and Application, *Nurse Practitioner* 10:38–42, 1985.

Weinberg, R., Jackson, A., and Kolodny, K. The Relationship of Massage and Exercise to Mood Enhancement, *Sport Psychologist* 2(3):202–211, 1988.

Wilkinson, S., et al. An Evaluation of Aromatherapy Massage in Palliative Care, *Palliative Medicine* 13(5):409–417, 1999.

Willis, D. A. Animal Therapy, *Rehabilitation Nursing* 22(2):78–81, 1997.

Woody, R. H. *The Use of Massage in Facilitating Holistic Health.* Thomas, Springfield, CA, 1980.

Yacenda, J. Sport Strokes, *Fitness Management* 5(9):38–39, 1989.

Ylinen, J., and Cash, M. *Sports Massage.* Hutchinson Educational, St. Paul, MN, 1988.

Zimmer, J. The Pleasure of Giving a Great Massage, *Health* April, 1985:52–53.

CHAPTER 24

T'ai Chi Ch'uan

*Tension is who you think you should be.
Relaxation is who you are.*

—T'ai Chi Saying

There is a life force or subtle energy that surrounds and permeates us all, which the Chinese call *Chi*. To harmonize with the universe, to move in unison with this energy, to move as freely as running water is to be at peace or one with the universe. This harmony of energy promotes tranquility and inner peace. This is the essence of **T'ai Chi ch'uan**: a harmony and balance with the vital life force of the natural world itself. The words *T'ai* and *Chi* can be translated several ways. One is the "supreme ultimate," a meaning symbolic of balance, power, and enlightenment. T'ai Chi, the softest of the martial arts, is also called a "moving meditation." Based on concepts similar to Feng Shui and similar to hatha yoga, it is a low-impact exercise that demonstrates unification or harmony of mind and body, and the *Chi* of the universe.

To understand *Chi*, it is helpful to examine the concept in the cultural context where it originated. The Chinese concept of health is quite different from that of the Western hemisphere. Westerners view health as the absence of disease and illness produced by bacteria and viruses, whereas the Chinese see it as an unrestricted current of subtle energy throughout the body. When *Chi*, or subtle energy, which flows through the body in a network of meridians, or "energy gates," is restricted or congested, the body is susceptible to physiological dysfunction. In Chinese medicine, it is not necessarily bacteria or viruses that cause physical dysfunction or disease because these are thought to be present everywhere. Rather, poor health is thought to be the result of low resistance, caused by non-harmonious (blocked) energy, to both internal and external factors that ultimately do one in. Stated another way, these "pathogens" are constantly present; it is low resistance to them that makes one vulnerable to disease. Just as acupuncture is used as a preventive intervention technique to unblock congested meridians to cure ailments, T'ai Chi ch'uan is a type of preventive exercise to maintain the peaceful flow of energy throughout the body and thus maintain good health. From a Chinese perspective, unrestricted flow of energy helps to maintain one's resistance to various influences, be they biological, psychological, or sociological in nature.

It may seem that the practice of self-defense is incongruent with relaxation. Upon closer examination, however, T'ai Chi reveals a profound expression of tranquility. It teaches one to remain calm and centered against the

> **T'ai Chi ch'uan:** A relaxation technique originating among the Chinese; a succession of movements to bring the body into harmony with the universal energy (*Chi*); a moving meditation.
>
> **Chi:** The universal life force of subtle energy that surrounds and permeates everything.

greatest opposition (stressors), to harmonize with aggression and fear, rather than fight it. As a physical exercise, it teaches how to conserve and concentrate energy rather than to dissipate it randomly. The integration of this life force into this moving meditation of self-defense suggests that T'ai Chi is not a violent exercise. Rather, it is an exercise to maintain balance in one's life. For this reason alone, the practice of T'ai Chi is a wonderful metaphor for conscious relaxation and the ability to move in balance and harmony with our environments. If you were to walk the streets of Beijing or Shanghai in the early morning hours, you would see thousands of people exercising together, practicing T'ai Chi as a mode of physical exercise, much as you would see people in the United States running or cycling.

Historical Perspective

The practice of T'ai Chi dates back thousands of years. Its origins blend the essence of Chinese philosophy with the substance of physical survival. Legend has it that thousands of years ago a man observed a fight between a crane and a serpent. With repeated jabs of his beak, the crane tried to defeat his opponent. But the snake, in a series of calculated maneuvers, shifted its body weight at the right moments and was able to remain free of harm until the crane became tired, gave up, and moved on. Stories have also been handed down through the ages that T'ai Chi developed as a unique style of boxing that emphasized internal strength mixed with flexibility and agility rather than the exhibition of brute force. As the art developed, subtle philosophical concepts were integrated with the movements as a way to teach and emphasize proficiency in mechanical skills, thus lending support to its understanding and mastery (Jou, 1988; Lo, 1979).

Philosophy of T'ai Chi Ch'uan

What makes T'ai Chi different from all other forms of self-defense, and perhaps unique unto itself, is its basis in philosophy. The practice of its physical movements is a wonderful metaphor for the essential mental attitude to successfully deal with life's daily stressors. The physical movements are fluid: They move *with* force, not against it. Many times, when we are confronted with situations we perceive to be threatening, our first instinct is to force a change or try to manipulate something we have no control over. T'ai Chi suggests quite literally going with the flow, swimming with the tide, not against it. The

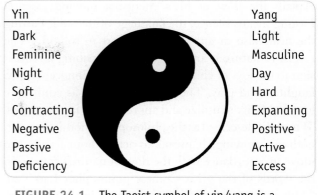

Yin	Yang
Dark	Light
Feminine	Masculine
Night	Day
Soft	Hard
Contracting	Expanding
Negative	Positive
Passive	Active
Deficiency	Excess

FIGURE 24.1 The Taoist symbol of yin/yang is a circle with two equal and opposite halves.

philosophy of T'ai Chi involves the manipulation of force by controlling oneself and yielding to become part of it.

As T'ai Chi developed, it quickly assimilated many philosophical concepts from Taoism, and to a lesser extent, Confucianism. Even the symbol used to represent T'ai Chi—a circular *mandala* of white and black halves with each half carrying a smaller circle of the other inside—represents the balance of opposites (**FIG. 24.1**). These opposites, **yin** and **yang**, symbolize (among other things) the positive and negative aspects in nature. Together, they represent wholeness and essential balance. T'ai Chi strives to attain the harmony of these forces through avoidance of extremes. The philosophical concepts of Taoism are embroidered with metaphorical imagery—light with darkness, good with evil, life with death—all of which express the concept of stillness in motion. Although not every concept can be categorized as "either-or," the theme of yin and yang, or wholeness, is to find peace by acknowledging the duality of these characteristics within yourself.

There are four basic philosophical concepts taught in T'ai Chi: fasting the heart, returning to nature, *Wu-wei*, and winning by losing. **Fasting the heart** is a concept to

Yin: Those complementary components in the Taoist philosophy of yin/yang expressed as dark, feminine, night, soft, etc.

Yang: Those complementary components in the Taoist philosophy of yin/yang expressed as light, masculine, day, hard, etc.

Fasting the heart: A T'ai Chi term that explains the flow of one's life energy as a moving essence, and finding comfort in solitude.

explain the flow of life's energy, a moving essence. Fasting means silence, the language of the soul. Fasting the heart also means to find comfort in solitude. The **return to nature** is another way of describing a regression to the joys of childhood, embracing innocence, joy, laughter, and play. These are traits that, as adults, we lose the ability to utilize and appreciate within ourselves. *Wu-wei* is described as the philosophy of nothing-doing, nothing-knowing. It means to act without forcing; to move in accordance with the flow of nature's course. In the words of the great Chinese philosopher Lao Tzu, "Although water is soft and weak, it invariably overcomes the rigid and strong" (Dreher, 1991). Often *Wu-wei* is expressed in the comparison of opposites. For example, to shrink, first you must stretch; to enervate, first you must energize; to take, first you must give. Another example is that of a Ping-Pong ball in water. No matter how many times you push it under, it always comes back up, and does so with little or no effort. The fourth component, **winning by losing**, advocates the success of failure. When failure is acknowledged, it becomes the first step to success. Winning by losing is an expression of unconditional acceptance. An additional concept of T'ai Chi is the realization that true understanding comes from emptying the mind (lowering the walls of the ego). This emptiness allows a liberation of the human spirit to unite with the universal life energy. Although this energy may seem elusive to those who have never practiced T'ai Chi, its effects cascade down through the body to influence the physiological systems as well.

Physiological and Psychological Benefits

Individuals who have practiced T'ai Chi, as well as those who instruct this traditional Chinese exercise, make several claims about the wonderful physical and mental benefits it has to offer.

> **Return to nature:** A T'ai Chi expression to explain the joys of childhood: innocence, laughter, and play.
>
> **Wu-wei:** A T'ai Chi term that signifies doing nothing, or action through nonaction, moving with the simple, subtle flow of nature.
>
> **Winning by losing:** A T'ai Chi expression that explains the benefits of failure as a stepping stone toward success.

As researchers begin to explore modalities in the cadre of integrative (complementary) medicine, interest in T'ai Chi shows promise for the ancient claims of long ago. Here are some highlights: T'ai Chi is well known for promoting balance, but a study by Michael Irwin and associates (2007) reveals that a 16-week T'ai Chi class can boost the immune system and augment the efficacy of vaccines for influenza. T'ai Chi also was proven to decrease nervous (sympathetic) tension in a group of elderly subjects (Motivala et al., 2006). One study by Jin (1988) investigated both physiological and psychological effects of T'ai Chi and found effects very similar to those produced by other types of aerobic exercises. In this study, heart rate, norepinephrine, cortisol, and mood were observed in both beginners and ardent followers (age range 15 to 75 years). These variables were measured three times daily for a period of several weeks. Data analysis showed a marked decrease in postexercise resting heart rate as well as stress hormones over the course of a day. As a result of this technique, subjects reported less physical tension and fatigue, less anger and anxiety, and less mood disturbance. From these observations it was concluded that T'ai Chi does promote a relaxing effect (**FIG. 24.2**). As reported by Koh (1981), a study by Munyi in 1963 indicated that habitual practice of T'ai Chi produced increased measures of muscular strength and flexibility compared to sedentary control subjects. Furthermore, in a study concluded in 1981 by Plummer to compare the effects of T'ai Chi to acupuncture, it was observed that both techniques promoted physical (postural) homeostasis and psychological homeostasis, which together enhanced emotional control and tranquility. T'ai Chi has been recommended as an ideal activity for the mobile aged population and is said to be as effective an exercise to promote relaxation as cross-country skiing, swimming, and bicycling (Meusel, 1986). Claims from the Far East include that T'ai Chi can cure hypertension, asthma, and insomnia, as well as prevent atherosclerosis and spinal deformity. To date, these claims have not been clinically proven or medically substantiated because they just have not been studied. Although these claims are yet unproven, it is believed by regular practitioners that T'ai Chi may play an important role in the prevention of disorders commonly associated with stress. Researchers also have focused on the effects of T'ai Chi and the prevention and reversal of osteoporosis (Gass, 2003).

The topic of T'ai Chi continues to spark much interest in the research community regarding its promising health benefits, particularly for the prevention of falls in

FIGURE 24.2

elderly people who might fracture their bones in such incidents (Büla et al., 2010; Campbell and Robertson, 2010). T'ai Chi is even thought to help people with Parkinson's disease (Klein, 2008). Touch researcher Tiffany Field studied the effects of T'ai Chi and yoga on anxiety, heart rate, electroencephalogram (EEG) readings, and math computations and noted significant positive effects on promoting relaxation with both modalities (Field, 2010). Tufts University medicine professor Chenchen Wang and his colleagues (2010) analyzed over 40 studies regarding the mental and physiological effects of T'ai Chi. According to his findings, T'ai Chi augments health in so many ways that the question becomes, Why isn't everyone practicing it? More information can be found at www.taichiresearch.com.

Although few studies have researched the effects of T'ai Chi on various health parameters, in the past decade numerous studies designed in China and Japan have measured the effects of **Qigong**. Like T'ai Chi, Qigong (pronounced "chee gong") is an energy-based exercise; however, Qigong places no focus or attention on the aspects of self-defense. Rather, the movement of *Chi* throughout the body is the sole emphasis of this practice. In simple terms, energy is moved through the body by meditation and breathing, which in turn are combined with a host of physical movements, similar to those observed in T'ai Chi. When practiced regularly, these movements create a sense of balance in the meridian system by opening blocks and clearing congestion in the meridian gates. With regular practice of Qigong, the energy system throughout the entire body operates at its optimal level.

In an exhaustive literature review on the medical applications of Qigong, Kenneth Sancier highlights several ways in which Qigong has been used in the clinical setting to improve various aspects of health and wellness. Sancier notes that Qigong has proven to bring about remarkable and significant results with hypertension, stroke, cardiovascular efficiency, bone density, sex hormone levels, cancer, and even the early stages of senility. Although the majority of these studies have been conducted in China, the statistics indicate that Qigong can be a significant factor in promoting health. Currently, similar studies in the United States are under way, with funding for one study supported by the National Institutes of Health's Center for Complementary and Alternative Medicine.

■ T'ai Chi Ch'uan and Chronic Pain

When engaging in T'ai Chi ch'uan, it is understood that one is employing the use of *Chi* or *Qi*. As such, creating a more harmonious flow of *Chi* through the body is in itself a means to reduce energy blocks, which results in a decrease in pain. Because of the subtleties involved with *Chi*, at first the results may seem less dramatic than those achieved with traditional pain relievers. For those who maintain a regular practice of T'ai

> **Qigong:** A form of Chinese energy exercise and energy healing, where *Qi* or *Chi* is directed through the body as a means to balance one's energy. Qigong healing may involve a Qigong healer to facilitate the energy healing process.

Chi or Qigong, however, an obvious change takes place over time to align not only the life force of energy, but also the musculo-skeletal structure that houses it. Case studies report that the pain from osteoarthritis is significantly reduced with the practice of T'ai Chi and Qigong (Cohen, 2003).

T'ai Chi Ch'uan as a Relaxation Technique

There are more than 100 positions or movements in T'ai Chi, with several similarities among some of them. Most people who learn T'ai Chi begin with formal lessons, either in a group or with private instruction. The purpose of this chapter is to provide exposure to some of its concepts and movements, and acquaint you with this exercise as an alternative relaxation technique. Keep in mind that initially T'ai Chi can be difficult to learn from reading and studying the movements in a book. It is my hope that this exposure may inspire you to take one or more lessons to further your appreciation of this exercise.

Before T'ai Chi can be practiced effectively, there are some important concepts to understand to make this exercise more enjoyable, which are taken from the *T'ai Chi Handbook* by Herman Kauz. As with yoga *asanas*, T'ai Chi movements may seem difficult at first. With time and practice, however, they will become so natural they will seem almost effortless. First and foremost, T'ai Chi is an egoless activity. That is, do not compare the precision of your movements with those of others who take part in this exercise for relaxation. And when you try the positions, go for the general movements first and then try to pick up the finer details later. There is no right or wrong, there only is.

1. *Breathe effortlessly.* Breathing should be natural. Some teachers instruct students to hold their tongue to the roof of the mouth, breathe through the nose, and allow the abdominal area to expand rather than the chest. When beginning, breathe in whatever fashion is easiest for you. With time you will find your breathing becoming more coordinated with the progression of each movement. Eventually you will probably adopt the suggested breathing style in coordination with the movements.

2. *Free the body of all unnecessary tension.* When watching someone perform T'ai Chi, the first word that comes to mind is *graceful.* When the body is relaxed, the flow of energy will move more freely. Tension in any body region inhibits energy movement. Use only the minimal amount of muscle tension to complete the movement.

3. *Maintain a stance perpendicular to the floor.* With a perpendicular stance, the balance of each position, as well as transition to the next position, is more easily attained. It is important to keep the spinal column completely aligned (perpendicular to the floor). A common metaphor used in teaching T'ai Chi is to move as if you were a marionette suspended by a string from the top of your head. Many instructors teach the 70/30 stance, where in transition from one movement to the next, the forward foot maintains approximately 70 percent of the body weight with the back foot maintaining 30 percent.

4. *Keep your center of gravity low.* Your center of gravity is approximately an inch or two below your belly button. Stand up, close your eyes, and sense your body's center of gravity. A lower center of gravity means a more stable base to move and position yourself. When performing these movements, bend the knees slightly, especially when shifting your weight from one leg to the other.

5. *Maintain even speed.* The graceful movements of T'ai Chi are a result of a continuous flow of movement like the gentle flow of water. The progression of these movements should be even, not sudden or jerky. Try to feel the surrounding space with your hands, as if you are swimming in air. Move arms and hands in unison with the body.

6. *Integrate the mind and body as one.* When performing T'ai Chi, the mind should move with the body. Concentration should be sharp. Try not to let your mind wander off to distant thoughts. If this should happen, quickly bring it back to your body movements.

T'ai Chi Ch'uan Movements

The following movements are the first eight positions in this moving meditation as illustrated in Kauz's *T'ai Chi Handbook.* Points of orientation will be north, south, east, and west. For simplicity, the starting position will begin facing north, wherever you decide that to be located. Most people learn T'ai Chi barefoot or in socks because this helps with initial foot placement. The feet also become more relaxed when less confined.

Position 1: **Starting posture** (FIG. 24.3). Stand erect with feet shoulder-width apart, arms by your side, palms facing back, chin up, and eyes looking directly ahead.

Position 2: **Beginning position** (FIG. 24.4). Raise your arms directly in front to about shoulder level, leading with the wrists. Elbows should be slightly bent, shoulders relaxed. Then, slowly allow arms and hands to return to the starting position below waist level, leading with the elbows.

Position 3: **Left-hand ward-off** (FIG. 24.5). Shift weight first to the left foot, allowing the left knee to bend slightly. Next, pivot onto the right foot, slowly rotating the body clockwise about 90 degrees. As you turn east, slowly raise the right hand to mid-chest level, palm facing down, while at the same time raising the left hand to waist level, palm facing up, as if carrying a beach ball in both hands. With completion of the pivot, the majority of your weight now rests on the right foot, and the left heel leaves the ground. Then, rotate the body back (counterclockwise) and return weight to the left foot. (The right foot remains pointed eastward.) Return the right arm to your side, while slowly raising the left arm to mid-chest level, palm facing in. Hips should remain directly under the shoulders.

Position 4: **Right-hand ward-off** (FIG. 24.6). With the majority of weight on your left foot, raise your right heel off the ground and turn your body clockwise, to the east. Raise the left hand to mid-chest level, palm facing down, while turning the

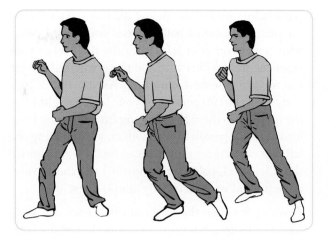

FIGURE 24.5

FIGURE 24.6

FIGURE 24.3

FIGURE 24.4

Starting posture: The stance that begins the first of many positions in the flow of the T'ai Chi exercise; balancing your weight on both feet and looking straight ahead.

Beginning position: From the starting position, one begins to move their hands upward to eye level, palms facing down.

Left-hand ward-off: The third step in the classic T'ai Chi movement with a specific series of hand motions and feet placement.

Right-hand ward-off: The fourth step in the classic T'ai Chi movement with a specific series of hand motions and feet placement.

right palm upward just below the waist. Again, hold the imaginary beach ball between your palms. With your weight on your left foot, raise the heel of your right foot and direct it to the place where the right toe was previously, facing east. As you rotate your body east, shift 70 percent of your body weight from the left foot to the right, keeping knees slightly bent, hips directly parallel to shoulders, and pivoting the left foot east. At the same time, raise the right hand to shoulder level, palm facing toward the chest. Move the left hand with your body at mid-chest level.

Position 5: **Grasp the bird's tail** (*roll back and press*) (FIG. 24.7). Now shift your body weight from the right to the left foot (70–30 percent). With this shift, begin to turn slightly north. Swing the left hand, palm facing in, slowly down past the waist and circle back, up, and over the left shoulder. Move the right hand, palm facing in, toward the chest. As the left hand comes back to mid-chest level, continue to rotate the body east again and transfer your body weight again to the right foot. Brush the left palm lightly against the right wrist at the same time.

Position 6: **Grasp the bird's tail** (*push*) (FIG. 24.8). Facing east, begin to separate the hands and lower them slowly to upper abdominal level, palms facing out. Shift your weight from the right foot to the left, as if you were slowly backing up. Then, reverse weight back to the right foot and extend your hands out slowly as if you were pushing an object away from your face. As you push, be conscious of directing energy in that direction.

Position 7: **The single whip** (FIG. 24.9). Shift your body weight from the right foot to the left, and rotate your body counterclockwise to the north-northwest. Swing arms and hands slowly in the same direction, keeping hands directly in front at mid-chest level. Place the right heel where the right toe was, now pointing north. Then, shift weight to the right foot, rotating slightly to the northeast. Swing the left hand slowly to waist level by the right hip,

> **Grasp the bird's tail:** The fifth (roll back and press) and sixth (push) steps in the classic T'ai Chi movement with a specific series of hand motions and feet placement.
>
> **The single whip:** The seventh step in the classic T'ai Chi movement with a specific series of hand motions and feet placement.

FIGURE 24.7

FIGURE 24.8

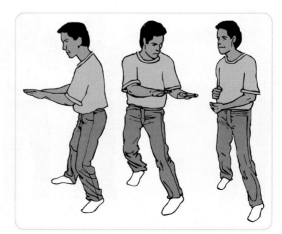

FIGURE 24.9

Stress with a Human Face

Betty Stewart had heard of T'ai Chi decades ago, but it wasn't until September 1994 that she began to practice it in earnest. In the early 1970s she was intrigued to try this form of relaxation, and even bought a video so she could teach herself, but she said that just didn't work. Then one day she noticed that a class in T'ai Chi was to be offered at the Prestige Club, a unique hospital-based health promotion program for seniors with a special focus on bridging standard and complementary forms of healing. Betty wasted no time in signing up.

What makes Betty's story so remarkable are the changes she saw soon after she began taking the class, as well as those that occurred after the first year. Prior to beginning the course, Betty, at the age of 79, was all of 55 inches tall. To the amazement of her physician, Betty has since added over an inch to her height. And unlike most people her age who lose inches to bone demineralization, Betty's bone density remained unchanged in the two years of doing T'ai Chi. Recently she told me, "There was a chance to be involved in a bone demineralization study, but I

didn't have time in my life to see if after four years of clinical trials, all I got was the placebo. I wanted the real thing—that's why I started T'ai Chi."

Aside from the benefits of bone integrity, Betty says there have been other benefits. "I have a much better sense of balance. Why, one day I tripped on an uneven sidewalk. Because I learned how to shift my weight, all that happened was a little bang, but no fracture. My coordination and concentration skills have also improved, as has my level of energy. You know, you cannot do T'ai Chi if your mind wanders. You lose track of where you are in the progression of movements."

Aside from the physical movements, Betty is attracted to the philosophy of this moving meditation. There is a real poetic quality to T'ai Chi, she says with a smile in her voice. "I can tell you about stress, too! Let's just say that both my husband and I have had our fair share of it these past few years. T'ai Chi has really kept me balanced. I think T'ai Chi is phenomenal and I recommend it to all your students."

palm facing up. Draw back the right arm to the right hip, leading with the elbow, and close the fingers as if dropping a coin into the palm of the left hand. Next, slowly rotate your body west, shifting weight from the right foot to the left by taking a step with the left foot. At the same time, raise the right hand to about shoulder level, and sweep the left hand slowly in an upward arc from right to left, twisting the wrist to allow the palm to face out as the hand comes to about shoulder level.

Position 8: **Lift hands** (**FIG. 24.10**). Slowly lift your right heel off the floor and place it once again where the right toe was pointing north. As the heel makes contact, begin to shift your weight from the left foot to the right, coming back to face north. Starting with hands loosely extended out to the sides, draw palms close together facing inward, and position the left hand near the right elbow.

Lift hands: The eighth step in the classic T'ai Chi movement, incorporating a series of specific hand motions and foot placement to facilitate optimal *Chi* movement.

FIGURE 24.10

■ Additional Comments on T'ai Chi Ch'uan

T'ai Chi is unique unto itself. To feel your body move in a guided motion generates a sense of inner peace that seems unparalleled among relaxation techniques. But to be effective, T'ai Chi takes continual practice, a half hour or so per day. Some advocate early morning practice as a fresh start to the day, while others like to end the day with this exercise. There really is no time that is best; choose whatever time fits into your regular schedule. This technique can certainly be done alone, but group sessions add a whole new element of grace and relaxation. Several YMCA, YWCA, and community programs offer morning sessions open to people of all abilities. Remember not to compare your technique with others: Make it an egoless activity. The practice also may necessitate additional lessons from a qualified instructor. Even the best instructors strive to improve their technique. When looking for a T'ai Chi instructor, be sure that his or her philosophy matches yours. Some instructors see T'ai Chi merely as a form of self-defense and teach it as such. Others teach it as a type of meditation, providing an atmosphere to enhance spiritual well-being as well as physical well-being. Sample several instructors before making a commitment to the advancement of your technique. Trust in the instructor is paramount in learning. Finally, this advice from my instructor, Steve Pearlman: "T'ai Chi classes should be lighthearted and fun. If you can have fun and be relaxed in a self-defense situation—in a situation of immediate physical harm—and you can learn to go with the flow, you can be relaxed anywhere. T'ai Chi teaches you how to be relaxed in all aspects of your life and how to stay relaxed in the face of stress."

■ Best Application of T'ai Chi Ch'uan

If you should find yourself getting bored with aerobic exercise or meditation and crave variety, try a session of T'ai Chi. Once you get beyond the idea that you may feel silly, this exercise can be dynamic in its ability to promote relaxation. Some people make T'ai Chi their only method of relaxation, whereas others use it to supplement their repertoire of techniques. When you first try it, remember that the nature of T'ai Chi is calm, not rushed. This moving meditation acts to defuse the emotions that disconnect us from the source of life's energy. To move with the force, not against it, is to abandon emotional attachment to the causes of stress. As a type of physical exercise, T'ai Chi requires its own time and space. Initially, implementation of this technique is not suitable for the overt confrontation of stress. But with practice and understanding, when balance is found, the physical arousal of stress is minimal when faced with a perceived threat.

To practice T'ai Chi, you need some room to move about, approximately five feet by five feet, although it can be done in less. Once the movements are committed to memory, they are easy to practice. But like any other skill, the benefits of this technique necessitate regular practice.

SUMMARY

- *Chi* is a Chinese term representing the universal life energy that surrounds and permeates everyone, the life force. T'ai Chi ch'uan is a form of exercise that is thought to help regulate this flow of universal energy.

- The Chinese believe that poor health is a result of blockages and congestion in the flow of internal energy, which in turn lowers one's physical resistance and makes one vulnerable to various pathogens.

- T'ai Chi, considered by many to be the softest of the martial arts, is called moving meditation, or a series of movements that act to help unify the life force energy with that of the person.

- T'ai Chi is deeply rooted in philosophy, primarily Taoism, but to a lesser extent, Confucianism. The premise of this exercise is to move with, rather than against, the flow of universal energy. The positions

(over 100 in all) reinforce the concept of consciously moving with, rather than against, perceived stressors in everyday life.

- There are four principles in T'ai Chi: fasting the heart, returning to nature, *Wu-wei*, and winning by losing.

- Studies investigating the physiological effects of T'ai Chi show that this technique is as effective as others in promoting relaxation.

- Qigong, a form of energy work, is often used as a mode of healing for chronic pain.

- When practicing T'ai Chi, breathe effortlessly, hold no excess muscular tension, maintain a perpendicular stance, keep your center of gravity low, move at a continuous speed, and integrate the mind and body as one.

STUDY GUIDE QUESTIONS

1. T'ai Chi is called a moving meditation; explain what this means.

2. Explain the philosophy of Taoism in Western terms as a means to promote relaxation.

3. List/explain both the physiological and the psychological effects of T'ai Chi.

REFERENCES AND RESOURCES

Alder, S. S. Seeking Stillness in Motion: An Introduction to T'ai Chi for Seniors, *Activities, Adaptations, and Aging* 3:1–14, 1983.

Bolen, J. S. *The Tao of Psychology.* Harper & Row, New York, 1979.

Büla, C. J., Monod, S., Hoskovec, C., and Rochat, S. Interventions Aiming at Balance Confidence Improvement in Older Adults: An Updated Review, *Gerontology* October 29, 2010.

Campbell, A. J., and Robertson, M. C. Comprehensive Approach to Fall Prevention on a National Level: New Zealand, *Clinical Geriatric Medicine* 26(4):719–731, 2010.

Capra, F. *The Tao of Physics,* 3rd ed. Shambhala Publications, Boston, 1991.

Channer, K. S., et al. Changes in Hemodynamic Parameters Following T'ai Chi Chuan and Aerobic Exercise in Patients Recovering from Acute Myocardial Infarction, *Postgraduate Medical Journal* 72(848):349–351, 1996.

Cohen, K. Personal communication. June 23, 2003.

Delza, S. *The T'ai Chi Experience: Reflections and Perceptions on Body-Mind Harmony.* State University of New York Press, New York, 1996.

Dreher, D. *The Tao of Inner Peace.* Harper & Row, New York, 1991.

Dunn, T. The Practice and Spirit of T'ai Chi Ch'uan, *Yoga Journal,* Nov./Dec., 1987.

Field, T., Diego, M., Hernandez-Reif, M. Tai Chi/Yoga Effects on Anxiety, Heart Rate, EEG, and Math Computations. *Complementary Therapy in Clinical Practice.* 16(4):235–238, 2010.

Gallagher, B. Tai Chi Chuan and Qigong: Physical and Mental Practice for Functional Mobility, *Topics in Geriatric Rehabilitation* 19(3):172–182, 2003.

Gass, R. Tai Chi Chuan and Bone Loss in Post Menopausal Women, *Archives of Physical Medicine and Rehabilitation.* 84:621, 2003.

Husted, C., et al. Improving Quality of Life for People with Chronic Conditions: The Example of T'ai Chi and Multiple Sclerosis, *Alternative Therapies in Health and Medicine* 5(5):70–74, 1999.

I Ching (Book of Changes). R. Wilhelm and C. Baynes, trans. Princeton University Press, Princeton, NJ, 1950.

Irwin, M. R., and Oxman, M. H. Augmenting Immune Response to Varicella Zoster Virus in Older Adults: A Randomized, Controlled Trial of Tai Chi, *Journal of the American Geriatric Society* 55(4):511–517, 2007.

Jacobson, B. H., et al. The Effect of T'ai Chi Chuan Training on Balance, Kinesthetic Sense and Strength, *Perceptual and Motor Skills* 8:27–33, 1997.

Jin, P. Changes in Heart Rate, Noradrenaline, Cortisol, and Mood during T'ai Chi, *Journal of Psychosomatic Research* 33:197–206, 1988.

Jou, T. H. *The Tao of T'ai Chi Ch'uan*. T'ai Chi Foundation, New York, 1988.

Kauz, H. *T'ai Chi Handbook*. Dolphin Books, New York, 1974.

Klein, P. J. Tai Chi in the Management of Parkinson's Disease and Alzheimer's Disease, *Medicine and Sport Science* 52: 173–181, 2008.

Koh, T. C. T'ai Chi Ch'uan, *American Journal of Chinese Medicine* 8:15–22, 1981.

Lang, C., Lai, J., and Chen, S. Tai Chi Chuan, *Sports Medicine* 32(4):3217–3224, 2002.

Lao Tzu. *Tao Te Ching One*. Gia-Fu Feng and Jane English, trans. Random House, New York, 1972.

Learning about Tai Chi Chuan, *Nursing* 32(12):86, 2002.

Li, J. X. Tai Chi: Physiological Characteristics and Beneficial Effects on Health, *British Journal of Sports Medicine* 35(3): 148, 2001.

Li, M., Chen, K., and Mo, Z. Use of Qigong Therapy in the Detoxification of Heroin Addicts, *Alternative Therapies* 8(1):50–59, 2002.

Lo, B. *The Essence of T'ai Chi Ch'uan*. North Atlantic Books, Berkeley, CA, 1979.

Lordi, J. Tai Chi and Its Applications for Massage Therapy, *Massage Therapy Journal* 42(2):44–53, 2003.

Meusel, H. Zur Enignung von Sportarten und Ubungsforman fur Altere (Sport and Exercise Training Suitable for Older People), *Zeitschruift fur Gerontologie* 19:376–386, 1986.

Miller, D., and Miller, J. An Ancient Art Can Change Your Running, *Runner's World,* March, 1982:58–61.

Ming-Dao, D. *Everyday Tao*. HarperCollins, San Francisco, 1996.

Motivala, S. J., Sollers, J., Thayer, J., and Irwin, M. R. Tai Chi Chih Acutely Decreases Sympathetic Nervous System Activity in Older Adults, *Journal of Gerontology and Biological Science Medicine* 61(11):1177–1180, 2006.

Perry, P. Grasp the Bird's Tail, *American Health* 5:58–63, 1986.

Plummer, J. P. Acupuncture and Homeostasis: Physiological, Physical (Postural), and Psychological, *American Journal of Chinese Medicine* 9:1–14, 1981.

Qin, L., et al. Regular Tai Chi Chuan Exercise May Retard Bone Loss in Postmenopausal Women, *Archives of Physical Medicine and Rehabilitation.* 83:1355–1359, 2002.

Sancier, K. Medical Applications of Qigong, *Alternative Therapies* 2(1):40–46, 1996.

Sancier, K. Personal communication, January 24, 1996.

Shapira, M., et al. Tai Chi Chuan Practice as a Tool for Rehabilitation of Severe Head Trauma: 3 Case Reports, *Archives of Physical Medicine and Rehabilitation.* 82:1283–1285, 2001.

Shrier, I. Tai Chi Retards Bone Loss and Improves Muscle Strength, *Physician and Sports Medicine* 31(4):16–17, 2003.

Suler, J. R. The T'ai Chi Images: A Taoist Model of Psychotherapeutic Change, *Psychologia—An International Journal of Psychology in the Orient* 34(1):18–27, 1991.

Wang, C., et al. Tai Chi on Psychological Well-Being: Systematic Review and Meta-analysis, *Complementary and Alternative Medicine* 10:23, 2010.

Wolf, S. L., et al. Exploring the Basis of T'ai Chi Chuan as a Therapeutic Exercise Approach, *Archives of Physical Medicine and Rehabilitation* 78:886–892, 1997.

Wong, A., Lin, Y., et al. Coordination Exercise and Postural Stability in Elderly People: Effect of Tai Chi Chuan, *Archives of Physical Medicine and Rehabilitation.* 82: 608–612, 2001.

Wu, M. Z. *Vital Breath of the Dao: Chinese Shamanic Tiger Qigong*. Dragon Door Publications, St. Paul, MN, 2006.

CHAPTER 25

Progressive Muscular Relaxation

Relaxation is the direct negative of nervous excitement. It is the absence of nerve-muscle impulse.

—Edmund Jacobson, M.D.

The body's muscles respond to thoughts of perceived threats with tension or contraction. Muscular tension is believed to be the most common symptom of stress, and although it may not send people to hospital emergency rooms like other stress-related disorders, its cumulative effects can be stiffness, pain, and discomfort. In extreme cases, it can distort and disalign posture and joint stability. The building blocks involved in muscular contraction are a motor end unit, a motor nerve fiber (neuron), a skeletal muscle fiber, and a stimulus from the nerve fiber to the muscle fiber called an action potential. Chemicals released from these neurons are referred to as neurotrophic substances, which flow from the nerve axon to the muscle fibers. Neurotransmitters secrete epinephrine, norepinephrine, and acetylcholine (ACh) to regulate and control muscle contraction.

Quotation from *Progressive Relaxation: A Physiological and Clinical Investigation of Muscular States and Their Significance in Psychology and Medical Practice* by Edmund Jacobson. Copyright © 1974. Reprinted by permission of the publisher, the University of Chicago Press.

The word *contraction* is often synonymous with shortening, but this is not always the case. Muscle fibers can, in fact, shorten like the barrel of a telescope, which is called **concentric contraction**. But some actually lengthen, in what is called **eccentric contraction**. Furthermore, muscles can contract without any noticeable motion; this type of contraction is called **isometric contraction**. The degree of intensity may vary considerably in isometric contraction, but tension at some level is exerted. Over time, this can result in stiffness and poor mobility of the joint to which the muscles are attached. It is primarily isometric contraction that is most commonly associated with the painful muscle

> **Concentric contraction:** A muscle contraction during which the length of the muscle shortens.
>
> **Eccentric contraction:** A muscle contraction during which the size of the muscle lengthens.
>
> **Isometric contraction:** A muscle contraction during which there is no visible change in the length of the muscle fiber.

tension produced by stress. With repeated excitatory neural stimulation, muscle tension can manifest in various ways, including tension headaches, stiff necks, lower-back pain, stomach cramps, and some forms of temporomandibular joint (TMJ) dysfunction. Often, muscle tension produced by thoughts in the unconscious mind occurs while we sleep, and it has been known to cause joint stiffness and even damaged connective tissue in the jaw, neck, shoulders, and lower back. Progressive muscular relaxation (PMR) is a technique specifically designed to help reduce muscle tension.

Historical Perspective

Early in the twentieth century, an American physician named Edmund Jacobson noticed that his patients suffered from a host of physical ailments, but they all seemed to share one symptom: muscle tension. The thought occurred to Jacobson that if muscle tension was reduced or eliminated, these somatic diseases might decrease or perhaps disappear altogether. In questioning his patients, he discovered that they were completely unaware of the levels of muscle tension in their bodies. Moreover, when patients were invited to relax, the suggestion produced only a partial state of relaxation. A slight degree of muscle tension, called **residual tension**, could still be detected.

Jacobson understood that the body cannot be tensed and relaxed at the same time. In an effort to teach his patients how to relax, he created a simple technique to increase physical neuromuscular awareness called **progressive muscular relaxation (PMR)**. In this exercise, patients were led through a series of steps in which they systematically contracted and relaxed each muscle group. Jacobson believed that if a comparison between tension and complete relaxation of muscle fibers could be recognized by the individual, the awareness would promote a deepened sense of relaxation, not only in the muscle itself but throughout the entire body. This technique, he advocated, could help restore the body's state of physical health; and this turned out to be the case in his patients who began to practice progressive muscular relaxation.

Jacobson presented his technique to the American public in his book *You Must Relax*, one of the first clinical attempts at

> **Residual tension:** A slight degree of muscle tension visible in some people who think they are relaxed.
>
> **Progressive muscular relaxation (PMR):** A relaxation technique; tensing and then relaxing the body's muscle groups in a systematic and progressive fashion to decrease muscle tension.

preventive medicine. He stated that neither the word *stress* nor *relaxation* was heard in American vocabulary prior to World War II. It was Jacobson's work in this field that made *relaxation* a household word. Because of Jacobson's professional background, the medical community unequivocally embraced this technique as its own. For several decades, this was the sole prescribed relaxation technique practiced in the United States, long before the introduction of yoga, Zen meditation, visualization, meditation, and other international techniques now recognized and accepted as bona fide modes of relaxation. In fact, when relaxation courses were first introduced in colleges and universities across the country, progressive muscular relaxation was often the sole technique taught. The Jacobson technique proved very easy to learn and teach; virtually anyone could and did teach it. Consequently, today there are many variations on this theme. Regardless of the variation, the basic process of progressive muscular relaxation remains the same: a progressive series of systematic phases combining isometric muscle contractions with periods of complete muscle relaxation. This technique, perhaps more than any other, illustrates the interception of the stress response by direct, conscious inhibition of the excitatory neural drive to the muscle fibers.

The original steps of Jacobson's progressive muscular relaxation included the following:

1. The progression of muscle groups should start with the lower extremities and move up to the head.

2. Muscle groups should be isolated during the contraction phase, leaving all remaining muscles relaxed.

3. The same muscle groups on both sides of the body should be contracted simultaneously.

4. The contraction should be held for 5 to 10 seconds, with a corresponding relaxation phase of about 45 seconds.

5. The individual should focus attention on the intensity of the contraction, sensing the tension level produced.

6. During the relaxation phase of each muscle group, special awareness of the feeling of relaxation should be focused on, comparing it to how the muscle felt when it was contracted.

Physiological Benefits

Research employing PMR has found that this technique is, indeed, beneficial in decreasing levels of muscle tension as well as increasing overall awareness of muscle tension.

This concept has been the premise of investigations measuring electromyographical (EMG) activity, the electrical conductance of muscle tissue. Biofeedback studies (Belar and Cohen, 1979; Hayes, 1975) in which electrodes were attached to various muscle sites including the forehead, jaw, neck, shoulder, and lower back to determine neuromuscular tension revealed that tension levels significantly decreased when this technique was practiced. Through biofeedback, individuals proficient in PMR learned to control the extent of neuromuscular electrical conduction, and to reach a **zero firing threshold** indicative of complete muscle relaxation. With regular daily practice, there was neuromuscular awareness. People became more attuned to muscular tension as it developed and were better able to release it. Although it may seem incongruent that PMR might be used to reduce the pain of a tension headache, a study by Anderson and Seniscal (2007) revealed that indeed the practice of PMR (with or without osteopathic treatment) showed a significant decrease in headache-free days for 29 patients.

Psychologists also suggest that this technique is effective in controlling muscle tension associated with anger, and some studies suggest cigarette smokers find this technique (without diaphragmatic breathing) more effective than meditation or mental imagery to "kick the habit" (Allen, 1983). Jacobson was of the opinion that once the body achieved a state of neuromuscular homeostasis, the mind would follow suit, allowing for a complete state of relaxation and rejuvenation. Currently, PMR is used to effectively intervene in physical disorders such as insomnia, hypertension, headaches, lower-back pain, and TMJ disorders.

Steps to Initiate Progressive Muscular Relaxation

The purpose of Jacobson's technique is to promote a profound sense of relaxation by comparing the contraction and relaxation phases of each selected muscle group. What makes this technique different from Eastern-based relaxation techniques is strong body awareness in the absence of internal self-talk or positive thoughts. There is no attempt to expand consciousness with this technique.

Position: (**FIG. 25.1**). Jacobson's relaxation technique can be performed in a comfortable sitting position; however, the best position to learn and practice PMR is lying comfortably on a carpeted floor. Your upper arms should rest on each side and your hands should meet on your stomach. Constricting clothing

FIGURE 25.1   Starting position.

should be loosened around your neck and waist. It is also suggested that you remove jewelry, watches, and glasses.

Breathing: The breathing technique with PMR is quite simple. Inhale as you contract the muscles, then exhale as you release the tension. The release of tension corresponding to relaxation of the diaphragm allows for a deeper sense of relaxation throughout the body.

Concentration and ambiance: Although concentration is important, interruptions during this technique seem less bothersome than during other meditation-based techniques, when unbroken concentration is more difficult to recapture. Nevertheless, you may wish to minimize distractions by designating a specific time and place to practice. Attention should be given to room temperature, because a cool environment may produce muscle tension (shivering). Once proficient in the technique, you can do it anywhere: while sitting in traffic, standing in line, or lying in bed trying to fall asleep. Benefits may appear soon after the completion of each session, with more profound physiological adaptations evident after prolonged practice (approximately 4 to 6 weeks). Jacobson believed the best prescription for this technique was three 5-minute daily sessions on a regular basis.

Alterations of several aspects of this technique have been introduced since its debut in 1929. Variations include (1) starting with the head and working down to the feet, (2) changing the intensity of the contraction phase, (3) diaphragmatic breathing after each muscle group, and (4) sitting instead of lying down. The original premise and process have not changed.

Remember that only the selected muscle group should be contracted, leaving the remainder of the body relaxed. It may seem hard at first not to involve surrounding muscles,

> **Zero firing threshold:** A term to signify complete muscular relaxation with no tension.

but with practice it will come. When finished with the progression, lie still on the floor for a few minutes and internalize all somatic sensations. Enjoy the full sense of relaxation. Then, begin to focus your thoughts on your current surroundings.

The following is a slight variation of Jacobson's original technique, which divides the contraction into three intensities—100, 50, and 5 percent—of 5 seconds each, followed by the relaxation phase after each. I have found this to be the most effective pattern. By sensing the differences between muscle contractions, you become more aware of your muscle-tension levels over the course of a day. The following instructions were written to be read yourself before you perform the technique, or to be read by a third party. Before you begin, find a comfortable position (preferably on your back on a carpeted floor), loosen any constrictive clothing, kick off your shoes, and begin to unwind.

1. *Face:* Tense the muscles of the forehead and eyes, as if you were pulling all your facial muscles to the center of your nose (FIG. 25.2). Pull really tight, as tight as you can, and hold it. Feel the tension you create in these muscles, especially the forehead and eyes. Now relax and exhale. Feel the absence of tension in these muscles, how loose and calm they feel. Try to compare this feeling of relaxation with the tension just produced. Now, contract the same muscles, but this time at 50 percent the intensity, and hold it. Then, relax and exhale. Feel how relaxed these muscles are. Compare this feeling to that during the last contraction. This comparison should make the muscles even more relaxed. Finally, contract the same facial muscles slightly,

FIGURE 25.2   Facial stretch.

at only 5 percent intensity. This is like feeling a slight warm breeze on your forehead and cheeks. Hold it. And relax. Take a comfortably slow and deep breath and, as you exhale, feel how relaxed the muscles are.

2. *Jaws:* Take a moment to feel the muscles of your jaws. Notice any tension, even the slightest amount. (The jaw muscles can harbor a lot of undetected muscle tension.) Now consciously tense the muscles of your jaws really tight, as tight as you can, and hold it. Now relax these muscles, exhale, and sense the tension disappearing completely. (You may even feel your mouth begin to open a little.) Feel the difference between how the muscles feel now compared to what you just experienced at 100 percent contraction. Feel the absence of tension. Now, contract these same muscles, but at half the full intensity. Hold the tension, keep holding; and now relax again. Feel how relaxed these muscles are. Compare this feeling of relaxation with what you felt at 50 percent intensity. Once again, contract the same muscles, but with only a 5 percent contraction—just the acknowledgment that these muscles can contract. Now hold it, keep holding, and relax. Release any remaining tension so that the muscles are completely loose and relaxed. Sense how relaxed the muscles are. To enhance this feeling of relaxation, take a comfortably slow, deep breath.

3. *Neck:* Concentrate on the muscles of your neck and isolate them from surrounding head and shoulder muscles. Take a moment to feel the muscles of your neck. Notice any tension. (The neck muscles can harbor a lot of undetected muscle tension.) Now consciously tense the muscles of your neck really tight, as tight as you can, and hold it, even tighter, and hold it. Now release the tension and completely relax these muscles. Sense the tension disappearing completely. Become aware of the difference between how these muscles feel now compared to how they felt at 100 percent contraction. Once again, contract these same muscles, but at 50 percent contraction. Hold this level of tension, keep holding, and now relax again. Feel how relaxed your neck muscles are. Compare this feeling of relaxation with what you felt at half intensity. Now, finally, contract these same muscles at only 5 percent, a very slight twinge up and down the sides of the neck with no motion whatsoever. Hold it, keep holding, and relax. Release any remaining tension so that the muscles

are completely relaxed. Feel just how relaxed these muscles are. To enhance the feeling of relaxation, take a comfortably slow, deep breath and sense how relaxed your neck muscles have become.

4. *Shoulders:* Concentrate on the muscles of your shoulders and isolate these from surrounding neck and upper arm muscles. Take a moment to sense the muscles of the deltoid region. Notice any degree of residual tension. (The shoulder muscles can also harbor a lot of undetected muscle tension, resulting in stiffness. Quite literally, your shoulders carry the weight of all your thoughts, the weight of your world.) Now, consciously tense the muscles of your shoulders really tight, as tight as you can, and hold it, even tighter, and hold it (**FIG. 25.3**). Now relax these muscles and sense the tension disappearing completely. Sense the difference between how these muscles feel now and how they felt during contraction. Once again, contract these same muscles, but this time at half the intensity. Hold the tension, keep holding; and now completely relax these muscles. Sense how relaxed your shoulder muscles are. Compare this feeling with what you felt at 50 percent intensity. Finally, contract these same muscles at only 5 percent, only just sensing clothing touching your shoulder muscles. Hold it, keep holding, and relax. Release any remaining tension so that these muscles are completely loose and relaxed. Feel just how relaxed these muscles are. To enhance this feeling of relaxation, take a comfortably slow, deep breath and sense how relaxed your shoulder muscles have become.

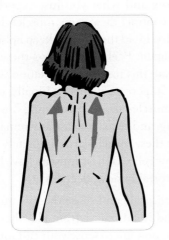

FIGURE 25.3   Shoulder stretch.

5. *Upper chest:* Concentrate on the muscles of your upper chest. Try to isolate these from the muscles of your neck, shoulders, and upper arms. Take a moment to feel these upper chest muscles. Sense the slightest tension these muscles may hold. Now, consciously tense your upper chest muscles really tight, as tight as you can, and hold it, even tighter, and hold it. Now, completely relax these muscles and sense the tension disappearing completely. Sense the difference between how loose these muscles feel now compared with what you just experienced at 100 percent contraction. Contract these same muscles, but at half the full intensity. Hold the tension, keep holding, and now relax again. Feel an even greater sense of relaxation in these muscles. Compare this feeling of relaxation with what you felt at 50 percent intensity. Finally, contract these same muscles at only 5 percent, merely feeling the fabric of clothing over these muscles. Now hold it, keep holding, and relax. Release any remaining tension so that the chest muscles hold absolutely no tension whatsoever. Feel how relaxed these muscles have become. To enhance the feeling, take a comfortably slow, deep breath.

6. *Hands and forearms:* Concentrate on the muscles of your hands and forearms. Take a moment to feel these muscles, including your fingers, palms, and wrists. Notice the slightest bit of tension. Now consciously tense the muscles of each hand and forearm really tight by making a fist, as tight as you can, and hold it as if you were hanging on for dear life. Make it even tighter, and hold it. Now release the tension and relax these muscles. Sense the tension disappear completely. Open the palm of each hand slowly, extend your fingers, and let them recoil just a bit. Sense the difference between how relaxed these muscles feel now compared with what you just experienced at 100 percent contraction. They should feel very relaxed. Now contract these same muscles at a 50 percent contraction. Hold the tension, keep holding, and relax again. Sense how relaxed these muscles are. Compare this feeling of relaxation with what you just felt. Now, contract these same muscles at only 5 percent, like holding an empty eggshell in the palm of your hand. Now hold it, keep holding, and relax. Release any remaining tension so that these muscles are completely relaxed. Feel just how relaxed these

muscles have become. To enhance this feeling of relaxation, take a comfortably slow, deep breath and sense how relaxed your forearm and hand muscles have become.

7. *Abdominals:* Really focus your attention on your abdominal muscles. Take a moment to sense any residual tension in these muscles or the organs they protect. Now, consciously tense your abdominal muscles really tight, as if you have an intense stomach cramp. Contract as tight as you can and hold it, even tighter, and hold it. Now relax these muscles and sense the tension disappearing completely. Feel the complete absence of tension. Compare the difference between how these muscles feel now with what you just experienced at 100 percent contraction. Once again, contract the same muscles, this time at half the full intensity. Hold the tension, keep holding, and now relax again. Feel how relaxed these muscles are. Compare this feeling of relaxation with what you felt at half intensity. When you compare the difference between tension levels and states of relaxation, a greater sense of relaxation will follow. Finally, contract these same muscles at only 5 percent, so that you barely feel the clothing over your stomach area. Just acknowledge that these muscles can contract. Now hold it, keep holding, and relax. Release any remaining tension so that the muscles are completely relaxed. Sense just how relaxed these muscles have become. Take a comfortably slow, deep breath and sense how relaxed your abdominal region has become.

8. *Lower back:* Isolate the muscles of your lower back. These muscles can get quite tense and cause much pain. Now, consciously tense these muscles by trying to press your lower back to the floor. Maintain this posture and hold really tight, as tight as you can, and hold it. Now, relax these muscles, allowing your back to curve naturally, and sense the tension disappearing completely. Sense how relaxed these muscles feel now and compare this with what you just experienced at 100 percent contraction. Once again, contract the same muscles, but at half the intensity. Hold the tension, keep holding, and now relax again. Feel how relaxed these muscles have become. Compare this feeling of relaxation with what you felt at 50 percent intensity. Once again, contract these same muscles, but this time at only 5 percent, a very slight twinge. Now hold it, keep holding, and relax. Release any remaining tension

so that these muscles are completely loose and relaxed. Feel just how relaxed your lower back has become. Now, take a comfortably slow, deep breath.

9. *Buttocks:* Concentrate on your buttock muscles. Notice any residual tension and release it. Now, consciously tense these muscles really tight, as tight as you can and hold it, even tighter, and hold it. Now, release the tension, relax the muscles, and sense the tension disappearing completely. Compare the difference between how these muscles feel now and what you just experienced at 100 percent contraction. Now contract these same muscles at a 50 percent contraction. Hold the tension, keep holding, and now relax again. Feel how relaxed these muscles are. Compare this feeling of relaxation with what you felt at half intensity. Now, finally, contract these same muscles at only 5 percent, showing no motion whatsoever. Now hold it, keep holding, and relax. Release any remaining tension so that these muscles are completely relaxed. Feel just how relaxed these muscles are. To enhance the feeling of relaxation, take a slow, deep breath and sense how relaxed these muscles have become.

10. *Thighs:* Concentrate on the muscles of your left and right thighs. Try not to involve your abdominal or buttock muscles. Take a moment to sense just the muscles of your thighs. Notice any residual tension that might be there and release it. Now, consciously contract these muscles as tight as you can and hold it, even tighter, and hold it. Now relax these muscles and sense the tension disappearing completely. Sense the difference between how these muscles feel now and what you just experienced. Once again, contract these same muscles, but at half the intensity. Hold the tension, keep holding, and now relax again. Feel how relaxed these muscles are. Compare this feeling of relaxation with what you felt at 50 percent intensity. Finally, contract these same muscles at only 5 percent. Now hold it, keep holding, and relax. Release any remaining tension so that these muscles are completely relaxed. Feel just how relaxed these muscles have become. Take a comfortably slow, deep breath.

11. *Calves:* Locate and sense the calf muscles of both legs and isolate these from all other leg muscles. Take a moment to sense your calf muscles. Notice if they have any residual tension. (These can be the tightest of all leg muscles.) Now, consciously tense

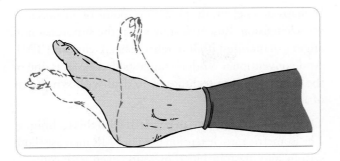

FIGURE 25.4   Pointing the toes to tighten calf muscles.

these muscles really tight by pointing your toes (**FIG. 25.4**). (If they should begin to cramp, release the tension by pulling your toes toward your knees.) Contract as tight as you can, and hold it, tighter. Now relax these muscles and sense the tension disappearing. Make a comparison between how relaxed these muscles now feel with the tension you just experienced at 100 percent contraction. Once again, contract these same muscles, but at a 50 percent contraction, like tip-toeing on a cold wood floor. Hold the tension, keep holding, and now relax again. Feel how relaxed these muscles are. Compare this feeling of relaxation with what you felt before. Now, contract these same muscles at only 5 percent, a very slight twinge with no motion whatsoever. Now hold it, keep holding, and relax. Release any remaining tension so that these muscles are completely relaxed. Feel just how relaxed your calf muscles are. To enhance this feeling of relaxation, take a comfortably slow, deep breath and sense how relaxed your calves have become.

12. *Feet:* Focus your attention on the muscles of your right and left feet. (Typically, the muscles of the feet are not tense, but when standing they can produce a lot of tension. In addition, in the confinement of shoes, they can become less than relaxed.) Now, consciously contract the muscles of your feet by scrunching your toes really tight, as tight as you can. Hold it, even tighter, and hold it. Now relax these muscles and sense the tension disappearing completely. (You may even feel your feet become warm as they relax.) Feel the difference between how these muscles feel now and what you just experienced at 100 percent contraction. Once again, contract these same muscles at half the intensity.

Hold the tension, keep holding, and now relax again. Feel how relaxed these muscles are. Compare this feeling of relaxation with the tension you felt at 50 percent intensity. Now, contract these same muscles at only 5 percent, a very slight twinge. Now hold it, keep holding, and relax. Release any remaining tension so that these muscles are completely relaxed. Sense how relaxed these muscles are. Finally, take a comfortably slow, deep breath and sense how relaxed your whole body is.

Your face and jaw muscles, your neck, shoulders, upper chest, arms and hands, your stomach and lower back, and your legs and feet—your whole body feels completely relaxed and calm. Now lie still, and enjoy the feeling of complete relaxation.

■ Best Application of Progressive Muscular Relaxation

Although Jacobson's technique was originally developed as a means to prevent the cumulative effects of stress, progressive muscular relaxation can also be used as an intervention technique when the body initiates the fight-or-flight response (**FIG. 25.5**). As variations of

"Just a suggestion, Boss: The next time you have a really stressful day, you may want to try some Progressive Muscular Relaxation before things get this bad."

FIGURE 25.5

PMR began to emerge, so too did the concept that this technique had the potential to reduce tension on the spot, in the midst of confronting a stressor, such as getting caught in traffic or standing in long shopping lines. As a preventive technique, however, the entire body must be systematically relaxed by progression through all the muscle groups, which may take up to 30 minutes. As an intervention technique, rather than going through the entire sequence of muscle groups, contract the hands or neck and shoulders—whatever muscle groups are tight—instead. This technique should be practiced not only in the morning or evening, but often during short (5-minute) PMR breaks over the course of a day.

Perhaps anger elicits the greatest response of unconscious muscle tension. Research shows that the suppression of anger can manifest itself in tension headaches and TMJ. And conventional wisdom suggests that PMR is one of the best relaxation techniques to deal with symptoms of anger.

There are some cautions to be noted with this technique. The isometric muscle tension used in PMR increases both systolic and diastolic blood pressure, even with contractions of short duration. Individuals with hypertension (elevated systolic and/or diastolic blood pressure) should refrain from using this technique because it will certainly aggravate their condition.

SUMMARY

- Muscle tension is the most common symptom of stress. This is so because the initial neural response to stress initiates muscular excitation to prepare the body to move for its physical survival.

- Muscles can contract in one of three ways: concentrically (shortening), eccentrically (lengthening), and isometrically (no visible change in length). Muscle tension produced through the stress response is primarily isometric in that there is very little, if any, noticeable change. Yet over time, muscles contracted isometrically begin to show signs of shortening.

- In the early twentieth century, Jacobson recognized that virtually all his patients shared the same symptom regardless of illness: muscle tension. He concluded that if people could reduce muscular tension, their susceptibility to disease would decrease.

- The relaxation technique he created, called progressive muscular relaxation, involves systematically tensing and relaxing the body's musculature, from the feet to the head.

- PMR was quickly accepted by the medical community in the United States as the best way to promote relaxation. Today there are several versions of this technique, all showing similar positive results.

- Research, specifically biofeedback using electromyography, has proved that this technique indeed helps reduce muscular tension.

STUDY GUIDE QUESTIONS

1. Explain the rationale for PMR as a relaxation technique.

2. Describe in simple terms how to do PMR for relaxation.

REFERENCES AND RESOURCES

Allen, K., and Shriver, M. Enhanced Performance Feedback to Strengthen Biofeedback Treatment Outcomes with Childhood Migraine, *Headache* 37:169–173, 1997.

Allen, R. *Human Stress: Its Nature and Control.* Burgess, Minneapolis, MN, 1983.

Anderson, R. E., and Seniscal, C. A Comparison of Selected Osteopathic Treatment and Relaxation for Tension-Type Headaches, *Headache* 47(3):450–451, 2007.

Belar, C., and Cohen, J. The Use of EMG Feedback and Progressive Muscular Relaxation in the Treatment of a Woman with Chronic Back Pain, *Biofeedback and Self-Regulation* 4:345–353, 1979.

Berkovec, T. D., and Fowles, D. C. Controlled Investigation of the Effects of Progressive and Hypnotic Relaxation on Insomnia, *Journal of Abnormal Psychology* 82:153–158, 1973.

Bernstein, D., and Berkovec, T. *Progressive Relaxation Training: A Manual for the Helping Professions.* Research Press, Champaign, IL, 1973.

Caroll, D., and Seers, K. Relaxation for the Relief of Chronic Pain: A Systematic Review, *Journal of Advanced Nursing* 27:467–487, 1998.

Charlesworth, E., and Nathan, R. *Stress Management: A Comprehensive Guide to Wellness.* Ballantine, New York, 1984.

Curtis, J., and Detert, R. *How to Relax.* Mayfield, Mountain View, CA, 1981.

Gard, C. How Biofeedback May Help You Chill Out, *Current Health* 2(24):30–32, 1998.

Gellhorn, E. The Physiological Basis of Neuromuscular Relaxation, *Archives of Internal Medicine* 102:392–399, 1958.

Gellhorn, E. The Influence of Baroreceptor Reflexes on the Reactivity of the Autonomic Nervous System, *Experientia* 12:259–260, 1957.

Girdano, D., and Everly, G. *Controlling Stress and Tension: A Holistic Approach.* Allyn and Bacon, Boston, 2000.

Greenberg, J. *Comprehensive Stress Management,* 10th ed. McGraw-Hill, New York, 2008.

Hayes, S. N. Electromyographical Biofeedback and Relaxation Instructions in the Treatment of Muscle Contraction Headaches, *Behavior Therapy* 6:672–678, 1975.

Herman, C., et al. Biofeedback Treatment for Pediatric Migraine: Prediction of Outcomes, *Journal of Consulting and Clinical Psychology* 65(4):611–616, 1997.

Jacobson, E. *Modern Treatment of Tense Patients.* Thomas, Springfield, IL, 1970.

Jacobson, E. *Progressive Relaxation.* University of Chicago Press, Chicago, 1929.

Jacobson, E. *You Must Relax.* McGraw-Hill, New York, 1978.

Marcus, A., and Smith, S. C. Biofeedback Helps Heart: A Successful Treatment for Chronic Heart Failure, *Prevention* 50:149–150, 1998.

Miller, E. *Letting Go of Stress.* Newman Communications, Albuquerque, NM, 1980. (audio tape, CD)

Mitchell, K., and Mitchell, D. Migraine: An Exploratory Treatment, Application of Programmed Behavior Therapy Techniques, *Journal of Psychosomatic Research* 15:137–157, 1978.

Rice, P. *Stress and Health,* 3rd ed. Wadsworth, Belmont, CA, 1998.

Robb, S., et al. Music-Assisted Progressive Muscle Relaxation, Progressive Muscle Relaxation, Music Listening, and Silence: A Comparison of Relaxation Techniques, *Journal of Music Therapy* 37(1):2–21, 2000.

Steinhaus, A. H., and Norris, J. E. *Teaching Neuromuscular Relaxation.* George Williams College, Chicago, IL, 1964.

Walker, C. E. *Learn to Relax: Thirteen Ways to Reduce Tension.* Prentice-Hall, Englewood Cliffs, NJ, 1975.

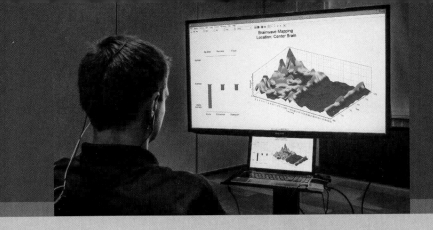

CHAPTER 26

Autogenic Training and Clinical Biofeedback

Open your mind to the power of self-suggestion.

—Johannes Schultz

The ability to control your body's physical reaction to stress is considered the epitome of stress management relaxation. Two techniques that specifically focus on this ability are known as autogenic training (AT) and biofeedback. Whereas autogenic training is a technique that can be done practically anywhere without the use of special equipment, biofeedback typically involves a machine of some kind to provide biological metric information. Both relaxation techniques discussed in this chapter highlight the importance of increasing the awareness of your body's physiology in an effort to return oneself back to homeostasis.

harm, it becomes a liability when the threats are to the ego and identity. So, when mental, emotional, or spiritual concerns threaten the psyche or ego, the body's responses need to be "retrained." By reprogramming the body's responses through self-generated thoughts or passive commands, physical effects are lessened considerably. We now know that mind-body integration is so profound that the antiquated survival mechanism can be overridden, much to our advantage, by conscious thoughts. Thus, the purpose of **autogenic training** is to reprogram the mind so as to override the stress response when physical arousal is not appropriate.

Autogenic Training

During physical arousal, heart rate, blood pressure, ventilation, and muscle tension can all increase in an effort to prepare the body to fight or flee. Although this aroused state is greatly appreciated under the threat of physical

Autogenic training: Introduced by Schultz and Luthe; a relaxation technique where the individual gives conscious messages to various body parts to feel warm and heavy; effects are thought to result from vasodilation to the specified body regions intended for warmth and heaviness.

Historical Perspective

Beliefs regarding the regulation of bodily functions began to change in the nineteenth century, when Europeans traveled the globe and returned recounting stories of human feats in far-off lands. Visitors to the Himalayas reported yogi masters who showed a remarkable ability to control their breathing, heart rate, and blood flow, to the point where they could be mistaken for dead. In a state of profound relaxation produced by meditation, these individuals exhibited incredible control over their body's physiological functions. These yogis appeared to have no magic powers. Rather, they employed exceptional concentration skills to send internal messages from the conscious mind to specific body parts to alter their physiological function. In essence, by believing in the possibility of control, they induced a self-hypnotic state that then produced deep relaxation (**FIG. 26.1**). (These observations were later documented at the Menninger Clinic by Elmer Green, Ph.D., in 1970 with the Hindu yogi Swami Rama.)

Meanwhile, on another continent at the turn of the twentieth century, **self-hypnosis** was being explored by a European brain physiologist, Oskar Vogt. Hypnosis, a trancelike state of consciousness, was already commonly practiced by doctors to better understand the relationship between the conscious and unconscious mind in their emotionally disturbed patients. But while working with several of his clients, Vogt discovered that if they were relaxed, some individuals could put themselves into this trancelike state. Vogt called this autohypnosis (Greenberg, 2010).

Building on this concept, the relaxation technique of autogenic training was introduced by two European physicians, Johannes Schultz and his protégé Wolfgang Luthe, in 1932. Although it was originally designed to calm the mind, patients often remarked on two other distinct physical sensations. The first was increased warmth of the extremities (the arms, hands, and feet). The second, which seemed to accompany the first, was an increased sense of heaviness in the extremities.

"You're getting pretty good at this stress management thing."

FIGURE 26.1

Schultz speculated that both phenomena were caused by vasodilation of blood vessels to localized musculature. It was this vasodilation that caused a change in the distribution of blood flow, bringing with it warmth from the body's core and a subtle but noticeable perception of heaviness. Although it seems that anyone can reap the benefits of self-hypnosis, Schultz and Luthe discovered several conditions that enhance this autogenic process. The term *training* was added when it was acknowledged that, like other skills, the more the technique was practiced, the better one's command over it, and the greater the relaxation response.

In their work with patients who mastered the autogenic technique, Schultz and Luthe (1959) concluded that it is most effective when the following factors are taken into consideration:

1. *The individual should be highly motivated and receptive to instructions and suggestions.* To master this technique, one must maintain a strong degree of self-confidence, faith, and willpower, knowing that the thoughts suggested in the conscious state will be passed from the mind through the body to produce the desired relaxation. Schultz and Luthe called this **passive concentration**.

2. *The individual should possess a strong sense of self-direction and control.* When practicing this technique, suggestions must be self-generated. In other words, one must take command or ownership of these thoughts to promote relaxation. Thus, the individual needs to take the initiative to organize thoughts and feed them systematically as the relaxation session unfolds. Individuals can be guided

---

Self-hypnosis: A form of relaxation; an individual provides himself/herself with suggestions to relax (as with the suggestions of autogenics) as opposed to having someone else provide the suggestions.

Passive concentration: A term coined by the creators of autogenic training to denote the conscious receptivity of self-generated thoughts.

through the process with a series of directions, but ultimately the choice to follow these directions is in the mind of each individual.

3. *The individual should position himself or herself comfortably.* It was noted by Schultz and Luthe that body position is very important to achieve success with this technique. From their observations, they advocated two positions. The most beneficial is lying on one's back on a carpeted surface, with arms resting by the sides and palms facing up. This position is most conducive to feeling the heaviness effects. If this position is not possible, then a comfortably seated position is the best alternative.

4. *The individual should maintain a strong sense of concentration and body awareness.* Loss of mental focus or concentration will impede the flow of messages from the mind to the body. The effectiveness of this technique is enhanced by using both an alert conscious state and imaginative thought processes from the unconscious to focus on specific body regions. Complete attention, like that used by yogis in Nepal, promotes a greater sense of mental control and state of relaxation.

5. *The individual should minimize sensory reception.* Sensory information through the eyes, ears, nose, mouth, and body surface can and will compete for attention at the conscious level. By learning to tune out information from these sources (e.g., closing the eyes), the mind can focus on internal sensations, making them more effective.

6. *The individual should focus on internal physiological processes.* Because the conscious mind normally allows the autonomic nervous system to operate vital body functions, initially the ability to tune into these is embryonic at best. With practice, though, a keen sense of internal physiological processes will develop. Repeated suggestions received by the deeper levels of the mind will eventually transfer to the body through neurobiochemical reactions associated with the relaxation response (**FIG. 26.2**).

Schultz and Luthe strongly believed that when these conditions are met, the stage is set for internal influences of both the conscious and unconscious mind to return the body to homeostasis through a balance of conscious mind-body awareness.

Unlike progressive muscular relaxation, in autogenic training there is no conscious, active effort to relax the muscles. Instead, emphasis is placed on making specific body regions

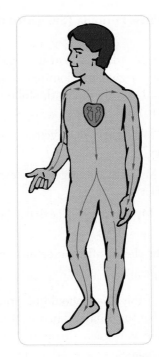

FIGURE 26.2 A person visualizing the flow of blood to the extremities.

warm and heavy through passive self-suggestions. In addition, greater degrees of body awareness and concentration are required to produce the desired relaxation effect. But because a passive attitude is adopted, you are in complete control and are able to stop at any time.

According to the International Committee for the Coordination of Clinical Application and Teaching of Autogenic Therapy (ICAT), the training sequence for autogenic training is a regimented 3-month training program. The systematic and progressive program begins with a breathing warm-up followed by one (or more) of seven phases. These phases include: (1) heaviness, (2) warmth, (3) calm heart, (4) breathing, (5) stomach, (6) cool forehead, and (7) completion. It is important to note that the suggested affirmations are divided into an inhale phase (e.g., "my right arm is") and an exhale phase (e.g., "limp and heavy"). Once competency is achieved in the first stage, which is 3 weeks in duration, you move on to the next phase; thus, the 3-month training program results in a daily routine that should be maintained to achieve a calm autogenic state under nearly any circumstance (Ernst, 2008). Following is a description of the specific step-by-step process for phase 1. (For a complete description of the program, please visit www.guideto psychology.com/autogen.htm.)

Phase 1: Heaviness Formula (Suggested practice time: 21 days)

After the breathing warm-up, begin this phase with your right (or dominant) arm. Breathe deeply and silently repeat the following affirmations six to eight times:

Inhale: "My right arm is getting," exhale: "limp and heavy"

Inhale: "My right arm is getting," exhale: "heavier and heavier"

Inhale: "My right arm," exhale: "is completely heavy"

Repeat the closing affirmation one time:

Inhale: "I feel," exhale: "supremely calm"

This segment of this phase should be practiced two to three times a day for 3 days. Then, continue with the following process with each affirmation repeated six to eight times for 3 days:

Inhale: "My left (or non-dominant) arm is getting," exhale: "limp and heavy"

Inhale: "Both my arms are getting," exhale: "limp and heavy"

Inhale: "My right leg is getting," exhale: "limp and heavy"

Inhale: "My left leg is getting," exhale: "limp and heavy"

Inhale: "Both my legs are getting," exhale: "limp and heavy"

Inhale: "My arms and legs are getting," exhale: "limp and heavy"

Inhale: "My arms and legs are getting," exhale: "heavier and heavier"

Inhale: "My arms and legs are," exhale: "completely heavy"

Repeat the closing affirmation one time:

Inhale: "I feel," exhale: "supremely calm"

> **Selected awareness:** The receptivity of the conscious mind to acknowledge and receive specific thoughts or messages.
>
> **Autogenic discharge:** Physical sensations such as muscle twitching, numbness, and perhaps some emotional responses (tears) released by the unconscious mind from autogenic training sessions.

Psychological and Physiological Responses

The autogenic technique uses what is called **selected awareness**, which refers to the receptivity of the conscious mind to acknowledgment and receipt of specific thoughts or messages. Ideally in the selected awareness process, the censorship role of the ego is eliminated and thoughts can travel freely from the conscious to the unconscious. Lack of censorship can improve dramatically the mind's ability to change or alter desired physiological functions. In a state of receptivity, too, sensations of pain are reduced, and sometimes eliminated altogether. In fact, there are volumes of anecdotal stories in newspapers around the world of people who have undergone incredible experiences, which under normal conditions would be impossible. For example, one runner reportedly ran the entire Boston Marathon feeling some pain in his leg, only to cross the finish line and collapse with a broken femur. Although barely understood scientifically, the powerful integration of conscious and unconscious thoughts allows for a greater state of psychic and physiological homeostasis.

Luthe (1969) also suggested that because the barriers between the conscious and unconscious mind are dismantled, there may be what he referred to as **autogenic discharge**, physical sensations such as muscle twitches, numbness, and emotional responses (e.g., crying), all triggered by the release of unconscious thoughts. These are said to be natural and healthy.

In its most characteristic sensations, warmth and heaviness, this technique can be compared to a muscle massage, although in this case, the muscles are massaged internally rather than on the surface of the skin. The body's muscles are connected to a multitude of nerve cells that regularly release catecholamines at their synaptic junctions to produce minimal tension, or optimal tonus. Under hypnosis, however, the muscles become saturated with blood in a resting state, so the tension decreases and a message is sent back to the brain via the afferent nervous system to stop neural firing. It's a win-win situation for both the muscles, which are allowed to relax, and the brain, which has less neurochemical work to do. The overall effect can be quite profound.

Several clinical tests measuring the effectiveness of this technique have revealed that a redistribution of blood flow indeed occurs in autogenic training, as well as many other changes. Decreases in heart rate, respiration, and muscle tension; increases in hemispheric alpha waves indicative of mental calmness; and even decreases in serum cholesterol levels have been clinically observed

Stress with a Human Face

A good magician never reveals his or her secrets, which is why going to a magic show can be as frustrating as it is entertaining. Trick after trick, you think to yourself, "How did he do that?" And the more amazing the stunt, the more baffled you become.

I once went to a magic show in college. The performer was renowned as an escape artist, and he announced that in the second half of the show he would escape from handcuffs and a locked trunk submerged in water. My friends and I were intrigued, to say the least.

After an amazing first act, I left my seat to stretch my legs. To my surprise, I met the star performer face to face as I walked outside the rear exit of the auditorium. I extended my hand to greet the magician and express my gratitude for a great show. As our hands clasped, I noticed that his palms and fingers were incredibly swollen, as if he had an acute case of poison ivy. After we exchanged polite comments, he went back to his dressing room and I went back to my seat.

I couldn't get over the feel of that handshake. It was like holding a balloon full of water. The escape act was very impressive and ended with thunderous applause. Walking home that night, I was still perplexed about how he got out of those handcuffs, but I was sure his spongy hands had something to do with it.

Years later, I learned that Houdini practiced a technique similar to autogenic training to effect his escapes. He was not only a master escape artist but apparently a master of relaxation as well.

(Greenberg, 2010). Since its introduction, the autogenic relaxation technique has been used successfully in the treatment of several manifestations of physical stress, including insomnia (Coates and Thoreson, 1978); migraines (Blanchard et al., 1985); muscle tension; Raynaud's syndrome (Keefe et al., 1980), a chronic condition of poor blood supply to the hands and feet; and perhaps most notably, hypertension (Silver, 1979).

But clinical laboratories and counseling centers are not the only sites where this technique has been employed. Houdini and several other magicians are known to have used the autogenic technique to "inflate" the size of their hands and wrists when handcuffed and locked up in a chest, then to reverse the process to escape the trap. National biathlon champion Kari Swenson, who was abducted by two men near Bozeman, Montana, in 1985, used this as a survival technique in an effort to minimize blood loss from her gunshot wound. In his book *Peace, Love, and Healing*, cancer surgeon Bernie Siegel wrote about the use of this technique with his patients during surgical procedures for which they were anesthetized. After giving them a clear understanding of the powers of the conscious and unconscious mind, Siegel asked his patients to shunt the flow of blood away from the operating site. After surgery he asked for their cooperation in healing the site. Siegel found that, when relaxed, patients can decrease blood flow in the area of the incision.

Moreover, he noted that patients who are receptive to this power of suggestion tend to recover much more quickly from their surgery. Siegel also recounted an episode where a patient showed signs of cardiac arrhythmia immediately following surgery. Siegel whispered in the patient's ear to sense his heart contracting in a relaxed rhythm, like a swing moving back and forth on a swing set. Sure enough, the dysrhythmia disappeared.

Since its acceptance as a bona fide relaxation technique, autogenic training has been utilized in many clinical settings and helped a number of patients with a host of stress-related physical problems. As a result of its widespread use, many variations have surfaced in the past 60 years, including its combination with complementary techniques such as diaphragmatic breathing and mental imagery.

Steps to Initiate Autogenic Training

Body Position. As Schultz and Luthe suggested, there are two recommended body positions (**FIG. 26.3**). The preferred position is lying on your back on a carpeted floor or bed, with your arms by your sides, palms facing up, and legs straight, heels resting evenly on the surface. Thin pillows or cushions may be used behind the head and knees for support as long as the body remains in comfortable vertebral alignment. If circumstances do not permit lying down, then a seated position

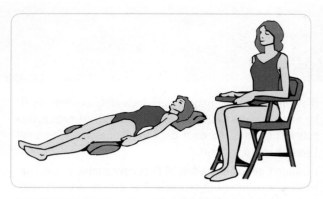

FIGURE 26.3 The two suggested body positions are (1) lying on your back on a comfortable floor surface, or if this is not possible, (2) sitting comfortably in a chair. Once you are proficient, any position will do.

in a chair is recommended. While seated, keep your head aligned over your body, with your arms either on your lap or supported by the frame of the chair. It is important to have your limbs supported so that they don't compete with the force of gravity and negate the effects you are trying to produce. Luthe suggests that if your head becomes too heavy, let it hang comfortably. Because several postural muscles are called upon when seated, it may be less effective than the reclining position. With practice, however, sitting will also produce the desired relaxation. It is also recommended to remove jewelry and loosen any restrictive clothing. Perhaps most important, refrain from eating a big meal before practicing this technique. This will compromise its effectiveness because when food is digested, blood concentrates in the gastrointestinal area and this will compete with the blood flow to the extremities.

Concentration and Awareness. Under normal conditions, attention is easily distracted by interruptions, from phone calls to random thoughts roaming the interiors of our minds. To minimize external distractions, find a quiet place and designate it as your relaxation space. By training your relaxation skills in the same location each

---

Indirect approach: A term used in autogenic training when you suggest to yourself that various body parts are warm and heavy.

Direct approach: A term used in autogenic training when you not only suggest the words *warm* and *heavy,* but also imagine the flow of blood to these body regions, such as hands or feet.

---

time, a comfort pattern is created for both mind and body. Next, control this environment by turning off the phone, closing the door, and making other necessary adjustments such as closing the window or blinds.

Now you can focus internally. When first trying this technique, you may find your mind drifting toward what seems like more important thoughts. But autogenic concentration concerns only the "here and now"— specifically, the present state of your body. If at first you find other thoughts competing for your attention, simply acknowledge them and then redirect your flow of consciousness back to your body. With practice, the frequency of competing thoughts will decrease and concentration will improve.

The concentration for relaxation skills is different from that required for driving a car, listening to a lecture, or watching a movie. Often those events require judgment and analysis. By contrast, during a state of relaxation, particularly autogenic training, concentration involves the right cerebral hemisphere's ability to receive and accept thoughts without judgment. In this technique, you must allow yourself to become open to suggestion and adopt a passive—but not defensive—frame of mind.

Other Suggestions. Despite dogmatic comments from members of the ICAT, the concepts and principles of autogenic training can be learned quickly by most people, and the short-term relaxation effects are often experienced immediately. However, like any skill, it will take several weeks of repeated and disciplined practice to feel the cumulative effects. When learning and practicing this technique, try to practice twice a day for 15 minutes each time so that a training effect does, indeed, occur.

Over the years, two general approaches to the autogenic relaxation technique have surfaced. The first is the **indirect approach**, wherein you simply suggest to yourself that certain body regions become warm and heavy. The second is a more **direct approach**, wherein you employ a greater sense of mental imagery by making reference to the specific physiological systems responsible for the sensations of warmth and heaviness.

Indirect Approach. As with most relaxation techniques (e.g., yoga, T'ai Chi), people adapt these for various target audiences. Over time, autogenic training has been adapted in a similar fashion. The following is an adaptation from the suggested 3-month intensive training program. This adaptation, "the indirect approach," involves very general instructions (affirmations) that you may repeat several times to yourself in an effort to increase body awareness and promote relaxation. There is little detail and internal visual imagery involved. The phases of these instructions are a feeling of heaviness, a feeling of warmth, a calmness of the heart, a calmness of breathing, and even a coolness of the forehead. Attention to each phase should continue for about one minute by repeating the instructions until the desired sensation is felt. This whole progression of phases should take approximately 15 minutes. When you are done, remain in position and try to lock the feeling of relaxation into your memory bank so you can recall it during times of stress and tension.

First, take a slow, deep breath and feel the sense of relaxation as you exhale. Do this once more, making the breath even slower and deeper than the last. Then, say the following thoughts to yourself:

Phase 1: Heaviness

- My arms and hands feel heavy.
- My legs and feet feel heavy.
- My arms and legs feel heavy.

Phase 2: Warmth

- My arms and hands feel warm.
- My legs and feet feel warm.
- My arms and legs feel warm.

Phase 3: Heart

- My heart is calm and relaxed.
- My heartbeat is slow and relaxed.

Phase 4: Breathing

- My breathing is slow and relaxed.
- My breathing is calm and comfortable.

Phase 5: Solar Plexus

- My stomach area is calm and relaxed.

Phase 6: Forehead

- My forehead is cool.
- My forehead is calm and relaxed.
- My entire body is calm and relaxed.

Direct Approach. The direct approach, also an adaptation from the original 3-month intensive training program, is a more detailed visual interpretation of the general instructions just listed. It is a slight variation

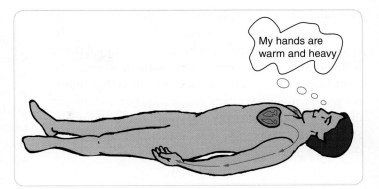

FIGURE 26.4   Visualizing blood flow to the arms and hands, the breath even slower and deeper. With each exhalation, feel how relaxed your body has become.

on the original technique offering added instructions for those who need more understanding of how the physiological changes occur. In the direct approach, the specific mechanisms involved in warmth and heaviness are focused on to initiate a stronger sense of relaxation (**FIG. 26.4**). You start out with diaphragmatic breathing to induce relaxation. When mind and body become relaxed through this technique, the mind becomes more receptive to additional thoughts (warmth and heaviness), and thus the selected awareness process is enhanced. The length of time required for this approach will vary. To begin, you may want to work on only one body region such as the arms and hands. With proficiency, you can add to the duration of each session. For a full experience of the direct approach, please visit the companion website for this text.

Adding Mental Imagery

As Aristotle once said, "The soul never thinks without a picture." When imagery is combined with autogenic training, it can produce profound physiological effects on the body. Imagery consisting of pictures or symbols that parallel and represent actual physiological responses seems to affect the body's functions in ways that words alone cannot. A host of stories shared in the medical community lend credence to this concept. Hypertensive patients who use mental imagery have shown significant decreases in blood pressure. For example, one client of mine used the image of a bottleneck traffic jam on a highway. By working to clear the jam in his mind and then visualizing only his car on the road, he was able to reduce his resting blood pressure to the point where he was taken off medication by his physician. This phenomenon can be explained through the specific cognitive functions of the right and left hemispheres of the brain. The left hemisphere, which controls verbal skills, is thought to communicate to the body in words. The right hemisphere, which is quite poor in verbal ability, but proficient with symbolic images, appears to communicate to the body visually. The combination of words and pictures seems to have a more profound effect on the body's physiology than do words alone.

The Use of Self-Hypnosis

The use of hypnosis has gained considerable acceptance (and found substantial success) in the field of psychology over the years as a means to enhance health and well-being in endeavors ranging from weight loss to smoking cessation. The premise of self-hypnosis, whether it is used specifically for relaxation, as with autogenic training, or to effect other changes in attitude and behavior, is similar to virtually every relaxation technique: a calm mind and a calm body. Relaxation induced with gentle diaphragmatic breathing sets the stage for a receptive mind, which can then rehearse affirmation statements for the desired attitudinal or behavioral change. Self-generated hypnotic suggestions take root only when the mind and body are calm, because the unconscious mind censors suggestions under any other circumstance (Vickers et al., 2001).

© Bradford Veley, Marquette, MI

FIGURE 26.5

Best Application of Autogenic Training

In its original design, autogenic training was created to be thorough in its attempt to relax the entire body. Sessions would last 20 to 40 minutes and could be done at any time of the day. Today, stress-management instructors advocate relaxing all body regions for the entire duration of each session to achieve full effectiveness. With proficiency, however, the ability to relax upon suggestion of warmth and heaviness can be immediate, which is especially useful in situations that trigger the stress response. The autogenic technique is as portable as the thoughts that create it. Some healthcare professionals even suggest periodic short "autogenic breaks" in the course of a busy day as a preventive approach to the cumulative effects of stress. The jury is still out on whether this technique is more advantageous for reducing anxiety or anger. It appears to be effective with both emotional responses, depending on the individual and circumstances. It's best to try it for yourself and find out how it can best work for you.

■ Clinical Biofeedback

Welcome to the techno-nano age of biometrics where anything is possible, and the future is now. Picture this: The shirt or blouse you wear contains thousands of tiny sensors that directly communicate your surface temperature, heart rate, blood pressure, muscle tension, and serum levels of cholesterol. The sensor on your computer mouse detects your skin temperature and the slightest beads of perspiration with a mere brush of your thumb. The lower left-hand corner of your computer screen displays a corresponding graph of your stress level with a suggestion to breathe deep to reduce your resting heart rate. Welcome to the age of nanobiofeedback, where your body's physiological parameters are less than a mouse click away, giving you more responsibility for your health status. Bed sheets, toothbrushes, bandages, smart wrist watches, and running shoes have all been created with artifical intelligence to help you regulate your body's physiological stress level and help you achieve homeostasis. Some (like court-ordered ankle bracelets) can even monitor your blood alcohol and send the information, via Wi-Fi, to a parole officer. Football helmets can transmit head blows and impact tackles to attending physicians. Toilets in Japan are now equipped to determine if one has diabetes through urine samples. Joysticks, thumb buttons, and eye motion sensors connected to video games are able to determine stress-prone thinking patterns. Even the Wii system is loosely based on biofeedback technology. Indeed, technology may give you stress, but technology can also provide the means to help you regulate it. The future is now.

These devices may seem like science fiction, but they exist today, funded in large part with your tax dollars for military purposes. Welcome to the first age of Biofeedback Bionics. Although you may not have access to the latest technology, biofeedback is as simple as monitoring your pulse and breaths per minute. When information is accessed through clinical (and now nano) instrumentation, it is referred to as **clinical biofeedback**. With the advancement of computer interface technology, some researchers now refer to biofeedback as *neurofeedback*.

The big craze these days are apps that monitor various aspects of your body's physiology in order to help you regulate your breathing, sleep, blood sugar, and eating habits. All of these apps fall into the biofeedback family, as they offer a way to measure a specific aspect of your body's physiological function and help bring you back to a sense of inner peace.

What Is Clinical Biofeedback?

Clinical biofeedback can be defined as the use of monitoring instruments to amplify the electrochemical energy produced by body organs. Normally individuals are not aware of producing this energy, but through biofeedback they can use information to gain voluntary control over various physiological processes. For example, let us say that you have just learned from your dentist that you apparently grind your teeth at night. Being unaware that your jaw muscles are clenched while you sleep makes the problem difficult to resolve. But the use of instrumentation to measure your physiological responses could show you the tension you produce in your jaw muscles while awake and thus teach you how to reduce it—and eliminate the wear and tear on your teeth.

What distinguishes clinical biofeedback from other techniques is that it allows a person to increase awareness of his or her own physiological responses (breathing, muscle tension, blood pressure, heart rate, and/or body temperature) by learning to monitor them through data gathered by a particular instrument. Through biofeedback training, a person can also learn to recondition the thought processes associated with increased autonomic nervous activity to relax. Some stressors are very obvious, as are our reactions to them. But others are more subtle, so much so that we condition ourselves to

ignore the effects they produce throughout our bodies. Clinical biofeedback has the advantage of magnifying a biological function to give you immediate evidence of changes in it, which in turn allows you to gain mastery over it as it is happening. And whereas most relaxation techniques are meant to have a general, overall effect, biofeedback is usually specific to one physiological parameter you want to target (e.g., tension in your jaw muscles). Athletes (amateur and professional) use all types of biofeedback equipment to enhance their athletic performance.

Clinical biofeedback typically employs sophisticated technological equipment in combination with one or more other relaxation techniques, including meditation, diaphragmatic breathing, mental imagery, autogenic training, and progressive muscular relaxation. When these relaxation techniques are performed in conjunction with data from an instrument revealing what the autonomic nervous system is really doing, the person gains a stronger "feel" for how to relax that body region.

Stress management is not the only area facilitated by this technique. Clinical biofeedback is also used in several types of psychotherapy (e.g., gestalt therapy) and some cases of physical rehabilitation of knee, lower back, and shoulder joints.

Once again, this technique emphasizes the importance of a strong mind-body-spirit connection. Clinical biofeedback is currently used in the treatment of migraine and tension headaches, ulcers, hypertension, bruxism, Raynaud's disease, and a host of other stress-related illnesses. Dr. Edward Blanchard of the Center for Stress and Anxiety Disorders in Albany, New York, has conducted numerous scientific investigations demonstrating the beneficial effects of biofeedback on several different maladies, substantiating the validity of this technique. His work is well respected throughout the allied health fields. But despite the fact that biofeedback is known to be effective in gaining control over specific biological functions, the exact mechanisms involved are as yet not completely understood (**FIG. 26.6**).

Clinical biofeedback: A process using one or more specially designed machines to amplify body signals (e.g., heart rate, muscle tension) and display these signals in a way that can be interpreted so that their intensity can be changed for the health of the individual.

FIGURE 26.6　These two spectacular images are from the Journey to the Wild Divine active feedback and Relaxing Rhythms active feedback programs by Wild Divine. Characters within the Journey help you to control your body's reactions. By increasing, decreasing, or synchronizing your body rhythms, you learn to master the Journey Events and progress through the program.

Historical Perspective

The term *biofeedback* was coined in the late 1960s by researcher Dr. Barbara Brown to describe biological feedback through electrical stimulation. This term was coined just prior to the first annual meeting of the Biofeedback Society in 1969 (Allen, 1983). Biofeedback includes information on any physiological parameter that can be electronically detected, amplified, and converted into visual or auditory stimuli. An individual can observe and interpret these stimuli, and thereby make appropriate changes to enhance his or her health. Although the name is rather new, the concepts of biofeedback date back to the classical conditioning theory of Pavlov (every stimulus produces a response through association) and operant conditioning theory of Thorndike (behaviors can be changed by redirected thought processes). Until 1960, it was strongly believed that the autonomic nervous system was reflexive in nature, influenced only by classical conditioning, not conscious thought. Like an autopilot computer program, the autonomic nervous system was thought to be under complete control of the lower brain centers. Basic physiological functions were called "involuntary" because it was believed that they could not be intentionally influenced or manipulated by the individual.

Clinical investigations with the yogi Swami Rama, conducted at the Menninger Clinic, as well as other studies by Miller (1968) began to show that conscious thought really can influence the physiological functions of the autonomic nervous system. In addition to significantly lowering his resting heart rate and breathing well below "normal homeostatic levels," Swami Rama was able to shift blood flow to various regions of his body. Similar studies showed that some people had the ability to change their brain waves at will. In fact, people who were taught autogenic training proved that with practice almost anyone could control these "involuntary" functions. And the more they practiced, the more control they seemed to exhibit. Biofeedback training is now considered a type of operant conditioning wherein, with the help of a trained therapist, an individual can learn

BOX 26.1　Insomnia and Biofeedback

Biofeedback has been used successfully in the treatment of insomnia. Through the use of EEGs and in some cases EMGs, patients are shown their brain waves (EEG) and muscle tension (EMG) and then taught how to reduce the neural firing. When this information is combined with other coping skills, including cognitive restructuring, visualization, and diaphragmatic breathing, patients are able to control their thoughts to produce a minimal level of brain activity, indicative of a presleep state. Research studies regarding insomnia and biofeedback include mostly case studies, but the body of evidence yielded by these investigations constitutes a critical mass of data to reveal that the use of biofeedback to train the mind is, indeed, a valuable skill to reduce problems associated with insomnia.

to control specific physiological functions by changing the thoughts and perceptions that produced them.

In his classic book *Mind as Healer, Mind as Slayer*, stress researcher Kenneth Pelletier states that biofeedback comprises three principles: (1) information can be obtained about specific organ activity, meaning that a machine can distinguish electrical conduction of heart muscle from that of brain and skeletal muscles; (2) every physiological change is paralleled by a change in attitude or consciousness, just as a change in feelings will produce a change in some biological function; and (3) people can be taught to control their autonomic nervous systems to influence these physiological changes directly. He adds that individuals must accept responsibility for their own health status—in this case, by learning to recondition thoughts and behaviors away from disease and toward health. This principle is closely related to Rotter's concept of locus of control, where a person learns to shift the focus of control from an external source (a stressor) to an internal source (his or her thoughts) to take control of physical health.

The HeartMath Institute has gained world renown for its well-designed research into heart rate variability. Based on the premise that both emotions and thoughts affect heart rate and other cardiovascular functions, a biofeedback program called the Em Wave PC Stress Relief System was developed by Doc Childre. The Em Wave PC Stress Relief System is an interactive computer learning system (**FIG. 26.7**) designed to teach participants to respond—rather than react—to situations that can promote stress.

Courtesy of HeartMath LLC

FIGURE 26.7 A client is taught to observe his heart rate activity through the HeartMath Institute's Em Wave PC Stress Relief System program.

Purpose of Biofeedback

To get an idea of our physical appearance, we gaze into a mirror at our hair, our complexion, and the clothing we wear. Mirrors offer a clear reflection of our physical exterior. The many physiological functions that take place inside our bodies are much more difficult to observe, yet equally necessitate our attention. For example, according to the Centers for Disease Control and Prevention (CDC) an estimated 33 percent of the U.S. population has hypertension, but blood pressure *cannot* be detected by physical appearance or by simply taking one's pulse. It must be monitored with a blood-pressure cuff, sphygmomanometer, and stethoscope. Physiological functions we cannot see, involving the nervous, endocrine, and immune systems, are strongly activated during the stress response. Whereas some people show the ability to scan their bodies and bring certain functions under control without the aid of a machine, most people need the additional help of biofeedback to do so. With enough practice, these people, too, can attain the ability to perceive and regulate their internal functions without the use of machines, or what is known as a **conditional response**.

Although the technology of clinical biofeedback may seem complex, the concept behind it is quite simple. Biofeedback is a **closed-loop feedback system**, where information taken from the system (the human body) is translated into a language understood by the five senses (**FIG. 26.8**). Biofeedback is like a horse-race track where the starting and finishing points are the same. In this case, the loop begins with the body, which is connected by wires to some type of electronic machine. The wires receive energy and send it to the machine, where it is converted to recognizable stimuli and then relayed back to the individual through one of the five senses. More technically, biochemical impulses generated by specific body organ tissue are transmitted via one or more electrodes attached to that body region and sent to an electronic receiver that converts the impulses to either visual or auditory stimuli. These stimuli can be in the form of colored lights, sounds, and/or parts such as needle pens that chart the data.

Conditional response: A learned response (in this case through biofeedback) to control various biological functions such as heart rate and blood pressure.

Closed-loop feedback system: A term used to describe the dynamics of biofeedback with its sensors attached to various parts of the human body.

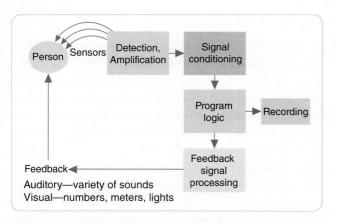

FIGURE 26.8   The biofeedback loop.

Biofeedback has been called an educational tool because it teaches people how to monitor and change the frequency and amplitude of the electronic signals by controlling (relaxing) the body region to which the electrodes are attached. The purpose of biofeedback, therefore, is to teach people how to "tune in" to their bodies so that they may regulate those physiological functions that are susceptible to increased metabolic activity caused by stress.

There are three distinct phases of biofeedback:

1. *Awareness of physiological response:* As mentioned before, the sensory stimulation deciphered by the biofeedback machine and decoded by one of the five senses helps one increase awareness of physiological adaptations to stress. Operating the instrument is a certified therapist who teaches the patient to interpret the amplified signals and thereby form an association between the flashing lights or beeping sounds and the body's current state of arousal.

Binary: One of two categories used to describe biofeedback; an example might include a device that lets one know of an effect of biofeedback on a specific biological function that results in lights appearing on a panel.

Proportional: One of two categories used to describe biofeedback; an example might be a device that lets one know the amount of physiological change, as determined by the pitch of a noise.

Electromyographic (EMG) biofeedback: Biofeedback that measures the electrical impulses from specific muscles.

---

2. *Control of physiological response:* The therapist guides the person through several types of relaxation techniques—meditation, mental imagery, and autogenic training, among others. At the same time, the person attempts to consciously manipulate his or her physiological response to bring a particular body organ or reaction to a state of homeostasis.

3. *Application of reconditioned response in everyday routines:* After much practice with biofeedback instrumentation, the individual then transfers the new skill to the office, home, car, or wherever he or she experiences the sensations of stress, by practicing the relaxation technique without using the equipment. This, of course, is the real test of the effectiveness of biofeedback training sessions.

Types of Biofeedback

There are many types of biofeedback equipment. Some are so small you can hold them in your hand, and others involve large (expensive) instrumentation in a wall unit. Different machines have been designed to receive the electrical signals from the heart, brain, muscles, skin, back, and so forth. The use of biofeedback is specific to the symptom(s) the patient exhibits in a particular body region. In general, though, instrumentation falls into two categories: **binary** and **proportional**. Binary equipment provides information that lets someone know only whether he or she is controlling a physiological function. An example would be a light that is off when someone's systolic blood pressure is above 130 mm Hg, and goes on when blood pressure goes below that number. Proportional biofeedback, by contrast, reveals the *amount of change* occurring during a session. An example is a machine that changes the pitch of a sound as a person becomes more relaxed. Because it provides more information to the patient, proportional biofeedback is thought to be more effective as a teaching tool. Regardless of instrumentation, biofeedback is effective because it is accurate and reliable.

Electromyographic (EMG) Biofeedback. This biofeedback modality monitors electrical impulses produced by muscle tissue (**FIG. 26.9**). Electrodes are placed on the skin over specific muscles that are prone to tension, such as the jaw, lower back, neck, and/or shoulders. For overall relaxation, the frontalis muscle on the forehead is used because this muscle has no direct connection to bone. Through the EMG, the patient first becomes aware of the current level of muscle tension by watching visual feedback or hearing auditory feedback. With the

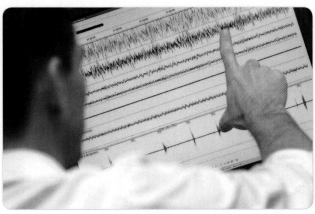

FIGURE 26.9   EMG biofeedback instruments.

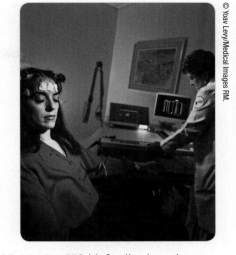

FIGURE 26.10   EEG biofeedback equipment.

aid of the therapist, the subject is then taught to relax the muscles that are diagnosed as tense, and to sense the difference between tension and relaxation, while monitoring visual and/or auditory data produced by the machine. EMG biofeedback is most commonly used for tension headaches and bruxism, or TMJ.

Electroencephalographic (EEG) Biofeedback. Like the heart and muscles, the brain produces electrical impulses. In 1924, Hans Berger created an instrument to detect and monitor brain waves, which he called the electroencephalogram (EEG) (**FIG. 26.10**). An EEG is recorded by applying electrodes to designated points on the scalp, which monitor electrical activity close to the surface of the brain. Through the use of EEG, it has been observed that the human brain produces different electrical rhythms during various states of consciousness. These brain waves are grouped and characterized by oscillations per second and amplitude. The four groups are beta waves (more than 15 cycles per second), which are associated with normal or waking consciousness; alpha waves (7–14 cycles per second), which are produced in an altered or relaxed state of consciousness; and theta (4–7 cycles per second) and delta (between 0.5 and 4 cycles per second) waves, which are observed in unconscious and sleeping states. Each type of brain wave is represented by a specific sound or pitch from the EEG. For the purpose of relaxation, the patient is taught to decrease the pitch associated with beta waves and increase the alpha sound. The primary purpose of this type of biofeedback is to alleviate the cognitive arousal observed in insomnia. So far, it seems to be of very little help in relieving tension headaches or other stress symptomology.

Cardiovascular (EKG) Biofeedback. Because there appears to be such a strong relationship between stress and coronary heart disease, cardiovascular biofeedback is often used to augment a patient's ability to control resting heart rate and blood pressure. Portable equipment is now available for cardiac patients so that they may monitor their heart rate on a regular basis. Portable blood pressure kits are also available for people with hypertension. In either case, patients are taught to employ relaxation skills when the biofeedback machine indicates that cardiovascular parameters are above preset resting levels.

But cardiovascular biofeedback is not used solely by people at risk for cardiac disease. Many Olympic and professional athletes also use portable heart-rate monitors to aid their training. Several of these consist of a belt worn around the upper chest and a receiver worn on the wrist like a watch (**FIG. 26.11**). The receiver is set to a target heart-rate range. If the athlete goes below or above this zone, the watch beeps, signifying that cardiovascular workload needs to be increased or decreased, respectively. In some cases, the receiver records heart rate for up to an hour, and these data can be retrieved and logged into a training diary.

> **Electroencephalographic (EEG) biofeedback:** Biofeedback that measures the electrical activity of the brain.
>
> **Cardiovascular (EKG) biofeedback:** Biofeedback that measures the electrical activity of the heart muscle in terms of amplitude and frequency of each heartbeat.

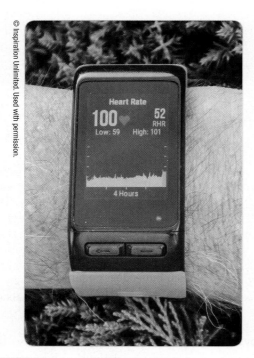

© Inspiration Unlimited. Used with permission.

FIGURE 26.11 A heart rate monitor.

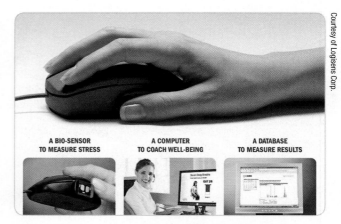

Courtesy of Logisens Corp.

FIGURE 26.12 The Logisens biosensor (located on the thumb placement of the mouse) detects one's stress level through electrodermal response. The Logisens biofeedback program educates the individual to monitor and control stress levels.

Another type of cardiovascular monitor measures temperature. **Thermal biofeedback**, as it is called, monitors the flow of blood to a specific area by the heat it gives off. Temperature receptors are applied to specific body parts (e.g., fingers and toes) so that changes in blood flow can be detected as changes in temperature. Thermal biofeedback is most often used in the treatment of migraine headaches and Raynaud's disease.

Electrodermal (EDR) Biofeedback. **Electrodermal (EDR) biofeedback**, also known as galvanic skin response (GSR), is used to measure electrical conduction in the skin itself (**FIG. 26.12**). The hands and fingers produce beads of sweat under stress, and the fact that water is a good conductor of electricity is the basis of the operation of the EDR instrument. The premise behind EDR is that electrical impulses produced by the skin are activated by the sympathetic nervous system. In this type of biofeedback, electrodes are lubricated with a conductance gel and placed on the skin, usually the index and ring fingers of the left hand. As in other forms of biofeedback,

the patient is then taught to decrease sympathetic activation through relaxation techniques. EDR is employed primarily to detect nervousness, and repeated use can help people learn to decrease anxiety. The same technology, incidentally, is used in polygraph (lie detector) tests.

Biofeedback and Chronic Pain

If you were to do an Internet search on the topic of biofeedback, the vast majority of studies turned up in the search would deal with the beneficial use of biofeedback for pain relief, whether for migraines, TMJ, lower-back pain, colitis, or a multitude of other chronic symptoms. Because biofeedback is meant to act as an amplification of the body's electrical responses, the regulation of pain is controlled through a conscious decrease of neural firing to the painful area. By using biofeedback technology to increase awareness of self-regulation, pain is brought under control and, in many cases, eliminated. For biofeedback to be fully effective, however, it must do more than simply decrease pain. When used properly with the aid of a certified biofeedback therapist, the causes of stress that manifest themselves as pain are addressed and resolved as well (Norris, 2012).

■ Best Application of Clinical Biofeedback

Clinical biofeedback, like muscle massage, is a technique that requires the assistance of a qualified instructor or therapist. The primary organization that certifies therapists in

> **Thermal biofeedback:** Biofeedback that measures the response from skin temperature.
>
> **Electrodermal (EDR) biofeedback:** Biofeedback that measures the sweat response from skin.

Stress with a Human Face

Sara began developing migraine headaches her senior year of high school. Not a week would pass without the effects of a severe migraine. She was placed on a prescription medicine, but it really didn't help much. Some headaches lasted a week and they felt like they were ripping her skull apart. Her first year in college was worse, sometimes with headaches so bad she curled up in bed for days. It was a program on the Discovery Channel one night that caught her attention. The program featured a technique called biofeedback. Although several people were interviewed for a host of maladies, it was the woman who suffered from migraines that caught her attention. "You become so desperate you are willing to try anything," she said. When the show was over, Sara Googled the word *biofeedback* and the name of her city to see what would show up. After spending an hour reading about biofeedback on the Internet and searching for a well-qualified technician in her area, she made a few phone calls the next day and set up an appointment. "What biofeedback does is put you in touch with your body. In order to listen to your body's signals, you have to pay attention and that's what biofeedback helps you do. Most people are so out of touch with their bodies, and I was one of those people. You can get so caught up in the day-to-day struggles that you lose touch with yourself, until it comes back to bite you in the butt." After several biofeedback sessions, Sara got her migraines under control to where she had only a couple per year, if that. "For me, it worked and I am grateful. Getting in touch with your body is not only beneficial, it's essential if you want to function in the fast-paced world we live in."

clinical biofeedback training is the Biofeedback Certificate Institute of America (BCIA). Since 1980, all therapists practicing biofeedback are required to have certification by one of these organizations. If you are interested in this mode of relaxation therapy because of recurring health problems, contact your primary care physician, local hospital, or psychological counseling center. You may also contact the Association for Applied Psychophysiology and Biofeedback at http://aapb.org. When you meet with a biofeedback therapist, he or she will determine how this treatment can alleviate your stress-related symptoms and which type of biofeedback is best suited to do this. The number of therapy sessions required depends on the type and severity of the symptoms. Once you are familiar with the technique, you will then be given "homework" assignments in which you are to practice the biofeedback therapy on your own for a specified length of time.

Occasionally there is concern about dependency on the biofeedback equipment to obtain a complete state of relaxation. If the therapist is good at instruction and you are conscientious about practicing your relaxation techniques, there really is no danger of biofeedback dependence. Keep your eyes open for new biofeedback gadgets that may soon become available for you to use by attaching them to your desktop or laptop computer to help you regulate your stress levels.

When biofeedback was first introduced into the world of clinical medicine, it was hailed as the most effective relaxation technique. Since that time, experts have learned that this technique holds no superiority over any other relaxation strategies or coping techniques. In many cases, it is effective for people with serious stress-related symptoms whom meditation or mental imagery alone does not seem to help. In any case, research has shown what many health practitioners and Eastern mystics already knew: We do indeed have conscious control of the autonomic nervous system, and that this control can affect health and well-being.

SUMMARY

- The term *autogenic training* refers to the body's ability to regulate specific physiological functions through conscious suggestion. This term is often used synonymously with the clinical term *self-regulation.*

- This relaxation technique was created by two German physicians, Schultz and Luthe, after learning that some of their patients could hypnotize themselves to achieve a profound state of relaxation. The primary effect was in peripheral body regions, which became warm and heavy. This effect is thought to be the result of changes in blood flow.

- Schultz and Luthe outlined six conditions they felt necessary for this technique to be effective. Among these are receptiveness to the self-suggestion to relax, positioning oneself comfortably, the ability to concentrate, and focusing on internal physiological processes.

- *Selected awareness* is a term used to explain how the mind focuses attention on the self-suggestion and receptivity that produce a sense of relaxation.

- Autogenic discharge refers to various sensory sensations and emotional responses triggered by this technique.

- The autogenic technique has been used in hospitals where patients have shunted blood away from surgical sites. It has also been reported to hasten recovery from surgery.

- There are two general approaches to this technique. In the direct method, the person consciously moves blood to the extremities where warmth and heaviness are desired. In the indirect method, the person focuses only on warmth and heaviness, not blood flow.

- Biofeedback is a process of gathering information about specific physiological functions such as heart rate, respiration, and body temperature. Clinical biofeedback uses sophisticated instrumentation to amplify and measure these functions so that they are easier to detect and interpret.

- The purpose of biofeedback is to teach people with stress-related disorders to recondition their responses so that they gain control over the physiological system responsible for their symptoms.

- Clinical biofeedback combines sophisticated technology and various other forms of relaxation, including diaphragmatic breathing, autogenic training, progressive muscular relaxation, and mental imagery, to strengthen the conditioned response.

- There are several types of clinical biofeedback, each monitoring a specific physiological system. These are electromyography (EMG), electroencephalography (EEG), electrocardiography (EKG), electrodermal (EDR), and thermal biofeedback.

- Clinical biofeedback is widely used and strongly recommended as a modality to decrease episodes of chronic pain.

- The research conducted on various aspects of clinical biofeedback has produced promising results. Biofeedback is now recognized as one of the most effective methods of relaxation.

STUDY GUIDE QUESTIONS

1. Explain the rationale for autogenic training as a relaxation technique.

2. Describe in simple terms how to do autogenic training for relaxation.

3. Define the concept of self-hypnosis.

4. Explain the rationale for biofeedback as a relaxation technique.

5. List three people who might use biofeedback in their lives.

6. Describe three types of biofeedback and explain how they would be used to promote relaxation.

REFERENCES AND RESOURCES

A Guide to Psychology and Its Practice. Autogenic Training. www.guidetopsychology.com/autogen.htm.

Allen, R. *Human Stress: Its Nature and Control.* Burgess Press, Minneapolis, MN, 1983.

Anderson, N., Lawrence, P., and Olson, T. Within-Subject Analysis of Autogenic Training and Cognitive Coping Training in the Treatment of Tension Headache Pain, *Journal of Behavioral Therapy and Experimental Psychiatry* 12: 219–223, 1981.

Association for Applied Psychophysiology and Biofeedback. http://aapb.org.

Basmanjian, J. *Biofeedback: Principles and Practice for Clinicians.* Williams & Wilkins, New York, 1989.

Beech, H. R., Burns, L. E., and Sheffield, B. F. *A Behavioral Approach to the Management of Stress: A Practical Guide to Techniques.* Wiley, Chichester, England, 1982.

Blanchard, E. B., and Haynes, M. R. Biofeedback Treatment of a Case of Raynaud's Disease, *Journal of Behavioral Therapy and Experimental Psychiatry* 6:230–234, 1975.

Blanchard, E. B., et al. Biofeedback and Relaxation Training with Three Kinds of Headaches: Treatment Effects and Their Predictions, *Journal of Consulting and Clinical Psychology* 50:562–575, 1982.

Blanchard, E. B., et al. Biofeedback and Relaxation Treatments for Headaches in the Elderly: A Caution and a Challenge, *Biofeedback and Self-Regulation* 10(1):68–73, 1985.

Brown, B. B. *Stress and the Art of Biofeedback.* Harper & Row, New York, 1977.

Budzynski, T., and Stoyva, J. Biofeedback Methods in the Treatment of Anxiety and Stress. In R. Wolfolk and D. Lehrer (eds.), *Principles and Practices of Stress Management,* Guilford Press, New York, 1984.

Burish, T. G. EMG Biofeedback Transfer of Teaching and Coping with Stress, *Psychosomatic Research* 24(2):85–96, 1980.

Carrol, D. *Biofeedback in Practice.* Longman, New York, 1984.

Carruthers, M. Autogenic Training, *Journal of Psychosomatic Research* 23:437–440, 1979.

Coates, T. J., and Thoreson, C. E. What to Use Instead of Sleeping Pills, *Journal of the American Medical Association* 240: 2311–2312, 1978.

Coutler, I., et al. Biofeedback Interventions for Gastrointestinal Conditions, *Alternative Therapies* 8(3):76–83, 2002.

Danskin, D. G., and Crow, M. *Biofeedback: An Introduction and Guide.* Mayfield, Palo Alto, CA, 1981.

Dhanani, N. M., Caruso, T. J., and Carinci, A. J. Complementary and Alternative Medicine for Pain: An Evidence-Based Review, *Current Pain Headache Reports* November 10, 2010.

DiCara, L. V. Learning in the Autonomic Nervous System, *Scientific American* 222(1):30–39, 1970.

Ernst, E. British Autogenic Society. 2008. www.autogenic -therapy.org.uk.

Everly, G. *A Clinical Guide to the Treatment of the Human Stress Response.* Plenum, New York, 2002.

Everly, G. *A Clinical Guide to the Treatment of the Human Stress Response.* Plenum, New York City, 2002.

Fisher-Williams, M. *A Textbook of Biological Feedback.* Human Sciences Press, New York, 1986.

Fuller, G. D. *Biofeedback: Methods and Procedures in Clinical Practice.* Biofeedback Press, San Francisco, 1977.

Gaarder, K., and Montgomery, P. *Clinical Biofeedback: A Procedural Manual.* Williams & Wilkins, Baltimore, MD, 1977.

Glanz, M., Klawansky, S., and Chalmers, T. Biofeedback Therapy in Stroke Rehabilitation: A Review, *Journal of the Royal Society of Medicine* 90:33–39, 1977.

Gorton, B. Autogenic Training, *American Journal of Clinical Hypnosis* 2:31–41, 1959.

Greenberg, J. *Comprehensive Stress Management*, 12th ed. McGraw-Hill, New York, 2010.

Green, E., and Green, A. *Beyond Biofeedback.* Delacorte Press, New York, 1977.

Green, E., Green, A., and Walters, E. D. Voluntary Control of Intense States: Psychological and Physiological, *Journal of Transpersonal Psychology* 2:1–26, 1970.

Keefe, J. F., Surwit, R. S., and Pilon, R. N. Biofeedback, Autogenic Training, and Progressive Muscular Relaxation in the Treatment of Raynaud's Disease: A Comparative Study, *Journal of Applied Behavior Analysis* 13:3–11, 1980.

Kirsch, I. Altered States, *Social Research* 68(3):795–809, 2001.

Luthe, W. *Autogenic Theory.* Grune and Stratton, New York, 1969.

Luthe, W. Method, Research, and Applications of Autogenic Training, *American Journal of Clinical Hypnosis* 5:17–23, 1962.

Marcer, D. *Biofeedback and Related Therapies in Clinical Practice.* Croom Helm, London, 1986.

Middaugh, S., and Pawlick, K. Biofeedback and Behavioral Treatment of Persistent Pain in the Older Adult: A Review and Study, *Applied Psychophysiology and Biofeedback* 27: 185–202, 2002.

Miller, E. *Letting Go of Stress.* Newman Communications, Albuquerque, NM, 1980.

Miller, N. E. Rx: Biofeedback, *Psychology Today,* February, 1985:54–59.

Miller, N. E. Visceral Learning and Other Additional Facts Potentially Applicable to Psychotherapy, *International Psychiatry Clinics* 5:294–312, 1968.

Miller, N. E. What Biofeedback Does (and Does Not Do), *Psychology Today*, November, 1989:22–24.

Norris, P. Personal communication. June 23, 2012.

Padgitt, S. Treating Insomnia with Biofeedback. www.brain wavecenter.com.

Pelletier, K. *Mind as Healer, Mind as Slayer.* Dell, New York, 1977.

Porter, G., and Norris, P. *Why Me? Harnessing the Healing Power of the Human Spirit.* Stillpoint Press, Walpole, NH, 1985.

Robbins, J. *A Symphony in the Brain: The Evolution of the New Brain Wave Biofeedback.* Atlantic Monthly Press, New York, 2000.

Rosenbaum, L. *Biofeedback Frontiers: Self-Regulation of Stress Reactivity.* AMS Press, New York, 1988.

Runick, B. *Biofeedback—Issues in Treatment Assessment.* National Institutes of Mental Health, Rockville, MD, 1980.

Schultz, J., and Luthe, W. *Autogenic Training: A Psychophysiological Approach to Psychotherapy.* Grune and Stratton, New York, 1959.

Schultz, J. *Das Autogene Training.* Geerg-Thieme, Verlag, Leipzig, Germany, 1932.

Schwartz, M. S. *Biofeedback: A Practitioner's Guide.* Guilford Press, New York, 1987.

Siegel, B. *Peace, Love, and Healing.* Perennial Press, New York, 1990.

Silver, B. V. Temperature Biofeedback and Regulation Training in the Treatment of Migraine Headaches, *Biofeedback and Self-Regulation* 4:359–366, 1979.

Stein, R. Number of Americans Who Have High Blood Pressure Up Sharply: 31 Percent of Adults Suffering from Hypertension, Study Finds, *Washington Post*, August 24, 2004. www.washingtonpost.com/wp-dyn/articles A27138 -2004Aug23.html.

Turk, D. G., Meichenbaum, D. H., and Berman, W. H. Application of Biofeedback for the Regulation of Pain: A Critical Review, *Psychological Bulletin* 86:1322–1338, 1979.

Vickers, A., Zollman, C., and Payne, D. Toolbox: Hypnosis and Relaxation Therapies, *Western Journal of Medicine* 175(4): 269–272, 2001.

Wall, S. E. An Overview of Biofeedback: Philosophy of Biofeedback and Consciousness (online). Available at http://www.7hz.com/Loverview.html.

Whitman, W. *Leaves of Grass.* Signet Books, 2000.

Whitney, E. High-Tech 'Band-Aids' Call Doctors, NPR, July 30, 2010. www.npr.org/templates/story/story.php?storyId =128877308.

Wisem, A. *Awakening the Mind: A Guide to Mastering the Power of Your Brain Waves.* Putnam, New York, 2002.

Yates, A. J. *Biofeedback and the Modification of Behavior.* Plenum Press, New York, 1980.

Physical Exercise, Nutrition, and Stress

A sound mind in a sound body.

—Juvenal

Perhaps the most telling sign of stress in the American population is our ever-expanding waist size. Obesity has reached epidemic proportions. The average American eats a lot more and exercises considerably less than his or her parents a generation ago and far less than his or her grandparents. One of the many examples of the stress/nutrition equation is that children are now being diagnosed with adult-onset diabetes, something unheard of a generation ago. In a rapidly paced world, people's lifestyles have changed dramatically over the past few decades, and with these changes various indices of health have spiraled down even further: cancer, diabetes, and scores of stress-related illnesses. Sadly, there is no quick fix for optimal health. But there are physical exercise and healthy eating habits.

Physical exercise not only utilizes the stress hormones for their intended purpose, but the cathartic release of stress is nearly unbeatable. Remember, though, there is a reason why exercise is called "work." Yet even work can have its rewards, and the health benefits of physical exercise and activity are worth their weight in gold. Let there be no doubt: Physical exercise is stress to the body. It is the fight-or-flight response in motion. Given the promise of physiological homeostasis, physical exercise might just be the closest thing we have to the fountain of youth. According to well-cited research, not only does physical exercise and activity enhance your health and longevity, it appears to increase brain cell tissue associated with memory, multitasking, and attention span (Carmichael, 2007; Ratey, 2008).

Given what experts call an overweight and sedentary population, one might conclude that Americans are headed down the wrong road. Getting back on track to a healthy lifestyle with a focus on physical activity, however, is just a mindset away, and best of all, the benefits are immeasurable. This chapter highlights exercise and nutrition as two additional stress-management relaxation techniques in an effort to maintain physiological homeostasis, physical well-being, and optimal health.

■ Physical Exercise and Stress

The ancient fight-or-flight response prepares the body for immediate physical movement. An increase in heart rate and blood pressure redistributes blood from the abdominal region to the large-muscle groups. Increased ventilation and circulation provide a greater supply of oxygen to the working muscles. The release of catecholamines and stress hormones activates the processes for metabolism of fats and carbohydrates, and these remain elevated long enough to ensure that muscles have adequate energy for contraction. Physical exercise strengthens the integrity of the body's physiological systems. Just as Selye observed physical deterioration from chronic distress, researchers in the field of exercise physiology have observed physical improvement from habitual exercise. There is adaptation to good stress as well as to bad stress.

The human body is a fantastic and complex phenomenon. There are several backup systems in the fight-or-flight response to ensure the best chance of physical survival. For example, there are at least four hormones responsible for increasing blood pressure to shunt blood from the body's core to the periphery. In addition, conversion of proteins to glucose substrates occurs to meet the body's energy demands.

Even though exercise perpetuates the stress response while one is in motion, when physical activity ceases, the body returns to homeostasis. In a well-trained individual, the rate of return is not only quicker, but also the degree of homeostasis attained is more complete than before the individual began to exercise. It seems that the body's natural inclination, when confronted with stress, is to move, be active, or exercise. To remain inactive results in an incredible strain on internal systems. When the body stays still, various organ tissues go into metabolic overdrive, like "flooring it" with the car in park for hours at a time. As a case in point, a classic study by Porter and Allsen (1978) showed that head basketball coaches had heart rates well above resting levels during games, in some cases as much as 253 percent (162 beats/minute) above resting pregame levels—for a 90-minute period.

In the past 50 years, since the recognition of coronary heart disease as America's number one cause of death and the factors putting one at risk, the effects of physical exercise on human anatomy and physiology have been studied feverishly. The overwhelming conclusion is that physical exercise is not merely good, it is a virtual necessity to maintain proper function of major physiological systems. Just as the body requires a state of calmness or homeostasis, it equally demands physical stimulation or it will go into dysfunction. In other words, use it or lose it. Given what we now know, it is obvious that there must be a balance between physical arousal (activity) and homeostasis (rest) for optimal wellness.

Unless you have been hiding in a cave for the past decade, you cannot help but hear news reports regarding the growing obesity problem in America. Obesity is not only a health issue; it can become a major stressor for those who are overweight and cannot lose those unwanted pounds. Whether the issue takes the form of obese children contracting adult-onset diabetes or news that Fenway Park needs to replace its bleachers with wider seats to accommodate patrons' wider rear ends, obesity and related health problems are clearly at epidemic proportions. Despite the claims made in pending lawsuits against various fast-food outlets, experts like Ken (*Aerobics*) Cooper, M.D., agree that caloric consumption is only half the problem. The human body was not designed to sit lethargically in front of a computer or TV for hours on end. Physical exercise (caloric expenditure) is necessary for physiological homeostasis.

The astonishing benefits of exercise on many aspects of health, from stress and depression to (Dahl, 2016) insomnia and longevity, have been researched for decades, and research continues to validate Ken Cooper's classic studies. Recent research by Mark Tarnopolsky at McMaster University in Toronto, Canada, confirms what the landmark studies revealed decades ago—that the combination of cardiovascular exercise and moderate strength training is the closest thing we have to the fountain of youth (Oacklander, 2016) with regard to the functioning of the cardiovascular, neuromuscular, immune, and endocrine systems.

Types of Physical Exercise

There are six components of fitness: cardiovascular endurance, muscular strength and endurance, flexibility, agility, power, and balance. (Some people include body composition as a seventh.) **Cardiovascular endurance** is the ability of the heart, lungs, and blood vessels to transport oxygenated blood to the working muscles for energy metabolism. **Muscular strength** is the ability to exert maximal force against a resistance, and **muscular endurance** is the ability to sustain repeated contractions over a prolonged period of time. **Flexibility** is defined as

---

Cardiovascular endurance: The ability of the heart, lungs, and blood vessels to supply oxygenated blood to the working muscles for energy metabolism.

Muscular strength: The ability to exert a maximal force against a resistance.

Muscular endurance: The ability to sustain repeated contractions over a prolonged period of time.

Flexibility: The ability to use a muscle group throughout its entire range of motion.

Sport	Calories Burned
TABLE 27.1 Energy Balance	
Swimming (freestyle)	249 kcal
Jogging	400 kcal
Golf	129 kcal
Racquetball	348 kcal
Aerobic dance	201 kcal
Cycling	460 kcal
Walking	280 kcal
Snowboarding	250 kcal
Inline skating	345 kcal

Calories burned during 30 minutes of various activities in a person weighing approximately 140 pounds.

FIGURE 27.1   Anaerobic exercise is important for muscle strength and toning, but a good exercise program should include a balance of aerobic and anaerobic exercise activities to stimulate both the cardiovascular and musculoskeletal systems of the body.

the ability to use a muscle group throughout its entire range of motion. These are thought to be the three most important components of fitness. **Agility** refers to maneuverability and coordination of fine and gross motor movements. **Power** is defined as force times distance over time; **balance** is the ability to maintain equilibrium in motion. Agility, power, and balance supplement the first three components. Some or all of these components are used in every type of physical activity.

Although there are many kinds of exercise (**TABLE 27.1**) —from swimming, to weightlifting, to golf—exercise physiologists classify all physical activity into two categories: anaerobic or aerobic. These two types of physical exertion nicely parallel the two aspects of the fight-or-flight response as well as the emotions they elicit.

Anaerobic Activities. **Anaerobic exercise** is defined as a physical motion intense in power and strength, yet short in duration (**FIG. 27.1**). Theoretically speaking, anaerobic activity is the type of movement or exercise used in the "fight" response. When expression of anger comes to mind, it is associated with power and strength. That is, when someone becomes angry and attempts to defend self or territory, it had better be forceful, quick, and decisive. Without these qualities, this half of the stress response proves ineffective for survival.

The word *anaerobic* means "without oxygen." There are two anaerobic energy systems: the **adenosine-triphosphate-creatine** (ATP-PC) system, which lasts only 1 to 10 seconds, and anaerobic glycolysis, or the **lactic acid** system, which continues after the ATP-PC

system for approximately 5 to 6 minutes. At this point, activity is either suspended because of extreme fatigue, or the aerobic energy system kicks in. Lactic acid has an incredibly fatiguing effect on muscle contraction. Because the full redistribution of blood takes 4 to 6 minutes, depending on the condition of the individual, initial oxygen supply is minimal at best. This means that the muscles required to do the work must metabolize energy sources (carbohydrates) using oxygen already stored in muscle cell tissue. Thus, anaerobic

Agility: Maneuverability and coordination of gross and fine motor movements.

Power: Force times distance over time.

Balance: The ability to maintain equilibrium in motion.

Anaerobic exercise: Physical work done in the absence of oxygen; activity that is powerful and quick but does not last more than a few minutes (e.g., weightlifting).

Adenosine-triphosphate-creatine: Chemical compound in muscles that produces energy (anaerobically) for muscle contraction.

Lactic acid: A by-product of the breakdown of ATP, which can also be used as a source of energy (anaerobic).

© Inspiration Unlimited. Used with permission.

FIGURE 27.2 Regular rhythmic aerobic exercise (e.g., swimming, jogging, walking) that maintains an elevated (target) heart rate for a set duration acts as a buffer to both physical and mental stress. In essence, aerobic exercise utilizes the stress hormones for their intended purpose rather than becoming a toxic hormonal cocktail in your body. The benefits of aerobic exercise are immeasurable.

exercise involves only short bursts of energy. Weight-lifting is perhaps the most common example of this type of activity. Sprints and some calisthenics also fall into this category. Anaerobic exercise employs the muscular strength and power (force over distance) components of fitness.

Aerobic Activities. Running, swimming, cycling, cross-country skiing, rhythmic dancing, and walking are examples of aerobic activities (**FIG. 27.2**). **Aerobic exercise,** or cardiovascular-endurance activities, are described as rhythmic or continuous in nature. They involve an equal supply and demand of oxygen in the working muscles. Aerobic work involves moderate intensity, but for a prolonged duration. Intensity is typically measured by heart rate (beats/minute) or volume of oxygen consumed (liters/minute). Aerobic exercise is the "flight" of the fight-or-flight response, and its primary energy source consists of fats. Theoretically speaking, aerobic exercise, as the flight response, is stimulated by fear and anxiety. These emotions make a person want to run for the hills, literally.

The word *aerobic* was coined many years ago to describe biological reactions using oxygen for metabolism. The

> **Aerobic exercise:** Rhythmic physical work using a steady supply of oxygen delivered to working muscles for a continuous period of not less than 20 minutes (e.g., jogging).

term was adapted by the fitness industry in the early 1970s by physician Kenneth Cooper, whose research on fitness-training effects (primarily running) set the national standard for fitness programming. Also in the 1970s, with the inspiration of Jackie Sorenson, originator of aerobic dance, the term *aerobics* started being used to describe a new activity, rhythmic (aerobic) dancing. Aerobic dancing soon became a popular alternative to jogging for men and women alike. Since then, *aerobics* has become a household word, not only across America, but also around the world. Today, the big push in aerobic exercise is to get people to move (any way possible). One of the most popular means is to use a pedometer attached to one's waist belt or pants to see if you can pass the sedentary benchmark of 2,000 to 3,000 steps (one mile) in the course of a day with the goal of reaching about 10,000 steps (5 miles) each day for optimal health.

Whereas anaerobic exercise stimulates muscular strength (hypertrophy of muscle fibers), aerobic exercise challenges the cardiovascular and pulmonary systems to increase endurance (and to some extent muscular endurance, depending on the nature of the activity). Volumes of research support the theory that cardiovascular-endurance exercise helps reduce the risk of heart disease by modifying several risk factors. These include (1) reduction of blood pressure; (2) reduction of cholesterol, specifically low-density lipoproteins (LDLs); (3) significant decreases in percentage of body fat; and (4) decreased physical arousal resulting from stress. For this reason, aerobic exercise tends to receive more favorable attention than anaerobic exercise. If it is true that epinephrine, the hormone associated with fear, is released three times as much and lasts much longer than norepinephrine, then perhaps the best technique to deal with fear is aerobic exercise. Note that aerobic exercise provides a great release for all shades of anger as well as anxiety.

The landmark position statement by the American College of Sports Medicine stated that for a fitness program to be effective it must integrate all primary components of fitness. Thus, a well-balanced exercise program should incorporate both anaerobic and aerobic exercise, as well as flexibility in the training regimen.

Physiological Effects of Physical Exercise

Exercise, like money in the bank, can be considered an investment in health. Unfortunately, unlike money, it accrues very little, if any, tangible interest. It is a pay-as-you-go plan. The short-term effects (neural and hormonal)

BOX 27.1   The Spark That Ignites the Brain

Like Paul Revere riding through the streets of Boston spreading a vital message, John Ratey, M.D., is also hitting the streets across America, spreading an equally important message: Aerobic exercise enhances brain cell activity. The message can be found in his book *Spark* (2008). He can be heard on television and radio talk shows.

National news headlines abound with increased cases of ADHD and Alzheimer's, poor national student achievement scores, and many other factors that hypothesize a decline of cognitive function across all age groups. Ratey explores the remarkable research compiled over the past several years to support the claims that aerobic exercise creates new brain cells, promotes neuroplasticity, increases academic scores, and sharpens mental acuity as well as generally slowing down the aging process. The message in a sound byte: Exercise is not only good for the body—it is great for the brain. The spark that ignites the brain's mental capabilities also helps neutralize the brain's response to stress. People who exercise simply deal better emotionally with stress than those who remain sedentary. This is a message worth paying attention to.

---

of a single bout of exercise last approximately 36 hours. There are also incredible long-term benefits, but one must continue training to keep them. Studies of inactive astronauts in space (Vailus, 1992), deconditioned runners (Coyle et al., 1984), and bed-rest patients (Lenzt, 1981) have shown that when a physical training program is interrupted or discontinued for longer than 2 weeks, approximately 10 percent of cardiovascular gains can be lost. In some cases, up to 40 percent is lost after a month's time, depending on the nature of the inactivity.

On the other hand, clinical studies by Davies and Knibbs (1971) and Shephard (1968) indicate that significant physiological changes begin to become evident between the sixth and eighth weeks of training. And the gains from cardiovascular exercise are quite impressive; they read like a list of who's who in physiological homeostasis. Cardiovascular efficiency can be equated with better health status. The following are some of its benefits:

1. Decreased resting heart rate
2. Decreased resting blood pressure
3. Decreased muscle tension
4. Better-quality sleep
5. Increased resistance to colds and illness
6. Decreased cholesterol and triglyceride levels

The following are additional benefits from habitual cardiovascular exercise:

1. Decreased body fat, improved body composition
2. Increased efficiency of heart
3. Decreased bone demineralization

4. Decreased rate of aging (several aspects)
5. Increased tolerance of heat and cold through acclimatization

In general, cardiovascular-endurance exercise acts as a catalyst to keep the body's physiological systems in balance. Through the multitude of mechanisms involved in energy metabolism, hormones, enzymes, and food substrates are used for their intended purpose. That is, minerals like calcium are absorbed by bone tissue where they are needed. But in a state of imbalance, other organs, like the lining of blood vessels, or in some cases mammary glands, begin to absorb these trace minerals and then show signs of dysfunction. Just how this unique balance is maintained is still under scientific investigation.

Is cardiovascular exercise a good investment in your health? Apparently so! Research completed at Stanford University by James Fries (Digitale, 2008) revealed that, indeed, regular participation in cardiovascular exercise (running) slows the aging process, in essence, negating the effect of stress. Tracking over 500 runners, Fries observed that regular exercise not only promotes fewer disabilities, but also the ultimate wellness goal: a longer, healthier life span.

Regarding the relationship between physical exercise and the relaxation response, one important concept to remember is **parasympathetic rebound**. In anticipation

Parasympathetic rebound: The parasympathetic effect of relaxation (homeostasis) after physical exercise. Typically the response is such that parameters such as heart rate and blood pressure dip below pre-exercise levels.

of movement, seconds before exercise begins, epinephrine and norepinephrine are released by order of the central nervous system. The level of catecholamines remains elevated throughout the duration of the activity. Upon completion of physical movement, the secretion of epinephrine and norepinephrine is inhibited by the parasympathetic nervous system, which initiates a calming response. In studies comparing stress-induced arousal (physical exercise) in athletically trained individuals versus sedentary ones, the trained subjects returned to their resting heart rate and serum catecholamine levels sooner than did their nonactive counterparts. In addition, the same values continued to decrease *below* prearousal levels in the conditioned individuals. These results indicate a very efficient calming mechanism by the parasympathetic nervous system.

Based on the landmark work of Bellet et al. (1969), Davies and Few (1974), Galbo and colleagues (1977), Sutton (1978), Tharp (1975), and Winder et al. (1973, 1982), the following conclusions have been drawn regarding the immediate, short-term, and long-term effects of cardiovascular exercise as a relaxation technique. First, it appears that a single bout of aerobic exercise "burns off" existing catecholamines and stress hormones by directing them toward their intended metabolic functions, rather than allowing them to linger in the body to undermine the integrity of vital organs and the immune system. This in itself can be considered a constructive intervention technique to counter daily stressors. Second, the training effect of aerobic exercise appears to prepare the body for future stressful episodes by decreasing the level of hormonal secretions when feelings of anger or fear manifest. In effect, exercise can be used as a preventive measure because it tends to minimize or neutralize physical arousal to nonphysical threats. Third, the long-term effect of exercise appears to be prolonged, efficient function of several organ systems, including the heart, lungs, blood vessels, kidneys, muscle, and skeletal tissue. Many researchers are of the opinion that although exercise training is not a panacea for the multitude of diseases and illnesses, nor is it the fountain of youth, its cumulative effects do appear to add to both the quality and quantity of life.

It has always been thought that keeping in good shape tends to retard the aging process, but research conducted at the University of Illinois (Barlow, 2003) confirms that, in terms of cognitive function, this supposition is indeed true (**FIG. 27.3**). Cardiovascular fitness improves cognition in three specific areas of the brain known to be

FIGURE 27.3   As we go through the aging process, exercise becomes increasingly more important, not only to maintain a healthy metabolic balance, but to provide a needed challenge to our cardiovascular and neuromusculoskeletal systems. Exercise may not be the fountain of youth, but it's the closest thing we have to it.

affected by the aging process. Through the use of magnetic resonance imaging, significant anatomical differences were observed in the gray and white matter of fit and sedentary individuals, with fit individuals showing less atrophy of these brain regions.

Theories of Athletic Conditioning

Numerous studies have been conducted to determine the minimal amount of exercise needed to maintain its benefits. The studies have investigated the intensity, frequency, and duration of aerobic exercise, specifically, because aerobic activity has the greatest effect on reducing the risks of heart disease. Every possible variable and permutation thereof has been examined, and a formula now accepted by the American College of Sports Medicine (ACSM) has set the standard for exercise programs for virtually all individuals. This is sometimes referred to as the all-or-none conditioning principle.

All-or-None Conditioning Principle. As stated in the ACSM guidelines, four major factors make up what is commonly called the FITT principle: frequency, intensity, time (duration), and type of exercise. Let's take a closer look.

- *Frequency:* The number of exercise sessions per week. The minimum number is three.

- *Intensity:* The challenge (stress) placed on a specific physiological system involved in an activity. In the case of the cardiovascular system, intensity is measured in terms of heart rate (the number of beats per minute) and should vary with age (**FIG. 27.4**). In a cardiovascular fitness program, the range is between 65 and 85 percent of maximal intensity, with an average intensity of 75 percent for healthy individuals. This is often called the **target heart rate** or target zone.

- *Time (duration):* The length of time involved in one exercise session. The minimum duration of an exercise session is suggested to be 20 to 30 minutes. Less than 20 minutes does not guarantee any benefits.

- *Type of exercise:* The type of activity chosen to challenge a particular physiological system. Walking, running, and swimming, for example, are types of aerobic exercises that adequately challenge the cardiovascular system. Weight-training, on the other hand, taxes the anaerobic energy system, despite claims to the contrary by several manufacturers of weight-training equipment. Only an Olympic-trained athlete could achieve cardiovascular benefits from a circuit-weight-training program. Likewise, running will tone and define muscles, but muscle hypertrophy is not of any benefit to cardiovascular endurance, so running is not considered superior to other forms of aerobic work.

Phases of a Workout. Just as there is a formula for calculating maximum cardiovascular benefits of exercise, there is also a formula for ensuring safe workouts. The components are a proper warm-up, a stimulus or conditioning period, and a cool-down.

- *Warm-up period:* The warm-up is the preparation for exercise. It usually lasts approximately 5 to 10 minutes, during which blood shifts from the gastrointestinal tract to the large muscle groups. Muscles are like sponges. When they are dry, they are difficult to stretch, which is why it is best to stretch at the end of the warm-up.

- *Stimulus period:* The stimulus period is the "meat" of the workout, during which physical exertion

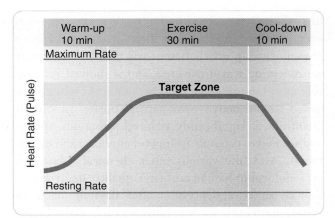

FIGURE 27.4 The target heart rate zone, or intensity of work needed to challenge the heart muscle for a more efficient cardiovascular system. Your exercise heart rate should be maintained for the duration of the workout.

All-or-none conditioning principle: A principle of exercise that states that to benefit from physical training, you must have the right intensity, frequency, and duration for each component of fitness challenged.

Frequency: The number of exercise sessions per week; the ideal number is three.

Intensity: The physical challenge (stress) placed on a specific physiological system for exercise.

Target heart rate: The ideal heart rate or target zone in which to identify the intensity of cardiovascular activity.

Time (duration): The number of minutes of exercise in one session; the ideal number is 30 minutes in the target zone, not including a warm-up or cool-down.

Type of exercise: The type of activity one chooses to engage in to work one or more physiological systems (e.g., walking, jogging, cycling).

Phases of a workout: Warm-up, stimulus period (target zone), and cool-down.

Warm-up period: The first phase of the workout, during which circulation is increased to the large muscles with some time for flexibility.

Stimulus period: Called the "meat" of the workout, during which one targets the specified intensity toward heart, lungs, and muscles (e.g., heart rate, sets, reps for weight lifting).

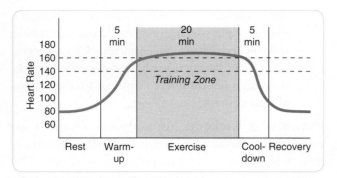

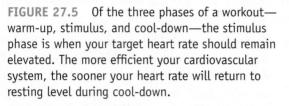

FIGURE 27.5   Of the three phases of a workout—warm-up, stimulus, and cool-down—the stimulus phase is when your target heart rate should remain elevated. The more efficient your cardiovascular system, the sooner your heart rate will return to resting level during cool-down.

(intensity) is used to maintain a challenge to the various physiological systems. The stimulus period should be a minimum of 20 minutes, regardless of which energy system (aerobic or anaerobic) is used (**FIG. 27.5**).

■   *Cool-down period:* The cool-down period allows for the body to gradually shift from a stressed state to a relaxation state, during which the blood is directed from the muscles to the body's core, rather than pooling in the extremities. A cool-down begins with decreased intensity of exercise followed by stretching for a total of 5 to 10 minutes.

Psychological Effects of Physical Exercise

When the fitness movement mushroomed in the late 1970s, the complexity of the many benefits reported caught some in the field of clinical medicine off guard. At the time, the most frequently prescribed drug in the country was the tranquilizer Valium. The Rolling Stones even wrote a hit song, "Mother's Little Helper," satirizing its widespread use.

But as people initiated running programs, they began to talk less and less about muscle soreness, weather conditions, and rude drivers; these concerns seemed to have relatively little importance. Instead, thoughts began to

> **Cool-down period:** A designated time right after the stimulus period to decrease circulation to the body's periphery and return to a resting state.

turn inward, and running began to take on a Zen-like quality. Moreover, it became a private time to sort out problems, resolve issues, and reflect about life in general, relationships, and the purpose of life. Running became a time for self-reflection and meditation. Many people stopped taking prescribed sedatives and tranquilizers; and some people even stopped going to their therapists. In time, members of the medical community also took up running. And some psychologists even changed counseling styles, taking their patients off the office couch and onto the sidewalk or high-school track.

As an investigative eye was kept on this national activity, reports soon filtered in that running could have an addictive quality. Specifically, it was learned that when running routines were interrupted for more than a few days, some individuals showed signs of withdrawal similar to those observed with chemical addictions. For his book *Positive Addiction*, William Glasser interviewed more than 700 long-distance runners to gain a better understanding of this phenomenon. His analysis revealed six important criteria for a physical activity to take on this addictive nature:

1. The activity must be done for at least an hour per day.

2. The activity must be done on a regular basis.

3. The activity must have a base of 6 months of training.

4. The activity must be well liked by the person doing it.

5. The activity must be noncompetitive.

6. The activity must be done alone, or perhaps with one other person.

Just when Glasser was conducting his research, other scientists were investigating the same concept from a physiological approach. In the early 1980s, a new human neuropeptide was discovered, and it showed remarkable morphine-like qualities. Beta-endorphin was soon hailed as the body's own natural opiate. In minute quantities, it significantly reduced sensations of pain and seemed to promote feelings of euphoria and exhilaration. And like various other chemical substances, beta-endorphin had an addictive quality; many people showed signs of depression after days of inactivity. What's more, this neuropeptide was released by other locations as well as the brain during physical activity, most notably running. Not everyone who ran, however, experienced this effect, perhaps because of the training effect. Today, the research into the runner's high not only focuses on endorphins, but a newly discovered substance called endocannabinoids, a neurotransmitter

---

BOX 27.2   Insomnia and Physical Exercise

One of the benefits of exercise that has been touted by exercise physiologists for years is the fact that regular rhythmical (cardiovascular) exercise promotes quality sleep and decreases symptoms of insomnia. The very nature of physical exercise increases one's metabolic activity, thus increasing one's body-core temperature. As the body returns to homeostasis after a vigorous workout, body-core temperature drops. During sleep, the body-core temperature is at its lowest point as a result of decreased metabolic activity. Research shows that the drop in body-core temperature that occurs when bedtime is four to six hours after a vigorous workout promotes drowsiness and deeper (delta waves) sleep than in nonactive individuals.

For this reason, it is suggested *not* to engage in strenuous physical activity shortly before bedtime. According to *Power Sleep* author James Maas, the best time to schedule a workout is around the noon hour or late afternoon, with morning exercise having the least effect on sleep quality. The best type of exercise to ensure a good night's sleep is cardiovascular in nature, including vigorous walking, jogging, swimming, or biking that elevates the heart rate to one's specific target zone for the desired duration. All types of rhythmic exercise utilize the cocktail of stress hormones for their intended purposes and help the body metabolize what's not used in this process as waste products for elimination.

---

that—unlike endorphins—can pass through the blood–brain barrier to increase pleasure and decrease pain (Ratey, 2008).

Although to date no songs have been written about **runner's high**, this phenomenon is now commonly accepted as the greatest psychological effect of exercise. But as it turns out, running is not the only physical activity during which beta-endorphin is released. Many other types of cardiovascular-endurance exercises, such as swimming and walking, potentially produce the same effect. What is necessary, regardless of the activity, is that the exercise be egoless, or noncompetitive.

Speculation now has it that activities with rhythmic, repetitive motion, such as swimming, running, walking, or cycling, offer a meditative form of conscious awareness. It has been suggested that such rhythmic activities may shift hemispheric dominance from the left to the right brain. Several long-distance runners interviewed by Fixx (1977) and Glasser (1976) stated that running heightened mental receptivity, resulting in greater imagination and creativity to apply to problem solving. Between this discovery and the other positive effects, psychologists took a new interest in cardiovascular exercise as a coping technique to reduce the psychological fallout from stress. Among the thousands of investigators to delve into the relationship between exercise and emotional health were Berger (1982, 1983), Berger and Motl (2001), Dishman (1981), Folkins and Sime (1981), Ismail and Young (1977), Morgan (1980, 1982, 1987), and Gosselin and Taylor (1999). The conclusion drawn from all this research is that athletic training or exercise is

viable as both a relaxation technique and a coping technique to deal with stress. The following are the reported psychological benefits of habitual exercise (particularly from jogging):

1. Improved self-esteem
2. Improved sense of self-reliance and self-efficacy
3. Improved mental alertness, perception, and information processing
4. Increased perceptions of acceptance by others
5. Decreased feelings of depression and anxiety
6. Decreased overall sense of stress and tension

Physical Exercise and Chronic Pain

Ten years ago, if you said the word "Pilates," you might have heard someone say, "Gesundheit." Today, most people know that Pilates is a form of muscle strength and flexibility exercises (**FIG. 27.6**). What many people don't know is that it is one of the best forms of exercise to help relieve chronic pain associated with the lower back and spine area (Ungaro, 2002; Stanmore, 2002). Developed as a series of exercises to strengthen the core muscles of the body's frame by Joe Pilates several decades ago, Pilates was originally used by dancers and athletes for both prevention and rehabilitation of athletic injuries. Today, like hatha yoga, Pilates classes are commonly taught at fitness clubs and Pilates centers around the country.

Runner's high: The euphoric feeling generated from beta-endorphins released from cardiovascular exercise.

Stress with a Human Face

There are basically two types of summer jobs where I come from: waiting tables or lifeguarding. I grew up doing the latter to finance my college education, and I also taught swimming lessons and coached several swim teams over the years. But when I chose a career in academia, lifeguarding and swim lessons became a distant memory—or so I thought. One day on campus, I was introduced to a nationally known figure, and soon found myself agreeing to give swim lessons once again.

At first Dan (not his real name) said his primary goal of getting in shape was to lose weight. Because of a back injury, running and biking were out of the question, so he chose swimming. But after he had progressed from blowing bubbles to swimming a quarter-mile, he confided that getting in shape was really secondary to clearing his mind and coping with stress. He needed not just physical conditioning, but some time alone to think and get his head straight, sort out problems, and access his intuition and creativity on a daily basis. But his fast-paced job in the nation's capital wasn't doing him any good, nor were his coronary risk factors (mainly hypertension). He knew there was only one solution: to take out his aggressions and anxieties in the pool.

Dan is up to a mile a day now, and his physical shape is superseded only by the smile on his face as he gets out of the water and heads for the showers. The risk factors are minimized, and he feels like a new man every day. On numerous occasions he has said that I literally saved his life. I know better than that. How does the expression go? You can lead a horse to water, but . . .

FIGURE 27.6 Pilates exercises have been proven to be quite effective for reducing chronic pain associated with weak muscles and poor posture.

Ironically, many episodes of chronic pain result from physical exercise—specifically, the overuse syndrome (too much, too often), which can lead to joint pain in the area of use. Common sense dictates that acute and chronic joint and muscle pain necessitates taking a break from the exercise that causes the pain. For this reason, it is good to have a complementary exercise or sport, such as swimming or walking, to fall back on if and when your primary mode of fitness is put on hiatus.

Steps to Initiate a Fitness Training Program

Although physical exercise is now praised as the wonder technique for stress reduction, it also poses a threat to physical well-being if not done correctly. The typical way many people approach something can be summarized in four words: too much, too soon (FIG. 27.7). Individuals get caught up in the whirlwind of excitement, and as a result often go overboard, thinking that if some is good, more is better. The result is burnout. When too-much/too-soon behavior is applied to physical exercise, it can result in injury, particularly muscle and tendon damage.

Let there be no doubt: Exercise is demanding work. And after cranking out 8 to 10 hours at the office, shop, or other place of business, the last thing a person wants is to go out and do more work. Motivation can be rather

FIGURE 27.7

elusive at the end of the day. Because the effects of exercise don't occur overnight, people can become quite disenchanted with the concepts of muscle fatigue and sweat. In fact, fitness club owners will tell you that motivation peaks about 3 to 7 days after the start of a fitness program and then rapidly declines. Without internal as well as external reinforcement, most exercise programs peter out before real physiological changes occur.

Exercise specialists and health educators have begun to incorporate goal setting into the design and prescription of exercise programming as a means to maintain motivation during this crucial period. Scientific research has unequivocally proven that physical exercise is necessary for optimal health. It should become a habit in everyone's lifestyle. The following are some suggestions regarding cardiovascular (aerobic) fitness to help guide you through the transition period.

1. *Start cautiously and progress moderately with your program.* The American College of Sports Medicine suggests that every person, particularly those over the age of 35, get a physical examination for medical clearance prior to starting a fitness program. As a part of the physical evaluation, you should be assessed for your fitness capacity and given an exercise prescription. The prescription includes a target heart rate, a mode of exercise, a selected intensity, frequency, and duration, as well as a review of the components of a workout and the design of health and fitness goals. Sometimes it helps to see physical exercise as a process, not an outcome. People who experience a natural high from exercise are in a

sense detached from the physical sensations and immediate rewards (e.g., losing weight). One rule of thumb to go by when working out is this: If you can't hold a conversation while exercising, you are pushing too hard. The no pain–no gain approach was discredited a long time ago.

2. *Pick an activity you really enjoy.* Not everyone is a jogger. If you have tried jogging and found it too difficult or displeasing, there are plenty of other aerobic activities to choose from. Perhaps the most underrated exercise is walking. Walking provides the same benefits as running if an adequate heart rate is maintained. Likewise, swimming is one of the best choices because it is cited as not only improving cardiovascular endurance, muscular endurance, and flexibility, but also being least likely to result in overuse injuries to muscle tissue and joints. Sometimes alternating activities is a great way to avoid burnout or staleness from the same sport (**FIG. 27.8**). Most important, pick an activity that is non-ego-involved and noncompetitive. Many people find that when the ego gets involved, the activity promotes, rather than reduces, feelings of stress.

3. *Select a time of day to exercise.* Make a commitment to allocate a special time each day just for this purpose, and make this time yours and yours alone, with no other responsibilities and commitments to take this time away from you. Mornings before work or school are often the easiest times to schedule exercise, and the immediate physiological effects certainly

© Photodisc

FIGURE 27.8 Noncompetitive exercising with a group of people serves as a great motivation factor to continue the activity.

help meet the challenges of the day. Sometimes early morning workouts mean sacrificing badly needed sleep; in this case, afternoon or evening is a good option. After a long and perhaps busy day, exercise is a great way to unwind and literally release pent-up energy. If neither of these options is workable, the lunch hour (the new executive recess) is always an alternative. And to be realistic, if you are like many people with busy schedules and no two days alike, the time for exercise may have to vary from day to day. Remember, you only need three days a week, half an hour each day to achieve and maintain the benefits of exercise. That is a total of one and a half hours per week.

4. *Exercise using the right clothes and equipment.* Perhaps the most important piece of equipment is a good pair of athletic shoes. The cost may be rather high, but quality shoes serve as a good insurance policy against injuries to the lower back, shins, ankles, feet, and most notably, knees. The knees are the weakest joint in the body. Poor shoes can decrease the stability of the tendons and ligaments supporting the knee, resulting in chronic knee pain known as **chondromalacia**. Also, cardiovascular exercise tends to significantly increase body-core temperature, so clothing should be layered so that it can be "peeled off" if you get overheated in the cool months.

Chondromalacia: Chronic knee pain, typically from excessive running and improper foot placement.

5. *Initiate a support group.* Although exercise is not always considered miserable, at times it does love company. There may be times when you would like nothing better than to exercise alone, but a companion certainly serves as a motivator for those days when the thought of exercising is not appealing.

6. *Set personal fitness goals for yourself.* Do you want to lose weight? Would you like to decrease your cholesterol levels? Would you like to have a "washboard" stomach? Do you want to reduce your resting blood pressure? Would you like to run a 10K road race? These are some commonly heard goals. Progression toward and accomplishment of health and fitness goals can be wonderful means of motivation. It is easy to see the progress you have made when you keep track of it. The most popular method for doing so is jotting a short note on a calendar. The companion to goal-setting is reward: When you accomplish a goal, treat yourself to something special.

7. *Care and prevention of injuries.* The best way to treat an injury is to prevent it, but if you encounter pain along the way, treat the injury immediately. The most common injuries occur to joints, where tendons begin to pull away from bone. If you feel pain in a joint, you should stop the activity and put ice on the joint as soon as possible. Some injuries, if caught early, may not need immediate medical attention. If pain persists after a day or two, however, see a physician. Not long ago, physicians knew very little about sports medicine, but today it is easier to find qualified care in this area. Please don't take an injury lightly.

These are some of the basic guidelines to follow when initiating a personal fitness program. But above all, use common sense. If you would like assistance in developing your personal fitness program, health clubs, community recreation centers, and YMCAs and YWCAs have qualified personnel to help you design a safe, quality program. Good luck and have fun!

Best Application of Physical Exercise and Activity

To get the most benefits from physical exercise, there must be the right intensity, frequency, and duration as well as the best mode of exercise for the individual involved. Physical activity of any type is best used as a postponed response to stress, unless the situation is right to put on your exercise clothes and run out the door.

BOX 27.3   Cortisol and Weight Gain

Is there a connection between chronic stress and obesity? Perhaps! There is speculation that cortisol, a hormone released from the adrenal gland during the stress response, may be related to the steady accumulation of body fat in one's lifetime. Given the amount of chronic stressors each American has today, and the incredible rate of obesity, there may indeed be a connection. Cortisol is responsible for a number of metabolic activities for fight-or-flight, including ensuring the release of glucose and free fatty acids into the blood for short- and long-term energy. If a person chooses not to fight or flee (anaerobic or aerobic exercise), watching hours of television instead, then the body may redistribute these energy nutrients as adipose tissue (fat). Additional speculation suggests that cortisol may be a principal hormone to regulate appetite under stress, to ensure that there is an adequate supply of both short- and long-term energy. It is well known that stress (acute and chronic) raises blood glucose levels of type 2 diabetics, hence making an exercise program all the more important for this target population.

Human physiology is much more complex than a single cause-and-effect scenario when it comes to cortisol, weight gain, and obesity, experts say. The combined effect of insulin and cortisol may be the culprit. Is cortisol the primary hormone responsible for weight gain? The jury is still out on this fact (Chang, 2006); however, given the dynamics of stress and the mind-body-spirit connection, one cannot understate its importance.

A training program that includes regular cardiovascular exercise helps to ensure that the hormones synthesized and released as a result of chronic stress are used for their intended purposes and then flushed out of the system with other metabolic waste products. Exercise also burns calories, making this a desired health package for everyone. It's no secret that the marketplace is becoming flooded with drugs and herbal products to minimize or block the effect of cortisol on appetite and weight gain. However, drugs and supplements can have several side effects, throwing your body's biochemistry out of balance. When performed correctly, the short- and long-term effects of exercise restore balance to mind, body, and spirit with no harmful side effects—and it's free.

Exercise—both aerobic and anaerobic—provides a wonderful catharsis of emotional frustrations. This includes both anger and anxiety. It is best to schedule a time to work out, and stick to it. Because injury or burnout can occur with a once-favorite activity, it is a good idea to have a backup sport.

How can you best find the means to balance your caloric intake and expenditure? Like most everything else in this book, it comes down to your attitude. Experts in the field of exercise physiology will tell you any activity is ideal, whether it's walking up stairs a few flights rather than taking the elevator, parking farther away from the entrance to the nearest store, or taking a Pilates class. Finding the balance between keeping active and sitting still transfers to the balance between a calm mind and a healthy body. Ultimately, the best application of physical exercise is to do some type of activity every day to flush the stress hormones out of your body.

Nutrition and Stress

Like millions of Americans, no doubt you take great pleasure in sitting down to a good meal. Food not only provides necessary nutrients to our body, but also provides emotional pleasure to the mind, particularly when these morsels taste really good. Experts have recognized for eons that food serves as a pacifier to calm nerves; as such, eating is not only a means for physical survival, but also is considered a popular relaxation technique (hence the expression "comfort food"). Yet for many people, eating as a coping technique is often abused. We eat to celebrate, we eat to relax, we eat out of frustration and boredom, and we eat to satisfy our hunger. Food and mood go together like peanut butter and jelly.

It is impossible to talk about proper nutrition without addressing the issue of stress. The two are inextricably linked. For that matter, it is impossible to talk about proper nutrition and ignore the issue of politics of special-interest groups and the power of the Food and Drug Administration, which work so diligently to control the dissemination of information leading to much inconsistent factual reporting and, thus, to even more stress for the consumer who tries to make sense of it all. One day there is a study reporting a particular finding, and the next day another study refutes the findings of the first study. It's no exaggeration to say that many people are confused and frustrated about the controversies in the field of nutrition—not to mention the ever-increasing number of popular diets, which in itself can prove stressful, especially in our weight-conscious culture. This section attempts to clarify some of the concepts regarding sound nutritional habits, how stress affects diet, and how diet affects stress and mood. In addition, this section contains information on an Eastern approach to eating called spiritual nutrition.

It is fair to say that the quantities of food in America are the envy of the world, yet the quality of our food choices are abysmal: high sugar, high fat, bleached flour, genetically modified organisms (GMOs), hormones, antibiotics, and untold amounts of petrochemicals introduced by means of fertilizers, herbicides, fungicides, and pesticides on and in our foods make healing more challenging today and give a whole new meaning to saying grace before a meal. Toxins (bio-ecological stressors) in our foods become stored in the body (now known as *bio-accumulation*) and compromise the immune system, leading to a plethora of health-related problems. When emotional stress is added to the equation, all of these health-related problems are magnified, with dire consequences. Specifically, stress compromises the ability to digest, absorb, metabolize, and eliminate nutrients (e.g., carbohydrates, fats, proteins, vitamins, minerals, and water) because the body's wisdom overrides these processes during fight or flight. By now, you should know the basics of nutrition (or can find this information easily elsewhere), but let's take a closer look at the relationship between nutrition and stress.

If we examine the dynamics of food, stress, and health, we see a confluence of factors that directly affect the immune system. In simplest terms, the relationship among nutrition, stress, and the immune system might best be illustrated through the use of four dominos (**FIG. 27.9**).

- *Domino 1:* Stress tends to deplete nutrients in the body. Water-soluble vitamins and several essential minerals are used for energy production in preparation for fight or flight, even if you sit still in front of a computer screen all day.

- *Domino 2:* Current American lifestyles under stress do not promote or reinforce good eating habits. Consequently, the nutrients depleted under chronic stress are not restored. (Comfort foods, junk foods, fast foods, and processed foods are high in calories and low in nutrients [empty calories]. This is often cited as a leading cause of obesity.) The body will do all it can to compensate for the

FIGURE 27.9 Dominos illustrate the delicate balance of stress and nutrition. When the first domino falls, it is typically not long before the others also tumble, compromising your health.

lack of nutrients, but eventually various aspects of health are compromised.

- *Domino 3:* Some food substances are known to increase sympathetic drive or other physiological responses that keep the stress response elevated. These include caffeine, processed sugar, processed flour, and salt. Some people use alcohol to relax, yet beyond moderation, alcohol presents many problems itself, including tilting this domino to fall on the next one.

- *Domino 4:* Many foods that are processed contribute to a cumulative effect of toxins. For example, residues of synthetic or petroleum-based fertilizers, herbicides, and pesticides found in many foods hinder the immune system from doing its job effectively. When this domino falls, one's health is greatly compromised (e.g., cancer, diabetes, colds, flus, etc.).

The fall of each domino increases the chance of health-related problems as a result of the confluence of stress-prone eating habits. This section highlights important aspects of these factors so that you can make choices about what you put in your mouth to nourish mind, body, and spirit.

Diet for a Stressed Planet

Because of the global economy and trade among nations, the choices of foods available today are unparalleled. At a grocery store it is not uncommon to see strawberries,

BOX 27.4   Eat for a Healthy Immune System

An old proverb states, "Let food be your medicine, and let medicine be your food." Unfortunately, rather than eating food as medicine, the vast majority of people today eat food as poison. Like toxins dumped into a river, the human body can take only so much before signs of disease and illness become manifest. The following is a list of suggestions to tip the scale back into balance and to promote a sense of health and well-being by engaging in a combination of behaviors that (1) enhances the natural abilities of the immune system and (2) decreases the amount of toxins that the immune system must assist in eliminating.

1. Consume a good supply of antioxidants (beta-carotene, vitamins C and E, and selenium). These fight the damage of free radicals, which destroy cell membranes, DNA, RNA, and mitochondria. Antioxidants can be found in fresh fruits, vegetables, and fresh herbs.

2. Consume a good supply of fiber (30–40 grams/day with organic vegetables). Fiber helps clean the colon of toxic materials that might otherwise be absorbed into the bloodstream. Fiber is found in fresh fruits, vegetables, and some grains.

3. Drink plenty of fresh, clean (filtered) water. (A good goal is nearly clear urine.) Being properly hydrated is essential for the elimination of toxins and metabolic by-products.

4. Decrease consumption of pesticides, fungicides, herbicides, and fertilizers found on and in produce, many of which are toxic or carcinogenic. (Eat organics whenever possible.)

5. Consume an adequate supply of complete proteins to ensure intake of essential amino acids. (White blood cells are made up of amino acids from protein sources.)

6. Decrease or eliminate the consumption of processed foods (e.g., junk food, fast food). Think outside "the box" to avoid overconsumption of additives and preservatives that are used merely to extend the shelf life of a product.

7. Decrease consumption of antibiotics and hormones (e.g., found in dairy, beef, and chicken products). These can have a negative effect on your body's physiology, including the elimination of the intestinal flora *Lactobacillus acidophilus*, leading to *Candida* infection.

8. Consume a good supply (and balance) of omega-3's (cold-water fish and flaxseed oil) and omega-6's (vegetable oils).

9. Decrease intake of saturated (solid) fats (meat and dairy products).

10. Decrease/avoid intake of trans fatty acids, listed as partially hydrogenated oils in most baked goods and boxed items.

11. Eat a variety of food colors (fruits and vegetables with bioflavonoids).

12. Consume a good balance of foods with proper pH. (Many processed and pasteurized foods are acidic, tipping the scales by creating a hospitable breeding ground for diseases such as cancer.)

13. Decrease intake of total percentage of fats. (High fat intake compromises the integrity of the lymphatic system, the highway taken by the immune system's cells.)

14. Replenish nutrients consumed by the stress response (e.g., B-complex vitamins, minerals).

15. Decrease consumption of simple sugars, including high-fructose corn syrup. (This not only takes a load off of the pancreas, but also is good for the immune system because cancerous tumors appear to like sugars.)

16. Decrease or avoid excitotoxins (aspartame, Nutrasweet, and MSG), which are believed to inhibit brain function.

17. Moderate your consumption of alcohol. (High alcohol intake compromises liver and immune system function.)

18. Prepare food in the best way possible (e.g., steam veggies, no microwave ovens).

19. Eat organic produce and free-range meats whenever possible.

20. Avoid genetically modified organisms (Frankenfoods), which are known to promote allergy problems.

21. Use herbal therapies to boost the immune system (e.g., Astragalus, echinacea, shiitake mushrooms, milk thistle).

Tip: Eat at least one meal a day for your immune system.

BOX 27.5 Insomnia and Nutrition

It's not uncommon to see students burning the midnight oil with a cup of coffee or caffeinated soda in hand. Perhaps more than any other foodstuff, caffeine intake greatly affects one's physiology—making it the number one thing to avoid if you are plagued by insomnia. Research reveals that caffeine intake decreases the amount of REM sleep, which has been noted as the most essential phase of each two-hour sleep cycle.

Why is drinking a glass of milk thought to send you trundling off to la-la land? The answer resides in the amino acid found in milk, called tryptophan. Tryptophan (also found in high concentrations in turkey meat) is known to induce sleep. For this reason, it is often used as a bedtime snack. With the popularity of natural remedies, the following herbs are renowned for their ability to decrease neural firing, thus relaxing the body in preparation for a good night's sleep: valerian, ginseng, passion flower, and kava kava (please take as directed). Finally, it should be noted that most processed foods contain a plethora of chemicals that undoubtedly have some impact on brain chemistry, including aspartame and MSG, and these should be avoided.

---

grapes, and a whole host of vegetables available year-round, not to mention a selection of meats, fish, and other foods imported from states and countries thousands of miles away. Quantities of food are abundant as well, but this does not necessarily mean the quality of food is superior to that of our grandparents. Across the planet, there is an alarming concern that the soil used to grow crops is severely depleted of its nutrients, resulting in a loss of nutrient density in foods and people experiencing the effects of malnourishment, even though the caloric intake is much greater than in the days of our grandparents.

The biggest nutrition problem in the United States is overconsumption, yet overconsumption does not necessarily mean an overabundance of the various nutrients that the body requires for optimal functioning (Wansink, 2006; Taubes, 2007). Foods high in fat and simple sugars and empty calories tend to rob the body of essential nutrients. Consequently, the body is operating under a nutritional deficiency, not nutritional abundance. Under these conditions, the body is stressed to maintain its integrity for metabolic functioning. Over time, one or more physiological systems may go into a state of dysfunction. In addition, it is no secret that when people are stressed, their eating habits are greatly compromised, perpetuating an already negative condition. Stated simply, a person under stress is extremely vulnerable to nutritional deficiency.

Under the most optimal conditions, stress can cause problems with the body's ability to digest and absorb nutrients, thus impeding the availability of the essential nutrients, particularly vitamins and minerals. As you will see, the physiological system most seriously affected by a poor nutritional state is the immune system. Following is a description of how stress affects our absorption of essential nutrients and, ultimately, our susceptibility to a wide range of illnesses.

Stress and Mineral Depletion. Research conducted by the U.S. Department of Agriculture (Sizer & Whitney, 2007) has revealed that, despite what appeared to be an adequate dietary intake, several levels of minerals have decreased as much as 33 percent in the past 20 years throughout various age ranges of people. A depletion of minerals decreases the integrity of the immune system, making one more susceptible to disease and illness. The following minerals are in deficit under conditions of chronic stress: magnesium, chromium, copper, iron, and zinc.

Stress and Vitamin Depletion. Four vitamins are also known to be greatly affected by chronic stress: the antioxidant vitamins A, C, and E, and the vitamin B complex.

The Antioxidants. The body encounters many environmental stressors in the course of a day, including particles known as free radicals. **Free radicals** are highly reactive oxygen particles most commonly found in air pollution, tobacco smoke, radiation, herbicides, and rancid fatty foods. Free radicals are also produced in the body under normal metabolic functioning. Left

---

Free radicals: Highly reactive oxygen molecules with an aberrant electron that can cause damage to cell membranes and DNA.

uncontrolled, free radicals will destroy various constituents of cells they come in contact with, including:

- *The cell membrane:* Free radicals change the permeability of the cell membrane, disturbing the transportation of essential nutrients into the cell as well as by-products out of the cell.

- *The mitochondria:* Free radicals destroy the constituents of the mitochondria (where cell respiration occurs) and compromise the energy capabilities of the cell.

- *DNA:* Free radicals attach to the DNA structure and inhibit the genetic code process that regulates cell reproduction and function.

- *RNA:* Free radicals distort the ability of the RNA to transmit messages throughout the CNS.

Under normal, healthy conditions, free radicals are removed (metabolized by beta-carotene and vitamins C and E). Under bouts of chronic stress, these vitamins are depleted or, in many cases, not even absorbed into the body so that free radicals are not destroyed. It has been noted that free radicals are often associated with the development of several diseases, including coronary heart disease and cancer.

Vitamin C. In addition to acting as an antioxidant, vitamin C is known to aid the immune system in battling colds and flu. Current estimates are that it takes about 200 mg of vitamin C to maintain the integrity of the immune system under stressful conditions. As a rule, people consume less than half that amount (about 60 mg per day, which is the Dietary Reference Intake [DRI]).

The Vitamin B Complex. Vitamin B requirements are known to increase during prolonged bouts of stress because they aid primarily in the function of the central nervous system, which is in a high state of arousal during periods of stress. The vitamin B complex includes thiamin (B_1), riboflavin (B_2), niacin (B_3), B_6, folate, biotin, pantothenic acid, and B_{12}. According to studies at Loma Linda University in California, decreases in B_6 vitamin levels correlate with decreased immune function (Webb, 2001).

A Word about Supplements

Years ago, when the soil used to grow crops was rich in nutrients, supplements were not necessary. Those who took them were looking for quick cures, trying to lose weight, or, in many cases, taking them in place of regular meals. For the average person, though, it was widely believed that if you ate well-balanced meals,

Courtesy of Jesse Geraci

FIGURE 27.10 The best source of vitamins is unprocessed food. Vitamin supplements are recommended for people who may not get essential nutrients, but vitamins should not be taken in place of a meal.

there really was no need to take supplements. The same cannot be said today! Because of soil depletion, combined with the rushed pace of life leading to greatly compromised dietary habits, taking supplements is not only recommended, it is often required to maintain optimal health (**FIG. 27.10**). Some facts to be aware of when choosing dietary supplements include the following:

- Not all **vitamin supplements** are created equal. Vitamin sources are either extracted from their original food sources or chemically synthesized. In the act of processing, vitamins may be *synthesized, crystallized, lyophilized (freeze-dried)*, or whole-food supplements. In the first two processes, extreme heat is used and, as a result, any beneficial qualities once present are most likely lost. In addition, the substance used in the process of binding the vitamins in a tablet is so strong that the body's enzymes cannot dissolve it. Consequently, the tablet is passed through the GI tract without ever being absorbed. Therefore, it is recommended that any vitamin supplement taken be lyophilized or made from whole-food extracts and that it be in the form of a powdered substance in a gel capsule for easy digestion and absorption.

Vitamin supplements: Processed pills containing various vitamins (e.g., A, B complex, C, E).

Taken in concentrated form, vitamin, mineral, and protein supplements can actually block the absorption rate (decrease bioavailability) of other essential nutrients (other vitamins and minerals), thereby negating any positive effect. Consult a certified nutritionist about taking supplements.

In large doses, the fat-soluble vitamins (A, D, E, and K) are toxic. Because vitamins B and C are water soluble, excess amounts of them will be excreted—making for very expensive urine.

Additional Stress and Nutritional Factors to Consider

Nutrition plays a crucial role in both minimizing and increasing the physiological arousal of the stress response. The stress response increases the rate of metabolism by activating the mobilization of carbohydrates and fats into the bloodstream for energy production. Additionally, several substances, when ingested, tend to mimic or induce the stress response or decrease the efficiency of the body's metabolic pathways, thus setting the stage for a more pronounced physiological reaction to stress. Likewise, the stress response can deplete necessary nutrients, vitamins, and minerals, creating a cyclical process of poor health. The relationship between stress and nutrition is profound for many reasons, including the following:

Stress increases the production of cortisol, which, in turn, increases the production of the chemical neuropeptide Y (NPY) in the brain. NPY is thought to be responsible for people cravings for carbohydrate-rich foods, particularly sweets (possibly a reason for weight gain). NPY levels are normally high in the morning. This, coupled with a stress-filled day, can create the urge for sweets all day long. Eating a good breakfast is believed to help maintain levels of NPY and keeps it in balance (Sommer, 1999).

According to nutritionist Elizabeth Sommer (1999), a low-fat diet stimulates the immune system, whereas a high-fat diet increases the risk of illness. Therefore, eating foods with high fat content may be convenient during a long working day, but the long-term effects are quite detrimental to optimal health.

An excess of simple sugars tends to deplete vitamin stores, particularly the vitamin B complex (niacin, thiamin, riboflavin, B_6, and B_{12}). White sugar (even bleached flour), flushed of its vitamin and mineral content, requires additional B-complex vitamins to be metabolized. These and other vitamins are crucial for the optimal functioning of the central nervous system. A depletion of the B-complex vitamins may manifest itself in fatigue, anxiety, and irritability. In addition, increased amounts of ingested simple sugars may cause major fluctuations in blood glucose levels, resulting in pronounced fatigue, headaches, and general irritability. *New York Times Magazine* investigative reporter Gary Taubes, author of the best-seller *Good Calories, Bad Calories* (2007), notes that refined sugars (not saturated fats) are the primary factor associated with obesity and many other chronic diseases.

Caffeine is a stimulant that arouses the sympathetic nervous system—most likely the reason people drink coffee in the morning to help wake up and get a start on the day (**FIG. 27.11**). Caffeine is quickly absorbed in the bloodstream and delivered to all parts of the body, with a direct effect on the brain. It is a well-known fact that caffeine is a diuretic. Also eliminated are various minerals such as calcium and magnesium. Food sources with caffeine that trigger the sympathetic nervous system are referred to as *sympathomimetic agents*. The substance in caffeine responsible for this effect is

FIGURE 27.11   You may consider coffee to be one of your essential food groups, but research reveals that more than two 8-ounce cups per day contains enough caffeine to trigger the fight-or-flight response. Caffeine is also found in tea, sodas, and chocolate. If you are stressed, coffee, tea, or soda is not a recommended beverage, despite cultural trends reinforcing this habit.

called **methylated xanthine**. This chemical stimulant with amphetamine-like characteristics triggers the sympathetic nervous system for a heightened state of arousal as well as stimulates the release of several stress hormones. The result is a heightened state of alertness, which makes the individual more susceptible to perceived stress. Caffeine is found in many foods, including chocolate, coffee, tea, and several types of soft drinks. According to current estimates, the average American consumes three 6-ounce cups of coffee per day. A 6-ounce cup of caffeinated coffee contains approximately 250 milligrams of caffeine, half the amount necessary to evoke an adverse arousal of the central nervous system. The body takes about 8 hours to metabolize one cup of coffee (Cherniske, 1998).

■ Chronic stress can cause a depletion of several vitamins necessary for energy metabolism, as well as a depletion of constituents required by the stress response itself. The synthesis of cortisol requires the presence of vitamins. The stress response activates several hormones responsible for mobilizing and metabolizing fats and carbohydrates for energy production. The breakdown of fats and carbohydrates requires the involvement of vitamins—specifically, vitamin C and B-complex vitamins. An inadequate supply of these vitamins may affect mental alertness and promote depression and insomnia. Stress is also associated with a depletion of calcium and the inability of bones to absorb calcium properly. This sets the stage for the development of osteoporosis, the demineralization of bone tissue. Vitamin supplementation is a controversial issue. When a balanced diet is consumed, there is typically an adequate supply of vitamins and nutrients for energy metabolism. However, a balanced diet is not the rule for the majority of Americans. Vitamin supplements may be recommended for individuals who are prone to excessive stress.

■ It seems that Americans have a love affair with salt. Some people even add salt to their food without tasting it. High sodium intake is associated with high blood pressure because sodium acts to increase water retention. As water volume increases in a closed system, blood pressure increases. If this condition persists, it may contribute to hypertension.

■ The excessive consumption of alcohol is thought to suppress the immune system by depleting

FIGURE 27.12   Think twice before you eat processed food.

water-soluble vitamins and minerals (primarily potassium, magnesium, calcium, and zinc), which are involved in the synthesis of components for the immune system. What is excess consumption of alcohol? Although this may vary from person to person, nutritionists suggest that more than one drink per day is excessive.

■ For years scientists have warned against the dangers of eating too many foods with cholesterol and saturated fat (**FIG. 27.12**), but the choices of foods that are offered as substitutes are proving to be no better and, in some cases, perhaps worse. Margarine is a processed form of corn oil; it is produced by changing the molecular structure through *hydrogenation*, in which the empty bonds are filled to turn the liquid oil into a solid at room temperature. Recently, scientists have observed an association between the hydrogenation process and the loss of integrity of the cell wall (through free radicals), setting the stage for the development of

Methylated xanthine: The active ingredient in caffeine, which triggers a sympathetic response.

© Losevsky Pavel/Shutterstock.

FIGURE 27.13 A stressed lifestyle can produce poor eating habits, which in turn can leave you with a nutrient deficiency and a compromised immune system. Get in the habit, no matter how busy your day, to eat one meal a day for your immune system.

cancer and coronary heart disease. As of November 2013, the Food and Drug Administration banned all foods with trans fats (hydrogenated oils) because of the chronic health risks associated with them.

- People who are constantly on the go rarely have time to prepare their own meals and may not eat regularly (**FIG. 27.13**). On average, many people eat one or two meals a day outside the home, which frequently leads to some rather unhealthy eating habits that will, over time, be the cause of stress. If you tend to eat out frequently—whether as a matter of convenience or social habit—you should be aware of these

---

Genetically modified organisms (GMOs): DNA manipulation of foods whereby the gene from one species is spliced into the DNA of a different species to enhance quality or shelf life. GMOs are currently associated with a host of food allergies. An example of this would be taking the genes from a flounder and splicing them into the DNA of a tomato.

Frankenfood: A name coined in Europe to promote the hidden dangers of genetically modified organisms (GMOs). GMOs are currently banned in Europe.

Spiritual nutrition: A term to suggest that the colors of specific fruits and vegetables augments the flow of subtle energy to the respective *chakras* represented by these colors (e.g., foods with the color red are beneficial for the root *chakra* and organs associated with this area).

---

facts. Food prepared in restaurants is generally high in sodium and sugar, and is particularly high in saturated fats. People like fatty foods because they taste good, and many of the selections on a menu are created with this in mind. Appetizers that are fried, salad dressings made with heavy oils, and rich desserts with heavy creams are where the fat calories are hidden. Fast food is even higher in fat, sodium, and sugars. If you must eat out, make a habit of skipping appetizers, soft drinks, and salad dressings; choosing fresh fruits and vegetables over fried foods; and passing on dessert.

A Word about Genetically Altered Foods

Research into various hybrids of plant species, such as peas, oranges, and lettuce, has been conducted for centuries, in the hopes of making more delicious and nutritious food. The line between science and science fiction became rather fuzzy in 2000 when it was reported that food scientists were splicing a unique gene from flounder (saltwater fish) into the DNA of tomatoes, and the genes of Brazil nuts into the DNA of corn. Scientists proceeded to alter the genetic makeup of corn by splicing Roundup, a synthetic pesticide, into the DNA of corn, which resulted in the mysterious death of thousands of migrating monarch butterflies (Teitel and Wilson, 1999). In the fall of 2000, corn taco shells were recalled from Taco John restaurants and corn flakes were recalled from grocery store shelves by Kellogg Corporation because of consumer alarm over **genetically modified organisms (GMOs) or** what some have labeled as **Frankenfood.** GMOs are considered by some people to be a bioecological stressor to the body. Over 65 percent of foods found in the grocery store are genetically modified (Glave, 2004; Mercola, 2008). Commercial foods and food products may not be labeled as containing "genetically altered" ingredients. Because of the possibility of severe allergic reactions to such foods, it is best to avoid them and choose whole foods with "certified organic" labels (**FIG. 27.14**).

Spiritual Nutrition

What does nutrition have to do with spirituality? On the surface, perhaps not much; but with closer examination we learn that some aspects of nutrition have a very strong spiritual and energy component. For instance, in the Eastern culture it is believed that there are several energy centers (called *chakras*), which run from the top of the head to the base of the spine. Each of the seven energy centers is associated with a color: red (base of spine), orange (navel), yellow (spleen), green (heart),

---

BOX 27.6   Food Allergies and GMOs

On Saturday, May 22, 2013, millions of people around the world gathered in a unified demonstration to protest against the American company Monsanto, which is notorious for its efforts to genetically modify food (e.g., splicing the herbicide Roundup into corn). Cross-species tinkering with DNA has harmful consequences. With the rise in GMO foods, there has also been a rise in food allergies. The proverbial question becomes this: When you place a gene of a flounder fish into a tomato plant, is it an animal or a vegetable? Less than a week after the global protests, scientists were quite surprised to find genetically modified wheat in a field in Oregon. Although genetically modified corn and soy are permitted by the U.S. government, genetically modified wheat is not. Wheat that is high in protein creates bigger yields for farmers and is considered more drought resistant. It also is considered harder to digest and absorb. It is estimated that over 30 percent of Americans are now gluten intolerant. (Gluten is the protein source in wheat, rye, and barley.) The Mayo Clinic estimates that one in 110 people have celiac disease (dire wheat intolerance). Wheat products include more than slices of bread and hamburger buns, including breadcrumbs in hamburgers, cereals, soups, imitation crab, mashed potatoes, some spices, and many sauces (Rizzo, 2013). Well beyond eggs, peanuts, and milk, people today suffer from a great many food allergies. GMO foods may be to blame, as these genetic "creations" are considered by some to be a foreign pathogen (a stressor) to the human immune system. It is estimated that over 65 percent of foods sold in grocery stores are genetically modified, yet not labeled as so due to powerful corporate lobbying efforts.

FIGURE 27.14   Organic foods that contain no herbicides, fungicides, pesticides, or synthetic fertilizers are highly recommended, particularly for anyone with a compromised immune system.

aqua-blue (throat), indigo blue (forehead), and violet (crown). It's not a coincidence that women are advised to drink cranberry juice for a urinary tract infection or that diabetics are advised to consume bilberries for their eyes to minimize the effects of retinopathy. The Ayurvedic principles from India suggest that people eat foods, specifically fruits and vegetables, that correspond to the colors of the energy centers. New research into light and color therapy suggests that every color has a vibrational frequency, and that when people or animals are denied full-spectrum lighting, the effects are evident in the functions of various organs. Eating foods that contain a specific frequency may, indeed, replenish what is not available through exposure to natural light. New research suggests that **bioflavonoids**, the "nonnutrients" in fruits and vegetables that are responsible for food color, act like antioxidants and seem to have an anti-cancer action (Simone, 1994; Kale et al., 2008).

The Taoist philosophy of the Chinese culture also advocates finding balance in the foods we eat, specifically in terms of acid (yin) and alkaline (yang) substances. Grains and animal foods (acids) should be balanced with seeds, vegetables, and salt (alkalines). According to this approach, the correct alkaline/acid balance is 80/20. The Chinese believe that a diet consisting of food heavy in acids creates an energy disturbance, resulting in poor health and disease.

In his book *Spiritual Nutrition and the Rainbow Diet*, Gabriel Cousens, M.D., highlights several ways to make our nutrition and eating habits more conducive to healthy living and more harmonious with the planet. His suggestions include the following:

1. Eat a great variety (full spectrum) of foods, noting color (outside), to nurture the care of specific organs associated with each *chakra* area.

> **Bioflavonoids:** Nonnutrients found in foods (fruits and vegetables) that contain antioxidants and seem to provide a means of fighting cancer and other illnesses. Bioflavonoids provide the colors in foods.

2. Avoid eating big meals prior to meditation because the stomach and the brain compete for blood flow, and when the stomach is full, more blood is needed for digestion. As a rule, undereat.

3. Drink plenty of water to cleanse the body of nutrients and toxins that are no longer needed.

4. In addition to digesting quality foods, good nutrition includes adequate sunlight (vitamin D), plenty of fresh air (oxygen), and plenty of fresh water to drink.

5. Learn what foods are associated with the acid/alkaline balance and make an effort to achieve this balance in your daily diet.

6. Learn to concentrate on the foods you are eating, noting the taste, texture, and temperature, and even the origin. According to the Eastern tradition, being mindful of the food we eat (mindfulness) is a spiritual experience.

Psychological Effects of Food

Brian Wansink begins his book *Mindless Eating* by describing a culture under the hypnotic effect of mass marketers vying to undermine your best eating habits by sabotaging your unconscious mind with subliminal messages to eat and eat and eat. When emotional stress is combined with this effort, the results can be alarming. It would be a simple world if eating were done solely to meet nutritional needs, but this is not the case. Often the act of eating is done for emotional reasons that have nothing to do with nutritional demands of the body. Food is often used as a means to pacify our minds and hearts, a behavior learned from day one at a mother's breast or with a bottle (FIG. 27.15). This pattern continues from infancy well into adulthood as we stuff our faces in an attempt to stuff our feelings or control them at some level. The consequences are serious, if not fatal. Experts in dietary behaviors will tell you that the problem of being overweight may look like a problem of overconsumption, but a closer examination reveals that there are some serious emotional issues under the surface. Likewise, eating disorders such as anorexia and bulimia may appear to suggest a problem with malnutrition, but the truth is that eating disorders are symptoms of much more serious unresolved emotional problems. Eating can be an outlet for unresolved anger (for example, guilt: the self-punisher or even the underhander who eats and drinks on an employer's expense account to seek revenge for working extra hours). But anger alone is not the cause

FIGURE 27.15 Eating a healthy meal can be considered a form of relaxation, particularly when done in the company of good friends. When dining with others, relax and enjoy the experience, keeping in mind that a strong social support group augments the relaxation potential.

of eating problems. Boredom, loneliness, procrastination, anxiety, and poor willpower also contribute to the blend of psychological and physiological interactions. In essence, food becomes a tranquilizer that calms nerves.

Cravings. The average person tends to gravitate toward one or more foods when feeling depressed or lonely. Food can become a "friend" when there are no other friends around. If at first we become acquainted with a particular food at a low point, we can become conditioned to return to that type of food when the situation arises again (comfort foods). Chocolate, french fries, diet sodas, potato chips, candy bars, popcorn, and ice cream are some foods people crave in times of stress. If you are like most people, you also crave a particular food or foods when you are stuck at the end of your emotional spectrum. What is your particular craving? What specific food calms your nerves or gives you a lift when things are not going as expected? Although it is acceptable to seek simple pleasures in food, problems arise when the occasional craving becomes a habit. An occasional craving is not bad, but it can become self-destructive if the behavior is not stopped or if help is not sought to regain emotional balance.

Eating Disorders. There is no simple solution to eating disorders because they involve various eating habits, perceptions of foods, personal history, social pressures, and personality—all of which add up to the monumental task of aligning these factors long enough to make some positive changes. Three of the most common eating disorders are anorexia, bulimia, and overeating.

Anorexia. Anorexics are classified into two groups: the individual who restricts food intake and starves herself and the bulimic who runs through cycles of gorging and then purging. Typically, anorexics are described as well-educated females with a middle- to upper-class background. The issue of starvation is centered on control—there is something the anorexic feels helpless about and self-starvation is a way to appease this condition, however remote or tangential. Anorexics have a very distorted body image, often seeing themselves as fat when they have little or no body fat. Aside from the obvious characteristic of extreme weight loss, anorexics are prone to insomnia, obsessive-compulsive disorder, stoicism, perfectionism, introversion, and, frequently, emotional inhibition. Statistics reveal that 1 out of every 100 adolescent girls is diagnosed with this condition (Levenkron, 2000; Gordon, 2000).

Bulimia. In the American culture, thinness is an obsession. This fact is validated by the plethora of women's magazines that feature thin models on the covers and convey the subliminal message that, unless you look like this, you are not pretty. Women who fall prey to the whims of these marketing attempts and social mores are often confronted with a dilemma, and food becomes the vehicle to control feelings of self-image, self-worth, and self-esteem. In an effort to control body weight, bulimics binge on an assortment of foods (typically junk food) and then purge (either by vomiting or using laxatives) in an attempt to satisfy the need to eat and also satisfy the need to control their weight. Bingeing efforts can be quite extreme: eating a whole gallon of ice cream or consuming an entire pizza or an entire box of cookies. The result of such behavior is the loss of control over caloric balance and the beginning of a cycle of bingeing and purging that frequently leads to malnutrition. Continued bulimia may result in tooth enamel erosion (from vomiting), bowel problems, constipation, irregular menstruation, electrolyte imbalance, and rips and tears in the GI tract.

Overeating. Excessive overeating may be a result of many factors, including guilt, loneliness, or nervousness. The use of food as a pacifier to calm the nerves becomes ingrained in the daily lifestyle. Overeating can also be a means to create a protective shell in an effort to keep people at a distance. This is often the case with people who were sexually abused or violently attacked as children. In many cases of overeating, low self-esteem is observed.

Is there a physiological explanation for eating disorders? Perhaps not, but there are links between eating and personality that can lead to a better understanding of how to deal with the problem. As the theme of this text suggests, all things connect and there is a direct link between the mind and the body, as evidenced by the hypothalamus. The hypothalamus, which registers emotional feelings, also controls appetite—the desire to consume food. When food is placed in the stomach, a calming message is sent to the hypothalamus to decrease the intensity of neural stimulation throughout the rest of the body. There is a profound connection between food and stress. Eating to pacify the nerves is such a common behavior that it is often overlooked in the field of stress management. But what is considered normal is not necessarily healthy. Take note (perhaps in a journal) of your eating behaviors in times of stress. From there, ask yourself whether eating is something you feel you have control over, or whether eating is something that is controlling you.

Recommendations for Healthy Eating Habits

Experts agree that the following dietary practices can minimize the body's arousal to stress and enhance optimal functioning.

Eat a Well-Balanced Diet. The typical American consumes too many fats and proteins and, frequently, not enough carbohydrates, specifically complex carbohydrates (Sizer and Whitney, 2007). An unbalanced diet leads to poor physical performance. At a young age it can retard the physical growth process. During the college years, both men and women seem to function at an acceptable level. But if habits are not corrected, the foundation is laid for a series of health-related problems later in life. Following is a comparison of the typical American diet and federal government–recommended daily allowances:

Typical American Diet	U.S. DRI Suggested Diet
Carbohydrates: 30–40%	Carbohydrates: 55–70%
Fats: 40–50%	Fats: 20–30%
Proteins: 20–30%	Proteins: 15–20%

Eat a Good Breakfast and Space Meals Evenly Throughout the Day. Americans typically skip breakfast, with college students being the worst offenders. The body operates on carbohydrates, and this is usually what breakfast foods consist of: breads, cereals, and fruits. When the body is not refueled after 8 to 10 hours

BOX 27.7 Food Label Warning

The following items have been noted to be dangers to your health and should be minimized or completely avoided in your diet.

Hydrogenated oils (trans fatty acids)

Partially hydrogenated oils (trans fatty acids)

Aspartame (Nutrasweet and AminoSweet)

Saturated fats

Sodium

Monosodium glutamate (MSG)

Caffeine

Red and blue dyes

Food prepared with more than 30 percent simple sugars or high-fructose corn syrup

Non-organic homogenized milk (contains hormones and steroids)

Nitrites

Nitrates

Steroids, pesticides, and hormones in meats and chicken

Olestra

Any artificial flavor or coloring

Any artificial preservative

- If you can't pronounce it, you probably shouldn't eat it.

of sleep, it doesn't function well. Symptoms of shortened attention span, early fatigue, and depression are common. When the mind is not alert, the body does not respond well to stress—it typically overreacts. Poor cognitive functioning can result in poor decision making, which can perpetuate the stress cycle. There is a new

Aspartame: Two amino acids that combine to make an artificially sweet taste, including one that is documented to affect brain chemistry and cognitive function. Like MSG, this substance is known as an "excitotoxin." (Aspartame is also marketed as Nutrasweet.)

Monosodium glutamate (MSG): A food brightener that is documented to affect brain chemistry and cognitive function. Like aspartame, this substance is known as an "excitotoxin." MSG is merely listed as "spice" on many condiments.

theory that humans should eat six small meals a day rather than three large ones for better metabolism (ClevelandClinic.org). Regardless of the number, meals should be spaced evenly throughout the day. An irregular eating schedule interrupts the body's natural rhythms.

Avoid or Minimize the Consumption of Caffeine and Sugar. Overconsumption of caffeine is unhealthy on many fronts. In the short term it can cause headaches, irritability, nervousness, sleeplessness, and in some cases gastrointestinal irritation. Caffeine should be avoided when you know you may encounter a stressor, and caffeine consumption is not recommended when performing relaxation techniques. Refined sugar can also lead to problems. Research (Sizer and Whitney, 2007) indicates that individuals consume their body weight in refined sugar each year. For reasons explained earlier, this is extremely unhealthy. Efforts should be made to decrease consumption of refined sugar.

Eat a Diet That Provides Adequate Levels of Vitamins and Minerals That Are Potentially Vulnerable to Stress. Vitamins are classified as either fat soluble (A, D, E, and K) or water soluble (B complex and C). The water-soluble vitamins tend to be targeted for destruction during the stress response. A well-balanced diet should exceed the minimum requirements of all of these vitamins, as well as the RDA of essential minerals. Poor nutritional habits compounded by chronic physical stress set the stage for vitamin depletion and deficiency. Caution is advised with vitamin supplementation. An overabundance of fat-soluble vitamins can lead to vitamin toxicity, while an excess of vitamins C and B complex is usually excreted, making for very expensive urine. Eat a well-balanced diet with whole and fresh foods and add a quality vitamin supplement (Sizer and Whitney, 2007).

Follow the U.S. Dietary Guidelines. Unlike developing nations that struggle to feed their citizens, the United States suffers from a problem of overconsumption. According to federal government sources, we as a nation overconsume calories in general and specifically fats, simple sugars, salt, and alcohol. These trends in the American diet are closely associated with six of the ten leading causes of death in this country, including coronary heart disease, diabetes, and cancer. Based on a review of these national eating behaviors, the following dietary guidelines were established by the U.S. Departments of Agriculture and Health and Human Services:

1. Aim for a healthy weight.

2. Be physically active each day.

3. Let the MyPlate food guidance system guide your food choices.

4. Choose a variety of grains daily, especially whole grains.

5. Choose a variety of fruits and vegetables daily.

6. Keep foods safe to eat.

7. Choose a diet that is low in saturated fat and cholesterol and moderate in total fat.

8. Choose beverages and foods to moderate your intake of sugars.

9. Choose and prepare foods with less salt.

10. If you drink alcoholic beverages, do so in moderation.

Additional Tips for Healthy Eating

Many of our eating habits were formed years ago and have become ingrained. When it comes to nutrition, there is no shortage of ideas and suggestions to follow to get back on the right track to eating better. Here are some additional tips:

- Thoroughly wash all pesticides from fruits and vegetables before eating. Studies show that individually, these pesticides are not harmful, but no studies have looked at the cumulative effects of various pesticides. It's a good idea to rinse all produce well. Eat organic produce whenever possible.

- Avoid canned fruits and vegetables when possible because, by the time they are eaten, vitamins and minerals have been absorbed into the water used to package the goods and are often discarded in preparation.

- Avoid nutritional supplements that advertise "time released." This phrase is a marketing gimmick that does not hold up under the constraints of human physiology.

- Consider alternative options for healthier meals when you are away from home. It is just as easy to go to a grocery store and pick up some produce as it is to pull into a fast-food restaurant.

- If you do choose to take a nutritional supplement, take it with food and water, not on an empty stomach.

- Eating a high-carbohydrate meal can make your blood glucose levels soar, only to fall down below resting levels soon thereafter. Eat some protein with the carbohydrates so that fatigue will not set in.

- If you are in the habit of eating while watching TV and you are hoping to lose weight, make a new habit to eat only in the kitchen area. TV commercials often send a message to eat even when you are not hungry. Hold fast to this rule: No eating in front of the TV.

- DRIs were designed to inform the general public about nutritional needs, yet these recommendations were not established for the optimal levels. Rather, what is listed are average amounts. Without pushing the limits of toxicity, you should consider slightly increasing your levels of nutrients, specifically vitamins and minerals.

- Switch from diet drinks that contain aspartame and caffeine to caffeine-free herbal teas or water when looking for a beverage and rehydration.

- If you are having problems sleeping at night, be careful to avoid foods that contain caffeine, and avoid eating a meal or snack before bedtime.

- Don't try to make several dietary changes all at once. Try making one change at a time (perhaps one each week) until you are at a level where it is comfortable to adopt a new eating behavior.

SUMMARY

- Physical exercise is a form of stress: the enactment of all the physiological systems that the fight-or-flight response triggers for physical survival.

- Physical exercise is classified as either anaerobic (fight) or aerobic (flight). Anaerobic (without oxygen) is a short, intense, and powerful activity, whereas aerobic exercise (with oxygen) is moderately intense activity for a prolonged period of time. Aerobic exercise is the better type to promote relaxation.

- The body adapts, either negatively or positively, to the stress placed upon it. Proper physical exercise will cause many adaptations that in the long term are thought to be effective in reducing the deleterious effects of stress by returning the body to a profound state of homeostasis. Physical exercise allows the body to use stress hormones for their intended purposes, detoxifying the body of stress hormones by utilizing them constructively.

- To get the benefits of physical exercise, four criteria must be met: intensity, duration, frequency of training, and mode of exercise. Together they are called the all-or-none principle, meaning that without meeting all four requirements few if any benefits will be gained. It takes between 6 and 8 weeks to see significant benefits in the body.

- The positive effects of physical exercise are lowering resting heart rate, resting blood pressure, and muscle tension, and a host of other functions that help maintain or regain physiological calmness.

- Exercise evokes not only physiological changes, but various psychological changes (e.g., runner's high) as well, again suggesting that mind and body act as one entity. Habitual physical exercise produces both physiological homeostasis and mental homeostasis. Individuals who engage in regular physical exercise report higher levels of self-esteem and lower incidences of depression and anxiety.

- Although the primary purpose of food is as a source of nutrients, many people use food as a means to fill an emotional void created by stress.

- Because of the global condition of soil depletion, even a healthy diet is considered deficient in the essential vitamins and minerals so that supplementation is encouraged.

- A malnourished diet—one that is deficient in essential amino acids, essential fats, vitamins, and minerals—is itself a stressor on the body.

- Research has shown that some foods actually induce a state of stress. Excess amounts of sugar, caffeine, salt, and foods poor in vitamins and minerals weaken the body's resistance to the stress response and may ultimately make a person more vulnerable to disease and illness.

- Not all supplements are created equal. Check to see that the processing does not destroy what it is intended to promote. Taken in excess, supplements can do more harm than good by inhibiting the proper digestion and absorption of essential nutrients.

- Food you eat can either boost or suppress the immune system.

- Food affects not only the physical body, but the mental, emotional, and spiritual aspects as well. The concept of spiritual nutrition suggests eating a wide variety of fruits, vegetables, and grains that nurture the health of the seven primary *chakras*. In addition, spiritual nutrition suggests ensuring a balance in all aspects of food, including the acid/base balance.

- Eating disorders are emotionally rather than physiologically based, ranging from bulimia and anorexia to overeating—all of which have serious consequences if not resolved.

- Change various aspects of your diet, including reducing or eliminating the consumption of caffeine, refined sugar, sodium, and fats, to reduce the risk of stress-related problems.

STUDY GUIDE QUESTIONS

1. Explain how physical exercise is stress but also helps reduce stress.

2. How does anaerobic exercise differ from aerobic exercise?

3. List five physiological effects of cardiovascular exercise.

4. List and explain the proven steps to begin and continue a successful exercise program.

5. How does stress affect eating habits?

6. How does stress affect digestion, absorption, and elimination?

7. How does stress affect the body's nutrients?

8. What foods trigger the stress response?

9. List three recommendations for healthy nutrition.

REFERENCES AND RESOURCES

American College of Sports Medicine. *Guidelines for Exercise Testing and Prescription,* 6th ed. Lippincott, New York, 2000.

American College of Sports Medicine. *Recommended Quantity and Quality of Exercise for Developing and Maintaining Cardiovascular and Muscular Fitness in Healthy Adults.* ACSM, Indianapolis, IN, April 1990.

Anoja, S., et al. Treatment of Insomnia: An Alternative Approach. www.thorne.com/altmedrev/fulltext/insomnia 5-3.html.

Antioxidants, *Journal of Nutrition* 133(5):1285–1291, 2003.

Aronson, D. Taking the Right Vitamins for You, *Natural Health* August 2003:67–77.

Aronson, V., and Fitzgerald, B. *Guidebook for Nutrition Counselors.* Prentice-Hall, Upper Saddle River, NJ, 1990.

Artal, M., and Sherman, C. Exercise and Depression, *Physician and Sports Medicine,* October 1998:55–60.

Barlow, J. Study Is First to Confirm Link Between Exercise and Changes in Brain. 2003. www.news.uiuc.edu/scitips/03 /0127exercise.html.

Bartholomew, J. B. Stress Reactivity after Maximal Exercise: The Effect of Manipulated Performance Feedback in Endurance Athletes, *Journal of Sports Science* 18(11):893, 2000.

Bein-Ari, E. T. Take Two Exercise Sessions and Call Me in the Morning, *BioScience* 50(1):96, 2000.

Bellet, S., et al. Effect of Physical Exercise on Adrenocortical Excretion, *Metabolism* 18:484–487, 1969.

Berger, B. G. Facts and Fancy: Mood Alteration through Exercise, *Journal of Physical Education, Recreation, and Dance* 53(9):47–48, 1982.

Berger, B. G. Stress Reduction through Exercise: The Mind-Body Connection, *Motor Skills: Theory into Practice* 7(2): 31–46, 1983.

Berger, B. G., and Motl, R. Physical Activity and Quality of Life. In R. Singer, et al. (eds.), *Handbook of Sport Psychology.* Wiley and Sons, New York, 2001.

Berger, B., et al. Comparison of Jogging, the Relaxation Response and Group Interaction for Stress Reduction, *Journal of Sport and Exercise Psychology* 10(4):431–447, 1988.

Blackburn, G. Nutritional Medicine: Eating Under Stress, *Prevention* 43(6):104, 1991.

Blaylock, R. *Excitotoxins: The Taste That Kills.* Health Press, Santa Fe, NM, 1994.

Carmichael, M. Stronger, Faster, Smarter: Exercise and the Brain, *Newsweek*, March 26, 2007:38–55.

Chang, L. *Stress Hormone: No Link to Obesity? MedicineNet .com,* February 3, 2006. www.medicinenet.com/script/main /art.asp?articlekey=57726.

Cherniske, S. *Caffeine Blues: Wake Up to the Hidden Dangers of America's #1 Drug.* Grand Central Publishing, New York, 1998.

Cleveland Clinic. www.clevelandclinic.org/health/healthinfo /docs/2500/2589.asp?index=9788.

Colcombe, S. J., et al. Aerobic Fitness Reduces Brain Tissue Loss in Aging Humans, *Journal of Gerontology* 58(2):176–180, 2003.

Collingwood, T. The Effects of Physical Training upon Behavior and Self-Attitudes, *Journal of Clinical Psychology* 28:583–585, 1971.

Colt, E., Wardlaw, S. L., and Franz, A. G. Effect of Running on Plasma B-Endorphin, *Life Science* 28:1637–1640, 1984.

Cooper, K. *The Aerobics Program for Total Wellbeing.* Bantam Books, New York, 1985.

Cooper, K. *The New Aerobics.* Evans, New York, 1970.

Cousens, G. *Conscious Eating.* North Atlantic Books, New York, 2000.

Cousens, G. *Spiritual Nutrition and the Rainbow Diet.* Cassandra Press, San Rafael, CA, 1986.

Cowley, G. Cancer and Diet, *Newsweek,* November 30, 1998: 60–68.

Coyle, E. G., et al. Time Course of Loss of Adaptations after Stopping Prolonged Intense Endurance Training, *Journal of Applied Physiology* 57(6):1857–1864, 1984.

Dahl, M. How Running and Meditation Change the Brains of the Depressed. *Science of Us*, March 24, 2016. http://nymag.com/scienceofus/2016/03/how-running-and-meditation-change-the-brains-of-the-depressed.html.

Davies, C., and Few, J. D. Effects of Exercise on Adrenocortical Function, *Journal of Applied Physiology* 35:887–891, 1974.

Davies, C., and Knibbs, A. The Training Stimulus: The Effects of Intensity, Duration, and Frequency of Effort on Maximum Aerobic Power Output, *Int Z Angew. Physiology* 29:299–305, 1971.

DeBenedette, V. Getting Fit for Life: Can Exercise Reduce Stress? *The Physician and Sports Medicine* 16:185–200, 1988.

Digitale, E. Running Slows Aging and Postpones Disability, Study Finds, *Stanford Report*, August 20, 2008. news.stanford.edu/news/2008/august20/med-aging-082008.html.

Dishman, R. K. Biological Influences on Exercise Adherence, *Research Quarterly for Exercise and Sport* 52(2):143–159, 1981.

Dishman, R. K., Ickes, W., and Morgan, W. P. Self-Motivation and Adherence to Habitual Physical Activity, *Journal of Applied Social Psychology* 1:115–125, 1980.

Dotson, G. Food in Treatment: Education for Self-Nurturance of the Body/Mind/Spirit, *Journal of Traditional Acupuncture,* Summer 1986:35–38.

Egoscue, P. *Pain Free.* Bantam Books, New York, 1998.

Farrell, P. A. Exercise and Endorphins: Male Responses, *Medicine and Science in Sports and Exercise* 17:89–92, 1985.

Fixx, J. *The Complete Book of Running.* Random House, New York, 1977.

Folkins, C. H. Psychological Fitness as a Function of Physical Fitness, *Archives of Physical Medicine and Rehabilitation* 53:503–508, 1972.

Folkins, C. H., and Sime, W. E. Physical Fitness Training and Mental Health, *American Psychologist* 36:373–389, 1981.

Galbo, H., et al. Diminished Hormonal Responses to Exercise in Trained Rats, *Journal of Applied Physiology* 43:953–958, 1977.

Getchel, B. *Physical Fitness: A Way of Life.* Wiley, New York, 1983.

Glasser, W. *Positive Addiction.* Harper & Row, New York, 1976.

Glave, M. P. Most Food in U.S. Grocery Stores Will Be Organic by 2020, *The Santa Fe New Mexican*, July 9, 2004. www.organicconsumers.org/organic/most071904.cfm.

Gordon, R. *Eating Disorders: Anatomy of a Social Epidemic.* Blackwell Publishing, New York, 2000.

Gosselin, C., and Taylor, A. Exercise as Stress Management Tool, *Stress News* 11(4), 1999. www.isma.org.uk/stressnw/exercise.htm.

Grossman, A. Endorphins: Opiates for the Masses, *Medicine and Science in Sport and Exercise* 17:74–80, 1985.

Husband, A. J., and Bryden, W. L. Nutrition, Stress and Immune Activities, *Proceedings of the Nutrition Society of Australia,* 20:60–70, 1996.

Ismail, A. H., and Young, R. J. Effect of Chronic Exercise on the Personality of Adults, *Annals of the New York Academy of Sciences* 301:958–969, 1977.

Kale, A., Gawande, S., and Kotwal, S. Cancer Phytotherapeutics: Role for Flavonoids at the Cellular Level, *Phytotherapy Research* 22(5):567–577, 2008.

Kemper, K., et al. Herbs and Other Dietary Supplements: Healthcare Professional's Knowledge, Attitude and Practices, *Alternative Therapies* 9(3):42–49, 2003.

Kesten, D. *Feeding the Body, Nourishing the Soul: Essentials of Eating for Physical, Emotional and Spiritual Wellbeing.* Conari Press, Berkeley, CA, 1997.

Kirby, J. Eat to Beat Stress, *American Health* December 1997:81.

Kozak, D. Keep Moving—Stay Happy, *Prevention* 53(2):39, 2001.

Lamb, D. *Physiology of Exercise.* Macmillan, New York, 1984.

Langer, S. Stressless: Natural Strategies to Help You Cope, *Better Nutrition* 60(11):38, 1998.

Lenzt, M. Selected Aspects of Deconditioning Secondary to Immobilization, *Nursing Clinics of North America* 16(4): 729–737, 1981.

Levenkron, S. *Anatomy of Anorexia.* W. W. Norton, New York, 2000.

Lyon, L. S. Psychological Effects of Jogging: A Preliminary Study, *Perceptual and Motor Skills* 47:1215–1218, 1978.

Maas, J. *Power Sleep.* Quill Books, New York, 2001.

McCaleb, R. Research and Reviews, *HerbalGram* 29:19–22, 1993.

Mercola, J. Genetically Modified (GM) Foods Prepare a Takeover, *Mercola*, 2008. http://articles.mercola.com/sites/articles/archive/2005/04/06/gm-foods-part-eight.aspx.

Mikevic, P. Anxiety, Depression, and Exercise, *Quest* 33(1): 140–153, 1982.

Mobily, K. Using Physical Activity and Recreation to Cope with Stress and Anxiety: A Review, *American Corrective Therapy Journal* 36(3):77–81, 1982.

Morgan, W., and Goldstein, S. (eds.). *Exercise and Mental Health.* Hemisphere, New York, 1987.

Morgan, W. P. Psychological Effects of Exercise, *Behavioral Medicine Update* 4:25–30, 1982.

Morgan, W. P., et al. Exercise as a Relaxation Technique, *Primary Cardiology* 6:48–57, 1980.

Morse, A., Walker, R., and Monroe, D. The Effect of Exercise on a Psychological Measure of the Stress Response, *Wellness Perspectives* 11(1):39–46, 1994.

Moss. M. *Salt, Sugar, Fat*. Random House, New York, 2013.

National Dairy Council. *Statement of Dietary Goals for the United States Submitted to the Select Committee on Nutrition and Human Needs, U.S. Senate*. The Council, Rosemont, IL, 1977.

Nieman, D. C. *The Exercise–Health Connection*. Human Kinetics, Champaign, IL, 1997.

Oaklander, M. The New Science of Exercise, *Time* pp. 54–60. September 12, 2016.

Pizzorno, J. Pow! Supercharge Your Immune System, *Natural Health,* Sept/Oct 1994:81–85.

Porter, D. T., and Allsen, P. E. Heart Rates of Basketball Coaches, *Physician and Sports Medicine,* October 1978:84–90.

President's Council on Physical Fitness and Sports. *Introduction to Running: One Step at a Time*. PCPFS, Washington, DC, 1980.

Ratey, J. *Spark: The Revolutionary New Science of Exercise and the Brain*. Little Brown, New York, 2008.

Reid, T. R. Caffeine: What's the Buzz, *National Geographic* January 2005.

Rizzo, J. Gut Reactions. *National Geographic*, April, 2013.

Robbins, J. *The Food Revolution*. Conari Press, Berkeley, CA, 2001.

Rubin, J. *Patient Heal Thyself*. Freedom Press, Topanga, CA, 2003.

Sachs, M., and Buffone, G. (eds.). *Running as Therapy: An Integrated Approach*. University of Nebraska Press, Lincoln, NE, 1984.

Shephard, R. *Exercise Physiology*. Decker, Toronto, 1987.

Shephard, R. Intensity, Duration, and Frequency of Exercise as Determinants of the Response to a Training Regimen, *Int Z Angew. Physiology* 26:272–278, 1968.

Simone, C. *Cancer and Nutrition: A Ten-Point Plan to Reduce Your Risk of Getting Cancer,* rev. ed. Avery Books, New York, 1994.

Sizer, F., and Whitney, E. *Hamilton and Whitney's Nutrition; Concepts and Controversies,* 11th ed. Brooks Cole, Belmont, CA, 2007.

Sleep Foundation. www.sleepfoundation.org.

Smith, L. *Dr. Lendon Smith's Low-Stress Diet*. McGraw-Hill, New York, 1985.

Snelling, A., Meholick, B., and Seaward, B. L. Counseling Fitness, *Fitness Management* 5(1):40–41, 1990.

Sobel, D., and Ornstein, R. Exercise Improves Sleep, *Mind/ Body Health Newsletter* VI:1–2, 1997.

Sommer, E. *Food and Mood*, 2nd ed. Henry Holt, New York, 1999.

Sorenson, J. *Aerobic Dancing*. Rawson-Wade, New York, 1979.

Stamford, B. The Adrenaline Rush, *Physician and Sports Medicine* 15:205–212, 1987.

Stanmore, T. *The Pilates Back Book: Heal Neck, Back and Shoulder Pain with Easy Pilates Stretches*. Fair Winds Press, Gloucester, MA, 2002.

Steinman, D. *Diet for a Poisoned Planet*. Random House, New York, 1990.

Sutton, J. R. Hormonal and Metabolic Responses to Exercise in Subjects of High and Low Work Capacity, *Medicine and Science in Sport* 10:1–6, 1978.

Taubes, G. *Good Calories, Bad Calories*. Knopf Books, New York, 2007.

Teitel, M., and Wilson, K. *Genetically Engineered Food: Changing the Nature of Nature*. Park Street Press, Rochester, VT, 1999.

Tharp, G. D. The Role of Glucocorticoids in Exercise, *Medicine and Science in Sports* 7:6–11, 1975.

Townsend Newsletter for Doctors and Patients. Pt. Townsend, WA 98368, www.tldp.com.

Ungaro, A. *Pilates: Body in Motion*. DK Publishing, New York, 2002.

Vailus, A. Effects of Weightlessness on Aerobic and Anaerobic Capacity, unpublished paper, Dept. of Health Fitness, American University, Washington, DC, 1992.

Wansink, B. *Mindless Eating: Why We Eat More Than We Think*. Bantam Books, New York, 2006.

Warner, M. *Pandora's Lunch Box*. Scribner, New York, 2013.

Waterman, R. *Nutrition and Stress*. www.umanitoba.ca/outreach /manitoba_womens_health/nstress.htm.

Watson, T., and Wu, C. Are You Too Fat? *U.S. News and World Report* 120(1):52–61, 1996.

Webb, D. Can B Vitamins Ease Holiday Nerves? *Prevention* December 2001:64–65.

Weil, A. *Eating Well for Optimal Health: The Essential Guide to Food, Diet and Nutrition*. Knopf, New York, 2000.

Weil, A. *Spontaneous Healing*. Fawcett Books, New York, 1995.

Willett, W., and Skerett, P. J. *Eat, Drink and Be Healthy*. Free Press, New York, 2005.

Wilson, V., Morley, N., and Bird, E. Mood Profiles of Marathon Runners, Joggers, and Nonexercisers, *Perceptual and Motor Skills* 50:117–118, 1980.

Winder, W. W., Beattie, M. A., and Holman, R. T. Endurance Training Attenuates Stress-Hormone Responses to Exercise in Fasted Rats, *American Journal of Physiology* 243: R179–R184, 1982.

Winder, W. W., and Heinger, R. W. Effect of Exercise on Degradation of Thyroxine in the Rat, *American Journal of Physiology* 224:572–575, 1973.

Wolfe, K., and Kern, D. *Create the Body Your Soul Desires*. Southern Century Press, Duluth, GA, 2003.

CHAPTER 28

Ecotherapy: The Healing Power of Nature

Forget not that the earth delights to feel your bare feet and the winds long to play with your hair.

—Kahil Gibran

To smell the fragrant scent of pines as you breathe in the fresh air on a morning hike exhilarates the senses. To feel the warm sunlight on your face as you stroll on a beach and gaze over the ocean fills your heart with a sense of wonder. And no words can adequately describe what you see and feel as you stand atop a mountain before you make your descent on groomed powder ski slopes. Ageless wisdom reminds us time and again that nature in all her glory is a remarkable healing force of homeostasis for mind, body, and spirit. Yet what seems like common sense has become lost in the madness of our current love affair with a 24/7, on-demand, instant-gratification world teeming with technology. With every click of a mouse, text message, Facebook update, Instagram post, and downloaded app, we are losing our inherent connection to the natural world. If Henry David Thoreau, author of the literary classic *Walden* (first published in 1854), were alive today, he would cover his face with disbelief. He's not alone. Experts from all corners of the world believe that our disconnect from nature has become a serious health problem (Sifferlin, 2016).

Consider this: Various estimates suggest that people today spend less than 5 percent of their day outdoors—a remarkable, if not drastic, change from the agrarian society of many decades ago. Moreover, studies investigating the impact of our highly industrialized environment on physical and mental health show that repeated exposure to artificial light, disturbing office noise, bad indoor air quality, chemical particulates from photocopier machines, and electromagnetic pollution all have a harmful effect on wellness. These variables are thought to be directly tied to the related epidemics of stress and chronic disease (Chalquist, 2009).

The abyss separating humankind from nature, however, didn't begin with the invention of the desktop computer or the Internet. For centuries, influential members of Western civilization have advocated a sense of superiority to and dominion over nature. This philosophy continues today, from genetically modified crops and cloning cows for beef steaks, to the installation of bright city lights, yet now there are serious unintended health consequences.

Although the negative health consequences of our deviation from nature are well documented, they can be counteracted. Enter ecotherapy, one of the newest (yet perhaps oldest) means of relaxation to be (re)introduced to humanity in the twenty-first century. **Ecotherapy** is a method of restoring optimal health and well-being through routine exposure to and experience in the natural world.

A Historical Perspective on Ecotherapy

For millennia, health experts of all kinds have known of and promoted the benefits of nature as healer, from ancient Zen gardens to European mineral baths. Frederick Law Olmstead specifically designed New York City's Central Park in 1858 to erase the ills of modern civilization from its citizens. Moreover, the establishment of our national park system was not merely to protect the wilderness, but to ensure our healthy relationship with it. The word *vacation* (to vacate one's urban home) entered the American lexicon after the Civil War, when an 1869 best-selling book written by William H. H. Murray titled *Adventures in the Wilderness* encouraged city slickers from Boston and New York to leave their rushed urban lifestyles and head to the Adirondack Mountains in upper New York state as a tonic for mind, body, and spirit (Perrottet, 2013).

It wasn't until the early 1990s, however, that the field of psychology took a deeper look at the effects of nature on mental health and the connection between psychology and environmentalism. This awareness first began in the city of San Francisco, which is named after St. Francis, the patron saint of nature and animals. Therapists began getting their clients off the couch and into the woods and parks for walks and precious moments of solitude. Before long an emerging field of psychotherapy developed under the umbrella term *ecotherapy*. Deep ecology, ecopsychology, green therapy, terra-psychology, and wilderness therapy fall under this umbrella, and the latest research in this area has given way to a few other related therapies: forest therapy, nature therapy, and even "avatar therapy" (a name based on James Cameron's mega-hit movie,

Avatar). A quick Google search of the term "ecotherapy" (and related terms) highlights the significance—if not the immensity—of this topic as it relates to stress levels and the personal health of human beings.

Several people have made significant contributions to the field of ecotherapy, including Theodore Roszak, Joanna Macy, Bill McKibben, Craig Chalquist, Elizabeth Roberts, Larry Robinson, and Linda Buzzell. These and other professionals showed great interest in the connection between the psyche and the natural world. They began to track patients' anxiety levels, grieving process, fear of death, and other spiritual concerns against rising concerns of deforestation, global warming, animal extinction, and other environmental problems. They found that worrying about environmental problems exacerbated patients' psychological conditions.

Although individuals alone cannot solve global environmental problems, they can influence their immediate environment. It became quite evident to these early researchers that bringing our relationship with nature back into balance can help the psyche. Everything from worksite infrastructure and hospital settings to school classroom environments, backyard gardens, animal therapy, and home design can be part of ecotherapy for people of all ages and demographics. Ecotherapy was first used among professionals in psychology, but this umbrella term now extends well beyond the domains of mental health to physical health and optimal well-being. Ecotherapy, as it turns out, is not merely a cognitive therapy recommended by counselors, therapists, and psychologists. Experts from a great many disciplines, including psychology, immunology, anthropology, outdoor recreation, and even theology, have come to the same conclusion: people need to get outside and expose themselves to nature regularly to reach optimal health. What was once taken for granted (spending time outdoors) is now recognized as an essential part of living a balanced life (**FIG. 28.1**). As emerging research in this new field suggests, the relaxing mind-body effects of being in nature cannot be understated. Simply stated: We are a part of nature, and it is a part of us.

A Nature Deficit Disorder?

Several years ago, a serious revelation came upon author and journalist Richard Louv. He realized that many kids of

> **Ecotherapy:** A method of restoring optimal health and well-being through routine exposure to and experience in the natural world.

FIGURE 28.1 Making a habit of spending quality alone time (solitude) in nature is a great way to calm the mind and bring a better sense of perspective to your life.

today's generation simply don't go outside to play, something that every kid did in his generation and perhaps hundreds of generations before him. (If kids do play outside, it's often through structured enrichment programs like soccer, rather than unstructured exploration.) Although some people might see this inactivity as one reason for childhood obesity, Louv had an entirely different concern: a disconnection from the natural world. It seemed impossible to believe that boys and girls would prefer to spend time indoors with technology rather than outside catching fireflies, watching meteor showers, following butterflies through fields of wildflowers, making snow angels, building forts, watching frogs, or fishing at the nearest pond. He discovered that, by and large, kids of the twenty-first century would rather play video games and watch television than spend actual time outside making discoveries in a field of grass or finding out what's hiding under a brookside rock. This phenomenon is a classic case of a "nature disconnect." The implications are startling.

Becoming well aware that people are not spending much time outdoors and the poor health implications of these

Nature deficit disorder: A term coined by Richard Louv to describe a now-common behavior (affliction) where people (particularly children) simply don't get outside enough, hence losing touch with the natural world and all of its wonder.

Biophilia: Human beings' emotional affiliation to other living organisms (e.g., plants, trees, animals, birds, dolphins and whales) and planet Earth as well.

findings, the gaming industry has taken notice. The 2016 video game Pokémon GO was designed specifically to get people outdoors (despite the mixed message of being outdoors with screen devices).

In his best-selling book, *Last Child in the Woods* (2005), Louv coined the term **nature deficit disorder**, a now-common behavior (affliction) where people simply don't get outside enough, hence losing touch with the natural world and all of its wonder and healing properties. He was quick to learn that it's not just kids who are afflicted; adults (parents) rarely get outside either, and kids model their behavior after their parents' behavior. Yale scholar Steven Kellert, author of *Birthright* (2012), cites that the average person spends over 95 percent of his or her day inside. Kellert explains that this behavior is against our nature; specifically, it goes against the wisdom of our DNA. Being in nature (e.g., forests, beaches, gardens, and parks) is as important as the air we breathe. Without it, health will suffer. Kellert's colleague and renowned Harvard naturalist E.O. Wilson recoined the term **biophilia** to describe human beings' emotional affiliation to other living organisms. Kellert embraces this idea, stating that humans have an inherent connection and affinity to the natural world. Once this birthright is abandoned or forfeited, health issues—both personal and planetary—ensue.

There was a time not too many decades ago when people couldn't wait to get away from their work in offices, as well as mills and factories, and head out of town on a vacation to the nearest seaside beach or mountain forest. It's been this way for over a hundred years. Renowned naturalist John Muir put it this way back in the late nineteenth century: "Thousands of tired, nerve-shaken, over-civilized people are beginning to find out that going to the mountains is going home; that wildness is necessity; that mountain parks and reservations are useful not only as fountains of timber and irrigating rivers, but as fountains of life." Things have only become more complex, high-tech, and stressful since he uttered these words. Moreover, people are now taking their smartphones and laptops (their virtual work desks) with them on vacations, denying themselves the true natural connection they should try to form.

Americans are not the only ones to be over-stressed at work and nature deprived. The Japanese are famous for putting in long hours at the office. In fact, they coined a term to describe those who literally die from job stress: *karoshi*. Many Europeans are equally nature deprived. In fact, in 2008 an odd milestone was achieved in the history

Stress with a Human Face

To get to the Rocky Mountain Wildlife Foundation (RMWF), a wolf rescue sanctuary, you head west on Route 24 from Colorado Springs. It's best to call for directions because some of the roads in these parts have yet to be charted on your favorite mapping site or GPS device. The reason to visit the sanctuary, of course, is to commune with wolves. If you're lucky, you might just get a wolf kiss.

Mark Johnson heads up the RMWF, a project he started in 2001. It began when he found himself the caretaker of a young wolf pup named Cheyenne. Mark's heart is as big as the Rocky Mountains themselves. His goal in raising Cheyenne was to teach people that wolves play an essential role in our ecosystem, and as such, they have much to teach us. Cheyenne became famous for her ability to befriend people, particularly people in need of physical, mental, or spiritual healing.

"Before she passed away, Cheyenne had met over 22,000 people and kissed over 1,900 people. She even had the unique ability to discern those people who had a chronic illness and spend extra time with them. She was a very special wolf with a very special healing energy," Mark said. Soon other wolf pups joined his pack, and the wolves' healing mission grew. One of Mark's proudest moments was taking two wolves, Cherokee and Lakota, to a federal prison and giving the inmates a chance to commune with nature. "It changes people's lives," he said.

As word spread about Cheyenne, Mark found himself taking care of more wolves and half-breeds (wolf and malamute or husky mixes). Some people might call Mark a wolf-whisperer, but he will tell you that he never whispers. He uses a combination of body language and voice commands—never any hand strikes. If you were to visit the wolf sanctuary today, Mark would first give you an educational lecture about wolves and the history of the RMWF. Afterward you would meet several wolves and wolf half-breeds, many of which long for your affection. If you're lucky, you might get a kiss or two, much like the one Lakota is giving Mark in the photo.

---

of humanity: for the first time ever, more people lived in urban cities than in rural areas. As more and more cultures adopt a Western lifestyle confined to an indoor routine, more cultures fall prey to this nature disconnect. As more people spend less time in nature, their indifference (some say apathy) regarding environmental issues dramatically increases. According to the 2008 *Proceedings of the National Academy of Sciences*, since the late 1980s, Americans have decreased their nature-based outdoor recreation by 35 percent (Cordell, 2008). Based on their compilation and analysis of the data, the authors predicted serious impending health issues (Cordell, 2008). Today, researchers from Japan, South Korea, China, and the United States are beginning to examine the effects of nature on various aspects of health, specifically stress levels. All over Japan you can now find "forest therapy" trails for what the Japanese call *shinrin-yoku*, or "forest bathing." The direct translation: Let nature enter your spirit through the five senses. Although many Americans run or walk outside, more often than not, they are tethered to their MP3 players or even their phones all the while (**FIG. 28.2**). With their mind still attached to work or other responsibilities, they negate the "outdoor effect" considerably (Reynolds, 2012).

Physiological Effects of Ecotherapy

In the thought-provoking book, *Your Brain on Nature* (2012), authors Eva Selhub and Alan Logan compile a strong body of research data from all corners of the earth and several disciplines to reveal just how important spending time in nature (or with representations of nature) is to your physical, mental, and emotional well-being. Highlights include the following:

- When people were shown images of nature, there was an increase of alpha waves in the brain with a corresponding increase in serotonin levels (the happy hormone).

- People who were shown photo images of nature reported a decreased sense of anger (whereas

FIGURE 28.2   A vacationer checks his text messages and voicemail while in Rocky Mountain National Park.

FIGURE 28.3   You don't have to be a tree hugger to gain the benefits of "forest bathing." A simple walk in the woods or park does wonders for one's health.

images of urban city life increased levels of frustration and corroborated with functional magnetic resonance imaging [fMRI] images of the amygdala region of the brain).

- Patients who had potted plants in their hospital rooms reported a greater sense of joy and happiness than those patients who had no plants. People who have plants in their houses show decreased stress levels and improved stress moderation.

- Functional MRI findings report that viewing aesthetically pleasing images of nature correspond to increased activity of the parahippocampal gyrus region of the brain, tissue that is rich in opioid receptors associated with the neuropeptide dopamine.

- A two-hour walk in the forest improves sleep quality (Morita et al., 2011).

"If simply viewed in isolation, it might be easy for critics to dismiss some of the research. But when viewed together [subjective and objective data] the picture of nature's influence emerges. Our perception of stress, our mental state, our immunity, our happiness, and our resiliency are all chemically influenced by the nervous system and its response to the natural environment" (Selhub and Logan, 2012).

It may seem intuitive that a walk in nature might decrease stress levels, but today many researchers are finding out exactly what happens to your body as you leave technology behind and acclimate to the rhythms of the natural world. Not only is the newest research fascinating, it also supports what philosophers and therapists have been saying for generations: repeated exposure to the natural elements is good for you. Here are some other recent findings:

- Leisurely walks in a forested area (**FIG. 28.3**) decreased cortisol levels by 12.4 percent as well as significantly decreased resting heart rate and blood pressure (Park, 2010; Miyazaki, 2011).

- Time spent in nature has been shown to increase the number of natural killer cells and anticancer proteins, sometimes by as much as 40 percent (Li et al., 2008).

- Exposure to phytoncides (aromatic scents) emitted by evergreen trees is associated with increased natural killer cells and decreased stress levels (Li et al., 2009).

- Exposing cancer cells grown in Petri dishes to phytoncides increased anticancer proteins and proteases, granzymes A and B, and perforin—substances known to destroy cancerous tumors (Li et al., 2009).

- Hospital patients who had a view of nature (e.g., trees) recovered more quickly from surgery than those who had a view of a brick wall (Ulrich, 1984).

- Exposure to sunlight increases the production of white blood cells, which boost the immune system, and red blood cells, which increase oxygen-carrying capacity (Williams, 2012).

- Repeated natural sunlight exposure (ultraviolet rays) converts cholesterol in your skin to vitamin D (hence sunlight's nickname, the "sunshine vitamin"). Lack of exposure to natural sunlight is known to increase cholesterol levels (Liberman, 1991).

Entrainment: A Symphony in Natural Rhythms

As the last person took their seat, the evening's keynote speaker, composer Steven Halpern, approached the stage and began to speak. It was the last keynote event at the Science and Consciousness Conference in Santa Fe, New Mexico. Halpern's presentation was on the topic of the healing power of music. For the next several minutes he explained that all aspects of nature have a healing rhythm, including the live potted plant on the stage next to the podium. Explaining some basic concepts of physics (such as that everything is energy and everything has a vibration), he began to speak about the vibrations one encounters in a forest, and how humans entrain on these vibrations (through sympathetic resonance) by direct contact. He then attached an electrode to a leaf of the potted plant. Through the magic of audio technology, with the electrode wires plugged into a transducer, a melody came from the speakers; it was an incredible harmonic melody that astounded the audience. "This is just one leaf of a plant," he said. "Can you imagine if I had an electrode attached to all the leaves? Can you imagine what your body senses at the energetic levels as you simply walk through a forest? This is the healing power of nature. Welcome to the healing power of entrainment in nature," he said.

Waterfalls, whale songs, and scores of other natural wonders that make up the world we live in produce a vibration of 7.8 Hz. Also known as the Schumann resonance, this energy vibration is now considered to be the vibration of homeostasis. When separated from this vibration (or when we are in closer proximity to a higher vibration, such as the constant hum of our laptop computers), our bodies become out of sync with the natural energetic rhythms that help keep our health in

check. This disruption affects everything from melatonin production for quality of sleep to the metabolic processes that regulate optimal health. Following the assumption that objects entrain to vibrations, the idea that spending time in nature to "bathe in the natural rhythms of the world" as a way to recalibrate the body's natural rhythms begins to make sense.

Circadian (Bio) Rhythms and Physical Health

You may have heard of the term "bio-rhythms" before, but the correct scientific term is "circadian rhythms." From the Latin root *circa,* which means "about a day," **circadian rhythms** are the various body rhythms that take place in a 24-hour period. Simply stated, circadian rhythms define the body's internal clock. It is this clock that regulates everything from the release of melatonin (the sleep hormone) in the evening to the increase in activity of the gastrointestinal tract. These rhythms are based on Earth's 24-hour rotation on its axis and the corresponding cycles of light and dark; these rhythms have been ingrained in our DNA since the dawn of humanity. In today's world, they are every bit as important as when humans first evolved, yet they are often disturbed, because of our reliance on artificial light and our frequent exposure to glowing television and computer screens.

Research in the field of circadian rhythms suggests that our bodies do best when kept to a regular schedule with regard to sleep, meals, and exercise—for example, eating breakfast, lunch, and dinner at the same times each day; going to bed and waking up at the same times every day; and exercising at approximately the same time every day. People who keep their body on a regular schedule and who are in tune with these rhythms tend to live longer, healthier lives.

Conversely, when we get off schedule, our body's physiology has a hard time adjusting—disrupting circadian rhythms is a form of stress. Over time the result is a greater propensity toward disease and illness as well as more rapid aging. Oncologists will tell you that cancer cells respond best to chemotherapy in the mid-morning

> **Circadian rhythms:** Biological rhythms that occur or cycle within a 24-hour period (e.g., body temperature) that create the body's internal clock, also known as chronobiology. These can be affected by stress, causing a disruption that is even more stressful to the body.

hours as compared to early evening hours. Athletes will tell you that their best competitions are held at the same time as their practice workouts. The human body craves habitual routines for optimal health.

Psychological Effects of Ecotherapy

A clever line for an outdoor camping ad states: *Think outside. No box required.* The message is simple: Get outside! One need look no further to see the healing power of nature than in the scores of poems, books, and essays from people of all walks of life describing nature's best attributes (BOXES 28.1 and 28.2). Throughout history, philosophers, sages, and wisdom keepers the world over have looked to nature to help solve all kinds of problems. If nothing more, the vastness of nature, not

---

BOX 28.1 The Voices of Healing Waters Are Many

The voices of healing waters are many,

Her streams echo to the rising cliffs she once trespassed,

Her waves sing a constant refrain to the beaches,

Her moist clouds whisper incessantly to the trees and mountains,

Soon cascading white ribbons refrain with misty rainbows,

There is music in all of these songs,

And this music dampens my dry heart like a spring rain.

Yet the song I like best is the silent melody of gentle falling snow,

Sometimes her voice is a thunderous roar that begs for my attention,

But mostly water's song is a celebration of life and I celebrate with it.

I long to hear the voices of water as I dangle my feet in a cool lake,

Or wade in the shallow ocean surf, or drink from a cold mountain stream.

The voices of healing waters are many and I sing with them.

—Brian Luke Seaward

BOX 28.2

You ask

why I perch

on a jade green mountain?

I laugh

but say nothing.

My heart, free

like a peach blossom,

in the flowering stream,

going by,

in the depths,

in another world,

not among men.

—Li Po (Ancient Chinese poet)

When the wind blows . . .

This is my medicine

When the sky rains,

This is my medicine

When the heavens are filled with snow,

This is my medicine

When the skies become clear after a storm,

This is my medicine

—Native American Prayer

---

to mention the stunning beauty, from her ocean beaches and cathedral forests to majestic mountain ranges, put into perspective the common, everyday problems of each individual. Being outdoors simply helps clear the mind and reduces personal issues to a manageable size. Perhaps John Muir said it best this way: "I only went out for a walk and finally concluded to stay out till sundown, for going out, I found, was really going in." Carl Jung also noticed that nature provided a canvas on which to explore the mind's landscape. He often wrote of the benefits of walks in nature and how immersion in nature benefits the yearning for wholeness; he offered dire warnings through his writings that when the connection to nature is severed, serious repercussions would result in harm to the psyche of the individual (Jung, 2002).

In the book *Refuge*, author and naturalist Terry Tempest Williams describes a parallel storyline between her mother's fight with cancer (which was a result of nuclear testing) and the Great Salt Lake floods that destroyed much wildlife in 1983. Williams is not alone in her attempt to connect the parallels of nature to our own lives. Over 2,000 years ago Chinese philosopher Lao Tzu created a philosophy of life based on living in the rhythms and cycles of nature, which he called Taoism and eloquently described in his classic book, *The Tao Te Ching*.

Do your physical surroundings affect your thoughts and behavior? Students of psychology might be interested to learn of the *Journal of Environmental Psychology*, which reports on the influences of nature, space, design, and architecture on various aspects of cognition, memory, attention span, concentration, and behavior. Recent investigations into the relationship between nature and cognition include work by Rachel and Stephen Kaplan from the University of Michigan that led to their "attention restoration" theory. Apartment dwellers who were given a view of the natural elements (e.g., trees) were reported to show significant increases in concentration skills when compared to residents who did not have natural element views. Through their extensive body of research, the Kaplans advocate nurturing a strong bond with nature as a means of promoting mental health (Kaplan, 1995, 2001).

Nature and the Art of Solitude

Experts in the field of sociology agree that modern life is not only fast-paced, but also crowded and noisy. Taking time to separate yourself from the cacophony of civilization and seek quiet solitude is a time-honored prescription for inner peace. In spending time alone, one gets the chance to clear the mind of mental clutter and put problems and issues in perspective. One also gains clarity in honoring the simplicity of life rather than the human-made complexities to which we have become so accustomed. Solitude is a different concept from isolation. Although many people have become isolated behind a computer screen, **solitude**—the intentional act of separation from friends and family—is anything but isolation. More than cleansing the mind, solitude becomes, for some, a spiritual experience. Early nineteenth-century British poet Lord Byron described it this way in his poem, *Solitude*:

> To sit on rocks, to muse o'er flood and fell,
>
> To slowly trace the forest's shady scene,

> Where things that own not man's dominion dwell,
>
> And mortal foot hath ne'er or rarely been;
>
> To climb the trackless mountain all unseen,
>
> With the wild flock that never needs a fold;
>
> Alone o'er steeps and foaming falls to lean;
>
> This is not solitude, 'tis but to hold
>
> Converse with Nature's charms, and view her stores unrolled.

Spiritual Moments

To have a hummingbird gently perch on your finger as it drinks nectar from the cup of your palm, to swim alongside a baby humpback whale in the crystal blue waters of Tahiti (**FIG. 28.4**), or to spot an elk or gaze at the aurora borealis with curtains of green, yellow, and red lights flashing across the winter sky is more than a brief connection to nature; by all accounts it's a spiritual experience. Quite simply, these moments take your breath away. In a stress-filled world it is easy to become myopic, if not egocentric, with a score of work and life responsibilities that obscure our vision to the bigger world we live in. These spiritual moments in nature serve as a gentle reminder that we are part of a much bigger universe; making this humbling realization

FIGURE 28.4 Swimming alongside a 2-week old, 12-foot baby humpback whale in the Tahitian island lagoon of Moorea is considered by many to be nothing less than a spiritual experience.

Solitude: The intentional act of seeking alone time in a quiet space, away from family, friends, and daily distractions as a means of seeking inner peace.

puts our lives back in perspective. The awareness of the diurnal cycles and seasonal changes offers a tangible reminder to move with the flow of nature, rather than in opposition to it. In survey after survey, people cite ocean beaches, lakes, and mountain streams as being the most relaxing places to be in nature—anywhere there is water. Just as the human body has rivers of energy called meridians, so too does the planet have rivers of energy (often located by bodies of water) called ley-lines. Although wisdom keepers will tell you that the entire planet is sacred, it is common to find many energetic spots on the planet deemed particularly spiritual that some call heaven on earth.

Earning "Nature Points"

No one is keeping score, but racking up nature points is a good idea as a means to bring balance back into your life. How often do you get outside? If you answer "Every day," but you are plugged into an electronic device or talking on your phone the whole time, you don't score any nature points. (However, using your phone to take a few photos of nature will earn you a few points.) There are no nature points for having a dog or cat, but if you walk your dog outside, you do get points. If you see (and even more importantly, can identify) wildlife species, you definitely get nature points. In what phase is the moon tonight? If you have to look at a calendar for the answer, no nature points. If you make a point to watch the Perseid meteor showers or lunar eclipse, this scores you lots of nature points.

Securing nature points outdoors involves the use of all five senses at the same time; it requires you to be fully present in the moment of the experience. And although there is no official scorecard for nature points, scoring lots of points each day makes you a winner.

Best Application of Ecotherapy

The message of ecotherapy is clear. We need to spend more time outside in nature. Going for a walk or a run in the woods, taking time to watch the sunset or sunrise, or turning off your smartphone or tablet and going outside at night to become familiar with the constellations, phases of the moon, and occasional meteor showers are just some of the many ways you can return to the surroundings of your natural world. So is getting a bird feeder in your backyard. In doing any one of these things, you begin to see your life in correct proportion to the bigger picture of life. Dedicating time each day outdoors, even if it involves nothing more than getting some exposure to the sun to recalibrate your circadian rhythms, is as important as brushing your teeth or paying your bills. Nature can be found anywhere, including city parks and local floral greenhouse nurseries. Find some nature near you, and get to know it!

SUMMARY

- For millennia, philosophers have touted nature as a great healing agent for mind, body, and spirit.

- Ecotherapy, originally a discipline of psychology, promotes mind-body-spirit health effects through the repeated exposure to nature.

- Nature deficit disorder is a term coined to explain the lack of exposure to nature due to people's love affair with technology.

- The physiological effects of spending time in nature include decreases in resting heart rate, blood pressure, and cortisol and increases in white blood cell count and biochemicals that have calming effects on the brain.

- Exposure to nature has a calming effect on the mind and human spirit. Being in the presence of a force greater than yourself puts things in perspective by reducing the scale of personal problems.

- Circadian rhythms are based on a 24-hour cycle of Earth's rotation on its axis; these rhythms affect countless physiological aspects of health, including sleep patterns and various metabolic processes.

- Nature affects us both objectively (e.g., raising dopamine and serotonin levels, and decreasing cortisol levels) and subjectively (giving us a feeling of peace, wonder, and awe).

- Routinely exposing yourself to nature enhances mental cognition, including attention span and possibly memory and concentration skills.

STUDY GUIDE QUESTIONS

1. What is ecotherapy?

2. What is nature deficit disorder?

3. What is biophilia?

4. List three effects of nature on human physiology.

5. How does the concept of entrainment correspond to ecotherapy?

6. How do disruptions of circadian rhythms affect health and stress levels?

7. Explain how ecotherapy affects both mind and body.

8. Describe how solitude can be therapeutic.

9. Give three examples of how you earn nature points in your present weekly routine. Then describe changes to your routine that would allow you to score more points in the future.

REFERENCES AND RESOURCES

Buzzell, L., and Chalquist, C. *Ecotherapy: Healing With Nature in Mind*. Sierra Club Books, San Francisco, 2009.

Chalquist, C. Ecotherapy: A Look at Ecotherapy Research Evidence. 2009. http://cliftoncommunitypartnership.org/uploads/articles/2009/08/2009080315530099/ecotheraphyeco.2009.0003.lowlink.pdf_v03.pdf.

Cordell, H. K. The Latest Trends in Nature-Based Outdoor Recreation. 2008. http://foresthistory.org/Publications/FHT/FHTSpring2008/Cordell.pdf.

Halpren, S. A Report on the Second Annual International Conference on Science and Consciousness (ICSC), Albuquerque, New Mexico, April 29–May 3, 2000. http://realityshifters.com/pages/articles/2000icscreport.html.

Jung, C. *The Earth Has a Soul: The Nature Writings of Jung* (edited by Sabini, M.). North Atlantic Books, Berkeley, CA, 2002.

Kaplan, R. The Nature of the View from Home. Psychological Benefits, *Environment and Behavior* 33(4):507–542, 2001.

Kaplan, S. The Restorative Benefits of Nature, *Journal of Environmental Psychology*. 15: 169–182, 1995.

Kellert, S. *Birthright: People and Nature in the Modern World*. Yale University Press, New Haven, CT, 2012.

Kellert, S. Living On Earth [Interview]. December 14, 2012.

Li, Q., et al. Effect of Phytoncide from Trees on Human Natural Killer Cell Function, *International Journal of Immunopathology Pharmacology* 4:951–959, 2009.

Li, Q., et al. A Forest Bathing Trip Increases Human Natural Killer Cell Activity and Expression of Anti-cancer Proteins in Female Subjects. *Journal of Biological Regulators and Homeostatic Agents* 22(1):45–55, 2008. http://www.ncbi.nlm.nih.gov/pubmed/18394317.

Liberman, J. *Light: Medicine of the Future*. Bear and Company, Sante Fe, NM, 1991.

Louv, R. *Last Child in the Woods*. Algonquin Books, Chapel Hill, NC, 2005.

Louv, R. *The Nature Principle; Reconnecting with Life in a Virtual World. Algonquin Books, Chapel Hill, NC,* 2011.

Mao, G. Effects of Short-Term Forest Bathing on Human Health in a Broad-Leaved Evergreen Forest in Zhejiang Province, China. *Biomedical Environmental Science* 25(3):317–324, 2012. http://www.ncbi.nlm.nih.gov/pubmed/22840583.

Miyazaki, Y. Science of Natural Therapy. 2011. http://www.marlboroughforestry.org.nz/mfia/docs/naturaltherapy.pdf.

Morita, E., et al. A Before and After Comparison of the Effects of Forest Walking on Sleep of a Community-Based Sample of People with Sleep Complaints. *Biopsychosocial Medicine* 5(13), 2011. http://www.ncbi.nlm.nih.gov/pmc/articles/PMC3216244/.

Park, B. J., et al. The Physiological Effects of *Shinrin-yoku* (Taking in the Forest Atmosphere or Forest Bathing): Evidence from Field Experiments in 24 Forests across Japan. *Environmental Health and Preventive Medicine* 15(1):18–26, 2010. https://www.ncbi.nlm.nih.gov/pmc/articles/PMC2793346/.

Perrottet, T. Birthplace of the American Vacation. *Smithsonian* 68–75, April 2013.

Reynolds, G. The 'Outside' RX: Six Natural Prescriptions for Improving your Body and Mind. *Outside,* December 2012. http://www.outsideonline.com/fitness/wellness/The-Outside-RX.html

Roberts, E., and Amidon, E. *Earth Prayers*. Harper Collins, New York, 1991.

Roszak, T. (Ed.). *Ecopsychology, Restoring the Earth, Healing the Mind*. San Francisco, Sierra Club Books, 1995.

Seaward, B. L. *A Beautiful World; The Earth Songs Journals*. White Light Publications, Boulder, CO, 2011.

Seaward, B. L. *Earth Songs: Mountains, Water and the Healing Power of Nature* (DVD). White Light Pictures, Boulder, CO, 2010.

Selhub, E., and Logan, A. *Your Brain on Nature*. John Wiley and Sons, New York, 2012.

Sifferlin, A. The Healing Power of Nature. *Time*, p. 24. July 25, 2016.

Swanson, J. *Communing with Nature: A Guidebook for Enhancing Your Relationship with the Living Earth*. Illahee Press, Corvalis, OR, 2001.

Ulrich, R. View Through a Window May Influence Recovery from Surgery. *Science* 224(4647):420–421,1984.

Williams, F. The Nature Cure: Take Two Hours of Pine Forest and Call Me in the Morning. *Outside*, 79–92, December 2012.

Williams, F. *The Nature Fix: Why Nature Makes Us Happier, Healthier, and More Creative*. W. W. Norton and Company, New York, 2017.

Williams, T. *Refuge*. Vintage Books, New York, 1992.

Creating Your Own Stress-Management Program

Human beings are like tea bags. You don't know your strength until you're put in hot water.

—Bruce Laingen
Former Chargé D'affaires,
American Embassy in Iran

Creating a stress-management program is a very individual undertaking. There is no set formula or series of dogmatic guidelines, only suggestions. If there is a secret to successful stress management, it is to cultivate and utilize your inner resources. Just like Dorothy, who all along had the ability to leave Oz and return home, you have the power of your inner resources. Inner resources are those abstract qualities and characteristics that become a tangible bridge over the chasm of chaos. These include, among others, intuition, creativity, willpower, faith, humor, love, courage, self-reliance, and optimism.

After these are nurtured, how does one access inner resources? The answer begins with awareness and the desire to grow. From this desire comes a greater consciousness of yourself and the events and circumstances in your environment. Ultimately, these circumstances contribute to your growth and maturation. Awareness and desire serve as catalysts for positive change.

No one relaxation technique works for everyone. Nor is one coping strategy applicable in every stressful situation. Both focus on a wide range of functions. Exposure to an array of coping strategies and relaxation techniques allows you to pick and choose those that are most appropriate and will ensure the greatest returns. The initial purpose of this book was to do just that: to provide as great an exposure as possible. Now, knowledge can certainly be gained by reading a book such as this; and our educational system is based on this premise. But it has been demonstrated time and time again that people are less likely to forget something when they have experienced it for themselves. Thus, putting the concepts in this book into practice is where the real learning will take place. *The Art of Peace and Relaxation Workbook*, which can be found online, is perhaps the best template to build your foundation of a personal stress management program.

The following are my best suggestions for constructing the best personal stress-management program:

1. *Make a habit of spending some quality time each day to get to know yourself.* Take perhaps half an hour every day for self-exploration, whether in the form of journal writing, art therapy, music therapy, exercise, or something else. Be selfish. Believe that you deserve this time, and you will find it takes priority in your life. Time management is one of the major cornerstones of a successful stress-management program; allocate time for this self-development. Keep in mind that there is a fixed amount of time in a day and that when a new activity is planned, an old one must be edited out of the daily agenda. Survey your daily routine to note where you can squeeze in a block of time for this purpose. If half an hour seems too long, start with five minutes and build from there. And remember that the occasion when you feel you do not have time for self-exploration is when you need it most.

2. *Make a habit of reading your emotional barometer.* Recognize the times when you feel angry, frustrated, anxious, and guilty. When you catch yourself feeling a certain emotion, ask yourself, What triggered this response? Why did this emotion surface? What is the most appropriate action or behavior to resolve the feeling? Emotional well-being is the ability to feel and express the full range of emotions, but it also means being able to control these emotions. On

average, people laugh 15 times a day. Make sure you fill this quota.

3. *Practice the art of unconditional love.* Self-esteem is so critical to effective stress management that it should be given top priority in the design of your stress-management program. Focus on your positive attributes, not what you perceive to be your negative ones, and work to enhance these. Don't just think of yourself as a physical entity; appreciate your intellectual, emotional, and spiritual aspects, as well. Self-esteem is the seed of unconditional love. To say hello, to smile, to share a song, to give positive feedback—these are all expressions of love. And when these behaviors are practiced, they seem to double our own sense of self-esteem and self-love.

4. *Nurture your creativity skills.* Creativity is second in importance only to self-esteem as a means to manage stress. Creativity plays a direct role in problem solving and an indirect role in distracting attention from stressful episodes during moments of "play." Don't let childhood memories suffocate your creative abilities.

5. *Balance all components of your well-being and take time to nurture them.* Stress is often expressed in terms of things being out of balance. In physiological terms, this is called lack of homeostasis. But our mental, emotional, and spiritual components can also lack homeostasis. Search out and practice ways to help you achieve mental homeostasis by learning how to either stimulate or desensitize your intellect, depending on its current state. Be attentive to your emotional component, as well, by being aware of emotional states as they arise. Learn to express, not suppress, your emotions, but do it in a way that is both therapeutic and diplomatic. Take good care of your body. Exercise it regularly. Feed it good nutrients, and get adequate amounts of sleep. Finally, give attention to your spirit by taking steps to enhance the maturation of your higher consciousness. Practice centering, emptying, grounding, and connecting on a regular basis. Search for and fulfill your purpose in life.

6. *Be like a child.* Children, like adults, experience acute stress, but they have not yet learned to be self-conscious about giggling or to suppress their tears. Before children are taught to conform to adult expectations, they are rich in curiosity, imagination, and creativity. These and other characteristics of young children can be relearned if we take the time to do so.

Designing and implementing a stress-management program of your own may not seem easy at first, but it doesn't have to be difficult. It just takes a little desire, some discipline, and the realization that you are worth the effort. Most important, you don't have to be hit with an avalanche of stressors to begin the process of creating a sense of calm in your life. You can begin right now, gradually, one step at a time.

The following strategic plan takes into account insights and wisdom from the previous chapters in the book. As you take yourself through the progression of steps, feel free to embellish this plan to make it as personal for your situation as possible.

Step 1. Identify Your Stressors. List your top five stressors (from most stressful to least stressful) and explain each with a sentence. The purpose of this exercise is to identify the problem, which is the first step in resolving it.

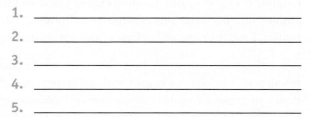

Step 2. Interventions. Now, look at your list of stressors. Ask yourself which problems trigger a sense of fear and mark these with an *F*. Next, ask yourself which of these issues promote feelings of anger (and remember—anger can surface in a great many ways, from impatience to rage and hostility). Place an *A* next to all of these. It's okay if you mark one or more items on your list with both an *A* and an *F*. Remember, after you have identified the underlying emotion associated with the problem, it becomes easier to address and resolve it.

Step 3. Integration. Stress affects all aspects of our being: mind, emotions, body, and spirit.

■ *Mind:* Do you feel overwhelmed or bored with your problems? If you feel overwhelmed, this is a sign that there is too much on your plate; some things need to be edited out or eliminated. If you feel bored, your threshold of stimulation probably is not being reached, and you might want to consider changing or adding something to achieve this balance. Mental well-being also involves attitudes and perceptions.

Describe one thing you can do to find mental balance. _____

_____

■ **Emotions:** The spectrum of stress-based emotions is rather wide, yet each emotion can be traced to some element of fear or anger. In the course of your day, ask yourself how you feel (not think, but feel). If you find that stress emotions occupy more than 50 percent of your time on a regular basis, this indicates an emotional imbalance.

Describe one thing you can do to find mental balance. _____

_____

■ **Body:** As you have learned throughout this book, stress can and will affect physical well-being. Do you have any health problems that you can associate with stress?

Describe one thing you can do to establish mental balance. _____

_____

■ **Spirit:** Take a look at your current list of stressors. How many of your stressors involve relationships, values (or value conflicts), and a meaningful purpose in life? Spiritual balance can be attained in a great many ways, from time spent alone in meditation to support groups or prayer.

Describe one thing you can do to find mental balance. _____

_____

Self-esteem is a part of spiritual well-being. Low self-esteem sets the stage for problems ranging from a bad hair day to the day from hell.

Describe one thing you can do to find mental balance. _____

_____

Step 4. Your Personal Stress-Management Strategy. *Coping skills* are mental and emotional skills that help you change a threatening perception to a nonthreatening perception. Humor, reframing, time management, creativity, prayer, and social orchestration are just a few examples of coping skills.

Take a look at the list of stressors that you completed in step 1. Try to match at least three effective coping skills with each stressor.

Skills that you are now using:

1. _____

2. _____

3. _____

4. _____

5. _____

6. _____

Skills that you would like to incorporate:

1. _____

2. _____

3. _____

4. _____

5. _____

6. _____

Relaxation skills include any and all activities that return you to a sense of calm and tranquillity.

Skills that you are now using:

1. _____

2. _____

3. _____

4. _____

5. _____

6. _____

Skills that you would like to incorporate:

1. _____

2. _____

3. _____

4. _____

5. _____

6. _____

Time management plays a huge role in putting stress-management strategies to work, especially relaxation techniques. Here is an important question to ask yourself: Where can I find a block of time (15 to 30 minutes) to sit or lie down comfortably and relax?

REFERENCES

Carlson, R. *Don't Sweat the Small Stuff*. Hyperion Books, New York, 1998.

Kirsta, A. *The Book of Stress Survival: How to Relax and Live Positively*. Simon and Schuster, New York, 1987.

Seaward, B. L. *The Art of Calm: Relaxation through the Five Senses*. Health Communications, Deerfield Beach, FL, 1999.

Wheeler, C. M. *10 Simple Solutions to Stress*. New Harbinger Publications, Oakland, CA, 2007.

Glossary

ABC rank-order method A time-management technique for which things are prioritized by order of importance.

Absurd or nonsense humor This type of humor is best exemplified by the works of Gary Larson's *The Far Side*. The comedian Steven Wright is also a prime example.

Acceptance Often the final outcome of reframing a situation: Accepting that which you cannot change and moving on with your life.

Acetylcholine A chemical substance released by the parasympathetic nervous system to help the body return to homeostasis from the stress response.

ACTH axis A physiological pathway whereby a message is sent from the hypothalamus to the pituitary and then on to the adrenal gland to secrete a flood of stress hormones for fight or flight.

Active imagination A term coined by Carl Jung describing a mental imagery process in which, in a lucid dream state or relaxed state, you consciously imagine (and resolve) the end of a recurring dream. Active imagination is a form of visualization.

Active meditation A term given to a physical activity (e.g., walking, swimming) that promotes a cleansing of the mind through repetitive motion.

Acute stress Stress that is intense in nature but short in duration.

Adaptation A behavior and attitude considered the epitome of the acceptance stage of grieving, in which a person adapts to the new situation and no longer views him- or herself as a victim.

Adaptors The most difficult type of nonverbal communication to decode, such as the folding of one's arms across the chest or the crossing of one's legs.

Adenosine-triphosphate-creatine Chemical compound in muscles that produces energy (anaerobically) for muscle contraction.

Adrenal cortex The portion of the adrenal gland that produces and secretes a host of corticosteroids (e.g., cortisol and aldosterone).

Adrenal gland The endocrine glands that are located on top of each kidney that house and release several stress hormones including cortisol and the catecholamines epinephrine and norepinephrine. The adrenal gland is known as "the stress gland."

Adrenal medulla The portion of the adrenal gland responsible for secreting epinephrine and norepinephrine.

Aerobic exercise Rhythmic physical work using a steady supply of oxygen delivered to working muscles for a continuous period of not less than 20 minutes (e.g., jogging).

Affect displays Facial expressions used to express a particular emotion (e.g., amazement).

Aggressive behavior style An aggression-based behavior that employs intimidation and manipulation.

Agility Maneuverability and coordination of gross and fine motor movements.

Agnostics Individuals who do not know if there is a higher source.

Alarm reaction The first stage of Selye's general adaptation syndrome, in which a threat is perceived and the nervous system is triggered for survival.

All-or-none conditioning principle A principle of exercise that states that to benefit from physical training, you must have the right intensity, frequency, and duration for each component of fitness challenged.

Allostatic load A term coined by stress researcher Bruce McEwen to replace the expression "stressed out"; the damage to the body when the allostatic (stress) response functions improperly or for prolonged states, causing physical damage to the body.

Altered state of consciousness A shift in one's thought process, typically from left-brain to right-brain thinking, to become more aware and more receptive.

Alternative medicine Modalities of healing (homeostasis) that include nearly all forms of stress management techniques. Also known as complementary or integrative medicine.

American Massage Therapy Association The governing body that accredits massage therapy schools and certifies graduates in massage therapy.

Anabolic functioning A physiological process in which various body cells (e.g., muscle tissue) regenerate or grow.

Anaerobic exercise Physical work done in the absence of oxygen; activity that is powerful and quick but does not last more than a few minutes (e.g., weightlifting).

Archetypes A Jungian term to describe primordial images that become symbolic forms with an inherent understanding among all people.

Aromatherapy The use of essential oils to promote relaxation through the sense of smell, often used in many types of body work as a complementary relaxation method.

Art of balance A term in hatha yoga that requires a balance of *asanas* on both the right and left sides of the body.

Art of breathing A term in hatha yoga that honors the importance of the pause of the breath (*pranayama*).

Art of conscious stretching An expression that suggests to yoga participants to be fully mindful as they assume and maintain an *asana*.

Art therapy A coping technique of self-expression and self-awareness employing various media to describe feelings and thoughts in ways that verbal language cannot.

Arteriosclerosis The third and final stage of coronary heart disease, wherein the arteries become hardened by cholesterol buildup, calcium deposits, and loss of elasticity.

Artist Von Oech's term to identify the second stage of the creative process, in which one plays with or incubates ideas that the explorer has brought back.

Artistic roadblocks The perceived inability to express oneself though creative expression (often based on fear).

Aspartame Two amino acids that combine to make an artificially sweet taste, including one that is documented to affect brain chemistry and cognitive function. Like MSG, this substance is known as an "excitotoxin." (Aspartame is also marketed as Nutrasweet.)

Assertive behavior style A behavior style that is neither passive nor aggressive, but one that is tolerant and considerate in the quest for individual rights.

Assertiveness The term given to a behavior that is neither passive nor aggressive, but proactively diplomatic.

Atheists Individuals who do not believe in a higher source.

Atherogenesis The first stage of coronary heart disease, wherein a fat streak appears on the inner lining of artery walls.

Atherosclerosis The second stage of coronary heart disease, wherein artery walls slowly become occluded by cholesterol-plaque buildup.

Attitudes These are beliefs about our values, often expressed as opinions.

Auditory imagery A term representing a means to imagine or recall a song or melody in one's head to promote relaxation.

Autogenic discharge Physical sensations such as muscle twitching, numbness, and perhaps some emotional responses (tears) released by the unconscious mind from autogenic training sessions.

Autogenic training Introduced by Schultz and Luthe; a relaxation technique in which the individual gives conscious messages to various body parts to feel warm and heavy; effects are thought to result from vasodilation to the specified body regions intended for warmth and heaviness.

Autoimmune diseases Diseases that occur because of an overactive immune system, which "attacks the body." Examples include lupus and rheumatoid arthritis.

Autonomic dysregulation Increased sensitivity to perceived threats resulting from heightened neural (sympathetic) responses speeding up the metabolic rate of one or more organs.

Autonomic nervous system (ANS) Often referred to as the automatic nervous system, the ANS consists of the sympathetic (arousal) and parasympathetic (relaxed) nervous systems. This part of the central nervous system requires no conscious thought; actions such as breathing and heart rate are programmed to function automatically.

Avoidance versus confrontation A dichotomy to describe how some people deal with stress.

Awareness Learning to become aware of a specific behavior in the effort to change it.

Awfulizing A mindset wherein one tends to see (or hope for) the bad in every situation.

Balance The ability to maintain equilibrium in motion.

Bandha A series of breathing exercises to unlock chronic pain.

Bathroom humor A form of humor often described as vulgar, crude, and tasteless, it derives its name from the use of various bodily functions known to occur in the bathroom.

Beginning position From the starting position, one begins to move his or her hands upward to eye level, palms facing down.

Behavior modification model A model that illustrates the steps taken to change a negative behavior into a positive one.

Behavioral changes One of three categories used in mental imagery (e.g., quitting smoking, improved athletic performance, weight-loss programming).

Behavioral substitution Substituting a new (positive) behavior for a less desirable one.

Behavioral therapy A therapy based on the work of John B. Watson, in which coping and relaxation techniques are used to desensitize oneself to stress.

Behaviors Actions (direct or indirect) that are based on conscious (sometimes unconscious) thoughts.

Belly breathing The most common form of relaxation by means of placing the emphasis of one's breathing on the lower stomach area (belly or diaphragm) rather than the upper chest (thoracic area), thereby decreasing sympathetic response and inducing a greater sense of relaxation.

Bhakti yoga One of five yogic paths; the path of devotion.

Binary One of two categories used to describe biofeedback; an example might include a device that lets one know of an effect of biofeedback on a specific biological function that results in lights appearing on a panel.

Biochemical theory A theory suggesting that music is received internally through the eardrum with sounds converted into neurochemicals that are registered by the brain, which one then finds either pleasant or unpleasant.

Bioflavonoids Nonnutrients found in foods (fruits and vegetables) that contain antioxidants and seem to provide a means of fighting cancer and other illnesses. Bioflavonoids provide the colors in foods.

Biophilia Human beings' affiliation to other living organisms (e.g., plants, trees, animals, birds, dolphins and whales) and planet earth, as well.

Bioplasma Another term for the etheric layer of energy closest to the physical body.

Biphasic Survivor personality traits; the ability to use both right-brain and left-brain thinking processes to successfully deal with a problem or stressors.

Bisociation The ability to perceive two aspects to a situation, in this case, resulting in a laugh.

Black Elk An early twentieth-century Native American elder whose perspective of spirituality is often cited as the clarion vision of our relationship with Mother Earth.

Black humor Humor about death and dying; thought to decrease fear of death.

Blaming Shifting the responsibility of a problem away from yourself.

Blog A term depicting someone's Internet journaling practice. Unlike a personal journal that is kept confidential, a blog is a public document to express opinions, beliefs, and newsworthy items of the author.

Blueprint aspect A term to suggest that the visualization has a goal to complete or accomplish; thus, the blueprint is the template for completion (e.g., a healed wound).

Borysenko, Joan An early pioneer in the field of psychoneuroimmunology who emphasized the importance of spirituality as part of the mind–body concept.

Bow Pose (Dhanurasana) A classic yoga *asana* intended to promote balance with the muscles of the lower back and stomach as well as neck and shoulders.

Boxing A scheduling technique used in time management for which the day is divided into 3- to 5-hour chunks of time devoted to accomplishing big projects.

Brief grief A concept that suggests that some grieving is appropriate and healthy versus unhealthy, prolonged grieving.

Broken heart syndrome A name given to the condition in which symptoms of a heart attack occur as a result of emotional stress; when stress hormones temporarily overwhelm heart tissue cells.

Buffer theory A theory suggesting that people invited to a support group act to buffer the participants from stress to lessen the impact.

Buzan writing style A specific journal approach to access the powers of both the right and left hemispheres of the brain through words and images.

Campbell, Joseph Renowned for his wisdom about human mythology gathered from all cultures over time, Campbell's greatest work illustrates the human experience as the hero's journey as exemplified in the template of every great story.

Cannon, Walter Twentieth-century Harvard physiologist who coined the term "fight or flight."

Cardiovascular (EKG) biofeedback Biofeedback that measures the electrical activity of the heart muscle in terms of amplitude and frequency of each heartbeat.

Cardiovascular endurance The ability of the heart, lungs, and blood vessels to supply oxygenated blood to the working muscles for energy metabolism.

Catabolic functioning A metabolic process in which metabolites are broken down for energy in preparation for, or in the process of, exercise (fight or flight).

Catastrophizing Making the worst out of every situation.

Catharsis Emotional release through crying, yelling, laughing, and the like.

Centering A time for soul searching, cultivating one's internal relationship.

Central nervous system (CNS) Consists of the brain and spinal column, whereas the peripheral nervous system (PNS) comprises all neural pathways to the extremities.

Cerebration A term used to describe the neurological excitability of the brain, associated with anxiety attacks and insomnia.

Chakras Chakra (pronounced "shock-ra") is a Sanskrit word for spinning wheel. Chakras are part of the subtle anatomy. The seven major chakras align from the crown of the head to the base of the spine and connect to various endocrine glands. Each major chakra is directly associated with various aspects of the mind-body-spirit dynamic. When a specific chakra is closed, distorted, or congested, the perception of stress, disease, or illness may ensue.

Chaotic antisocial The first stage of Peck's hierarchy of spiritual growth in which one's spiritual essence is lacking (spiritual bankruptcy).

Chi The universal life force of subtle energy that surrounds and permeates everything.

Chondromalacia Chronic knee pain, typically from excessive running and improper foot placement.

Chopra, Deepak A contemporary physician and metaphysician originally from India, he presents and integrates the ageless wisdom of spirituality, quantum physics, and medicine.

Chronic stress Stress that is not as intense as acute stress but that lingers for a prolonged period of time (e.g., financial problems).

Circadian rhythms Biological rhythms that occur or cycle within a 24-hour period (e.g., body temperature) that create the body's internal clock, also known as chronobiology. These can be affected by stress, causing a disruption that is even more stressful to the body.

Civility The practice of good manners and appropriate behavior.

Classical conditioning A learned behavior to a stimulus with regard to involuntary functions, such as becoming hungry when the clock strikes 12 noon.

Clinical biofeedback A process using one or more specially designed machines to amplify body signals (e.g., heart rate, muscle tension) and display these signals in a way that can be interpreted so that their intensity can be changed for the health of the individual.

Closed-loop feedback system A term used to describe the dynamics of biofeedback with its sensors attached to various parts of the human body.

Clustering A scheduling technique used in time management for which errands are grouped by location (e.g., dry cleaners, post office, pharmacy).

Cobra (Bhujanghasana) A classic yoga *asana* intended to promote balance with the lower back.

Codependency A stress-prone personality with many traits and behaviors that seem to increase the likelihood of perceived stress and the inability to cope effectively with it; addictive in nature; based on the need to make others dependent to receive self-validation.

Cognitive-dissonance theory A theory suggesting that the collective energy of one's support group supersedes any individual's negative experience of stress.

Cognitive distortion Distorting a situation beyond how bad it actually is.

Cognitive restructuring A coping technique; substituting negative, self-defeating thoughts with positive, affirming thoughts that change perceptions of stressors from threatening to nonthreatening.

Collective unconscious A term coined by psychologist Carl Jung; the deepest level of consciousness, which connects all people together as one; divine consciousness.

Color therapy A type of mental imagery exercise for which color is imagined as an agent for tranquility (e.g., green) or healing (e.g., blue).

Combative versus preventive Another dichotomy to describe how some people deal with stress.

Compensation The ability to cultivate and utilize one's strengths in times of need rather than claim victimization.

Compensation theory A theory suggesting that support groups compensate for various emotional losses one experiences during stress.

Concentric contraction A muscle contraction during which the length of the muscle shortens.

Conditional response A learned response (in this case through biofeedback) to control various biological functions such as heart rate and blood pressure.

Conditioned response A response learned over time to a particular (negative) situation, such as displaying caution or apprehension about something perceived as stressful.

Conflict-management styles There are five conflict-management styles: withdrawal, surrender, hostile aggression, persuasion, and dialogue.

Conflict resolution The resolution of arguments displayed as three styles: content conflict, value conflict, and ego conflict.

Connecting A realization that we are all connected, and the connection is made and nurtured through love.

Conventional sense of humor A term to describe more than one person laughing at the same thing, all agreeing to its humor.

Cool-down period A designated time right after the stimulus period to decrease circulation to the body's periphery and return to a resting state.

Coping responses Positive skills to cope with stress.

Corpse Pose (Shavasana) This is the typical position assumed at the close of each yoga session to restore energy.

Corticosteroids Stress hormones released by the adrenal cortex, such as cortisol and cortisone.

Cortisol A stress hormone released by the adrenal glands that helps the body prepare for fight or flight by promoting the release of glucose and lipids in the blood for energy metabolism.

Corumination Stress-based conversations between women as a means of coping by finding support among friends.

Cousins, Norman (1915–1990) An author of the classic book *Anatomy of an Illness* (1976), he used humor to help heal himself from a serious disease and brought the importance of humor to the national consciousness in terms of mind-body-spirit healing, paving the way for the field of psychoneuroimmunology.

Creation spirituality A term coined by theologian Matthew Fox to describe the paths of human spirituality blending the laws of physics and theology.

Creative problem solving A coping technique utilizing creative abilities to describe a problem, generate ideas, select and refine a solution, implement the solution, and evaluate its effectiveness.

Creative sense of humor This describes a person who thinks of jokes or funny things, but may be too shy to share them.

Cultural roadblocks Cultural thinking patterns that limit our ability to take in new ideas, leading to asymmetrical thinking.

Daily life hassles Occasional hassles, like locking your keys in your car; when combined with many other annoyances in the course of a day, these create a critical mass of stress.

Deceptive procrastinator Someone who attempts to work on projects, but only scratches the surface, stalling on the completion of tasks.

Decibels A unit of measurement (named in honor of Alexander Graham Bell) to denote the level of sound/noise measured as pressure through air.

Decoding A process in which the listener attempts to understand what the speaker has encoded in his or her verbal message.

Defense mechanisms Described by Sigmund Freud; unconscious thinking patterns of the ego to either decrease pain or increase pleasure.

Delegation Relinquishing control of a responsibility by turning it over to someone else.

Denial In some cases, this is the first step toward changing a negative behavior; one of the primary defense mechanisms noted by Freud in which one disbelieves what occurred when personally threatened.

Depression A state of mind in which thoughts are clouded by feelings of despair. Physiologists suggest that depression is caused by a chemical imbalance; psychologists suggest that depression is the result of unresolved stress emotions (anger turned inward).

Descartes, René A seventeenth-century scientist and philosopher credited with the reductionistic method of Western science (also known as the Cartesian principle). He is equally renowned for his influential philosophy of the separation of mind and body as well as the statement, "I think, therefore I am."

Desires In the Buddhist perspective of stress, desires are conditions and expectations that are associated with goals. Desires with attachments cause stress.

Detached observation A term derived from inclusive meditation during which the individual observes him- or herself meditating, in essence detaching from the ego's desire.

Diaphragmatic breathing The most basic relaxation technique; breathing from the lower stomach or diaphragm rather than the thoracic area.

Direct approach A term used in autogenic training when you not only suggest the words *warm* and *heavy* but also imagine the flow of blood to these body regions such as hands or feet.

Direct-effect theory A theory suggesting that social contact serves to provide uplifting aspects to the individual and thus pleasure to the ego.

Displacement The transference of emotional pain (usually anger) from a threatening source (one's boss) to a nonthreatening source (one's cat).

Distractions Material possessions (greed or wealth) and/or behaviors (addictions) that distract one from making progress on the spiritual path. Distractions begin as attractions, pulling one off the spiritual path indefinitely.

Distress The unfavorable or negative interpretation of an event (real or imagined) to be threatening that promotes continued feelings of fear or anger; more commonly known simply as stress.

Divine personification A term signifying one's evolving perception or image of the divine, whatever this happens to be.

Divinity theory The belief that humor is a gift from God.

Double entendre A joke that has two meanings.

Dream incubation A process in which an idea to be used as dream material is consciously seeded to prompt the unconscious mind during sleep; a technique effective to help resolve stressors.

Dream therapy A coping technique in which dreams, including recurring dreams, are explored and deciphered to help understand acute or chronic stressors.

Dry humor Often found in storytelling (e.g., Garrison Keillor, Mark Twain), in which the humor is subtle and clever.

Eccentric contraction A muscle contraction during which the size of the muscle lengthens.

Ecotherapy A method of restoring optimal health and well-being through routine exposure to and experience in the natural world.

Effleurage The first of five progressive steps/hand maneuvers in the Swedish massage that consists of long strokes along the length of the muscle tissue.

Ego A term coined by Freud naming the part of the psyche that not only triggers the stress response when threatened, but also defends against all enemies, including thoughts and feelings generated from within.

Egosyntonic A visualization expression meaning that images created/suggested in the visualization process must fit with the values and ideals that are most beneficial.

Einstein, Albert A world-renowned theoretical physicist who revolutionized perceptions of reality with the equation $E = mc^2$, suggesting that everything is energy. His later years focused on a spiritual philosophy including pacifism.

Electrodermal (EDR) biofeedback Biofeedback that measures the sweat response from skin.

Electroencephalographic (EEG) biofeedback Biofeedback that measures the electrical activity of the brain.

Electromyographic (EMG) biofeedback Biofeedback that measures the electrical impulses from specific muscles.

Emblems Physical gestures that tend to replace words, such as the thumbs-up signal.

Emotional literacy A term used in reference to one's ability to express oneself in an emotionally healthy way. Someone who routinely "goes ballistic" would be said to lack emotional literacy.

Emotional roadblocks Obstacles to the creative process, in the guise of fear, such as the fear of making a mistake (failure), rejection, or the unknown.

Emotional well-being The ability to feel and express the full range of human emotions and to control these feelings, not be controlled by them.

Emptying Also known as the "dark night of the soul" and the winter of discontent. The emptying process is a time to release, detach, and let go of thoughts, attitudes, perceptions, and beliefs that no longer serve you.

Enablers A term coined in the alcohol recovery movement, referring to a person who enables a spouse, parent, or child to continue either a substance or process addiction.

Encoding The process in which the speaker attempts to frame his or her thoughts and perceptions into words.

Endogenous-overreactive An overreactive immune system affected by internal pathogens (e.g., rheumatoid arthritis and ulcers).

Endogenous-underreactive An underreactive immune system affected by internal pathogens (e.g., cancer).

Energy psychology A term used to describe the collaboration of subtle energy (chakras, meridians, and the human energy field) with psychological issues and trauma involving certain aspects of stress.

Enhanced receptivity In the practice of meditation, one's mind opens to become more receptive to ideas that are often censored by the ego during normal consciousness.

Entrainment In physics, the mutual phase locking of like oscillations; in human physiology, organs or organisms giving off strong vibrations influencing organs or organisms with weaker vibrations to match the stronger rate of oscillation; thought to conserve energy.

Environmental disconnect A state in which people have distanced themselves so much from the natural environment that they cannot fathom the magnitude of their impact on it.

Environmental roadblocks Personal constraints such as time, money, or a host of responsibilities that impede the creative process.

Epigenetic theory A theory subscribed to by cell biologist Bruce Lipton. The theory states that DNA is greatly affected by the cell's environment, not just the unfolding of the genetic code. Lipton states that emotional stress is part of the cell's environment.

Epinephrine A special neurochemical referred to as a catecholamine that is responsible for immediate physical readiness for stress including increased heart rate and blood pressure. It works in unison with norepinephrine.

Essentic forms Musical patterns (vibrations) that are thought to influence neuropeptide activity and thus metabolic activity in the body.

Etheric energy The layer of energy closest to the physical body (also known as the etheric body).

Eustress Good stress; any stressor that motivates an individual toward an optimal level of performance or health.

Evaluation The process of observing and analyzing a newly adopted behavior, to see if the new behavior works.

Exclusive meditation A form of meditation wherein concentration is focused on one object (e.g., *mantra*, *tratak*) to the exclusion of all other thoughts, to increase self-awareness and promote relaxation.

Execution The third of three aspects essential for effective time management, in which tasks are actually completed.

Exogenous-overreactive An overreactive immune system affected by external pathogens (e.g., allergies).

Exogenous-underreactive An underreactive immune system affected by external pathogens (e.g., colds and flu).

Exploders People exhibiting a mismanaged-anger style by exploding and intimidating others as a means to control them.

Explorer Von Oech's term to identify the first stage of the creative process in which one begins to look for new ideas by venturing outside one's comfort level.

Exposure desensitization A process of learning to destress from something by brief, yet safe, encounters with the stressor.

External relationships One's relationships with others (e.g., family, friends, and colleagues) as well as the earth, water, and air we breathe.

Faith An optimistic attitude adopted to cope with stress for which one perceives a connection to something bigger than oneself (e.g., a divine source).

Fasting the heart A T'ai Chi term that explains the flow of one's life energy as a moving essence, and finding comfort in solitude.

Fear of death Anxious feelings about death and the dying process.

Fear of failure Anxious feelings of not meeting your own expectations.

Fear of isolation Anxious feelings of being left alone.

Fear of rejection Anxious feelings of not meeting the expectations of others.

Fear of the loss of self-dominance Anxious feelings of losing control of your life.

Fear of the unknown Anxious feelings about uncertainty and future events.

Fight-or-flight response A term coined by Walter Cannon; the instinctive physiological responses preparing the body, when confronted with a threat, to either fight or flee; an evolutionary survival dynamic.

Fish (Matsyasana) A classic yoga *asana* intended to promote balance with the lower back.

Fist over Head (Araha Chakrasana) A classic yoga *asana* intended to promote balance with arms and shoulders.

Flexibility The ability to use a muscle group throughout its entire range of motion.

Flexible optimism A term coined by Seligman to convey that we can all harness the power of optimism into positive thinking.

Flotation tanks A moderate sensory deprivation tank in which a person floats on his or her back in warm water to calm the nervous system through decreased stimulation.

Focusing The ability to recognize the body signals of oncoming stress (e.g., muscle tension, increased breathing, sweating).

Forgiveness A coping technique for anger-related stressors for which a shift in attitude is adopted toward those against whom a grudge was previously held.

Formal-institutional The second stage of Peck's hierarchy of spiritual growth, in which one tends to find comfort in the guidelines of religious institutions.

Fox, Matthew A Christian theologian renowned for his theory of creation spirituality and many other concepts. He was silenced by the Vatican in 1989 for one year followed by excommunication in 1999. He is now an Episcopal minister in California.

Frankenfood A name coined in Europe to promote the hidden dangers of genetically modified organisms (GMOs). GMOs are currently banned in Europe.

Frankl, Viktor (1905–1997) World-renowned psychiatrist and survivor of the Nazi Auschwitz Concentration Camp who coined the term "logo therapy" to describe a purpose in life focus. Author of the best-seller *Man's Search for Meaning*.

Free radicals Highly reactive oxygen molecules with an aberrant electron that can cause damage to cell membranes and DNA.

Freeze response Part of the stress response wherein the individual neither fights nor flees but freezes like a deer caught in headlights, paralyzed as if the person has forgotten to run.

Frequency The number of exercise sessions per week; the ideal number is three.

Friction The third of five progressive steps/hand maneuvers in the Swedish massage, also known as kneading the muscle tissue.

General adaptation syndrome A term coined by Hans Selye; the three distinct physiological phases in reaction to chronic stress: the alarm phase, the resistance phase, and the exhaustion phase.

Genetically modified organisms (GMOs) DNA manipulation of foods whereby the gene from one species is spliced into the DNA of a different species to enhance quality or shelf life. GMOs are currently associated with a host of food allergies. An example of this would be taking the genes from a flounder and splicing them into the DNA of a tomato.

Glucocorticoids A family of biochemical agents that includes cortisol and cortisone, produced and released from the adrenal gland.

Good-sport sense of humor This describes someone who can take a practical joke without suing.

Grasp the bird's tail The fifth (roll back and press) and sixth (push) steps in the classic T'ai Chi movement with a specific series of hand motions and feet placement.

Grounding The point at which new insights may be revealed to assist a person to move from point A to point B.

Guided mental imagery An exercise in which one is guided through a series of suggestions provided by an instructor, therapist, or counselor to enhance one's imagination.

Hardy personality A term coined by Maddi and Kobasa; personality characteristics that, in combination, seem to buffer against stress: control, commitment, and challenge.

Hatha yoga One of five yogic paths; the path of physical balance.

Head of Cow (Gomukhasana) A classic yoga *asana* intended to promote balance with arms and shoulders.

Helpless-hopeless personality Describes a person who has given up on life, or aspects of it, as a result of repeated failure.

Hero's journey Mythologist Joseph Campbell's classic template of the human journey with three stages: departure, initiation, and return.

Hertz (Hz) A physics term describing the number of oscillations or vibrations produced per second.

Hierarchy of needs Maslow's concept of a stair-step approach of consciousness (thoughts and behaviors), ranging from physiological needs to self-transcendence.

Hobby A pleasurable pursuit or interest outside one's daily work responsibilities through which one begins to make order out of chaos (e.g., botanical gardening).

Holistic medicine A healing approach that honors the integration, balance, and harmony of mind, body, spirit, and emotions to promote inner peace. Every technique used in stress management is considered to support the concept of holistic medicine.

Homeostasis A physiological state of complete calmness or rest; markers include resting heart rate, blood pressure, and ventilation.

HPA axis The hypothalamic-pituitary-adrenal axis, a term synonymous with the ACTH axis.

Human energy field Subtle human anatomy that goes by many names, from the electromagnetic field around an object to a colorful aura. The human energy field is thought to be composed of layers of consciousness that surround and permeate the physical body.

Human Triangle (Trikonasana) A classic yoga *asana* intended to promote balance with the upper torso.

Humor A perception of something funny or comical; not a mood, but a perception that can trigger a feeling or mood of joy and happiness. Also, the defense mechanism noted by Freud that both decreases pain and increases pleasure.

Humor therapy A coping technique; the use of humor and comic relief as a means to relieve and reduce emotional stress by focusing on the funny, humorous, and positive aspects of life.

Hydrotherapy The use of baths, hot tubs, Jacuzzis, and flotation tanks to augment the sense of touch to promote relaxation.

Hypothalamus Often called the "seat of the emotions," the hypothalamus is involved with emotional processing. When a thought is perceived as a threat, the hypothalamus secretes a substance called corticotrophin-releasing factor (CRF) to the pituitary gland to activate the fight-or-flight response.

Idiosyncratic A term meaning self-generated, such as images used in visualization that are created by the person performing the visualization.

Illusion of control A term used in association with codependent behavior, thinking that one can control (manipulate) things/others that one really cannot.

Illustrators Movements or postures used in combination with verbal conversation, such as various hand motions.

Immediate (effects of stress) A neural response to cognitive processing in which epinephrine and norepinephrine are released, lasting only seconds.

Immune dysregulation An immune system wherein various functions are suppressed; now believed to be affected by emotional negativity.

Immunoenhancement A term used to describe various stress management techniques that appear to boost the immune system.

Important-versus-urgent method A prioritization time-management technique in which tasks are categorized.

Inclusive meditation A form of meditation in which all thoughts are invited into awareness without emotional evaluation, judgment, or analysis. Zen meditation is an example.

Incongruity theory A theory that states the reason we laugh is because when two concepts come together in our head and they don't make sense, we get a chuckle.

Increased awareness The first step of an effective coping technique when one becomes more aware of the situation.

Indirect approach A term used in autogenic training when you suggest to yourself that various body parts are warm and heavy.

Individuation A term coined by Carl Jung to describe self-realization, a process leading to wholeness.

Ineffability Experiences that cannot be expressed verbally; especially common during meditation.

Information processing The second step of an effective coping technique when one works toward resolution of the problem.

Information-processing model A model that reveals how we potentially perceive sensory information, for better or worse.

Information seeking A common coping technique; searching for detailed information to increase awareness about a situation that has become a perceived threat.

Infradian rhythms Biological rhythms that occur less than once in a 24-hour period (e.g., women's menstrual period). These can be affected by stress.

Insightful meditation An expression given to any type of meditation (inclusive or exclusive) whereby a person, after clearing the mind of interrupting thoughts and ego chit-chat, begins to expand his or her awareness to the intuition, or the deep-seated wisdom of the collective unconscious, thus giving insight into the person's life.

Insightful internal relationship How well do you know and love yourself? What is your relationship with your higher self?

Insomnia Poor-quality sleep, abnormal wakefulness, or the inability to sleep.

Instinctual tension A Freudian term used to highlight the tension between the mind's impulses and the body's response, suggesting that stress is humanly inherent.

Instrumental coping The implementation of a series of effective coping skills to alter one's reaction to stress.

Intellectual/expressive roadblocks Obstacles to the creative process; in this case, created by the language we use that gives bias to our way of thinking (e.g., doorway versus entrance).

Intensity The physical challenge (stress) placed on a specific physiological system for exercise.

Intercessory prayer One style of prayer for which the individual seeks assistance from a higher (divine) source to intervene or assist with his or her problems.

Intermediate stress effects The hormonal response triggered by the neural aspects of the adrenal medulla that are released directly into the blood, lasting minutes to hours.

Internal body images One of three categories used in mental imagery for the purpose of healing disease or illness (e.g., shrinkage of cancerous tumors, mending broken bones).

Irony A type of humor in which the opposite from what was originally expected occurs.

Irrational An overwhelming feeling of anxiety based on a false perception.

Isometric contraction A muscle contraction during which there is no visible change in the length of the muscle fiber.

Jesus of Nazareth A remarkable spiritual leader with a timeless message of compassion, forgiveness, and integrity.

Jnana yoga One of five yogic paths; the path of knowledge.

Jonah complex A term coined by Abraham Maslow to illustrate the fear of not maximizing one's potential.

Journal writing A coping technique; expression of thoughts, feelings, memories, and ideas in written form, either prose or poetry, to increase self-awareness.

Judge Von Oech's term to identify the third stage of the creative process in which one selects the best idea and prepares it for manifestation.

Jung, Carl A twentieth-century psychiatrist who, under the initial tutelage of Sigmund Freud, forged a new premise of psychology honoring the importance of the human spirit. He became the second greatest influence in the field of psychology.

Karma yoga One of five yogic paths; the path of action.

Kinesthetic A visualization expression meaning the actual involvement through the five senses in the practice of this technique.

Kirlian photography A technique developed by Russian Semyon Kirlian enabling the viewer to see the electromagnetic energy given off by an object such as the leaf of a tree or human hand. This technique is one of several technologies that substantiates the human energy field.

Kneading Also known as friction in Swedish massage, when hands knead the muscle tissue to promote relaxation.

Koan An unsolvable riddle that aims to shift one's consciousness from analytical thoughts to profound contemplation.

Kübler-Ross (MD), Elisabeth (1926–2004) Psychiatrist renowned for her stages of grieving (denial, anger, bargaining, withdrawal, and acceptance) and death with dignity.

Kundalini yoga One of five yogic paths; the path of spiritual awakening.

Lactic acid A by-product of the breakdown of ATP, which can also be used as a source of energy (anaerobic).

Law of Detachment A reminder to release and let go of all thoughts that hold back our human potential.

Law of Dharma or Life Purpose This law invites contemplation of one's purpose in life.

Law of Giving A reminder to live life with an open heart to give and receive freely.

Law of Intention and Desire A reminder to set our intentions for both big and small goals yet not become encumbered by the ego's desires.

Law of Karma (or Cause and Effect) A reminder that we reap what we sow.

Law of Least Effort A reminder to go with the flow with things that we cannot control as well as to live in harmony with nature.

Law of Pure Potentiality A reminder to be silent and look within for guidance and insights rather than validation through external means.

Lazarus, Richard Renowned stress researcher credited with the concept of daily life hassles.

Left-hand ward-off The third step in the classic T'ai Chi movement with a specific series of hand motions and feet placement.

Leftover guilt A term coined by psychologist Wayne Dyer explaining the ill effects of unresolved guilt left over from an early childhood experience.

Leukocytes The family of cells that constitute the major component of the immune system.

Life-change units A unit of measurement that corresponds to items on the Social Readjustment Rating Scale.

Life-of-the-party sense of humor The class clown, the person who gets all the laughs.

Lifestyle behavior trap A behavior in which people have a hard time saying no and end up overwhelmed with multiple responsibilities.

Lift hands The eighth step in the classic T'ai Chi movement, incorporating a series of specific hand motions and foot placement to facilitate optimal *Chi* movement.

Light therapy An extension of color therapy for which full-spectrum lighting or one color from the light spectrum is used to promote homeostasis and healing.

Limbic system The midlevel of the brain, including the hypothalamus and amygdala, which is thought to be responsible for emotional processing.

Locus of control A sense of who or what is in control of one's life; people with an internal locus of control take responsibility for their actions; those with an external locus of control place responsibility on external factors like luck or the weather; the latter is associated with the helpless-hopeless personality, a stress-prone personality.

Logotherapy A term coined by psychiatrist Viktor Frankl describing the search for meaning in one's life.

Love The emotion studied and advocated by Leo Buscaglia as being the cornerstone to self-esteem and ultimately altruism.

Lymphocytes Immune system cells that are housed throughout the lymphatic system, with two percent in circulation at any one time.

Magnifying A term to describe blowing things out of proportion.

Mandala A circular-shaped object used as a visual mantra for the purpose of clearing the mind of unnecessary (ego-based) thoughts.

Mantra Typically a one-syllable word (e.g., *om*, *peace*, *love*) or a short phrase that acts like a broom to sweep the mind of nonessential (ego-based) thoughts.

Massage therapy A relaxation technique; the manipulation of skin, muscles, ligaments, and connective tissue for the purpose of releasing muscle tension and increasing physical comfort of musculature and surrounding joints.

Mechanistic model A health model based on the concept that the body is a machine with parts that can be repaired or replaced.

Meditation A practice of increased concentration that leads to increased awareness; a solitary practice of reflection on internal rather than external stimuli.

Melatonin A hormone secreted in the brain that is related to sleep, mood, and perhaps several other aspects of physiology and consciousness.

Mental imagery Using the imagination to observe, in the first person, images created by the unconscious mind; falls into three categories: (1) images that replicate peaceful scenes to promote relaxation, (2) images that substitute a less desirable behavior with a more healthy one, and (3) images that help to heal damaged body tissue.

Mental well-being The ability to gather, process, recall, and communicate information.

Meridian A river of energy with hundreds of interconnected points throughout the body, used in the practice of acupuncture and shiatsu massage.

Metadisease A concept by Maslow that depicts origins of physical disease as being based in unresolved emotional issues.

Metamessages The underlying intention of verbal communication when people are indirect with their comments thus adding to miscommunication.

Metaphysical theory A theory that suggests that music is a gift from God.

Methylated xanthine The active ingredient in caffeine, which triggers a sympathetic response.

Mindfulness A type of meditation in which all senses concentrate on the activity being performed during the present moment, like eating an apple or washing the dishes.

Mineralocorticoids A class of hormones that maintain plasma volume and electrolyte balance, such as aldosterone.

Misoneism A term coined by Carl Jung to explain the fear or hatred of anything new (fear of the unknown).

Modeling The ability to emulate or imitate our behaviors from the observation of others we respect (e.g., parents, schoolteachers, and peers).

Modified behaviors The third step of an effective coping technique when one works toward a sense of resolution.

Monosodium glutamate (MSG) A food brightener that is documented to affect brain chemistry and cognitive function. Like aspartame, this substance is known as an "excitotoxin." MSG is merely listed as "spice" on many condiments.

Mother Earth spirituality The expression used to describe the Native American philosophy with the divine through all of nature.

Mountain Pose (Tadasana) A classic yoga *asana* intended to promote balance and stability.

Mozart effect A term coined by renowned music therapist Don Campbell to illustrate the lifelong effect of classical music on healing, learning, and behavior.

Multitasking Acting on many responsibilities at one time (driving and talking on a cell phone) to save time, yet potentially compromising the integrity of both outcomes.

Muscular endurance The ability to sustain repeated contractions over a prolonged period of time.

Muscular strength The ability to exert a maximal force against a resistance.

Music therapy The ability to listen to, sing, or perform music as a means to promote relaxation and homeostasis.

Myofascial release Deep-tissue massage created by John Barnes to release tension by working with the myofascial (soft connective) tissue.

Mystical (peak) sensation A euphoric experience during which one feels a divine or spiritual connection with all life.

Mystic-communal The fourth stage of Peck's spiritual hierarchy in which one perpetually and joyfully seeks life's answers in the mystical divine universe.

Nadam An auditory mantra for which a repetitive sound is used to help clear the mind of unnecessary (ego-based) thoughts.

Natural killer (NK) cells Large lymphocytes that can detect endogenous antigens, thus helping to destroy mutant cells.

Nature Deficit Disorder A term coined by Richard Louv to describe a now-common behavior (affliction) in which people (particularly children) simply don't get outside enough, hence losing touch with the natural world and all of its wonder.

Neoplasms Another term for cancerous tumors.

Networking Establishing and nurturing personal and professional relationships to assist with the completion of personal responsibilities.

Neurolinguistic programming (NLP) A program designed to look at how our thoughts control our language and how our language influences our behavior.

Neuropeptides Unique messenger hormones produced in the brain (and other organs of the body) that fit into the receptor sites of lymphocytes.

Neurotheology A name coined to describe how the brain is hardwired to perceive metaphysical or mystical experiences of a divine nature.

Neustress Any kind of information or sensory stimulus that is perceived as unimportant or inconsequential.

Newton, Issac An eighteenth-century physicist who advocated the mechanistic paradigm of the universe, which was then adapted to the human body.

Nocebos A bona fide, effective medicine that does *not* work because the patient doesn't believe that it will.

Nonlocal mind A term given to consciousness that resides outside the brain (possibly outside the human energy field), which may explain premonitions, distant healing, and prayer.

Nonverbal communication All types of communication that do not involve words, including body language and facial expressions.

Nonverbal expression Many thoughts and feelings cannot be expressed verbally, giving rise to art therapy as a means of nonverbal expression.

Noo-dynamics A term coined by Viktor Frankl describing a state of tension, a spiritual dynamic, that motivates one to find meaning in life. The absence of noo-dynamics is an existential vacuum.

Norepinephrine A special neurochemical referred to as a catacholamine that is responsible for immediate physical readiness to stress, including increased heart rate and blood pressure. It works in unison with epinephrine.

Occupational stress Job-related stress, which often comes from occupational duties for which people perceive themselves as having a great deal of responsibility yet little or no authority or decision-making latitude.

Oncogene A gene in the DNA double-helix strand thought to be responsible for producing a mutant (cancerous) cell.

One Knee to Chest (Pawan Muktasana) A classic yoga *asana* intended to promote balance with the lower back.

Opening-up meditation *See* Inclusive meditation.

Operant conditioning A learned behavior that stems from a voluntary function or something about which we make a conscious decision.

Palliative coping A positive emotional regulation process during a stressful encounter (e.g., responding, not reacting).

Paradigm shift Moving from one perspective of reality to another.

Paralanguage A term used to describe speaking aspects such as volume, tone, and pitch that actually color verbal language.

Parasympathetic The branch of the central nervous system that specifically calms the body through the parasympathetic response.

Parasympathetic rebound The parasympathetic effect of relaxation (homeostasis) after physical exercise. Typically the response is such that parameters such as heart rate and blood pressure dip below preexercise levels.

Pareto principle Also known as the 80/20 Rule, this time-management technique prioritizes tasks by the satisfaction factor.

Parody A style of humor in which something or someone is made fun of. Self-parody is thought to be the best type of humor to reduce stress.

Passive-aggressive A mismanaged-anger style (*see* Underhanders) in which people seek revenge while at the same time fronting a smile.

Passive behavior style A behavior influenced by intimidation that can often lead to feelings of resentment and victimization.

Passive concentration A term coined by the creators of autogenic training to denote the conscious receptivity of self-generated thoughts.

Peaceful resolution The ultimate goal of any effective coping technique allowing one to move on with life.

Peck, M. Scott A contemporary psychiatrist who reintroduced the aspect of human spirituality and psychology with his classic book, *The Road Less Traveled*.

Perception distortion A sense during meditation (an altered state) in which, for example, one's arms and legs seem extremely heavy.

Perceptual roadblocks Obstacles to the creative process, placed by the ego, in the role of the judge.

Perennial philosophy A term used by Aldous Huxley to describe human spirituality, a transcendent reality beyond cultures, religions, politics, and egos.

Perfectionism Perpetually imposing above-human standards on oneself.

Perfectionist A person who is obsessed with the details of every task, aiming for quality, yet who ends up getting caught up with the details and missing the whole picture.

Personal cosmology Fox's term to explain one's personal relationship with the divine that dwells in each of us.

Personal unconscious A repository of personal thoughts, perceptions, feelings, and memories.

Personality traits Thoughts and behaviors that combine to form or color one's personality; in this case, cognitive traits associated with survival.

Pessimism Looking at the worst of every situation.

Pet therapy The use of hand contact with pets to promote relaxation among hospital patients, nursing home patients, and now everyday pet owners who claim better health through decreased resting heart rate and blood pressure values.

Petrissage The second of five progressive steps/hand maneuvers in the Swedish massage, it consists of a series of rolls, rings, and squeezes made by the fingertips or palm of the hand.

Phases of a workout Warm-up, stimulus period (target zone), and cool-down.

Physical well-being The optimal functioning of the body's eight physiological systems (e.g., respiratory, skeletal).

Pitch The human ear detects vibrations or oscillations as pitch.

Pituitary gland An endocrine gland ("master gland") located below the hypothalamus that, upon command from the hypothalamus, releases ACTH and then commands the adrenal glands to secrete their stress hormones.

Placebos A nonmedicine (e.g., sugar pill) that can prove to be as effective as the medicine it is supposed to represent. Healing occurs as a matter of belief.

Poetry therapy A therapeutic tool; a modality of writing poetry to enhance both increased awareness and emotional catharsis of a variety of issues.

Polarized thinking A condition in which things are always viewed in extremes, either extremely good or horribly bad.

Polyphasia A trait of thinking or doing many activities at once, also known as multitasking. This is also a trait of the Type A personality.

Positive psychology A field of modern psychology emphasizes the brighter side of human behavior with a specific focus on (1) positive emotions, (2) positive personality traits, and (3) positive institutions.

Post-traumatic stress disorder (PTSD) The mental, emotional, and physical repercussions experienced after an extremely stressful experience (e.g., war combat, natural disasters, rape and sexual abuse, car accidents).

Poverty consciousness A term used to describe an attitude or perception held by a person reinforcing the idea that he or she never has enough money, which in turn becomes a self-fulfilling prophecy.

Power Force multiplied by distance over time.

Pranayama A Sanskrit term to describe diaphragmatic breathing that restores one's vital life force of energy.

Pranayama A yogic term describing the concept of breath control during each of the *asanas* (yoga postures).

Predictive encoding A mental training strategy to utilize the unconscious mind for better performance; an academic term for *mental imagery*.

Present-centeredness An altered state in which one is fully aware of the present moment with no regard to past or future time periods.

Primary creativity Maslow's term for the first stage of the creative process in which ideas are conceived.

Principle of Cyclical Growth A Taoist concept suggesting that everything is cyclic: the moon, tides, seasons, and all aspects of human life.

Principle of Dynamic Balance A Taoist concept revealing the opposites that make up the balance of life.

Principle of Harmonious Action A Taoist concept that reminds us to work in harmony with nature, not in opposition to it or control over it.

Principle of Oneness A Taoist concept of oneness with nature serving as a reminder of our oneness with it.

Prioritization The first of three aspects necessary in effective time management, for which tasks are given priority for completion.

Process addiction The addiction to a behavioral process such as shopping, intercourse, gambling, television watching, cutting, and codependent behaviors.

Procrastinator Someone who employs diversions and avoidance techniques rather than tackling a host of responsibilities.

Progressive muscular relaxation (PMR) A relaxation technique; tensing and then relaxing the body's muscle groups in a systematic and progressive fashion to decrease muscle tension.

Projection The act of attributing one's thoughts and feelings to other people so that they are less threatening to the ego.

Prolonged effect of stress Hormonal effects that may take days or perhaps more than a week to be fully realized from the initial stress response.

Proportional One of two categories used to describe biofeedback; an example might be a device that lets one know the amount of physiological change, as determined by the pitch of a noise.

Psychic equilibrium A term coined by Carl Jung to describe the balance of thought (and subsequent health-wholeness) between the conscious and unconscious minds, by having the conscious mind become multilingual to the many languages of the unconscious mind (e.g., dream interpretation).

Psychoneuroimmunology The study of the effects of stress on disease; treats the mind, central nervous system, and immune system as one interrelated unit.

Psychophysiology A field of study based on the principle that the mind and body are one, where thoughts and perceptions affect potentially all aspects of physiology.

Psychosomatic A term coined from Franz Alexander's term *organ neurosis*, used to describe a host of physical illnesses or diseases caused by the mind and unresolved emotional issues.

Psychospirituality A focus in the field of psychology, influenced by Carl Jung, to acknowledge the spiritual dimension of the psyche.

Puns A type of wordplay that may leave people sighing rather than laughing.

Qigong A form of Chinese energy exercise and energy healing, in which *Qi* or *Chi* is directed through the body as a means to balance one's energy. Qigong healing may involve a Qigong healer to facilitate the energy healing process.

Quick-witted humor A style of humor that is based on quick wit without using sarcasm. Quick-witted humor often involves clever wording or phrasing that catches you off guard and leaves you impressed. Examples include the works of Mark Twain and NPR's "Car Talk" radio show.

Rage reflex A concept coined by Darwin that reflects the aggressive (fight) nature of all animals as a means of survival.

Rational emotive behavior therapy (REBT) Developed by Albert Ellis as a means to help people cope with anxiety by changing the perceptions associated with the stressor.

Rational A term to mean useful, as in rational fear of poisonous snakes.

Rationalization The reinterpretation of the current reality to match one's liking; a reinterpretation of the truth.

Reactionaries A term associated with the codependent personality illustrating a behavior of reacting, rather than responding, to stress.

Reconstruction The reinterpretation (from negative to neutral or positive) of a stressor (also known as reframing).

Reframing The name given to the thought process by which a negative perception is substituted for a neutral or positive one, without denying the situation.

Regulators Nonverbal messages used to regulate or even manipulate a conversation, including eye movements and other types of body language.

Relaxation response A term coined by Dr. Herbert Benson, who Americanized TM to make it more accessible to the Western world.

Release/relief theory Freud's theory of laughter is based on his concept that all laughter is the result of suppressed sexual tension, thus relieving it through humor.

Repression The involuntary removal of thoughts, memories, and feelings from the conscious mind so they are less threatening to the ego.

Residual tension A slight degree of muscle tension visible in some people who think they are relaxed.

Restrictive meditation A form of meditation wherein concentration is focused on one object (e.g., *mantra*, *tratak*) to the exclusion of all other thoughts, to increase self-awareness and promote relaxation.

Retail therapy The behavior attributed to people who go shopping to alleviate their stress. The consequence is buying things they don't really need or cannot always afford.

Reticular activating system (RAS) The neural fibers that link the brain to the spinal column.

Return to nature A T'ai Chi expression to explain the joys of childhood: innocence, laughter, and play.

Right-hand ward-off The fourth step in the classic T'ai Chi movement with a specific series of hand motions and feet placement.

Roadblocks A metaphor to explain how stressors act as obstructions on the human journey or spiritual path, yet these are not meant to be avoided—rather they are meant to be dismantled, circumnavigated, or transcended so that one can move on with one's life.

Rolfing Deep-tissue massage created by Ida Rolf to promote better posture by working with the soft connective tissue around and between muscles.

Runner's high The euphoric feeling generated from beta-endorphins released from cardiovascular exercise.

Salute to the Sun (surya namaskar) One of the most classic and symbolic series of hatha yoga *asanas*, often performed at the beginning and/or end of each yoga session.

Sapir-Whorf hypothesis The idea that our perception of reality is based largely on the words we use to communicate or express ourselves.

Sarcasm Thought to be the lowest form of humor, the word *sarcasm* means to tear flesh. Because sarcasm is a latent form of anger, it promotes rather than reduces stress.

Satire A written or dramatic form of parody. Examples include the works of Bill Maher, Louis C. K., and the movie *Shrek*.

Scheduling The second of three aspects necessary in effective time management, for which prioritized tasks are scheduled for completion.

Schismogenesis A term coined by Deborah Tannen suggesting that exaggerated conversation styles become intensified under stress, thus adding to miscommunication.

Schumann's resonance A physics term given to the actual vibration of the planet Earth: 7.8 Hertz.

Seasonal affective disorder (SAD) The physiological response to lack of sunlight that results in feelings of depression.

Secondary creativity Maslow's term for the last stage of the creative process in which a strategy is played out to have the selected idea come to fruition.

Secondary PTSD The emotional and financial stress of the family members and friends of those with PTSD.

Selected awareness The receptivity of the conscious mind to acknowledge and receive specific thoughts or messages.

Self-actualization The fifth level of Maslow's hierarchy of needs, at which one experiences a sense of personal fulfillment.

Self-disclosure The process in which a person reveals various aspects of him- or herself that are not readily apparent.

Self-efficacy A term coined by Albert Bandura to describe a sense of faith that produces a "can-do" attitude.

Self-esteem The sense of underpinning self-values, self-acceptance, and self-love; thought to be a powerful buffer against perceived threats.

Self-hypnosis A form of relaxation; an individual provides him- or herself with suggestions to relax (as with the suggestions of autogenics) as opposed to having someone else provide the suggestions.

Self-imposed guilt A term coined by psychologist Wayne Dyer to describe the guilt one places on oneself when a personal value has been compromised or violated.

Self-punishers People exhibiting a mismanaged-anger style by denying a proper outlet of anger, replacing it with guilt. Self-punishers punish themselves by excessive eating, exercise, sleeping, cutting, or even shopping.

Self-regulation The ability to control various aspects of human physiology; a self-produced or self-generated activity (e.g., self-hypnosis).

Self-talk The perpetual conversation heard in the mind, usually negative and coming from the critical (ego), which rarely has anything good to say.

Self, *the* (two versions, Tibetan psychology) The *Self* is the higher self or the true self; the *self* is identified as the false self or the ego-driven self.

Self-transcendence A sense of becoming one with something bigger than oneself; a mystical experience that occurs in meditation. Also the sixth and highest stage of Maslow's hierarchy of needs, at which one offers oneself altruistically to the service of others. Mother Teresa, Jane Goodall, Jimmy Carter, and Desmond Tutu serve as examples of this stage.

Seligman, Martin Renowned psychologist and proponent of the field of Positive Psychology.

Sensation seeker Also known as Type R personality, these courageous people confront stress by calculating their risks in extreme situations and then proceeding with gusto.

Senses of humor A frame of mind as part of one's personality in how one uses humor and laughter in one's life.

Sensory overload An inundation of information that overwhelms the mind.

Serenity Prayer A popular short prayer encouraging acceptance and wisdom, attributed to Reinhold Niebuhr.

Serotonin A neurotransmitter that is associated with mood. A decrease in serotonin levels is thought to be related to depression. Serotonin levels are affected by many factors including stress hormones and the foods you consume.

Seville Statement A statement drafted in Seville, Spain, endorsing the belief that aggression is neither genetically nor biologically determined in human beings.

Shallow effect A shallow understanding of complicated issues that is caused by information grazing. Jumping from website to website and cherry-picking information compromises one's ability to concentrate or focus on something long enough to fully understand all of its implications.

Shiatsu A type of massage, also known as acupressure, for which pressure is placed on various points (*tsubos*) to release blocked energy and thus promote relaxation.

Should-ing Reprimanding yourself for things you "should" have done.

Single whip The seventh step in the classic T'ai Chi movement characterized by a specific series of hand motions and feet placement.

Sit and Reach (Paschimottasana) A classic yoga *asana* intended to promote balance with the hamstrings and lower back.

Skeptical The third stage of Peck's spiritual hierarchy, at which one shuns all religious dogma.

Slapstick Originating from vaudeville, a physical farce such as getting a pie thrown in the face or slipping on a banana peel.

Sleep hygiene Factors that affect one's quality of sleep, from hormonal changes and shift-work to excessive caffeine intake.

Social orchestration A coping technique; either (1) changing stress-producing factors in the environment or (2) changing the entire stress-producing environment; the path of least resistance (as distinguished from avoidance).

Social Readjustment Rating Scale An inventory of life events that may be perceived to be stressful, used to determine one's level of stress.

Social support A coping technique; those groups of friends, family members, and others whose company acts to buffer against and dissipate the negative effects of stress.

Sociology The study of human social behavior within families, organizations, and institutions; the study of the individual in relationship to society as a whole.

Solitude The intentional act of seeking alone time in a quiet space, away from family, friends, and daily distractions as a means of seeking inner peace.

Somatizers People exhibiting an anger style by suppressing rather than expressing feelings of anger. *Soma* means body, and when anger is suppressed, unresolved anger issues appear as symptoms of disease and illness.

Spinal Twist (Ardha Matsyendrasana) A classic yoga *asana* intended to promote balance with the upper and lower back and hips.

Spiritual bankruptcy A term to convey the lack of spiritual direction, values, or less than desirable behaviors, suggesting moral decay.

Spiritual dormancy A state in which someone chooses not to recognize the importance of the spiritual dimension of life, individually and socially.

Spiritual health A term to describe the use of our inner resources to help us cope with stress and dismantle the roadblocks on the path of life.

Spiritual hunger A term to illustrate the quest for understanding of life's biggest questions, the bigger picture, and how each of us fits into it.

Spiritual nutrition A term to suggest that the colors of specific fruits and vegetables augments the flow of subtle energy to the respective *chakras* represented by these colors (e.g., foods with the color red are beneficial for the root *chakra* and organs associated with this area).

Spiritual optimism Joan Borysenko's description of an intuitive knowledge that love is *the* universal energy.

Spiritual pessimism Joan Borysenko's description of an attitude that nurtures low self-esteem, guilt, and other less-than-becoming behaviors.

Spiritual potential A term coined by the author to describe the potential we all have as humans to cope with stress through the use of our inner resources (e.g., humor, compassion, patience, tolerance, imagination, and creativity).

Spiritual well-being The state of mature higher consciousness deriving from insightful relationships with oneself and others, a strong value system, and a meaningful purpose in life.

Spontaneous remission The sudden (sometimes gradual) disappearance of a nonmedically treated disease, most often observed with cancerous tumors, but other diseases, as well.

Sports massage A combination of Swedish massage, shiatsu, and some type of deep-tissue body work now popular among professional and amateur athletes.

Stage of exhaustion The third and final stage of Selye's general adaptation syndrome, in which one or more target organs show signs of dysfunction.

Stage of resistance The second stage of Selye's general adaptation syndrome, in which the body tries to recover.

Stages of grieving A process outlined by Elisabeth Kübler-Ross regarding the mental preparation for death, including denial, anger, bargaining, depression, and acceptance.

Starting posture The stance that begins the first of many positions in the flow of the T'ai Chi exercise; balancing your weight on both feet and looking straight ahead.

Stimulus period Called the "meat" of the workout, during which one targets the specified intensity toward heart, lungs, and muscles (e.g., heart rate, sets, reps for weight lifting).

Straightforward procrastinator A person who knowingly avoids completing a task.

Stress The experience of a perceived threat (real or imagined) to one's mental, physical, or spiritual well-being, resulting from a series of physiological responses and adaptations.

Stressor Any real or imagined situation, circumstance, or stimulus that is perceived to be a threat.

Stress reaction The body's initial (central nervous system) reaction to a perceived threat.

Stress response The release of epinephrine and norepinephrine to prepare various organs and tissues for fight or flight.

Substance addiction The addiction to a host of substances, from nicotine and caffeine to alcohol and various drugs.

Subtle anatomy Also called energy anatomy, subtle anatomy comprises the human energy field (aura), the *chakra* system, and the meridian system of energetic pathways that supply energy (also known as *chi* or *prana*) to the organs and physiological systems with which they connect.

Subtle energy A series of layers of energy that surround and permeate the body; thought to be associated with layers of consciousness constituting the human energy field.

Superiority theory First coined by Plato describing the reason why people laugh is at other people's expense.

Supportive-expressive group therapy A term coined by Dr. David Spiegel for women with breast cancer to share their experiences, grief, and healing with others going through the same experience.

Survival skills A term associated with codependency in which certain behaviors are adopted in adolescence to "survive" demanding, alcoholic, or abusive parents.

Survivor personality The traits that comprise a unique winning attitude to overcome adversity and challenges, no matter what the odds may be, so that one comes out the victor, not the victim.

Swedish massage The most common and well-known type of massage in Western culture that uses a variety of hand motions (e.g., kneading, stroking, and karate-type chops) to relieve the tension for muscle tissue, often expressed as knots.

Sympathetic The branch of the central nervous system that triggers the fight-or-flight response when some element of threat is present.

Sympathetic resonance A resonating vibration given off by one object that is picked up by another object in close proximity. Tuning forks are a classic example.

Synchronicity A term coined by Carl Jung to explain the significance of two seemingly unrelated events that, when brought together, have a significant meaning.

Synesthesia A cross-wiring of one's senses (during an altered state) during which one smells sounds or sees noises.

Systematic desensitization A term coined by psychologist Joseph Wolpe to describe a process of progressive tolerance to stress by gaining a greater sense of comfort with the unknown through repeated exposure and visualization.

T'ai Chi ch'uan A relaxation technique originating among the Chinese; a succession of movements to bring the body into harmony with the universal energy (*Chi*); a moving meditation.

Tapotement The fourth of five progressive steps/hand maneuvers in the Swedish massage that look like karate chops on the belly of the muscle.

Target heart rate The ideal heart rate or target zone in which to identify the intensity of cardiovascular activity.

Target organs Any organ or tissue receiving excess neural or hormonal stimulation that increases metabolic function or abnormal cell growth; results in eventual dysfunction of the organ.

T-cytotoxic cells Best known as the cells that attack and destroy tumorous cells by releasing cytokines.

Technostress A term used to define the result of a fast-paced life dependent on various means of technology, including computers, cell phones and smartphones, personal digital assistants, texting, and email—all of which were supposed to give people more leisure time. Instead, people have become slaves, addicted to the constant use of these devices and technologies.

Tend and befriend A theory presented by Shelley Taylor stating that women who experience stress don't necessarily run or fight, but rather turn to friends to cope with unpleasant events and circumstances.

T-helpers Also known as CD4, these cells help in the production of antibodies released by T-cells.

Theory of motivation Maslow's theory associated with personality and behavior, based on his theory of the hierarchy of needs.

Therapeutic touch An energy-based healing modality using the science of subtle energy to restore homeostasis (also similar to Reiki and healing touch).

Thermal biofeedback Biofeedback that measures the response from skin temperature. These can be affected by stress.

Thigh Stretch (Bandha Konasana) A classic yoga *asana* intended to promote balance with the leg muscles.

Thought stopping A coping technique by which one consciously stops the run of negative thoughts going through one's head.

Thyroxine axis A chain of physiological events stemming from the release of thyroxine.

Tickler notebook A personal collection of humorous items (e.g., cards, letters, JPEGs, jokes) to lighten your spirits.

Time (duration) The number of minutes of exercise in one session; the ideal number is 30 minutes in the target zone, not including a warm-up or cool-down.

Time distortion As an altered state, one's perception of time is changed or distorted so that a segment of time seems either longer or shorter than it actually is.

Time juggler Someone who multitasks, overbooks, and double-books oneself and bargains for time, often dropping responsibilities in the process.

Time management The prioritization, scheduling, and execution of daily responsibilities to a level of personal satisfaction. Effective time management does not mean you have more time; it means you make better use of the time you have.

Time mapping A time-management technique; breaking down the day into 15- to 30-minute segments and assigning a task or responsibility to each segment.

Time urgency A characteristic or behavior of someone who displays Type A personality, someone who is constantly time conscious.

Time-trap procrastinator A person who does other tasks, such as laundry, thus keeping busy while still avoiding the more important responsibilities.

Tinnitus The clinical name given to the symptom of ringing, hissing, or buzzing in the ears.

Toxic thoughts Repeated negative thought processing that tends to pollute our view of our lives and ourselves.

Tragic optimism A term coined by psychiatrist Viktor Frankl to explain the mindset of someone who can find value and meaning in the worst situation.

Tranquil natural scenes One of three categories used in mental imagery (e.g., ocean beach, mountain vista, old-growth forest, lavender gardens).

Transcendence A means to rise above the mundane existence to see a higher order to things, often used to describe human spirituality.

Transcendental Meditation (TM) This meditation is the epitome of exclusive meditation in which all thoughts are eliminated save the mantra itself.

Transpersonal psychology A discipline in the field of psychology that recognizes the spiritual dimension of the human condition.

Transpsychological A term used to describe the therapeutic effects of self-discovery through active awareness in journaling.

Tratak A visual type of mantra, such as a seashell, a colorfully designed mandala, or any object that is used by the eyes to focus attention and ignore distracting thoughts.

Trigger point therapy Applied pressure to and manipulation of hyper-irritable points of the muscle that are causing radiating pain in a region; used in sports massage.

Tsubos The specific point on the meridian that is used in acupressure to release tension.

T-suppressors Also known as CD8, these cells decrease the production of antibodies, thus keeping a healthy balance of T-cells.

Two Knees to Chest (Apanasana) A classic yoga *asana* intended to promote balance with the lower back.

Type A personality This personality, once associated with time urgency, is now associated with unresolved anger issues.

Type of exercise The type of activity one chooses to engage in to work one or more physiological systems (e.g., walking, jogging, cycling).

Tzu, Lao An ancient Chinese philosopher and writer. He is the author of the acclaimed book *Tao Teh Ching*, a manifesto for human spirituality based on the concept of balance with nature. Lao Tzu is believed to be the creator of the concept of Taoism.

Ultradian rhythms Biological rhythms that occur many times in a 24-hour period (e.g., hunger pangs).

Unconditional love An altruistic love expressed by Jesus of Nazareth, for which nothing is expected in return.

Underhanders People exhibiting a mismanaged anger style by seeking revenge and retaliation. This passive-aggressive anger style is a means to control others, but in a very subtle way.

Unwarranted fear Similar to an irrational fear, an instance when anxiety overcomes one's thoughts based on a non-physical threat to one's existence.

Values Abstract, intangible concepts of importance or meaning, such as time, health, honesty, and creativity, that are symbolized by material possessions.

Vasopressin axis A chain of physiological events stemming from the release of vasopressin or antidiuretic hormone (ADH).

Via creativa Fox's term to describe a breakthrough or moment of enlightenment.

Via negativa Fox's term to describe the act of emptying and letting go of unnecessary thoughts and feelings.

Via positiva Fox's term to describe a sense of awe and wonder of creation.

Via transformativa Fox's term to describe the euphoria from the realization of insights and the responsibility to share these with others.

Vibration The fifth of five progressive steps/hand maneuvers in the Swedish massage that resembles a type of shaking gesture to promote increased circulation.

Victimization A mindset of continually seeing yourself as a victim.

Vision quest A Native American custom of a retreat in nature during which one begins or continues to search for life's answers.

Visualization A directed exercise in mental imagery; consciously creating images of success, healing, or relaxation for the purpose of self-improvement.

Vitamin supplements Processed pills containing various vitamins (e.g., A, B complex, C, E).

von Bingen, Hildegard An early Christian mystic who added a feminine voice to a male-dominated Christian theology.

Warm-up period The first phase of the workout, during which circulation is increased to the large muscles with some time for flexibility.

Warrior The last stage in von Oech's creative process template, in which the idea is taken to the street and campaigned to the rest of the world for its merits.

Wellness paradigm The integration, balance, and harmony of mental, physical, emotional, and spiritual well-being through taking responsibility for one's own health; posits that the whole is greater than the sum of the parts.

Winning by losing A T'ai Chi expression that explains the benefits of failure as a stepping stone toward success.

Workaholism A personality style that inhibits good time-management skills with excessive hours devoted to work, often at the expense of other responsibilities.

Writer's block The inability to write down one's thoughts and feelings, usually attributed to fear (e.g., fear of failure).

Wu-wei A T'ai Chi term that signifies doing nothing, or action through nonaction, moving with the simple, subtle flow of nature.

X-factor A term coined by psychologist Leo Buscaglia to describe that special quality that makes each one of us unique. By focusing on our X-factor and not our faults and foibles, we enhance our self-esteem.

Yang Those complementary components in the Taoist philosophy of yin/yang expressed as light, masculine, day, hard, and so on.

Yerkes-Dodson principle The theory that some stress (eustress) is necessary for health and performance but that beyond an optimal amount, both will deteriorate as stress increases.

Yin Those complementary components in the Taoist philosophy of yin/yang expressed as dark, feminine, night, soft, and so forth.

Yoga A Sanskrit word that means union, specifically the union of mind, body, and spirit.

Yoga Sutras The ancient yogic text attributed to Patanjali, who described each of the yoga *asanas*.

Zen (Zazen) meditation A form of meditation wherein one learns to detach from one's emotional thoughts by becoming the observer of those thoughts.

Zero firing threshold A term to signify complete muscular relaxation with no tension.

Index

Note: Page numbers followed by b, f, or t
indicate material in boxes, figures,
or tables, respectively.

A

AA. *See* Alcoholics Anonymous
ABC rank-order method, 334
abdominal muscles, 480
absorption, 519
absurd humor, 276
academic deadlines, college stress, 17
"Accentuate the Positive, Eliminate
the Negative," 221
acceptance
defined, 224
as stage of grieving, 107
of thoughts, 224
acetylcholine (ACh), 49
Achterberg, Jeanne, 78, 413, 415, 420
ACS. *See* American Cancer Society
ACTH. *See* adrenocorticotropic
hormone
action potential, 475
active imagination, 105, 412
active meditation, 375
acupressure. *See* shiatsu
acupuncture, 75, 75f
acute stress, 9
Adams, Kathleen, 243, 251
Adams, Patch, 286
adaptation, 107
adaptors, 317
Adcock, C. L., 449
ADD. *See* attention deficit disorder
addictive personality, 151
Addison's disease, 51b
adenosine-triphosphate-creatine
(ATP-PC), 505
ADH. *See* antidiuretic hormone
adrenal cortex, 50, 51f, 53
adrenal fatigue/failure, 51b
adrenal gland, 50, 51f
adrenal medulla, 52
adrenocorticotropic hormone
(ACTH), 46
axis, 53–54, 54f
Adventures in the Wilderness (Murray), 533
aerobic exercise, 506, 506f, 512–514
affect displays, 317

affectionate writing, 244
Agassi, Andre, 222
age of self-expression, 255
Ageless Body, Timeless Mind (Chopra), 183
aggression. *See* anger
aggressive behavior style, 235
agility, 505
agnostics, 353
AIS. *See* American Institute of Stress
alarm reaction, 13
alcohol, excessive consumption of, 521
Alcoholics Anonymous (AA), 175,
345, 419
aldosterone, 51
Alexander, Franz, 62
Alexie, Sherman, 278
all-or-none conditioning principle, 509
Allen, Steve, Jr., 272
Allen, Woody, 296
allergies, 87–88, 88f
allostatic load, 56
Alone Together (Turkle), 31
Alpert, Mark, 436
alpha thinking, 372
alpha waves, 383
Alter Ego: Avatars and Their Creators
(Cooper and Spaight), 163
altered state of consciousness, 383–385
alternate nostril breathing exercise,
366, 366f
alternative medicine, 21
Amabile, Teresa, 296
ambiance, relaxation technique, 477
American Art Therapy Association,
255, 256
American Cancer Society (ACS), 4, 89
American College of Sports Medicine
(ACSM), 508, 509
American Heart Association, 4, 85, 372
American Holistic Medical Association,
73, 74
American Indians
medicine wheel, 178, 180f
mental imagery, 411
music, use of, 428
vision quest, 178, 193–194
American Institute of Stress (AIS), 3, 9,
62, 70
American Massage Therapy Association
(AMTA), 446, 451

American Psychological Association
(APA), 119
AMTA. *See* American Massage Therapy
Association
amygdala, 46b
An Inconvenient Truth (Gore), 168
anabolic functioning, 49
anaerobic exercise, 505–506, 505f
Anatomy of an Illness (Cousins),
269, 281, 429
Andrew, Kelly, 406
anger, 264
anatomy of, 126–134
catharsis, myth of, 129–131
conflicts, recommendations to
resolve, 130
depression a by-product of, 138–139
forms of, 126–127
gender differences, 127–129
mismanagement styles, 131–132
exploders, 131
self-punishers, 131
somatizers, 131
underhanders, 132
physiological responses, 129
as stage of grieving, 107
strategies for handling, 132–135
Anger Advantage, The (Cox, Bruckner,
and Stabb), 128
Anger Kills (Williams), 130
Anger—The Misunderstood Emotion
(Travis), 130
anorexia, 525
antibodies, protein, 64
antidiuretic hormone (ADH), 46, 53
antigens, 63
antioxidants, 518
anxiety breathing, 363
APA. *See* American Psychological
Association
Apanasana, 403, 403f
Araha Chakrasana, 402, 403f
archetypes, 173
Ardha Matsyendrasana, 404, 404f
Aristotle, 119, 428, 491
Arlen, Harold, 221
aromatherapy, 455–456, 456f
art of balance, 399, 399f
art of breathing, 397–398, 398f
art of conscious stretching, 398, 398f

Art of Happiness, The (Dalai Lama), 120
Art of Peace and Relaxation Workbook, The, 543
art therapy
    applications, 265
    clinical use of, 257–262
    defined, 255
    doodles, 261–262, 262*f*
    interpretations, 265
    materials for, 262–263
    origins of, 256–257
    steps to initiate, 262–265
    themes, 263–264
    used to treat migraine headache, 261*f*
arteriosclerosis, 86
artist, 295
artistic roadblock, 262
As Above, So Below (Miller), 168
asanas, 402–405
Ascent to Truth, The (Merton), 185
ashrams, 395
Ashtanga yoga, 406*t*
aspartame, 518*b*, 526*b*, 526
Assaglioli, Robert, 412
assertive behavior style, 235
assertiveness
    defined, 235
    skills, 236–238
    training, 138
astragalus, 517*b*
AT. *See* autogenic training
At a Journal Workshop (Progoff), 243
atheists, 353
atherogenesis, 86
atherosclerosis, 86
athletic conditioning, theories of, 508–510
attending, communication and, 318–319
attention deficit disorder (ADD),
        meditation and, 388*b*
attitudes, 230
attribution theory, 219
auditory imagery, 439–440
auric field. *See* human energy field
Authentic Happiness (Seligman), 119
auto-hypnosis, 486
autogenic discharge, 488
autogenic training (AT)
    application of, 492
    definition, 486
    historical use of, 486–488
    mental imagery and, 491–492
    psychological and physiological
        responses, 488–491
    self-hypnosis, use of, 492

steps to initiate
    body position, 489–490, 490*f*
    concentration and awareness, 490
    direct approach, 491
    indirect approach, 490–491
    use of, 492
autoimmune diseases, 66
autonomic dysregulation, 63, 63*t*
autonomic nervous system (ANS)
    defined, 46
    disease and, 413
    sympathetic and parasympathetic,
        47–50, 48*f*
avatar therapy, 533
avoidance
    vs. confrontation coping style, 210
    as defense mechanism, 343
awareness
    autogenic training, 490
    behavior modification model and, 232
    increased, 211
    selected, 488
awfulizing, 222
Ax, Albert, 129
Ayurvedic medicine, 182
Ayurvedic principles, 523

B

B-cells, 63, 64
B-complex vitamins, depletion, 521
Bach, Edward, 455
Bach, Richard, 300
back pain, 397
Bad Santa, 277
Bahr, Raymond, 438
balance, 505
    T'ai Chi and, 465, 467
    time management and, 336, 337*f*
    yoga and, 399, 399*f*
Ban Ki-Moon, 36
Bandha, 364, 364*f*
Bandha Konasana, 403, 403*f*
Bandler, Richard, 219
Bandura, Albert, 210, 215
bandwidth, 33
bargaining, as stage of grieving, 107
Barnes, John, 454
Barr, Frank, 433
bathroom humor, 278
baths, 457
BCIA. *See* Biofeedback Certificate
        Institute of America
Beattie, Melodie, 152

Beck, A. T., 215
Becker, Dana, 29
Becker, Robert, 76
beginning position, T'ai Chi, 469
behavior modification, 211
    assertiveness, 235–236
    as component of personality, 230–231
    coping and, 210–212
    model, 231–235
    steps, 238
    theories of, 230
    Type A personality and, 148–151
behavioral changes, mental imagery for,
        416–419
behavioral substitution, 233
behavioral therapy, 138
behaviors
    defined, 230
    styles of, 235–236
    time management and, 331–333
Bell, Alexander Graham, 295, 430
belly breathing, 362, 367*f*
Benjamin, Harold, 137
Benson, Herbert, 181, 352, 376, 385, 386
Bentov, Itzhak, 190, 363, 433
Berger, Hans, 497
Bernard, Claude, 61
beta-endorphin, 457–458, 510
bhakti yoga, 395
Bhujanghasana, 403, 403*f*
Biaggio, Mary Kay, 128
binary biofeedback, 496
bio-accumulation, 516
bioavailability, 520
biochemical theory, 431–436
    entrainment theory, 433–435
    metaphysical theory, 435–436
bioecological influences, 10–11
biofeedback. *See* clinical biofeedback
Biofeedback Certificate Institute of
        America (BCIA), 499
bioflavonoids, 523
Biology of Belief, The (Lipton), 69
biophilia, 534
bioplasma, 71
Birren, Faber, 421
bisociation, 273
Bizarro, 274
Black Elk, 177–179, 201, 411
Black Elk Speaks (Neihardt), 178, 411
black humor, 277
Blake, William, 295
Blalock, Edwin, 67
blaming, 221

Blanchard, Edward, 493

blocked heart chakra, symptoms of, 73

blog, 248

blueprint aspect, 414

body images, mental imagery to change internal, 419–421

body language, 237, 317, 317f
  communication, absence of, 311

body position, autogenic training, 489–490

body, stress, 545

bodywork, 447

Bohm, Dave, 190

Boiling Point, 127

Bolen, Jean, 190

Bonham, Tal, 272, 274

Bonny, Helen, 437

Booth, Leo, 171

Borysenko, Joan, 62, 77, 181–182, 192, 193, 194, 222, 223, 224, 354

Borysenko model, 63–67, 63t, 64f, 66t

Borysenko, Myrin, 63

boundaries, 33

Bow Pose (*Dhanurasana),* 404, 404f

Bowling for Columbine (Moore), 135

boxing, 335b

Braden, Gregg, 39

brain, 507b
  cognitive functions of, 382t
  imaging research, 56–57, 386–387, 412
  insomnia and, 54b
  levels, 45–47
  split-brain theory, 379–382

brain imaging research, meditation and, 386–387

Branden, Nathaniel, 161

breathing. *See also* diaphragmatic breathing
  anxiety, 363
  belly, 362
  clouds exercise, 366, 366f
  energy, 366–367, 367f
  technique with PMR, 477
  yoga and, 397–398, 398f

Brennen, Barbara Ann, 458

Breuer, Joseph, 412

brevity *vs.* integrity, 311

brief grief, 222

Brody, Jane, 38

bronchial asthma, 84

Brosse, Therese, 385

brow chakra, 74

Brown, Barbara, 494

Brown, Jackson H., 354

Bruckner, K., 128

Buchwald, Art, 281

Buddhism, 120

buffer theory, 346

building community, 196

bulimia, 525

Burfoot, Amby, 360

Burnham, Sophie, 354

Burns, David, 220

Burns, Robert, 261

Buscaglia, Leo, 112–115, 113f

Bush, George H. W., 271

Bush, George W., 271

buttock muscles, 480

Buzan diagram, 250, 250f

Buzan, Tony, 250

Buzan writing style, 250

Byrd, Randolph, 190, 352

C

caffeine, 518b, 520–521, 526

calcium, depletion of, 521

calf muscles, 480–481, 481f

Campbell, Don, 438

Campbell, Joseph, 186–188, 201, 294

cancer, 89
  art therapy and, 257–262
  mental imagery and, 411–413

Candid Camera, 269

Cannon, Walter, 6, 27, 46, 63

Capra, Fritjof, 191

carbohydrates, 520, 525

carcinogens, 89

cardiovascular (EKG) biofeedback, 497–498

cardiovascular endurance, 504

cardiovascular exercise, 507–508, 511

Carey, Ken, 185

Carr, Nicholas, 31–32

Carter, Jimmy, 271, 371

Cassel, J., 346

Cassileth, Barrie, 413

Castaneda, Carlos, 172

cat back arch, 400b

catabolic functioning, 48

catastrophizing, 221

catecholamines, effect of, 66

catharsis, myth of, 129–131

Cava, Marco della, 32

CD4. *See* T-helpers

CD8. *See* T-suppressors

cell membrane, free radicals and, 519

cell memory, 80

centering process, 192, 192f

Centers for Disease Control and Prevention, 2

central nervous system (CNS), 45–47

cerebration, 55

chakras, 72–76, 74f

chamomile, 456

change
  inevitable, 292
  rate of, 3
  stages of, 233–234
  times of, 2–5

Channon, L. D., 449

chaotic antisocial individual, 175

Chapin, Harry, 299

CHD. *See* coronary heart disease

chemotherapy, 415

Cheng, Nien, 160

chest expansion, 400b

Chi, 464. *See also* T'ai Chi ch'uan

childbirth, 362

Childre, D. L., 130, 495

cholesterol, 86

chondromalacia, 514

Chopra, Deepak, 62, 182–184, 193, 201

Christianity, 184

chronic fatigue syndrome, 51b

chronic pain. *See* pain, chronic

chronic stress, 9
  on B-cells, 63–64

chronic stressors, 9–10

Churchill, Winston, 278

circadian rhythms, 10, 537–538

CISM. *See* critical incidence stress management

civility, decline in, 33–35

classical conditioning theory, 230, 494

Clemes, Harris, 161, 162

clinical biofeedback, 493
  application of, 498–499
  chronic pain and, 498
  historical use of, 494–495
  insomnia and, 494b
  phases of, 496
  purpose of, 495–496
  types of equipment, 496–498

Clinton, Bill, 271

closed-loop feedback system, 495, 496f

clothes
  exercise and, 514
  nonverbal communication, 316–317

cloud issues, 33

clustering, 336

Clynes, Manfred, 432

Co-dependence: Misunderstood, Mistreated (Schaef), 154

co-rumination, 8

Cobra (*Bhujanghasana*), 403, 403*f*
codependency, 151
Codependent No More (Beattie), 152
codependent personality, 151–155
cognitive-based theory, 273
cognitive-dissonance theory, 346
cognitive distortion, 214, 220*b*
cognitive restructuring
    acceptance, 224
    behavior modification and, 232
    choosing thoughts, 221–224
    defined, 215
    information-processing model,
        215–216, 215*f*
    optimism and pessimism, 224*b*
    steps for initiating, 225
    tips for, 226
    toxic thoughts, 217–221
Cognitive Surplus (Shirky), 30
Colbert, Stephen, 275, 278
colds, 87
colitis, 88–89
collective unconscious, 103
College Dropout (Kanye), 241
college stress, 17, 19
color therapy, 421
combative *vs.* preventive coping
        style, 210
comic relief. *See* humor therapy
communication
    absence of body language, 311
    basics of, 313–314
    brevity *vs.* integrity, 311
    conflict-management styles, 320
    conflict resolution, 319, 319*f*
    forms of, 309
    high-tech, 309–310
    of ideas and feelings, 315
    information overload, 311–312, 321
    listening, attending, and responding
        skills, 318–319
    nonverbal, 316–317
    resolve problems, 312
    screen time *vs.* direct eye contact,
        311–312
    steps to enhance, 320–322, 321*f*
    styles, 314
    technology gap, 310, 310*f*
    verbal, 314–315
    without emotions, 310
community building, 194
compensation, 158
compensation theory, 346
competitiveness, 149, 150

complementary medicine, 22
Complete Book of Running, The
        (Fixx), 360
computer dating, 33
concentration
    autogenic training, 490
    relaxation technique, 477
concentration meditation. *See* exclusive
        meditation
concentric contraction, 475
conditional response, 495
conditioned response, 134
conflict-management styles, 320
conflict resolution, 319, 319*f*
confrontation, avoidance *vs.*, 210
connecting process, 194, 194*f*
conscious mind, 102–104
consciousness, 70
    altered state of, 383–385
    movement, 168
    stretching, art of, 398, 398*f*
    turning point in, 169–171
content conflict, 319
contraction, muscular, 475
controlled aggression, 127
conventional sense of humor, 279
conversational styles, 317
Cook-Medley Hostility Index, 149
cool-down period, exercise and, 510
Cooper, Kenneth, 504, 506
Cooper, Robbie, 163
coping
    defined, 210
    instrumental, 210
    palliative, 210
    personality and, 210–211
    skills, 545
    strategies, 210–212, 214–226, 269–287,
        291–304
    styles, 210–211
coping responses, 210
coping techniques, 251, 263
    communication skills, 308–322
    dream therapy, 349–350
    forgiveness, 348–349
    hobbies, 347–348, 347*f*
    information seeking, 342–343
    journal writing, 243–246
    prayer and faith, 351–354
    social orchestration, 343–345
    social-support groups, 345–347
coronary heart disease (CHD), 4, 86*f*
    hostility and, 129, 149
    stages of, 86

statistics on, 4
    stress and, 85
    Type A personality and, 149
Corpse Pose (*shavasana*), 394, 404, 404*f*
corticosteroids, 50
corticotropin-releasing factor (CRF),
        50, 53
cortisol, 51
    weight gain and, 515*b*
Course in Miracles, A, 185
Cousens, Gabriel, 523
Cousins, Norman, 68, 269, 270, 271,
        281, 282, 429
Covey, Stephen, 334
Cox, Deborah, 128
CQ. *See* creative intelligence (CQ)
cravings, 524
Creation of Health, The (Shealy and Myss),
        72, 74
creation spirituality, 180, 180*f*
creative intelligence (CQ), 292
creative problem solving, 291–304
    action, evaluation and analysis of, 303
    applications, 304
    defined, 302
    description of, 302–303
    generating ideas, 303
    idea, implementation, 303
    map of, 303, 303*f*
creative sense of humor, 279
creativity. *See also* creative problem
        solving
    importance of, 292
    myths of, 296–299
    obstacles to, 299–301
    primary, 294
    process of, 293–299
    role of, 293
    secondary, 294
Creativity in Business (Ray and Myers), 295
credit cards, 326–327
critical incidence stress management
        (CISM), 14*b*
Cross Currents (Becker), 76
crown chakra, 74, 74*f*
cultural differences, 37
cultural roadblocks, 301
curing, 21
Cut-Thru (Childre), 130
cyber bullying, 33, 41
cyber hacking, 33
cymatics, 436*f*
cytokines, 64
Czimbal, B., 447

D

Dacher, Elliot, 74
daily life hassles, 12
Daily Show, 31
DailyBeast.com, 31
Dalai Lama, 120, 139, 187, 198, 198*f,*
    274, 286
Dance of Anger, The (Lerner), 127, 128
"Dark Continent," 187
Davidson, Jeff, 338
Davidson, Richard, 386
Davis, William, 437
daydreaming, 383, 415–416, 415*f*
De Becker, Gavin, 135
death
    and dying process, work of
        Kübler-Ross, 106–108
    fear of, 137
    leading causes of, 3–4
deceptive procrastinator, 332
decibels, 430
decision making, time management, 339
decoding, 314
defense mechanisms, 100, 101
dehydroepiandrosterone (DHEA), 49*b*
Delaney, Gayle, 349, 350
delegation, 337
Delmonte, Michael, 385
denial
    behavior modification model and, 232
    as defense mechanism, 100
    as stage of grieving, 107
Denollet, Johan, 151, 152
depression, 139, 257
    a by-product of anger and fear, 138–139
    exercise and, 139
    as stage of grieving, 107
    Type D personality and, 151
"dermapoint massage," to forearm and
        trapezius muscles, 449
Descartes, René, 19, 20*f,* 44, 62
desensitization, systematic and
        exposure, 138
desires, 120
desk/cubicle yoga asanas, 400*b*
Destructive Emotions (Goleman), 135
detached observation, 377
detachment, law of, 184
Dhanurasana, 404, 404*f*
Dharma, law of, 184
DHEA. *See* dehydroepiandrosterone
*Diagnostic and Statistical Manual of Mental
        Disorders (DSM),* 14*b,* 126

dialogue, conflict-management style, 320
Diamond, Jared, 38
Diamond, John, 433
diaphragmatic breathing, 171,
        362–367, 379
    and chronic pain, 364
    defined, 362
    insomnia and, 364*b*
    mystery of breathing, 363–364
    steps to initiate
        comfortable position, 364, 364*f*
        concentration, 364–365
        visualization, 366–367
diary, 242
Dickinson, Emily, 244
DiClemente, Carlo, 233
diet. *See* nutrition
Different Drum, The (Peck), 175
digestion, 519, 524
direct approach, 491
direct-effect theory, 346
direct eye contact, screen time *vs.,* 311
diseases, caused by stress, 3
displacement, 101
distractions, 200, 373
distress, 8
diversions, 332
divine mystery, 199, 201*f*
divine personification, 195
divinity theory, 274, 274*f*
DNA, 61, 64, 68, 519
domesticating the ego, 377
dominant rhythm style (DRS), 432
Dominguez, Joe, 327
Donne, John, 28–29, 313
doodles, 261–262, 262*f*
dopamine, 30
Dossey, Larry, 19, 62, 181, 190, 200
double entendre, 276
dream(s)
    Freud and, 349
    incubation, 349
    interpretation, 103
    journal, 250–251
    Jung and, 102–106, 173–174, 174*f,*
        265, 349
    therapy, 349–350
Dreher, Diane, 188
DRS. *See* dominant rhythm style
Drummond, Henry, 185
Drury, Nevill, 429
dry humor, 278
duration, exercise and, 509, 509*f,* 513
Dyer, Wayne, 110–112, 110*f*

E

Eagle Man, 178
*Earth in the Balance: Ecology and the
        Human Spirit* (Gore), 168
Eastern-based relaxation techniques, 477
eating disorders, 524
ECaP. *See* exceptional cancer patients
eccentric contraction, 475
echinacea, 517*b*
Eckhart, Meister, 180
Eckman, Paul, 412
ecotherapy, 533
    application of, 540
    circadian rhythms, 537–538
    entrainment, 537
    historical perspective, 533
    nature deficit disorder, 533–535
    physical health, 537–538
    physiological effects, 535–537
    psychological effects, 538–539
    securing nature points, 540
    solitude, nature and art of, 539
    spiritual moments, 539–540
Eden, Donna, 73
EDR biofeedback. *See* electrodermal
        biofeedback
EEG. *See* electroencephalogram
effective coping, 252
effective holistic stress management, 23
effective stress-management program, 9
effleurage, 451, 452*f*
ego, 99
    conflict, 319
    defense mechanisms of, 108
    mass marketing and your, 326–327
    overprotection of, 101
egosyntonic, 414
80/20 rule, 334
Einstein, Albert, 20, 189, 201, 354
    path of, 189–191
Eisenberg, David, 22
electrodermal (EDR) biofeedback, 498
electroencephalogram (EEG), 379
    biofeedback, 497, 497*f*
electromagnetic field. *See* human
        energy field
electromyography (EMG)
    activity, 477
    biofeedback, 496–497, 497*f*
ELF. *See* extremely low frequencies
elimination, 511*b,* 517*b*
Elizabeth, Queen of England, 270, 272
Ellis, Albert, 98, 215

Em Wave PC Stress Relief System, 138, 495, 495*f*
"email stress," 30
emblems, 316
EMG. *See* electromyography
emotional baggage, 77
emotional expression, 244
"emotional hijacking," 135
Emotional Intelligence (Goleman), 135
emotional literacy, 127
emotional roadblocks, 301
emotional stress, 14*b*, 66, 516
emotional well-being, 22
emotions, 126
　　stress, 545
empathy, communication, 318
emptying process, 192–193, 193*f*
　　of spiritual well-being, 337
enablers, 152
encoding, 314
　　predictive, 411
End of Stress as We Know It, The (McEwen), 56
endocrine system, 49*b*, 50–52
endogenous-overreactive, 87
endogenous-underreactive, 87
energy
　　anatomy. *See* subtle anatomy
　　breathing exercise, 366–367, 367*f*
　　etheric, 71
　　psychology, 72
　　subtle, 71, 80, 190
energy balance, 505*t*
energy psychology, 72
enhanced receptivity, 384
enlightenment, 193, 379*f*
"entitlement generation," 125, 127
entrainment
　　of oscillation, 434
　　sonic, 76
　　theory, 433–435
environmental disconnect, 35–39
environmental roadblocks, 301
epigenetic theory, 69
epinephrine, 48–50, 52
equipment, exercise and, 514
essentic forms, 432
Esterling, B. A., 68
estrogen, 8
etheric energy, 71
ethics, 33
ethnic issues, stress and, 40
etiology, 62
Europe's Age of Exploration, 242

eustress, 8, 139, 168
evaluation, behavior modification model and, 233
Everly, George, 44, 379
exceptional cancer patients (ECaP), 259
exclusive meditation, 373–375
execution, 336
"Exercise Against Depression" (Artal and Sherman), 139
exercises
　　applications, 514–515
　　benefits, 503, 504
　　chronic pain and, 511–512
　　depression and, 139
　　insomnia and, 511*b*
　　phases, 509, 510*f*
　　physiological effects of, 506–508
　　physiologists, 398
　　psychological effects, 510–511
　　steps to initiate fitness training program, 512–514
　　stress and, 503–504
　　theories of athletic conditioning, 508–510
　　types, 504–506
　　visualization, 366–367
exhaustion stage, 13
existential vacuum, 109
exogenous-overreactive, 87
exogenous-underreactive, 87
exploders, 131
explorer, 294–295
exposure desensitization, 138
exposure technique to promote relaxation, 421
expressive roadblocks, 301
expressive writing, 244
external relationships, 194–196
extremely low frequencies (ELF), 76, 77
Eye Yoga, 400*b*
Eyre, Chris, 278

F

face-to-face communication skills
　　basics of, 313–314
　　steps to enhance, 320–323, 321*f*
　　styles, 320
face-to-face time, spending less, 35*f*
Facebook, 243
facial expressions, 317
facial stretch, 478, 478*f*
failure, fear of, 136
faith, 351–354. *See also* prayer

Faith Factor, The (Matthews), 353
Fanning, Patrick, 411
Far Side, The, 276
Faraday, Ann, 350
Farmer, Gary, 278
Farther Reaches of Human Nature, The (Maslow), 117
fasting the heart, 465
fat-soluble vitamins, 520, 526
fatigue syndrome, chronic, 51*b*
fats, 522, 526
FDA. *See* Food and Drug Administration
fear
　　anatomy of, 134–138
　　depression a by-product of, 138–139
　　human, 135–137
　　irrational, 135
　　rational, 135
　　strategies to overcome, 138
　　unwarranted, 135
fear of death, 137
fear of failure, 136
fear of isolation, 137
fear of rejection, 136
fear of the loss of self-dominance, 137
fear of the unknown, 136–137
Feeling Good Handbook, The (Burns), 220*b*
feet, muscles of, 481–482
Fetzer Institute, 113
Field, The (McTaggart), 71
Field, Tiffany, 448, 467
Fields, W. C., 282
fight-or-flight response, 6, 47
　　stages of, 7
Fighting Cancer from Within (Rossman), 420
finances, management of, 326
financial aid and school loans, college stress, 17
Fish (*Matsyasana*), 404, 404*f*
Fist over Head (*Araha Chakrasana*), 402, 403*f*
fitness training program, 512–514
FITT principle, 509
fix-or-replace method, 19
Fixx, Jim, 360, 511
flexibility, 504
flexible optimism, 221
flotation tanks, 457
Floyd, Pink, 429
fMRI. *See* functional magnetic resonance imaging
focusing, 158
Food and Drug Administration (FDA), 80

Food, Inc., 38
foods. *See also* nutrition
 allergies, 523*b*
 genetically altered, 522
 label warning, 526*b*
 organic, 523*f*
 psychological effects of, 524–525
forearms muscle, 479–480
forest therapy, 535
forgiveness, 348–349
Forgiveness (Simon and Simon), 348
formal-institutional individual, 176
Foster, Steven, 243
Fowler, James, 175
Fox, Matthew, 179, 192, 193, 195, 201
 path of, 179–181
Framingham Anger Scales Inventory, 128
frankenfood, 522
Frankl, Viktor, 171, 194, 197, 198, 222, 280
 theory of, 108–110, 108*f*
Frederickson, Barbara, 219
free radicals, 517*b,* 518
freeze response, 6
Freinkel, Susan, 38
frequency, exercise and, 509
frequency following response, 434
Freud, Sigmund
 analysis of guilt, 111*f*
 art therapy, 265
 catharsis, 129
 compare human psyche to egg, 99, 99*f*
 denial of reality, 216
 dreams, 349
 fear, 134
 imagination, 412
 release/relief theory of humor, 273–274
 theory of, 99–101, 99*f*
friction, 452, 452*f*
Friedman, Erika, 458
Friedman, Meyer, 148–150
Fries, James, 507
From Victim to Victor (Benjamin), 137
Fry, William, 282
Full Catastrophe Living (Kabat-Zinn), 380*b*
functional magnetic resonance imaging
 (fMRI), 46*b,* 232, 386, 536
Funt, Alan, 269
Future Shock (Toffler), 27, 292

G

Gallwey, Timothy, 418
galvanic skin response (GSR), 498
gamma globulins, 64

Garfield, Patrick, 349
GAS. *See* general adaptation syndrome
Gauthier, P., 449
Gaynor, Mitchell, 440
Gelb, Michael, 293
gender differences
 anger and, 127–129
 communication styles and, 313*b*
gender stress, 40–41
general adaptation syndrome (GAS), 13
generation gap, 310
generational social factors, 8
genetically modified organisms (GMOs),
 10, 516, 522, 523*b*
Geography of Bliss, The (Weiner), 140
Gerber model, 70–78
Gerber, Richard, 61, 69–78, 191
germ theory, 61
Getting Well Again (Simonton and
 Simonton), 419, 421
Gibran, Kahlil, 371
glands, 50
Glaser, Ron, 68
Glasser, William, 510
globulins, 64
glucocorticoids, 51
GMOs. *See* genetically modified
 organisms
Golden Rule, 35*b*
Goldman, Jonathan, 435
Goleman, Daniel, 135
Gomukhasana, 402, 403*f*
Good Calories, Bad Calories (Taubes), 520
good-quality journal writing, 252
good-sport sense of humor, 279
Goodall, Jane, 187
Google, 338–339
Gordon, James, 62
Gore, Al, 168
Grad, Bernard, 75
grand perspective mental video, 387
Grasp the bird's tail position, T'ai
 Chi, 470
Gray, Harry, 296
Great Recession, 2, 325
Green, Elmer, 75–76, 486
Greenfield, Susan, 30
grieving
 brief, 222
 stages of, 106–107, 222
Grinder, John, 219
grounding process, 193–194, 193*f*
GSR. *See* galvanic skin response
guided mental imagery, 411

guilt
 leftover, 111
 self-imposed, 111
 sin of, 111
Guilt Is the Teacher, Love Is the Lesson
 (Borysenko), 181
gut feeling, 73

H

Halpern, Steven, 429, 430, 433
Han, Kim, 75
hands muscle, 479–480
Hands of Light (Brennen), 458
happiness, 139–141, 261
hardy personality, 156–158
Harold and Maude, 277
hatha yoga, 394
 application of, 405–406
 and chronic pain, 397
 asanas, 402–405
  balance, 399, 399*f*
  breathing, 397–398, 398*f*
 guidelines, 405
 historical perspective, 395–396
 insomnia and, 399*b*
 physiological and psychological benefits,
  396–397
 steps to initiate, 397–405
 types of, 406*t*
Hawking, Stephen, 38
Head First (Cousins), 281
Head of Cow (*Gomukhasana*), 402, 403*f*
headache
 migraine, 84
 tension, 84
HEAL method, 348
healing, 21–22
 images, 263–265
 process, 420*f,* 421
Healing and the Mind, 22
Healing Power of Humor, The (Klein), 280
Healing Power of Sound, The (Gaynor), 421
Healing Words (Dossey), 190
health, defined, 21
heart chakra, 73–74
Heart Math Institute, 138
heart rate
 monitor, 498*f*
 music and, 432–433
 target, 509
Heart's Code, The (Pearsall), 80
Helicobacter, 89
helpless-hopeless personality, 119, 155–156

hemispheric cognitive functions, 257
Hero with a Thousand Faces, The (Campbell), 186
hero's journey, 186
hertz, 429
hierarchy of needs, Maslow's, 74, 115
high-tech communication, 309–310
    anger and fear influences with, 310–312
    benefits of, 322
high-tech miscommunication, 310
Hildegard von Bingen, 177, 201
    path of, 177
Hippocrates, 349, 447
histamines, 87
Ho Scale, 149
hobbies, 347–348, 347f
Hodge, David, 352
Hoff, Benjamin, 188
holistic approach, to stress management, 19–23
holistic medicine, 5
Holmes, Peter, 456
Holmes, Thomas, 11, 28
homeostasis, 61
    defined, 6
    lack of, 544
Hoover, J. Edgar, 315
Hope, Bob, 270
Hopper, Grace, 296
hormonal imbalance, 49b
hormones, 49b, 50
hostile aggression, conflict-management style, 320
hostility
    Cook-Medley Hostility Index, 149
    coronary heart disease and, 129, 149
    Type A personality and, 149
hot tubs, 457
Houdini, 489
Houston, Jean, 39
How to Know God (Chopra), 184
How to Put More Time in Your Life (Scott), 330
How to Think Like Leonardo da Vinci (Gelb), 293
HPA axis. *See* hypothalamicpituitary-adrenal axis
huffingtonpost.com, 31
human energy field, 70, 71f, 75
Human Genome Project, 33, 61
human potential movement, 168
human spirituality, 168
    stress and, 201b
Human Triangle (*Trikonasana*), 403, 403f

humanistic journal therapy, 243
humor
    defined, 101, 270, 274
    Freud and, 101
    network access, 286
    physiology of, 281–282
    senses of, 275–280
    theories of, 272–274
    types of, 275–280
Humor: God's Gift (Bonham), 274
humor therapy, 270, 280, 281
    applications, 286–287
    as coping technique, 270–287
    Cousins, example of, 269–270
    defined, 270, 281
    historical perspectives, 270–272
    steps to initiate, 282–286
Hundredth Monkey theory, 373
Hunt, Valerie, 75
Huxley, Aldous, 168
Huygens, Christian, 434
hydrogenation, 521
hydrotherapy, 457
hyperproductivity, 329
hypertension, 51, 54
hypnosis, 79, 486
hypothalamicpituitary-adrenal (HPA) axis, 53
hypothalamus, 46, 50, 53
    role in physiological responses, 129

I

IBS. *See* irritable bowel syndrome
ICAT. *See* International Committee for the Coordination of Clinical Application and Teaching of Autogenic Therapy
identify theft, 33
idiosyncratic, 414
Ievleva, L., 413
illusion of control, 154
illustrators, 316–317
imagery, auditory, 439–440
imagination. *See also* mental imagery
    active, 105, 412
immediate, 49
    stress effects, 49, 52, 52t
immune dysregulation, 63, 63t
immune system
    eating for healthy, 517b
    effects on, 66
    purpose of, 63
    related disorders, 87–90

immunoenhancement, 68, 81
immunoglobulins (Ig), 64
immunoregulatory cells, 64
immunosuppression, 68
important-versus-urgent method, 334, 335b
inclusive/opening-up meditation, 373, 376–377
incongruity (surprise) theory, 272–273
increased awareness, 211
indirect approach, 490–491
individuation, 102
ineffability, 384
influenza, 87
information overload, 32
information processing, 211
    model, 215–216, 215f
information seeking, 342–343
infradian rhythms, 10
injuries, care and prevention of, 514
innate stress, 99
Inner Game of Tennis, The (Gallwey), 418
Inner Work (Johnson), 350
insightful internal relationship, 195
insightful meditation, 373, 376
insomnia, 14b
    brain physiology and, 54b
    and clinical biofeedback, 494b
    defined, 15
    diaphragmatic breathing and, 364b
    exercise and, 511b
    meditation and, 377b
    nutrition and, 518b
    stress and, 15
    and yoga, 399b
instinctual tension, 99, 99f
Institute for Research on Unlimited Love, 113
Institute of Noetic Sciences, 78
instrumental coping, 210
integration, 544–545
integrative medicine, 21
integrity, brevity *vs.*, 311
intellectual/expressive roadblocks, 301
intensity, exercise and, 509
Intensive Journal Workshop, 242–243
intention and desire, law of, 183
Intention Experiment, The (McTaggart), 353
intercessory prayer, 351
intermediate stress effects, 52, 52t
internal body images, 419–421
internal relationships, 195

International Committee for the Coordination of Clinical Application and Teaching of Autogenic Therapy (ICAT), 487, 490
International Labour Organization, 338
International Society for the Study of Subtle Energy and Energy Medicine (ISSSEEM), 76
Internet
  journal writing (blog), 248
  personality and, 163
  technostress, 29–33
Internet service providers, 339
interventions, 199–200, 544
  technique, 481
irony, 277
irrational fear, 135
irritable bowel syndrome (IBS), 85
Irwin, Michael, 466
isolation, fear of, 137
isometric contraction, 475
isometric muscle tension, 482
ISSSEEM. *See* International Society for the Study of Subtle Energy and Energy Medicine
It's Always Something (Radner), 281, 420
Ivy, J., 241, 244
Iyengar yoga, 406*t*

J

Jacobson, Edmund, 347, 476
Jacobson's relaxation technique, 477
Jacuzzi, Candido, 457
Jaffe, Dennis, 235
Jampolsky, Gerald, 185
Japanese Reiki method, 458
JAQ. *See* Jenkins Activity Questionnaire
Jasnoski, M., 413
jaw muscle, 478
Jenkins Activity Questionnaire (JAQ), 148
Jenkins, David, 148
Jermott, J. B., 68
Jesus of Nazareth, 184, 194, 201
  path of, 184–186, 185*f*
jnana yoga, 395
jogging, 511
Johnson, Charles M., 294
Johnson, Jack, 294
Johnson, Robert, 350
Joint Commission, 201
jokes, 271
Jonah complex, 136

journal writing, 244*f*
  application of, 252
  art of, 245*f*, 247
  consensus of therapists, 247–248
  as coping technique, 243–246
  defined, 241
  effects of, 243
  historical perspective, 242–243
  immediate effects, 245
  Internet, 248
  long-term effects, 245
  purpose of, 252
  steps to initiate, 247–251
  styles, 250–251
  summary excerpts, 246*b*
  therapeutic benefits, 243
  tips for, 251
joy, 139
Joyful Christ, The (Samra), 274
Judd, Naomi, 435
judge, 294, 295
Jung, Carl Gustav, 136, 173, 181, 199, 201
  art therapy, 251
  centering process, 192
  collective unconscious, 173, 173*f*, 191, 194
  compared mind to iceberg, 102, 103*f*
  divine mystery, 199
  dreams, 102–106, 173, 173*f*, 265, 349
  imagination, 412
  individuation, 102
  misoneism, 136
  path of, 173–175
  spiritual crisis, 174, 196
  spiritual evolution, 195
  theory of, 102–106, 102*f*
Jungian psychology, 242, 243
juniper, 456

K

Kabat-Zinn, Jon, 387
Kant, Immanuel, 273
karma
  law of, 183
  yoga, 395
Kauz, Herman, 468
Kaymen, Leslie, 217, 218
Keillor, Garrison, 278
Kellert, Steven, 534
Kennedy, John F., 185, 354
Kennedy, Robert F., Jr., 27
Kent, Jaylene, 79

Ki-Moon, Ban, 36
Kick in the Seat of the Pants, A (von Oech), 294
Kiecolt-Glaser, J., 66, 81, 244, 396, 456
killer cells, 64
Kindlon, D., 127
kinesthetic, 414
King, Martin Luther, Jr., 198, 198*f*
King, Serge Kahili, 5
Kirlian photography, 71, 71*f*
Kirlian, Semyon, 71
Kirschvink, Joseph, 76
Klein, Allen, 271, 278
kneading, 452, 452*f*
koan, 378
Kobasa, Suzanne, 156–158
Koestler, A., 273
Kolpakov, S., 449
Koonce, Gene, 77*f*
Kramer, Edith, 256
Krieger, Dolores, 75, 458
Kübler-Ross, Elisabeth, 90, 106–108, 106*f*, 137, 348
Kugler, J., 413
Kundalini energy. *See* root chakra
kundalini yoga, 395

L

lack of homeostasis, 544
lactic acid, 505
Lallas, Nitsa, 34
Lao Tzu, 170, 183, 195, 201, 224, 466
  path of, 188–189
Larson, Gary, 276
Lazarus, Richard, 98
Laskow, Leonard, 75
Last Child in the Woods (Louv), 35, 534
Laugh after Laugh (Moody), 279
lavender, 456
law
  of detachment, 184
  of dharma or life purpose, 184
  of giving, 183
  of intention and desire, 183–184
  of karma (cause and effect), 183
  of least effort, 183
  of pure potentiality, 183
Lazarus, Arnold, 235
Lazarus, Richard, 5, 12, 181, 210, 211
LCUs. *See* Life-Change Units
Learned Optimism (Seligman), 119, 220
least effort, law of, 183
Lee, Roberta, 28

left-hand ward-off position, 469
leftover guilt, 111
leisure time, less of, 3
Leno, Jay, 279
Leonardo da Vinci, 293
Lerner, Harriet, 127–128
less family time, 33
letters, use of unsent, 251
leukocytes, 64
Levick, Myra, 257
Levine, Robert, 329
Levitin, Daniel, 431
Lewis, C. S., 185
Lewis, H. A., 196
Lewis, Nolan, 256
Liberman, Jacob, 216, 421
Lidell, L., 405
Life and Death in Shanghai (Cheng), 146
Life-Change Units (LCUs), 11
life of the party sense of humor, 279–280
lifestyle behaviors, 17, 19
    college stress, 17
    diseases, caused by stress, 3
    trap, 332
lift hands position, T'ai Chi, 471
Light: Medicine of the Future (Liberman), 421
light therapy, 421
Lilly, John C., 457
limbic system, 45, 45f, 46
Lincoln, Abraham, 141, 271
Ling, Peter Heinrik, 451
Lingerman, H. A., 440
Lipton, Bruce, 39, 69–70, 217
Lipton model, 69–70
listening, communication and, 318–319
locus of control, 156
logotherapy, 108, 109
Lopez, George, 278
Louv, Richard, 35, 533
love
    defined, 112, 113
    self, 112–115
    unconditional, 184, 185f
Love, Medicine, and Miracles (Siegel), 80
lower back
    arch, 400b
    muscles, 480
lupus, 88
Luskin, Fred, 348
Luthe, Wolfgang, 486–487, 489
Lyle, Daniel B., 76
lymphocytes, 64

M

Maas, James, 511
MacDonald, Tim, 5
Maddi, Salvatore, 156–158
magnetic resonance imaging (MRI), 80, 431
magnetite, 76
magnifying, 221
Make Anger Your Ally (Warren), 131
mala, 375
Maltz, Maxwell, 162–163
Man and His Symbols (Jung), 104, 350
mandala, 374, 374f, 465
Man's Search for Meaning (Frankl), 108–109, 221, 280
mantras, 373–376, 419
Marketon, Webster, 65
Marshall, Barry, 89
Marx Brothers, 269
Marx, Groucho, 278
Marx-Hubbard, Barbara, 39
M*A*S*H, 277
Maslow, Abraham, 112, 115f, 121, 194, 197, 199
    creativity and, 294, 304
    hierarchy of needs, 74, 115, 116f
    Jonah complex, 136
    "peak experiences," 168
    self-actualization, 115–118, 158
    valuelessness, 197
massage therapy
    chronic pain and, 459
    defined, 446
    historical perspective, 447
    need for human touch, 447–448
    physiological and psychological benefits, 458–459
    research, 448–449
    types, 449–458
Matheny, K., 210
Matsyasana, 404, 404f
Matthews, D. A., 353
Matthews, James Owen, 435
Mayer, Marissa, 313
McClellan, Randall, 431
McClelland, David, 282
McEwen, Bruce, 46, 56
McGaa, Ed (Eagle Man), 178
McGary, Gladys Taylor, 62
McGhee, P., 272, 275
McKechnie, A., 449
McMeekin, Gail, 296

McPherson, John, 276
McTaggart, Lynne, 71, 353
meaningful purpose in life, 109, 197–198, 197f, 198f
mechanistic model, 19, 73
medications, over-the-counter, 88
medicine wheel, 178, 180f
meditation
    active, 375
    ADD and, 388b
    altered state of consciousness, 383–385
    applications, 389
    brain imaging research and, 386–387
    chronic pain and, 387
    continuum, 379
    defined, 371
    effects, 385–386
    exclusive, 373–375
    historical use, 371–373
    inclusive/opening-up, 373, 376–377
    insightful, 373
    insomnia and, 377b
    neuroplasticity, 386
    opening-up, 373, 376–377
    position, 375
    prayer and, 351–354
    purpose, 371
    relaxation response, 376
    restrictive, 373
    split-brain theory, 379–382
    steps to initiate, 387–388
    transcendental, 375–376
    types, 373–379
    Zen, 377–379
Megatrends 2000 (Naisbitt), 447
Meichenbaum, D. H., 215
melatonin, 49, 49b, 54b
Memories, Dreams, Reflections (Jung), 174, 191
mental imagery, 264
    application, 423
    athletes, 418f
    autogenic training and, 491–492
    chronic pain and, 421–422
    defined, 411
    guided, 411, 412–413
    historical perspective, 411–412
    research, 412–415
    steps to initiate, 422–423
mental repetition, 373
mental well-being, 22
Mercer, Johnny, 221
meridian system, 72
Merritt, Stephanie, 436, 439

Merton, Thomas, 185
Mesmer, Anton, 76
meta-disease, 118
metamessages, 314
metaphysical theory, 435–436
metastasis, 89
Metcalf, Linda, 250
methylated xanthine, 521
Middelton-Moz, Jane, 127
Miller, Ronald, 168
Miller, William, 234
mind, 376, 387–388, 388*f*
    art of, 380*b*–381*b*
    role. *See* psychology, theories of
    stress, 544–545
Mind as Healer, Mind as Slayer
        (Pelletier), 495
mind-body connection, 98
mind-body-spirit healing
    Borysenko model, 63–67
    Gerber model, 70–78
    Lipton model, 69–70
    Pelletier premodel, 78–81
    Pert model, 67–69
Mind, Music, and Imagery (Merritt), 436
Mind over Medicine (Rankin), 218
Minding the Body, Mending the Mind
        (Borysenko), 222
Mindless Eating (Wansink), 524
mineral depletion, 518
mineralocorticoids, 51
minerals, 516, 518, 526–527
Minnesota Multiphasic Personality
        Inventory (MMPI), 149
Mipham, Sakyong, 120
miscommunication, high-tech, 310
misoneism, 136
Mitchell, Edgar, 39
mitochondria, free radicals and, 519
MMPI. *See* Minnesota Multiphasic
        Personality Inventory
mode of exercise, 514
modeling, 231
Modern Man in Search of a Soul (Jung), 174
modified behaviors, 211
Molecules of Emotion (Pert), 69
money
    management, 326
    problems, 327–328
monosodium glutamate (MSG), 526, 526*b*
Monroe, Robert, 434
Monty Python's Flying Circus, 278
Moody, Raymond, 270, 279
Moore, Michael, 135

moroccan blue, 456
morphogenic field theory, 373
Morrison, Morris, 244
Mother Earth spirituality, 178, 180*f*
Mother Earth Spirituality (McGaa
        or Eagle Man), 178
Mother Teresa, 81, 187, 198, 198*f,* 282
Motivation and Personality (Maslow), 116
motivation, theory of, 115
motivational interviewing, 234
Motoyama, Hiroshi, 75
Moundeville, Henri de, 270
Mountain Pose (*Tadasana),* 402, 402*f*
moving meditation, 464
Moyers, Bill, 22, 186
Mozart effect, 438
MPD. *See* multiple personality disorder
MRI. *See* magnetic resonance imaging
Muir, John, 534, 538
multiple personality disorder (MPD), 78
multitasking, 53*b,* 149, 339, 371
Murray, Edward, 129
muscle
    fibers, 476
    groups, 476
    tension, 449, 459*f,* 459
muscular endurance, 504
muscular relaxation. *See* progressive
        muscular relaxation
muscular strength, 504
music, qualities of, 432*b*
music therapy
    applications, 441
    biochemical theory, 431–436
    chronic pain and, 440
    defined, 427
    entrainment theory, 433–435
    historical use of, 428–429
    metaphysical theory, 435–436
    psychological effects, 436–439
    recommended CDs for
        relaxation, 438*t*
    as relaxation technique, 431
    sound to noise to music, 429–431
    steps to initiate, 440–441
    visualization and auditory
        imagery, 439–440
Musicophilia (Sacks), 429
Myers, Rochelle, 295
myofascial release, 454, 459*f*
Myss, Caroline, 72–74
mystic-communal individual, 176–177
mystical (peak) sensation, 118
myth/mythology, 186–188

N
NACoA. *See* National Association
        for Children of Alcoholics
nadam, 374, 376
Naisbitt, John, 447
Naliboff, B. D., 449
NAMT. *See* National Association
        for Music Therapy
Naparstek, Belleruth, 412
National Association for Children
        of Alcoholics (NACoA), 155
National Association for Holistic
        Aromatherapy, 455
National Association for Music Therapy
        (NAMT), 429
National Center for Health Statistics, 3
National Geographic, 36
National Institute for Mental Health, 67
National Institutes of Health, 372, 457
National Outdoor Leadership School
        (NOLS), 161
National Safety Council, 40
natural killer (NK) cells, 64*f,* 65
natural rhythms, 537
natural scenes, mental imagery and
        use of, 416
nature deficit disorder, 35, 533–535
nature therapy, 533
nature *vs.* nurture debate, 61, 62
Naumberg, Margaret, 256
near-death experiences (NDEs), 170
neck muscles, 478–479
needs, Maslow's hierarchy of, 74, 115
negative thinking, 217–218
Neihardt, John G., 178
neocortical level of brain, 45*f,* 46–47
neoplasms, 66
nervous system, 63
    autonomic, 46, 47–50
    central, 45–47
    peripheral, 45, 46
    related disorders, 84–87
neuroendocrine pathways, 52–55
neurofeedback, 493
neurolinguistic programming (NLP),
        217, 219
neuromarketing, 326
neuropeptides, 67, 67*f,* 510
neuroplasticity, 30, 57, 386
neustress, 8
New Age movement, 168
New Age music, 429

New Earth, A (Tolle), 170
New England Journal of Medicine, 22, 269
New York State Psychiatric Unit, 256
New York Times, 30, 34, 520
Newberg, A., 386
Newton, Isaac, 19, 20*f*
Niebuhr, Reinhold, 224
NK cells. *See* natural killer cells
NLP. *See* neurolinguistic programming
nocebos, 80
noise, 429–431
NOLS. *See* National Outdoor Leadership School
noncompetitive exercising, 514*f*
nonlocal mind, 191
nonphysical elements, nonverbal communication, 317
nonsense humor, 276
nonverbal communication, 316–317
nonverbal expression, 258, 265
noo-dynamics, 109
norepinephrine, 48, 52, 54, 88
Norris, Patricia, 411, 414, 420
Northrup, Christiane, 73
nutrient density, 518
nutrition
    additional nutritional factors, 520–522
    dangerous items in diet, 526*b*
    eating disorders, 524–525
    genetically altered foods, 522
    healthy immune system and, 517*b*
    insomnia and, 518*b*
    psychological effects of food, 524–525
    recommendations, 525–527
    spiritual, 522–524
    stress and, 515–516
    for stressed planet, 516–519
    tips, 527
    well-balanced, 525

O

Obama, Barack, 271
obesity, 504
occupational stress, 39–40
On Death and Dying (Kübler-Ross), 106
oncogene, 89
One Knee to Chest (*Pawan Muktasana*), 403, 403*f*
One Nation Under Stress (Becker), 29
Onion, The, 275
Open (Agassi), 222
opening-up meditation, 373, 376–377

Opening Up: The Healing Power of Confiding in Others (Pennebaker), 249
operant conditioning, 231, 494
optimism
    defined, 224*b*
    flexible, 221
    learned, 220
    spiritual, 182
    tragic, 109
organ neurosis, 62
organic foods, 523*f*
organizational skills, development of, 337
Orlick, T., 413
Orman, Suze, 328
Ornish, Dean, 73, 151, 372
Ornstein, Robert, 12, 381
osteoporosis, 466, 521
Outward Bound, 160, 243
over-the-counter medications, 88
overeating, 525

P

Page, Christine, 39
pain, chronic
    breathing and, 364
    clinical biofeedback and, 498
    exercise and, 511–512
    knee, 514
    massage therapy and, 459
    meditation and, 387
    mental imagery, 421–422
    music therapy and, 440
    T'ai Chi and, 467–468
    yoga and, 397
palliative coping, 210
palmarosa, 456
paradigm shift, 19
paralanguage, 317
paralysis by analysis, 249
parasympathetic nervous system, 47–50, 48*f*
parasympathetic rebound, 507
Pareto principle, 334
Parker, Dorothy, 277
Parnes, Sidney, 301, 439
Parody, 275–276
partially hydrogenated oils, 517*b*, 526*b*
Paschimottasana, 403, 404*f*
passive-aggressive behavior, 132
passive behavior style, 235
passive concentration, 486
Pasteur, Louis, 61–62

Path of Prayer, The (Burnham), 354
Pauling, Linus, 294
Pavlov, Ivan, 230, 494
Pawan Muktasana, 403, 403*f*
Peace, Love, and Healing (Siegel), 489
peaceful resolution, 211
Pearlman, Steve, 472
Pearsall, Paul, 80
Peck, M. Scott, 175–177, 192–194, 196, 199, 201
peer groups, college stress, 18
peer pressure, college stress, 18
Pelletier, Kenneth, 11, 62–63, 78–81, 495
Pelletier premodel, 78–81
Pennebaker, James, 243–244, 249
Peper, Erik, 412
perception distortion, 384
perceptual roadblocks, 301
perennial philosophy, 168
perfectionism, 221, 332–333
peripheral nervous system (PNS), 45, 46
personal cosmology, 181
personal house-cleaning technique, 337
personal space, need for, 317
personal stress-management strategy, 545–546
personal unconscious, 102
personal value system, 196–197
personality
    behavior as component of, 230–231
    defined, 147
    technology and, 163
    traits, 158–160
    personality types
        codependent, 151–155
        coping strategies and, 211
        hardy, 156–158
        helpless-hopeless, 119
        sensation seeker, 160–161
        survivor, 158–160
        time management and, 330–333
        Type A, 148–151, 331
        Type D, 151
persuasion, conflict-management style, 320
Pert, Candace, 67–69
Pert model, 67–69, 67*f*
pessimism
    defined, 221, 224*b*
    spiritual, 182
pet therapy, 457–458
petrissage, 451–452, 452*f*
Pew Research Center (PRC), 169
phases of workout, 509–510, 510*f*

physical elements, nonverbal communication, 316–317

physical exercise. *See* exercises

physical repetition, 374

physical well-being, 22

physiology of stress, 55*b*

    autonomic nervous system, 46, 47–50

    central nervous system, 45–47

    endocrine system, 50–52

    neuroendocrine pathways, 52–55

Pilates exercises, 511–512, 512*f*

Pilates, Joe, 511

Pingdom, 30

Piraro, Dan, 197*f,* 276, 521

pitch, 429

pituitary gland, 46, 50

placebos, 80

Plastic: A Toxic Love Story (Freinkel), 38

Plato, 270, 272, 428

PMR. *See* progressive muscular relaxation

PNI. *See* psychoneuroimmunology

PNI: The New Mind-Body HealingProgram (Dacher), 74

PNS. *See* peripheral nervous system

Poetry as Therapy (Morrison), 244

polarized thinking, 221

polite eye contact, maintenance of, 312

political incivility, 34*b*

polyphasia, 148, 331

Popp, Fritz-Albert, 68

Porter, Garrett, 420*f*

Positive Addiction (Glasser), 510

positive attitude, 422

positive psychology, 119

post-traumatic stress disorder (PTSD), 14*b,* 48, 56, 105, 260, 396, 413, 427

potentiality, law of pure, 183

poverty

    consciousness, 327

    psychology of, 327

power, 505

    motivation, 68

Power of Myth, The, 186, 187

Power of Now, The (Tolle), 377

Power Sleep (Maas), 511

Power yoga, 406*t*

Prairie Home Companion, 278

pranayama, 171, 362, 374, 395, 397, 398*f*

prayer(s)

    and meditation, 351

    for nonbelievers, 353

    research on, 352–353

    types of, 351

    ways to, 354

predictive encoding, 411

preparatory-loss depression, 107

present-centeredness, 384

Present Shock: When everything happens now (Rushkoff), 27, 328

presenteeism, 39

Pressman, P., 353

preventive, combative *vs.,* 210

primary creativity, 294

principles, Tao

    cyclical growth, 189

    dynamic balance, 188–189

    harmonious action, 189

    oneness, 188

prioritization, 334

privacy, 33, 311

process addiction, 153, 417

Prochaska, James, 233, 234

procrastinators, 332

professional muscle massage, 446

professional pursuits, college stress, 17

Progoff, Ira, 242

Progoff 's method of journal writing, 242

progressive muscular relaxation (PMR), 476

    application, 481–482

    benefits, 476–477

    historical perspective, 476

    steps to initiate, 477–481

Project Adventure, 160–161

projection, 100

prolonged effect of stress, 52, 52*t*

Prophet, The (Gibran), 371

proportional biofeedback, 496

proprioceptive method, 250

proteins, 504, 517*b,* 525

psychic equilibrium, 104, 174

Psycho-Cybernetics (Maltz), 162, 163

psychointrapersonal influences, 11

Psychology of Consciousness, The (Ornstein), 381

psychology, theories of

    Buddhism, 120

    Buscaglia, 112–115

    Dyer, 110–112

    Frankl, 108–110

    Freud, 99–101

    Jung, 102–106

    Kübler-Ross, 106–108

    Maslow, 115–118

    mind and stress, Tibetan perspective of, 120

    Seligman, 118–120

Psychology Today, 127, 280, 281

psychoneuroimmunology (PNI), 62, 270, 282

    Borysenko model, 63–67

    Gerber model, 70–78

    Lipton model, 69–70

    Pelletier premodel, 78–81

    Pert model, 67–69

psychophysiology, 44, 55–56

psychosomatic diseases, 46, 62

psychospirituality, 173

PTSD. *See* post-traumatic stress disorder

puns, 278

Puzo, Mario, 296

Pythagoras, 428

Q

Qigong, 467

Quantum Healing, Perfect Health (Chopra), 183

quick-witted humor, 278

R

race, stress and, 40–41

radiation treatment, 415

Radner, Gilda, 281, 420

rage reflex, 126

Rahe, Richard, 28

Raising Cain (Kindlon and Thompson), 127

raja yoga, 395

Ralston, Aron, 158–160

Rama, Swami, 395, 397, 405, 494

Ramos, Joseph, 18

Rankin, Lissa, 218

RAS. *See* reticular activating system

Ratey, John, 507*b*

rational emotive behavior therapy (REBT), 98, 215

rational fear, 135

rationalization, 100, 216

Ray, Michael, 295

reactionaries, 154

reactive depression, 107

Reagan, Ronald, 271

Reason for Hope (Goodall), 187

REBT. *See* rational emotive behavior therapy

Rechtschaffen, Stephan, 329

reconstruction, 158

Recovering the Soul (Dossey), 190

reductionist model, 19

reflections, 246*b*
reframing, 223
regulators, 317
Reiki, Japanese, 458
Rein, Glen, 75
Reivich, K., 158
rejection, fear of, 136
relationships, internal and external, 194–196
relative inviability, 89
relaxation
    changing views of, 5
    skills, 545
relaxation response, 376
        relaxation techniques, 84, 85, 88, 258, 262, 360–361, 512
        autogenic training, 485–499
        behavioral changes, 416–419
        clinical biofeedback, 492–498
        daydreaming, 415
        diaphragmatic breathing, 362–367
        internal body images, 419–421
        massage therapy, 446–459
        meditation, 370–389
        mental imagery and visualization, 410–423
        music therapy, 427–441
        progressive muscular relaxation, 475–482
        promotion, 417*b*
        purpose of, 360
        T'ai Chi Ch'uan, 464–472
        tranquil natural scenes, 416
        yoga, 394–406
Relaxation Response, The (Benson), 376
release/relief theory, 273
Religions, Values, and Peak Experiences (Maslow), 116
Renewing Values in America (Lallas), 34
repetitions
    mental, 373
    physical, 374
    sounds, 374
    tactile, 375
repression, 100
residual tension, 476
resiliency, 156–158
resistance stage, 13
responding skills, communication and, 318–319
restrictive meditation, 373
retail therapy, 326
Retallack, Dorothy, 434

reticular activating system (RAS), 45
retirement, stress and, 109
return to nature, 466
rheumatoid arthritis, 88
Richtel, Matt, 30
Rider, Mark, 432
right-hand ward-off position, T'ai Chi, 469
RMWF. *See* Rocky Mountain Wildlife Foundation
RNA, free radicals and, 519
Road Less Traveled, The (Peck), 175
roadblocks, 199–200
    artistic, 262
    cultural, 301
    emotional, 301
    environmental, 301
    intellectual/expressive, 301
    perceptual, 301
    to time management, 330–331, 331*f*
Roar of Silence, The (Campbell), 438
Robin, Vicki, 327
Rocky Mountain Wildlife Foundation (RMWF), 535
Roesch, Robert, 330
Rogers, Will, 278
Rokeach, Milton, 196, 230
role playing, 163
Rolf, Ida, 453
rolfing, 453–454, 453*f*
Rolf's theory, 453
Rolling Thunder, 178
Rollnick, Stephan, 234
roommate dynamics, college stress, 17
root chakra, 73
Rorschach ink-blot test, 412
Rosch, Paul, 39, 40, 70
Rosen, L., 32
Rosen, R., 364
Rosenfeld, R., 379
Rosenman, Ray, 148–150
Rossman, Marty, 420, 421
Rotter, Julian, 156
"royal path" (raja yoga), 395
Rubik, Beverly, 74
Rumyantseva, S., 449
runner's high, 360, 511
Rushkoff, Douglas, 27, 328

S

S-IgA. *See* secretory immunoglobulin
Sacks, Oliver, 429, 435
sacral chakra, 73

SAD. *See* seasonal affective disorder
Sajady, Mas, 80*f*
Salter, Andrew, 235
Salute to the Sun (*Surya Namaskar*), 399–402, 400*f*, 401*f*, 402*f*
Samra, Cal, 274
Sancier, Kenneth, 467
Sapir-Whorf hypothesis, 315
Sapolsky, Richard, 62
Sapolsky, Robert, 6, 56
sarcasm, 278
SARS, 62
Sartoris, Elizabeth, 39
Saturday Night Live, 272, 275
Scary Movie, 277, 280
Schaef, Ann Wilson, 153–155, 171, 194, 199
Schafer, Louis, 277
Schafer, W., 221
scheduling, 334–336, 335*b*
schismogenesis, 314
schizophrenia, 351
Schlitz, Marilyn, 353
Schmale, Arthur, 155–156
Schmid, Charles, 440
Schultz, Johannes, 486–487, 489
Schumann's resonance, 433
Scivias (Hildegard von Bingen), 177
Scott, Dru, 330
Scozzarro, Gianni, 316
screen time *vs.* direct eye contact, 311
seasonal affective disorder (SAD), 10, 54
"seasons of the soul," 192*f*
Seattle, Chief, 178, 179*b,* 194
secondary appraisal, 210
secondary creativity, 294
secondary PTSD, 14*b*
secretory immunoglobulin (S-IgA), 68, 282
selected awareness, 488
selective serotonin reuptake inhibitors (SSRIs), 54*b*
self, 120
self-actualization, 115–118, 158
self-disclosure, 315
self-dominance, fear of loss, 137
self-efficacy, 210
self-esteem, 114, 149, 151, 161–163, 544, 545
self-expression, 257
self-fulfilling prophecy, 222
self-hypnosis, 486
    use of, 492

self-image, 162–163

self-imposed guilt, 111

self-love, 112–115

self-mutilation, 131

self-punishers, 131

self-reflection, 372

self-regulation, 486

self-talk, 221

self-transcendence, 116, 384

Seligman, Martin E., 118–120, 119*f,* 155, 220

Selye, Hans, 2, 4, 5, 6, 13, 22, 27, 44, 51*b,* 56, 63, 119, 194, 198, 504

Sen, Amartya, 327

seniors, T'ai Chi and, 471

sensation seekers, 160–161

senses of humor, 279–280

sensory overload, 370

Serenity Prayer, 224

serotonin, 49, 49*b*

Seven Spiritual Laws of Success, The (Chopra), 183

Seville Statement, 126

sex hormone, 49*b*

Shackleton, Ernest, 159

shallow effect, 31

Shallows: What the Internet Is Doing to Our Brains, The (Carr), 31

shavasana, 394, 404, 404*f*

Shealy, Norm, 72–73

Sheldrake, Rupert, 373

shiatsu, 74–75, 450–451, 451*f*

Shirky, Clay, 30

shoulding, 221

shoulder muscles, 479, 479*f*

shoulders to ear stretch, 400*b*

Siebert, Al, 158, 159–160

Siegel, Bernie, 80, 90, 259–260, 262–263, 282, 420, 489

Silva, José, 372

Silva method, 372

Silverman, Sarah, 278

Simbo, Juliet Mamie, 37

Simeons, A.T.W., 6

Simon, Neil, 278

Simon, Sidney, 348

Simon, Suzanne, 348

Simonton, O. Carl, 90, 258, 412, 419, 420, 421

Simonton, Stephanie, 258, 412

single whip position, T'ai Chi, 470

Singletary, Michelle, 328

Sit and Reach (*Paschimottasana*), 403, 404*f*

sitting mountain pose, 400*b*

Sivananda Companion to Yoga, The (Lidell), 405

Six Pillars of Self-Esteem (Branden), 161

60 Minutes, 271

skeptical individual, 175–176

Skinner, B. F., 231

Skog, Susan, 139

slapstick comedy, 276

sleep hygiene, 16, 16*b*

sleep, time management, 339

smartphones, 308, 310–312

Sobel, D., 12

social affiliation hormone, 8

social engineering. *See* social orchestration

social influences, 11

Type A personality and, 148–151

social media, 31*f*

"social networking,", 29, 29*f*

social orchestration, 343–345

Social Readjustment Rating Scale (SRRS), 11, 28, 106

social-support groups, 345–347

sociology

civility, decline in, 33–35

defined, 28

environmental disconnect, 35–39

occupational stress, 39–40

race and gender stress, 40–41

techno-stress, 29–33

sodium intake, 521

solar plexus chakra, 73–74

solitude, 539

self-actualization characteristics, 116

somatizers, 131

Sommer, Elizabeth, 520

Sorenson, Jackie, 506

Sound Health (Halpern), 441

sounds, 429–431

loudness of, 431*t*

repeated, 374

waves, 430*f,* 431*f*

Space, Time, and Medicine (Dossey), 190

Spaight, Tracy, 163

Spark (Ratey), 507*b*

Spear, Deena, 440

spectrum meditation, 437*t*

Spend Well, Live Right (Singletary), 328

Sperry, Roger, 103, 295, 381

Spiegel, D., 346

Spinal Twist (*Ardha Matsyendrasana*), 404, 404*f*

Spindrift Organization, 190, 354

Spinner, Jackie, 261

spirit, stress, 545

spiritual bankruptcy, 169

spiritual conversion, 174

spiritual dormancy, 169

spiritual evolution, 195

spiritual health, 199

spiritual hunger, defined, 169

spiritual nutrition, 516, 522–524

Spiritual Nutrition and the Rainbow Diet (Cousens), 523

spiritual optimism, 182

spiritual pessimism, 182

spiritual potential, 199

spiritual well-being

defined, 22

model, 194–202

spirituality

common bonds of, 191–194

creation, 180, 180*f*

current research on, 200–202

defined, 171–172

model of, for stress management, 194–202

Mother Earth, 178, 180*f*

theories of, 172–191

split-brain theory, 379

Spontaneous Evolution (Lipton), 39

spontaneous remission, 78–79

sports massage, 454–455, 459*f*

SQUID. *See* superconducting quantum interference device

SRRS. *See* Social Readjustment Rating Scale

Stabb, S., 128, 133

stage of exhaustion, 13

stage of resistance, 13

stages of grieving, 106–107

Stalking the Wild Pendulum (Bentov), 190, 433

Starseed (Carey), 185

starting position

relaxation technique, 477, 477*f*

T'ai Chi, 469

Stein, Joel, 15

Steptoe, Andrew, 218

Stewart, Betty, 471

Stewart, Jon, 31

stimulus generalization, 427

stimulus period, exercise and, 509

Sting, 39, 295, 371

straightforward procrastinator, 332

Stratton, Valerie, 437

stress, 234–235
  awareness chart, 121*f*
  definitions of, 2, 5–6
  diseases caused by, 3
  gland. *See* adrenal gland
  impact of societal, 28
  inoculation, 215
  occupational, 39–40
  physiology of. *See* physiology of stress
  race and gender, 40–41
  reaction, 6
  superstress, 28
  techno-stress, 29–33
  and type 2 diabetes, 82*b*
  types of, 8–10
stress-and-disease phenomenon, 62
stress-management
  courses, 245
  critical incidence, 14*b*
  holistic approach to, 19–23
  model of spirituality for, 194–202
  program, 543–546
  techniques, 22
  therapy programs, 23
Stress of Life, The (Selye), 4, 22
stress-related hormones, effect of, 66
stress response, 6–8
  defined, 6
  description, 6
  pathways, 52*t*
Stress without Distress (Selye), 198
stressed planet, diet for, 516–518
stressors, 544
  bioecological, 10–11
  defined, 10
  psychointrapersonal, 11
  social, 11
    in America, 11–13
  types, 10–11
stretching, yoga and, 398, 398*f*
structured interview, 148
substance addiction, 161
subtle anatomy, 72
subtle energy, 71, 80, 190
Suedfeld, Peter, 160
suffering, 108–109
summarization, communication, 319
Sundram, Joseph, 130
superconducting quantum interference
    device (SQUID), 80
superiority theory, 272
superstress, 28
supplements, vitamins, 519
supportive-expressive group therapy, 346

supraconsciousness, 379*f*
surrender, conflict-management
    style, 320
survival skills, 153, 161
survivor personality, 160
Survivor Personality, The (Siebert), 159
Surya Namaskar, 399–402, 400*f,*
    401*f,* 402*f*
Swedish massage, 451–453, 452*f*
Swenson, Kari, 489
swimming, 512
switching, 433
Sylvia, Claire, 80
sympathetic nervous system, 47–50, 48*f*
sympathetic resonance, 76
sympathomimetic agents, 520
synchronicity, 174
synesthesia, 384
systematic desensitization, 138, 412,
    417–418

T

T-cells, 64
  cytotoxic, 64, 64*f*
  examination of, 64
  family of, 64*f*
T-helpers (CD4), 64, 64*f*
T-lymphocytes. *See* T-cells
T-suppressors (CD8), 64, 64*f*
Tachiki, K. H., 449
tactile repetition, 375
Tadasana, 402, 402*f*
T'ai Chi ch'uan
  applications of, 472
  chronic pain and, 467–468
  defined, 464
  historical perspective of, 465
  movements, 468–471
  philosophy of, 465–466
  physiological and psychological
    benefits of, 466–467
  as relaxation technique, 468
T'ai Chi Handbook (Kauz), 468
Tannen, Deborah, 314, 318
Tao of Inner Peace, The (Dreher), 188
Tao of Physics, The (Capra), 191
Tao of Pooh (Hoff), 188
Tao of Psychology, The (Bolen), 190
Tao Teh Ching, 188, 224
Taoism, principles of, 188
tapotement, 452, 453*f*
target heart rate, 509, 509*f*

target organs, 50, 82, 84–90
  and immune system–related disorders,
    87–90
  and nervous system–related disorders,
    84–87
Tarlton, Richard, 270
Taubes, Gary, 520
Tavris, Carol, 129, 130
Taylor, Shelly, 211, 342, 413
TBI. *See* traumatic brain injury
Teach Only Love (Jampolsky), 185
Teachings of Don Juan, The
    (Castaneda), 172
technostress, 29–33
  aspects of, 32–33
  defined, 30
technology
  and generational divide, 33
  impact of societal stress, 28
  personality and, 163
technology gap, 310, 310*f*
technophile, 332
Technostress (Weil and Rosen), 32
television, time management, 338
Templeton, John, 113
temporomandibular joint dysfunction
    (TMJD), 84–85, 476
  forms of, 85*f*
tend and befriend, 7–8
territorial space, nonverbal
    communication, 317
text messages, 310–312
TFAs. *See* trans fatty acids
thalamus, 46
That's Not What I Meant (Tannen), 314
Thaut, Michael, 437
theory of motivation, 115
theory of specific etiology, 61
therapeutic journal writing, 241
therapeutic touch (TT), 458
thermal biofeedback, 498
Thigh Stretch (*Bandha Konasana*),
    403, 403*f*
thigh muscle, 480
This Is Your Brain on Music (Levitin), 431
Thompson, M., 127
Thoreau, Henry David, 532
thought(s)
  choosing, 221–224
  stopping, 221
  toxic, 217–221
three-C's method, 335
throat chakra, 74
thyroid gland, 50

thyrotropic hormone (TTH), 55
thyrotropic hormone–releasing
　　　factor (TRF), 55
thyroxine axis, 53, 55
tickler notebook, 285
time
　　distortion, 383
　　exercise and duration, 509
　　historical concepts of, 328–330, 330f
　　juggler, 331
　　mapping, 336
　　urgency, 148, 149
time management
　　additional ideas, 336–339
　　applications, 339
　　defined, 330
　　personality styles and behaviors,
　　　　331–333
　　roadblocks to, 330–331, 331f
　　steps to initiate, 334–336
time robbers, 331
Time Shifting (Rechtschaffen), 329
time-trap procrastinator, 332
time wasters, 331
tinnitus, 430
TM. *See* transcendental meditation
TMJD. *See* temporomandibular
　　　joint dysfunction
Toffler, Alvin, 27, 292
Tolle, Eckhart, 170, 377, 388
Tomatis, Alfred, 436
Tomlin, Lily, 351
Torrance, Paul, 292
touch. *See also* massage therapy
　　communication and, 316
　　need for human, 447–448
　　tactile repetition, 375
　　therapeutic, 458
　　vitamin T, 448, 448t
"touch-conscious" society, 446
"touch it once" rule, 312
toxic thoughts, 217–221
toxins, 516
tragic optimism, 109
Training Your Creative Mind
　　　(VanGundy), 301
tranquil natural scenes, 416
trans fatty acids (TFAs), 517, 526b
transcendence, 171
transcendental meditation (TM), 183,
　　　375–376
transpersonal psychology, 173
transpsychological, 243
tratak, 374

Trauma Recovery Institute, 14b
traumatic brain injury (TBI), 413
Travis, John, 22
TRF. *See* thyrotropic
　　　hormone–releasing factor
trigger point therapy, 455
triiodothyronine, 55
Trikonasana, 403, 403f
trunk-rotation, 400b
"trusting hormone," 8
tsubos, 451
TT. *See* therapeutic touch
TTH. *See* thyrotropic hormone
Turkle, Sherry, 31, 32
Turning the Mind into an Ally
　　　(Mipham), 120
Twain, Mark, 273, 274, 278
12 Secrets of Highly Creative Women,
　　　The (McMeekin), 296
Twitter, 243
Two Knees to Chest (*Apanasana*), 403, 403f
type 2 diabetes, stress and, 82b
Type A personality, 148–151, 331
Type D personality, 151
type of exercise, 509
Typhoid Mary, 62

U

ulcers, 88–89
Ulman, Eleanor, 256
ultradian rhythms, 10
unconditional love, 184, 185f
unconscious
　　collective, 103, 173, 173f, 191, 194
　　mind, 104
　　personal, 103–104
　　resistance, 216
underhanders, 132
"unhealthy rumination," 8
unified field theory, 20f
unknown, fear of, 136–137
unsent letters, 251
unwarranted fear, 135
upper chest muscle, 479
U.S. Department of Labor and Statistics
　　　reports, 4
U.S. Dietary Guidelines, 526

V

Vacation Deprivation survey, 5
vacation time, changes in, 5

values
　　conflicts, 197, 319
　　defined, 230
　　personal, 197
Van de Castle, Robert, 349
VanGundy, Arthur, 301
vasopressin, 46
vasopressin axis, 54
vegetative level of brain, 45
verbal communication, 314–315
Vernejoul, Pierre de, 75
vetiver, 456
via creativa, 180
via negativa, 180
via positiva, 180
via transformativa, 180–181
V.I.B.E. machine, 77f
vibration, 453, 453f
vibrational medicine, 421
Vibrational Medicine (Gerber), 70
Vibrational Medicine for the 21st Century
　　　(Gerber), 70
victimization, 219, 220
Virshup, Evelyn, 258, 263
vision quest, 178, 193, 194
Vision Quest (Foster), 243
visual concentration, 374
visualization
　　defined, 411
　　exercises, 366–367
　　music and, 439–440
　　phases of, 365
Visualization for Change (Fanning), 411
vitamin B complex, 519
vitamin C, 519
vitamin D deficiency, 38
vitamin T (touch), 448, 448t
vitamins, 526
　　depletion, 518–520
　　supplements, 519–520, 519f
Vivekananda, Swami, 395
Vogt, Oskar, 486
von Oech, Roger, 294, 296
Vonnegut, Kurt, 282, 294

W

walking, 512
Wallace, Robert Keith, 376, 385
Wansink, Brian, 524
warm-up period, exercise and, 509
Warren, Neil, 131
warrior, 294, 296–297

water, 516, 517*b*
water shortages, 36
water-soluble vitamins, 516, 521
Watson, Andrew, 429
Watson, John B., 138
Watson, Lyle, 373
Watson, Thomas J., 300
Weber, Karl, 38
weight gain, cortisol and, 515*b*
Weil, Andy, 62
Weil, M., 32
Weinberg, R., 449
well-balanced diet, 525
Wellness Community, 137
wellness paradigm, 21, 21*f*, 22, 23
West, Kanye, 241
Western Collaborative Groups Study, 148
Whack on the Side of the Head,
    A (von Oech), 299
white noise, 430
WHO. *See* World Health Organization
whole systems theory, 20
Why God Won't Go Away (Newberg), 387
Why Me? (Porter and Norris), 420
Why Zebras Don't Get Ulcers (Sapolsky),
    56, 62
Wi-Fi, stress, 33
Williams, Redford, 130
Williams, Robin, 429
Wilson, E. O., 38
winning by losing, 465–466

withdrawal, conflict-management
    style, 320
Wittstein, Ilan, 87
Wolpe, Joseph, 138, 412
Woman's Journey to God, A
    (Borysenko), 182
women, nutritional needs for, 525
Women's Anger Project, 128
Women's Bodies, Women's Wisdom
    (Northrup), 73
work, stress and, 39–40
workaholism, 331
World Health Organization (WHO),
    19, 171
worrying, art of, 111–112
Wright, Steven, 171, 276
Writer's block, 248–249
writing meditation, 245
Writing the Mind Alive (Metcalf), 250
wu wei, 189, 465

X

X-factor, 114

Y

yang, 465, 465*f*
Yerkes-Dodson principle, 9, 9*f*
yin, 465, 465*f*

yoga
    centers, 395
    defined, 394
    hatha yoga. *See* hatha yoga
    insomnia and, 399*b*
"*Yoga in America*", 395
Yoga Sutras, 395
You Must Relax (Jacobson), 347, 476
Your Brain on Nature (Selhub), 535
Your Erroneous Zones (Dyer), 110, 112
Your Money or Your Life (Dominguez and
    Robin), 327
Your Sacred Self (Dyer), 112

Z

Zadikov, Maggie, 448
Zalanowski, Anthony, 437
Zaltman, Gerald, 326
Zen (Zazen) meditation, 377–379
zero firing threshold, 477
Ziv, Avner, 272, 273, 281
Zombieland, 277
Zuckerman, M., 160